Cover art: *Evening on Crow Reservation, Montana* (oil on canvas), Sharp, Joseph Henry (1859–1953) / Private Collection / Photo © Christie's Images / Bridgeman Images

About the Cover Image

Evening on Crow Reservation, Montana, Sharp, Joseph Henry (1859–1953)

From an early age, John Henry Sharp was fascinated by American Indians. Born in Ohio in 1859 to Irish immigrants, Sharp lost his hearing in an accident but his powers of observation remained acute. After visiting Taos, New Mexico in 1893, he illustrated the everyday life of members of the Pueblo Nation. He lived among the Crow Indians in Montana and painted them as well as the Sioux and Nez Perce. President Theodore Roosevelt commissioned him to paint the native survivors of the Little Big Horn battle of 1876. In his portrayals of American Indians, Sharp departed from the prevailing policies of the U. S. government that emphasized assimilation. His depiction of this Crow reservation, probably painted around 1920, demonstrates Sharp's respect for the perseverance of American Indians and their fervent efforts to retain their own society and culture.

Guide to Analyzing Primary and Secondary Sources

In their search for an improved understanding of the past, historians look for a variety of evidence—written sources, visual sources, and material artifacts. When they encounter any of these primary sources, historians ask certain key questions. You should ask these questions too. Sometimes historians cannot be certain about the answers, but they always ask the questions. Indeed, asking questions is the first step in writing history. Moreover, facts do not speak for themselves. It is the task of the historian to organize and interpret the facts in a reasoned and verifiable manner. The books and articles that they publish are secondary sources, which are created after the events or conditions they are studying. These secondary sources then become the basis for teaching and for other historians to use in researching and writing their own studies. Because they are interpretative and open for debate, secondary sources allow historians to move forward by modifying explanations of the past. Thus, historical interpretations are constantly being revised, and *Exploring American Histories*, 3e offers students opportunities to appreciate this dynamic quality.

Analyzing a Written Primary Source

- What kind of source is this? For example, is it a diary, letter, speech, sermon, court opinion, newspaper article, witness testimony, poem, memoir, or advertisement?
- Who wrote the source? How can you identify the author? Was the source translated by someone other than the author or speaker (for example, American Indian speeches translated by whites)?
- When and where was it written?
- Why was the source written? Is there a clear purpose?
- Who was, or who might have been, its intended audience?
- What point of view does it reflect?
- What can the source tell us about the individual(s) who produced it and the society from which he, she, or they came?
- How might individuals' race, ethnicity, class, gender, age, and region have affected the viewpoints in the sources?
- In what ways does the larger historical context help you evaluate individual sources?

Analyzing a Visual or Material Primary Source

- What kind of visual or material source is this? For example, is it a map, drawing or engraving, a physical object, painting, photograph, census record, or political cartoon?
- Who made the image or artifact, and how was it made?
- When and where was the image or artifact made?
- Can you determine if someone paid for or commissioned it? If so, how can you tell that it was paid for or commissioned?
- Who might have been the intended audience or user? Where might it have originally been displayed or used?
- What message or messages is it trying to convey?
- How might it be interpreted differently depending on who viewed or used it?
- What can the visual or material source tell us about the individual who produced it and the society from which he or she came?
- In what ways does the larger historical context help you evaluate individual sources?

Comparing Multiple Primary Sources

- In what ways are the sources similar in purpose and content? In what ways are they different?
- How much weight should one give to who wrote or produced the source?
- Were the sources written or produced at the same time or at different times? If they were produced at different times, does this account for any of the differences between or among the sources?
- What difference does it make that some sources (such as diaries and letters) were intended to be private and some sources (such as political cartoons and court opinions) were meant to be public?
- How do you account for different perspectives and conclusions? How might these be affected by the author's relative socioeconomic position or political power in the larger society?
- Is it possible to separate fact from personal opinion in the sources?
- Can the information in the sources under review be corroborated by other evidence? What other sources would you want to consult to confirm your conclusions?

Cautionary Advice for Interpreting Primary Sources

- A single source does not tell the whole story, and even multiple sources may not provide a complete account. Historians realize that not all evidence is recoverable.
- Sources have biases, whether they appear in personal or official accounts. Think of biases as particular points of view, and try to figure out how they influence the historical event and the accounts of that event.
- Sources reflect the period in which they were written or produced and must be evaluated within the historical time frame from which they came. Explain how people understood the world in which they lived, and be careful to avoid imposing contemporary standards on the past. Nevertheless, remember that even in a particular time period people disagreed over significant principles and practices such as slavery, imperialism, and immigration.
- Sources often conflict or contradict each other. Take into account all sides. Do not dismiss an account that does not fit into your interpretation; rather, explain why you are giving it less weight or how you are modifying your interpretation to conform to all the evidence.

Analyzing Secondary Sources

- Secondary sources are written or produced by people who did not participate in or experience first-hand the events that they are analyzing. Secondary sources in history usually appear as scholarly books and articles. Secondary sources underscore that history is an ever-changing enterprise.
- Identify the author's main interpretations.
- Describe the evidence the author uses to make that interpretation.
- Evaluate how well the evidence supports the author's interpretation.
- Describe whether the author considers alternative explanations and points of view.
- Compare the author's account with any other sources you have read.
- Assess whether the author has the credentials for making reliable historical judgments.
- Evaluate whether there is anything in the author's background or experience that might have influenced the author's point of view and interpretation.
- Identify the main audience that the author is addressing.

Comparing Secondary Sources

- Explain how two sources differ in interpretation. To what extent, if any, do they agree?
- Historians are products of their own times. Identify the date of publication for each of the sources and explain how the particular time periods might have shaped the authors' arguments.
- Compare the approaches each author takes to reach an interpretation. Describe whether they are looking at the events mainly from a political, social, cultural, or economic perspective.
- Compare the secondary sources with other secondary sources on the same subject, such as the historical narrative in this textbook.
- Taking these considerations into account, explain which secondary source you find more convincing or how the two interpretations might be combined.

Cautionary Advice for Analyzing Secondary Sources

- The secondary sources in this book are excerpts from longer books or articles. The selections are meant to provide a representative view of the authors' main interpretations and perspectives on the subject. Nevertheless, these excerpts do not show the broad sweep of evidence from which the authors draw their conclusions.
- No excerpt can provide a full appreciation of how historians gather evidence and present and defend their interpretations in a reliable manner. Only a more extensive reading of the secondary source can provide sufficient evidence for judging whether the author has presented a convincing account.
- As with primary sources, secondary sources have biases. Think of biases as particular points of view, and try to figure out how they influence the historical interpretation and the accounts of an event or development.
- Secondary sources often conflict with or contradict each other. Do not dismiss an account that does not fit with your perspective; rather, explain why you are giving it more or less weight or how you are modifying your interpretation to conform to all the arguments made by the authors of the secondary sources.
- Secondary sources reflect the period in which they are written or produced and must be evaluated within the historical time frame from which they originate. This doesn't mean that a newer book or article is more accurate than an older one. Interpretations may differ because new facts have been uncovered, but they are just as likely to change according to the contemporary concerns and perspectives of the authors. Moreover, even in the same time period historians often disagree over controversial subjects due to different viewpoints on politics, religion, race, ethnicity, region, class, and gender.

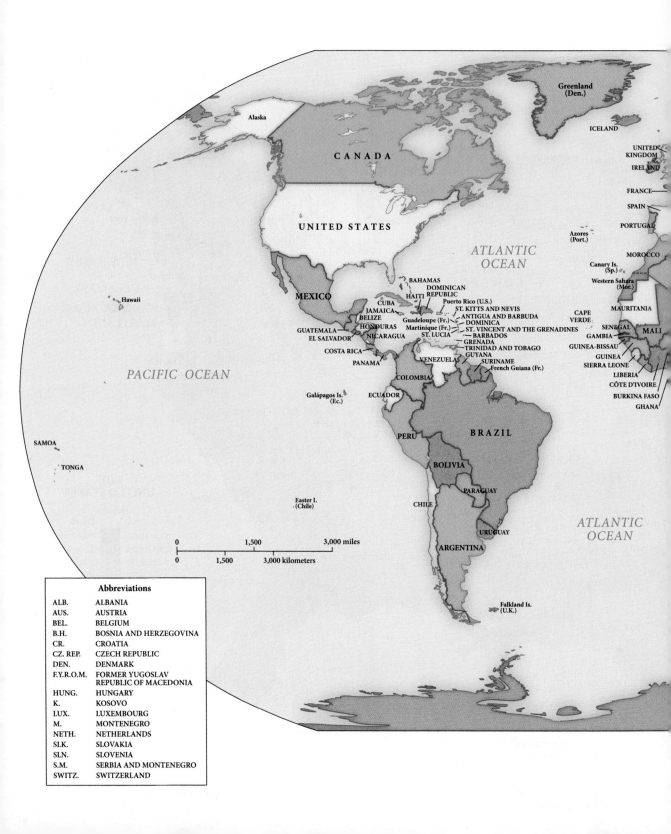

Alaska

Greenland
(Den.)

ICELAND

UNITED
KINGDOM

IRELAND

CANADA

FRANCE

SPAIN

PORTUGAL

ATLANTIC
OCEAN

Azores
(Port.)

MOROCCO

UNITED STATES

Canary Is.
(Sp.)

Western Sahara
(Mor.)

Hawaii

BAHAMAS
DOMINICAN
REPUBLIC
HAITI
Puerto Rico (U.S.)

MEXICO

CUBA

JAMAICA

ST. KITTS AND NEVIS
ANTIGUA AND BARBUDA
Guadeloupe (Fr.)
DOMINICA

MAURITANIA

BELIZE

Martinique (Fr.)
ST. VINCENT AND THE GRENADINES

CAPE
VERDE

GUATEMALA

HONDURAS

ST. LUCIA
BARBADOS

SENEGAL

MALI

EL SALVADOR

NICARAGUA

GRENADA
TRINIDAD AND TOBAGO

GAMBIA

COSTA RICA

GUYANA

GUINEA-BISSAU

PANAMA

VENEZUELA

SURINAME
French Guiana (Fr.)

GUINEA

SIERRA LEONE

COLOMBIA

LIBERIA

CÔTE D'IVOIRE

PACIFIC OCEAN

Galápagos Is.
(Ec.)

ECUADOR

BURKINA FASO

GHANA

PERU

BRAZIL

SAMOA

BOLIVIA

TONGA

Easter I.
(Chile)

PARAGUAY

CHILE

ATLANTIC
OCEAN

URUGUAY

0	1,500	3,000 miles

ARGENTINA

0	1,500	3,000 kilometers

Falkland Is.
(U.K.)

Abbreviations	
ALB.	ALBANIA
AUS.	AUSTRIA
BEL.	BELGIUM
B.H.	BOSNIA AND HERZEGOVINA
CR.	CROATIA
CZ. REP.	CZECH REPUBLIC
DEN.	DENMARK
F.Y.R.O.M.	FORMER YUGOSLAV REPUBLIC OF MACEDONIA
HUNG.	HUNGARY
K.	KOSOVO
LUX.	LUXEMBOURG
M.	MONTENEGRO
NETH.	NETHERLANDS
SLK.	SLOVAKIA
SLN.	SLOVENIA
S.M.	SERBIA AND MONTENEGRO
SWITZ.	SWITZERLAND

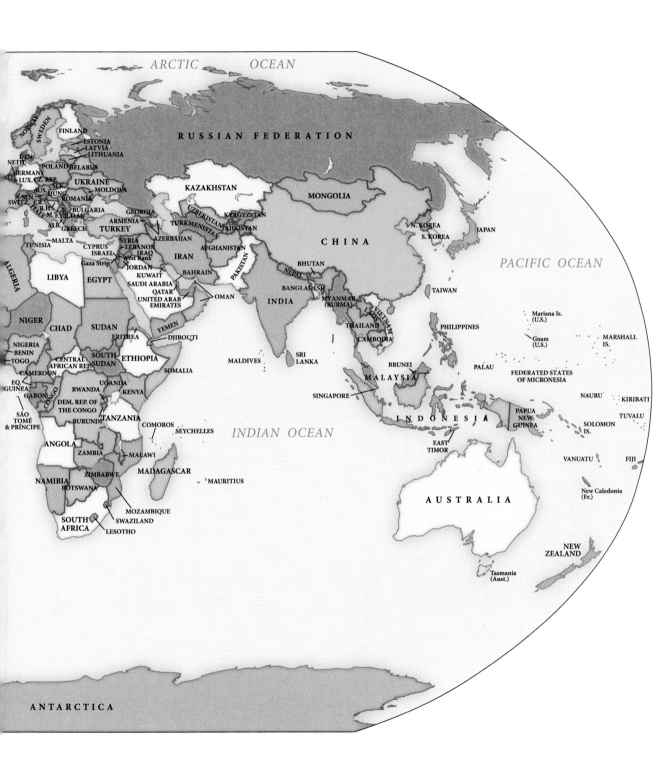

Exploring American Histories

A SURVEY WITH SOURCES

THIRD EDITION

Exploring American Histories

A SURVEY WITH SOURCES

THIRD EDITION

Nancy A. Hewitt

Rutgers University

Steven F. Lawson

Rutgers University

 bedford/st.martin's
Macmillan Learning

Boston | New York

To Mary and Charles Takacs, Florence and Hiram Hewitt, Sarah and Abraham Parker, Lena and Ben Lawson, who made our American Histories possible.

For Bedford/St. Martin's

Vice President, Editorial, Macmillan Learning Humanities: Edwin Hill

Publisher for History: Michael Rosenberg

Senior Executive Editor for History: William J. Lombardo

Executive Development Managers: Laura Arcari, Maura Shea

Senior Content Project Manager: Kerri A. Cardone

Editorial Assistant: Stephanie Sosa

Media Editor: Tess Fletcher

Senior Workflow Content Manager: Lisa McDowell

Senior Production Supervisor: Robert Cherry

Marketing Manager: Melissa Rodriguez

Copy Editor: Harold Johnson

Cartography: Mapping Specialists, Ltd.

Photo Researchers: Naomi Kornhauser, Christine Buese

Permissions Editor: Kalina Ingham

Art Director: Diana Blume

Text Design: Jerilyn Bockorick, Cenveo Publisher Services

Cover Design: William Boardman

Cover Art/Cover Photo: Evening on Crow Reservation, Montana (oil on canvas), Sharp, Joseph Henry (1859–1953) / Private Collection / Photo © Christie's Images / Bridgeman Images

Composition: Lumina Datamatics, Inc.

Printing and Binding: LSC Communications, Crawfordsville

Manufactured in the United States of America.

1   2   3   4   5   6   23   22   21   20   19   18

For information, write: Bedford/St. Martin's, 75 Arlington Street, Boston, MA 02116 (617-399-4000)

ISBN-13: 978-1-3191-0637-9 (Combined Edition)
ISBN-13: 978-1-3191-0640-9 (Volume 1)
ISBN-13: 978-1-3191-0642-3 (Volume 2)

Acknowledgments

Text acknowledgments and copyrights appear at the back of the book on pages C-1–C-2, which constitute an extension of the copyright page. Art acknowledgments and copyrights appear on the same page as the art selections they cover.

Why This Book This Way?

We are delighted to publish the third edition of *Exploring American Histories*. Users of the first two editions have told us our book gives them and their students opportunities to actively engage with both the narrative of American history and primary sources from that history in a way previously not possible. Our book offers a new kind of U.S. history survey text, one that makes a broad and diverse American history accessible to a new generation of students and instructors interested in a more engaged learning and teaching style. To accomplish this, we carefully weave an unprecedented number of written and visual primary sources, representing a rich assortment of American perspectives, into each chapter.

We know that students in the introductory survey course often need help in developing the ability to think critically about primary sources. Accordingly, in this third edition we have done even more to ensure students can move easily and systematically from working with single and paired sources (**Guided Analysis** and **Comparative Analysis**) to tackling a set of sources from varied perspectives (**Primary Source Project**). Students will also have the chance to evaluate how historians use primary sources to construct their own interpretations in our new Secondary Source Analysis. We have also strengthened our digital tools and instructor resources so faculty have more options for engaging students in active learning and assessing their progress, whether it be with traditional lecture classes, smaller discussion-oriented classes, "flipped" classrooms, or online courses.

In this edition, we add a **Secondary Source Analysis** that extends the building-block approach to working with sources by offering differing perspectives on important historical issues or events. For example, in chapter 13 historians debate "Why Union Soldiers Fought the Civil War" and in chapter 22 they debate "New Deal or Raw Deal?" With a brief introduction that frames the issue and prompts that ask students to think critically about the source and topic in context, students are invited into the discussion.

A Unique Format That Places Primary Sources at the Heart of the Story

Students learn history most effectively when they read a historical narrative in conjunction with primary sources. Sources bring the past to life in ways that narrative alone cannot, while the narrative offers the necessary framework, context, and chronology that sources by themselves do not typically provide. We believe that the most appealing entry to the past starts with individuals and how people in their daily lives connect to larger political, economic, cultural, and international developments. This approach makes history relevant and memorable.

Throughout our teaching experience, the available textbooks left us unsatisfied, compelling us to assign additional books, readers, and sources we found on the Web. However, these supplementary texts raised costs for our students, and too often students had difficulty seeing how the different readings related to one another. Simply remembering what materials to bring to class became unwieldy. So we decided to write our own book that would provide everything we would want to use in class, in one place. Many texts include some primary sources, but the balance between narrative (too much) and primary sources (too few) was off-kilter, so we carefully crafted the narrative to make room for us to include more primary sources and integrate them in creative ways that help students make the necessary connections and that spur them to think critically. *Exploring American Histories* is comprehensive in the essentials of American history, but with a carefully selected amount of detail that is more in tune with what instructors can realistically expect their students to comprehend. Thus, the most innovative aspect of *Exploring American Histories* is its format, which provides just the right balance between narrative and primary sources.

Abundant Primary Sources Woven Throughout the Narrative. In *Exploring American Histories*, we have selected an extensive and varied array of written and visual primary source material—more than 200 sources in all—and we have integrated them at key points as teaching moments within the text. We underscore the importance of primary sources by opening each chapter with a facsimile of some portion of a primary source that appears subsequently within the chapter. These **"Windows to the Past"** are designed to pique students' curiosity for working with sources.

To help students move seamlessly between narrative and sources, we embed **Explore** prompts at key junctures in the narrative, which describe what the sources illuminate. Such integration is designed to help students make a firm connection between the narrative of history and the evidence upon which it is built. These primary sources connect directly with discussions in the narrative and give a real sense of multiple viewpoints that make history come alive. By integrating sources and narrative, we help students engage divergent experiences from the past and give them the skills to think critically about sources and their interpretation. Because of our integrated design, every source flows from the narrative, and each source is clearly cross-referenced within the text so that students can easily incorporate them into their reading as well as reflect on our interpretation.

Progression in Primary Source Work. We continue to offer, with a slight modification, our unique building-blocks approach to the primary sources. Each chapter contains 7 to 8 substantial, featured primary sources—both written and visual—with a distinctive pedagogy aimed at helping students make connections between the sources and the text's major themes.

In every chapter we offer a progression of primary sources that moves from a single source with guiding annotations, to paired sources that lead students to understand each source better through comparison. Although we have eliminated the "Solo Analysis" feature (see below "Helping Students Work with Primary Sources"), each chapter still culminates with a "Primary Source Project" (previously called "Document Project")—a set of interrelated sources that addresses an important topic or theme related to the chapter. Instructors across the country confirm that with *Exploring American Histories* we have made teaching the breadth and diversity of American history and working with primary sources easier and more rewarding than ever.

Variety of Primary Sources and Perspectives. Because the heart of *Exploring American Histories* remains its primary sources, we carefully selected sources from which students can evaluate the text's interpretations and construct their own versions of history. These firsthand accounts include maps, engravings, paintings, illustrations, sermons, speeches, translations, letters, diaries, journals, memoirs, census reports, newspaper articles, political cartoons, laws, wills, court cases, petitions, advertisements, photographs, and blogs. In selecting sources, we have provided manifold perspectives on critical issues, including both well-known sources and those that are less familiar. In all time periods, some groups of Americans are far better represented in primary sources than others. Those who were wealthy, well educated, and politically powerful, produced and preserved many primary sources about their lives, and their voices are well represented in this textbook. But we have also provided sources by American Indians, enslaved Africans, free blacks, colonial women, rural residents, immigrants, working people, and young people. Moreover, the lives of those who left few primary sources of their own can often be illuminated by reading sources written by elites to see what information they yield, intentionally or unintentionally, about less well-documented groups. The questions that we ask about these sources are intended to help students read between the lines or see beyond the main image to uncover new meanings.

In weaving a wide variety of primary sources into the narrative, we challenge students to consider diverse viewpoints. For example, in chapter 5, students read contradictory testimony and examine an engraving to analyze the events that became known as the Boston Massacre. In chapter 12, they compare the views on the Fugitive Slave Law of a black abolitionist and the president of the United States. In chapter 18, students have to reconcile two very different views by a Chinese immigrant and a Supreme Court justice concerning the status of Chinese Americans in the late nineteenth century. In chapter 28, we ask readers to reconsider the depiction of the 1980s as a conservative decade in light of widespread protests challenging President Reagan's military build-up against the Soviet Union.

Flexibility for Assignments. We recognize from the generous feedback reviewers have offered us that instructors want flexibility in assigning primary sources. Our book easily allows faculty to assign all the primary sources in a chapter or a subset depending on the activities they have planned. With this range of choices, instructors are free to teach their courses just as they like and to tailor them to their students. Even if not featured on specific course assignments, these sources expose students to the multitude of voices from the past and hammer home the idea that history is not just a story passed on from one person to another but a story rooted in historical evidence. For instructors who value even more options, we again make available with the third edition a **companion primary source reader** that provides an additional primary source project for each chapter. This reader, *Thinking through Sources: Exploring American Histories,* can be packaged with the book at no additional cost to students.

Narrative Approach: Diverse Stories

Recent historical scholarship has transformed our vision of the past, most notably by dramatically increasing the range of people historians study, and thus deepening and complicating traditional understandings of change over time. The new research has focused particularly on gender, race, ethnicity, class, and region and historians have produced landmark work in women's history, African American history, American Indian history, Latino history, Asian American history, labor history, and histories of the West and the South.

Throughout the narrative we acknowledge recent scholarship by highlighting the theme of diversity and recognizing the American past as a series of interwoven stories made by a great variety of historical actors. We do this within a strong national framework that allows our readers to see how the numerous stories fit together and to understand why they matter. Our approach to diversity also allows us to balance the role of individual agency with larger structural forces as we push readers to consider the many forces that create historical change. Each chapter opens with **Comparing American Histories**, a pair of biographies that showcase individuals who experienced and influenced events in a particular period, and then returns to them throughout the chapter to strengthen the connections and highlight their place in the larger picture. These biographies cover both well-known Americans—such as Daniel Shays, Frederick Douglass, Andrew Carnegie, and Eleanor Roosevelt—and those who never gained fame or fortune—such as the Cherokee chief John Ross, activist Amy Post, labor organizer Luisa Moreno, and World War II internee Fred Korematsu. Introducing such a broad range of biographical subjects illuminates the many ways that individuals shaped and were shaped by historical events. This strategy also makes visible throughout the text the intersections where history from the top down meets history from the bottom up, and the relationships between social and political histories and economic, cultural, and diplomatic developments.

Helping Students Work with Primary Sources

In this third edition, we have strengthened the building-blocks approach by replacing the "Solo Analysis" with the new **Secondary Source Analysis** feature, discussed below. We have retained the following elements of the building-blocks approach so that students can increase their confidence and skills in analyzing primary sources:

- Each chapter begins with **Guided Analysis** of a textual or visual source, with a headnote offering historical context and questions in the margins to help students consider a specific phrase or feature and analyze the source as a whole. These targeted questions are intended to guide students in reading and understanding a primary source. A **Put It in Context** question prompts students to consider the source in terms of the broad themes of the chapter.

- Next, each chapter contains **Comparative Analysis**, a paired set of primary sources that show contrasting or complementary perspectives on a particular issue. This task marks a step up in difficulty from the previous Guided Analysis by asking students to analyze sources through their similarities and differences. These primary sources are introduced by a single headnote and are followed by **Interpret the Evidence** and **Put It in Context** questions that prompt students to analyze and compare the items and place them in a larger historical framework.

- Finally, a **Primary Source Project** at the end of every chapter provides the capstone of our integrated primary-sources approach. Each Primary Source Project brings together four or five sources focused on a critical issue central to that chapter. It is introduced by a brief overview and ends with **Interpret the Evidence** and **Put It in Context** questions that ask students to draw conclusions based on what they have learned in the chapter and read or seen in the sources.

We understand that the instructor's role is crucial in teaching students how to analyze primary-source materials and develop interpretations. Instructors can use the primary sources in many different ways—as in-class discussion prompts, for take-home writing assignments, and even as the basis for exam questions—and also in different combinations with primary sources throughout or across chapters being compared and contrasted with one another. The instructor's manual for *Exploring American Histories* provides a wealth of creative suggestions for using the primary source program effectively. As authors of the textbook, we have written a section, entitled **"Teaching American Histories with Primary Sources,"** which provides ideas and resources for both new and experienced faculty. It offers basic guidelines for teaching students how to analyze sources critically and suggests ways to integrate selected primary sources into lectures, discussions, small group projects, and writing assignments. We also suggest ideas for linking in-text primary sources with the opening biographies, maps, and illustrations in a particular chapter and for using the **Primary Source Projects** to help students understand the entangled histories of the diverse groups that comprise North America and the United States. (See the Versions and Supplements description on pages xxvii–xxxi for more information on all the available instructor resources.)

In the third edition, we have retained the handy guide to analyzing primary sources. This checklist at the front of the book gives students a quick and efficient lesson on how to read and analyze sources and what kinds of questions to ask in understanding them. We know that many students find primary sources intimidating. Eighteenth and nineteenth century sources contain spellings and language often difficult for modern students to comprehend. Yet, students also have difficulty with contemporary primary sources because in the digital age of Facebook and Twitter they are exposed to information in tiny fragments and without proper verification. Thus, the checklist will guide students in how to approach sources from any era and what to look for in exploring them. Because we are adding secondary sources to this edition, we have expanded the guide and renamed it, **Guide to Analyzing Primary and Secondary Sources,** to include an examination of secondary sources.

New Secondary Source Analysis

We are delighted to include a new feature in the third edition. Although our book highlights primary sources and their interrelationship with the narrative, reviewers persuaded us to add excerpts from notable secondary sources in each chapter. These selections furnish students with examples of how historical scholarship, built upon the analysis of primary sources, offer different interpretations of the same topic. They reinforce the idea that history is not fixed and changes over time. They also help students to get a glimpse into the debates among historians over important events and issues. To this end, the book contains a total of fifty-eight excerpts from books and journal articles. Each chapter provides two excerpts on a significant topic related to the overall coverage of the chapter. The selections differ in interpretation, approach, and the period in which they were written. Each secondary source feature is put into context by a brief introduction to the subject under discussion. These features are then followed by questions under the headings, **Examine the Sources** and **Put It in Context**, which ask students to compare the two secondary sources and how they reflect what they have read in the primary sources and in the narrative of the textbook. For example, for the early republic, chapter 7 provides selections on partisanship in the 1800 election by Eric Burns and John Ferling. Chapter 11, on the expansion of slavery, contrasts a view of enslaved family life offered by Robert Fogelman and Stanley Engerman with one by Deborah Gray White. With respect to the Progressive Era, chapter 19 offers divergent excerpts on reform in the South by C. Vann Woodward and Glenda Elizabeth Gilmore. Chapter 23 on World War II compares a selection on FDR and the Holocaust by David Wyman with that of Richard Breitman and Allan J. Lichtman.

Helping Students Understand the Narrative

We know that students need help making sense of their reading. As instructors, we have had students complain that they cannot figure out what's important in the textbooks we assign. For many of our students, especially those just out of high school, their college history survey textbook is likely the most difficult book they have ever encountered. Students come to the U.S. history survey with different levels of preparation. We understand the challenges our students face, so in addition to the extensive sources program, we have included the following pedagogical features designed to help students get the most from the narrative:

- **Learning Objectives** in the chapter openers prepare students to read the chapter with clear goals in mind.
- Clear **chapter overviews** and **conclusions** preview and summarize the chapters to help students identify main developments.
- **Review and Relate** questions help students focus on main themes and concepts presented in each major section of the chapter.
- **Key terms** in boldface highlight important content. All terms are explained in the narrative as well as defined in a glossary at the end of the book.
- A full-page **Chapter Review** lets students review key terms, important concepts, and notable events.

New Coverage and Updates to the Narrative

As a consequence of the constructive feedback we have received from many reviewers, in this third edition we present an even more rounded view of the history of the United States.

Enriched Diversity and Increased Focus on the West. We continue to pay significant attention to African Americans and women throughout the text and to expand coverage on the histories of American Indians, Hispanic and Latino Americans, and Asian Americans. We have not confined our discussion of these subjects to a few chapters, but we have placed them throughout the book and integrated them into the narrative and sources. For the third edition, in Volume 1, there is updated information on the peopling of the Americas in chapter 1 as well as greater coverage of native peoples' response to the Spanish conquest; additional attention to Indian-French encounters in chapters 3 and 4;

expanded discussion of the roles of native peoples in the late colonial and revolutionary eras in chapters 5 and 6 and in the early nineteenth century in chapter 11. In Volume 2, we have updated the struggles of American Indians in chapter 15, which covers Westward expansion. We have also added new material on Mexican Americans and immigration in the 1920s (chapter 21) and Native Americans in relationship to World War II (chapter 23) and the 1960s (chapter 26). In addition, the impact of the closing of the western frontier in the 1890s on U.S. imperialism is explored in chapter 20, and the political influence of the modern West is discussed in chapter 28 with respect to rising conservatism. With these additions, the American West appears in nearly every chapter.

Updated and Expanded Coverage. We have also absorbed the most recent scholarship to ensure that the most useful and accurate textbook is placed in the hands of students. In addition to more expansive attention to regional, racial, and ethnic diversity, we revised our approach to a number of other historical developments. Chapter 1 once again incorporates the most recent research on the settlement of the Americas while chapter 2 adds coverage of the experiences of a black indentured servant. Chapter 4 addresses transatlantic print culture and the complex ways that both Enlightenment thought and religious revivals shaped popular protests and politics, while chapter 5 discusses more fully the tensions among colonists over British versus American identities and loyalties. The sources of anti-authoritarian and anti-British ideas are explored in more detail in chapter 6 while the discussion of Romanticism as well as religious revitalization is expanded in chapter 8. The environment is given greater coverage in chapters 9 and 10. Chapter 10 also adds new material on the market revolution and its effects on middle-class and working-class families as well as a new Guided Analysis based on the 1850 federal census. Chapter 16 on industrial America shows how the growth of large-scale business organizations fostered the expansion of a managerial class as well as the creation of new middle-class clerical jobs for both men and women. There is new material in chapter 23 on the role played

by female codebreakers during World War II as well as on the innovative military strategy of "island-hopping "in the Pacific theater. The brutal treatment of Allied prisoners of war by the Japanese military also has been added to this chapter. One story rarely told appears in chapter 25 on the 1950s. The courageous efforts of an African American family to integrate suburban Levittown, Pennsylvania, are described and placed in the context of racial conflicts in the North. Likewise, chapter 26 on the 1960s makes an often overlooked connection between the moderate Republican President Dwight Eisenhower and the young radicals of the Students for a Democratic Society in challenging the military-industrial complex.

New Maps and Visuals. We have placed additional maps throughout the text to give students even more opportunity to learn how to read and think about these important historical tools. In Volume 1, we have added maps on the West Indies and Carolina in the Seventeenth Century (chapter 2), Religious Diversity in 1750 (chapter 4), and the Underground Railroad (chapter 10). In Volume 2, we have added maps on the Great Railroad Strike of 1877 (chapter 17), the immigrant population as of 1910 (chapter 18), the location of national parks during the Progressive era (chapter 19), European alliances during World War I (chapter 20), the shift from rural to urban population in the 1920s (chapter 21), the Dust Bowl during the Great Depression (chapter 22), and conflict between the U.S. and Cuba in the early 1960s (chapter 26). We have also changed about one-quarter of the illustrations accompanying the text from the previous edition.

Modification to Learning Objectives and Primary Source Project Questions. We have reviewed the **Learning Objectives** for each chapter in order to strengthen them. In doing so, we have focused more on stimulating student thinking about the key issues around which each chapter is organized. We are attempting to get students to practice some of the skills used by historians: description, identification, explanation, analysis, and evaluation. We have also added a key central question located at the beginning of each **Primary Source Project** to provide a framework for approaching the project. In addition, to enhance analytic and comparative skills we have reformulated some of the **Interpret the Evidence** and **Put it in Context** questions that follow the Primary Source Projects.

Adjustments to Chapter Organization and Focus. Based on reviewers' comments, we also reframed and re-organized several chapters. In Volume 1, chapters 10 and 11 have been flipped. Students are now introduced to the market revolution and social movements, including abolition, in the North in chapter 10, (Social and Cultural Ferment in the North, 1820–1850). Chapter 11 (Slavery Expands South and West) then focuses on the expansion of slavery and its effects on regional development, the national economy and politics, and the daily lives of southern blacks and whites. Chapters 27 (The Swing toward Conservatism, 1968–1980) and 28 (The Triumph of Conservatism, the End of the Cold War, and the Rise of the New World Order, 1980–1992) have been reorganized along chronological lines to reduce the overlap in time periods that previously existed. Chapter 27 now traces domestic and foreign affairs primarily during the 1970s. In reorganizing this chapter, we have replaced the opening **Comparing American Histories** biography of Anita Hill, who gained public attention in the 1980s, with that of Louise Day Hicks, the Boston antibusing leader who reached national prominence in the 1970s. We have rearranged chapter 28 to cover domestic and global events through the 1980s. In this way, we are offering students a sharper understanding of the interplay of events inside the U.S. with those on the world stage.

The final chapter of a history textbook is necessarily and continuously evolving, and for this edition we have added material on the extremely divisive 2016 presidential election and Donald Trump's victory over Hillary Clinton. This chapter now covers President Trump's first year in office and his efforts to roll back the accomplishments of his predecessor, Barack Obama. The new material traces the rise of the reactionary alt-right and its appeal, to racial, ethnic, and gender grievances as well as the manipulation of digital social media in shaping the results. This updated chapter further explores revelations about Russian efforts to interfere in the election and U.S. responses to them. Also covered is the rise of the #MeToo movement consisting of an extraordinary number of women coming forward to voice widespread experience with sexual harassment in the workplace and elsewhere. While revelations during the campaign of Trump's inappropriate sexual behavior in the past stunned some Americans, it was testimonies about similar behavior among movie moguls, actors, television personalities, and other politicians that sparked a social movement. These events are still unfolding and the new additions are intended to provide students a framework for understanding these controversial issues as they evolve.

Promoting Active Learning in the Digital Age

As all instructors know, students can often "do the assignment" or read the required chapter and yet have little understanding of it when they come to class. The problem, frequently, is passive studying—a quick once-over, perhaps some highlighting of the text—but little sustained involvement with the material. A central pedagogical problem in all teaching is how to encourage more active, engaged styles of learning. We want to enable students to manipulate the information of the book, using its ideas and data to answer questions, to make comparisons, to draw conclusions, to criticize assumptions, and to infer implications that are not explicitly disclosed in the text itself.

Exploring American Histories seeks to promote active learning in various ways. Most obviously, the primary and secondary sources in the companion reader ***Thinking through Sources for Exploring American Histories*** (also available on LaunchPad) invite students to engage actively with documents and images alike, assisted by abundant questions to guide that engagement.

In addition, whenever an instructor assigns the **LaunchPad e-Book** (which can be bundled for free with the print book), students have at their disposal all the resources of the comprehensive print text (*Exploring American Histories: A Survey with Sources*), including its special features and its primary and secondary sources. But they also gain access to **LearningCurve**, an online adaptive learning tool that helps students actively rehearse what they have read and foster a deeper understanding and retention of the material. With this adaptive quizzing, students accumulate points toward a target score as they go, giving the interaction a game-like feel. Feedback for incorrect responses explains why the answer is incorrect and directs students back to the text to review before they attempt to answer the question again. The end result is a better understanding of the key elements of the text. Instructors who actively assign LearningCurve, report that their students come to class prepared for discussion and their students enjoy using it. In addition, LearningCurve's reporting feature allows instructors to quickly diagnose which concepts students are struggling with so they can adjust lectures and activities accordingly.

Further opportunities for active learning are available with the special online activities accompanying *Thinking through Sources for Exploring American Histories* in **LaunchPad**. When required by instructors, the wrap-around pedagogy that accompanies the sources virtually ensures active learning. These activities supply a distinctive and sophisticated pedagogy of self-grading exercises that help students not only understand the sources but also think critically about them. More specifically, a short **quiz after each source** offers students the opportunity to check their understanding of materials that often derive from quite distant times and places. Some questions focus on audience, purpose, point of view, limitations, or context, while others challenge students to draw conclusions about the source or to compare one source with another. And a **Draw Conclusions from the Evidence activity** challenges students to assess whether a specific piece of evidence drawn from the sources supports or challenges a stated conclusion. Collectively these assignments create an active learning environment where reading with a purpose is reinforced by immediate feedback and support. This feedback for

each rejoinder creates an active learning environment where students are rewarded for reaching the correct answer through their own process of investigation. LaunchPad is thus a rich asset for instructors who want to support students in all settings, from traditional lectures to "flipped" classrooms.

For instructors who need a mobile and accessible option for delivering adaptive quizzing with the narrative alone, Macmillan's new **Achieve Read & Practice** e-Book platform offers an exceptionally easy-to-use and affordable option. This simple product pairs the Value Edition with the power of LearningCurve's quizzing, all in a format that students can use wherever they go. Available for the first time with this edition, Achieve Read & Practice's interactive e-Book, adaptive quizzing, and gradebook are built with an intuitive interface that can be read on mobile devices and are fully accessible and available at an affordable price.

To learn more about the benefits of LearningCurve, LaunchPad, Achieve Read & Practice, and the different versions to package with these digital tools, see the Versions and Supplements section on page xxvii.

Acknowledgments

We wish to thank the talented scholars and teachers who were kind enough to give their time and knowledge to help us with our revision, as well as those who provided advice in preparation for previous editions. Historians who provided special insight for the third edition include the following:

Rob Alderson, *Perimeter College at Georgia State University*
Chad Gregory, *Tri-County Technical College*
Larry Grubbs, *Georgia State University*
Don Knox, *Wayland Baptist University*
Leslie Leighton, *Georgia State University*
Amani Marshall, *Georgia State University*
Ricky Moser, *Kilgore College*
David Soll, *University of Wisconsin, Eau Claire*
Ramon Veloso, *Palomar College*

We are also grateful to those who provided ideas and suggestions for previous editions:

Benjamin Allen, *South Texas College*
Daniel Allen, *Trinity Valley Community College*
Leann Almquist, *Middle Georgia State University*
Christine Anderson, *Xavier University*
Uzoamaka Melissa C. Anyiwo, *Curry College*
Rebecca Arnfeld, *California State University, Sacramento*
David Arnold, *Columbia Basin College*
Brian Alnutt, *Northampton Community College*
Anthony A. Ball, *Housatonic Community College*
Terry A. Barnhart, *Eastern Illinois University*
John Belohlavek, *University of South Florida*
Edwin Benson, *North Harford High School*
Paul Berk, *Christian Brothers University*
Deborah L. Blackwell, *Texas A&M International University*
Jeff Bloodworth, *Gannon University*
Carl Bon Tempo, *University at Albany–SUNY*
Thomas Born, *Blinn College*
Margaret Bramlett, *St. Andrews Episcopal High School*
Martha Jane Brazy, *University of South Alabama*
Lauren K. Bristow, *Collin College*
Tsekani Browne, *Duquesne University*
Jon L. Brudvig, *Dickinson State University*
Richard Buckelew, *Bethune-Cookman University*
Timothy Buckner, *Troy University*
Dave Bush, *Shasta College*
Monica Butler, *Seminole State College of Florida*
Barbara Calluori, *Montclair State University*

Julia Schiavone Camacho, *The University of Texas at El Paso*
Jacqueline Campbell, *Francis Marion University*
Amy Canfield, *Lewis-Clark State College*
Michael Cangemi, *Binghamton University*
Roger Carpenter, *University of Louisiana, Monroe*
Dominic Carrillo, *Grossmont College*
Mark R. Cheathem, *Cumberland University*
Keith Chu, *Bergen Community College*
Laurel A. Clark, *University of Hartford*
Myles L. Clowers, *San Diego City College*
Remalian Cocar, *Georgia Gwinnett College*
Lori Coleman, *Tunxis Community College*
Wilbert E. Corprew, *SUNY Broome*
Hamilton Cravens, *Iowa State University*
Audrey Crawford, *Houston Community College*
Vanessa Crispin-Peralta, *Moorpark College*
John Crum, *University of Delaware*
David Cullen, *Collin College*
Gregory K. Culver, *Austin Peay State University*
Alex G. Cummins, *St. Johns River State College*
Robert Chris Davis, *Lone Star College – Kingwood*
Susanne Deberry-Cole, *Morgan State University*
Julian J. DelGaudio, *Long Beach City College*
Patricia Norred Derr, *Kutztown University*
Thomas Devine *California State University, Northridge*
Tom Dicke, *Missouri State University*
Andy Digh, *Mercer University*
Gary Donato, *Massachusetts Bay Community College*
John Donoghue, *Loyola University Chicago*
Timothy Draper, *Waubonsee Community College*

David Dzurec, *University of Scranton*

Susan Eckelmann, *University of Tennessee, Chattanooga*

George Edgar, *Modesto Junior College*

Keith Edgerton, *Montana State University Billings*

Taulby Edmondson, *Virginia Tech*

Ashton Ellett, *University of Georgia*

Blake Ellis, *Lone Star College*

Christine Erickson, *Indiana University–Purdue University Fort Wayne*

Keona K. Ervin, *University of Missouri*

Todd Estes, *Oakland University*

Gabrielle Everett, *Jefferson College*

Julie Fairchild, *Sinclair Community College*

Robert Glen Findley, *Odessa College*

Randy Finley, *Georgia Perimeter College*

Tiffany Fink, *Hardin-Simmons University*

Kirsten Fischer, *University of Minnesota*

Michelle Fishman-Cross, *College of Staten Island*

Roger Flynn, *TriCounty Technical College*

Jeffrey Forret, *Lamar University*

Jonathan Foster, *Great Basin College*

Kristen Foster, *Marquette University*

Sarah Franklin, *University of North Alabama*

Michael Frawley, *University of Texas of the Permian Basin*

Susan Freeman, *Western Michigan University*

Nancy Gabin, *Purdue University*

Kevin Gannon, *Grand View University*

Benton Gates, *Indiana University–Purdue University Fort Wayne*

Bruce Geelhoed, *Ball State University*

Mark Gelfand, *Boston College*

Robert Genter, *Nassau Community College*

Jason George, *The Bryn Mawr School*

Judith A. Giesberg, *Villanova University*

Dana Goodrich, *Northwest Vista College*

Sherry Ann Gray, *Mid-South Community College*

Patrick Griffin, *University of Notre Dame*

Audrey Grounds, *University of South Florida*

Abbie Grubb, *San Jacinto College - South*

Kenneth Grubb, *Wharton County Junior College*

Aaron Gulyas, *Mott Community College*

Scott Gurman, *Northern Illinois University*

Melanie Gustafson, *University of Vermont*

Ashley Haines, *Mt. San Antonio College*

Dennis Halpin, *Virginia Tech*

Hunter Hampton, *University of Missouri*

Tona Hangen, *Worcester State University*

Brian Hart, *Del Mar College*

Paul Hart, *Texas State University*

Paul Harvey, *University of Colorado Colorado Springs*

Stephen Henderson, *William Penn University*

Kimberly Hernandez, *University of Wisconsin-Milwaukee*

Lacey A. Holley-McCann, *Columbia State Community College*

Woody Holton, *University of Richmond*

Vilja Hulden, *University of Arizona*

Creed Hyatt, *Lehigh Carbon Community College*

Colette A. Hyman, *Winona State University*

Brenda Jackson-Abernathy, *Belmont University*

Joe Jaynes, *Collin College*

Troy R. Johnson, *California State University, Long Beach*

Shelli Jordan-Zirkle, *Shoreline Community College*

Stephen Katz, *Community College of Philadelphia*

Lesley Kauffman, *San Jacinto College-Central*

Jennifer Kelly, *The University of Texas at Austin*

Kelly Kennington, *Auburn University*

Andrew E. Kersten, *University of Wisconsin–Green Bay*

Tina M. Kibbe, *Lamar University*

Melanie Kiechle, *Virginia Tech*

Janilyn M. Kocher, *Richland Community College*
Max Krochmal, *Duke University*
Peggy Lambert, *Lone Star College*
Stephanie Lamphere, *Sierra College*
Jennifer R. Lang, *Delgado Community College*
Todd Laugen, *Metropolitan State University of Denver*
Carolyn J. Lawes, *Old Dominion University*
John Leazer, *Carthage College*
Marianne Leeper, *Trinity Valley Community College*
Alan Lehmann, *Blinn College – Brenham*
John S. Leiby, *Paradise Valley Community College*
Mitchell Lerner, *The Ohio State University*
Carole N. Lester, *University of Texas at Dallas*
Amanda Littauer, *Northern Illinois University*
Matthew Loayza, *Minnesota State University, Mankato*
Gabriel J. Loiacono, *University of Wisconsin Oshkosh*
Carmen Lopez, *Miami Dade College*
Robert Lyle, *University of North Georgia*
John F. Lyons, *Joliet Junior College*
Lorie Maltby, *Henderson Community College*
Christopher Manning, *Loyola University Chicago*
Amani Marshall, *Georgia State University*
Phil Martin, *San Jacinto College - South*
David Mason, *Georgia Gwinnett College*
Marty D. Matthews, *North Carolina State University*
Eric Mayer, *Victor Valley College*
Suzanne K. McCormack, *Community College of Rhode Island*
David McDaniel, *Marquette University*
J. Kent McGaughy, *Houston Community College, Northwest*
Alan McPherson, *Howard University*
Sarah Hand Meacham, *Virginia Commonwealth University*
Jason Mead, *Johnson University*
Brian Craig Miller, *Emporia State University*
Robert Miller, *California State University, San Marcos*

Brett Mizelle, *California State University, Long Beach*
Mark Moser, *The University of North Carolina at Greensboro*
Ricky Moser, *Kilgore College*
Jennifer Murray, *Coastal Carolina University*
Peter C. Murray, *Methodist University*
Steven E. Nash, *East Tennessee State University*
Chris Newman, *Elgin Community College*
David Noon, *University of Alaska Southeast*
Richard H. Owens, *West Liberty University*
Alison Parker, *College at Brockport, SUNY*
Craig Pascoe, *Georgia College*
David J. Peavler, *Towson University*
Linda Pelon, *McLennan Community College*
Laura A. Perry, *University of Memphis*
Wesley Phelps, *University of St. Thomas*
Jamie Pietruska, *Rutgers University*
Sandra Piseno, *Clayton State University*
Merline Pitre, *Texas Southern University*
Eunice G. Pollack, *University of North Texas*
Kimberly Porter, *University of North Dakota*
Cynthia Prescott, *University of North Dakota*
Gene Preuss, *University of Houston*
Sandra Pryor, *Old Dominion University*
Rhonda Ragsdale, *Lone Star College*
Ray Rast, *Gonzaga University*
Michaela Reaves, *California Lutheran University*
Peggy Renner, *Glendale Community College*
Steven D. Reschly, *Truman State University*
Barney J. Rickman, *Valdosta State University*
Pamela Riney-Kehrberg, *Iowa State University*
Paul Ringel, *High Point University*
Jason Ripper, *Everett Community College*
Timothy Roberts, *Western Illinois University*
Glenn Robins, *Georgia Southwestern State University*
Alicia E. Rodriquez, *California State University, Bakersfield*
Mark Roehrs, *Lincoln Land Community College*

Patricia Roessner, *Marple Newtown High School*

John G. Roush, *St. Petersburg College*

James Russell, *St. Thomas Aquinas College*

Eric Schlereth, *The University of Texas at Dallas*

Gregory L. Schneider, *Emporia State University*

Debra Schultz, *Kingsborough Community College, CUNY*

Ronald Schultz, *University of Wyoming*

Stanley K. Schultz, *University of Wisconsin–Madison*

Scott Seagle, *University of Tennessee at Chattanooga*

Donald Seals, *Kilgore College*

Sharon Shackelford, *Erie Community College*

Donald R. Shaffer, *American Public University System*

Gregory Shealy, *Saint John's River State College*

Cathy Hoult Shewring, *Montgomery County Community College*

Jill Silos-Rooney, *Massachusetts Bay Community College*

David J. Silverman, *The George Washington University*

Beth Slutsky, *California State University, Sacramento*

Andrea Smalley, *Northern Illinois University*

Karen Smith, *Emporia State University*

Molly Smith, *Friends School of Baltimore*

Suzie Smith, *Trinity Valley Community College*

Troy Smith, *Tennessee Tech University*

David L. Snead, *Liberty University*

David Snyder, *Delaware Valley College*

David Soll, *University of Wisconsin - Eau Claire*

Gary Sprayberry, *Columbus State University*

Jodie Steeley, *Merced College*

Bethany Stollar, *Tennessee State University*

Bryan E. Stone, *Del Mar College*

Jason Stratton, *Bakersfield College*

Emily Straus, *SUNY Fredonia*

Kristen Streater, *Collin College*

Joseph Stromberg, *San Jacinto College - Central*

Jean Stuntz, *West Texas A&M University*

Sarah Swedberg, *Colorado Mesa University*

Nikki M. Taylor, *University of Cincinnati*

Heather Ann Thompson, *Temple University*

Timothy Thurber, *Virginia Commonwealth University*

Christopher Thrasher, *Calhoun Community College*

T. J. Tomlin, *University of Northern Colorado*

Jeffrey Trask, *Georgia State University*

Laura Trauth, *Community College of Baltimore County–Essex*

Russell M. Tremayne, *College of Southern Idaho*

Laura Tuennerman-Kaplan, *California University of Pennsylvania*

Linda Upham-Bornstein, *Plymouth State University*

Mark VanDriel, *University of South Carolina*

Kevin Vanzant, *Tennessee State University*

Ramon C. Veloso, *Palomar College*

Morgan Veraluz, *Tennessee State University*

Vincent Vinikas, *The University of Arkansas at Little Rock*

David Voelker, *University of Wisconsin–Green Bay*

Melissa Walker, *Converse College*

William Wantland, *Mount Vernon Nazarene University*

Ed Wehrle, *Eastern Illinois University*

David Weiland, *Collin College*

Eddie Weller, *San Jacinto College-South*

Shane West, *Lone Star College-Greenspoint Center*

Geoffrey West, *San Diego Mesa College*

Kenneth B. White, *Modesto Junior College*

Matt White, *Paris Junior College*

Anne Will, *Skagit Valley College*

John P. Williams, *Collin College*

Zachery R. Williams, *University of Akron*

Gregory Wilson, *University of Akron*

Kurt Windisch, *University of Georgia*

Jonathan Wlasiuk, *The Ohio State University*

Timothy Wright *Shoreline Community College*

Timothy L. Wood, *Southwest Baptist University*

Nancy Beck Young, *University of Houston*

Maria Cristina Zaccarini, *Adelphi University*

Nancy Zens, *Central Oregon Community College*

Jean Hansen Zuckweiler, *University of Northern Colorado*

We especially want to thank Julia Bowes, our research assistant for the third edition, who left no library shelf untouched in her quest to locate the secondary sources that we have excerpted. We also appreciate the help the following scholars, archivists, and students gave us in providing the information we needed at critical points in the writing of this text: Lori Birrell, Leslie Brown, Andrew Buchanan, Gillian Carroll, Susan J. Carroll, Jacqueline Castledine, Derek Chang, Paul Clemens, Dorothy Sue Cobble, Jane Coleman-Harbison, Alison Cronk, Kayo Denda, Elisabeth Eittreim, David Foglesong, Phyllis Hunter, Tera Hunter, Molly Inabinett, Kenneth Kvamme, William Link, James Livingston, Julia Livingston, Justin Lorts, Melissa Mead, Gilda Morales, Andrew Preston, Vicki L. Ruiz, Julia Sandy-Bailey, Susan Schrepfer, Bonnie Smith, Melissa Stein, Margaret Sumner, Camilla Townsend, Jessica Unger, Anne Valk, and Melinda Wallington.

We want to thank Rob Heinrich and Julia Sandy for compiling the primary source projects for the original companion source reader, *Thinking through Sources: Exploring American Histories.* Stephanie Sosa at Bedford/St. Martin's deftly orchestrated the development of the new edition of the reader collaborating with us to locate interesting and varied sources that aptly fit with the themes of the third edition, and we owe her our thanks.

We would particularly like to applaud the many hardworking and creative people at Bedford/St. Martin's who guided us through the labyrinthine process of writing this third edition. No one was more important to us than Laura Arcari and Maura Shea, our editors. We could not have had a better team than Edwin Hill, Michael Rosenberg, William Lombardo, Stephanie Sosa, Tess Fletcher, Kerri Cardone, Melissa Rodriguez, Christine Buese, and Kalina Ingham. The team at Bedford/St. Martin's also enlisted help from Naomi Kornhauser and Elaine Kosta, for which we are grateful. We will always remain thankful to Sara Wise and Patricia Rossi for their advice about and enthusiasm for a primary source-based American History textbook and to Joan Feinberg, who had the vision that guided us through every page of this book. Finally, we would like to express our gratitude to our friends and family who have encouraged us through all three editions and have even read the book without it being assigned.

Nancy A. Hewitt and Steven F. Lawson

Adopters of *Exploring American Histories* and their students have access to abundant print and digital resources and tools, the acclaimed Bedford Series in History and Culture volumes, and much more. The LaunchPad course space for *Exploring American Histories* provides access to the narrative as well as a wealth of primary sources and other features, along with assignment and assessment opportunities at the ready. Achieve Read & Practice supplies adaptive quizzing and our mobile, accessible Value Edition e-Book, in one easy-to-use, affordable product. See below for more information, visit the book's catalog site at macmillanlearning.com, or contact your local Bedford/St. Martin's sales representative.

Get the Right Version for Your Class

To accommodate different course lengths and course budgets, *Exploring American Histories* is available in several different versions and formats to best suit your course needs. The comprehensive *Exploring American Histories* includes a full-color art program and a robust set of features. The Value Edition offers a trade-sized two-color option with the full narrative and selected art and maps (without the primary documents) at a steep discount. The Value Edition is also offered at the lowest price point in loose-leaf format, and both versions of the book are available as e-Books. For the best value of all, package a new print book with LaunchPad or Achieve Read & Practice at no additional charge to get the best each format offers. LaunchPad users get a print version for easy portability with an interactive e-Book for the full-feature text and course space, along with LearningCurve and loads of additional assignment and assessment options. Achieve Read & Practice users get a print version with a mobile, interactive Value Edition e-Book plus LearningCurve adaptive

quizzing in one exceptionally affordable, easy-to-use product.

- **Combined Volume** (Chapters 1–29): available in paperback, Value Edition, loose-leaf, and e-Book formats and in LaunchPad and Achieve Read & Practice.
- **Volume 1: To 1877** (Chapters 1–14): available in paperback, Value Edition, loose-leaf, and e-Book formats and in LaunchPad and Achieve Read & Practice.
- **Volume 2: Since 1865** (Chapters 14–29): available in paperback, Value Edition, loose-leaf, and e-Book formats and in LaunchPad and Achieve Read & Practice.

As noted below, any of these volumes can be packaged with additional titles for a discount. To get ISBNs for discount packages, visit macmillanlearning.com for the comprehensive version or Value Edition or contact your Bedford/St. Martin's representative.

LaunchPad Assign LaunchPad— an Assessment-Ready Interactive e-Book and Course Space

Available for discount purchase on its own or for packaging with new books at no additional charge, LaunchPad is a breakthrough solution for history courses. Intuitive and easy-to-use for students and instructors alike, LaunchPad is ready to use as is, and can be edited, customized with your own material, and assigned quickly. *LaunchPad for Exploring American Histories* includes Bedford/St. Martin's high-quality content all in one place, including the full interactive e-Book and the companion reader *Thinking through Sources for Exploring American Histories*, plus LearningCurve adaptive quizzing, guided reading activities designed to help students read actively for key concepts, auto-graded quizzes for each primary source, Thinking through Sources activities that use the document projects in the companion source reader to prompt students to build arguments and practice historical reasoning, and chapter summative quizzes. Through a wealth of formative and summative assessments, including the adaptive learning program of LearningCurve (see the full description ahead), students gain confidence and get into their reading before class. These features, plus additional primary source documents, video sources and tools for making video assignments, map activities, flashcards, and customizable test banks, make LaunchPad an invaluable asset for any instructor.

LaunchPad easily integrates with course management systems, and with fast ways to build assignments, rearrange chapters, and add new pages, sections, or links, it lets teachers build the courses they want to teach and hold students accountable. For more information, visit **launchpadworks.com** or to arrange a demo, contact us at **historymktg@macmillan.com**.

☑ Assign LearningCurve So Your Students Come to Class Prepared

Students using LaunchPad or Achieve Read & Practice receive access to LearningCurve for *Exploring American Histories*. Assigning LearningCurve in place of reading quizzes is easy for instructors, and the reporting features help instructors track overall class trends and spot topics that are giving students trouble so they can adjust their lectures and class activities. This online learning tool is popular with students because it was designed to help them rehearse content at their own pace in a nonthreatening, game-like environment. The feedback for wrong answers provides instructional coaching and sends students back to the book for review. Students answer as many questions as necessary to reach a target score, with repeated chances to revisit material they haven't mastered. When LearningCurve is assigned, students come to class better prepared.

ⓜ Achieve READ & PRACTICE Assign Achieve Read & Practice So Your Students Can Read and Study Wherever They Go

Available for discount purchase on its own or for packaging with new books at no additional charge, Achieve Read & Practice is Bedford/St. Martin's most affordable digital solution for history courses. Intuitive and easy-to-use for students and instructors alike, Achieve Read & Practice is ready to use as is, and can be assigned quickly. *Achieve Read & Practice for Exploring American Histories* includes the Value Edition interactive e-Book, LearningCurve formative quizzing, assignment tools, and a gradebook. All this is built with an intuitive interface that can be read on mobile devices, and is fully accessible and available at a discounted price so anyone can use it. Instructors can set due dates for reading assignments and LearningCurve quizzes in just a few clicks, making it a simple and affordable way to engage students with the narrative and hold students accountable for course reading so they will come to class better prepared. For more information, visit **macmillanlearning.com/ReadandPractice**.

iClicker, Active Learning Simplified

iClicker offers simple, flexible tools to help you give students a voice and facilitate active learning in the classroom. Students can participate with the devices they already bring to class using our iClicker Reef mobile apps (which work with smart phones, tablets, or laptops) or iClicker remotes. We've now integrated iClicker with Macmillan's LaunchPad to make it easier than ever to synchronize grades and promote engagement—both in and out of class. iClicker Reef access cards can also be packaged with LaunchPad or your textbook at a significant savings for your students. To learn more, talk to your Macmillan Learning representative or visit us at **www.iclicker.com**.

Take Advantage of Instructor Resources

Bedford/St. Martin's has developed a rich array of teaching resources for this book and for this course. They range from lecture and presentation materials and assessment tools to course management options. Most can be found in LaunchPad or can be downloaded or ordered from the Instructor's Resources tab of the book's catalog site at macmillanlearning.com.

Bedford Coursepack for Blackboard, Canvas, Brightspace by D2L, or Moodle. We can help you integrate our rich content into your course management system. Registered instructors can download coursepacks that include our popular free resources and book-specific content for *Exploring American Histories*. Visit macmillanlearning.com to find your version or download your coursepack.

Instructor's Resource Manual. The instructor's manual offers both experienced and first-time instructors tools for presenting textbook material in engaging ways. It includes content learning objectives, annotated chapter outlines, and strategies for teaching with the textbook, plus suggestions on how to get the most out of LearningCurve, and a survival guide for first-time teaching assistants. In addition, a guide for teaching with documents, written by the textbook authors, provides detailed advice for getting the most out of the book's sources in the classroom.

Guide to Changing Editions. Designed to facilitate an instructor's transition from the previous edition of *Exploring American Histories* to this new edition, this guide presents an overview of major changes as well as of changes in each chapter.

Online Test Bank. The test bank includes a mix of fresh, carefully crafted multiple-choice, matching, short-answer, and essay questions for each chapter. Many of the multiple-choice questions feature a map, an image, or a primary-source excerpt as the prompt. All questions appear in Microsoft Word format an in easy-to-use test bank software that allows instructors to add, edit, re-sequence, filter by question type or learning objective, and print questions and answers. Instructors can also export questions into a variety of course management systems.

The Bedford Lecture Kit: **Lecture Outlines, Maps, and Images.** Look good and save time with *The Bedford Lecture Kit*. These presentation materials include fully customizable multimedia presentations built around chapter outlines that are embedded with maps, figures, and images from the textbook and are supplemented by more detailed instructor notes on key points and concepts.

Print, Digital, and Custom Options for More Choice and Value

For information on free packages and discounts up to 50%, visit macmillanlearning.com, or contact your local Bedford/St. Martin's sales representative.

Thinking through Sources for Exploring American Histories, **Third Edition.** This companion reader provides an additional primary source project with four to five written and visual sources focused on a central topic to accompany each chapter of *Exploring American Histories*. To aid students in approaching and interpreting the sources, the project for each chapter contains an introduction, document headnotes, and questions for discussion. Available free when packaged with the print book and included in the LaunchPad e-Book. Also available on its own as a downloadable e-Book.

Bedford Tutorials for History. Designed to customize textbooks with resources relevant to individual courses, this collection of brief units, each 16 pages long and loaded with examples, guides students through basic skills such as using historical evidence effectively, working with primary sources, taking effective notes, avoiding plagiarism and citing sources, and more. Up to two tutorials can be added to a Bedford/St. Martin's history survey title at no additional charge, freeing you to spend your class time focusing on content and interpretation. For more information, visit macmillanlearning.com/historytutorials.

Bedford Document Collections. This source collection provides a flexible and affordable online repository of discovery-oriented primary-source projects ready to assign. Each curated project — written by a historian about a favorite topic — poses a historical question and guides students step by step through analysis of primary sources. Examples include What Caused the Civil War?; The California Gold Rush: A Trans-Pacific Phenomenon; and, War Stories: Black Soldiers and the Long Civil Rights Movement. For more information, visit macmillanlearning.com/bdc/ushistory/catalog. You can also select up to two document projects from the collection to add in print for free to customize your Bedford/St. Martin's textbook. Additional document projects can be added for a reasonable cost. For more information, visit macmillanlearning.com/custombdc/ushistory or contact your Bedford/St. Martin's representative.

Bedford Select for History. This custom option allows you to create the ideal textbook for your course with only the chapters you need. Starting from the Value Edition of *Exploring American Histories*, you can rearrange chapters, delete unnecessary chapters, select chapters of primary sources from *Thinking through Sources for Exploring American Histories* and add document projects from the Bedford Document Collections, or choose to improve your students' historical thinking skills with the Bedford Tutorials for History. In addition, you can add your own original content to create just the book you're looking for. With Bedford Select, students pay only for material that will be assigned in the course, and nothing more. Order your textbook every semester, or modify from one term to the next. It is easy to build your customized textbook, without compromising the quality and affordability you've come to expect from Bedford/St. Martin's.

The Bedford Series in History and Culture. More than 100 titles in this highly praised series combine first-rate scholarship, historical narrative, and important primary documents for undergraduate courses. Each book is brief, inexpensive, and focused on a specific topic or period. Recently published titles include: *The Chinese Exclusion Act and Angel Island: A Brief History with Documents*, by Judy Yung; *The Life of P.T. Barnum,*

Written by Himself, With Related Documents, edited with an introduction by Stephen Mihm; and *The California Gold Rush: A Brief History with Documents*, by Andrew C. Isenberg. For a complete list of titles, visit macmillanlearning.com. Package discounts are available.

Rand McNally Atlas of American History. This collection of more than eighty full-color maps illustrates key events and eras from early exploration, settlement, expansion, and immigration to U.S. involvement in wars abroad and on U.S. soil. Introductory pages for each section include a brief overview, timelines, graphs, and photos to quickly establish a historical context. Free when packaged.

The Bedford Glossary for U.S. History. This handy supplement for the survey course gives students historically contextualized definitions for hundreds of terms— from *abolitionism* to *zoot suit*—that they will encounter in lectures, reading, and exams. Free when packaged.

Trade Books. Titles published by sister companies Hill and Wang; Farrar, Straus and Giroux; Henry Holt and Company; St. Martin's Press; Picador; and Palgrave Macmillan are available at a 50% discount when packaged with Bedford/St. Martin's textbooks. For more information, visit macmillanlearning.com/tradeup.

A Pocket Guide to Writing in History. This portable and affordable reference tool by Mary Lynn Rampolla provides reading, writing, and research advice useful to students in all history courses. Concise yet comprehensive advice on approaching typical history assignments, developing critical reading skills, writing effective history papers, conducting research, using and documenting sources, and avoiding plagiarism—enhanced with practical tips and examples throughout—have made this slim reference a best-seller. Package discounts are available.

A Student's Guide to History. This complete guide to success in any history course provides the practical help students need to be successful. In addition to introducing students to the nature of the discipline, author Jules Benjamin teaches a wide range of skills from preparing for exams to approaching common writing assignments, and explains the research and documentation process with plentiful examples. Package discounts are available.

Going to the Source: The Bedford Reader in American History. Developed by Victoria Bissell Brown and Timothy J. Shannon, this reader combines a rich diversity of primary and secondary sources with in-depth instructions for how to use each type of source. Mirroring the chronology of the U.S. history survey, each of the main chapters familiarizes students with a single type of source—from personal letters to political cartoons—while focusing on an intriguing historical episode such as the Cherokee Removal or the 1894 Pullman Strike. The reader's wide variety of chapter topics and sources provoke students' interest as it teaches them the skills they need to successfully interrogate historical sources. Package discounts are available.

America Firsthand. With its distinctive focus on first person accounts from ordinary people, this primary documents reader by Anthony Marcus, John M. Giggie, and David Burner, offers a remarkable range of perspectives on America's history from those who lived it. Popular Points of View sections expose students to different perspectives on a specific event or topic. Package discounts are available.

BRIEF CONTENTS

CONTENTS

9 Defending and Redefining the Nation

1809–1832 *281*

10 Social and Cultural Ferment in the North

1820–1850 *317*

11 Slavery Expands South and West

1830–1850   *353*

12 Imperial Ambitions and Sectional Crises
1842–1861 *389*

13 Civil War
1861–1865 *421*

14 Emancipation and Reconstruction

1863–1877 *455*

17   Workers and Farmers in the Age of Organization

1877–1900   *561*

COMPARING AMERICAN HISTORIES
John McLuckie and Mary Elizabeth Lease   *562*

18   Cities, Immigrants, and the Nation

1880–1914   *595*

COMPARING AMERICAN HISTORIES
Beryl Lassin and Maria Vik Takacs   *596*

19 Progressivism and the Search for Order
1900–1917 *629*

22 Depression, Dissent, and the New Deal

1929–1940   *737*

23 World War II

1933–1945   *775*

25 Troubled Innocence
1945–1961   *849*

26 Liberalism and Its Challengers
1960–1973   *885*

MAPS, FIGURES, AND TABLES

Maps

Figures and Tables

How to Use This Book

Use the chapter tools to focus on what's important as you read.

Learning Objectives preview what is important to take away from each section of the chapter.

A pair of Comparing American Histories biographies at the start of each chapter personalizes the history of the period, and the chapter touches on these stories throughout to bring history to life.

At the end of each major section and repeated in the chapter review, the Review & Relate questions review key concepts.

LEARNING OBJECTIVES

After reading this chapter you should be able to:

- Analyze the ways that social and cultural leaders worked to craft an American identity and how that was complicated by racial, ethnic, and class differences.
- Interpret how the Democratic-Republican ideal of limiting federal power was transformed by international events, westward expansion, and Supreme Court rulings between 1800 and 1808.
- Explain the ways that technology reshaped the American economy and the lives of distinct groups of Americans.

COMPARING AMERICAN HISTORIES

When Parker Cleaveland graduated from Harvard University in 1799, his parents expected him to pursue a career in medicine, law, or the ministry. Instead, he turned to teaching. In 1805 Cleaveland secured a position in Brunswick, Maine, as professor of mathematics and natural philosophy at Bowdoin College. A year later, he married Martha Bush. Over the next twenty years, the Cleavelands raised eight children on the Maine frontier, entertained visiting scholars, corresponded with families at other colleges, and boarded dozens of students. While Parker taught

(*left*) **Parker Cleaveland.** Courtesy the Bowdoin College Library, Brunswick, Maine, USA
(*right*) **Shoshone woman.** (No image of Sacagawea exists.) Joslyn Museum, Omaha, Nebraska, USA/Alecto Historical Editions/Bridgeman Images

246

those students math and science, Martha trained them in manners and morals. The Cleavelands also served as a model of new ideals of companionate marriage, in which husbands and wives shared interests and affection.

Professor Cleaveland believed in using scientific research to benefit society. When Brunswick workers asked him to identify local rocks, Parker began studying geology and chemistry. In 1816 he published his *Elementary Treatise on Mineralogy and Geology*, providing a basic text for students and interested adults. He also lectured throughout New England, displaying mineral samples and performing chemical experiments.

The Cleavelands viewed the Bowdoin College community as a laboratory in which distinctly American values and ideas could be developed and sustained. So, too, did the residents of other college towns. Although less than 1 percent of men in the United States attended universities at the time, frontier colleges were considered important vehicles for bringing virtue—especially the desire to act for the public good—to the far reaches of the early republic. Yet several of these colleges were constructed with the aid of slave labor, and all were built on land bought or confiscated from Indians.

The purchase of the Louisiana Territory by President Thomas Jefferson in 1803 marked a new American frontier and ensured further encroachments on native lands. The territory covered 828,000 square miles and stretched from the Mississippi River to the Rocky Mountains and from New Orleans to present-day Montana. The area was home to tens of thousands of Indian inhabitants.

In 1800 a Hidatsa raiding party swept into a Shoshone village and seized captives, including a girl about twelve years old. The girl, Sacagawea, and her fellow captives were marched hundreds of miles to a Hidatsa-Mandan village on the Missouri River. Eventually Sacagawea was sold to a French trader, Toussaint Charbonneau, along with another young Shoshone woman, and both became his wives.

In November 1804, an expedition led by Meriwether Lewis and William Clark set up winter camp near the Hidatsa village where Sacagawea lived. The U.S. government had sent Lewis and Clark to

---

freely, and deals were made.

Examine the Sources

1. How do Hatch and Porterfield differ in their interpretations of the relationships between religion and politics?
2. Drawing upon evidence in Chapters 7 and 8, evaluate the strengths and weaknesses of Hatch's and Porterfield's presentations.

Put It in Context

How would you analyze religion's relationship to political transformations in the early republic?

Use the integrated, stepped approach to primary sources to strengthen your interpretive skills while bringing history to life.

Step 1: Guided Analysis

Near the start of each chapter, a **Guided Analysis** of a textual or visual source with annotated questions in the margins models how to analyze a specific phrase or detail of the source as well as the source as a whole.

Red Explore callouts highlight connections between the narrative and specific sources and help you move easily to the sources and back.

GUIDED ANALYSIS

Plea from the Scottsboro Prisoners, 1932

In 1931, nine black youths were arrested in Scottsboro, Alabama and charged with raping two white women. They were quickly convicted, and eight were sentenced to death. (One of the nine, Roy Wright, was twelve years old, and the prosecution did not seek the death penalty.) In this letter to the editor of the *Negro Worker*, a Communist magazine, the Scottsboro Nine plead their innocence and ask for help. A year had passed since their arrest and trial, which would account for their ages in the following statement recorded as between thirteen to twenty. Only those sentenced to death signed the letter.

Source 22.1

Why do you think they mention their ages?

What tactics did Alabama officials use on the prisoners? What was their purpose?

Why do the Scottsboro prisoners repeatedly emphasize that they were workers?

We have been sentenced to die for something we ain't never done. Us poor boys have been sentenced to burn up on the electric chair for the reason that we is workers—and the color of our skin is black. We like any one of you workers is none of us older than 20. Two of us is 14 and one is 13 years old.

What we guilty of? Nothing but being out of a job. Nothing but looking for work. Our kinfolk was starving for food. We wanted to help them out. So we hopped a freight—just like any one of you workers might a done—to go down to Mobile to hunt work. We was taken off the train by a mob and framed up on rape charges.

At the trial they gave us in Scottsboro we could hear the crowd yelling, "Lynch the Niggers." We could see them toting those big shotguns. Call 'at a fair trial? And while we lay here in jail, the boss-man make us watch 'em burning up other Negroes on the electric chair. "This is what you'll get," they say to us.

Working class boys, we asks you to save us from being burnt on the electric chair. We's only poor working class boys whose skin is black. . . . Help us boys. We ain't done nothing wrong.
[Signed] Andy Wright, Olen Montgomery, Ozie Powell, Charlie Weems, Clarence Norris, Haywood Patterson, Eugene Williams, Willie Robertson

Source: "Scottsboro Boys Appeal from Death Cells to the 'Toilers of the World,'" *The Negro Worker* 2, no. 5 (May 1932): 8–9.

Put It in Context
Why was it unlikely that black men in Alabama could receive a fair trial on the charge of raping a white woman?

Explore ▸

See Source 22.1 for a letter from the Scottsboro prisoners.

See also the **Guide to Analyzing Primary Sources** at the front of the book for additional help with sources.

Step 2: Comparative Analysis

Next, each chapter progresses to the more complex **Comparative Analysis**, a paired set of documents that reveal contrasting or complementary perspectives on a particular issue or event.

COMPARATIVE ANALYSIS

Letters to Eleanor Roosevelt

During the 1930s Americans wrote to President Roosevelt and the First Lady in unprecedented numbers, revealing their personal desperation and their belief that the Roosevelts would respond to their individual pleas. Though most requested government assistance, not all letter writers favored the New Deal. In the following letters written to Eleanor Roosevelt, high school student Mildred Isbell from Albertville, Alabama asks the First Lady for personal help, while Minnie Hardin of Columbus, Indiana expresses her frustration with direct relief programs.

Source 22.2

Mildred Isbell to Mrs. Roosevelt, January 1, 1936

Dear Mrs. Roosevelt,

My life has been a story to me and most of the time a miserable one. When I was 7 years old my father left for a law school and never returned. This leaving my mother and 4 children. He left us a small farm, but it could not keep us up. For when we went back to mother's people the renters would not give us part, and we were still dependent. I have been shoved to pillar to post that I feel very relieved to get off to my sel[...]

I am now 15 y[...] grade. I have alwa[...] had a chance as al[...] complete my educ[...] school I guess if th[...] bought. (Don't thi[...] Mother has been a[...] keep us to gather.[...] made it.

Mrs Roosevelt, don't think I am just begging, but that is all you can call it I guess. There is no harm in asking I guess eather. Do you have any old clothes you have throwed back. You don't realize how honored I would feel to be wearing your clothes. I don't have a coat at all to wear. The clothes may be too large but I can cut them down so I can wear them. Not only clothes but old shoes, hats, hose, and under wear would be appreciated so much. I have three brothers that [...]

Source 22.3

Minnie Hardin to Mrs. Roosevelt, December 14, 1937

Mrs. Roosevelt:

I suppose from your point of view the work relief, old age pensions, slum clearance, and all the rest seems like a perfect remedy for all the ills of this country, but I would like for you to see the results, as the other half see them.

We have always had a shiftless, never-do-well class of people whose one and only aim in life is to live without work. I have been rubbing elbows with this class for nearly sixty years and have tried to help some of the most promising and have seen others try to help them, but it can't be done. We cannot help those who will not try to help themselves and if they do try, a square deal is all they need, and by the way that is all this country needs or ever has needed: a square deal for all

and then, let each paddle their own canoe, or sink.

There has never been any necessity for any one who is able to work, being on relief in this locality, but there have been many eating the bread of charity and they have lived better than ever before. I have had taxpayers tell me that their children came from school and asked why they couldn't have nice lunches like the children on relief. The women and children around here have had to work at the fields to help save the crops and several women fainted while at work and at the same time we couldn't go up or down the road without stumbling over some of the reliefers, moping around carrying dirt from one side of the road to the other and back again, or else asleep.

Interpret the Evidence

1. How does each writer explain the source of poverty and the attitudes of poor people?
2. If Minnie Hardin were answering Mildred Isbell's letter, what would she say to her?

Put It in Context

How did the New Deal tackle poverty?

Step 3: Secondary Source Analysis

Next you will encounter the **Secondary Source Analysis**, comprised of two secondary sources by historians that inform each other, offering differing perspectives on an important historical issue or event.

Examine the Sources questions help you evaluate and compare the historians' interpretations.

SECONDARY SOURCE ANALYSIS

New Deal or Raw Deal

The Great Depression posed major challenges for the U.S. government and its citizens. Depressions had struck many times throughout American history but none had been so severe or long lasting. Grasping that the economic collapse was not just the ordinary rise and fall of the business cycle, Franklin Roosevelt's New Deal brought the federal government into the lives of Americans to a greater extent than ever before. Yet the New Deal did not end the depression nor did it redistribute wealth and power more equally among the various segments of the population. The key question for historians remains, what did it do and how much reform did it bring to those who needed it most?

Source 22.4

William E. Leuchtenburg, The Roosevelt Reconstruction, 1963

Franklin Roosevelt re-created the modern Presidency. He took an office which had lost much of its prestige and power in the previous twelve years and gave it an importance which went well beyond what even Theodore Roosevelt and Woodrow Wilson had done.... Under Roosevelt, the White House became the focus of all government—the fountainhead of ideas, the initiator of action, the representative of the national interest.

Despite this encroachmen[t] on traditional business prerog[ative] Deal could advance impressive[ly] regarded as a "savior of capital[ism]" sense of the land, of family, an[d] community marked him as a m[an of] ingrained conservative traits. [In those] years, the government sought [in] Roosevelt's words, "to energize[...]

enterprise." The RFC financed business, housing agencies underwrote home financing, and public works spending aimed to revive the construction industry. . . . Yet such considerations should not obscure the more important point: that the New Deal, however conservative it was in some respects and however much it owed to the past, marked a radically new departure. . . . The New Deal achieved a more just society by recognizing

Source 22.5

Barton J. Bernstein, The Conservative Achievements of Liberal Reform, 1969

The liberal reforms of the New Deal did not transform the American system; they conserved and protected American corporate capitalism, occasionally by absorbing parts of threatening programs. There was no significant redistribution of power in American society, only limited recognition of other organized groups, seldom of unorganized peoples. Neither the bolder programs advanced by New Dealers nor the final legislation greatly extended the beneficence of government beyond the middle classes or draw upon the wealth of the few for the needs of the many. Designed to maintain the American system, liberal activity was directed toward essentially conservative goals. Experimentalism was most frequently limited to means; seldom did it extend to ends. Never questioning private enterprise, it operated within safe channels, far short of Marxism or even of native American radicalisms that offered structural critiques and structural solutions.

The New Deal was [not] . . . "a half-way revolution," as William Leuchtenburg concludes. Not only was the extension of representation to new groups less than full-fledged partnership, but the New Deal neglected many Americans— sharecroppers, tenant farmers, migratory workers and farm laborers, slum dwellers, unskilled workers, and unemployed Negroes. They were left outside the new order. . . . Yet by the power of rhetoric and through the appeals of political organization, the Roosevelt government managed to win or retain the allegiance of these people. Perhaps this is one of the crueler ironies of liberal politics, that the marginal men trapped in hopelessness were seduced by rhetoric, by the style and movement, of efforts seldom reaching beyond words.

Source: Barton J. Bernstein, "The New Deal: The Conservative Achievements of Liberal Reform," in *Towards a New Past: Dissenting Essays in American History*, edited by Barton J. Bernstein (New York, Vintage Books, 1969), 264, 281.

Examine the Sources

1. Compare the similarities and differences between the Leuchtenburg and Bernstein interpretations of Roosevelt and the New Deal.
2. Based on evidence in this chapter, evaluate the credibility of each interpretation.

Put it in Context

Explain why it was possible for President Roosevelt to get so much of his New Deal legislation passed.

Finally, for the opportunity to draw deeper conclusions, a **Primary Source Project** of 4-5 sources focused on a central topic concludes each chapter.

PRIMARY SOURCE PROJECT 8

The Corps of Discovery: Paeans to Peace and Instruments of War

▶ How did the Corps of Discovery influence relations between Indian nations and non-Indian explorers, between traders and settlers, and among Indian nations?

From 1804 to 1806, the Corps of Discovery mapped vast regions of the West, documented plants and animals, and initiated trade relations with Indian nations. When the Corps built its winter camp at Fort Mandan in October 1804, its members hoped to develop commercial relations with local Mandan, Hidatsa, and Arikara villages. Most of these tribes had been ravaged by smallpox in the early 1780s and were now subject to raids by more powerful nations in the region. Meriwether Lewis and William Clark hoped to persuade all of these nations that peaceful relations would benefit them politically and economically. To aid negotiations, the Corps offered gifts to the Indian leaders they encountered (Source 8.6). The Mandan, however, expected more gifts than the expedition could offer. Although Lewis and Clark assured Mandan leaders they would benefit from future trade with and protection from the United States, the Indians had heard such promises before and were wary of giving away vital food as winter descended (Source 8.7).

Worried about surviving the winter, Lewis and Clark finally found an unexpect[ed] the Mandan. When their men smithy in December 1804, they ans would exchange almost hatchets, especially those (Sources 8.8 and 8.9).

In April the Corps moved Idaho and traded with Shoshon[e]

The Shoshone were engaged in a long and l[ucrative] trade in horses with the Comanche, who ha[d split] from the Shoshones, moved south, and dev[eloped] ties with the Spanish. But the Shoshone had a [hard] time getting guns, a concern they expressed t[o Lewis] (Source 8.10). While Lewis and Clark adv[ocated] peace among Indian nations, one of their most [valued] trade items was weaponry.

Source 8.6

William Clark, Journal | October 12, 1804

As the Corps of Discovery traveled up the Mis[souri] River from St. Louis, they stopped at Indian vi[llages] along the way to advocate peace; offer prese[nts] from President Jefferson; and learn about loc[al] plants, animals, and potential trade items. In [his] journal entry for October 12, William Clark de[scribed] a visit to a Ricara (Arikara) village near where [the] Corps planned to stay for the winter.

After breakfast, we went on shore to the house of the chief of the second village named [ ] [w]e found his chiefs and [ ] a present of about seven [ ] of leggings, a twist of their [ ] of two different specie[s] [ ] delivered a speech [ma]de for the presents an[d] [ ]e had given him; his int[ ] [ ]er [the president of the] [ ]ar of the Sioux; and

Source 8.7

Charles McKenzie | Narrative of a Fur Trader, November 1804

Charles McKenzie was a Scotsman working as a clerk for the Hudson Bay Company. He arrived with six traders at a Hidatsa village in November 1804. Over time, McKenzie adopted Indian dress, married an Indian woman, and became an advocate for Indian concerns. Here he recounts Lewis's frustration in his efforts to gain favor with local Indians as well as Mandan concerns about the Corps' lack of generosity.

Source 8.9

William Clark | Journal, January 28, 1805, and Meriwether Lewis, Journal, February 1, 1805

By early 1805 it was clear to Lewis and Clark that metal goods, especially axes or hatchets, were the most valuable means of obtaining the corn and other items they needed from the Mandans and neighboring Indians. These two short entries, by Clark and then Lewis, describe the value of the trade in hatchets to the Corps and their continued commitment to peace among Indian nations.

Source 8.8

William Clark | Journal, November 18, 1804

By November 1804, the Corps had built and settled into Fort Mandan, at the convergence of the Missouri and Knife Rivers, for the winter. Lewis and Clark became increasingly aware that their trade with particular groups, like the Mandans, might shift the balance of power in the region. But given the extended journey ahead, they were limited in what goods they could give or trade with local Indians even as they sought to reassure them of U.S.

Use the Chapter Review to identify significant historical developments and how they fit together over time.

Review the **Timeline of Events**, which shows the relationship among chapter events.

Study the **Key Terms** list to see if you can define each term and describe its significance.

Answer the **Review & Relate questions**, which prompt you to recall major concepts in each section.

TIMELINE OF EVENTS

1931	Scottsboro Nine tried for rape
1932–1939	Dust Bowl storms
1932	Reconstruction Finance Corporation created
	River Rouge autoworkers' strike
	Farm Holiday Association formed
	Bonus Army marches
1933	Roosevelt moves to stabilize banking and financial systems
	Agricultural Adjustment Act passed
	Federal Emergency Relief Administration created
	Tennessee Valley Authority created
	National Recovery Administration created
	Civilian Conservation Corps created
1934	Indian Reorganization Act passed
	Francis Townsend forms Old-Age Revolving Pensions Corporation
	Huey Long establishes Share Our Wealth movement
	Securities and Exchange Commission created
1935	Charles E. Coughlin organizes National Union for Social Justice
	Works Progress Administration created
	Social Security Act passed
	National Labor Relations Act passed
	Congress of Industrial Organizations founded
1937	Sit-down strike against General Motors
	Roosevelt proposes to increase the size of the Supreme Court
1938	Fair Labor Standards Act passed

KEY TERMS

Scottsboro Nine, *743*
Bonus Army, *749*
New Deal, *751*
Federal Deposit Insurance Corporation (FDIC), *751*
Agricultural Adjustment Act, *751*
Tennessee Valley Authority (TVA), *752*
National Recovery Administration (NRA), *752*
Civilian Conservation Corps (CCC), *753*
Works Progress Administration (WPA), *758*
Social Security Act, *759*
National Labor Relations Act, *760*
sit-down strike, *761*
Fair Labor Standards Act, *762*
Indian Reorganization Act (IRA), *763*
court-packing plan, *766*
conservative coalition, *766*

REVIEW & RELATE

1. How did President Hoover respond to the problems and challenges created by the Great Depression?
2. How did different segments of the American population experience the depression?
3. What steps did Roosevelt take to stimulate economic recovery and provide relief to impoverished Americans during his first term in office?
4. What criticisms did Roosevelt's opponents level against the New Deal?
5. Why and how did the New Deal shift to the left in 1934 and 1935?
6. Despite the president's landslide victory in 1936, why did the New Deal stall during Roosevelt's second term in office?

Mapping Global Frontiers

to 1590

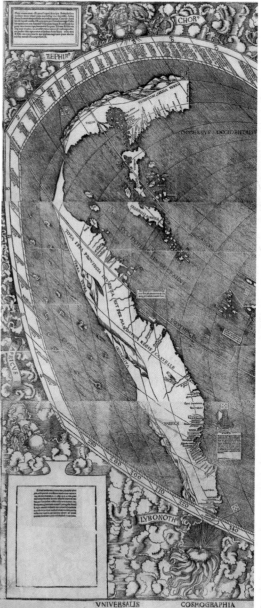

Geography and Maps Division, Library of Congress

WINDOW TO THE PAST

Universalis Cosmographia, 1507

This image of the Americas was engraved on one of the first world maps of the sixteenth century. The elongated shape was based on information supplied by early European explorers. ▸ To discover more about what this primary source can show us, see Source 1.1 on page 12.

After reading this chapter you should be able to:

- Describe the diverse societies that populated the Americas prior to European exploration.

- Explain the reasons for European exploration and expansion, and compare the impact of this expansion on Europe and Africa.

- Evaluate the reasons for Europeans' success in reaching the Americas, and compare the impact of the Columbian Exchange on American Indians, Africans, and Europeans.

- Analyze how the Spanish created an empire in the Americas, and describe the impact of Spain's empire building on Indian empires and European nations.

COMPARING AMERICAN HISTORIES

In 1519 a young Indian woman named Malintzin was thrust into the center of dramatic events that transformed not only her world but also the world at large. As a young girl, Malintzin, whose birth name is lost to history, lived in the rural area of Coatzacoalcos on the frontier between the expanding kingdom of the Mexica and the declining Mayan states of the Yucatán peninsula. Raised in a noble household, Malintzin was fluent in Nahuatl, the language of the Mexica.

In 1515 or 1516, when she was between the ages of eight and twelve, Malintzin was taken by or given to Mexica merchants, perhaps as a peace offering to

(left) **Portrait of Malintzin (detail).** Gianni Dagli Orti/Rex/Shutterstock

(right) ***Universalis Cosmographia,* 1507 (detail).** Geography and Maps Division, Library of Congress

stave off military attacks. She then entered a well-established trade in slaves, consisting mostly of women and girls, who were sent eastward to work in the expanding cotton fields or the households of their owners. She may also have been forced into a sexual relationship with a landowner. Whatever her situation, Malintzin learned the Mayan language during her captivity.

In 1517 Mayan villagers sighted Spanish adventurers along local rivers and drove them off. But in 1519 the Spaniards returned. The Maya's lightweight armor made of dense layers of cotton, cloth, and leather and their wooden arrows were no match for the invaders' steel swords, guns, and horses. Forced to surrender, the Maya offered the Spaniards food, gold, and twenty enslaved women, including Malintzin. The Spanish leader, Hernán Cortés, baptized the enslaved women and assigned each of them Christian names, although the women did not consent to this ritual. Cortés then divided the women among his senior officers, giving Malintzin to the highest-ranking noble.

Already fluent in Nahuatl and Mayan, Malintzin soon learned Spanish. Within a matter of months, she became the Spaniards' chief translator. As Cortés moved into territories ruled by the Mexica (whom the Spaniards called Aztecs), his success depended on his ability to understand Aztec ways of thinking and to convince subjugated groups to fight against their despotic rulers. Malintzin thus accompanied Cortés at every step, including his triumphant conquest of the Aztec capital in the fall of 1521.

At the same time that Malintzin played a key role in the conquest of the Aztecs, Martin Waldseemüller sought to map the frontiers along which these conflicts erupted. Born in present-day Germany in the early 1470s, Waldseemüller enrolled at the University of Fribourg in 1490, where he probably studied theology. He would gain fame, however, as a cartographer, or mapmaker.

In 1507 Waldseemüller and Mathias Ringmann, working at a scholarly religious institute in St. Dié in northern France, produced a map of the world, a small globe, and a Latin translation of the four voyages of the Italian explorer Amerigo Vespucci. The map and the globe, entitled *Universalis Cosmographia,* depict the "known" world as well as the "new" worlds recently discovered by European explorers. The latter include an elongated territory labeled *America*, in honor of Amerigo, who first recognized that the lands Columbus reached were part of a separate continent. It was set between the continents of Africa and Asia. The map, covering some 36 square feet, offered a view of the world never before attempted.

In 1516 Waldseemüller produced an updated map of the world, the *Carta Marina*. Apparently in response to challenges regarding Vespucci's role in discovering new territories, he substituted the term *Terra Incognita* ("unknown land") for the region he had earlier labeled America. But the 1507 map had already circulated widely, and *America* became part of the European lexicon. ■

A comparison of the personal histories of Malintzin and Martin Waldseemüller highlights the profound consequences of contact between the peoples of Europe and those of the Americas. The Mexica, or Aztec, and the Spanish were most affected during this period, but France and England would soon also seek footholds in the Americas. For millennia, travel and communication between the two sides of the Atlantic had been extremely limited. Then, in the sixteenth century — and despite significant obstacles — animals, plants, goods, ideas, and people began circulating between Europe and what became known as America. Malintzin and Waldseemüller, in their very different ways, helped map the frontiers of this global society and contributed to the dramatic transformations that followed.

Native Peoples in the Americas

The first people in the Americas almost certainly arrived as migrants from northeast Asia, but the timing of such migrations remains in doubt. They likely began at least 25,000 years ago. It is also difficult to estimate the population of the Americas before contact with Europeans. Estimates range from 37 million to 100 million. It is clear, however, that the vast majority of people lived within a few hundred miles of the equator, and the smallest number — perhaps 4 to 7 million — lived in present-day North America. By the fifteenth century, like other regions of the world, the Americas were home to diverse societies, ranging from coastal fishing villages to nomadic hunter-gatherers to settled horticulturalists to large city-centered empires.

Native Peoples Develop Diverse Cultures. The settlement of the Americas was encouraged by the growth of glaciers on the North American continent between about 38,000 and 14,000 B.C.E. This development led to a dramatic drop in sea levels and created a land bridge in the Bering Strait, between present-day Siberia and Alaska, called **Beringia**. The first migrations may have occurred about 20,000 to 25,000 years ago, during a warming trend when melting glaciers retreated from large areas of land. During the warming trend, some settlers probably traveled from the northeastern region of the Asian Steppe (southern Siberia) to Beringia, following herds of mammoths, musk oxen, and woolly rhinoceroses. Then, 15,000 to 20,000 years ago, descendants of some of these settlers followed coastal pathways and the Pacific shore line, taking advantage of the rich maritime resources. These coastal journeys may help explain how Asiatic migrants peopled vast areas of South America in just a few thousand years. As immense expanses of ice returned to many regions some 13,000 years ago, the routes that migrants could follow shifted and forced many groups to push inland as well as further south.

Whether over land or sea, most early groups traveled southward. Those moving inland had to skirt melting glaciers to find better hunting grounds and more abundant plant life. When the mammoths and other large game disappeared from large areas about 10,000 years ago, people became more dependent on smaller game, fish, roots, berries, and other plant foods to survive. At the same time, new groups of migrants headed east from Beringia. These included Inuit and Aleut peoples who arrived in present-day Alaska thousands of years after more southern areas had been settled (Map 1.1).

Between 8000 and 2000 B.C.E., some communities in the Americas began establishing agricultural systems that encouraged more stable settlements and population growth. **Horticulture** — a form of agriculture in which people work small plots of land with simple tools — became highly developed in the area of present-day Mexico. There men and women developed improved strains of maize (or Indian corn). They also cultivated protein-rich beans, squash, tomatoes, potatoes, and manioc (a root vegetable, also known as cassava or yucca root). The combination of beans, squash, and corn offered an especially nutritious diet while maintaining the fertility of the soil. Moreover, high yields produced surplus food that could be stored or traded to neighboring communities.

By 500 C.E., complex societies, rooted in intensive agriculture, began to thrive in the equatorial region. Between 500 and 1500 C.E., the spread of maize cultivation northward into the present-day American Southwest and beyond fostered economic developments that necessitated irrigation and led to the diversification of native societies. Small bands of hunters and gatherers continued to thrive in deserts and forests while impressive civilizations arose on swamplands and grasslands, and in the mountains.

The Aztecs, the Maya, and the Incas.
Three significant civilizations had emerged by the early sixteenth century: Aztec and Mayan societies in the equatorial region and the Inca society along the Pacific coast in present-day Peru. Technologically advanced and with knowledge of mathematics and astronomy, these societies were characterized by vast mineral wealth, large urban centers, highly ritualized religions, and complex political systems. Unlike their counterparts in Europe, Asia, and Africa, they did not develop the wheel to aid in transportation, nor did they have steel tools and weapons. Since most of their commerce was carried out over land or along rivers and coastlines, they did not build large boats. They also lacked horses, which had disappeared from the region thousands of years earlier. Still, the Aztecs, Maya, and Incas established grand cities and civilizations.

Around 1325 C.E., the **Aztecs**, who called themselves Mexica, built their capital, Tenochtitlán, on the site of present-day Mexico City. As seminomadic warriors who had invaded and then settled in the region, the Aztecs drew on local residents' knowledge of irrigation and cultivation and adopted their written language. Aztec commoners, who tilled communally owned lands, were ruled over by priests and nobles. The nobles formed a warrior class and owned vast estates on which they employed both serfs and slaves captured from non-Aztec communities in the region. Priests promised fertility — for the land and its people — but demanded human sacrifices, including thousands of men and women from captured tribes. To sustain their society, Aztecs extended their trade networks, offering pottery, cloth, and leather goods in exchange for textiles and obsidian to make

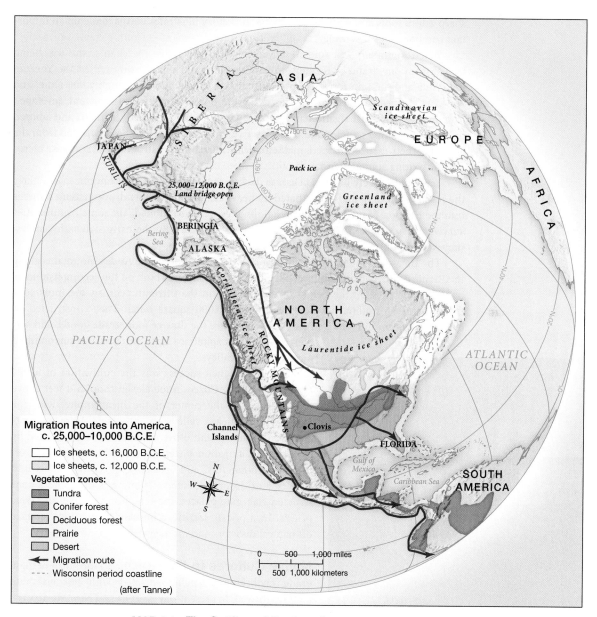

MAP 1.1   The Settling of the Americas

Beginning about 25,000 B.C.E., Asian peoples likely migrated to America across a land bridge after expanding glaciers lowered sea levels. Others probably followed the coastline in boats. As glaciers retreated over several centuries, they opened corridors along which people migrated, leaving traces in archaeological sites in present-day Wisconsin, New Mexico, Florida, Central America, and Chile.

sharp-edged tools and weapons. As Malintzin's story illustrates, slaves made up an important component of this trade.

When Malintzin was sold to a Mayan village by Aztec merchants, she was being traded from one grand civilization to another. The **Maya** had slowly settled the Yucatán peninsula and the rain forests of present-day Guatemala between roughly 900 B.C.E. and 300 C.E. They established large cities that were home to skilled artisans and developed elaborate systems for irrigation and water storage. Farmers worked the fields and labored to build huge stone temples and palaces for rulers who claimed to be descended from the gods. Learned men developed mathematical calculations, astronomical systems, hieroglyphic writing, and a calendar.

Yet the Mayan civilization began to decline around 800 C.E. An economic crisis, likely the result of drought and exacerbated by heavy taxation, probably drove peasant families into the interior. Many towns and religious sites were abandoned. Yet some communities survived the crisis and reemerged as thriving city-states. By the early sixteenth century, they were trading with the Aztecs.

The **Incas** developed an equally impressive civilization in the Andes Mountains along the Pacific coast. The Inca empire, like the Aztec empire, was built on the accomplishments of earlier societies. At the height of their power, in the fifteenth century, the Incas controlled some 16 million people spread over 350,000 square miles. They constructed an expansive system of roads and garrisons to ensure the flow of food, trade goods, and soldiers from their capital at Cuzco through the surrounding mountains and valleys.

The key to Inca success was the cultivation of fertile mountain valleys. Cuzco, some eleven thousand feet above sea level, lay in the center of the Inca empire, with the Huaylas and Titicaca valleys on either side. Here residents cultivated potatoes and other crops on terraces watered by an elaborate irrigation system. Miners dug gold and silver from the mountains, and artisans crafted the metals into jewelry and decorative items. Thousands of laborers constructed elaborate palaces and temples. And like the Aztec priests, Inca priests sacrificed humans to the gods to stave off natural disasters and military defeat.

Native Cultures to the North. To the north of these grand civilizations, smaller societies with less elaborate cultures thrived. In present-day Arizona and New Mexico, the

Female Figurine, Peru, c. 1430–1532 This figurine made of gold depicts a Mamacona, who was similar to a nun in Incan society. Daughters of the nobility or young women of exceptional beauty lived in temple sanctuaries and dedicated themselves to the sun god, Inti. They served the Inca people and priests. The multicolored woolen robe and gold pin indicate this woman's special status. Werner Forman/Universal Images Group/Getty Images

Mogollon and Hohokam established communities around 500 C.E. The Mogollon were expert potters, while the Hohokam, migrating north from Mexico, developed extensive irrigation systems. Farther north, in present-day Utah and Colorado, the ancient Pueblo people built adobe and masonry homes cut into cliffs around 750 C.E. After migrating south and constructing large buildings that included administrative offices, religious centers, and craft shops, the Pueblo returned to their cliff dwellings in the 1100s for protection from invaders. There, drought eventually caused them to disperse into smaller groups.

Farther north on the plains that stretched from present-day Colorado into Canada, hunting societies developed around herds of bison. A weighted spear-throwing device, called an *atlatl*, allowed hunters to capture smaller game, while nets, hooks, and snares allowed them to catch birds, fish, and small animals. Societies in the Great Plains as well as the Great Basin (between the Rockies and the Sierra Nevada) generally remained small and widely scattered. Given the arid conditions in these regions, communities needed a large expanse of territory to ensure their survival as they followed migrating animals or seasonal plant sources. Here the adoption of the bow and arrow, in about 500 C.E., proved the most significant technological development.

Other native societies, like the Mandan, settled along rivers in the heart of the continent (present-day North and South Dakota). The rich soil along the banks fostered farming, while forests and plains attracted diverse animals for hunting. Around 1250 C.E., however, an extended drought forced these settlements to contract, and competition for resources increased among Mandan villages and with other native groups in the region.

Hunting-gathering societies also emerged along the Pacific coast, where the abundance of fish, small game, and plant life provided the resources to develop permanent settlements. The Chumash Indians, near present-day Santa Barbara, California, harvested resources from the land and the ocean. Women gathered acorns and pine nuts, while men fished and hunted. The Chumash, whose villages sometimes held a thousand inhabitants, participated in regional exchange networks up and down the coast.

Even larger societies with more elaborate social, religious, and political systems developed near the Mississippi River. A group that came to be called the **Hopewell people** established a thriving culture there in the early centuries C.E. The river and its surrounding lands provided fertile fields and easy access to distant communities. Centered in present-day southern Ohio and western Illinois, the Hopewell constructed towns of four to six thousand people. Artifacts from their burial sites reflect extensive trading networks that stretched from the Missouri River to Lake Superior, and from the Rocky Mountains to the Appalachian region and Florida.

Beginning around 500 C.E., the Hopewell culture gave birth to larger and more complex societies that flourished in the Mississippi River valley and to the south and east. As bows and arrows spread into the region, people hunted more game in the thick forests. But Mississippian groups also learned to cultivate corn. The development of corn as a staple crop allowed the population to expand dramatically, and more complex political and religious systems developed in which elite rulers gained greater control over the labor of farmers and hunters. Mississippian peoples created massive earthworks sculpted in the shape of serpents, birds, and other creatures. Some earthen sculptures stood higher than 70 feet and stretched longer than 1,300 feet. Mississippians also constructed huge temple mounds that could cover nearly 16 acres.

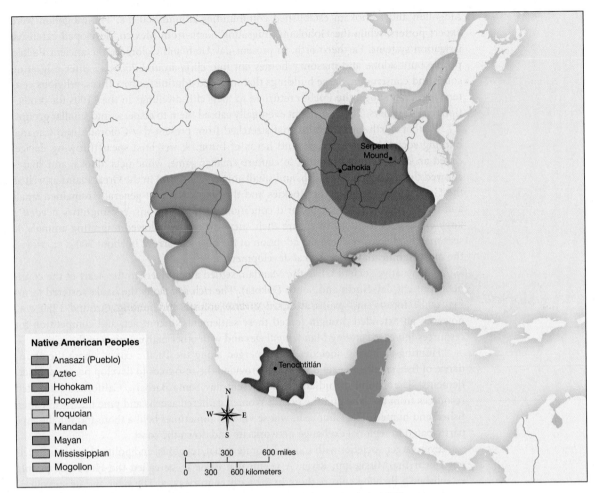

MAP 1.2 Native American Peoples, c. 500–1500 C.E.

Many distinct cultures developed in the Americas in the ten centuries before 1500. Some societies, like the Mississippians, developed extensive trade networks over land or along rivers and coastlines. Societies in the same region often learned from those who preceded them, such as the Aztec from the Maya, but other groups battled over scarce resources.

By about 1100 C.E., the Cahokia people established the largest Mississippian settlement, which may have housed ten to thirty thousand inhabitants (Map 1.2). Powerful chieftains extended their trade networks from the Great Lakes to the Gulf of Mexico, conquered smaller villages, and created a centralized government. But in the 1200s environmental factors affected the Cahokian people, too. Deforestation, drought, and perhaps disease as well as overhunting diminished their strength, and many settlements dispersed. After 1400, increased warfare and political turmoil joined with environmental changes to cause Mississippian culture as a whole to decline.

Serpent Mound Memorial   This mound, located in Locust Grove, Ohio, was likely constructed sometime between 950 and 1200 C.E. by the Mississippian society. A sun-worshipping culture, the Mississippians aligned the head of the serpent with the sunset of the summer solstice (June 20 or 21). Goods found at such sites indicate that Hopewell networks were further extended by the Mississippians. Tony Linck/SuperStock

REVIEW & RELATE

- Compare and contrast the Aztecs, Incas, and Maya. What similarities and differences do you note?

- How did the societies of North America differ from those of the equatorial zone and the Andes?

Europe Expands Its **Reach**

The complex societies that emerged in the Americas were made possible by an agricultural revolution that included the establishment of crop systems, the domestication of animals, and the development of tools. These developments had occurred between 4000 and 3000 B.C.E. in the Fertile Crescent of the Middle East and in China. The increased productivity in these areas ensured population growth and allowed attention to science, trade, politics, religion, and the arts. Over millennia, knowledge from these civilizations made its way into Europe. At the height of the Roman empire in the early centuries C.E., dense global trade networks connected the peoples of Europe, Africa, and Asia. With the decline of Roman power in western Europe, those connections broke down, but commercial ties continued to thrive among diverse peoples surrounding the Mediterranean Sea. Portuguese explorers, denied access to that rich Mediterranean world by the politics of the period, instead sought trade routes along the coast of Africa. Increased trade with African kingdoms by Portugal and other European societies included the purchase of slaves. This lucrative and devastating form of commerce would expand dramatically as European nations colonized the Americas.

The Mediterranean World.

Beginning in the seventh century Islam proved one of the most dynamic cultural, political, and military forces in the world. By the ninth century, Islamic (also known as Muslim) regimes created an Arab empire that controlled most of southwest Asia and North Africa and conquered parts of the Iberian peninsula in Europe. In the eleventh and twelfth centuries, Catholic leaders launched several military and religious campaigns to reclaim Jerusalem and other sites associated with Jesus for the Church. Later known as the **Crusades**, these campaigns largely failed, but they enhanced the roles of Italian merchants, who profited from both outfitting Crusaders and opening new trade routes to the East. Moreover, these campaigns inspired explorers and adventurers throughout Europe.

Europeans also learned of successful civilizations in the Middle East, where inhabitants had managed to survive droughts and other ecological crises, largely because of their productive economic systems. In the Mediterranean world, this productivity depended on technological advances in irrigation and navigation and a vast network of slave-trading centers and enslaved laborers. It was the productivity of agriculture — developed centuries earlier than in Europe or America — that allowed societies along the southern Mediterranean, in northern Africa, and in southwest Asia to excel in astronomy, mathematics, architecture, and the arts.

Medieval European states proved far less adept at staving off human and environmental disasters than their counterparts to the south. Besieged by drought and disease as well as wars and peasant rebellions, rulers across the continent expended most of their resources on trying to sustain their population and protect their borders. In the 1340s, as Europeans began to trade with various regions of Asia, fleas on rats carried the bubonic plague and similar epidemic diseases on board ships and into European seaports. From the 1340s to the early fifteenth century, the bubonic plague — later called the **Black Death** — periodically ravaged European cities and towns. During the initial outbreak between 1346 and 1350, about 36 million people — half of Europe's population — perished. At the same time, France and England engaged in a century-long war that added to the death and destruction.

By the early fifteenth century, the plague had retreated from much of Europe, and the climate had improved. Only then were European peoples able to benefit significantly from the riches of the East. Smaller populations led to an improved standard of living. Then rising birthrates and increased productivity, beginning in Italian city-states, fueled a resurgence of trade with other parts of the world. The profits from agriculture and commerce allowed the wealthy and powerful to begin investing in the arts and luxury goods. Indeed, a cultural **Renaissance** (from the French word for "rebirth") flourished in the Italian city-states and then spread to France, Spain, the Low Countries, and central Europe.

The cultural rebirth went hand in hand with political unification as more powerful rulers extended their control over smaller city-states and principalities. A vibrant and religiously tolerant culture had existed in Muslim Spain from the eighth to the tenth century, but that was followed by a long period of persecution of Christians. When Christians began reconquering Spain after 1200, Muslims and Jews alike became targets. Then in 1469, the marriage of Isabella of Castile and Ferdinand II of Aragon sealed the unification

Explore ▶

For one cartographer's vision
of the world during this
period, see Source 1.1.

of Christian Spain. By 1492 their combined forces expelled the last Muslim conquerors from the Iberian peninsula. Promoting Catholicism to create a more unified national identity, Isabella and Ferdinand launched an Inquisition against supposed heretics and executed or expelled some 200,000 Jews as well. Despite the brutality of the reconquest and the Inquisition, Catholic Spain had the wealth and military power to forge its own trade networks with North Africa, India, and other Asian lands.

Yet Italy controlled the most important routes through the Mediterranean, so leaders in Spain and neighboring Portugal sought alternate paths to riches. Their efforts were aided by explorers, missionaries, and merchants who traveled to Morocco, Turkey, India, and other distant lands. They brought back trade goods and knowledge of astronomy, shipbuilding, mapmaking, and navigation that allowed Iberians to venture farther south along the Atlantic coast of Africa and, eventually, west into the uncharted Atlantic Ocean.

Portugal Pursues Long-Distance Trade.

Cut off from the Mediterranean by Italian city-states and Muslim rulers in North Africa, Portugal looked toward the Atlantic. Although a tiny nation, Portugal benefited from the leadership of its young prince, Henry, who launched explorations of the African coast in the 1420s, hoping to find a passage to India via the Atlantic Ocean. Prince Henry — known as Henry the Navigator — gathered information from astronomers, geographers, mapmakers, and craftsmen in the Arab world and recruited Italian cartographers and navigators along with Portuguese scholars, sailors, and captains. He then launched a systematic campaign of exploration, observation, shipbuilding, and long-distance trade that revolutionized Europe and shaped developments in Africa and the Americas.

Prince Henry and his colleagues developed ships known as caravels — vessels with narrow hulls and triangular sails that were especially effective for navigating the coast of West Africa. His staff also created state-of-the-art maritime charts, maps, and astronomical tables; perfected navigational instruments; and mastered the complex wind and sea currents along the African coast. Soon Portugal was trading in gold, ivory, and slaves from West Africa.

In 1482 Portugal built Elmina Castle, a trading post and fort on the Gold Coast (present-day Ghana). Further expeditions were launched from the castle; five years later, a fleet led by Bartolomeu Dias rounded the Cape of Good Hope, on the southernmost tip of Africa. This feat demonstrated the possibility of sailing directly from the Atlantic to the Indian Ocean. Vasco da Gama followed this route to India in 1497, returning to Portugal in 1499, his ships laden with valuable cinnamon and pepper.

By the early sixteenth century, Portuguese traders had wrested control of the India trade from Arab fleets. They established fortified trading posts at key locations on the Indian Ocean and extended their expeditions to Indonesia, China, and Japan. Within a decade, the Portuguese had become the leaders in international trade. Spain, England, France, and the Netherlands competed for a share of this newfound wealth by developing long-distance markets that brought spices, ivory, silks, cotton cloth, and other luxury goods to Europe.

With expanding populations and greater agricultural productivity, European nations developed more efficient systems of taxation, built larger military forces, and adapted gunpowder to new kinds of weapons. The surge in population provided the men to labor on

GUIDED ANALYSIS

Martin Waldseemüller and Mathias Ringmann | *Universalis Cosmographia*, 1507

In 1507 German cartographers Waldseemüller and Ringmann produced a map of the "known" world, which included those areas in the Western Hemisphere recently discovered by European explorers. They were the first to use the term *America*, and their *Universalis Cosmographia* was also the first map to show the Americas as separate from Asia. The map was printed from wood engravings and produced in twelve sections covering 36 square feet.

Source 1.1

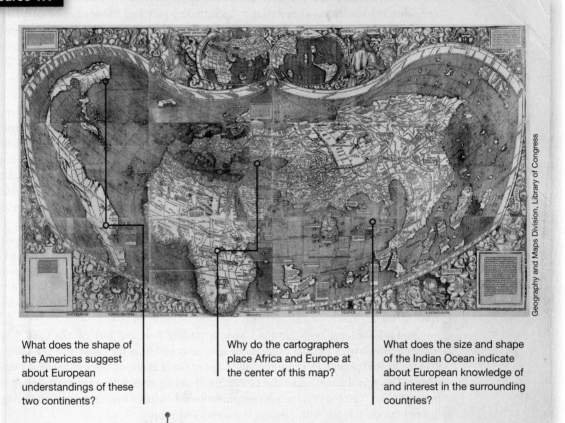

Geography and Maps Division, Library of Congress

What does the shape of the Americas suggest about European understandings of these two continents?

Why do the cartographers place Africa and Europe at the center of this map?

What does the size and shape of the Indian Ocean indicate about European knowledge of and interest in the surrounding countries?

Put It in Context

How does this new map of the world both reflect and reinforce European nations' growing interest in trade with Africa and Asia?

merchant vessels, staff forts, and protect trade routes. More people began to settle in cities, which grew into important commercial centers. Slowly, a form of capitalism based on market exchange, private ownership, and capital accumulation and reinvestment developed across much of Europe.

European Encounters with West Africa.

African slaves were among the most lucrative goods traded by European merchants. Slavery had been practiced in Europe, America, Africa, and other parts of the world for centuries. But in most times and places, slaves were captives of war or individuals sold in payment for deaths or injuries to conquering enemies. Under such circumstances, slaves generally retained some legal rights, and bondage was rarely permanent and almost never inheritable. With the advent of large-scale European participation in the African slave trade, however, the system of bondage began to change, transforming Europe and Africa and eventually the Americas.

In the fifteenth century, Europeans were most familiar with North Africa, a region deeply influenced by Islam and characterized by large kingdoms, well-developed cities, and an extensive network of trading centers. In northeast Africa, including Egypt, city-states flourished, with ties to India, the Middle East, and China. In northwest Africa, Timbuktu linked North Africa to empires south of the Great Desert as well as to Europe. Here African slaves labored for wealthier Africans in a system of bound labor long familiar to Europeans.

As trade with western Africa increased, however, Europeans learned more about communities that lived by hunting and subsistence agriculture. By the mid-sixteenth century, European nations established competing forts along the African coast from the Gold Coast and Senegambia in the north to the Bight of Biafra and West Central Africa farther south. The men and women shipped from these forts to Europe generally came from communities that had been raided or conquered by more powerful groups. They arrived at the coast exhausted, hungry, dirty, and with few clothes. They worshipped gods unfamiliar to Europeans, and their cultural customs and social practices seemed strange and primitive. Over time, it was the image of the West African slave that came to dominate European visions of the entire continent.

As traders from Portugal, Spain, Holland, and England brought back more stories and more African slaves, these negative portraits took deeper hold. Woodcuts and prints circulated in Europe showing half-naked Africans who were portrayed more like apes than humans. Biblical stories also reinforced notions of Africans as naturally inferior to Europeans. In the Bible, Ham had sinned against his father, Noah. Noah then cursed Ham's son Canaan to a life of slavery. Increasingly, European Christians considered Africans the "sons of Ham," infidels rightly

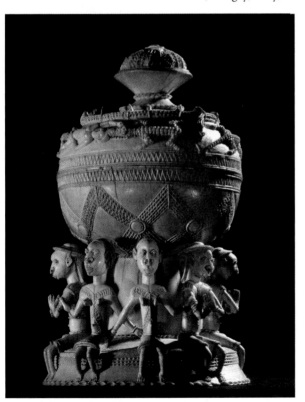

African Salt Cellar   This ivory salt cellar was carved in the fifteenth or sixteenth century in Sierra Leone, on the West African coast and was made for sale to Portuguese traders. The artisan depicted traditional geometric designs and African reptiles but clothed the four male and four female African figures in items of European dress. Werner Forman Archive / Bridgeman Images

assigned by God to a life of bondage. This self-serving idea was used to justify the enslavement of black men, women, and children.

Of course, these images of West Africa failed to reflect the diverse peoples who lived in and the diverse societies that developed in the area's tropical rain forests, plains, and savannas. As the slave trade expanded in the sixteenth and seventeenth centuries, it destabilized large areas of western and central Africa, with smaller societies decimated by raids and even larger kingdoms damaged by the extensive commerce in human beings.

Still, rulers of the most powerful African societies helped shape the slave trade. For instance, because women were more highly valued by Muslim traders in North Africa and Asia, African traders steered women to these profitable markets. At the same time, African societies organized along matrilineal lines — where goods and political power passed through the mother's line — often tried to protect women against enslavement. Other groups sought to limit the sale of men.

Ultimately, men, women, and children were captured by African as well as Portuguese, Spanish, Dutch, and English traders. Still, Europeans did not institute a system of perpetual slavery, in which enslavement was inherited from one generation to the next. Instead, Africans formed another class of bound labor, alongside peasants, indentured servants, criminals, and apprentices. Crucially, distinctions among bound laborers on the basis of race did not exist. Wealthy Englishmen, for instance, viewed both African and Irish laborers as ignorant and unruly heathens. However, as Europeans began to conquer and colonize the Americas and demands for labor increased dramatically, ideas about race and slavery would change significantly.

REVIEW & RELATE

- How and why did Europeans expand their connections with Africa and the Middle East in the fifteenth century?

- How did early European encounters with West Africans influence Europeans' ideas about African peoples and reshape existing systems of slavery?

Worlds Collide

In the 1520s and 1530s, Spain and Portugal chartered traders to ship enslaved Africans to the Caribbean, Brazil, Mexico, and Peru. The success of this trade relied heavily on the efforts of European cartographers, who used information from explorers and adventurers to map these areas. The maps illustrate the growing connections among Europe, Africa, and the Americas even as they also reflect the continued dominance of the Mediterranean region, the Middle East, India, and China in European visions of the world. Yet that world was changing rapidly as Europeans introduced guns, horses, and new diseases to the Americas and came in contact with previously unknown flora and fauna. The resulting exchange of plants, animals, and germs transformed the two continents as well as the wider world.

Europeans Cross the Atlantic.   The first Europeans to discover lands in the western Atlantic were Norsemen. In the late tenth century, Scandinavian seafarers led by Erik the Red reached Greenland. Sailing still farther west, Erik's son Leif led a party that discovered an area in North America that they called Vinland, near the Gulf of St. Lawrence. The

Norse established a small settlement there around 1000 C.E., and people from Greenland continued to visit Vinland for centuries. By 1450, however, the Greenland settlements had disappeared.

Nearly a half century after Norse settlers abandoned Greenland, a Genoese navigator named Christopher Columbus visited the Spanish court of Ferdinand and Isabella and proposed an **Enterprise of the Indies**. Portuguese explorers used this name for the region that included present-day South Asia and Southeast Asia and surrounding islands. Because Italian city-states controlled the Mediterranean and Portugal dominated the routes around Africa, Spain sought a third path to the rich Eastern trade. Columbus claimed he could find it by sailing west across the Atlantic to Japan, China, or the Indies themselves.

Columbus's 1492 proposal was timely. Having just expelled the last Muslims and Jews from Granada and imposed Catholic orthodoxy on a now-unified nation, the Spanish monarchs sought to expand their empire. After winning Queen Isabella's support, the Genoese captain headed off in three small ships with ninety men. They stopped briefly at the Canary Islands and then headed due west on September 6, 1492.

Columbus had calculated the distance to Japan, which he judged the nearest island, based on Ptolemy's division of the world into 360 degrees of north-south lines of longitude. But in making his calculations, Columbus made a number of errors that led him to believe that it was possible to sail from Spain to Asia in about a month. The miscalculations nearly led to mutiny, but disaster was averted when a lookout finally spotted a small island on October 12. Columbus named the island San Salvador and made contact with local residents, whom he named Indians in the belief that he had found East Indies islands near Japan or China. Columbus was impressed with their warm welcome and considered the gold jewelry Indians wore as a sign of great riches in the region.

> **Explore ▶**
>
> Read two accounts by early explorers of their encounters with native peoples in Sources 1.2 and 1.3.

Columbus and his crew were welcomed as heroes when they returned to Spain in March 1493. Their discovery of islands seemingly unclaimed by any known power led the pope to confer Spanish sovereignty over all lands already claimed or to be claimed 100 leagues west of the Cape Verde Islands. A protest by Portugal soon led to a treaty that moved the line 270 leagues farther west, granting Portugal control of territory that became Brazil and Spain control of the rest of what became known as South America.

Europeans Explore the Americas. Columbus made three more voyages to the Caribbean to claim land for Spain and sought to convince those who accompanied him to build houses, plant crops, and cut logs for forts. But the men had come for gold, and when the Indians stopped trading willingly, the Spaniards used force to claim their riches. Columbus sought to impose a more rigid discipline but failed. On his final voyage, he introduced a system of *encomienda*, by which leading men received land and the labor of all Indians residing on it. By the time of Columbus's death in 1506, the islands he had discovered were dissolving into chaos as traders and adventurers fought with Indians and one another over the spoils of conquest. By then, no one believed that Columbus had discovered a route to China, but few people understood the revolutionary importance of the lands he had found.

Nonetheless, Columbus's voyages inspired others to head across the Atlantic (Map 1.3). In 1497 another Genoese navigator, John Cabot (or Caboto), sailing under the English flag,

---

COMPARATIVE ANALYSIS

Who Are These Native People?

European explorers portrayed native peoples in disparate ways, shaped by individual experiences and the larger context in which they wrote. When Christopher Columbus landed in the West Indies in October 1492, he kept a journal that highlighted the value of his discoveries to his Spanish sponsors, including friendly and submissive natives. Nearly thirty years later, when Ferdinand Magellan landed in the present-day Philippines, his crew had already suffered disease, starvation, and desertion and soon became embroiled in a deadly conflict between native groups. Antonio Pigafetta, a paying passenger on that voyage, described this more brutal encounter in his journal for April 1521.

Source 1.2

Christopher Columbus | Description of His First Encounter with Indians, 1492

I [believed] . . . that we might form great friendship, for I knew that they were a people who could be more easily freed and converted to our holy faith by love than by force, gave to some of them red caps, and glass beads to put round their necks, and many other things of little value, which gave them great pleasure, and made them so much our friends that it was a marvel to see. They afterwards came to the ship's boats where we were, swimming and bringing us parrots, cotton threads in skeins, darts, and many other things; and we exchanged them for other things that we gave them, such as glass beads and small bells. In fine [In short], they took all, and gave what they had with good will. It appeared to me to be a race of people very poor in everything.

They go as naked as when their mothers bore them, and so do the women, although I did not see more than one young girl. . . . They have no iron, their darts being wands without iron, some of them having a fish's tooth at the end. . . . They should be good servants and intelligent, for I observed that they quickly took in what was said to them, and I believe that they would easily be made Christians, as it appeared to me that they had no religion. I, our Lord being pleased, will take hence, at the time of my departure, six natives for your Highnesses, that they may learn to speak.

Source: *The Journal of Christopher Columbus (during His First Voyage, 1492–93) and Documents Relating to the Voyages of John Cabot and Gaspar Corte Real* (London: Hakluyt Society, 1893), 37–38.

---

reached an island off Cape Breton in the North Atlantic, where he discovered good cod fishing but met no local inhabitants. Over the next several years, Cabot and his son Sebastian made more trips to North America, but England failed to follow up on their discoveries.

More important at the time, Portuguese and Spanish mariners continued to explore the western edges of the Caribbean. Amerigo Vespucci, a Florentine merchant, joined one such voyage in 1499. It was Vespucci's account of his journey that led Martin Waldseemüller to identify the new continent he charted on his 1507 *Universalis Cosmographia* as "America." Meanwhile, Spanish explorers subdued tribes like the Arawak and Taino in the Caribbean

Source 1.3

Antonio Pigafetta | Journal, 1521

When day came, our men leaped into the water up to our thighs, forty-nine of them. . . . The boats could not come in closer because of certain rocks in the water. . . . [When the natives saw that we were firing muskets without any result] . . . they cried out determined to stand firm . . . shooting so many arrows and hurling bamboo lances, charred pointed stakes, stones and mud at the Captain [Magellan] that he could scarce defend himself. When the Captain saw this he sent some men to burn their houses to frighten them. And when they saw their houses burning they were all the more fierce. . . . And so great a number came upon us that they pierced the right leg of the Captain with a poisoned arrow, wherefore he ordered that they gradually retreat. . . . [But] they had so many spears, darts and stones that they [the soldiers] could not withstand them, and the artillery of the fleet was so far away that it could not help them. And our men withdrew to the shore, fighting all the while. . . . They [the natives] recognized the Captain and so many assailed him that twice they knocked his sallet [helmet] from his head. And he, like a good knight, continued to stand firm with a few others, and they fought thus for more than an hour. . . . An Indian threw his bamboo spear into his [the Captain's] face and he immediately killed him [the native] with his own spear. . . . And the Captain tried to draw his sword and was able to draw it only half way, because he had been wounded in the arm with a spear. . . . The Christian king [a rival chief who converted to Christianity] would have helped us but . . . the Captain bade him not to leave the ship. . . . When the king learned that the Captain was dead he grieved much, and not without cause.

Source: *The Voyage of Magellan, the Journal of Antonio Pigafetta*, trans. Paula Spurlin Paige (Englewood Cliffs, NJ: Prentice-Hall, 1969), 76–78.

Interpret the Evidence

1. How might Columbus's journal entry, which was circulated among clerics and officials in Spain, have shaped Spanish views about native peoples in the 1490s?
2. What does Pigafetta's description of the battle between Magellan's forces and native warriors suggest about how Spanish explorers viewed the native peoples they encountered in the Philippines? How does the response of the Christianized chief complicate our understanding of Spanish-native encounters?

Put It in Context

How might changing expectations and perceptions of native peoples between the 1490s and the 1520s have affected the actions of explorers as they encountered groups in newly discovered locations?

and headed toward the mainland. In 1513 Vasco Nuñez de Balboa traveled across the Isthmus of Darien (now Panama) and became the first known European to see the Pacific Ocean. That same year, the Spanish explorer Juan Ponce de León launched a search for gold and slaves along a peninsula he named Florida and claimed for Spain.

Ferdinand Magellan launched an even more impressive expedition in August 1519 when he, with the support of Charles V of Spain, sought a passageway through South America to Asia. In October 1520, after fifteen months of struggle and travail, his crew discovered a strait at the southernmost tip of South America that connected the Atlantic

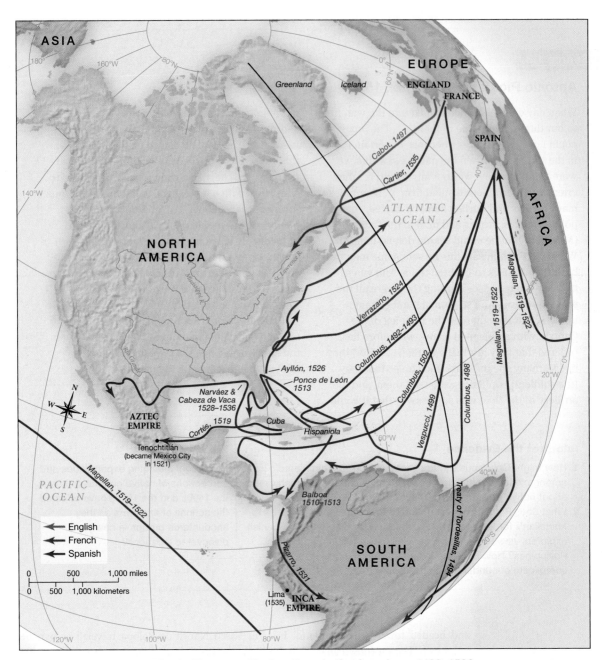

MAP 1.3   European Explorations in the Americas, 1492–1536

Early explorers, funded by Spain, sought trade routes to Asia or gold, silver, and other riches in the Americas. The success of these voyages encouraged adventurous Spaniards to travel throughout the West Indies, South America, and regions immediately to the north. It also inspired the first expeditions by the French and the English in North America.

and Pacific Oceans. Ill with scurvy and near starvation, the crew reached Guam and then the Philippines in March 1521. Magellan died there a month later, but one of his five ships and eighteen of the original crew finally made it back to Seville in September 1522, having successfully circumnavigated the globe. Despite the enormous loss of life and equipment, Magellan's lone ship was loaded with valuable spices and detailed information for cartographers, and his venture allowed Spain to claim the Philippine Islands.

Mapmaking and Printing.
Waldseemüller's 1507 map reflected the expanding contacts among Europe, Africa, and the Americas. Over the following decades, cartographers charted newly discovered islands, traced coastlines and bays, and situated each new piece of data in relation to lands already known.

The dissemination of geographical knowledge was greatly facilitated by advances in information technology. The Chinese had developed a form of printing with wood blocks in the tenth century, and woodcut pictures appeared in Europe in the fifteenth century. In the 1440s, German craftsmen invented a form of movable metal type in which each letter was created in a separate mold. This allowed printers to rearrange the type for each page and create multiple copies of a single manuscript more quickly and more cheaply than ever before. Between 1452 and 1455, Johannes Gutenberg, a German goldsmith, printed some 180 copies of the Bible with movable type. Although this was not the first book printed using the new system, Gutenberg's Bible marked a revolutionary change in the production and circulation of written texts.

Innovations in printing helped publicize Portuguese and Spanish explorations, the travels of European adventurers, and the atlases created by Waldseemüller and other cartographers. Italian craftsmen contributed by manufacturing paper that was thinner and cheaper than traditional vellum and parchment. Books were still expensive, and they could be read only by the small minority of Europeans who were literate. Still, mechanical printing rapidly increased the speed with which knowledge was circulated. The enhanced ability to exchange ideas encouraged their expression and ensured the flow of information among scholars and rulers across Europe.

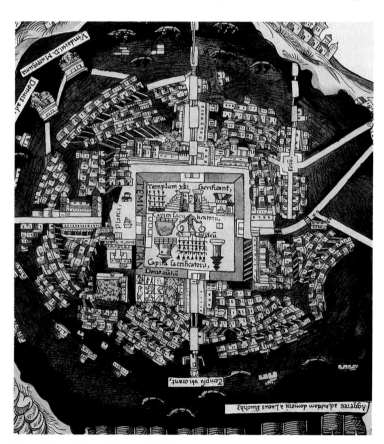

The Aztec City of Tenochtitlán   German geographers drew this map of Tenochtitlán in 1524 based on Aztec sources. At its peak, the city contained some 100,000 people. Temples, a marketplace, schools, the palace of the Aztec chief Montezuma, and a ball-game court stood at its center. The Aztecs viewed Tenochtitlán as the intersection of the secular and divine worlds. Bildarchiv Preussischer Kulturbesitz/Dietmar Katz/Art Resource, NY

The peoples of the Americas had their own ways of charting land, waterways, and boundary lines and of circulating information. The Maya, for instance, developed a system of glyphs — images that represented prefixes, suffixes, numbers, people, or words. Scribes carved glyphs into large flat stones, or *stela*, providing local residents with histories of important events. In settled farming villages, this system communicated information to a large portion of the population. But it could not serve, as printed pages did, to disseminate ideas more widely. Similarly, the extant maps created by the Maya, Aztecs, and other native groups tended to focus on specific locales. Still, we know that these groups traded across long distances, so they must have had some means of tracing rivers, mountains, and villages beyond their own communities.

The Columbian Exchange.

The Spaniards were aided in their conquest of the Americas as much by germs as by maps, guns, or horses. Because native peoples in the Western Hemisphere had had almost no contact with the rest of the world for millennia, they lacked immunity to most germs carried by Europeans. Disease along with warfare first eradicated the Arawak and Taino on Hispaniola, wiping out some 300,000 people. In the Inca empire, the population plummeted from about 9 million in 1530 to less than half a million by 1630. Among the Aztecs, the Maya, and their neighbors, the population collapsed from some 40 million people around 1500 to about 3 million a century and a half later. The germs spread northward as well, leading to catastrophic epidemics among the Pueblo peoples of the Southwest and the Mississippian cultures of the Southeast.

These demographic disasters — far more devastating even than the bubonic plague in Europe — were part of what historians call the **Columbian exchange**. But this exchange also involved animals, plants, and seeds and affected Africa and Asia as well as Europe and the Americas. The transfer of flora and fauna and the spread of diseases transformed the economies and environments of all four continents. Initially, the catastrophic decline in Indian populations ensured the victory of Spain and other European powers over American populations. Africans' partial immunity to malaria and yellow fever then made them attractive to Europeans seeking laborers for Caribbean islands after the native population was decimated. At the same time, African coconuts and bananas were traded to Europe, while European traders provided their African counterparts with iron and pigs. Asia also participated in the exchange, introducing both Europe and Africa not only to the bubonic plague but also to sugar, rice, tea, and highly coveted spices.

America provided Europeans with high-yielding, nutrient-rich foods like maize and potatoes, as well as new indulgences like tobacco and cacao. The conquered Inca and Aztec empires also provided vast quantities of gold and silver, making Spain the treasure-house of Europe and ensuring its dominance on the continent for several decades. Sugar was first developed in the East Indies, but it also became a source of enormous profits once it took root on Caribbean islands, which became known as the West Indies. Moreover, when mixed with cacao, sugar created an addictive drink known as chocolate.

In exchange for products that America offered to Europe and Africa, these continents sent rice, wheat, rye, lemons, and oranges as well as horses, cattle, pigs, chickens, and honeybees to the Western Hemisphere (Map 1.4). The grain crops transformed the American landscape, particularly in North America, where wheat became a major food source.

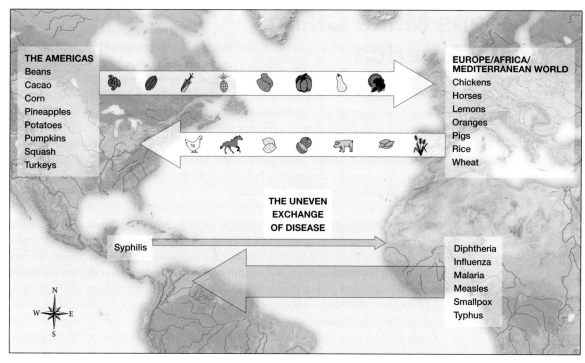

MAP 1.4   The Columbian Exchange, Sixteenth Century

When Europeans made contact with Africa and the Americas, they initiated an exchange of plants, animals, and germs that transformed all three continents. The contact among these previously isolated ecosystems caused dramatic transformations in food, labor, and mortality. American crops changed eating habits across Europe, while diseases devastated native populations even as foreign grains and domesticated animals thrived in the Americas.

Cattle and pigs, meanwhile, changed native diets, while horses inspired new methods of farming, transportation, and warfare throughout the Americas.

The Columbian exchange benefited Europe far more than the Americas. Initially, it also benefited Africa, providing new crops with high yields and rich nutrients. Ultimately, however, the spread of sugar and rice to the West Indies and European cravings for tobacco and cacao increased the demand for labor, which could not be met by the declining population of Indians. This situation ensured the expansion of the African slave trade to the Americas. The consequences of the Columbian exchange were thus monumental for the peoples of all three continents.

REVIEW & RELATE

- What were the short-term consequences in both Europe and the Americas of Columbus's voyages?

- How did the Columbian exchange transform both the Americas and Europe?

Europeans Make Claims to **North America**

With the help of native translators, warriors, and laborers, Spanish soldiers called **conquistadors** conquered some of the richest and most populous lands in South America in the early sixteenth century. Others then headed north, hoping to find gold in the southern regions of North America or develop new routes to Asia. At the same time, rulers of other European nations began to fund expeditions to North America. France and England both launched efforts to claim colonies in the Americas, though they failed to find the riches Spain had acquired. By the late sixteenth century, Spanish supremacy in the Americas and the wealth acquired there transformed the European economy. But conquest also raised critical questions about Spanish responsibilities to God and humanity.

Spaniards Conquer Indian Empires.

Although rulers in Spain supposedly set the agenda for American ventures, it was difficult to control the campaigns of their emissaries at such a distance. The Spanish crown held the power to grant successful leaders vast amounts of land and Indian labor via the encomienda system. But the leaders themselves then divided up their prizes to reward those who served under them, giving them in effect an authority that they sometimes lacked in law. This dynamic helped make Cortés's conquest of the Aztecs possible.

Diego de Velásquez, the Spanish governor of Cuba, granted Cortés the right to explore and trade along the coast of South America. He gave him no authority, however, to attack native peoples in the region or claim land for himself. But seeing the possibility for gaining great riches, Cortés forged alliances with local rulers willing to join the attack against the Aztec chief, Montezuma. From the perspective of local Indian communities, Cortés's presence offered an opportunity to strike back against the brutal Aztec regime.

Despite their assumption of cultural superiority, many Spaniards who accompanied Cortés were astonished by Aztec cities, canals, and temples, which rivaled those in Europe. Seeing these architectural wonders may have given some soldiers pause about trying to conquer the Indian kingdom. But when Montezuma presented Cortés with large quantities of precious objects, including gold-encrusted jewelry, as a peace offering, he alerted Spaniards to the vast wealth awaiting them in the Aztec capital.

When Cortés and his men marched to Tenochtitlán in 1519, Montezuma was indecisive in his response. After an early effort to ambush the Spaniards failed, the Aztec leader allowed Cortés to march his men into the capital city, where they took Montezuma hostage. In response, Aztec warriors attacked the Spaniards, but Cortés and his men managed to fight their way out of Tenochtitlán. They suffered heavy losses and might have been crushed by their Aztec foes but for the alliances forged with native groups in the surrounding area. Given time to regroup, the remaining Spanish soldiers and their allies attacked the Aztecs with superior steel weapons, horses, and trained dogs and gained a final victory.

The Spanish victory was also aided by the germs that soldiers carried with them. Smallpox swept through Tenochtitlán in 1521, killing thousands and leaving Montezuma's army dramatically weakened. This human catastrophe as much as military resources and strategies allowed Cortés to conquer the capital that year. He then claimed the entire region as New Spain, assigned soldiers to construct the new capital of Mexico City, and asserted Spanish authority over the native groups that had allied with him.

An Aztec with Smallpox   Smallpox followed the Spanish conquest, killing thousands of native peoples. In the sixteenth century, Bernardino de Sahagún, a missionary and educator, learned Nahuatl and wrote an illustrated history of New Spain with the aid of indigenous students. This illustration shows a woman with smallpox aided by a native healer. But the incurable disease ultimately led to death or disfigurement. Granger, NYC

As news of Cortés's victory spread, other Spanish conquistadors sought gold and glory in the Americas. Most important, in 1524 Francisco Pizarro conquered the vast Inca empire in present-day Peru. Once again, the Spaniards were aided by the spread of European diseases and conflicts among peoples subjected to Inca rule. This victory ensured Spanish access to vast supplies of silver in Potosí (in present-day Bolivia) and the surrounding mountains. It also ensured the spread of enslaved African labor from plantation agriculture to mining. Spain was now in control of the most densely populated regions of South America, which also contained the greatest mineral wealth. Still, the diversity of populations in these regions — wealthy Spanish *encomenderos*, much poorer Spanish soldiers, Indians, and Africans — concerned authorities. In response, the Spanish developed a caste system the defined the status of these diverse populations and ensured that Spaniards remained at the top of the hierarchy even as wealthy landowners distinguished themselves from their poorer countrymen. In one decade, life for Aztecs and other Indians as well as the Spanish changed dramatically. **See Primary Source Project 1: Indian and Spanish Encounters in the Americas, 1519–1530, page 32.**

Spanish Adventurers Head North. In 1526, a company of Spanish women and men traveled from the West Indies as far north as the Santee River in present-day South Carolina. They planned to settle in the region and then search for gold and other valuables. The effort failed, but two years later Pánfilo de Narváez — one of the survivors — led four hundred soldiers from Cuba to Florida's Tampa Bay. Seeking precious metals, the party instead confronted hunger, disease, and hostile Indians. The ragtag group continued to journey along the Gulf coast, until only four men, led by Álvar Núñez Cabeza de Vaca, made their way from Galveston Bay back to Mexico City. In both cases, native peoples effectively defended their political sovereignty, economic prosperity, and religious beliefs.

A decade later, in 1539, a survivor of Narváez's ill-fated venture—a North African named Esteban—led a party of Spaniards from Mexico back north. Lured by tales of Seven Golden Cities, the party instead encountered Zuñi Indians, who attacked the Spaniards and killed Esteban. Still, the men who returned to Mexico passed on stories of large and wealthy cities. Hoping to find fame and fortune, Francisco Vásquez de Coronado launched a grand expedition northward in 1540. Angered when they failed to discover fabulous wealth, Coronado and his men terrorized the region, burning towns, killing residents, and stealing goods before returning to Mexico.

Hernando de Soto headed another effort to find wealth in North America. An experienced conquistador, de Soto received royal authority in 1539 to explore Florida. That spring he established a village near Tampa Bay with more than six hundred Spanish, Indian, and African men, and a few women. A few months later, de Soto and the bulk of his company traveled up the west Florida coast with Juan Ortiz, a member of the Narváez expedition and an especially useful guide and interpreter. That winter, the expedition traveled into present-day Georgia and the Carolinas in an unsuccessful search for riches (Map 1.5).

On their return trip, de Soto's men engaged in a brutal battle with local Indians led by Chief Tuskaloosa. Although the Spaniards claimed victory, they lost a significant number of men and horses and most of their equipment. Fearing that word of the disaster would reach Spain, de Soto steered his men away from supply ships in the Gulf of Mexico and headed back north. The group traveled into present-day Tennessee, then turned west, and in May 1541 became the first Europeans to report seeing the vast Mississippi River. Crossing it, they journeyed on into Arkansas, Oklahoma, and Texas. By the winter of 1542, the expedition had lost more men and supplies to Indians, and de Soto had died. The remaining members finally returned to Spanish territory in the summer of 1543.

The lengthy journey of de Soto and his men brought European diseases into new areas, leading to epidemics and the depopulation of once-substantial native communities. At the same time, the Spaniards left horses and pigs behind, creating new sources of transportation and food for native peoples. Although most Spaniards considered de Soto's journey a failure, the Spanish crown claimed vast new territories. Two decades later, in 1565, Pedro Menéndez de Avilés established a mission settlement on the northeast coast of Florida, named St. Augustine. It became the first permanent European settlement in North America. Still, unlike the conquest of central and South America, the colonization of North America forced Spaniards to accept some of the native people's political and economic systems, religious beliefs, and even gender roles. When they refused to do so, open rebellions often resulted.

Europeans Compete in North America.

Spain's early ventures in North America helped inspire French and English explorers to establish their own footholds on the continent. The French entered the race for empire in 1524, when an Italian navigator named Giovanni da Verrazano led a French company along the coast of North America. Landing initially near Cape Fear on the Carolina coast, the expedition headed north, sailing into what would become New York harbor. Verrazano then continued north, claiming lands all along the coast for France.

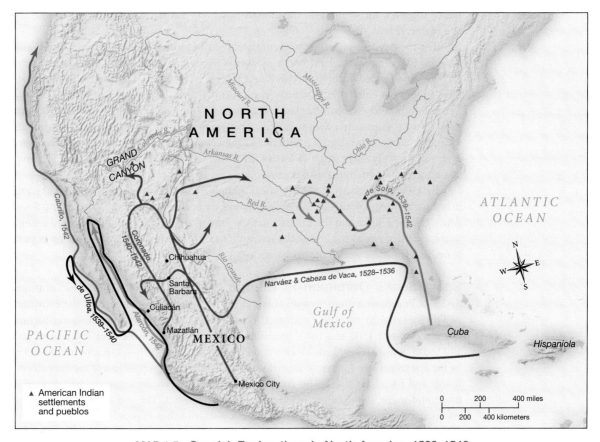

MAP 1.5 Spanish Explorations in North America, 1528–1542

Spanish explorers in North America hoped to find gold and other treasures. Instead, they encountered difficult terrain and native peoples hostile to Spanish intruders. Many Spaniards died on these expeditions, and they failed to discover new sources of wealth. But they laid the foundations for Spanish settlements in Florida, northern Mexico, and California while devastating local Indian populations.

A decade later, in 1534, the Frenchman Jacques Cartier sailed to the Gulf of St. Lawrence. In two subsequent expeditions, Cartier pushed deeper into the territory known as Canada. Although he failed to discover precious metals or the elusive passage to the Pacific Ocean, he did trade for furs with local Indians. Cartier also inspired a French nobleman, the Sieur de Roberval, and several hundred followers to attempt a permanent settlement at Quebec in 1542. But the project was abandoned within a year because of harsh weather, disease, and high mortality.

English interest in North America was ignited by Spanish and French challenges to claims Cabot had made along the North Atlantic coast in the 1490s. To secure these rights, the English needed to colonize the disputed lands. Since the English crown did not have funds to support settlement, the earliest ventures were financed by minor noblemen who hoped to gain both wealth and the crown's favor. The earliest of these, in Newfoundland and Maine, failed.

The most promising effort to secure an English foothold was organized by Sir Walter Raleigh. Claiming all the land north of Florida for England, Raleigh called the vast territory Virginia (after Elizabeth I, "the Virgin Queen"). In 1585 Raleigh sent a group of soldiers to found a colony on Roanoke Island, off the coast of present-day North Carolina. The colony would establish England's claims and allow English sailors stationed there to seize Spanish ships laden with valuables. This venture lasted less than a year. But in 1587 Raleigh tried again, sending a group of 117 men, women, and children to Roanoke. However, when supply ships came to fortify the settlement in 1590, the settlers had all disappeared, and their fate remains unknown.

By 1590, then, nearly a century after Columbus's initial voyage, only Spain had established permanent colonies in the Americas, mostly in the West Indies, Mexico, and South America. The French and the English, despite numerous efforts, had not sustained a single ongoing settlement by the end of the sixteenth century. Yet neither nation gave up hope of benefiting from the wealth of the Americas.

Spain Seeks Dominion in Europe and the Americas.

The continued desire of European nations to gain colonies in the Americas resulted from the enormous wealth garnered by Spanish conquests. That wealth transformed economies throughout Europe. Between 1500 and 1650, Spanish ships carried home more than 180 tons of gold and 16,000 tons of silver from Mexico and Potosí. About one-fifth of this amount was taken by the Spanish crown for taxes; the rest was dispersed among supporters of the expeditions; family and friends of those who conquered lands, gained *encomiendas*, or participated in trade; and soldiers and sailors who returned from America. The money was spent mainly on luxury goods imported from the Americas, Asia, or other European nations. Very little of this wealth was invested in improving conditions at home. Indeed, the rapid infusion of gold and silver fueled inflation, making it harder for ordinary people to afford the necessities of life.

In one area, however, employment for the poor expanded rapidly. Spain's King Philip II (r. 1556–1598) used American gold and silver to fund a variety of military campaigns, ensuring an endless demand for soldiers and sailors. The king, a devout Catholic, claimed to be doing God's work as Spain conquered Italy and Portugal, including the latter's colonies in Africa, and tightened its grip on the Netherlands, which had been acquired by Spain through marriage in the early sixteenth century.

Despite the obvious material benefits, the Spaniards were not blind to the enormous human costs of colonization, and the conquest of the Americas inspired heated debates within Spain. Catholic leaders believed that the conversion of native peoples to Christianity was critical to Spanish success in the Americas. However, most royal officials and colonial agents viewed the extraction of precious metals as far more important. They argued that cheap labor was essential to creating wealth. Yet brutal conditions led to the death of huge numbers of Indians, which made it nearly impossible to convert others to Catholicism.

By 1550, tales of the widespread torture and enslavement of Indians convinced the Spanish king Carlos V (r. 1519–1556) to gather a group of theologians, jurists, and philosophers at Valladolid to discuss the moral and

Explore ▶

Read two historians' interpretations of Indian responses to Spanish rule in Secondary Sources 1.4 and 1.5.

Spanish Torturing Indians   In the late 1500s, Theodor de Bry and his sons created a series of detailed and graphic engravings of interactions between Spanish soldiers and American Indians based on reports from explorers and missionaries. Some portrayed Spaniards torturing Indians. These popular illustrations led critics to protest the Spanish conquest of the Americas, which they labeled the "Black Legend." Beinecke Rare Book and Manuscript Library, Yale University.

legal implications of conquest. Bartolomé de Las Casas took a leading role in defending the rights of Indians. A former conquistador and Dominican friar, Las Casas had spent many years preaching to Indians in America. He asked, "And so what man of sound mind will approve a war against men who are harmless, ignorant, gentle, temperate, unarmed, and destitute of every human defense?" Las Casas reasoned that even if Spain defeated the Indians, the souls of those killed would be lost to God, while among the survivors "hatred and loathing of the Christian religion" would prevail. He even suggested replacing Indian labor with African labor, apparently less concerned with the souls of black people.

Juan Ginés de Sepúlveda, the royal historian, attacked Las Casas's arguments. Although he had never set foot in America, he read reports of cannibalism and other violations of "natural law" among native peoples. Since the Indians were savages, the civilized Spaniards were obligated to "destroy barbarism and educate these people to a more humane and virtuous life." If they refused such help, Spanish rule "can be imposed upon them by force of arms." Although Ginés de Sepúlveda spoke for the majority at Valladolid,

SECONDARY SOURCE ANALYSIS

Indians in the New Spanish Empire

While Theodor De Bry depicted and Bartolomé de Las Casas denounced the cruelty Spanish conquistadores visited on Indians in the Americas, most Indians who survived the conquest were forced to accommodate to their new rulers. Many had already been conquered and even enslaved by more powerful Indian societies like the Aztec or Maya. Finding a way to survive did not mean that Indians wholly accepted Spanish authority, but it did require wielding more subtle forms of resistance or finding ways to benefit from the new imperial system.

Source 1.4

Camilla Townsend | An Indian Woman Aids in the Conquest of Mexico, 2006

It was not simply that the Spanish needed their translators in order to find their way and obtain requisite food and water. They needed them for far more than this—for the conquest itself. . . .

[Malintzin] knew that her survival was dependent on the Spaniards' survival, so she was motivated to observe them carefully; undoubtedly her years as a slave had honed her skills in that regard. . . . [B]y all accounts she learned Spanish and Spanish ways quickly. . . . By 1524 . . . Malintzin did all his [Cortés'] translation between Spanish, Nahuatl, and Maya.

For Malintzin could do more than repeat what others said in a foreign vocabulary. . . . [S]he could speak in different registers and thus make a necessary point more effectively. . . . [The] Spaniards who depended on her competence seemed to like and admire her.

Bernal Diaz [a Spanish conquistador who wrote a history of the conquest] . . . conveys that she spoke to them archly or coquettishly if need be—in other words, that she knew how to handle her Spanish male audience. Such an approach, however, would never have worked with her Nahua audiences, who were also largely male. With them, . . . she spoke like . . . "a lady of power," not . . . like a playful girl. A playful girl should respect her elders, not tell them what to do. She knew this and adjusted her tone accordingly.

She was to need all her skills, linguistic and otherwise, as they [the Spanish army] marched from the sea to Tenochtitlan.

Source: Camilla Townsend, *Malintzin's Choices: An Indian Woman in the Conquest of Mexico* (Albuquerque: University of New Mexico Press, 2006), 58–59.

Las Casas and his supporters continued to press their case as Spain expanded its reach into North America.

At the same time, American riches increasingly flowed beyond Spain's borders. The Netherlands was a key beneficiary of this wealth, becoming a center for Spanish shipbuilding and trade. Still, the Dutch were never completely under Spanish control, and they traded gold, silver, and other items to France, England, and other European nations. Goods also followed older routes across the Mediterranean to the Ottoman empire, where traders could make huge profits on exotic items from the Americas. Thus, while some Europeans

Source 1.5

Jane E. Mangan | Indians Seek to Benefit from Spanish Conquest, 2005

History has made Potosí as infamous for its forced labor draft, known as the *mita*, as it was famous for its silver. . . . [T]he Spanish victimization of native Andeans through the mita is indisputable. . . .

The early modern Dutch engraver Theodor de Bry provided one of the most enduring visual images of the mine labor. . . . because it portrayed the Indians' victimization by the Spanish. . . . [But] had de Bry's European contemporaries been able to turn their view 180 degrees from the mines and face the town center of Potosí, an equally compelling . . . scene would have appeared. Sixteenth-century Potosí resident Luis Capoche['s] . . . view of the bustling marketplace highlights . . . areas where Andean historians have modified a De Bry-like image of Indians as victims of Spanish colonization. . . . Economic historians have revealed that highland native Andean groups, like the Lupaqas and the Carangas, made a business trading coca, foodstuffs, and llamas. . . . [H]istorians of mining and labor have shown how Indians stole silver to sell for profit (and thus boosted the brisk exchange in the marketplace). . . .

In the same era that Capoche observed the market plaza, Cuzco native Catalina Palla marketed bread and coca on credit to indigenous residents of Potosí. The mother of several children with Spanish men, Palla dressed in finely woven native textiles known as *cumbi*. Engaged in urban and economic and social exchanges that included both native Andeans and Spaniards, Palla was representative of an urban marketeer. . . .

[Yet others], like Bartolina, brewed *chicha* [corn beer] for the Spaniard Francisca Nieto for pitiful wages. . . ."

Source: Jane E. Mangan, *Trading Roles: Gender, Ethnicity, and the Urban Economy in Colonial Potosí* (Durham, N.C.: Duke University Press, 2005), 4–5 and 7.

Examine the Sources

1. Evaluate the effectiveness of Townsend's and Mangan's interpretations about Indian responses to Spanish conquest, identifying differences and similarities in their arguments.
2. Many of the sources on native peoples come from Spanish observers. What are the challenges in using these sources to understand native experiences in Mexico and Potosí?

Put It in Context

How does recognizing the ways that Indian women and men accommodated to Spanish authority shape your overall evaluation of the Spanish conquest of the Aztecs and the Incas?

suffered under Spanish power, others benefited from the riches brought to the continent. By the late sixteenth century, the desire for a greater share of those riches revitalized imperial dreams among the French and English as well as the Dutch.

REVIEW & RELATE

What motivated the Spanish to conquer and colonize the Americas?

What were the consequences in Europe of Spain's acquisition of an American empire?

Conclusion: A **Transformed America**

For centuries, Asian peoples migrated to the Americas by land and sea. They developed an astonishing array of cultures and societies, from small hunting-and-gathering bands to complex empires. In the fourteenth and fifteenth centuries, extensive commercial and political networks existed among the Mississippians, the Aztecs, and the Incas, although only the latter two continued to thrive by the late 1400s. In southern Europe, too, during the fifteenth century, economic, cultural, and political advances fueled interest in long-distance trade and exploration. Italy and Portugal led these efforts, but their monopoly of trade routes across the Mediterranean and around Africa to Asia forced Spain to look west in hopes of gaining access to China and the Indies. In doing so, the Spanish unexpectedly came into contact with the Americas.

When Spanish explorers happened upon Caribbean islands and the nearby mainland, they created contacts between populations that would be dramatically transformed in a matter of decades. While native residents of the Americas were sometimes eager to trade with the newcomers and to form alliances against their traditional enemies, they fought against those they considered invaders. Yet some of the most significant invaders — plants, pigs, and especially germs — were impossible to defend against. Even Europeans seeking peaceful relations with native inhabitants or bent on conversion rather than conquest brought diseases that devastated local populations, and plants and animals that transformed their landscape, diet, and traditional ways of life.

Waldseemüller died in 1521 or 1522, so he did not see the most dramatic changes that his remarkably accurate maps inspired. Malintzin, however, experienced those changes firsthand. She watched as disease ravaged not only rural villages but even the capital city of Tenochtitlán. She encountered horses, pigs, attack dogs, and other European animals. She ate the foods and wore the clothes that her Spanish captors provided. In 1522, Malintzin gave birth to Cortés's son; two years later, she served as interpreter when he ventured north to conquer more territory. In 1526 or 1527, however, she married a Spanish soldier, Juan Jaramillo, settled in Mexico City, and bore two more children. As more and more Spaniards, including the first women, settled in New Spain, Malintzin realized that her children would grow up in a world very different from the one in which she was raised.

From 1490 to 1590, the most dramatic and devastating changes for native peoples occurred in Mexico, the West Indies, Central America, and South America. But events there also presaged what would happen throughout the Americas. As Spanish conquistadors ventured into Florida and the Gulf Coast and French and English explorers sought to gain footholds along the Atlantic seaboard, they carried sufficient germs, seeds, and animals to transform native societies even before Europeans established permanent settlements in North America.

In the century to come, contacts and conflicts between native peoples and Europeans would escalate as France, England, and the Netherlands joined Spain in colonizing North America. Conflicts among European nations also multiplied as they struggled to control land, labor, and trade. Moreover, as Indian populations died out in some regions and fended off conquest in others, Europeans turned increasingly to the trade in Africans to provide the labor to produce enormously profitable items like sugar, coffee, and tobacco.

TIMELINE OF **EVENTS**

25,000–13,000 B.C.E.	First northeast Asians migrate to the Americas
900 B.C.E.–300 C.E.	Maya settle Yucatán peninsula
500 C.E.	Mogollon and Hohokam settle in southwestern North America; spread of maize cultivation northward begins
500–1400	Mississippian peoples establish complex cultures
800	Mayan civilization begins to decline
1000	Norse settle in North America
1325	Aztecs build Tenochtitlán
1340s	Black Death (bubonic plague) in Europe
1400–1500	Inca empire reaches its height
1440s	Portuguese begin to trade along the coast of West Africa
1452–1455	Johannes Gutenberg prints Bibles using movable type
1469	Unification of Spain
1487	Bartolomeu Dias rounds the Cape of Good Hope
1492	Spain expels Muslim conquerors and Jews
	Christopher Columbus's first voyage to the Americas
1497	Vasco da Gama sails to India
1507	Martin Waldseemüller and Mathias Ringmann publish *Universalis Cosmographia*
1519	Malintzin captured by Spaniards
1519–1521	Hernán Cortés conquers the Aztecs
1519–1522	Ferdinand Magellan's fleet circumnavigates the globe
1524	Francisco Pizarro conquers the Incas
1587	English settle Roanoke Island

KEY **TERMS**

Beringia, *3*

horticulture, *4*

Aztecs, *4*

Maya, *6*

Incas, *6*

Hopewell people, *7*

Crusades, *10*

Black Death, *10*

Renaissance, *10*

Enterprise of the Indies, *15*

encomienda, *15*

Columbian exchange, *20*

conquistadors, *22*

REVIEW & RELATE

1. Compare and contrast the Aztecs, Incas, and Maya. What similarities and differences do you note?
2. How did the societies of North America differ from those of the equatorial zone and the Andes?
3. How and why did Europeans expand their connections with Africa and the Middle East in the fifteenth century?
4. How did early European encounters with West Africans influence Europeans' ideas about African peoples and reshape existing systems of slavery?
5. What were the short-term consequences in both Europe and the Americas of Columbus's voyages?
6. How did the Columbian exchange transform both the Americas and Europe?
7. What motivated the Spanish to conquer and colonize the Americas?
8. What were the consequences in Europe of Spain's acquisition of an American empire?

Indian and Spanish Encounters in the Americas, 1519–1530

▶ Evaluate the significance of the cultural misunderstandings between Indians and the Spanish in shaping political, social, and economic relations in the early sixteenth century.

The arrival of Europeans in the Americas in the fifteenth century reshaped the society, culture, and economy of the entire world. For the Indians who had inhabited the region for thousands of years, these encounters began a story of devastation. Europeans came in search of wealth and glory (see Source 1.8). They brought with them superior firepower and, more significantly, deadly diseases that led to the dramatic decline of the Indian population. After the Spanish explorer Hernán Cortés conquered the Aztec city of Tenochtitlán in 1521, Spain emerged as the world's preeminent empire.

On the local level, the Columbian exchange of plants, animals, diseases, and ideas between Europe, Africa, and the Americas meant a clash of distinct cultures (see Sources 1.7 and 1.9). The Spanish questioned the Indians' religions, social norms, and work habits. They sought to impose Catholicism and control the Indians' labor, and they used extreme means to reach these ends (Source 1.6). The Indians tried to resist the imposition of Spanish culture, but a variety of factors related to differences in power, cultural views, and economic systems among the many Indian societies that occupied present-day Mexico and the Gulf Coast undermined their efforts.

The following documents explore early contact between Europeans, specifically the Spanish, and American Indians, primarily the Aztecs. As you read, consider the many levels of cultural misunderstanding and misinterpretation that occurred when these worlds collided.

Source 1.6

Hernán Cortés | Letter to King Charles I, 1520

Hernán Cortés wrote a series of letters to the Spanish king Charles I detailing his experiences and progress in Mexico. In the following excerpt from his second letter, Cortés explains how the Indians refused to accept Catholicism and the rule of the Spanish king. He then describes military actions that he carried out against the Indians.

When I undertook to [read] my requirements in due form, through the interpreters whom I had brought with me, and . . . the more diligent I was to admonish and require them to keep the peace, just so much the more diligent were they in committing hostilities upon us, and, seeing that neither requirements nor protests were of any avail, we began to defend ourselves as best we could, and thus they kept us fighting, until we found ourselves in the midst of an hundred thousand warriors, who surrounded us on all sides. This went on all day long, until about an hour before sunset, when they retired. In this fight I did them a good deal of harm with about half a dozen cannon, and five or six muskets, forty archers, and thirteen horsemen . . . without our receiving any hurt from them. . . . And it truly appeared that it was God who battled for us, because amongst such a multitude of people, so courageous and skilled in fighting, and with so many kinds of offensive arms, we came out unhurt.

That night I fortified myself in a small tower of their idols, which stood on a small hill, and afterwards, at daybreak, I left two hundred men and all the artillery in the camp. As I was the attacking party I went out towards evening with the horsemen, and a hundred foot soldiers, and four hundred Indians whom I had brought from Cempoal, and three hundred from Yztacmastitan. Before the enemy had time to assemble, I set fire to five or six small places of about a hundred houses each, and brought away about four hundred prisoners, both men and women, fighting my way back to my camp without their doing me any harm. At daybreak the following morning, more than a hundred and forty-nine thousand men, covering all the country, attacked our camp so determinedly that some of them penetrated into it, rushing about, and thrusting with their swords at the Spaniards. We mustered against them, and Our Lord was pleased so to aid us, that, in about four hours, we managed that they should no more molest us in our camp. . . .

The next day I again went out before daybreak, in another direction, without having been observed by the enemy, taking with me the horsemen, a hundred foot-soldiers, and the friendly Indians. I burned more than a hundred villages, one of which had more than three thousand houses, where the villagers fought with me, though there were no other people there. As we carried the banner of the Holy Cross, and were fighting for our Faith, and in the service of Your Sacred Majesty, to Your Royal good fortune God gave us such a victory that we slew many people without our own sustaining any injury. . . .

Messengers came from the chiefs the next day, saying that they wished to become vassals of Your Highness and my friends, beseeching me to pardon their past fault; and they brought me provisions, and certain feather-work which they use, and esteem and prize. I answered that they had behaved badly, but that I was satisfied to be their friend, and pardon them for all they had done. . . .

When we had somewhat rested, I made a sally [foray] one night . . . taking a hundred foot[men], the friendly Indians, and the horsemen; and about a league from our camp five horses and mares fell, unable to go on, so I sent them back. Although those who accompanied me, said that I ought to return, as this was an evil omen, I still pushed ahead, confiding in God's supremacy above everything. Before daybreak I fell upon two towns, in which I slaughtered many people, but I did not want to burn the houses, so as to avoid attracting the attention of other people who were very near. When day dawned I fell upon another large town, . . . and, as I had surprised them, I found them unarmed, and the women and children, running naked through the streets; and we did them some harm. Seeing they could offer no resistance, a certain number of the inhabitants came to beseech me not to do them further injury, for they desired to become vassals of Your Highness, and my friends.

Source: Francis Augustus MacNutt, ed. and trans., *Fernando Cortés: His Five Letters of Relation to the Emperor Charles V* (Cleveland: Arthur H. Clark, 1908), 201–3, 205–6.

Source 1.7

Aztec Priests | Respond to the Spanish, 1524

As Indian resistance to the *requerimiento* — the requirement for obedience to the Catholic Church — indicated, most Aztecs did not want to renounce their own religion in favor of Catholicism. In 1524 twelve Franciscan friars organized a series of meetings with Aztec political and religious leaders, who defended the legitimacy of their own customs. In the 1560s another friar published the notes from these meetings, providing insight into how Aztec leaders viewed the differences between their own beliefs and those of the Spanish.

You say that we [the Aztecs] do not recognize the being that is everywhere, lord of heaven and earth. You say our gods are not true gods. The new words that you utter are what confuse us; due to them we feel foreboding. Our makers [our ancestors] who came to live on earth never uttered such words. They gave us their *laws*, their ways of doing things. They believed in the gods, served them and honored them. They are the ones who taught us everything, the gods' being served and respected. Before them we eat earth [kiss the ground]; we bleed; we pay our debts to the gods, offer incense, make

33

sacrifice. . . . Indeed, we live by the grace of those gods. They rightly made us out of the time, the place where it was still dark. . . . They give us what we go to sleep with, what we get up with [our daily sustenance], all that is drunk, all that is eaten, the produce, corn, beans, green maize, chia. We beg from them the water, the rain, so that things grow upon the earth.

The gods are happy in their prosperity, in what they have, always and forever. Everything sprouts and turns green in their home. What kind of place is the land of Tlaloc [the god of rain]? Never is there any famine there, nor any illness, nor suffering. And they [the gods] give people virility, bravery, success in the hunt, [bejeweled] lip rings, blankets, breeches, cloaks, flowers, tobacco, jade, feathers and gold.

Since time immemorial they have been addressed, prayed to, taken as gods. It has been a very long time that they have been revered. . . . These gods are the ones who established the mats and thrones [that is, the inherited chieftainships], who gave people nobility, and kingship, renown and respect.

Will we be the ones to destroy the ancient traditions of the Chichimeca, the Tolteca, the Colhuaca? [No!] It is our opinion that there is life, that people are born, people are nurtured, people grow up, [only] by the gods' being called upon, prayed to. Alas, o our lords, beware lest you make the common people do something bad. How will the poor old men, the poor old women, forget or erase their upbringing, their education? May the gods not be angry with us. Let us not move towards their anger. And let us not agitate the commoners, raise a riot, lest they rebel for this reason, because of our saying to them: address the gods no longer, pray to them no longer.

Source: Camilla Townsend, ed. and trans., *American Indian History: A Documentary Reader* (Malden, MA: Wiley-Blackwell, 2009), 29–30.

Hernán Cortés and Malintzin Meet Montezuma at Tenochtitlán, 1519

This image, depicting Cortés and Malintzin meeting Montezuma in November 1519, is one of eighty illustrations from a sixteenth-century mural cycle detailing the conquest of Mexico and its aftermath. The originals were painted by Tlaxcalan artists and represent an Indian perspective on these events. Malintzin is standing between Cortés (seated) and Montezuma (in gold robe). The Spanish and Aztec leaders are accompanied by leading warriors.

Gianni Dagli Orti/Rex/Shutterstock

34

Álvar Núñez Cabeza de Vaca | *La Relación*, c. 1528

In 1528 a group of Spaniards sailed from Cuba to Tampa Bay in present-day Florida. After failing to find great riches, the survivors tried to return to Cuba but were washed ashore at Galveston Bay. Álvar Núñez Cabeza de Vaca and three other men survived the expedition, but only after enduring a nine-year, six-hundred-mile trek across Texas and Mexico and enslavement by Indians. In an account of his journey, Cabeza de Vaca described his experiences on the Isla de Malhado (Island of Misfortune) off the coast of Texas.

All the people of this country go naked; only the women cover part of their bodies with a kind of wool that grows on trees. The girls go about in deer skins. They are very liberal towards each other with what they have. There is no ruler among them. All who are of the same descendancy [ancestry] cluster together. There are two distinct languages spoken on the island; those of one language are called Capoques, those of the other Han. They have the custom, when they know each other and meet from time to time, before they speak, to weep for half an hour. After they have wept the one who receives the visit rises and gives the other all he has. The other takes it, and in a little while goes away with everything. Even sometimes, after having given and obtained all, they part without having uttered a word. There are other very queer customs, but having told the principal ones and the most striking, I must now proceed to relate what further happened to us. . . .

I had to remain with those same Indians of the island for more than one year, and as they made me work so much and treated me so badly I determined to flee and go to those who live in the woods on the mainland, and who are called those from Charruco. . . .

Among many other troubles I had to pull the eatable roots out of the water and from among the canes where they were buried in the ground, and from this my fingers had become so tender that the mere touch of a straw caused them to bleed. . . . This is why I went to work and joined the other Indians. Among these I improved my condition a little by becoming a trader, doing the best in it I could, and they gave me food and treated me well.

They entreated me to go about from one part to another to get the things they needed, as on account of constant warfare there is neither travel nor barter in the land.

So, trading along with my wares I penetrated inland as far as I cared to go and along the coast as much as forty or fifty leagues. My stock consisted mainly of pieces of seashells and cockles, and shells with which they cut a fruit which is like a bean, used by them for healing and in their dances and feasts. This is of greatest value among them, besides shell-beads and other objects. These things I carried inland, and in exchange brought back hides and red ochre with which they rub and dye their faces and hair; flint for arrow points, glue and hard canes wherewith to make them, and tassels made of the hair of deer, which they dye red. This trade suited me well because it gave me liberty to go wherever I pleased; I was not bound to do anything and no longer a slave. Wherever I went they treated me well, and gave me to eat for the sake of my wares. My principal object in doing it, however, was to find out in what manner I might get further away. . . .

My sufferings, while trading thus, it would take long to tell; danger, hunger, storms and frost overtaking me often in the open field and alone, and from which through the mercy of God, Our Lord, I escaped. For this reason I did not go out trading in winter, it being the time when the Indians themselves remain in their huts and abodes, unable to go out or assist each other.

Nearly six years I spent thus in the country, alone among them and naked, as they all were themselves.

Source: Adolph F. Bandelier, ed., *The Journey of Álvar Núñez Cabeza de Vaca and His Companions from Florida to the Pacific, 1528–1536* (New York: A. S. Barnes, 1905), 71–76.

Interpret the Evidence

1. How does Hernán Cortés treat his Indian adversaries (Source 1.6) and how does he justify this treatment and to whom? What conflicts among the Indians themselves are revealed in Cortés's letter?

2. How do the Aztec priests respond to Spanish criticisms of their religion? Why do they refuse to abandon their gods (Source 1.7)?

3. What does the mural image, created by Tlaxcalan Indians, suggest about the relative power of Montezuma and Cortés at this meeting and the possibilities for conflict or cooperation between them (Source 1.8)? Given the information in Sources 1.6 and 1.7, what concerns might Malintzin, as the translator, have about conveying information to each leader?

4. What does Álvar Núñez Cabeza de Vaca find surprising about Indian culture, and how might that reflect differences between the Spanish and Indians (Source 1.9)? How does his story differ from the information provided in Sources 1.6, 1.7, and 1.8?

Put It in Context

What do these sources reveal about Spanish-Indian relations throughout the conquest period? How did news of these encounters shape debates among Spanish religious leaders over the conquest in the 1550s?

What roles did religion, military power, and economic interests play in the differing perspectives among the Indians, among Spaniards, and between the Indians and the Spanish?

Colonization and Conflicts

1580–1680

WINDOW TO THE PAST

William Nahaton, Petition to Free an Indian Slave, 1675

William Nahaton, a Christianized Indian in Massachusetts Bay, sent this petition to gain the release of a relative whom he feared would be sold into slavery by the English. While hundreds of native people were sold into slavery, petitions for their release were rare. This petition offers important insights into the views of an Indian who had chosen to adopt many English ways.

▸ To discover more about what this primary source can show us, see Source 2.6 on page 65.

Massachusetts Archives Collection. 30:176. Petition from William Nahaton, 1675. SC1/series 45X. Courtesy of the Massachusetts Archives, Boston, Massachusetts.

After reading this chapter you should be able to:

- Discuss the impact of the Reformation and Counter-Reformation on European nations and their imperial goals in the American colonies.

- Evaluate the ways that England's hopes for its North American colonies were transformed by relations with Indians, upheavals among indentured servants, the development of tobacco, and the emergence of slavery.

- Analyze the influence of Puritanism on New England's development and how religious and political upheavals in England fueled Puritan expansion and conflicts with Indians in the colonies.

COMPARING AMERICAN HISTORIES

Born in 1580 to a yeoman farm family in Lincolnshire, John Smith left England as a young man "to learne the life of a Souldier." After fighting and traveling in Europe, the Mediterranean, and North Africa for several years, Captain Smith returned to England around 1605. There he joined the Virginia Company, whose wealthy investors planned to establish a private settlement on mainland North America. In April 1607, Captain Smith and 104 men arrived in Chesapeake Bay, where they founded Jamestown, named in honor of King James I, and claimed the land for themselves and their country. However, the area was already controlled by a powerful Indian leader, Chief Powhatan.

(left) **John Smith** Beinecke Rare Book and Manuscript Library, Yale University
(right) **Anne Hutchinson** Schlesinger Library, Radcliffe Institute, Harvard University/Bridgeman Images

In December 1607, when Powhatan's younger brother discovered Smith and two of his Jamestown comrades in the chief's territory, the Indians executed the two comrades but eventually released Smith. It is likely that before sending him back to Jamestown, Powhatan performed an adoption ceremony in an effort to bring Smith and the English under his authority. A typical ceremony would have involved Powhatan sending out one of his daughters — in this case, Pocahontas, who was about twelve years old — to indicate that the captive was spared. Refusing to accept his new status, if he understood it, Smith returned to Jamestown and urged residents to build fortifications for security.

The following fall, the colonists elected Smith president of the Jamestown council. Smith insisted that intimidating the Indians was the way to win Powhatan's respect. He also demanded that the English labor on farms and fortifications six hours a day. Many colonists resisted. Those who claimed the status of gentlemen considered manual labor beneath them, and the many who were adventurers sought wealth and glory, not hard work. The Virginia Company soon replaced Smith with a new set of leaders. In October 1609, angry and bitter, he returned to England.

Captain Smith published his criticisms of Virginia Company policies in 1612, which brought him widespread attention. He then set out to map the Atlantic coast farther north. In 1616 Smith published a tract that emphasized the similarity of the area's climate and terrain to the British Isles, calling it New England. He argued that colonies there could be made commercially viable but that success depended on recruiting settlers with the necessary skills and offering them land and a say in the colony's management.

English men and women did settle New England in the 1620s, but they sought religious sanctuary, not commercial success or military dominance. Yet they, too, suffered schisms in their ranks. Anne Hutchinson, a forty-five-year-old wife and mother, was at the center of one such division. Born in Lincolnshire in 1591, Anne was well educated when she married William Hutchinson, a merchant, in 1612. The Hutchinsons and their children began attending Puritan sermons and by

1630 embraced the new faith. Four years later, they followed the Reverend John Cotton to Massachusetts Bay.

The Reverend Cotton soon urged Anne Hutchinson to use her exceptional knowledge of the Bible to hold prayer meetings in her home on Sundays for pregnant and nursing women who could not attend regular services. Hutchinson, like Cotton, preached that individuals must rely solely on God's grace rather than a saintly life or good works to ensure salvation.

Hutchinson began challenging Puritan ministers who opposed this position, charging that they posed a threat to their congregations. She soon attracted a loyal and growing following that included men as well as women. Puritan leaders met in August 1637 to denounce Hutchinson's views and condemn her meetings. In November 1637, after she refused to recant, she was put on trial. Hutchinson mounted a vigorous defense. Unmoved, the Puritan judges convicted her of heresy and banished her from Massachusetts Bay. Hutchinson and her family, along with dozens of followers, then settled in the recently established colony of Rhode Island. ■

Comparing the American histories of John Smith and Anne Hutchinson illustrates the diversity of motives that drew English men and women to North America in the seventeenth century. Smith led a group of artisans, gentlemen, and adventurers whose efforts to colonize Virginia were in many ways an extension of a larger competition between European states. Hutchinson's journey to North America was rooted in the Protestant Reformation, which divided Europe into rival factions. Yet as different as these two people were, both furthered English settlement in North America even as they generated conflict within their own communities. Communities like theirs also confronted the expectations of diverse native peoples and the colonial aspirations of other Europeans while reshaping North America between 1550 and 1680.

Religious and Imperial Transformations

The Puritans were part of a relatively new religious movement known as **Protestantism** that had emerged around 1520. Protestants challenged Catholic policies and practices but did not form a single church of their own. Instead, a number of theologians formed distinct denominations in various regions of Europe. Catholics sought to counter their claims by revitalizing their faith and reasserting control. These religious conflicts shaped developments in North America as the Spanish, French, Dutch, and English competed for lands and sometimes souls.

The Protestant Reformation.

Critiques of the Catholic Church multiplied in the early sixteenth century, driven by papal involvement in conflicts among monarchs and corruption among church officials. But the most vocal critics focused on immorality, ignorance, and absenteeism among clergy. These anticlerical views appeared in popular songs and printed images as well as in learned texts by theologians such as Martin Luther.

Luther, a professor of theology in Germany, believed that faith alone led to salvation, which could be granted only by God. He challenged the Catholic Church's claim that individuals could achieve salvation by buying indulgences, which were documents that absolved the buyer of sin. The church profited enormously from these sales, but they suggested that God's grace could be purchased. In 1517 Luther wrote an extended argument against indulgences and sent it to the local bishop. Although intended for learned clerics and academics, his writings soon gained a wider audience.

Luther's followers, who protested Catholic practices, became known as Protestants. His teachings circulated widely through sermons and printed texts, and his claim that ordinary people should read and reflect on the Scriptures appealed to the literate middle classes. Meanwhile his attacks on indulgences and corruption attracted those who resented the church's wealth and priests' lack of attention to their flocks. In Switzerland, John Calvin developed a version of Protestantism in which civil magistrates and reformed ministers ruled over a Christian society. Calvin argued that God had decided at the beginning of time who was saved and who was damned. Calvin's idea, known as predestination, energized Protestants who understood salvation as a gift from an all-knowing God in which the "works" of sinful humans played no part.

The Protestant Reformation quickly spread through central and northern Europe. England, too, came under the influence of Protestantism in the 1530s, although for different reasons. When the pope refused to annul the marriage of King Henry VIII (r. 1509–1547) and Catherine of Aragon, Henry denounced papal authority and established the **Church of England**, or Anglicanism, with himself as "defender of the faith." Despite the king's conversion to Protestantism, the Church of England retained many Catholic practices.

In countries like Spain and France with strong central governments and powerful ties to the Catholic Church, a strong Catholic Counter-Reformation largely quashed Protestantism. At the same time, Catholic leaders initiated reforms to counter their critics. In 1545 Pope Paul II called together a commission of cardinals, known as the Council of Trent (1545–1563), which initiated a number of reforms, such as the founding of seminaries to train priests and the return of monastic orders to their spiritual foundations.

Religious upheavals in Europe turned many eyes toward North America. Protestant and Catholic leaders urged followers to spread their faith across the Atlantic, while religious minorities sought a safe haven free from persecution. Just as important, political struggles erupted between Catholic and Protestant rulers in Europe following the Reformation. The resulting economic and military crises pushed (or forced) people to seek new opportunities in the Americas. Thus, in a variety of ways, religious transformations in Europe fueled the construction of empires in America.

Spain's Global Empire Declines.

As religious conflicts escalated in Europe, the Spaniards in America continued to push north from Florida and Mexico in hopes of expanding their empire. The nature of Spanish expansion, however, changed. As a result of the Council of Trent and the Catholic Counter-Reformation, Spain increasingly emphasized its religious mission. Thus Spanish authorities decided in 1573 that missionaries rather than soldiers should direct all new settlements. Franciscan priests began founding missions on the margins of Pueblo villages north of Mexico. They named the area Nuevo México (New Mexico), and many learned Indian languages. Over the following decades, as many as twenty thousand Pueblos officially converted to Catholicism, although many still retained traditional beliefs and practices. Missionaries made a considerable effort to eradicate such beliefs and practices, including flogging ceremonial leaders, but to no avail.

At the same time, the Franciscans tried to force the Pueblo people to adopt European ways. They insisted that men rather than women farm the land and that the Pueblos speak,

San Esteban del Rey Mission
Opened in 1644 after fourteen years of construction, this Spanish mission in present-day New Mexico provided instruction in Christianity and Hispanic customs for the Acoma (Pueblo) people. To this end, Spanish missionaries prohibited traditional Pueblo practices such as performing dances and wearing masks. The mission was one of the few to survive Pueblo revolts in the late seventeenth century. © age fotostock/ SuperStock

cook, and dress like the Spaniards. Yet the missionaries largely ignored Spanish laws intended to protect Indians from coerced labor, demanding that the Pueblos build churches, provide the missions with food, and carry their goods to market. Wealthy land-owners who followed the missionaries into New Mexico also demanded tribute in the form of goods and labor.

Then in 1598 Juan de Oñate, a member of a wealthy mining family, established a trading post and fort in the upper Rio Grande valley. The 500 soldiers who accompanied him seized corn and clothing from Pueblo villages and murdered or raped those who resisted. When the Spanish force was confronted by Indians at the Acoma pueblo, 11 soldiers were killed. The Spanish retaliated, slaughtering 500 men and 300 women and children. Fearing reprisals from outraged Indians, most Spanish settlers withdrew from the region.

In 1610 the Spanish returned, founded Santa Fe, and established a network of missions and estates owned by *encomenderos*, Spanish elites granted land and the right to exploit local Indian labor. This time the Pueblo people largely accepted the new situation. In part, they feared military reprisals if they challenged Spanish authorities. But they were also facing drought, disease, and raids by hostile Apache and Navajo tribes. The Pueblos hoped to gain protection from Spanish soldiers and priests. Yet their faith in the Franciscans' spiritual power soon began to fade when conditions did not improve. Although Spain maintained a firm hold on Florida and its colonies in the West Indies, it began focusing most of its efforts on staving off growing resistance among the Pueblo people. Thus as other European powers expanded their reach into North America, the Spaniards were left with few resources to protect their eastern frontier.

France Enters the Race for Empire. In the late sixteenth century, French, Dutch, and English investors became increasingly interested in gaining a foothold in North America. But until Catholic Spain's grip on the Atlantic world was broken, other nations could not hope to compete for an American empire. It was the Protestant Reformation that helped shape the alliances that shattered Spain's American monopoly. As head of the Church of England, Queen Elizabeth I (King Henry VIII's daughter, r. 1558–1603) sought closer political and commercial ties with Protestant nations like the Netherlands. The queen also assented to, and benefited from, Francis Drake's raids on Spanish ships. In 1588 King Philip II of Spain (r. 1556–1598) decided to punish England for its attacks against Spanish shipping and intervention in the Netherlands and sent a massive armada to spearhead the invasion of England. Instead, the English, aided by Dutch ships, defeated the armada and ensured that other nations could compete for riches and colonies in North America.

Although French rulers shared Spain's Catholic faith, the two nations were rivals, and the defeat of the armada provided them as well as the Dutch and English with greater access to North American colonies. Moreover, once in North America, the French adopted attitudes and policies that were significantly different from those of Spain. This was due in part to their greater interest in trade than in conquest. The French had fished the North Atlantic since the mid-sixteenth century, but in the 1580s they built stations along the Newfoundland coast for drying codfish. French traders then established relations with local Indians, exchanging iron kettles and other European goods for valuable beaver skins.

By the early seventeenth century, France's King Henry IV (r. 1589–1610) sought to profit more directly from the resources in North America. With the Edict of Nantes (1598), the king ended decades of religious wars by granting political rights and limited toleration to French Protestants, known as Huguenots, many of whom had earlier sought refuge in North America. Now he could focus on developing the increasingly lucrative trade in American fish and furs. Samuel de Champlain founded the first permanent French settlement in North America in 1608 at Quebec. Accompanied by several dozen men, Champlain joined a Huron raid on the Iroquois, who resided south of the Great Lakes. By using guns, the French helped ensure a Huron victory and a powerful ally for the French. But the battle also fueled lasting bitterness among the Iroquois.

Trade relations flourished between the French and their Indian allies, but relatively few French men and even fewer French women settled in North America in the seventeenth century. Government policies discouraged mass migration, and peasants were also concerned by reports of short growing seasons and severe winters in Canada. Cardinal Richelieu, the king's chief minister, urged priests and nuns to migrate to New France, but he barred continued emigration by Huguenots, which further limited colonization. Thus into the 1630s, French settlements in North America consisted largely of fishermen, fur traders, and Catholic missionaries.

Fur traders were critical to sustaining the French presence and warding off encroachment by the English. They journeyed throughout eastern Canada, aided by the Huron tribe. Some Frenchmen took Indian wives, who provided them with both domestic labor and kinship ties to powerful trading partners. Despite Catholic criticism of these marriages, they enhanced French traders' success and fostered alliances among the Ojibwe and Dakota nations to the west. These alliances, in turn, created a middle ground in which economic and cultural exchanges led to a remarkable degree of mutual adaptation. French traders benefited from Indian women's skills in preparing beaver skins for market as well as from Indian canoes, while natives adopted iron cooking pots and European cloth.

In their ongoing search for new sources of furs, the French established a fortified trading post at Montreal in 1643, and over the next three decades

Explore ▶

In Source 2.1, read a Catholic nun's report of a Huron woman's complaints about the Jesuits.

GUIDED ANALYSIS

A French Nun Reports a Huron Woman's View of the Jesuits, 1640

Jesuit missionaries and Ursuline nuns brought the Catholic faith to Indians in New France along with germs and guns. In this letter, the nun Marie de L'Incarnation writes to her superiors about the views expressed by an elderly and respected Huron woman. She conveys a report she heard about this woman, who told her village that the Jesuits, known as Black Robes, were destroying their communities. L'Incarnation summarizes and then analyzes the Huron woman's speech.

Source 2.1

What is the Huron woman's evidence of the Jesuits' danger to her people?

What are the sources, in her experience, of the Jesuits' power to do harm?

How does Marie de L'Incarnation interpret the message of this Huron woman?

It's the Black Robes who are making us die by their spells. Listen to me, I will prove it by reasons that you will recognize as true. They set themselves up in a village where everyone is feeling fine; no sooner are they there, but everyone dies except for three or four people. They move to another place, and the same thing happens. They visit cabins in other villages, and only those where they have not entered are exempt from death and illness. Don't you see that when they move their lips in what they call prayer, spells are coming out of their mouths? It's the same when they read their books. They have big pieces of wood [guns] in their cabins by which they make noise and send their magic everywhere. If they are not promptly put to death, they will end up ruining the country, and no one will be left, young or old. . . .

When she stopped speaking, everyone agreed that this was true, . . . [and] it seemed true . . . , for wherever the [Jesuit] Fathers went, God permitted death to accompany them so as to render more pure the faith of those who converted.

Source: Marie de L'Incarnation, *Correspondance*, ed. Dom Guy Oury (Abbaye de Saint-Pierre, 1971), trans. Natalie Zemon Davis, *Women on the Margins: Three Seventeenth-Century Lives* (Cambridge, MA: Harvard University Press, 1995), 111–12.

Put It in Context

How might this account of a Huron woman's perspective have been transformed in its retelling and translation? Despite these changes, what can it tell us about Huron interactions with Catholic priests and nuns in the early 1600s?

they continued to push farther west. However, as they extended the fur trade beyond the St. Lawrence River valley, the French left their Huron allies behind. The Iroquois wanted to keep the Huron tribe from trading their high-quality furs to the Dutch. With guns supplied by Dutch merchants, the Iroquois could fend off economic competition and secure captives to restore their population, which was decimated by disease. The result was a series of devastating assaults on Huron villages.

The ongoing wars among native rivals limited the ability of France to capitalize on its North American colonies. Indeed, the only hope of maintaining profits from the fur trade was to continue to move westward. But in doing so, the French carried European diseases into new areas, ignited warfare among more native groups, and stretched their always small population of settlers ever thinner. Still, French explorers, traders, and priests extended their reach across Canada and by 1681 had moved southward along the Mississippi to a territory they named Louisiana in honor of King Louis XIV (r. 1643–1715).

The conflicts between commerce and conversion so evident in Spanish America were far less severe in New France. French traders relied on Indian allies, and some French Jesuit priests also sought to build on native beliefs and to learn the Indians' language and customs. Although Catholics assumed that their own religious beliefs and cultural values were superior to those of the Indians, many sought to engage Indians on their own terms. Thus one French Jesuit employed the Huron belief that "our souls have desires which are inborn and concealed" to explain Christian doctrines of sin and salvation to potential converts. Still, French traders and missionaries carried deadly germs, and Catholics sought conversion, not mutual adaptation. Thus while Indians clearly benefited from their alliances with the French in the short term, the long-term costs would prove devastating.

The Dutch Expand into North America.

The Protestant Dutch made no pretense of bringing religion to Indians in America. From the beginning, their goals were primarily economic. As Spain's shipbuilding center, the Netherlands benefited from the wealth pouring in from South America, and an affluent merchant class emerged. But the Dutch also embraced Calvinism and sought to separate themselves from Catholic Spain. In 1581 the Netherlands declared its independence from King Philip II (r. 1556–1598), although Spain refused to recognize the new status for several decades. Still, by 1600 the Netherlands was both a Protestant haven and the trading hub of Europe. Indeed, the Dutch East India Company controlled trade routes to much of Asia and parts of Africa.

With the technology and skills developed under Spanish control, the Dutch decided to acquire their own American colonies. In 1609 the Dutch established a fur-trading center on the Hudson River in present-day New York. The small number of Dutch traders developed especially friendly relations with the powerful Mohawk nation, and in 1614 the trading post was relocated to Fort Orange, near present-day Albany.

In 1624, to fend off French and English raids on ships sent downriver from Fort Orange, the Dutch established New Amsterdam on Manhattan Island, which they purchased from the Lenape Indians. The new settlement was organized by the Dutch West India Company, which had been chartered three years earlier. New Amsterdam was the centerpiece of the larger New Netherland colony and attracted a diverse community of traders, fishermen, and farmers. It was noted for its representative government and religious toleration.

The European settlers of New Netherland, which became part of the Middle Colonies, may have gotten along with one another, but the same could not be said for settlers and local Indians. Tensions increased as Dutch colonists carved out farms north of New Amsterdam where large communities of Algonquian Indians lived. In 1639 conflict escalated when Governor William Kieft demanded an annual tribute in wampum or grain. Local Algonquians resisted, raiding Dutch farms on the frontier and killing at least two colonists. Then in 1643 Kieft launched a surprise attack on an Indian encampment on Manhattan Island, murdering eighty people, mostly women and children. Outraged Algonquians burned and looted homes north of the city, killed livestock, and murdered settlers. For two decades, sporadic warfare continued, but eventually the Algonquians were defeated.

New Amsterdam   This engraving on copper offers one of the oldest extant images of New Amsterdam. It captures the thriving commercial center of New Netherland at the tip of Manhattan. It also illustrates the importance of enslaved Africans to the colony's success and the significant role played by Dutch women as well as men in its economic development.
New York Public Library, USA/Bridgeman Images

At the same time, the Dutch eagerly traded for furs with Mohawk Indians along the upper Hudson River. The Mohawks were a powerful tribe that had the backing of the even more powerful Iroquois Confederacy. Their ties to Indian nations farther west allowed them to provide beaver skins to Dutch traders long after beavers had died out in the Hudson valley. Still, the Mohawk people did not deceive themselves. As one chief proclaimed in 1659, "The Dutch say we are brothers and that we are joined together with chains, but that lasts only so long as we have beavers."

Meanwhile reports of atrocities by both Indians and the Dutch circulated in the Netherlands. These damaged New Amsterdam's reputation and slowed migration dramatically. A series of wars with their former ally England further weakened Dutch power in America. In 1664, the England sent a naval convoy to take New Amsterdam. Exhausted by decades of unrelenting conflict, the Dutch surrendered New Amsterdam to the English without a fight.

REVIEW & RELATE

How did the Protestant Reformation shape the course of European expansion in the Americas?

How did the French and Dutch colonies in North America differ from the Spanish empire to the south?

The **English Seek** an **Empire**

The English, like the French and the Dutch, entered the race for an American empire well after the Spanish. England did not have a permanent settlement in the Americas until the founding of **Jamestown** at the mouth of Chesapeake Bay in 1607. In the 1620s, the English also established settlements in the West Indies, which quickly became the economic engine of English colonization. Expansion into these areas demanded new modes of labor to ensure a return on investment. Large numbers of indentured servants crossed the Atlantic, while growing numbers of Africans were forced onto ships for sale in the Americas. meanwhile, the rapid expansion of English settlement fostered conflicts with Indian nations and fueled tensions among settlers themselves.

The English Establish Jamestown. England's success in colonizing North America depended in part on a new economic model in which investors purchased shares in joint-stock companies that could raise large amounts of money quickly. If the venture succeeded, investors shared the profits. If they failed, no investor suffered the whole loss. In 1606 a group of London merchants formed the Virginia Company, and King James I granted them the right to settle a vast area of North America, from present-day New York to North Carolina.

Some of the men that the Virginia Company recruited as colonists were gentlemen who hoped to get rich through the discovery of precious metals. They also recruited skilled artisans and laborers to launch the settlement, many of whom hoped to gain wealth and status. Some men who planned to stay for an extended period even brought their wives, which was almost unheard of among Spanish and French explorers and missionaries. Arriving on the coast of North America in April 1607, the colonists established Jamestown on a site they chose mainly for its easy defense since it lay within territory controlled by a large confederation of Indians. Although bothered by the settlement's mosquito-infested environment, the colonists variously focused their energies on constructing buildings, producing food, and searching for gold and silver.

The Englishmen quickly made contact with the Indian chief Powhatan. He presided over the confederation of some 14,000 Algonquian-speaking Indians from twenty-five to thirty tribes, which surrounded

A Susquehannock Warrior   John Smith published a remarkably accurate map of Virginia in 1612. It included major geographical features and the names of some 200 Indian towns. Smith placed a sketch of a Susquehannock warrior in the upper right-hand corner; at his feet, Smith noted that the Susquehannock were "a Gyant-like people." This map was widely used for seven decades. Beinecke Rare Book and Manuscripts Library, Yale University

the small Jamestown settlement. The **Powhatan Confederacy** was far more powerful than the English settlers, and, indeed, for the first two years the settlers depended on the Indians to survive. A shortage of food, caused by a severe drought between 1606 and 1612, affected both Indians and the English. It was exacerbated in Jamestown by some colonists' refusal to engage in manual labor. Moreover, the nearby water was tainted by salt from the ocean, and diseases that festered in the low-lying area killed more than half of the original settlers.

Despite the Englishmen's aggressive posture, Powhatan assisted the new settlers in hopes they could provide him with English cloth, iron hatchets, and even guns. His capture and subsequent release of John Smith in 1607 suggests his interest in developing trade relations with the newcomers even as he sought to subordinate them. But leaders like Captain Smith considered Powhatan and his warriors a threat rather than an asset. When unable to feed themselves that first year, Jamestown residents raided Indian villages for corn and other food, making Powhatan increasingly wary. The settlers' decision to construct a fort under Smith's direction only bolstered the Indians' concern.

Meanwhile the Virginia Company devised a plan to stave off the collapse of its colony. It started selling seven-year joint-stock options to raise funds and recruited new settlers to produce staple crops, glassware, or other items for export. Interested individuals who could not afford to invest cash could sign an indenture for service in Virginia. After seven years, these indentured servants would gain their freedom and receive a hundred acres of land. In June 1609, a new contingent of colonists attracted by this plan — five hundred men and a hundred women — sailed for Jamestown.

The new arrivals, however, had not brought enough supplies to sustain the colony through the winter. Powhatan did offer some aid, but Indians, too, suffered from shortages in the winter of 1609–1610. A "starving time" settled on Jamestown. By the spring of 1610, seven of every eight settlers who had arrived in Jamestown since 1607 were dead.

That June, the sixty survivors decided to abandon Jamestown and sail for home. But they changed their minds when they met three English ships in the harbor loaded with supplies and three hundred more settlers. Emboldened by fresh supplies and an enlarged population, Jamestown's new leaders adopted an aggressive military posture, attacking native villages, burning crops, killing many Indians, and taking others captive. They believed that such brutality would convince neighboring tribes to obey English demands for food and labor.

Tobacco Fuels Growth in Virginia. It was not military aggression, however, but the discovery of a viable cash crop that saved the colony. Orinoco tobacco, grown in the West Indies and South America, sold well in England and Europe. Virginia colonist John Rolfe began to experiment with its growth in 1612, just as the drought lifted. Production of the leaf soared as eager investors poured seeds, supplies, and labor into Jamestown. Exports multiplied rapidly, from 2,000 pounds in 1615 to 40,000 pounds five years later and an incredible 1.5 million pounds by 1629.

Tobacco cultivation exacerbated tensions between the English and the Indians. As production increased and prices declined, farmers could increase their profits only by obtaining more land and more laborers. That is why the Virginia Company was willing to offer land to indentured laborers who spent seven years clearing new fields and creating more plantations. Yet in most cases, the land the Virginia Company offered these

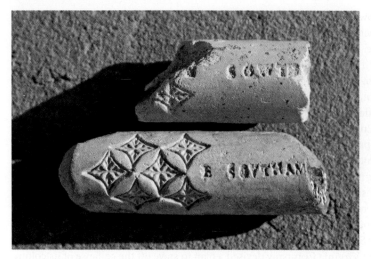

Clay Tobacco Pipe, James Fort, Virginia   Robert Cotton, a pipe maker from England, arrived in Jamestown in 1608. He copied Indian designs in crafting pipes from Virginia clay. Cotton added decorations and the names of leading men before the clay was fired. These fragments, discovered at an archaeological dig, suggest the importance of local artisans in Jamestown and the interplay of Indian and English styles. Courtesy Jamestown Rediscovery (Historic Jamestowne)

would-be colonists was already settled by members of the Powhatan Confederacy. Thus the rapid increase in tobacco cultivation intensified competition between colonists and Indians.

Nonetheless, Powhatan tried one last time to create an alliance between his confederacy and the English settlers. Perhaps he was encouraged by the return of rain, assuming that increased productivity would ensure better trade relations with the English. In 1614 he agreed to allow his daughter Pocahontas to marry John Rolfe. Pocahontas converted to Christianity and two years later traveled to England with Rolfe and their infant son. While there, she fell ill and died in 1617. Rolfe returned to Virginia just as relations with the Powhatan Confederacy began to change. In 1618 Powhatan died, and his younger brother Opechancanough took over as chief.

A year later, in 1619, the English crown granted Virginia the right to establish a local governing body, the **House of Burgesses**. Its members could make laws and levy taxes, although the English governor or the company council in London held veto power. The Virginia Company also resolved to recruit more female settlers as a way to increase the colony's population. More young women and men arrived as **indentured servants**, working in the fields and homes of more affluent Englishmen for a set period of time in exchange for passage to America. A Dutch ship carried the first boatload of twenty Africans to Jamestown that same year, bound as indentured servants to farmers desperate for labor.

Although the English colony still hugged the Atlantic coast, its expansion increased conflict with native inhabitants. In March 1622, after repeated English incursions on land cleared and farmed by Indians, Chief Opechancanough and his allies launched a surprise attack that killed nearly a third of the colonists. In retaliation, Englishmen assaulted native villages, killed inhabitants, burned cornfields, and sold captives into slavery.

The English proclaimed victory in 1623, but hostilities continued for nearly a decade. In 1624, in the midst of the crisis, King James annulled the Virginia Company charter and took control of the colony. He appointed the governor and a small advisory council, required that legislation passed by the House of Burgesses be ratified by the Privy Council,

Engraving of Pocahontas, 1616
Simon van de Passe created this portrait of Pocahontas during her visit to England in 1616. The engraving was commissioned by the Virginia Company to promote settlement in Jamestown. It was the only portrait of Pocahontas made before her death in London. While van de Passe clothes her in English aristocratic style, he retains her dark complexion and direct gaze. Library of Congress, 3a10723

and demanded that property owners pay taxes to support the Church of England. These regulations became the model for royal colonies throughout North America.

Still, royal proclamations could not halt Indian opposition. In 1644 Opechancanough launched a second uprising against the English, killing hundreds of colonists. After two years of bitter warfare, Chief Opechancanough was finally captured and then killed. With the English population now too large to eradicate, the Chesapeake Indians finally submitted to English authority in 1646.

Expansion, Rebellion, and the Emergence of Slavery. By the 1630s, despite continued conflicts with Indians, Virginia was well on its way to commercial success. The most successful tobacco planters used indentured servants, including some Africans as well as thousands of English and Irish immigrants. Between 1640 and 1670, some 40,000 to 50,000 of these migrants settled in Virginia and neighboring Maryland (Map 2.1). Maryland was founded in 1632 when King Charles I, the successor to James I, granted most of the territory north of Chesapeake Bay to Cecilius Calvert and appointed him Lord Baltimore. Calvert was among the minority of English who remained a Catholic, and he planned to create Maryland as a refuge for his persecuted co-worshippers. Appointing his brother Leonard Calvert as governor, he carefully prepared for the first settlement. The Calverts recruited artisans and

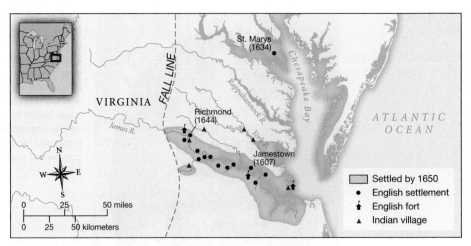

MAP 2.1 The Growth of English Settlement in the Chesapeake, c. 1650

With the success of tobacco, English plantations and forts spread along the James River and north to St. Mary's. By 1650 most Chesapeake Indian tribes had been vanquished or forced to move north and west. The fall line, which marked the limit of navigable waterways, kept English settlements close to the Atlantic coast but also ensured easy shipment of goods.

farmers (mainly Protestant) as well as wealthy merchants and aristocrats (mostly Catholic) to settle the colony. Although conflict continued to fester between the Catholic elite and the Protestant majority, Governor Calvert convinced the Maryland assembly to pass the Act of Religious Toleration in 1649, granting religious freedom to all Christians.

Taken together, Maryland and Virginia formed the Chesapeake region of the English empire. Both colonies relied on tobacco to produce the wealth that fueled their growth, and both introduced African labor to complement the supply of white indentured servants. Still, neither colony had yet developed a legal code of slavery. From 1650 on, however, improved economic conditions in England meant fewer English men and women were willing to gamble on a better life in North America. Even though the number of African laborers remained small until late in the century, colonial leaders considered measures to increase their control over the African population. In 1660 the House of Burgesses passed an act that allowed black laborers to be enslaved and in 1662 defined slavery as an inherited status passed on from mothers to children. In 1664 Maryland followed suit. The slow march toward full-blown racial slavery had begun. In legalizing human bondage, Virginia legislators followed a model established in Barbados, where the booming sugar industry spurred the development of plantation slavery. By 1660 Barbados had become the first English colony with a black majority population. Twenty years later, there were seventeen slaves for every white indentured servant on Barbados. The growth of slavery on the island depended almost wholly on imports from Africa since slaves there died faster than they could reproduce themselves. In the context of high death rates, brutal working conditions, and massive imports, Barbados systematized its slave code, defining enslaved Africans as chattel — that is, as mere property more akin to livestock than to human beings.

While African slaves would become, in time, a crucial component of the Chesapeake labor force, indentured servants made up the majority of bound workers

Explore ▶

In Sources 2.2 and 2.3, analyze the experiences of indentured servants in Maryland.

in Virginia and Maryland for most of the seventeenth century. They labored under harsh conditions, and punishment for even minor infractions could be severe. They were beaten, whipped, and branded for a variety of behaviors. Some white servants made common cause with black laborers who worked side by side with them on tobacco plantations. They ran away together, stole goods from their masters, and planned uprisings and rebellions.

By the 1660s and 1670s, the population of former servants who had become free formed a growing and increasingly unhappy class. Most were struggling economically, working as common laborers or tenants on large estates. Those who managed to move west and claim land on the frontier were confronted by hostile Indians like the Susquehannock. Virginia governor Sir William Berkeley, who levied taxes to support nine forts on the frontier, had little patience with the complaints of these colonists. The labor demands of wealthy tobacco planters needed to be met, and frontier settlers' call for an aggressive Indian policy would hurt the profitable deerskin trade with the Algonquian Indians.

In late 1675, conflict erupted when frontier settlers attacked Indians in the region. Unlike colonial leaders back east, men on the frontier generally considered all Indians hostile. Rather than attacking only the Susquehannock nation, they also assaulted Indian communities allied with the English. When a large force of local Virginia militiamen did surround a Susquehannock village, they ignored pleas for peace and murdered five chiefs. Susquehannock warriors retaliated with raids on frontier farms. Despite the outbreak of open warfare, Governor Berkeley still refused to send troops, so disgruntled farmers turned to Nathaniel Bacon. Bacon came from a wealthy family and was related to Berkeley by marriage. But he defied the governor's authority and called up an army to attack Indians across the colony. **Bacon's Rebellion** had begun. Frontier farmers formed an important part of Bacon's coalition. But affluent planters who had been left out of Berkeley's inner circle also joined Bacon in hopes of gaining access to power and profits. And bound laborers, black and white, assumed that anyone who opposed the governor was on their side.

In the summer of 1676, Governor Berkeley declared Bacon guilty of treason. Rather than waiting to be captured, Bacon led his army toward Jamestown. Berkeley then arranged a hastily called election to undercut the rebellion. Even though Berkeley had rescinded the right of men without property to vote, Bacon's supporters won control of the House of Burgesses, and Bacon won new adherents. These included "news wives," lower-class women who spread information (and rumors) about oppressive conditions to aid the rebels. As Bacon and his followers marched across Virginia, his men plundered the plantations of Berkeley and his supporters. In September they reached Jamestown after the governor and his administration fled across Chesapeake Bay. The rebels burned the capital to the ground, victory seemingly theirs.

Only a month later, however, Bacon died of dysentery, and the movement he formed unraveled. Governor Berkeley quickly reclaimed power. He hanged twenty-three rebel leaders and incited his followers to plunder the estates of planters who had supported Bacon. But he could not undo the damage to Indian relations on the Virginia frontier. Bacon's army had killed or enslaved hundreds of once-friendly Indians and left behind a tragic and bitter legacy.

Another important consequence of the rebellion was that wealthy planters and investors realized the depth of frustration among poor whites who were willing to make

COMPARATIVE ANALYSIS

Indentured Servants in the Chesapeake

Indentured servants, who generally worked for tobacco farmers in seventeenth-century Maryland and Virginia, had little control over their lives. They could ask local courts or county councils, however, to intervene if they were severely abused. In Document 2.2 Sarah Tailer accuses her master and mistress of physical abuse. Although she did not win this case, evidence of repeated abuse led the court to free her two years later. In Document 2.3, the Virginia General Assembly (also known as the House of Burgesses) granted freedom to Elizabeth Key, the daughter of a white father and an enslaved mother. An Assembly Committee accepted Key's claim that she had been an indentured servant, not a slave.

Source 2.2

Sarah Tailer Charges Captain and Mrs. Thomas Bradnox with Abuse, 1659

A Court holden on Kent the first day of October 1659

Sarah Tailer Complaineth to the Majestrate mr Joseph [W]ickes of divers wronges & abuses given her by her Master and Mrs, Capt Thomas Bradnox & Mary his wife. . . .

John Jenkins sworne in Court Examined saith That he never saw Capt Bradnox or his wife strike his Servant Sarah Tailer with either Bulls pisle [whip] or Rope but he saw the said Sarah have a blacke place crosse one of her shoulders & this Deponent heard her Mrs give her som bad words. . . .

Tobias [W]ells on oath saith that he saw Sarah Tailer Stript & on her backe he saw severall blacke spotts and on her Arme a great black spott about as broad as his hand. . . .

Mr Joseph [W]ickes doth Informe the Court that Mrs Mary Bradnox broake the peace in strikeinge her Sarvant before him beinge a Majestrate, And on the time when the said Sarvant was there to make her Complaint which the said [M]r [W]ickes could not in Justice passe by or suffer, which was one blow or stroke with a Ropes ende.

Source: J. Hall Pleasants, ed., *Archives of Maryland*, vol. 54, *Proceedings of the County Courts of Kent, 1648–1676* (Baltimore: Maryland Historical Society, 1937), 167–69.

common cause with their black counterparts. Having regained power, the planter elite worked to crush any such interracial alliance. Virginia legislators began to improve the conditions and rights of poor white settlers while imposing new restrictions on blacks. At nearly the same time, in an effort to meet the growing demand for labor in the West Indies and the Chesapeake, King Charles II chartered the Royal African Company in 1672 to carry enslaved Africans to North America.

The English Compete for West Indies Possessions.
While tobacco held great promise in Virginia, investors were eager to find other lucrative exports. Some turned their sights on the West Indies. In the 1620s, the English developed more permanent settlements on St. Christopher, Barbados, and Nevis (Map 2.2). Barbados quickly became the most attractive of these West Indies colonies. English migrants settled

Source 2.3

Report of a Committee of the Assembly Concerning the Freedom of Elizabeth Key, 1656

It appeareth to us that shee is the daughter of Thomas Key [a white planter] . . . by a fine imposed upon the said Thomas for getting her mother with Child. . . . That she hath bin by verdict of a Jury . . . in the County of Northumberland found to be free by several oaths. . . . That by the Comon Law the Child of a Woman slave begot by a freeman ought to bee free. That she hath bin long since Christened. . . . That Thomas Key sould her only for nine years to Col Higginson with several conditions to use her more Respectfully than a Comon servant or a slave. . . . For theise reasons, wee conceive the said Elizabeth ought to bee free and that her last Master should give her Corn and Cloathes and give her satisfaction for the time shee hath served longer then Shee ought to have done.

Source: "A Report of a Committee from the Assembly Concerning the Freedome of Elizabeth Key," in Warren M. Billings, ed., *The Old Dominion in the Seventeenth Century: A Documentary History of Virginia, 1609–1689* (Chapel Hill: University of North Carolina Press, 1975), 167.

Interpret the Evidence

1. What does the case of Sarah Tailer suggest about the ability of white indentured servants to use the courts to address their grievances?
2. How did the Northumberland County Court and the Assembly Committee justify granting freedom to Elizabeth Key?

Put It in Context

How do these court cases help us understand legal efforts in the 1660s to redefine the status of blacks and the gradual replacement of indentured servants with slaves thereafter?

Barbados in growing numbers, bringing in white indentured servants, many Irish and Scotch, to cultivate tobacco and cotton and raise livestock.

In the 1630s, falling tobacco prices resulted in economic stagnation on Barbados. By that time, however, a few forward-looking planters were already considering another avenue to wealth: sugarcane. English and European consumers absorbed as much sugar as the market could provide, but producing sugar was difficult, expensive, and labor-intensive. In addition, the sugar that was sent from America needed further refinement in Europe before being sold to consumers. The Dutch had built the best refineries in Europe, but their small West Indies colonies could not supply sufficient raw material. By 1640 they formed a partnership with English planters, offering them the knowledge and financing to cultivate sugar on Barbados, which then would be refined in the Netherlands. That decision reshaped the economic and political landscape of North America and intensified competition for both land and labor.

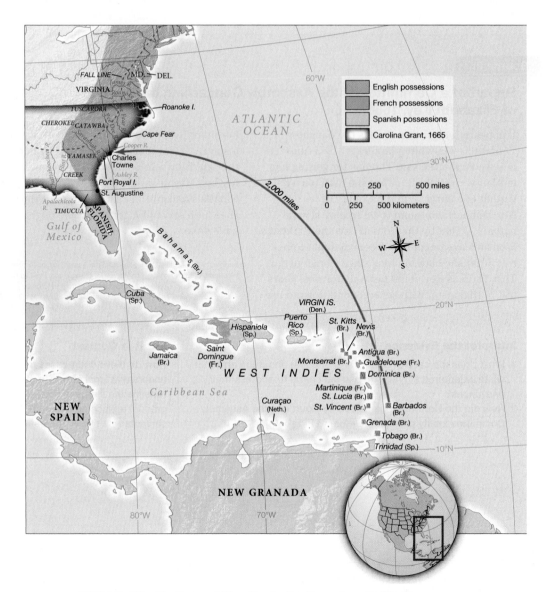

MAP 2.2 West Indies and Carolina in the Seventeenth Century

Beginning in the 1630s, sugar cultivation transformed West Indies colonies. The British consumed sugar in large quantities, ensuring the economic success of Barbados and its neighbors and a vast increase in the enslaved population. In the 1660s, Barbados planters obtained a charter for Carolina and sent many early settlers — white planters and merchants as well as enslaved laborers — to this mainland colony.

REVIEW & RELATE

● How did the Virginia colony change and evolve between 1607 and the 1670s?

● How did the growth of the English colonies on the mainland and in the West Indies shape conflicts in Virginia and demands for labor throughout North America?

Sugar Manufacturing in the West Indies   This seventeenth-century engraving, which was later colorized, depicts the use of enslaved labor in the production of sugar in the West Indies. The Dutch, English, and French used slaves to plant sugarcane and then cut, press, and boil it to produce molasses. The molasses was turned into rum and refined sugar, both highly profitable exports. Sarin Images, Granger, NYC

Pilgrims and Puritans Settle New England

Along with merchants, planters, and indentured servants, religious dissenters also traveled to North America. Critics of the Church of England formed a number of congregations in the early seventeenth century, and some sought refuge in New England. One such group, the **Pilgrims** (also known as Separatists), landed on the Massachusetts coast in 1620 and established a permanent settlement at Plymouth. Their goal was to establish a religious community wholly separate from the Anglican Church. The Puritans, who hoped to purify rather than separate from the Church of England, arrived a decade later with plans to develop their own colony. Over the next two decades, New England colonists prospered, but they also confronted internal dissent and conflicts with local Indians.

Pilgrims Arrive in Massachusetts. In the 1610s, to raise capital, the Virginia Company began offering legal charters to groups of private investors, who were promised their own tract of land in the Virginia colony with minimal company oversight. One such charter was purchased by a group of English Pilgrims who wanted to form a separate church and community in a land untainted by Catholicism, Anglicanism, or European cosmopolitanism. Thirty-five Pilgrims from Leiden in the Dutch Republic and several dozen from England set sail on the *Mayflower* from Plymouth, England, in September 1620.

Battered by storms, the ship veered off course, landing at Cape Cod in present-day Massachusetts in early December. Before leaving the ship, the settlers, led by William Bradford, signed a pact to form a "civill body politick," which they considered necessary because they were settling in a region where they had no legal authority. The pact, known as the **Mayflower Compact**, was the first written constitution adopted in North America. It followed the Separatist model of a self-governing religious congregation.

After several forays along the coast, the Pilgrims located an uninhabited village surrounded by cornfields where they established their new home, Plymouth. Uncertain of native intentions, the Pilgrims were unsettled by sightings of Indians. They did not realize that a smallpox epidemic in the area only two years earlier had killed nearly 90 percent of the local Wampanoag population. Indeed, fevers and other diseases proved far more deadly to the settlers than did Indians. By the spring of 1621, only half of the 102 Pilgrims remained alive.

Desperate to find food, the survivors were stunned when two English-speaking Indians — Samoset and Squanto — appeared at Plymouth that March. Both had been captured as young boys by English explorers, and they now negotiated a fragile peace between the Pilgrims and Massasoit, chief of the Wampanoag tribe. Although concerned by the power of English guns, Massasoit hoped to create an alliance that would assist him against his traditional native enemies. With Wampanoag assistance, the surviving Pilgrims soon regained their health.

In the summer of 1621, reinforcements arrived from England, and the next year the Pilgrims received a charter granting them rights to Plymouth Plantation and a degree of self-government. Although some Pilgrims hoped to convert the Indians, other leaders favored a more aggressive stance toward hostile Indians. One Indian nation, the Massachusetts, posed an especially serious threat. So in 1623 Captain Miles Standish led an attack on a Massachusetts tribal village after kidnapping and killing the chief and his younger brother. Standish's strategy, though controversial, ensured that Massasoit, the colonists' Wampanoag ally, was now the most powerful chief in the region.

The Puritan Migration.

As the Pilgrims gradually expanded their colony during the 1620s, a new group of English dissenters, the **Puritans**, made plans to develop their own settlement. Puritans believed that their country's church and government had grown corrupt and was being chastened by an all-powerful God. During the early seventeenth century, the English population boomed but harvests failed, leading to famine, crime, unemployment, and inflation. The enclosure movement, in which landlords fenced in fields and hired a few laborers and tenants to replace a large number of peasant farmers, increased the number of landless vagrants. At the same time, the English cloth industry nearly collapsed under the weight of competition from abroad. In the Puritans' view, all of these problems were divine punishments for the nation's sins.

The Puritans envisioned New England as a safe haven from God's wrath. Under Puritan lawyer John Winthrop's leadership, a group of affluent Puritans obtained a royal charter for the Massachusetts Bay Company, established in 1623 by English investors hoping to gain wealth through the establishment of North American colonies. However, New England was more than just a place of safety to the Puritans. Unlike the Pilgrims, they believed that England and the Anglican Church could be redeemed. By prospering spiritually and materially in America, they could establish a model "City upon a Hill" that would then inspire reform among residents of the mother country.

About one-third of English Puritans chose to leave their homeland for North America. They were better supplied, more prosperous, and more numerous than either their Pilgrim or Jamestown predecessors. Following John Smith's recommendations, the settlers, arriving on seventeen ships, included ministers, merchants, craftsmen, and farmers. Many Puritans sailed with entire families. The community benefited from being well supplied, including women who traditionally nursed their families, and settling in a cold climate that reduced the spread of disease. These factors ensured the rapid growth of the colony.

The first Puritan settlers arrived on the coast north of Plymouth in 1630 and named their community Boston, after the port city in England from which they had departed. Once established, they relocated the Massachusetts Bay Company's capital and records to New England, thereby converting their commercial charter into the founding document of a self-governing colony. They instituted a new kind of polity in which adult male church members participated in the election of a governor, deputy governor, and legislature. Although the Puritans suffered a difficult first winter, they quickly recovered and soon cultivated sufficient crops to feed themselves and a steady stream of new migrants. During the 1630s, some eighteen thousand Puritans migrated to New England. Even without a cash crop like tobacco or sugar, the Puritan colony flourished.

Eager to take advantage of the abundant land, the close-knit community spread quickly beyond its original boundaries. The legislature was thus forced early on to develop policies for establishing townships with governing bodies that supported a local church and school. By the time the migration of Puritans slowed around 1640, the settlers had turned their colony into a thriving commercial center. They shipped codfish, lumber, grain, pork, and cheese to England in exchange for manufactured goods and to the West Indies for rum and molasses. This trade, along with the healthy climate, relatively egalitarian distribution of property, and more equal ratio of women to men, ensured a stable and prosperous colony.

Puritans also sought friendly relations with some local natives, particularly the neighboring Massachusetts tribe, who were longtime enemies of the Pilgrims' allies, the Wampanoags. Many Puritans hoped that their Indian neighbors might be converted to Christianity. Puritan missionaries taught their pupils how to read the Bible, and a few students attended Harvard College, founded in 1636. In an effort to wean converts from their traditional customs and beliefs, missionary John Eliot created "praying towns." There Christian Indians could live among others who shared their faith while being protected from English settlers seeking to exploit them. Yet most "praying Indians" continued to embrace traditional rituals and beliefs alongside Christian practices.

The Puritan Worldview.
Opposed to the lavish rituals and hierarchy of the Church of England and believing that few Anglicans truly felt the grace of God, Puritans set out to establish a simpler form of worship. They focused on their inner lives and on the purity of their church and community. Puritans followed Calvin, believing in an all-knowing God whose true Word was presented in the Bible. The biblically sanctioned church was a congregation formed by a group of believers who made a covenant with God. Only a small minority of people, known as Saints, were granted God's grace.

Whether one was a Saint and thereby saved was predetermined by and known only to God. Still, some Puritans believed that the chosen were likely to lead a saintly life. Visible signs included individuals' passionate response to the preaching of God's Word, their sense

Mrs. Elizabeth Freake and Baby Mary
This anonymous 1674 portrait shows Elizabeth Freake, the wife of merchant John Freake, and their eighth child, Mary. Large families helped ensure Puritan expansion and financial success. Here Elizabeth and her daughter capture Puritan simplicity in their white head coverings and aprons. But they display their family's wealth and John Freake's commercial ties through their silk gowns and embroidered cloth. Worcester Art Museum, Massachusetts, USA/Bridgeman Images

of doubt and despair over their own soul, and that wonderful sense of reassurance that came with God's "saving grace." God's hand in the world appeared in nature as well. Comets and eclipses were considered "remarkable providences." But so too, was a smallpox epidemic that killed several thousand Massachusetts Indians in 1633–1634 and thereby opened up land for Puritan settlers.

Shared religious beliefs helped forge a unified community where faith guided civil as well as spiritual decisions. While ministers were discouraged from holding political office, political leaders were devout Puritans who were expected to promote a godly society. Such leaders determined who got land, how much, and where; they also served as judge and jury for those accused of crimes or sins. Their leadership was largely successful. Even if colonists differed over who should get the most fertile strip of land, they agreed on basic principles. Still, almost from the beginning, certain Puritans challenged some of the community's fundamental beliefs and, in the process, the community itself.

Explore ▶

Explore two perspectives on North American colonies as models of Britain and models for America in Secondary Sources 2.4 and 2.5.

Dissenters Challenge Puritan Authority. In the early 1630s, Roger Williams, a Salem minister, criticized Puritan leaders for not being sufficiently pure in their rejection of the Church of England and the English monarchy. He preached that not all the Puritan leaders were Saints and that some were bound for damnation. By 1635 Williams was forced out of Salem and moved south with his followers to found Providence in the area that became Rhode Island. Believing that there were very few Saints in the world, Williams and his followers accepted that one must live among those who were not saved. Thus unlike Massachusetts Bay, Providence welcomed Quakers, Baptists, and Jews to the community, and Williams's followers insisted on a strict separation of church and state. Williams also forged alliances with the Narragansetts, the most powerful Indian nation in the region.

A year after Williams's departure, Anne Hutchinson was accused of sedition, or trying to overthrow the government by challenging colonial leaders. She was put on trial in November 1637. An eloquent orator, Hutchinson ultimately claimed that her authority to challenge the Puritan leadership came from "an immediate revelation" from God, "the voice of his own spirit to my soul." Since Puritans believed that God spoke only through the intermediary of properly appointed male ministers, her claim was condemned as heretical.

Hutchinson was seen as a threat not only because of her religious beliefs but also because she was a woman. The Reverend Hugh Peter, for example, reprimanded her at trial: "You have stept out of your place, you have rather bine a Husband than a Wife and a preacher than a Hearer; and a Magistrate than a Subject." Many considered her challenge to Puritan authority especially serious because she also challenged traditional gender hierarchies. After being banished from Massachusetts Bay, Hutchinson and her followers joined Williams's Rhode Island colony.

Wars in Old and New England.

As Anne Hutchinson and Roger Williams confronted religious leaders, Puritans and Pilgrims faced serious threats from their Indian neighbors as well. The Pequot nation, which was among the most powerful tribes in New England, had been allies of the English for several years. Yet some Puritans feared that the Pequots, who opposed the colonists' continued expansion, "would cause all the Indians in the country to join to root out all the English." Using the death of two Englishmen in 1636 to justify a military expedition against the Pequots, the colonists went on the attack. The Narragansetts, whom Roger Williams had befriended, allied with the English in the **Pequot War**. After months of bloody conflict, the English and their Indian allies launched a brutal attack on a Pequot fort in May 1637 that left some four hundred men, women, and children dead.

Puritans in England were soon engaged in armed conflict as well, but this time against other Englishmen. Differences over issues of religion, taxation, and royal authority had strained relations between Parliament and the crown for decades, as James I (r. 1603–1625) and his son Charles I (r. 1625–1649) sought to consolidate their own power at Parliament's expense. In 1642 the relationship between Parliament and King Charles I broke down completely, and the country descended into civil war. Oliver Cromwell, a Puritan, emerged as the leader of the Protestant parliamentary forces, and after several years of fighting, he claimed victory. Charles I was executed, Parliament established a republican commonwealth, and bishops and elaborate rituals were banished from the Church of England. Cromwell ruled England as a military dictator until his death in 1658. By then, much of England had tired of religious conflict and Puritan rule, so Charles I's son, Charles II (r. 1660–1685), was invited to return from exile on the continent and restore the monarchy and the Church of England. In 1660, when Charles II acceded to the throne, the Puritans recognized that their only hope for building a godly republic lay in North America.

Colonial Models of and for English Society

From the late nineteenth century to the 1970s, most historians of colonial North America argued that New England offered a closer model *of* the home country, England, than did other colonies and that it served as an important model *for* American society generally. In recent decades, some scholars have instead claimed that the colonial Chesapeake more closely mirrored not only seventeenth-century English society but also England's other colonies in Ireland and the West Indies. They suggest that the focus on New England, where the number of slaves was far smaller than elsewhere in the British colonies, allowed colonial historians to marginalize the role of slavery in American society. Others acknowledge the distinctiveness of New England's colonial development but still highlight the importance of Puritan legacies and New England colonists' relations with Indians.

Source 2.4

Jack P. Greene, The Chesapeake as Model of and for English Society, 1988

As long as they could continue to believe that New England, the region of colonial British America in which black slavery was least well entrenched, was indeed the most direct and important source of later American sociocultural patterns, historians could continue to perpetuate the comforting illusion that slavery . . . had never been central to American culture but had always only been a marginal institution confined to the cultural peripheries of the colonial British American world. . . .

[Yet] between 1630 and 1660, the Chesapeake colonies represented a much closer approximation of old England than did the puritan colonies of Connecticut and Massachusetts Bay. . . .

In its permissiveness, lack of social cohesion, . . . slowly developing community spirit, religious pluralism, secular orientation, competitiveness, acquisitiveness, high levels of property concentration, . . . reliance upon dependent servant labor, treatment of labor as a disposable commodity, mobility, strong orientation for large-scale production for the market . . . , Chesapeake society reflected, and in only a few instances to an exaggerated degree, characteristics that were deeply and undeniably English. . . .

Chesapeake society before 1660 exhibited impulses and social and cultural configurations that were broadly representative of those in the first generations of settlement all over the early modern English world — with the notable exception of the orthodox New England colonies.

Source: Jack P. Greene, *Pursuits of Happiness: The Social Development of Early Modern British Colonies and the Formation of American Culture.* (Chapel Hill: University of North Carolina Press, 1988), 35–36, 53.

During the civil war of the 1640s, English settlements had quickly spread as a result of both natural increase and migration. English communities stretched from Connecticut through Massachusetts and Rhode Island and into Maine and what became New Hampshire. The English king and Parliament, embroiled in war, paid little attention to events in North America, allowing these New England colonies to develop with little oversight. In 1664, after the restoration of the monarchy, the English wrested control of New Amsterdam from the Dutch and renamed it New York. By 1674 the English could claim dominance — in population, trade, and politics — over the other European powers vying for empires along the northern Atlantic coast.

Source 2.5

Alan Taylor, New England Puritans Develop Anglo-American Ideals, 2001

The Puritans understood in spiritual terms many causes that we might define as "economic." They interpreted the wandering beggars, increased crime, cloth trade depression, and famine [in England] as divine afflictions meant to punish a guilty land that wallowed in sin. . . .

To redeem their hope for a brighter future, many Puritans sought a distant refuge. . . .

By colonial standards, New England attracted an unusual set of emigrants. . . . Most seventeenth-century English emigrants were poor young single men who lacked prospects in the mother country. Seeking regular meals in the short term and a farm in the long, they gambled their lives as indentured servants in the Chesapeake or the West Indies. In contrast, most of the New England colonists could pay their own way and emigrated as family groups. . . .

Compared with other colonial regions, New England was a land of relative equality, broad (albeit moderate) opportunity, and thrifty, industrious, and entrepreneurial habits that sustained an especially diverse and complex economy. . . . And nowhere else in colonial America did colonists enjoy readier access to public worship and nearly universal education. That those ideals remain powerful in our own culture attests to the enduring importance of the Puritan legacy. But those accomplishments also had a dark side, especially the intolerance of dissenters. . . . And, . . . the pursuit of Puritan ideals and Puritan prosperity depended upon dispossessing the Indians and transforming their land.

Source: Alan Taylor, *American Colonies: The Settling of North America.* (New York: Penguin Books, 2001), 167, 169, and 186.

Examine the Secondary Sources

1. How do Green and Taylor understand the relationship of the Chesapeake and New England colonies, respectively, to England? To British North America?
2. Based on the descriptions offered by Green and Taylor, which elements of Chesapeake and New England society are most similar to Great Britain and which are most characteristic of British North America?

Put It in Context

Were the differences among the English colonies greater than the differences between the English colonies and those of the French and the Dutch?

The spread of English control was still contested, however, by diverse Indian groups. In New England, only 15,000 to 16,000 native people remained by 1670, a loss of about 80 percent over fifty years. Meanwhile the English population reached more than 50,000, with settlers claiming ever more land. In 1671 the English demanded that the Wampanoags, who had been their allies since the 1620s, surrender their guns and be ruled by English law. Instead, many Indians hid their weapons and, over the next several years, raided frontier farms and killed several settlers. English authorities responded by hanging three Wampanoag men.

By 1675 the Wampanoag chief Metacom, called King Philip by the English, came to believe that Europeans had to be forced out of New England if Indians were going to survive. As conflict escalated between the English and the Wampanoags, Metacom gained the support of the Narragansett and Nipmuck Indians. Together warriors from the three tribes attacked white settlements throughout the region, burning fields, killing male settlers, and taking wives and children captive.

Initially, the English were convinced they could win an easy victory over their Indian foes and insisted on calling the conflict King Philip's War, using the local chief's English name. There was no easy victory, however, and the war, called **Metacom's War** by Wampanoags, dragged on and became increasingly brutal on both sides. Some 1,000 English settlers were killed and dozens were taken captive during the war. Metacom's forces attacked Plymouth and Providence and marched within twenty miles of Boston. The English meanwhile made an alliance with Mohawks, Pequots, Mohegans, and praying Indians (mostly Christian Wampanoags) in the region, who ambushed Narragansett forces. The English attacked enemy villages, killing hundreds of Indians and selling hundreds more into slavery in the West Indies, including Metacom's wife and son. Indian losses were catastrophic on both sides of the conflict, as food shortages and disease combined with military deaths to kill as many as 4,500 men, women, and children. About a quarter of the remaining Indian population of New England died in 1675–1676.

The war finally ended when Wampanoag, Narragansett, and Nipmuck forces ran short of guns and powder and the Mohawks ambushed and killed Metacom. **See Primary Source Project 2: Metacom's War, page 65.** The remaining Algonquian-speaking Indians moved north and gradually intermarried with tribes allied with the French. As the carnage of the war spilled into New York, Iroquois leaders and colonists met at Albany in 1677 in hopes of salvaging their lucrative fur trade. There they formed an alliance, the Covenant Chain, to forestall future conflict. In the following decades, furs and land would continue to define the complex relations between Indians and Europeans across the northern regions of North America.

REVIEW & RELATE

- How did Puritan religious views shape New England's development?

- Why did conflict between New England settlers and the region's Indians escalate over the course of the seventeenth century?

Conclusion: European Empires in North America

When John Smith died in 1631, the English were just beginning to establish colonies in North America. Smith realized early on that a successful empire in Virginia required a different approach than the Spanish had taken in Mexico and Peru. North American colonies demanded permanent settlement, long-term investment, and hard work. Liberal land policies, self-government, and trade formed the touchstones of colonies along the north Atlantic coast. Colonies in New England, established by Pilgrims and Puritans, were especially successful. These religious dissenters benefited from liberal land policies, self-government, and trade. In addition, their large families, diverse skills, and settlement in relatively healthy northern climes aided their success.

European colonists found ways to prosper in Virginia, Quebec, and New Amsterdam as well as Massachusetts Bay, but they still faced daunting choices. Most important, should they create alliances with local Indians for sustenance and trade, or should they seek to dominate them and take what they needed? Smith, Miles Standish, and many others supported an aggressive policy, much like that of Spain. In Virginia this policy ended the most serious threats from the Powhatan Confederacy by the 1640s. But many Europeans, especially in New England, New Amsterdam, and Canada, advocated a less violent approach. A few French Jesuit priests and Puritans like Roger Williams focused on the spiritual and material benefits of conversion. Far more argued that building alliances was the most effective means of advancing trade and gaining land, furs, and other goods valued by Europeans.

Throughout the early and mid-seventeenth century, English, Dutch, and French colonists profited from trade relations and military alliances with Indian nations. Nonetheless, European demands for land fueled repeated conflicts with tribes like the Pequot in the 1630s and the Wampanoag and Narragansett in the 1670s. The exhaustion of furs along the Atlantic coast only increased the vulnerability of those Indians who could no longer provide this valuable trade item. Already devastated by European-borne diseases, their very survival was at stake. Indians in New Amsterdam as well as New England resisted the loss of their land and livelihood, often with violence. Such violence led to the death of Anne Hutchinson. In 1642 she and her six youngest children moved to the outskirts of New Netherland after the death of her husband. A year later, Anne and all but one of her children were massacred by Indians outraged by Dutch governor William Kieft's 1643 slaughter of peaceful Indians on Manhattan Island.

Still, as European settlements reached deeper into North America in the late seventeenth century and early eighteenth century, their prosperity continued to depend on trade goods and land that were often in Indian hands. At the same time, a growing demand for labor led wealthier settlers to seek an increased supply of indentured servants from Europe and enslaved workers from Africa. Over the next half century, relations between wealthy and poor settlers, between whites and blacks, between settlers and Indians, and among the European nations that vied for empire would grow only more complicated.

CHAPTER 2 REVIEW

TIMELINE OF EVENTS

1517	Protestant Reformation begins
1530s	England breaks with the Roman Catholic Church
1545–1563	Council of Trent
1598	Acoma pueblo uprising, Edict of Nantes
1607	Jamestown founded
1608	French settle in Quebec
1609	Dutch settle on the Hudson River
1612–1614	Tobacco cultivation begins in Virginia
1619	First Africans arrive in Virginia
1620	Pilgrims found Plymouth settlement
1624	Dutch establish New Amsterdam
1630	Puritans found Massachusetts Bay colony
1632	Maryland founded
1635	Roger Williams moves to Rhode Island
1636–1637	Pequot War
1637	Anne Hutchinson banished from Massachusetts Bay colony
1642–1649	English civil war
1660	Monarchy restored in England
1660–1664	Virginia and Maryland establish lifelong, inherited slavery
1664	Dutch surrender New Amsterdam to the English
1675–1676	Metacom's War
1676	Bacon's Rebellion

KEY TERMS

Protestantism, *39*

Church of England, *40*

Jamestown, *46*

Powhatan Confederacy, *47*

House of Burgesses, *48*

indentured servants, *48*

Bacon's Rebellion, *51*

Pilgrims, *55*

Mayflower Compact, *56*

Puritans, *56*

Pequot War, *59*

Metacom's War, *62*

REVIEW & RELATE

1. How did the Protestant Reformation shape the course of European expansion in the Americas?

2. How did the French and Dutch colonies in North America differ from the Spanish empire to the south?

3. How did the Virginia colony change and evolve between 1607 and the 1670s?

4. How did the growth of the English colonies on the mainland and in the West Indies shape conflicts in Virginia and demands for labor throughout North America?

5. How did Puritan religious views shape New England's development?

6. Why did conflict between New England settlers and the region's Indians escalate over the course of the seventeenth century?

Metacom's War

▶ How does Metacom's War illuminate differences among Indians and among the English as well as those between the Indians and the English?

Despite decades of relative peace between Indians and colonists, tensions escalated during the 1660s. Metacom, whom colonists called King Philip, became grand sachem (primary chief) of the Wampanoag Confederacy in 1662, when New England Indians had lost both land and population. Especially troubled by English encroachments on native lands, King Philip forged an alliance that brought together two-thirds of the region's Indian population, including the Narragansett. This New England Confederation coordinated attacks on white settlements, burning fields, taking captives, and killing male colonists.

In 1675 Indian attacks on New England towns escalated. The English, in turn, sold Indians into slavery (Source 2.6). As relations between settlers and Indians deteriorated, the Rhode Island colony sent representatives to meet with King Philip in June. Some colonists and Indian leaders also met independently to discuss the growing conflict (Sources 2.7 and 2.8). However, these diplomatic efforts failed, and Indian attacks increased throughout the summer. In September, the New England Confederation declared war. Fighting continued for a year, leading to the deaths of 1,000 colonists and more than 4,000 Indians. Edward Randolph, a customs agent, criticized both colonists and Indians for their parts in the conflict (Source 2.9). The English finally gained the upper hand in August 1676 with the help of Indian allies. Then soldiers led by Captain Benjamin Church ambushed King Philip near Bristol, Rhode Island. The killing of Metacom/King Philip by John Alderman, an Indian ally of the colonists, signaled the end of the war. Six years later, Mary Rowlandson, who had been captured in 1675, published an account of her captivity, which was widely read by New Englanders (Source 2.10).

Because there are fewer Indian sources, historians have struggled to develop a balanced picture of the war. William Nahaton (Source 2.6) provides the view of a Christianized Indian, and some other documents offer information about Indian perceptions of the war even though written by the English.

Source 2.6

William Nahaton | Petition to Free an Indian Slave, 1675

The English sold a number of Indians into slavery before and during Metacom's War. Many English colonists petitioned the government of Massachusetts Bay to stop this practice. As the following document indicates, Indians also tried to find recourse through petitions. William Nahaton, an Indian who had embraced Christianity, sent this petition to convince colonial leaders to release a relative who was about to be sold into slavery in the West Indies.

To the honored counsel now siting at boston to the humble petition of william [n]ahaton hee humbly sheweth.

I have seing a woman taken by the mohegins and now brought to boston which woman although she did belong to [King] phillip his Company yet shee is a kinn to me and all so to john hunter as severall of the indians of punkapoag do know[.] my humble and right request there fore to the Renowned Counsel is that if it may stand with there pleasure and with out furtur inconvenience her Life may be spared and her Liberty granted under such conditions as the honored Counsel see most fit: shee being a woman whatever her mind hath been it is very probable she hath not dun much mischefe and if the honored counsel shall plese so grant me that favor I shall understand to leve her at punkapoag[.] . . . I shall obtaine so much favor from the honored counsel which will further oblige him who is your honored to command william [n] ahaton.

Source: Massachusetts State Archives, Massachusetts Archives, Series 45X, Vol. 176.

Source 2.7

Benjamin Church | A Visit with Awashonks, Sachem of the Sakonnet, 1716

Benjamin Church was an aide to Plymouth governor Josiah Winslow. But Church was also viewed as a fair man by local Indian leaders. Thus in June 1675, before the outbreak of war, Awashonks, the sachem of the Sakonnet Indians, invited Church to meet with her. He offered his advice on how best to secure the protection of her people. Although the Sakonnets initially allied with King Philip, they later switched to the English side. Meanwhile, as captain in the Plymouth militia, Church adopted Indian fighting tactics, and his unit conducted many successful raids, eventually ambushing King Philip. In 1716 Church's son, Thomas, published an account of the war from his father's notes.

The next Spring advancing, while Mr. Church was diligently settling his new Farm, stocking, leasing, and disposing of his Affairs, and had a fine prospect of doing no small things; and hoping that his good success would be inviting unto other good Men to become his Neighbours; Behold! The rumor of a War between the English and the Natives gave check to his projects. People began to be very jealous of the Indians, and indeed they had no small reason to suspect that they had form'd a design of War upon the English. Mr. Church had it daily suggested to him that the Indians were plotting a bloody design. That Philip the great Mount-hope Sachem was leader therein: and so it prov'd, he was sending his Messengers to all the Neighbouring Sachems, to ingage them in a Confederacy with him in the War.

Among the rest he sent Six Men to Awashonks Squaw-Sachem of the Sogkonate [Sakonnet] Indians, to engage her in his Interests: Awashonks so far listened unto them as to call her Subjects together, to make a great Dance, which is the custom of that Nation when they advise about Momentous Affairs. But what does Awashonks do, but sends away two of her Men that well understood the English Language . . . to invite Mr. Church to the Dance. Mr. Church upon the Invitation, immediately takes with him Charles Hazelton his Tennants Son, who well understood the Indian Language, and rid [rode] down to the Place appointed: Where they found hundreds of Indians gathered together from all Parts of her Dominion. Awashonks her self in a foaming Sweat was leading the Dance. But she was no sooner sensible of Mr. Churches arrival, but she broke off, sat down, calls her Nobles round her, orders Mr. Church to be invited into her presence. Complements being past, and each one taking Seats. She told him, King Philip had sent Six Men of his with two of her People that had been over at Mount-hope, to draw her into a confederacy with him in a War with the English. . . .

Then Mr. Church turn'd to Awashonks, and told her, if Philip were resolv'd to make War, her best way would be to knock those Six Mount-hopes on the head, and shelter her self under the Protection of the English: upon which the Mount-hopes were for the present Dumb. . . .

Then he told Awashonks he thought it might be most advisable for her to send to the Governour of Plymouth, and shelter her self, and People under his Protection. She lik'd his advice, and desired him to go on her behalf to the Plymouth Government, which he consented to: And at parting advised her what ever she did, not to desert the English Interest, to joyn with her Neighbours in a Rebellion which would certainly prove fatal to her. He mov'd none of his Goods from his House that there might not be the least umbrage from such an Action. She thank'd him for his advice, and sent two of her Men to guard him to his House; which when they came there, urged him to take care to secure his Goods, which he refused for the reasons before mentioned. But desired the Indians that if what they feared should happen, they would take care of what he left, and directed them to a Place in the woods where they should dispose them; which they faithfully observed.

Source: Benjamin Church, *The History of King Philip's War* (Boston: John Kimball Wiggin, 1865), 5–11.

John Easton | A Relation of the Indian War, 1675

As relations between English settlers and Indians grew more tense, a meeting was arranged for June 1675 between Metacom and John Easton, attorney general of the Rhode Island colony. At this meeting, Metacom related the Indians' many complaints, which included the sale of liquor to Indians, the destruction of their crops, and their mistreatment under the colonial justice system. This meeting was unsuccessful in preventing further violence, however, and by the end of the month Metacom's War began.

Another Grievance was, when their King sold Land, the English would say, it was more than they agreed to, and a Writing must be prove against all them, and some of their Kings had dun Rong [done wrong] to sell so much. He left his Peopell [people] none, and some being given to Drunknes the English made them drunk and then cheated them in Bargains, but now their Kings were forewarned not for to part with Land, for nothing in Comparison to the Value thereof. Now home [some] the English had owned for King or Queen, they would disinherit, and make another King that would give or sell them these Lands; that now they had no Hopes left to keep any Land. Another Grievance, the English Catell [cattle] and Horses still increased; that when they removed 30 Miles from where English had any thing to do, they could not keep their Corn from being spoiled, they never being used to fence, and thought when the English bought Land of them they would have kept their Catell upon their owne Land. Another Grievance, the English were so eager to sell the Indians Lickers [liquor], that most of the Indians spent all in Drunknes, and then ravened upon the sober Indians, and they did believe often did hurt the English Cattel, and their King could not prevent it.

Source: John Easton, "A Relation of the Indian War," in *A Narrative of the Causes Which Led to Philip's Indian War, of 1675 and 1676* (Albany: J. Munsell, 1858), 13–15.

Edward Randolph | Report on the War, 1676

Edward Randolph was an English customs official sent to the colonies to investigate colonial compliance with English laws. He criticized the Puritan colonies for pursuing political autonomy, like coining money and administering their own oath of allegiance, and called for greater control by Parliament. Randolph's reports to his superiors in London also described the outbreak of violence. He reported on what he saw as the causes of the war, criticizing the actions of both colonists and Indians.

Various are the reports and conjectures of the causes of the late Indian wars. Some impute it to an imprudent zeal in the magistrates of Boston to Christianize those heathens, before they were civilized, and enjoining them to the strict observation of their laws, which, to people so rude and licentious hath proved even intolerable; and that the more, for while the magistrates, for their profit, severely put the laws in execution against the Indians, the people on the other side, for lucre [money] and gain, intice and provoke the Indians to the breach thereof, especially to drunkenness, to which these people are so generally addicted, that they will strip themselves to the skin to have their fill of rum and brandy.

The Massachusetts government having made a law that every Indian being drunk should pay ten shillings or be whipped, according to the discretion of the magistrate, many of these poor people willingly offered their backs to the lash, to save their money. Upon the magistrate finding much trouble and no profit to arise to the government by whipping, did change that punishment of the whip into ten days' work, for such as would not or could not pay the fine of ten shillings; which did highly incense the Indians. . . .

Others impute the cause to arise from some injuries offered to the Sachem Philip; for he being possessed of a tract of land called Mount Hope, a very fertile, pleasant and rich soil, some English had a mind to dispossess him thereof, who, never wanting some pretence or other to attain their ends, complained of injuries done by Philip and his Indians to their stock and cattle. Whereupon the Sachem [King] Philip was often summoned to appear before the magistrates, sometimes imprisoned, and never released but upon parting with a considerable part of his lands.

But the government of the Massachusetts . . . do declare [the following acts] are the great and provoking evils which God hath given the barbarous heathen commission to rise against them: . . .

For men wearing long hair and perriwigs made of women's hair.

For women wearing borders of hair and cutting, curling and laying out their hair and disguising themselves by following strange fashions in their apparel.

For profaneness of the people in not frequenting their [church] meetings, and others going away before the blessing is pronounced.

For suffering the Quakers to dwell among them, and to set up their thresholds by God's thresholds, contrary to their old laws and resolutions, with many such reasons.

But whatever was the cause, the English have contributed very much to their misfortunes, for they first taught the Indians the use of arms and admitted them to be present at all their musters and trainings, and showed them how to handle, mend and fix their muskets, and have been constantly furnished with all sorts of arms by permission of the government, so that the Indians are become excellent fire-men.

Source: John Norris McClintock, *History of New Hampshire* (Boston: B. B. Russell, 1888), 79–80.

Source 2.10

Mary Rowlandson | Narrative of Captivity, 1682

In February 1675, the Wampanoags and their allies attacked Lancaster, Massachusetts, setting fire to the town and killing many residents. Mary Rowlandson and her three children were captured and forced to flee with the Indians as they tried to outrun colonial forces. Mary's six-year-old daughter, Sarah, died, but she and her other children survived and were sold for ransom after eleven weeks and reunited with her husband, Joseph. After the war, she published an account of her captivity that highlighted the ways in which her Puritan faith helped her survive the ordeal. The book became one of the most popular publications of its era.

Upon a *Friday*, a little after noon we came to this River. When all the company was come up, and were gathered together, I thought to count the number of them, but they were so many, and being somewhat in motion, it was beyond my skil. In this travel, because of my wound, I was somewhat favored in my load; I carried only my knitting work and two quarts of parched meal: Being very faint I asked my mistress to give me one spoonfull of the meal, but she would not give me a taste. They quickly fell to cutting dry trees, to make Rafts to carry them over the river: and soon my turn came to go over: By the advantage of some brush which they had laid upon the Raft to sit upon, I did not wet my foot (which many of themselves at the other end were mid-leg deep) which cannot but be acknowledged as a favour of God to my weakened body, it being a very cold time. I was not before acquainted with such kind of doings or dangers. *When thou passeth through the waters I will be with thee, and through the rivers they shall not overflow thee*, Isai. 43.2. A certain number of us got over the River that night, but it was the night after the Sabbath before all the company was got over. On the *Saturday* they boyled [boiled] an old Horses leg which they had got, and so we drank of the broth, as soon as they thought it was ready, and when it was almost all gone, they filled it up again.

The first week of my being among them, I hardly ate any thing; the second week, I found my stomach grow very faint for want of something; and yet it was very hard to get down their filthy trash: but the third week, though I could think how formerly my stomach would turn against this or that, and I could starve or die before I could eat such things, yet they were sweet and savory to my taste. I was at this time knitting a pair of white cotton stockins for my mistriss and had not yet wrought upon a Sabbath day; when the Sabbath came they bade me go to work; I told them it was the Sabbath-day, and desired them to let me rest, and told them I would do as much more tomorrow; to which they answered me, they would break my face. And here I cannot but take notice of the strange providence of God in preserving the heathen: They were many hundreds, old and young, some sick, and some lame, many had *Papooses* [infants] at their backs, the greatest number at this time with us, were *Squaws*, and they travelled with

all they had, bag and baggage, and yet they got over this River aforesaid; and on *Munday* they set their *Wigwams* on fire, and away they went: On that very day came the English Army after them to this River, and saw the smoak of their *Wigwams*, and yet this River put a stop to them. God did not give them courage or activity to go over after us; we were not ready for so great a mercy as victory and deliverance; if we had been, God would have found out a way for the *English* to have passed this River, as well as for the *Indians* with their *Squaws* and *Children*, and all their Luggage. . . .

On Munday *(as I said) they set their* Wigwams *on fire, and went away.* It was a cold morning, and before us there was a great Brook with ice on it; some waded through it, up to the knees & higher, but others went till they came to a Beaver dam, and I amongst them, where through the good providence of God, I did not wet my foot. I went along that day mourning and lamenting, leaving farther my own Country, and travelling into the vast and howling *Wilderness*, and I understood something of *Lot's* Wife's Temptation, *when she looked back.* We came that day to a great Swamp, by the side of which we took up our lodging that night. When I came to the brow of the hill, that looked toward the Swamp, I thought we had been come to a great *Indian* Town (though there were none but our own Company). The *Indians* were as thick as the trees: it seemed as if there had been a thousand Hatchets going at once: if one looked before one, there was nothing but *Indians*, and behind one, nothing but *Indians*, and so on either hand, I my self in the midst, and no Christian soul near me, *and yet how hath the Lord preserved me in safety! Oh the experience that I have had of the goodness of God, to me and mine!*

Source: Henry S. Nourse, ed., *The Narrative of the Captivity and the Restoration of Mrs. Mary Rowlandson* (Lancaster, MA, 1903), 17–20.

Interpret the Evidence

1. What does William Nahaton's petition (Source 2.6) reveal about English leaders' main goal when dealing with the Indians, Christian and non-Christian?

2. What types of complaints did the Wampanoag have against the English, and which seem the most grievous (Sources 2.7, 2.8, and 2.9)? What do these complaints reveal about how the colonists viewed the Wampanoag?

3. What does Benjamin Church's meeting with Awashonks (Source 2.7) suggest about the difficult choices faced by some Indians and some colonists as war approached?

4. What does Edward Randolph's description of the causes of the war (Source 2.9) reveal about how the conflict might be viewed by Englishmen who were not colonists? How do his perceptions compare with those of Benjamin Church and John Easton (Sources 2.7 and 2.8)?

5. How does Mary Rowlandson employ religion to explain the events that happen to her during her captivity (Source 2.10)? What does the enormous popularity of her book indicate about the place of religion and of Indians in New England in the 1680s?

Put It in Context

Metacom's War was one of the bloodiest in American history. From these documents, how do you explain its ferociousness?

What does the war and its outcome suggest about the trajectory of Indian-English relations from 1620 to 1680?

Colonial America amid Global Change

1680–1754

WINDOW TO THE PAST

Plan of a Slave Ship, 1794

By the mid-eighteenth century, slave traders were designing ships specifically for the purpose of transporting captured Africans to the Americas for sale. This image of the English slave ship *Brooks*, based on a ship maker's diagram, was initially created as a broadside in 1789 by English opponents of the slave trade to highlight the trade's brutality. Nonetheless, it shows how slave traders sought to use every available space to carry more Africans into slavery in the Americas throughout the 1700s. ▸ To discover more about what this primary source can show us, see Source 3.2 on page 88.

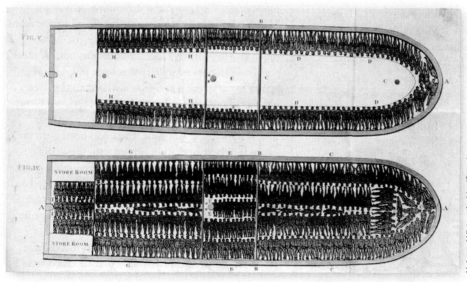

Universal History Archive/Getty Images

After reading this chapter you should be able to:

- Compare the development of Spanish, French, and English colonies from the late sixteenth to the mid-seventeenth century.

- Analyze the effects of European wars on relations among different groups of European colonists and between colonists and diverse Indian nations in North America.

- Examine how the American colonies became part of a global trading network.

- Describe the changing character of labor in the English colonies and the rise of slavery.

COMPARING AMERICAN HISTORIES

In 1729, at age thirty, William Moraley Jr. signed an indenture to serve a five-year term as a "bound servant" in the "American Plantations." This was not what his parents had imagined for him. The son of a journeyman watchmaker, Moraley received a good education and was offered a clerkship with a London lawyer. But Moraley preferred London's pleasures to legal training. At age nineteen, out of money, he was forced to return home and become an apprentice watchmaker for his father. Moraley made a poor apprentice, and in 1725, fed up with his son's lack of enterprise, Moraley's father rewrote his will, leaving him just 20 shillings. When Moraley's father died

(left) **Indentured Servant** (No image of William Moraley exists) Granger, NYC

(right) **Fabric dyed with indigo** (No image of Eliza Lucas Pinckney exists) Cooper Hewitt, Smithsonian Design Museum/Art Resource, NY (detail)

unexpectedly, his wife gave her son 20 pounds, and in 1728 Moraley headed back to London.

But times were hard in London, and Moraley failed to find work. After being imprisoned for debt, he sold his labor for five years in return for passage to America. Arriving in the colonies in December 1729, Moraley was indentured to Isaac Pearson, a Quaker clockmaker and goldsmith in Burlington, New Jersey. Preferring to live in a large city like Philadelphia, Moraley ran away but was soon captured. Most runaway servants had their contracts extended, but Moraley did not. For the next three years, he worked for Pearson alongside another indentured servant and an enslaved boy. Pearson allowed Moraley to travel the countryside fixing clocks and watches, and the servant observed the far worse conditions of enslaved workers. Perhaps having recouped his investment, Pearson released Moraley from his contract two years early.

Moraley spent the next twenty months traveling the northern colonies, but found no steady employment. Hounded by creditors, he returned to England, penniless and unemployed. In 1743, hoping to cash in on popular interest in adventure tales, he published an account of his travels. In the book, entitled *The Infortunate, the Voyage and Adventures of William Moraley, an Indentured Servant*, he offered a poor man's view of eighteenth-century North America. Like so much else in Moraley's life, the book was not a success.

In 1738, while Moraley was back in England trying to carve out a career as a writer, sixteen-year-old Eliza Lucas, the eldest daughter of Colonel George Lucas, arrived at Wappoo, her father's estate near Charleston, South Carolina. Eliza had been born on Antigua, where her father served with the British army and owned a sugar plantation. The move north, made necessary by her mother's ill health, created an unusual opportunity for Eliza, who was left in charge of the estate when Colonel Lucas was called back to Antigua in May 1739.

For the next five years, Eliza Lucas managed Wappoo and two other Carolina plantations owned by her father. Rising each day at 5 a.m., she checked on the fields and the enslaved laborers who worked them, balanced the books, nursed her mother, taught her younger sister to read, and wrote to her younger brothers at school in England. She also befriended neighboring planters, including Charles Pinckney, whom she would later marry, adding her landholdings to his.

While still single, Eliza improved the value of her family's estates by experimenting with new crops. With her father's enthusiastic support, she cultivated indigo, a plant used for making textile dyes. When her experiments proved successful, Eliza Lucas encouraged other planters to follow her lead, and with financial aid from the colonial legislature and Parliament, indigo became a profitable export from South Carolina, second only to rice. ∎

Comparing the American histories of William Moraley and Eliza Lucas illuminates profound shifts in global trading patterns that resulted in the circulation of labor and goods among Asia, Africa, Europe, and the Americas. Between 1680 and 1750, indentured servants, enslaved Africans, planters, soldiers, merchants, and artisans traveled along these new trade networks. So, too, did sugar, rum, tobacco, indigo, cloth, and a host of other items. As England, France, and Spain expanded their empires, colonists developed new crops for export and increased the demand for manufactured goods from home. Yet the vibrant, increasingly global economy was fraught with peril. Economic crises, the uncertainties of maritime navigation, and outbreaks of war caused constant disruptions. For some, the opportunities offered by colonization outweighed the dangers; for others, fortune was less kind, and the results were disappointing, even disastrous.

Europeans Expand Their Claims

Beginning with the restoration of the monarchy in 1660, English kings began granting North American land and commercial rights to men who were loyal to the crown. France and Spain also expanded their empires in North America, and all three would frequently come into conflict with each other in the late seventeenth and early eighteenth centuries. At the same time, American Indians challenged various European efforts to displace them from their homelands.

English Colonies Grow and Multiply. Shortly after Charles II (r. 1660–1685) was restored to the English throne, Connecticut and Rhode Island requested and received royal charters that granted them some local authority. Because the charters could be changed only with the agreement of both parties, Connecticut and Rhode Island maintained this local autonomy throughout the colonial period. In other colonies, however, Charles II asserted his authority by rewarding loyal supporters with land grants and commercial rights, which could more easily be changed or revoked than royal charters could. He also appointed his supporters to the newly formed Councils for Trade and Plantations, and provided them other privileges. He gave his brother James, the Duke of York, control over all the lands between the Delaware and Connecticut Rivers, once known as New Netherland, but now known as New York. He then conveyed the adjacent lands to investors who established the colonies of East and West Jersey. Finally, Charles II repaid debts to Admiral Sir William Penn by granting his son huge tracts of land in the Middle Atlantic region. Six years later, William Penn Jr. left the Church of England and joined the Society of Friends, or Quakers. This radical Protestant sect was severely persecuted in England, so the twenty-two-year-old Penn turned his holdings into a Quaker refuge named Pennsylvania.

Between 1660 and 1685, York, Penn, and other English gentlemen were established as the proprietors of a string of **proprietary colonies** from Carolina to New York. Although Charles II could have intruded into the government of these colonies, he rarely did. Instead, local conditions largely dictated what was possible. Most proprietors envisioned the creation of a manorial system in their colony, one in which they and other gentry presided over workers producing goods for export. In practice, however, a range of relationships emerged between property owners and workers. For instance, small farmers and laborers in northern Carolina rose up and forced proprietors there to offer land at reasonable prices and a semblance of self-government. In the southern part of Carolina, however, English planters with West Indies connections dominated. They created a mainland version of Barbados by introducing enslaved Africans as laborers, carving out plantations, and trading with the West Indies.

William Penn provided a more progressive model of colonial rule. He established friendly relations with the local Lenni-Lenape Indians and drew up a Frame of Government in 1681 that recognized religious freedom for all Christians. It also allowed all property-owning men to vote and hold office. Under Penn's leadership, Pennsylvania attracted thousands of middling farm families, most of them Quakers, as well as artisans and merchants.

Charles's death in 1685 marked an abrupt shift in crown-colony relations. Charles's successor, James II (r. 1685–1688), instituted a more authoritarian regime both at home and abroad. He consolidated the colonies in the Northeast and established tighter controls. His royal officials banned town meetings, challenged land titles granted under the original colonial charters, and imposed new taxes. Fortunately for the colonists, the Catholic James II alienated his subjects in England as well as in the colonies, inspiring a bloodless coup in 1688, the so-called **Glorious Revolution**. His Protestant daughter Mary and her husband, William of Orange (r. 1689–1702), then ascended the throne, introducing more democratic systems of governance in England and the colonies. Two years later, John Locke, a physician and philosopher, wrote a widely circulated treatise supporting the initiatives of William and Mary by insisting that government depended on the consent of the governed.

Eager to restore political order and create a commercially profitable empire, William and Mary established the new colony of Massachusetts (which included Plymouth, Massachusetts Bay, and Maine) and restored town meetings and an elected assembly. But the 1692 charter also granted the English crown the right to appoint a royal governor and officials to enforce customs regulations. It ensured religious freedom to members of the Church of England and allowed all male property owners (not just Puritans) to be elected to the assembly. In Maryland, too, the crown imposed a royal governor and replaced the Catholic Church with the Church of England as the established religion. And in New York, wealthy English merchants won the backing of the newly appointed royal governor, who instituted a representative assembly and supported a merchant-dominated Board of Aldermen. Thus, taken as a whole, William and Mary's policies instituted a partnership between England and colonial elites by allowing colonists to retain long-standing local governmental institutions but also asserting royal authority to appoint governors and ensure the influence of the Church of England (Table 3.1).

TABLE 3.1 **English Colonies Established in North America, 1607–1750**

Colony	Date	Original Colony Type	Religion	Status in 1750
Virginia	1624	Royal	Church of England	Royal
Massachusetts	1630	Charter	Congregationalist	Royal with charter
Maryland	1632	Proprietary	Catholic	Royal
Connecticut	1662	Charter	Congregationalist	Charter
Rhode Island	1663	Charter	No established church	Charter
Carolina	1663	Proprietary	Church of England	
North	1691	Proprietary		Royal
South	1691	Proprietary		Royal
New Jersey	1664	Proprietary	Church of England	Royal
New York	1664	Proprietary	Church of England	Royal
Pennsylvania	1681	Proprietary	Quaker	Proprietary
Delaware	1704	Proprietary	Lutheran/Quaker	Proprietary
Georgia	1732	Charter	Church of England	(Royal 1752)
New Hampshire (separated from Massachusetts)	1691	Royal	Congregationalist	Royal

In the early eighteenth century, England's North American colonies took the form that they would retain until the revolution in 1776. In 1702 East and West Jersey united into the colony of New Jersey. Delaware separated from Pennsylvania in 1704. By 1710 North Carolina became fully independent of South Carolina. Finally, in 1732, the colony of Georgia was chartered as a buffer between Spanish Florida and the plantations of South Carolina. At the same time, settlers pushed back the frontier in all directions.

The Pueblo Revolt and Spain's Fragile Empire.

Meanwhile Spain's forces in North America were spread dangerously thin. In Florida, Indians resisted the spread of cattle ranching in the 1670s. Some moved their settlements north to the Carolina border, wooed by the English who eagerly exchanged European goods for deerskins. The efforts of the English to interfere with Spanish-Indian trade networks fueled growing tensions along this Anglo-Spanish frontier. In New Mexico, open conflict erupted between Spanish and Pueblo peoples when war broke out in Europe in 1702. Tensions between Spanish missionaries and *encomenderos* and the Pueblo nation had simmered for decades (see "Spain's Global Empire Declines" in chapter 2). Relations worsened in the 1670s when a drought led to famine among many area Indians and brought a revival of Indian rituals that the Spaniards considered threatening. Meanwhile, Spanish forces were failing to protect the Pueblos against devastating raids by Apache and Navajo warriors, while Catholic prayers proved unable to stop Pueblo deaths in a 1671 epidemic.

When some Pueblos returned to their traditional priests, Spanish officials hanged three Indian leaders for idolatry and whipped and incarcerated forty-three others. Among those punished was Popé, a militant Pueblo who upon his release began planning a broad-based revolt. On August 10, 1680, seventeen thousand Pueblo Indians initiated a coordinated assault on numerous Spanish missions and forts. They destroyed buildings and farms, burned crops and houses, and smeared excrement on Christian altars. The Spaniards retreated to Mexico without launching any significant counterattack.

Still, the Spaniards returned in the 1690s and reconquered parts of New Mexico, aided by growing internal conflict among the Pueblos and raids by the Apache. The governor general of New Spain worked hard to subdue the province and in 1696 crushed the rebels and opened new lands for settlement. Meanwhile Franciscan missionaries improved relations with the Pueblos by allowing them to retain more indigenous practices.

Yet despite the Spanish reconquest, in the long run the **Pueblo revolt** limited Spanish expansion by strengthening other indigenous peoples in the region. In the aftermath of the revolt, some Pueblo refugees moved north and taught the Navajo how to grow corn, raise sheep, and ride horses. Through the Navajo, the Ute, Shoshone, and Comanche peoples also gained access to horses. By the 1730s, the Comanches launched mounted bison hunts as well as raids on other Indian nations. At Taos, they traded Indian captives into slavery for more horses and guns. Thus the Pueblos provided other Indian nations with the means to support larger populations, wider commercial networks, and more warriors, allowing them to continue to contest Spanish rule.

At the same time, Spain sought to reinforce its claims to Texas (named after the Tejas Indians) in response to French settlements in the lower Mississippi valley. In the early eighteenth century, Spanish missions and forts appeared along the route from San Juan Batista to the border of present-day Louisiana. Although small and scattered, these outposts were meant to ensure Spain's claim to Texas. But the presence of large and powerful Indian nations, including the Caddo and the Apache, forced Spanish residents to accept many native customs in order to maintain their presence in the region.

Ambush of the Villasur Expedition, c. 1720 An unknown artist painted this battle scene on buffalo hide. In 1720, Spanish soldiers and Pueblo warriors tried to expel the French from the lower Mississippi River valley. Instead, French soldiers and their Indian allies ambushed the expedition and killed forty-five men. Two of the dead, Spanish Father Juan Minguez and Pueblo leader Joseph Naranjo, are shown here in the center. Palace of the Governors Photo Archive (NMHM/DCA), negative 149804

France Seeks Land and Control. Louis XIV of France (r. 1643–1715) claimed absolute power derived from what he believed was his divine right to rule. One of his missions was to extend the boundaries of France's North American colonies. However, French efforts were focused more on exploration and trade than on settlement. In 1682 French adventurers and their Indian allies journeyed from the *Pays d'en Haut*, the Upper Country surrounding the Great Lakes, down the Mississippi River. Led by the French explorer René-Robert Cavelier, Sieur de La Salle, the party traveled to the Gulf of Mexico and claimed all the land drained by the river's tributaries for France. The new territory of Louisiana promised great wealth, but its development stalled when La Salle failed in his attempt to establish a colony.

Still eager for a southern outlet for furs, the French did not give up. After several more attempts at colonization in the early eighteenth century, French settlers maintained a toehold along Louisiana's Gulf coast. Most important, Pierre LeMoyne d'Iberville and his brother established forts at Biloxi and Mobile bays, where they traded with local Choctaw Indians. They recruited settlers from Canada and France, and these two small outposts survived despite conflicts among settlers, pressure from the English and the Spanish, a wave of epidemics, and a lack of supplies from France. Nevertheless, Louisiana counted only three hundred French settlers by 1715.

Continuing to promote commercial relations with diverse Indian nations, the French built a string of missions and forts along the upper Mississippi and Illinois Rivers. The most important of these, Kaskaskia (just south of Cahokia), became a multicultural community of diverse Indian groups, French fur traders, and Jesuit missionaries. These outposts in the continent's interior allowed France to challenge both English and Spanish claims to North America. In addition, extensive trade with a range of Indian nations ensured that French power was far greater than the small number of French settlers suggests.

REVIEW & RELATE

- What role did the crown play in the expansion of the English North American colonies in the second half of the seventeenth century?

- How did the development of the Spanish and French colonies in the late seventeenth century differ from that of the English colonies?

European Wars and American Consequences

Developments in North America in the late seventeenth and early eighteenth centuries were driven as much by events in Europe as by those in the colonies. From 1689 until 1713, Europe was in an almost constant state of war, with continental conflicts spilling over into colonial possessions in North America. The result was increased tensions between colonists of different nationalities, Indians and colonists, and colonists and their home countries.

Colonial Conflicts and Indian Alliances. France was at the center of much of the European warfare of the period. Louis XIV hoped to expand France's borders and gain supremacy in Europe. To this end, he built a powerful professional army under state authority. Having gained victories in the Spanish Netherlands, Flanders, Strasbourg, and Lorraine, the French army seemed invincible.

Between 1689 and 1697, France and England fought their first sustained war in North America, **King William's War**. The war began over conflicting French and English interests on the European continent, but it soon spread to the American frontier when English and Iroquois forces attacked French and Huron settlements around Montreal and northern New York.

Although neither side had gained significant territory when peace was declared in 1697, the war had important consequences. Many colonists serving in the English army died of battle wounds, smallpox, and inadequate rations. Those who survived resented their treatment and the unnecessary deaths of so many comrades. The Iroquois fared even worse. Their fur trade was devastated, and hundreds of Mohawks and Oneidas were forced to flee from France's Indian allies along the eastern Great Lakes. "French Indians" and Iroquois continued to attack each other after the peace settlement, but in 1701 the Iroquois agreed to end the raids and remain neutral in all future European conflicts. Wary of further European entanglements, Iroquois leaders focused on rebuilding their tattered confederacy.

A second protracted conflict, known as the **War of the Spanish Succession** (1702–1713) or Queen Anne's War, had even more devastating effects on North America. The conflict erupted in Europe when Charles II of Spain (r. 1665–1700) died without an heir, launching a contest for the Spanish kingdom and its colonies. France and Spain squared off against England, the Netherlands, Austria, and Prussia. In North America, however, it was England alone that faced France and Spain, with each nation hoping to gain additional territory. Both sides recruited Indian allies.

After more than a decade of savage fighting, Queen Anne's War ended in 1713 with the Treaty of Utrecht, which sought to secure a prolonged peace by balancing the interests of the great powers in Europe and their colonial possessions. Yet England benefited the most in North America. At the same time, it consolidated power at home by incorporating Scotland into Great Britain through the 1707 Act of Union. Just six years later, France surrendered Newfoundland, Nova Scotia, and the Hudson Bay Territory to England, while Spain granted England control of St. Kitts in the West Indies, Gibraltar, and Minorca as well as the right to sell African slaves in its American colonies. Yet neither the treaty nor Britain's consolidation forestalled further conflict. Indeed, Spain, France, and Britain all strengthened fortifications along their North American borders (Map 3.1).

Indians Resist European Encroachment.
The European conflicts in North America put incredible pressure on Indian peoples to choose sides. It was increasingly difficult for native peoples in colonized areas to remain autonomous, yet Indian nations were not simply pawns of European powers. Some actively sought European allies against their native enemies, and nearly all desired European trade goods like cloth, guns, and horses. As colonial expansion and trade led to war, however, the power of young male warriors increased in many tribes. In societies like the Cherokee and Iroquois, in which older women had long held significant economic and political authority, this change threatened traditional gender and generational relations. Moreover, struggles among English, French, and Spanish forces both reinforced conflicts among Indian peoples that existed before European settlement and created new ones.

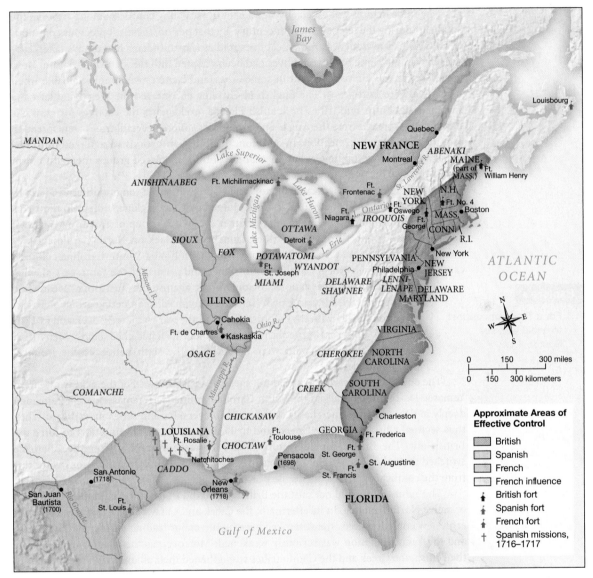

MAP 3.1　European Empires and Indian Nations in North America, 1715–1750

European nations competed with one another and with numerous Indian nations for control of vast areas of North America. Although wars continually reshaped areas under European and Indian control, this map shows the general outlines of the empires claimed by each European nation, the key forts established to maintain those claims, and the major Indian nations in each area.

The trade in guns was especially significant in escalating conflicts among tribes in the Southeast during the late seventeenth century. By that period, the most precious commodity Indians had to trade was Indian captives sold as slaves. Indians had always taken captives in war, but some of those captives had been adopted into the victorious nation. Now, however, war was almost constant in some areas, and captives were more valuable when sold as slaves to Europeans. The English in Carolina encouraged the Westo and later the Savannah nation to raid tribes in Spanish Florida, exchanging the captives for guns. As slave raiding spread across the Anglo-Spanish borders, more peaceful tribes were forced to acquire guns for self-protection. In addition, many Indian nations were forced off traditional lands by slave-raiding Indian foes. Some of these displaced groups merged to form new tribes, like the Yamasee in the Southeast.

By the 1710s, the vicious cycle of guns and slaves convinced some southern Indians to develop a pan-Indian alliance similar to that forged by New England Indians in the 1670s (see "Wars in Old and New England" in chapter 2). First, a group of Tuscarora warriors, hoping to gain support from other tribes, launched an attack on North Carolina settlements in September 1711. In the **Tuscarora War** that followed, South Carolina colonists came to the aid of their North Carolina countrymen and persuaded the Yamasee, Catawba, and Cherokee nations to join forces against the Tuscarora. Meanwhile political leaders in North Carolina convinced a competing group of Tuscarora to ally with the colonists. By 1713 the war was largely over, and in 1715 the Tuscarora signed a peace treaty and forfeited their lands. Many then migrated north and were accepted as the sixth nation of the Iroquois Confederacy.

Explore ▶

For a Tuscarora appeal to avoid war, see Source 3.1.

The end of the Tuscarora War did not mean peace, however. For the next two years, a Yamasee-led coalition attacked the South Carolina militia. The Yamasee people remained deeply in debt to British merchants as the trade in deerskins and slaves moved west. They thus secured allies among the Creeks and in 1715 launched an all-out effort to force the British out. The British gained victory in the **Yamasee War** only after the Cherokee switched their allegiance to the colonists in early 1716. The final Indian nations withdrew from the conflict in 1717, and a fragile peace followed.

The Yamasee War did not oust the British, but it did transform the political landscape of native North America. In its aftermath, the Creek and Catawba tribes emerged as powerful new confederations, the Cherokee became the major trading partner of the British, and the Yamasee nation was seriously weakened. Moreover, as the Cherokee allied with the British, the Creek and the Caddo tribes strengthened their alliance with the French.

Despite the British victory, colonists on the Carolina frontier faced raids on their settlements for decades to come. In the 1720s and 1730s, settlers in the Middle Atlantic colonies also experienced fierce resistance to their westward expansion. And attacks on New Englanders along the Canadian frontier periodically disrupted settlement there. Still, many Indian tribes were pushed out of their homelands. As they resettled in new regions, they alternately allied and fought with native peoples already living there. At the same time, the trade in Indian slaves expanded in the west as the French and the Spanish competed for economic partners and military allies.

Conflicts on the Southern Frontier.

Conflicts on the Southern Frontier. Indians were not the only people to have their world shaken by war. By 1720 years of warfare and upheaval had transformed

GUIDED ANALYSIS

The Tuscarora Appeal to the Pennsylvania Government, 1710

Shortly before the outbreak of a pan-Indian war led by the Tuscarora, a delegation from that nation traveled to Pennsylvania to negotiate with British colonial officials and representatives of the Iroquois Confederacy. The views of Tuscarora representatives Iwaagenst Terrutawanaren and Teonnottein are summarized below by two white officials, John French and Henry Worley, who sought to present the arguments of the Indians. The Pennsylvania government subsequently denied their requests. The Iroquois were apparently more sympathetic since, when the war ended in 1715, the Tuscarora became the sixth nation of the Iroquois Confederacy.

Source 3.1

What groups did the Tuscarora representatives speak for, and what does this suggest about political dynamics within the Tuscarora nation?

What are the most important demands of the Tuscarora?

What is the most immediate concern of the Tuscarora?

At Conestogo, June 8th, 1710.

The Indians were told that according to their request we were come from the Govr. and Govmt. to hear what proposals they had to make anent [about] a peace, according to the purport of their Embassy from their own People.

They signified to us by a Belt of Wampum, which was sent from their old Women, that those Implored their friendship of the Christians & Indians of this Govmt., that without danger or trouble they might fetch wood & Water.

The second Belt was sent from their Children born, & those yet in the womb, Requesting that Room to sport & Play without danger of Slavery, might be allowed them.

The third Belt was sent from their young men fitt to Hunt, that privilege to leave their Towns, & seek provision for their aged, might be granted to them without fear of Death or Slavery.

The fourth was sent from the men of age, Requesting that the Wood, by a happy peace, might be as safe for them as their forts.

The fifth was sent from the whole nation, requesting peace, that thereby they might have Liberty to visit their Neighbours.

The sixth was sent from their Kings and Chiefs, Desiring a lasting peace with the Christians & Indians of this Govmt., that thereby they might be secured against those fearful apprehensions they have for these several years felt. . . .

These Belts (they say) are only sent as an Introduction, & in order to break off hostilities till next Spring, for then their Kings will come and sue for the peace they so much Desire.

Source: Sherman Day, *Historical Collections of the State of Pennsylvania* (Philadelphia: George W. Gorton, 1853), 391–92.

Put It in Context

To what extent does the Tuscarora appeal illuminate important concerns of other Indian tribes in the early 1700s?

the mind-set of many colonists. Although most considered themselves loyal British subjects, many believed that British proprietors remained largely unconcerned with the colonies' welfare. Others resented the British army's treatment of colonial militia and Parliament's unwillingness to aid settlers against Indian attacks. Moreover, the growing numbers of settlers who arrived from other parts of Europe had little investment in British authority.

The impact of Britain's ongoing conflicts with Spain during the 1730s and 1740s illustrates this development. Following the Yamasee War, South Carolina became a royal colony, and its profitable rice and indigo plantations spread southward. Then, in 1732, Parliament established Georgia (named after King George II, r. 1727–1760) on lands north of Florida as a buffer between Carolina colonists and their longtime Spanish foes.

Spanish authorities were furious at this expansion of British territorial claims. Thus in August 1739, a Spanish naval ship captured an English ship captain who was trading illegally in the Spanish West Indies and severed his ear. In response, Great Britain attacked St. Augustine and Cartagena (in present-day Colombia), but its troops were repulsed. In 1742 Spain sent troops into Georgia, but the colonial militia pushed back the attack. By then, the American war had become part of a more general European conflict. Once again France and Spain joined forces while Great Britain supported Germany in Europe. When the war ended in 1748, Britain had ensured the future of Georgia and reaffirmed its military superiority. Once again, however, victory cost the lives of many colonial settlers and soldiers, and some colonists began to wonder whether their interests and those of the British government were truly the same.

Southern Indians were also caught up in ongoing disputes among Europeans. While both French and Spanish forces attacked the British along the Atlantic coast, they sought to outflank each other in the lower Mississippi River valley and Texas. With the French relying on Caddo, Choctaw, and other Indian allies for trade goods and defense, the Spaniards needed to expand their alliances beyond those with the Tejas. In 1749, when Spaniards agreed to stop kidnapping and enslaving Apache women and children, they were able to negotiate peace with that powerful Indian nation.

The British meanwhile became increasingly dependent on a variety of European immigrants to defend colonial frontiers against the French, Spaniards, and Indians. Certainly many Anglo-Americans moved westward as coastal areas became overcrowded, but frontier regions also attracted immigrants from Scotland and Germany who sought refuge and economic opportunity in the colonies. Many headed to the western regions of Virginia and Carolina and to Georgia in the 1730s and 1740s. Meanwhile, South Carolina officials recruited Swiss, German, and French Huguenot as well as Scots-Irish immigrants in the 1740s. Small communities of Jews settled in Charleston as well. Gradually many of these immigrants moved south into Georgia, seeking more and cheaper land. Thus when Spanish, French, or Indian forces attacked the British colonial frontier, they were as likely to face Scots-Irish and German immigrants as Englishmen.

REVIEW & RELATE

How did the European wars of the late seventeenth and early eighteenth centuries impact relations between colonists and England?

How were Indian alliances, with other Indians and with European nations, shaped by the trade in slaves and guns and by wars between European powers?

The **Benefits** and **Costs** of **Empire**

The combined forces of global trade and international warfare altered the political and economic calculations of imperial powers. This was especially true for British North America, where colonists settled as families and created towns that provided key markets for Britain's commercial expansion. Over the course of the eighteenth century, British colonists became increasingly avid consumers of products from around the world. Meanwhile the king and Parliament sought greater control over these far-flung commercial networks.

Colonial Traders Join Global Networks. In the late seventeenth and early eighteenth centuries, trade became truly global. Not only did goods from China, India, the Middle East, Africa, and North America gain currency in England and the rest of Europe, but the tastes of European consumers also helped shape goods produced in other parts of the world. For instance, by the early eighteenth century the Chinese were making porcelain teapots and bowls specifically for the English market. The trade in cloth, tea, tobacco, and sugar was similarly influenced by European tastes. The exploitation of African laborers contributed significantly to this global commerce. They were a crucial item of trade in their own right, and their labor in the Americas ensured steady supplies of sugar, rice, tobacco, and indigo for the world market.

By the early eighteenth century, both the volume and the diversity of goods multiplied. Silk, calico, porcelain, olive oil, wine, and other items were carried from the East to Europe and the American colonies, while cod, mackerel, shingles, pine boards, barrel staves, rum, sugar, rice, and tobacco filled ships returning west. A healthy trade also grew up within North America as New England fishermen, New York and Charleston merchants, and Caribbean planters met one another's needs. Salted cod and mackerel flowed to the Caribbean, and rum, molasses, and slaves flowed back to the mainland. This commerce required ships, barrels, docks, warehouses, and wharves, all of which ensured a lively trade in lumber, tar, pitch, and rosin (Map 3.2).

The flow of information was critical to the flow of goods and credit. By the early eighteenth century, coffeehouses flourished in port cities around the Atlantic, providing access to the latest news. Merchants, ship captains, and traders met in person to discuss new ventures and to keep apprised of recent developments. British and American periodicals reported on parliamentary legislation, commodity prices in India and Great Britain, the state of trading houses in China, the outbreak of disease in foreign ports, and stock ventures in London. Still, these markets were volatile. In 1720 shares in the British South Seas Company, which had risen to astronomical heights, collapsed. Thousands of investors, including William Moraley's father, lost a great deal of money.

Imperial Policies Focus on Profits. European sovereigns worked to ensure that this international trade and their colonial possessions benefited their own European treasuries. In the late seventeenth century, both Louis XIV and his English rivals embraced a system known as **mercantilism**, which centered on the maintenance of a favorable balance of trade, with more gold and silver flowing into the home country than flowed out. In France, finance minister Jean-Baptiste Colbert honed the system. Beginning in the 1660s, he taxed foreign imports while removing all barriers to trade within French territories. Colonies provided valuable raw materials that could be used to produce manufactured items for sale to foreign nations and to colonists.

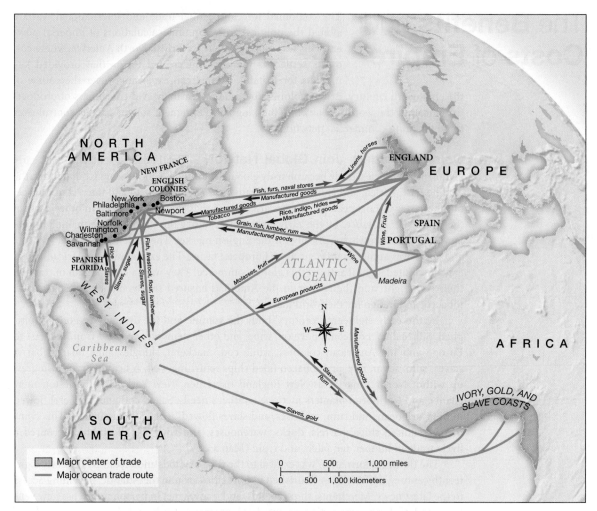

MAP 3.2   North Atlantic Trade in the Eighteenth Century

North Atlantic trade provided various parts of the British empire with raw materials, manufactured goods, and labor. Many ships traveled between only two regions because they were equipped to carry particular kinds of goods — slaves, grains, or manufactured goods. Ultimately, however, people and goods were exchanged among four key points: the West Indies, mainland North America, West Africa, and Great Britain.

While France's mercantile system was limited by the size of its empire, England benefited more fully from such policies. The English crown had access to a far wider array of natural resources from which to manufacture goods and a larger market for these products. Beginning in 1660, Parliament passed a series of **Navigation Acts** that required merchants to conduct trade with the colonies only in English-owned ships. In addition, certain items imported from foreign ports had to be carried in English ships or in ships with predominantly English crews. Finally, a list of "enumerated

Industrious Americans in Boston 1770   This English engraving appeared as a broadsheet in London. It depicts American colonists engaged in agricultural and artisanal labors on the outskirts of Boston. The anonymous artist titled his image "Political electricity," and intended it as a warning to the British government that industrious Americans might one day rebel against parliamentary policies that sought to limit colonial productivity and profits. © Pictorial Press Ltd./Alamy

articles" — including tobacco, cotton, sugar, and indigo — had to be shipped from the colonies to England before being reexported to foreign ports. Thus the crown benefited directly or indirectly from nearly all commerce conducted by its colonies. But colonies, too, often benefited, as when Parliament helped subsidize the development of indigo in South Carolina.

In 1663 Parliament expanded its imperial reach through additional Navigation Acts, which required that goods sent from Europe to English colonies also pass through British ports. And a decade later, ship captains had to pay a duty or post bond before carrying enumerated articles between colonial ports. These acts ensured not only greater British control over shipping but also additional revenue for the crown as captains paid duties in West Indies, mainland North American, and British ports. Beginning in 1673, England sent customs officials to the colonies to enforce the various parliamentary acts. By 1680, London, Bristol, and Liverpool all thrived as barrels of sugar and tobacco and stacks of deer and beaver skins were unloaded and bolts of dyed cloth and cases of metal tools and guns were put on board for the return voyage. As mechanization and manufacturing expanded in England, Parliament sought to keep the profits at home by quashing nascent industries in the colonies. It thus prohibited the sale of products such as American-made textiles (1699), hats (1732), and iron goods (1750). In addition, Parliament worked to restrict trade among the North American colonies, especially between those on the mainland and in the West Indies.

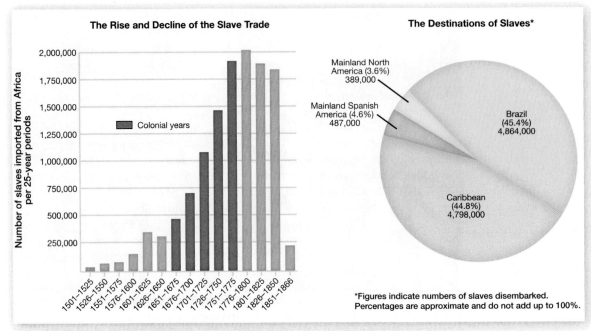

FIGURE 3.1   The Slave Trade in Numbers, 1501–1866

Extraordinary numbers of Africans were shipped as slaves to other parts of the world from the sixteenth to the nineteenth century. The slave trade transformed mainland North America, Brazil, and the West Indies. What broad patterns about the African slave trade can you infer from this data?

Source: Estimates Database. 2009. Voyages: Trans-Atlantic Slave Trade Database, http://www.slavevoyages.org/tast/assessment/estimates.faces. Accessed June 15, 2010.

Despite the increasing regulation, American colonists could own British ships and transport goods produced in the colonies. Indeed, by the mid-eighteenth century, North American merchants oversaw 75 percent of the trade in manufactures sent from Bristol and London to the colonies and 95 percent of the trade with the West Indies. Ironically, then, a system established to benefit Great Britain ended up creating a mercantile elite in British North America. Most of those merchants traded in goods, but some traded in human cargo.

The Atlantic Slave Trade. Parliament chartered the Royal African Company in 1672 as Britain expanded its role in the Atlantic slave trade. Between 1700 and 1808, some 3 million captive Africans were carried on British and Anglo-American ships, about 40 percent of the total of those sold in the Americas in this period (Figure 3.1). Half a million Africans died on the voyage across the Atlantic. Huge numbers also died in Africa, while being marched to the coast or held in forts waiting to be forced aboard ships. Yet despite this astounding death rate, the slave trade yielded enormous profits and had far-reaching consequences: The Africans whom British traders bought and sold transformed labor systems in the colonies, fueled international trade, and enriched merchants, planters, and their families and communities.

European traders worked closely with African merchants to gain their human cargo, trading muskets, metalware, and linen for men, women, and children. Originally many of those sold into slavery were war captives. But by the time British and Anglo-American merchants became central to this notorious trade, their contacts in Africa were procuring labor in any way they could. Over time, African traders moved farther inland to fill the demand, devastating large areas of West Africa, particularly the Congo-Angola region, which supplied some 40 percent of all Atlantic slaves.

The trip across the Atlantic, known as the **Middle Passage**, was a brutal and often deadly experience for Africans. Exhausted and undernourished by the time they boarded the large oceangoing vessels, the captives were placed in dark and crowded holds. Most had been poked and prodded by slave traders, and some had been branded to ensure that a trader received the exact individuals he had purchased. Once in the hold, they might wait for weeks before the ship finally set sail. By that time, the foul-smelling and crowded hold became a nightmare of disease and despair. There was never sufficient food or fresh water for the captives, and women especially were subject to sexual abuse by crew members. Many captives could not communicate with each other since they spoke different languages, and none of them knew exactly where they were going or what would happen when they arrived.

Explore ▶

Examine two sources that reveal the horrors of the Middle Passage in Sources 3.2 and 3.3.

Those who survived the voyage were likely to find themselves in the slave markets of Barbados or Jamaica, where they were put on display for potential buyers. Once purchased, the slaves went through a period of seasoning as they regained their strength, became accustomed to their new environment, and learned commands in a new language. Some did not survive seasoning, falling prey to malnutrition and disease or committing suicide. Others adapted to the new circumstances and adopted enough European or British ways to carry on even as they sought means to resist the shocking and oppressive conditions.

Seaport Cities and Consumer Cultures. The same trade in human cargo that brought misery to millions of Africans provided traders, investors, and plantation owners with huge profits that helped turn America's seaport cities into centers of culture and consumption. Charleston was one of the main ports receiving African slaves in the early 1700s, and Eliza Lucas was impressed with its prosperous character. Arriving in 1738, she noted that "the Metropolis is a neat pretty place. The inhabitants [are] polite and live in a very gentile [genteel] manner." North American seaports, with their elegant homes, fine shops, and lively social seasons, did capture the most dynamic aspects of colonial life. Although cities like New York, Boston, Philadelphia, Baltimore, and Charleston contained less than 10 percent of the colonial population, they served as focal points of economic, political, social, and cultural activity.

Affluent urban families created a consumer revolution in North America. Changing patterns of consumption challenged traditional definitions of status. Less tied to birth and family pedigree, status in the colonies became more closely linked to financial success and a genteel lifestyle. Successful men of humble origins and even those of Dutch, Scottish, French, and Jewish heritage might join the British-dominated colonial gentry.

Of those who made this leap in the early eighteenth century, Benjamin Franklin was the most notable. Franklin was apprenticed to his brother, a printer, an occupation that matched his interest in books, reading, and politics. At age sixteen, Benjamin published

> ### COMPARATIVE ANALYSIS

The Middle Passage

To increase their profits, slave traders built ships specifically to transport Africans. They were designed to hold as many people as possible at the least expense. The image of the slave ship *Brooks* vividly portrays the profit motive in transporting human cargo while *The Interesting Narrative of the Life of Olaudah Equiano* captures the horrific personal experience. Unusually for a slave, Equiano learned to read and write and purchased his freedom in 1766. His narrative likely combines his own experience with that of other slaves. Both documents were widely used by British abolitionists in late eighteenth-century campaigns against the slave trade.

> ### Source 3.2

Plan of a Slave Ship, 1794

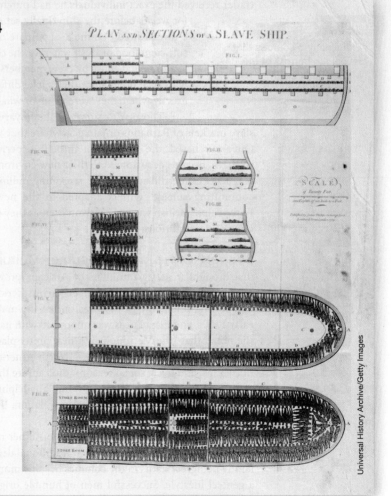

Universal History Archive/Getty Images

Source 3.3

The Interesting Narrative of the Life of Olaudah Equiano, 1789

At last, when the ship we were in had got in all her cargo, they made ready with many fearful noises, and we were all put under deck, so that we could not see how they managed the vessel. . . . [N]ow that the whole ship's cargo were confined together, it became absolutely pestilential. The closeness of the place, and the heat of the climate, added to the number in the ship, which was so crowded that each had scarcely room to turn himself, almost suffocated us. This produced copious perspirations, so that the air soon became unfit for respiration, from a variety of loathsome smells, and brought on a sickness among the slaves, of which many died, thus falling victims to the improvident avarice, as I may call it, of their purchasers. This wretched situation was again aggravated by the galling of the chains, now become insupportable; and the filth of the necessary tubs, into which the children often fell, and were almost suffocated. The shrieks of the women, and the groans of the dying, rendered the whole a scene of horror almost inconceivable.

Happily perhaps for myself I was soon reduced so low here that it was thought necessary to keep me almost always on deck; and from my extreme youth I was not put in fetters. . . . One day, when we had a smooth sea and moderate wind, two of my wearied countrymen who were chained together (I was near them at the time), preferring death to such a life of misery, somehow made through the nettings and jumped into the sea: immediately another quite dejected fellow, who, on account of his illness, was suffered to be out of irons, also followed their example. . . . Those of us that were the most active were in a moment put down under the deck, and there was such a noise and confusion amongst the people of the ship as I never heard before, to stop her, and get the boat out to go after the slaves. However two of the wretches were drowned, but they got the other, and afterwards flogged him unmercifully for thus attempting to prefer death to slavery.

Source: *The Interesting Narrative of the Life of Olaudah Equiano, or Gustavus Vassa, The African, Written by Himself* (London, 1789), 78–82.

Interpret the Evidence

1. What aspects and challenges of the slave trade does the plan of a slave ship emphasize?
2. How does the narrative of Olaudah Equiano complement and deepen our understanding of the image of the ship?

Put It in Context

What do these sources reveal about the role of the Middle Passage in transforming African captives into slaves?

A View of Charleston, South Carolina, c. 1760s This eighteenth-century oil painting by English artist Thomas Mellish offers a view of Charleston harbor c. 1760s. A ship flying an English flag looms in the foreground. The other ships and small boats along with the substantial buildings surrounding the harbor reflect Charleston's stature as one of the main commercial centers of the North American colonies. Ferens Art Gallery, Hull Museums, UK/Bridgeman Images

(anonymously) his first essays in his brother's paper, the *New England Courant*. Two years later, a family dispute led Benjamin to try his luck in New York and then Philadelphia. His fortunes were fragile, but unlike William Moraley Jr., he combined hard work with a quick wit, good luck, and political connections, which together led to success. In 1729 Franklin purchased the *Pennsylvania Gazette* and became the colony's official printer.

While Franklin worried about the concentration of wealth in too few hands, most colonial elites in the early eighteenth century happily displayed their profits. Leading merchants in Boston, Salem, New York, and Philadelphia emulated British styles and built fine homes that had separate rooms for sleeping, eating, and entertaining guests. Mercantile elites also redesigned the urban landscape, donating money for brick churches and stately town halls. They constructed new roads, wharves, and warehouses to facilitate trade, and they invested in bowling greens and public gardens.

The spread of international commerce created a lively cultural life and great affluence in colonial cities. The colonial elite replicated British fashions, including elaborate tea rituals. In Boston, the wives of merchants served fine teas imported from East Asia in cups and saucers from China while decorated bowls held sugar from the West Indies. However, the emergence of a colonial aristocracy also revealed growing inequality. Wealthy urban merchants and professionals lived alongside a middling group of artisans and shopkeepers and a growing class of unskilled laborers, widows, orphans, the elderly, the disabled, and the unemployed. In seaport cities, enslaved laborers might live in their owners' homes or be relegated to separate and impoverished communities. In New York City, which boasted the second largest slave market in the mainland colonies in the 1710s, blacks were regularly buried outside the city limits. The frequent wars of the late seventeenth and early eighteenth centuries contributed to these economic and social divisions by boosting the profits of merchants, shipbuilders, and artisans. They temporarily improved the wages of seamen as well. But in their aftermath, rising prices, falling wages, and a lack of jobs led to the concentration of wealth in fewer hands.

REVIEW & RELATE

- What place did North American colonists occupy in the eighteenth-century global trade network?

- How and with what success did the British government maintain control over the colonial economy and ensure that it served Britain's economic and political interests?

Labor in **North America**

What brought the poor and the wealthy together was the demand for labor. Labor was sorely needed in the colonies, but this did not mean that it was easy to find steady, high-paying employment. Many would-be laborers had few skills and faced fierce competition from other workers for limited, seasonal manual labor. Moreover, a majority of European immigrants and nearly all Africans arrived in America with significant limits on their freedom.

Finding Work in the Colonies. The demand for labor did not necessarily help free laborers find work. Many employers preferred indentured servants, apprentices, or others who came cheap and were bound by contract. Others employed criminals or purchased slaves, who would provide years of service for a set price. Free laborers who sought a decent wage and steady employment needed to match their desire to work with skills that were in demand.

When William Moraley ended his indenture and sought work, he discovered that far fewer colonists than Englishmen owned timepieces, leaving him without a useful trade. So he tramped the countryside, selling his labor when he could, but found no consistent employment. Thousands of other men and women, most without Moraley's education or skills, also found themselves at the mercy of unrelenting economic forces.

Many poor men and women found jobs building homes, loading ships, or spinning yarn. But they were usually employed for only a few months a year. The rest of the time they scrounged for bread and beer, begged in the streets, or stole what they needed. Most lived in ramshackle buildings filled with cramped and unsanitary rooms. Children born into such squalid circumstances were lucky to survive their first year. Those raised in seaport cities might earn a few pence running errands for captains or sailors, but they would never have access to the bounteous goods unloaded at the docks.

By the mid-eighteenth century, older systems of labor, like indentured servitude, began to decline in many areas. In some parts of the North and across the South, white servants were gradually replaced by African slaves (Figure 3.2). At the same time, farm families who could not usefully employ all their children began to bind out sons and daughters to more prosperous neighbors. Apprentices, too, competed for positions. Unlike most servants, apprentices contracted to learn a trade. They trained under the supervision of a craftsman, who gained cheap labor by promising to teach a young man (and most apprentices were men) his trade. But master craftsmen limited the number of apprentices they accepted to maintain the value of their skills.

Another category of laborers emerged in the 1720s. A population explosion in Europe and the rising price of wheat and other items convinced many people to seek passage to America. Shipping agents offered them loans for their passage that were repaid when the immigrants found a colonial employer who would redeem (that is, repay) the agents. In turn, these **redemptioners**, who often traveled with families, labored for the employer for

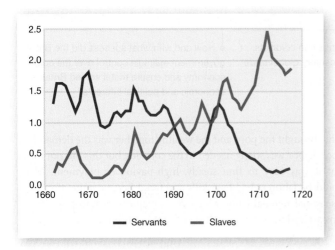

FIGURE 3.2   Indentured Servants and Slaves in Six Maryland Counties, 1662–1717

This chart illustrates a dramatic shift in the Chesapeake labor force between 1662 and 1717. Although based on a study of estate inventories from six Maryland counties, what does the trend shown here suggest about the larger transition in the use of white indentured servants and black slaves on Chesapeake farms? Based on Gloria L. Main, *Tobacco Colony: Life in Early Maryland, 1650–1720* (Princeton: Princeton University Press, 1982), 26.

a set number of years. The redemption system was popular in the Middle Atlantic colonies, especially among German immigrants who hoped to establish farms on the Pennsylvania frontier. While many succeeded, their circumstances could be extremely difficult.

Large numbers of convicts, too, entered the British colonies in the eighteenth century. Jailers in charge of Britain's overcrowded prisons offered inmates the option of transportation to the colonies. Hundreds were thus bound out each year to American employers. The combination of indentured servants, redemptioners, apprentices, and convicts ensured that as late as 1750 the majority of white workers — men and women — in the British colonies were bound to some sort of contract.

Sometimes white urban workers also competed with slaves, especially in the northern colonies. Africans and African Americans formed only a small percentage of the northern population, just 5 percent from Pennsylvania to New Hampshire in 1750. In the colony of New York, however, blacks formed about 14 percent of inhabitants. While some enslaved blacks worked on agricultural estates in the Hudson River valley and New Jersey, even more labored as household servants, dockworkers, seamen, and blacksmiths in New York City alongside British colonists and European immigrants.

Coping with Economic Distress.

Some white workers who were bound by contracts felt common cause with their black counterparts. But whites had a far greater chance of gaining their freedom even before slavery was fully entrenched in colonial law. Still, several challenges confronted white servants, apprentices, redemptioners, and convicts looking to purchase land, open a shop, or earn a decent wage. First, white women and men who gained their freedom from indentures or other contracts had to compete for jobs with a steady supply of redemptioners, convicts, and apprentices as well as other free laborers. Second, by the early eighteenth century, many areas along the Atlantic coast faced a land shortage that threatened the fortunes even of long-settled families. Finally, a population boom in Britain's North American colonies produced growing numbers of young people seeking land and employment. Thus many free laborers migrated from town to town and from country to city seeking work. They hoped to find farmers who needed extra hands for planting and harvesting, ship captains and contractors who would hire them to load or unload cargo or assist in the construction of homes and churches, or wealthy families who needed cooks, laundresses, or nursemaids.

Seasonal and temporary demands for labor created a corps of transient workers. Many New England towns developed systems to "warn out" those who were not official residents. Modeled after the British system, warning-out was meant to ensure that strangers did not become public dependents. Still, being warned did not mean immediate removal. Sometimes transients were simply warned that they were not eligible for poor relief. At other times, constables returned them to an earlier place of residence. In many ways, warning-out served as an early registration system, allowing authorities to encourage the flow of labor, keep residents under surveillance, and protect the town's coffers. But it rarely aided those in need of work.

Residents who were eligible for public assistance might be given food and clothing or boarded with a local family. Many towns began appointing Overseers of the Poor to deal with the growing problem of poverty. By 1750 every seaport city had constructed an almshouse that sheltered residents without other means of support. In 1723 the Bridewell prison was added to Boston Almshouse, built in 1696. Then in 1739 a workhouse was opened on the same site to employ the "able-bodied" poor in hopes that profits from it would help fund the almshouse and prison. Still, these efforts at relief fell far short of the need, especially in hard economic times.

Rural Americans Face Changing Conditions.

While seaport cities and larger towns fostered a growing cohort of individuals who lived outside traditional households, families remained the central unit of economic organization in rural areas, where the vast majority of Americans lived. Yet even farms were affected by the transatlantic circulation of goods and people.

In areas along the Atlantic coast, rural families were drawn into commercial networks in a variety of ways. Towns and cities needed large supplies of vegetables, meat, butter, barley, wheat, and yarn. Farm families sold these goods to residents and bought sugar, tea, and other imported items that diversified their diet. Few rural families purchased ornamental or luxury items, but cloth or cheese bought in town saved hours of labor at home. Just as important, coastal communities like Salem, Massachusetts and Wilmington, Delaware that were once largely rural became thriving commercial centers in the late seventeenth century.

In New England, the land available for farming shrank as the population soared. In the original Puritan colonies, the population rose from 100,000 in 1700 to 400,000 in 1750, and many parents were unable to provide their children with sufficient land for profitable farms. The result was increased migration to the frontier, where families were more dependent on their own labor and a small circle of neighbors. And even this option was not accessible to all. Before 1700, servants who survived their indenture had a good chance of securing land, but by the mid-eighteenth century only two of every ten were likely to become landowners.

Explore ▶

Read two historical interpretations of white settlers in colonial Pennsylvania in Secondary Sources 3.4 and 3.5.

In the Middle Atlantic region, the population surged from 50,000 in 1700 to 250,000 in 1750. The increase was due in part to the rapid rise in wheat prices, which leaped by more than 50 percent in Europe. Hoping to take advantage of this boon, Anglo-Americans, Germans, Scots-Irish, and other non-English groups flooded into the region in the early eighteenth century. By the 1740s, German families had created self-contained communities in western Pennsylvania, New York's Mohawk River valley, and the Shenandoah

Individualism and Community in Colonial North America

The majority of Europeans who entered the British North American colonies between 1680 and 1750 came as indentured servants, slaves, or other forms of bound labor. Others, however, came as independent farmers, artisans, or merchants seeking economic advancement, religious liberty, or political sanctuary. This latter group has received a great deal of attention from scholars searching for the historical roots of a distinctive American sense of individualism or of the nation's ethnic, cultural, and religious diversity. The Middle Colonies have been the focus of much of this scholarship since they attracted a large number of economically independent immigrants from a range of ethnic and religious groups.

Source 3.4

James T. Lemon, Individualism Flourishes in Pennsylvania, 1972

[The] supporters of individualism were not only the more affluent citizens [of Pennsylvania] but also those who moved elsewhere to seek better opportunities for their families. Undoubtedly their views were fostered by a sense that the environment was "open." As individuals, they were ready in spirit to conquer the limitless continent, to subdue the land. . . . We can see the early signs of liberal North America in Pennsylvania as much as anywhere. . . .

The migrants were . . . largely from the middle stratum of western European society. Because they came from the middle class, these settlers brought with them certain characteristics that came to mark Pennsylvania's society. . . . These migrants sought a better life, possessed certain skills, and were neither wealthy nor poverty stricken, at least when they left their homeland. . . . [F]or nearly a century after 1680 [Pennsylvania] possessed a reputation for providing the best chance in the western world for an improved standard of living and life free of external restraint.

The balance was shifting away from the community toward the individual . . . and this led to significant results in early Pennsylvania. Most people sought sites on good land or as near as possible to Philadelphia, the focus of trade; most organized family farms rather than cooperative or manorial farms; and most responded to the demands of the market, which was reflected in the use of the land.

Source: James T. Lemon, *The Best Poor Man's Country: A Geographical Study of Early Southeastern Pennsylvania.* (Baltimore, Md.: John Hopkins University Press, 1972), xv–xvi, 5–7.

Valley of Virginia. They worshipped in German churches, read German newspapers, and preserved German traditions. Meanwhile Scots-Irish immigrants established churches and communities in New Jersey, central Pennsylvania, and western Maryland and Virginia (Map 3.3).

In the South, immigrants could acquire land more easily, but their chances for economic autonomy were increasingly influenced by the spread of slavery. As hundreds and then thousands of Africans were imported into the Carolinas in the 1720s and 1730s, economic and political power became more entrenched in the hands of planters and merchants. Increasingly, they controlled the markets, wrote the laws, and set the terms by which white as well as black families lived. Farms along inland waterways and on the frontier were crucial in providing food and other items for urban residents and for planters with large

Source 3.5

James A. Henretta, Ethnic and Religious Bonds Foster Community, 1978

[V]oluntary concentrations of like-minded settlers indicate the importance of communal values, of people who preferred to share a religious or ethnic identity. . . .

Most of the German immigrants who arrived in Lancaster, Pennsylvania, in 1744 settled on the lots laid out by Dr. Adam Simon Kuhn, the leading German resident, rather than on land offered by the English proprietor, Alexander Hamilton. These linguistic and religious ties extended beyond settlement patterns to encompass economic relationships. . . . [T]he main business connections of the merchants of Lancaster, whether they were Jewish or Quaker or German, were with their co-religionists in Philadelphia. . . .

[T]he weight of the evidence indicates that these decisions were not made for narrowly economic or utilitarian reasons: the felt need to maintain a religious or ethnic identity was as important a consideration as the fertility of the soil or the price of the land in determining where a family would settle. . . . These ethnic, linguistic, or religious ties did not reflect a coherent ideological system, a planned communitarian culture similar to the highly organized Moravian settlement at Bethlehem, Pennsylvania. These bonds among families, neighbors, and fellow church members were informal; nonetheless, they circumscribed the range of individual action among the inhabitants of Pennsylvania and laid the foundations for a rich and diverse cultural existence.

Source: James A. Henretta, "Families and Farms: Mentalité in Pre-Industrial America," *William and Mary Quarterly* 35:1 (1978), 4–5.

Examine the Sources

1. How do Lemon and Henretta differ in their historical interpretations of white settlers in colonial Pennsylvania?
2. Explain how the experiences of New England and Chesapeake colonists might be used to support and/or complicate Lemon's and Henretta's interpretations.

Put It In Context

Analyze how the experiences of slaves and indentured servants challenge the interpretation of Lemon or Henretta. How might the Tuscarora Indians in Source 3.1 have responded to the visions of colonial Pennsylvania offered by Lemon and Henretta?

labor forces. But farm families depended on commercial and planter elites to market their goods and help defend their communities against hostile Indians or Spaniards.

Slavery Takes Hold in the South. The rise of slavery reshaped the South in numerous ways. A major shift from white indentured servants to black slaves began in Virginia after 1676 and soon spread across the Chesapeake (see Figure 3.2). The Carolinas, meanwhile, developed as a slave society from the start. Slavery in turn allowed for the expanded cultivation of cash crops like tobacco, rice, and indigo, which promised high profits for planters as well as merchants. But these developments also made southern elites more dependent on the global market and limited opportunities for poorer whites and all

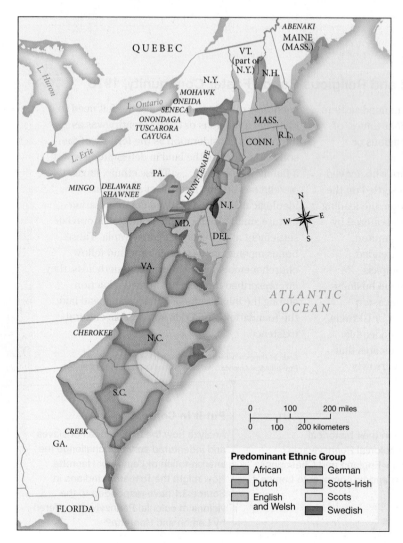

MAP 3.3 Ethnic and Racial Diversity in British North America, 1750

By 1750 British North America was a far more diverse region than it had been fifty years earlier. In 1700 the English dominated most regions, while the Dutch controlled towns and estates in the Hudson River valley. By 1750, however, growing numbers of African Americans, German and Scots-Irish immigrants, and smaller communities of other ethnic groups predominated in various regions.

blacks. They also ensured that Indians and many whites were pushed farther west as planters sought more land for their ventures.

In the 1660s, as tobacco cultivation spread across the Chesapeake, the Virginia Assembly passed a series of laws that defined slavery as a distinct status based on racial identity and passed on through future generations. The enactment of these **slave laws** was driven largely by the growing need for labor, which neither enslaved Indians nor indentured servants could fill. Modeling their laws on statutes passed earlier in Barbados, political leaders ensured that Africans and their descendants would spend their entire lives laboring for white owners. Slavery became a status inherited through the mother; the status could not be changed by converting to Christianity; and masters were granted the right to kill slaves who resisted their authority. In 1680 the Assembly made it illegal for "any negro or other slave to carry or arme himself with any club, staffe, gunn, sword, or any other weapon of defence or offence." Nor

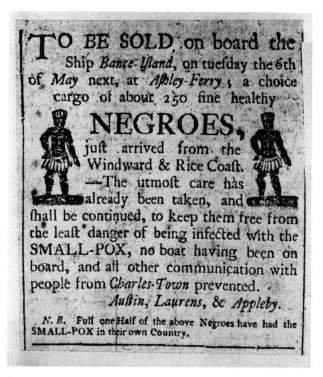

TO BE SOLD, on board the
Ship *Bance-Yland*, on tuefday the 6th
of *May* next, at *Afhley-Ferry*, a choice
cargo of about 250 fine healthy

NEGROES,

juft arrived from the
Windward & Rice Coaft.
—The utmoft care has
already been taken, and
fhall be continued, to keep them free from
the leaft danger of being infected with the
SMALL-POX, no boat having been on
board, and all other communication with
people from *Charles-Town* prevented.
                    Auftin, Laurens, & Appleby.

N. B. Full one Half of the above Negroes have had the
SMALL-POX in their own Country.

Sale of Slaves in Charleston, South Carolina Henry Laurens, one of the major slave traders in Charleston, formed a partnership with two other men to import enslaved Africans to North America. This ad focuses on the health of the 250 Africans they are offering for sale, half of whom have developed immunity to smallpox. Being from the Rice Coast, they were also likely skilled in cultivating rice. Library of Congress, 3a52072

could slaves leave their master's premises without a certificate of permission. Increasingly harsh laws in Virginia and Maryland coincided with a rise in the number of slaves imported to the colonies. The statutes also ensured the decline of the free black population in the Chesapeake. In 1668 one-third of all Africans and African Americans in Virginia and Maryland were still free, but the numbers dwindled year by year. Once the Royal African Company started supplying the Chesapeake with slaves directly from Africa in the 1680s, the pace of change quickened. By 1750, 150,000 blacks resided in the Chesapeake, and only about 5 percent remained free. **See Primary Source Project 3: Tobacco and Slaves, page 101.**

Direct importation from Africa had other negative consequences on slave life. Far more men than women were imported, skewing the sex ratio in a population that was just beginning to form families and communities. Women, like men, performed heavy field work, and few bore more than one or two children. When these conditions, along with brutal work regimens, sparked resistance by the enslaved, fearful whites imposed even stricter regulations, further distinguishing between white indentured servants and enslaved blacks.

While slavery in the Carolinas was influenced by developments in the Chesapeake, it was shaped even more directly by practices in the British West Indies. Many wealthy families from Barbados, Antigua, and other sugar islands—including that of Colonel Lucas—established plantations in the Carolinas. At first, they brought slaves from the West Indies to oversee cattle and pigs and assist in the slaughter of livestock and curing of meat for shipment back to the West Indies. Some of the slaves grew rice, using techniques learned in West Africa, to supplement their diet. Owners soon realized that rice might prove very profitable. Although not widely eaten in Europe, rice could provide cheap and nutritious food for sailors, orphans, convicts, and peasants. Relying initially on Africans' knowledge, planters began cultivating rice for export. (See Map 2.2 in chapter 2.)

The need for African rice-growing skills and the fear of attacks by Spaniards and Indians led Carolina owners to grant slaves rights unheard of in the Chesapeake or the West Indies. Initially slaves were allowed to carry guns and serve in the militia. For those who nonetheless ran for freedom, Spanish and Indian territories offered refuge. Still, most stayed, depending for support on bonds they had developed in the West Indies. The frequent absence of owners also offered Carolina slaves greater autonomy.

Yet as rice cultivation expanded from the 1690s through the early 1700s, slavery in the Carolinas turned more brutal. The Assembly enacted harsher and harsher slave codes to ensure control of the growing labor force. No longer could slaves carry guns, join militias, meet in groups, or travel without a pass. At the same time, the increase in the direct import of slaves skewed gender balances and disrupted older community networks. New military patrols by whites enforced laws and labor practices. Some plantations along the Carolina coast turned into virtual labor camps, where thousands of mostly male slaves worked under harsh conditions with no hope of improvement.

By 1720 blacks outnumbered whites in the Carolinas, and fears of slave rebellions inspired South Carolina officials to impose even harsher laws and more brutal enforcement measures. When indigo joined rice as a cash crop in the 1740s, the demand for slave labor increased further. Although far fewer slaves—about 40,000 by 1750—resided in South Carolina than in the Chesapeake, they constituted more than 60 percent of the colony's total population.

Africans Resist Their Enslavement. Enslaved laborers in British North America resisted their subjugation in a variety of ways. They sought to retain customs, foods, belief systems, and languages from their homelands. They tried to incorporate work patterns passed down from one generation to the next into new environments. They challenged masters and overseers by refusing to work, breaking tools, feigning illness, and other means of disputing whites' authority. Some ran for freedom, others fought back in the face of punishment, and still others used arson, poison, or other means to defy owners. A few planned revolts.

The consequences for resisting were severe, from whipping, mutilation, and branding to summary execution. Fearful of rebellion, whites often punished people falsely accused of planning revolts. Yet some slaves did plot insurrections against their owners or whites in general, and both southern and northern colonies lived with the threat of slave rebellion. In New York City in 1712, several dozen enslaved Africans and Indians set fire to a building. When whites rushed to the scene, the insurgents attacked them with clubs, pistols, axes, and staves, killing 8 and injuring many more. The rebels were soon defeated by the militia, however. Authorities executed 18 insurgents, burning several at the stake as a warning to others, while 6 of those imprisoned committed suicide. In 1741 a series of suspicious fires in the city led to accusations against a white couple who owned an alehouse where blacks gathered to drink. To protect herself from prosecution, an Irish indentured servant testified that she had overheard discussions of an elaborate plot involving black and white conspirators. Frightened of any hint that poor whites and blacks might make common cause, authorities immediately arrested suspects and eventually executed 34 people, including 4 whites. They also banished 72 blacks from the city. Among those executed was Cuffee, a slave who claimed that "a great many people have too much, and others too little."

The most serious slave revolt, however, erupted in South Carolina, just a few miles from Wappoo, the Lucas plantation. A group of recently imported Africans led the **Stono rebellion** in 1739. On Sunday, September 9, a group of enslaved men stole weapons from a country store and killed the owners. They then marched south, along the Stono River, beating drums and recruiting others to join them. Torching plantations and killing whites along the route, they had gathered more than fifty insurgents when armed whites overtook them. In the ensuing battle, dozens of rebels died. The militia, along with Indians hired to assist them, killed another twenty over the next two days and then captured a group of forty, who were executed without trial.

This revolt reverberated widely in a colony where blacks outnumbered whites nearly two to one, direct importation from Africa was at an all-time high, and Spanish authorities in Florida promised freedom to runaway slaves. In 1738 the Spanish governor formed a black militia company, and he allowed thirty-eight fugitive families to settle north of St. Augustine and build Fort Mose for their protection. When warfare erupted between Spain and Britain over commercial rivalries in 1739, the Carolina slaves may have seen their chance to gain freedom en masse. But as with other rebellions, this one failed, and the price of failure was death.

REVIEW & RELATE

What were the sources of economic inequality in North America in the early eighteenth century?

How did the laws and conditions under which poor black and white workers lived during the late seventeenth and early eighteenth centuries differ?

Conclusion: Changing Fortunes in British North America

Global commerce, international wars, and immigration reshaped the economy and geography of North America between 1680 and 1750. Many colonists and some Indians thrived as international trade boomed. In seaport cites, a consumer revolution transformed daily life, fueling the emergence of a colonial elite and the demand for skilled artisans. Others found greater opportunities by pushing inland and establishing farms and communities along new frontiers. But many people failed to benefit from these changes. Indians were often dispossessed of their land as white settlers pushed west. Many indentured servants found it impossible to obtain land or decent wages after they gained their independence. Still, even if white servants and unskilled workers struggled amid periodic economic upheavals, they had the benefit of freedom. Black workers were increasingly forced into slavery, with the shrinking percentage of free blacks suffering from intensifying discrimination against the race as a whole. The consequences of international trade and imperial conflicts only widened the gap between economically successful and impoverished or enslaved Americans.

Increased mechanization and the growth of manufacturing in England shaped the lives of working people on both sides of the Atlantic Ocean. William Moraley Jr., for example, lived out his life in Newcastle-upon-Tyne, making and repairing watches at a time when cheap watches were being turned out in large numbers. Yet these economic changes had far more positive effects for some colonists. The mechanization of cloth production in England demanded vast amounts of raw material from the English countryside and the colonies. It ensured, for example, the profitability of indigo. This crop benefited South Carolina planters like Eliza Lucas and — after her marriage in 1744 — her husband, Charles Pinckney, a successful planter himself. Still, profits from indigo could be gained only through the labor of hundreds of slaves.

Eliza Pinckney's sons became important leaders in South Carolina, and despite their English education and the benefits they gained through British trade, both developed a strong belief in the rights of the colonies to control their own destinies. Like many American colonists, they were spurred by the consumer revolution, geographical expansion, growing ethnic diversity, and conflicts with Indian and European enemies to develop a mind-set that differed significantly from their counterparts in England. Yet this turn away from the religious and political beliefs that had sustained them for generations soon spurred a series of revivals that initially reinforced the importance of faith but ultimately challenged the authority of traditional institutions.

CHAPTER 3 REVIEW

TIMELINE OF EVENTS

1660	Monarchy restored in England
1660–1673	Navigation Acts
1660–1685	Charles II grants North American proprietorships
1672	Royal African Company chartered
1680	Pueblo revolt
1688	Glorious Revolution
1689–1697	King William's War
1691–1710	North Carolina separates from South Carolina
1692	Colony of Massachusetts established
1700–1750	New England colonial population quadruples
	Middle Atlantic colonial population quintuples
1700–1808	British ships carry 3 million African slaves to the Americas
1702	East and West Jersey unite into New Jersey
1702–1713	War of the Spanish Succession
1704	Delaware separates from Pennsylvania
1711–1713	Tuscarora War
1715–1717	Yamasee War
1732	Colony of Georgia established
1739	Stono rebellion
1749	Spanish settlers in Texas make peace with the Apache

KEY TERMS

proprietary colonies, *74*

Glorious Revolution, *74*

Pueblo revolt, *76*

King William's War, *78*

War of the Spanish Succession, *78*

Tuscarora War, *80*

Yamasee War, *80*

mercantilism, *83*

Navigation Acts, *84*

Middle Passage, *87*

redemptioners, *91*

slave laws, *96*

Stono rebellion, *98*

REVIEW & RELATE

1. What role did the crown play in the expansion of the English North American colonies in the second half of the seventeenth century?

2. How did the development of the Spanish and French colonies in the late seventeenth century differ from that of the English colonies?

3. How did the European wars of the late seventeenth and early eighteenth centuries impact relations between colonists and England?

4. How were Indian alliances, with other Indians and with European nations, shaped by the trade in slaves and guns and by wars between European powers?

5. What place did North American colonists occupy in the eighteenth-century global trade network?

6. How and with what success did the British government maintain control over the colonial economy and ensure that it served Britain's economic and political interests?

7. What were the sources of economic inequality in North America in the early eighteenth century?

8. How did the laws and conditions under which poor black and white workers lived during the late seventeenth and early eighteenth centuries differ?

Tobacco and Slaves

▶ Explain the roles that legislators, planters, and enslaved workers played in the production of tobacco and describe the challenges they faced.

Tobacco was a popular commodity among Europeans, and they relied on colonies like Virginia and Maryland to provide it. Consumption and production expanded dramatically between the 1670s and the 1750s. The 17.5 million pounds of tobacco exported from the Chesapeake in 1672 leapt to nearly 51 million pounds by 1750. While many small farmers cultivated tobacco with only the aid of family members or indentured servants, increased demand drove others to seek new sources of labor. Laws that codified the status of slaves encouraged more planters to invest in Africans (Source 3.6).

Many planters worried about how to balance proper care of slaves, in whom they had invested significant capital, with the need for discipline (Sources 3.7 and 3.9). At the same time, tobacco planters sought to promote a positive image that would appeal to consumers and English authorities (Source 3.8). While large slave owners could find themselves deeply in debt when prices fell, they were still likely to gain the greatest profits from the tobacco trade.

As tobacco production increased in Virginia, so did the importation of enslaved Africans. While 4,000 Africans were imported in the 1690s, more than 15,000 arrived in the 1730s. By 1740, natural reproduction added to the steady rise in Virginia's African American population. The vast majority of black Virginians were enslaved, and the greatest number worked in tobacco. While much of the work of clearing fields, weeding, and hoeing was considered unskilled, the cutting, stemming, and packing of tobacco leaf required considerable skill (Sources 3.8 and 3.9). In response to the arduous labor and harsh discipline, some slaves ran away and others organized collective escapes (Source 3.10). However, most of Virginia's enslaved workers remained locked into the tobacco cycle, along with their children and grandchildren.

Source 3.6

Virginia Slave Laws, 1662 and 1667

As the demand for labor on tobacco farms increased in the mid-seventeenth century and the flow of white indentured servants to Virginia slowed, tobacco planters imported more Africans to fill their labor needs. In the 1660s Virginia legislators passed a series of laws to clarify the status of this new category of worker. Several were based on laws in effect in the West Indies, including the 1662 law that defined slavery as an inherited position.

[1662]
WHEREAS some doubts have arisen whether children got by any Englishman upon a negro woman should be slave or free, *Be it therefore enacted and declared by this present grand assembly*, that all children borne in this country shall be held bond or free only according to the condition of the mother, *And* that if any christian shall commit fornication with a negro man or woman, he or she so offending shall pay double the fines imposed by the former act.

[1667]

WHEREAS some doubts have risen whether children that are slaves by birth, and by the charity and piety of their owners made pertakers of the blessed sacrament of baptisme, should by vertue of their baptisme be made free; *It is enacted and declared by this grand assembly, and the authority thereof,* that the conferring of baptisme doth not alter the condition of the person as to his bondage or freedome; that diverse masters, freed from this doubt, may more carefully endeavour the propagation of christianity by permitting children, though slaves, or those of greater growth if capable to be admitted to that sacrament.

Source: William W. Hening, ed., *The Statutes at Large; Being a Collection of All Laws of Virginia, from the First Session of the Legislature in the Year 1619* (Samuel Pleasants, 1810), 2:170, 260.

Source 3.7

Joseph Ball Instructs His Nephew on Managing Enslaved Workers, 1743

Joseph Ball of Stratford, England, owned a tobacco plantation named Morattico in Lancaster County, Virginia. He lived in England, where he practiced law, so he employed his nephew Joseph Chinn to manage his estate. Ball sent Chinn detailed instructions about handling crops, livestock, the overseer, and the slaves. He also visited Morattico regularly. This letter from February 1743 focuses on Chinn's care of the slaves.

will have what Goods I send to Virginia to the use of my Plantation there, kept in my House at Morattico.

If I should not send Goods enough, you must Supply the rest out of the stores there with my Tobacco.

The Coarse Cotton . . . was assign'd for blankets for my Negroes: there must be four yards a half to each Blanket. They that have [now] two blankets already; that is one tolerable one, and one pretty good one, must have what is wanting to make it up, 4½ yards in a blanket. And Everyone of the workers must have a Good Suite of the Welsh Plain

[wool] made as it should be. Not to[o] Scanty, nor bobtail'd. And Each of the Children must have a Coat of Worser Cotton . . . and two shirts or shifts of ozenbrig [coarse linen] and the Workers must Each of them have Summer Shirtfs of the brown Rolls. And All the workers must have Good strong Shoes, & stockings; and they that go after the Creatures [livestock], or Much in the Wet, must have two pair of Shoes . . . and all must be done in Good time; and not for Winter to be half over before they get their summer Clothes; as the Common Virginia fashion is.

If any of the Negroes should be sick, let them ly by a Good fire; and have fresh Meat & brot[h]; and blood, and vomit [purge] them, as you shall think proper. . . . I would have no Doctor unless in very violent Cases: they Generally do more harm than Good. . . .

Let not the overseers abuse my People. Nor let them abuse their overseer.

Let the Breeding Wenches have Baby Clothes, for wh[ic]h you may tear up old sheets, or any other old Linen . . . (I shall Send things proper hereafter) and let them have Good Midwives; and what is necessary. Register all the Negro Children that shall be born and after keep an account of their ages among my Papers.

Source: Joseph Ball Letterbook, 1743–1759, in *Correspondence of Joseph Ball, 1743–1780*, Library of Congress.

Source 3.8

Enslaved Blacks Working on a Tobacco Plantation, c. 1750

This wood engraving, created by nineteenth-century English author and engraver Frederick W. Fairholt, was based on a mid-eighteenth-century drawing. Fairholt published it in his 1859 book, *Tobacco, Its History and Associations*. Fairholt depicts bare-chested slaves packing tobacco leaves in hogsheads and rolling them to waiting ships while well-dressed whites oversee their work. The overhead banner reminds readers that Indians introduced tobacco to the English.

Peter Newark American Pictures/Bridgeman Images

Richard Corbin Describes How to Become a Successful Planter, 1759

Richard Corbin (c. 1708–1790) owned tobacco plantations in King and Queen County, Virginia, and served as a burgess and receiver general of Virginia. Here he writes to his new manager, James Semple, describing his duties as well as the work of overseers and slaves. Corbin describes the crucial processes in preparing cut leaves for market — "striking" them down from the rafters where they are hung to cure; "stripping" the leaves from the stalk; and "stemming," or rolling, individual leaves, which are then "prized" or packed in a hogshead.

As it will be Necessary to . . . Suggest to you my Thoughts upon the business you have undertaken, I shall endeavor to be particular and Circumstanial. . . .

Observe a prudent and a Watchful Conduct over the Overseers that they attend their business with diligence; keep the Negroes in good order and enforce obedience by the Example of their own Industry, wch [which] is a more effectual method in every respect . . . than Hurry and Severity; the ways of Industry are constant and regular, not to be in a hurry at one time and do nothing at another, but to be always Usefully and Steadily employed. . . .

Take an Exact account of all the Negroes & Stocks [animals] at each Plantation and send to me; & tho[ugh] once a year may be sufficient to take this acct, yet it will be advisable to see them once a Month at least, as such an Inspection will fix more closely the overseers attention to these points.

As complaints have been made by the Negroes in respect to their provision of corn, I must desire you to put that matter under such a Regulation, as your own Prudence will dictate. . . . The allowance to be sure is Plentiful and they ought to have their Belly full but care must be taken with this Plenty that no Waiste [waste] is Committed. . . .

Tob[acc]o h[ogs]h[ea]ds [large casks] should always be provided the 1st Week in Sept; every morning of that month is fit for Striking & Stripping;

every morning therefore of this month, they should Strike as much Tob[acc]o as they can strip whilst the Dew is upon the Ground and what they Strip in the morning must be Stem'd in the Evening; this method constantly practiced, the Tobacco will be prised before Christmas, Weigh well, and at least one hhd in Ten gained by finishing the Tob[acc]o thus early.

Source: Richard Corbin to Mr. James Semple, January 1, 1759, Richard Corbin Letterbook, Manuscript DMS 1971.5, John D. Rockefeller, Jr. Library, Colonial Williamsburg Foundation.

Source 3.10

Lieutenant Governor William Gooch to the Board of Trade, London, 1729

William Gooch served as lieutenant governor and governor of the Virginia colony from 1727 to 1749. His success depended in large part on his support for Virginia's tobacco planters, who comprised the colony's ruling elite. His frequent letters to the Board of Trade in London addressed planters' and the board's concerns regarding trade relations, debt collection, the quality of tobacco, and, in the letter below, resistance among some enslaved workers.

Some time after my last [letter] a number of negroes, about fifteen, belonging to a new plantation, . . . formed a design to withdraw from their master and to fix themselves in the fastnesses of the neighbouring mountains: they had found means to get into their possession some arms and ammunition, and they took along with them some provisions, their cloaths, bedding and working tools; but the Gentleman to whom they belonged with a party of men made such diligent pursuit after them, that he soon found them out in their settlement, a very obscure place among the mountains, where they had already begun to clear the ground, and obliged them after exchanging a shot or two by which one of the slaves was wounded, to surrender and return back, and so prevented for this time a design which might have proved as dangerous to this country, as is that of the negroes in the mountains of Jamaica to the inhabitants of that island. Tho' this attempt has happily been defeated, it ought nevertheless to awaken us into some effectual measures for preventing the like hereafter, it being certain that a very small number of negroes once settled in those parts, would very soon be encreas'd by the accession of other runaways and prove dangerous neighbours to our frontier inhabitants.

Source: Lt. Gov. William Gooch to Board of Trade, June 29, 1729, *Calendar of State Papers, Colonial Series, America and the West Indies, 1728–1729* (London, 1937), 414–15, in Paul G. E. Clemens, ed., *The Colonial Era: A Documentary Reader* (Malden, MA: Blackwell, 2008), 135–36.

Interpret the Evidence

1. Why did Virginia lawmakers decide that slave status should pass through the mother's (rather than father's) line and would be unaffected by baptism (Source 3.6)?
2. What do the descriptions of slave life and labor by Joseph Ball and Richard Corbin reveal about the attitudes of Virginia planters toward enslaved workers (Sources 3.7 and 3.9)? Because no slaves left us direct descriptions of their lives, what limitations do these sources present for historians?
3. How does the engraving (Source 3.8) portray the roles of planters, managers, and enslaved workers? What are the most notable differences between the black and white figures in this image?
4. What issues about slave life on a tobacco plantation are raised by Lieutenant Governor William Gooch (Source 3.10), and how do they compare with the image presented in the engraving (Source 3.8) and the writings by planters (Sources 3.7 and 3.9)?

Put It in Context

What were the relationships among the growing demand for tobacco, the actions of Virginia politicians and planters, and the lives of enslaved laborers?

What were the greatest challenges faced by white colonists (slave owners and non-slave owners) and by black laborers as the Atlantic slave trade expanded between 1680 and 1750?

Religious Strife and Social Upheavals

1680–1754

WINDOW TO THE PAST

Abigail Faulkner Appeals Her Conviction for Witchcraft, 1692

Abigail Faulkner, the daughter of a minister and wife of a large landowner, was convicted of witchcraft in Salem, Massachusetts, but maintained her innocence. Any woman sentenced to death had her execution postponed if she was pregnant. Faulkner used the delay in carrying out her death penalty to petition the Massachusetts governor for her release based on what she considered insufficient evidence.

▶ To discover more about what this primary source can show us, see Source 4.1 on page 110.

After reading this chapter you should be able to:

- Explain the relationships among religious, economic, and political tensions and accusations of witchcraft.

- Describe family dynamics, particularly between husbands and wives, and how they changed over time and differed by class and region.

- Understand the ways that economic developments and increasing diversity fueled conflicts in early eighteenth-century colonial society.

- Explain the emergence of the Great Awakening and identify its critics and legacies.

- Describe how the Great Awakening shaped political developments in the 1730s and 1740s.

COMPARING AMERICAN HISTORIES

The son of a Scots-Irish clergyman, Gilbert Tennent was born in Vinecash, Ireland, in 1703 and at age fifteen moved with his family to Philadelphia. After receiving an M.A. from Yale College in 1725, Gilbert was ordained a Presbyterian minister in New Brunswick, New Jersey, with little indication of the role he would play in a major denominational schism.

Tennent entered the ministry at a critical moment, when leaders of a number of denominations had become convinced that the colonies were descending into spiritual apathy. Tennent dedicated himself to sparking a rebirth of Christian

(left) **Gilbert Tennent**. Granger, NYC
(right) **Gravestone of Sarah Grosvenor**. Jessica C. Linker

commitment, and by the mid-1730s the pastor had gained fame as a revival preacher. At the end of the decade, he journeyed through the middle colonies with Englishman George Whitefield, an Anglican preacher known for igniting powerful revivals. Then in the fall of 1740, following the death of his wife, Tennent launched his own evangelical "awakenings."

Revivals inspired thousands of religious conversions across denominations, but they also fueled conflicts within established churches. Presbyterians in Britain and America disagreed about whether only those who had had a powerful, personal conversion experience were qualified to be ministers. Tennent made his opinion clear by denouncing unconverted ministers in his sermons, a position that led to his expulsion from the Presbyterian Church in 1741. But many local churches sought converted preachers, and four years later a group of ejected pastors formed a rival synod that trained its own evangelical ministers.

While ministers debated the proper means of saving sinners, ordinary women and men searched their souls. In Pomfret, Connecticut, Sarah Grosvenor certainly feared for hers in the summer of 1742 when the unmarried nineteen-year-old realized she was pregnant. Her situation was complicated by her status in the community. She was the daughter of Leicester Grosvenor, an important landowner, town official, and member of the Congregational Church.

The pew next to Sarah and her family was occupied by Nathaniel Sessions and his sons, including the twenty-six-year-old Amasa, who had impregnated Sarah. Many other young women became pregnant out of wedlock in the 1740s, but families accepted the fact as long as the couple married before the child was born. In Sarah's case, however, Amasa refused to marry her and suggested instead that she have an abortion.

Although Sarah was reluctant to follow this path, Amasa insisted. When herbs traditionally used to induce a miscarriage failed, Amasa introduced Sarah to John Hallowell, a doctor who claimed he could remove the fetus with forceps. After admitting her agonizing situation to her older sister Zerviah and her cousin Hannah, Sarah allowed Hallowell to proceed. He finally induced a miscarriage, but Sarah soon grew feverish, suffered convulsions, and died ten days later.

Apparently Sarah's and Amasa's parents were unaware of the events leading to her demise. Then in 1745, a powerful religious revival swept through the region, and Zerviah and Hannah suffered great spiritual anguish. It is likely they finally confessed their part in the affair since that year officials brought charges against Amasa Sessions and John Hallowell for Sarah's death. At the men's trial, Zerviah and Hannah testified about their roles and those of Sessions and Hallowell. Still, their spiritual anguish did not lead to earthly justice. Hallowell was found guilty but escaped punishment by fleeing to Rhode Island. Sessions was acquitted and remained in Pomfret, where he married and became a prosperous farmer. ■

Comparing the American histories of Gilbert Tennent and Sarah Grosvenor reveals the power of the religious forces — later called the Great Awakening — that swept through the colonies in the early eighteenth century. Those forces are best understood in the context of larger social, economic, and political changes. Many young people became more independent of their parents and developed tighter bonds with siblings, cousins, and neighbors their own age. Towns and cities developed clearer hierarchies by class and status, which could protect wealthier individuals from being punished for their misdeeds. A double standard of sexual behavior became more entrenched as well, with women subject to greater scrutiny than men for their sexual behavior. Of course, most young women did not meet the fate of Sarah Grosvenor. Still, pastors like Gilbert Tennent feared precisely such consequences if the colonies — growing ever larger and more diverse — did not reclaim their religious foundations.

An **Ungodly Society?**

As American colonists became more engaged in international and domestic commerce, spiritual commitments appeared to wane. In New England, Congregational ministers condemned the apparent triumph of worldly ambition over religiosity. Nonetheless, some ministers saw economic success as a reward for godly behavior even as they worried that wealth and power opened the door to sin. In the late seventeenth century, these anxieties deepened when accusations of witchcraft erupted across southern New England.

The Rise of Religious Anxieties.
In 1686 the Puritan minister Samuel Sewell railed against the behavior of Boston mercantile elites. Citing examples of their depravity in his diary, including drunkenness and cursing, he claimed that such "high-handed wickedness has hardly been heard of before." Sewell was outraged as well by popular practices such as donning powdered wigs in place of God-given hair, wearing scarlet and gold jackets rather than simple black cloth, and offering toasts rather than prayers.

While Sewell spoke for many Puritans concerned with the consequences of commercial success, other religious leaders tried to meld old and new. The Reverend Cotton Mather complained that many colonists showed greater interest in the latest fashions than in the state of their souls. Yet he was attracted by the luxuries available to colonists and hoped to make his own son "a more finished Gentleman." Mather was also fascinated by new scientific endeavors and supported inoculations for smallpox, which others viewed as challenging God's power.

Certainly news of the Glorious Revolution in England (1688) offered Puritans hope of regaining their customary authority (see "English Colonies Grow and Multiply" in chapter 3). But the outbreak of King William's War in 1689 quickly ended any notion of an easy return to peace and prosperity. Instead, continued conflicts and renewed fears of Indian attacks on rural settlements heightened the sense that Satan was at work in the region. Soon, accusations of witchcraft joined outcries against other forms of ungodly behavior.

Cries of Witchcraft.

Belief in witchcraft had been widespread in Europe and England for centuries. It was part of a general belief in supernatural causes for events that could not otherwise be explained—severe storms, a suspicious fire, a rash of deaths among livestock. When a community began to suspect witchcraft, they often pointed to individuals who challenged cultural norms. Women who were quarrelsome, eccentric, poor, or simply too independent were easy to imagine as cavorting with evil spirits and invisible demons.

Witchcraft accusations tended to be most common in times of change and uncertainty. Over the course of the seventeenth century, colonists had begun to spread into new areas seeking more land and greater economic opportunities. But expansion brought with it confrontations with Indians, exposure to new dangers, and greater vulnerability to a harsh environment. As the stress of expansion mounted, witchcraft accusations emerged. Some 160 individuals, mostly women, were accused of witchcraft in Massachusetts and Connecticut and 15 were put to death between 1647 and 1691. Many of the accused were poor, childless, or disgruntled women, but widows who inherited property also came under suspicion, especially if they fought for control against male relatives and neighbors.

The social and economic complexities of witchcraft accusations are well illustrated by the most famous American witch-hunt, the Salem witch trials of the early 1690s. In 1692 residents of Salem, Massachusetts confronted conflicts between long-settled farmers and newer mercantile families, political uncertainties following the Glorious Revolution, ongoing threats from Indians, and quarrels over the choice of a new minister. These tensions were brought to a head when the Reverend Samuel Parris's daughter and niece learned voodoo lore and exotic dances from the household's West Indian slave, Tituba. The daughters and servants of neighboring families also became entranced by Tituba's tales and began to tell fortunes, speak in gibberish, and contort their bodies into painful positions. When the girls were questioned about their strange behavior, they pointed not only to Tituba but also to other people in the community. They first accused an elderly female pauper and a homeless widow of bewitching them, but later singled out respectable churchwomen as well as a minister, a wealthy merchant, and a four-year-old child.

Within weeks, more than one hundred individuals, 80 percent of them women, stood accused of witchcraft. Governor William Phips established a special court to handle the cases, over which the Reverend Samuel Sewell presided. Twenty-seven of the accused came to trial, and twenty were found guilty based on testimony from the girls and on **spectral evidence**, that is, evidence that came to the girls in dreams or visions. In court, the young accusers were seen writhing, shaking, and crying out in pain as spirits of the accused, invisible to everyone else, came to them in visions and pinched, choked, and bit them. Based on such evidence, nineteen people were hanged, and one was pressed to death with stones.

Explore ▶

Read the appeal of a woman accused of witchcraft in Source 4.1.

But when accusations reached into prominent Salem and Boston families, Governor Phips ended the proceedings and released the remaining suspects. In the following months, leading ministers and colonial officials condemned the use of spectral evidence, and some of the young accusers recanted their testimony.

The Salem trials illuminate far more than beliefs in witchcraft. The trials pitted the daughters and servants of prosperous farmers against the wives and widows of recently arrived merchants. The accusers included young women like nineteen-year-old Mercy Lewis, who was bound out as a servant when her parents were killed by Indians. Fear of attack from hostile Indians, hostile officials in England, or hostile neighbors fostered anxieties in Salem, as it did in many colonial communities. Other anxieties also haunted the accusers. A shortage of land led many New England men to seek their fortune farther west, leaving young women with few eligible bachelors to choose from. Marriage prospects were affected as well by battles over inheritance. Thomas Putnam Jr., who housed three of the accusers, was in the midst of one such battle, which left his three sisters — the accusers' aunts — in limbo as they awaited legacies that could enhance their marriage prospects. As young women in Salem forged tight bonds in the face of such uncertainties, they turned their anger not against men, but instead against older women, including respectable "goodwives" like Abigail Faulkner.

REVIEW & RELATE

● What factors led to a rise in tensions within colonial communities in the early 1700s?

● How did social, economic, and political tensions contribute to an increase in accusations of witchcraft?

Family and Household Dynamics

Concerns about marriage, property, and inheritance were not limited to Salem or to New England. As the American colonies became more populous and the numbers of women and men more balanced, husbands gained greater control over the behavior of household members, and the legal and economic rewards available to most women declined. Yet some women improved their situation by wielding their skills as midwives, brewers, or even plantation managers to benefit their families.

Women's Changing Status. In most early American colonies, the scarcity of women and workers ensured that many white women gained economic and legal leverage. In the first decades of settlement in the Chesapeake, where women were in especially short supply and mortality was high, young women who arrived as indentured servants and completed their term might marry older men of property. If the husbands died first, widows often took control of the estate and passed on the property to their children. Even in New England, where the numbers of men and women were more balanced from the beginning, the crucial labor of wives in the early years of settlement was sometimes recognized by their control of family property after a husband's death.

By the late seventeenth century, however, as the sex ratio in the Chesapeake evened out, women lost the opportunity to marry "above their class" (see Table 4.1). And across the colonies, widows lost control of family estates. Even though women still performed

GUIDED ANALYSIS

Abigail Faulkner Appeals Her Conviction for Witchcraft, 1692

While most women accused of witchcraft in Salem were marginal to society, Abigail Faulkner was the daughter of a minister and the wife of a large landowner. Nonetheless, she was declared guilty on the basis of spectral evidence and the charges made by "bewitched" girls. When Faulkner's execution was postponed, she petitioned Governor Phips to release her. Faulkner was released, but only after Massachusetts officials stepped in and ended the trials.

Source 4.1

What evidence does Faulkner provide of her innocence?

What saved Faulkner from being executed initially?

How does Faulkner try to persuade Governor Phips of the need for immediate action?

The humblee Petition of Abigall: Falkner unto his Excellencye S'r W'm Phipps knight and Govern'r of their Majestyes Dominions in America: humbly sheweth

That your poor and humble Petitioner having been this four monthes in Salem Prison and condemned to die having had no other evidences against me but the Spectre Evidences and the Confessors w'ch Confessors have lately since I was condemned owned to my selfe and others and doe still own that they wronged me and what they had said against me was false: and that they would not that I should have been put to death for a thousand worldes for they never should have enjoyed themselves againe in this world; w'ch undoubtedly I shouled have been put to death had it not pleased the Lord I had been with child. Thankes be to the Lord I know my selfe altogether Innocent & Ignorant of the crime of witchcraft w'ch is layd to my charge: as will appear at the great day of Judgment (May it please yo'r Excellencye) my husband about five yeares a goe was taken w'th fitts w'ch did very much impaire his memory and understanding but w'th the blessing of the Lord upon my Endeavors did recover of them againe but now through greife and sorrow they are returned to him againe as bad as Ever they were: I having six children and having little or nothing to subsist on being in a manner without a head [husband] to doe any thinge for my selfe or them and being closely confined can see no otherwayes but we shall all perish Therfore may it please your Excellencye your poor and humble petition'r doe humbly begge and Implore of yo'r Excellencye to take it into yo'r pious and Judicious consideration that some speedy Course may be taken w'th me for my releasement.

Source: Paul Boyer and Stephen Nissenbaum, eds., *The Salem Witchcraft Papers, Verbatim Transcripts of the Legal Documents of the Salem Witchcraft Outbreak of 1692* (New York: Da Capo Press, 1977), 1:333–34.

Put It in Context

How might the conviction of a woman like Abigail Faulkner have helped bring an end to the Salem witch trials?

TABLE 4.1　Sex Ratios in the White Population for Selected Colonies, 1624–1755

Date	Colony	White Male Population	White Female Population	Females per 100 Males
1624–1625	Virginia	873	222	25
1660	Maryland	c. 600	c. 190	32
1704	Maryland	11,026	7,136	65
1698	New York	5,066	4,677	92
1726	New Jersey	15,737	14,124	90
1755	Rhode Island	17,860	17,979	101

vital labor, the spread of indentured servitude and slavery lessened the recognition of their contributions, while in urban areas the rise of commerce highlighted their role as consumers rather than as producers. As a result, most wives and daughters of white settlers were assigned primarily domestic roles. They also found their legal and economic rights restricted to those accorded their female counterparts in Great Britain.

According to English common law, a wife's status was defined as *feme covert*, which meant that she was legally covered over by (or hidden behind) her husband. The husband controlled his wife's labor, the house in which she lived, the property she brought into the marriage, and any wages she earned. He was also the legal guardian of their children, and through the instrument of a will he could continue to control the household after his death.

With the growth and diversity of colonial towns and cities, the **patriarchal family** — a model in which fathers held absolute authority over wives, children, and servants — came to be seen as a crucial bulwark against disorder. Families with wealth were especially eager to control the behavior of their sons and daughters as the parents sought to build social, commercial, and political alliances. The refusal of Amasa Sessions to marry Sarah Grosvenor, for instance, may have resulted from his father's expectation of a better match.

> **Explore ▶**
>
> Compare the images of elite women conveyed in a family portrait and a personal letter in Source 4.2 and 4.3.

Working Families. Still, for most colonial women and men, daily rounds of labor shaped their lives more powerfully than legal statutes or inheritance rights. Husbands and wives depended on each other to support the family. By the early eighteenth century, many colonial writers promoted the idea of marriage as a partnership, even if the wife remained the junior partner.

This concept of marriage as a partnership took practical form in communities across the colonies. In towns, the wives of artisans often learned aspects of their husband's craft and assisted their husbands in a variety of ways. Given the overlap between homes and workplaces in the eighteenth century, women often cared for apprentices, journeymen, and laborers as well as their own children. Husbands meanwhile labored alongside their subordinates and represented their families' interests to the larger community. Both spouses were expected to provide models of godliness and to encourage prayer and regular church attendance among household members.

On farms, where the vast majority of colonists lived, women and men played crucial if distinct roles. In general, wives and daughters labored inside the home as well as in the

Elite Women's Lives in the North American Colonies

By the 1740s, elite women were viewed as paragons of piety and domesticity. Yet many contributed wealth and management skills to family enterprises. The painting by Robert Feke (Source 4.2) portrays Isaac Royall of Medford, Massachusetts, with his wife, Elizabeth, and his daughter, sister, and sister-in-law. Isaac's estate was built on his deceased father's trade in rum, sugar, and slaves from Antigua. Elizabeth cared for the family and its staff, including several slaves. In Source 4.3, twenty-year-old Eliza Lucas, born on Antigua, describes her typical routine. Although young and single, she managed her father's South Carolina plantations, adding substantially to the family's wealth.

Source 4.2

Isaac Royall and His Family, 1741

Historical & Special Collections, Harvard Law School Library

Source 4.3

Eliza Lucas | Letter to Miss Bartlett, London, c. 1742

Why, my dear Miss B, will you so often repeat your desire to know how I triffle away my time. . . . [H]ere it is.

In general then I rise at five o'Clock in the morning, read till Seven, then take a walk in the garden or field, see that the Servants [slaves] are at their respective business, then to breakfast. The first hour after breakfast is spent at my musick, the next is constantly employed in recolecting something I have learned least . . . , such as French and short hand. . . . I devote the rest of the time till I dress for dinner to our little Polly and two black girls who I teach to read, and if I have my papa's approbation (my Mamas I have got) I intend [them] for school mistres's for the rest of the Negroe children. . . . [After dinner, musick and then] the rest of the afternoon in Needle work till candle light, and from that time to bed read or write. . . . I have

particular matter for particular days. . . . Mondays my musick Master is here. Tuesday my friend Mrs. Chardon (about 3 miles distant) and I are constantly engaged to each other, she at our house one Tuesday—I at hers the next, and this is one of the happiest days I spend at Woppoe. Thursday the whole day . . . is spent in writing, either on the business of the plantation, or letters to my friends. Every other Fryday . . . we go a vizeting so that I go abroad once a week and no oftener. . . .

O! I had like to forgot the last thing I have done a great while. I have planted a large figg orchard with design to dry and export them. . . . [W]as I to tell you how great an Estate I am to make this way . . . you would think me far gone in romance.

Source: Eliza Lucas Pinckney Letterbook, 1739–1762, South Carolina Historical Society.

Interpret the Evidence

1. What do the positions of the Royall family members, their clothing, and the furnishings indicate about the family's and the women's status?
2. How does Eliza Lucas's description of her activities compare with those you imagine the Royall women perform? In what ways do these sources reflect or challenge patriarchal ideals?

Put It in Context

How did the profits of slavery and the slave trade shape the lives of elite women in northern and southern colonies?

surrounding yard with its kitchen garden, milk house, chicken coop, dairy, or washhouse. Husbands and sons worked the fields, kept the livestock, and managed the orchards. Many families supplemented their own labor with that of servants, slaves, or hired field hands. And surplus crops and manufactured goods such as cloth or sausage were exchanged with neighbors or sold at market, creating an economic network of small producers.

Indeed, in the late seventeenth and early eighteenth centuries, many farm families in long-settled areas participated in a household mode of production. Men lent each other tools and draft animals and shared grazing land, while women gathered to spin, sew, and quilt. Individuals with special skills like midwifery or blacksmithing assisted neighbors, adding farm produce or credit to the family ledger. One woman's cheese might be bartered for another woman's jam. A family that owned the necessary equipment might brew barley and malt into beer, while a neighbor with a loom would turn yarn into cloth. The system of exchange, managed largely through barter, allowed individual households to function even as they became more specialized in what they produced. Whatever cash was obtained could be used to buy sugar, tea, and other imported goods.

Harvest Scene   Mary Woodhull was born on Long Island in 1743 and created this colorful needlepoint sampler sometime before her marriage to Amos Underhill. Such decorative samplers were often hung in the family parlor to illustrate the young woman's ideals and skills to prospective husbands. Interestingly here, both the woman and the man are holding scythes used to cut the grain. Granger Collection, NYC

Reproduction and Women's Roles.
Maintaining a farm required the work of both women and men, which made marriage an economic as well as a social and religious institution. In the early eighteenth century, more than 90 percent of white women married. By 1700 a New England wife who married at age twenty and survived to forty-five bore an average of eight children, most of whom lived to adulthood. In the Chesapeake, mortality rates remained higher and the sex ratio still favored men. It took another generation for southern white women to come close to the reproductive rates of their northern counterparts.

Fertility rates among enslaved Africans and African Americans were much lower than those among whites in the early eighteenth century, and fewer infants survived to adulthood. It was not until the 1740s that the majority of slaves were born in the colonies rather than imported as some southern slave owners began to realize that encouraging reproduction made good economic sense. Still, enslaved women, most of whom worked in the fields, gained only minimal relief from their labors during pregnancy.

Colonial mothers who were free combined childbearing and child rearing with a great deal of other work. While some affluent families could afford wet nurses and nannies, most women fended for themselves or hired temporary help for particular tasks. In rural areas, mothers with babies on hip and children under foot hauled water, fed chickens, collected eggs, picked vegetables, prepared meals, spun thread, and manufactured soap and candles. Children were at constant risk of disease and injury, but were spared the overcrowding, the raw sewage, and the foul water that marked most cities in this period.

Infants were the most vulnerable to disease, and parents were relieved when their children passed their first birthdays. Colonists feared the deaths of mothers as well. In 1700 roughly one out of thirty births ended in the mother's death. Women who bore six to eight children thus faced death on a regular basis. One minister urged pregnant women to prepare their souls, "For ought you know your Death has entered into you."

When a mother died while her children were still young, her husband was likely to remarry soon afterward in order to maintain the family and his farm or business. Even though fathers held legal guardianship over their children, there was little doubt that child rearing, especially for young children, was women's work. Many husbands acknowledged this role, prayed for their wife while in labor, and sought to ease her domestic burdens near the end of a pregnancy. But some women drew little help or protection from their husbands.

The Limits of Patriarchal Order.
While most white families accepted the idea of female subordination in return for patriarchal protection, there were signs of change in the early eighteenth century. Sermons against fornication; ads for runaway spouses, servants, and slaves; reports of domestic violence; poems about domineering wives; petitions for divorce; and legal suits charging rape, seduction, or breach of contract make clear that ideals of patriarchal authority did not always match the reality. It is impossible to quantify the frequency with which women contested their subordination, but a variety of evidence points to increasing tensions around issues of control — by husbands over wives, fathers over children, and men over women.

Women's claims about men's misbehavior were often demeaned as gossip, but gossip could be an important weapon for those who had little chance of legal redress. In colonial communities, credit and trust were central to networks of exchange, so damaging a man's reputation could be a serious matter. Still, gossip was not as powerful as legal sanctions.

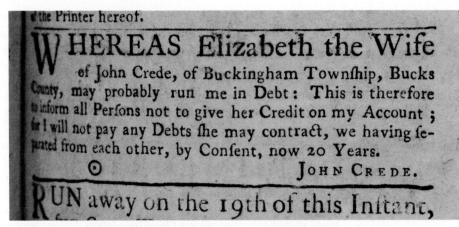

the Printer hereof.

WHEREAS Elizabeth the Wife of John Crede, of Buckingham Townſhip, Bucks County, may probably run me in Debt: This is therefore to inform all Perſons not to give her Credit on my Account ; for I will not pay any Debts ſhe may contra&, we having ſeparated from each other, by Conſent, now 20 Years.

☉   JOHN CREDE.

RUN away on the 19th of this Inſtant,

Advertising a Married Couple's Separation   Although it was difficult to obtain a legal divorce, husbands and wives sometimes abandoned each other or agreed to separate. In this June 1743 notice in the *Pennsylvania Gazette*, John Crede notified merchants and other creditors that he would not pay debts contracted by his wife, Elizabeth, from whom he claimed to have been separated for twenty years. Library of Congress

Thus some women who bore illegitimate children, suffered physical and sexual abuse, or were left penniless by a husband who drank might seek assistance from the courts.

Divorce was as rare in the colonies as it was in England. In New England, colonial law allowed for divorce, but few were granted and almost none to women before 1750. In other colonies, divorce could be obtained only by an act of the colonial assembly and was therefore confined to the wealthy and powerful. If a divorce was granted, the wife usually received an allowance for food and clothing. Yet without independent financial resources, she nearly always had to live with relatives. Custody of any children was awarded to fathers who had the economic means to support them, although infants or young girls might be assigned to live with the mother. A quicker and cheaper means of ending an unsatisfactory marriage was to abandon one's spouse. Again wives were at a disadvantage since they had few means to support themselves or their children. Colonial divorce petitions citing desertion and newspaper ads for runaway spouses suggest that husbands fled in at least two-thirds of such cases.

In the rare instances when women did obtain a divorce, they had to bring multiple charges against their husbands. Domestic violence, adultery, or abandonment alone was insufficient to gain redress. Indeed, ministers and relatives were likely to counsel abused wives to change their behavior or suffer in silence. Even evidence of brutal assaults on a wife rarely led to legal redress because husbands had the legal right to "correct" their wives and children and because physical punishment was widely accepted.

Single women also faced barriers in seeking legal redress. By the late seventeenth century, church and civil courts in New England gave up on coercing sexually active couples to marry. Judges, however, continued to hear complaints of seduction or breach of contract brought by the fathers of single women who were pregnant but unmarried. Had Sarah Grosvenor survived the abortion, her family could have sued Amasa Sessions on the grounds that he gained "carnal knowledge" of her through "promises of marriage." If the

TABLE 4.2   Sexual Coercion Cases Downgraded in Chester County, Pennsylvania, 1731–1739

Date	Defendant/Victim	Charge on Indictment in Testimony	Charge in Docket
1731	Lawrence MacGinnis/Alice Yarnal	Assault with attempt to rape	None
1731	Thomas Culling/Martha Claypool	Assault with attempt to rape	Assault
1734	Abraham Richardson/Mary Smith	Attempted rape	Assault
1734	Thomas Beckett/Mindwell Fulfourd	Theft (testimony of attempted rape)	Theft
1734	Unknown/Christeen Pauper	(Fornication charge against Christeen)	None
1735	Daniel Patterson/Hannah Tanner	Violent assault to ravish	Assault
1736	James White/Hannah McCradle	Attempted rape/adultery	Assault
1737	Robert Mills/Catherine Parry	Rape	None
1738	John West/Isabella Gibson	Attempt to ravish/assault	Fornication
1739	Thomas Halladay/Mary Mouks	Assault with intent to ravish	None

Source: Sharon Block, *Rape and Sexual Power in Early America* (Chapel Hill: University of North Carolina Press). Data from Chester County Quarter Sessions Docket Books and File Papers, 1730–1739.

plaintiffs won, the result was no longer marriage, however, but financial support for the child. In 1730 in Concord, Massachusetts, Susanna Holding sued a farmer, Joseph Bright, whom she accused of fathering her illegitimate child. When Bright protested his innocence, Holding found townsmen to testify that the farmer, "in his courting of her . . . had designed to make her his Wife." In this case, the abandoned mother mobilized members of the community, including men, to uphold popular understandings of patriarchal responsibilities. Without such support, women were less likely to win their cases.

Women who were raped faced even greater legal obstacles than those who were seduced and abandoned. In most colonies, rape was a capital crime, punishable by death, and all-male juries were reluctant to find men guilty. Unlikely to win and fearing humiliation in court, few women charged men with rape. Yet more did so than the records might show since judges and justices of the peace sometimes downgraded rape charges to simple assault or fornication, that is, sex outside of marriage (Table 4.2).

Young white women had the best chance of gaining support and redress for seduction or rape if they confided in their parents or other elders. But by the mid-eighteenth century, young people were seeking more control over their sexual behavior and marriage prospects, and certain behaviors — for example, sons settling in towns distant from the parental home, younger daughters marrying before their older sisters, and single women finding themselves pregnant — increased noticeably. In part, these trends were natural consequences of colonial growth and mobility. The bonds that once held families and communities together began to loosen. But in the process, young women's chances of protecting themselves against errant and abusive men diminished. Just as important, even when they faced desperate situations, young women like Sarah Grosvenor increasingly turned to sisters and friends rather than fathers or ministers.

Poor women, especially those who labored as servants, had even fewer options. Servants faced tremendous obstacles in obtaining legal independence from masters or mistresses who beat or sexually assaulted them. Colonial judges and juries generally refused to declare a man who was wealthy enough to support servants guilty of criminal acts against them. Moreover, poor women generally and servants in particular were regularly depicted as lusty and immoral, making it unlikely that they would gain the sympathy of white judges or juries. Slaves faced many of the same obstacles and had even less hope of prevailing against brutal owners. Thus for most servants and slaves, running away was their sole hope for escaping abuse; however, if they were caught, their situation would likely worsen. Even poor whites who lived independently had little chance of addressing issues of domestic violence, seduction, or rape through the courts.

REVIEW & RELATE

- Why and how did the legal and economic status of colonial women decline between 1650 and 1750?

- How did patriarchal ideals of family and community shape life and work in colonial America? What happened when men failed to live up to those ideals?

Diversity and Competition in Colonial Society

As the English colonies in North America expanded, divisions increased between established families living in long-settled regions — whether on rural farmsteads or in urban homesteads — and the growing population of women and men with few resources. Although most colonists still hoped to own their own land and establish themselves as farmers, artisans, or shopkeepers, fewer were likely to succeed than in the past. By 1760 half of all white men in North America were propertyless. This growing class cleavage was accompanied by increasing racial, national, and religious diversity, which also fostered economic competition and conflict.

Population Growth and Economic Competition. After 1700, the population grew rapidly across the colonies. In 1700 about 250,000 people lived in England's North American colonies. By 1725 that number had doubled, and fifty years later it had reached 2.5 million. Much of the increase was due to natural reproduction, but in addition nearly 250,000 immigrants and Africans arrived in the colonies between 1700 and 1750.

Because more women and children arrived than in earlier decades, higher birthrates and a more youthful population resulted. At the same time, most North American colonists enjoyed a better diet than their counterparts in Europe and had access to more abundant natural resources. Thus colonists in the eighteenth century began living longer, with more adults surviving to watch their children and grandchildren grow up.

However, as the population soared, the chance for individuals to obtain land or start a business of their own diminished. Those who had established businesses early generally expanded to meet new needs, making it more difficult for others to compete. Those bent on making their living from the land often found the soil exhausted in long-settled regions. On the frontier, settlers might have to carve out farms amid forests, swamps, or areas already claimed by Indian, French, or Spanish residents. While owning land did not

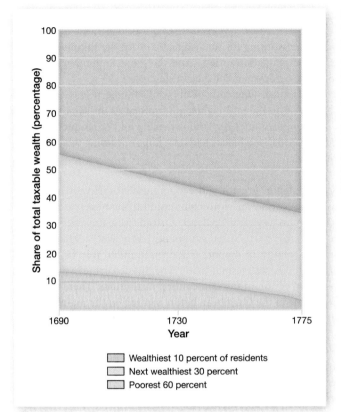

FIGURE 4.1   Wealth Inequality in Northern Cities, 1690–1775

During the eighteenth century, the wealth of merchants rose much faster than that of artisans and laborers. This table tracks the percent of wealth held by three groups of taxable residents in major northern cities from the late seventeenth century to the eve of the American Revolution. Over this period, how did the wealth of the top 10 percent of this population change in relation to the next wealthiest 30 percent and the poorest 60 percent?

Data from Gary B. Nash, *The Urban Crucible: Social Change, Political Consciousness, and the Origins of the American Revolution* (Cambridge, MA: Harvard University Press, 1979).

Wealthiest 10 percent of residents
Next wealthiest 30 percent
Poorest 60 percent

automatically lead to prosperity, those who were landless had to find work as tenant farmers, laborers, or in other unskilled occupations. In the South Carolina backcountry, a visitor in the mid-eighteenth century noted that many residents "have nought but a Gourd to drink out of, nor a Plate, Knive or Spoon, a Glass, Cup, or anything."

In prosperous parts of the Middle Atlantic colonies like Pennsylvania, many landless laborers abandoned rural life and searched for urban opportunities. They moved to Philadelphia or other towns and cities in the region, seeking jobs as dockworkers, street vendors, or servants, or as apprentices in one of the skilled trades. But newcomers found the job market flooded and the chances for advancement growing slim (Figure 4.1).

In the South, too, divisions between rich and poor became more pronounced in the early decades of the eighteenth century. Tobacco was the most valuable product in the Chesapeake, and the largest tobacco planters lived in relative luxury. They developed mercantile contacts in seaport cities on the Atlantic coast and in the Caribbean and imported luxury goods from Europe. They also began training some of their slaves as domestic workers to relieve wives and daughters of the strain of household labor.

Small farmers could also purchase and maintain a farm based on the profits from tobacco. In 1750 two-thirds of white families farmed their own land in Virginia, a larger percentage than in northern colonies. An even higher percentage did so in the Carolinas.

Yet small farmers became increasingly dependent on large landowners, who controlled markets, political authority, and the courts. Many artisans, too, depended on wealthy planters for their livelihood, either working for them directly or for the shipping companies and merchants that relied on plantation orders. And the growing number of tenant farmers relied completely on large landowners for their sustenance.

Some southerners fared far worse. One-fifth of all white southerners owned little more than the clothes on their backs in the mid-eighteenth century. At the same time, free blacks in the South found their opportunities for landownership and economic independence increasingly curtailed, while enslaved blacks had little hope of gaining their freedom and held no property of their own.

Increasing Diversity. Population growth and economic divisions were accompanied by increased diversity in the North American colonies. Indentured servants arrived from Ireland, Scotland, and Germany as well as England. Africans were imported in growing numbers and entered a more highly structured system of slavery, whether laboring on southern farms, on northern estates, or in seaport cities. In addition, free families and redemptioners from Ireland, Scotland, the German states, and Sweden came in ever-larger numbers and developed their own communities and cultural institutions. There were also more colonists who had spent time in the Caribbean before settling on the mainland, and the frontiers of British North America were filled with American Indians and French and Spanish settlers as well.

As the booming population demanded more land, colonists pushed westward to find territory that either was not claimed by others or could be purchased. At the beginning of the eighteenth century, German and Scots-Irish immigrants joined Anglo-American settlers in rural areas of New Jersey, Pennsylvania, and Delaware. Many immigrants to Pennsylvania settled in areas like Shamokin that were dotted with Iroquois, Algonquian, and Siouan towns and negotiated with Indians to obtain farmland. At the same time, Delaware and Shawnee groups, who were pushed out of New Jersey and the Ohio Valley by pressure from settlers, also moved into Pennsylvania. They negotiated with colonists, the colonial government, and other Indian groups to establish communities for themselves. All along the Pennsylvania frontier, the lines between Indian and immigrant settlements blurred. Still, many communities prospered in the region, with white settlers exchanging European and colonial trade goods for access to Indian-controlled orchards, waterways, and lands (Map 4.1).

In the 1720s and 1730s, however, Scots-Irish settlers flooded into Pennsylvania when bad harvests and high rents caused them to flee oppressive conditions back home. The new immigrants overwhelmed native communities that had welcomed earlier settlers. The death of William Penn in 1718 exacerbated the situation as his sons and closest advisers struggled to gain control over the colony. Indians were increasingly pushed to the margins as growing numbers of European settlers moved into frontier territories.

Expansion and Conflict. As more and more colonists sought economic opportunities on the frontier, conflicts erupted regularly between earlier British and newer immigrant settlers as well as among immigrant groups. In Pennsylvania, Dutch, Scots-Irish, and German colonists took each other to court, sued land surveyors, and even burned down cabins built by their immigrant foes. For longtime British settlers, such acts only

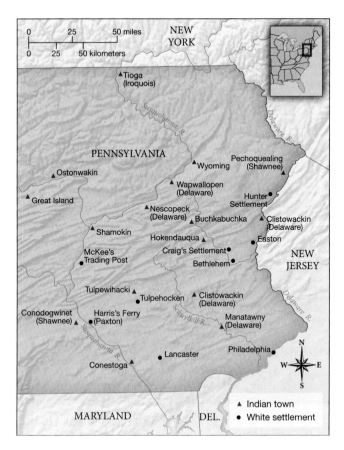

MAP 4.1   Frontier Settlements and Indian Towns in Pennsylvania, 1700–1740

German and Scots-Irish immigrants to Pennsylvania mingled with Indian settlements in the early eighteenth century as Delaware and Shawnee groups were pushed west from New Jersey. In the 1720s and 1730s, however, European migration escalated dramatically in the fertile river valleys. In response, once-independent Indian tribes joined the Delaware and Shawnee nations to strengthen their position against the influx of colonists.

From *At the Crossroads: Indians & Empires on a Mid-Atlantic Frontier, 1700–1763* by Jane T. Merritt, Published for the Omohundro Institute of Early American History and Culture. Copyright © 2003 by the University of North Carolina Press. Used by permission of the publisher. www.uncpress.unc.edu.

reinforced their sense that recent immigrants were a threat to their society. In 1728 James Logan, William Penn's longtime secretary, complained that the "Palatines [Germans] crowd in upon us and the Irish yet faster." For Logan, these difficulties were exacerbated by what he considered the "idle," "worthless," and "indigent" habits of Scots-Irish and other recent arrivals.

Anglo-Americans hardly set high standards themselves, especially when negotiating with Indians. Even in Pennsylvania, where William Penn had established a reputation for (relatively) fair dealing, the desire for Indian land led to dishonesty and trickery. Conflicts among Indian nations aided colonial leaders in prying territory from the Indians. Hoping to assert their authority over the independent-minded Delaware Indians, Iroquois chiefs insisted that they held rights to much of the Pennsylvania territory and therefore must be the ones to negotiate with colonial officials. Those colonial authorities, however, produced a questionable treaty supposedly drafted by Penn in 1686 that allowed them to claim large portions of the contested territory. James Logan "discovered" a copy of this treaty, which allowed the English to control an area that could be walked off in a day and a half. Seeking to maintain control of at least some territory, the Iroquois finally agreed to this **Walking Purchase**. The Delaware tribe, far smaller, was then pressured into letting Pennsylvania

Bethlehem, Pennsylvania, 1757   This painting by Nicholas Garrison shows Bethlehem sixteen years after its settlement by German Moravians. The Moravians fled religious persecution in Germany in the early 1700s and established communal societies in Pennsylvania and New Jersey. Moravians pooled their labor and resources so they could sustain farms and shops, establish separate schools for their children, and missionize among local Indians. Art Resource, NY

officials walk off the boundaries. By the time the Delaware acquiesced in the fall of 1737, Pennsylvania surveyors had already marked off the "shortest and best course," which allowed them to extend the boundaries by at least thirty miles beyond those set in the original, and questionable, treaty.

The rapid expansion of the colonial population ensured that conflicts between Indian and colonial leaders over land rights would continue to erupt. Meanwhile migrants and immigrants on the Anglo-American frontier claimed land simply by taking control of it, building houses, and planting crops. This led to conflicts with Indian communities that considered the territory their own, with English officials who demanded legal contracts and deeds, and among immigrants who settled in the same area.

These conflicts contrasted with developments around the Great Lakes where French traders and Algonquian inhabitants forged military and economic alliances. In this region, called *Pays d'en Haut* (upper country) by the French, colonists and Indians sought diplomatic solutions to problems to

Explore ▶

Compare two perspectives on French Indian relations in New France in Sources 4.4 and 4.5.

protect mutually beneficial trade relations and fend off challenges from other European and indigenous groups.

Some religiously minded immigrants also worked to improve relations with Indians in Pennsylvania, at least temporarily. The tone had been set by William Penn's Quakers, who generally accepted Indian land claims and tried to pursue honest and fair negotiations. German Moravians who settled in eastern Pennsylvania in the 1740s also developed good relations with area tribes. On Pennsylvania's western frontier, Scots-Irish Presbyterians established alliances with Delaware and Shawnee groups. These alliances, however, were rooted less in religious principles than in the hope of profiting from the fur trade as Indians sought new commercial partners when their French allies became too demanding.

Still, as tensions escalated between English and French officials in the region, conflicts intensified among the various immigrant and religious communities and with Indians. The distinct religious traditions and the dramatically different visions of Indian-settler relations drawn from these traditions also sharpened boundaries within and between colonial communities. German Moravians and Scots-Irish Presbyterians in Pennsylvania established churches and schools separate from their Quaker neighbors, while Puritan New Englanders remained suspicious of Quakers as well as other Protestant sects. Moravians and other German sects also flourished in Georgia and the Carolinas, and nearly all sought to isolate themselves from the influences of other religious and ethnic groups.

Some religious groups were isolated as much by force as by choice. While most early Irish immigrants were Protestant, by the early eighteenth century more Irish Catholics began to arrive. Then in 1745 some forty thousand Scots who had supported the Catholic monarchs in England prior to the Glorious Revolution were shipped to the Carolinas after a failed rebellion. Even long-settled Catholics, like those in Maryland, were looked on with suspicion by many Protestants. Although only a few hundred Jewish families resided in the colonies by 1750, they formed small but enduring communities in a number of seaport cities, where they established synagogues and developed a variety of mercantile ventures.

Africans, too, brought new ideas and practices to North America. Transported by force to an unknown land, they may have found religious faith particularly important. Enslaved blacks included some Catholics from regions long held by the Portuguese and a few thousand Muslims, but many Africans embraced religions that were largely unknown to their Anglo-American masters.

As religious affiliations in the colonies multiplied, they reinforced existing concerns about spiritual decline. Moreover, spiritual differences often exacerbated cleavages rooted in nationality, class and race. And they heightened concerns among many well-established families over the future of British culture and institutions in North America.

REVIEW & RELATE

How and why did economic inequality in the colonies increase in the first half of the eighteenth century?

How did population growth and increasing diversity contribute to conflict among and anxieties about the various groups inhabiting British North America?

SECONDARY SOURCE ANALYSIS

Finding a Middle Ground in New France

Scholars have generally emphasized conflict, including open warfare, between American Indians and European colonists. More recently, historians of the early colonial period have explored the effects of the Columbian Exchange, especially of germs and epidemics, on Indian-European relations. A third framework for analyzing these relations developed in the early 1990s when historians explored areas of North America where native peoples, traders, and settlers sought accommodations that would allow the development of economic and military alliances. Such accommodations in the *Pays d'en Haut*, the Upper Country of New France, allowed some Indian nations to thrive while others fell victim to these new alliances.

Source 4.4

Richard White, Cultural Accommodation on the Middle Ground, 1991

The process of accommodation described [here] certainly involves cultural change, but it takes place on what I call the middle ground. The middle ground is the place in between: in between cultures, peoples, and in between empires and the nonstate world of villages. It is a place where many of the North American subjects and allies of empire lived. It is the area between the historical foreground of European invasion and occupation and the background of Indian defeat and retreat. On the middle ground diverse peoples adjust their differences through what amounts to a process of creative, and often expedient, misunderstandings. People try to persuade others who are different from themselves by appealing to what they perceive to be the values and practices of those others. They often misinterpret and distort both the values and the practices of those they deal

with, but from these misunderstandings arise new meanings and through them new practices—the shared meanings and practices of the middle ground. This accommodation took place for long periods of time in large parts of the colonial world where whites could neither dictate to Indians nor ignore them. Whites needed Indians as allies, as partners in exchange, as sexual partners, as friendly neighbors. . . .

The world of the *pays d'en haut* . . . is a joint Indian-white creation. Within it well-known European and Anglo-American names appear: . . . Sir Jeffrey Amherst, William Johnson, Daniel Boone, George Washington, . . . and Thomas Jefferson, So, too, do well-known Indian names such as Pontiac and Tecumseh.

Source: Richard White, *The Middle Ground* (Cambridge, UK: Cambridge University Press, 1991), ix and xiii.

Religious Awakenings

Whether rooted in fears that worldly concerns were overshadowing spiritual devotion or that growing religious diversity was undermining the power of the church, many Protestant ministers lamented the state of faith in eighteenth-century America. Church leaders in Britain and the rest of Europe shared their fears. Ministers eager to address this crisis of faith — identified in the colonies as **New Light clergy** — worked together to reenergize the faithful and were initially welcomed, or at least tolerated, by more traditional **Old Light clergy**. But by the 1740s, fears that the passionate New Light clergy had gone too far led to a backlash.

Source 4.5

Brett Rushforth, Indian Slavery and Cultural Accommodation, 2014

This study explores the relationship between indigenous and Atlantic slaveries in New France, a colony centered on the Saint Lawrence River and stretching westward to a region the French called the *Pays d'en Haut*, or Upper Country. . . . Between about 1660 and 1760, French colonists and their Native allies enslaved thousands of Indians, keeping them in the towns and villages of New France, or shipping them to the French Caribbean. . . . Unlike many American colonies, where Indian slaves were replaced by Africans in the early stages of settlement, Native slavery predominated in New France throughout the colony's final century. . . .

The slave trade grew from, and indeed offers a strong example of, these intercultural negotiations in the *Pays d'en Haut*. As the region's Natives encountered French traders and eventually settlers in the second half of the seventeenth century, they greeted them with rituals and gifts to signal their friendship and to invite the newcomers into an alliance. Among the most significant of these gifts were enslaved enemies, offered as a sign of trust and evidence of Native power. From these beginnings, Natives and the French developed a sustained slave trade built upon decades of small-scale exchanges of bodies, goods, and ideas. Slavery reveals a somber dimension to cultural accommodation in the *Pays d'en Haut*, showing that its success was often founded on a shared commitment to violence. Yet even this violence was a product of mutual adaptation and produced new cultural forms that persisted for generations.

Source: Brett Rushforth, *Bonds of Alliance: Indigenous and Atlantic Slaveries in New France* (Chapel Hill: University of North Carolina Press, 2014), 10–11.

Examine the Sources

1. To what degree does Rushforth's interpretation of Indian cultural accommodation support White's thesis about the middle ground?
2. Explain how one specific event or development from this chapter not explicitly mentioned in the excerpts above could be used to support White's or Rushforth's interpretation.

Put It in Context

Compare relations between Indians and colonists in British North America with those in New France as analyzed by White and Rushforth.

The Roots of the Great Awakening. By the eighteenth century, the **Enlightenment**, a European cultural movement that emphasized rational and scientific thinking over traditional religion and superstition, had taken root in the colonies, particularly among elites. The development of a lively print culture spread the ideas of Enlightenment thinkers like the English philosopher John Locke, the German intellectual Immanuel Kant, and the French writer Voltaire across the Atlantic. These thinkers argued that through reason humans could discover the laws that governed the universe and thereby improve society. Benjamin Franklin, a leading printer in Philadelphia, was one of the foremost advocates of Enlightenment ideas in the colonies. His experiments with electricity reflected his faith in rational thought, and his publication of the *Pennsylvania Gazette* and *Poor Richard's Almanac* spread such ideas throughout the colonies in the 1720s and 1730s.

As more colonists were influenced by Enlightenment thought, they became more accepting of religious diversity, which had spread as settlers from diverse countries and denominations arrived in the English colonies. At the same time, Enlightenment ideas could undermine the religious vitality of the colonies. Many Enlightenment thinkers believed in a Christian God but rejected the revelations and rituals that defined traditional church practices and challenged ministerial claims that God was directly engaged in the daily workings of the world.

There were, however, countervailing forces. The German **Pietists** in particular challenged Enlightenment ideas that had influenced many Congregational and Anglican leaders in Europe. Pietists decried the power of established churches and urged individuals to follow their hearts rather than their heads in spiritual matters. Persecuted in Germany, Pietists migrated to Great Britain and North America, where their ideas influenced Scots-Irish Presbyterians and members of the Church of England. John Wesley, the founder of Methodism and a professor of theology at Oxford University, taught Pietist ideas to his students, including George Whitefield. Like the German Pietists, Whitefield considered the North American colonies a perfect venue for restoring intensity and emotion to religious worship.

Some colonists had begun rethinking their religious commitments before Whitefield or the Pietists arrived. By 1700 both laymen and ministers voiced growing concern with the state of colonial religion. Preachers educated in England or at colonial colleges like Harvard and William and Mary often emphasized learned discourse over passion. At the same time, there were too few clergy to meet the demands of the rapidly growing population in North America. In many rural areas, residents grew discouraged at the lack of ministerial attention. Meanwhile urban churches increasingly reflected the class divisions of the larger society, with wealthier members paying substantial rents to seat their families in the front pews. Farmers and shopkeepers rented the cheaper pews in the middle of the church, while the poorest congregants sat on free benches at the very back or in the gallery. Educated clergy might impress the richest parishioners with their learned sermons, but they did little to move the spirits of the congregation at large.

In 1719 the Reverend Theodorus Frelinghuysen, a Dutch Reformed minister in New Jersey, began emphasizing parishioners' emotional investment in Christ. The Reverend William Tennent, the father of Gilbert Tennent, arrived in neighboring Pennsylvania with his family about the same time. He despaired that Presbyterian ministers were too few in number to reach the growing population and, like Frelinghuysen, feared that their approach was too didactic. Tennent soon established his own one-room academy to train his sons and other young men for the ministry. Though disparaged by Presbyterian authorities, the school attracted devout students.

Jonathan Edwards, a Congregational minister in Northampton, Massachusetts, joined Enlightenment ideas with religious fervor. A brilliant scholar who studied natural philosophy and science as well as theology, Edwards viewed the natural world as powerful evidence of God's design. He came to view the idea that God elected some individuals for salvation and others for damnation as a source of mystical joy. Although Edwards wrote erudite books and essays, he proclaimed that "our people do not so much need to have their heads stored [with knowledge] as to have their hearts touched." From 1733 to 1735, his sermons on God's absolute sovereignty over man initiated a revival in Northampton that reached hundreds of parishioners.

A few years earlier, Gilbert Tennent had begun urging his flock in New Brunswick, New Jersey to embrace "a true living faith in Jesus Christ." He took his lead from Frelinghuysen, who viewed conversion as a three-step process: Individuals must be convinced of their sinful nature, experience a spiritual rebirth, and then behave piously as evidence of their conversion. Tennent embraced these measures, believing they could lance the "boil" of an unsaved heart and apply the "balsam" of grace and righteousness. Then in 1739 Tennent met Whitefield, who launched a wave of revivals that revitalized and transformed religion across the colonies.

An Outburst of Revivals.

Whitefield was perfectly situated to extend the series of revivals that scholars later called the **Great Awakening**. Gifted with a powerful voice, he understood that the expanding networks of communication and travel — developed to promote commerce — could also be used to promote religion. Advertising in newspapers and broadsides and traveling by ship, coach, and horseback, Whitefield made seven trips to the North American colonies beginning in 1738. He reached audiences from Georgia to New England to the Pennsylvania backcountry and inspired ministers in the colonies to expand upon his efforts.

In 1739 Whitefield launched a fifteen-month preaching tour that reached tens of thousands of colonists. Like Edwards, Frelinghuysen, and Tennent, he asked individuals to invest less in material goods and more in spiritual devotion. If they admitted their depraved and sinful state and truly repented, God would hear their prayers. Whitefield danced across the platform, shouted and raged, and gestured dramatically, drawing huge crowds everywhere he went. He attracted 20,000 people to individual events, at a time when the entire city of Boston counted just 17,000 residents.

New Light ministers carried on Whitefield's work throughout the 1740s, honing their methods and appeal. Less concerned with denominational affiliation than with core beliefs, they denounced urbane and educated clergy, used extemporaneous oratorical styles and outdoor venues to attract crowds, and invited colonists from all walks of life to build a common Christian community. Some became itinerant preachers, preferring to carry their message throughout the colonies than be constrained by a single church. [Map 4.2]

New Light clergy brought young people to religion by the thousands. In addition, thousands of colonists who were already church members were "born again," recommitting themselves to their faith. Poor women and men who felt little connection to preaching when they sat on the back benches eagerly joined the crowds at outdoor revivals, where they could stand as close to the pulpit as a rich merchant.

Religious Dissension.

Initially, the Great Awakening drew support from large numbers of ministers because it increased religious enthusiasm and church attendance throughout the colonies. After decades of decline, religion once again took center stage. But the early embrace by Old Light clergy diminished as revivals spread farther afield, as

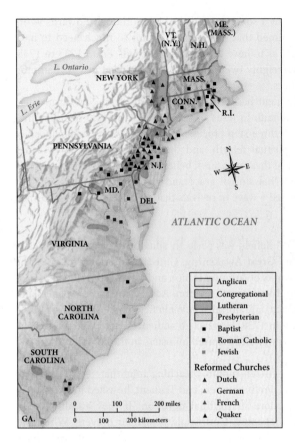

MAP 4.2   Religious Diversity in 1750

Despite the universal appeal of Whitefield and other New Light ministers, religious diversity had increased by 1750. Baptist churches multiplied in New England, where Congregationalists long held sway, while Presbyterian and Lutheran churches spread across the South where Anglicanism was the established church. Non-evangelical houses of worship, such as Quaker meeting houses and Jewish synagogues, also gradually increased in number.

critiques of educated clergy became more pointed, and as worshippers left established congregations for new churches. A growing number of ministers and other colonial leaders began to fear that revivalists were providing lower-class whites, free blacks, women, and even slaves with compelling critiques of those in power. As the Great Awakening peaked in 1742, a backlash developed among more settled ministers and their congregations. **See Primary Source Project 4: Awakening Religious Tensions, page 136.**

Itinerant preachers traveling across the South seemed especially threatening as they invited blacks and whites to attend revivals together and proclaimed their equality before God. Although New Light clergy rarely attacked slavery directly, they implicitly challenged racial hierarchies. Revivalists also attracted African Americans and Indians by emphasizing communal singing and emotional expressions of the spirit, which echoed traditional African and Indian practices.

In the North, too, Old Light ministers and local officials began to question New Light techniques and influences. One of the most radical New Light preachers, James Davenport, attracted huge crowds when he preached in Boston in the early 1740s. Drawing thousands of colonists to Boston Common day after day, Davenport declared that the people "should drink rat poison rather than listen to corrupt, unconverted clergy." Boston officials finally called a grand jury into session to silence him "on the charge of having said that Boston's ministers were leading the people blindfold to hell."

Even some New Light ministers, including Tennent, considered Davenport extreme. Yet revivals continued throughout the 1740s. Still, over time they lessened in intensity as churches and parishioners settled back into a more ordered religious life. Moreover, the central tenets of revivalist preaching—criticisms of educated clergy, itinerancy, and extemporaneous preaching—worked against the movement's institutionalization. The Great Awakening echoed across the colonies for at least another generation, but its influence was felt more often in attitudes and practices than in institutions.

For example, when, in 1750, King George II (r. 1727–1760) threatened to appoint an Anglican bishop for the North American colonies, many North American ministers, both Old Light and New, resisted the appointment. Most colonists had become used to religious diversity and toleration, at least for Protestants, and had little desire to add church officials to the existing hierarchies of colonial authorities. In various ways, revivalists also highlighted the democratic tendencies in the Bible, particularly in the New Testament. Even as they proclaimed God's wrath against sinners, they also preached that a lack of wealth and power did not diminish a person in God's eyes. And revivalists honed a style of passionate and popular preaching that would shape American religion as well as politics for centuries to come. This mode of communication had immediate application as colonists mobilized to resist what they saw as tyrannical actions by colonial officials and others in authority.

REVIEW & RELATE

- What was the relationship between the Enlightenment and the religious revivals of the early eighteenth century?

- What was the immediate impact of the Great Awakening, and what were its legacies for American religious and social life?

Political Awakenings

The effects of eighteenth-century religious awakenings rippled out from churches and revivals to influence social and political relations. New Light clergy allowed colonists to view their resistance to traditional authorities as part of their effort to create a better and more just world. Experiences of self-government, Enlightenment ideas, and protests against perceived corruption in the imperial system also led some colonists to question the right of those in power to impose their will on the community as a whole.

Changing Political Relations. The settlements of the seventeenth century could be regulated with a small number of officials, and in most colonies male settlers agreed on who should rule. However, with geographical expansion, population growth, and commercial development, colonial officials — whether appointed by the crown or selected by local residents — found themselves confronted with a more complex, and more contentious, situation. In New England, most colonies developed participatory town meetings that elected members to their colonial legislatures. In the South, wealthy planters exercised greater authority locally and colony-wide, but they still embraced ideals of self-governance and political liberty.

Throughout the British American colonies, officials were usually educated men who held property and had family ties to other colonial elites. Although ultimate political authority — or sovereignty — rested with the king and Parliament, many decisions were made by local officials because the king and Parliament were too distant to have a hand in daily colonial life. Another factor that weakened the power of royal officials was the tradition of town meetings and representative bodies, like the Virginia House of Burgesses, that gave colonists a stake in their own governance. Officials in England and the colonies assumed that most people would defer to those in authority, and they minimized resistance by holding public elections in which freemen cast ballots by voice vote. Not surprisingly, those with wealth and power continued to win office.

Still, evidence from throughout the colonial period indicates that deference to authority was not always sufficient to maintain order. Roger Williams and Anne Hutchinson, Bacon's Rebellion, the Stono rebellion, the Salem witchcraft trials, and the radical

Boston Town Hall Boston's Town Hall and the broad avenue on which it sat was engraved by the German artist Franz Xavier Habermann, who specialized in scenes of urban North America. The buildings reflect a European view of the city's affluence in the mid-eighteenth century, as do the clothes worn by the two gentlemen talking over their walking sticks. Bibliotheque Nationale, Paris, France/Bridgeman Images Private Collection/Bridgeman Images

preaching of James Davenport make clear that not everyone willingly supported their supposed superiors. These episodes of dissent and protest were widely scattered across time and place. But as the ideas disseminated by New Light clergy and Enlightenment thinkers converged with changing political relations, resistance to established authority became more frequent and more collective.

Dissent and Protest. Protests against colonial elites multiplied from the 1730s on. The issues and methods varied, but they indicate a growing sense of political and economic autonomy among North American colonists. Some protests focused on royal officials like governors and Royal Navy captains; others focused on local authorities, merchants, or large landowners. Whatever the target of resistance, protests demonstrated colonists' belief that they had rights that were worth protecting, even against those who held legitimate authority. Just as importantly, dissenters included the poor, women, and African Americans as well as property-owning white men.

Access to reasonably priced food, especially bread, inspired regular protests in the eighteenth century. During the 1730s, the price of bread—a critical staple in colonial diets — rose despite falling wheat prices and a recession in seaport cities. Bread rioters attacked grain warehouses, bakeries, and shops, demanding more bread at lower prices. In New England, such uprisings were often led by women, who were responsible for putting bread on the table. When grievances involved domestic or consumer issues, women felt they had the right to make their voices heard, a right reinforced by evangelical clergy's insistence on their moral obligations to society.

Public markets were another site where struggles over food led to collective protests. In 1737, for instance, Boston officials decided to construct a public market and charge fees to farmers who sold their goods there. Small farmers, who were used to selling produce from the roadside for free, clashed with officials and with larger merchants over the venture. Many Boston residents supported the protesters because the market fees would lessen competition and raise prices for consumers. Adopting a rational approach to voice their concerns, residents petitioned city officials. When that had no effect, however, opponents demolished the market building and stalls in the middle of the night. Local authorities could find no witnesses to the crime.

Access to land was also a critical issue in the colonies. Beginning in the 1740s, protests erupted on estates in New Jersey and along the Hudson River in New York over the leasing policies of landlords as well as the amount of land controlled by speculators. Here, again, when tenants and squatters petitioned colonial officials and received no response, they took collective action. They formed associations, targeted specific landlords, and then burned barns, attacked livestock, and emptied houses and farm buildings of furniture and tools. Embracing Enlightenment ideas of "natural law," they also established regional committees to hear grievances and formed "popular" militia companies and courts to mete out justice to recalcitrant land owners. When landlords and colonial officials called out local militia to arrest the perpetrators, they failed to consider that militia members were often the same poor men whose protests they ignored.

In seaport cities, a frequent source of conflict was the **impressment** of colonial men who were seized and forcibly drafted into service in the Royal Navy. Viewed as a sign of the corrupt practices of imperial authorities, the challenge to impressment energized diverse groups of colonists. Sailors, dockworkers, and men drinking at taverns along the shore feared being pressed into military service, while colonial officials worried about labor shortages. Those officials petitioned the British government to stop impressment, but working men who faced the navy's high mortality rates, bad food, rampant disease, and harsh discipline took action on their own behalf. Asserting their growing sense of political liberty, they fought back against both colonial and British authorities. In 1747 in Boston, a general impressment led to three days of rioting. An observer noted that "Negros, servants, and hundreds of seamen seized a naval lieutenant, assaulted a sheriff, and put his deputy in stocks, surrounded the governor's house, and stormed the Town House (city hall)." Such riots did not end the system of impressment, but they showed that many colonists now refused to be deprived of what they considered their natural rights.

The religious upheavals and economic uncertainties of the 1730s and 1740s led colonists to challenge colonial and British officials with greater frequency than in earlier decades and to justify their actions in evangelical or Enlightenment terms. Still, most protests also accentuated class lines as, small farmers, craftsmen, and the poor fought against merchants, landowners, and local officials. However, the resistance to impressment proved that colonists could mobilize across economic differences when British policies affected diverse groups of colonial subjects.

Transforming Urban Politics. The development of cross-class alliances in the 1730s and 1740s was also visible in the more formal arena of colonial politics. Beginning in the 1730s, some affluent political leaders in cities like New York and Philadelphia began to seek support from a wider constituency. In most cases, it was conflicts among the elite that led to these appeals to the "popular" will. In 1731, for instance, a new royal charter confirmed New York City's existence as a "corporation" and stipulated the rights of freemen (residents who could vote in local elections after paying a small fee) and freeholders (individuals, whether residents or not, who held property worth £40 and could vote on that basis). A large number of artisans, shopkeepers, and laborers acquired the necessary means to vote, and shopkeepers and master craftsmen now sat alongside wealthier men on the Common Council. Yet most laboring men did not participate actively in elections until 1733, when local elites led by Lewis Morris sought to mobilize the mass of voters against royal officials, like Governor William Cosby, appointed in London.

Morris, a wealthy man and a judge, joined other colonial elites in believing that the royal officials recently appointed to govern New York were tied to ministerial corruption in England. Morris, as chief justice of the provincial court, ruled against Governor Cosby in a suit the new governor brought against his predecessor. Cosby then suspended Morris from office. In the aftermath, Morris and his supporters — the Morrisites — took his case to the people, who were suffering from a serious economic depression. Morrisites launched an opposition newspaper, published by apprentice printer John Peter Zenger, to mobilize artisans, shopkeepers, and laborers around an agenda to stimulate the economy and elect men supportive of workers to the city's common council.

In his *New-York Weekly Journal*, Zenger leaped into the political fray, accusing Governor Cosby and his cronies of corruption, incompetence, election fraud, and tyranny. The vitriolic attacks led to Zenger's indictment for seditious libel and his imprisonment in November 1734. At the time, libel related only to whether published material undermined government authority, not whether it was true or false. But Zenger's lead attorney, Andrew Hamilton of Philadelphia, argued that truth must be recognized as a defense against charges of libel. Appealing to a jury of Zenger's peers, Hamilton proclaimed, "It is not the cause of a poor printer, nor of New York alone, which you are now trying. . . . It is the best cause. It is the cause of liberty." In response, jurors ignored the law as written and acquitted Zenger.

Although the decision in the Zenger case did not lead to a change in British libel laws, it did signal the willingness of colonial juries to side with fellow colonists against king and Parliament in at least some situations. Building on their success, Morris and his followers continued to gain popular support. In 1737 his son, Lewis Morris Jr., was appointed speaker of the new Assembly, and the Assembly appointed Zenger as its official printer. But soon the group fell into disarray when royal officials offered political prizes to a few of their leaders. Indeed, the elder Morris accepted appointment as royal governor of New Jersey, after which he switched allegiances and became an advocate of executive authority. Nonetheless, the political movement he led had aroused ordinary freemen to participate in elections, and newspapers and pamphlets now readily attacked corrupt officials and threats to the rightful liberties of British colonists.

Even as freemen gained a greater voice in urban politics, they could challenge the power of economic and political leaders only when the elite were divided. Moreover, the rewards they gained sometimes served to reinforce class divisions. Thus many city workers had benefited when the elder Morris used his influence to ensure the building of the city's first permanent almshouse in 1736. The two-year project employed large numbers of artisans and laborers in a period of economic contraction. Once built, however, the almshouse became a symbol of the growing gap between rich and poor. Its existence was also used by future city councils as a justification to eliminate other forms of relief, leaving the poor in worse shape than before.

The rising inequality of wealth was especially apparent in the largest cities of British North America — New York, Philadelphia, Boston, and Charleston — but economic distinctions were also growing in smaller cities and towns. As the price of some goods, such as sugar and tobacco, fell in the 1750s, more colonists were able to afford them. At the same time, the expansion of transatlantic trade ensured that wealthier colonists had growing access to silver plates, clocks, tea services, bed and table linens, and other luxury goods. With British exporters extending more credit to colonial merchants and affluent white consumers, the division between rich and poor became increasingly visible to colonists of all backgrounds.

REVIEW & RELATE

- How did ordinary colonists, both men and women, black and white, express their political opinions and preferences in the first half of the eighteenth century?

- How did politics bring colonists together across economic lines in the first half of the eighteenth century? How did politics highlight and reinforce class divisions?

Conclusion: A Divided Society

By 1754 religious and political awakenings had transformed colonists' sense of their relation to spiritual and secular authorities. Both Gilbert Tennent and Sarah Grosvenor were caught up in these transitions. As a man and a minister, however, Tennent had far more power to control his destiny than did Grosvenor. While wives and daughters in elite families benefited from their wealth and position, they were also constrained by the strictures of the patriarchal family. Women who were poor, indentured, or enslaved were forced into the greatest dependency on male employers and civic officials. But even women in farm and artisanal families depended on loving husbands and fathers to offset the strictures of patriarchal authority. While few colonists conceived of themselves as part of a united body politic, women probably identified most deeply with their family, town, or church. Yet men, too, thought of themselves as English, or Scots-Irish, or German, rather than more broadly American. At best, they claimed identity as residents of Massachusetts, New Jersey, or South Carolina rather than British North America.

Between the 1680s and the 1750s, the diversity and divisions among colonists increased as class, racial, religious, and regional differences multiplied across the colonies. Immigrants from Germany, Ireland, and Scotland created their own communities; religious awakenings led to cleavages among Protestants and between them and other religious groups; and economic inequality deepened in seacoast cities. At the same time, conflicts between Indians and settlers intensified along the frontier as growing numbers of enslaved Africans reshaped economic and social relations in the urban North and the rural South.

By midcentury, the colonies as a whole had been transformed in significant ways. Religious leaders had gained renewed respect, colonial assemblies had wrested more autonomy from royal hands, freemen participated more avidly in political contests and debates, printers and lawyers insisted on the rights and liberties of colonists, and local communities defended those rights in a variety of ways. When military conflicts brought British officials into more direct contact with their colonial subjects in the following decade, they sought to check these trends, with dramatic consequences.

TIMELINE OF EVENTS

1688	Glorious Revolution
1692	Salem witch trials
1700–1750	250,000 immigrants and Africans arrive in the colonies
1700–1775	Population of British North America grows from 250,000 to 2.5 million
1720–1740	Influx of Scots-Irish to Pennsylvania
1734	John Peter Zenger acquitted of libel
1737	Iroquois and Delaware acquiesce to Walking Purchase
	Protest against public market in Boston
1739	George Whitefield launches preaching tour of the colonies
1745	40,000 Scottish Catholics shipped to the Carolinas after failed rebellion
1747	Rioting in Boston against impressment
1750	Colonists resist appointment of an Anglican bishop for North America

KEY TERMS

spectral evidence, *108*

patriarchal family, *111*

Walking Purchase, *121*

New Light clergy, *124*

Old Light clergy, *124*

Enlightenment, *125*

Pietists, *126*

Great Awakening, *127*

impressment, *131*

REVIEW & RELATE

1. What factors led to a rise in tensions within colonial communities in the early 1700s?

2. How did social, economic, and political tensions contribute to an increase in accusations of witchcraft?

3. Why and how did the legal and economic status of colonial women decline between 1650 and 1750?

4. How did patriarchal ideals of family and community shape life and work in colonial America? What happened when men failed to live up to those ideals?

5. How and why did economic inequality in the colonies increase in the first half of the eighteenth century?

6. How did population growth and increasing diversity contribute to conflict among and anxieties about the various groups inhabiting British North America?

7. What was the relationship between the Enlightenment and the religious revivals of the early eighteenth century?

8. What was the immediate impact of the Great Awakening, and what were its legacies for American religious and social life?

9. How did ordinary colonists, both men and women, black and white, express their political opinions and preferences in the first half of the eighteenth century?

10. How did politics bring colonists together across economic lines in the first half of the eighteenth century? How did politics highlight and reinforce class divisions?

Awakening Religious Tensions

▶ Evaluate the relationship between the Great Awakening and the Enlightenment in the British American colonies.

The Great Awakening and the Enlightenment were two of the most influential developments in the early eighteenth-century colonies. Although often considered as oppositional, some New Light ministers embraced Enlightenment ideas, and some advocates of the Enlightenment respected popular New Light preachers (Source 4.7). Ultimately, conflicts over the Great Awakening came mainly from Old Light preachers who feared the disruption of traditional church structures and discipline and from civic leaders who feared the social disruption fostered by New Light revivals.

Certainly there were significant differences between the rational approach of scientific observers like Benjamin Franklin and the passion of preachers like George Whitefield and Jonathan Edwards (Sources 4.6, 4.7, 4.8, and 4.10). Differences were at least as great between New Light and Old Light ministers. Old Light ministers initially embraced the Awakening as a way to revive religiosity in the colonies. But as revivalist preachers grew more popular and outspoken, Old Lights became increasingly uneasy. By 1742 the controversial actions of itinerant preachers like James Davenport led Old Light ministers as well as newspaper editors and civic leaders to critique the movement as a whole (Source 4.9). One concern of many critics was the challenge the Awakening posed to established relations of class and status. At mass revivals, women and men, old and young, upper and lower classes, and even blacks and whites mingled. And sermons often included pointed critiques of colonial elites (Sources 4.9 and 4.10). Thus New Light preachers revitalized but also challenged established churches and the established order.

Source 4.6

Nathan Cole | On George Whitefield Coming to Connecticut, 1740

As the Great Awakening swept through British North America in the 1730s and 1740s, thousands flocked to revivals led by traveling ministers. George Whitefield, an English evangelical preacher, launched an extensive speaking tour of the colonies from 1739 to 1740. In the following passage, Nathan Cole, a Connecticut farmer, describes his own reaction and that of the crowd assembled at Wethersfield to hear Whitefield preach.

We went down in the Stream; I heard no man speak a word all the way three mile but every one pressing forward in great haste and when we got down to the old meeting house there was a great multitude; it was said to be 3 or 4000 of people assembled together. We got off from our horses and shook off the dust and the ministers were then coming to the meeting house. I turned and looked toward the great river and saw the ferry boats running swift forward and backward bringing over loads of people; the oars rowed nimble and quick. Every thing men horses and boats all seemed to be struggling for life; the land and the banks over the river looked black with people and horses all along the 12 miles. I see no man at work in his field but all seemed to be gone — when I saw Mr. Whitefield come upon the Scaffold [platform] he looked almost angelical, a young slim slender youth before some thousands of people and with a bold undaunted countenance, and my hearing how God was with him every where as he came along it solemnized my mind and put me in a trembling fear before he began to preach; for he looked as if he was clothed with authority from the great God, and a sweet solemn solemnity sat upon his brow. And my hearing him preach gave me a heart wound; by God's blessing my old foundation was broken up and I saw that my righteousness would not save me; then I was convinced of the doctrine of Election and went right to quarreling with God about it because all that I could do would not save me; and he had decreed from Eternity who should be saved and who not.

Source: George Leon Walker, *Some Aspects of the Religious Life of New England* (New York: Silver, Burnett, 1897), 91–92.

Source 4.7

Benjamin Franklin | On George Whitefield, the Great Revivalist, 1739

Benjamin Franklin, the Philadelphia printer, inventor, and politician, was an ardent advocate of the Enlightenment. But he was also interested in popular causes and thus attended one of Whitefield's sermons in Philadelphia in 1739, and several thereafter. While Franklin remained a religious skeptic, he and Whitefield became friends. In his *Autobiography* Franklin printed several of Whitefield's sermons and described the preacher's power.

In 1739 arriv'd among us from England the Rev. Mr. Whitefield, who had made himself remarkable there as an itinerant Preacher. . . . The Multitudes of all Sects and Denominations that attended his Sermons were enormous and it was [a] matter of Speculation to me who was one of the Number, to observe the extraordinary Influence of his Oratory on his Hearers, and how much they admir'd and respected him, notwithstanding his common Abuse of them, by assuring them they were naturally *half Beasts and half Devils*. It was wonderful to see the Change soon made in the Manners of our Inhabitants; from being thoughtless or indifferent about Religion, it seem'd as if all the World were growing Religious. . . .

He us'd indeed sometimes to pray for my Conversion, but never had the Satisfaction of believing that his Prayers were heard. . . .

He had a loud and clear Voice, and articulated his Words and Sentences so perfectly that he might be heard and understood at a great Distance, especially as his Auditors [audience], however numerous, observ'd the most exact Silence. He preach'd one Evening from the Top of the Court House Steps, which are in the middle of Market Street, and on the West Side of Second Street which crosses it at right angles. Both Streets were fill'd with his Hearers to a considerable distance. Being among the hindmost in Market Street, I had the Curiosity to learn how far he could be heard, by retiring backwards down the Street towards the River; and I found his Voice distinct till I came near Front Street. . . . Imagining then a Semicircle, of which my Distance should be the Radius, and that it were fill'd with Auditors, . . . I computed that he might well be heard by more than Thirty Thousand. . . .

His delivery . . . was so improv'd by frequent Repetitions that every Accent, every Emphasis, every Modulation of Voice, was so perfectly well turn'd and well plac'd, that without being interested in the Subject, one could not help being pleas'd with the Discourse, a Pleasure of much the same kind with that receiv'd from an excellent Piece of Music. This is an Advantage itinerant Preachers have over those who are stationary: as the latter cannot well improve their Delivery of a Sermon by so many Rehearsals.

Source: *The Autobiography of Benjamin Franklin, The Unmutilated and Correct Version*, comp. and ed. John Bigelow (New York: G. P. Putnam's Sons, 1912), 220–25.

Jonathan Edwards | Sinners in the Hands of an Angry God, 1741

Before enrolling at Yale College at age twelve, Jonathan Edwards studied natural history and wrote an essay titled "The Flying Spider." However, his adult fame came from his theological works; his ministry at Christ Church in Northampton, Massachusetts; and his sermons, which he delivered in a quiet yet emotive voice. He first delivered "Sinners in the Hands of an Angry God" at a revival in Enfield, Connecticut, in 1741. Religious opposition to the revivals eventually forced Edwards from his Northampton pulpit, but he continued to publish and to preach, including to New England Indians.

There is nothing that keeps wicked Men at any one Moment, out of Hell, but the meer Pleasure of GOD.

By the meer Pleasure of God, I mean his sovereign Pleasure, his arbitrary Will, restrained by no Obligation, hinder'd by no manner of Difficulty, any more than if nothing else but God's meer Will had in the least Degree, or in any Respect whatsoever, any Hand in the Preservation of wicked Men. . . .

He is not only able to cast wicked Men into Hell, but he can most easily do it. . . .

We find it easy to tread on and crush a Worm that we see crawling on the Earth; so 'tis easy for us to cut or singe a slender Thread that any Thing hangs by; thus easy is it for God when he pleases to cast his Enemies down to Hell. . . .

[What] Use may be of [an] *Awakening* to unconverted Persons in this Congregation[?] . . . That World of Misery, that Lake of burning Brimstone is extended abroad under you. . . .

You probably are not sensible of this. . . . [But] if God should let you go, you would immediately sink and swiftly descend & plunge into the bottomless Gulf, and your healthy Constitution, and your own Care and Prudence, and best Contrivance, and all your Righteousness, would have no more Influence to uphold you and keep you out of Hell, than a Spider's Web would have to stop a falling Rock. . . .

The God that holds you over the Pit of Hell, much as one holds a Spider, or some loathsome Insect, over the Fire, abhors you, and is dreadfully provoked. . . .

[But] now you have an extraordinary Opportunity, a Day wherein CHRIST has flung the Door of Mercy wide open, and stands in the Door calling and crying with a loud Voice to poor Sinners. . . .

And you that are *young* Men, and *young* Women, will you neglect this precious Season that you now enjoy, when so many others of your Age are renouncing all youthful Vanities, and flocking to CHRIST? You especially have now an extraordinary Opportunity; but if you neglect it, it will soon be with you as it is with those Persons that spent away all the precious Days of Youth in Sin, and are now come to such a dreadful pass in blindness and hardness. . . .

Therefore let every one that is out of CHRIST, now awake and fly from the Wrath to come. The Wrath of almighty GOD is now undoubtedly hanging over great Part of this Congregation: Let every one fly out of *Sodom: Haste and escape for your Lives, look not behind you, escape to the Mountain, least you be consumed.*

Source: Jonathan Edwards, *"Sinners in the Hands of an Angry God," A Sermon Preached at Enfield, July 8, 1741* (Boston: S. Kneeland and T. Grant, 1741), 5, 12–13, 15, 23–24, 25.

Newspaper Report on James Davenport, 1743

James Davenport, whose popular sermons denounced Old Light clergy as corrupt and worldly, was a controversial New Light minister. During the early 1740s, his behavior became increasingly erratic, culminating in a public burning of "immoral" books in New London, Connecticut, in 1743. Davenport also urged his audience to throw luxury items and clothing into the fire. Davenport even took off his own pants and threw them into the fire. His actions, and the ensuing controversy, caused some New Light ministers to turn against Davenport, and by 1744 he issued a public apology for his behavior. The following selection from a Boston newspaper describes the incident in New London.

Multitudes hasten'd toward the Place of Rendezvous, directing themselves by the Clamor and Shouting, which together, with the ascending Smoak [smoke] bro't them to one of the most public Places in the Town, and there found these good People encompassing a Fire which they had built up in the Street, into which they were casting Numbers of Books, principally on Divinity, and those that were well-approved by Protestant Divines, viz. . . . Mr. Russel's Seven Sermons, one of Dr. Colman's, and one of Dr. Chauncy's Books, and many others. Nothing can be more astonishing than their insolent Behaviour was during the Time of their Sacrifice, as 'tis said they call'd it; whilst the Books were in the Flames they cry'd out, *Thus the Souls of the Authors of those Books, those of them that are dad [dead], are roasting in the Flames of Hell; and that the Fate of those surviving, would be the same, unless speedy Repentance prevented:* On the next Day they had at the same Place a second Bonfire of the like Materials, and manag'd in the same manner. Having given this fatal Stroke to Heresy, they made ready to attack Idolatry, and sought for Direction, as in the Case before; and then Mr. [Davenport] told them to look at Home first, and that they themselves were guilty of idolizing their Apparel, and should therefore divest themselves of those Things especially which were for Ornament, and let them be burnt: Some of them in the heighth of their Zeal, conferred not with Flesh and Blood, but fell to stripping and cast their Cloaths [clothes] down at their Apostle's Feet; one or two hesitated about the Matter, and were so bold as to tell him they had nothing on which they idoliz'd: He reply'd, that such and such a Thing was an Offence to him; and they must down with them. . . . Next Mr. [Davenport] pray'd himself; and now the Oracle spake clear to the Point, without Ambiguity, and utter'd that *the Things must be burnt;* and to confirm the Truth of the Revelation, took his wearing Breeches, and hove them with Violence into the Pile, saying, *Go you with the Rest.*

Source: "Religious Excess at New London," *Boston Weekly Post-Boy*, March 28, 1743, in *The Great Awakening: Documents on the Revival of Religion, 1740–1745*, ed. Richard L. Bushman (New York: Institute of Early American History and Culture, 1970), 51–52.

George Whitefield Preaching, c. 1760

Paintings and engravings of the Great Awakening highlighted the most famous preachers and the diverse women and men who attended revivals. This painting by English artist John Collet captures an outdoor revival and shows Whitefield's appeal to a mixed audience of women and men. Collet was known for his satirical images of English life, so it is not clear whether the inclusion of working people and dogs is meant to illustrate or demean Whitefield's broad appeal.

Private Collection/Bridgeman Images

Interpret the Evidence

1. How does Benjamin Franklin's description of George Whitefield compare to Nathan Cole's, and how might the Enlightenment have influenced Franklin's view (Sources 4.6 and 4.7)?

2. What aspects of God's will and human sin does Jonathan Edwards emphasize in his sermon? How is Edwards's interest in science revealed in Source 4.8?

3. Why does James Davenport (Source 4.9) encourage his followers to burn religious books by Old Light ministers as well as items considered idolatrous, and how does the Boston newspaper respond to the resulting bonfires?

4. How does the image in Source 4.10 compare to the descriptions by Cole, Franklin, and the Boston newspaper (Sources 4.6, 4.7, and 4.9)? What aspects of these descriptions and of Edwards's sermon (Source 4.8) do Old Light ministers and civic leaders find threatening?

Put It in Context

How do these documents help explain the appeal of the Great Awakening, particularly to women, workers, and other non-elites? What legacies — ideas or practices — remained after the revivals ended?

War and Empire

1754–1774

WINDOW TO THE PAST

The Stamp Act Repealed, 1766

In 1765 the British Parliament passed the Stamp Act, which imposed a tax on a variety of paper items and documents in the American colonies to help pay debts from the French and Indian War. But the Stamp Act aroused widespread protests in the colonies, forcing its repeal in 1766. This political cartoon depicts a funeral service for the American stamps held by its British supporters. ▶ To discover more about what this primary source can show us, see Source 5.3 on page 161.

Library of Congress, 3g02568

After reading this chapter you should be able to:

■ Describe the causes and consequences of the French and Indian War.

■ Explain how British policies following the French and Indian War fostered colonial grievances.

■ Analyze the major British policies from 1764 to 1774 and how colonial responses to them became more unified.

COMPARING AMERICAN HISTORIES

Praised as the father of the United States, George Washington remained a loyal British subject for forty-three years. He was born in 1732 to a prosperous farm family in eastern Virginia. When his father died in 1743, George became the ward of his half-brother Lawrence, who took control of the family's Mount Vernon estate. Lawrence's father-in-law, William Fairfax, was an agent for Lord Fairfax, one of the chief proprietors of the colony. When George was sixteen, William hired him to help survey Lord Fairfax's land on Virginia's western frontier.

As a surveyor, George journeyed west, coming into contact with Indians, both friendly and hostile, as well as other colonists seeking land. George began investing in western properties, but when Lawrence Washington died in 1752, George suddenly became head of a large estate. He gradually expanded Mount

Vernon's boundaries and its enslaved workforce, increasing its profitability.

George was soon appointed Lieutenant Colonel in the Virginia militia, and in the fall of 1753 Virginia's governor sent him to warn the French against encroaching on British territory in the Ohio River valley. The French commander rebuffed Washington and, within six months, gained control of a British post near present-day Pittsburgh, Pennsylvania and named it Fort Duquesne. With help from Indians hostile to the French, Washington's surprise attack on Fort Duquesne in May 1754 led the governors of Virginia and North Carolina to provide the newly promoted Colonel Washington with more troops. The French then responded with a much larger force that compelled Washington to surrender.

Washington's fortunes and his family increased when he married the wealthy widow Martha Dandridge Custis in 1759. With more land to defend, Washington supported efforts to extend Britain's North American empire westward to create a protective buffer against European and Indian foes.

Like Washington, Hermon Husband hoped to improve his lot through hard work and new opportunities on the frontier. Born to a modest farm family in Maryland in 1724, he was swept up by George Whitefield's preaching in 1739, but eventually joined the Society of Friends, or Quakers. Although his farm in Maryland was thriving, Husband explored prospects on the North Carolina frontier. In 1762 he settled with his family at Sandy Creek.

There Husband again proved a successful farmer, but he began to speak against wealthy landowners and speculators who made it difficult for small farmers to obtain sufficient land. He also challenged established leaders in the local Quaker community, or meeting, and was among a number of worshippers disowned from the Cane Creek Friends Meeting in 1764. Disputes within radical Protestant congregations were not unusual in this period, as members with deep religious convictions chose the liberty of their individual conscience over church authority.

In 1766 local farmers joined Husband in organizing the Sandy Creek Association, through which they sought to increase their political clout in order to combat corruption among local officials.

(left) **George Washington.** Granger, NYC
(right) **Hermon Husband's Deed.** Courtesy of the State Archives of North Carolina

The association disbanded after two years, but its ideas lived on in a group called the Regulation, which brought together frontier farmers to "regulate" government abuse. The Regulators petitioned the North Carolina Assembly and Royal Governor William Tryon, demanding legislative reforms and suing local officials for extorting labor, land, and money from poorer residents.

Husband quickly emerged as one of the organization's chief pamphleteers, articulating the demands of the Regulators and echoing other colonial protesters of the period. Governor Tryon viewed the Regulators as threatening the colony's peace and order and, in 1768 and 1771, had Husband and other Regulators arrested. This confirmed the group's belief that they could not receive fair treatment at the hands of colonial officials. They then turned to extralegal methods to assert their rights, such as taking over courthouses so that legal proceedings against debt-ridden farmers could not proceed. ■

Comparing the American histories of Washington and Husband demonstrates how colonists' lives were shaped by both opportunities and conflicts. Mid-eighteenth-century colonial America offered greater opportunities for social advancement and personal expression than anywhere in Europe, but collective efforts to take advantage of these opportunities often led to tension and discord. Frontier conflicts foreshadowed a broader struggle for land and power within the American colonies. Religious and economic as well as political discord intensified in the mid-eighteenth century as upheavals among colonists increasingly occurred alongside challenges to British authority. Whatever their grievances, most colonists worked hard to reform systems they considered unfair or abusive before resorting to more radical means of instituting change.

Imperial Conflicts and Indian Wars, 1754–1763

The war that erupted in the Ohio valley in 1754 sparked an enormous shift in political and economic relations in colonial North America. What began as a small-scale, regional conflict expanded into a brutal and lengthy war around the world. Known as the French and Indian War in North America and as the Seven Years' War in Great Britain and Europe, the extended conflict led to a dramatic expansion of British territory in North America and to increasing demands from American colonists for more control over their own lives.

The Opening Battles. Even before Washington and his troops were defeated in July 1754, the British sought to protect the colonies against threats from the French and the Indians. To limit such threats, the British were especially interested in cementing an alliance with the powerful Iroquois Confederacy, composed of six northeastern tribes. Thus the British invited an official delegation from the Iroquois to a meeting in June 1754 in Albany, New York with representatives from several colonies. Benjamin Franklin of Philadelphia had drawn up a Plan of Union that would establish a council of representatives from the various colonial assemblies to debate issues of frontier defense, trade, and territorial expansion and to recommend terms mutually agreeable to colonists and Indians. Their deliberations were to be overseen by a president-general appointed and supported

Join or Die Benjamin Franklin created the first political cartoon in American history to accompany an editorial he wrote in the *Pennsylvania Gazette* in 1754. Franklin's cartoon urged the mainland British colonies to unite politically during the French and Indian War. Legend had it that a snake could come back to life if its severed sections were attached before dusk. Library of Congress, 3g05315

by the British crown. Despite the proposed council's mandate, Franklin excluded Iroquois or other Indian representatives from participation.

The **Albany Congress** created new bonds among a small circle of colonial leaders, but it failed to establish a firmer alliance with the Iroquois or resolve problems of colonial governance. The Mohawk warrior and sachem Hendrick Peters Theyanoguin urged British representatives at the Congress to take more forceful action, including military action, against its enemies. His views were reported in the British and colonial press. By July, Iroquois delegates, angered by Franklin's plan, left the Congress and broke off talks with the British. The Plan of Union was also rejected by the individual colonies because they were unwilling to give up any of their autonomy in military, trade, and political matters to some centralized body. Meanwhile officials in the royal government worried that the debates might force its hand in dealing with the French and their Indian allies.

If war was going to erupt between the British and the French, the Iroquois and other Indian tribes could not afford to have the outcome decided by imperial powers alone. For most Indians, contests among European nations for land and power offered them the best chance of survival in the eighteenth century. They gained leverage as long as various imperial powers needed their trade items, military support, and political alliances. This leverage would be far more limited if one European nation controlled most of North America.

Still, Indian tribes adopted different strategies. The Delaware, Huron, Miami, and Shawnee nations, for example, allied themselves with the French, hoping that a French victory would stop the far more numerous British colonists from invading their settlements in the Ohio River valley. Members of the Iroquois Confederacy, on the other hand, tried to play one power against the other, hoping to win concessions from the British in return for their military support. The Creek, Choctaw, and Cherokee nations also sought to perpetuate the existing stalemate among European powers by bargaining alternately with the British in Georgia and the Carolinas, the French in Louisiana, and the Spaniards in Florida. Faced with incursions into their lands, some Indian tribes, like the Abenaki in northern New England, launched preemptive attacks on colonial settlements.

The British government soon decided it had to send additional troops to defend its American colonies against attacks from Indians and intrusions from the French. General Edward Braddock and two regiments arrived in 1755 to expel the French from Fort Duquesne. At the same time, colonial militia units were sent to battle the French and their Indian allies along the New York and New England frontiers. Colonel Washington joined Braddock as his personal aide-de-camp. Within months, however, Braddock's forces were ambushed, bludgeoned by French and Indian forces, and Braddock was killed.

Other British forces fared little better during the next three years. Despite having far fewer colonists in North America than the British, the French had established extensive trade networks that helped them sustain a protracted war with support from numerous Indian nations. Alternating guerrilla tactics with conventional warfare, the French captured several important forts, built a new one on Lake Champlain, and moved troops deep into British territory. The ineffectiveness of the British and colonial armies also encouraged Indian tribes along the New England and Appalachian frontiers to reclaim land from colonists. Bloody raids devastated many outlying settlements, leading to the death and capture of hundreds of Britain's colonial subjects.

A Shift to Global War. As the British faced defeat after defeat in North America, European nations began to contest imperial claims elsewhere in the world. In 1756 France and Great Britain officially declared war against each other. Eventually Austria, Russia, Sweden, most of the German states, and Spain allied with France, while Portugal and Prussia sided with Great Britain. Naval warfare erupted in the Mediterranean Sea and the Atlantic and Indian Oceans. Battles were also fought in Europe, the West Indies, India, and the Philippines. By the end of 1757, Britain and its allies had been defeated in nearly every part of the globe. The war appeared to be nearing its end, with France in control.

Then in the summer of 1757, William Pitt took charge of the British war effort. He transformed the political and military landscape in the American colonies, while Prussian forces held the line in Europe. Pouring more soldiers and arms into the North American campaign along with young and ambitious officers like Colonel Henry Bouquet, Pitt energized colonial and British troops.

By the summer of 1758, the tide began to turn. In July, British generals recaptured the fort at Louisburg on Cape Breton Island, a key to France's defense of Canada. Then British troops with Bouquet and Washington's aid seized Fort Duquesne, which was renamed Fort Pitt. Other British forces captured Fort Frontenac along the

Colonel George Washington   This 1772 oil painting by Charles Willson Peale portrays George Washington as a colonel in the Virginia militia. Washington commanded this militia during the French and Indian War following the death of General Braddock. After the war, Washington prospered as a planter and land speculator. Granger, NYC

St. Lawrence River, while Prussia defeated France and its allies in Europe and Britain gained key victories in India (Map 5.1). In 1759 General Jeffrey Amherst captured Forts Ticonderoga and Crown Point on Lake Champlain while General James Wolfe attacked a much larger French force in Quebec. Despite heavy casualties, including Wolfe himself, the British won Quebec and control of Canada.

The Costs of Victory. Despite Wolfe's dramatic victory, the war dragged on in North America, Europe, India, and the West Indies for three more years. By then, however, King George III had tired of Pitt's grand, and expensive, strategy and dismissed him. He then opened peace negotiations with France and agreed to give up a number of conquered

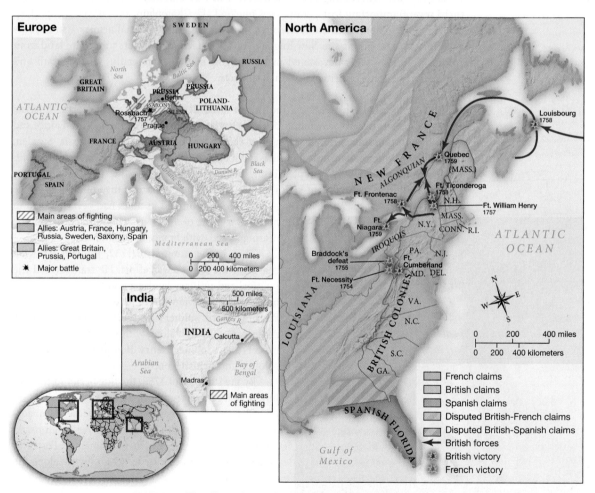

MAP 5.1 The French and Indian War, 1754–1763

Clashes between colonial militia units and French and Indian forces erupted in North America in 1754. The conflict helped launch a wider war that engulfed Europe as well as the West Indies and India. In the aftermath of this first global war, Britain gained control of present-day Canada and India, but France retained its West Indies colonies.

territories in order to finalize the **Peace of Paris** in 1763. Other countries were ready to negotiate as well. To regain control of Cuba and the Philippines, Spain ceded Florida to Great Britain. While France was expelled from North America, it rewarded Spanish support by granting Spain Louisiana and all French lands west of the Mississippi River. Despite these concessions, the British empire reigned supreme, regaining control of India as well as North America east of the Mississippi, all of Canada, and a number of Caribbean islands.

The wars that erupted between 1754 and 1763 reshaped European empires, transformed patterns of global trade, and initially seemed to tighten bonds between North American residents and the mother country. Yet the Peace of Paris did not resolve many of the problems that had plagued the colonies before the war, and it created new ones as well.

The incredible cost of the war raised particularly difficult problems. Over the course of the war, the national debt of Great Britain had more than doubled. At the same time, as the North American colonies grew and conflicts erupted along their frontiers, the costs of administering these colonies increased fivefold. With an empire that stretched around the globe, the British crown and Parliament were forced to consider how to pay off war debts, raise funds to administer their far-flung territories, and keep sufficient currency in circulation for expanding international trade. Just as important, the Peace of Paris ignored the claims of Indian tribes to the territories that France and Spain turned over to Great Britain. Nor did the treaty settle contested claims among the colonies themselves over lands in the Ohio River valley and elsewhere along British North America's new frontiers.

Battles and Boundaries on the Frontier.

The sweeping character of the British victory encouraged thousands of colonists to move farther west, into lands once controlled by France. This exacerbated tensions that were already rising on the southern and western frontiers of British North America.

In late 1759, for example, the Cherokee nation, reacting to repeated incursions on its hunting grounds, dissolved its long-term trade agreement with South Carolina. Cherokee warriors attacked backcountry farms and homes, leading to counterattacks by British troops. The fighting continued into 1761, when Cherokees on the Virginia frontier launched raids on colonists there. General Jeffrey Amherst then sent 2,800 troops to invade Cherokee territory and end the conflict. The soldiers sacked fifteen villages; killed men, women, and children; and burned acres of fields.

Although British raids diminished the Cherokees' ability to mount a substantial attack, sporadic assaults on frontier settlements continued for years. These conflicts fueled resentments among backcountry settlers not only against Indians but also against political leaders in eastern parts of the colonies who rarely provided sufficient resources for frontier defense.

A more serious conflict erupted in the Ohio River valley when Indians realized the consequences of British victories. When the British captured French forts along the Great Lakes and in the Ohio valley in 1760, they immediately antagonized local Indian groups by hunting and fishing on tribal lands and depriving villages of much-needed food. British traders also defrauded Indians on numerous occasions and ignored traditional obligations of gift giving.

The harsh realities of the British regime led some Indians to seek a return to ways of life that preceded the arrival of white men. An Indian visionary named Neolin preached that Indians had been corrupted by contact with Europeans and urged them to purify themselves by returning to their ancient traditions, abandoning white ways, and reclaiming their lands. Neolin was a prophet, not a warrior, but his message inspired others, including an Ottawa leader named Pontiac.

When news arrived in early 1763 that France was about to cede all of its North American lands to Britain and Spain, Pontiac convened a council of more than four

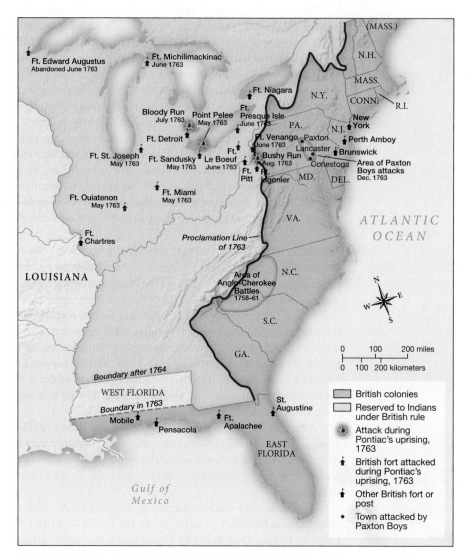

MAP 5.2 British Conflicts with Indians, 1758–1763, and the Proclamation Line

The entrance of British troops into former French territory in the Ohio River valley following the French and Indian War fueled conflicts with Indian nations. Colonists in Pennsylvania and the Carolinas also battled with Indians, including tribes who were allies or remained neutral during the war. Parliament established the Proclamation Line to limit westward expansion and thereby diminish such hostilities.

hundred Ottawa, Potawatomi, and Huron leaders near Fort Detroit. Drawing on Neolin's vision, he proclaimed, "It is important my brothers, that we should exterminate from our land this nation [Britain], whose only object is our death. You must all be sensible," he continued, "that we can no longer supply our wants the way we were accustomed to do with our Fathers the French." Pontiac then mobilized support to drive out the British. In May 1763, Pontiac's forces laid siege to Detroit and soon gained the support of eighteen Indian nations. They then attacked Fort Pitt and other British frontier outposts as well as white settlements along the Virginia and Pennsylvania frontier (Map 5.2).

Accounts of violent encounters with Indians on the frontier circulated throughout the colonies and sparked resentment among settlers as well as British troops. Many colonists did not distinguish between friendly and hostile Indians. In December 1763, a group of men from Paxton Creek, Pennsylvania raided families of peaceful, Christian Conestoga Indians near Lancaster, killing thirty. Protests from eastern colonists infuriated the Paxton Boys, who then marched on Philadelphia demanding protection from "savages" on the frontier.

Although violence on the frontier slowly subsided, neither side had achieved victory. Without French support, Pontiac and his followers had to retreat. Meanwhile, Benjamin Franklin negotiated a truce between the Paxton Boys and the Pennsylvania authorities, but it did not settle the fundamental issues over protection of western settlers. Convinced that it could not endure further costly frontier clashes, the British crown issued a proclamation in October 1763 forbidding colonial settlement west of a line running down the Appalachian Mountains to create a buffer between Indians and colonists. But Parliament also ordered Colonel Bouquet to subdue hostile Indians in the Ohio region.

The **Proclamation Line of 1763** denied colonists the right to settle west of the Appalachian Mountains. Imposed by the British government following the Peace of Paris, the Proclamation Line frustrated colonists who sought the economic benefits won by a long and bloody war. Small farmers, backcountry settlers, and squatters who had hoped to improve their lot by acquiring rich farmlands

The Indians Delivering Up English Captives, 1766 This hand-colored engraving was based on a Benjamin West sketch made in 1764 when Colonel Henry Bouquet led an army of 1,500 men into the Ohio territory. His mission was to force the Shawnee and Delaware to accept the Peace of Paris and release all English captives. The image suggests that not all captives wanted to leave their Indian families. Library of Congress 3b49465

were told to stay put. Meanwhile Washington and other wealthy speculators managed to acquire additional western lands, certain that the Proclamation was merely "a temporary expedient to quiet the Minds of the Indians."

Conflicts over Land and Labor Escalate.

Conflicts among colonists and with Britain were not confined to frontier regions. Land riots directed against the leasing policies of landlords and the greed of speculators had plagued New York's Hudson valley and New Jersey before the war, and these struggles continued into the 1760s. New clashes also occurred in the Carolinas as settlers like Hermon Husband stood up to landlords and government officials.

Even before the French and Indian War ended, the owners of large estates along the Hudson River in New York State raised rents and reduced the rights of tenants. In the early eighteenth century, the titles to some of these estates were challenged by small landowners and tenants, but even where legitimate titles existed, tenants declared a moral right to own the land they had long farmed. The manors and estates of the Hudson valley, they claimed, were more appropriate to a feudal government than to an enlightened empire.

Farmers in neighboring New Hampshire were drawn into battles over land when the king's Privy Council in London decided in 1764 that the Green Mountains belonged to New York rather than New Hampshire. Landlords along the Hudson River hoped to expand eastward into this region, but the farmers already living there claimed they had bought the land in good faith and deserved to keep it. These farmers launched guerrilla warfare against New York authorities and large landowners as well as against New York farmers who claimed land that New Hampshire families had cleared and settled. These Green Mountain Boys, led by Ethan Allen, refused to recognize New York authorities as legitimate and established their own local governments and popular courts.

Inspired by the Green Mountain Boys and uprisings in New Jersey, tenants in the Hudson valley banded together in 1765 and 1766. Under the leadership of Irish immigrant William Prendergast, a group of tenants calling themselves Levellers refused to pay rent and instead claimed freehold title to the land they farmed. New York tenants petitioned the colonial assembly and sought redress in a variety of ways. But landowners refused to negotiate, and Prendergast concluded that "there was no law for poor men."

Explore ▶

Read part of Hermon Husband's account of the Regulator's grievances in Source 5.1.

In many ways, the beliefs of Allen, Prendergast, and their followers echoed those of Hermon Husband and the North Carolina **Regulators**. All of these groups developed visible, well-organized networks of supporters, targeted specific landlords, sought redress first through colonial courts and assemblies, and then established popular militias and other institutions to govern themselves and to challenge those in authority.

REVIEW & RELATE

- How did the French and Indian War and the subsequent peace treaty affect relations among Britain, American Indian nations, and American colonies?

- How did the French and Indian War and the increasing power of large landowners contribute to conflict between average colonists and colonial elites?

GUIDED ANALYSIS

Hermon Husband | Causes of Armed Resistance in North Carolina, 1770

Frontier settler Hermon Husband owned substantial land, but most of his neighbors were poor families who had cleared vacant lands in the southern backwoods. They planned to gain legal title when agents for Earl Granville, Lord Proprietor of a large tract in North Carolina, arrived, but the agents failed to appear. Having paid taxes and fees on their land, many farmers joined the Regulators to resist what they saw as abusive practices. In a 1770 pamphlet, *An Impartial Relation*, Husband summarized his understanding of the causes of the Regulator uprising.

Source 5.1

What justifies the right of people to clear and cultivate vacant land before gaining legal title to it?

What actions by the Earl of Granville, his agents, and North Carolina officials does Husband consider abusive?

To whom is Husband addressing his pamphlet and how does he explain the actions of poor families who oppose British authorities?

[I]t has been the Opinion of all the several Legislative Bodies, both of Great-Britain and her Colonies, that peaceable Possession, especially of back waste vacant Lands, is a Kind of Right, always looked upon quite sufficient to entitle them to the Preference or Refusal of a farther [legal] Title. . . . This method has been used from New-England to Georgia, some Hundreds of Years Past. . . .

Now the Earl of Granville's Office, shut in such a manner, that no one in the Province knew but it would open again every year. . . . [B]ut four or five years being now elapsed, there is so much of the Lands seated under these Circumstances [cleared and cultivated], that Individuals in Power, and who has Money, are Marking them out for a Prey. . . .

It is to be feared too many of our Rulers have an eye to make a Prey of these poor People, because an Opinion seems to be propagated, that it is Criminal to cut a Tree down off the vacant Lands. Whether this Notion took its Rise from the great Men's making Tar and Turpentine on vacant Lands . . . or from the Motive's above mentioned [powerful men seeking improved lands], I would advise no honest Man to suffer such an Opinion to take Place with him; for the Thing is so inhuman and base, that you will not find a man but he will deny and clear himself, or hide such a Design as long as he can. . . .

Who can justify the Conduct of any Government who have countenanced and encouraged so many Thousands of poor Families to bestow their All, and the Labour of many Years, to improve a Piece of waste Land, with full Expectation of a Title, to deny them Protection from being rob[b]ed of it all by a few roguish Individuals, who never bestowed a Farthing thereon?

Source: Hermon Husband, *Impartial Relation of the First Rise and Cause of the Recent Differences in Publick Affairs, in the Province of North Carolina; and of the Past Tumults and Riots that Lately Happened in that Province* (North Carolina, 1770), 74, 77–78.

Put It in Context

How do Husband's complaints against colonial officials and elites compare with those of Hudson River tenants and the Green Mountain Boys?

Postwar British Policies and Colonial Unity

Even as ordinary colonists challenged the authority of economic and political elites, colonial leaders tried to persuade the disaffected to turn their anger against royal authorities in Britain. By highlighting colonists' rights as British subjects, local traditions of self-rule, and Enlightenment ideas, these leaders slowly gained support. Some of them even joined earlier opponents like Hermon Husband in arguing for the rights of the individual. The imposition of new British policies in the decade following the French and Indian War, from 1764 to 1774, was equally important in nurturing common grievances and uniting colonists across regional and economic differences. For instance, the Proclamation Line of 1763 inspired widespread dissent as poor farmers, large landowners, and speculators sought to expand westward. A second policy, impressment, by which the Royal Navy forced young colonial men into military service, also aroused anger across regions and classes. At the same time, the Great Awakening provided colonists with shared ideas about moral principles and new techniques for mass communication. Finally, Britain's efforts to repay its war debts by taxing colonists and its plan to continue quartering troops in North America led colonists to forge intercolonial protest movements.

Common Grievances. Like the Proclamation Line, which denied all colonists the right to settle beyond the Appalachian Mountains, the policy of impressment affected port city residents of all classes. Impressment had been employed by the British during the extended wars of the eighteenth century to procure seamen. While plucking poor men from ports throughout the British empire, the Royal Navy faced growing resistance to this practice in the American colonies from merchants and common folk alike.

Seamen and dockworkers had good reason to fight off impressment agents. Men in the Royal Navy faced low wages, bad food, harsh punishment, rampant disease, and high mortality. As the practice escalated with each new war, the efforts of British naval officers

Impressment by the British This eighteenth-century engraving depicts the harsh impressment of men into the British navy. Set in England, this illustration shows that impressment was widely practiced at home. Thus the British government did not single out colonists for special mistreatment.
© Mary Evans/The Image Works

and impressment agents to capture new "recruits" met violent resistance, especially in the North American colonies where several hundred men might be impressed at one time. In such circumstances, whole communities joined in the battle.

In the aftermath of the French and Indian War, serious impressment riots erupted in Boston, New York City, and Newport, Rhode Island. Increasingly, poor colonial seamen and dockworkers made common cause with owners of merchant ships and mercantile houses in protesting British policy. Colonial officials — mayors, governors, and customs agents — were caught in the middle. Some insisted on upholding the Royal Navy's right of impressment; others tried to placate both naval officers and local residents; and still others resisted what they saw as an oppressive imposition on the rights of colonists. Both those who resisted British authority and those who sought a compromise had to gain the support of the lower and middling classes to succeed.

Employers and politicians who opposed impressment gained an important advantage if they could direct the anger of colonists away from themselves and toward British policies. The decision of British officials to continue quartering troops in the colonies gave local leaders another opportunity to join forces with ordinary colonists. Colonial towns and cities were required to quarter (that is, house and support) British troops even after the Peace of Paris was signed. While the troops were intended to protect the colonies, they also provided reinforcements for impressment agents and surveillance over other illegal activities like smuggling and domestic manufacturing. Thus a range of issues and policies began to bind colonists together through common grievances against the British Parliament.

Forging Ties across the Colonies.
The ties forged between poorer and wealthier colonists over issues of westward expansion, impressment, and quartering grew stronger in the 1760s, but they tended to be localized in seaport cities or in specific areas of the frontier. Creating bonds across the colonies required considerably more effort in a period when communication and transportation beyond local areas were limited. Means had to be found to disseminate information and create a sense of common purpose if the colonists were going to persuade Parliament to take their complaints seriously. One important model for such intercolonial communication was the Great Awakening.

By the 1750s, the Great Awakening seemed to be marked more by dissension than by unity as new denominations continued to split from traditional churches. For example, in the Sandy Creek region of North Carolina, home to Hermon Husband, radical Protestants formed the Separate Baptists, who proclaimed a message of absolute spiritual equality. From the late 1750s through the 1770s, Separate Baptists converted thousands of small farmers, poor whites, and enslaved women and men and established churches throughout Virginia, Georgia, and the Carolinas.

Like Separate Baptists, Methodists, Dunkards, Moravians, and Quakers also offered southern residents religious experiences that highlighted spiritual equality. Some dissenting preachers invited slaves and free blacks to attend their services alongside local white farmers, farmwives, and laborers. Slaveholders and other elite southerners considered such practices outrageous and a challenge to the political as well as the social order.

Most women and men who converted to Separate Baptism, Methodism, or other forms of radical Protestantism did not link their religious conversion directly to politics. But as more and more ordinary colonists and colonial leaders voiced their anger at offensive British policies, evangelical techniques used to rouse the masses to salvation became important for mobilizing colonists to protest.

Thus even though the Great Awakening had spent its religious passion in most parts of North America by the 1760s, the techniques of mass communication and critiques of opulence and corruption it initiated provided emotional and practical ways of forging ties among widely dispersed colonists. Many evangelical preachers had condemned the lavish lifestyles of colonial elites and the spiritual corruption of local officials. Now in the context of conflicts with Great Britain, colonial leaders used such rhetoric to paint Parliament and British officials as aristocrats with little faith and less compassion.

The public sermons and mass gatherings used during the Great Awakening to inspire loyalty to a greater moral cause could now be translated into forms applicable to political protest. The efforts of Great Britain to assert greater control over its North American colonies provided colonial dissidents an opportunity to test out these new ways to forge inter-colonial ties.

Great Britain Seeks Greater Control.
Until the French and Indian War, British officials and their colonial subjects coexisted in relative harmony. Economic growth led Britain to ignore much of the smuggling and domestic manufacturing that took place in the colonies, since such activities did not significantly disrupt Britain's mercantile policies (see "Imperial Policies Focus on Profits" in chapter 3). Similarly, although the king and Parliament held ultimate political sovereignty, or final authority, over the American colonies, it was easier to allow some local control over political decisions, given the communication challenges created by distance.

This pattern of **benign** (or "salutary") **neglect** led some American colonists to view themselves as more independent of British control than they really were. Many colonists came to see smuggling, domestic manufacturing, and local self-governance as rights rather than privileges. Thus when British officials decided to assert greater control, many colonists protested.

To King George III and to Parliament, asserting control over the colonies was both right and necessary. In 1763 King George appointed George Grenville to lead the British government. As Prime Minister and Chancellor of the Exchequer, Grenville faced an economic depression in England, rebellious farmers opposed to a new tax on domestic cider, and growing numbers of unemployed soldiers returning from the war. He believed that regaining political and economic control in the colonies could help resolve these crises at home.

Eighteenth-century wars, especially the French and Indian War, cost a fortune. British subjects in England paid taxes to help offset the nation's debts, even though few of them benefited as directly from the British victory as did their counterparts in the American colonies. The colonies would cost the British treasury more if the crown could not control colonists' movement into Indian territories, limit smuggling and domestic manufacturing, and house British troops in the colonies cheaply.

To reassert control, Parliament launched a three-pronged program. First, it sought stricter enforcement of existing laws and established a Board of Trade to centralize policies and ensure their implementation. The **Navigation Acts**, which prohibited smuggling, established guidelines for legal commerce, and set duties on trade items, were the most important laws to be enforced. Second, Parliament extended wartime policies into peacetime. For example, the Quartering Act of 1765 ensured that British troops would remain in the colonies to enforce imperial policy. Colonial governments were expected to support them by allowing them to use vacant buildings and providing them with food and supplies.

The third part of Grenville's colonial program was the most important. It called for the passage of new laws to raise funds and reestablish the sovereignty of British rule. The first revenue act passed by Parliament was the American Duties Act of 1764, known as the **Sugar Act**. It imposed an **import duty**, or tax, on sugar, coffee, wines, and other luxury items. The act actually reduced the import tax on foreign molasses, which was regularly smuggled into the colonies from the West Indies, but insisted that the duty be collected. The crackdown on smuggling increased the power of customs officers and established the first vice-admiralty courts in North America to ensure that the Sugar Act raised money for the crown. That same year, Parliament passed the Currency Act, which prohibited colonial assemblies from printing paper money or bills of credit. Taken together, these provisions meant that colonists would pay more money into the British treasury even as the supply of money (and illegal goods) diminished in the colonies.

Some colonial leaders protested the Sugar Act through speeches, pamphlets, and petitions, and Massachusetts established a **committee of correspondence** to circulate concerns to leaders in other colonies. However, dissent remained disorganized and ineffective. Nonetheless, the passage of the Sugar and Currency Acts caused anxiety among many colonists, which was heightened by passage of the Quartering Act the next year. Colonial responses to these developments marked the first steps in an escalating conflict between British officials and their colonial subjects.

REVIEW & RELATE

- How did Britain's postwar policies lead to the emergence of unified colonial protests?

- Why did British policymakers believe they were justified in seeking to gain greater control over Britain's North American colonies?

Resistance to Britain Intensifies

Over the next decade, between 1764 and 1774, the British Parliament sought to extend its political and economic control over the American colonies, and the colonists periodically resisted. With each instance of resistance, Parliament demanded further submission to royal authority. With each demand for submission, colonists responded with greater assertions of their rights and autonomy. Still, no one imagined that a revolution was in the making.

The Stamp Act Inspires Coordinated Resistance. Grenville decided next to impose a stamp tax on the colonies similar to that long used in England. The stamp tax required that a revenue stamp be affixed to all transactions involving paper items, from newspapers and contracts to playing cards and diplomas. Grenville announced his plans in 1764, a full year before Parliament enacted the **Stamp Act** in the spring of 1765. The tax was to be collected by colonists appointed for the purpose, and the money was to be spent within the colonies at the direction of Parliament for "defending, protecting and securing the colonies." To the British government, the Stamp Act seemed completely fair. After all, Englishmen paid on average 26 shillings in tax annually, while Bostonians averaged just 1 shilling. Moreover, the act was purposely written to benefit the American colonies.

The colonists viewed it in a more threatening light. The Stamp Act differed from earlier parliamentary laws in three important ways. First, by the time of its passage, the colonies were experiencing rising unemployment, falling wages, and a downturn in trade. All of these developments were exacerbated by the Sugar, Currency, and Quartering Acts passed by Parliament the previous year. Second, critics viewed the Stamp Act as an attempt to control the *internal* affairs of the colonies. It was not an indirect tax on trade, paid by importers and exporters, but a direct tax on daily business. Third, such a direct intervention in the economic affairs of the colonies unleashed the concerns of both local officials and ordinary residents that Parliament was taxing colonists who had no representation in its debates and decisions.

By announcing the Stamp Act a year before its passage, Grenville allowed colonists plenty of time to organize their opposition. In New York City, Boston, and other cities, merchants, traders, and artisans formed groups dedicated to the repeal of the Stamp Act. Soon Sons of Liberty, Daughters of Liberty, Sons of Neptune, Vox Populi, and similar organizations emerged to challenge the imposition of the Stamp Act. Even before the act was implemented, angry mobs throughout the colonies attacked stamp distributors. Some were beaten, others tarred and feathered, and all were forced to take an oath never to sell stamps again.

Colonists lodged more formal protests with the British government as well. The Virginia House of Burgesses, led by Patrick Henry, acted first. It passed five resolutions, which it sent to Parliament, denouncing taxation without representation. The Virginia Resolves were reprinted in many colonial newspapers and repeated by orators to eager audiences in Massachusetts and elsewhere. At the same time, the Massachusetts House adopted a circular letter—a written protest circulated to the other colonial assemblies—calling for a congress to be held in New York City in October 1765 to consider the threat posed by the Stamp Act.

In the meantime, popular protests multiplied. The protests turned violent in Boston, where **Sons of Liberty** leaders like Samuel Adams, a Harvard graduate and town official, organized mass demonstrations. Adams modeled his oratory on that of itinerant preachers, but with a political twist. Other activists used more visual means of inspiring their audiences. At dawn on August 14, 1765, the Boston Sons of Liberty hung an effigy of stamp distributor Andrew Oliver on a tree and called for his resignation. A mock funeral procession, joined by farmers, artisans, apprentices, and the poor, marched to Boston Common. The crowd, led by shoemaker and French and Indian War veteran Ebenezer Mackintosh, carried the fake corpse to the Boston stamp office and destroyed the building. Demonstrators saved pieces of lumber, "stamped" them, and set them on fire outside Oliver's house. Oliver, wisely, had already left town.

Oliver's brother-in-law, Lieutenant Governor Thomas Hutchinson, arrived at the scene and tried to quiet the crowd, but he only angered them further. They soon destroyed Oliver's stable house, coach, and carriage, which the crowd saw as signs of aristocratic opulence.

The battle against the Stamp Act unfolded across the colonies with riots, beatings, and resignations reported from Newport, Rhode Island, to New Brunswick, New Jersey, to Charles Town (later Charleston), South Carolina. On November 1, 1765, when the Stamp Act officially took effect, not a single stamp agent remained in his post in the colonies.

Protesters carefully chose their targets: stamp agents, sheriffs, judges, and colonial officials. Even when violence erupted, it remained focused, with most crowds destroying stamps and stamp offices first and then turning to the private property of Stamp Act supporters. These protests made a mockery of notions of deference toward British rule. But they also revealed growing autonomy on the part of middling- and working-class colonists who attacked men of wealth and power, sometimes choosing artisans rather than wealthier men as their leaders. However, this was not primarily a class conflict because many wealthier colonists made common cause with artisans, small farmers, and the poor. Indeed, colonial elites considered themselves the leaders, inspiring popular uprisings through the power of their political arguments and oratorical skills. Still, they refused to support actions they considered too radical.

It was these more affluent protesters who dominated the Stamp Act Congress that met in New York City in October 1765. It brought together twenty-seven delegates from nine colonies. The delegates petitioned Parliament to repeal the Stamp Act, arguing that taxation without representation was tyranny. Delegates then urged colonists to boycott British goods and refuse to pay the stamp tax. Yet they still proclaimed their loyalty to king and country.

The question of representation became a mainstay of colonial protests. Whereas the British accepted the notion of "virtual representation," by which members of Parliament gave voice to the views of particular classes and interests, the North American colonies had developed a system of representation based on locality. According to colonial leaders, only members of Parliament elected by colonists could represent their interests.

Even as delegates at the Stamp Act Congress declared themselves loyal, if disaffected, British subjects, they participated in the process of developing a common identity in the American colonies. Christopher Gadsden of South Carolina expressed the feeling most directly. "We should stand upon the broad common ground of natural rights," he argued. "There should be no New England man, no New-Yorker, known on the continent, but all of us Americans."

Eventually the British Parliament was forced to respond to colonial protests and even more to rising complaints from English merchants and traders whose business had been damaged by the colonists' boycott. Parliament repealed the Stamp Act in March 1766, and King George III granted his approval a month later. Victorious colonists looked forward to a new and better relationship between themselves and the British government.

From the colonists' perspective, the crisis triggered by the Stamp Act demonstrated the limits of parliamentary control. Colonists had organized effectively and forced Parliament to repeal the hated legislation. Protests had raged across the colonies and attracted support from a wide range of colonists. Individual leaders, like Patrick Henry of Virginia and Samuel Adams of Massachusetts, became more widely known through their fiery oratory and their success in appealing to the masses. The Stamp Act agitation also demonstrated the growing influence of ordinary citizens who led parades and demonstrations and joined in attacks on stamp agents and the homes of British officials. And the protests revealed the growing power of the written word and printed images in disseminating ideas among colonists. Broadsides, political cartoons, handbills, newspapers, and pamphlets circulated widely, reinforcing discussions and proclamations at taverns, rallies, demonstrations, and more formal political assemblies.

For all the success of the Stamp Act protests, American colonists still could not imagine in 1765 that protest would ever lead to open revolt against British sovereignty. More well-to-do colonists were concerned that a revolution against British authority might fuel

A Patriot Merchant's Mansion   Jeremiah Lee, the wealthiest merchant in Massachusetts, moved his family into a newly built Marblehead mansion in 1768. It was decorated with hand-carved moldings, furniture made by colonial craftsmen, and hand-painted wallpaper from England. Despite his strong ties to British commercial circles, he was an ardent patriot and friend of Samuel Adams and used his wealth to promote the colonists' cause. Lucinda Lambton, Bridgeman Images

a dual revolution in which small farmers, tenants, servants, slaves, and laborers would rise up against their political and economic superiors in the colonies. Even most middling- and working-class protesters believed that the best solution to the colonies' problems was to gain greater economic and political rights within the British empire, not to break from it.

The Townshend Act.   The repeal of the Stamp Act in March 1766 led directly to Parliament's passage of the Declaratory Act. That act declared that Parliament had the authority to pass any law "to bind the colonies and peoples of North America" closer to Britain. No new tax or policy was established; Parliament simply wanted to proclaim Great Britain's political supremacy in the aftermath of the successful stamp tax protests.

Following this direct assertion of British sovereignty, relative harmony prevailed in the colonies for more than a year. Then in June 1767, a new chancellor of the Exchequer, Charles Townshend, rose to power in England. He persuaded Parliament to return to the model offered by the earlier Sugar Act. The **Townshend Act**, like the Sugar Act, instituted an import tax on a range of items sent to the colonies, including glass, lead, paint, paper, and tea.

Now, however, even an indirect tax led to immediate protests and calls for a boycott of taxed items. In February 1768, Samuel Adams wrote a circular letter reminding colonists of the importance of the boycott, and the Massachusetts Assembly disseminated it to other colonial assemblies. In response, Parliament posted two more British army regiments in Boston and New York City to enforce the law. Angry colonists did not retreat when confronted by this show of military force. Instead, a group of outspoken colonial leaders demanded that colonists refuse to import goods of any kind from Britain.

Explore ▶

See Sources 5.2 and 5.3 for two different types of dissent.

In 1767 and 1768, John Dickinson, a prominent Pennsylvania attorney and Quaker, published a series of letters attacking the Townshend Act. He presented himself as an ordinary colonist by using the pen name "A Farmer." Arguing that any duty on goods was a tax, he insisted, "Those who are taxed without their own consent, given by themselves, or their representatives, are slaves. We are taxed without our own consent given by ourselves, or our representatives. We are therefore — I speak it with grief — I speak it with indignation — we are slaves." Clearly, a boycott was necessary to demonstrate colonists' rights as British subjects.

This boycott depended especially on the support of women, who were often in charge of the day-to-day purchase of household items. Wives and mothers were expected to boycott a wide array of British goods, and even single women and widows who supported themselves as shopkeepers were expected not to sell British goods. Women were called upon as well to provide substitutes for boycotted goods. Many wives and mothers produced homespun shirts and dresses and brewed herbal teas to replace British products.

Despite the hardships, many colonial women, including twenty-two-year-old Charity Clarke, embraced the boycott. She wrote to a friend in England, "If you English folks won't give us the liberty we ask . . . I will try to gather a number of ladies armed with spinning wheels [along with men] who shall learn to weave & keep sheep, and will retire beyond the reach of arbitrary power." Other women also organized spinning bees in which dozens of participants produced yards of homespun cloth, the wearing of which symbolized female commitment to the cause.

Refusing to drink tea offered another way for women to protest parliamentary taxation. In February 1770, more than "300 Mistresses of Families, in which number the Ladies of the Highest Rank and Influence," signed a petition in Boston and pledged to abstain from drinking tea. Dozens of women from less prosperous families signed their own boycott agreement.

The Boston Massacre.
Boston women's refusal to drink tea and their participation in spinning bees were part of a highly publicized effort to make their city the center of opposition to the Townshend Act. Printed propaganda, demonstrations, rallies, and broadsides announced to the world that Bostonians rejected Parliament's right to impose its will, or at least its taxes, on the American colonies. Angry over Parliament's taxation policies, Boston men also considered the soldiers, who moonlighted for extra pay, as economic competitors. Throughout the winter of 1769–1770, boys and young men reacted by harassing the growing number of British soldiers stationed in the city.

On the evening of March 5, 1770, young men began throwing snowballs at the lone soldier guarding the Boston Customs House. An angry crowd began milling about, now joined by a group of sailors led by Crispus Attucks, an ex-slave of mixed African and Indian ancestry. The guard called for help, and Captain Thomas Preston arrived at the scene with seven British soldiers. He appealed to the "gentlemen" present to disperse the crowd. Instead, the harangues of the crowd continued, and snowballs, stones, and other projectiles flew in greater numbers. Then a gun fired, and soon more shooting erupted. Eleven men in the crowd were hit, and four were "killed on the Spot," including Attucks.

Despite confusion about who, if anyone, gave the order to fire, colonists expressed outrage at the shooting of ordinary men on the streets of Boston. Samuel Adams and other Sons of Liberty recognized the incredible potential for anti-British propaganda. Adams organized a mass funeral for those killed, and thousands watched the caskets being paraded through the city. Newspaper editors and broadsides printed by the Sons of Liberty labeled the shooting a "massacre." But when the accused soldiers were tried in Boston for the so-called **Boston Massacre**, the jury acquitted six of the eight of any crime. Still, ordinary colonists as well as colonial leaders were growing more convinced that British rule had become tyrannical and that such tyranny must be opposed. **See Primary Source Project 5: The Boston Massacre, page 169.**

COMPARATIVE ANALYSIS

Protesting the Stamp Act

The announcement of the Stamp Act in 1764 ignited widespread protests throughout the colonies. Colonial governments petitioned Parliament for its repeal, crowds attacked stamp agents and distributors, broadsides and newspapers denounced "taxation without representation," and boycotts and mass demonstrations were organized in major cities. As the first document shows, London merchants also protested, arguing that they were losing revenue because of colonial boycotts of British goods. The second document celebrates the repeal of the Stamp Act by depicting a funeral for the act led by its supporters. Dr. William Scott, who published letters supporting the Stamp Act in a London newspaper, leads the procession.

Source 5.2

London Merchants Petition to Repeal the Stamp Act, 1766

And that, in consequence of the trade between the colonies and the mother country, as established and permitted for many years, and of the experience which the petitioners have had of the readiness of the Americans to make their just remittances to the utmost of their real ability, they have been induced to make and venture such large exportations of British manufactures, as to leave the colonies indebted to the merchants of Great Britain in the sum of several millions sterling; at that at this time the colonists, when pressed for payment, appeal to past experience, in proof of their willingness; but declare it is not in their power, at present, to make good their engagements, alleging, that the taxes and restrictions laid upon them, and the extension of the jurisdiction of vice admiralty courts established by some late acts of parliament, particularly . . . by an act passed in the fifth year of his present Majesty, for granting and applying certain stamp duties, and other duties, in the British colonies and plantations in America, with several regulations and restraints, which, if founded in acts of parliament for defined purposes, are represented to have been extended in such a manner as to disturb legal commerce and harass the fair trader, have so far interrupted the usual and former most fruitful branches of their commerce, restrained the sale of their produce, thrown the state of the several provinces into confusion, and brought on so great a number of actual bankruptcies, that the former opportunities and means of remittances and payments are utterly lost and taken from them; and that the petitioners are, by these unhappy events, reduced to the necessity of applying to the House, in order to secure themselves and their families from impending ruin; to prevent a multitude of manufacturers from becoming a burthen to the community, or else seeking their bread in other countries, to the irretrievable loss of this kingdom; and to preserve the strength of this nation entire.

Source: Guy Steven Callender, *Selections from the Economic History of the United States, 1765–1860* (Boston: Ginn, 1909), 146–147.

Source 5.3

The Repeal, 1766

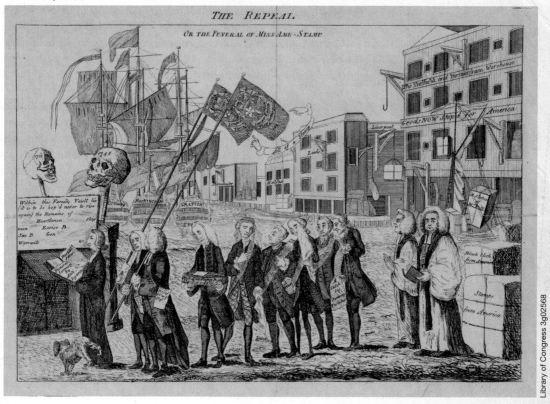

Library of Congress 3g02568

Interpret the Evidence

1. How do the petition and the cartoon emphasize the economic arguments against the Stamp Act? What role, if any, do arguments about political representation play in these documents?

2. Who do you think was the intended audience for each of these documents? What evidence can you find in each document to support your answer?

Put It in Context

What do these documents suggest about the more general relations among the colonies, British merchants, and Parliament in 1766?

To ensure that colonists throughout North America learned about the Boston Massacre, committees of correspondence formed once again to spread the news. These committees became important pipelines for sending information about plans and protests across the colonies. They also circulated an engraving by Bostonian Paul Revere that suggested the soldiers purposely shot at a peaceful crowd.

Parliament was already considering the repeal of the Townshend duties, and in the aftermath of the shootings, public pressure increased to do so. Merchants in England and North America insisted that parliamentary policies had resulted in economic losses on both sides of the Atlantic. In response, Parliament repealed all of the Townshend duties except the import tax on tea, which it retained to demonstrate its political authority to tax the colonies.

Continuing Conflicts at Home.

As colonists in Boston and other seaport cities rallied to protest British taxation, other residents of the thirteen colonies continued to challenge authorities closer to home. In the same years as the Stamp Act and Townshend Act protests, tenants in New Jersey and the Hudson valley continued their campaign for economic justice. So, too, did Hermon Husband and the Regulators. Conflicts escalated when the North Carolina Assembly, dominated by the eastern slaveholding elite, approved a measure in 1768 to build a stately mansion for Governor Tryon with public funds. Outraged frontier farmers withheld their taxes, took over courthouses, and harassed corrupt local officials. While Governor Tryon claimed that Parliament abused its power in taxing the colonies, he did not recognize such abuses in his own colony. Instead, he increasingly viewed the Regulators as traitors. In spring 1771, he recruited a thousand militiamen to quell what he considered open rebellion on the Carolina frontier. The Regulators amassed two thousand farmers to defend themselves, although Husband, a pacifist, was not among them. But when twenty Regulators were killed and more than a hundred wounded at the Battle of Alamance Creek in May 1771, he surely knew many of the fallen. Six of the defeated Regulators were hanged a month later. Many local residents harbored deep resentments against colonial officials for what they viewed as the slaughter of honest, hardworking men. Hermon Husband fled the Carolina frontier and headed north.

Resentments against colonial leaders were not confined to North Carolina. An independent Regulator movement had emerged in South Carolina in 1767. Far more effective than their North Carolina counterparts, South Carolina Regulators seized control of the western regions of the colony, took up arms, and established their own system of frontier justice. In 1769 the South Carolina Assembly negotiated a settlement with the Regulators, establishing new parishes in the colony's interior that ensured greater representation for frontier areas and extending colonial political institutions, such as courts and sheriffs, to the region.

Tea and Widening Resistance.

For a brief period after the Boston Massacre, conflicts within the colonies generally overshadowed protests against British policies. During this period, the tea tax was collected, the increased funds ensured that British officials in the colonies were less dependent on local assemblies to carry out their duties, and general prosperity seemed to lessen the antagonism between colonists and royal authorities. In May 1773, however, all that changed. That month Parliament passed a new act that granted the revered but financially struggling East India Company a monopoly on shipping and selling tea in the colonies. Although this did not add any new tax or raise the price of tea, it did fuel a new round of protests.

Explore ▶

See Sources 5.4 and 5.5 for different perspectives on how colonists' identities changed in the 1760s and 1770s.

Samuel Adams, Patrick Henry, Christopher Gadsden, and other radicals had continued to view the tea tax as an illegal imposition on colonists and refused to pay it as a matter of principle. They had established committees of correspondence to keep up the pressure for a colony-wide boycott, and Adams published and circulated "Rights of the Colonies," a pamphlet that listed a range of grievances against British policies. Their concerns became the basis for a new round of protests when Parliament, many of whose members invested in the East India Company, granted its monopoly. By eliminating colonial merchants from the profits to be made on tea and implementing a monopoly for a single favored company, Parliament pushed merchants into joining with radicals to demand redress.

Committees of correspondence quickly organized another colony-wide boycott. In some cities, like Charleston, South Carolina, tea was unloaded from East India Company ships but never sold. In others, like New York, the ships were turned back at the port. Only in Boston, however, did violence erupt as ships loaded with tea sat anchored in the harbor. On the night of December 16, 1773, the Sons of Liberty organized a "tea party." After a massive rally against British policy, a group of about fifty men disguised as Indians boarded the British ships and dumped forty-five tons of tea into the sea.

Although hundreds of spectators knew who had boarded the ship, witnesses refused to provide names or other information to British investigators. The Boston Tea Party was a direct challenge to British authority and resulted in large-scale destruction of valuable property.

Parliament responded immediately with a show of force. The **Coercive Acts**, passed in 1774, closed the port of Boston until residents paid for the tea, moved Massachusetts court cases against royal officials back to England, and revoked the colony's charter in order to strengthen the authority of royal officials and weaken that of the colonial assembly. The British government also approved a new Quartering Act, which forced Boston residents to accommodate more soldiers in their own homes or build more barracks.

The royal government passed the Coercive Acts to punish Massachusetts and to discourage similar protests in other colonies. Instead, the legislation, which colonists called the **Intolerable Acts**, spurred a militant reaction. Committees of correspondence spread news of the fate of Boston and of Massachusetts. Colonial leaders, who increasingly identified themselves as patriots, soon formed committees of safety—armed groups of colonists who gathered weapons and munitions and vowed to protect

A SOCIETY of PATRIOTIC LADIES,
AT
EDENTON in NORTH CAROLINA.

Plate V.

The Edenton Proclamation, 1774   In Edenton, North Carolina, a group of women published a proclamation in 1774 stating their allegiance to the cause of liberty by refusing to serve or drink British tea. Their public statement received much attention in the American and the British press. This political cartoon, which satirizes the women who signed the declaration, appeared in several London newspapers. Library of Congress, LC-DIG-ppmsca-19468

SECONDARY SOURCE ANALYSIS

Colonial Identities in Eighteenth Century British North America

In the 1760s and early 1770s, colonists on mainland North America increasingly resisted Parliament's imposition of policies they considered burdensome and unfair. The great distance between England and mainland North America had allowed colonists to develop relatively autonomous institutions and ideas over the previous century. In this same period, a growing proportion of colonists emigrated from places other than the British Isles. Still, many colonists were closely bound to Britain and British culture by familial and religious ties, commercial exchanges, books and newspapers, and rituals like tea drinking. Historians have asked whether, as political relations between Britain and its mainland colonies frayed in the 1760s and 1770s, the balance between colonists' British and American identities shifted, and have come to differing conclusions.

Source 5.4

Gordon Wood, Britain's Influence on Colonial Identities, 1993

In our enthusiasm to contrast the "traditional" society of the mother country with the "modernity" of the colonies, we have often overlooked how dominantly British and traditional the colonists' culture was; indeed, in some respects colonial society was more traditional than that of the mother country. Most colonial leaders in the mid-eighteenth century thought of themselves not as Americans but as Britons. They read much the same literature, the same law books, the same history, as their brethren at home, and they drew most of their conceptions of society and their values from their reading. Whatever sense of unity the disparate colonies of North America had came from their common tie to the British crown and from their membership in the British empire. Most colonists knew more about events in London than they did about occurrences in neighboring colonies. They were provincials living on the edges of a pan-British world, and all the more British for that.

Source: Gordon Wood, *The Radicalism of the American Revolution.* Vintage Books, 1993, p. 12

themselves against British encroachments on their rights and institutions. Other colonies sent support, both political and material, to Massachusetts and instituted a boycott of British goods. All ranks of people throughout the colonies joined the boycott.

At the same time, a group of patriots meeting in Williamsburg, Virginia in the spring of 1774 called for colonies to send representatives to a **Continental Congress** to meet in Philadelphia the following September to discuss relations between the North American colonies and Great Britain.

By passing the Coercive Acts, Parliament had hoped to dampen the long-smoldering conflict with the colonies. Instead, it flared even brighter, with radical leaders committing

Source 5.5

Jon Butler, American Influences on Colonial Identities, 2000

The transformation of the [British mainland] colonies between 1680 and 1770 exhibited the settlers' increasing fascination with power and authority, a determination to make the world anew in yet untested images. Men and women of all kinds pressed on to control their own destiny, sometimes collectively, sometimes individually as America's population, economy, secular life, and religion became more complex and variegated. Colonists created a far more independent economy than their "colonial" status might have suggested was desirable or possible. Most European settlers extended and enlivened traditional religious expression in the New World. Africans and American Indians shaped new cultures and modes of living under extraordinarily difficult conditions. Provincial politics gave European settlers persuasive control over colonial affairs. A vigorous secular life emulated European models but moved to New World rhythms and concerns.

Modernity could also support and even create new problems that would afflict America and much of the modern world for decades, even centuries. Most spectacularly, the slaveholding that overwhelmed Spanish America and the British Caribbean by the 1650s, was perfected in the British mainland colonies after 1680. . . .

The result was America in its aspirations, its character, its flaws, and its achievements—a surprising America that seventeenth-century immigrants never imagined. The transformations occurring between 1680 and 1770 made the term "America" increasingly indelible. They made the direction of American history unmistakable, even if they did not make it inevitable.

Source: Jon Butler, *Becoming America: The Revolution Before 1776.* Harvard University Press, 2000, pp. 3 and 4

Examine the Sources

1. How do Wood and Butler differ in their historical interpretation of colonial identity in the eighteenth century?
2. Which colonial leaders discussed in this chapter support the main arguments of Wood? Which support the main arguments of Butler?

Put It in Context

3. How might Wood's and Butler's views of colonial identities have differed if they focused on specific populations within the colonies, such as those living on the frontier, women, blacks, or poor colonists?

themselves to the use of violence, moderate merchants and shopkeepers making common cause with radicals, and ordinary women and men embracing a boycott of all British goods.

The Continental Congress and Colonial Unity. When the Continental Congress convened in Philadelphia in September 1774, fifty-six delegates represented every colony but Georgia. Many of these men—and they were all men—had met before. Some had worked together in the Stamp Act Congress in 1765; others had joined forces in the intervening years on committees of correspondence or in petitions to Parliament. Still, the representatives disagreed on many fronts. Some were radicals like Samuel Adams, Patrick

Henry, and Christopher Gadsden. Others held moderate views, including George Washington and John Dickinson of Pennsylvania. And a few, like John Jay of New York, voiced more conservative positions.

Despite their differences, all the delegates agreed that the colonies must resist further parliamentary encroachments on their liberties. They talked not of independence but rather of reestablishing the freedoms that colonists had enjoyed in an earlier period. Washington voiced the sentiments of many. Although opposed to the idea of independence, he echoed John Locke by refusing to submit "to the loss of those valuable rights and privileges, which are essential to the happiness of every free State, and without which life, liberty, and property are rendered totally insecure."

To demonstrate their unified resistance to the Coercive Acts, delegates called on colonists to continue the boycott of British goods and to end all colonial exports to Great Britain. Committees were established in all of the colonies to coordinate and enforce these actions. Delegates also insisted that Americans were "entitled to a free and exclusive power of legislation in their several provincial legislatures." By 1774 a growing number of colonists supported these measures and the ideas on which they were based.

The delegates at the Continental Congress could not address all the colonists' grievances, and most had no interest in challenging race and class relations within the colonies themselves. Nonetheless, it was a significant event because the congress drew power away from individual colonies and local organizations and placed the emphasis instead on colony-wide plans and actions. To some extent, the delegates also shifted leadership of the protests away from more radical artisans, like Ebenezer Mackintosh, and put planning back in the hands of men of wealth and standing. Moreover, even as they denounced Parliament, many representatives felt a special loyalty to the king and sought his intervention to rectify relations between the mother country and the colonies.

REVIEW & RELATE

- How and why did colonial resistance to British policies escalate in the decade following the conclusion of the French and Indian War?

- How did internal social and economic divisions shape the colonial response to British policies?

Conclusion: Liberty within Empire

From the Sugar Act in 1764 to the Continental Congress in 1774, colonists reacted strongly to parliamentary efforts to impose greater control over the colonies. Their protests grew increasingly effective as colonists developed organizations, systems of communication, and arguments to buttress their position. Residents of seacoast cities like Boston and New York City developed especially visible and effective challenges, in large part because they generally had the most to lose if Britain implemented new economic, military, and legislative policies.

In frontier areas, such as the southern backcountry, the Hudson valley, and northern New England, complaints against British tyranny vied with those against colonial land speculators and officials throughout the 1760s and 1770s. Still, few of these agitators questioned the right of white colonists to claim Indian lands or enslave African labor. In this sense, at least, most frontier settlers made common cause with more elite colonists, including the many planters and large landowners who attended the Continental Congress.

One other tie bound the colonists together in 1774. No matter how radical the rhetoric, the aim continued to be resistance to particular policies, not independence from the British empire. Colonists sought greater liberty within the empire. Only on rare occasions did a colonist question the fundamental framework of imperial governance. And despite some colonists' opposition to certain parliamentary acts, many others supported British policies. Indeed, the majority of colonists did not participate in protest activities. Most small farmers and backcountry settlers were far removed from centers of protest activity, while poor families in seaport cities who purchased few items to begin with had little interest in boycotts of British goods. Finally, some colonists hesitated to consider open revolt against British rule for fear of a revolution from below. The activities of land rioters, Regulators, evangelical preachers, female petitioners, and African American converts to Christianity reminded more well-established settlers that the colonies harbored their own tensions and conflicts.

The fates of George Washington and Hermon Husband suggest the uncertainties that plagued the colonies and individual colonists in 1774. As Washington returned to his Virginia estate from the Continental Congress, he began to devote more time to military affairs. He took command of the volunteer militia companies in the colonies and chaired the committee on safety in his home county. Although still opposed to rebellion, he was nonetheless preparing for it. Hermon Husband, on the other hand, had watched his rebellion against oppressive government fail at the Battle of Alamance Creek. When the Continental Congress met in Philadelphia, he was working to reestablish his farm and family on the Pennsylvania frontier. Whether ruled by Great Britain or eastern colonial elites, Husband was most concerned with the rights of poor farmers and working people. Yet he and Washington would have agreed with the great British parliamentarian Edmund Burke, who, on hearing of events in the American colonies in 1774, lamented, "Clouds, indeed, and darkness, rest upon the future."

CHAPTER **5** REVIEW

TIMELINE OF **EVENTS**

KEY **TERMS**

REVIEW & RELATE

1. How did the French and Indian War and the subsequent peace treaty affect relations among Britain, American Indian nations, and American colonies?

2. How did the French and Indian War and the increasing power of large landowners contribute to conflict between average colonists and colonial elites?

3. How did Britain's postwar policies lead to the emergence of unified colonial protests?

4. Why did British policymakers believe they were justified in seeking to gain greater control over Britain's North American colonies?

5. How and why did colonial resistance to British policies escalate in the decade following the conclusion of the French and Indian War?

6. How did internal social and economic divisions shape the colonial response to British policies?

The Boston Massacre

▶ Why did these individuals portray the events of March 5, 1770 so differently, and what do these differences suggest about how the Boston Massacre escalated tensions between British officials and colonists?

The Boston Massacre was a critical episode in the American independence movement. The origins of this skirmish between Bostonians and British troops lay in the passage of the Townshend Act in 1767, three years before the so-called massacre. The following documents reveal the chaos of that night from the differing perspectives of Bostonians and British soldiers.

There was widespread resistance to the Townshend duties, including public demonstrations, petitions, and boycotts against British goods. The situation in Boston became so tense that four thousand British troops were brought in to enforce the Townshend Act. In late February 1770, a British sympathizer tore down an anti-British poster, and an angry mob then threw stones at his house and hit his wife. The homeowner fired into the crowd and killed an eleven-year-old boy. A mass funeral for the boy set the stage for the events of March 5.

On that chilly evening, an exchange between young men and a British officer outside the Customs House escalated with supporters joining both sides. Church bells were rung, bringing more colonial sailors and soldiers to the scene (Source 5.5). Captain Thomas Preston, the officer in charge, called in reinforcements to regain control (Source 5.8). As Bostonians overwhelmed the British regulars, someone fired his gun. A number of British soldiers then followed suit, killing four men immediately, including Crispus Attucks, and seriously injuring two others (Sources 5.6 and 5.9). Some colonial leaders used the event to promote the patriot cause (Sources 5.7 and 5.8).

Within the month, as contradictory accounts circulated, Preston and eight British soldiers were indicted for murder. They were tried in October 1770. Unable to find attorneys, Preston appealed directly to patriot John Adams, who agreed to take the case to ensure a fair trial. Adams provided a strong defense (Source 5.10), resulting in the acquittal of Preston, who was tried separately, and of six of the other eight soldiers. Two soldiers were found guilty of murder, a charge later reduced to manslaughter.

Source 5.6

Deposition of William Wyatt, March 7, 1770

Just two days after the Boston Massacre, city officials began deposing dozens of witnesses to the event. They later published their descriptions as part of a pamphlet that criticized the event as a "Horrid Massacre." The following selection is from the testimony of William Wyatt and describes his version of the scene just as British soldiers were loading their weapons.

That last Monday evening, being the fifth day of March current, I was in Boston, down on Treat's wharf, where my vessel was lying, and hearing the bells ring, supposed there was a fire in the town, whereupon I hastened up to the

Town-house, on the south side of it, where I saw an officer of the army lead out of the guard-house there seven or eight soldiers of the army, and lead them down in seeming haste, to the Custom-house on the north side of King street, where I followed them, and when the officer had got there with the men, he bid them face about. I stood just below them on the left wing, and the said officer ordered his men to load, which they did accordingly, with the utmost dispatch, then they remained about six minutes, with their firelocks rested and bayonets fixed, but not standing in exact order. I observed a considerable number of young lads, and here and there a man amongst them, about the middle of the street, facing the soldiers, but not within ten or twelve feet distance from them; I observed some of them, viz., the lads, etc., had sticks in their hands, laughing, shouting, huzzaing, and crying fire; but could not observe that any of them threw anything at the soldiers, or threatened any of them. Then the said officer retired from before the soldiers and stepping behind them, towards the right wing, bid the soldiers fire; they not firing, he presently again bid 'em fire, they not yet firing, he stamped and said, "Damn your bloods, fire, be the consequence what it will"; then the second man on the left wing fired off his gun, then, after a very short pause, they fired one after another as quick as possible, beginning on the right wing; the last man's gun on the left wing flashed in the pan, then he primed again, and the people being withdrawn from before the soldiers, most of them further down the street, he turned his gun toward them and fired upon them. Immediately after the principal firing, I saw three of the people fall down in the street; presently after the last gun was fired off, the said officer, who had commanded the soldiers (as above) to fire, sprung before them, waving his sword or stick, said, "Damn ye, rascals, what did ye fire for?" and struck up the gun of one of the soldiers who was loading again, whereupon they seemed confounded and fired no more.

Source: *A Short Narrative of the Horrid Massacre in Boston Perpetrated in the Evening of the Fifth Day of March, 1770, by the Soldiers of the 29th Regiment* (Boston, 1770), republished with additional material by John Doggett Jr. (New York, 1849), 72.

Source 5.7

Account of Boston Massacre Funeral Procession, March 12, 1770

One week after the Boston Massacre, a massive public funeral was held for the four victims who had already died: Samuel Gray, Samuel Maverick, James Caldwell, and Crispus Attucks. Shops were closed, church bells marked the event in Boston and nearby Charlestown and Roxbury, and Bostonians of all ranks attended the funeral.

Last Thursday, agreeable to a general request of the inhabitants, and by the consent of parents and friends, were carried to their grave in succession, the bodies of Samuel Gray, Samuel Maverick, James Caldwell, and Crispus Attucks, the unhappy victims who fell in the bloody massacre of the Monday evening preceding!

On this occasion most of the shops in town were shut, all the bells were ordered to toll a solemn peal, as were also those in the neighboring towns of Charlestown, Roxbury, etc. The procession began to move between the hours of 4 and 5 in the afternoon; two of the unfortunate sufferers, Messrs. James Caldwell and Crispus Attucks, who were strangers [not residents of Boston], borne from Faneuil Hall, attended by a numerous train of persons of all ranks; and the other two, Mr. Samuel Gray, from the house of Mr. Benjamin Gray (his brother), on the north side of the Exchange, and Mr. Maverick, from the house of his distressed mother, Mrs. Mary Maverick, in Union Street, each followed by their respective relations and friends: The several hearses forming a junction in King Street, the theatre of the inhuman tragedy! proceeded from thence through the Main Street, lengthened by an immense concourse of people, so numerous as to be obliged to follow in ranks of six, and brought up by a long train of carriages belonging to the principal gentry of the town. The bodies were deposited in one vault in the middle burying ground. The aggravated circumstances of their death, the distress and sorrow visible in every countenance, together with the peculiar solemnity with which the whole funeral was conducted, surpass description.

Source: *Boston Gazette and Country Journal*, March 12, 1770.

Paul Revere | Etching of the Boston Massacre, 1770

Published three weeks after the Boston Massacre, Paul Revere's famous etching of the event stirred anti-British sentiment among the colonists. Revere had produced an earlier sketch that showed the position of Attucks, Caldwell, and the other men killed near the Customs House. The etching that circulated widely, however, was based on an engraving by another artist, Henry Pelham, which depicted an organized line of British soldiers firing into a crowd of unarmed colonists. At the time of the Boston Massacre, Revere was a prominent silversmith and a member of the Sons of Liberty.

Account of Captain Thomas Preston, June 25, 1770

Captain Thomas Preston, the officer in charge on March 5, was tried separately from the other soldiers. His trial centered on whether he had ordered his men to fire on the crowd. Assuming that defendants in criminal trials would perjure themselves to gain an acquittal, English legal custom prohibited them from testifying. But Preston presented his version of events to British authorities just a week after the event, strenuously denying the charges against him. That account was published in the *Boston Gazette* on March 12, 1770; later appeared in London papers; and was republished in the *Boston Evening-Post* on June 25, 1770.

On Monday night about Eight o' Clock two Soldiers were attacked and beat. But the Party of the Towns-People, in order to carry Matters to the utmost Length, broke into two Meeting-Houses, and rang the Alarm Bells, which I supposed was for Fire as usual, but was soon undeceived. About Nine some of the Guard came to and informed me, the Town-Inhabitants were assembling to attack the Troops, and that the Bells were ringing as the Signal for that Purpose, and not for Fire, and the Beacon intended to be fired to bring in the distant People of the Country. This, as I was Captain of the Day, occasioned my repairing immediately to the Main-Guard. In my Way there I saw the People in great Commotion, and heard them use the most cruel and horrid Threats against the Troops. In a few Minutes after I reached the Guard, about an hundred People passed it, and went towards the Custom-House, where the King's Money is lodged. They immediately surrounded the Sentinel posted there, and with Clubs and other Weapons threatened to execute their Vengeance on him. I was soon informed by a Townsman, their Intention was to carry off the Soldier from his Post, and probably murder him. On which I desired him to return for further Intelligence; and he soon came back and assured me he heard the Mob declare they would murder him. This I feared might be a Prelude to their plundering the King's Chest. I immediately sent a non-commissioned Officer and twelve Men to protect both the Sentinel and the King's-Money, and very soon followed myself, to prevent (if possible) all Disorder; fearing lest the Officer and Soldiery by the Insults and Provocations of the Rioters, should be thrown off their Guard and commit some rash Act. They soon rushed through the People, and, by charging their Bayonets in half Circle, kept them at a little Distance. Nay, so far was I from intending the Death of any Person, that I suffered the Troops to go to the Spot where the unhappy Affair took Place, without any Loading in their Pieces, nor did I ever give Orders for loading them. This remiss Conduct in me perhaps merits Censure; yet it is Evidence, resulting from the Nature of Things, which is the best and surest that can be offered, that my Intention was not to act offensively, but the contrary Part, and that not without Compulsion. The mob still increased, and were more outrageous, striking their clubs or bludgeons one against another, and calling out, "Come on you rascals, you bloody backs, you lobster scoundrels, fire if you dare, G–d damn you, fire and be damned; we know you dare not"; and much more such language was used. At this time I was between the soldiers and the mob, parleying with and endeavouring all in my power to persuade them to retire peaceably; but to no purpose. They advanced to the points of the bayonets, struck some of them, and even the muzzles of the pieces, and seemed to be endeavouring to close with the soldiers. On which some well-behaved persons asked me if the guns were charged. I replied, yes. They then asked me if I intended to order the men to fire. I answered no, by no means; observing to them that I was advanced before the muzzles of the men's pieces, and must fall a sacrifice if they fired; that the soldiers were upon the half-cock and charged bayonets, and my giving the word fire under those circumstances would prove me no officer. While I was thus speaking, one of the soldiers, having received a severe blow with a stick, stepped a little on one side and instantly fired, on which turning to and asking him why he fired without orders, I was struck with a club on my arm, which for some time deprived me of the use of it, which blow, had it been placed on my head, most probably would have destroyed me. On this a general attack was made on the men by a great number of heavy clubs, and snowballs being thrown at them, by which all our lives were in imminent danger; some persons at the same time from behind calling out, "Damn your bloods, why don't you fire?" Instantly three or four of the soldiers fired, one after another, and directly after three more in the same confusion and hurry.

The mob then ran away, except three unhappy men who instantly expired, in which number was Mr. Gray, at whose rope-walk the prior quarrel took place; one more is since dead, three others are dangerously, and four slightly wounded. The whole of this melancholy affair was transacted in almost 20 minutes. On my asking the soldiers why they fired without orders, they said they heard the word "Fire" and supposed it came from me. This might be the case, as many of the mob called out "Fire, fire," but I assured the men that I gave no such order, that my words were, "Don't fire, stop your firing."

Source: *Supplement to the Boston Evening-Post*, June 25, 1770.

Source 5.10

John Adams | Defense of the British Soldiers at Trial, October 1770

A descendant of Puritans, John Adams was a Harvard graduate, Enlightenment thinker, and lawyer. He wrote some of the most important legal defenses of colonial rights in response to Parliament's passage of the Stamp Act. A staunch patriot, Adams agreed to defend the British soldiers because he believed that everyone deserved a fair trial. This decision did not injure Adams's reputation. Indeed, he was elected to the Massachusetts General Court (legislature) while preparing for the trial.

I shall endeavour to make some few observations on the testimonies of the witnesses, such as will place the facts in a true point of light. . . .

The next witness is Dodge, he says, there were fifty people near the soldiers pushing at them; now the witness before says, there were twelve sailors with clubs, but now here are fifty more aiding and abetting of them, ready to relieve them in case of need; now what could the people expect? It was their business to have taken themselves out of the way; some prudent people by the Town-house told them not to meddle with the guard, but you hear nothing of this from these fifty people; no, instead of that, they were huzzaing and whistling, crying damn you, fire! why don't you fire? So that they were actually assisting these twelve sailors that made the attack; he says the soldiers were pushing at the people to keep them off, ice and snow balls were thrown, and I heard ice rattle on their guns, there were some clubs thrown from a considerable distance across the street. . . .

. . . When the multitude was shouting and huzzaing, and threatening life, the bells ringing, the mob whistling, screaming, and rending like an Indian yell, the people from all quarters throwing every species of rubbish they could pick up in the street, and some who were quite on the other side of the street throwing clubs at the whole party, Montgomery in particular smote with a club and knocked down, and as soon as he could rise and take up his firelock, another club from afar struck his breast or shoulder, what could he do? Do you expect he should behave like a stoic philosopher lost in apathy? . . . It is impossible you should find him guilty of murder. You must suppose him divested of all human passions, if you don't think him at the least provoked, thrown off his guard, and into the furor brevis [brief madness], by such treatment as this. . . .

. . . Facts are stubborn things; and whatever may be our wishes, our inclinations, or the dictates of our passions, they cannot alter the state of facts and evidence: nor is the law less stable than the fact; if an assault was made to endanger their lives, the law is clear, they had a right to kill in their own defence; if it was not so severe as to endanger their lives, yet if they were assaulted at all, struck and abused by blows of any sort, . . . this was a provocation, for which the law reduces the offence of killing, down to manslaughter, in consideration of those passions in our nature, which cannot be eradicated. To your candor and justice I submit the prisoners and their cause.

Source: Frederick Kidder, *History of the Boston Massacre, March 5, 1770* (Albany, NY: J. Munsell, 1870), 249, 252, 257–58.

Interpret the Evidence

1. What are the major similarities and differences between the testimonies of William Wyatt and Captain Preston (Sources 5.6 and 5.9)?

2. How does Revere's portrayal (Source 5.8) compare with the testimonies of Wyatt (Source 5.6) and Preston (Source 5.9)? Who was the primary audience for Revere's engraving?

3. How might the funeral procession (described in Source 5.7) have incited popular sentiment against the British before March 5?

4. Why does John Adams challenge the eyewitness accounts of the event (Source 5.10) and how is he able to convince a Boston jury to acquit most of the British soldiers?

Put It in Context

What events occurred between March 1770 and March 1774 that heightened the meaning of the Boston Massacre for colonial patriots?

Evaluate how the deaths of the five colonists and the outcome of the trial changed the way patriots and ordinary colonists viewed the British authorities.

The American Revolution

1775–1783

6

WINDOW TO THE PAST

Colonists Topple a King, 1776

On July 9, the day that New York's Provincial Congress approved the Declaration of Independence, a group of city residents gathered at a major intersection and pulled a statue of King George III to the ground. Soldiers and civilians, white and black, joined the effort to topple the king symbolically as colonists launched an effort to defeat the British by force of arms. ▸ To discover more about what this primary source can show us, see Source 6.2 on page 184.

Slaves Destroy Statue of King George III in New York City, July 1776 (detail)

After reading this chapter you should be able to:

- Explain the relationship between the beginning of armed conflict and patriots' decision to declare independence.

- Understand the choices of colonists, American Indians, and African Americans to support or oppose independence.

- Analyze the military strategies of the British and the Americans in 1776–1777, the roles that various allies played, and the importance of women and other groups on the home front.

- Explain the major accomplishments of and conflicts within the new state and federal governments during the Revolution.

- Analyze the shift of warfare to the South and West from 1778 to 1781; the importance of American Indians, foreign allies, and colonial soldiers in patriot victories there; and the challenges Americans faced once they defeated the British.

COMPARING AMERICAN HISTORIES

One of the foremost pamphleteers of the patriot cause, Thomas Paine was born in 1737 in England, where his parents trained him as a corset maker. Eventually he left home and found work as a seaman, a teacher, and a tax collector. He drank heavily and beat both his wives. Yet he also taught working-class

(left) **Thomas Paine.** Library of Congress, 3g02542
(right) **Deborah Sampson.** Granger Collection, NYC

children to read and pushed the British government to improve the working conditions and pay of tax collectors. In 1772 Paine was fired from his government job, but a pamphlet he wrote had caught the eye of Benjamin Franklin, who persuaded him to try his luck in the colonies.

Arriving in Philadelphia in November 1774 at age thirty-seven, Paine secured a job on the *Pennsylvania Magazine.* The newcomer quickly gained in-depth political knowledge of the intensifying conflicts between the colonies and Great Britain. He also gained patrons for his political tracts among Philadelphia's economic and political elite. When armed conflict with British troops erupted in April 1775, colonial debates over whether to declare independence intensified. Pamphlets were a popular means of influencing these debates, and Paine wrote one entitled *Common Sense* to tip the balance in favor of independence.

Published in January 1776, *Common Sense* proved an instant success. It provided a rationale for independence and an emotional plea for creating a new democratic republic. Paine urged colonists to separate from England and establish a political structure that would ensure liberty and equality for all Americans. "A government of our own is our natural right," he concluded. "'Tis time to part."

When *Common Sense* was published, sixteen-year-old Deborah Sampson was working as an indentured servant to Jeremiah and Susanna Thomas in Marlborough, Massachusetts. Jeremiah Thomas thought education was above the lot of servant girls, but Sampson insisted on reading whatever books she could find. However, her commitment to American independence likely developed less from reading and more from the fighting that raged in Massachusetts and drew male servants and the Thomases' five sons into the Continental Army.

When Deborah Sampson's term of service ended in 1778, she sought work as a weaver and then a teacher. In March 1782 she disguised herself as a man and enlisted in the Continental Army. Her height and muscular frame allowed her to fool local recruiters, and she accepted the bounty paid to those who enlisted. But Deborah never reported for duty, and when her charade was discovered, she was forced to return the money.

In May 1782 Sampson enlisted a second time under the name Robert Shurtliff. For the next year, Sampson, disguised as Shurtliff, marched, fought, and lived with her Massachusetts regiment. Her ability to carry off the deception was helped by lax standards of hygiene: Soldiers rarely undressed fully to bathe, and most slept in their uniforms.

Even after the formal end of the war in March 1783, Sampson/Shurtliff continued to serve in the Continental Army. That fall, she was sent to Philadelphia to help quash a mutiny by Continental soldiers angered over the army's failure to provide back pay. While there, Sampson/Shurtliff fell ill with a raging fever, and a doctor at the army hospital discovered that "he" was a woman. The doctor reported the news to General John Paterson, and Sampson was honorably discharged, having served the army faithfully for more than a year. ∎

Comparing the American histories of Thomas Paine and Deborah Sampson demonstrates how the American Revolution transformed individual lives as well as the life of the nation. Paine had failed financially and personally in England but gained fame in the colonies through his skills as a patriot pamphleteer. Sampson, who was forced into an early independence by her impoverished family, excelled as a soldier. Still, while the American Revolution offered opportunities for some colonists, it promised hardship for others. Most Americans had to choose sides long before it was clear whether the colonists could defeat Great Britain, and the long years of conflict (1775–1783) took a toll on families and communities across the thirteen colonies. Moreover, even with English converts like Paine and homegrown supporters like Sampson, the patriots would need foreign allies to achieve victory. And even battlefield victory could not ensure political stability in the new nation.

The Question of Independence

The Continental Congress that met to protest the Coercive Acts adjourned in October 1774, but delegates reconvened in May 1775. During the intervening months, patriot leaders honed their arguments for resisting British tyranny, and committees of correspondence circulated the latest news. While some patriots began advocating resistance in the strongest terms, the eruption of armed clashes between British soldiers and local farmers created the greatest push for independence. It also led the Continental Congress to establish the Continental Army in June 1775. A year later, in July 1776, the congress declared independence.

Armed Conflict Erupts. As debates over independence intensified, patriots along the Atlantic coast expanded their efforts. The Sons of Liberty and other patriot groups spread propaganda against the British, gathered and stored weapons, and organized and trained local militia companies. In addition to boycotting British goods, female patriots manufactured bandages and bullets. Some northern colonists freed enslaved African Americans who agreed to enlist in the militia. Others kept close watch on the movements of British troops.

On April 18, 1775, Boston patriots observed British movement in the harbor. British soldiers were headed to Lexington, intending to confiscate guns and ammunition hidden there and in neighboring Concord and perhaps arrest patriot leaders. To warn his fellow patriots, Paul Revere raced to Lexington on horseback but was stopped on the road to Concord by the British. By that time, however, a network of riders was spreading the alarm and alerted Concord residents of the impending danger.

Early in the morning of April 19, the first shots rang out on the village green of Lexington. After a brief exchange between British soldiers and local militiamen—known as minutemen for the speed with which they assembled—eight colonists lay dead. The British troops then marched on Concord, where they burned colonial supplies. However, patriots in nearby towns had now been alerted. Borrowing guerrilla tactics from American Indians, colonists hid behind trees, walls, and barns and battered the British soldiers as they marched back to Boston, killing 73 and wounding 200.

Word of the conflict traveled quickly. Outraged Bostonians attacked British troops and forced them to retreat to ships in the harbor. The victory was short-lived, however, and the British soon regained control of Boston. But colonial forces entrenched themselves on hills just north of the city. Then in May, Ethan Allen and his Green Mountain Boys joined militias from Connecticut and Massachusetts to capture the British garrison at Fort Ticonderoga, New York. The battle for North America had begun.

The Battle of Bunker Hill   On June 16, 1775, 2,500 British infantry sought to dislodge 1,500 patriot volunteers from Breeds Hill, 600 yards below Charlestown's strategic Bunker Hill. Although the British managed to root out the patriots during a third assault, more than a thousand British soldiers were wounded or killed. British General Thomas Gage lost his command, and the Royal Army no longer seemed invincible. akg-images

When the **Second Continental Congress** convened in Philadelphia on May 10, 1775, the most critical question for delegates like Pennsylvania patriot John Dickinson was how to ensure time for discussion and negotiation. Armed conflict had erupted, but should, or must, revolution follow? Other delegates, including Patrick Henry, insisted that independence was the only appropriate response to armed attacks on colonial residents.

Just over a month later, on June 16, British forces under General Sir William Howe attacked patriot fortifications on Breed's Hill and Bunker Hill, north of Boston. The British won the **Battle of Bunker Hill** when patriots ran out of ammunition. But the redcoats—so called because of their bright red uniforms—suffered twice as many casualties as the patriots. The victory allowed the British to maintain control of Boston for nine more months, but the heavy losses emboldened patriot militiamen.

Building a Continental Army.

The Battle of Bunker Hill convinced the Continental Congress to establish an army for the defense of the colonies. They appointed forty-three-year-old George Washington as commander in chief, and he headed to Massachusetts to take command of militia companies already engaged in battle. Since the congress had not yet proclaimed itself a national government, Washington depended largely on the willingness of local militias to accept his command and of individual colonies to supply soldiers, arms, and ammunition. Throughout the summer of 1775, Washington wrote numerous letters to patriot political leaders detailing the army's urgent need for men and supplies. He also sought to remove incompetent officers and improve order among the troops, who spent too much time carousing.

As he worked to forge a disciplined army, Washington and his officers developed a twofold military strategy. They sought to drive the British out of Boston and to secure the colonies from attack by British forces and their Indian allies in New York and Canada. In November 1775, American troops under General Richard Montgomery captured Montreal. However, the difficult trek in cold weather and the spread of smallpox decimated the patriot reinforcements led by General Benedict Arnold, and American troops failed to dislodge the British from Quebec.

Despite the disastrous outcome of the Canadian invasion, the Continental Army secured important victories in the winter of 1775–1776. To improve Washington's position in Massachusetts, General Henry Knox retrieved weapons captured at Fort Ticonderoga. In March, Washington positioned the forty-three cannons on Dorchester Heights and surprised the British with a bombardment that drove them from Boston and forced them to retreat to Nova Scotia.

Reasons for Caution and for Action.

When the British retreated from Boston, the war had already spread into Virginia. In spring 1775, local militias forced Lord Dunmore, Virginia's royal governor, to take refuge on British ships in Norfolk harbor. Dunmore encouraged white servants and black slaves to join him there, and hundreds of black men fought with British troops when the governor led his army back into Virginia in November 1775. After the Battle of Great Bridge, Dunmore reclaimed the governor's mansion and issued an official proclamation that declared "all indent[ur]ed Servants, Negroes or others (appertaining to Rebels)" to be free if they were "able and willing to bear Arms" for the British.

Dunmore's Proclamation, offering freedom to slaves who fought for the crown, reinforced other challenges to social hierarchies. During the 1760s, Baptist preachers had repudiated class and racial distinctions, and even in the South, they invited poor whites and enslaved blacks to their services. By 1775, 15 percent of whites in Virginia and hundreds of African Americans had joined Baptist churches. In England itself, a group of radicals drew on anti-authoritarian ideas developed during the English Civil War (1642–1651) to criticize British rule over its expanding empire. Through pamphlets and newspapers, their ideas circulated widely in the colonies. In addition, Enlightenment thinkers generally emphasized individual talent over inherited privilege, a view reinforced by the success of a man like Thomas Paine.

Still, many delegates at the Continental Congress, which included large planters, successful merchants, and professional men, hesitated to act. They held out hope for a negotiated settlement that would increase the colonies' political liberty without disrupting social and economic hierarchies. However, the king and Parliament refused to compromise in any way with colonies they considered in rebellion. Instead, in December 1775, the king prohibited any negotiation or trade with the colonies, increasing the leverage of radicals who argued independence was a necessity. The January 1776 publication of Thomas Paine's **Common Sense** bolstered their case. Paine wielded both biblical references and Enlightenment ideas in his best-selling pamphlet. It impressed patriot leaders as well as ordinary farmers and artisans, who debated his ideas at taverns and coffeehouses.

Explore ▶

Read some of Paine's arguments in Source 6.1.

By the spring of 1776, a growing number of patriots believed that independence was necessary. Colonies began to take control of their legislatures and instruct their delegates to the Continental Congress to support independence. Meanwhile, the congress requested economic and military assistance from France. And in May, the congress advised colonies that had not yet done so to establish independent governments.

Still, many colonists opposed the idea of breaking free from Britain. Charles Inglis, the rector at Trinity Church in New York City, insisted that "limited monarchy is the form of government which is most favorable to liberty."

Declaring Independence.   As colonists argued back and forth, Richard Henry Lee of Virginia introduced a motion to the Continental Congress in early June 1776 resolving that "these United Colonies are, and of right ought to be, Free and Independent States." A heated debate followed in which Lee and John Adams argued passionately for independence. Eventually, even more cautious delegates, like Robert Livingston of New York, were convinced. Livingston concluded that "they should yield to the torrent if they hoped to direct it." He then joined Adams, Thomas Jefferson, Benjamin Franklin, and Roger Sherman on a committee to draft a formal statement justifying independence.

The thirty-three-year-old Jefferson took the lead in preparing the declaration, building on ideas expressed by Paine, Adams, and Lee. He also drew on language used in dozens of "declarations" written by town meetings, county officials, and colonial assemblies, particularly the Virginia Declaration of Rights drafted by George Mason in May 1776. Several of these documents insisted on religious freedom since the power of faith strengthened the view of many Americans that they were uniquely blessed with liberty. Another principle central to these documents was the contract theory of government, proposed by the seventeenth-century British philosopher John Locke. Locke argued that sovereignty resided in the people, who submitted voluntarily to laws and authorities in exchange for protection of their life, liberty, and property. The people could therefore reconstitute or overthrow a government that abused its powers. Jefferson summarized this argument and then listed the

Thomas Paine | *Common Sense*, January 1776

Thomas Paine's *Common Sense* was the most widely read pamphlet supporting American independence. Paine's plain style and use of biblical allusions appealed to ordinary people and ignited the Revolutionary movement. As a government employee in England, Paine had been hired, transferred, dismissed, rehired, and dismissed again, which likely influenced his critique of the monarchy. But he offered a broader vision as well, providing colonists with a new understanding of the relationship between a government and its citizens.

Source 6.1

How does Paine characterize the role of the King in England?

In England a King hath little more to do than to make war and give away places; which, in plain terms, is to impoverish the nation, and set it together by the ears. A pretty business, indeed, for a man to be allowed eight hundred thousand sterling a year for, and worshipped into the bargain! Of more worth is one honest man to society, and in the sight of God, than all the crowned ruffians that ever lived. . . .

But where, say some, is the King of America? I will tell you, friend, he reigns above, and does not make havock of mankind like the royal brute of Great Britain. Yet that we may not appear to be defective even in earthly honors, let a day be solemnly set apart for proclaiming the charter; let it be brought forth, placed on the divine law, the word of God: let a crown be placed thereon, by which the world may know that so far we approve of monarchy, that in America,

What does Paine consider the proper relationship between the law and political authority?

THE LAW IS KING. For as in absolute governments the King is law, so in free countries the Law *ought* to be King; and there ought to be no other. But lest any ill use should afterwards arise, let the crown, at the conclusion of the ceremony, be demolished, and scattered among the people whose right it is.

A government of our own is our natural right; and when a man seriously reflects on the precariousness of his human affairs, he will become convinced, that it is infinitely wiser and safer, to form a

What system of government does Paine advocate for the American colonies?

constitution of our own in a cool deliberate manner, while we have it in our power, than to trust such an interesting event to time and chance.

Source: Thomas Paine, *Common Sense; Addressed to the Inhabitants of America* (London: H. D. Symonds, 1792), 11, 20.

Put It in Context

To whom was this 1776 pamphlet addressed, and how did it influence colonial support for independence from Britain?

abuses and crimes perpetrated by King George III against the colonies, which justified the patriots' decision to break their contract with British authorities.

Once prepared, the **Declaration of Independence** was debated and revised. In the final version, all references to slavery were removed. But delegates agreed to list among the abuses suffered by the colonies the fact that the king "excited domestic insurrections amongst us," referring to the threat posed by Dunmore's Proclamation. On July 2, 1776, delegates from twelve colonies approved the Declaration, with only New York abstaining. Independence was publicly proclaimed on July 4 when the Declaration was published as a broadside to be circulated throughout the colonies.

REVIEW & RELATE

- What challenges did Washington face when he was given command of the Continental Army?

- How and why did proponents of independence prevail in the debates that led to the Declaration of Independence?

Choosing Sides

Probably no more than half of American colonists actively supported the patriots. Perhaps a fifth actively supported the British. The rest tried to stay neutral or were largely indifferent unless the war came to their doorstep. Both patriots and loyalists included men and women from all classes and races and from both rural and urban areas.

Recruiting Supporters. Men who took up arms against the British before independence was declared and the women who supported them clearly demonstrated their commitment to the patriot cause. In some colonies, patriots organized local committees, courts, and assemblies to assume governance should British officials lose their authority. At the same time, white servants and enslaved blacks in Virginia who fled to British ships or marched with Lord Dunmore made their loyalties known as well. Some Indians, too, declared their allegiance early in the conflict. In May 1775, Colonel Guy Johnson, the British superintendent for Indian affairs, left Albany, New York and sought refuge in Canada. He was accompanied by 120 British loyalists and 90 Mohawk warriors led by their mission-educated chief, Joseph Brant (Thayendanegea).

Colonel Guy Johnson and Karonghyontye (Captain David Hill), 1776   Benjamin West painted this portrait of Colonel Johnson, British superintendent of Indian affairs, with the Mohawk chief Karonghyontye. Johnson directed joint Mohawk and British attacks against patriots during the Revolution. His red coat and musket are combined with moccasins, a wampum belt, and an Indian blanket while Karonghyontye holds a peace pipe, representing the Mohawk-British alliance before and during the war. National Gallery of Art, Washington DC, USA/Bridgeman Images

The Continental Congress, like Johnson, recognized the importance of Indians to the outcome of any colonial war. It appointed commissioners from the "United Colonies" to meet with representatives of the Iroquois Confederacy in August 1775. While Brant's group of Mohawk warriors were already committed to the British, some Oneida Indians, influenced by missionaries and patriot sympathizers, wanted to support the colonies. Others, however, urged neutrality, at least for the moment.

Once independence was declared, there was far more pressure to choose sides. The stance of political and military leaders and soldiers was clear. But to win against Great Britain required the support of a large portion of the civilian population as well. As battle lines shifted back and forth across New England, the Middle Atlantic region, and the South, civilians caught up in the fighting were faced with difficult decisions.

Many colonists who remained loyal to the king found safe haven in cities like New York, Newport, and Charleston, which remained under British control throughout much of the war. **Loyalist** men were welcomed by the British army. Still, those who made their loyalist sympathies clear risked a good deal. When British troops were forced out of cities or towns they had temporarily occupied, many loyalists faced harsh reprisals. Patriots had no qualms about invading the homes of loyalists, punishing women and children, and destroying or confiscating property.

Many loyalists were members of the economic and political elite. Others came from ordinary backgrounds. Tenants, small farmers, and slaves joined the loyalist cause in defiance of their landlords, large property owners, and wealthy planters. Many poorer loyalists lived in the Hudson valley, their sympathy for the British heightened by the patriot commitments of the powerful men who controlled the region. When the fighting moved south, many former Regulators also supported the British, who challenged the domination of patriot leaders among North Carolina's eastern elite.

Explore ▶

For images of African Americans' varied responses to the war, see Sources 6.2 and 6.3.

Perhaps most important, the majority of Indian nations ultimately sided with the British. The Mohawk, Seneca, and Cayuga nations in the North and the Cherokee and Creek nations in the South were among Great Britain's leading allies. Although British efforts to limit colonial migration, such as the Proclamation Line of 1763, had failed, most Indian nations still believed that a British victory offered the only hope of ending further encroachments on their territory.

Choosing Neutrality.
Early in the war, many Indian nations proclaimed their neutrality. This included the Delaware and Shawnee in the Ohio River valley and the Oneida in Connecticut. The Oneida's chief warriors declared that the English and patriots were "*two brothers of one blood. We are unwilling to join on either side in such a contest.*" But patriots often refused to accept Indian neutrality. Indeed, colonial troops killed the Shawnee chief Cornstalk under a flag of truce in 1777, leading that nation to ally, finally, with the British.

Colonists who sought to remain neutral during the war also faced hostility. Some 80,000 Quakers, Mennonites, Amish, Shakers, and Moravians considered war immoral and embraced neutrality. These men refused to bear arms, hire substitutes, or pay taxes to new state governments. The largest number of religious pacifists lived in Pennsylvania. Despite Quakerism's deep roots there, pacifists were treated as suspect by both patriots and loyalists.

African Americans in New York City Amid the Upheavals of 1776

On July 9, the day New York's Provincial Congress approved the Declaration of Independence, a rowdy crowd of soldiers and civilians toppled a statue of King George III. However, an etching of the event presents it as the work of African Americans, with most whites simply observing (Source 6.2). In a second etching, by François Xavier Haberman (Source 6.3), Manhattan burns only days after British troops occupied the city. The fire, which may have been purposely set, burnt a mile-long swath. Here, redcoats beat suspected patriots while white and black residents carry items from burning buildings.

Source 6.2

Slaves Destroy Statue of King George III in New York City, July 1776

Library of Congress, LC-DIG-ppmsca-17521

Source 6.3

A Fire Burns British-Occupied New York City, September 1776

Library of Congress, 3b48304

Interpret the Evidence

1. Why might an American artist depict the destruction of the statue of King George III as the work mainly of blacks? What roles are whites playing in this portrayal?
2. What meanings might be attached to black and white residents carrying items out of burning buildings after the British occupation of Manhattan? Why are the blacks here and in Source 6.2 shown as barely clothed?

Put It in Context

Given the limited choices available to most African Americans during the American Revolution, what advantages or disadvantages were created when the patriots or the British gained control of areas where they lived?

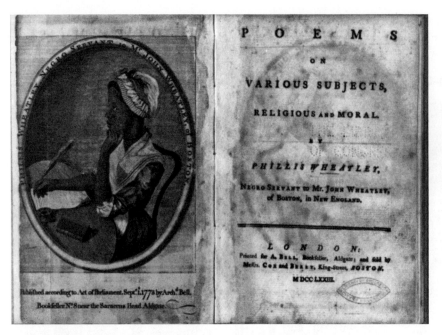

Phillis Wheatley   This portrait of Phillis Wheatley appears facing the title page of her book of poems, printed in London in 1773. It was painted by another Boston slave, Scipio Moorhead. Phillis Wheatley converted to Christianity and sided with the patriots in the Revolution. She won her freedom but never gained sufficient support to publish another book of poems. Library of Congress, 3b04682

Explore ▶

For two historians' perspectives on what led colonists to revolt against British rule, see Sources 6.4 and 6.5

In June 1778, Pennsylvania authorities jailed nine Mennonite farmers who refused to take an oath of allegiance to the revolutionary government. Their worldly goods were sold by the state, leaving their wives and children destitute. Quakers were routinely fined and imprisoned for refusing to support the patriot cause and harassed by British authorities in the areas they controlled. At the same time, Quaker meetings regularly disciplined members who offered aid to either side. Betsy Ross was among those disowned Quakers. Her husband joined the patriot forces, and she sewed flags for the Continental Army and Navy.

Committing to Independence.
After July 4, 1776, the decision to support independence took on new meaning. If the United States failed to win the war, all those who actively supported the cause could be considered traitors. The families of Continental soldiers faced especially difficult decisions as the conflict spread and soldiers moved farther and farther from home. Men too old or too young to fight proved their patriotism by gathering arms and ammunition and patrolling local communities.

Some female patriots accompanied their husbands or fiancés as camp followers, cooking, washing clothes, nursing, and providing other services for soldiers. Most patriot women remained at home, however, and demonstrated their commitment by raising funds, gathering information, and sending clothes, bedding, and other goods to soldiers at the front. The Continental Army was desperately short of supplies from the beginning of the war. Northern women were urged to increase cloth production, while southern women were asked to harvest crops for hungry troops. The response was overwhelming. Women in Hartford, Connecticut produced 1,000 coats and vests and 1,600 shirts in 1776 alone. Across the colonies, women collected clothing door-to-door and opened their homes to sick and wounded soldiers.

Some African American women also became ardent patriots. Phillis Wheatley of Boston, whose owners taught her to read and write, published a collection of poems in 1776 and sent a copy to General Washington. She urged readers to recognize Africans as children of God. Rewarded with freedom by her master, Wheatley was among a small number of blacks who actively supported the patriot cause. Still, the vast majority of blacks labored as slaves. While some escaped and joined the British in hopes of gaining their freedom, most were not free to choose sides.

REVIEW & RELATE

- How did colonists choose sides during the Revolutionary War? What factors influenced their decisions?
- Why would some Indian tribes try to stay neutral during the conflict? Why did most of those who chose sides support the British?

Fighting for Independence, 1776–1777

After July 4, 1776, battles between British and colonial troops intensified, but it was not until December that the patriots celebrated a major military victory. The rebellion faced a formidable set of challenges. Over the course of the eighteenth century, Great Britain had developed the world's most powerful military force, including a huge navy. Moreover, once independence was declared, the colonists lost their main trading partner and had to find ways to sustain their economy while funding a war. To succeed, the patriots needed support from men and women on the home front as well as the battlefront and assistance from Europeans experienced in fighting the British. It took two yearsfor the patriots and the Continental Army to gain traction against British forces.

British Troops Gain Early Victories. In the summer of 1776, when General Washington tried to lead his army out of Boston to confront British troops set to invade New York City, many soldiers deserted and returned home. They believed that New York men should defend New York. Among the soldiers who remained with Washington, many were landless laborers whose wives and sisters followed the troops as their only means of support. Although Washington considered these camp followers undesirable, the few hundred women provided critical services to ordinary soldiers. Ultimately, Washington arrived in New York with 19,000 men, many of whom were poorly armed and poorly trained and some of whom were coerced into service by local committees of safety.

Meanwhile, throughout the summer British ships sailed into New York harbor or anchored off the coast of Long Island. General Howe, hoping to overwhelm the colonists, ordered 10,000 troops to march into the city in the weeks immediately after the Declaration of Independence was signed. Still, the Continental Congress rejected Howe's offer of peace and a royal pardon.

So Howe prepared to take control of New York City by force and then march up the Hudson valley, isolating New York and New England from the rest of the rebellious colonies. He was aided by some 8,000 Hessian mercenaries (Germans being paid to fight for the British). On August 27, 1776, British forces clashed with a far smaller contingent of Continentals on Long Island. More than 1,500 patriots were killed or wounded in the fierce fighting.

SECONDARY SOURCE ANALYSIS

Americans Decide to Revolt against British Rule

Historians have long debated why, between the years 1774 and 1776, a large number of American colonists decided to revolt against British rule. Until 1774, colonists protested British policies, such as taxes or impressment, but hoped to reform, not overthrow, the imperial system. By 1776, however, a significant percentage of American colonists changed course and demanded independence from the British Crown. The question for historians is what are the most important factors that account for this change.

Source 6.4

Bernard Bailyn, The Importance of Ideas, 1967

[T]he American Revolution was above all else an ideological, constitutional, political struggle. . . . [The pamphlets read for this study] confirmed . . . my belief that the intellectual developments in the decade before Independence led to a radical idealization and conceptualization of the previous century and half of American experience, and that it was this intimate relationship between Revolutionary thought and the circumstances in eighteenth-century America that endowed the Revolution with its peculiar force and made it so profoundly a transforming event. . . .

The pamphlets . . . reveal the influence of Enlightenment thought, and . . . show the effective force of certain religious ideas, of the common law, and also of classical literature; but they reveal most significantly the close integration of these elements . . . [with] still another tradition. . . . This distinctive influence had been transmitted most directly to the colonists by a group of early eighteenth-century radical publicists and opposition politicians in England who carried forward into the eighteenth century . . . the peculiar strain of anti-authoritarianism bred in the upheaval of the English Civil War. . . .

[T]he fear of a comprehensive conspiracy against liberty throughout the English-speaking world—a conspiracy believed to have been nourished in corruption, and of which, it was felt oppression in America was only the most immediately visible part—lay at the heart of the Revolutionary movement. . . .

For the primary goal of the American Revolution . . . was not the overthrow or even the alteration of the existing social order but the preservation of political liberty. . .

Source: Bernard Bailyn, *The Ideological Origins of the American Revolution* (Cambridge: Belknap Press of Harvard University Press, 1967), pp. vi–ix and 19.

By November, the British had captured Fort Lee in New Jersey and attacked the Continental Army at Fort Washington, north of New York City. Meanwhile Washington led his weary troops and camp followers into Pennsylvania, while the Continental Congress, fearing a British attack on Philadelphia, fled to Baltimore.

Although General Howe might have ended the patriot threat right then by an aggressive campaign, he wanted to wear down the Continental Army and force the colonies to sue for peace. Washington did not have the troops or arms to launch a major assault, and

Source 6.5

Timothy H. Breen, Insurgents Mobilize, 2010

The [essence] of our Revolution—indeed, of any successful revolution—was the willingness of a sufficient number of people to take up arms against an unelected imperial government that no longer served the common good. This moment occurred in America sometime in mid-1774. . . .

Insurgencies are not movements for the faint of heart. They certainly involve a lot more than a commitment to a set of intellectual principles. What is demanded of us, therefore, is a greater appreciation of the kinds of passions that have energized insurgencies throughout world history. Our revolutionary lexicon will include popular anger and rage, and a feeling of betrayal—harsh concepts perhaps, but ones that better reflect the actual revolutionary process than do those encountered in abstract histories of political thought.

The argument is not that insurgents did not have ideas about politics. They did. But these were ideas driven by immediate passions; they were amplified through fear, fury and resentment. Moreover, evangelical religion played a much larger role in motivating revolutionary resistance than most historians have recognized. . . .

To be sure, the insurgents did not fight for democracy, but by inviting so many new participants into the political process on the local level and by rejecting a monarchical system of government, with its attendant aristocratic privilege, they transformed the colonial political culture. Thousands of Americans . . . invented new, highly effective forms of popular resistance. . . .

Revolutions do not sustain themselves through ideas alone. . . . [T]he evidence of ordinary Americans mobilizing in response to parliamentary insults and an army of occupation, forging common bonds of sympathy throughout all thirteen colonies, and creating an infrastructure to support and drive forward revolution in the years ahead of the Declaration of Independence is overwhelming.

Source: Timothy H. Breen, *American Insurgents, American Patriots: The Revolution of the People* (New York: Hill & Wang, 2010), pp. 10–12 and 16.

Examine the Sources

1. How do Bailyn and Breen differ in their interpretation of why Americans chose to revolt against British rule in the mid-1770s?
2. What evidence from this chapter supports the view of Bailyn or Breen as to why so many Americans embraced the idea of revolution from 1774 to 1776?

Put It in Context

How would you weigh the importance of the ideas promoted by patriot leaders and the anger and resentment that fueled popular support not only during 1774–1776 but also over the course of the Revolutionary War?

---

he hoped that the British would accept American independence once they saw the enormous effort it would take to defeat the colonies. So the war continued.

Patriots Prevail in New Jersey. The Continental Army did not gain a single military victory between July and December 1776. Fortunately for Washington, Howe followed the European tradition of waiting out the winter months and returning to combat after the spring thaw. This gave the patriots the opportunity to regroup, repair weapons and wagons, and recruit soldiers. Yet Washington was reluctant to face the cold and discomfort of winter with troops discouraged by repeated defeats and retreats.

Camped in eastern Pennsylvania, Washington learned that Hessian troops had been sent to occupy the city of Trenton, New Jersey, just across the Delaware River. On Christmas Eve, Washington attacked Trenton in an icy rain, and the Continentals quickly routed the surprised Hessians. They then marched on Princeton and defeated regular British troops on January 3, 1777. The British army soon retreated from New Jersey, settling back into New York City, and the Continental Congress returned to Philadelphia. By mid-January 1777, it seemed clear to both sides that the conflict would be harder, more costly, and more deadly than anyone had imagined.

A Critical Year of Warfare.
The British army emerged from winter camp in spring 1777. Its regular army units, American loyalists, Indian allies, Hessians, and naval men-of-war were concentrated largely in New York City and Canada. The Continental forces, numbering fewer than 5,000 men, were then entrenched near Morristown, New Jersey. With his troops ravaged by smallpox over the winter, Washington feared that an aggressive British assault might succeed.

Meanwhile, the Continental Congress had returned to Philadelphia, but members feared that the British would seek to capture the city and split the United States in two. General Howe did indeed plan on capturing Philadelphia, hoping to force a patriot surrender. Although Washington's force was too small to defeat Howe's army, it delayed his advance by guerrilla attacks and skirmishes. En route, Howe learned that he was expected to reinforce General John Burgoyne's soldiers, who were advancing south from Canada. Instead he continued to Philadelphia and captured it in September 1777. Meanwhile Burgoyne and his 7,200 troops regained control of Fort Ticonderoga on July 7. He continued south, but by late July his forces had to stop until supplies from Canada and reinforcements from Howe and General Barry St. Leger reached them.

St. Leger was marching his troops east through New York State, and Joseph Brant and his sister Molly Brant were gathering a force of Mohawk, Seneca, and Cayuga warriors to support them. But on August 6, they suffered a stunning defeat. In the **Battle of Oriskany** in New York, a band of German American farmers led by General Nicholas Herkimer held off the British advance, allowing General Arnold to reach nearby Fort Stanwix with reinforcements. On August 23, the British and Indian troops retreated to Canada (Map 6.1).

When General Howe's reinforcements also did not materialize, Burgoyne faced a brutal onslaught from patriot forces. In September patriots defeated the British at Freeman's Farm, with the British suffering twice the casualties of the Continentals. Fighting intensified in early October, when Burgoyne lost a second battle at Freeman's Farm. Ten days later, he surrendered his remaining army of 5,800 men to General Gates at nearby Saratoga, New York.

The Continental Army's victory in the **Battle of Saratoga** stunned the British. It undercut the significance of Howe's victory at Philadelphia and indicated the general's misunderstanding of the nature of the war he was fighting. Meanwhile, the patriot victory energized Washington and his troops as they dug in at Valley Forge for another long winter. It also gave Benjamin Franklin, the Continental Congress envoy to Paris, greater leverage for convincing French officials to support American independence.

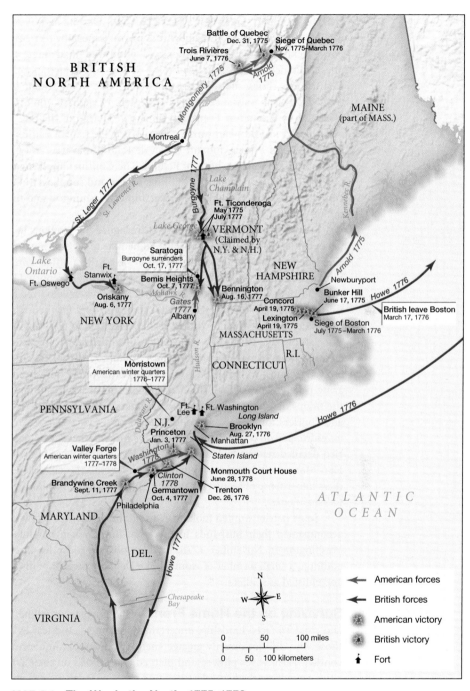

MAP 6.1   The War in the North, 1775–1778
After early battles in Massachusetts, patriots invaded Canada but failed to capture Quebec. The British army captured New York City in 1776 and Philadelphia in 1777, but New Jersey remained a battle zone through 1778. Meanwhile General Burgoyne secured Canada for Britain and then headed south, but his forces were defeated by patriots at the crucial Battle of Saratoga.

Patriots Gain Critical Assistance. Despite significant Continental victories in the fall of 1777, the following winter proved especially difficult. The quarters at **Valley Forge** were again marked by bitter cold, poor food, inadequate clothing, and scarce supplies. A French volunteer arrived to see "a few militia men, poorly clad, and for the most part without shoes; many of them badly armed." Many recent recruits were also poorly trained. Critical assistance arrived with Baron Friedrich von Steuben, a Prussian officer recruited by Benjamin Franklin, who took charge of drilling soldiers. Other officers experienced in European warfare also joined the patriot cause that winter: the Marquis de Lafayette of France, Johann Baron de Kalb of Bavaria, and Thaddeus Kosciusko and Casimir Count Pulaski, both of Poland. The Continental Army continued to be plagued by problems of recruitment, discipline, wages, and supplies. But the contributions of foreign volunteers, along with the leadership of Washington and his officers, sustained the military effort.

Patriots on the home front were also plagued by problems in 1777–1778. Families living in battlefield areas were especially vulnerable to the shifting fortunes of war. When British troops captured Philadelphia in fall 1777, a British officer commandeered the home of Elizabeth Drinker, a Quaker matron. An angry Drinker reported that the officer moved in with "3 Horses 2 Cows 2 Sheep and 3 Turkeys." Women who lived far from the conflict were isolated from such intrusions but were forced to fend for themselves with husbands at the front. Meanwhile, wives of patriot leaders, anxious to end the conflict, formed voluntary associations, like the Ladies Association of Philadelphia, to provide critical resources for the army. **See Primary Source Project 6: Women in the Revolution, page 204.**

While most women worked tirelessly on the home front, some cast their fate with the army. Camp followers continued to provide critical services to the military and suffered, as the troops did, from scarce supplies and harsh weather. Some women also served as spies and couriers for British or Continental forces. Lydia Darragh, a wealthy Philadelphian, eavesdropped on conversations among the British officers who occupied her house and carried detailed reports to Washington hidden in the folds of her dress. Others, like Nancy Hart Morgan of Georgia, took more direct action. Morgan lulled half a dozen British soldiers into a sense of security at dinner, hid their guns, and shot two before neighbors came to hang the rest.

Some patriot women took up arms on the battlefield. A few, such as Margaret Corbin, accompanied their husbands to the front lines. When her husband was killed at Fort Washington in November 1776, Corbin took his place loading and firing cannons. In addition, a small number of women, like Deborah Sampson, disguised themselves as men and enlisted as soldiers.

Surviving on the Home Front. Whether black or white, enslaved or free, women and children faced hardship, uncertainty, loneliness, and fear as a result of the war. Even those who did not directly engage enemy troops took on enormous burdens during the conflict. Farm wives plowed and planted and carried on their domestic duties as well. In cities, women worked ceaselessly to find sufficient food, wood, candles, and cloth to maintain themselves and their children.

As the war intensified, Continental and British forces slaughtered cattle and hogs for food, stole corn and other crops or burned them to keep the enemy from obtaining supplies, looted houses and shops, and kidnapped or liberated slaves and servants. Some home invasions turned savage. Both patriot and loyalist papers in New York, Philadelphia, and Charleston reported cases of rape.

In these desperate circumstances, many women asserted themselves in order to survive. When merchants hoarded goods in order to make greater profits from rising prices, housewives raided stores and warehouses and took the supplies they needed. Others learned as much as they could about family finances and submitted reports to local officials when their houses, farms, or businesses were damaged or looted. Growing numbers of women banded together to assist one another, help more impoverished families, and supply troops with badly needed clothes, food, bandages, and bullets.

REVIEW & RELATE

- How did the patriot forces fare in 1776? How and why did the tide of war turn in 1777?
- What role did colonial women and foreign men play in the conflict in the early years of the war?

Governing in Revolutionary Times

Amid the constant upheavals of war, patriot leaders established new governments. At the national level, responsibilities ranged from coordinating and funding military operations to developing diplomatic relations with foreign countries and Indian nations. At the state level, constitutions had to be drafted and approved, laws enforced, and military needs assessed and met. Whether state or national, new governments had to assure their followers that they were not simply replacing old forms of oppression with new ones. Yet few states moved to eliminate the most oppressive institution in the nation, slavery.

Colonies Become States. For most of the war, the Continental Congress acted in lieu of a national government while the delegates worked to devise a more permanent structure. But the congress had depended mainly on states for funds and manpower. Delegates did draft the **Articles of Confederation** in 1777, creating a central government with limited powers. They submitted them to the states for approval, and eight of the thirteen states ratified the plan for a national government by mid-1778. But nearly three more years passed before the last state, Maryland, approved the Articles.

Without a formal central government, state governments played crucial roles throughout the war. Even before the Continental Congress declared American independence, some colonies had forced royal officials to flee and established new state governments. Some states abided by the regulations in their colonial charters or by English common law. Others created new governments based on a written constitution.

These constitutions reflected the opposition to centralized power fueled by the struggle against British tyranny. In Pennsylvania, patriots developed one of the most democratic constitutions. The governor was replaced by an executive council. The legislature consisted of a single house elected by popular vote. Legislators could only serve for four in any seven years to discourage the formation of a political aristocracy. Although Pennsylvania's constitution was among the most radical, all states limited centralized power in some way.

Thus, most states, adopting Virginia's model, included in their constitutions a bill of rights that ensured citizens freedom of the press, freedom of elections, speedy trials by one's peers, humane punishments, and the right to form militias. Some states also insisted on people's freedom of speech and assembly, the right to petition and to bear arms, and equal protection of the laws. The New Jersey constitution of 1776 enfranchised all free inhabitants who met the property qualifications, thereby allowing some single and widowed women and free blacks to vote. However, most new state constitutions allowed only white men with property to vote, and nearly all granted significant power to the legislative branch, where white men of property dominated.

Patriots Divide over Slavery.

Although state constitutions were revolutionary in many respects, few of them addressed the issue of slavery. Only Vermont abolished slavery in its 1777 constitution. Legislators in Pennsylvania approved a gradual abolition law by which slaves born after 1780 could claim their freedom at age twenty-eight. In Massachusetts, two slaves sued for their freedom in county courts in 1780–1781. Quock Walker, who had been promised his emancipation by a former master, sued his current master to gain his freedom. About the same time, an enslaved woman, Mum Bett, who was the widow of a Revolutionary soldier, initiated a similar case. Mum Bett won her case and changed her name to Elizabeth Freeman. When Walker's owner appealed the local court's decision to free his slave, the Massachusetts Supreme Court cited Mum Bett's case and ruled that slavery conflicted with the state constitution.

In southern states like Virginia, the Carolinas, and Georgia, however, life for slaves grew increasingly harsh during the war. Because British forces promised freedom to blacks who fought with them, slave owners and patriot armies in the South did everything possible to ensure that African Americans did not make it behind British lines. When the British retreated, some generals, like Lord Dunmore and Sir Henry Clinton, took black volunteers with them. But thousands more were left behind to fend for themselves.

Nonetheless, the American Revolution dealt a blow to human bondage. For many blacks, Revolutionary ideals required the end of slavery. Northern free black communities grew rapidly during the war,

The Marquis de La Fayette with an Aide-de-Camp This eighteenth-century portrait of the Marquis de Lafayette was painted by a Frenchman during the Revolution. It shows him with his aide-de-camp, probably from the French West Indies. Lafayette joined the Continental Army in September 1777, led patriot forces in numerous battles, camped at Valley Forge, and trapped British forces under General Cornwallis at the decisive Siege of Yorktown. Musée de la Ville de Paris, Musée Carnavalet, Paris, France/Archives Charmet/Bridgeman Images

especially in seaport cities. In the South, too, thousands of slaves gained freedom, either by joining the British army or by fleeing in the midst of battlefield chaos. As many as one-quarter of South Carolina's slaves had emancipated themselves by the end of the Revolution. Yet as the Continental Congress worked toward developing a framework for a national government, few delegates considered the abolition of slavery a significant issue.

France Allies with the Patriots.

The Continental Congress considered an alliance with France far more critical to patriot success than the issue of slavery. France's long rivalry with Britain made it a likely ally, and the French government had secretly provided funds to the patriots early in the war. In December 1776, the Continental Congress sent Benjamin Franklin to Paris to serve as its unofficial liaison. Franklin was enormously successful, securing supplies and becoming a favorite among the French aristocracy and ordinary citizens alike.

But the French were initially unwilling to forge a formal compact with the upstart patriots. Only after the patriot victory at Saratoga in October 1777 did King Louis XVI agree to an alliance. In February 1778, Franklin secured an agreement that approved trading rights between the United States and all French possessions. France then recognized the United States as an independent nation, relinquished French territorial claims on mainland North America, and sent troops to reinforce the Continental Army. In return, the United States promised to defend French holdings in the Caribbean. A year later, Spain allied itself with France to protect its own North American holdings.

British leaders responded by declaring war on France. Yet doing so ensured that military conflicts would spread well beyond North America and military expenditures would skyrocket. French forces attacked British outposts in Gibraltar, the Bay of Bengal, Senegal in West Africa, and Grenada in the West Indies. At the same time, the French supplied the United States with military officers, weapons, funds, and critical naval support.

Faced with this new alliance, Britain's prime minister, Lord North (1771–1782), decided to concentrate British forces in New York City. This tactic forced the British army to abandon Philadelphia in summer 1778. For the remainder of the war, New York City provided the sole British stronghold in the North, serving as a supply center and prisoner-of-war camp.

Raising Armies and Funds.

The French alliance did create one unintended problem for the Continental Army. When Americans heard that France was sending troops, fewer men volunteered for military service. Local officials had the authority to draft men into the army or to accept substitutes for draftees. In the late 1770s, some draftees forced enslaved men to take their place; others hired landless laborers, the handicapped, or the mentally unfit as substitutes.

As the war spread south and west in 1778–1779, Continental forces were stretched thin, and enlistments faltered further. Soldiers faced injuries, disease, and shortages of food and ammunition. They also risked capture by the British, one of the worst fates to befall a Continental. Considered traitors by the British, most captives were held on ships in New York harbor. They faced filthy accommodations, a horrid stench, inadequate water, and widespread disease and abuse. Altogether, between 8,000 and 11,500 patriots died in British prisons in New York—more than died in battle.

Even if the British had allowed the Continental Congress to aid prisoners, it could do little, given the financial problems it faced. With no authority to impose taxes on American citizens, the congress had to borrow money from wealthy patriots, accept loans from France and the Netherlands, and print money of its own—some $200 million by 1780. However, money printed by the states was used far more widely than were Continental dollars. "Continentals" depreciated so quickly that by late 1780 it took one hundred continentals to buy one silver dollar's worth of goods. In 1779, with the cost of goods skyrocketing, housewives, sailors, and artisans in Philadelphia and other cities attacked merchants who were hoarding goods, forcing officials to distribute food to the poor.

The congress finally improved its financial standing slightly by using a $6 million loan from France to back certificates issued to wealthy patriots. Meanwhile states raised money through taxes to provide funds for government operations, backing for its paper money, and other expenses. Most residents found such taxes incredibly burdensome given wartime inflation, and even the most patriotic began to protest increased taxation. Thus the financial status of the new nation remained precarious.

Indian Affairs and Land Claims.
The congress also sought to settle land claims in the western regions of the nation and build alliances with additional Indian nations. The two issues were intertwined, and both were difficult to resolve. Most Indian nations had long-standing complaints against colonists who intruded on their lands, and many patriot leaders made it clear that independence would mean further expansion.

In the late 1770s, British forces and their Indian allies fought bitter battles against patriot militias and Continental forces all along the frontier. Each side destroyed property, ruined crops, and killed civilians. In the summer and fall of 1778, Indian and American civilians suffered through a series of brutal attacks in Wyoming, Pennsylvania; Onoquaga, New York; and Cherry Valley, New York. Patriots and Indians also battled along the Virginia frontier after pioneer and militia leader Daniel Boone established a fort there in 1775. In the South, 6,000 patriot troops laid waste to Cherokee villages in the Appalachian Mountains in retaliation for the killing of white intruders along the Watauga River by a renegade Cherokee warrior, Dragging Canoe.

Regardless of Indian rights, much western land had already been claimed by individual states like Connecticut, Georgia, New York, Massachusetts, and Virginia. These states hoped to use western lands to reward soldiers and expand their settlements. However, states without such claims, like Maryland, argued that if such lands were "wrested from the common enemy by the blood and treasure of the thirteen States," they should be considered "common property, subject to be parcelled out by Congress into free and independent governments." In 1780 New York State finally ceded its western claims to the Continental Congress, and Connecticut and Massachusetts followed suit.

With land disputes settled, Maryland ratified the Articles of Confederation in March 1781. A new national government was finally formed, unifying the rebellious states just as it appeared they would gain their independence. Still, the congress's guarantee that western lands would be "disposed of for the common benefit of the United States" ensured continued conflicts with Indians as the Confederation government took charge.

REVIEW & RELATE

What values and concerns shaped state governments during the Revolutionary War?

What issues and challenges did the Continental Congress face even after the French joined the patriot side?

Winning the War and the Peace, 1778–1783

From 1778 to 1781, the battlefront in the Revolution moved south and west. The king, who believed that southern colonists' sympathies were more loyalist than patriot, insisted on pursuing a southern strategy. At the same time, patriot conflicts with Britain and its Indian allies intensified along the western frontier. The patriots' eventual victory rested on a combination of superb strategy, their French and Spanish allies, and the continued support of affluent men and women. Still, even after Britain's surrender in October 1781, the war dragged on while peace terms were negotiated. The celebrations following the signing of a peace treaty were themselves tempered by protests among Continental soldiers demanding back pay and by the realization of the new nation's looming problems.

Fighting in the West. While the congress debated the fate of western land claims, battles continued in the Ohio and Mississippi River valleys. The British commander at Fort Michilimackinac on Lake Huron recruited Sioux, Chippewa, and Sauk warriors to attack Spanish forces along the Mississippi, while soldiers at Fort Detroit armed Ottawa, Fox, and Miami warriors to assault American settlers flooding into the Ohio River valley. British forces also moved deeper into this region, establishing a post at Vincennes on the Wabash River.

The response to these British forays was effective, if not well coordinated. In 1778 a patriot surveyor, George Rogers Clark of Virginia, organized an expedition to counter Indian raids in the West and to reinforce Spanish and French allies in the upper Mississippi valley. He fought successfully against British and Indian forces at Kaskaskia and Cahokia on the Mississippi River. Then Clark launched a surprise attack on British forces at Vincennes. Although Detroit remained in British hands, Spanish troops defeated British-allied Indian forces at St. Louis, giving the patriots greater control in the Ohio River valley (Map 6.2).

Patriot General John Sullivan employed the same tactic in central New York, leading a 1779 campaign to wipe out British allies by destroying Mohawk, Seneca, Cayuga, and Onondaga villages. As Mary Jemison, an Irish immigrant captured by Indians in 1755, recalled, "they destroyed every article of the food kind that they could lay their hands on. A part of our corn they burnt, and threw the remainder into the river. They burnt our houses, killed what few cattle and horses they could find, destroyed our fruit trees, and left nothing but the bare soil and timber." Sullivan temporarily ended attacks by Britain's Iroquois allies and disrupted supplies sent out by British forces at Fort Niagara. However, over the next two years, Iroquois warriors and British troops attacked several white settlements in central and eastern New York, killing or capturing dozens of American colonists. In 1782, such retaliatory violence in Ohio led to an atrocity at a Moravian mission. There Pennsylvania militiamen massacred 160

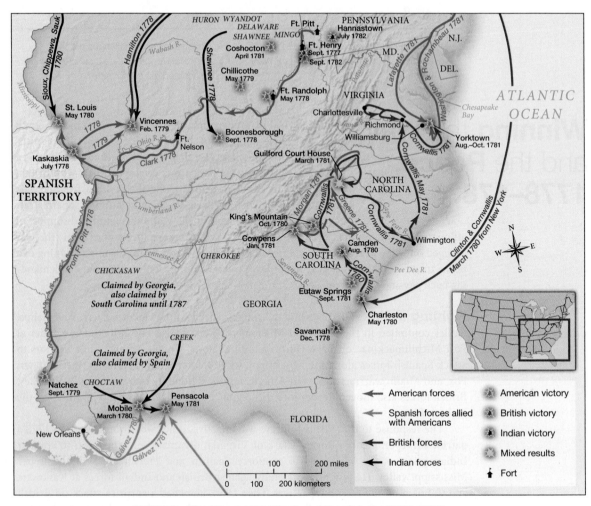

MAP 6.2 The War in the West and the South, 1777–1782

Between 1780 and 1781, major battles between Continental and British troops took place in Virginia and the Carolinas, and the British general Cornwallis finally surrendered at Yorktown, Virginia in October 1781. But patriot forces also battled British troops and their Indian allies from 1777 to 1782 in the Ohio River valley, the lower Mississippi River, and the Gulf coast.

Delaware men, women, and children. They had refused to fight on either side but had assisted patriots as guides and spies.

Battles between Indian nations and American settlers did not end with the American Revolution. For the moment, however, the patriots and their allies had defeated British and Indian efforts to control the Mississippi and Ohio River valleys.

War Rages in the South. Meanwhile British troops sought to regain control of southern states from Georgia to Virginia. British troops captured Savannah, Georgia in 1778 and soon extended their control over the entire state. When General Clinton was called north later that year, he left the southern campaign in the hands of Lord Charles Cornwallis.

In May 1780, General Cornwallis reclaimed Charleston, South Carolina. He then evicted patriots from the city, purged them from the state government, gained military control of the state, and imposed loyalty oaths on all Carolinians able to fight. To aid his efforts, local loyalists organized militias to battle patriots in the interior. Banastre Tarleton led one especially vicious company of loyalists who slaughtered civilians and murdered many who surrendered. In retaliation, patriot planter Thomas Sumter organized 800 men who showed a similar disregard for regular army procedures, raiding largely defenseless loyalist settlements near Hanging Rock, South Carolina in August 1780.

As retaliatory violence erupted in the interior of South Carolina, General Gates marched his Continental troops south to join 2,000 militiamen from Virginia and North Carolina. But his troops were exhausted and short of food, and on August 16 Cornwallis won a smashing victory against the combined patriot forces at Camden, South Carolina (see Map 6.2). Soon after news of Gates's defeat reached General Washington, he heard that Benedict Arnold, commander at West Point, had defected to the British.

Suddenly, British chances for victory seemed more hopeful. Cornwallis was in control of Georgia and South Carolina, and local loyalists were eager to gain control of the southern countryside. Meanwhile Continental soldiers in the North mutinied in early 1780 over enlistment terms and pay. Patriot morale was low, funds were scarce, and civilians were growing weary of the war.

"Crossing the Peedee River" Francis Marion, known as "the Swamp Fox," and his militia waged guerilla war against the British in South Carolina. They wreaked havoc by conducting quick surprise attacks. In this 1850 painting, Marion, a Patriot icon, is crossing the river with horses, soldiers, equipment, and enslaved laborers. He sits on the reddish-brown horse with his uniform visible under his brown cloak. William T. Ranney (1813-1857); Marion Crossing the Peedee; 1850; Oil on canvas; Amon Carter Museum of American Art, Fort Worth, Texas; 1983.126

Yet somehow the patriots prevailed. A combination of luck, strong leadership, and French support turned the tide. In October 1780, when Continental hopes looked especially bleak, a group of 800 frontier sharpshooters routed loyalist troops at King's Mountain in South Carolina. The victory kept Cornwallis from advancing into North Carolina and gave the Continentals a chance to regroup.

Shortly after the battle at King's Mountain, Washington sent General Nathanael Greene to replace Gates as head of southern operations. Taking advice from local militia leaders like Daniel Morgan and Francis Marion, Greene divided his limited force into even smaller units. Marion and Morgan each led 300 Continental soldiers into the South Carolina backcountry, picking up hundreds of local militiamen along the way. At the village of Cowpens, Morgan inflicted a devastating defeat on Tarleton's much larger force.

Despite their victory, Continental forces were spread thin and retreated in order to regroup. Cornwallis, enraged at the patriot victory, pursued these Continental forces, but his troops had outrun their cannons, and Greene circled back and attacked them at Guilford Court House. Although Cornwallis eventually forced the far smaller Continental company to withdraw from the battlefield, British troops suffered enormous losses. In August 1781, frustrated at the ease with which patriot forces still found local support in the South, he hunkered down in Yorktown on the Virginia coast and waited for reinforcements from New York.

Washington now coordinated strategy with his French allies. Comte de Rochambeau marched 5,000 troops south from Rhode Island to Virginia as General Lafayette led his troops south along Virginia's eastern shore. At the same time, French naval ships headed north from the West Indies. One unit cut off a British fleet trying to resupply Cornwallis by sea. Another joined up with American privateers to bombard Cornwallis's forces. By mid-October, British supplies had run out, and it was clear that reinforcements would not be forthcoming. On October 19, 1781, the British army admitted defeat.

An Uncertain Peace. The Continental Army had managed the impossible. It had defeated the British army and won the colonies' independence. Yet even with the surrender after the **Battle of Yorktown**, the war continued in fits and starts. Peace negotiations in Paris dragged on as French, Spanish, British, and American representatives sought to settle a host of issues. Meanwhile, British forces challenged Continental troops in and around New York City.

Some Continental soldiers continued to fight, but others focused on the long-festering issue of overdue wages. When the congress decided in June 1783 to discharge the remaining troops without providing back pay, a near mutiny erupted in Pennsylvania. Nearly three hundred soldiers marched on the congress in Philadelphia. Washington sent troops, including Deborah Sampson/Robert Shurtliff, to put down the mutiny. Bloodshed was avoided when the Pennsylvania soldiers agreed to accept half pay and certificates for the remainder. Despite this compromise, the issue of back pay would continue to plague the nation.

Meanwhile patriot representatives in Paris—Benjamin Franklin, John Adams, and John Jay—continued to negotiate peace terms. Rising antiwar sentiment on the British home front forced the government's hand. But the Comte de Vergennes, the French foreign minister, opposed the Americans' republican principles and refused to consider the American delegates as his political equals. Given the importance of the French to the American victory, the congress had instructed its delegates to defer to French wishes. This blocked the American representatives from signing a separate peace with the British.

Eventually, however, U.S. delegates finalized a treaty that secured substantial benefits for the young nation. The United States gained control of all lands south of Canada and north of Louisiana and Florida stretching to the Mississippi River. In addition, the treaty recognized the United States to be "free Sovereign and independent states." Spain signed a separate treaty with Great Britain in which it regained control of Florida. Despite their role in the war, none of the Indian nations that occupied the lands under negotiation were consulted.

When the **Treaty (Peace) of Paris** was finally signed on September 2, 1783, thousands of British troops and their supporters left the colonies for Canada, the West Indies, or England. British soldiers on the western frontier were supposed to be withdrawn at the same time, but they remained for many years and continued to foment hostilities between Indians in the region and U.S. settlers along the frontier.

The evacuation of the British also entailed the exodus of thousands of African Americans who had fought against the patriots. At the end of the war, British officials granted certificates of manumission (freedom) to more than 1,300 men, 900 women, and 700 children. Most of these freed blacks settled in Nova Scotia, where they received small allotments of land from the British, but they generally lacked the resources to make such homesteads profitable. Despite these obstacles, some created a small Afro-Canadian community in Nova Scotia, while others migrated to areas considered more hospitable to black residents, such as Sierra Leone.

A Surprising Victory. Americans had managed to defeat one of the most powerful military forces in the world. That victory resulted from the convergence of many circumstances. Certainly Americans benefited from fighting on their own soil. Their knowledge of the land and its resources as well as earlier experiences fighting against Indians and the French helped prepare them for battles against the British.

Just as important, British troops and officers were far removed from centers of decision making and supplies. Even supplies housed in Canada could not be easily transported the relatively short distance into New York. British commanders were often hesitant to make decisions independently, but awaiting instructions from England proved costly on several occasions, especially since strategists in London often had little sense of conditions in America.

Both sides depended on outsiders for assistance, but here, too, Americans gained the advantage. The British army relied heavily on German mercenaries, Indian allies, and freed blacks to bolster its regular troops. In victory, such "foreign" forces were relatively reliable, but in defeat, many of them chose to look out for their own interests. The patriots meanwhile marched with French and Spanish armies well prepared to challenge British troops and motivated to gain advantages for France and Spain if Britain was defeated.

Perhaps most important, a British victory was nearly impossible without conquering the American colonies one by one. Because a large percentage of colonists supported the patriot cause, British troops had to contend not only with Continental soldiers but also with an aroused citizenry fighting for its independence.

REVIEW & RELATE

• How and why did the Americans win the Revolutionary War?

• What uncertainties and challenges did the new nation face in the immediate aftermath of victory?

Conclusion: Legacies of the Revolution

After the approval of the Declaration of Independence, Thomas Hutchinson, the British official who had gained fame during the Stamp Act upheavals in Boston, charged that patriot leaders had "sought independence from the beginning." But the gradual and almost reluctant move from resistance to revolution in the American colonies suggests otherwise. When faced with threats from British troops, a sufficient number of colonists took up arms to create the reality of war, and this surge of hostilities finally gave the advantage to those political leaders urging independence.

The victory over Great Britain won that independence but left the United States confronting difficult problems. Most soldiers simply wanted to return home and reestablish their former lives. But the government's inability to pay back wages and the huge debt the nation owed to private citizens and state and foreign governments hinted at difficult economic times ahead. And these problems affected American Indians and African Americans as well as whites. Using western lands to reward officers and soldiers who had not received full pay intensified conflicts along the new nation's western frontier. Warfare between settlers and Indians west of the Appalachian Mountains, from the Ohio River valley to Georgia, continued for decades. At the same time, slaveowners seeking more fertile fields also expanded into the trans-Appalachian region. By 1800 they had carried tens of thousands of enslaved blacks into Kentucky, Tennessee, and the Mississippi Territory. Separated from families back east, slaves on the frontier engaged in backbreaking labor without the support or camaraderie of the communities left behind.

Although faced with far better opportunities than enslaved laborers, many white soldiers still found the adjustment to postwar life difficult. Like many other soldiers, Deborah Sampson embraced a conventional life after the war. She married a farmer, Benjamin Gannett, and had three children. But times were hard. A decade after she was discharged, Massachusetts finally granted her a small pension for her wartime service. Deborah Gannett earned some money by lecturing on her wartime adventures and received a small federal pension in 1804. Many men waited at least as long to receive any compensation for their wartime service while they struggled to reestablish farms and businesses and pay off debts accrued while fighting for independence.

Political leaders tried to address the concerns of former soldiers and ordinary citizens while they developed a new government. Within a few years of achieving independence, financial distress among small farmers and tensions with Indians on the western frontier intensified concerns about the ability of the confederation government to secure order and prosperity. While some patriots demanded a new political compact to strengthen the national government, others feared replicating British tyranny.

In the decade following the Revolution, leading patriots engaged in heated disagreements over the best means to unify and stabilize the United States. However, key leaders like Thomas Jefferson, Benjamin Franklin, and John Adams were living abroad as ambassadors, strengthening U.S. ties to Britain and France. In 1787 Thomas Paine, too, left for England, where he wrote pamphlets supporting the French Revolution. He eventually moved to France, but his radical political ideas led to his imprisonment there, and he returned to the United States upon his release. Even here, however, Paine was maligned for his attacks on organized religion and private property. Thus he played no part in the intense debates about how to secure the political future of the United States while holding on to the republican impulses that drove Americans to revolution.

TIMELINE OF EVENTS

April 19, 1775	Battles of Lexington and Concord
June 1775	Continental Congress establishes Continental Army
June 16, 1775	Battle of Bunker Hill
August 1775	Representatives of Continental Congress and Iroquois Confederacy meet
November 1775	Lord Dunmore issues his proclamation
January 1776	Thomas Paine publishes *Common Sense*
July 4, 1776	Continental Congress publicly declares independence
July to mid-December 1776	British forces defeat Continental Army
December 1776– January 1777	Patriot victories at Trenton and Princeton
October 1777	Patriot victory at Saratoga
Winter 1777–1778	Continental Army encamps at Valley Forge
1778	Articles of Confederation ratified by eight states
February 1778	France declares alliance with the United States
Summer 1779	Patriot forces destroy Iroquois villages
1780	Elizabeth "Mum Bett" Freeman sues for freedom
1780–1781	Iroquois warriors and British troops attack New York settlements
March 1781	Articles of Confederation ratified
October 19, 1781	British surrender at Yorktown, Virginia
September 2, 1783	Treaty (Peace) of Paris

KEY TERMS

Second Continental Congress, *179*

Battle of Bunker Hill, *179*

Dunmore's Proclamation, *179*

Common Sense, *180*

Declaration of Independence, *182*

loyalist, *183*

Battle of Oriskany, *190*

Battle of Saratoga, *190*

Valley Forge, *192*

Articles of Confederation, *193*

Battle of Yorktown, *200*

Treaty (Peace) of Paris, *201*

REVIEW & RELATE

1. What challenges did Washington face when he was given command of the Continental Army?

2. How and why did proponents of independence prevail in the debates that led to the Declaration of Independence?

3. How did colonists choose sides during the Revolutionary War? What factors influenced their decisions?

4. Why would some Indian tribes try to stay neutral during the conflict? Why did most of those who chose sides support the British?

5. How did the patriot forces fare in 1776? How and why did the tide of war turn in 1777?

6. What role did colonial women and foreign men play in the conflict in the early years of the war?

7. What values and concerns shaped state governments during the Revolutionary War?

8. What issues and challenges did the Continental Congress face even after the French joined the patriot side?

9. How and why did the Americans win the Revolutionary War?

10. What uncertainties and challenges did the new nation face in the immediate aftermath of victory?

Women in the Revolution

▶ What did women gain from the opportunities created by the American Revolution, and which women gained, or lost, the most?

The Revolutionary War had a tremendous impact on the lives of women, just as women helped shape the course of that conflict. As in all wars, women faced the fear and hardships brought on by absent men, inadequate supplies, roaming enemy soldiers, and nearby battles. But the war also expanded opportunities for women in the public sphere. They ran family farms and shops, raised money, and produced homespun goods for the Continental Army while defending themselves and their homes. Some women spied on enemy encampments, provided medical care for soldiers, and even fought alongside men on the battlefield. Many women gained new skills, felt pride in their independence and abilities, and, like their male counterparts, gained satisfaction and sometimes fame in supporting the cause in which they believed. Although many cast their efforts in a political light, patriot leaders failed to treat them as equal partners in the revolution.

The following documents reflect a wide variety of women's Revolutionary-era experiences. Some women, like Christian Barnes (Source 6.6), remained loyal to Great Britain and suffered attacks by patriot neighbors and soldiers. Bett, however, an enslaved African, turned revolutionary rhetoric to her advantage and sued for her own independence (Source 6.10). Abigail Adams, wife of the patriot leader John Adams, sought greater rights for all women, though she could only plead with her husband to take action (Source 6.8). Other women with connections to patriot political and military leaders carried messages behind British lines and raised funds for

Continental troops (Sources 6.7 and 6.9). Women contributed significantly to the patriot victory, but they also faced serious challenges.

Source 6.6

Christian Barnes | Letter to Elizabeth Inman, April 29, 1775

As the conflict intensified between Great Britain and America, colonists were forced to choose sides. Whether patriots or loyalists, women were often terrorized by enemy soldiers. One such woman was Christian Barnes, the wife of a well-known loyalist who fled to Marlborough, Massachusetts to avoid capture by the colonial government. The following selection is from a letter written by Barnes in the spring of 1775, in which she describes a frightening visit by a colonial soldier.

It is now a week since I had a line from my dear Mrs. Inman, in which time I have had some severe trials, but the greatest terror I was ever thrown into was on Sunday last. A man came up to the gate and loaded his musket, and before I could determine which way to run he entered the house and demanded a dinner. I sent him the best I had upon the table. He was not contented, but insisted upon bringing in his gun and dining with me; this terrified the young folks, and they ran out of the house. I went in and endeavored to pacify him by every method in my power, but I found it was to no purpose. He still continued to abuse me, and said that when he had eat his dinner he should want a horse and if I did not let him have one he would blow my brains out. He pretended to have an order from the General for one of my horses, but did not produce it. His language was so dreadful and his looks so frightful that I could not remain in the house, but fled to the store and locked myself in. He followed me and declared he would break the door open. Some people very luckily passing to meeting prevented his doing any mischief and staid by me until he was out of sight, but I did not recover from my fright for several days. The sound of drum or the sight of a gun put me into such a tremor that I could not command myself. I have met with but little molestation since this affair, which I attribute to the protection sent me by Col. Putnam and Col. Whitcomb. I returned them a card of thanks for their goodness tho' I knew it was thro' your interest I obtained this favor. . . . The people here are weary at his [Mr. Barnes's] absence, but at the same time give it as their opinion that he could not pass the guards. . . . I do not doubt but upon a proper remonstrance I might procure a pass for him through the Camp from our two good Colonels. . . . I know he must be very unhappy in Boston. It was never his intention to quit the family.

Source: Nina M. Tiffany, ed., *Letters of James Murray, Loyalist* (Boston, 1901), 187–88.

Source 6.7

Deborah Champion | Letter to Patience, October 2, 1775

Deborah Champion was the daughter of Henry Champion, a high-ranking officer in the Continental Army. In the fall of 1775, she traveled from Connecticut to Boston to deliver secret messages from her father to George Washington. Accompanied by a family slave named Aristarchus, she was stopped by British troops several times during her journey. Several days after her return home, she described the adventure in a letter to a friend, excerpted here.

Father laid his hand on my shoulder, (a most unusual caress with him) and said almost solemnly, "Deborah I have need of thee. Hast thee the courage to go out and ride, it may be even in the dark and as fast as may be, till thou comest to Boston town?" He continued, "I do not believe Deborah, that there will be actual danger to threaten thee, else I would not ask it of thee, but the way is long, and in part lonely. I shall send Aristarchus with thee and shall explain to him the urgency of the business. Though he is a slave, he understands the mighty matters at stake, and I shall instruct him yet further. There are reasons why it is better for you a woman to take the despatches I would send than for me to entrust them to a man; else I should send your brother Henry. Dare you go? . . ."

Everywhere we heard the same thing, love for the Mother Country, but stronger than that, that she *must* give us our rights, that we were fighting not for independence, though that might come and would be the war-cry if the oppression of unjust taxation was not removed. Nowhere was a cup of imported tea offered us. It was a glass of milk, or a cup of "hyperion" the name they gave to a tea made of raspberry leaves. We heard that it would be almost impossible to avoid the British, unless by going so far out of the way that too much time would be lost, so plucked up what courage I could as darkness began to come on at the close of the second day. I secreted the papers in a small pocket in a saddle bag under some eatables that mother had put up. We decided to ride all night. Providentially the moon just past full, rose about 8 o'clock and it was not unpleasant, for the roads were better. I confess that I began to be weary. It was late at night or rather very early in the morning, that I heard a sentry call and knew that if at all the danger point was reached. I pulled my calash [a large hood] as far over my face as I could, thanking my wise mother's forethought, and went on with what boldness I could muster. I really believed I heard Aristarchus' teeth chatter as he rode to my side and whispered "De British missus for sure." Suddenly I was ordered to halt. As I could not help myself I did so. A soldier in a red coat appeared and suggested that I go to headquarters for examination. I told him "It was early to wake his Captain and to please let me pass for I had been sent in urgent haste to see a friend in need," which was true, if a little ambiguous. To my joy he let me go saying "Well, you are only an old woman any way." Evidently as glad to be rid of me as I of him.

Source: Deborah Champion to Patience, 2 October 1775, in *Women's Letters: America from the Revolutionary War to the Present*, ed. Lisa Grunwald and Stephen J. Adler (New York: Dial Press, 2005), 25–28.

Abigail Adams | Letter to John Adams, March 31, 1776

Abigail Adams wrote detailed letters to John Adams while he was serving as a delegate to the Continental Congress in Philadelphia. She moved to Braintree, Massachusetts during the British occupation of Boston but described conditions in the city and surrounding area. She often highlighted the difficulties that the civilian population faced and their responses to them. But Abigail Adams also discussed specifically political matters, as here where she calls on her husband to grant women more legal rights under the new government.

D o not you want to see Boston; I am fearfull of the small pox, or I should have been in before this time. I got Mr. Crane to go to our House and see what state it was in. I find it has been occupied by one of the Doctors of a Regiment, very dirty, but no other damage has been done to it . . . am determined to get it cleand as soon as possible. . . .

I feel very differently at the approach of spring to what I did a month ago. We knew not then whether we could plant or sow with safety, . . . but now we feel as if we might sit under our own vine and eat the good of the land. . . .

I long to hear that you have declared an independency—and by the way in the new Code of Laws which I suppose it will be necessary for you to make I desire you would Remember the Ladies, and be more generous and favourable to them than your ancestors. Do not put such unlimited power into the hands of the Husbands. Remember all Men would be tyrants if they could. If perticuliar care and attention is not paid to the Laidies we are determined to foment a Rebelion, and will not hold ourselves bound by any Laws in which we have no voice, or Representation.

That your Sex are Naturally Tyrannical is a Truth so thoroughly established as to admit of no dispute, but such of you as wish to be happy willingly give up the harsh title of Master for the more tender

and endearing one of Friend. Why then, not put it out of the power of the vicious and the Lawless to use us with cruelty and indignity with impunity.

Source: Abigail Adams to John Adams, March 31–April 5, 1776, Adams Family Papers, Massachusetts Historical Society, Digital Adams Project, http://www.masshist.org/digitaladams/archive/doc?id=L17760331aa&bc=%2Fdigitaladams%2Farchive%2Fbrowse%2Fletters_1774_1777.php.

Esther De Berdt Reed | The Sentiments of an American Woman, 1780

Esther De Berdt Reed lived in England until her marriage to merchant Joseph Reed in 1770. Joseph was a leading Philadelphia patriot and was elected president (governor) of Pennsylvania during the war. In June 1780, Esther Reed, the mother of five young children and recently recovered from smallpox, called on women to aid the Continental Army. Her broadside "The Sentiments of an American Woman" was the foundation of the Ladies Association of Philadelphia, whose members raised large sums by soliciting contributions from women door-to-door.

W ho knows if persons disposed to censure, and sometimes too severely with regard to us, may not disapprove our appearing acquainted even with the actions of which our sex boasts? We are at least certain, that he cannot be a good citizen who will not applaud our efforts for the relief of the armies which defend our lives, our possessions, our liberty? . . .

We know that at a distance from the theatre of war, if we enjoy any tranquility, it is the fruit of your watchings, your labours, your dangers. If I live happy in the midst of my family; if my husband cultivates his field, and reaps his harvest in peace; if, surrounded with my children, I myself nourish the youngest, and press it to my bosom, without being affraid of seeing myself separated from it, by a ferocious enemy; if the house in which we dwell; if our barns, our orchards are safe at the present time from the hands of those incendiaries, it is to you that we owe it. And shall we hesitate to evidence to you our gratitude? Shall we hesitate to wear a cloathing more simple; hair dressed less elegant, while at the price of this small privation, we shall deserve your benedictions. Who, amongst us, will not renounce with the highest pleasure, those vain ornaments, when she shall consider that the valiant defenders of America will be able to draw some advantage from the money which she may have laid out in these; that they will be better defended from the rigours of the seasons, that after their painful toils, they will receive some extraordinary and unexpected relief; that these presents will perhaps be valued by them at a greater price, when they will have it in their power to say: *This is the offering of the Ladies.* The time is arrived to display the same sentiments which animated us at the beginning of the Revolution, when we renounced the use of teas, however agreeable to our taste, rather than receive them from our persecutors; when we made it appear to them that we placed former necessaries in the rank of superfluities, when our liberty was interested; when our republican and laborious hands spun the flax, prepared the linen intended for the use of our soldiers; when exiles and fugitives we supported with courage all the evils which are the concomitants of war. Let us not lose a moment; let us be engaged to offer the homage of our gratitude at the altar of military valour, and you, our brave deliverers, while mercenary slaves combat to cause you to share with them, the irons with which they are loaded, receive with a free hand our offering, the purest which can be presented to your virtue,

BY AN AMERICAN WOMAN

Source: Esther De Berdt Reed, "The Sentiments of an American Woman" (Philadelphia: John Dunlop, 1780).

Source 6.10

Elizabeth "Mum Bett" Freeman, 1811

Bett, a slave, sued her owner John Ashley, Esq., for her freedom with the aid of lawyer Theodore Sedgwick. She may have been inspired to act by her mistress's beating of her sister Lizzie or by overhearing conversations about the new Massachusetts state constitution, which declared "all men . . . free and equal." A jury at the Berkshire County Court of Common Pleas set her free in 1781, after which she worked for the Sedgwick family for three decades. This portrait was painted by Susan Anne Ridley Sedgwick, Theodore's daughter-in-law, when Freeman, then known as Mum Bett, was sixty-nine years old.

© Massachusetts Historical Society, Boston, MA, USA/Bridgeman Images

Interpret the Evidence

1. What types of activities did female patriots undertake in the service of American independence (Sources 6.7, 6.8, 6.9, and 6.10)? What challenges did female loyalists face (Source 6.6)?

2. How did assumptions about the proper roles of elite white women prior to the war shape their experiences during the Revolution and affect the ways they described those experiences (Sources 6.6, 6.7, 6.8, and 6.9)?

3. How did Deborah Champion, Abigail Adams, Esther De Berdt Reed, and Bett (Elizabeth Freeman) create new opportunities for themselves during the Revolution (Sources 6.7, 6.8, 6.9, and 6.10)?

4. What dangers or constraints did women face during the war, and how did they justify the public actions they took?

Put It in Context

How would you compare white women's experiences of the American Revolution to those of African American and American Indian women and to the experiences of white men?

How did the efforts of patriot women shape the outcome of the war?

7

Forging a New Nation

1783–1800

WINDOW TO THE PAST

Eleventh Pillar Of The Great National Dome

During 1788, the thirteen states held conventions to decide whether to ratify the plan for the federal government laid out under the new Constitution. Newspapers followed the proceedings closely, and many created visual images to track the progress of ratification. The *Massachusetts Centinel*, shown here, used Greek pillars to represent each state. ▶ To discover more about what this primary source can show us, see Source 7.10 on page 244.

After reading this chapter you should be able to:

- Analyze the major threats to the new nation after the Revolution.

- Explain which groups of Americans were marginalized in this period and how they responded to the changes that occurred.

- Describe the chief debates over the Constitution and its ratification.

- Evaluate the ways that the young nation's economic policies affected its relations with European nations abroad and on the U.S. frontier and fostered competing political views.

- Describe how the presidency of John Adams exacerbated differences between Federalists and Democratic-Republicans and led to Thomas Jefferson's election in 1800.

COMPARING AMERICAN HISTORIES

One of six children born to Irish parents in Hopkinton, Massachusetts, Daniel Shays received little formal education. In 1772, age twenty-five, he married, had a child, and settled into farming. But in April 1775, he, his father, and his brother raced toward Concord to meet the British forces. By June, he was among the patriots defending Bunker Hill.

After distinguished service in the Continental Army, Shays purchased a farm in Pelham, Massachusetts

(*left*) **Daniel Shays**. Granger, NYC
(*right*) **Alexander Hamilton**. Library of Congress, 3g06423

in 1780 and hoped to return to a normal life. Instead, economic turmoil roiled the region and the nation. Many farmers had fallen into debt while fighting for independence. They returned to an economic recession and increased taxes as state governments labored to repay wealthy creditors and fund their portion of the federal budget. In western Massachusetts, many farmers faced eviction. Shays kept his farm and represented his town at county conventions that petitioned the state government for economic relief. However, the legislature largely ignored the farmers' concerns.

In 1786, angered by the state's failure to act, armed groups of farmers attacked courthouses throughout western Massachusetts. Although a reluctant leader, Shays headed the largest band of more than a thousand farmer-soldiers. In January 1787, this group headed to the federal arsenal at Springfield, Massachusetts to seize guns and ammunition. The farmers were routed by state militia and pursued by governor James Bowdoin's army. Many rebel leaders were captured; others, including Shays, escaped to Vermont and New York. Four were convicted and two were hanged before Bowdoin granted amnesty to the others in hopes of avoiding further conflict.

This uprising, known as Shays's Rebellion, alarmed many state and national leaders who feared such insurgencies might emerge elsewhere. Among those outraged by the rebels was Alexander Hamilton, a young New York politician. Hamilton was born illegitimate and impoverished in the British West Indies. Orphaned at eleven, he was apprenticed to a firm of merchants that sent him to the American colonies. There Hamilton was drawn into the activities of radical patriots and joined the Continental Army in 1776.

During the war, Hamilton fell in love with Elizabeth Schuyler, who came from a wealthy New York family. They married in December 1780. After the war, Hamilton used military and marital contacts to establish himself as a lawyer and financier in New York City. In 1786, Hamilton was elected to the New York State legislature, where he focused on improving the state's finances, and served as a delegate to a convention on interstate commerce held in Annapolis, Maryland. Hamilton and several other delegates advocated a stronger central government. They pushed through a resolution calling for a second convention "to render the constitution of the Federal Government adequate to the exigencies of the Union."

Although the initial response to the call was lukewarm, the eruption of Shays's Rebellion and the government's financial problems soon convinced many political leaders that change was necessary. Although Hamilton played only a small role in the 1787 convention in Philadelphia, he worked tirelessly for ratification of the Constitution drafted there. When the new federal government was established in 1789, Hamilton became the nation's first secretary of the treasury. ■

Comparing the histories of Daniel Shays and Alexander Hamilton demonstrates that the patriots may have come together to win the Revolutionary War but that they did not share a common vision of the new nation. Despite the suppression of Shays's Rebellion, the grievances that fueled the uprising persisted and Americans differed significantly over how best to resolve them. By 1787, demand for a stronger central government led to the ratification of a new U.S. Constitution. Hamilton played a leading role in advocating and establishing the new government, particularly by seeking to stabilize and strengthen the national economy. While many political and economic elites applauded his efforts, other national leaders and many ordinary citizens opposed them. These differences, exacerbated by foreign and frontier crises, eventually led to the development of competing political parties and the first contested presidential election in American history.

Financial, Frontier, and Foreign Problems

The United States faced serious financial instability in its formative years. The situation was so desperate that Continental Army officers threatened to march on the confederation congress if they did not receive their pay. Other issues also threatened the emerging nation. Conflicts between settlers and Indians in western areas forced the confederation government to attend more closely to its frontier territories. Meanwhile, Spain closed the port of New Orleans to U.S. trade as individual states struggled to regulate domestic and foreign commerce. Off the coast of North Africa, Barbary pirates attacked U.S. merchant ships. Clearly, diplomatic relations with European powers were crucial but difficult, given America's outstanding war debts and the relative weakness of the confederation government.

Continental Officers Threaten Confederation.
As the American Revolution ground to an end, issues of military pay sparked conflict. Uprisings by ordinary soldiers were common but successfully put down. Complaints from Continental officers, however, posed a greater problem. In 1780 they had extracted a promise from the Continental Congress for half pay for life but had received no compensation since. Officers encamped at Newburgh, New York, awaiting a peace treaty, petitioned the confederation government in December 1782 for back pay for themselves and their soldiers, again with no success. By March 1783, most soldiers had returned home without pay, but some five hundred officers remained at

Newburgh. Many confederation leaders were sympathetic to the officers' plight and hoped to use pressure from this formidable group to enhance the powers of the congress.

Alexander Hamilton had been pressing state governments to grant the confederation congress a new duty of 5 percent on imported goods, thereby providing the federal government with an independent source of revenue. Perhaps threats of an uprising by officers could convince states like New York to agree to the collection of this import duty. Quietly encouraged by political supporters, dissident officers circulated veiled threats of a military takeover. However, on March 15 the officers were confronted by General George Washington. In an emotional speech, he urged them to respect civilian control of the government. Most officers quickly retreated from their "infamous propositions." At the same time, congressional leaders promised the officers full pay for five years. However, lacking sufficient funds, they could provide only "commutation certificates," promising future payment.

Indians, Land, and the Northwest Ordinance.

One anonymous petitioner at Newburgh suggested that the officers move as a group to "some unsettled country" and let the confederation fend for itself. In reality, no such unsettled country existed beyond the thirteen states. Numerous Indian nations and growing numbers of American settlers claimed control of western lands. In 1784 some two hundred Indian leaders from the Iroquois, Shawnee, Creek, Cherokee, and other nations gathered in St. Louis, where they complained to the Spanish governor that the Americans were "extending themselves like a plague of locusts."

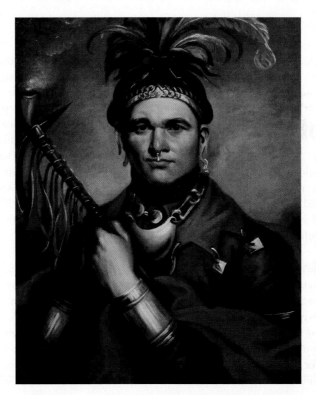

Cornplanter, Seneca Chief Cornplanter, son of a white father and Seneca mother, fought with the British during the Revolution. Afterward, however, he argued that Indians must adapt to American control. He helped negotiate three treaties that ceded large tracts of Indian land to the U.S. government, arousing opposition from more militant leaders. This 1796 portrait by an Italian artist suggests his mixed heritage. New York Historical Society/ Getty Images

Despite the continued presence of British and Spanish troops in the Ohio River valley, the United States hoped to convince Indian nations that it controlled the territory. In October 1784, U.S. commissioners met with Iroquois delegates at Fort Stanwix, New York and demanded land cessions in western New York and the Ohio valley. When the Seneca chief Cornplanter and other leaders refused, the commissioners insisted that "you are a subdued people" and must submit. An exchange of gifts and captives taken during the Revolution finally ensured the deal. Indian leaders not at the meeting disavowed the **Treaty of Fort Stanwix**. But the confederation government insisted it was legal, and New York State began surveying and selling the land. With a similar mix of negotiation and coercion, U.S. commissioners signed treaties at Fort McIntosh, Pennsylvania (1785), and Fort Finney, Ohio (1786), claiming lands held by the Wyandots, Delawares, Shawnees, and others.

Explore ▶

See Source 7.1 for a pan-Indian perspective on relations with the U.S. government.

As eastern Indians were increasingly pushed into the Ohio River valley, they crowded onto lands already claimed by other nations. Initially, these migrations increased conflict among Indians, but eventually some leaders used this forced intimacy to launch pan-Indian movements against further American encroachment on their land.

Indians and U.S. political leaders did share one concern: the vast numbers of squatters, mainly white men and women, living on land to which they had no legal claim. In fall 1784 George Washington traveled west to survey nearly thirty thousand acres of territory he had been granted as a reward for military service. He found much of it occupied by squatters who refused to acknowledge his ownership. Such flaunting of property rights deepened his concerns about the weaknesses of the confederation government.

The confederation congress was less concerned about individual property rights and more with the refusal of some states to cede the western lands they claimed to federal control. Slowly, between 1783 and 1785, the congress finally persuaded the two remaining states with the largest claims, Virginia and Massachusetts, to relinquish all territory north of the Ohio River (Map 7.1).

To regulate this vast territory, Thomas Jefferson drafted the **Northwest Ordinance** in 1785. It provided that the territory be surveyed and divided into adjoining townships. He hoped to carve nine small states out of the region to enhance the representation of western farmers and to ensure the continued dominance of agrarian views in the national government. The congress revised his proposal, however, stipulating that only three to five states be created from the vast territory and thereby limiting the future clout of western settlers in the federal government.

The population of the territory grew rapidly, with speculators buying up huge tracts of land and selling smaller parcels to eager settlers. In response, congressional leaders modified the Northwest Ordinance in 1787, clarifying the process by which territories could become states. The congress appointed territorial officials and guaranteed residents the basic rights of U.S. citizens. After a territory's population reached 5,000, residents could choose an assembly, but the territorial governor retained the power to veto legislation. When a prospective state reached a population of 60,000, it could apply for admission to the United States. Thus the congress established an orderly system by which territories became states in the Union.

The 1787 ordinance also tried to address concerns about race relations in the region. It encouraged fair treatment of Indian nations but did not include any means of enforcing

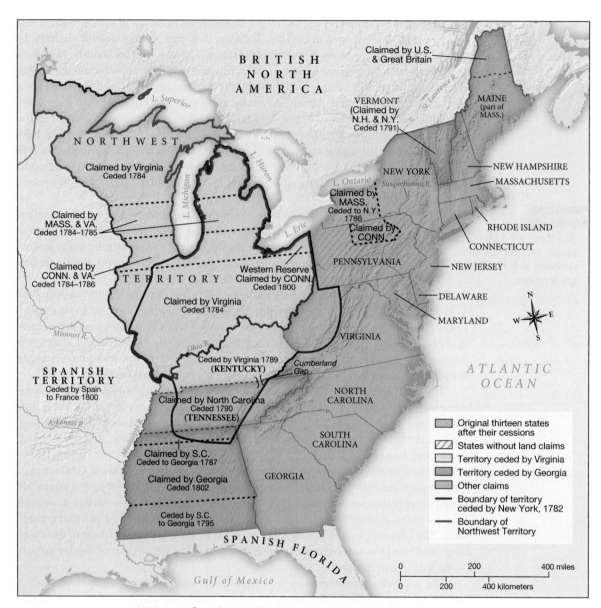

MAP 7.1   Cessions of Western Land, 1782–1802

Beginning under the Articles of Confederation, political leaders sought to resolve competing state claims to western territory based on colonial charters. The confederation congress and, after ratification of the Constitution, the U.S. Congress gradually persuaded states to cede their claims and create a "national domain," part of which was then organized as the Northwest Territory.

> **GUIDED ANALYSIS**

United Indian Nations Council | Message to Congress, 1786

Following the Revolutionary War, one of the most pressing issues that the confederation government faced was the disposition of western lands. Although the U.S. government negotiated with a number of Indian tribes to gain clear title to western lands, it often negotiated in secret with only a few leaders and backed negotiations with the threat of force. A pan-Indian council meeting was called in 1786 at which various leaders stated their concerns about the confederation government's actions. The speech was addressed to the confederation congress and expressed the Indians' united stance and their hopes for fair and open dealings with the United States.

Source 7.1

To the Congress of the United States of America:

Brethren of the United States of America: It is now more than three years since peace was made between the King of Great Britain and you, but we, the Indians, were disappointed, finding ourselves not included in that peace, according to our expectations: for we thought that its conclusion would have promoted a friendship between the United States and Indians, and that we might enjoy that happiness that formerly subsisted between us and our elder brethren. . . . In the course of our councils, we imagined we hit upon an expedient that would promote a lasting peace between us.

> How would you characterize the tone of this speech? What might this suggest about the Indians' purpose and audience?

   Brothers: We are still of the same opinion as to the means which may tend to reconcile us to each other; and we are sorry to find, although we had the best thoughts in our minds, during the beforementioned period, mischief has, nevertheless, happened between you and us. We are still anxious of putting our plan of accommodation into execution, and we shall briefly inform you of the means that seem most probable to us of effecting a firm and lasting peace and reconciliation: the first step towards which should, in our opinion, be, that all treaties carried on with the United States, on our parts, should be with the general voice of the whole confederacy, and carried on in the most open manner, without any restraint on either side; and especially as landed matters are often the subject of our councils with you, a matter of the greatest importance and of general concern to us, in this case we hold it indispensably necessary that any cession of our lands should be made in the most public manner, and by the united voice of the confederacy; holding all partial treaties as void and of no effect.

> What kinds of "mischief" do you think the Indians are referring to here?

> What do the Indians consider the most important ways to ensure fair treaty negotiations?

Source: *American State Papers, Class II: Indian Affairs* (Washington, 1832), 1:8.

Put It in Context

Why have Indians chosen to send this message to the congress from the United Indian Nations Council rather than from their individual nations?

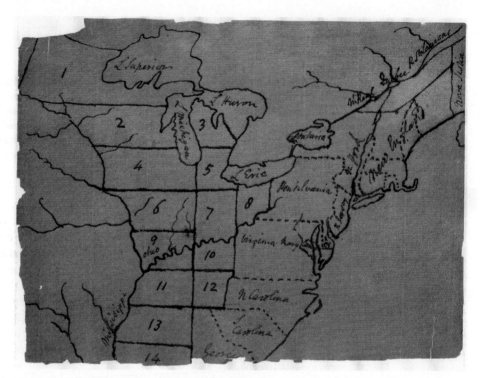

Thomas Jefferson's Map of Western Territories   Jefferson drew this 1784 map of the western territories, showing nine states in the region north of the Ohio River. He proposed giving land to settlers to encourage rapid settlement and discourage speculation and suggested prohibiting slavery in the region. Land taxes would provide funds to the federal government. Congress revised his plan significantly before adopting the Northwest Ordinance in 1785. Clements Library, University of Michigan

such treatment and failed to resolve Indian land claims. It also abolished slavery throughout the Northwest Territory but mandated the return of fugitive slaves to their owners to forestall a flood of fugitives.

The 1787 legislation did not address territory south of the Ohio River. As American settlers streamed into areas that became Kentucky and Tennessee, they confronted Creek, Choctaw, and Chickasaw tribes, well supplied with weapons by Spanish traders, as well as Cherokee who had sided with the British during the Revolution. Conflicts there were largely ignored by the national government for the next quarter century.

Depression and Debt.   Disputes over western lands were deeply intertwined with the economic difficulties that plagued the new nation. Victory in the Revolution was followed by years of economic depression and mushrooming debt. While the war fueled the demand for domestic goods and ensured high employment, both the demand and the jobs declined in peacetime. International trade was also slow to recover from a decade of disruption. Meanwhile the nation was saddled with a huge war debt. Individuals, the states, and the federal government all viewed western lands as a solution to their problems. Farm families could start over on "unclaimed" land; states could distribute land in lieu of cash to veterans or creditors; and congress could sell land to fund its debts. Yet there was never enough land to meet these conflicting needs, nor did the United States hold secure title to the territory.

Some national leaders, including Hamilton, focused on other ways of repaying the war debt. Fearing that wealthy creditors would lose faith in a nation that could not repay its debts, they urged states to grant the federal government a percentage of import duties as a way to increase its revenue. But states had their own problems. Legislators in Massachusetts and other states passed hard-money laws that required debts to be repaid in gold or silver rather than in paper currency. Affluent creditors favored these measures to ensure repayment in full. But small farmers, including veterans, who had borrowed paper money during the war, now had to repay those loans in hard currency as the money supply shrank. Taxes, too, were rising as states sought to cover the interest on wartime bonds held by wealthy investors.

Failures of American diplomacy weakened the nation's economy further. In 1783 the British Parliament denied the United States the right to trade with the British West Indies. The following year, Spain, seeking leverage over disputed western territories, prohibited U.S. ships from accessing the port of New Orleans. Spain and Great Britain also threatened U.S. sovereignty by conspiring with American citizens on the frontier and promising them protection from Indians. At the same time, British troops remained in forts on America's western frontier and urged Indians to harass settlers there.

REVIEW & RELATE

What challenges did the new nation face in the immediate aftermath of the Revolutionary War?
How did farmers, financial leaders, foreign nations, and Indians react to government efforts to address challenges after the Revolution?

On the Political Margins

A young nation, the United States was forced to the political margins in international affairs. At the same time, some groups within the nation were marginalized as well. Small farmers suffered in the postwar period, but they were not alone. Church leaders who had enjoyed government support in the colonial period now had to compete for members and funds. African Americans, whose hopes for freedom had been raised by the Revolution, continued to fight for full-fledged citizenship and an end to slavery. Women, too, faced challenges as they sought to enhance their role in the nation.

Separating Church and State. Government support of churches ended in most states with the establishment of the United States. Anglican churches had long benefited from British support and taxed residents to support their ministry during the Revolution. But in 1786, the Virginia Assembly approved the Statute of Religious Freedom, which made church attendance and support voluntary. Many other states followed Virginia's lead and removed government support for established churches.

Churches that had dominated the various colonies now faced greater competition. Especially in frontier areas, Baptists and Methodists, the latter of which broke off from the Anglican Church in 1784, gained thousands of converts. The Society of Friends, or Quakers, and the Presbyterians also gained new adherents, while Catholics and Jews experienced greater tolerance than in the colonial era. This diversity ensured that no single religious voice or perspective dominated the new nation. Instead, all denominations competed for members, money, and political influence.

Some Protestant churches were also challenged from within by free blacks who sought a greater role in church governance. In 1794 Richard Allen, who had been born a slave, led a small group of Philadelphia blacks in founding the first African American church in the United States. Initially, this African Methodist Episcopal Church remained within the larger Methodist fold. By the early 1800s, however, Allen's church served as the basis for the first independent black denomination.

African Americans Struggle for Rights. It was no accident that the first independent black church was founded in Philadelphia, which attracted large numbers of free blacks after Pennsylvania adopted a gradual emancipation law in 1780. Although the northern states with the largest enslaved populations—New York and New Jersey—did not pass such laws until 1799 and 1804, the free black population increased throughout the region.

Many free blacks were migrants from the South, where tens of thousands of enslaved women and men gained their freedom during or immediately following the Revolution. A few slave owners took Revolutionary ideals to heart and emancipated their slaves following the war. Many others emancipated slaves in their wills. In addition, several states prohibited the importation of slaves from Africa during or immediately following the Revolution. At the same time, however, the enslaved population continued to grow rapidly, and southern legislators soon made it difficult for owners to free their slaves and for free blacks to remain in the region.

The limits on emancipation in the South only nurtured the growth of free black communities in the North, especially in seaport cities like Philadelphia, New York, and New Bedford. Most African Americans focused on finding jobs, supporting families, and securing the freedom of enslaved relatives. Others, like Richard Allen, sought to establish churches, schools, and voluntary societies and claim a political voice. Some northern states, such as New Jersey, granted property-owning blacks the right to vote. Others, such as Pennsylvania, did not specifically exclude them.

Some whites aided blacks in their struggles. The Society of Friends, the only religious denomination to oppose slavery in the colonial period, became more outspoken. By the 1790s, many Friends, also known as Quakers, had freed their slaves and withdrawn from the slave trade. Anthony Benezet, a writer and educator, advocated tirelessly for the abolition of slavery and directed one of several schools for blacks founded by the Society of Friends.

Explore ▶

Compare the claims for rights made by a northern woman and southern free blacks in Sources 7.2 and 7.3.

Women Seek Wider Roles. Quaker women as well as men testified against slavery in the 1780s, writing statements on the topic in separate women's meetings. Although few other women experienced such spiritual autonomy, many gained a greater sense of economic and political independence during the Revolution.

Abigail Adams had written her husband John in 1776, "[I]f perticuliar care and attention is not paid to the Laidies we are determined to foment a Rebelion" (see Source 6.8 in chapter 6). While she and other elite women sought a more public voice, only New Jersey granted women—widowed or single and property-owning—the right to vote. The vast majority of women could shape political decisions only by influencing their male relatives and friends. Fortunately, many leaders of the early Republic viewed wives and mothers as necessary to the development of a strong nation. In 1787 Benjamin Rush, in his *Essay on*

Female Education, developed a notion of **republican motherhood**. He claimed that women could best shape political ideas and relations by "instructing their sons in principles of liberty and government." To prepare young women for this role, Rush suggested educating them in literature, music, composition, geography, history, and bookkeeping.

Judith Sargent Murray offered a more radical approach to women's education, arguing that "girls should be enabled to procure for themselves the necessaries of life; independence should be placed within their grasp" (see Source 7.2). A few American women in the late eighteenth century did receive broad educations, and some ran successful businesses; wrote plays, poems, and histories; and established urban salons where women and men discussed the issues of the day. In 1789 Massachusetts became the first state to institute free elementary education for all children, and female academies also multiplied in this period. While schooling for affluent girls was often focused on preparing them for domesticity, the daughters of artisans and farmers learned practical skills so they could assist in the family enterprise.

While women's influence was praised in the post-Revolutionary era, state laws rarely expanded women's rights. All states limited women's economic autonomy, although a few allowed married women to enter into business. Divorce was also legalized in many states but was still available only to the wealthy and well connected. Meanwhile women were excluded from juries, legal training, and, with rare exceptions, voting rights.

African American and Indian women lived under even more severe constraints than white women. Most black women were enslaved, and those who were free could usually find jobs only as domestic servants or agricultural workers. Among Indian nations, years of warfare enhanced men's role as warriors and diplomats while restricting women's political influence. U.S. government officials and Protestant missionaries encouraged Indians to embrace gender roles that mirrored those of Anglo-American culture, further diminishing women's roles. Indian women forced to move west also lost authority tied to their traditional control of land, crops, and households.

Indebted Farmers Fuel Political Crises.

Unlike blacks, Indians, and women, many farmers and workingmen could hope to

Judith Sargent Stevens, later Murray, c. 1772 Born into a wealthy Massachusetts family, Judith Sargent was allowed to study alongside her brother until she married John Stevens at age 18. In the 1770s, she wrote well-received essays on social and political topics and later promoted women's education and independence. Widowed at 35, she soon married Universalist minister John Murray and continued to publish into her sixties. Terra Foundation for American Art, Chicago/Art Resource, NY

COMPARATIVE ANALYSIS

Women and Free Blacks Claim Rights in the Nation

Limited in their civil and political rights and educational and economic opportunities, some women and African Americans demanded change. Northern white women focused especially on gaining access to a more rigorous education. In the first selection, Judith Sargent Murray insists that women are rational creatures who could make important contributions to society. Blacks had far fewer opportunities since the vast majority were enslaved and illiterate. Even free blacks faced numerous restrictions on their activities. In the second selection, three free black men in Charleston, South Carolina petition the state legislature for increased judicial rights.

Source 7.2

Judith Sargent Murray | On the Equality of the Sexes, 1790

Are we [women] deficient in reason? . . . [I]f an opportunity of acquiring knowledge hath been denied us, the inferiority of our sex cannot fairly be deduced from thence. . . . May we not trace its source in the difference of education, and continued advantages? Will it be said that the judgment of a male of two years old, is more sage than that of a female's of the same age? . . . But from that period what partiality! . . . As their years increase, the sister must be wholly domesticated, while the brother is led by the hand through all the flowery paths of science. . . . Now, was she permitted the same instructors as her brother, . . . for the employment of a rational mind an ample field would be opened. In astronomy she might catch a glimpse of the immensity of the Deity, and thence she would form amazing conceptions of the august and supreme Intelligence. In geography she would admire Jehovah in the midst of his benevolence; thus adapting this globe to the various wants and amusements of its inhabitants. In natural philosophy she would adore the infinite majesty of heaven, clothed in condescension; and as she traversed the reptile world, she would hail the goodness of a creating God. . . . Will it be urged that those acquirements would supersede our domestick duties. I answer that every requisite in female economy is easily attained; and, with truth I can add, that when once attained, they require no further mental attention. Nay, while we are pursuing the needle, or the superintendency of the family, I repeat, that our minds are at full liberty for reflection; that imagination may exert itself in full vigor; and that if a just foundation is early laid, our ideas will then be worthy of rational beings. . . . [I]s it reasonable, that a candidate for immortality . . . be allowed no other ideas, than those which are suggested by the mechanism of a pudding, or the sewing the seams of a garment?

Source: *Massachusetts Magazine*, March 1790, 132–35.

expand their political role in the new nation. Under constitutions written during the Revolution, most state governments broadened the electorate, allowing men with less property (or in some cases no property) to vote and hold office. They also increased representation from western areas.

Still, the economic interests of small farmers and workers diverged sharply from those of wealthy merchants and large landowners. As conflicts between debtors and creditors

Source 7.3

Petition from Free Blacks of Charleston, 1791

That in the enumeration of free citizens by the Constitution of the United States for the purpose of representation of the Southern states in Congress your memorialists [petitioners] have been considered under that description as part of the citizens of this state.

Although by the fourteenth and twenty-ninth clauses in an Act of Assembly made in the year 1740 . . . commonly called the Negro Act, now in force, your memorialists are deprived of the rights and privileges of citizens by not having it in their power to give testimony on oath in prosecutions on behalf of the state; from which cause many culprits have escaped the punishment due to their atrocious crimes, nor can they give their testimony in recovering debts due to them, or in establishing agreements made by them within the meaning of the Statutes of Frauds and Perjuries in force in this state except in cases where persons of color are concerned, whereby they are subject

to great losses and repeated injuries without any means of redress.

That by the said clauses in the said Act, they are debarred of the rights of free citizens by being subject to a trial without the benefit of a jury and subject to prosecution by testimony of slaves without oath by which they are placed on the same footing.

Your memorialists show that they have at all times since the independence of the United States contributed and do now contribute to the support of the government by cheerfully paying their taxes proportionable to their property with others who have been during such period, and now are, in full enjoyment of the rights and immunities of citizens, inhabitants of a free independent state.

Source: Petition of Thomas Cole, Peter Bassnett Matthewes, and Matthew Webb to the South Carolina Senate, January 1, 1791, Records of the General Assembly, no. 181.

Interpret the Evidence

1. What kind of rights do Judith Sargent Murray and the free blacks in Charleston claim for women and free African Americans, respectively?
2. What explains the differences in the rights demanded by Murray and the black petitioners and the ways they justify those claims?

Put It in Context

What do these documents reveal about the positions of white women and free black men during the formation of the United States?

escalated between 1783 and 1787, state governments came down firmly on the side of the wealthy. But indebted farmers did not give up. They voted, petitioned, and protested to gain more favorable policies. When that failed, debt-ridden farmers in New Hampshire marched on the state capital in September 1786, demanding reform. But they were confronted by cavalry units, who quickly seized and imprisoned their leaders.

Daniel Shays   This sketch is the only eighteenth-century illustration in existence of Daniel Shays (on the left in this detail). He stands with Jacob Shattuck, another antigovernment leader. The picture appeared in a pro-Constitution Boston almanac, which ridiculed the two rebels by showing them in fancy uniforms and holding swords, in contrast to what would have been their usual homespun appearance. National Portrait Gallery, Smithsonian Institution/Art Resource, NY

Assaults on national authority worried many political leaders far more than farmers' uprisings. The continued efforts of Great Britain and Spain to undercut U.S. sovereignty and ongoing struggles with Indian nations posed especially serious threats. When James Madison and Alexander Hamilton attended the 1785 convention in Annapolis to address problems related to interstate commerce, they discovered that their concerns about the weakness of the confederation were shared by many large landowners, planters, and merchants. Despite these concerns, state legislatures were reluctant to give up the powers conferred on them under the Articles of Confederation.

Still, it was **Shays's Rebellion**, the armed uprising of indebted farmers in western Massachusetts in 1786 to 1787, that crystallized fears among prominent patriots about the limits of the confederation model. On December 26, 1786, Washington wrote Henry Knox to express his concerns about the rebellion and upheavals along the frontier: "If the powers [of the central government] are inadequate, amend or alter them; but do not let us sink into the lowest states of humiliation and contempt." Hamilton agreed, claiming that Shays's Rebellion "marked almost the last stage of national humiliation."

REVIEW & RELATE

- How did America's experience of the Revolutionary War change the lives of African Americans and women?

- What do uprisings by farmers and debtors tell us about social and economic divisions in the early Republic?

Reframing the American Government

The delegates who met in Philadelphia in May 1787 did not agree on the best way to reform the government. Some delegates, like James Monroe of Virginia, hoped to strengthen the existing government by amending the Articles of Confederation. Others joined with Madison and Hamilton, who argued for a new governmental structure. Once representatives agreed to draft a new constitution, they still disagreed over questions of representation, the powers of state and national governments, and the limits of popular democracy. Significant compromises had to be reached on these issues to frame a new Constitution.

Other issues arose once the Constitution was ratified and George Washington was inaugurated as president. The government needed to be organized and staffed. A system for levying, collecting, and distributing funds had to be put in place. Diplomatic relations with foreign powers and Indian nations needed to be reestablished. A bill of rights, demanded by many state ratifying conventions, had to be drafted and approved. Finally, both proponents and opponents of the Constitution had to be convinced that this new government could respond to the varied needs of its citizens.

The Constitutional Convention of 1787.
The fifty-five delegates who attended the Philadelphia convention were composed of white, educated men of property, mainly lawyers, merchants, and planters. Only eight had signed the Declaration of Independence eleven years earlier. The elite status of the delegates and the absence of many leading patriots raised concern among those who saw the convention as a threat to the rights of states and of citizens. Not wanting to alarm the public, delegates agreed to meet in secret until they had hammered out a new framework of government.

On May 25, the convention opened, and delegates quickly turned to the key question: Revise the Articles of Confederation or draft an entirely new document? The majority of men came to Philadelphia with the intention of amending the Articles. However, a core group who sought a more powerful central government had met before the convention and drafted a plan to replace the Articles. This **Virginia Plan** proposed a strong centralized state, including a bicameral (two-house) legislature in which representation was to be based on population. Members of the two houses would select the national executive and the national judiciary, and would settle disputes between states. Although most delegates opposed the Virginia Plan, it launched discussions in which strengthening the central government was assumed to be the goal.

Discussions of the Virginia Plan raised another issue that nearly paralyzed the convention: the question of representation. Heated debates pitted large states against small states, even though political interests were not necessarily determined by size. Yet delegates held on to size as the critical issue in determining representation. In mid-June, William Patterson introduced the **New Jersey Plan**, which highlighted the needs of smaller states. In this plan, Congress would consist of only one house, with each state having equal representation.

With few signs of compromise, the convention finally appointed a special committee to hammer out the problem of representation. Their report broke the logjam. Members of the House of Representatives were to be elected by voters in each state; members of the Senate would be appointed by state legislatures. Representation in the House would be determined by population—counted every ten years in a national census—while in the Senate, each state, regardless of size, would have equal representation. While the Senate had more authority than the House in many areas, only the House could introduce funding bills.

Included within this compromise was one of the few direct considerations of slavery at the Philadelphia convention. With little apparent debate, the committee decided that representation in the House of Representatives was to be based on an enumeration of the entire free population and three-fifths of "all other persons," that is, slaves. If delegates had moral scruples about this **three-fifths compromise**, most found them outweighed by the urgency of settling the troublesome question of representation.

Still, slavery was on the minds of delegates. In the same week that the Philadelphia convention tacitly accepted the institution of slavery, the confederation congress in New York City outlawed slavery in the Northwest Territory. News of that decision likely inspired representatives from Georgia and South Carolina to insist that the Constitution protect the slave trade. Delegates in Philadelphia agreed that the importation of slaves would not be interfered with for twenty years. Another provision guaranteed the return of fugitive slaves to their owners. At the same time, northern delegates insisted that the three-fifths formula be used in assessing taxation as well as representation, ensuring that the South paid for the increased size of its congressional delegation with increased taxes.

Two other issues provoked considerable debate in the following weeks. All delegates supported federalism, a system in which states and the central government shared power, but they disagreed over the balance of power between them. They also disagreed over the degree of popular participation in selecting national leaders. The new Constitution increased the powers of the central government significantly. For instance, Congress would now have the right to raise revenue by levying and collecting taxes and tariffs and coining money; raise armies; regulate interstate commerce; settle disputes between the states; establish uniform rules for the naturalization of immigrants; and make treaties with foreign nations and Indians. But Congress could veto state laws only when those laws challenged "the supreme law of the land," and states retained all rights that were not specifically granted to the federal government.

One of the important powers retained by the states was the right to determine who was eligible to vote, but the Constitution regulated the influence eligible voters would have in national elections. Members of the House of Representatives were to be elected directly by popular vote for two-year terms. Senators—two from each state—were to be selected by state legislatures for a term of six years. Selection of the president was even further removed from voters. The president would be selected by an electoral college, and state legislatures would decide how to choose its members. Finally, the federal judicial system was to be wholly removed from popular influence. Justices on the Supreme Court were to be appointed by the president and approved by the Senate. Once approved, they served for life to protect their judgments from the pressure of popular opinion. In addition, the Constitution created a separation of powers between these three branches—congressional, executive, and judicial—that limited the authority of each.

With the final debates concluded, delegates agreed that approval by nine states, rather than all thirteen, would make the Constitution the law of the land. Some delegates sought formal reassurance that the powers granted the federal government would not be abused and urged inclusion of a bill of rights, like the Virginia Declaration of Rights. But weary men eager to finish their business voted down the proposal. On September 17, 1787, the Constitution was approved and sent to the states for ratification.

Americans Battle over Ratification.
The confederation congress sent the document to state legislatures and asked them to call conventions to consider ratification. These conventions could not modify the document, but only accept or reject it. Thousands of copies of the Constitution also circulated in newspapers and as broadsides. Pamphleteers, civic

leaders, and ministers proclaimed their opinions publicly while ordinary citizens in homes, shops, and taverns debated the wisdom of establishing a stronger central government.

Fairly quickly, two sides emerged. The **Federalists**, who supported ratification, came mainly from urban and commercial backgrounds and lived in towns and cities along the Atlantic coast. They viewed a stronger central government as essential to the economic and political stability of the nation. Their opponents were generally more rural, less wealthy, and more likely to live in interior or frontier regions. Labeled **Antifederalists**, they opposed increasing the powers of the central government.

The pro-Constitution position was presented in a series of editorials that appeared in New York newspapers in 1787 to 1788 and published collectively as *The Federalist Papers*. The authors James Madison, John Jay, and Alexander Hamilton articulated broad principles embraced by most supporters of the Constitution. Most notably, in *Federalist* No. 10, Madison countered the common wisdom that small units of government were most effective in representing the interests of their citizens and avoiding factionalism. He argued that in large units groups with competing interests had to collaborate and compromise, providing the surest check on the "tyranny of the majority." **See Primary Source Project 7, Debating the Constitution in New York State, page 240.**

Still, Antifederalists worried that a large and powerful central government could lead to tyranny. Small farmers claimed that a strong congress filled with merchants, lawyers, and planters was likely to place the interests of creditors above those of ordinary (and indebted) Americans. Even some wealthy patriots, like Mercy Otis Warren of Boston, feared that the Constitution would empower a few individuals who cared little for the "true interests of the people." And the absence of a bill of rights concerned many Americans.

Federalists worked in each state to soften their critics by persuasive arguments, flattering hospitality, and the promise of a bill of rights once the Constitution was ratified. They gained strength from the quick ratification of the Constitution by Delaware, Pennsylvania, New Jersey, Georgia, and Connecticut by January 1788. Federalists also gained the support of influential newspapers based in eastern cities and tied to commercial interests.

Still, the contest in many states was heated. In Massachusetts, Antifederalists, including leaders of Shays's Rebellion, gained the majority among convention delegates. Federalists worked hard to overcome the objections of their opponents, even drafting a preliminary bill of rights. On February 6, Massachusetts delegates voted 187 to 168 in favor of ratification. Maryland and South Carolina followed in April and May. A month later, New Hampshire Federalists won a close vote, making it the ninth state to ratify the Constitution.

However, two of the most populous and powerful states—New York and Virginia—had not yet ratified. Passionate debates erupted in both ratifying conventions, and Federalists decided it was prudent to wait until these states acted before declaring victory. After promising that a bill of rights would be added quickly, Virginia Federalists finally won the day by a few votes. A month later, New York approved the Constitution by a narrow margin. The divided nature of the votes, and the fact that two states (North Carolina and Rhode Island) had still not ratified, meant that the new government would have to prove itself quickly (Table 7.1).

Organizing the Federal Government.

Most political leaders hoped that the partisanship of the ratification battle would fade away with the Constitution approved. The electoral college's unanimous decision to name George Washington the first president

TABLE 7.1   Votes of State-Ratifying Conventions

State	Date	For	Against
Delaware	December 1787	30	0
Pennsylvania	December 1787	46	23
New Jersey	December 1787	38	0
Georgia	January 1788	26	0
Connecticut	January 1788	128	40
Massachusetts	February 1788	187	168
Maryland	April 1788	63	11
South Carolina	May 1788	149	73
New Hampshire	June 1788	57	47
Virginia	June 1788	89	79
New York	July 1788	30	27
North Carolina	November 1788	194	77
Rhode Island	May 1790	34	32

and John Adams as vice president helped calm the political turmoil. The two took office in April 1789, launching the new government.

To bring order to his administration, Washington appointed respected men to head three departments—State, War, and Treasury. Thomas Jefferson was named secretary of state; Henry Knox, secretary of war; and Alexander Hamilton, secretary of the treasury. He also appointed Edmund Randolph as attorney general, the first step toward establishing a Department of Justice.

Congress, meanwhile, worked to establish a judicial system. The Constitution called for a Supreme Court but provided no specific guidelines. The Judiciary Act of 1789 established a Supreme Court composed of six justices along with thirteen district courts and three circuit courts to hear cases appealed from the states. Congress also quickly produced a bill of rights. Representative James Madison gathered more than two hundred resolutions passed by state ratifying conventions and honed them down to twelve amendments, which Congress approved and submitted to the states for ratification. In 1791 ten of the amendments were ratified, and these became the **Bill of Rights**. It guaranteed the rights of individuals and states in the face of a powerful central government, including freedom of speech, the press, religion, and the right to petition.

Hamilton Forges an Economic Agenda.
The new government's leaders recognized that without a stable economy, the best political structure could falter. Thus Hamilton's appointment as secretary of the treasury was especially significant. In formulating his economic policy, Hamilton's main goal was to establish the nation's credit. Paying down the debt and establishing a national bank would strengthen the United States in the eyes of the world and tie wealthy Americans more firmly to the federal government.

Federal Hall   This drawing shows Federal Hall, located on Wall Street in New York City. The building housed the Stamp Act Congress in 1765 and the confederation congress from 1785 to 1788. In 1789 it became the seat of Congress under the new Constitution (the capital was later moved to Philadelphia in December 1790), and the site of President Washington's first inauguration. Granger

Hamilton advocated funding the national debt at face value and assuming the remaining state debts as part of the national debt. To pay for this policy, he planned to raise revenue through government bonds and new taxes. Hamilton also called for the establishment of a central bank to carry out the financial operations of the United States. In three major reports to Congress—on public credit and a national bank in 1790 and on manufactures in 1791—he laid out a system of state-assisted economic development.

Hamilton's proposal to repay at face value the millions of dollars in securities issued by the confederation was particularly controversial. Thousands of soldiers, farmers, and shopkeepers had been paid with these securities during the war; but needing money in its aftermath, most sold them to speculators for a fraction of their value. These speculators would make enormous profits if the securities were paid off at face value. One of the policy's most ardent critics, Patrick Henry, claimed that Hamilton's policy was intended "to erect, and concentrate, and perpetuate a large monied interest" that would prove "fatal to the existence of American liberty." Despite such passionate opponents, Hamilton gained the support of Washington and other key Federalists.

The federal government's assumption of the remaining state war debts also faced fierce opposition, especially from southern states like Virginia that had already paid off their debt. Hamilton again won his case, though this time only by agreeing to "redeem" (that is, reimburse) states that had repaid their debts. In addition, Hamilton and his supporters had to agree to move the nation's capital from Philadelphia to a more central location along the Potomac River.

Funding the national debt, assuming the remaining state debts, and redeeming state debts already paid would cost $75.6 million (about $1.5 billion today). But Hamilton believed maintaining some debt was useful. He thus proposed establishing a Bank of the United States, funded by $10 million in stock to be sold to private stockholders and the national government. The bank would serve as a repository for federal revenues and grant loans and sell bills of credit to merchants and investors, thereby creating a permanent national debt. This, he argued, would bind investors to the United States, turning the national debt into a "national blessing."

Not everyone agreed. Jefferson and Madison argued vehemently against the Bank of the United States, noting that there was no constitutional sanction for a federal bank. Hamilton fought back, arguing that Congress had the right to make "all Laws which shall be necessary and proper" for carrying out the provisions of the Constitution. Once again, he prevailed. Congress chartered the bank for a period of twenty years, and Washington signed the legislation into law.

The final piece of Hamilton's plan focused on raising revenue. Congress quickly agreed to pass tariffs on a range of imported goods, which generated some $4 million to $5 million annually. Some congressmen viewed these tariffs as a way to protect new industries in the United States, from furniture to shoes. Excise taxes placed on a variety of consumer goods, most notably whiskey, generated another $1 million each year.

Hamilton's financial policies proved enormously successful in stabilizing the American economy, repaying outstanding debts, and tying men of wealth to the new government. The federal bank effectively collected and distributed the nation's resources. Commerce flourished, revenues rose, and confidence revived among foreign and domestic investors. And while the United States remained an agricultural nation, Hamilton's 1791 "Report on the Subject of Manufactures" foreshadowed the growing significance of industry, which gradually lessened U.S. dependence on European nations.

REVIEW & RELATE

- What issues attracted the most intense debate during the drafting and ratification of the Constitution? Why?

- How did Hamilton's policies stabilize the national economy, and why did they nonetheless arouse opposition?

Years of Crisis, 1792–1796

By 1792 Hamilton had succeeded in implementing his plan for U.S. economic development. Yet as Washington began his second term in the spring of 1793, signs of strain appeared throughout the nation. The French Revolution posed challenges to foreign trade and diplomacy. Migration to the frontier increased, which intensified conflicts between Indians and white settlers and increased hostilities between the United States and Great Britain. Yellow fever swept through Philadelphia and other cities, causing fear and disrupting political and economic life. Finally, the excise tax on whiskey fueled armed protests among frontier farmers. This cluster of crises split the Federalists into warring factions during Washington's second term.

Foreign Trade and Foreign Wars. Jefferson and Madison led the opposition to Hamilton's policies. Their supporters were mainly southern Federalists who envisioned the country's future rooted in agriculture, not the commerce and industry supported by Hamilton and his allies. Jefferson agreed with the Scottish economist Adam Smith that an international division of labor could best provide for the world's people. Americans could supply Europe with food and raw materials in exchange for manufactured goods. When wars in Europe, including a revolution in France, disrupted European agriculture in the 1790s, Jefferson's views were reinforced.

Although trade with Europe remained the most important source of goods and wealth for the United States, some merchants expanded into other parts of the globe. In the mid-1780s, the first American ships reached China, where they traded ginseng root and sea otter pelts for silk, tea, and chinaware. Still, events in Europe had a far greater impact on the United States at the time than those in the Pacific world.

The French Revolution (1789–1799) was especially significant for U.S. politics. The ideals of freedom of speech, assembly, and religion declared in the American Declaration of

Americans Trade with China This painting by a Chinese artist c. 1800 shows the Hongs at Canton, where ships from foreign countries arrived to unload and load goods. The foreign ships were limited to this small area outside Canton's city walls. There each nation established a trading post identified by its national flag and overseen by a Chinese merchant. © Sotheby's/akg-images

Independence resonated with French men and women who opposed the tyrannical rule of their King, Louis XVI. The resulting uprising disrupted French agriculture, increasing demand for American wheat, while the efforts of French revolutionaries to institute an egalitarian republic gained support from many Americans. The followers of Jefferson and Madison formed Republican societies, and members adopted the French term *citizen* when addressing each other. At the same time, the importance of workers and farmers among France's revolutionary forces reinforced critiques of the "monied power" that drove Federalist policies.

In late 1792, as French revolutionary leaders began executing thousands of their opponents in the Reign of Terror, wealthy Federalists grew more anxious. The beheading of King Louis XVI horrified them, as did the revolution's condemnation of Christianity. When France declared war against Prussia, Austria, and finally Great Britain, merchants worried about the impact on trade. In response, President Washington proclaimed U.S. neutrality in April 1793, prohibiting Americans from providing support or war materials to any belligerent nations—including France or Great Britain.

While the Neutrality Proclamation limited the shipment of certain items to Europe, Americans simultaneously increased trade with colonies in the British and French West Indies. Indeed, U.S. ships captured much of the lucrative sugar trade. At the same time, farmers in the Chesapeake and Middle Atlantic regions filled the growing demand for wheat in Europe, causing their profits to climb.

Yet these benefits did not bring about a political reconciliation. Although Jefferson condemned the French Reign of Terror, he protested the Neutrality Proclamation by resigning his cabinet post. Tensions escalated when the French envoy to the United States, Edmond Genêt, sought to enlist Americans in the European war. Republican clubs poured out to hear him speak and donated generously to the French cause. But the British also ignored U.S. neutrality. The Royal Navy stopped U.S. ships carrying French sugar and seized more than 250 vessels. The British also supplied Indians in the Ohio River valley with guns and encouraged them to raid U.S. settlements.

More concerned with addressing issues with Britain, President Washington sent John Jay to England to resolve concerns over trade with the British West Indies, compensation for seized American ships, the continued British occupation of frontier forts, and southerners' ongoing demands for reimbursement of slaves evacuated by the British during the Revolution. Jay returned from England in 1794 with a treaty, but it was widely criticized in Congress and the popular press. While securing limited U.S. trading rights in the West Indies, it failed to address British reimbursement for captured cargoes or slaves and granted Britain eighteen months to leave frontier forts. It also demanded that U.S. planters repay British firms for debts accrued during the Revolution. While the **Jay Treaty** was eventually ratified, it remained a source of contention among Federalists.

The Whiskey Rebellion.

Despite these foreign crises, it was the effect of Federalist policies on the American frontier that crystallized opposing factions. In the early 1790s, Republican societies from Maine to Georgia demanded the removal of British and Spanish troops from frontier areas, while frontier farmers lashed out at enforcement of the so-called whiskey tax. Many farmers on the frontier grew corn and turned it into whiskey to make it easier to transport and more profitable to sell. The whiskey tax hurt these farmers, hundreds of whom petitioned the federal government for relief.

Western Pennsylvania farmers were particularly incensed and rallied in 1792 and 1793 to protest the tax and those who enforced it. Former North Carolina Regulator Hermon

"An Exciseman," c. 1791   This early cartoon depicts an excise agent, carrying two casks of whiskey to "Squire Vultures," with whom he intends to divide his take. He is pursued by two farmers opposed to the whiskey tax, who yell, "let us tar and feather the rascal." The exciseman is eventually hung over a barrel of whiskey, which is set on fire and explodes. Fotosearch/Getty Images

Husband was one of the most outspoken critics of the new excise tax (see American Histories in chapter 5). Adopting tactics from Stamp Act protests and Shays's Rebellion, farmers blocked roads, burned sheriffs in effigy, marched on courthouses, and assaulted tax collectors. Government operations in Philadelphia were largely paralyzed by a yellow fever epidemic from August to November 1793, but the lack of response only fueled the rebels' anger. By 1794 all-out rebellion had erupted.

Washington, Hamilton, and their supporters worried that the rebellion could spread and that it might encourage Indians to rise up as well. Since Spanish and British soldiers were eager to foment trouble along the frontier, the **Whiskey Rebellion** might spark their intervention as well. These Federalists also suspected that pro-French immigrants from Scotland and Ireland helped fuel the insurgency.

Unlike 1786, however, when the federal government had no power to intervene in Shays's Rebellion, Washington now federalized militias from four states, calling up nearly thirteen thousand soldiers to quash the uprising. The army that marched into western Pennsylvania in September 1794 vastly outnumbered the "whiskey rebels" and easily suppressed the uprising. Having gained victory, the federal government prosecuted only two of the leaders, who although convicted were later pardoned by Washington.

Washington proved that the Constitution provided the necessary powers to put down internal threats. Yet in doing so, the administration horrified many Americans who viewed the force used against the farmers as excessive. Jefferson and Madison voiced this outrage from within the Federalist government. The Revolutionary generation had managed to compromise on many issues, from representation and slavery to the balance between federal and state authority. But now Hamilton's economic policies had led to a frontier uprising, and Washington had used a federal army to destroy popular dissent. The Federalists were on the verge of open warfare themselves.

Further Conflicts on the Frontier.   In one area, Federalists shared a common concern: the continued threats to U.S. sovereignty by Indian, British, and Spanish forces. In 1790 Congress had passed the Indian Trade and Intercourse Act to regulate

Indian-white relations on the frontier and to ensure fair and equitable dealings. However, the act was widely ignored.

The government's failure to stem the flood of settlers into the Ohio and Mississippi River valleys proved costly. In 1790 Little Turtle, a war chief of the Miami nation, gathered a large force of Shawnee, Delaware, Ottawa, Chippewa, Sauk, Fox, and other Indians. This pan-Indian alliance successfully attacked federal troops in the Ohio valley that fall. A year later, the allied Indian warriors defeated a large force under General Arthur St. Clair (Map 7.2). The

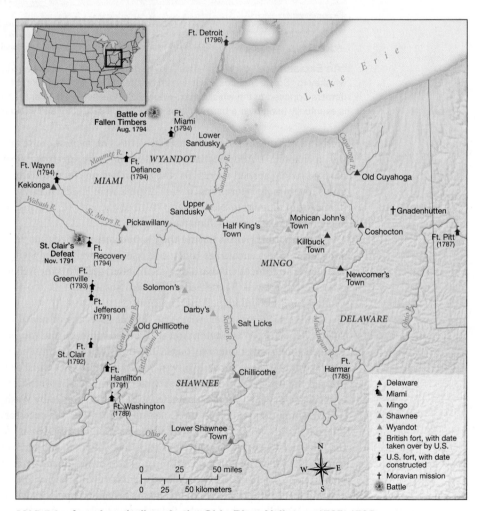

MAP 7.2   American Indians in the Ohio River Valley, c. 1785–1795

Until the mid-eighteenth century, despite conflicts, Indian tribes in the Ohio River valley forged trade and diplomatic relations with various colonial powers. But once the United States established the Northwest Territory in 1785, conflicts between Indians and U.S. settlers and soldiers escalated dramatically. As tribes created pan-Indian alliances, the United States constructed numerous forts in the region.

stunning defeat shocked Americans. In the meantime, Spanish authorities negotiated with Creeks and Cherokees to attack U.S. settlements on the southern frontier.

Washington decided to deal with problems in the Northwest Territory first, sending 2,000 men under the command of General Anthony Wayne into the Ohio frontier. In August 1794, Wayne's forces attacked 1,500 to 2,000 Indians gathered at a British fort. In the Battle of Fallen Timbers, the pan-Indian warriors, led by Little Turtle, suffered a bitter defeat. A year later, the warring Indians in the Northwest Territory signed the **Treaty of Greenville**, granting the United States vast tracts of land.

Amid this turmoil, in November 1794, John Jay signed his controversial treaty with Great Britain. With Britain agreeing to withdraw its forces from the U.S. frontier by 1796, the treaty may have helped persuade Indian nations to accept U.S. peace terms at Greenville. Nonetheless, the Jay Treaty's requirement that Americans make "full and complete compensation" to British firms for Revolutionary War debts without the British compensating U.S. merchants or slave owners for their losses nearly led Congress to reject it. In June 1795, however, the Senate finally approved the treaty without a vote to spare. Before Jay's controversial treaty took effect, Spain agreed to negotiate an end to hostilities on the southern frontier of the United States. Envoy Thomas Pinckney negotiated that treaty, which recognized the thirty-first parallel as the boundary between U.S. and Spanish territory in the South and opened the Mississippi River and the port of New Orleans to U.S. shipping. Many Federalists, especially from the West and South, who opposed the Jay Treaty supported the **Pinckney Treaty**, which was ratified in 1796.

REVIEW & RELATE

- How did events overseas shape domestic American politics and frontier policy in the 1790s?

- What common concerns underlay the Whiskey Rebellion and Shays's Rebellion? How did the U.S. government deal differently with each?

The **First Party System**

In September 1796, when President Washington decided not to run again, he offered a Farewell Address in which he warned against the "spirit of party." "It agitates the community with ill-founded jealousies and false alarms," he claimed, and "kindles the animosity of one part against another." By then, however, Jefferson, Madison, and other opponents of Hamilton's economic policies, Washington's assault on the whiskey rebels, and Jay's Treaty had already formed a distinct party. They called themselves **Democratic-Republicans** and supported Jefferson for president. The electoral college, hoping to bring the warring sides together, chose Federalist John Adams as president and Thomas Jefferson as vice president. The two disagreed fundamentally on a wide range of issues, and events soon heightened these divisions. Foreign crises once again fueled political antagonisms, and in this charged atmosphere, Federalists in Congress passed two acts in 1798 relating to aliens (immigrants) and to sedition (activities that promote civil disorder). Instead of resolving tensions, however, these laws exacerbated opposition to Federalist rule. By 1800, partisan differences had crystallized, and the Democratic-Republicans threatened to oust the Federalists from power.

The Adams Presidency. The election of 1796 was the first to be contested by candidates identified with opposing parties. Federalists supported John Adams for president and Thomas Pinckney for vice president. The Democratic-Republicans chose Thomas Jefferson and Aaron Burr of New York to represent their interests. When the electoral college was established, political parties did not exist and, in fact, were seen as promoting conflict. Thus electors were asked to choose the best individuals to serve, regardless of their views. In 1796 they picked Adams for president and Jefferson for vice president, perhaps hoping to lessen partisan divisions by forcing men of different views to compromise. Instead, the effects of an administration divided against itself were nearly disastrous, and opposing interests became more thoroughly entrenched.

Adams and Jefferson had disagreed on almost every major policy issue during Washington's administration. Not surprisingly, the new president rarely took advice from his vice president. At the same time, Adams retained most of Washington's appointees, who often sought advice from Hamilton, undercutting Adams's authority. Worse still, the new president had poor political instincts and faced numerous challenges.

At first, foreign disputes enhanced the authority of the Adams administration. The Federalists remained pro-British, and French seizures of U.S. ships threatened to provoke war. In 1798 Adams tried to negotiate compensation for the losses suffered by merchants. When an American delegation arrived in Paris, however, three French agents demanded a bribe to initiate talks.

Adams made public secret correspondence from the French agents, whose names were listed only as X, Y, and Z. Americans, including Democratic-Republicans, expressed outrage at this French insult to U.S. integrity, which became known as the **XYZ affair**. Congress quickly approved an embargo act that prohibited trade with France and permitted privateering against French ships. For the next two years, the United States fought an undeclared war with France.

Despite praise for his handling of the XYZ affair, Adams feared dissent from opponents at home and abroad. Consequently, the Federalist majority in Congress passed a series of security acts in 1798. The Alien Act allowed the president to order the imprisonment or deportation of noncitizens and was directed primarily at Irish and Scottish dissenters who criticized the government's pro-British policies. Congress also approved the Naturalization Act, which raised the residency requirement for citizenship from five to fourteen years. Finally, Federalists pushed through the Sedition Act, which outlawed "false, scandalous, or malicious statements against President or Congress." In the following months, nearly two dozen Democratic-Republican editors and legislators were arrested for sedition, and some were fined and imprisoned.

Democratic-Republicans were understandably infuriated by the **Alien and Sedition Acts**. They considered the attack on immigrants an attempt to limit the votes of farmers, artisans, and frontiersmen, who formed the core of their supporters. The Sedition Act threatened Democratic-Republican critics of Federalist policies and the First Amendment's guarantee of free speech. Jefferson and Madison encouraged states to pass resolutions that would counter this violation of the Bill of Rights. Using language drafted by the two Democratic-Republican leaders, legislators passed the **Virginia and Kentucky Resolutions**, which declared the Alien and Sedition Acts "void and of no force." They protested against the "alarming infractions of the Constitution," particularly the freedom of speech that "has

Matthew Lyon and Roger Griswold This political cartoon depicts a fight on the floor of the House of Representatives in February 1798 between Representatives Matthew Lyon of Vermont, a Democratic-Republican brandishing tongs, and Roger Griswold of Connecticut, a Federalist waving a cane. A newspaper editor and a critic of the Alien and Sedition Acts, Lyon was later convicted of sedition but won reelection while in jail. Library of Congress, LC-DIG-ppmsca-19356

been justly deemed, the only effectual guardian of every other right." Virginia even claimed that states had a right to nullify any powers exercised by the federal government that were not explicitly granted to it.

Although the Alien and Sedition Acts curbed dissent in the short run, they reinforced popular concerns about the power wielded by the Federalists. Combined with the ongoing war with France, continuing disputes over taxes, and relentless partisan denunciations in the press, these acts set the stage for the presidential election of 1800.

The Election of 1800.

By 1800 Adams had negotiated a peaceful settlement of U.S. conflicts with France, considering it one of the greatest achievements of his administration. However, other Federalists, including Hamilton, disagreed and continued to seek open warfare and an all-out victory. Thus the Federalists faced the election of 1800 deeply divided. Democratic-Republicans meanwhile united behind Jefferson and portrayed the Federalists as the "new British" tyrants.

For the first time, congressional caucuses selected candidates for each party. The Federalists agreed on Adams and Charles Cotesworth Pinckney of South Carolina. The Democratic-Republicans again chose Jefferson and Burr as their candidates. The campaign was marked by bitter accusations and denunciations.

In the first highly contested presidential election, the different methods states used to record voters' preferences gained more attention. Only five states determined members of the electoral college by popular vote. In the rest, state legislatures appointed electors. Created at a time when political parties were considered injurious to good

Explore ▶

For two historians' views on partisan attacks in the Presidential election of 1800, see Sources 7.4 and 7.5.

The Election of 1800 Initiates Partisan Campaigning

While the election of 1796 was the first to involve candidates chosen by opposing parties, it was decidedly civil compared to that of 1800. Partisan differences intensified as divisions over domestic and foreign policies led each side to view the other as a threat to fundamental American values. Historians agree that the election of 1800—between Federalist John Adams and Democratic-Republican Thomas Jefferson—marks a critical moment in U.S. history because it necessitated the peaceful transfer of power from one political party to another. Yet it was also the first campaign in which partisan newspapers circulated vitriolic claims about the opposition.

Source 7.4

Eric Burns, Federalists Attack Thomas Jefferson, 2006

[W]ould Federalists willingly and peacefully hand power over to their political enemies . . . , men whom they not only loathed but also considered dangerous to the republic, to private property, to economic growth and a strong central government, to everything they cherished and respected?

The answer, at least as far as federalist newspapers were concerned, was no. And to try to make sure that they would not have to report on the transfer of power to those whom they despised, they began devoting their pages to the most dire of predictions. "Should the infidel Jefferson be elected to the Presidency," wrote the *Hudson Bee* . . . , "the *seal of death* is that moment set on our holy religion, our churches will be prostrated, and some infamous prostitute, under the title the Goddess of Reason, will preside in the Sanctuaries now devoted to the Most High." . . .

The [Democratic-]Republican counterattack was surprisingly feeble. Some papers praised Jefferson, in colorless language for the most part, for his perceptiveness and eloquence and experience. Other papers attacked Adams, but without much fire; one said that the incumbent wanted to start an American aristocracy by marrying one of his sons to a daughter of [King] George III. . . . Apparently at least some of the anti-federalist newspapers were confident of a Jeffersonian victory.

Source: Eric Burns, *Infamous Scribblers: The Founding Fathers and the Rowdy Beginnings of American Journalism.* New York: Public Affairs, Perseus Book Group, 2006, pp. 369 and 371.

government, the electoral college was not prepared for the situation it faced in January 1801. Federalist and Democratic-Republican caucuses nominated one candidate for president and one for vice president on party tickets. As a result, Jefferson and Burr received exactly the same number of electoral college votes, and the House of Representatives then had to break the tie. There Burr sought to gain the presidency with the help of Federalist representatives ardently opposed to Jefferson. But Alexander Hamilton stepped in and warned against Burr's leadership. This helped Jefferson emerge victorious, but it also inflamed animosity between Burr and Hamilton that eventually led Burr to kill Hamilton in a duel in 1804.

President Jefferson labeled his election a revolution achieved not "by the sword" but by "the suffrage of the people." The election of 1800 was hardly a popular revolution, given

Source 7.5

John Ferling, Democratic-Republicans Attack John Adams, 2013.

While most of the candidates avoided the hustings [public platforms], party activists were busy. For the most part, both sides spread their messages through pamphlets, broadsides, and newspapers. The Federalists had a decided edge in the press, but [Democratic-]Republican newspapers had climbed up from 15 percent of the total in 1796 to nearly one-third by 1800. The [Democratic-] Republicans were better organized for disseminating information, as they established committees of correspondence to funnel publications to the hinterland. . . .

Some [Democratic-]Republican penmen limned [depicted]Adams as a monarchist . . . , but their essayists focused mostly on the Federalist program. One writer after another attacked the Alien and Sedition Acts, the taxes levied to pay for the debt . . . , and the very existence of a standing army. Much of their ink was [also] spilled on Hamilton's economic program. . . .

The abuse . . . directed against Hamilton paled in comparison to the calumny heaped on Jefferson. . . . Federalists charged that Jefferson's residence in France had transformed him into a dangerous radical. . . . A Federalist newspaper in Virginia alleged that Jefferson had a slave mistress. . . . [And] Federalists twisted Jefferson's advocacy of religious freedom in *Notes on the State of Virginia* to brand him an atheist.

Source: John Ferling, *Jefferson and Hamilton: The Rivalry That Forged a Nation.* New York: Bloomsbury Press, 2014, 320–321.

Examine the Sources

1. How do Ferling and Burns differ in their assessments of Federalist and Democratic-Republican attacks on each other's presidential candidates?
2. How effective are Ferling and Burns in using primary sources to make their argument? Do you find one argument more compelling than the other, and if yes, why?

Put It in Context

Given the fierce attacks on Jefferson, what explains his victory in the 1800 election?

---

the restrictions on suffrage and the methods of selecting the electoral college. Still, between 1796 and 1800, partisan factions had been transformed into opposing parties, and the United States had managed a peaceful transition from one party to another.

REVIEW & RELATE

What were the main issues dividing the Federalists and the Democratic-Republicans?

What do the Alien and Sedition Acts and the election of 1800 tell us about political partisanship in late-eighteenth-century America?

Conclusion: A Young Nation Comes of Age

In the 1780s and 1790s, the United States faced numerous obstacles to securing its place as a nation. Financial hardship, massive debts, hostile Indians, and European diplomacy had to be addressed by a federal government that, under the Articles of Confederation, was relatively weak. By 1787 concerns about national security, fueled by rebellious farmers and frontier conflicts, persuaded some political leaders to advocate a new governmental structure. While it required numerous compromises among groups with competing ideas and interests, the Constitution was drafted and, after a fierce battle in important states, ratified.

With the federal government's power strengthened, George Washington took office as the first American president. His administration sought to enhance U.S. power at home and abroad. Secretary of the treasury Alexander Hamilton proposed a series of measures to stabilize the American economy, pay off Revolutionary War debts, and promote trade and industry. However, these policies also aroused opposition, with leaders like Jefferson and Madison and ordinary farmers and frontiersmen questioning the benefits of Hamilton's economic priorities. Differences over the French Revolution also led to heated debates, while the imposition of an excise tax on whiskey fueled open rebellion on the Pennsylvania frontier. Although a majority of Federalists supported Hamilton and an alliance with Britain, they faced growing opposition from those who advocated agrarian ideals and supported the French Revolution.

While conflicts among Federalists drew many Americans into debates over government programs, large groups remained marginalized or excluded from the political system. Indians, African Americans, and women had little voice in policies that directly affected them. Even white workingmen and farmers found it difficult to influence political priorities and turned to petitions, protests, and even armed uprisings to demonstrate their views.

By 1796, Jefferson and Madison, who led the opposition among Federalists, had formed a separate political party, the Democratic-Republicans. They considered passage of the Alien and Sedition Acts as a direct attack on their supporters, and in 1800 wrested control of Congress and the presidency from the Federalists. Still, this peaceful transition in power boded well for the young United States.

Despite political setbacks, the Federalist legacy remained powerful. Hamilton's policies continued to shape national economic growth, and Federalists retained political power in the Northeast for decades. Meanwhile the benefits that small farmers and frontiersmen like Daniel Shays hoped to gain under Democratic-Republican rule proved largely elusive. Marginalized Americans such as Indians and African Americans also benefited little from the transition to Democratic-Republican leadership. Indeed, the growth of slavery and U.S. westward expansion created new burdens for these groups.

Yet the Democratic-Republican Party would not be seriously challenged for national power until 1824, giving it nearly a quarter century to implement its vision of the United States. Members of this heterogeneous party would now have to learn to compromise with each other if they were going to achieve their goal of limited federal power in an agrarian republic.

TIMELINE OF **EVENTS**

1783	Continental Army officers threaten to mutiny
1784	Treaty of Fort Stanwix
1785	Northwest Ordinance passed
	Annapolis Convention
1786–1787	Shays's Rebellion
1787	Constitutional Convention in Philadelphia
	Northwest Ordinance revised
1788	U.S. Constitution ratified
1789	Alexander Hamilton named secretary of the treasury
	Judiciary Act of 1789 passed
1789–1799	French Revolution
1790–1794	Little Turtle leads pan-Indian alliance in the Ohio valley
1791	Bill of Rights ratified
1793	Neutrality Proclamation
	Yellow fever epidemic paralyzes U.S. capital in Philadelphia
1794	Whiskey Rebellion
	African Methodist Episcopal Church founded
1796	Jay Treaty and Pinckney Treaty ratified
	Democratic-Republican Party established
1798	Alien and Sedition Acts passed

KEY **TERMS**

Treaty of Fort Stanwix, *213*

Northwest Ordinance, *213*

republican motherhood, *219*

Shays's Rebellion, *222*

Virginia Plan, *223*

New Jersey Plan, *223*

three-fifths compromise, *224*

Federalists, *225*

Antifederalists, *225*

Bill of Rights, *226*

Jay Treaty, *230*

Whiskey Rebellion, *231*

Treaty of Greenville, *233*

Pinckney Treaty, *233*

Democratic-Republicans, *233*

XYZ affair, *234*

Alien and Sedition Acts, *234*

Virginia and Kentucky Resolutions, *234*

REVIEW & RELATE

1. What challenges did the new nation face in the immediate aftermath of the Revolutionary War?

2. How did farmers, financial leaders, foreign nations, and Indians react to government efforts to address challenges after the Revolution?

3. How did America's experience of the Revolutionary War change the lives of African Americans and women?

4. What do uprisings by farmers and debtors tell us about social and economic divisions in the early Republic?

5. What issues attracted the most intense debate during the drafting and ratification of the Constitution? Why?

6. How did Hamilton's policies stabilize the national economy, and why did they nonetheless arouse opposition?

7. How did events overseas shape domestic American politics and frontier policy in the 1790s?

8. What common concerns underlay the Whiskey Rebellion and Shays's Rebellion? How did the U.S. government deal differently with each?

9. What were the main issues dividing the Federalists and the Democratic-Republicans?

10. What do the Alien and Sedition Acts and the election of 1800 tell us about political partisanship in late-eighteenth-century America?

Debating the Constitution in New York State

▶ As Americans considered the proposed Constitution, which groups sought to increase and which groups sought to restrict federal power and why?

Although the Constitution was eventually approved by all thirteen states, the battle over its ratification revealed a deeply divided nation. Antifederalist delegates dominated conventions in Massachusetts, Virginia, and New York; and when Massachusetts and Virginia finally ratified the Constitution by close votes, the New York convention was still in session.

As elsewhere, New York delegates debated questions of representation, the increased powers of the federal government, and a bill of rights. Before the convention opened, James Madison, Alexander Hamilton, and John Jay offered fellow New Yorkers pro-Constitution arguments in *The Federalist Papers* (Source 7.6). At the convention, Hamilton emphasized the need for a strong central government in which checks and balances limited the power of any single branch and insisted on accommodating the views of diverse groups, including southern slaveholders (Source 7.8).

A secretary recorded the speeches of Hamilton and other delegates. Melancton Smith was a large landowner and a New York City merchant, but he led the state's Antifederalists and questioned the expansion of federal power and the limits on representation (Source 7.7). John Williams, a farmer from rural Washington County and thus a more typical Antifederalist, criticized the Constitution more adamantly. He distrusted federal power, disliked the system of representation, and worried about America's moral decline (Source 7.9).

However, the Federalists eventually prevailed, with Hamilton, Smith, and twenty-eight other delegates voting yes and Williams one of the twenty-seven no votes. The slim victory elated the Federalist newspaper, the *Massachusetts Centinel*, which tracked each state that ratified the Constitution (Source 7.10).

The intensity of these debates highlights the competing ideas and interests among Americans. It also shows the willingness of Federalists to compromise on issues like a bill of rights while insisting on creating a new political structure.

Source 7.6

James Madison | *Federalist* 10, The Union as a Safeguard Against Domestic Faction and Insurrection, November 1787

James Madison wrote the most significant of the pro-Constitution essays known collectively as *The Federalist Papers*. In this tenth essay, Madison challenged the widely held belief that republican governments were mostly likely to succeed when they were small and compact. He argued instead that a large and diverse population in which various factions competed for support would keep any one faction from subverting the freedom of other groups.

To the People of the State of New York:

AMONG the numerous advantages promised by a well-constructed Union, none deserves to be more accurately developed than its tendency to break and control the violence of faction. The friend of popular governments never finds himself so much alarmed for their character and fate, as when he contemplates their propensity to this dangerous vice. He will not fail, therefore, to set a due value on any plan which, without violating the principles to which he is attached, provides a proper cure for it. . . .

By a faction, I understand a number of citizens, whether amounting to a majority or a minority of the whole, who are united and actuated by some common impulse of passion, or of interest, adversed to the rights of other citizens, or to the permanent and aggregate interests of the community. . . .

The latent causes of faction are . . . sown in the nature of man; and we see them everywhere brought into different degrees of activity, according to the different circumstances of civil society. . . . But the most common and durable source of factions has been the various and unequal distribution of property. Those who hold and those who are without property have ever formed distinct interests in society. Those who are creditors, and those who are debtors, fall under a like discrimination. A landed interest, a manufacturing interest, a mercantile interest, a moneyed interest, with many lesser interests, grow up of necessity in civilized nations, and divide them into different classes, actuated by different sentiments and views. . . .

[I]t may be concluded that a pure democracy, by which I mean a society consisting of a small number of citizens, who assemble and administer the government in person, can admit of no cure for the mischiefs of faction. A common passion or interest will, in almost every case, be felt by a majority of the whole; a communication and concert result from the form of government itself; and there is nothing to check the inducements to sacrifice the weaker party or an obnoxious individual. . . .

A republic, by which I mean a government in which the scheme of representation takes place, opens a different prospect, and promises the cure for which we are seeking. . . .

[T]he greater number of citizens and extent of territory which may be brought within the compass of republican than of democratic government . . . is th[e] circumstance principally which renders factious combinations less to be dreaded in the former than in the latter. The smaller the society, the fewer probably will be the distinct parties and interests composing it; the fewer the distinct parties and interests, the more frequently will a majority be found of the same party; and the smaller the number of individuals composing a majority, and the smaller the compass within which they are placed, the more easily will they concert and execute their plans of oppression. Extend the sphere, and you take in a greater variety of parties and interests; you make it less probable that a majority of the whole will have a common motive to invade the rights of other citizens; or if such a common motive exists, it will be more difficult for all who feel it to discover their own strength, and to act in unison with each other. . . .

The influence of factious leaders may kindle a flame within their particular States, but will be unable to spread a general conflagration through the other States. A religious sect may degenerate into a political faction in a part of the Confederacy; but the variety of sects dispersed over the entire face of it must secure the national councils against any danger from that source.

Source: *New York Packet*, November 23, 1787, Library of Congress.

Source: *New York Packet*, November 23, 1787, Library of Congress.

Source 7.7

Melancton Smith | Antifederalist Argument at the New York State Convention, June 1788

Melancton Smith was unusually wealthy for an Antifederalist delegate to the New York ratifying convention. Smith also worked alongside Alexander Hamilton in the New York Manumission Society, which encouraged the gradual abolition of slavery. But while Hamilton accepted the three-fifths compromise as necessary, Smith found it odious. He also embraced the traditional view that republics were best governed by smaller governmental bodies.

I n the discussion of this question, he [Smith] was disposed to make every reasonable concession, and, indeed, to sacrifice every thing for a union, except the liberties of his country. . . .

The defects of the Old Confederation needed as little proof as the necessity of an Union. But there was no proof in all this that the proposed Constitution was a good one. Defective as the Old Confederation is, . . . no one could deny but it was possible we might have a worse government. . . .

241

He would agree with the honorable gentlemen [Hamilton] that perfection in any system of government was not to be looked for. . . . But he would observe, that this observation applied with equal force against changing any systems, especially against material and radical changes. Fickleness and inconstancy, he said, were characteristic of a free people; and in framing a Constitution for them, it was, perhaps the most difficult thing to correct this spirit, and guard against the evil effects of it. . . .

He would now proceed to state his objections to the clause just read, (section 2, of article 1, clause 3). . . . In the first place, the rule of apportionment of the representatives is to be according to the whole number of the white inhabitants, with three fifths of all others, that is in plain English, each state is to send Representatives in proportion to the number of freemen, and three fifths of the slaves it contains. He could not see any rule by which slaves were to be included in the ratio of representation. The principle of a representation, being that every free agent should be concerned in governing himself, it was absurd to give that power to a man who could not exercise it. . . . The very operation of it was to give certain privileges to those people who were so wicked as to keep slaves. He knew it would be admitted that this rule of apportionment was founded on unjust principles, but that it was the result of accommodation; which, he supposed, we should be under the necessity of admitting, . . . though utterly repugnant to his feelings. . . .

[And] how was the will of the community to be expressed? . . . [W]e may approach a great way towards perfection by increasing the representation and limiting the powers of Congress. He considered that the great interests and liberties of the people could only be secured by the State Governments. He admitted, that if the new government was only confined to great national objects, it would be less exceptionable; but it extended to every thing dear to human nature. . . . [F]or that power which had both the purse and the sword had the government of the whole country, and might extend its powers to any and to every object.

Source: New York State Ratification Convention, Minutes, June 20, 1788.

Source 7.8

Alexander Hamilton | Federalist Argument at the New York State Convention, June 1788

Alexander Hamilton directly countered Melancton Smith's claims about the three-fifths compromise and the benefits of relying on state governments. Noting that many states failed to provide their share of troops or funds when requisitioned by the confederation government, Hamilton feared that without a stronger central government, the United States would be weakened economically and militarily.

I will not agree with gentlemen who trifle with the weaknesses of our country; and suppose, that they are enumerated to answer a party purpose, and to terrify with ideal dangers. No; I believe these weaknesses to be real, and pregnant with destruction. Yet, however weak our country may be, I hope we never shall sacrifice our liberties. . . .

Sir, it appears to me extraordinary, that, while gentlemen in one breath acknowledge that the old confederation requires many material amendments, they should in the next deny, that its defects have been the cause of our political weakness, and the consequent calamities of our country. . . . [T]he states have almost uniformly weighed the requisitions by their own local interests; and have only executed them so far as answered their particular conveniency or advantage. Hence there have ever been thirteen different bodies to judge of the measures of Congress, and the operations of government have been distracted by their taking different courses. . . .

Shall we take the old Confederation, as the basis of a new system? . . . certainly not. Will any man who entertains a wish for the safety of his country, trust the sword and the purse with a single Assembly organized on principles so defective — so rotten? Though we might give to such a government certain powers with safety, yet to give them the full and unlimited powers of taxation and the national forces would be to establish a despotism; the definition of which is, a government in which all power is concentrated in a single body. . . . These considerations show clearly, that a government totally different must be instituted. . . . [T]he convention . . . therefore formed two branches, and divided the powers, that each might be a check upon the other. . . .

Sir, the natural situation of this country seems to divide its interests into different classes. . . . It became necessary, therefore, to compromise; or the Convention must have dissolved without effecting any thing. . . .

The first thing objected to is that clause which allows a representation for three fifths of the negroes. . . . It is the unfortunate situation of the Southern States to have a great part of their population, as well as property, in blacks. The regulation complained of was one result of the spirit of accommodation, which governed the Convention; and without this indulgence, no union could possibly have been formed. But, Sir, considering some peculiar advantages which we derive from them, it is entirely just that they should be gratified. The Southern States possess certain staples, tobacco, rice, indigo, &c. which must be capital objects in treaties of commerce with foreign nations; and the advantages which they necessarily procure in these treaties, will be felt throughout all the States. . . . [Moreover] representation and taxation go together, and one uniform rule ought to apply to both. Would it be just to compute these slaves in the assessment of taxes; and discard them from the estimate in the apportionment of representatives?

Source: New York State Ratification Convention, Minutes, June 20, 1788.

Source 7.9

John Williams | Antifederalist Argument at the New York State Convention, June 1788

One of four delegates from the northern counties of Washington and Clinton, John Williams represented the interests of rural farmers. An ardent Antifederalist, he preferred that political power be focused at local and state levels. But he also expressed deep concern about the loss of traditional values like thrift and hard work, making the nation vulnerable to mercantile and foreign interests.

I believe that this country has never before seen such a critical period in political affairs. We have felt the feebleness of those ties, by which the States are held together, and the want of that energy which is necessary to manage our general concerns. . . .

Indeed, Sir, it appears to me, that many of our present distresses flow from a source very different from the defects in the Confederation. Unhappily for us, immediately after our extrication from a cruel and unnatural war, luxury and dissipation overran the country, banishing all that economy, frugality, and industry, which had been exhibited during the war. . . .

Let us, then, abandon all those foreign commodities which have hitherto deluged our country; which have loaded us with debt, and which, if continued, will forever involve us in difficulties. How many thousands are daily wearing the manufactures of Europe, when by a little industry and frugality, they might wear those of their own country! . . . What dissipation is there from the immoderate use of spirits! Is it not notorious that men cannot be hired, in time of harvest, without giving them, on an average, a pint of rum per day? . . . And, what is worse, the disposition of eight tenths of the commonalty is such, that, if they can get credit, they will purchase unnecessary articles, even to the amount of their crop, before it becomes merchantable. . . . [T]he best government ever devised, without economy and frugality will leave us in a situation no better than the present. . . .

[L]et us examine whether it [the Constitution] be calculated to preserve the invaluable blessings of liberty, and secure the inestimable rights of mankind. . . . [I]f it be found to contain principles that will lead to the subversion of liberty, . . . let us insist upon the necessary alterations and amendments. . . .

In forming a constitution for a free country like this, the greatest care should be taken to define its powers, and guard against an abuse of authority. The Constitution should be so formed as not to swallow up the State governments: the general government ought to be confined to certain national objects; and the States should retain such powers, as concern their own internal police. . . . The number of representatives is, in my opinion, too small to resist corruption. Sir, how guarded is our State Constitution on this head! The number of senate and house of representatives proposed in the Constitution does not surpass those of our State. How great the disparity, when compared with the aggregate number of the United States! . . . Can it be supposed that six men can be a complete representation of the various orders of people of this State?

Source: New York State Ratification Convention, Minutes, June 21, 1788.

The Eleventh Pillar of the Great National Dome, 1788

Throughout 1788, newspapers like the *Massachusetts Centinel* traced the results of ratifying conventions state by state. A graphic represented each state that ratified the Constitution as a pillar of the new federal superstructure. The addition of New York State is accompanied by flowery verse above and below "the beauteous DOME."

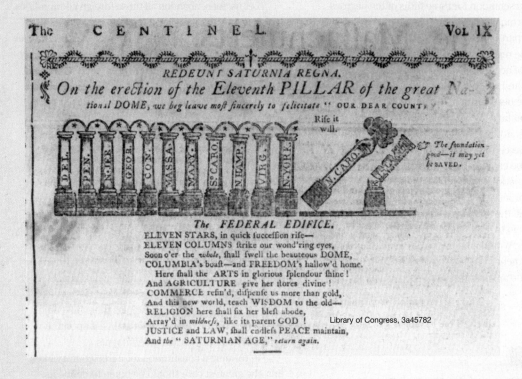

The CENTINEL. VOL IX

REDEUNT SATURNIA REGNA.

On the erection of the Eleventh PILLAR of the great National DOME, we beg leave most sincerely to felicitate " OUR DEAR COUNTRY."

Rise it
will.

The foundation
good—it may yet
be SAVED.

The FEDERAL EDIFICE.
ELEVEN STARS, in quick succession rise—
ELEVEN COLUMNS strike our wond'ring eyes,
Soon o'er the *whole*, shall swell the beauteous DOME,
COLUMBIA's boast—and FREEDOM's hallow'd home.
  Here shall the ARTS in glorious splendour shine !
And AGRICULTURE give her stores divine !
COMMERCE refin'd, dispense us more than gold,
And this new world, teach WISDOM to the old—
RELIGION here shall fix her blest abode,
Array'd in *mildness*, like its parent GOD !
JUSTICE and LAW, shall endless PEACE maintain,
And the " SATURNIAN AGE," return again.

Library of Congress, 3a45782

Interpret the Evidence

1. How do Melancton Smith, Alexander Hamilton, and John Williams each view the problems that exist under the confederation government (Sources 7.7, 7.8, and 7.9)?

2. What does James Madison see as the major source of factions in the United States, and how does he think they can most effectively be contained (Source 7.6)?

3. What are the main arguments for and against the three-fifths compromise in the Constitution (Sources 7.7, 7.8, and 7.9)? What other issues of representation inspired debate?

4. Are there any shared beliefs between the Federalists and Antifederalists in New York (Sources 7.6, 7.7, 7.8, and 7.9)? How might these contribute to Smith's decision to vote yes on ratification?

5. What does the Massachusetts Centinel's representation of ratification in New York State (Source 7.10) suggest about that newspaper's point of view?

Put It in Context

In what ways does the ratification process in New York State reflect larger debates and divisions in the United States in the 1780s?

The Early Republic

1790–1820

WINDOW TO THE PAST

William Clark, Journal, January 28, 1805

William Clark kept a detailed journal of the 1804–1806 expedition he and Meriwether Lewis led to explore the American West. They were aided by many different Indian groups, especially the Mandan Indians along the Missouri River. They camped near the Mandan in the winter of 1804, before heading into the Rocky Mountains. Here Clark draws a Mandan war hatchet, which was crucial to the tribe's defense. ▸ To discover more about what this primary source can show us, see Source 8.9 on pages 278–79.

American Philosophical Society

After reading this chapter you should be able to:

- Analyze the ways that social and cultural leaders worked to craft an American identity and how that was complicated by racial, ethnic, and class differences.

- Interpret how the Democratic-Republican ideal of limiting federal power was transformed by international events, westward expansion, and Supreme Court rulings between 1800 and 1808.

- Explain the ways that technology reshaped the American economy and the lives of distinct groups of Americans.

COMPARING AMERICAN HISTORIES

When Parker Cleaveland graduated from Harvard University in 1799, his parents expected him to pursue a career in medicine, law, or the ministry. Instead, he turned to teaching. In 1805 Cleaveland secured a position in Brunswick, Maine, as professor of mathematics and natural philosophy at Bowdoin College. A year later, he married Martha Bush. Over the next twenty years, the Cleavelands raised eight children on the Maine frontier, entertained visiting scholars, corresponded with families at other colleges, and boarded dozens of students. While Parker taught

(*left*) **Parker Cleaveland.** Courtesy the Bowdoin College Library, Brunswick, Maine, USA
(*right*) **Shoshone woman.** (No image of Sacagawea exists.) Joslyn Museum, Omaha, Nebraska, USA/Alecto Historical Editions/Bridgeman Images

those students math and science, Martha trained them in manners and morals. The Cleavelands also served as a model of new ideals of companionate marriage, in which husbands and wives shared interests and affection.

Professor Cleaveland believed in using scientific research to benefit society. When Brunswick workers asked him to identify local rocks, Parker began studying geology and chemistry. In 1816 he published his *Elementary Treatise on Mineralogy and Geology*, providing a basic text for students and interested adults. He also lectured throughout New England, displaying mineral samples and performing chemical experiments.

The Cleavelands viewed the Bowdoin College community as a laboratory in which distinctly American values and ideas could be developed and sustained. So, too, did the residents of other college towns. Although less than 1 percent of men in the United States attended universities at the time, frontier colleges were considered important vehicles for bringing virtue—especially the desire to act for the public good—to the far reaches of the early republic. Yet several of these colleges were constructed with the aid of slave labor, and all were built on land bought or confiscated from Indians.

The purchase of the Louisiana Territory by President Thomas Jefferson in 1803 marked a new American frontier and ensured further encroachments on native lands. The territory covered 828,000 square miles and stretched from the Mississippi River to the Rocky Mountains and from New Orleans to present-day Montana. The area was home to tens of thousands of Indian inhabitants.

In 1800 a Hidatsa raiding party swept into a Shoshone village and seized captives, including a girl about twelve years old. The girl, Sacagawea, and her fellow captives were marched hundreds of miles to a Hidatsa-Mandan village on the Missouri River. Eventually Sacagawea was sold to a French trader, Toussaint Charbonneau, along with another young Shoshone woman, and both became his wives.

In November 1804, an expedition led by Meriwether Lewis and William Clark set up winter camp near the Hidatsa village where Sacagawea lived. The U.S. government had sent Lewis and Clark to document flora and fauna in the Louisiana Territory, enhance trade, and explore routes to the Northwest. Charbonneau, who spoke French and Hidatsa, and Sacagawea, who spoke several Indian languages, joined the expedition as interpreters in April 1805.

The only woman in the party, Sacagawea traveled with her infant son strapped to her back. Although no portraits of her exist, her presence was crucial, as Clark noted in his journal: "The Wife of Chabono our interpreter we find reconsiles all the Indians, as to our friendly intentions." Sacagawea did help persuade Indian leaders to assist the expedition, but her extensive knowledge of the terrain and fluency in Indian languages were equally important. ∎

Comparing the American histories of Parker Cleaveland and Sacagawea highlights the distinct ways that individuals contributed to the development of the United States and of national identities. Cleaveland gained fame as part of a generation of intellectuals who symbolized Americans' ingenuity. Although Sacagawea was not considered learned, her understanding of Indian languages and western geography was crucial to Lewis and Clark's success. Like many other Americans, Sacagawea and Cleaveland forged new identities as the young nation developed. Still, racial, class, and gender differences made it impossible to create a single American identity. At the same time, Democratic-Republican leaders sought to shape a new national identity by promising to limit federal power and enhance state authority and individual rights. Instead, western expansion, international crises, and Supreme Court decisions all contributed to the growth of federal power.

The **Dilemmas** of **National Identity**

In his inaugural address in March 1801, President Thomas Jefferson argued that the vast distance between Europe and the United States was a blessing, allowing Americans to develop their own unique culture and institutions. For many Americans, education offered one means of ensuring a distinctive national identity. Public schools could train American children in republican values, while the wealthiest among them could attend private academies and colleges. Newspapers, sermons, books, magazines, and other printed works could also help forge a common identity among the nation's far-flung citizens. Even the presence of Indians and Africans contributed to art and literature that were uniquely American. In addition, the construction of a new capital city to house the federal government offered a potent symbol of nationhood.

Yet these developments also illuminated political and racial dilemmas in the young nation. The decision to move the U.S. capital south from Philadelphia was prompted by concerns among southern politicians about the power of northern economic and political elites. The very construction of the capital, in which enslaved and free workers labored side by side, highlighted racial and class differences. Educational opportunities differed by race and class as well as by sex. How could a singular notion of American identity be forged in a country where differences of race, class, and sex loomed so large?

Education for a New Nation. The desire to create a specifically American culture began as soon as the Revolution ended. In 1783 Noah Webster, a schoolmaster, declared that "America must be as independent in *literature as in Politics*, as famous for *arts* as for *arms."* To promote his vision, Webster published the *American Spelling Book* (1810) and the *American Dictionary of the English Language* (1828). Webster's books were widely used in the nation's expanding network of schools and academies and led to more standardized spelling and pronunciation of commonly used words.

Before the Revolution, public education for children was widely available in New England and the Middle Atlantic region. In the South, only those who could afford private schooling—perhaps 25 percent of the boys and 10 percent of the girls—received any formal instruction. Few young people enrolled in high school in any part of the colonies. Following the Revolution, state and national leaders proposed ambitious plans for public education, and in 1789 Massachusetts became the first state to demand that each town provide free schools for local children, though attendance policies were decided by the towns.

The American colonies boasted nine colleges that provided higher education for young men, including Harvard, Yale, King's College (Columbia), Queen's College (Rutgers), and the College of William and Mary. After independence, many Americans worried that these institutions were tainted by British and aristocratic influences. New colleges based on republican ideals needed to be founded.

Frontier towns offered opportunities for colleges to enrich the community and benefit the nation. The relative isolation of these villages ensured that students would focus on education. And frontier colleges provided opportunities for ethnic and religious groups

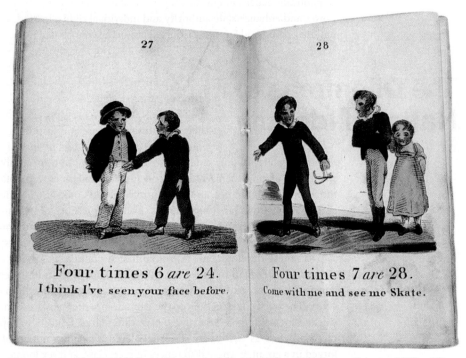

Marmaduke Multiply's Merry Method of Making Minor Mathematics, c. 1815   After Noah Webster introduced his *American Spelling Book* in 1810, math instructors introduced books for young people like the one shown here. The book uses rhymes and colorful illustrations to teach students multiplication tables. More and more educational books for children were published as public schools multiplied in the decades following the Revolution. Granger

outside the Anglo-American mainstream—like Scots-Irish Presbyterians—to cement their place in American society. The young nation benefited as well, albeit at the expense of Indians and their lands. For example, the founding of Franklin College in Athens, Georgia encouraged white settlement in the state's interior, an area still largely populated by the Creek and Cherokee.

Frontier colleges were organized as community institutions composed of extended families, where administrators, faculty, and their wives guided students, hosted social events, and hired local workers, including servants and slaves. Women were viewed as exemplars of virtue in the new nation, and professors' wives served as maternal figures for young adults away from home. Families of modest means could send their sons to these less expensive colleges, depending on faculty couples to expand their intellect and provide moral guidance. In some towns, students at local female academies joined college men at chaperoned events to cultivate proper relations between the sexes.

Literary and Cultural Developments.
Older universities also contributed to the development of a national identity. A group known as the Hartford Wits, most of them Yale graduates, gave birth to a new literary tradition. Its members identified mainly as Federalists and published paeans to democracy, satires about Shays's Rebellion, and plays about the proper role of the central government in a republican nation. Developments in Europe, particularly liberal social ideas and Romantic beliefs in human perfectibility, also shaped American art, literature, philosophy, and architecture in the early nineteenth century. European Romantics, like the English poet William Wordsworth, the German philosopher Immanuel Kant, and the French painter Eugène Delacroix, challenged Enlightenment ideas of rationality by insisting on the importance of human passion, the mysteries of nature, and the virtues of common folk.

American novelists in the early republic drew on these ideas as they sought to educate readers about virtue. Advances in printing and the manufacture of paper increased the circulation of novels, a literary genre developed in Britain and continental Europe at the turn of the eighteenth century. Improvements in girls' education then produced a growing audience for novels among women. American authors like Susanna Rowson and Charles Brockden Brown placed ordinary women and men in moments of high drama that tested their moral character. Novelists also emphasized new marital ideals, by which husbands and wives became affectionate partners and companions in creating a home and family.

Washington Irving was one of the most well-known literary figures in the early republic. He wrote a series of popular folktales, including "The Legend of Sleepy Hollow" and "Rip Van Winkle," that were published in his *Sketchbook* in 1820. They drew on the Dutch culture of the Hudson valley region and often poked fun at more celebratory tales of early American history. In one serious essay, Irving challenged popular accounts of colonial wars that ignored courageous actions by Indians while applauding white atrocities.

Still, books that glorified the nation's past were also enormously popular. Just as European Romantics emphasized individual, especially heroic, action, so too did America's earliest historical writers. Among the most influential were Mason Weems, author of the *Life of Washington* (1806), a celebratory if fanciful biography, and Mercy Otis Warren, who wrote a three-volume *History of the Revolution* (1805). The influence of American authors increased as residents in both urban and rural areas purchased growing numbers of books.

Artists, too, devoted considerable attention to historical themes, though in the late eighteenth century, they tended more to Enlightenment perspectives. Charles Willson

Peale painted Revolutionary generals while serving in the Continental Army and became best known for his portraits of George Washington. Samuel Jennings offered a more radical perspective on the nation's character by incorporating women and African Americans into works like *Liberty Displaying the Arts and Sciences* (1792), but highlighted the importance of learning and rationality. So, too, did William Bartram, the son of a botanist. He

Explore ▸

See Source 8.1 for one artist's image of republican education.

journeyed through the southeastern United States and Florida, and published beautiful, and scientifically accurate, engravings of plants and animals in his *Travels* (1791). Engravings were less expensive than paintings so circulated more widely, and many highlighted national symbols like flags, eagles, and Lady Liberty.

In 1780, the Massachusetts legislature established the American Academy of Arts and Sciences to promote American literature and science. Six years later, Philadelphia's American Philosophical Society created the first national prize for scientific endeavor. Philadelphia was also home to the nation's first medical college, founded at the University of Pennsylvania. Frontier colleges like Bowdoin also promoted new scientific discoveries. As in the arts, American scientists built on developments in continental Europe and Britain but prided themselves on contributing their own expertise.

Religious Renewal.
Amid the wave of scientific discoveries, religious leaders sought to renew American spirituality. However, this spiritual renewal was rooted less in established churches and educated ministers than in new religious organizations and popular preachers. Methodist and Baptist churches were especially vital to this development. In 1780, only fifty Methodist churches existed in the United States. By 1820, it was the largest denomination in the nation, followed closely by Baptists. Believing that everyone could gain salvation, the two denominations appealed to small farmers, workers, and the poor as well to women and African Americans. In some cases, women and blacks joined this popular ministry, and a few attracted followings independent of any church. Jemima Wilkinson, a white woman who called herself "the Publick Universal Friend," developed a gender-neutral persona. Proclaiming herself the "Spirit of Light," she preached throughout the Northeast.

In rural and frontier areas, Baptists, Methodists, and Presbyterians organized camp meetings, where a dozen or more preachers, many without formal training, tapped into deep wells of spirituality. The first camp meeting, held in Cane Ridge, Kentucky in 1801, attracted some 10,000 men and women. Whites and blacks, enslaved and free, attended these meetings and were encouraged to dance, shout, sing, and pray. For the next two decades, camp meetings continued to attract large crowds across the South and West.

The Racial Limits of an American Culture.
American Indians received significant attention from writers and scientists. White Americans in the early republic often wielded native names and symbols as they sought to create a distinct national identity. Some Americans, including whiskey rebels, followed in the tradition of the Boston Tea Party, dressing as Indians to protest economic and political tyranny (see "The Whiskey Rebellion" in Chapter 7). But more affluent whites also embraced Indian names and symbols. Tammany societies, which promoted patriotism and republicanism in the late eighteenth century, were named after a mythical Delaware chief called Tammend. They attracted large numbers of lawyers, merchants, and skilled artisans.

GUIDED ANALYSIS

Samuel Jennings | Liberty Displaying the Arts and Sciences, 1792

Samuel Jennings was born in Philadelphia and attended the College of Philadelphia before the Revolution. He taught drawing and painted portraits before moving to London to study with Benjamin West in 1787. There his allegorical paintings were exhibited at the Royal Academy. Jennings painted this image for the newly established Library Company of Philadelphia, many of whose directors were Quakers who opposed slavery. The directors requested that he include Lady Liberty with her cap on the end of a pole.

Source 8.1

The Library Company of Philadelphia

Which arts and sciences are displayed in this painting?

What does the broken chain at the feet of Lady Liberty indicate?

What distinguishes the black people inside and outside the building?

Put It in Context

What does this painting suggest about how Jennings and the Library Company directors envisioned American identities in the early republic?

Poets, too, focused on American Indians. In his 1787 poem "Indian Burying Ground," Philip Freneau offered a sentimental portrait that highlighted the lost heritage of a nearly extinct native culture in New England. The theme of lost cultures and heroic (if still savage) Indians became even more pronounced in American poetry in the following decades. Such sentimental portraits of American Indians were decidedly less popular along the nation's frontier, where Indians continued to fight for their lands and rights.

Sympathetic depictions of Africans and African Americans by white artists and authors appeared less frequently. Most were produced in the North and were intended for the rare patrons who opposed slavery. Typical images of blacks, and of Indians as well, were far more demeaning. When describing Indians in frontier regions, white Americans generally focused on their savagery and their duplicity. Most images of Africans and African Americans exaggerated their perceived physical and intellectual differences from whites, to imply an innate inferiority.

Whether their depictions were realistic, sentimental, or derogatory, Africans, African Americans, and American Indians were almost always presented to the American public through the eyes of whites. Educated blacks like the Reverend Richard Allen of Philadelphia or the Reverend Thomas Paul of Boston wrote mainly for black audiences or corresponded privately with sympathetic whites. Similarly, cultural leaders among American Indians worked mainly within their own nations either to maintain traditional languages and customs or to introduce their people to Anglo-American ideas and beliefs.

The improved educational opportunities available to white Americans generally excluded blacks and Indians. Most southern planters had little desire to teach their slaves to read and write. Even in the North, states did not generally incorporate black children into their plans for public education. African Americans in cities with large free black populations established the most long-lived schools for their race. The Reverend Allen opened a Sunday school for children in 1795 at his African Methodist Episcopal Church, and other free blacks formed literary and debating societies. Still, only a small percentage of African Americans received an education equivalent to that available to whites in the early republic.

U.S. political leaders were more interested in the education of American Indians, but government officials left their schooling to religious groups. Several denominations sent missionaries to the Seneca, Cherokee, and other tribes, and a few successful students were then sent to American colleges to be trained as ministers or teachers for their own people. This was important since few whites bothered to learn Indian languages.

The divergent approaches that whites took to Indian and African American education demonstrated broader assumptions about the two groups. Most white Americans believed that Indians were untamed and uncivilized, but not innately different from Europeans. Africans and African Americans, on the other hand, were assumed to be inferior, and most whites believed that no amount of education could change that. As U.S. frontiers expanded, white Americans considered ways to "civilize" Indians and incorporate them into the nation. But the requirements of slavery made it much more difficult for whites to imagine African Americans as anything more than lowly laborers, despite free blacks who clearly demonstrated otherwise.

Aware of the limited opportunities available in the United States, some African Americans considered the benefits of moving elsewhere. In the late 1780s, the Newport African Union Society in Rhode Island developed a plan to establish a community for American

Benjamin Banneker's *Pennsylvania, Delaware, Maryland, and Virginia Almanac*, 1795   Benjamin Banneker (here spelled Bannaker) was a free black from Baltimore County, Maryland. Largely self-educated, he was a talented astronomer who compiled almanacs that included annual calendars, tide charts, lunar and solar observations, and statistical charts. Almanacs were widely used by farmers, sailors, and the general public. Banneker's almanac included his portrait to highlight his achievements as a black man.
Granger

blacks in Africa. Many whites, too, viewed the settlement of blacks in Africa as the only way to solve the nation's racial dilemma.

Over the next three decades, the idea of emigration (as blacks viewed it) or colonization (as whites saw it) received widespread attention. Those who opposed slavery hoped to persuade slave owners to free or sell their human property on the condition that they be shipped to Africa. Others assumed that free blacks could find opportunities in Africa that were not available to them in the United States. Still others simply wanted to rid the nation of its race problem by ridding it of blacks. In 1817 a group of southern slave owners and northern merchants formed the **American Colonization Society (ACS)** to establish colonies of freed slaves and free-born American blacks in Africa. Although some African Americans supported this scheme, northern free blacks generally opposed it, viewing colonization as an effort originating "more immediately from prejudice than philanthropy." Ultimately the plans of the ACS proved impractical. Particularly as cotton production expanded from the 1790s on, few slave owners were willing to emancipate their workers.

A New Capital for a New Nation.   The construction of Washington City, the new capital, provided an opportunity to highlight the nation's distinctive culture and identity. But here, again, slavery emerged as a crucial part of that identity. The capital was situated along the Potomac River between Virginia and Maryland, an area where more than 300,000 enslaved workers lived. Between 1792 and 1809, hundreds of enslaved men and a few women were hired out by their owners, who were paid $5 per month for each individual's labor. Enslaved men cleared trees and stumps, built roads, dug trenches, baked bricks, and cut and laid sandstone while enslaved women cooked, did laundry, and nursed the sick and injured. A small number performed skilled labor as carpenters or assistants to stonemasons and surveyors. Some four hundred slaves worked on the Capitol building alone, more than half the workforce.

The United States Capitol   This watercolor by William Russell Birch presents a view of the Capitol in Washington, D.C., before it was burned down by the British during the War of 1812. Birch had emigrated from England in 1794 and lived in Philadelphia. As this painting suggests, neither the Capitol nor the city was as yet a vibrant center of republican achievements. Library of Congress, LC-DIG-ppmsca-22593

Free blacks also participated in the development of Washington. Many worked alongside enslaved laborers, but a few held important positions. Benjamin Banneker, for example, a self-taught clock maker, astronomer, and surveyor, was hired as an assistant to the surveyor Major Andrew Ellicott. In 1791 Banneker helped to plot the 100-square-mile site on which the capital was to be built.

African Americans often worked alongside Irish immigrants, whose wages were kept in check by the availability of slave labor. Most workers, regardless of race, faced poor housing, sparse meals, malarial fevers, and limited medical care. Despite these obstacles, in less than a decade, a system of roads was laid out and cleared, the Executive Mansion was built, and the north wing of the Capitol was completed.

More prosperous immigrants and foreign professionals were also involved in creating the U.S. capital. Irish-born James Hoban designed the Executive Mansion. A French engineer developed the plan for the city's streets. A West Indian physician turned architect drew the blueprints for the Capitol building, the construction of which was directed by Englishman Benjamin Latrobe. Perhaps what was most "American" about the new capital was the diverse nationalities and races of those who designed and built it.

Washington's founders envisioned the city as a beacon to the world, proclaiming the advantages of the nation's republican principles. But its location on a slow-moving river and its clay soil left the area hot, humid, and dusty in the summer and muddy and damp in the winter and spring. When John Adams and his administration moved to Washington in June 1800, they considered themselves on the frontiers of civilization. The tree stumps that remained on the mile-long road from the Capitol to the Executive Mansion made it nearly impossible to navigate in a carriage. On rainy days, when roads proved impassable, officials walked or rode horses to work. Many early residents painted Washington in harsh tones. New Hampshire congressional representative Ebenezer Matroon wrote a friend, "If I wished to punish a culprit, I would send him to do penance in this place . . . this swamp— this lonesome dreary swamp, secluded from every delightful or pleasing thing."

Despite its critics, Washington was the seat of federal power and thus played an important role in the social and political worlds of American elites. From January through March, the height of the social season, the wives of congressmen, judges, and other officials created a lively schedule of teas, parties, and balls in the capital city. When Thomas Jefferson became president, he opened the White House to visitors on a regular basis. Yet for all his republican principles, Jefferson moved into the Executive Mansion with a retinue of slaves.

In decades to come, Washington City would become Washington, D.C., a city with broad boulevards decorated with beautiful monuments to the American political experiment. And the Executive Mansion would become the White House, a proud symbol of republican government. Yet Washington was always characterized by wide disparities in wealth, status, and power, which were especially visible when slaves labored in the Executive Mansion's kitchen, laundry, and yard. President Jefferson's efforts to incorporate new territories into the United States only exacerbated these divisions by providing more economic opportunities for planters, investors, and white farmers while ensuring the expansion of slavery and the decimation of American Indians.

REVIEW & RELATE

- How did developments in education, literature, and the arts contribute to the emergence of a distinctly American identity?

- How did blacks and American Indians both contribute to and challenge the predominantly white view of American identity?

Extending Federal Power

Thomas Jefferson, like other Democratic-Republicans, envisioned the United States as a republic composed of small, independent farmers who had little need and less desire for expansive federal power. Despite Jefferson's early efforts to impose this vision on the government, developments in international affairs soon converged with Supreme Court rulings to expand federal power. But Jefferson, too, contributed to this expansion. Imagining the nation's extensive frontiers as a boon to its development, he purchased the Louisiana Territory from France in 1803. The purchase and development of this vast territory increased federal authority. It also raised new questions about the place of Indians and African Americans in a republican society.

A New Administration Faces Challenges. In 1801 Democratic-Republicans worked quickly to implement their vision of limited federal power. Holding the majority in Congress, they repealed the whiskey tax and let the Alien and Sedition Acts expire. Jefferson significantly reduced government expenditures, and immediately set about slashing the national debt, cutting it nearly in half by the end of his second term. Democratic-Republicans also worked to curb the powers granted to the Bank of the United States and the federal court system.

Soon, however, international upheavals forced Jefferson to make fuller use of his presidential powers. The U.S. government had paid tribute to the Barbary States of North Africa during the 1790s to gain protection for American merchant ships. The new president opposed this practice and in 1801 refused to continue the payments. The Barbary pirates quickly resumed their attacks, and Jefferson was forced to send the U.S. Navy and Marine Corps to retaliate. Although a combined American and Arab force did not achieve their objective of capturing Tripoli, the Ottoman viceroy agreed to negotiate a new agreement with the United States. Seeking to avoid all-out war, Congress accepted a treaty with the Barbary States that reduced the tribute payment.

Jefferson had also followed the developing crisis in the West Indies during the 1790s. In 1791 slaves on the sugar-rich island of Saint Domingue launched a revolt against French rule. Inspired in part by the American Declaration of Independence, the **Haitian Revolution** escalated into a complicated conflict in which free people of color, white slave owners, and slaves formed competing alliances with British and Spanish forces as well as with leaders of the French Revolution. Finally, in December 1799, Toussaint L'Ouverture, a military leader and former slave, claimed the presidency of the new Republic of Haiti. But Napoleon Bonaparte seized power in France that same year and sent thousands of troops to reclaim the island. Toussaint was shipped off to France, where he died in prison. Many Haitians fled to the United States, but other Haitian rebels continued the fight.

Explore ▶

See Sources 8.2 and 8.3 for two views on the revolution in Haiti.

In the United States, reactions to the revolution were mixed, but southern whites feared that it might incite rebellions among their slaves. In 1800 Gabriel, an enslaved blacksmith in Richmond, Virginia, plotted such a rebellion. Inspired by both the American and Haitian revolutions, supporters rallied around the demand for "Death or Liberty." Gabriel's plan failed when informants betrayed him to authorities. Nonetheless, news of the plot traveled across the South and terrified white residents. Their anxieties were probably heightened when in November 1803, prolonged fighting, yellow fever, and the loss of sixty thousand soldiers forced Napoleon to admit defeat in Haiti. Haiti became the first independent black-led nation in the Americas.

Acquiring the Louisiana Territory.

In France's defeat Jefferson saw an opportunity to gain navigation rights on the Mississippi River, which the French controlled. This was a matter of crucial concern to Americans living west of the Appalachian Mountains. Jefferson sent James Monroe to France to offer Napoleon $2 million to ensure Americans the right of navigation and deposit (i.e., offloading cargo from ships) on the Mississippi. To Jefferson's surprise, Napoleon offered instead to sell the entire Louisiana Territory for $15 million.

The president agonized over the constitutionality of this **Louisiana Purchase**. Since the Constitution contained no provisions for buying land from foreign nations, a strict interpretation would prohibit the purchase. In the end, though, the opportunity proved too tempting, and the president finally agreed to buy the Louisiana Territory. Jefferson justified his decision by arguing that the territory would allow for the removal of more Indians from east of the Mississippi River, end European influence in the region, and expand U.S. trade networks. Opponents viewed the purchase as benefiting mainly agrarian interests and suspected Jefferson of trying to offset Federalist power in the Northeast. Neither party seemed especially concerned about the French, Spanish, or native peoples living in the region. They came under U.S. control when the Senate approved the purchase in October 1803. And the acquisition proved popular among ordinary Americans, most of whom focused on the opportunities it offered rather than the expansion of federal power it ensured.

At Jefferson's request, Congress had already appropriated funds for an expedition known as the **Corps of Discovery** to explore territory along the Missouri River. That expedition could now explore much of the Louisiana Territory. The president's personal secretary, Meriwether Lewis, headed the venture and invited fellow Virginian William Clark to serve as co-captain. The two set off with about forty-five men on May 14, 1804. For two years, they traveled thousands of miles up the Missouri River, through the northern plains, over the Rocky Mountains, and beyond the Louisiana Territory to the Pacific coast. Sacagawea and her husband joined them in April 1805 as they headed into the Rocky Mountains. Throughout the expedition, members meticulously recorded observations about local plants and animals as well as Indian residents, providing valuable evidence for young scientists like Parker Cleaveland and fascinating information for ordinary Americans. **See Primary Source Project 8: The Corps of Discovery: Paeans to Peace and Instruments of War, page 276.**

Sacagawea was the only Indian to travel as a permanent member of the expedition, but many other native women and men assisted the Corps when it journeyed near their villages. They provided food and lodging for the Corps, hauled baggage up steep mountain trails, and traded food, horses, and other items. The one African American on the expedition, a slave named York, also helped negotiate trade with local Indians. York, who realized his value as a trader, hunter, and scout, asked Clark for his freedom when the expedition ended in 1806. York did eventually become a free man, but it is not clear whether it was by Clark's choice or York's escape.

Other expeditions followed Lewis and Clark's venture. In 1806 Lieutenant Zebulon Pike led a group to explore the southern portion of the Louisiana Territory (Map 8.1). After traveling from St. Louis to the Rocky Mountains, the expedition entered Mexican territory. In early 1807, Pike and his men were captured by Mexican forces. They were returned to the United States at the Louisiana border that July. Pike had learned a great deal about lands that would eventually become part of the United States and about Mexican desires to overthrow Spanish rule, information that proved valuable over the next two decades.

Early in this series of expeditions, in November 1804, Jefferson easily won reelection as president. His popularity among farmers, already high, increased when Congress reduced the minimum allotment for federal land sales from 320 to 160 acres. This act allowed more farmers to purchase land on their own rather than via speculators. Yet by the time of Jefferson's second inauguration in March 1805, the president's vision of limiting federal power had been shattered by his own actions and those of the Supreme Court.

The Supreme Court Extends Its Reach.

In 1801, just before the Federalist-dominated Congress turned over power to the Democratic-Republicans, it passed a new

> **COMPARATIVE ANALYSIS**

White Responses to Black Rebellion

White southerners who feared the effect of the Haitian Revolution were nonetheless shocked when Gabriel, an enslaved blacksmith, plotted a rebellion in Virginia. Upon the plot's discovery, thirty blacks were tried and convicted, and twenty-seven executed for conspiring to rebel. In the first document, President Jefferson expresses concern about slave rebellions but also about the punishment of insurgents. The second document, by Leonore Sansay, the wife of a Saint-Domingue planter, captures the situation in Haiti in 1802 as France fought to reclaim its colony. Sansay, who had earlier met Vice President Aaron Burr, writes to him about conditions on the island.

> **Source 8.2**

Thomas Jefferson | Letter to U.S. Minister to Great Britain Rufus King, July 1802

The course of things in the neighboring islands of the West Indies appears to have given a considerable impulse to the minds of the slaves in different parts of the U.S. A great disposition to insurgency has manifested itself among them, which, in one instance, in the state of Virginia, broke out into actual insurrection. This was easily suppressed; but many of those concerned, (between 20 and 30, I believe) fell victims to the law. So extensive an execution could not but excite sensibility in the public mind, and beget a regret that the laws had not provided, for such cases, some alternative, combining more mildness with equal efficacy. The legislature of the state, at a subsequent meeting, took the subject into consideration, and have communicated to me . . . their wish that some place could be provided, out of the limits of the U.S., to which slaves guilty of insurgency might be transported; and they have particularly looked to Africa as offering the most desirable receptacle. We might for this purpose, enter into negotiations with the natives, on some part of the coast, to obtain a settlement and, by establishing an African company, combine with it commercial operations, which might not only reimburse expenses but procure profit also.

Source: Paul Leicester Ford, ed., *The Writings of Thomas Jefferson* (New York, 1896), 8:161–64.

Judiciary Act. The act created six additional circuit courts and sixteen new judgeships, which President Adams filled with Federalist "midnight appointments" before he left office. Jefferson accused the Federalists of having "retired into the judiciary" and worried that "from that battery all the works of Republicanism are to be beaten down and destroyed." Meanwhile John Marshall, chief justice of the United States (1801–1835), insisted that the powers of the Supreme Court must be equal to and balance those of the executive and legislative branches.

One of the first cases to test the Court's authority involved a dispute over President Adams's midnight appointments. Jefferson's secretary of state, James Madison, refused to deliver the appointment papers to several of the appointees, including William Marbury. Marbury and three others sued Madison to receive their commissions. In ***Marbury v. Madison***

Source 8.3

Leonora Sansay | Letter to Aaron Burr, November 1802

The so much desired general Rochambeau is at length here. His arrival was announced . . . by the firing of cannon. . . . Nothing is heard of but the public joy. He is considered as the guardian, as the saviour of the people. Every proprietor feels himself already in his habitation [plantation] and I have even heard some of them disputing about the quality of the coffee they expect soon to gather. . . .

The arrival of General Rochambeau seems to have spread terror among the negroes[.] I wish they were reduced to order so that I might see the so much vaunted habitations where I should repose beneath the shade of orange groves, walk on carpets of rose leaves and Frenchipone; be fanned to sleep by silent slaves. . . .

What a delightful existence! . . .

But the moment of enjoying these pleasures is, I fear, far distant. The negroes have felt during ten years the blessing of liberty, for a blessing it certainly is, however acquired, and then will not easily be deprived of it. They have fought and vanquished French troops, and their strength has increased from a knowledge of the weakness of their opposer, and the climate itself combats for them. . . .

Every evening several old Creoles . . . assemble at our house, and talk of their affairs. One of them . . . now lives in a miserable hut. . . . Yet he still hopes for better days, in which hope they all join him.

Source: Mary Hassal [Leonora Sansay], *Secret History of the Horrors of St. Domingo, in a Series of Letters Written by a Lady at Cape François to Colonel Burr* (Philadelphia: Bradford & Inskelp, 1808), 430–32.

Interpret the Evidence

1. How does Thomas Jefferson view the influence of West Indies rebellions on U.S. slaves, and why is he reluctant to respond to conspiracies by executing large numbers of insurgents?
2. How would you compare Leonora Sansay's response to black rebellion in Saint-Domingue/Haiti with Jefferson's response to conspiracies in Virginia? What accounts for the similarities and differences?

Put It in Context

How might reports of the Haitian Revolution and the Virginia rebellion have contributed to debates over the future of slavery in the early years of the United States?

(1803), the Supreme Court ruled that it was not empowered to force the executive branch to give Marbury his commission. But in his decision, Chief Justice Marshall declared that the Supreme Court did have the duty "to say what the law is." He thus asserted a fundamental constitutional power: that the Supreme Court had the authority to decide which federal laws were constitutional. The following year, the Court also claimed the right to rule on the constitutionality of state laws. In doing so, the justices rejected Democratic-Republicans' claim that state legislatures had the power to repudiate federal law. Instead, the Supreme Court declared that federal laws took precedence over state laws.

Over the next dozen years, the Supreme Court continued to assert Federalist principles. In 1810 it insisted that it was the proper and sole arena for determining matters of constitutional interpretation. Then in 1819, the highest court reinforced its loose

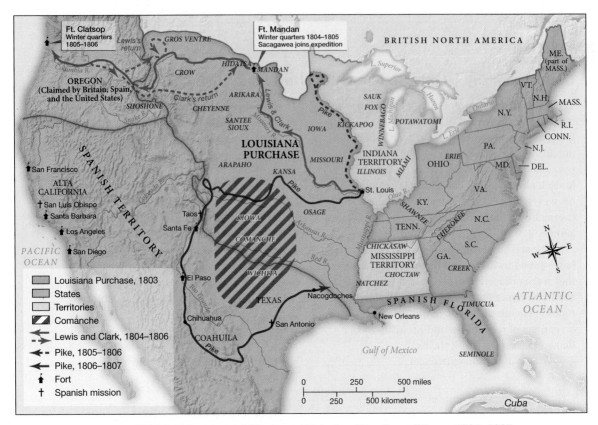

MAP 8.1   Lewis and Clark and Zebulon Pike Expeditions, 1804–1807

The expeditions led by Meriwether Lewis, William Clark, and Zebulon Pike illustrate the vast regions explored in just four years after the U.S. purchase of the Louisiana Territory. Journeying through and beyond the borders of that territory, the explorers gathered information about Indian nations, plants, animals, and the natural terrain even as Comanche and Shoshone nations, with access to horses, transformed the region.

interpretation of the Constitution's implied powers clause in *McCulloch v. Maryland*. This clause gave the federal government the right to "make all laws which shall be necessary and proper" for carrying out the explicit powers granted to it by the Constitution. Despite Democratic-Republicans' earlier opposition to a national bank, Congress chartered the Second Bank of the United States in 1816, and its branch banks issued notes that circulated widely in local communities. Legislators in Maryland, believing that branch banks had gained excessive power, approved a tax on their operations. Marshall's Court ruled that the establishment of the bank was "necessary and proper" for the functioning of the national government and rejected Maryland's right to tax the branch bank, claiming that "the power to tax involves the power to destroy."

By 1820 the Supreme Court, under the forceful direction of John Marshall, had established the power of judicial review—the authority of the nation's highest court to rule on cases involving states as well as the nation. From the Court's perspective, the judiciary was as important an institution in framing and preserving a national agenda as Congress or the president.

Democratic-Republicans Expand Federal Powers.

Although Democratic-Republicans generally opposed Marshall's rulings, they, too, continued to expand federal power. Once again, international developments drove the Jefferson administration's political agenda. By 1805 the security of the United States was threatened by continued conflicts between France and Great Britain. Both sought alliances with the young nation, and both ignored U.S. claims of neutrality. Indeed, each nation sought to punish Americans for trading with the other. Britain's Royal Navy began stopping American ships carrying sugar and molasses from the French West Indies and, between 1802 and 1811, impressed more than eight thousand sailors from such ships, including many American citizens. France claimed a similar right to stop U.S. ships that continued to trade with Great Britain.

Unable to convince foreign powers to recognize U.S. neutrality, Jefferson and Madison pushed for congressional passage of an embargo that they hoped would, like colonial boycotts, force Great Britain's hand. In 1807 Congress passed the **Embargo Act**, which prohibited U.S. ships from leaving their home ports until Britain and France repealed their

OGRABME, or, The American Snapping-turtle.

Opposition to the Embargo Act   Although Congress repealed the Embargo Act in 1809, lawmakers still barred the United States from trading with Great Britain and France, both of which attacked American shipping in violation of U.S. neutrality. This political cartoon by Alexander Anderson criticizes the embargo, which proved costly to merchants, sailors, and dockworkers. Here a merchant carrying a barrel of goods curses the snapping turtle "Ograbme," which is *embargo* spelled backward. New York Historical Society/Bridgeman Images

restrictions on American trade. Although the act kept the United States out of war, it had a devastating impact on national commerce.

New England merchants immediately voiced their outrage, and some began sending goods to Europe via Canada. In response, Congress passed the Force Act, granting extraordinary powers to customs officials to end such smuggling. The economic pain caused by the rapid decline in trade spread well beyond the merchant class. Parker Cleaveland was forced to sell his home to the Bowdoin trustees and become their tenant. Farmers and urban workers as well as southern planters suffered the embargo's effects more directly. Exports nearly stopped, and sailors and dockworkers faced escalating unemployment. With the recession deepening, American concerns about the expansion of federal power reemerged. Congress and the president had not simply regulated international trade; they had brought it to a halt.

Still, despite the failure of the Embargo Act, many Americans viewed Jefferson favorably. He had devoted his adult life to the creation of the United States. He had purchased the Louisiana Territory, opening up vast lands to American exploration and development. This geographical boon encouraged inventors and artisans to pursue ideas that would help the early republic take full advantage of its resources and recover from its current economic plight. Some must have wondered, however, how a Democratic-Republican president had so significantly expanded the power of the federal government.

REVIEW & RELATE

- How did the Federalist-dominated courts and the Democratic-Republican president and Congress each contribute to the expansion of the federal government?

- How did the purchase of the Louisiana Territory from France and international conflicts with France and Britain shape domestic issues in the late eighteenth and early nineteenth centuries?

Remaking America's Economic Character

As the United States expanded geographically, technological ingenuity became a highly valued commodity. The spread of U.S. settlements into new territories necessitated improved forms of transportation and communication and increased demands for muskets and other weapons to protect the nation's frontier. The growing population also fueled improvements in agriculture and manufacturing to meet demands for clothing, food, and farm equipment. Continued conflicts with Great Britain and France also highlighted the need to develop the nation's natural resources and technological capabilities. Yet even though American ingenuity was widely praised, the daily lives of most Americans changed slowly. And for some, especially enslaved women and men, technological advances only added to their burdens.

U.S. Population Grows and Migrates. Although Democratic-Republicans initially hoped to limit the powers of the national government, the rapid growth of the United States pulled in the opposite direction. An increased population, combined with the exhaustion of farmland along the eastern seaboard, fueled migration to the West as well as the growth of cities. These developments heightened conflicts with Indians and over slavery, but they also encouraged innovations in transportation and communication and improvements in agriculture and manufacturing.

As white Americans encroached more deeply on lands long settled by native peoples, Indian tribes were forced ever westward. As early as 1800, groups like the Shoshone, who originally inhabited the Great Plains, had been forced into the Rocky Mountains by Indians moving into the plains from the Mississippi and Ohio valleys (Map 8.2). Sacagawea must have realized that the expedition she accompanied would only increase pressure on the Shoshone and other nations as white migration escalated.

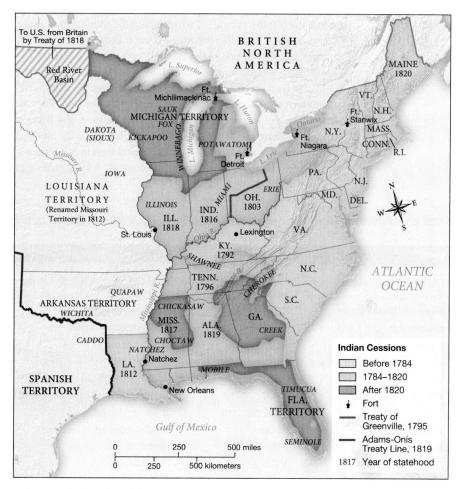

MAP 8.2 Indian Land Cessions, 1790–1820

With the ratification of the Constitution, the federal government gained greater control over Indian relations, including land cessions. At the same time, large numbers of white settlers poured into regions west of the Appalachian Mountains. The U.S. government gained most Indian land by purchase or treaty, but these agreements were often the consequence of military victories by the U.S. Army.

Although the vast majority of Americans continued to live in rural areas, a growing number moved to cities as eastern farmland lost its fertility and young people sought job opportunities in manufacturing, skilled trades, and service work. Cities were defined at the time as places with 8,000 or more inhabitants, but New York City and Philadelphia both counted more than 100,000 residents by 1810. In New York, immigrants, most of them Irish, made up about 10 percent of the population in 1820 and twice that percentage five years later. At the same time, the number of African Americans in New York City increased to more than 10,000. Cities began to emerge along the nation's frontier as well. After the Louisiana Purchase, New Orleans became a key commercial center while western migration fueled cities like Cincinnati. Even smaller frontier towns, like Rock Island, Illinois, served important functions for migrants traveling west. Trading posts appeared across the Mississippi valley, which eased the migration of thousands headed farther west. They served as sites of exchange between Indians and white Americans and created the foundations for later cities (Table 8.1).

Most Americans who headed west hoped to benefit from the increasingly liberal terms for land offered by the federal government. Yeomen farmers sought sufficient acreage to feed their families and grow some crops for sale. They were eager to settle in western sections of the original thirteen states, in the Ohio River valley, or in newly opened territories along the Missouri and Kansas Rivers. In the South, small farmers had to compete with slave-owning planters who headed west in the early nineteenth century. Migrants to the Mississippi valley also had to contend with a sizable population of Spanish and

TABLE 8.1   Prices at George Davenport's Trading Post, Rock Island, Illinois, c. 1820

Item	Price	Item	Price
Ax	$6.00	Large copper kettle	$30.00
Beaver trap	$8.00	Lead	$0.20 per pound
Black silk handkerchief	$2.00	Lead shot for guns	$1.00 per 5 pounds
Breechcloth	$3.00	Medium copper kettle	$10.00
Bridles	$2.00–$10.00	Muskrat spear	$2.00
Chain for staking down traps	$0.75 per 6 feet	Muskrat trap	$5.00
Combs	$1.00 per pair	Muslin or calico shirt	$3.00
File (for sharpening axes)	$2.00	Ordinary butcher knife	$0.50
Flannel	$1.00 per yard	Sheet iron kettle	$10.00
Flannel mantle	$3.00	Small copper kettle	$3.00
Gunflints	$1.00 per 15	Spurs	$6.00 per pair
Hand-size mirrors	$0.25	Tin kettle	$14.00
Heavy wool cloth	$10.00 per yard	Tomahawk	$1.50
Hoe	$2.00	Trade gun	$20.00–$25.00
Horn of gunpowder	$1.50	Wool blanket	$4.00
Horses	$35.00–$50.00	Wool mantle (short cloak or shawl)	$4.00

Source: Will Leinicke, Marion Lardner, and Ferrel Anderson, *Two Nations, One Land* (Rock Island, IL: Citizens to Preserve Black Hawk Park, 1981).

French residents, as well as Chickasaw and Creek Indians in the South and Shawnee, Chippewa, Sauk, and Fox communities farther north.

The development of roads and turnpikes hastened the movement of people and the transportation of goods. Frontier farmers wanted to get their produce to eastern markets quickly and cheaply. Before completion of the Lancaster Turnpike in Pennsylvania, it cost as much to carry wheat overland the sixty-two miles to Philadelphia as it did to ship it by sea from Philadelphia to London. Those who lived farther west faced even greater challenges. With the admission of Kentucky (1792), Tennessee (1796), and Ohio (1803) to the Union, demands for congressional support for building transportation routes grew louder. By 1819 five more states had been admitted along the Mississippi River, from Louisiana to Illinois.

During Jefferson's administration, secretary of the treasury Albert Gallatin urged Congress to fund roads and canals to enhance the economic development of the nation. He advocated a "great turnpike road" along the Atlantic seaboard from Maine to Georgia as well as roads to connect the four main rivers that flowed from the Appalachians to the Atlantic Ocean. Although traditionally such projects were funded by the states, in 1815 Congress approved funds for a **National Road** from western Maryland through southwestern Pennsylvania to Wheeling, West Virginia. This so-called Cumberland Road was completed in 1818 and later extended into Ohio and Illinois.

Carrying people and goods by water remained faster and cheaper than transporting them over land, but rivers ran mainly north and south. In addition, although loads could be delivered quickly downstream, the return voyage was long and slow. While politicians advocated the construction of canals along east-west routes to link river systems, inventors and mechanics focused on building boats powered by steam to overcome the problems of sending goods upriver.

In 1804 Oliver Evans, a machinist in Philadelphia, invented a high-pressure steam engine attached to a dredge that cleaned the silt around the docks in Philadelphia harbor. He had insufficient funds, however, to pursue work on a steam-powered boat. Robert Fulton, a New Yorker, improved on Evans's efforts, using the low-pressure steam engine developed in England. In 1807 Fulton launched the first successful steamboat, the *Clermont*, which traveled some 150 miles up the Hudson River from New York City to Albany in only thirty-two hours. The powerful Mississippi River proved a greater challenge, but by combining Evans's high-pressure steam engine with a flat-bottom hull that avoided the river's sandbars, mechanics who worked along the frontier improved Fulton's design and launched the steamboat era in the West.

Technology Reshapes Agriculture and Industry.

Advances in agricultural and industrial technology paralleled the development of roads and steamboats. And new inventions spurred others, inducing a **multiplier effect** that inspired additional dramatic changes. Two inventions in particular—the cotton gin and the spinning machine—transformed the deeply intertwined realms of southern agriculture and northern industry.

American developments were closely tied to the earlier rise of industry in Great Britain. By the 1770s, British manufacturers had built spinning mills in which steam-powered machines spun raw cotton into yarn. Eager to maintain their monopoly on industrial technology, the British made it illegal for engineers to emigrate. They could not stop everyone

Robert Fulton's *Clermont*, c. 1813 This painting of the *Clermont* by an unknown artist was published as a lithograph in France c.1830, suggesting Europeans' interest in American innovations. As the illustrations shows, early steamboats included paddle wheels and sails to guide their travels. Here the *Clermont* plies the Hudson River alongside sail boats as it passes a cluster of houses on the far shore. Granger

who worked in a cotton mill, however, from leaving. At age fourteen, Samuel Slater was hired as an apprentice in an English mill that used a yarn-spinning machine designed by Richard Arkwright. Slater was promoted to supervisor of the factory but in 1789, at age twenty-one, he emigrated to America, seeking greater opportunities. While working in New York City, he learned that Moses Brown, a wealthy Rhode Island merchant, was eager to develop a machine like Arkwright's. Funded by Rhode Island investors and assisted by local craftsmen, Slater designed and built a spinning mill in Pawtucket.

The mill opened in December 1790 and began producing yarn, which was then woven into cloth in private shops and homes. By 1815 a series of cotton mills dotted the Pawtucket River. These factories offered workers, most of whom were the wives and children of farmers, a steady income, and they ensured employment for weavers in the countryside. They also increased the demand for cotton in New England just as British manufacturers sought new sources of the crop as well.

Ensuring a steady supply of cotton required another technological innovation, this one created by Eli Whitney. After graduating from Yale, Whitney agreed to serve as a private tutor for a planter family in South Carolina. On the ship carrying him south, Whitney met the widow Catherine Greene, who invited him to stay at her Mulberry Plantation near Savannah, Georgia. There local planters complained to him about the difficulty of making a profit on cotton. Long-staple cotton, grown in the Sea Islands, yielded enormous profits, but the soil in most of the South could sustain only the short-staple variety, which required hours of intensive labor to separate its sticky green seeds from the cotton fiber.

In 1793, in as little as ten days, Eli Whitney built a machine that could speed the process of deseeding short-staple cotton. Using mesh screens, rollers, and wire brushes,

Whitney's **cotton gin** could clean as much cotton fiber in one hour as several workers could clean in a day. Recognizing the gin's value, Whitney received a U.S. patent, but because the machine was easy to duplicate, he never profited from his invention.

Fortunately, Whitney had other ideas that proved more profitable. In June 1798, amid U.S. fears of a war with France, the U.S. government granted him an extraordinary contract to produce 4,000 rifles in eighteen months. Adapting the plan of Honoré Blanc, a French mechanic who devised a musket with interchangeable parts, Whitney demonstrated the potential for using machines to produce various parts of a musket, which could then be assembled in mass quantities. With Jefferson's enthusiastic support, the federal government extended Whitney's contract, and by 1809 his New Haven factory was turning out 7,500 guns annually. Whitney's factory became a model for the **American system of manufacturing**, in which water-powered machinery and the division of production into several small tasks allowed less skilled workers to produce mass quantities of a particular item. Moreover, the factories developed by Whitney and Slater became training grounds for younger mechanics and inventors who devised improvements in machinery or set out to solve new technological puzzles. Their efforts also transformed the lives of generations of workers—enslaved and free—who planted and picked the cotton, spun the yarn, wove the cloth, and sewed the clothes that cotton gins and spinning mills made possible.

Transforming Domestic Production.

Slater and Whitney were among the most influential American inventors, but both required the assistance and collaboration of other inventors, machinists, and artisans to implement their ideas. The achievement of these enterprising individuals was seen by many Americans as part of a larger spirit of inventiveness and technological ingenuity that characterized U.S. identity. Although many Americans built on foreign ideas and models, a cascade of inventions did appear in the United States between 1790 and 1820.

Cotton gins and steam engines, steamboats and interchangeable parts, gristmills and spinning mills, clocks and woodworking lathes—each of these items and processes was improved over time and led to myriad other inventions. For instance, in 1811 Francis Cabot invented a power loom for weaving, a necessary step once spinning mills began producing more yarn than hand weavers could handle. Eventually clocks would be used to routinize the labor of workers in those mills so that they all arrived, ate lunch, and left at the same time.

Despite these rapid technological advances, the changes that occurred in the early nineteenth century were more evolutionary than revolutionary. Most political leaders and social commentators viewed gradual improvement as a blessing. For many Americans, the ideal situation consisted of either small mills scattered through the countryside or household enterprises that could supply neighbors with finer cloth, wool cards, sturdier chairs, or other items that improved household comfort and productivity.

The importance of domestic manufacturing increased after passage of the Embargo Act as imports of cloth and other items fell dramatically. Small factories, like those along the Pawtucket River, increased their output, and so did ordinary housewives. Blacksmiths, carpenters, and wheelwrights busily repaired and improved the spindles, looms, and other equipment that allowed family members to produce more and better cloth from wool, flax, and cotton. These developments allowed some Americans, especially in towns and cities, to achieve a middling status between poorer laborers and wealthier elites. In this middling sector of society, new ideas about companionate marriage, which emphasized mutual obligations, may have encouraged husbands and wives to work more closely in domestic enterprises. While husbands generally carried out the heavier or more skilled parts of home manufacturing, like weaving, wives spun yarn and sewed together sections of cloth into finished goods.

At the same time, daughters, neighbors, and servants remained critical to the production of household items. In early nineteenth-century Hallowell, Maine, Martha Ballard labored alongside her daughters and a niece, producing cloth and food for domestic consumption, while she supplemented her husband's income as a surveyor by working as a midwife. Yet older forms of mutuality also continued, with neighbors sharing tools and equipment and those with specialized skills assisting neighbors in exchange for items they needed. Perhaps young couples imagined themselves embarking on more egalitarian marriages than those of their parents, but most still needed wider networks of support.

In wealthy households north and south, servants and slaves took on a greater share of domestic labor in the late eighteenth and early nineteenth centuries. Most female servants in the North were young and unmarried. Some arrived with children in tow or became pregnant while on the job, a mark of the rising rate of out-of-wedlock births following the Revolution. Meanwhile in the South, if household slaves became pregnant their children added to the owner's labor supply. Moreover, on larger plantations, owners increasingly assigned a few enslaved women to spin, cook, wash clothes, make candles, and wait on table. Plantation mistresses might also hire the wives of small farmers and landless laborers to spin cotton into yarn, weave yarn into cloth, and sew clothing for slaves and children. While mistresses in both regions still engaged in household production, they expanded their roles as domestic managers.

However, most Americans at the turn of the nineteenth century continued to live on family farms, to produce or trade locally to meet their needs, and to use techniques handed down for generations. Yet by 1820 their lives, like those of wealthier Americans, were transformed by the expanding market economy, which over the next twenty years would inspire a market revolution. Gradually, more and more families would sew clothes with machine-spun thread made from cotton ginned in the American South, work their fields with newly invented cast-iron plows, and vary their diet by adding items shipped from other regions by steamboat.

Technology, Cotton, and Slaves. Some of the most dramatic technological changes occurred in agriculture, and none was more significant than the cotton gin, which led to the vast expansion of agricultural production and slavery in the South. This in turn fueled regional specialization, ensuring that residents in one area of the nation—the North, South, or West—depended on those in other areas. Southern planters relied on a growing demand for cotton from northern merchants and manufacturers. At the same time, planters, merchants, manufacturers, and factory workers became more dependent on western farmers to produce grain and livestock to feed the nation.

As cotton gins spread across the South, cotton and slavery expanded into the interior of many southern states as well as into the lower Mississippi valley. While rice and sugar were also produced in the South, cotton quickly became the most important crop. In 1790 southern farms and plantations produced about 3,000 bales of cotton, each weighing about 300 pounds. By 1820, with the aid of the cotton gin, the South produced more than 330,000 bales annually (Table 8.2). For southern blacks, increased production meant increased burdens. Because seeds could be separated from raw cotton with much greater efficiency, farmers could plant vastly larger quantities of the crop. Although family members, neighbors, and hired hands performed this work on small farms with only a few or no slaves, wealthy planters, with perhaps a dozen slaves, took advantage of rising cotton prices in the early eighteenth century to purchase more slaves.

The dramatic increase in the amount of cotton planted and harvested each year was paralleled by a jump in the size of the slave population. Thus, even as northern states began to abolish the institution, southern planters significantly increased the number of slaves they held. In 1790 there were fewer than 700,000 slaves in the United States. By

The Cotton Gin, 1793   This colored lithograph by an anonymous American artist shows Eli Whitney's cotton gin at the center of complex transactions. Enslaved women and men haul and gin cotton. Meanwhile the planter appears to be bargaining with a cotton factor, or agent, who likely wants to purchase his crop for a northern manufacturer. Private Collection/Peter Newark American Pictures/Bridgeman Images

TABLE 8.2 **Growth of Cotton Production in the United States, 1790–1830**

Year	Production in Bales
1790	3,135
1795	16,719
1800	73,145
1805	146,290
1810	177,638
1815	208,986
1820	334,378
1825	532,915
1830	731,452

Source: Lewis Cecil Gray, *History of Agriculture in the Southern United States to 1860*, vol. 2 (Gloucester, MA: Peter Smith, 1958).

1820 there were nearly 1.5 million. Despite this population increase, growing competition for field hands drove up the price of slaves, which roughly doubled between 1795 and 1805.

Although the international slave trade was banned in the United States in 1808, some planters smuggled in women and men from Africa and the Caribbean. Most planters, however, depended on enslaved women to bear more children, increasing the size of their labor force through natural reproduction. In addition, planters in the Deep South—from Georgia and the Carolinas west to Louisiana—began buying slaves from farmers in Maryland and Virginia, where cotton and slavery were less profitable. Expanding slave markets in New Orleans and Charleston marked the continued importance of this domestic or internal slave trade as cotton moved west.

In the early nineteenth century, most white southerners believed that there was enough land to go around. And the rising price of cotton allowed small farmers to imagine they would someday be planters. Some southern Indians also placed their hopes in cotton. Cherokee and Creek Indians cultivated the crop, even purchasing black slaves to increase production. Some Indian villages now welcomed ministers to their communities, hoping that embracing white culture might allow them to retain their current lands. Yet other native residents foresaw the increased pressure for land that cotton cultivation produced and organized to defend themselves from whites' invasion. Regardless of the policies adopted by Indians, cotton and slavery expanded rapidly into Cherokee- and Creek-controlled lands in the interior of Georgia and South Carolina. And the admission of the states of Louisiana, Mississippi, and Alabama between 1812 and 1819 marked the rapid spread of southern agriculture farther west.

Enslaved men and women played critical roles in the South's geographical expansion. Without their labor, neither cotton nor sugar could have become mainstays of the South's economy. The heavy work of carving out new plantations led most planters to select young slave men and women to move west, breaking apart families in the process. Some slaves resisted their removal and, if forced to go, used their role in the labor process to limit owners' control. Slaves resisted by working slowly, breaking tools, and feigning illness or injury. Other enslaved women and men hid out temporarily as a respite from brutal work regimes or harsh punishments. Still others ran to areas controlled by Indians, hoping for better treatment, or to regions where slavery was no longer legal.

Yet given the power and resources wielded by whites, most slaves had to find ways to improve their lives within the system of bondage. The end of the international slave trade helped blacks in this regard since planters had to depend more on natural reproduction to increase their labor supply. To ensure that slaves lived longer and healthier lives, planters were forced to provide better food, shelter, and clothing. Some slaves gained leverage to fish, hunt, or maintain small gardens to improve their diet. With the birth of more children, southern blacks also developed more extensive kinship networks, which often allowed other family members to care for children if their parents were compelled to move west. Enslavement was still brutal, but slaves made small gains that improved their chances of survival.

Explore ▶

Sources 8.4 and 8.5 offer distinct views of the interplay of religion and politics in the early republic

To find release from the oppressive burdens of daily life, southern slaves not only joined the camp meetings and religious revivals that burned across the southern frontier in the late eighteenth and early nineteenth century but also established their own religious ceremonies. These were often held in the woods or swamps at night, away from the prying eyes of planters and overseers.

Evangelical religion, combined with revolutionary ideals promoted in the United States and Haiti, proved a potent mix, and planters rarely lost sight of the potential dangers this posed to the system of bondage. Outright rebellions occurred only rarely, yet victory in Haiti and Gabriel's conspiracy in Virginia reminded slaves and owners alike that uprisings were possible. Clearly, the power of new American identities could not be separated from the dangers embedded in the nation's oppressive racial history.

REVIEW & RELATE

- How did new inventions and infrastructure improvements contribute to the development of the American economy?

- Why did slavery expand and become more deeply entrenched in southern society in the early nineteenth century? What fears did this reinforce?

Conclusion: New Identities and New Challenges

The geographical and economic expansion that marked the period from 1790 to 1820 inspired scientific and technological advances as well as literary and artistic tributes to a distinctly American identity. For young ambitious men like Parker Cleaveland, Eli Whitney, Washington Irving, and Meriwether Lewis, the opportunities that opened in education, science, literature, and exploration offered possibilities for fame and financial success. While Whitney, Irving, and Lewis traveled

Religion and Politics in the Early Republic

By the 1790s, the disestablishment of state churches and the guarantee of religious freedom led to a proliferation of denominations that attracted people from diverse backgrounds. Some denominations recognized the ministry of individuals without formal training, known as lay preachers. Extended camp meetings gained popularity across the South and the frontier, with women and African Americans participating alongside white men. Historians have studied the relationships of these developments with the changing political landscape of the Early Republic, particularly the rise of Jeffersonians who demanded limited government and individual liberty.

Source 8.4

Nathan O. Hatch, Religion as a Democratizing Force, 1989

These religious leaders [of the 1780s and 1790s] were fierce independents and localists. . . . Their gospel of the backcountry resonated with the powerful Anti-Federalist and Jeffersonian persuasions. . . .

[T]he most powerful popular movements in the early republic were expressly religious. . . . It was lay preachers . . . who most effectively constructed new frames of reference for people living in a period of profound transition. Religious leaders from the rank and file were phenomenally successful in reaching out to marginal people, in promoting self-education and sheltering participants from the indoctrination of elite orthodoxies, in binding people together in supportive communities, and in identifying the aspirations of common people with the will of God. . . .

This groundswell shook churches to the foundation. . . . Traditional elites, keenly aware of the fragile authority of "college learnt merchants of the gospel," scrambled to consolidate the position of orthodox churches. . . . [Yet] nurtured by sources as contradictory as George Whitfield and Tom Paine, many deeply religious people were set adrift from ecclesiastical establishments at the same time they demanded that the church begin living up to its spiritual promise. . . .

This awakening developed inversely to that commonly depicted, however. Instead of fostering a unified, cohesive movement, it splintered American Christianity and magnified the diversity of institutions claiming to be the church. It sprang from a populist upsurge rather from changing mores of established parishes. . . .

Their success may have been the most profoundly democratic upheaval in the early republic. . . .

Source: Nathan O. Hatch, *The Democratization of American Christianity* (Yale University Press, 1989), pp. 34 and 224–226.

Amanda Porterfield, Religion Sows Doubt and Nurtures Partisanship, 2012

The 1790s saw rising panic about how to get along in the new world of American liberty, where old traditions of decorum had broken down,. . .. As old traditions fell away, uncertainty about how to conduct oneself, cynicism with respect to other people, and ambivalence about the effects of American independence all contributed to the uneasy atmosphere of mistrustful doubt. . . .

Promoting the supreme authority of God's law, churches not only exerted moral authority as interpreters of divine governance but also fostered distrust of secular reason and government. . . .

The spike in religion's popularity around 1800 [thus] coincided with political upheavals and new forms of political organization. . . .

As public life in every region of the new republic became increasingly politicized . . . political activists channeled mistrust along partisan lines. . . . Taverns became headquarters for a new breed of political organizers who planned public events and worked to recruit voters. Alcohol flowed freely, and deals were made.

Religious organizations grew on both sides of the partisan political divide, and revivals flourished even more exuberantly outside New England, in regions where Jefferson and his party were more popular. New Light Presbyterianism from North Carolina ignited the Great Revival of 1801 in the Kentucky Cumberland, and that amazing event shaped religious expectations throughout the West and in many parts of the South. . . .

Evangelical religion surged in the context of bitter partisan conflict, the growth of libertarian policies [those opposed to federal government intervention] with respect to slavery and Indian rights, and profound ambivalence toward authority. . . .

Religion came to designate a diffuse realm, protected by the state, where people built communities, conceived relationships with God, and lamented the corruption of the state and of profane, mistrustful society. . . .

Source: Amanda Porterfield, *Conceived in Doubt: Religion and Politics in the New American Nation* (University of Chicago Press, 2012), pp. 2-4 and 11-12.

Examine the Sources

1. How do Hatch and Porterfield differ in their interpretations of the relationships between religion and politics?
2. Drawing upon evidence in Chapters 7 and 8, evaluate the strengths and weaknesses of Hatch's and Porterfield's presentations.

Put It in Context

How would you analyze religion's relationship to political transformations in the early republic?

widely, Cleaveland remained a professor of mathematics, mineralogy, and chemistry at Bowdoin, dying in Brunswick, Maine in 1858.

Lewis's efforts to open up the Louisiana Territory transformed the lives of many Americans. Along with the construction of roads, the invention of steamboats, and the introduction of iron plows, his Corps of Discovery opened up new lands for farming and also fueled the rise of western cities. Many white families sought fertile land, abundant wildlife, or opportunities for trade on the frontier. Yet these families often had to purchase land from speculators or compete with wealthy planters. And those who carved out farms might face Indians angered by the constant encroachment of white Americans on their lands.

New opportunities also appeared in eastern towns and cities as investors, inventors, and skilled artisans established factories and improved transportation. White women of middling or elite status could attend female academies, enter marriages based on ideals of companionship and mutual responsibilities, purchase rather than make cotton thread and cloth, and retain servants to perform the heaviest work. Yet these changes occurred gradually and unevenly. And while poorer white women might more easily find jobs in cotton mills or as servants, the pay was low and the hours long.

Transformations in white society introduced even more difficult challenges for African Americans. Despite the introduction of gradual emancipation in the North and the end of the international slave trade, slavery continued to grow. The invention of the cotton gin ensured the expansion of cotton cultivation into new areas, and many slaves were forced to move west and leave family and friends behind. Enslaved women and men honed means of survival and resistance, but few could imagine a revolution like the one that took place in Haiti.

At the same time, all along the expanding U.S. frontier, American Indians faced continued pressure to leave their lands, embrace white culture, or both. In 1810 Sacagawea, Charbonneau, and their son Baptiste apparently traveled to St. Louis at the invitation of William Clark, who offered to pay for Baptiste's schooling. Sacagawea left Baptiste in Clark's care, and it is not clear whether she ever saw her son again. William Clark wrote "Se car ja we au Dead" on the cover of his cash book for 1825–1828, suggesting that she died during those years. By then, the Shoshone and Hidatsa were facing the onslaught of white settlement. They, along with Indians living in areas like Georgia, the Carolinas, and Tennessee, continued to resist U.S. expansion and struggled to control the embattled frontier.

Indeed, the United States remained embattled throughout the early years of the republic. From 1790 to 1820, Great Britain, France, and the Barbary States of North Africa constantly challenged U.S. sovereignty from abroad while debates over slavery and conflicts over Indian lands multiplied at home. Moreover, as federal power expanded under Democratic-Republican rule, some Americans continued to worry about protecting the rights of states and of individuals. The American identities forged in the early republic would be continually tested as new challenges emerged and older conflicts intensified in the following decades.

TIMELINE OF **EVENTS**

1789 Massachusetts institutes free public elementary education

1790 Samuel Slater's spinning mill opens

1790–1820 Cotton production in the South increases from 3,000 to 330,000 bales annually

U.S. slave population rises from 700,000 to 1.5 million

1791–1803 Haitian Revolution

1792–1809 New capital of Washington City constructed

1793 Eli Whitney invents cotton gin

1801 Judiciary Act

U.S. forces challenge Barbary pirates

Thousands attend camp meeting in Cane Ridge, Kentucky

1803 Louisiana Purchase

Marbury v. Madison

1804–1806 Corps of Discovery explores Louisiana Territory and Pacific Northwest

1807 Robert Fulton launches first successful steamboat

Embargo Act

1810 Population of New York and Philadelphia each exceeds 100,000

1817 American Colonization Society founded

1819 *McCulloch v. Maryland*

1820 Washington Irving publishes *Sketchbook*

1828 Noah Webster publishes *American Dictionary of the English Language*

KEY **TERMS**

American Colonization Society (ACS), *253*

Haitian Revolution, *256*

Louisiana Purchase, *256*

Corps of Discovery, *257*

Judiciary Act, *258*

Marbury v. Madison, *258*

McCulloch v. Maryland, *260*

Embargo Act, *261*

National Road, *265*

multiplier effect, *265*

cotton gin, *267*

American system of manufacturing, *267*

REVIEW & RELATE

1. How did developments in education, literature, and the arts contribute to the emergence of a distinctly American identity?

2. How did blacks and American Indians both contribute to and challenge the predominantly white view of American identity?

3. How did the Federalist-dominated courts and the Democratic-Republican president and Congress each contribute to the expansion of the federal government?

4. How did the purchase of the Louisiana Territory from France and international conflicts with France and Britain shape domestic issues in the late eighteenth and early nineteenth centuries?

5. How did new inventions and infrastructure improvements contribute to the development of the American economy?

6. Why did slavery expand and become more deeply entrenched in southern society in the early nineteenth century? What fears did this reinforce?

The Corps of Discovery: Paeans to Peace and Instruments of War

▶ How did the Corps of Discovery influence relations between Indian nations and non-Indian explorers, between traders and settlers, and among Indian nations?

From 1804 to 1806, the Corps of Discovery mapped vast regions of the West, documented plants and animals, and initiated trade relations with Indian nations. When the Corps built its winter camp at Fort Mandan in October 1804, its members hoped to develop commercial relations with local Mandan, Hidatsa, and Arikara villages. Most of these tribes had been ravaged by smallpox in the early 1780s and were now subject to raids by more powerful nations in the region. Meriwether Lewis and William Clark hoped to persuade all of these nations that peaceful relations would benefit them politically and economically. To aid negotiations, the Corps offered gifts to the Indian leaders they encountered (Source 8.6). The Mandan, however, expected more gifts than the expedition could offer. Although Lewis and Clark assured Mandan leaders they would benefit from future trade with and protection from the United States, the Indians had heard such promises before and were wary of giving away vital food as winter descended (Source 8.7).

Worried about surviving the winter, Lewis and Clark finally found an unexpected item to trade with the Mandan. When their men finished building a smithy in December 1804, they discovered that Indians would exchange almost any item for metal hatchets, especially those designed for battle (Sources 8.8 and 8.9).

In April the Corps moved west into present-day Idaho and traded with Shoshone leaders for horses.

The Shoshone were engaged in a long and lucrative trade in horses with the Comanche, who had split from the Shoshones, moved south, and developed ties with the Spanish. But the Shoshone had a harder time getting guns, a concern they expressed to Lewis (Source 8.10). While Lewis and Clark advocated peace among Indian nations, one of their most desired trade items was weaponry.

Source 8.6

William Clark, Journal | October 12, 1804

As the Corps of Discovery traveled up the Missouri River from St. Louis, they stopped at Indian villages along the way to advocate peace; offer presents from President Jefferson; and learn about local plants, animals, and potential trade items. In his journal entry for October 12, William Clark describes a visit to a Ricara (Arikara) village near where the Corps planned to stay for the winter.

After breakfast, we went on shore to the house of the chief of the second village named Lassel, where we found his chiefs and warriors. They made us a present of about seven bushels of corn, a pair of leggings, a twist of their tobacco, and the seeds of two different species of tobacco. The chief then delivered a speech expressive of his gratitude for the presents and the good counsels which we had given him; his intention of visiting his great father [the president of the United States] but for fear of the Sioux; and requested us to take one of the Ricara chiefs up to the Mandans and negociate a peace between the two nations. . . . After we had answered and explained the magnitude and power of the United States, the three chiefs came with us to the boat. We gave them some sugar, a little salt, and a sun-glass. Two of them left us, and the chief of the third [village] . . . accompanied us to the Mandans.

[T]he Ricaras . . . were originally colonies of Pawnees, who established themselves on the Missouri. . . . From that situation, a part of the Ricaras emigrated to the neighbourhood of the Mandans, with whom they were then in alliance. The rest of the nation continued near the Chayenne [Cheyenne] till the year 1797, in the course of which, distressed by their wars with the Sioux, they joined their countrymen near the Mandans. Soon after a new war arose between the Ricaras and the Mandans, in consequence of which the former came down the river to their present position. . . .

They [the Ricara] express a disposition to keep at peace with all nations, but they are well armed with fusils [muskets], and being much under the influence of the Sioux, who exchanged the goods which they got from the British for Ricara corn, their minds are sometimes poisoned and they cannot always be depended on.

Source: William Clark Journal, October 12, 1804, *History of the Expeditions of Captains Lewis and Clark, 1804-5-6, Reprinted from the Edition of 1814, with Introduction and Index by James K. Hosmer* (Chicago: A. C. McClurg, 1902), 1:110–11, 114.

Source: William Clark Journal, October 12, 1804, *History of the Expeditions of Captains Lewis and Clark, 1804-5-6, Reprinted from the Edition of 1814, with Introduction and Index by James K. Hosmer* (Chicago: A. C. McClurg, 1902), 1:110–11, 114.

Source 8.7

Charles McKenzie | Narrative of a Fur Trader, November 1804

Charles McKenzie was a Scotsman working as a clerk for the Hudson Bay Company. He arrived with six traders at a Hidatsa village in November 1804. Over time, McKenzie adopted Indian dress, married an Indian woman, and became an advocate for Indian concerns. Here he recounts Lewis's frustration in his efforts to gain favor with local Indians as well as Mandan concerns about the Corps' lack of generosity.

Here we also found a party of forty Americans under the command of Captains Lewis and Clark exploring a passage by the Mississouri [Missouri] to the Pacific Ocean—they came up the River in a Boat of twenty oars accompanied by two *Peroque*s [open boats or canoes]. Their fortifications for winter Quarters were already complete—they had held a council with the Mandanes, and distributed many presents; but most of the Chiefs did not accept any thing from them. Some time after Captain Lewis with three Interpreters paid a visit to the *Gros Ventres* [Hidatsa] Village. . . . [N]ext morning he came to the village where I was—and observed to me that he was not very graciously received at the upper Village. . . .

After haranguing the Indians and explaining to them the purport of his [Lewis's] expedition to the Westward, several of them accepted clothing—but notwithstanding they could not be reconciled to like these strangers as they called them:—"Had these Whites come amongst us, Said the Chiefs, with charitable views they would have loaded their Great Boat with necessaries [trade items]. It is true they have ammunition but they prefer throwing it away idly [shooting in the air] than sparing a shot of it to a poor Mandane." . . . "Had I these White warriors in the upper plains, said the *Gros Ventres* Chief, my young men on horseback would soon do for them, as they would do for so many wolves—for, continued he, there are only two sensible men among them—the worker of Iron, and the mender of Guns."

The American Gentlemen gave flags and medals to the Chiefs on condition that they should not go to war unless the enemy attacked them in their Villages. Yet the Chief of the wolves, whose brother had been killed in the fall previous to our arrival, went soon after with a party of fifty men to revenge his death.

Source: W. Raymond Wood and Thomas D. Thiessen, eds., *Early Fur Trade on the Northern Plains: Canadian Traders among the Mandan and Hidatsa Indians, 1738–1818* (Norman: University of Oklahoma Press, 1985), 232–33.

Source: W. Raymond Wood and Thomas D. Thiessen, eds., *Early Fur Trade on the Northern Plains: Canadian Traders among the Mandan and Hidatsa Indians, 1738–1818* (Norman: University of Oklahoma Press, 1985), 232–33.

William Clark | Journal, November 18, 1804

By November 1804, the Corps had built and settled into Fort Mandan, at the convergence of the Missouri and Knife Rivers, for the winter. Lewis and Clark became increasingly aware that their trade with particular groups, like the Mandans, might shift the balance of power in the region. But given the extended journey ahead, they were limited in what goods they could give or trade with local Indians even as they sought to reassure them of U.S. support.

To-day we had a cold windy morning; the Black Cat [a Mandan chief] came to see us, and occupied us for a long time with questions on the usages [customs] of our country. He mentioned that a council had been held yesterday to deliberate on the state of their affairs. It seems that not long ago a party of Sioux fell in with some horses belonging to the Minnetarees and carried them off, but in their flight they were met by some Assiniboins, who killed the Sioux and kept the horses. A Frenchman, too, who had lived many years among the Mandans, was lately killed on his route to the British factory [trading post] on the Assiniboin . . . , all of which being discussed, the council decided that they would not resent the recent insults from the Assiniboins . . . until they had seen whether we had deceived them or not in our promises of furnishing them with arms and ammunition. They had been disappointed in their hopes of receiving them from Mr. Evans, and were afraid that we, too, like him, might tell them what was not true. We advised them to continue at peace, that supplies of every kind would no doubt arrive for them, but that time was necessary to organize the trade. The fact is that the Assiniboins treat the Mandans as the Sioux do the Ricaras; by their vicinity to the British they get all the supplies, which they withhold or give at pleasure to the remoter Indians; the consequence is that, however badly treated, the Mandans and Ricaras are very slow to retaliate lest they should lose their trade altogether.

Source: William Clark Journal, November 18, 1804, *History of the Expeditions of Captains Lewis and Clark, 1804-5-6*, Reprinted from the Edition of 1814, with Introduction and Index by James K. Hosmer (Chicago: A. C. McClurg, 1902), 1:136–37.

William Clark | Journal, January 28, 1805, and Meriwether Lewis, Journal, February 1, 1805

By early 1805 it was clear to Lewis and Clark that metal goods, especially axes or hatchets, were the most valuable means of obtaining the corn and other items they needed from the Mandans and neighboring Indians. These two short entries, by Clark and then Lewis, describe the value of the trade in hatchets to the Corps and their continued commitment to peace among Indian nations.

American Philosophical Society

28th January

Attempt to cut through the ice to get our Boat and Canoes out without success. Several Indians here wishing to get war hatchets made [image of one drawn here]. The man sick yesterday is getting well Mr. Jessome [Jessaume], our interpreter was taken very unwell this evening. Warm day.

1st February

A cold, windy day. . . . One of the Minnetaree chiefs . . . came to see us and procure a war hatchet; he also requested that we would suffer him to go to war against the Sioux and Ricaras, who had killed a Mandan some time ago; this we refused for reasons which we explained to him. He acknowledged that we were right, and promised to open his ears to our counsel.

Source: William Clark Journal, January 28, 1805, Codex C: 158 American Philosophical Society, Courtesy of the American Philosophical Society Library; and Meriwether Lewis Journal, February 1, 1805, *History of the Expeditions of Captains Lewis and Clark, 1804-5-6, Reprinted from the Edition of 1814, with Introduction and Index by James K. Hosmer* (Chicago: A. C. McClurg, 1902), 1:168.

Source 8.10

Meriwether Lewis | Journal, August 20, 1805

The Corps was eager to encounter the Shoshone nation in hopes of getting horses and aid in crossing the mountains and the Columbia River. Sacagawea had been raised as a Shoshone, and her brother Câmeahwait was now a Shoshone chief. He and Sacagawea were shocked and excited to see each other again, and Lewis was moved by their reunion. But he was more interested in the relations between the Shoshone and tribes to the east as well as Spanish traders to the south.

can discover that these people are by no means friendly to the Spaniards. Their complaint is, that the Spaniards will not let them have fire arms and amunition, that they put them off by telling them that if they suffer them to have guns they will kill each other, thus leaving them defenceless and an easy prey to their bloodthirsty neighbours to the East of them, who being in possession of fire arms hunt them up and murder them without rispect to sex or age and plunder them of their horses on all occasions. They told me that to avoid their enemies who were eternally harrassing them that they were obliged to remain in the interior of these mountains at least two thirds of the year where the[y] suffered as we then saw great heardships for the want of food sometimes living for weeks without meat and only a little fish roots and berries. But this added Câmeahwait, with his ferce eyes and lank jaws grown meager for the want of food, would not be the case if we had guns, we could then live in the country of buffaloe and eat as our enimies do and not be compelled to hide ourselves in these mountains and live on roots and berries as the bear do. We do not fear our enimies when placed on an equal footing with them. I told them that the Minnetares Mandans & Recares of the Missouri had promised us to desist from making war on them & that we would indevour to find the means of making the Minnetares . . . or as they call them Pahkees desist from waging war against them also. That after our finally returning to our homes towards the rising sun whitemen would come to them with an abundance of guns and every other article necessary to their defence and comfort, and that they would be enabled to supply themselves with these articles on reasonable terms in exchange for the skins of the beaver Otter and Ermin so abundant in their country. They expressed great pleasure at this information and said they had been long anxious to see the whitemen that traded guns; and that we might rest assured of their friendship and that they would do whatever we wished them.

Source: Reuben Gold Thwaites, ed., *Original Journals of the Lewis and Clark Expedition, 1804–1808* (New York: Dodd, Mead, 1904), 383–84.

Interpret the Evidence

1. How do European traders and American explorers view the connection between trade with and peaceful relations among Indian nations (Sources 8.6 and 8.7)?

2. Describe William Clark's perspective on relations among Indian nations in the region (Source 8.8). Then evaluate the effects of his and Lewis's willingness to trade war hatchets for food on their desire for peace among these Indian nations (Sources 8.9 and 8.10)?

3. Analyze Lewis's goal in promising guns to the Shoshone when the Corps encountered Indian nations living in Spain's commercial sphere (Source 8.10)?

4. What can we learn about Indian attitudes toward European traders, American explorers, and other Indian nations from sources written by white men (Source 8.6 to 8.10)?

Put It in Context

What were the most significant problems faced by Indians as more European and American explorers and traders entered the region explored by the Corps of Discovery?

Defending and Redefining the Nation

1809–1832

WINDOW TO THE PAST

Crowds Celebrate a Presidential Inauguration

When Andrew Jackson was elected president in 1828, he decided to open the traditional White House reception to ordinary women and men. Some people applauded his democratic inclusion; others were appalled by the "mob scene." The event drew attention in Great Britain as well as the United States. This 1829 image is from *President's Levee*, drawn by Robert Cruikshank, a British satirical artist. ▶ To discover more about what this primary source can show us, see Source 9.10 on page 315.

Granger, NYC

After reading this chapter you should be able to:

■ Analyze the intertwined effects of conflicts on the frontier and with Britain and on U.S. federal policies and the lives of white and Indian Americans.

■ Describe the role of state and federal governments in the nation's expansion and how expansion affected relations among increasingly distinct regions.

■ Evaluate how the panic of 1819 and the Missouri Compromise affected and were affected by the nation's economic expansion and political divisions.

■ Discuss how expanded voting rights for white working men, new racial restrictions, and continued debates over federal power led to political realignment.

■ Explain the challenges that President Jackson faced in implementing federal policies on the tariff, the national bank, and the removal of the Cherokee.

COMPARING AMERICAN HISTORIES

Dolley Payne was raised on a Virginia plantation. But her Quaker parents, moved by the Society of Friends' growing antislavery sentiment, decided to free their slaves. In 1783, when Dolley was fifteen, the Paynes moved to Philadelphia. There, Dolley's father suffered heavy economic losses, and Dolley lost her first husband and her younger son to yellow fever. In 1794

(*left*) **Dolley Madison.** Library of Congress, 3b15638
(*right*) **John Ross.** Library of Congress, 3g03156

the young widow met and married Virginia congressman James Madison. When the newly elected president Thomas Jefferson appointed James secretary of state in 1801, the couple moved to the new capital city of Washington.

Since Jefferson and his vice president, Aaron Burr, were widowers, Dolley Madison served as hostess for White House affairs. When James Madison succeeded Jefferson as president in 1809, he, too, depended on his wife's social skills and networks. Dolley held lively informal receptions to which she invited politicians, diplomats, cabinet officers, and their wives. These social events helped bridge the ideological differences that continued to divide Congress and proved crucial in creating a unified front when Congress declared war on Great Britain in 1812.

During the War of 1812, British forces attacked Washington City and burned the Executive Mansion, now called the White House. With the president away, his wife was left to secure important state papers, emerging as a symbol of national courage at a critical moment in the conflict. When peace came the following year, Dolley Madison quickly reestablished a busy social calendar to help mend conflicts that had erupted during the war.

In 1817, at the end of the president's second term, the Madisons left Washington just as a young trader named John Ross entered the political arena. Born in 1790 in the Cherokee nation, John (also known as Guwisguwi) was the son of a Scottish trader and his wife, who was both Cherokee and Scottish. John Ross was raised in an Anglo-Indian world in eastern Tennessee, where he played with Cherokee children and attended tribal events but was educated by private tutors and in Protestant missionary schools. At age twenty, Ross was appointed as a U.S. Indian agent among the Cherokee and during the War of 1812 served as an adjutant (or administrative assistant) in a Cherokee regiment.

After the war, Ross focused on business ventures in Tennessee, including the establishment of a plantation. He also became increasingly involved in Cherokee political affairs, using his bilingual skills and Protestant training to represent Indian interests to government officials. In 1819 Ross was elected president of the Cherokee legislature. In the 1820s he moved to Georgia, where he served as president of the

Cherokee constitutional convention in 1827. Having overseen the first written constitution produced by an Indian nation, Ross was then elected principal chief in 1828. Over the next decade, he battled to retain the Cherokee homeland against the pressures of white planters and politicians. ■

Comparing the American histories of Dolley Madison and John Ross demonstrates that, while American politics was a white man's game, it was possible for those on the political margins to influence national developments. Both Madison and Ross sought to defend and expand the democratic ideals that defined the young nation. The First Lady helped to nurture a bipartisan political culture in Washington, which was particularly important following the War of 1812. Dolley Madison also struggled with the issue of slavery, an issue that fueled tensions among Democratic-Republicans when Missouri sought admission to statehood in 1819. Missouri's admission resulted from the nation's rapid geographical expansion. Its economic development proved more volatile, however, with the nation suffering its first major recession in 1819. Working men then demanded the right to vote to protect their economic interests. The Cherokee also asserted their rights. Ross encouraged Cherokees to embrace Anglo-American culture as a path to inclusion. But he could not overcome the power of planters and politicians to wrest valuable territory from his tribe. President Andrew Jackson, elected in 1828, ensured Cherokee removal and supported slavery. Yet he was lauded as a democratic hero for his frontier background and promotion of workingmen's rights. The United States successfully defended itself against British intervention, but still could not agree on which Americans truly belonged in the nation.

Conflicts at Home and Abroad

When Thomas Jefferson completed his second term as president in March 1809, he was succeeded by his friend and ally James Madison. Like Jefferson, Madison sought to end foreign interference in American affairs and to resolve conflicts between Indians and white residents on the nation's frontier. By 1815 the United States had weathered a series of domestic and foreign crises, including another war with Britain, but American sovereignty remained fragile. At the same time, even though Madison (like Jefferson) believed in a national government with limited powers, he, too, found himself expanding federal authority.

Tensions at Sea and on the Frontier. When President Madison took office, Great Britain and France remained embroiled in the Napoleonic Wars in Europe and refused to modify their policies toward American shipping or to recognize U.S. neutrality. American ships were subject to seizure by both nations, and British authorities continued to impress "deserters" into the Royal Navy. Just before Madison's inauguration in March 1809, Congress replaced the Embargo Act with the **Non-Intercourse Act**, which restricted trade only with France and Britain and their colonies. Although the continued embargo against Britain encouraged U.S. manufacturing and the act allowed trade with other European nations, many Americans still opposed Congress using its power to restrict their right to trade.

In the midst of these crises, Madison also faced difficulties in the Northwest Territory. In 1794 General Anthony Wayne had won a decisive victory against a multi-tribe coalition at the **Battle of Fallen Timbers**. But this victory inspired two forceful native leaders to create a pan-Indian alliance in the Ohio River valley. The Shawnee prophet Tenskwatawa and his half-brother Tecumseh, a warrior, encouraged native peoples to resist white encroachments on their territory and to give up all aspects of white society and culture, including liquor and other popular trade goods. They imagined an Indian nation that stretched from the Canadian border to the Gulf of Mexico.

Although powerful Creek and Choctaw nations in the lower Mississippi valley refused to join the alliance, Indians in the upper Midwest rallied around the brothers. In 1808 Tenskwatawa and Tecumseh established Prophet Town along the Tippecanoe River in Indiana Territory. The next year, William Henry Harrison, the territorial governor, tricked several Indian leaders into signing a treaty selling three million acres of land to the United States for only $7,600. An enraged Tecumseh dismissed the treaty, claiming the land belonged to all the Indians together.

Explore ▶

Read part of Tecumseh's response to Harrison in Source 9.1.

In November 1811, fearing the growing power of the Shawnee leaders, President Madison ordered Harrison to attack Prophet Town. With more troops and superior weapons, the U.S. army defeated the allied Indians forces and burned Prophet Town to the ground. The rout damaged Tenskwatawa's stature as a prophet, and he and his supporters fled to Canada, where skirmishes continued along the U.S.-Canadian border.

War Erupts with Britain. Convinced that British officials in Canada fueled Indian resistance, many Democratic-Republicans demanded an end to British intervention on the western frontier as well as British interference in transatlantic trade. Some called for the United States to declare war. Yet merchants in the Northeast, who hoped to renew trade with Great Britain and the British West Indies, feared the commercial disruptions that war entailed. Thus New England Federalists adamantly opposed a declaration of war.

For months, Madison avoided taking a clear stand on the issue. On June 1, 1812, however, with diplomatic efforts exhausted, Madison sent a secret message to Congress outlining U.S. grievances against Great Britain. Within weeks, Congress declared war by sharply divided votes in the House of Representatives and the Senate.

Supporters claimed that a victory over Great Britain would end threats to U.S. sovereignty and raise Americans' stature in Europe. However, the nation was ill prepared to launch a major offensive against such an imposing foe given cuts in federal spending, falling tax revenues, and diminished military resources. The U.S. navy, for example, established under President Adams, had been reduced to only six small gunboats by President Jefferson. Democratic-Republicans had also failed to recharter the Bank of the United States when it expired in 1811, so the nation lacked a vital source of credit. Nonetheless, many in Congress believed that Britain would be too engaged by the ongoing conflict with France to attack the United States.

Meanwhile U.S. commanders devised plans to attack Canada, but the U.S. army and navy proved no match for Great Britain and its Indian allies. Instead, Tecumseh, who was appointed a brigadier general in the British army, helped capture Detroit. Joint British and Indian forces also launched successful attacks on Fort Dearborn, Fort Mackinac, and other points along the U.S.-Canadian border.

Even as U.S. forces faced numerous defeats in the summer and fall of 1812, American voters reelected James Madison as president. While Madison won most western and southern states, where the war was most popular, he lost in New England and New York, where Federalist opponents held sway.

GUIDED ANALYSIS

Tecumseh | Speech to William Henry Harrison, 1810

In 1809 William Henry Harrison, governor of the Indiana Territory, negotiated a treaty with a coalition of native leaders to cede three million acres to the United States. Unhappy with this treaty, two Shawnee brothers, Tecumseh and Tenskwatawa, united with other Indian nations to resist white settlement of the region. In August 1810 Tecumseh confronted Harrison at Vincennes in the Indiana Territory and urged him to return the land. Harrison refused, and in the fall of 1811 U.S. troops attacked and defeated the Shawnees at Prophet Town.

Source 9.1

Why does Tecumseh consider white Americans untrustworthy?

How does Tecumseh's view of Indian land differ from that negotiated in the treaty?

How does Tecumseh compare U.S. actions toward Indians with Indian actions toward whites?

Brother. Since the peace was made you have kill'd some of the Shawanese, Winebagoes, Delawares, and Miamies and you have taken our lands from us, and I do not see how we can remain at peace with you if you continue to do so. You have given goods to the Kickapoos for the sale of their lands . . . which has been the cause of many deaths among them. You have promised us assistance but I do not see that you have given us any.

You try to force the red people to do some injury. It is you that is pushing them on to do mischief. You endeavor to make distinctions, you wish to prevent the Indians to do as we wish them: to unite and let them consider their land as the common property of the whole.

You take tribes aside and advise them not to come into this measure [coalition] and untill our design is accomplished we do not wish to accept of your invitation to go and visit the President.

The reason I tell you this is you want by your distinctions of Indian tribes in allotting to each a particular track of land to make them to war with each other. You never see an Indian come and endeavour to make the white people do so. You are continually driving the red people when at last you will drive them into the great Lake where they can't eather stand or work.

Source: Logan Esarey, ed., *Messages and Letters of William Henry Harrison* (Indianapolis: Indiana Historical Commission, 1922), 1:465.

Put It in Context

What does Tecumseh reveal about the complex relationships between American Indian nations and the U.S. government in the 1810s?

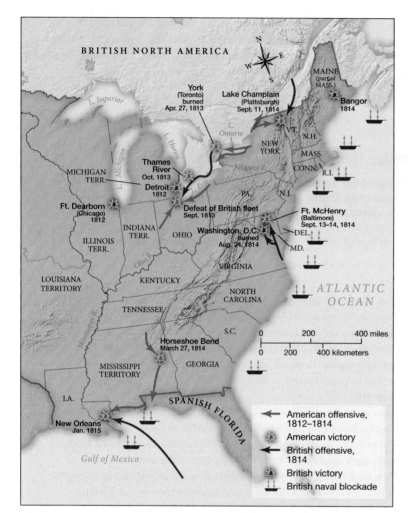

MAP 9.1   The War of 1812

Most conflicts in this war occurred in the Great Lakes region or around Washington, D.C. Yet two crucial victories occurred in the South. At Horseshoe Bend, troops under General Andrew Jackson and aided by Cherokee warriors defeated Creek allies of the British. At New Orleans, Jackson beat British forces shortly after a peace agreement was signed in Europe.

After a year of fighting, U.S. forces drove the British back into Canada in 1813 (Map 9.1). A naval victory on Lake Erie led by Commodore Oliver Perry proved crucial to U.S. success. Soon after, Tecumseh was killed in battle and U.S. forces burned York (present-day Toronto). Yet just as U.S. prospects in the war improved, New England Federalists demanded retreat. The war devastated the New England maritime trade, causing economic distress throughout the region. In 1813, state legislatures in New England withdrew their support for any invasion of "foreign British soil," and Federalists in Congress sought to block war appropriations and the deployment of local militia units into the U.S. army.

New England Federalists were not powerful enough to change national policy, but they called a meeting at Hartford, Connecticut in 1814 to "deliberate upon the alarming state of public affairs." Some participants at the **Hartford Convention** called for New England's secession from the United States. Most supported amendments to the U.S. Constitution that would constrain federal power by limiting presidents to a single term and ensuring they were elected from diverse states (ending Virginia's domination of the office). Other amendments would require a two-thirds majority in Congress to declare war or prohibit trade.

The Hartford resolutions gained increased attention as British forces launched new attacks into the United States and British warships blockaded U.S. ports. In August 1814, the British sailed up the Chesapeake. As American troops retreated, Dolley Madison and a family slave, Peter Jennings, gathered up government papers and valuable belongings before fleeing the White House. The redcoats then burned and sacked Washington City. U.S. troops quickly rallied, defeating the British in Maryland and expelling them from Washington and New York.

Meanwhile news arrived in March 1814 that Andrew Jackson and his Tennessee militiamen had defeated a force of Creek Indians, important British allies. Cherokee warriors (including John Ross), longtime foes of the Creek, joined the fight. At the **Battle of Horseshoe Bend**, in present-day Alabama, the combined U.S.-Cherokee forces slaughtered eight hundred Creek warriors. Although some Americans were appalled at the slaughter, in the resulting treaty the Creek nation lost two-thirds of its tribal domain.

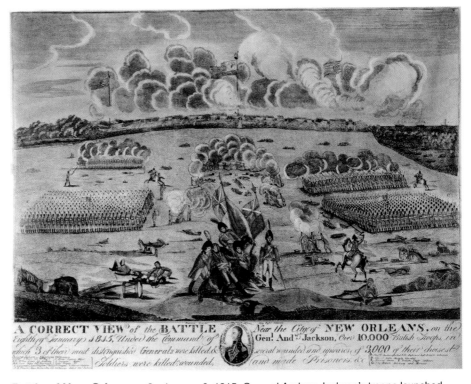

Battle of New Orleans On January 8, 1815, General Andrew Jackson's troops launched grapeshot and canister bombs against British forces in New Orleans in this final battle of the War of 1812. Jackson's troops included Indian allies, backcountry immigrants, and French-speaking black soldiers. This engraving by Francisco Scacki shows the slain British commander, Major General Sir Edward Pakenham, in the center foreground. Granger

Despite sporadic victories, the United States was no closer to winning the war when the British defeated Napoleon in June 1814. Six months later, the British fleet landed thousands of seasoned troops at New Orleans. Still, the British were losing steam as well, and representatives of the two countries met in Ghent, Belgium to negotiate a peace settlement. On Christmas Eve 1814, the **Treaty of Ghent** was signed, returning to each nation the lands it controlled before the war.

News of the treaty had not yet reached the United States in January 1815, when U.S. troops under General Andrew Jackson attacked and routed the British army at New Orleans. The victory cheered Americans, who, unaware that peace had already been achieved, made Jackson a national hero.

Although the War of 1812 achieved no formal territorial gains, it did represent an important defense of U.S. sovereignty and garnered international prestige for the young nation. In addition, Indians on the western frontier lost a powerful ally when British representatives at Ghent failed to act as advocates for their allies. Thus, in practical terms, the U.S. government gained greater control over vast expanses of land in the Ohio and Mississippi River valleys.

REVIEW & RELATE

• How were conflicts with Indians in the West connected to ongoing tensions between the United States and Great Britain on land and at sea?

• What were the long-term consequences of the War of 1812?

National Expansion and Regional Economies

By further expanding federal powers, the War of 1812 reinforced political changes that had been under way for more than a decade. At the Hartford Convention, Federalists who had once advocated broad national powers called for restrictions on federal authority. By contrast, Democratic-Republicans, who initially demanded restraints on federal power, now applauded its expansion. Indeed, Democratic-Republicans in Congress sought to use federal authority to settle boundary disputes in the West, make investments in transportation, and reestablish a national bank. Some state governments also invested in roads and canals. Federal power was again asserted to settle disputes with Britain and Spain over U.S. borders in the North and the South. At the same time, more secure borders and state and federal investments in transportation fueled overseas trade and the development of increasingly distinct regional economies.

Governments Fuel Economic Growth. In 1800 Thomas Jefferson captured the presidency by advocating a reduction in federal powers and a renewed emphasis on the needs of small farmers and workingmen. Once in power, however, Jefferson and his Democratic-Republican supporters faced a series of economic and political developments that led many to embrace a loose interpretation of the U.S. Constitution and support federal efforts to aid economic growth.

"Erie-Canal, Lockport," c. 1850   This steel engraving, based on an 1839 painting, depicts one of five locks that lifted boats sixty feet over a limestone ridge near the western end of the canal. The remarkable engineering feat required 1200 laborers to blast the ridge, clear the rocks, and build the locks. The village of Lockport, which emerged at the site, grew rapidly after 1825. akg-images

Population growth and commercial expansion encouraged these federal efforts. In 1811 the first steamboat traveled down the Mississippi from the Ohio River to New Orleans; over the next decade, steamboat traffic expanded. This development helped western and southern residents but hurt trade on overland routes between northeastern seaports and the Ohio River valley. The federal government began construction of the Cumberland Road in 1811 to reestablish this regional connection by linking Maryland and Ohio. Congress passed additional bills to fund ambitious federal transportation projects, but President Madison vetoed much of this legislation, believing that it overstepped even a loose interpretation of the Constitution.

After the War of 1812, however, Democratic-Republican representative Henry Clay of Kentucky sketched out a plan to promote U.S. economic growth and advance commercial ties throughout the nation. Called the **American System**, it combined federally funded internal improvements, such as roads and canals, to aid farmers and merchants with federal tariffs to protect U.S. manufacturing. Western expansion fueled demand for these internal improvements. The non-Indian population west of the Appalachian Mountains more than doubled between 1810 and 1820, from 1,080,000 to 2,234,000. Many veterans of the War of 1812 settled there after receiving 160-acre parcels of land in the region as payment for service. Congress admitted four new states to the Union in just four years: Indiana (1816), Mississippi (1817), Illinois (1818), and Alabama (1819).

Congress also negotiated with Indian nations to secure trade routes farther west. In the 1810s, Americans began trading along an ancient trail from Missouri to Santa Fe, a town in northern Mexico. But the trail cut across territory claimed by the Osage Indians. In 1825 Congress approved a treaty with the Osage to guarantee right of way for U.S. merchants. The Santa Fe Trail soon became a critical route for commerce between the United States and Mexico.

East of the Appalachian Mountains, state governments funded most internal improvement projects. The most significant of these was New York's **Erie Canal**, a 363-mile waterway stretching from the Mohawk River to Buffalo that was completed in 1825. Self-taught men directed this extraordinary engineering feat by which thousands of workers carved a swath forty feet wide and four feet deep through limestone cliffs, mountains, forests, and swamps. The canal, which rises 566 feet along its route, required the construction of 83 locks to lift and lower boats. The arduous and dangerous work was carried out mainly by Irish, Welsh, and German immigrants, many of whom settled along its route. Tolls on the Erie Canal quickly repaid the tremendous financial cost of its construction. Freight charges and shipping times plunged. And by linking western farmers to the Hudson River, the Erie Canal ensured that New York City became the nation's premier seaport (Map 9.2).

The Erie Canal's success inspired hundreds of similar projects in other states. Canals carried manufactured goods from New England and the Middle Atlantic states to rural households in the Ohio River valley. Western farmers, in turn, shipped agricultural products back east. Canals also linked smaller cities within Pennsylvania and Ohio, facilitating the rise of commercial and manufacturing centers like Harrisburg, Pittsburgh, and Cincinnati. Moreover, canals allowed vast quantities of coal to be transported out of the Allegheny Mountains, fueling industrial development throughout the Northeast.

Americans Expand the Nation's Borders.
In 1816, in the midst of the nation's economic resurgence, James Monroe won an easy victory in the presidential election over Rufus King, a New York Federalist. To improve relations with Britain and resolve problems on the frontier, Monroe sent John Quincy Adams to London. He negotiated treaties that limited U.S. and British naval forces on the Great Lakes, set the U.S.-Canadian border at the forty-ninth parallel, and established joint British-U.S. occupation of the Oregon Territory. In 1817 and 1818, the Senate approved these treaties, which further restricted Indian rights and power.

President Monroe harbored grave concerns about the nation's southern boundary as well. He sought to limit Spain's power in North America and stop Seminole Indians in Florida and Alabama from claiming lands the defeated Creeks ceded to the United States. Shifting from diplomacy to military force, in 1817 the president sent General Andrew Jackson to force the Seminoles back into central Florida. But he ordered Jackson to avoid direct conflict with Spanish forces for fear of igniting another war. However, in spring 1818 Jackson attacked two Spanish forts, hanged two Seminole chiefs, and executed two British citizens.

Jackson's attacks spurred outrage among Spanish and British officials and many members of Congress. The threat of conflict with Britain, Spain, and the Seminole tribe prompted President Monroe to establish the nation's first peacetime army. In the end, the British chose to ignore the execution of citizens engaged in "unauthorized" activities, while Spain decided to sell the Florida Territory to the United States. Indeed, in the

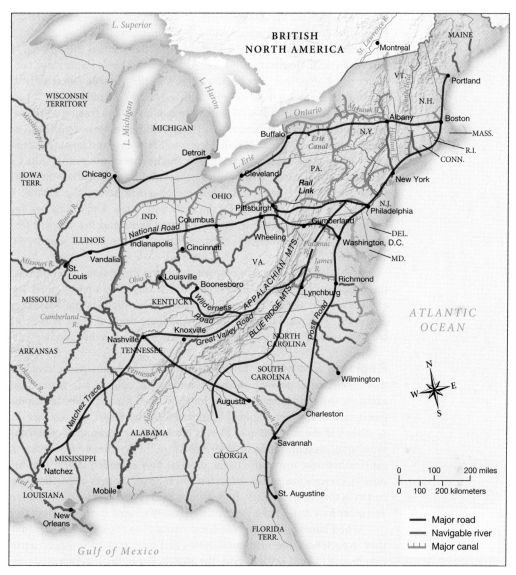

MAP 9.2   Roads and Canals to 1837

During the 1820s and 1830s, state and local governments as well as private companies built roads and canals to foster migration and commercial development. The Erie Canal, completed in 1825, was the most significant of these projects. Many other states, particularly in the Northeast and the old Northwest, sought to duplicate that canal's success over the following decade.

Adams-Onís Treaty (1819), negotiated by John Quincy Adams, Spain ceded all its lands east of the Mississippi to the United States.

Success in acquiring Florida encouraged the administration to look for other opportunities to limit European influence in the Western Hemisphere. By 1822 Argentina, Chile, Peru, Colombia, and Mexico had all overthrown Spanish rule. That March, President

Monroe recognized the independence of these southern neighbors, and Congress quickly established diplomatic relations with the new nations. The following year, President Monroe added a codicil to a treaty with Russia that claimed that the Western Hemisphere was part of the U.S. sphere of influence. Although the United States did not have sufficient power to enforce what later became known as the **Monroe Doctrine**, it had declared its intention to challenge Europeans for authority in the Atlantic world.

By the late 1820s, U.S. residents were moving to and trading with newly independent Mexican territories. Southern whites began settling on Mexican lands in east Texas, while traders traveled the Santa Fe Trail. Meanwhile New England manufacturers and merchants began sending goods via clipper ships to another Mexican territory, Alta California.

Some Americans looked even farther afield. In the early nineteenth century, U.S. ships carried otter pelts and other merchandise across the Pacific, returning with Chinese porcelains and silks. In the early 1800s, the Alta California and China trades converged, expanding the reach of U.S. merchants and the demand for U.S. manufactured goods. Some Americans then set their sights on Pacific islands, especially Hawaii and Samoa.

Expanded trade routes along with wartime disruptions of European imports fueled the expansion of U.S. manufacturing, which improved opportunities for entrepreneurs and workers. By 1813 the area around Providence, Rhode Island boasted seventy-six spinning mills. Two years later, Philadelphia claimed pride of place as the nation's top industrial city, turning out glass, chemicals, metalwork, and leather goods.

Regional Economic Development.

The roads, rivers, canals, and steamboats that connected a growing nation meant that people in one region could more easily exchange the goods they produced for those they needed. This development fostered the emergence of distinct, regional economies. In the South, for instance, vast Indian land cessions and the acquisition of Florida ensured the expansion of cotton cultivation. At the same time, overcultivation in older regions of the Southeast forced many planters to relocate further west and south. In the process, they extended slavery into new lands to produce cash crops like cotton, sugar, and rice. Small farmers often planted as much land in cotton as they could manage. Both groups used profits from these staple crops to buy grain and other food items from the West and manufactured shoes and cloth from the North.

When James and Dolley Madison returned to their plantation, Montpelier, in 1817, they experienced the new possibilities and problems of southern agriculture. Plantation homes in long-settled areas like Montpelier in the Virginia piedmont became more fashionable as they incorporated luxury goods imported from China and Europe. But the soil in the region, depleted of nutrients, limited the profits from tobacco and made a shift to cotton impossible. As agricultural production declined, some Virginia planters made money by selling slaves to planters farther south and west. However, James Madison refused to break up slave families who had worked his plantation for decades and had no desire to relocate. Thus the Madisons were forced to reduce their standard of living.

However, many white Americans benefited from the expansion of southern agriculture west of the Appalachians. Southern farmers and planters who cultivated cotton made substantial profits in the 1810s. So did western farmers, who shipped vast quantities of agricultural produce to the South. Towns like Cincinnati, located across the Ohio River from Kentucky, sprang up as regional centers of commerce. Americans living in the Northeast increased their commercial connections with the South as well. Northern merchants became more deeply engaged in the southern cotton trade, opening warehouses in cities like Savannah and Charleston and sending agents into the countryside to bargain for cotton to be spun into thread in mills powered by water.

The southern cotton boom thus fueled northern industrial growth, the improvement of roads, the expansion of canals, and the building of larger and faster ships. Factory owners and merchants in New England could ship growing quantities of yarn, thread, and cloth along with shoes, tools, and leather goods to the South. Meanwhile, merchants in Philadelphia and Pittsburgh built ties to western farmers, exchanging manufactured goods for agricultural products. Over time America's regional economies became not only more distinctive but also increasingly interdependent.

REVIEW & RELATE

- What role did government play in early-nineteenth-century economic development?

- How and why did economic development contribute to regional differences and shape regional ties?

Economic and Political Crises

Even as regional economies ensured economic interdependence, they highlighted political differences. For instance, the growth in trade between regions led to an increase in commercial institutions, such as banks, the largest of which were established in the North. When the nation's first severe recession hit in 1819, many southern planters and midwestern farmers blamed it on the banks. In reality, falling prices for cotton and wheat abroad as well as overextension of credit by U.S. banks contributed to the recession. Whatever the cause, the interdependence of regional economies ensured that everyone suffered. At the same time, these economies were built on distinct forms of labor, with the South becoming more dependent on slavery and the North less so. When Missouri, situated between the old Northwest Territory and expanding southern cotton lands, applied for statehood in 1819, these regional differences set off a furious national debate over slavery.

The Panic of 1819. The **panic of 1819** resulted primarily from irresponsible banking practices in the United States and was deepened by the declining overseas demand for American goods, especially cotton. Beginning in 1816, American banks, including the newly chartered Second Bank of the United States, loaned huge sums to settlers seeking land on the frontier and merchants and manufacturers expanding their businesses. Many loans were not backed by sufficient collateral because many banks assumed that continued economic growth would ensure repayment. Then, as agricultural production in Europe revived with the end of the Napoleonic Wars, the demand for American foodstuffs dropped sharply. Farm income plummeted by roughly one-third in the late 1810s.

In 1818 the directors of the Second Bank, fearing a continued expansion of the money supply, tightened the credit they provided to branch banks. This sudden effort to curtail credit led to economic panic. Some branch banks failed immediately. Others survived by calling in loans to companies and individuals, who in turn demanded repayment from those to whom they had extended credit. The chain of indebtedness pushed many people to the brink of economic ruin just as factory owners cut their workforce and merchants

Auction in Chatham Street, New York, 1820   Widespread unemployment between 1819 and 1823 resulted in evictions for thousands of families. Public auctions of the furniture, dishes, and other household goods of evicted families were held regularly in cities across the country. This depiction of an 1820 auction in New York's Chatham Square was painted by E. Didier in 1843, during the next major economic panic. © Museum of the City of New York, USA/Bridgeman Images

decreased orders for new goods. Individuals and businesses faced bankruptcy and foreclosure, and property values fell sharply.

Bankruptcies, foreclosures, unemployment, and poverty spread across the country. Cotton farmers were especially hard hit by declining exports and falling prices. Planters who had gone into debt to purchase land in Alabama and Mississippi were unable to pay their mortgages. Many western residents, who had invested all they had in new farms, lost their land or simply stopped paying their mortgages. This further strained state banks, some of which collapsed, leaving the national bank holding mortgages on vast amounts of western territory.

Many Americans viewed banks as the cause of the panic. Some states defied the Constitution and the Supreme Court by trying to tax Second Bank branches or printing state banknotes with no specie (gold or silver) to back them. Some Americans called for government relief, but there was no system to provide the kinds of assistance needed. When Congress debated how to reignite the nation's economy, regional differences quickly appeared. Northern manufacturers called for even higher tariffs to protect them from foreign competition, but southern planters argued that high tariffs raised the price of manufactured goods while agricultural profits declined. Meanwhile, workingmen and small farmers feared that their economic needs were being ignored by politicians tied to bankers, planters, manufacturers, and merchants.

By 1823 the panic had largely dissipated, but the prolonged economic crisis shook national confidence, and citizens became more skeptical of federal authority and more suspicious of banks. From 1819 until the Civil War, one of the greatest limitations on national growth remained the cycle of economic expansion and contraction.

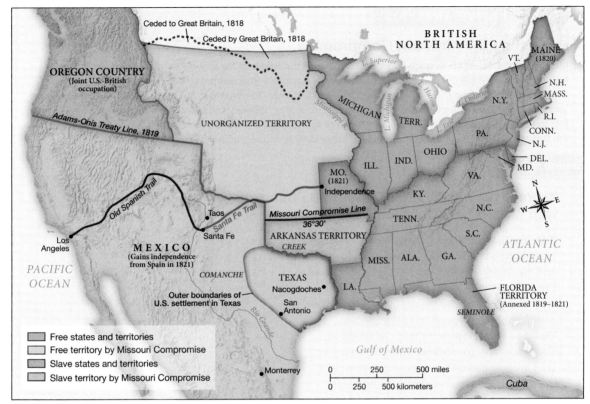

MAP 9.3   The Missouri Compromise and Westward Expansion, 1820s

The debate over the Missouri Compromise occurred as the United States began expanding farther westward. Within a few years of its adoption, the growth of U.S. settlements in eastern Texas and increased trade with a newly independent Mexico suggested the importance of drawing a clear boundary between slave and free states.

Slavery in Missouri.

A second national crisis highlighted regional systems of labor. In February 1819 the Missouri Territory applied for statehood. New York congressman James Tallmadge Jr. proposed that Missouri be admitted only if it banned further importation of slaves and passed a gradual emancipation law. Southern congressmen blocked Tallmadge's proposals, but the northern majority in the House of Representatives then rejected Missouri's admission.

Southern politicians were outraged, claiming that since the Missouri Territory allowed slavery, so should the state of Missouri. With cotton production moving ever westward, southern congressmen wanted to ensure the availability of new lands. They also wanted to ensure the South's power in Congress. Because the northern population had grown more rapidly than that in the South, by 1819 northern politicians controlled the House of Representatives. The Senate, however, was evenly divided. If northerners could block the admission of slave states like Missouri while allowing the admission of free states, the balance of power in the Senate would tip in the North's favor.

Explore ▶

Compare two critiques of the Missouri Compromise in Sources 9.2 and 9.3.

COMPARATIVE ANALYSIS

Protesting the Missouri Compromise

Missouri's statehood application sparked a crisis over the future of slavery in America, and the resulting Missouri Compromise did little to ease the fears of Americans who wanted to contain its spread. Timothy Claimright and Thomas Jefferson both opposed the Missouri Compromise, but they offered different reasons for doing so. Claimright, of Brunswick, Maine, argues in this poetic broadside that his home state should not join the Union if it means inviting the admission of Missouri as a slave state. Jefferson predicts in a letter that the temporary solution of the compromise will lead only to future tragedy.

Source 9.2

Timothy Claimright | Maine Not to Be Coupled with the Missouri Question, 1820

If the South will not yield, to the West be it known,
That Maine will declare for a *King* of her own;
And *three hundred thousand* of freemen demand
The justice bestow'd on each State in the land.
Free whites of the East are not blacks of the West,
And Republican souls on this principle rest,
That if no respect to their rights can be shown,
They know how to vindicate what are their own. . . .
They are founded on freedom, humanity's right,
Ordained by God against slavery to fight.
And Heaven born liberty sooner than yield,
The whites of Missouri shall dress their own field.
We are hardy and healthy, can till our own soil,
In labour delight; make a pleasure of toil. . . .
They too lazy to work, drive slaves, whom they fear;
We school our own children, and brew our own beer.
We do a day's work and go fearless to bed;
Tho' lock'd up, they dream of slaves, whom they dread. . . .
They may boast of their blacks; we boast of our plenty,
And swear to be free, eighteen hundred and twenty. . . .
A Sister in Union admit her, as free;
To be coupled with slaves, she will never agree.

Source: Timothy Claimright, *Maine Not to Be Coupled with the Missouri Question* (Brunswick, ME, 1820), Library of Congress Ephemera Collection.

eliminated property qualifications for white men, raised property qualifications for African American voters.

When African American men protested their disfranchisement, some whites spoke out on their behalf. They claimed that denying rights to men who had in no way abused the privilege of voting set "an ominous and dangerous precedent." In response, opponents

Source 9.3

Thomas Jefferson | Letter to John Holmes, 1820

Monticello, April 22, 1820

I thank you, dear Sir, for the copy you have been so kind as to send me of the letter to your constituents on the Missouri question. It is a perfect justification to them. I had for a long time ceased to read newspapers, or pay any attention to public affairs, confident they were in good hands, and content to be a passenger in our bark [ship] to the shore from which I am not distant. But this momentous question, like a fire-bell in the night, awakened and filled me with terror. I considered it at once as the knell of the Union. It is hushed, indeed, for the moment. But this is a reprieve only, not a final sentence. A geographical line, coinciding with a marked principle, moral and political, once conceived and held up to the angry passions of men, will never be obliterated; and every new irritation will mark it deeper and deeper. I can say, with conscious truth, that there is not a man on earth who would sacrifice more than I would to relieve us from this heavy reproach, in any *practicable* way. The cession of that kind of property [slavery], for so it is misnamed, is a bagatelle [an insignificant thing] which would not cost me a second thought, if, in that way, a general emancipation and *expatriation* could be effected; and, gradually, and with due sacrifices, I think it might be. But as it is, we have the wolf by the ears, and we can neither hold him, nor safely let him go. Justice is in one scale, and self-preservation in the other.

Source: Thomas Jefferson Randolph, ed., *Memoirs, Correspondence, and Private Papers of Thomas Jefferson* (London: Henry Colburn and Richard Bentley, 1829), 4:332.

Interpret the Evidence

1. In opposing the Missouri Compromise, how does Claimright differentiate Maine and other northern states from the slave societies of the South?

2. How does Jefferson's opposition to the Missouri Compromise differ from Claimright's and why does Jefferson believe it would exacerbate the conflict over slavery?

Put It in Context

How might supporters of the Missouri Compromise have responded to the concerns of Claimright and Jefferson?

of black suffrage offered explicitly racist justifications. Some argued that black voting would lead to interracial socializing, even marriage. Others feared that black voters might hold the balance of power in close elections, forcing white civic leaders to accede to their demands. Gradually, racist arguments won the day, and by 1840, 93 percent of free blacks in the North were excluded from voting.

For southern planters, the decision on Missouri defined the future of slavery. With foreign trade in slaves outlawed, planters relied on natural increase and trading slaves from older to newer areas of cultivation to meet the demand for labor. Moreover, free blacks packed the congressional galleries in Washington to listen to congressmen debate Missouri statehood, leading supporters of slavery to worry that any signs of weakness would fuel resistance to slavery. Recent attacks on Georgia plantations by a coalition of fugitive slaves and Seminole Indians lent power to such fears.

In 1820 Representative Henry Clay of Kentucky forged a compromise that resolved the immediate issues and promised a long-term solution. Maine was to be admitted as a free state and Missouri as a slave state, thereby maintaining the balance between North and South in the U.S. Senate (Map 9.3). At the same time, Congress agreed that the southern border of Missouri—latitude 36°30'—was to serve as the boundary between slave and free states throughout the Louisiana Territory.

The **Missouri Compromise** ended the crisis for the moment. Still, the debates made clear how quickly a disagreement over slavery could escalate into clashes that threatened the survival of the nation.

REVIEW & RELATE

- How did regional interdependency contribute to the panic of 1819?

- What regional divisions did the conflict over slavery in Missouri reveal?

The **Expansion** and **Limits** of **American Democracy**

With the panic of 1819 and the debates over Missouri shaking many Americans' faith in their economic and political leaders and the frontier moving ever westward, the nation was ripe for change. Workingmen, small farmers, and frontier settlers, who had long been locked out of the electoral system by property qualifications and eastern elites, demanded the right to vote. The resulting political movement ensured voting rights for nearly all white men during the 1820s. Yet African Americans lost political and civil rights in the same period; and Indians fared poorly under the federal administrations brought to power by this expanded electorate. While some white women gained greater political influence as a result of the voting rights gained by fathers and husbands, they did not achieve independent political rights. Finally, as a wave of new voters entered the political fray, ongoing conflicts over slavery, tariffs, and the rights of Indian nations transformed party alignments.

Expanding Voting Rights. Between 1788 and 1820, the U.S. presidency was dominated by Virginia elites and after 1800 by Democratic-Republicans. With little serious political opposition at the national level, few people bothered to vote in presidential elections. Far more people engaged in political activities at the state and local levels. Many towns attracted large audiences to public celebrations on the Fourth of July and election days. Female participants sewed symbols of their partisan loyalties on their clothes and joined in parades and feasts organized by men.

Election Day in Philadelphia, 1815   This engraving, based on a painting by German immigrant John Lewis Krimmel, depicts an election-day celebration in Philadelphia in 1815. The image highlights the widespread popular participation of men, women, and children in political events even before the expansion of voting rights for white men in the 1820s. Art Collection 3/Alamy Stock Photo

The panic of 1819 stimulated even more political activity as laboring men, who were especially vulnerable to economic downturns, demanded the right to vote so they could hold politicians accountable. In New York State, Martin Van Buren, a rising star in the Democratic-Republican Party, led the fight to eliminate property qualifications for voting. At the state constitutional convention of 1821, the committee on suffrage argued that the only qualification for voting should be "the virtue and morality of the people." By the word people, Van Buren and the committee meant white men.

> **Explore ▶**
>
> Examine two historians' interpretations of the expansion of voting rights in Sources 9.4 and 9.5.

Despite opposition from powerful and wealthy men, by 1825 most states along the Atlantic seaboard had lowered or eliminated property qualifications on white male voters. Meanwhile states along the frontier that had joined the Union in the 1810s established universal white male suffrage from the beginning. And by 1824 three-quarters of the states (18 of 24) allowed voters, rather than state legislatures, to elect members of the electoral college.

Yet as white workingmen gained political rights in the 1820s, democracy did not spread to other groups. Indian nations were considered sovereign entities, so Indians voted in their own nations, not in U.S. elections. Women were excluded from voting because of their perceived dependence on men. And African American men faced increasing restrictions on their political rights. No southern legislature had ever granted blacks the right to vote, and northern states began disfranchising them as well in the 1820s. In many cases, expanded voting rights for white men went hand in hand with new restrictions on black men. In New York State, for example, the constitution of 1821, which

Expanding American Democracy for Whom?

President Andrew Jackson's victory in the 1828 presidential election has been viewed by most historians as directly tied to the expansion of male voting rights over the preceding decade. That expansion continued through the 1840s as nearly every state eliminated property requirements for white male voters. As the electorate grew, political contests became increasingly partisan and voters turned out at higher rates across the young nation. Yet this democratic expansion did not include all Americans. Indeed, some historians have noted that expanded voting rights for white men went hand-in-hand with greater limits on black men, increasing racial inequities in the electorate.

Source 9.4

Alexander Keyssar, Broadening the Franchise, 2000

The much-celebrated broadening of the suffrage during the first half of the nineteenth century . . . was spawned . . . by the convergence of different factors, present in varying combinations in individual states. . . . Most fundamentally . . . all of the states that had property requirements in 1790 witnessed an increase in the number and proportion of adult males who were unable to meet those requirements. . . .

[T]he disfranchised were unable to precipitate change by themselves. When the right to vote was enlarged, it happened because some men who were already enfranchised. . . . saw themselves as having a direct interest in enlarging the electorate. One such interest was military preparedness. . . . [A]fter the War of 1812, many middle-class citizens concluded that extending the franchise to the "lower orders" would enhance their own security and help to preserve their way of life, by assuring that such men would continue to serve in the army and the militias. . . . .

In the South, the issue had an added twist: enfranchising all white Southerners was a means of making sure that poor whites would serve in militia patrols guarding against slave rebellions. . . . [And] it would contribute to white solidarity. . . . Economic self-interest also played a role in the expansion of the franchise. . . . As territories began to organize themselves into states, inhabitants of sparsely populated regions embraced white manhood suffrage, . . . believ[ing] that a broad franchise would encourage settlement and in so doing . . . stimulate economic development. . . . After 1840, similar concerns helped to propel the alien suffrage laws. . . . Granting full political rights to immigrants appeared to be economically advantageous as well as democratic. . . .

Source: Alexander Keyssar, *The Right to Vote: the Contested History of Democracy in the United States* (New York: Basic Books, 2000) pp. 34, 35, 37, 38.

Racial Restrictions and Antiblack Violence.

Restrictions on voting followed other constraints on African American men and women. As early as 1790, Congress limited naturalization (the process of becoming a citizen) to white aliens, or immigrants. It also excluded blacks from enrolling in federal militias. In 1820 Congress authorized city officials in Washington, D.C. to adopt a separate legal code governing free blacks and slaves. This federal legislation encouraged states, in both the North and the South, to add

Source 9.5

James Oliver Horton and Lois E. Horton, The Limits of Democratic Expansion, 1997

The expansion of the franchise for white men, however, was often accompanied by the restriction or elimination of the franchise for black men. . . . In 1822, Rhode Island's legislature disenfranchised blacks in that state for the first time. In New York the constitution of 1777 had guaranteed all men who could meet the property restrictions, including free blacks, the right to vote. . . . [T]hrough the early years of the nineteenth century . . . Federalists . . . foiled several attempts to institute racial restrictions. The War of 1812 was a turning point. . . . Discredited by their opposition to the war, Federalists lost control of state politics and were unable to stop Republicans . . . from limiting the black vote . . . . [B]lack males were required to . . . have more than $250 in property before they could vote. . . . As the roster of eligible white voters expanded in every state, . . . a new political grassroots style brought General Andrew Jackson to the presidency in 1828. Political parties vied for the votes of common working people, and candidates portrayed themselves as ordinary men. . . . This "age of the common man" was the age of the common white man, as black men . . . lost the franchise in many states. Party politics became a struggle between white men for the support and loyalty of other white men. Although the Jacksonians' political ideology was populist in that it attacked a somewhat vague "privilege," [it] incorporate[ed] a growing belief in white superiority and [a] distinctly racial orientation. . . .

Source: James Oliver Horton and Lois E. Horton, *In Hope of Liberty: Culture, Community and Protest Among Northern Free Blacks 1700–1860* (New York: Oxford University Press, 1997), p. 168.

Examine the Sources

1. How do Keyssar and Horton and Horton differ in their interpretation of the role of race in the expansion of voting rights in the early nineteenth century?
2. What evidence can you find in this chapter that supports Keyssar or Horton and Horton's interpretations?

Put It in Context

How do the explanations of Keyssar and Horton and Horton for the changes in voting rights differ from that provided by the author of this chapter (see "Expanding Voting Rights" on pp. 296–299)?

their own restrictions, including the segregation of public schools, transportation, and accommodations. Some northern legislatures even denied African Americans the right to settle in their state.

In addition, blacks faced mob and state-sanctioned violence across the country. In 1822 officials in Charleston, South Carolina accused Denmark Vesey, a free black, of following the revolutionary leader Toussaint L'Ouverture's lead and plotting a conspiracy to free the city's slaves. Vesey had helped to organize churches, mutual aid societies, and other black institutions. His accomplishments were considered threatening to the future of slavery by challenging assumptions about black inferiority. Vesey may have organized a plan to free slaves in the city, but it is also possible that white officials concocted the plot to terrorize blacks. Despite scant evidence, Vesey and thirty-four of his alleged co-conspirators were found guilty and hanged. The African Methodist Episcopal Church where they supposedly planned the insurrection was demolished. Northern blacks also suffered from violent attacks by whites. For example, in 1829 white residents of Cincinnati attacked black neighborhoods, and more than half of the city's black residents fled. Many of them resettled in Ontario, Canada. They were soon joined by Philadelphia blacks who had been attacked by groups of white residents in 1832. Such attacks continued in northern cities throughout the 1830s.

Political Realignments. Restrictions on black political and civil rights converged with the continued decline of the Federalists. Federalist majorities in New York State had approved the gradual abolition law of 1799. In 1821 New York Federalists advocated equal rights for black and white voters as long as property qualifications limited suffrage to respectable citizens. But Federalists were losing power, and the concerns of African Americans were low on the Democratic-Republican agenda.

Struggles within the Democratic-Republican Party now turned to a large extent on the limits of federal power. Many Democratic-Republicans had come to embrace a more expansive view of federal authority and a looser interpretation of the U.S. Constitution. Others argued forcefully for a return to limited federal power and a strict construction of the Constitution. At the same time, rising young politicians—like Martin Van Buren and Andrew Jackson—and newly enfranchised voters sought to seize control of the party from its longtime leaders.

CLASS No. 1.

Comprises those prisoners who were found guilty and executed.

Prisoners Names.	Owners' Names.	Time of Commit.	How Disposed of.
Peter	James Poyas	June 18	
Ned	Gov. T. Bennett,	do.	Hanged on Tuesday
Rolla	do.	do	the 2d July, 1822,
Batteau	do.	do.	on Blake's lands,
Denmark Vesey	A free black man	22	near Charleston.
Jessy	Thos. Blackwood	23	
John	Elias Horry	July 5	Do. on the Lines near
Gullah Jack	Paul Pritchard	do.	Ch.; Friday July 12.
Mingo	Wm. Harth	June 21	
Lot	Forrester	27	
Joe	P. L. Jore	July 6	
Julius	Thos. Forrest	8	
Tom	Mrs. Russell	10	
Smart	Robt. Anderson	do.	
John	John Robertson	11	
Robert	do.	do.	
Adam	do.	do.	
Polydore	Mrs. Faber	do.	Hanged on the Lines
Bacchus	Benj. Hammet	do.	near Charleston,
Dick	Wm. Sims	13	on Friday, 26th
Pharaoh	— Thompson	do.	July.
Jemmy	Mrs. Clement	18	
Mauidore	Mordecai Cohen	19	
Dean	— Mitchell	do.	
Jack	Mrs. Purcell	12	
Bellisle	Est. of Jos. Yates	18	
Naphur	do.	do.	
Adam	do.	do.	
Jacob	John S. Glen	16	
Charles	John Billings	18	
Jack	N. McNeill	22	
Cæsar	Miss Smith	do.	
Jacob Stagg	Jacob Lankester	23	Do. Tues. July 30.
Tom	Wm. M. Scott	24	
William	Mrs. Garner	Aug. 2	Do. Friday, Aug. 9.

Record of Thirty-five Men Executed for Conspiring to Revolt against Their Masters   This official record of executions related to an alleged 1822 slave conspiracy lists the name of Denmark Vesey, the only free black man accused, fifth. The enslaved men are listed next to their owners' names, including the governor of South Carolina, twenty-one other men, and six women. There were no appeals of their convictions, and the hangings took place quickly. Granger, NYC

The election of 1824 brought these conflicts to a head, splitting the Democratic-Republicans into rival factions that by 1828 coalesced into two distinct entities: the **Democrats** and the **National Republicans**. Unable to agree on a single presidential candidate in 1824, the Democratic-Republican congressional caucus fractured into four camps backing separate candidates: John Quincy Adams, Andrew Jackson, Henry Clay, and Secretary of the Treasury William Crawford.

As the race developed, Adams and Jackson emerged as the two strongest candidates. John Quincy Adams's stature rested on his diplomatic achievements and the reputation of his father, former president John Adams. He favored internal improvements and protective tariffs that would bolster northern industry and commerce. Jackson, on the other hand, relied largely on his fame as a war hero and Indian fighter to inspire popular support. He advocated limited federal power.

As a candidate who appealed to ordinary voters, Jackson held a decided edge. Outgoing and boisterous, Jackson took his case to the people. Emphasizing his humble origins, he appealed to small farmers and northern workers. Just as important, Jackson gained the support of Van Buren, who also wanted to expand the political clout of the "common [white] man" and limit the reach of a central government that was becoming too powerful.

The four presidential candidates created a truly competitive race, and turnout at the polls increased significantly. Jackson won the popular vote by carrying Pennsylvania, New Jersey, the Carolinas, and much of the West and led in the electoral college with 99 electors. But with no candidate gaining an absolute majority in the electoral college, the Constitution called for the House of Representatives to choose the president from the three leading contenders—Jackson, Adams, and Crawford. Clay, who came in fourth, asked his supporters to back Adams, ensuring his election. Once in office, President Adams appointed Clay secretary of state. Jackson claimed that the two had engineered a "corrupt bargain," but Adams and Clay, who shared many ideas, formed a logical alliance.

Once in office, President Adams ran into vigorous opposition in Congress led by Van Buren. John C. Calhoun, a South Carolina Senator who had been elected vice president, also opposed Adams's policies. Van Buren argued against federal funding for internal improvements since New York State had financed the Erie Canal with its own monies. Calhoun, meanwhile, joined other southern politicians in opposing any expansion of federal power for fear it would then be used to restrict the spread of slavery.

The most serious battle in Congress, however, involved tariffs. The tariff of 1816 had excluded most cheap English cotton cloth from the United States to aid New England manufacturing. In 1824 the tariff was extended to more expensive cotton and woolen cloth and to iron goods. During the presidential campaign, Adams and Clay appealed to northern voters by advocating even higher duties on these items. When Adams introduced tariff legislation that extended duties to raw materials like wool, hemp, and molasses, he gained support from both Jackson and Van Buren, who considered these tariffs beneficial to farmers on the frontier. Despite the opposition of Vice President Calhoun and congressmen from southeastern states, the tariff of 1828 was approved, raising duties on imports to an average of 62 percent.

The tariff of 1828, however, was Adams's only notable legislative victory. His foreign policy was also stymied by a hostile Congress. Adams thus entered the 1828 election campaign with little to show in the way of domestic or foreign achievements, and Jackson and his supporters took full advantage of the president's political vulnerability.

The Presidential Election of 1828.

The election of 1828 tested the power of the two major factions in the Democratic-Republican Party. President Adams followed the traditional approach of "standing" for office. He told supporters, "If my country wants my services, she must ask for them." Jackson and his supporters chose instead to "run" for office. They took their case directly to the voters, introducing innovative techniques to create enthusiasm among the electorate.

Van Buren managed the first truly national political campaign in U.S. history, seeking to re-create the original Democratic-Republican coalition among farmers, northern artisans, and southern planters while adding a sizable constituency of frontier voters. He was aided in the effort by Calhoun, who again ran for vice president and supported the Tennessee war hero despite their disagreement over tariffs. Jackson's supporters organized state nominating conventions rather than relying on the congressional caucus. They established local Jackson committees in critical states like Virginia and New York. They organized newspaper campaigns and developed a logo, the hickory leaf, based on the candidate's nickname, "Old Hickory."

Jackson traveled the country to build loyalty to himself as well as to his party. His Tennessee background, rise to great wealth, and reputation as an Indian fighter ensured his popularity among southern and western voters. He also reassured southerners that he advocated "judicious" duties on imports, suggesting that he might try to lower the 1828 rates. At the same time, his support of the tariff of 1828 and his military credentials created enthusiasm among northern workingmen and frontier farmers.

President Adams's supporters demeaned the "dissolute" and "rowdy" men who attended Jackson rallies. They also launched personal attacks on the candidate and on his wife, Rachel. They questioned the timing of her divorce from her first husband and remarriage to Jackson. A Cincinnati newspaper headline asked: "Ought a convicted adulteress and her paramour husband be placed in the highest offices of this free and Christian land?" **See Primary Source Project 9: The Election of 1828, page 311.**

Adams distanced himself from his own campaign. He sought to demonstrate his statesmanlike gentility by letting others speak for him. This strategy worked well when only men of wealth and property could vote. But with an enlarged electorate and an astonishing turnout of more than 50 percent of eligible voters, Adams's approach failed and Jackson became president (Figure 9.1).

The election of 1828 formalized a new party alignment. During the campaign Jackson and his supporters referred to themselves as "the Democracy" and forged a new national Democratic Party. In response Adams's supporters and the remaining diehard Federalists renamed themselves National Republicans. The competition between **Democrats and National Republicans** heightened interest in national politics among ordinary voters and ensured that the innovative techniques introduced by Jackson would be widely adopted in future campaigns.

REVIEW & RELATE

- How and why did the composition of the electorate change in the 1820s?

- How did Jackson's 1828 campaign represent a significant departure from earlier patterns in American politics?

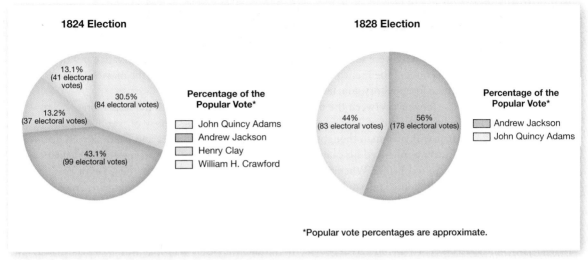

FIGURE 9.1   The Elections of 1824 and 1828

Andrew Jackson lost the 1824 election to John Quincy Adams when the decision was thrown into the House of Representatives. In 1828 Jackson launched the first popular campaign for president, mobilizing working-class white men who were newly enfranchised. Three times as many men—more than one million voters—cast ballots in 1828 than in 1824, ensuring Jackson's election as president. How did the greater number of candidates running in 1824 complicate the Electoral College system of selecting a president?

Jacksonian Politics in Action

Jackson hoped to make government more responsive to the needs of white workers and frontier farmers. But the president's notion of democracy did not extend to Indians or African Americans. During his presidency, Indian nations actively resisted his efforts to take more of their land, and blacks continued to resist their enslavement. Of more immediate importance, once President Jackson had to take clear positions on tariffs and other controversial issues, he could not please all of his constituents. He also confronted experienced adversaries like Henry Clay, Daniel Webster, and John Quincy Adams, who was elected to the House of Representatives from Massachusetts in 1830. The president thus faced considerable difficulty in translating popular support into public policy.

A Democratic Spirit?   On March 4, 1829, crowds of ordinary citizens came to see Jackson's inauguration. Jackson's wife, Rachel, had died of heart failure shortly after his election, leaving her husband devastated. Now Jackson, dressed in a plain black suit, walked alone to the Capitol as vast throngs of supporters waved and cheered. A somber Jackson read a brief inaugural address, took the oath of office, and then rode his horse through the crowds to the White House.

The size and enthusiasm of the crowds soon shattered the decorum of the inauguration. Author Margaret Bayard Smith reported mobs "scrambling, fighting, [and] romping" through the White House reception. Jackson was nearly crushed to death by "rabble" eager to shake his hand. Tubs of punch laced with rum, brandy, and champagne were finally placed on the lawn to draw the crowds outdoors.

While Jackson and his supporters viewed the event as a symbol of a new democratic spirit, others were less optimistic. Bayard Smith and other conservative political leaders saw echoes of the French Revolution in the unruly behavior of the masses. Supreme Court justice Joseph Story, too, feared "the reign of King 'Mob.'"

Tensions between the president and the capital's traditional leaders intensified when Jackson appointed Tennessee senator John Eaton as secretary of war. Eaton had had an affair with a woman thought to be of questionable character and later married her. When Jackson announced his plans to appoint Eaton to his cabinet, congressional leaders urged him to reconsider. When the president appointed Eaton anyway, the wives of Washington's leading politicians snubbed Mrs. Eaton. This time Jackson was outmaneuvered in what became known as the **Petticoat Affair**, and Eaton was eventually forced from office.

In the aftermath of Eaton's resignation, Jackson asked his entire cabinet to resign so he could begin anew. Afterward, however, his legislative agenda stalled in Congress, and National Republicans regained the momentum they had lost with Adams's defeat. The Petticoat Affair reinforced concerns that the president used his authority to reward his friends, as did his reliance on an informal group of advisers, known as the Kitchen Cabinet. While his administration opened up government posts to a wider range of individuals, ensuring more democratic access, Jackson often selected appointees based on personal ties. He believed that "to the victor goes the spoils," and the resulting **spoils system**— continued by future administrations—assigned federal posts as gifts for partisan loyalty rather than as jobs that required experience or expertise.

Confrontations over Tariffs and the Bank.

The Democratic Party that emerged in the late 1820s was built on an unstable foundation. The coalition that formed around Jackson included northern workers who benefited from high tariffs as well as southern farmers and planters who did not. It brought together western voters who sought federal support for internal improvements and strict constructionists who believed such expenditures were unconstitutional. In nearly every legislative battle, then, decisiveness aroused conflict. In 1830 Congress passed four internal improvement bills with strong support from National Republicans. Jackson vetoed each one, which pleased his southern constituency but not his frontier supporters.

Southern congressmen, however, were more interested in his stand on tariffs. The tariff of 1828 still enraged many southern planters and politicians, but most believed that once Jackson reached the White House, he would reverse course and reduce this **Tariff of Abominations**. Instead, he avoided the issue, and southern agriculture continued to suffer. Agricultural productivity in Virginia and other states of the Old South was declining from soil exhaustion, while prices for cotton and rice had not fully recovered after the panic of 1819. At the same time, higher duties on manufactured items raised prices for southerners on many goods.

Even as Calhoun campaigned with Jackson in 1828, the South Carolinian developed a philosophical argument to negate the effects of high tariffs on his state. In *The South Carolina Exposition and Protest*, published anonymously in 1828, Calhoun argued that states should have the ultimate power to determine the constitutionality of laws passed by Congress. When Jackson, after taking office, realized that his vice president advocated **nullification**—the right of individual states to declare individual laws void within their borders—it further damaged their relationship, which was already frayed by the Eaton affair.

When Congress debated the tariff issue in 1830, South Carolina senator Robert Hayne defended nullification. Claiming that the North intended to crush the South economically, he argued that only the right of states to nullify federal legislation could protect southern society. In response, Massachusetts Senator Daniel Webster denounced nullification and the states' rights doctrine on which it was built. Jackson further antagonized southern political leaders by supporting Webster's position.

Matters worsened in 1832 when Congress confirmed the high duties set four years earlier. In response South Carolina held a special convention that approved an Ordinance of Nullification. It stated that duties on imports would not be collected in the state after February 1, 1833, and threatened secession if federal authorities tried to collect them.

The tariff crisis thus escalated in the fall of 1832 just as Jackson faced reelection. The tariff debates had angered many southerners, and Calhoun refused to run again as his vice president. Fortunately for Jackson, opponents in Congress had provided him with another issue that could unite his supporters and highlight his commitment to ordinary citizens: the renewal of the charter of the Bank of the United States.

Clay and Webster persuaded Nicholas Biddle, head of the bank, to request an early recharter of the bank. Jackson's opponents in Congress knew they had the votes to pass a new charter in the summer of 1832, and they hoped Jackson would veto the bill and thereby split the Democratic Party just before the fall elections. The Second Bank was a political quagmire. The bank had stabilized the economy during the 1820s by regularly demanding specie (gold or silver) payments from state-chartered banks. This kept those banks from issuing too much paper money and thereby prevented inflation and higher prices. This tight-money policy also kept banks from expanding too rapidly in the western states. Most financial elites applauded the bank's efforts, but its policies aroused hostility among the wider public. When state-chartered banks closed because of lack of specie, ordinary Americans were often stuck with worthless paper money. Tight-money policies also made it more difficult for individuals to get credit to purchase land, homes, or farm equipment.

As the president's opponents had hoped, Congress approved the new charter, and Jackson vetoed it. Yet rather than dividing the Democrats, Jackson's veto gained enormous support from voters across the country. In justifying his action, the president cast the Second Bank as a "monster" that was "dangerous to the liberties of the people"—particularly farmers, mechanics, and laborers—while promoting "the advancement of the few." Finally, Jackson noted that since wealthy Britons owned substantial shares of the bank's stock, national pride demanded ending the Second Bank's reign over the U.S. economy. Jackson rode the enthusiasm for his bank veto to reelection over National Republican candidate Henry Clay. Within a year, the Second Bank was dead, deprived of government deposits by Jackson.

Soon after his reelection, however, the president faced a grave political crisis related to the tariff issue. Jackson now supported lower tariffs, but he was adamant in his opposition to nullification. In early 1833, he persuaded Congress to pass a Force Bill, which gave him authority to use the military to enforce national laws in South Carolina. At the same time, Jackson made clear that he would work with Congress to reduce tariffs, allowing South Carolina to rescind its nullification ordinance without losing face. Open conflict was averted, but the question of nullification was not resolved.

Contesting Indian Removal.

On another long-standing issue—the acquisition of Indian land—Jackson gained the support of white southerners and most frontier settlers. Yet not all Americans agreed with his effort to force Indians off their lands. In the 1820s nations like the Cherokee gained the support of Protestant missionaries who hoped to "civilize" Indians by converting them to Christianity and "American" ways. In 1819 Congress had granted these groups federal funds to advance these goals. Jackson, however, was unsupportive of such efforts and sided with political leaders who sought to force eastern Indians to accept homelands west of the Mississippi River.

In 1825, three years before Jackson was elected president, Creek Indians in Georgia and Alabama were forcibly removed to the Unorganized Territory (previously part of Arkansas Territory and later called Indian Territory) based on a fraudulent treaty. Jackson supported this policy. When he became president, politicians and settlers in Georgia, Florida, the Carolinas, and Illinois demanded federal assistance to force Indian communities out of their states.

The largest Indian nations vehemently protested their removal. The Cherokee, who had fought alongside Jackson at Horseshoe Bend, adopted a republican form of government in 1827 based on the U.S. Constitution. John Ross served as the president of the Cherokee constitutional convention and a year later was elected principal chief. He and the other chiefs then declared themselves a sovereign nation within the borders of the United States. The Georgia legislature rejected Cherokee claims of independence and argued that Indians were simply guests of the state, a position that gained added significance when gold was discovered in Cherokee territory in 1829. Ross appealed to Jackson to recognize Cherokee sovereignty, but the president was affronted by what he saw as a challenge to his authority. He urged Congress to pass the **Indian Removal Act** in 1830, by which the Cherokee and other Indian nations would be forced to exchange their lands in the Southeast for a "clear title forever" on territory west of the Mississippi River. The majority of Cherokees refused to accept these terms.

As the dispute between the Cherokee nation and Georgia unfolded, Jackson made clear his intention to implement the Indian Removal Act. In 1832 he sent federal troops into western Illinois to force Sauk and Fox peoples to move farther west. Instead, whole villages, led by Chief Black Hawk, fled to the Wisconsin Territory. Black Hawk and a thousand warriors confronted U.S. troops at Bad Axe, but the Sauk and Fox warriors were decimated in a brutal daylong battle. The survivors were forced to move west. Meanwhile the Seminole Indians prepared to go to war to protect their territory, while John Ross pursued legal means to resist removal through state and federal courts. The contest for Indian lands continued well past Jackson's presidency, but the president's desire to force indigenous nations westward would ultimately prevail.

REVIEW & RELATE

- What did President Jackson's response to the Eaton affair and Indian removal reveal about his vision of democracy?

- Which of Jackson's policies benefited or antagonized which groups of southerners?

Conclusion: The Nation Faces New Challenges

From the 1810s through the early 1830s, the United States was buffeted by a series of crises. Although early in the period geographical expansion and economic growth led the federal government to invest in internal improvements, the War of 1812 soon threatened the nation's stability and revealed significant regional divisions. The panic of 1819 then threw the nation into economic turmoil and led to demands for expanded voting rights for white men, while African American men experienced increased restrictions on their political participation. Regional differences rooted in different natural resources and economic priorities—manufacturing in the North, cotton and rice cultivation in the South, and family agriculture in the Midwest—were increasing in the 1810s. They led to greater interdependence across regions, but distinct economic needs and uncertainties intensified political debates over issues like tariffs. The admission of Missouri similarly heightened debates over slavery as white southerners saw themselves losing out to the North in population growth and political representation. At the same time, continued western expansion escalated conflicts with a diverse array of Indian nations.

In navigating these difficult issues, some Americans sought to find a middle ground. Dolley Madison worked to overcome partisan divisions through social networking. After the death of her husband, James, in 1836, she returned to Washington and transformed her home into a center of elite social life. Although her son's mismanagement of Montpelier forced her to sell the beloved estate, Dolley secured her old age when Congress purchased President James Madison's papers from her. Similarly, John Ross wielded his biracial heritage to seek rights for Indians within a white-dominated world. He served as both a lobbyist for Cherokee interests in Washington and an advocate of acculturation to Anglo-American ways among the Cherokee. However, congressional passage of the Indian Removal Act challenged Ross's efforts to maintain his tribe's sovereignty and homeland. Henry Clay, too, was widely known for helping to forge compromises on issues like slavery and tariffs. In the 1820s, he brought a deeply divided Congress together, hoping that political leaders could eventually develop permanent solutions.

Despite the efforts of Madison, Ross, Clay, and others, differences often led to division in the 1820s and 1830s. Indeed, Clay's success in ensuring John Quincy Adams's selection as president in 1824 only furthered partisan divisions, leading to the emergence of two distinct political parties: the Democrats and the National Republicans. Andrew Jackson, who led the new Democratic Party, transformed the process of political campaigning. He gave voice to white workers and frontier farmers, but he also introduced the spoils system to government, smashed the Second Bank of the United States, and forced thousands of Indians off their lands. Indian removal, in turn, fostered the expansion of white settlement southward and westward, contributing to the growth of slavery.

Dolley Madison, who lived into the late 1840s, and John Ross, who survived the Civil War, observed the continuing conflicts created by geographical expansion and partisan agendas. Ross, however, faced much more difficult circumstances as the Cherokee nation divided over whether to accept removal and continued to face internal dissent and pressure from the federal government for years.

Despite the dramatically different backgrounds and careers of Madison and Ross, both worked to bridge differences in the young nation, and both defended it against attack. Ultimately, however, neither had the power to overcome the partisan rivalries and economic crises that shaped the young nation or to halt the rising social, economic, and political tensions that would plague Americans in the decades to come.

CHAPTER 9 REVIEW

TIMELINE OF EVENTS

1809	Non-Intercourse Act
1811	First steamboat travels down the Mississippi
	William Henry Harrison defeats Shawnees at Prophet Town
June 1812	War of 1812 begins
1814	Hartford Convention
March 1814	Battle of Horseshoe Bend
August 1814	British burn Washington City
December 1814	Treaty of Ghent
1815	Battle of New Orleans
1817–1818	Andrew Jackson fights Spanish and Seminole forces in Florida
1818	Great Britain and United States agree to joint occupation of Oregon Territory
1819	Adams-Onís Treaty
1819–1823	Panic of 1819
1820	Missouri Compromise
1821	White traders begin using Santa Fe Trail
1822	Denmark Vesey accused of organizing a slave uprising
1823	Monroe Doctrine articulated
1825	Erie Canal completed
1828	Tariff of 1828 (Tariff of Abominations)
	John Ross elected principal chief of the Cherokee nation
1829	Petticoat Affair
1830	Indian Removal Act
1832	South Carolina passes Ordinance of Nullification
1833	Force Bill

KEY TERMS

Non-Intercourse Act, *283*

Battle of Fallen Timbers, *284*

Hartford Convention, *286*

Battle of Horseshoe Bend, *287*

Treaty of Ghent, *288*

American System, *289*

Erie Canal, *290*

Adams-Onís Treaty, *291*

Monroe Doctrine, *292*

panic of 1819, *293*

Missouri Compromise, *298*

Democrats and National Republicans, *304*

Petticoat Affair, *306*

spoils system, *306*

Tariff of Abominations, *306*

nullification, *306*

Indian Removal Act, *308*

REVIEW & RELATE

1. How were conflicts with Indians in the West connected to ongoing tensions between the United States and Great Britain on land and at sea?

2. What were the long-term consequences of the War of 1812?

3. What role did government play in early-nineteenth-century economic development?

4. How and why did economic development contribute to regional differences and shape regional ties?

5. How did regional interdependency contribute to the panic of 1819?

6. What regional divisions did the conflict over slavery in Missouri reveal?

7. How and why did the composition of the electorate change in the 1820s?

8. How did Jackson's 1828 campaign represent a significant departure from earlier patterns in American politics?

9. What did President Jackson's response to the Eaton affair and Indian removal reveal about his vision of democracy?

10. Which of Jackson's policies benefited or antagonized which groups of southerners?

The Election of 1828

> ▶ **How did the campaigns of 1828 appeal to people's passions, and why did this benefit Andrew Jackson?**

Following the bargain that brought John Quincy Adams to power in 1824, followers of Andrew Jackson had four years to plan for the next election. In the interim Adams did little to distinguish himself in office. During the campaign season of 1828, supporters of Jackson and Adams debated political programs and ideas, but they spent even more energy discussing the personal character of the candidates. Adams did not campaign directly. But his supporters held conventions and wrote editorials in which they smeared Jackson in a number of ways (Sources 9.6 and 9.7). They even accused him of adultery and bigamy for marrying Rachel Donelson, whose divorce from a previous husband was never officially finalized. They also ridiculed Jackson's supporters as rowdy and unrefined—charges many of those supporters likely embraced (Source 9.10).

Jackson's campaign took an even more active approach. Spearheaded by vice presidential candidate Martin Van Buren, "Jackson men" fanned out across the country, organizing rallies and drumming up grassroots support. They portrayed Jackson as "Old Hickory," a patriotic war hero who understood the importance of expanding American democracy and winning popular support (Source 9.8). They also assailed Adams for his elite upbringing, inherited career, and undemocratic vision and charged his supporters with slandering Jackson (Sources 9.8 and 9.9). In the end, Jackson prevailed. He easily won the popular election and the electoral college vote by a count of 178 to 83. Jackson did particularly well in the South and

West, where he benefited from voter rolls significantly expanded by the elimination or decrease in property requirements.

While some earlier campaigns had featured attacks on candidates' qualifications, the campaign of 1828 set a new standard for future contests. The following documents reveal how the character of candidates came to dominate political discourse as partisan differences sharpened. While Jackson supporters reveled in his military victories, for instance, opponents were often appalled.

Source 9.6

Proceedings of the Anti-Jackson Convention in Richmond, 1828

Across the country, voters held rallies and conventions to declare their support for candidates. At an "Anti-Jackson" convention in Richmond, Virginia, participants listed a litany of reasons why Jackson was not fit to hold the nation's highest office. The following document is an excerpt from the official publication of the convention's proceedings.

It is not in wantonness, that we speak.—but in the sadness of our hearts, we are compelled to declare,—that while we yield our confidence to the present Chief Magistrate in very different degrees, we are unanimous, and unhesitating in the opinion, that Andrew Jackson is altogether unfit for the Presidency, and that his election would be eminently dangerous,—that while we cheerfully accord to him his full share of the glory, which renders the anniversary of the 8th of January a day of joy and triumph to our land,—we must, in the most solemn manner, protest against a claim to civil rule, founded exclusively upon military renown,—and avow, that nothing has occurred in the history of our country, so much calculated to shake our confidence in the capacity of the people for self-government, as the efforts, which have been made, and are yet making, to elevate to the first office in the nation, the man, who, disobeying the orders of his superiors, trampling on the laws and constitution of his country, sacrificing the liberties and lives of men, has made his own arbitrary will, the rule of his conduct. . . .

Gen. Jackson has lived beyond the age of 60 years, and was bred to the profession best calculated to improve and display the faculties, which civil employment requires;—yet the history of his public life, in these employments, is told in a few brief lines, on a single page of his biography. He filled successively, for very short periods,—the office of member of the Tennessee Convention, which formed their State constitution,—representative and senator in Congress,—judge of the supreme court of Tennessee,—and again senator, in the Congress of the United States. Here was ample opportunity for distinction, if he had possessed the talent, taste and application suited for civil eminence. But he resigned three, and passed through all these stations, acknowledging his unfitness in two instances,—manifestly feeling it in all,—and leaving no single act, no trace behind, which stamps his qualification above mediocrity.

For civil government,—and in no station more emphatically, than in that of President of the United States,—a well governed temper is of admitted importance; Gen. Jackson's friends lament the impetuosity of his, and all the work has evidence of its fiery misrule.

To maintain peace and harmony, in the delicate relations existing between the government of the Union and the various State governments, in our confederacy, requires a courtesy and forbearance in their intercourse, which no passions should disturb. . . .

[Our claims] in accusing General Jackson of being unmindful of their [law and constitution] voice . . . will be acknowledged by impartial posterity, when they review the history of his Indian campaigns—and especially when they read the stories, of the cold blooded massacre, at the Horseshoe [Bend]—and of the decoyed and slaughtered [Seminole] Indians at St. Mark's [Florida]. . . .

[W]e regard Gen. Jackson, as wholly disqualified for the Presidency, and look to the prospect of his election with forebodings.

Source: *Proceedings of the Anti-Jackson Convention, Held at the Capitol in the City of Richmond, with Their Address to the People of Virginia* (Richmond: Franklin Press, 1828), 17–19.

Source 9.7

John Binns | Monumental Inscriptions, 1828

The 1828 election was fought with words and images. Adams supporters seized on the controversy surrounding Jackson's ordering of six executions during the War of 1812. The men who were eventually executed were tried and convicted of leaving their unit at Mobile, Alabama in summer 1814. John Binns, a Philadelphia journalist, created the following "coffin handbill" to dramatize this story. Numerous versions of the anti-Jackson handbill appeared throughout the campaign season. The headline and the text from two of the coffins are transcribed below.

Paragraph Below the Headline

These Inscriptions, compiled from authentic sources, but principally from OFFICIAL DOCUMENTS, communicated by the Department of War to *Congress*, on the 25th of January, 1828, are, in this form, submitted to the serious consideration of the AMERICAN PEOPLE, under the firm conviction, that the facts embodied in them, ought to, and will, produce a cool and deliberate examination of the qualifications, from Nature and Education, of General ANDREW JACKSON, for the high Civil Station to which he aspires, and to attain which he electioneers with a boldness and pertinacity, unexampled in this Republic. If he shall be found guilty of having ILLEGALLY AND WANTONLY SHED THE BLOOD OF HIS COUNTRYMEN AND FELLOW SOLDIERS, ENTRUST NOT THE LIBERTY AND HAPPINESS OF THIS MOST FREE AND MOST HAPPY COUNTRY TO HIS KEEPING.

MONUMENTAL INSCRIPTIONS!

Library of Congress 3a44143r

of his fate, During which time, He buried himself in writing to his AFFLICTED WIFE, Consoling her, and urging her to bring up his *Nine* Children in the love and foot (?) of THE LORD. An outraged country erects this Monument July 4, 1828.

Coffin from bottom row, right

THIS MARBLE CELL CONTAINS THE MOULDERING REMAINS OF THE GALLANT DAVID HUNT, *He was the Son of a Soldier of the Revolution.* A Volunteer in the Creek War, He faithfully served his country until his Tour of Duty had expired, When he left the Camp, And returned to the home of his Brave Parent; Where learning that his tour of duty had possibly not expired He returned to the Camp and to his Duty, The Veteran Father saying, "Go my Son, I am sure no harm can come to you; I too have been a soldier, and under WASHINGTON A soldier returning to duty which he had left in error always found mercy." *But the Son never more saw the face of his Venerable Father!* He was Arrested, Tried, and SHOT TO DEATH BY ORDER OF GEN. ANDREW JACKSON *On the 21st February, 1815.* The Militia of his Native State erected this simple slab to his Memory on the 4th of July, 1828.

Coffin from bottom row, center

SACRED TO THE MEMORY OF JOHN HARRIS. *He was a Preacher of the Gospel of Christ to the Heathen in the Wilderness.* His temporal substance was destroyed by Fire. TO EARN BREAD For a Wife and Nine Children, he entered as a SUBSTITUTE In the Militia during the Creek War. *He sought information from his Colonel as to his legal Tour of Duty.* IT WAS WITHHELD FROM HIM. He was instructed by his Officers that his Tour of duty would Expire on the 20th September; On that day he surrendered his musket to his Captain, took from him a receipt for it, Departed from Camp, and Returned to the wretched hovel which contained his family. Fearing that he might have erred, he VOLUNTARILY RETURNED TO CAMP, And offered to do duty, if he had mistaken his rights. FOR THESE ACTS HE WAS Arrested, Tried, and by the Orders of GEN. ANDREW JACKSON, SHOT TO DEATH On the 21st of February, 1815, Having only Four Days Notice

Source 9.8

New Jersey Pro-Jackson Convention, 1828

Jackson's supporters organized a greater number of rallies and conventions than Adams's supporters did and campaigned from the western frontier to the East Coast. The following excerpt comes from the proceedings of a pro-Jackson convention in Trenton, New Jersey.

I t is true, no titled honors cluster around his brow. He received not his education in the colleges of foreign potentates, nor was it ever his lot to mingle with princes and imbibe the corruption of their Courts. *He is an American, and nothing but an American.* Without the aid of family or patronage, his intrinsic merit alone, has placed him before the American people, as worthy of the highest honours of the country. And notwithstanding the unprincipled attacks of hireling presses, aided by all the efforts of a sinking administration, his talents and services are daily better appreciated. His entire devotion to his country's welfare; his stern integrity; his unbending republican simplicity; his enlarged and national views, commend themselves to the intelligence and affections of a free and generous people.

Andrew Jackson was rocked in the cradle of the Revolution. His mind is deeply imbued with the spirit and principles, which, at that day, pervaded the community, and gave a tone to public feeling. While yet a boy, he stood forth in defense of his country's rights, and gave earnest of that lofty spirit of independence, which has ever since characterized the man, whether in the field, the senate chamber, or the retirement of domestic life. . . .

But, Fellow-Citizens, notwithstanding General Jackson has long been known to the American people, as a firm and incorruptible patriot; an honest and able politician, and a virtuous man, yet, a system of warfare has been opened upon him, at which candour and decency must blush and be ashamed. It can find no apology, save in that phrenzy of desperation which excites pity rather than contempt. He has been openly accused of adultery, cruelty, murder; and, last of all, of such gross ignorance as scarcely to be able to read or write! Yes, the man whom you have delighted to honor; and who in 1824, received a much larger proportion of the votes for President, than any other candidate, is now discovered to be the most base, infamous and ignorant of men!! "'Tis strange—'tis passing strange!'" . . .

Slanders like these, so gross, so palpable, carry their own refutation with them. They can have no weight with sensible and reflecting men, and on such they were not intended to operate. But they are oft repeated, and reiterated by every press in the interest of the administration. And we grieve to say, that even our members of Congress, our Senators, and the heads of the departments, aid in their circulation.

And why is it that such desperate efforts are made to tarnish the fame of General Jackson? It is because he is sustained by the people, and is advancing with sure and rapid strides in their affections. It is that ill-gotten power may be retained, until the line of safe precedents shall be better established. Those who are now in power, are aware, that they have been weighed and found wanting. Fear hath taken hold of them, and their hour is at hand. Hence it is that every means is resorted to, and truth and honesty sacrificed, to accomplish their unhallowed purpose.

Source: *Proceedings and Address of the New-Jersey State Convention, Assembled at Trenton, on the Eighth Day of January, 1828* (Trenton: Joseph Justice, 1828), 15, 18–19.

Source 9.9

Resolution of the Albany County Republican Convention, 1828

Adams's family connections had certainly benefited his political career, but they also left him vulnerable to criticism. Many of Jackson's supporters linked the younger Adams, a former Federalist, with the unpopular, one-term administration of his father. A pro-Jackson convention in Albany, New York claims that Adams's background makes him an ineffective president. It also focuses on the War of 1812, in which then–Secretary of State John Quincy Adams served as a peace negotiator.

Resolved, That we oppose the re-election of John Quincy Adams—

Because we believe him to be now, as in all his early hostility to Jefferson and the democracy, imbued with the principles and wedded to the distinctions of the aristocracy—

Because he came to the democratic party, with tales of treason against his former political associates, but with unchanged principles and with personal views—

Because, his ends being selfish, he was willing to prey upon any party that chanced to be predominant—. . .

Because, in that eventful period, when his patriot competitor devoted his whole energies to his country, and, instead of accusing his government of feebleness and penury and holding out the disgraceful language of fear and submission, raising the banner of his country, and inviting to its defence, by the most elevated examples of constancy, devotion and courage, the brave volunteers and militia of the west, freely pledging his private fortune for a people whom he loved, and for hearths that were assailed, showing himself at every point of danger, exciting all to the noble discharge of their duty, animating them by his presence and relieving them by his sacrifices, passing days of fatigue and sleepless nights in preparing for the gallant resistance which the invader afterwards met with at his hands and the hands of his undaunted compatriots, and appearing in that hour of peril in the midst of the conflict, holding to all the inspired and encouraging language, *"Remember that our watch-word is victory or death: our country must*

and shall be defended: we will enjoy our liberty or perish in the last ditch,"—John Quincy Adams predicted our overthrow without raising a finger to avert it, and declared that it could not be expected that "we should resist the mass of force which the gigantic power of Britain had collected to crush us at a blow!"—...

Because, bred amongst the aristocracy and educated in foreign courts, his habits and principles are not congenial with the spirit of our institutions and the notions of a democratic people.

Source: *The Striking Similitude between the Reign of Terror of the Elder Adams, and the Reign of Corruption of the Younger Adams: An Address Adopted by the Albany Republican County Convention* (Albany, NY: D. M'Glashan, 1828), 1.

Source 9.10

President Andrew Jackson's First Inauguration, 1829

This illustration by the British satirical artist Robert Cruikshank, entitled *President's Levee, or All Creation Going to the White House*, depicts crowds attending Andrew Jackson's White House inaugural reception in 1829. As Margaret Bayard Smith, a well-connected Washington insider, described the scene, "The *Majesty of the People* had disappeared, and a rabble, a mob, of boys, negros, women, children, scrambling, fighting, romping. What a pity! what a pity!"

Granger

315

Interpret the Evidence

1. Why, according to the Richmond Convention, was Andrew Jackson unfit for president (Source 9.6)? How does the Trenton Convention description of Jackson differ from that offered by the Richmond convention (Sources 9.6 and 9.8)?

2. What was the purpose of the coffin handbill (Source 9.7)? How do the descriptions of the men executed contrast with Jackson's supposed support for ordinary workingmen?

3. How do the Trenton and Albany Conventions' critiques of Adams compare (Sources 9.8 and 9.9)?

4. Why does Cruikshank focus on the outside of the White House in his image of the inauguration (Source 9.10)? How might the various convention delegates and John Binns respond to this illustration?

Put It in Context

In what ways does the election of 1828 confirm or contest the claim that Andrew Jackson was an advocate for ordinary Americans?

How do these sources reflect the popular campaign style that Jackson introduced into presidential elections?

Social and Cultural Ferment in the North

1820–1850

1850 Census of the Isaac Post Family in Rochester, New York

In the 1850 federal census, the U.S. government began listing the name of every household member with their age, sex, race and occupation. This information allows historians to calculate household and family size, occupational patterns, the class character of particular neighborhoods, and other demographic and economic patterns. Despite cultural ideals that emphasized the importance of the nuclear family, many middle-class households, like that of the Posts, included other relatives, boarders and servants.

▶ To discover more about what this primary source can show us, see Source 10.1 on page 325.

Dwelling-houses numbered in the order of visitation.	Families numbered in the order of visitation.	The Name of every Person whose usual place of abode on the first day of June, 1850, was in this family.	Age.	Sex.	White, black, or mulatto.
1	**2**	**3**	**4**	**5**	**6**
		Margaret Hennesy	20	f	
		Elizabeth Vannen	23	f	
285	338	Isaac Post	50	m	
		Amy "	45	f	
		Jacob K. "	20	m	
		Joseph "	16	m	
		Willett "	3	m	
		Sarah S. Hallowell	30	f	
		Ansel Brown	28	m	
		Elizabeth "	28	f	
		Bindut Head	23	f	

DESCRIPTION.

United States Census Bureau

After reading this chapter you should be able to:

- Explain the growth of and changes in northern cities, including issues of immigration, class stratification, and gender roles.

- Analyze how industrialization transformed workers' lives, was affected by the boom and bust economic cycle, and contributed to class and ethnic tensions.

- Describe the range and appeal of religious movements that emerged in the 1830s and 1840s.

- Evaluate the emergence of reform movements and the strategies they embraced.

- Explain the various forms of antislavery activism and their impact on other social and political changes.

COMPARING AMERICAN HISTORIES

The great revival preacher Charles Grandison Finney was born in 1792 and raised in rural New York State. As a young man, Finney studied the law. But in 1821, like many others of his generation, he experienced a powerful religious conversion. No longer interested in a legal career, he turned to the ministry instead.

After being ordained in the Presbyterian Church, Finney joined "New School" ministers who rejected the more conservative traditions of the Presbyterian Church and embraced a vigorous evangelicalism. In the early 1830s the Reverend Finney traveled throughout New York State preaching about Christ's

(*left*) **Charles Grandison Finney** Oberlin College Archives
(*right*) **Amy Kirby Post** Courtesy of the Department of Rare Books and Special Collections, University of Rochester River Campus Libraries

place in a changing America. He held massive revivals in cities along the Erie Canal, most notably in Rochester, New York. He achieved his greatest success in places experiencing rapid economic development and an influx of migrants and immigrants, where the clash of cultures and classes fueled fears of moral decay.

Finney urged Christians to actively seek salvation. Once individuals reformed themselves, he said, they should work to abolish poverty, intemperance, prostitution, and slavery. He expected women to participate in revivals and good works but advised them to balance these efforts with their domestic responsibilities.

In many ways, Amy Kirby Post fit Finney's ideal. Born into a farm family in Jericho, New York, she found solace in spirituality and social reform. Like many other people in this period, Amy experienced the loss of loved ones. In 1825, at age twenty-three, Amy's fiancé died, and two years later she lost the sister to whom she was closest. The next year, Amy married a widower, Isaac Post. She mothered his two young children and bore five children of her own, two of whom died young. Yet Amy Post did not embrace evangelical revivals, but focused instead on the quiet piety preferred by her Quaker community.

Still, the personal upheavals Amy experienced in her twenties occurred amid heated controversies within the Society of Friends (Quakers). Elias Hicks claimed that the Society had abandoned its spiritual roots and become too much like a traditional church. His followers, called Hicksites, insisted that Quakers should reduce their dependence on disciplinary rules, elders, and preachers and rely instead on the "Inner Light"—the spirit of God dwelling within each individual. When the Society of Friends divided into Hicksite and Orthodox branches in 1827, Amy Kirby and Isaac Post joined the Hicksites.

In 1836 Amy Post moved with her husband and children to Rochester, New York. In a city marked by the spirit of Finney's revivals, Quakers emphasized quiet contemplation rather than emotional conversions, but the Society of Friends allowed members, including women, to preach when moved by the spirit. Quaker women also held separate meetings to discipline female congregants, evaluate marriage proposals, and write testimonies on important religious and social issues.

Amy Post's spiritual journey was increasingly shaped by the rising tide of abolition. Committed to ending slavery, she joined hundreds of local evangelical women in signing an 1837 antislavery petition. Five years later, she helped found the Western New York Anti-Slavery Society, which included Quakers and evangelicals, women and men, and blacks and whites. Post's growing commitment to abolition caused tensions in the Hicksite meeting since some members opposed working in "worldly" organizations alongside non-Quakers. In 1848 Post and other radical Friends formed a new, more activist-oriented Quaker meeting and embraced women's rights as well as abolition. ∎

Comparing the American histories of Charles Finney and Amy Post shows how individuals responded to and helped shape the dynamic religious, social, and economic developments of the early nineteenth century. Finney changed the face of American religion, aided by masses of evangelical Protestants. The transportation revolution, the expansion of the market economy, and the rise of cities, especially in the northern United States, benefitted many Americans. However, they also made problems like poverty, unemployment, alcohol abuse, crime, and prostitution more visible, drawing people to Finney's message. Like many Americans, Amy Post migrated with her family along improved roads and canals to seek better economic opportunities. But as the moral stain of slavery continued to grow, she joined other Quakers and some northern blacks in refusing to purchase any slave-produced goods. Bursting traditional religious bonds, she also reconsidered what it meant to do God's work. For both Finney and Post, Rochester—the fastest-growing city in the nation between 1825 and 1835—exemplified the possibilities and the problems created by the market revolution, urban expansion, and rapid social change.

The Market Revolution

Commercial and industrial development, immigration from Europe, and migration from rural areas led to the rapid growth of cities in the northern United States from 1820 on. Such growth both built on and furthered the expansion of roads and canals, which were funded by federal and state governments in the 1810s and 1820s. By linking northern industries with western farms and southern plantations, these innovations in transportation fueled a **market revolution** as the manufacture of goods became better organized and innovations in industry, agriculture, and communication increased efficiency and productivity. These changes fostered urbanization, which, in turn, reinforced economic growth and innovation. However, it also created social upheaval. Cultural divisions intensified in urban areas where Catholics and Protestants, workers and the well-to-do, immigrants, African Americans, and native-born whites lived side by side. Class dynamics also changed with the development of a clear middle class of shopkeepers, professionals, and clerks.

Creating an Urban Landscape. Across the North, urban populations boomed. As commercial centers, seaports like New York and Philadelphia were the most populous cities in the early nineteenth century. Between 1820 and 1850, the number of cities with 100,000 inhabitants increased from two to six; five were seaports. The sixth was the river port of Cincinnati, Ohio. Smaller boomtowns, like Rochester, New York, emerged along inland waterways as the completion of the Erie Canal in 1825 spurred agriculture and industry.

Development along the Erie Canal illustrates the ways that advancements in transportation transformed the surrounding landscape and ecology. As soon as the first stretch was completed in 1819, its economic benefits became clear. As the 40-foot-wide canal was extended across central and western New York State, settlers rushed to establish farms, mills, and ports. They chopped down millions of trees to construct homes and businesses and to open land for farms and orchards. Farmers shipped grain, cattle, and hogs to eastern markets or to emerging cities like Rochester. There millers and butchers turned them into flour, beef, and pork, products that were now easier and cheaper to ship further onward.

As the population in western New York and along the Great Lakes increased, residents demanded more and more manufactured goods. This demand fueled the growth of factories, especially in New England. Cotton, lumber, and flour mills were constructed near waterfalls for power, transforming isolated villages into mill towns while endangering the natural habitats of fish and wildlife. As thousands of newcomers cleared more and more land in Ohio and Michigan, they expanded trade between areas fueled by the Erie Canal and the Great Lakes and older towns from New England to New York City. Moreover, Midwesterners could ship food south via the Ohio and Mississippi Rivers in exchange for southern cotton, rice, and sugar.

Business and political leaders in Philadelphia and Baltimore, seeing the economic benefits created by the Erie Canal, demanded state funding for canals linking them to the Midwest. Where state funding proved insufficient, they persuaded English bankers and merchants to invest in American canals as well as railroads, which were just beginning to compete with waterways as a method to transport people and goods.

The Lure of Urban Life.   As transportation improved and the economy expanded, cities across the North increased not only in size but also in diversity. During the 1820s, some 150,000 European immigrants entered the United States; during the 1830s, nearly 600,000; and during the 1840s, more than 1,700,000. This surge of immigrants included more Irish and German settlers than ever before as well as large numbers of Scandinavians. Many settled along the eastern seaboard. Others migrated west, including thousands of Irish immigrants who labored in difficult and dangerous conditions to build the Erie Canal. Many Irish workers quit these jobs and settled in local communities along the canal's route. Others added to the growth of frontier cities such as Cincinnati, St. Louis, and Chicago.

Late eighteenth-century Irish immigrants, many of whom were Protestants, were joined by hundreds of thousands more in the 1830s and 1840s, when Irish Catholics poured into the United States. The Irish countryside was then plagued by bad weather, a potato blight, and harsh economic policies imposed by the English government. In 1845 to 1846 a full-blown famine forced thousands more Irish Catholic families to emigrate. Young Irish women, who could easily find work as domestics or seamstresses, emigrated in especially large numbers. Poor harvests, droughts, failed revolutions, and repressive landlords convinced large numbers of Germans, including Catholics, Lutherans, and Jews, and Scandinavians to flee their homelands as well. By 1850 the Irish made up about 40 percent of immigrants to the United States, and Germans nearly a quarter (Figure 10.1).

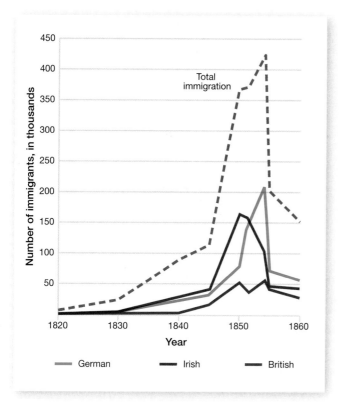

FIGURE 10.1   Immigration to the United States, 1820–1860

Famine, economic upheaval, and political persecution led masses of people from Ireland, Germany, and Britain to migrate to the United States from the 1820s through the 1850s. The vast majority settled in cities and factory towns in the North or on farms in the Midwest. An economic recession in the late 1850s finally slowed immigration, though only temporarily. What does this graph tell us about the growing diversity of the U.S. population?

These immigrants provided an expanding pool of cheap labor as well as skilled artisans who further fueled northern commerce and industry. Banks, mercantile houses, and dry-goods stores multiplied. Urban industrial enterprises included both traditional workshops and mechanized factories. Credit and insurance agencies emerged to aid entrepreneurs in their ventures. The increase in business also drove the demand for ships, commercial newspapers, warehouses, and other commercial necessities, which created a surge in jobs for many urban residents.

Businesses focused on leisure also flourished. In the 1830s theater became affordable to working-class families, who attended comedies, musical revues, and morality plays. They also joined middle- and upper-class audiences at productions of Shakespeare and contemporary dramas. Minstrel shows mocked self-important capitalists but also portrayed African Americans in crude caricatures. One of the most popular characters was Jim Crow, who appeared originally in an African American song. In the 1820s he was incorporated into a song-and-dance routine by Thomas Rice, a white performer who blacked his face with burnt cork.

The lures of urban life were especially attractive to the young. Single men and women and newly married couples flocked to cities. By 1850 half the residents of New York, Philadelphia, and other seaport cities were under sixteen years old. Young men sought work in factories, construction, and the maritime trades or in banks and commercial houses, while young women competed for jobs as seamstresses and domestic servants.

Jenny Lind at Castle Garden, 1850   American showman P. T. Barnum convinced Swedish opera star Jenny Lind to tour the United States in 1850. Huge crowds greeted her arrival in New York harbor and packed her concerts, leading reporters to describe the phenomenon as "Lind mania." In this lithograph, Nathaniel Currier captures the crowd at her first appearance at Castle Garden in New York. Granger

The Roots of Urban Disorder. While immigrant labor stimulated northern economic growth, immigrant families transformed the urban landscape. They crowded into houses and apartments and built ethnic institutions, including synagogues and convents—visible indicators of the growing diversity of northern cities. While most native-born Protestants applauded economic growth, cultural diversity aroused anxieties. Anti-Catholicism and anti-Semitism flourished in the 1830s and 1840s. Crude stereotypes portrayed Jews as manipulative moneylenders and Catholic nuns and priests as sexually depraved. Ethnic groups also battled stereotypes. Irishmen, for example, were often pictured as habitual drunkards.

Still, rising immigration did not deter rural Americans from seeking economic opportunities in the city. Native-born white men often set out on their own, but most white women settled in cities under the supervision of a husband, landlady, or employer. African Americans, too, sought greater opportunities in urban areas. In the 1830s, more blacks joined Philadelphia's vibrant African American community, attracted by its churches, schools, and mutual aid societies. New Bedford, Massachusetts, a thriving whaling center, recruited black workers and thus attracted fugitive slaves as well.

Yet even as cities welcomed many migrants and immigrants, newcomers also faced dangers. Racial and ethnic minorities regularly met discrimination and hostility. Physical battles erupted between immigrant and native-born residents, Protestant and Catholic gangs, and white and black workers. Criminal activity flourished as well, and disease spread quickly through densely populated neighborhoods. When innovations in transportation made it possible for more affluent residents to distance themselves from crowded inner cities, they moved to less congested neighborhoods on the urban periphery. Horse-drawn streetcar lines, first built in New York City in 1832, hastened this development.

By the 1840s, economic competition intensified, fueling violence among those driven to the margins. Native-born white employers and workers pushed Irish immigrants to the bottom of the economic ladder, where they competed with African Americans. Yet Irish workers insisted that their whiteness gave them a higher status than even the most skilled blacks. When black temperance reformers organized a parade in Philadelphia in August 1842, white onlookers—mostly Irish laborers—attacked the marchers, and the conflict escalated into a riot.

Americans who lived in small towns and rural areas regularly read news of urban violence and vice. Improvements in printing created vastly more and cheaper newspapers, while the construction of the first telegraph in 1844 ensured that news could travel more quickly from town to town. Tabloids wooed readers with sensational stories of crime, sex, and scandal. Even more respectable newspapers reported on urban mayhem, and religious periodicals warned parishioners against urban immorality. In response to both a real and a perceived increase in crime, cities replaced voluntary night watchmen with paid police forces.

The New Middle Class. Members of the emerging middle class, which developed first in the North, included ambitious businessmen, successful shopkeepers, doctors, and lawyers as well as teachers, journalists, ministers, and other salaried employees. At the top rungs, successful entrepreneurs and professionals adopted affluent lifestyles. At the lower rungs, a growing cohort of salaried clerks and managers hoped that their hard work, honesty, and thrift would be rewarded with upward mobility.

Explore ▶

See Source 10.1 for a statistical portrait of a middle-class family.

Education, religious affiliation, and sobriety were important indicators of middle-class status. A well-read man who attended a well-established church and drank in strict moderation was marked as belonging to this new rank. He was also expected to own a comfortable home, marry a pious woman, and raise well-behaved children. The rise of the middle class inspired a flood of advice books, ladies' magazines, religious periodicals, and novels advocating new ideals of womanhood. These publications emphasized the centrality of child rearing and homemaking to women's identities. This **cult of domesticity** ideally restricted wives to home and hearth, where they provided their husbands with respite from the cares and corruptions of the world.

In reality, however, entrance to the middle class required the efforts of wives as well as husbands. While upper middle-class men were expected to provide financial security, women helped cement social and economic bonds by entertaining the wives of business associates, serving in charitable and temperance societies, and organizing Sabbath schools. Families struggling to enter the middle class might take in boarders or extended family members to help secure their financial status. The adoption of new marital ideals of affection and companionship also made the boundaries between public and domestic life more fluid. In many middle-class families, husbands and wives both participated in church, civic, and reform activities, even if many did so through single-sex organizations. At the same time, husbands joined in domestic activities in the evening, presiding over dinner or reading to children.

Shoe Shopping from *Godey's Lady's Book* In the 1830s and 1840s, women's magazines appeared to promote new ideals of middle-class womanhood and to guide them as consumers. This 1848 image of women shopping for shoes from *Godey's Lady's Book* encouraged female outings to elegant emporiums. The lavish engravings created by *Godey's* quickly made it the best-selling "ladies" magazine in the United States. Archive Photos/Getty Images

The ideal of separate spheres of work and home had even less relevance to the millions of women who toiled on farms and factories or as domestic servants, providing goods and services for middle-class and elite families. In turn, those middle-class families played a crucial role in the growing market economy and the jobs it created. Wives and daughters were responsible for much of the family's consumption. They purchased cloth, rugs, chairs, clocks, and housewares, and, if wealthy enough, European crystal and Chinese porcelain figures. Middling housewives bought goods once made at home, such as butter and candles, and arranged music lessons and other educational opportunities for their children.

Although increasingly recognized for their ability to consume wisely, middle-class women also performed significant domestic labor. While many could afford servants, they often joined domestics and daughters in household tasks. Except for those in the upper middle class, most women still cut and sewed garments, cultivated gardens, canned fruits and vegetables, cooked at least some meals, and entertained guests. As houses expanded in size and clothes became fancier, domestic servants shouldered the most laborious and time-consuming chores, but many mothers and daughters still performed domestic labor as well. However, such work was increasingly invisible, focused inwardly on the family rather than outwardly as part of the market economy.

1850 U.S Census of the Isaac and Amy Post Household

In 1850, for the first time, the federal census listed each member of the household by name as well as by age, sex, race (then labeled "Color"), and place of birth. Some census takers noted the relationship of each household member to the family head. This census taker did not, nor did he note Color. That information appears in brackets and came from other genealogical records. Census records provide portraits of individual households at a moment in time and allow historians to compare families and households across place well as time.

Source 10.1

1850 US Census of the Isaac and Amy Post Household

Names of Residents in Household	Relation to Head of Household	Age/Sex/Color*	Occupation for Males over 15 Years	Place of Birth
Isaac Post	[Head]	50/male/[white]	Druggist	New York
Amy Post	[wife]	45**/female/[white]		New York
Jacob K. Post	[son]	20/male/[white]	Clerk	New York
Joseph Post	[son]	16/male/[white]	Clerk	New York
Willet Post	[son]	3/male/[white]		New York
Sarah Hallowell	[sister-in-law]	30/female/[white]		New York
Ansel Bowen	[boarder]	28/male/[white]	Teacher	New York
Elizabeth Bowen	[boarder]	28/female/[white]		New York
Bridget Head	[servant]	23/female/[white]		Ireland
Mary Ann Pitkin	[boarder]	10/female/[black]		New York

*The options for "Color": in the 1850 Census were "White, Black, and Mulatto." The bracketed information is from the 1855 N.Y. State Census and Rochester city directories.

**Amy Post was 47 in summer 1850, not 45.

Source: Seventh U.S. Federal Census, 1st Ward, Rochester, N.Y., 2 August 1850.

How many different families are represented in the Isaac and Amy Post household?

How would you characterize the relationships among the women in the household, and what kind of work did they likely perform?

What do the occupations of the men in the household tell us about these families' class status?

Put It in Context

How do the families represented in the Post household conform to ideals about the middle-class family?

Middle-class men contributed to the consumer economy by creating and investing in industrial and commercial ventures. Moreover, in carrying out business and professional obligations, many enjoyed restaurants, the theater, or sporting events. Men attended plays and lectures with their wives and visited museums and circuses with their children. They also purchased hats, suits, mustache wax, and other accouterments of middle-class masculinity.

REVIEW & RELATE

- How did the market revolution, including improvements like the Erie Canal, reshape the landscape and lives of Americans in the North?

- As northern cities became larger and more diverse in the first half of the nineteenth century, what changes and challenges did urban residents face and what values and beliefs did the new middle class embrace?

The **Rise** of **Industry**

In the mid-nineteenth century, industrial enterprises in the Northeast transformed the nation's economy even though they employed less than 10 percent of the U.S. labor force. In the 1830s and 1840s, factories grew considerably in size, and some investors, especially in textiles, constructed factory towns. New England textile mills relied increasingly on the labor of girls and young women, while urban workshops hired children, young women and men, and older adults. Although men still dominated the skilled trades, making chairs, clocks, shoes, hats, and fine clothing, employment in these trades slowly declined as industrial jobs expanded. An economic panic in 1837 exacerbated this trend and increased tensions that made it more difficult for workers to organize across differences of skill, ethnicity, race, and sex.

Factory Towns and Women Workers. In the late 1820s investors and manufacturers joined forces to create factory towns in the New England countryside. The most famous mill town, Lowell, Massachusetts, was based on an earlier experiment in nearby Waltham. In the Waltham system, every step of the production process was mechanized; planned communities included factories, boardinghouses, government offices, and churches. Agents for the Waltham system recruited the daughters of New England farm families as workers, assuring parents that they would be watched over by managers and foremen as well as landladies. The young women were required to attend church and observe curfews, and their labor was regulated by clocks and bells to ensure discipline and productivity.

Farm families needed more cash because of the growing market economy, and daughters in the mills could contribute to family finances and save money for the clothes and linens required for married life. Factory jobs also provided an alternative to marriage as young New England men moved west and left a surplus of women behind. Boardinghouses provided a relatively safe, all-female environment for the young mill workers, and sisters and neighbors often lived together. Despite nearly constant supervision, many rural women viewed factory work as an adventure. They could set aside a bit of money for themselves, attend lectures and concerts, meet new people, and acquire a wider view of the world.

During the 1830s, however, working conditions began to deteriorate. Factory owners cut wages, lengthened hours, and sped up machines. Boardinghouses became overcrowded, and company officials regulated both rents and expenses so that higher prices for lodging did not necessarily mean better food or furnishings. Factory workers launched numerous strikes in the 1830s against longer hours, wage cuts, and speedups in factory production. The solidarity required to sustain these strikes was forged in boardinghouses and at church socials as well as on the factory floor. At age twelve, Harriet Robinson led a walkout at the Lowell Mills in 1836. In her memoir, written in 1898, she noted, "As I looked back at the long line that followed me, I was more proud than I have ever been since at any success I have achieved."

Despite mill workers' solidarity, it was difficult to overcome the economic power wielded by manufacturers. Working women's efforts at collective action were generally short-lived, lasting only until a strike was settled. Then employees returned to their jobs until the next crisis hit. And as competition increasingly cut into profits, owners resisted mill workers' demands more vehemently. When the panic of 1837 intensified fears of job loss, women's organizing activities were doomed until the economy recovered.

The Decline of Craft Work and Workingmen's Responses.
While the construction of factory towns expanded economic opportunities for young women, the gradual decline of time-honored crafts narrowed the prospects for workingmen. Craft workshops gradually increased in size and hired fewer skilled workers and more men who performed single tasks, like attaching soles to shoes. Many tasks also became mechanized during the nineteenth century. The final product was less distinctive than an entire item crafted by a skilled artisan, but it was less expensive and available in mass quantities.

The shift from craft work to factory work threatened to undermine workingmen's skills, pay, and labor conditions. Masters began hiring foremen to regulate the workforce and installing bells and clocks to regulate the workday. As this process of **deskilling** transformed shoemaking, printing, tailoring, and other trades, laboring men fought to maintain their status.

Some workers formed mutual aid societies to provide assistance in times of illness, injury, or unemployment. Others participated in religious revivals or joined fraternal orders to find the camaraderie they once enjoyed at work. The expansion of voting rights in the 1820s offered another avenue for action. The first workingmen's political party was founded in Philadelphia in 1827, and working-class men in the North joined forces to support politicians sympathetic to their needs. Most workingmen's parties focused on practical proposals: government distribution of free land in the West, abolishing compulsory militia service and imprisonment for debt, public funding for education, and regulations on banks and corporations. Although the electoral success of these parties was modest, in the 1830s Democrats and Whigs adopted many of their proposals.

Workingmen also formed unions to demand better wages and working conditions. In the 1820s and 1830s, skilled journeymen held mass meetings to protest employers' efforts to lengthen the workday, merge smaller workshops into larger factories, and cut wages. In New York City in 1834, labor activists formed a citywide federation, the General Trades Union, which provided support for striking workers. The National Trades Union was established later that year, with delegates representing more than twenty-five thousand workers across the North. These organizations aided skilled workers but refused admission to women and unskilled men.

It proved difficult to establish broader labor organizations, however. Most skilled workers considered unskilled workers as competitors, not allies. Many workingmen feared women workers would undercut their wages and so refused to organize alongside them. And anti-immigrant and racist beliefs among many native-born Protestant workers interfered with organizing across racial and ethnic lines. With the onset of the panic of 1837, the common plight of workers became clearer. But the economic crisis made unified action nearly impossible as individuals sought to hold on to what little they had.

The Panic of 1837. The panic of 1837 began in the South but hit northern cotton merchants hard (see "Van Buren and the Panic of 1837" in chapter 11). With cotton shipments sharply curtailed, textile factories drastically cut production, unemployment rose, and merchants and investors went broke. Those still employed saw their wages cut in half. In Rochester, the Posts temporarily moved in with family members and their oldest son left school to help save their pharmacy from foreclosure. Petty crime, prostitution, and violence also rose as men and women struggled to make ends meet.

In Lowell, hours increased and wages fell. Just as important, the process of deskilling intensified. Factory owners considered mechanization one way to improve their economic situation. A cascade of inventions, including power looms, steam boilers, and the steam press, transformed industrial occupations and led factory owners to invest more of their limited resources in machines. At the same time, the rising tide of immigrants provided a

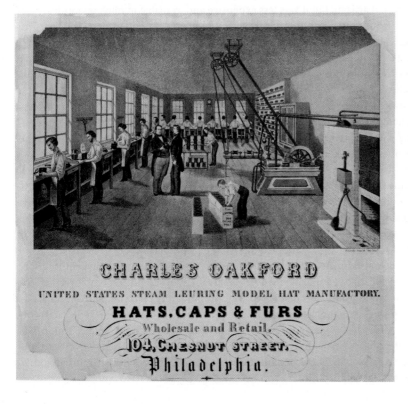

Hat Manufacturing, 1850 This 1850 lithograph advertises Charles Oakford's hat factory in Philadelphia. Like many industries, hat making became increasingly mechanized in the 1840s. Here Oakford talks with a client in the center of the room, across from his steam-powered lathe, while workers stand at stations shaping and stacking hats. A boy packs the merchandise into a box ready for shipping. © Philadelphia History Museum at the Atwater Kent/The Bridgeman Art Library

ready supply of relatively cheap labor. Artisans tried to maintain their traditional skills and status, but in many trades they were fighting a losing battle.

By the early 1840s, when the panic subsided, new technologies did spur new jobs. Factories demanded more workers to handle machines that ran at a faster pace. In printing, the steam press allowed publication of more newspapers and magazines, creating positions for editors, publishers, printers, engravers, reporters, and sales agents. Similarly, mechanical reapers sped the harvest of wheat and inspired changes in flour milling that required engineers to design machines and mechanics to build and repair them.

These changing circumstances fueled new labor organizations as well. Many of these unions comprised a particular trade or ethnic group, and almost all continued to address primarily the needs of skilled male workers. Textile operatives remained the one important group of organized female workers. In the 1840s, workingwomen joined with workingmen in New England to fight for a ten-hour day. Slowly, however, farmers' daughters left the mills as desperate Irish immigrants flooded in and accepted lower wages.

For most women in need, charitable organizations offered more support than unions. Organizations like Philadelphia's Female Association for the Relief of Women and Children in Reduced Circumstances provided a critical safety net for many poor families since public monies for such purposes were limited. Although most northern towns and cities now provided some form of public assistance, they never had sufficient resources to meet local needs in good times, much less the extraordinary demands posed by the panic.

REVIEW & RELATE

- How and why did American manufacturing change during the first half of the nineteenth century?

- How did new technologies, immigration, and the panic of 1837 change the economic opportunities and organizing strategies for northern workers?

Saving the Nation from Sin

In the first half of the nineteenth century, men and women of all classes and races embraced the Protestant religious revival known as the **Second Great Awakening** to express deeply held beliefs and reclaim a sense of the nation's godly mission. Yet evangelical Protestantism was not the only religious tradition to thrive in this period. Catholic churches and Jewish synagogues multiplied with immigration, and in the North Quaker meetings and Unitarian congregations flourished as well. New religious groups also attracted thousands of followers while transcendentalists sought deeper engagements with nature as another path to spiritual renewal.

The Second Great Awakening.
Although diverse religious traditions flourished in the United States, evangelical Protestantism proved the most powerful in the 1820s and 1830s. Evangelical churches hosted revivals, celebrated conversions, and organized prayer and missionary societies. This second wave of religious revivals began in Cane Ridge, Kentucky in 1801, and took root across the South. It then spread northward, transforming Protestant churches and the social fabric of northern life.

Ministers like Charles Grandison Finney adopted techniques first wielded by southern Methodists and Baptists: plain speaking, powerful images, and mass meetings. But Finney molded these techniques for a more affluent audience and held his "camp meetings" in established churches. By the late 1820s, boomtown growth along the Erie Canal aroused deep concerns among religious leaders about the rising tide of sin. In response, the Reverend Finney arrived in Rochester in September 1830. He began preaching in local Presbyterian churches, leading crowded prayer meetings that lasted late into the night. Individual supplicants walked to special benches designated for anxious sinners, who were prayed over in public. Female parishioners played crucial roles, encouraging their husbands, sons, friends, and neighbors to submit to God.

Thousands of Rochester residents joined in the evangelical experience as Finney's powerful message engulfed other denominations (Map 10.1). The significance of these revivals went far beyond an increase in church membership. Finney converted "the great mass of the most influential people" in the city: merchants, lawyers, doctors, master craftsmen, and shopkeepers. Equally important, he proclaimed that if Christians were "united all over the world the Millennium [Christ's Second Coming] might be brought about in three months." Preachers in Rochester and the surrounding towns took up his call, and converts committed themselves to preparing the world for Christ's arrival.

Developments in Rochester were replicated in cities across the North. Presbyterian, Congregational, and Episcopalian churches overflowed with middle-class and wealthy Americans, while Baptists and Methodists ministered to more laboring women and men. Black Baptists and Methodists evangelized in their own communities, combining powerful preaching with rousing spirituals. In Philadelphia, African Americans built fifteen churches between 1799 and 1830. A few black women joined men in evangelizing to their fellow African Americans.

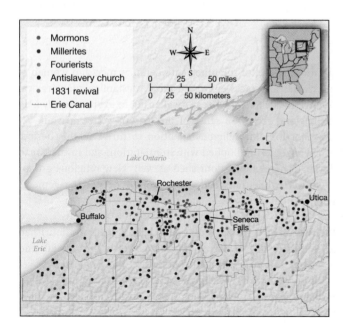

MAP 10.1   Religious Movements in the Burned-Over District, 1831–1848

Western and central New York State was burned over by the fires of religious revivalism in the 1830s and 1840s. But numerous other religious groups also formed or flourished in the region in these decades, including Quakers, Mormons, and Millerites. In the 1840s, Fourierist phalanxes, the Oneida community, and other utopian experiments were established here.

Source: Whitney R. Cross, *The Burned-Over District: The Social and Intellectual History of Enthusiastic Religion in Western New York, 1800–1850* (Ithaca, NY: Cornell University Press, 1950).

Tens of thousands of black and white converts embraced evangelicals' message of moral outreach. No reform movement gained greater impetus from the revivals than **temperance**, whose advocates sought to moderate and then ban the sale and consumption of alcohol. In the 1820s Americans fifteen years and older consumed six to seven gallons of distilled alcohol per person per year (about double the amount consumed today). Middle-class evangelicals, who once accepted moderate drinking as healthful, now insisted on eliminating alcohol consumption altogether.

New Visions of Faith and Reform.
Although enthusiasm for temperance and other reforms waned during the panic of 1837 and many churches lost members, the Second Great Awakening continued in its aftermath. But now evangelical ministers competed for souls with a variety of other religious groups, many of which supported good works and social reform. The Society of Friends, the first religious group to refuse fellowship to slaveholders, expanded throughout the early nineteenth century, but largely in the North and Midwest. Having divided in 1827 and again in 1848, the Society of Friends continued to grow. So, too, did its influence in reform movements as activists like Amy Post carried Quaker testimonies against alcohol, war, and slavery into the wider society. Unitarians also combined religious worship with social reform. They differed from other Christians by believing in a single unified higher spirit rather than the Trinity of the Father, the Son, and the Holy Spirit. Emerging mainly in New England in the early nineteenth century, Unitarian societies slowly spread west and south in the 1830s. Opposed to evangelical revivalism and dedicated to a rational approach to understanding the divine, Unitarians attracted prominent literary figures such as James Russell Lowell and Harvard luminaries like William Ellery Channing.

Other churches grew as a result of immigration. Dozens of Catholic churches were established to meet the needs of Irish and some German immigrants. With the rapid increase in Catholic churches, Irish priests multiplied in the 1840s and 1850s, and women's religious orders became increasingly Irish as well. At the same time, synagogues, Hebrew schools, and Hebrew aid societies signaled the growing presence of Jewish immigrants, chiefly from Germany, in the United States. These religious groups were less active in social reform and more focused on assisting their own congregants in securing a foothold in their new home.

Entirely new religious groups also flourished in the 1840s. One of the most important was the Church of Jesus Christ of Latter-Day Saints, or Mormons, founded by Joseph Smith. Smith began to receive visions from God at age fifteen and was directed to dig up gold plates inscribed with instructions for redeeming the Lost Tribes of Israel. *The Book of Mormon* (1830), supposedly based on these inscriptions, served, along with the Bible, as the scriptural foundation of the Church of Jesus Christ of Latter-Day Saints, which Smith led as the Prophet.

Smith founded not only a church but a theocracy (a community governed by religious leaders). In the mid-1830s Mormons established a settlement at Nauvoo, Illinois and recruited followers—black and white—from the eastern United States and England. When Smith voiced antislavery views, some local residents expressed outrage. But it was his claim to revelations sanctioning polygamy that led local authorities to arrest him and his brother. When a mob then lynched the Smith brothers, Brigham Young, a successful missionary, took over as Prophet. In 1846 he led 12,000 followers west, 5,000 of whom settled near the Great Salt Lake, in what would soon become the Utah Territory. Isolated from anti-Mormon mobs, Young established a thriving theocracy. In this settlement, leaders practiced polygamy and denied black members the right to become priests.

New religious groups also formed by separating from established denominations. William Miller, a prosperous farmer and Baptist preacher, claimed that the Bible proved that the Second Coming of Jesus Christ would occur in 1843. Thousands of Americans joined the Millerites. When various dates for Christ's Second Coming passed without incident, however, Millerites developed competing interpretations for the failure and divided into distinct groups. The most influential group formed the Seventh-Day Adventist Church in the 1840s.

Transcendentalism. Another important movement for spiritual renewal was rooted in the transcendent power of nature. The founder of this transcendentalist school of thought was Ralph Waldo Emerson. Raised a Unitarian, Emerson began challenging the church's ideas. His 1836 essay entitled "Nature" expounded his newfound belief in a Universal Being. This Being existed as an ideal reality beyond the material world and was accessible through nature. Emerson's natural world was distinctly American and suggested

Thomas Cole, *View of the Round-Top in the Catskills Mountains*, 1827 Thomas Cole was born in England in 1801, migrated to America in 1818, and lived for many years in Catskill, New York with his wife and children until his death in 1848. Many of his paintings captured a romantic view of nature that combined a hint of wildness with the beauty of mountain mists and sunlit rivers shown here. Bridgeman Images/Museum of Fine Arts, Boston, Massachusetts, USA / Gift of Martha C. Karolik for the M. and M. Karolik / Bridgeman Images

that moral perfection could be achieved in the United States. Emerson expressed his ideas in widely read essays and books and in popular lectures.

Emerson's hometown of Concord, Massachusetts served as a haven for writers, poets, intellectuals, and reformers who were drawn to **transcendentalism**. In 1840 Margaret Fuller, a close friend of Emerson, became the first editor of *The Dial*, a journal dedicated to transcendental thought. In 1844 she moved to New York City, where Horace Greeley hired her as a critic at the *New York Tribune*. She soon published a book, *Woman in the Nineteenth Century* (1845), which combined transcendental ideas with arguments for women's rights.

Henry David Thoreau also followed the transcendentalist path. He grew up in Concord and read "Nature" while a student at Harvard in the mid-1830s. In July 1845 Thoreau moved to a cabin near Walden Pond and launched an experiment in simple living. A year later he was imprisoned overnight for refusing to pay his taxes as a protest against slavery and the Mexican-American War. In the anonymous *Civil Disobedience* (1846), Thoreau argued that individuals of conscience had the right to resist government policies they believed to be immoral. Five years later, he published *Walden*, which highlighted the interplay among a simple lifestyle, natural harmony, and social justice.

Like Emerson, many American artists embraced the power of nature. Led by Thomas Cole, members of the Hudson River School painted romanticized landscapes from New York's Catskill and Adirondack Mountains. Some northern artists also traveled to the West, painting the region's grand vistas. Pennsylvanian George Catlin portrayed the dramatic scenery of western mountains, gorges, and waterfalls and also painted moving portraits of Plains Indians.

REVIEW & RELATE

What impact did the Second Great Awakening have in the North?

What new religious organizations and viewpoints emerged in the first half of the nineteenth century, *outside* of Protestant evangelical denominations?

Organizing for Change

Both religious commitments and secular problems spurred social activism in the 1830s and 1840s. In cities, small towns, and rural communities, Northerners founded organizations, launched campaigns, and established institutions to better the world around them. Yet even Americans who agreed that society needed to be reformed still often disagreed over priorities and solutions. Moreover, while some activists employed moral arguments to persuade Americans to follow their lead, others insisted that laws that imposed reform were the only effective means of change.

Varieties of Reform. Middle-class Protestants formed the core of many reform movements in the mid-nineteenth-century North. They had more time and money to devote to social reform than did their working-class counterparts and were less tied to traditional ways than their wealthy neighbors. Nonetheless, workers and farmers, African Americans and immigrants, Catholics and Jews also participated in efforts to improve society.

Reformers used different techniques to pursue their goals. Since women could not vote, for example, they were excluded from direct political participation. Instead, they established charitable associations, distributed food and medicine, constructed asylums, circulated petitions, organized boycotts, arranged meetings and lectures, and published newspapers and pamphlets. Other groups with limited political rights—African Americans and immigrants, for instance—embraced similar modes of action and also formed mutual aid societies. Native-born white men wielded these forms of activism and, in addition, organized political campaigns and lobbied legislators. The reform techniques chosen were also affected by the goals of a particular movement. Moral suasion worked best with families, churches, and local communities, while legislation was more likely to succeed if the goal involved transforming people's behavior across a whole state or region.

Reformers often used a variety of tactics to support a single cause, and many changed their approach over time. For instance, reformers who sought to eradicate prostitution in the 1830s prayed in front of urban brothels and attempted to rescue "fallen" women. They soon launched *The Advocate of Moral Reform*, a monthly journal filled with morality tales, advice to mothers, and lists of men who visited brothels. In small towns, moral reformers sought to alert young women and men to the dangers of city life. By the 1840s, urban reformers opened Homes for Virtuous and Friendless Females to provide safe havens for vulnerable women. And across the country, moral reformers began petitioning state legislators to make punishments for men who hired prostitutes as harsh as those for prostitutes themselves.

The Problem of Poverty.

Poverty had existed since the colonial era, but the panic of 1837 aroused greater public concern. Leaders of both government and private charitable endeavors increasingly linked relief to the moral character of those in need. Affluent Americans had long debated whether the poor would learn habits of industry and thrift if they were simply given aid without working for it. The debate was deeply gendered. Women and children were considered the worthiest recipients of aid, and middle- and upper-class women the appropriate dispensers of charity. Successful men, meanwhile, often linked poverty to weakness and considered giving pennies to a beggar an unmanly act that indulged the worst traits of the poor.

Explore ▶

See Sources 10.2 and 10.3 for the views of two reformers on ways to uplift the poor.

While towns and cities had long relegated the poorest residents to almshouses or workhouses, charitable societies in the early nineteenth century sought to change the conditions that produced poverty. As the poor increased with urban growth, northern charitable ladies began visiting poor neighborhoods, offering blankets, clothing, food, and medicine to needy residents. But the problem seemed intractable, and many charitable organizations began building orphan asylums, hospitals, and homes for working women to provide deserving but vulnerable individuals with resources to improve their life chances.

The "undeserving" poor faced grimmer choices. They generally received assistance only through the workhouse or the local jail. By the 1830s images of rowdy men who drank or gambled away what little they earned, prostitutes who tempted respectable men into vice, and immigrants who preferred idle poverty to virtuous labor became stock figures in debates over the causes of and responses to poverty.

At the same time, young poor women—at least if they were white and Protestant—were increasingly portrayed as the victims of immoral men or unfortunate circumstance. In fictional tales, naive girls were seduced and abandoned by manipulative men. One of the first mass-produced books in the United States, Nathaniel Hawthorne's *The Scarlet Letter* (1850), was set in Puritan New England but addressed contemporary concerns about the seduction of innocents. It illustrated the social ostracism and poverty suffered by a woman who bore a child out of wedlock.

Other fictional tales placed the blame for fallen women on foreigners, especially Catholics. Such works drew vivid portraits of young nuns ravished by priests and then thrown out pregnant and penniless. These stories heightened anti-Catholic sentiment, which periodically boiled over into attacks on Catholic homes, schools, churches, and convents.

At the same time, economic competition intensified conflicts between immigrants and native-born Americans. By the 1840s Americans who opposed immigration took the name **nativists** and launched public political campaigns that blamed foreigners for poverty and crime. Samuel F. B. Morse, the inventor of the telegraph, was among the most popular anti-immigrant spokesmen. Irish Catholics were often targeted in attacks against immigrants. In May 1844 working-class nativists clashed with Irishmen in Philadelphia after shots were fired from a firehouse. A dozen nativists and one Irishman were killed the first day. The next night, nativists looted and burned Irish businesses and Catholic churches.

Many nativists blamed poverty among immigrants on their drinking habits. Others considered alcohol abuse, whether by native-born or immigrant Americans, the root cause not only of poverty but of many social evils.

The Temperance Movement.

Temperance advocates first organized officially in 1826 with the founding of the American Temperance Society. This all-male organization was led by clergy and businessmen but focused on alcohol abuse among

Drunkard's Home, 1850   Temperance societies undertook a variety of activities to publicize the dangers of alcohol. This engraved illustration is from *The National Temperance Offering*, published by the Sons of Temperance, one of the oldest temperance organizations in the United States. It suggests the harm men's alcohol abuse creates for working-class women and children.
From *The National Temperance Offering, and Sons and Daughters of Temperance Gift*, Clifton Waller Barrett Library of American Literature, Albert and Shirley Small Special Collections Library, University of Virginia

How Can We Help the Poor?

Americans who sought to uplift the poor offered various solutions. Some supported workhouses; others provided clothes and medicine to the "deserving" poor; and still others established employment agencies for single women and widows. The sources below capture the views of two affluent northern reformers. Matthew Carey, a prominent publisher and civic leader in Philadelphia, challenged reformers to address the dire plight of working women. Emily G. Kempshall, a longtime officer of the Rochester Female Charitable Society, lost faith in the ability of female benevolence to improve the situation of impoverished families and resigned in 1838.

Source 10.2

Matthew Carey | *Appeal to the Wealthy of the Land*, 1833

Let us now turn to the appalling case of seamstresses, . . . [who are] Beset . . . by poverty and wretchedness, with scanty and poor fare, miserable lodgings, clothing inferior in quality . . . , without the most distant hope of amelioration of condition, by a course of unrelenting and unremitting industry. . . .

IT is frequently asked—what remedy can be found for the enormous and cruel oppression experienced by females employed as seamstresses . . . ? . . . [A] complete remedy for the evil is . . . impracticable. I venture, to suggest a few palliatives.

1. Public opinion, a powerful instrument, ought to be brought to bear on the subject. All honourable members of society, male and female, ought to unite in denouncing those who "grind the faces of the poor." . . .

2. Let the employments of females be multiplied as much as possible . . . especially in shop-keeping in retail stores. . . .

4. Let the Provident Societies, intended to furnish employment for women in winter, be munificently supported; and let those Societies give fair and liberal wages. . . .

6. Let schools be opened for instructing poor women in cooking. Good cooks are always scarce. . . .

8. Ladies who can afford it, ought to give out their sewing and washing, and pay fair prices. . . .

9. In the towns in the interior of the state, and in those in western states, there is generally a want of females as domestics, seamstresses, etc. . . . [The rich should] provide for sending some of the superabundant poor females of our cities to those places.

Source: Matthew Carey, *Appeal to the Wealthy of the Land, Ladies as well as Gentlemen* (Philadelphia: L. Johnson, 1833), 13, 15, 33–34.

working-class men. Religious revivals inspired the establishment of some 5,000 local chapters, and black and white men founded other temperance organizations as well. Over time, the temperance movement changed its goal from moderation to total abstinence, targeted middle-class and elite as well as working-class men, and welcomed women's support. Wives and mothers were expected to persuade male kin to stop drinking and sign a temperance pledge. Women founded dozens of temperance societies in the

Source 10.3

Emily G. Kempshall | Letter to the Rochester Female Charitable Society, 1838

[T]he Board . . . have asked my reasons for withdrawing my . . . members[hip]. . . . I reply . . . that I look upon the funds of your society, however judiciously distributed, among the destitute sick of our city, as being wholly inadequate to meet their necessities. . . . I dare not draw a single Dollar, to relieve one poor family, lest in doing this I rob another poorer family, perhaps of what they must have. . . . I know [also] . . . that whole Districts are appointed to females as visitors of the S[ociety] where no decent female should go, to look after and try to assist, their vile and degraded inhabitants. . . .

And now were I addressing the . . . Common Council of this City I would say, "Give the ladies power to point, in their visits of mercy, to a work House, where idle drunken fathers and mothers must go and work.". . . [T]his being granted, the idle Drunken inhabitants . . . Being safely . . . out of the way of the sick members of their own families . . . the objection to becoming a visitor . . . will be lessened at once. . . .

[H]as not the day gone by, when your Flag of Charity may wave over its Lake, River, Canal, and Rail Road, inviting the outcasts of every city in the Union, . . . to seek . . . their subsistence from your bounty. . . . And so while your Banner, whose merciful insignia on the one side is Relief for the destitute sick, has been held up as a beacon of hope, it is painful to tell them to read the other side where want of funds has written Despair of further Relief.

Source: Emily G. Kempshall to President of the Female Charitable Society of Rochester, January 30, 1838, Rochester Female Charitable Society Papers, Rare Books and Special Collections, University of Rochester, Rochester, New York.

Interpret the Evidence

1. How are poor women and families portrayed by Matthew Carey and Emily Kempshall, both leaders in benevolent reform in their cities? Who would Kempshall send to a workhouse if one existed in Rochester?

2. How might Carey and Kempshall respond to each other's assessments of aiding the poor?

Put It in Context

What do these documents suggest about class tensions and conflicts in northern cities? How might the panic of 1837 have affected such conflicts?

1830s, which funded the circulation of didactic tales, woodcuts, and etchings about the dangers of "demon rum."

Some workingmen viewed temperance as a way to gain dignity and respect. For Protestants, in particular, embracing temperance distinguished them from Irish Catholic workers. A few working-class temperance advocates criticized liquor dealers, whom they claimed directed "the vilest, meanest, most earth-cursing and hell-filling business ever followed." More turned to self-improvement. In the 1840s small groups of laboring men formed Washingtonian societies—named in honor of the nation's founder—to help each other stop excessive drinking. Martha Washington societies appeared shortly thereafter, composed of the wives, mothers, and sisters of male alcoholics.

Despite the rapid growth of temperance organizations, moral suasion failed to reduce alcohol consumption significantly. As a result, many temperance advocates turned to legal reform. In 1851 Maine was the first state to legally prohibit the sale of alcoholic beverages. By 1855 twelve more states had restricted the manufacture or sale of alcohol. Yet these stringent measures inspired a backlash. Hostile to the imposition of middle-class Protestant standards on the population at large, Irish workers in Maine organized the Portland Rum Riot in 1855. It led to the Maine law's repeal the next year. Still, the diverse strategies used by temperance advocates gradually reduced, but did not eliminate, the consumption of beer, wine, and spirits across the United States.

Utopian Communities.

While most reformers reached out to the wider society to implement change, some activists established self-contained communities to serve as models for others. The architects of these **utopian societies**, most formed in the North and Midwest, gained inspiration from European intellectuals and reformers as well as American religious and republican ideals.

In the 1820s Scottish and Welsh labor radicals such as Frances Wright, Robert Owen, and his son Robert Dale Owen established several utopian communities in the United States. They perceived the young republic as open to experiments in communal labor, gender equality, and (in Wright's case) racial justice. Their efforts ultimately failed, but they did arouse impassioned debate.

Then in 1841, former Unitarian minister George Ripley established a transcendentalist community at Brook Farm in Massachusetts. Four years later, Brook Farm was reorganized according to the principles of the French socialist Charles Fourier. Fourier believed that cooperation across classes was necessary to temper the conflicts inherent in capitalist society. He developed a plan for communities, called phalanxes, where residents chose jobs based on individual interest but were paid according to the contribution of each job to the community's well-being. Fourier also advocated equality for women. More than forty Fourierist phalanxes were founded in the northern United States during the 1840s.

A more uniquely American experiment, the Oneida community, was established in central New York by John Humphrey Noyes in 1848. He and his followers believed that Christ's Second Coming had already occurred and embraced the communalism of the early Christian church. Noyes required members to relinquish their private property to the community and to embrace the notion of "complex marriage," in which women and men were free to have sexual intercourse with any consenting adult. He also introduced a form of birth control that sought to ensure women's freedom from constant childbearing and instituted communal child-rearing practices. Divorce and remarriage were also permitted. Despite the public outrage provoked by Oneida's economic and sexual practices, the community recruited several hundred residents and thrived for more than three decades.

"Women Drawing Water, Bishop Hill Colony," c. 1860 This painting by Olaf Kraus captures the collective labor that characterized communal life at Bishop Hill Colony, Illinois. This utopian community was founded in 1846 by Eric Jansen, a critic of the Lutheran Church in Sweden. Forced to emigrate, he recruited 1400 other dissidents to join him on the American prairie. Kraus painted several scenes while living at Bishop Hill. Granger Collection

REVIEW & RELATE

How did efforts to alleviate poverty and temper alcohol consumption reflect the range of reform tactics and participants during the 1830s and 1840s?

What connections can you identify between utopian communities and mainstream reform movements in the first half of the nineteenth century?

Abolitionism Expands and **Divides**

For a small percentage of Northerners, slavery was the ultimate injustice. While most Northerners considered it sufficient to rid their own region of human bondage, antislavery advocates argued that the North remained complicit in the institution. After all, slaves labored under brutal conditions to provide cotton for New England factories, sugar and molasses for northern tables, and profits for urban traders. Free blacks were the earliest advocates of abolition, but their role in the movement generated conflict as more whites joined in the 1830s. The place of the church, of women, and of politics in antislavery efforts also stirred controversy. By the 1840s abolitionists disagreed over whether to focus on abolishing slavery in the South or simply preventing its extension into western territories. These debates often weakened individual organizations but expanded the range of antislavery associations and campaigns.

The Beginnings of the Antislavery Movement. In the 1820s African Americans and a few white Quakers led the fight to abolish slavery. They published pamphlets, lectured to small audiences, and helped runaway slaves reach freedom. In 1829 David Walker wrote the most militant antislavery statement, ***Appeal . . . to the Colored Citizens of the World***. The free son of an enslaved father, Walker left his North Carolina home for Boston in the 1820s and became a writer for *Freedom's Journal*, the country's first newspaper published by African Americans. In his *Appeal*, Walker warned that slaves would claim their freedom by force if whites did not agree to emancipate them. Some northern blacks feared Walker's radical *Appeal* would unleash a white backlash, while Quaker abolitionists like Benjamin Lundy, editor of the *Genius of Universal Emancipation*, admired Walker's courage but rejected his call for violence. Nonetheless the Appeal circulated widely among free and enslaved blacks, with copies spreading from northern cities to Charleston, Savannah, New Orleans, and Norfolk.

William Lloyd Garrison, a white Bostonian who worked on Lundy's newspaper, was inspired by Walker's radical stance. In 1831 he launched his own abolitionist newspaper, the ***Liberator***. He urged white antislavery activists to embrace the goal of immediate emancipation without compensation to slave owners, a position first advocated by the English Quaker Elizabeth Heyrick.

The *Liberator* demanded that whites take an absolute stand against slavery but use moral persuasion rather than armed force to halt its spread. With like-minded black and white activists in Boston, Philadelphia, and New York City, Garrison organized the **American Anti-Slavery Society (AASS)** in 1833. By the end of the decade, the AASS boasted branches in dozens of towns and cities across the North. Members supported lecturers and petition drives, criticized churches that refused to denounce slavery, and proclaimed the U.S. Constitution a proslavery document. Some Garrisonians also participated in the work of the **underground railroad**, a secret network of activists who assisted fugitives fleeing enslavement (Map 10.2).

In 1835 Sarah and Angelina Grimké joined the AASS and soon began lecturing for the organization. Daughters of a prominent South Carolina planter, they had moved to Philadelphia and converted to Quakerism. As white Southerners, their denunciations of slavery carried particular weight. Yet as women, their public presence aroused fierce opposition. In 1837 Congregationalist ministers in Massachusetts decried their presence in front of "promiscuous" audiences of men and women, but 1,500 female millworkers still turned out to hear them at Lowell's city hall.

Maria Stewart, a free black widow in Boston, spoke out against slavery even earlier. In 1831 to 1832, she lectured to mixed-sex and interracial audiences, demanding that northern blacks take more responsibility for ending slavery and fighting racial discrimination. In 1833 free black and white Quaker women formed an interracial organization, the Philadelphia Female Anti-Slavery Society, which advocated the boycott of cotton, sugar, and other slave-produced goods.

The abolitionist movement quickly expanded to the frontier, where debates over slave and free territory were especially intense. In 1836 Ohio claimed more antislavery groups than any other state, and Ohio women initiated a petition drive to abolish slavery in the District of Columbia. The petition campaign, which spread across the North, inspired the first national meeting of women abolitionists in 1837. Other antislavery organizations, like the AASS, recruited male and female abolitionists, black and white. And still others remained all-white, all-black, and single-sex.

Abolition Gains Ground and Enemies.
The growth of the abolitionist movement shocked many Northerners, and in the late 1830s violence often erupted in response to antislavery agitation. Northern manufacturers and merchants were generally hostile, fearing abolitionists' effect on the profitable trade in cotton, sugar, cloth, and rum. And white workingmen feared increased competition for jobs. In the 1830s mobs routinely attacked antislavery meetings, lecturers, and presses. At the 1838 Antislavery Convention

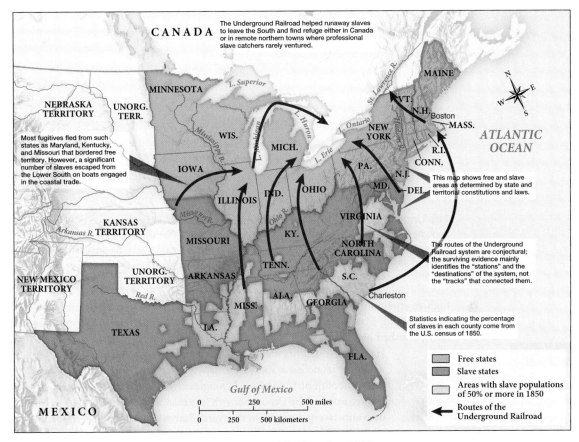

The Underground Railroad helped runaway slaves to leave the South and find refuge either in Canada or in remote northern towns where professional slave catchers rarely ventured.

Most fugitives fled from such states as Maryland, Kentucky, and Missouri that bordered free territory. However, a significant number of slaves escaped from the Lower South on boats engaged in the coastal trade.

This map shows free and slave areas as determined by state and territorial constitutions and laws.

The routes of the Underground Railroad system are conjectural; the surviving evidence mainly identifies the "stations" and the "destinations" of the system, not the "tracks" that connected them.

Statistics indicating the percentage of slaves in each county come from the U.S. census of 1850.

Free states
Slave states
Areas with slave populations of 50% or more in 1850
Routes of the Underground Railroad

0   250   500 miles
0   250   500 kilometers

MAP 10.2   The Underground Railroad c. 1850

Free blacks and their white allies aided men and women who fled slavery from the 1790s on. By 1840, the system became more organized with individual conductors offering safe havens along well-worn routes. Former fugitives, most famously Harriet Tubman, joined the effort and provided advice to those deciding whether to stay in the states or continue on to Canada.

of American Women at Philadelphia's Pennsylvania Hall, mobs forced black and white women to flee and then burned the hall to the ground.

Massive antislavery petition campaigns in 1836 and 1837 generated opposition in and between the North and South. Thousands of abolitionists, including Amy Post and her husband, Isaac, signed petitions to ban slavery in the District of Columbia, end the internal slave trade, and oppose the annexation of Texas. Some evangelical women considered such efforts part of their Christian duty, but most ministers (including Finney) condemned antislavery work as outside women's sphere. Most female evangelicals retreated in the face of clerical disapproval, but others continued their efforts alongside their non-evangelical sisters. **See Primary Source Project 10: Religious Faith and Women's Activism, page 348.** Meanwhile incensed Southern politicians persuaded Congress to pass the gag rule in 1836, which tabled all antislavery petitions without discussion.

But gag rules did not silence abolitionists. Indeed new groups of activists, especially fugitive slaves, offered potent personal tales of the horrors of bondage. The most famous

The Underground Railroad in Action Once Frederick Douglass moved to Rochester, New York, he became central to efforts to assist fugitive slaves. He relied on networks of black and white abolitionists to hide fugitives until they could be sent to Canada. Since hiding fugitives was illegal, notes like this one to Amy Post are rare. Most were destroyed once fugitives reached freedom. Courtesy of the Department of Rare Books and Special Collections, University of Rochester River Campus Libraries

fugitive abolitionist was Frederick Douglass, a Maryland-born slave who in 1838 fled to New Bedford, Massachusetts. He met Garrison in 1841, joined the AASS, and four years later published his life story, *Narrative of the Life of Frederick Douglass, as Told by Himself.*

Explore ▶

Compare opposing views of the origins of the abolition movements in Sources 10.4 and 10.5.

Having revealed his identity as a former slave, Douglass sailed for England, where he launched a successful two-year lecture tour. While he was abroad, British abolitionists purchased Douglass's freedom from his owner, and Douglass returned to the United States a free man. In 1847 he decided to launch his own antislavery newspaper, the *North Star*, a decision that Garrison and other white AASS leaders opposed. Douglass moved to Rochester, where he had earlier found free black and white Quaker allies, including Amy Post.

While eager to have fugitive slaves tell their dramatic stories, many white abolitionists did not match Post's vigorous support of African Americans who asserted an independent voice. Some abolitionists opposed slavery but still believed that blacks were racially inferior; others supported racial equality but assumed that black abolitionists would defer to white leaders. Thus several affiliates of the AASS refused to accept black members. Ultimately, the independent efforts of Douglass and other black activists expanded the antislavery movement even as they made clear the limits of white abolitionist ideals.

Conflicts also arose over the responsibility of churches to challenge slavery. The major Protestant denominations included southern as well as northern churches. If mainstream churches—Presbyterians, Baptists, Methodists—refused communion to slave owners, their southern branches would secede. Still, from the 1830s on, abolitionists pressured churches to take Christian obligations seriously and denounce human bondage. Individual congregations responded, but aside from the Society of Friends, larger denominations failed to follow suit.

In response, abolitionists urged parishioners to break with churches that admitted slaveholders as members. Antislavery preachers pushed the issue, and some worshippers "came out" from mainstream churches to form antislavery congregations. White Wesleyan Methodists and Free Will Baptists joined African American Methodists and Baptists in insisting that their members oppose slavery. Although these churches remained small, they served as a living challenge to mainstream denominations.

Abolitionism and Women's Rights. Women were increasingly active in the AASS and the "come outer" movement, but their growing participation aroused opposition even among abolitionists. By 1836 to 1837, female societies formed the backbone of many antislavery petition campaigns. More women also joined the lecture circuit, including Abby Kelley, a fiery orator who demanded that women be granted an equal role in the movement. But when Garrison and his supporters appointed Kelley to the AASS business committee in May 1839, angry debates erupted over the propriety of women participating "in closed meetings with men." Of the 1,000 abolitionists in attendance, some 300 walked out in protest. The dissidents, including many evangelical men, soon formed a new organization, the American and Foreign Anti-Slavery Society, which excluded women from public lecturing and office holding but encouraged them to support men's efforts.

Those who remained in the AASS then continued to expand the roles of women. In 1840 local chapters appointed a handful of female delegates, including Lucretia Mott of Philadelphia, to the World Anti-Slavery Convention in London. The majority of men at the meeting, however, rejected the female delegates' credentials. Women were then forced to watch the proceedings from a separate section of the hall, confirming for some that women could be effective in campaigns against slavery only if they gained more rights for themselves.

Finally, in July 1848, a small circle of women, including Lucretia Mott and a young American she met in London, Elizabeth Cady Stanton, organized the first convention focused explicitly on women's rights. Held in Stanton's hometown of Seneca Falls, New York, the convention attracted three hundred women and men. James Mott, husband of Lucretia, presided over the convention, and Frederick Douglass spoke, but women dominated the proceedings. One hundred participants, including Amy Post, signed the **Declaration of Sentiments**, which called for women's equality in everything from education and employment to legal rights and voting. Two weeks later, Post helped organize a second convention in Rochester, where participants took the radical action of electing a woman, Abigail Bush, to preside. Here, too, Douglass spoke alongside other black abolitionists and local working women.

Although abolitionism provided much of the impetus for the women's rights movement, other movements also contributed. Strikes by seamstresses and mill workers in the 1830s and 1840s highlighted women's economic needs. Utopian communities experimented with gender equality, and temperance reformers focused attention on domestic violence and sought changes in divorce laws. A diverse coalition also advocated for married women's property rights in the mid-1840s. Women's rights were debated among New York's Seneca Indians as well. Like the Cherokee, Seneca women had lost traditional rights over land and tribal policy as their nation adopted Anglo-American ways. In the summer of 1848, the creation of a written constitution threatened to enshrine these losses in writing. The Seneca constitution did strip women of their dominant role in selecting chiefs but protected their right to vote on the sale of tribal lands. Earlier in 1848, revolutions had erupted against repressive regimes in France and elsewhere in Europe. Antislavery newspapers like the *North Star* covered developments in detail, including European women's demands for political and civil recognition. The meetings in Seneca Falls and Rochester drew on these ideas and influences even as they focused primarily on the rights of white American women.

The Rise of Antislavery Parties. As women's rights advocates demanded female suffrage, debates over the role of partisan politics in the antislavery campaign intensified. Keeping slavery out of western territories depended on the actions of Congress, as did

SECONDARY SOURCE ANALYSIS

Religion, Race, and the Call to End Slavery

In the 1830s, as reform movements surged across the North, some opponents of slavery began demanding an immediate end to human bondage. These *immediatists*, as they were known, including allies of white editor and activist William Lloyd Garrison and of Frederick Douglass and other outspoken fugitive slaves, challenged the economic and political structures and moral values that supported slavery. Historians have sought the roots of this new form of abolitionism in religious movements, in the transportation and communication revolutions, and in the increase in free black communities and the number of fugitive slaves in this period.

Source 10.4

Lawrence J. Friedman, The Religious Roots of Immediate Abolition, 1982

[I]mmediatist abolitionists showed a decidedly different cast of mind and personality from that of antislavery gradualists. Immediatists refused to temporize with evil. . . . They sensed that by plying slow, calculating gradualist measures such as African colonization . . . in the hope of ending slavery eventually, one compromised with sin. . . .

Like missionaries who champion temperance, Sabbath observation, [and] Bible and tract distribution, . . . immediatists constantly sought rapport with those whom they sought to proselytize; they embraced fellow immediatist abolitions, more moderate antislavery Northerners, and even a few Southerners. . . . [T]hey attempted to win these elements over to immediatist abolitionism through missionary appeals. . . .

For the most part, they were not radicals but representatives of the broad Northern middle-class benevolent reform community, subscribers to the pervasive values of market capitalism and Christian self-help. It is certainly noteworthy that members of their highly diverse local constituencies sometimes did not share their class allegiance of all of their ideological proclivities. . . . But the most revealing aspects of the immediatist experience concern the ways in which they reflected the values of the Northern middle class generally and the evangelical missionary community in particular, as well as those factors that caused them to depart in important respects from those who they most closely resembled.

Source: Lawrence J. Friedman, *Gregarious Saints: Self and Community in American Abolitionism, 1830–1870* (Cambridge: Cambridge University Press, 1982), pp. 1, 3, 4.

abolishing slavery in the nation's capital and ending the internal slave trade. Moral suasion had seemingly done little to change minds in Congress or in the South. To force abolition onto the national political agenda, the **Liberty Party** was formed in 1840. Many Garrisonians were appalled at the idea of participating in national elections when the federal government supported slavery in numerous ways, from the three-fifths compromise to allowing slavery in newly acquired territories. Still, the Liberty Party gained significant support among abolitionists in New York, the Middle Atlantic states, and the Midwest.

The Whigs and Democrats generally avoided the antislavery issue to keep their southern and northern wings intact, but that strategy became more difficult once the Liberty Party entered campaigns. In 1840 the party won less than 1 percent of the popular vote but organized rallies that attracted large crowds. In 1844 the party more than doubled its votes,

Source 10.5

Manisha Sinha, The Black Roots of Immediate Abolition, 2016

Slave resistance . . . lay at the heart of the abolition movement. . . . The enslaved inspired the formation of the first Quaker-dominated abolition and manumission [emancipation] societies as well as the first landmark [court] cases that inaugurated emancipation in the Western world. The actions of slave rebels and runaways, black writers and community leaders, did not lie outside of but shaped abolition and its goals. . . . Fugitive slaves united all factions of the movement and led abolitionists to justify revolutionary resistance to slavery. . . .

Black abolitionists were integral to the broader interracial milieu of the movement. . . . Black and white abolitionists also went beyond a simple appeal to the American republican tradition that sought to include African Americans in its promise. They generated a powerful critique of the slaveholding Republic and constructed a counternarrative that highlighted its origins in the slave trade and slavery. . . .

The abolition movement, in which the disenfranchised . . . played a seminal role was driven by passionate outsiders. Women were abolition's foot soldiers, and more controversially, its leaders and orators. . . . Its [the movement's] steady radicalization on women's rights, organized religion, politics and direct action made it quickly outgrow the empire of religious benevolence and moral reform. . . .

From the early Quaker and black protests against slavery to the rise of the Anglo-American movement against the slave trade . . . to the golden age of abolitionism in the years before the Civil War, abolitionists were united in their devotion to the slave's cause.

Source: Manisha Sinha, *The Slave's Cause: The History of Abolition* (New Haven: Yale University Press, 2016), pp. 1–3, 5.

Examine the Sources

1. How do Friedman and Sinha differ in their interpretations of the composition of the abolition movement?
2. Drawing upon evidence in this chapter, how would you evaluate the strengths and weaknesses of Friedman's and Sinha's presentations?

Put It in Context

How did religion and race shape the wide range of reform movements that erupted between 1820 and 1850?

---

which was sufficient to deny Henry Clay a victory in New York State and thus ensure the election of James K. Polk (see "Expanding to Oregon and Texas" in chapter 11).

When President Polk led the United States into war with Mexico, interest in an antislavery political party surged. In 1848 the Liberty Party gained the support of antislavery Whigs, also called Conscience Whigs; northern Democrats who opposed the extension of slavery into the territories; and African American leaders like Frederick Douglass, who broke with Garrison on the utility of electoral politics. Seeing a political opportunity, more practically minded political abolitionists founded the **Free-Soil Party**, which quickly subsumed the Liberty Party. Free-Soilers focused less on the moral wrongs of slavery than on the benefits of keeping western territories free for northern whites seeking economic opportunity. The Free-Soil Party nominated Martin Van Buren, a former Democrat, for president in 1848 and won 10 percent of the popular vote. But once again, the result was to send a slaveholder to the White House—Zachary Taylor, a Mexican War hero. Nonetheless, the Free-Soil Party had expanded beyond the Liberty Party, raising fears in the South and in the two major parties that the battle over slavery could no longer be contained.

REVIEW & RELATE

- How did the American Anti-Slavery Society differ from earlier abolitionist organizations?

- How did conflicts over gender, race, and tactics shape the development of the abolitionist movement in the 1830s and 1840s?

Conclusion: From the North to the Nation

Charles Grandison Finney followed these political developments from Oberlin College, where he served as president in the 1840s. Skeptical that electoral politics could transform society, he continued to view individual conversions as the wellspring of change. As the nation expanded westward, he trained ministers to travel the frontier converting American Indians to Christianity and reminding pioneering families of their religious obligations. Amy Post took a more militant stand, rejecting any participation in a government that accepted slavery and fomented war. She disagreed with Frederick Douglass's decision to support the Liberty Party, but he argued that moral persuasion alone would never convince planters to end slavery.

The efforts of the tens of thousands of Northerners inspired by religious and reform movements between 1820 and 1850 had a greater impact because of the growth of cities and improvements in transportation and communication. It was far easier by the 1830s for evangelicals, Quakers, Mormons, transcendentalists, utopian communalists, and other activists to spread their ideas through sermons, lectures, newspapers, pamphlets, and conventions.

Urban development was driven by the migration of native-born Americans from rural areas and small towns as well as the increase in immigration from Ireland, Germany, and other European nations. The panic of 1837 fueled an economic crisis that lasted several years and temporarily stalled the market revolution. But the panic also inspired many Americans to organize against poverty, intemperance, prostitution, and other urban problems. At the same time, the concentration of workers, immigrants, and free blacks in cities allowed them to unite and claim rights for themselves. For workers, the need to organize was heightened by the growth of factories and factory towns even as the increasing diversity of the labor force aroused tensions among distinct racial and ethnic groups. Thus numerous attacks occurred against free blacks who competed for jobs with immigrants and poor whites even as the antislavery movement expanded across the North.

Of the numerous reform movements that emerged in this period, abolitionism carried the most powerful national implications by 1850. The growth of abolitionist sentiment was related in part to the rapid expansion of slavery. Yet the increase in the size of southern plantations and their spread westward also ensured a steady supply of raw materials, such as cotton, that drove commercial and industrial development across the North. Ultimately, however, the most significant transformations fueled by slavery occurred across the South.

TIMELINE OF **EVENTS**

1820–1850	Northern cities grow; immigration surges
1823	Lowell mills built
1826	American Temperance Society founded
1827	First workingmen's political party founded
1829	David Walker publishes *Appeal . . . to the Colored Citizens of the World*
1830	Joseph Smith publishes *The Book of Mormon*
1830–1831	Second Great Awakening in Rochester, New York
1833	William Lloyd Garrison founds American Anti-Slavery Society (AASS)
1834	National Trades Union founded
1837–1842	Panic of 1837
1839	American Anti-Slavery Society splits over the role of women
1840	Liberty Party formed
	World Anti-Slavery Convention, London
1844	Congress funds construction of the first telegraph line
May 1844	Anti-immigrant violence in Philadelphia
1845	Frederick Douglass publishes *Narrative of the Life of Frederick Douglass*
	Margaret Fuller publishes *Woman in the Nineteenth Century*
1845–1846	Irish potato famine
1846	Henry David Thoreau publishes *Civil Disobedience*
1848	Free-Soil Party formed
July 1848	Seneca Falls Woman's Rights Convention
1851	Maine prohibits the sale of alcoholic beverages

KEY **TERMS**

market revolution, *319*

cult of domesticity, *323*

deskilling, *327*

Second Great Awakening, *329*

temperance, *331*

transcendentalism, *333*

nativists, *335*

utopian societies, *338*

Appeal . . . to the Colored Citizens of the World, *339*

Liberator, *340*

American Anti-Slavery Society (AASS), *340*

underground railroad, *340*

Declaration of Sentiments, *343*

Liberty Party, *344*

Free-Soil Party, *345*

REVIEW & RELATE

1. How did the market revolution, including improvements like the Erie Canal, reshape the landscape and lives of Americans in the North?

2. As northern cities became larger and more diverse in the first half of the nineteenth century, what changes and challenges did urban residents face and what values and beliefs did the new middle class embrace?

3. How and why did American manufacturing change during the first half of the nineteenth century?

4. How did new technologies, immigration, and the panic of 1837 change the economic opportunities and organizing strategies for northern workers?

5. What impact did the Second Great Awakening have in the North?

6. What new religious organizations and viewpoints emerged in the first half of the nineteenth century, *outside* of Protestant evangelical denominations?

7. How did efforts to alleviate poverty and temper alcohol consumption reflect the range of reform tactics and participants during the 1830s and 1840s?

8. What connections can you identify between utopian communities and mainstream reform movements in the first half of the nineteenth century?

9. How did the American Anti-Slavery Society differ from earlier abolitionist organizations?

10. How did conflicts over gender, race, and tactics shape the development of the abolitionist movement in the 1830s and 1840s?

Religious Faith and Women's Activism

▶ In what ways did religion limit or expand women's roles and their participation in reform movements in the 1830s?

During the 1830s, religious revivals and growing religious diversity raised new questions about women's place in public life. In many white evangelical churches, women played prominent roles during revivals, leading prayer circles and persuading others to seek salvation. Still, male ministers retained sole authority and often emphasized women's subjection during the conversion process (Source 10.6). While accepting their subordinate role, many evangelical women nevertheless labored on behalf of temperance, moral reform, and even abolition (Source 10.7).

Male ministers also dominated black churches, but a few black women were recognized as itinerant evangelicals by the 1830s. It was Maria Stewart, however, a free black widow and evangelical convert, who spoke out most publicly about slavery, racial prejudice, and the challenges facing northern African American communities (Source 10.8).

Quaker, Unitarian, Catholic, and Jewish women also combined faith and social activism. They, too, advocated temperance, expanded charitable efforts, and promoted moral uplift. Quaker women also played prominent roles in the antislavery movement alongside white men and African Americans. These efforts generated heated debates over women's sphere. When Sarah and Angelina Grimké, daughters of a South Carolina slave owner, moved to Philadelphia and converted to Quakerism, the American Anti-Slavery Society invited them to lecture on behalf of abolition. Their 1837 lecture tour attracted large mixed-sex audiences, leading Congregational ministers in New England

to denounce their unwomanly conduct (Source 10.9). While many white evangelical women then retreated from antislavery activities, Quaker and black evangelical women continued their activities and Sarah Grimké published a spirited defense of women's antislavery activism (Source 10.10). Like Stewart, Grimké linked female efforts on behalf of racial advancement to women's need for more rights for themselves.

Source 10.6

Charles G. Finney | An Influential Woman Converts, 1830

Women were among the earliest converts in the Reverend Charles Finney's revivals in Rochester, New York. Many then persuaded friends and relatives to seek salvation. In describing the conversion of Mrs. Selah Mathews, Finney reinforces conventional ideas about female subordination while recognizing Mrs. Mathews's influence among local elites. Mrs. Mathews later joined a short-lived female antislavery society and worked on behalf of moral reform.

The wife of a prominent lawyer . . . was one of the first converts. She was a woman of high standing, a lady of culture and extensive influence. . . .

Mrs. M[athews] had been a gay, worldly woman, and very fond of society. She afterward told me that when I first came there, she greatly regretted it, and feared [that] . . . a revival would greatly interfere with the pleasures and amusements that she had promised herself that winter. On conversing with her I found that the Spirit of the Lord was indeed dealing with her. . . . She was bowed down with great conviction of sin. . . . I pressed her earnestly to renounce sin, and the world, and self, and everything for Christ. . . . [W]e knelt down to pray; and my mind being full of the subject of the pride of her heart . . . I very soon introduced the text: "Except ye be converted and become as little children, ye shall in no wise enter into the kingdom of heaven." . . . [A]lmost immediately I heard Mrs M[athews] . . . repeating that text:

"Except ye be converted and become as little children—as little children—Except ye be converted and become as little children." I observed that her mind was taken with that, and the Spirit of God was pressing it upon her heart. I therefore continued to pray, holding that subject before her mind. . . .

. . . Her heart broke down, her sensibility gushed forth, and before we rose . . . , she was indeed a little child. . . . From that moment she was out-spoken in her religious convictions, and zealous for the conversion of her friends.

Source: Charles G. Finney, *The Memoirs of Rev. Charles G. Finney, Written by Himself* (New York: F. H. Revell, 1876), 287–88.

Source 10.7

Elizabeth Emery and Mary P. Abbott | Founding a Female Anti-Slavery Society, 1836

Many women who converted during the Second Great Awakening engaged in social activism. Some believed they were called to rid America of the sin of slavery. Women in Andover, Massachusetts organized a Female Anti-Slavery Society. Elizabeth Emery and Mary Abbott, two leaders in the society, wrote a letter to the *Liberator*, expressing their belief in Christian women's moral responsibility to end slavery.

Mr. Editor:

In these days of women's doings, it may not be amiss to report the proceedings of some ladies in Andover. . . .

The call of our female friends across the waters—the energetic appeal of those untiring sisters in the work of emancipation in Boston—above all, the sighs, the groans, the deathlike struggles of scourged sisters in the South—these have moved our hearts, our hands. We feel that woman has a place in this Godlike work, for woman's woes, and woman's wrongs, are borne to us on every breeze that flows from the South; woman has a place, for she forms a part in God's created intelligent instrumentality to reform the world. . . . When man proves recreant [remiss] to his duty and faithless to his Maker, woman, with her feeling heart, should rouse him—should start his sympathies—should cry in his ear, and raise such a storm of generous sentiment, as shall never let him sleep again. We believe God gave woman a heart to feel—an eye to weep—a hand to work—a tongue to speak. Now let her use that tongue to speak on slavery. Is it not a curse—a heaven-daring abomination? Let her employ that hand, to labor for the slave. Does not her sister in bonds, labor night and day without reward? Let her heart grieve, and her eye fill with tears, in view of a female's body dishonored—a female's mind debased—a female's soul forever ruined! Woman nothing to do with slavery! Abhorred the thought!! We will pray to abhor it more and more. Is not woman abused—woman trampled upon—woman spoiled of her virtue, her probity, her influence, her joy! And this, not in India—not in China—not in Turkey—not in Africa but in America—in the United States of America. . . .

As Christian women, we will do a Christian woman's duty. . . .

Our preamble gives our creed:

"We believe American Slavery is a sin against God—at war with the dictates of humanity, and subversive of the principles of freedom, because it regards rational beings as goods and chattel; robs them of compensation for their toil—denies to them the protection of law—disregards the relation of husband and wife, brother and sister, parent and child; shuts out from the intellect the light of knowledge; overwhelms hope in despair and ruins the soul—thus sinking to the level of brutes, more than one million of American females, who are created in God's image, a little lower than the angels', and consigns them over to degradation, physical, social, intellectual, and moral.

Source: Elizabeth Emery and Mary P. Abbott, "Letter to *The Liberator,*" *Liberator*, August 27, 1836, 138.

Maria Stewart | On Religion and the Pure Principles of Morality, 1831

Maria Stewart was orphaned in 1808 at age five. She then worked as a servant for fifteen years, gaining an education by attending Sunday school. Married at twenty-three and widowed at twenty-six, she experienced a religious conversion the next year and began speaking publicly in 1831 to mixed-sex, largely black audiences. She urged black women to claim their God-given rights and improve themselves and their community. When some black Bostonians criticized her views, Stewart moved to New York City and later Washington, D.C.

O ye daughters of Africa, awake! awake! arise! no longer sleep nor slumber, but distinguish yourselves. Show forth to the world that ye are endowed with noble and exalted faculties. . . .

I am of a strong opinion, that the day on which we unite, heart and soul, and turn our attention to knowledge and improvement, that day the hissing and reproach among the nations of the earth against us will cease. . . .

. . . Why cannot we do something to distinguish ourselves, and contribute some of our hard earnings that would reflect honor upon our memories, and cause our children to arise and call us blessed? Shall it any longer be said of the daughters of Africa, they have no ambition . . . ? By no means. Let every female heart become united; and let us raise a fund ourselves; and at the end of one year and a half, we might be able to lay the corner-stone for the building of a High School . . . and God would raise us up, and enough to aid us in our laudable designs. . . .

How long shall the fair daughters of Africa be compelled to bury their minds and talents beneath a load of iron pots and kettles? . . . How long shall a mean set of men flatter us with their smiles, and enrich themselves with our hard earnings; their wives' fingers sparkling with rings, and they themselves laughing at our folly? Until we begin to promote and patronize each other. . . . We have never had an opportunity of displaying our talents; therefore the world thinks we know nothing. . . . Do you ask the disposition I would have you possess?

Possess the spirit of independence. The Americans do, and why should not you? Possess the spirit of men, bold and enterprising, fearless and undaunted. Sue for your rights and privileges. . . . That day we, as a people, harken unto the voice of the Lord our God, . . . and we shall begin to flourish.

Source: Maria Stewart, "Religion and the Pure Principles of Morality," in *Meditations from the Pen of Mrs. Maria W. Stewart. . . . First Published by W. Lloyd Garrison & Knapp* (Washington, DC: Enterprise, 1879), 25, 31–32.

Congregational Pastoral Letter, 1837

White women's increased involvement in abolitionism generated considerable controversy. In August 1837 Congregational Church leaders circulated a letter to ministers throughout New England. They were outraged by Angelina and Sarah Grimké's lecturing on antislavery to mixed-sex audiences and condemned both them and women's public activism generally.

W e invite your attention to the dangers which at present seem to threaten the female character with wide-spread and permanent injury. The appropriate duties and influence of woman are clearly stated in the New Testament. Those duties and that influence are unobtrusive and private, but the source of mighty power. When the mild, dependent, softening influence of woman upon the sternness of man's opinions is fully exercised, society feels the effects of it in a thousand ways. The power of woman is in her dependence, flowing from the consciousness of that weakness which God has given her for her protection. . . . There are social influences which females use in promoting piety and the great objects of Christian benevolence which we cannot too highly commend. We appreciate the unostentatious prayers and efforts of woman in advancing the cause of religion at home and abroad; in Sabbath-schools; . . . and in all such associated effort as becomes the modesty of her sex. . . .

But when she assumes the place and tone of man as a public reformer, our care and protection of her seem unnecessary; . . . and her character becomes unnatural. If the vine, whose strength and beauty is to lean upon the trellis-work and half conceal its clusters, thinks to assume the independence and the overshadowing nature of the elm, it will not only cease to bear fruit, but fall in shame and dishonor into the dust. We cannot, therefore, but regret the mistaken conduct of those who encourage females to bear an obtrusive and ostentatious part in measures of reform, and countenance any of that sex who so far forget themselves as to incinerate in the character of public lecturers and teachers. . . . We especially deplore the intimate acquaintance and promiscuous conversation of females with regard to things "which ought not to be named"; by which that modesty and delicacy . . . which constitutes the true influence of woman in society, is consumed, and the way opened . . . for degeneracy and ruin.

Source: "Pastoral Letter of the General Association of Massachusetts to the Congregational Churches under Their Care," *Liberator*, August 11, 1837.

Source: "Pastoral Letter of the General Association of Massachusetts to the Congregational Churches under Their Care," *Liberator*, August 11, 1837.

Source 10.10

Sarah Grimké | Response to the Pastoral Letter, 1837

In response to the ministers' criticism, Sarah Grimké wrote a letter to the *Liberator* that she later published in a book of essays. Having converted to Quakerism, she and her sister felt obligated to speak out against the evils of slavery, which they had witnessed firsthand on their father's South Carolina plantation. The criticisms leveled at them inspired Sarah to develop arguments in support of women's rights as well as abolition.

Dear Friend,

. . . I am persuaded that when the minds of men and women become emancipated from the thraldom [bondage] of superstition and "traditions of men," the sentiments contained in the Pastoral Letter will be recurred to with as much astonishment as the opinions of Cotton Mather and other distinguished men of his day, on the subject of witchcraft. . . .

But to the letter. It says, "We invite your attention to the dangers which at present seem to threaten the female character with wide-spread and permanent injury." I rejoice that they have called the attention of my sex to this subject, because I believe if woman investigates it, she will soon discover that danger is impending, though from a totally different source . . . —danger from those who, having long held the reins of *usurped* authority, are unwilling to permit us to fill that sphere which God created us to move in, and who have entered into league to crush the immortal mind of woman. I rejoice, because I am persuaded that the rights of woman, like the rights of slaves, need only be examined to be understood and asserted. . . .

"The appropriate duties and influence of women are clearly stated in the New Testament. Those duties are unobtrusive and private, but the sources of *mighty power.* . . ." No one can desire more earnestly than I do, that woman may move exactly in the sphere which her Creator has assigned her; and I believe her having been displaced from that sphere has introduced confusion into the world. It is, therefore, of vast importance to herself and to all the rational creation, that she should ascertain what are her duties and her privileges as a responsible and immortal being. . . .

But . . . her light is not to shine before man like that of her brethren; but she is passively to let the lords of the creation, as they call themselves, put the bushel over it, lest peradventure [perhaps] it might appear that the world has been benefitted by the rays of *her* candle. So that her quenched light, according to their judgment, will be of more use than if it were set on the candlestick. "Her influence is the source of mighty power." This has ever been the flattering language of man since he laid aside the whip as a means to keep woman in subjection. He spares her body; but the war he has waged against her mind, her heart, and her soul, has been no less destructive to her as a moral being. . . . She has surrendered her dearest RIGHTS, and been satisfied with the privileges which man has assumed to grant her. . . . He has adorned the creature whom God gave him as a companion, with baubles and gewgaws [showy things], turned her attention to personal attractions, offered incense to her vanity, and made her the instrument of his selfish gratification. . . .

We are told, "the power of woman is in her dependence, flowing from a consciousness of that weakness which God has given her for her protection." If physical weakness is alluded to, I cheerfully concede the superiority . . . but if they mean to intimate, that mental or moral weakness belongs to woman, more than to man, I utterly disclaim the charge. . . . [N]o where does God say that he made any distinction between us, as moral and intelligent beings. . . .

As to the pretty simile . . . , "If the vine whose strength and beauty is to lean upon the trellis work, and half conceal its clusters. . . ." etc. I shall only remark that it might well suit the poet's fancy . . . ; but it seems to me utterly inconsistent with the dignity of a Christian body, to endeavor to draw such an anti-scriptural distinction between men and women. Ah! how many of my sex feel . . . , under the gentle appellation of protection, that what they have leaned upon has proved a broken reed at best, and oft a spear.

Source: Sarah Grimké, *Letters on the Equality of the Sexes and the Condition of Woman* (Boston: Isaac Knapp, 1838), 14–18, 21.

Interpret the Evidence

1. What does Charles Finney's account of Mrs. Mathews's conversion indicate about the subordination and influence of evangelical women (Source 10.6)? How does it compare in intent and attitudes with the Pastoral Letter (Source 10.9)?

2. Why do Elizabeth Emery and Mary Abbott describe enslaved women as their sisters (Source 10.7)? Would Maria Stewart agree with their view (Source 10.8)?

3. Who is Stewart's audience and why does she highlight the actions and character of free black women (Source 10.8)?

4. How do white and black women activists justify women's roles in the abolitionist movement, and who are they trying to persuade (Sources 10.6, 10.7, and 10.9)?

Put It in Context

How do the arguments of Emery, Abbott, Stewart, and Grimké challenge dominant beliefs about men's and women's proper spheres in the mid-nineteenth century?

Why did evangelical ministers denounce the Grimkés' speeches before mixed-sex audiences but not Stewart's?

Slavery Expands South and West

1830–1850

WINDOW TO THE PAST

The Slave Market

Few Americans and even fewer Europeans ever entered a slave market where black men, women and children were auctioned off to the highest bidder. They did, however, see etchings, engravings, and paintings of the market created by artists. Some emphasized the horrors of the market; others, like German painter Friedrich Schulz, softened the reality through rich colors and respectable dress. ▶ To discover more about what this primary source can show us, see Source 11.9 on pages 385–86.

Hirshhorn Museum & Sculpture Garden, Washington D.C., USA/Bridgeman Images

After reading this chapter you should be able to:

- Explain the development of a plantation society and the impact on planters and their families as well as slaves and their families.

- Discuss the importance of slave labor and the development of a distinctive slave culture, including forms of slave resistance.

- Analyze the differences among southern whites as slavery expanded and compare the techniques used by planters to control blacks and non-slaveholding whites.

- Evaluate the challenges that Indians, the panic of 1837, Texas independence, and the Whig Party posed for the Democratic Party.

- Evaluate the ways that the idea of manifest destiny shaped national elections and intensified debates over slavery.

COMPARING AMERICAN HISTORIES

Although James Henry Hammond became a wealthy plantation owner, he initially planned to pursue the law. Born in 1807 near Newberry, South Carolina, Hammond opened a law practice in Columbia, the state capital, in 1828. Two years later, bored by his profession, he established a newspaper, the *Southern Times*. Writing bold editorials that supported

(left) **James Henry Hammond** Documenting the American South, University Library, The University of North Carolina at Chapel Hill, http://docsouth.unc.edu/fpn/clay/ill18.html

(right) **Solomon Northup** Documenting the American South, University Library, The University of North Carolina at Chapel Hill, http://docsouth.unc.edu/fpn/northup/frontis.html

nullification of the "Tariff of Abominations," Hammond quickly gained attention. He soon married Catherine Fitzsimmons, the daughter of a wealthy, politically connected family. The marriage made Hammond the master of Silver Bluff, a 7,500-acre plantation worked by 147 slaves. A successful planter and agricultural reformer, Hammond was elected to the U.S. House of Representatives in 1834.

In 1836 Hammond campaigned successfully for congressional passage of the so-called gag rule, ensuring that antislavery petitions would be tabled rather than read on the floor of the House. Soon afterward, he took ill and resigned from Congress but returned to politics in 1842 as South Carolina's governor. His ambitions were stymied again, however, when Catherine discovered that her husband had made sexual advances on his four nieces, aged thirteen to sixteen. Fearing public exposure, Hammond withdrew from politics, but then joined southern intellectuals in arguing that slavery was a positive good rather than a necessary evil.

Solomon Northup was an African American who endured the ravages of slavery and held a distinctly different view of the institution than James Henry Hammond. His father, Mintus, was born into slavery but freed by his owner's will. He moved to Minerva, New York, married and had a son, Solomon, in 1808. At the age of twenty-one, the free-born Northup married Anne Hampton and worked transporting goods on the region's waterways. He was also hired as a fiddle player, while Anne worked as a cook. In 1834 the couple moved to Saratoga Springs, where they raised their three children until tragedy struck.

In March 1841 Northup met two white circus performers who hired him to play the fiddle for them on tour. They paid his wages up front and told him to obtain documents proving his free status. After reaching Washington, D.C., however, Northup was drugged, chained, and sold to James Birch, a notorious slave trader. Northup was resold in New Orleans to William Ford, who changed his name to Platt. Ford put him to work as a raftsman while Northup tried unsuccessfully to get word to his wife.

In 1842 Ford sold "Platt" to a neighbor, John Tibeats, who, unlike Ford, whipped and abused his workers. When Tibeats attacked Northup with an ax, he fought back and fled to Ford's house. His former owner shielded him from Tibeats's wrath and arranged his sale to the planter Edwin Epps. For the next ten years, Northup worked the cotton fields and played the fiddle at local dances.

Finally, in 1852 Samuel Bass, a Canadian carpenter who openly acknowledged his antislavery views, came to work on Epps's house. Northup persuaded Bass to send a letter to his wife in Saratoga Springs. Anne Northup, astonished to hear that her husband was still alive, took the letter to lawyer Henry Northup, the son of Mintus's former owner. After months of legal efforts, a local judge freed Solomon Northup in January 1853. ∎

Comparing the American histories of James Henry Hammond and Solomon Northup illuminates the struggle over slavery from two distinctive perspectives. Between 1820 and 1850 slave labor became central to the South's economic success and an important factor in fueling the market revolution across the nation. In this same period, however, slave ownership became concentrated in the hands of a small proportion of white families. These wealthy and powerful planter families gained increased authority over free blacks and non-slave-owning whites as well as slaves. The concentration of more slaves on each plantation did strengthen African American communities, although it did not negate the brutality they faced. At the same time, the volatility of the cotton market fueled economic instability, triggering the economic panic in 1837. Planters insisted that only expanding into new lands to cultivate more cotton could ensure economic growth. In response, Democratic administrations in Washington, D.C. forcibly removed Indians from the Southeast, supported independence for Texas, and proclaimed war on Mexico. However, these policies only intensified conflicts with Indian nations, heightened political tensions over slavery, and inspired the emergence of the Whig Party.

Planters Expand the Slave System

The cotton gin, developed in the 1790s, ensured the growth of southern agriculture into the 1840s. As the cotton kingdom spread west, **planters**, those who owned the largest plantations, forged a distinctive culture around the institution of slavery. But this slave-based agricultural economy limited the development of cities, technology, and educational institutions, leaving the South increasingly dependent on the North and West for many of its needs. In addition, westward expansion extended the trade in slaves within the South, shattering black families. Still, southern planters viewed themselves as national leaders, both the repository of traditional American values and the engine of economic progress.

A Plantation Society Develops in the South.
Plantation slavery existed throughout the Americas in the early nineteenth century. Extensive plantations worked by large numbers of slaves existed in the West Indies and South America. In the U.S. South, however, the volatile cotton market and a scarcity of fertile land kept most plantations relatively small before 1830. But over the next two decades, territorial expansion and the profits from cotton, rice, and sugar allowed successful southern planters to build grand houses and purchase a variety of luxury goods.

As plantations grew, a wealthy aristocracy sought to ensure productivity by employing harsh methods of discipline. Although James Henry Hammond imagined himself a progressive master, he used the whip liberally, hoping thereby to ensure that his estate generated sufficient profits to support a lavish lifestyle.

Increased attention to comfort and luxury helped make the heavy workload of plantation mistresses tolerable. Mistresses were expected to manage their own families and the domestic slaves as well as the feeding, clothing, and medical care of the entire labor force. They also organized social events, hosted relatives and friends for extended stays, and sometimes directed the plantation in their husband's absence.

Still, plantation mistresses were relieved of the most arduous labor by enslaved women, who cooked, cleaned, and washed for the family, cared for the children, and even nursed the babies. Wealthy white women benefited from the best education, the greatest access to music and literature, and the finest clothes and furnishings. Yet the pedestal on which plantation mistresses stood was shaky, built on a patriarchal system in which husbands and fathers held substantial power. For example, most wives tried to ignore the sexual relations that husbands initiated with female slaves. Catherine Hammond did not. She moved to Charleston with her two youngest daughters when she discovered James's sexual abuse of an enslaved mother and daughter. Others, however, took out their anger and frustration on slave women already victimized by their husbands. Moreover, some mistresses owned slaves themselves, gave them as gifts or bequests to family members and friends, and traded them on the open market.

Not all slaveholders were wealthy planters like the Hammonds, with fifty or more slaves and extensive landholdings. Far more planters in the 1830s and 1840s owned between twenty and fifty slaves, and an even larger number of farmers owned just three to six slaves. As Hammond wrote a friend in 1847, "The planters here are essentially what the nobility are in other countries. They stand at the head of society & politics."

Urban Life in the Slave South.

The insistence on the supremacy of slave owners had broad repercussions. The richest men in the South invested in slaves, land, and household goods, with little left to develop industry, technology, or urban institutions. The largest factory in the South, the Tredegar Iron Works in Richmond, Virginia, employed several hundred free and enslaved African Americans by 1850. Most southern industrialists, however, like South Carolina textile manufacturer William Gregg, employed poor white women and children. But neither Tredegar nor a scattering of textile mills fundamentally reshaped the region's economy.

The South also fell behind in urban development. The main exception was port cities. Yet even in Baltimore, Charleston, and Savannah, commerce was often directed by northern agents, especially cotton brokers. In addition, nearly one-third of southern whites had no access to cash and instead bartered goods and services, further restricting the urban economy.

Southern cities did attract many free blacks. The growing demand for cheap domestic labor in urban areas and planters' greater willingness to emancipate less valuable single female slaves meant that free black women generally outnumbered men in southern cities. These women worked mainly as washerwomen, cooks, and general domestics, while free black men labored as skilled artisans, dockworkers, or sailors. Free blacks competed for these jobs with slaves and growing numbers of European immigrants who flocked to

New Orleans, 1841   New Orleans was one of the few major urban areas in the South and, like Baltimore and Charleston, prospered through its seaport. The port of New Orleans attracted sailing ships engaged in foreign commerce, steamships carrying goods along the Mississippi River, and slave traders from across the eastern United States. The New York Public Library/Art Resource, NY

southern cities in the 1840s and 1850s. The presence of immigrants and free blacks and the reputation of ports as escape hatches for runaway slaves ensured that cities remained suspect in the South.

The scarcity of cities and industry also curtailed the development of transportation. State governments invested little in roads, canals, and railroads. Most small farmers traded goods locally, and most planters used the South's extensive river system to ship goods to commercial hubs. Only Virginia and Maryland, with their proximity to the nation's capital, developed extensive road and rail networks.

The Consequences of Slavery's Expansion.
Outside the South, industry and agriculture increasingly benefited from technological innovation. Planters, however, continued to rely on intensive manual labor. Even reform-minded planters focused on fertilizer and crop rotation rather than machines to enhance productivity. The limited use of new technologies—such as iron plows or seed drills—resulted from a lack of investment capital and planters' refusal to purchase expensive equipment that they feared might be broken or purposely sabotaged by slaves. Instead, they relied on continually expanding the acreage under cultivation.

One result of these practices was that a declining percentage of white Southerners came to control vast estates with large numbers of enslaved laborers. Between 1830 and

1850, the absolute number of both slaves and owners grew. But slave owners became a smaller proportion of all white Southerners because the white population grew faster than the number of slave owners. At the same time, distinctions among wealthy planters, small slaveholders, and whites who owned no slaves also increased.

The concern with productivity and profits and the concentration of more slaves on large plantations did have some benefits for black women and men. The end of the

Slave Population, 1820
• One dot equals 200 slaves

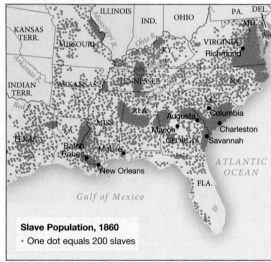

Slave Population, 1860
• One dot equals 200 slaves

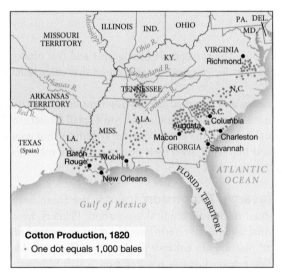

Cotton Production, 1820
• One dot equals 1,000 bales

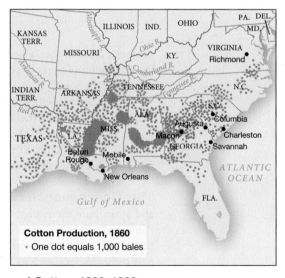

Cotton Production, 1860
• One dot equals 1,000 bales

MAP 11.1   The Spread of Slavery and Cotton, 1820–1860

While tobacco, rice, and sugar remained important crops in a few states, cotton became the South's and the nation's major export. The need to find more fertile fields led planters to migrate to Alabama, Mississippi, and Louisiana. As a result of cotton's success, the number of enslaved people increased dramatically, the internal slave trade expanded, and labor demands intensified.

international slave trade in 1808 forced planters to rely more heavily on natural reproduction to increase their labor force. Thus many planters thought more carefully about how they treated their slaves, who were increasingly viewed as "valuable property." It was no longer good business to work slaves to death or cripple them by severe punishments.

Nonetheless, owners continued to whip slaves and made paltry investments in their diet and health care. Most slaves lived in small houses with dirt floors and little furniture and clothing. They ate a diet high in calories, especially fats and carbohydrates, but with little meat, fish, fresh vegetables, or fruits. The high mortality rate among slave infants and children—more than twice that of white children to age five—reflected this limited care.

The spread of slavery into Mississippi, Louisiana, Alabama, Missouri, and eventually Texas affected both white and black families, though again not equally. The younger sons of wealthy planters were often forced to move to the frontier, and their families generally lived in rough quarters on isolated plantations. A woman traveler noted that the men "think only of making money, and their houses are hardly fit to live in." A planter's wife complained, "Mississippi and Alabama are a dreary waste." Such moves were far more difficult for slaves, however. Between 1830 and 1850, more than 440,000 slaves were forced to move from the Upper South to the Lower South (Map 11.1), often tearing them away from their families. On the southern frontier, they endured especially harsh conditions as they cleared and cultivated new lands.

Explore ▶

See Source 11.1 for one visitor's description of a slave pen in Washington, D.C.

By the 1830s, slave markets blossomed in key cities across the South. Solomon Northup was held in one in Washington, D.C., where a woman named Eliza watched as her son Randall was "won" by a planter from Baton Rouge. She promised "to be the most faithful slave that ever lived" if he would also buy her and her daughter. The slave trader threatened the desperate mother with a hundred lashes, and her tears could not change the outcome. As slavery spread westward, such scenes were repeated thousands of times.

REVIEW & RELATE

- What role did the planter elite play in southern society and politics?

- What were the consequences of the dominant position of slave-based plantation agriculture for the southern economy?

Slave Society and Culture

Because slave labor formed the backbone of the southern economy, enslaved workers gained some leverage against owners and overseers. But blacks did not simply define themselves in relation to whites. They also developed relationships, identities, and cultural practices within the slave quarters. Many also found small ways to resist their enslavement on an everyday basis. Others resisted more openly, and a small number organized rebellions against their masters.

Slaves Fuel the Southern Economy. The labor of enslaved blacks drove the nation's economy as well as the South's. In 1820 the South produced some 500,000 bales of cotton, much of it exported to England. By 1850 the region produced nearly 3 million bales, feeding textile mills in New England and abroad. A decade later, cotton accounted for nearly two-thirds of the U.S. export trade and added nearly $200 million a year to the American economy.

GUIDED ANALYSIS

Edward Strutt Abdy | Description of Washington, D.C., Slave Pen, 1833

Slavery and the slave trade had always been legal in Washington, D.C., and enslaved laborers cleared land and constructed buildings. As the debate over slavery increased in the nineteenth century, abolitionists often highlighted the incongruence of slavery in the capital city of American democracy. Visitors wrote with disgust about slave auctions held within sight of the Capitol steps. In the 1830s the English writer Edward Strutt Abdy toured the United States and described the scene at a slave pen.

Source 11.1

How does Abdy describe the construction of the slave pen and its relation to the U.S. Capitol?

How are whites and blacks described?

How might northern and southern audiences have reacted to this description of a slave pen? How might readers in Great Britain, where slavery had just been abolished, have responded?

One day I went to see the "slaves' pen"—a wretched hovel, "right against" the Capitol, from which it is distant about half a mile, with no house intervening. The outside alone is accessible to the eye of a visitor; what passes within being reserved for the exclusive observation of its owner (a man of the name of Robey) and his unfortunate victims. It is surrounded by a wooden paling fourteen or fifteen feet in height, with the posts outside to prevent escape, and separated from the building by a space too narrow to admit of a free circulation of air. At a small window above, which was unglazed and exposed alike to the heat of summer and the cold of winter, so trying to the constitution, two or three sable faces appeared, looking out wistfully to while away the time and catch a refreshing breeze; the weather being extremely hot. In this wretched hovel, all colors, except white—the only guilty one—both sexes, and all ages, are confined, exposed indiscriminately to all the contamination which may be expected in such society and under such seclusion. The inmates of the gaol, of this class I mean, are even worse treated; some of them, if my informants are to be believed, having been actually frozen to death, during the inclement winters which often prevail in the country. While I was in the city, Robey had got possession of a woman, whose term of slavery was limited to six years. It was expected that she would be sold before the expiration of that period, and sent away to a distance, where the assertion of her claim would subject her to ill-usage. Cases of this kind are very common.

Source: Edward Strutt Abdy, *Journal of a Residence and Tour in the United States of North America, from April, 1833, to October, 1834* (London: John Murray, 1835), 2:96–97.

Put It in Context

How did the spread of cotton to the south and west fuel the development of slave traders and slave pens?

Plantation Slaves at Work   Slaves performed a wide variety of labor, such as planting and harvesting crops, domestic work, and blacksmithing. This panel painted by William Henry Brown in about 1842 shows slaves, perhaps an enslaved family, behind a wagon hauling cotton. Although most tasks were physically demanding, workers who carried goods to market at least had the chance to briefly leave the plantation. The Historic New Orleans Collection/Bridgeman Images

Enslaved laborers, of course, saw little of this wealth. Carpenters, blacksmiths, and other skilled slaves were sometimes hired out and allowed to keep a small amount of the money they earned. They traveled to nearby households, compared their circumstances to those on other plantations, and sometimes made contact with free blacks. Some skilled slaves also learned to read and write and had access to tools and knowledge denied to field hands. Still, they were constantly hounded by whites who demanded travel passes and deference, and they were often suspected of involvement in rebellions.

Household slaves sometimes received old clothes and bedding or leftover food from their owners. Yet they were under the constant surveillance of whites, and women especially were vulnerable to sexual abuse. Moreover, the work they performed was physically demanding. Fugitive slave James Curry recalled that his mother, a cook in North Carolina, rose early each morning to milk cows, bake bread, and churn butter. She was responsible for meals for her owners and the slaves. In summer, she cooked her last meal around eight o'clock, after which she milked the cows again. Then she returned to her quarters, put her children to bed, and often fell asleep while mending clothes.

Once slaves reached the age of ten to twelve, they were put to work full-time, usually in the fields. Although field labor was defined by its relentless pace and drudgery, it also brought together large numbers of slaves for the entire day and thus helped forge bonds among laborers on the same plantation. Songs provided a rhythm for their work and offered slaves the chance to communicate their frustrations or hopes.

Field labor was generally organized by task or by gang. Under the task system, typical on rice plantations, slaves could return to their quarters once the day's task was completed. This left time for slaves to cultivate gardens, fish, or mend clothes. In the gang system, widely used on cotton plantations, men and women worked in groups under the supervision of a driver. Often working from sunup to sundown, they swept across fields hoeing, planting, or picking. **See Primary Source Project 11: Lives in Slavery, page 384.**

Developing an African American Culture.
Amid hard work and harsh treatment, slaves created social bonds and a rich culture of their own. Thus African Americans continued for generations to employ African names, like Cuffee and Binah. Even if masters gave them English names, they might use African names in the slave quarters to sustain family memories and community networks. Elements of West African and Caribbean languages, agricultural techniques, medical practices, forms of dress, folktales, songs and musical instruments, dances, and courtship rituals demonstrated the continued importance of these cultures to African Americans. This hybrid culture was disseminated as slaves hauled cotton to market, forged families across plantation boundaries, or were sold farther south. It was also passed across generations through storytelling, music, rituals, and healthcare. Most slave births were attended by black midwives, and African American healers sought southern equivalents to herbal cures used in West Africa.

Religious practices offer an important example of this blended slave culture. Africans from Muslim communities often continued to pray to Allah even if they were also required to attend Protestant churches, while black Protestant preachers developed rituals that combined African and American elements. In the early nineteenth century, many slaves eagerly embraced the evangelical teachings offered by Baptist and Methodist preachers, which echoed some of the expressive spiritual forms in West Africa. On Sundays, slaves who listened in the morning to white ministers proclaim slavery as God's will might gather in the evening to hear their own preachers declare God's love and the possibilities of liberation, at least in the hereafter. Slaves often incorporated drums, dancing, or other West African elements into these worship services.

Although most black preachers were men, a few enslaved women gained a spiritual following. Many female slaves embraced religion enthusiastically, hoping that Christian baptism might substitute for West African rituals that protected newborn babies. Enslaved women sometimes called on church authorities to intervene when white owners, overseers, or even enslaved men abused them. They also considered the church one means of sanctifying slave marriages that were not recognized legally.

Resistance and Rebellion.
Many slave owners worried that black preachers and West African folktales inspired blacks to resist enslavement. Fearing defiance, planters went to incredible lengths to control their slaves. Although they were largely successful in quelling open revolts, they were unable to eliminate more subtle forms of opposition, like slowing the pace of work, feigning illness, and damaging equipment. More overt forms of resistance—such as truancy and running away, which disrupted work and lowered profits—also proved impossible to stamp out.

"A Slave Wedding," c. 1800   This rare water color painting of an African American wedding probably dates from the turn of the nineteenth century. The distance between the slave quarters and the plantation house suggests this may be a South Carolina scene. The enslaved women and men are dressed in their finest clothing and the musicians appear to be playing African-style instruments made from gourds. MPI/Getty Images

The forms of everyday resistance slaves employed varied in part on their location and resources. Skilled artisans, mostly men, could do more substantial damage because they used more expensive tools, but they were less able to protect themselves through pleas of ignorance. Field laborers could often damage only hoes, but they could do so regularly without exciting suspicion. House slaves could burn dinners, scorch shirts, break china, and even poison owners. Often considered the most loyal slaves, they were also among the most feared because of their intimate contact with white families. Single male slaves were the most likely to run away, planning their escape to get as far away as possible before their absence was noticed. Women who fled plantations were more likely to hide out for short periods in the local area. Eventually, isolation, hunger, or concern for children led most of these truants to return if slave patrols did not find them first.

Despite their rarity, efforts to organize slave uprisings, such as the one supposedly hatched by Denmark Vesey in 1822, continued to haunt southern whites. Rebellions in the West Indies, especially the one in Saint Domingue (Haiti), also echoed through the early nineteenth century. Then in 1831 a seemingly obedient slave named Nat Turner organized a revolt in rural Virginia that stunned whites across the South. Turner was a religious visionary who believed that God had given him a mission. On the night of August 21, he and his followers killed his owners, the Travis family, and then headed to nearby plantations in Southampton County. The insurrection led to the deaths of 57 white men, women, and children and liberated more than 50 slaves. But on August 22, outraged white militiamen burst on the scene and eventually captured the black rebels. Turner managed to hide out for two months but was eventually caught, tried, and hung. Virginia executed 55 other African Americans suspected of assisting Turner.

Nat Turner's rebellion instilled panic among white Virginians, who beat and killed some 200 blacks with no connection to the uprising. White Southerners worried they might be killed in their sleep by seemingly submissive slaves. News of the rebellion traveled through slave communities as well, inspiring both pride and anxiety. The execution of Turner and his followers reminded African Americans how far whites would go to protect the institution of slavery.

A mutiny on the Spanish slave ship *Amistad* in 1839 reinforced white Southerners' fears of rebellion. When Africans being transported for sale in the West Indies seized control of the ship near Cuba, the U.S. navy captured the vessel and imprisoned the enslaved rebels. But international treaties outlawing the Atlantic slave trade and pressure applied by abolitionists led to a court case in which former president John Quincy Adams defended the right of the Africans to their freedom. The widely publicized case reached the U.S. Supreme Court in 1841, and the Court freed the rebels. While the ruling was cheered by abolitionists, white Southerners were shocked that the justices would liberate enslaved men.

REVIEW & RELATE

- How did enslaved African Americans create ties of family, community, and culture?
- How did enslaved African Americans resist efforts to control and exploit their labor?

Planters Tighten Control

Fears of rebellion led to stricter regulations of black life, and actual uprisings temporarily reinforced white solidarity. Yet yeomen farmers, poor whites, and middle-class professionals all voiced some doubts about the ways in which slavery affected southern society. To ensure white unity, planters wielded their economic and political authority, highlighted bonds of kinship and religious fellowship, and promoted an ideology of white supremacy. Their efforts intensified as northern states and other nations began eradicating slavery.

Harsher Treatment for Southern Blacks. Slave revolts led many southern states to impose harsher controls; however, Nat Turner's rebellion led some white Virginians to question slavery itself. In December 1831, the state assembly established a special committee to consider the crisis. Representatives from western counties, where slavery was never profitable, argued for gradual abolition laws and the colonization of the state's black population in Africa. Hundreds of women in the region sent petitions to the Virginia legislature supporting these positions.

While advocates of colonization gained significant support, eastern planters vehemently opposed abolition or colonization, and leading intellectuals argued for the benefits of slavery. Professor Thomas Dew, president of the College of William and Mary, insisted that slaveholders performed godly work in raising Africans from the status of brute beast to civilized Christian. "Every one acquainted with southern slaves," he claimed, "knows that the slave rejoices in the elevation and prosperity of his master." In the fall of 1832 the Virginia legislature embraced Dew's proslavery argument, rejected gradual emancipation, and imposed new restrictions on slaves and free blacks.

From the 1820s to the 1840s, more stringent codes were passed across the South. Most southern legislatures prohibited owners from manumitting their slaves, made it illegal for whites to teach slaves to read or write, placed new limits on independent black churches, abolished slaves' limited access to courts, outlawed slave marriage, banned antislavery literature, defined rape as a crime only against white women, and outlawed assemblies of more than three blacks without a white person present.

States also regulated the lives of free blacks. Some prohibited free blacks from residing within their borders, others required large bonds to ensure good behavior, and most forbade free blacks who left the state from returning. The homes of free blacks could be raided at any time, and the children of free black women were subject to stringent apprenticeship laws that kept many in virtual slavery.

Such measures proved largely successful in controlling slaves, but there was a price to pay. Restricting education and mobility for blacks often hindered schooling and transportation for poor whites as well. Moreover, characterizing the region's primary labor force as savage and lazy discouraged investment in industry and other forms of economic development. And the regulations increased tensions between poorer whites, who were often responsible for enforcement, and wealthy whites, who benefited most clearly from their imposition.

White Southerners without Slaves.

Yeomen farmers, independent owners of small plots who owned few or no slaves, had a complex relationship with the South's plantation economy. Many were related to slave owners, and they often depended on planters to ship their crops to market. Some made extra money by hiring themselves out to planters. Yet yeomen farmers also recognized that their economic interests and daily experiences often diverged from those of planters. This was particularly clear on slavery's frontier, where many yeoman farmers had to carve fields out of forests without the benefit of enslaved workers. They joined with friends and neighbors for barn raisings, corn shuckings, quilting bees, and other collective endeavors that combined labor with sociability. Church services and church socials also brought small farm families together.

While most yeomen farmers believed in slavery, they sometimes challenged planters' authority and assumptions. In the Virginia slavery debates, for example, small farmers from western districts advocated gradual abolition. As growing numbers gained the right to vote in the 1830s and 1840s, they voiced their concerns in county and state legislatures. They advocated more liberal policies toward debtors and demanded greater representation in state legislatures. They also protested planters' obstruction of common lands and waterways, such as building dams upriver that deprived farmers downriver of fishing rights. Yeomen farmers questioned certain ideals embraced by elites. Although plantation mistresses considered manual labor beneath them, the wives and daughters of many small farmers worked in the fields, hauled water, and chopped wood. Still, yeomen farmers' ability to diminish planter control was limited by the continued importance of cotton to the southern economy.

White Southerners who owned no property at all had fewer means of challenging planters' power. These poor whites depended on hunting and fishing in frontier areas, performing day labor on farms and plantations, or working on docks or as servants in southern cities. Poor whites competed with free blacks and slaves for employment and often harbored resentments as a result. Yet some, including poor immigrants from Ireland, Wales, and Scotland, built alliances with blacks based on their shared economic plight.

Some poor whites remained in the same community for decades, establishing themselves on the margins of society. They attended church regularly, performed day labor for

North Carolina Emigrants, 1845 James Henry Beard, who later gained fame for his portraits of political leaders and of dogs, captures in this painting a family of poor whites hoping to find better opportunities farther west. The family was fortunate to own a cow, but the children are barefoot and the mother cradles her infant on a horse that carries all their worldly possessions. Cincinnati Art Museum, Ohio, USA / Gift of the Procter & Gamble Company/Bridgeman Images

affluent families, and taught their children to defer to those higher on the social ladder. Other poor whites moved frequently and survived by combining legal and illegal ventures. They might perform day labor while also stealing food from local farmers. These men and women often had few ties to local communities and little religious training or education. Although poor whites unnerved southern elites by flouting the law and sometimes befriending poor blacks, they could not mount any significant challenge to planter control.

The South's small but growing middle class distanced themselves from poorer whites in pursuit of stability and respectability. They worked as doctors, lawyers, teachers, and shopkeepers and often looked to the North for models to emulate. Many were educated in northern schools and developed ties with their commercial or professional counterparts in that region. They were avid readers of newspapers, religious tracts, and literary periodicals published in the North. And like middle-class Northerners, southern businessmen often depended on their wives' social and financial skills to succeed.

Nonetheless, middle-class southern men shared many of the social attitudes and political priorities of slave owners. They participated alongside planters in benevolent, literary, and temperance societies and agricultural reform organizations. Most middle-class

Southerners also adamantly supported slavery. In fact, some suggested that bound labor might be useful to industry. Despite the emergence of a small middle class, however, the gap between rich and poor continued to expand in the South.

Planters Seek to Unify Southern Whites.

Planters faced another challenge as nations in Europe and South America began to abolish slavery. Antislavery views, first widely expressed by Quakers, gained growing support among evangelical Protestants in Great Britain and the United States and among political radicals in Europe. Slave rebellions in Saint Domingue and the British West Indies in the early nineteenth century intensified these efforts. In 1807 the British Parliament forbade the sale of slaves within its empire and in 1834 emancipated all those who remained enslaved. France followed suit in 1848. As Spanish colonies such as Mexico and Nicaragua gained their independence in the 1820s and 1830s, they, too, eradicated the institution. Meanwhile gradual abolition laws in the northern United States slowly eliminated slavery there. Although slavery continued in Brazil and in Spanish colonies such as Cuba, and serfdom remained in Russia, international attitudes toward human bondage were shifting.

In response, planters wielded their political and economic power to forge tighter bonds among white Southerners. According to the three-fifths compromise in the U.S. Constitution, areas with large slave populations gained more representatives in Congress than those without. The policy also applied to state elections, giving such areas disproportionate power in state politics. In addition, planters used their resources to provide credit for those in need, offer seasonal employment for poorer whites, transport crops to market for yeomen farmers, and help out in times of crisis. Few whites could afford to antagonize these affluent benefactors.

Wealthy planters also emphasized ties of family and faith. James Henry Hammond, for example, regularly assisted his siblings and other family members financially. Many slave owners worshipped alongside their less well-to-do neighbors, and both the pastor and the congregation benefited from maintaining good relations with the wealthiest congregants. Most church members, like many relatives and neighbors, genuinely admired and respected planter elites who looked out for them.

While planters continued to insist that slavery and the right of states to enforce their own labor systems were protected by the U.S. Constitution, they did not take white solidarity for granted. From the 1830s on, they relied on the ideology of **white supremacy** to cement the belief that all whites, regardless of class or education, were superior to all blacks. Following on Thomas Dew, southern elites argued with growing vehemence that the moral and intellectual failings of blacks meant that slavery was not just a necessary evil but a positive good. At the same time, they insisted that blacks harbored deep animosity toward whites, which could be controlled only by regulating every aspect of their lives. Combining racial fear and racial pride, planters forged bonds with poor and middling whites to guarantee their continued dominance. They continued to seek support from state and national legislators as well.

REVIEW & RELATE

What groups made up white southern society? How did their interests overlap or diverge?

How and why did the planter elite seek to reinforce white solidarity?

Democrats Face Political and Economic Crises

Southern planters depended on federal power to expand and sustain the system of slavery. Despite differences on tariffs, both President Andrew Jackson and his successor, Martin Van Buren, stood with southern planters in support of Indian removal and independence for Texas from Mexico. But Van Buren faced a more well-organized opposition in the **Whig Party**, which formed in 1834. When later that decade U.S. rebels in Texas faced powerful resistance from Mexican and Comanche forces and a prolonged and severe economic panic gripped the nation, the Whigs found their opportunity to end Democratic control of the federal government. Over the next two decades, a **Second Party System** formed that pitted Whigs against Democrats on a wide range of economic, cultural, and political issues.

The Battle for Texas. As southern agriculture expanded westward, some whites looked toward Texas for fresh land. White Southerners had begun moving into eastern Texas in the early nineteenth century, but the Adams-Onís Treaty of 1819 guaranteed Spanish control of the territory. Then in 1821 Mexicans overthrew Spanish rule and claimed Texas as part of the new Republic of Mexico. But Mexicans faced serious competition from Comanche Indians, who controlled vast areas in northern Mexico and launched frequent raids into Texas.

Eager to increase settlement in the area and to create a buffer against the Comanches, the Mexican government granted U.S. migrants some of the best land in eastern Texas. It hoped these settlers would eventually spread into the interior, where Comanche raids had devastated Mexican communities. To entice more Southerners, the Mexican government negotiated a special exemption for U.S. planters when it outlawed slavery in 1829. But rather than spreading into the interior, American migrants stayed east of the Colorado River, out of reach of Comanche raids and close to U.S. markets in Louisiana.

Moreover, U.S. settlers resisted assimilation into Mexican society. Instead, they continued to worship as Protestants, speak English, send their children to separate schools, and trade mainly with the United States. By 1835 the 27,000 white Southerners and their 3,000 slaves far outnumbered the 3,000 Mexicans living in eastern Texas.

Forming a majority of the east Texas population and eager to expand their plantations and trade networks, growing numbers of U.S. settlers demanded independence. Then in 1836 Mexicans elected a strong nationalist leader, General Antonio López de Santa Anna, as president. He sought to calm **Tejanos** (Mexican Texans) angered by their vulnerability to Comanche attacks and to curb U.S. settlers seeking further concessions. However, when Santa Anna appointed a military commander to rule Texas, U.S. migrants organized a rebellion and, on March 2, declared their independence. Some elite Tejanos, long neglected by authorities in Mexico City, sided with the rebels. But the rebellion appeared to be short-lived. On March 6, 1836, General Santa Anna crushed settlers defending the **Alamo** in San Antonio. Soon thereafter, he captured the U.S. settlement at Goliad.

At this point, Santa Anna was convinced that the uprising was over. But the U.S. government, despite its claims of neutrality, aided the rebels with funds and army officers. American newspapers picked up the story of the Alamo and published accounts of the battle, describing the Mexican fighters as brutal butchers bent on saving Texas for the pope. These stories, though more fable than fact, increased popular support for the war at a time when many Americans were increasingly hostile to Catholic immigrants in the United States.

As hundreds of armed volunteers headed to Texas, General Sam Houston led rebel forces in a critical victory at San Jacinto in April 1836. While the Mexican government refused to recognize rebel claims, it did not try to regain the lost territory. Few of the U.S. volunteers arrived in time to participate in the fighting, but some settled in the newly liberated region. The Comanche nation quickly recognized the Republic of Texas and developed trade relations with residents to gain access to the vast U.S. market. Still, Santa Anna's failure to recognize Texas independence kept the U.S. government from granting the territory statehood for fear it would lead to war with Mexico.

Explore ▶

See Sources 11.2 and 11.3 for opposing views on Texas independence and annexation.

President Jackson also worried that admitting a new slave state might split the national Democratic Party before the fall elections. To limit debate on the issue, Congress passed a **gag rule** in March 1836 that tabled all antislavery petitions without being read. Nevertheless, thousands of antislavery activists still flooded the House of Representatives with petitions opposing the annexation of Texas.

Indians Resist Removal.

At the same time as the United States and Mexico battled over Texas, the United States also faced continued challenges from Indian nations. After passage of the Indian Removal Act in 1830, Congress hoped to settle the most powerful eastern Indian tribes on land west of the Mississippi River. But some Indian peoples resisted. While federal authorities forcibly removed the majority of Florida Seminoles to Indian Territory between 1832 and 1835, a minority fought back. Jackson and his military commanders expected that this **Second Seminole War** would be short-lived. However, they misjudged the Seminoles' strength; the power of their charismatic leader, Osceola; and the resistance of black fugitives living among the Seminoles.

The conflict continued long after Jackson left the presidency. During the seven-year guerrilla war, 1,600 U.S. troops died. U.S. military forces defeated the Seminole in 1842 only by luring Osceola into an army camp with false promises of a peace settlement. Instead, officers took him captive, finally breaking the back of the resistance. Still, to end the conflict, the U.S. government had to allow fugitive slaves living among the Seminoles to accompany the tribe to Indian Territory.

Unlike the Seminole, members of the Cherokee nation challenged removal by peaceful means, believing that their prolonged efforts to coexist with white society would ensure their success. Indian leaders like John Ross had urged Cherokees to embrace Christianity, white gender roles, and a republican form of government as the best means to ensure control of their communities. Large numbers had done so, but in 1829 and 1830, Georgia officials sought to impose new regulations on the Cherokee living within the state's borders. Tribal leaders took them to court, demanding recognition as a separate nation and using evidence of their Americanization to claim their rights. In 1831 *Cherokee Nation v. Georgia* reached the Supreme Court, which denied a central part of the Cherokee claim. It ruled that all Indians were "domestic dependent nations" rather than fully sovereign governments. Yet the following year, in *Worcester v. Georgia*, the Court declared that the state of Georgia could not impose *state* laws on the Cherokee, for they had "territorial boundaries, within which their authority is exclusive," and that both their land and their rights were protected by the federal government.

COMPARATIVE ANALYSIS

Two Views on Texas Independence

In March 1836, U.S.-born Texans declared an independent republic. Under attack by Mexican forces at the Alamo, twenty-six–year-old Colonel William Travis and others appealed for reinforcements (Source 11.2). While all the men were killed, their appeals inspired hundreds of U.S. volunteers to join military efforts in Texas. They contributed to winning Texas independence, but that victory fueled intense debates over the question of annexation. Abolitionist and Quaker editor Benjamin Lundy was among those who argued that annexation would benefit the "Slaveholding Interest" (Source 11.3). These men offer competing perspectives on the relationship between Texas independence and national honor.

Source 11.2

Colonel William Travis | Appeal for Reinforcements, March 3, 1836

I hope your honorable body will hasten on reinforcements, ammunition, and provisions to our aid. . . . At least five hundred pounds of cannon powder, and two hundred rounds of six, nine, twelve, and eighteen pound balls—ten kegs of rifle powder, and a supply of lead, should be sent to this place without delay, under a sufficient guard.

If these things are promptly sent and large reinforcements are hastened to this frontier, this neighborhood will be the great and decisive battle ground. The power of Santa Ana is to be met here, or in the colonies; we had better meet them here, than to suffer a war of desolation to rage in our settlements. A blood-red banner waves from the church of Bejar, and in the camp above us, in token that the war is one of vengeance against rebels; they have declared us such, and demanded that we should surrender at discretion, or that this garrison should be put to the sword. Their threats have had no influence on me, or my men, but to make all fight with desperation, and that high souled courage which characterizes the patriot, who is willing to die in defence of his country's liberty and his own honor.

The citizens of this municipality are all our enemies except those who have joined us heretofore; . . . those who have not joined us in this extremity, should be declared public enemies, and their property should aid in paying the expenses of the war.

The bearer of this will give your honorable body a statement more in detail should he escape through the enemies lines.

God and Texas—Victory or Death!!
Your obedient ser't
W. Barrett Travis, Lieut. Col. Comm.

Source: *Telegraph and Texas Register*, March 12, 1836, 3.

President Jackson, who sought Cherokee removal, argued that only the tribe's removal west of the Mississippi River could ensure its "physical comfort," "political advancement," and "moral improvement." Most southern whites, seeking to mine gold and expand cotton production in Cherokee territory, agreed. But Protestant women and men in the North launched a massive petition campaign in 1830 supporting the Cherokees' right to their land. The Cherokee themselves forestalled action through Jackson's second term.

Source 11.3

Benjamin Lundy | The War in Texas, 1836

It is generally admitted that the war in Texas has assumed a character which must seriously affect both the interests and honor of this nation. It implicates the conduct of a large number of our citizens, and even the policy and measures of the government are deeply involved in it. . . . The great fundamental principles of universal liberty—the perpetuity of our free republican institutions—the prosperity, the welfare, and the happiness of future generations—are measurably connected with the prospective issue of this fierce and bloody conflict.

But the prime cause and the real objects of this war are not distinctly understood by a large portion of the honest, disinterested, and well-meaning citizens of the United States. . . . [M]any of them have been deceived and misled by the misrepresentations of those concerned in it, and especially by hireling writers for the newspaper press. They have been induced to believe that the inhabitants of Texas were engaged in a legitimate contest for the maintenance of the sacred principles of Liberty, and the natural,

inalienable Rights of Man: whereas . . . the immediate cause and the leading object of this contest originated in a settled design, among the slaveholders of this country (with land speculators and slave-traders), to wrest the large and valuable territory of Texas from the Mexican Republic, in order to re-establish the SYSTEM OF SLAVERY; to open a vast and profitable SLAVE-MARKET therein; and, ultimately, to annex it to the United States. . . . The Slaveholding Interest is now paramount in the Executive branch of our national government; and its influence operates, indirectly, yet powerfully, through that medium, in favor of this Grand Scheme of Oppression and Tyrannical Usurpation. Whether the national Legislature will join hands with the Executive, and lend its aid to this most unwarrantable, aggressive attempt, will depend on the VOICE OF THE PEOPLE, expressed in their primary assemblies, by their petitions, and through the ballot-boxes.

Source: Benjamin Lundy, *The War in Texas* (Philadelphia: Merrihew and Gunn, 1836), 3.

Interpret the Evidence

1. According to William Travis, why was it crucial for the United States to defend the Alamo and Texas independence?
2. How would you compare Travis's appeal for aid with Benjamin Lundy's claims about the rationale for the war and the interests supporting independence? How does each define U.S. national interests?

Put It in Context

What do the battle for Texas independence and debates over Texas annexation reveal about sectional divisions in the United States in the 1830s and 1840s?

In December 1835, however, U.S. officials convinced a small group of Cherokee men—without tribal sanction—to sign the **Treaty of New Echota**. It proposed the exchange of 100 million acres of Cherokee land in the Southeast for $68 million and 32 million acres in Indian Territory. Outraged Cherokee leaders like John Ross lobbied Congress to reject the treaty. But in May 1836, Congress approved the treaty by a single vote and set the date for final removal two years later (Map 11.2).

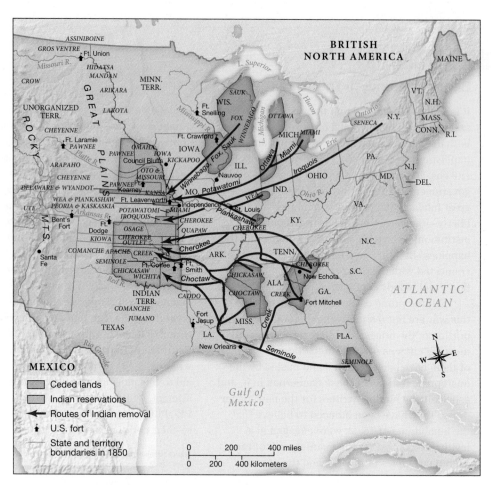

MAP 11.2   Indian Removals and Relocations, 1820s–1840s

In the 1820s and 1830s, the federal government used a variety of tactics, including military force, to expel Indian nations residing east of the Mississippi River. As these tribes resettled in the West, white migration along the Oregon and other trails began to increase. The result, by 1850, was the forced relocation of many western Indian nations as well.

In 1838, the U.S. army forcibly removed Cherokees who had not yet resettled in Indian Territory. That June, General Winfield Scott, assisted by 7,000 U.S. soldiers, forced some 15,000 Cherokees into forts and military camps. Indian families spent the next several months without sufficient food, water, sanitation, or medicine. In October, when the Cherokees finally began the march west, torrential rains were followed by snow. Although the U.S. army planned for a trip of less than three months, the journey actually took five months. As supplies ran short, many Indians died. The remaining Cherokees completed this **Trail of Tears**, as it became known, in March 1839. But thousands remained near starvation a year later.

Following the Trail of Tears, Seneca Indians petitioned the federal government to stop their removal from western New York. Federal agents had negotiated the Treaty of Buffalo

Cherokee Removal, 1838   This woodcut appeared in a U.S. geography textbook about 1850. The title "Indian Emigrants" and the image of Cherokee disembarking from a steamboat falsely suggest that the emigration was voluntary and the means of travel relatively easy. The U.S. fort on the hill symbolizes the role of the federal government in forcing the Cherokee to move west of the Mississippi. Sarin Images/Granger

Creek with several Iroquois leaders in 1838. But some Seneca chiefs claimed the negotiation was marred by bribery and fraud. With the aid of Quaker allies, the Seneca petitioned Congress and the president for redress. Perhaps reluctant to repeat the Cherokee and Seminole debacles, Congress approved a new treaty in 1842 that allowed the Seneca to retain two of their four reservations in western New York.

Van Buren and the Panic of 1837.

Although Jackson proposed the Indian Removal Act, it was President Martin Van Buren who confronted ongoing challenges from Indian nations. When Van Buren ran for president in 1836, the Whigs hoped to defeat him by bringing together diverse supporters: evangelical Protestants who objected to Jackson's Indian policy, financiers and commercial farmers who advocated internal improvements and protective tariffs, merchants and manufacturers who favored a national bank, and Southerners who were antagonized by the president's heavy-handed use of federal authority. But the Whigs could not agree on a single candidate, and this lack of unity allowed Democrats to prevail. Although Van Buren won the popular vote by only a small margin (50.9 percent), he secured an easy majority in the electoral college.

Inaugurated on March 4, 1837, President Van Buren soon faced a major financial crisis. The **panic of 1837** started in the South and was rooted in the changing fortunes of American cotton in Great Britain. During the 1820s and 1830s, British banks lent large sums to states such as New York to fund internal improvements, which drove the market revolution but also fueled inflation. The British also invested heavily in cotton plantations, and southern planters used the funds to expand production and improve shipping facilities.

In late 1836, the Bank of England, faced with bad harvests at home and a declining demand for textiles, tightened credit to limit the flow of money out of the country. This forced British investors to call in their loans, which drove up interest rates in the United States just as cotton prices started to fall. Some large American cotton merchants were forced to declare bankruptcy. The banks where they held accounts, many in the South, then failed—ninety-eight of them in March and April 1837 alone.

The economic crisis hit the South hard. Cotton prices continued to fall, cut by nearly half in less than a year. Land values declined dramatically, port cities came to a standstill, and cotton communities on the southern frontier collapsed. Because regional economies were increasingly intertwined, the panic radiated throughout the United States. Northern brokers, shippers, and merchants were devastated by losses in the cotton trade, and northern banks were hit by unpaid debts incurred for canals and other internal improvements. In turn, entrepreneurs who borrowed money to expand their businesses defaulted in large numbers, and shopkeepers, artisans, factory workers, and farmers in the North and Midwest suffered unemployment and foreclosures.

In the North and West, many Americans blamed Jackson's war against the Bank of the United States for precipitating the panic, and Americans everywhere were outraged at Van Buren's refusal to intervene in the crisis. While it is unlikely that any federal policy could have resolved the nation's economic problems, the president's apparent disinterest in the plight of the people inspired harsh criticisms from ordinary citizens as well as political opponents. Worse, despite brief signs of recovery in 1838, the depression deepened in 1839 and continued for four more years.

The Whigs Win the White House. Eager to exploit the weakness of Van Buren and the Democrats, the Whig Party organized its first national convention in fall 1840 and united behind military hero William Henry Harrison. Harrison was born to a wealthy planter family in Virginia, but he was portrayed as a self-made man who lived in a simple log cabin in Indiana. His running mate, John Tyler, another Virginia gentleman and a onetime Democrat, joined the Whigs because of his opposition to Jackson's stand on nullification. Whig leaders hoped he would attract southern votes. Taking their cue from the Democrats, the Whigs organized rallies, barbecues, parades, and mass meetings. They turned the tables on their foe by portraying Van Buren as an aristocrat and Harrison as a war hero and friend of the common man. The Whigs supported American innovation and the entrepreneurial spirit, proclaimed prosperous farmers and skilled workers the backbone of the country, and insisted on their moral and religious superiority to Democrats. At the same time, eager to remind voters that Harrison had defeated Tenskwatawa at the Battle of Tippecanoe, the Whigs adopted the slogan "Tippecanoe and Tyler Too."

The Whigs also welcomed women into the campaign. By 1840 thousands of women had circulated petitions against Cherokee removal, organized temperance and antislavery societies, promoted religious revivals, and joined charitable associations. They embodied the kind of moral force that the Whig Party claimed to represent. In October 1840, Whig senator Daniel Webster spoke to a gathering of 1,200 women, calling on them to encourage their brothers and husbands to vote for Harrison.

The Whig strategy paid off handsomely on election day. Harrison won easily, and the Whigs gained a majority in Congress. Yet the election's promise was shattered when Harrison died of pneumonia a month after his inauguration. Whigs in Congress now had to deal with John Tyler, whose sentiments were largely southern and Democratic. Vetoing many Whig efforts at reform, Tyler allowed the Democratic Party to regroup and set the stage for close elections in 1844 and 1848.

REVIEW & RELATE

- How did westward expansion affect white Southerners, white Northerners, enslaved blacks, and American Indians in the 1830s and 1840s?

- What economic and political developments led to a Whig victory in the election of 1840?

The **National Government Looks** to the **West**

Despite the Whig victory in 1840, planters wielded considerable clout in Washington, D.C., because of the importance of cotton to the U.S. economy. In turn, Southerners needed federal support to expand into more fertile areas. The presidential election of 1844 turned on this issue, with Democratic candidate James K. Polk demanding continued expansion into Oregon and Mexico. Once Polk was in office, his claims were contested not only by Britain and Mexico but also by the Comanche. After the United States won vast Mexican territories in 1848, conflicts with Indians and debates over slavery only intensified.

Expanding to Oregon and Texas. Southerners eager to expand the plantation economy were at the forefront of the push for territorial expansion. Yet expansion was not merely a southern strategy. Northerners demanded that the United States reject British claims to the Oregon Territory, and some northern politicians and businessmen advocated acquiring Hawaii and Samoa to benefit U.S. trade. In 1844 the Democratic Party built on these expansionist dreams to recapture the White House.

The Democrats nominated a Tennessee congressman and governor, James K. Polk. The Whigs, unwilling to nominate Tyler for president, chose Kentucky senator Henry Clay. Polk declared himself in favor of the annexation of Texas. Clay, meanwhile, waffled on the issue. This proved his undoing when the Liberty Party, a small antislavery party founded in 1840, denounced annexation. Liberty Party candidate James G. Birney captured just enough votes in New York State to throw the state and the election to Polk.

In February 1845, a month before Polk took office, Congress passed a joint resolution annexing the Republic of Texas. That summer, John L. O'Sullivan, editor of the *Democratic Review*, captured the American mood by declaring that nothing must interfere with "the fulfillment of our manifest destiny to overspread the continent allotted by Providence." This vision of **manifest destiny**—of the nation's God-given right to expand its borders— defined Polk's presidency.

With the Texas question seemingly resolved, President Polk turned his attention to Oregon, which stretched from the forty-second parallel to latitude 54°40' and was jointly occupied by Great Britain and the United States. In 1842, three years before Polk took office, glowing reports of the mild climate and fertile soil around Puget Sound had inspired thousands of farmers and traders to flood into Oregon's Willamette Valley. Alarmed by this "Oregon fever," the British tried to confine Americans to areas south of the Columbia River. But U.S. settlers demanded access to the entire territory. President Polk encouraged migration into Oregon but was unwilling to risk war with Great Britain. Instead, diplomats negotiated a

Astoria, Oregon, 1848 In 1845 the British army sent Lieutenant Henry Warre to the Oregon Country to gather intelligence on American settlements in case of war with the United States. Warre sketched Astoria, which lies at the mouth of the Columbia River. The first permanent settlement in the Oregon Country, it was established by John Jacob Astor's Pacific Fur Company in 1811. Sarin Images/Granger

treaty in 1846 that extended the border with British Canada (the forty-ninth parallel) to the Pacific Ocean. Over the next two years, Congress admitted Iowa and Wisconsin to statehood, reassuring northern residents that expansion benefited all regions of the nation.

Some Americans hoped to gain even more territory by pushing Mexicans out of northern Mexico and California. Spanish missions and forts, built in the late eighteenth century, dotted the Pacific Coast from San Diego to San Francisco. When Mexico achieved independence in 1821, it took control of this missionary and military network. Diseases carried by the Spanish and forced labor in their missions and forts had decimated some Indian tribes in the region. As Mexican soldiers took control, some married into Indian families, gaining land and social status and nurturing compound cultures. More often, however, diseases, guns, thefts of food and animals, sexual assault, and forced labor continued to debilitate native peoples.

Indians in the lands newly claimed by the U.S. government faced some of these same dangers. In addition, as the U.S. government forced eastern tribes to move west of the Mississippi, tensions increased among Indian nations (see Map 11.2). When the Cherokee and other southeastern tribes were removed to Indian Territory, for example, they confronted tribes such as the Osage. Pushed into the Southwest, the Osage came into conflict with the Comanche, who had earlier fought the Apache for control of the southern plains. Other Indian nations were pushed onto the northern plains from the Old Northwest. When tribes like the Mandan were decimated by smallpox in the 1830s, the Sioux came to dominate the region.

The flood of U.S. migrants into Texas and the southern plains transformed relations among Indian nations as well as between Indians and Mexico. In the face of Spanish and then Mexican claims on their lands, for example, the Comanche forged alliances with former foes like the Wichita and the Osage. The Comanche also developed commercial ties with tribes in Indian Territory and with both Mexican and Anglo-American traders. They thereby hoped to benefit from the imperial ambitions of the United States and Mexico while strengthening bonds among Indians in the region.

Comanche expansion was especially problematic for Mexico. The young nation did not have sufficient resources to sustain the level of gift giving that Spanish authorities had used to maintain peace. As a result, Comanche warriors launched continual raids against Tejano settlements in Texas. But the Comanche also developed commercial relations with residents of New Mexico, who flaunted trade regulations promulgated in Mexico City. By 1846 Comanche trade and diplomatic relations with New Mexican settlements had seriously weakened the hold of Mexican authorities on their northern provinces.

Pursuing War with Mexico. At the same time, with Texas now a state, Mexico faced growing tensions with the United States. Conflicts centered on Texas's western border. Mexico insisted on the Nueces River as the boundary line, while Americans claimed all the land to the Rio Grande. In January 1846, Polk secretly sent emissary John Slidell to negotiate a border treaty with Mexico. But Polk also sent U.S. troops under

"Hanging of the San Patricios," 1847   In 1846–1847 more than two hundred immigrants, most of them Irish Catholics who defected from U.S. Army units, joined the Mexican Army. They formed the Batallón de San Patricios, which fought fiercely in many battles. When dozens were captured after the Battle of Chapultepec, the soldiers were convicted of desertion. Samuel Chamberlain painted one of two mass hangings that followed. Herbert Orth/The LIFE Images Collection/ Getty Images

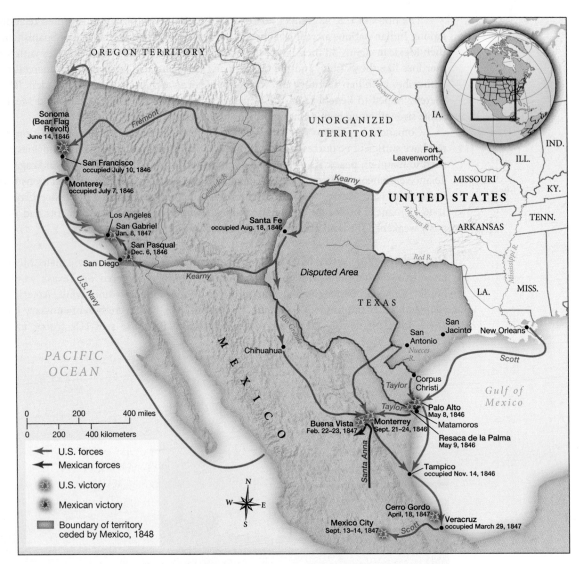

MAP 11.3 The Mexican-American War, 1846–1848

Although a dispute over territory between the Nueces River and the Rio Grande initiated the Mexican-American War, most of the fighting occurred between the Rio Grande and Mexico City. In addition, U.S. forces in California launched battles to claim independence for that region even before gold was discovered there.

General Zachary Taylor across the Nueces River. Mexican officials refused to see Slidell and instead sent their own troops across the Rio Grande. Meanwhile, U.S. naval commanders prepared to seize San Francisco Bay from the Mexicans if war was declared. The Mexican government responded by sending more troops into the disputed Texas territory.

When fighting erupted near the Rio Grande in May 1846 (Map 11.3), Polk claimed that "American blood had been shed on American soil" and declared a state of war. Many

Whigs in Congress opposed the declaration, arguing that the president had provoked the conflict. However, antiwar Whigs failed to convince the Democratic majority, and Congress voted to finance the war. Although northern abolitionists protested the war, most Americans—North and South—considered westward expansion a boon.

Once the war began, battles erupted in a variety of locations. In May 1846, U.S. troops defeated Mexican forces in Palo Alto and Resaca de la Palma. A month later, the U.S. army captured Sonoma, California with the aid of local settlers. John Frémont then led U.S. forces to Monterey, where the navy launched a successful attack and declared the California territory part of the United States. That fall, U.S. troops gained important victories at Monterrey, Mexico, just west of the Rio Grande, and Tampico, along the Gulf coast.

Despite major U.S. victories, Santa Anna, who reclaimed the presidency of Mexico during the war, refused to give up. In February 1847, his troops attacked U.S. forces at Buena Vista and nearly secured a victory. Polk then agreed to send General Winfield Scott to Veracruz with 14,000 soldiers. Capturing the port in March, Scott's army marched on to Mexico City. After a crushing defeat of Santa Anna at Cerro Gordo, the president-general was removed from power and the new Mexican government sought peace.

With victory ensured, U.S. officials faced a difficult decision: How much Mexican territory should they claim? The U.S. army in central Mexico faced continued guerrilla attacks. Meanwhile Whigs and some northern Democrats denounced the war as a southern conspiracy to expand slavery. In this context, Polk agreed to limit U.S. claims to the northern regions of Mexico. The president signed the **Treaty of Guadalupe Hidalgo** in February 1848, committing the United States to pay Mexico $15 million in return for control over Texas north and east of the Rio Grande plus California and the New Mexico territory.

Debates over Slavery Intensify.

News of the U.S. victory traveled quickly across the United States. In the South, planters imagined slavery spreading into the lands acquired from Mexico. Northerners, too, applauded the expansion of U.S. territory but focused on California as a center for agriculture and commerce. Still, the acquisition of new territory heightened sectional conflicts. Debates over slavery had erupted during the war, fueled by abolitionist outrage, and a few northern Democrats joined Whigs in denouncing "the power of SLAVERY" to "govern the country, its Constitutions and laws." In August 1846, Democratic congressman David Wilmot of Pennsylvania proposed outlawing slavery in all territory acquired from Mexico so that the South could not profit from the war. While the **Wilmot Proviso** passed in the House, southern and proslavery northern Democrats defeated it in the Senate.

Explore ▶

For two historians' interpretations of family life under slavery, see Sources 11.4 and 11.5.

The presidential election of 1848 opened with the unresolved question of whether to allow slavery in the territories acquired from Mexico. With Polk declining to run for a second term, Democrats nominated Lewis Cass, a Michigan senator and ardent expansionist. Hoping to keep northern antislavery Democrats in the party, Cass argued that residents in each territory should decide whether to make the region free or slave. This strategy put the slavery question on hold but satisfied almost no one.

The Whigs, too, hoped to avoid the slavery issue for fear of losing southern votes. They nominated Mexican-American War hero General Zachary Taylor, a Louisiana slaveholder who had no declared position on slavery in the western territories. But they sought to reassure

SECONDARY SOURCE ANALYSIS

Families in Slavery

Abolitionist claims about the destructive effects of slavery on enslaved families informed scholarly assessments in the twentieth century. So, too, did studies of World War II concentration camps, which claimed that victims were infantilized by their total lack of power. In 1959, the historian Stanley Elkins argued that prolonged bondage had similar effects on slaves and limited their ability to forge emotional bonds. Six years later, scholar Daniel Patrick Moynihan claimed that slavery spawned female-dominated households, which helped explain the "pathology" of black families in the present. Later historians challenged these views in different and sometimes contradictory ways.

Source 11.4

Robert William Fogel and Stanley L. Engerman, Planters Shape Slave Families, 1974

For better or worse, the dominant role in slave society was played by men, not women. It was men who occupied virtually all of the managerial slots available to slaves. There were very few female overseers or drivers. Men occupied nearly all the artisan crafts. . . .

While females worked along with males in the field, their role was strictly delimited. . . . Just as some jobs on the plantation were confined strictly to men, others were confined strictly to women. . . .

There was also a division of labor within the slave family, a division that began with courtship. It was the male who, at least on the surface, initiated the period of courtship. And it was the man who secured the permission of the planter to marry. After marriage, the tasks of cooking, ordinary household cleaning, laundering, and care of the children fell to the mother.

Planters recognized husbands as the head of the family. Slave families were listed in their record books with the husband at the top of the list. Houses were assigned by the names of husbands and the semiannual issues of clothing to families were made in the name of husbands. . . .

While both moral convictions and good business practice generally led planters to encourage the development of stable nuclear families, . . . there is considerable evidence that the nuclear form was not merely imposed on slaves. Slaves apparently abandoned the African family forms [such as multi-generational families living together] because they did not satisfy the needs of blacks who lived and worked under conditions and in a society much different from those which their ancestors experienced. The nuclear family took root among blacks because it did satisfy those needs.

Source: Robert William Fogelman and Stanley L. Engerman, *Time on the Cross: The Economics of American Negro Slavery* (Boston: Littleton, Brown and Company, 1974), pp. 139, 141, 142–143.

their northern wing by nominating Millard Fillmore of Buffalo, New York, for vice president. As a member of Congress in the 1830s, Fillmore had opposed the annexation of Texas.

The Liberty Party, disappointed in the Whig ticket, decided to run its own candidate for president. Its leaders hoped to expand their support by reconstituting themselves as the Free-Soil Party. This party focused more on excluding slaves from western territories than on the moral injustice of slavery. The party nominated former president Martin Van Buren and appealed to small farmers and urban workers who hoped to benefit from western expansion.

Source 11.5

Deborah Gray White, The Roles of Enslaved Women, 1985

[R]evisionist historians have had difficulty reconciling the slave woman's reality with Western cultural mores that dictate a subordinate familial role for women within the family. They have ignored that slave women played important provider roles and that, short of brute force, bondmen lacked the leverage by which to impose subordinate status on their wives. The extensive female network has also gone unrecognized by those who have assumed that slave woman's primary source of emotional support came from bonded men.... [T]he stark reality is that slave women were not sheltered from life's ugliness nor dependent on their men for subsistence goods and services. . . .

Therefore, slave families were unusually egalitarian. Equality could not have been based on sameness because . . . many jobs and responsibilities still belonged by definition to one sex or the other. This suggests that equality in the slave family was founded on complementary roles, roles that were different yet so critical to slave survival that they were of equal necessity. . . .

Nevertheless, relationships between mother and child still superseded those between husband and wife. Slaveholder practices encouraged the primacy of the mother-child relationship, and in the mores of the slave community motherhood ranked above marriage. In fact, women in their roles as mothers were the central figures in the nuclear slave family. . . .

What black women did was very much in the pattern of their female African ancestors who had for generations stood at the center of the African family. . . . Acting out a very traditional role, they made themselves a real bulwark against the destruction of the slave family's integrity.

Source: Deborah Gray White, *Ar'n't I a Woman? Female Slaves in the Plantation South* (New York: W.W. Norton & Company, 1985), pp. 158, 159, 160.

Examine the Sources

1. How do Fogel and Engerman differ from White in their interpretation of family life among the enslaved?
2. What kind of evidence do these historians draw on in making their arguments, and which interpretation do you find more compelling and why?

Put It in Context

In what ways did slaves and plantation owners shape black family life, and how did the expansion of slavery affect familial relationships?

Once again, the presence of a third party affected the outcome of the election. While Whigs and Democrats tried to avoid the slavery issue, Free-Soilers demanded attention to it. By focusing on the exclusion of slavery in western territories rather than its abolition, the party won more adherents in northern states. Indeed, Van Buren won enough northern Democrats so that Cass lost New York State and the 1848 election. Zachary Taylor and the Whigs won, but only by placing a southern slaveholder in the White House.

REVIEW & RELATE

How did the battle over Texas affect relations among Indian nations, among white Americans, and between Indians and whites?

How did the Mexican-American War reshape national politics and intensify debates over slavery?

Conclusion: Geographical Expansion and Political Division

By the mid-nineteenth century, the United States stood at a crossroads. Most Americans considered expansion advantageous and critical to revitalizing the economy. Planters certainly considered it critical to slavery's success. Yet as the number of slaves and the size of plantations grew, planters also sought to impose stricter controls over blacks, enslaved and free, and to bind non-slaveowning whites more firmly to their interests. Enslaved blacks, meanwhile, developed an increasingly rich culture by combining traditions and rituals from Africa and the Caribbean with U.S. customs and beliefs. This African American culture served as one form of resistance against slavery's brutality. Many enslaved laborers resisted in other ways as well: sabotaging tools, feigning illness, running away, or committing arson or theft. Smaller numbers engaged in outright rebellions.

While most white Northerners were willing to leave slavery alone where it already existed, many hoped to keep it out of newly acquired territories. In this sense, the removal of the Cherokee did not disturb Northerners since it was largely white yeoman farmers who would benefit from access to their land. Still many northern whites, including evangelical women, opposed removal on moral grounds. When it came to the Mexican-American War, more Northerners—black and white—feared victory would mainly benefit southern planters. The vast lands gained from Mexico in 1848 intensified debates over slavery and led small but growing numbers of white Northerners to join African Americans, American Indians, and Mexicans in protesting U.S. expansion. Even some yeomen farmers and middle-class professionals in the South questioned whether extending slavery benefited the region economically and politically.

It was the panic of 1837, however, that opened the way for a new political alignment. The extended depression allowed the newly formed Whig Party to gain support for its economic and reform agenda. In 1840 Whigs captured the White House and Congress, and a new antislavery force, the Liberty Party, emerged as well. But just four years later, James K. Polk's support of westward expansion and manifest destiny returned Democrats to power. The political volatility continued when the U.S. victory in the war with Mexico intensified debates over slavery in the territories, fracturing the Democratic Party and inspiring the founding of the Free-Soil Party.

Political realignments continued over the next decade, fueled by growing antislavery sentiment in the North and proslavery beliefs in the South. In 1853 Solomon Northup horrified thousands of antislavery readers with his book *Twelve Years a Slave*, which vividly described life in bondage. Such writings alarmed planters like James Henry Hammond, who continued to believe that slavery was a divine blessing. Yet in insisting on the benefits of slave labor, the planter elite inspired further conflict with Northerners, whose lives were increasingly shaped by commercial and industrial developments and the expansion of free labor.

CHAPTER **11** REVIEW

TIMELINE OF EVENTS

KEY TERMS

REVIEW & RELATE

1. What role did the planter elite play in southern society and politics?

2. What were the consequences of the dominant position of slave-based plantation agriculture for the southern economy?

3. How did enslaved African Americans create ties of family, community, and culture?

4. How did enslaved African Americans resist efforts to control and exploit their labor?

5. What groups made up white southern society? How did their interests overlap or diverge?

6. How and why did the planter elite seek to reinforce white solidarity?

7. How did westward expansion affect white Southerners, white Northerners, enslaved blacks, and American Indians in the 1830s and 1840s?

8. What economic and political developments led to a Whig victory in the election of 1840?

9. How did the battle over Texas affect relations among Indian nations, among white Americans, and between Indians and whites?

10. How did the Mexican-American War reshape national politics and intensify debates over slavery?

Lives in Slavery

▶ What forms of subjugation and resistance characterized the lives of slaves between 1820 and 1860?

S laves lived under a system of severe subjugation and routinely suffered brutal working conditions, violence, and the devastating separation of families (Sources 11.6, 11.7, 11.8, and 11.9). Yet many slaves found ways to resist their bondage and carve out autonomous spaces. They feigned illness, ran away or hid for a few days, and developed a distinctive African American culture (Source 11.10).

A rich body of slave narratives has helped historians understand slave life. During the nineteenth century a few escaped slaves published books about their lives. Often sponsored or encouraged by white abolitionists, these books highlighted the humanity of blacks and the horrors of slavery. Frederick Douglass, William Wells Brown, Solomon Northup, and Harriet Jacobs all published narratives that revealed hidden aspects of slaves' experience (Sources 11.6, 11.7, and 11.8). In the twentieth century the Works Progress Administration, a federal program to provide work during the Great Depression of the 1930s, hired mostly white writers to conduct interviews with ex-slaves. Although recorded some seventy years after slavery's end, the interviews with people such as Mary Reynolds (Source 11.10) offer valuable insight into the lives of slaves who had no way to record their stories during the slave era.

Whites also documented the lives of the enslaved in the nineteenth century. Both abolitionists and planters wrote extensively about slavery, though from opposing perspectives. Many Europeans were fascinated by American slavery, and some captured the institution in books and paintings (Source 11.9). These white-produced sources can be valuable when analyzed in the context of slaves' stories about their own lives.

Source 11.6

William Wells Brown | Memories of Childhood

William Wells Brown was born into slavery in 1814 on a Missouri farm and later worked on Mississippi riverboats. He escaped in 1834, fleeing first to Cleveland and then to western New York and Boston. He became a popular antislavery lecturer and published his narrative in 1847. While he focuses here on his time as a household slave, he also recalls the cries of his mother being whipped in the fields.

[T]he field hands . . . were summoned to their unrequited toil every morning at four o'clock, by the ringing of a bell. . . . They were allowed half an hour to eat their breakfast, and get to the field. At half past four, a horn was blown by the overseer, which was the signal to commence work; and every one that was not on the spot at the time, had to receive ten lashes from the negro-whip, . . . The handle was about three feet long, with the butt-end filled with lead, and the lash six or seven feet in length, made of cowhide, with platted wire on the end of it. This whip was put in requisition very frequently and freely, and a small offence on the part of a slave furnished an occasion for its use. . . . I was a house servant—a situation preferable to that of a field hand, as I was better fed, better clothed, and not obliged to rise at the ringing of the bell, but about half an hour after. I have often laid and heard the crack of the whip, and the screams of the slave. My mother was a field hand, and one morning was ten or fifteen minutes behind the others in getting into the field. As soon as she reached the spot where they were at work, the overseer commenced whipping her. She cried, "Oh! pray—Oh! pray—Oh! pray"— . . . . I heard her voice, and knew it, and jumped out of my bunk, and went to the door. Though the field was some distance from the house, I could hear every crack of the whip, and every groan and cry of my poor mother. . . . The cold chills ran over me, and I wept aloud. After giving her ten lashes, the sound of the whip ceased, and I returned to my bed, and found no consolation but in my tears. It was not yet daylight.

Source: William Wells Brown, *Narrative of William W. Brown, A Fugitive Slave, Written by Himself* (Boston: Anti-Slavery Office, 1847), 14–16.

Source 11.7

Harriet Jacobs | A Girl Threatened by Sexual Exploitation

Harriet Jacobs was born into slavery in 1813 in Edenton, North Carolina. She made a daring escape in 1835 but remained hidden for seven years in a crawlspace in the house of her grandmother, a free black woman. She finally reached the North in 1842 and became active in abolitionist circles. In her 1861 autobiography, published under the pseudonym Linda Brent, Jacobs describes in harrowing detail her master's attempted sexual exploitation.

But I now entered on my fifteenth year—a sad epoch in the life of a slave girl. My master began to whisper foul words in my ear. Young as I was, I could not remain ignorant of their import. I tried to treat them with indifference or contempt. The master's age, my extreme youth, and the fear that his conduct would be reported to my grandmother, made him bear this treatment for many months. He was a crafty man, and resorted to many means to accomplish his purposes. Sometimes he had stormy, terrific ways, that made his victims tremble; sometimes he assumed a gentleness that he thought must surely subdue. Of the two, I preferred his stormy moods, although they left me trembling. He tried his utmost to corrupt the pure principles my grandmother had instilled. He peopled my young mind

with unclean images. . . . I turned from him with disgust and hatred. But he was my master. I was compelled to live under the same roof with him— where I saw a man forty years my senior daily violating the most sacred commandments of nature. He told me I was his property; that I must be subject to his will in all things. My soul revolted against the mean tyranny. But where could I turn for protection? No matter whether the slave girl be as black as ebony or as fair as her mistress. In either case, there is no shadow of law to protect her from insult, from violence, or even from death; all these are inflicted by fiends who bear the shape of men. The mistress, who ought to protect the helpless victim, has no other feelings towards her but those of jealousy and rage. . . .

Even the little child, who is accustomed to wait on her mistress and her children, will learn, before she is twelve years old, why it is that her mistress hates such and such a one among the slaves. Perhaps the child's own mother is among those hated ones. . . . She will become prematurely knowing in evil things. Soon she will learn to tremble when she hears her master's footfall. She will be compelled to realize that she is no longer a child. If God has bestowed beauty upon her, it will prove her greatest curse. That which commands admiration in the white woman only hastens the degradation of the female slave.

Source: Linda Brent [Harriet Jacobs], *Incidents in the Life of a Slave Girl* (Boston: Published for the Author, 1861), 44–46.

Source 11.8

Solomon Northup | Endless Labor and Constant Fear

Solomon Northup, who was born free in New York State in 1808, was kidnapped and sold into slavery in 1841. After he regained his freedom in 1853, he wrote an autobiography, *Twelve Years a Slave*, about his experiences under slavery. In this excerpt, he describes the labor regimen of his owner, Edwin Epps, a planter in southern Louisiana.

The hands are required to be in the cotton field as soon as it is light in the morning, and, with the exception of ten or fifteen minutes, which is given them at noon to swallow their allowance of cold bacon, they are not permitted to be a moment idle until it is too dark to see, and when the moon is full, they often times labor till the middle of the night. They do not dare to stop even at dinner time, nor return to the quarters, however late it be, until the order to halt is given by the driver.

The day's work over in the field, the baskets are . . . carried to the gin-house, where the cotton is weighed. No matter how fatigued and weary he may be—no matter how much he longs for sleep and rest—a slave never approaches the gin-house with his basket of cotton but with fear. If it falls short in weight—if he has not performed the full task appointed him, he knows that he must suffer. And if he has exceeded it by ten or twenty pounds, in all probability his master will measure the next day's task accordingly. . . . Most frequently they have too little, and therefore it is they are not anxious to leave the field. After weighing, follow the whippings; and then the baskets are carried to the cotton house, and their contents stored away like hay, all hands being sent in to tramp it down. . . .

This done, the labor of the day is not yet ended, by any means. Each one must then attend to his respective chores. One feeds the mules, another the swine—another cuts the wood, and so forth; besides, the packing is all done by candle light. Finally, at a late hour, they reach the quarters, sleepy and overcome with the long day's toil. Then a fire must be kindled in the cabin, the corn ground in the small hand-mill, and supper, and dinner for the next day in the field, prepared. All that is allowed them is corn and bacon, which is given out at the corncrib and smoke-house every Sunday morning. . . . That is all—no tea, coffee, sugar, and with the exception of a very scanty sprinkling now and then, no salt. . . .

The softest couches in the world are not to be found in the log mansion of the slave. The one whereon I reclined year after year, was a plank twelve inches wide and ten feet long. My pillow was a stick of wood. The bedding was a coarse blanket, and not a rag or shred beside. Moss might be used, were it not that it directly breeds a swarm of fleas. . . .

An hour before day light the horn is blown. . . . Then the fears and labors of another day begin.

Source: Solomon Northup, *Twelve Years a Slave* (Auburn, NY: Derby and Miller, 1853), 167–69, 171.

Source 11.9

Friedrich Shulz, *The Slave Market*

American slave markets regularly appeared in etchings, engravings, and paintings in the nineteenth century. Several images were produced by European artists traveling through the South. The German artist Friedrich Shulz (1825–1875) visited the United States in the 1840s or 1850s and painted this image of a slave auction. The beautiful colors and rich tones belie the tragic scenes taking place in this southern market.

Hirshorn Museum & Sculpture Garden, Washington, D.C., USA/Bridgeman Images

Source 11.10

Mary Reynolds | Recalling Work, Punishment, and Faith c. 1850s

Ex-slaves interviewed in the 1930s offered a wealth of information. Mary Reynolds claimed to be more than a hundred years old when interviewed in 1937, but her memories were vivid. She was one of the older interviewees and thus had experienced slavery longer than many who told their stories in this period. Here she recalls life with her parents and sisters on the Kilpatrick family plantation in Black River, Louisiana.

Massa Kilpatrick wasn't no piddlin' man. He was a man of plenty. He had a big house. . . . He was a medicine doctor and they was rooms in the second story for sick folks what come to lay in. It would take two days to go all over the land he owned. He had cattle and stock and sheep and more'n a hundred slaves and more besides. He bought the bes' of niggers near every time the spec'lators come that way. He'd make a swap of the old ones and give money for young ones what could work. . . .

He raised corn and cotton and cane and 'taters and goobers [potatoes and peanuts], 'sides the peas and other feedin' for the niggers. I 'member I helt a hoe handle mighty onsteady when they put a old women to larn me and some other chillun to scrape the fields. . . . She say, "For the love of Gawd, you better larn it right, or Solomon will beat the breath out you body." Old man Solomon was the nigger driver. . . .

The times I hated most was pickin' cotton when the frost was on the bolls. My hands git sore and crack open and bleed. We'd have a li'l fire in the fields and iffen the ones with tender hands couldn't stand it no longer, we'd run and warm our hands a li'l bit. . . .

Sometimes massa let niggers have a li'l patch. They'd raise 'taters or goobers . . . to help fill out on the victuals. . . .

Once in a while they's give us a li'l piece of Sat'day evenin' to wash out clothes. . . . When they'd git through with the clothes on Sat'day evenin's the niggers . . . brung fiddles and guitars and come out and play. The others clap they hands and stomp they feet and we young'uns cut a step round. I was plenty biggity and like to cut a step.

We was scart of Solomon and his whip, though, and he didn't like frolickin'. He didn't like for us niggers to pray, either. We never heared of no church, but us have prayin' in the cabins. . . . I know that Solomon is burnin' in hell today, and it pleasures me to know it.

Once my maw and paw taken me and Katherine after night to slip to 'nother place to a prayin' and singin'. A nigger man with white beard told us a day am comin' when niggers only be slaves of Gawd. We prays for the end of Trib'lation and the end of beatin's and for shoes that fit our feet. We prayed that us niggers could have all we wanted to eat and special for fresh meat. . . .

When we's comin' back from that prayin', I thunk I heared the nigger [tracking] dogs and somebody on horseback. . . . Maw listens and say, "Sho 'nough, them dogs am runnin' and Gawd help us!" Then she and paw . . . take us to a fence corner and stands us up 'gainst the rails and say don't move. . . . They went to the woods, so the hounds chase them and not git us. Me and Katherine stand there, holdin' hands, shakin' so we can hardly stand. We hears the hounds come nearer, but we don't move. They goes after paw and maw, but they circles round to the cabins and gits in. Maw say its the power of Gawd.

Source: Ex-Slave Stories: Mary Reynolds, in "Born in Slavery: Slave Narratives from the Federal Writers' Project, 1936–1938," American Memory, Library of Congress, Texas, vol. 16, pt. 3, pp. 238–41.

Interpret the Evidence

1. What do these documents tell us about the working lives of slaves? What differences and similarities do they reveal across age, sex, and region (Sources 11.6, 11.8, and 11.10)?

2. How does the likely audience for each of these sources affect the way that black writers and the black interviewee portray life in bondage? How might the German artist's portrayal be affected by his likely audience?

3. What were the greatest threats or fears confronted by the enslaved people in these documents and how did they seek to survive or resist these conditions?

4. How did enslaved women and men create a sense of community and culture, and what does this tell us about their views of slaveowners and other whites?

5. In reading across these documents, how does the experience of slavery change over the course of a person's lifetime?

Put It in Context

How would proslavery Southerners respond to the experiences revealed in these documents?

What do the examples of resistance suggest about white efforts to control slaves' behavior?

Imperial Ambitions and Sectional Crises

1842–1861

WINDOW TO THE PAST

William C. Nell, Meeting of Colored Citizens of Boston, September 30, 1850

William C. Nell, a free black Bostonian and well-known abolitionist, fought for the racial integration of schools and government jobs and wrote a history of African Americans in the American Revolution. He also worked for abolitionist newspapers, including the *Liberator*. In September 1850, he served as secretary for a meeting of black activists who encouraged residents to defend themselves should slave catchers appear in Boston.

▶ To discover more about what this primary source can show us, see Source 12.2 on page 402.

Resolved, That the Fugitive Slave Bill, recently adopted by the United States Congress, puts in imminent jeopardy the lives and liberties of ourselves and children; it deprives us of a trial by jury, when seized by the infernal slave-catcher, and by high penalties forbids the assistance of those who would otherwise obey their heart-promptings in our behalf; in making it obligatory upon the marshals to become bloodhounds in pursuit of human prey; leaving us no alternative (thus left without protection) but to be prepared in the emergency for self-defence; therefore, assured that God has no attribute which can take sides with the oppressors, we have counted the cost, and as we prefer *liberty* to *life*, we mutually pledge to defend ourselves and each other in resisting this God-defying and inhuman law, at any and every sacrifice, invoking Heaven's defence of the right.

Library of Congress

After reading this chapter you should be able to:

- Compare the experiences of different groups living in and migrating to the West.

- Explain how geographical expansion heightened sectional conflicts and how those conflicts shaped and were shaped by federal policies like the Compromise of 1850 and the Fugitive Slave Act.

- Analyze the ways that the spread of antislavery sentiments, partisan politics, and federal court decisions intensified sectional divisions.

- Evaluate the importance of John Brown's raid and the election of Abraham Lincoln as President in convincing southern states to secede from the Union.

COMPARING AMERICAN HISTORIES

John C. Frémont, a noted explorer and military leader, rose from humble beginnings. He was born out of wedlock to Anne Beverley Whiting Pryor of Savannah, Georgia, who abandoned her wealthy husband and ran off with a French immigrant. Frémont attended the College of Charleston, where he excelled at mathematics, but was eventually expelled for neglecting his studies. At age twenty, in 1833, he was hired to teach aboard a navy ship through the help of an influential South Carolina politician. He then obtained a surveying position to map new railroad lines and Cherokee lands in Georgia and was

(*left*) **John C. Frémont** Library of Congress
(*right*) **Dred Scott** LC-DIG-ppmsca-03210 and Library of Congress, 3a0841

finally appointed a second lieutenant in the Corps of Topographical Engineers.

In 1840 Lieutenant Frémont moved to Washington, D.C., where he worked on maps and reports based on his surveys. The following year, he eloped with Jessie Benton, the daughter of Missouri senator Thomas Hart Benton. Despite the scandal, Senator Benton supported his son-in-law's selection for a federally funded expedition to the West. In 1842 Frémont and his guide, Kit Carson, led twenty-three men along the emerging Oregon Trail. Two years later, John returned to Washington, where Jessie helped him turn his notes into a vivid report on the Oregon Territory and California. Congress published the report, which inspired a wave of hopeful migrants to head west.

Frémont's success was tainted, however, by a quest for personal glory. On a federal mapping expedition in 1845, he left his post and headed to Sacramento, California. In the winter of 1846, he stirred support among U.S. settlers there for war with Mexico. His brash behavior nearly provoked a bloody battle. Frémont then fled to the Oregon Territory, where he and Kit Carson initiated conflicts with local Indians. As the United States moved closer to war with Mexico, Frémont returned to California to support Anglo-American settlers' efforts to declare the region an independent republic. After the war, Frémont worked tirelessly for California's admission to the Union and served as one of the state's first senators. With his wife's encouragement, he embraced abolition and in 1856 was nominated for president by the new Republican Party.

Dred Scott also traveled the frontier in the 1830s and 1840s, but not of his own free will. Born a slave in Southampton, Virginia around 1800, he and his master, Peter Blow, moved west to Alabama in 1818 and then to St. Louis, Missouri, in 1830. Three years later, Blow sold Scott to Dr. John Emerson, an assistant surgeon in the U.S. army. In 1836 Emerson took Scott to Fort Snelling in the Wisconsin Territory, a free territory. There Scott met Harriet Robinson, a young African American slave. Her master, an Indian agent, allowed the couple to marry in 1837 and transferred ownership of Harriet to Dr. Emerson. When Emerson moved back to

St. Louis, the Scotts returned with him. After the doctor's death in 1843, the couple was hired out to local residents by Emerson's widow.

In April 1846, the Scotts initiated lawsuits to gain their freedom. The Missouri Supreme Court had ruled in earlier cases that slaves who resided for any time in free territory must be freed, and the Scotts had lived and married in Wisconsin. In 1850 the Missouri Circuit Court ruled in the Scotts' favor. However, the Emerson family appealed the decision to the state supreme court, with Harriet's case to follow the outcome of her husband's. Two years later, that court ruled against all precedent and overturned the lower court's decision. Dred Scott then appealed to the U.S. Supreme Court, but it, too, ultimately ruled against the Scotts, leaving them enslaved. ■

Comparing the American histories of John Frémont and Dred Scott demonstrates how the explosive combination of westward expansion and growing regional divisions over the issue of slavery divided the nation by 1861. Whereas Frémont joined expeditions to map and conquer the West, Scott followed the migrations of slave owners and soldiers. Both Frémont and Scott were supported by strong women, and both men advocated government action to end slavery. Only Frémont, however, had the right to vote, run for office, and join the Republican Party. From their different positions, these two men reflected the dramatic changes that occurred as westward expansion pushed the issues of empire and slavery to the center of national debate.

Claiming the West

During the 1830s and 1840s, national debates over slavery intensified. The most important battles now centered on western territories gained through victory in the war with Mexico. Before 1848, government-sponsored expeditions had opened up vast new lands for American pioneers seeking opportunity, and migrants moved west in growing numbers. Then, following the Mexican-American War and the discovery of gold in California, tens of thousands of men rushed to the Pacific coast seeking riches. But the West was already home to a diverse population that included Indians, Mexicans, Mormons, and missionaries. Pioneers converged, and often clashed, with these groups.

Traveling the Overland Trail. In the 1830s a growing number of migrants followed overland trails to the far West. In 1836 Narcissa Whitman and Eliza Spaulding joined a group traveling to the Oregon Territory, the first white women to make the trip. They accompanied their husbands, both Presbyterian ministers, who hoped to convert the region's Indians. Their letters to friends and co-worshippers back east described the rich lands and needy souls in the Walla Walla valley. Such missives were widely shared and encouraged further migration.

The panic of 1837 also prompted families to head west. Thousands of U.S. migrants and European immigrants sought better economic prospects in Oregon, the Rocky Mountain region, and the eastern plains, while Mormons continued to settle in Salt Lake City. Some pioneers opened trading posts where Indians exchanged goods with Anglo-American settlers or with merchants back east. Small settlements developed around these posts and near the expanding system of U.S. forts that dotted the region.

For many pioneers, the journey on the **Oregon Trail** began at St. Louis. From there, they traveled by wagon train across the Great Plains and the Rocky Mountains to the Pacific coast. By 1860 some 350,000 Americans had made the journey, claimed land from the Mississippi River to the Pacific, and transformed the United States into an expanding empire.

Because the journey west required funds for wagons and supplies, most pioneers were of middling status. The majority of pioneers made the three- to six-month journey with family members, to help share the labor. Men, mainly farmers, comprised some 60 percent of these western migrants, but women and children traveled in significant numbers, often alongside relatives or neighbors from back east. Some courageous families headed west alone, but most traveled in wagon trains—from a few wagons to a few dozen—that provided support and security.

Explore ▶

See Source 12.1 for one account of the journey west.

Traditional gender roles often broke down on the trail, and even conventional domestic tasks posed novel problems. Women had to cook unfamiliar food over open fires in all kinds of weather and with only a few pots and utensils. They washed laundry in rivers or streams and on the plains hauled water from great distances. Wood, too, was scarce on the plains, and women and children gathered buffalo dung (called "chips") for fuel. Men frequently had to gather food rather than hunt and fish, or they had to learn to catch strange (and sometimes dangerous) animals, such as jack rabbits and rattlesnakes. Few men were prepared for the dangerous work of floating wagons across rivers. Nor were many of them expert in shoeing horses or fixing wagon wheels, tasks that were performed by skilled artisans at home.

Emigrant Party Headed to California, 1850   This hand-colored engraving of a wagon train heading through a mountain pass shows the presence of many family groups and the need for many adults and children to walk and carry goods for parts of the journey. Presenting a wide rolling trail on a clear day, it does not capture the many obstacles faced by pioneers crossing the Rocky Mountains. Library of Congress, LC-DIG-ppmsca-02887

Expectations changed dramatically when men took ill or died. Then wives often drove the wagon, gathered or hunted for food, and learned to repair axles and other wagon parts. When large numbers of men were injured or ill, women might serve as scouts and guides or pick up guns to defend wagons under attack by Indians or wild animals. Yet despite their growing burdens, pioneer women gained little power over decision making. Moreover, the addition of men's jobs to women's responsibilities was rarely reciprocated. Few men cooked, did laundry, or cared for children on the trail.

GUIDED ANALYSIS

Elizabeth Smith Geer | Oregon Trail Diary, 1847

Like thousands of other families, Elizabeth and Cornelius Smith and their seven children set out for the Oregon Territory in the spring of 1847. They fared well through the summer, but in the fall heavy rains made things difficult. In November Cornelius became sick, but the Smiths arrived in Portland, Oregon by Thanksgiving. However, Cornelius died two months later, and in 1849 Elizabeth married Joseph Geer, the father of ten children whose wife also died after journeying across the Oregon Trail.

Source 12.1

November 18.

It rains and snows. We start around the falls this morning with our wagons. We have five miles to go. I carry my babe and lead, or rather carry another, through snow, mud, and water almost to my knees. It is the worst road a team could possibly travel. I went ahead with my children and I was afraid to look behind me for fear of seeing the wagons overturn into the mud and water with everything in them. My children gave out with cold and fatigue and could not travel, and the boys had to unhitch the oxen and bring them and carry the children on to camp. I was so cold and numb that I could not tell by the feeling that I had any feet. We started this morning at sunrise and did not camp until after dark, and there was not one dry thread on one of us—not even on the babe. I had carried my babe and I was so fatigued that I could scarcely speak or step. When I got here I found my husband lying in Welch's wagon very sick. He had brought Mrs. Polk down the day before and was taken sick. We had to stay up all night for our wagons were left halfway back. I have not told half we suffered. I am not adequate to the task.

How did weather affect the ability of families to travel on the Oregon Trail?

How did children both assist and create problems for their parents?

How did the roles of husbands and wives change during the journey?

Source: Theodore Thurston Geer, *Fifty Years in Oregon* (New York: Neale, 1912), 146.

Put It in Context

Despite widespread fear of Indian attacks on the trail, what were the most serious dangers that men and women pioneers faced on the journey west?

In one area, however, relative equality reigned. Men and women were equally susceptible to disease, injury, and death during the journey. Accidents, gunshot wounds, drownings, broken bones, and infections affected people on every wagon train. Some groups were struck as well by deadly epidemics of measles or cholera. In addition, about 20 percent of women on the overland trail became pregnant, which posed even greater dangers than usual given the lack of medical services and sanitation. About the same percentage of women lost children or spouses on the trip west. Overall, about one in ten to fifteen migrants died on the western journey.

The Gold Rush.

Despite the hazards, more and more Americans traveled overland to the Pacific coast, although only a few thousand Americans initially settled in California. Some were agents sent there by eastern merchants to purchase fine leather made from the hides of Spanish cattle. Several agents married into families of elite Mexican ranchers, known as Californios, and adopted their culture, even converting to Catholicism.

However, the Anglo-American presence in California changed dramatically after 1848 when gold was discovered at Sutter's Mill in northeastern California. Beginning in 1849 news of the discovery brought tens of thousands of settlers from the eastern United States, South America, Europe, and Asia. In the **gold rush,** "forty-niners" raced to claim riches in California, and men vastly outnumbered women.

The rapid influx of gold seekers heightened tensions between newly arrived whites, local Indians, and Californios. Forty-niners confiscated land owned by Californios,

Gold Rush Miners, 1849
These prospectors were two of some 80,000 who traveled to California after gold was discovered. While many Chinese miners were run off their claims, these two men, dressed in a mix of Chinese and American attire, panned for gold with the tools of their trade—pickax, hoe, and pan. A shed in the background may have served as their home. Granger Collection/NYC

shattered the fragile ecosystem in the California mountains, and forced Mexican and Indian men to labor for low wages or a promised share in uncertain profits. New conflicts erupted when migrants from Asia and South America joined the search for wealth. Forty-niners from the United States regularly stole from and assaulted these foreign-born competitors.

The gold rush also led to the increased exploitation of women as thousands of male migrants demanded food, shelter, laundry, and medical care. While some California women earned a good living by renting rooms, cooking meals, washing clothes, or working as prostitutes, many faced exploitation and abuse. Indian and Mexican women were especially vulnerable to sexual harassment and rape, while Chinese women were imported specifically to provide sexual services for male miners.

Chinese men were also victims of abuse by whites, who ran them off their claims. Yet some Chinese men used the skills traditionally assigned them in their homeland—cooking and washing clothes—to earn a far steadier income than prospecting for gold could provide. Other men also took advantage of the demand for goods and services. Levi Strauss, a German Jewish immigrant, moved from New York to San Francisco to open a dry-goods store in 1853. He soon made his fortune producing canvas and then denim pants that could withstand harsh weather and long wear.

A Crowded Land.
While U.S. promoters of migration continued to depict the West as open territory, it was in fact the site of competing national ambitions in the late 1840s. Despite granting statehood to Texas in 1845 and winning the war against Mexico in 1848, the United States had to battle for control of the Great Plains with powerful Indian nations, like the Sioux and Cheyenne (Map 12.1).

Although attacks on wagon trains were rare, Indians did threaten frontier settlements throughout the 1840s and 1850s. Settlers often retaliated, and U.S. army troops joined them in efforts to push Indians back from areas newly claimed by whites. Yet in many parts of the West, Indians were as powerful as whites, and they did not cede territory without a fight. The Reverend Marcus Whitman and his wife, Narcissa, became victims of their success in promoting western settlement when pioneers brought a deadly measles epidemic to the region, killing thousands of Cayuse and Nez Percé Indians. In 1847, convinced that whites brought disease but no useful medicine, a group of Cayuse Indians killed the Whitmans and ten other white settlers.

Yet violence against whites could not stop the flood of migrants into the Oregon Territory. Indeed, attacks by one Indian tribe were often used to justify assaults on any Indian tribe. Thus John Frémont and Kit Carson, whose party was attacked by Modoc Indians in Oregon in 1846, retaliated by destroying a Klamath Indian village and killing its inhabitants. The defeat of Mexico and the discovery of gold in California only intensified such conflicts.

Although Indians and white Americans were the main players in many battles, Indian nations also competed with each other. In the southern plains, drought and disease exacerbated those conflicts in the late 1840s and dramatically changed the balance of power there. In 1845 the southern plains were struck by a dry spell, which lasted on and off until the mid-1860s. In 1848, smallpox ravaged Comanche villages, and a virulent strain of cholera was introduced into the region the next year by forty-niners traveling to California. In the late 1840s, the Comanche nation was the largest Indian group, with about twenty thousand members; by the mid-1850s, less than half that number remained.

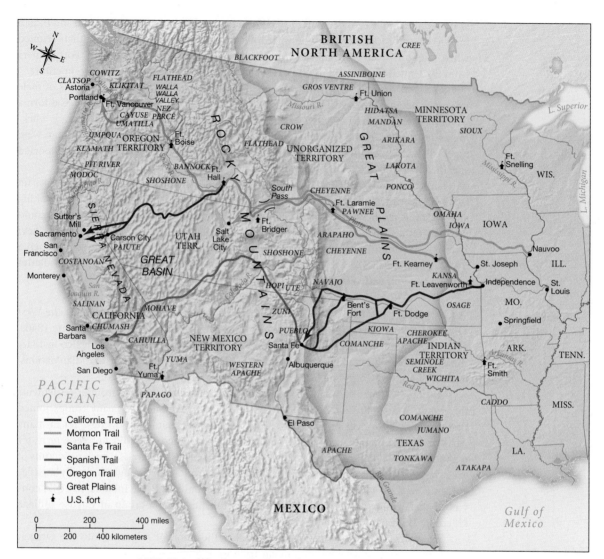

MAP 12.1   Western Trails and Indian Nations, c. 1850

As wagon trains and traders journeyed west in rapidly growing numbers during the 1830s and 1840s, the United States established forts along the most well-traveled routes. At the same time, Indians claimed or were forced into new areas through the pressure of Indian removals, white settlement, and the demands of hunting, trade, and agriculture.

Yet the collapse of the Comanche empire was not simply the result of outside forces. As the Comanche expanded their trade networks and incorporated smaller Indian nations into their orbit, they overextended their reach. Most important, they allowed too many bison to be killed to meet the needs of their Indian allies and the demand of Anglo-American and European traders. The Comanche also herded growing numbers of horses, which required expansive grazing lands and winter havens in the river valleys and forced the bison onto more marginal lands. Opening the Santa Fe Trail to commerce multiplied the problems by destroying vegetation and polluting springs, thereby diminishing resources in more of the region. The prolonged drought completed the depopulation of the bison on the southern plains. Without bison, the Comanche lost a trade item critical to sustaining their commercial and political control. As the Comanche empire collapsed, former Indian allies sought to advance their own interests. These developments reignited Indian wars on the southern plains as tens of thousands of pioneers poured through the region.

African Americans also participated in these western struggles. Many were held as slaves by southeastern tribes forced into Indian Territory, while others were freed and married Seminole or Cherokee spouses. The Creeks proved harsh masters, prompting some slaves to escape north to free states or south to Mexican or Comanche territory. Yet as southern officers in the U.S. army moved to frontier outposts, they carried more slaves into the region. Many, including Dr. John Emerson, changed posts frequently, taking slaves like Dred Scott into both slave and free territories. Still, it was white planters who brought the greatest numbers of African Americans into Texas, Missouri, and Kansas, pushing the frontier of slavery ever westward. At the same time, some free blacks joined the migration voluntarily in hopes of finding better economic opportunities and less overt racism in the West.

REVIEW & RELATE

- Why did Americans go west in the 1830s and 1840s, and what was the journey like?

- What groups competed for land and resources in the West? How did disease, drought, and violence shape this competition?

Expansion and the Politics of Slavery

The place of slavery in the West aroused intense political debates as territories in the region began to seek statehood. Debates over the eradication of slavery and limits on its expansion had shaped the highly contested presidential election of 1848. After the Mexican-American War, the debate intensified and focused more specifically on slavery's westward expansion. Each time a territory achieved the requirements for statehood, a new crisis erupted. To resolve these crises required strong political leadership, judicial moderation, and a spirit of compromise among the American people. None of these conditions prevailed. Instead, passage of the Fugitive Slave Act in 1850 aroused deeper hostilities, and President Franklin Pierce (1853–1857) encouraged further expansion but failed to address the crises that ensued.

California and the Compromise of 1850. In the winter of 1849, just before President Zachary Taylor's March inauguration, California applied for admission to the Union as a free state. Some California political leaders opposed slavery on principle. Others wanted to "save" the state for whites by outlawing slavery, discouraging free black migration, and restricting the rights of Mexican, Indian, and Chinese residents. Yet the internal debates among Californians were not uppermost in the minds of politicians. Southerners were concerned about the impact of California's free-state status on the sectional balance in Congress, while northern Whigs were shocked when President Taylor suggested that slavery should be allowed anywhere in the West.

The United States Senate, A.D. 1850 This print captures seventy-three-year-old Henry Clay presenting his Compromise of 1850 to colleagues in the Old Senate Chamber. An aged John C. Calhoun, seated to the left of the Speaker's chair, denounced the compromise, as did antislavery Whigs and Free-Soilers. Daniel Webster, sitting to the left of Clay, offered a passionate defense but failed to gain the compromise's passage. Library of Congress, 3g01724

Other debates percolated in Congress at the same time. Many Northerners were horrified by the spectacle of slavery and slave trading in the nation's capital and argued that it damaged America's international reputation. Southerners, meanwhile, complained that the Fugitive Slave Act of 1793 was being widely ignored in the North. A boundary dispute between Texas and New Mexico irritated western legislators, and Texas continued to claim that debts it accrued while an independent republic and during the Mexican-American War should be assumed by the federal government.

Senator Henry Clay of Kentucky, the Whig leader who had hammered out the Missouri Compromise in 1819 and 1820, again tried to resolve the many conflicts that stalled congressional action. He offered a compromise by which California would be admitted as a free state; the remaining land acquired from Mexico would be divided into two territories—New Mexico and Utah—and slavery there would be decided by popular sovereignty; the border dispute between New Mexico and Texas would be decided in favor of New Mexico, but the federal government would assume Texas's war debts; the slave trade (but not slavery) would be abolished in the District of Columbia; and a new and more effective fugitive slave law would be approved. Although Clay's compromise offered something to everyone, his colleagues did not immediately embrace it.

By March 1850, after months of passionate debate, the sides remained sharply divided, as did their most esteemed leaders. John C. Calhoun, a proslavery senator from South Carolina, refused to support any compromise that allowed Congress to decide the fate of slavery in the western territories. William H. Seward, an antislavery Whig senator from New York, proclaimed he could not support a compromise that forced Northerners to help hunt down fugitives from slavery. While Daniel Webster, a Massachusetts Whig, urged fellow senators to support the compromise to preserve the Union, Congress adjourned with the fate of California undecided.

Before the Senate reconvened in September 1850, however, the political landscape changed in unexpected ways. Henry Clay retired the previous spring, leaving the Capitol with his last great legislative effort unfinished. On March 31, 1850, Calhoun died; his absence from the Senate made compromise more likely. Then in July, President Taylor died unexpectedly, and his vice president, Millard Fillmore, became president. Fillmore then appointed Webster as secretary of state, removing him from the Senate as well.

In fall 1850, with President Fillmore's support, a younger cohort of senators and representatives steered the **Compromise of 1850** through Congress, one clause at a time. This tactic allowed legislators to support only those parts of the compromise they found palatable. In the end, all the provisions passed, and Fillmore quickly signed the bills into law.

The Compromise of 1850, like the Missouri Compromise thirty years earlier, fended off a sectional crisis but signaled future problems. Would popular sovereignty prevail when later territories sought admission to the Union, and would Northerners abide by a fugitive slave law that called on them to aid directly in the capture of runaway slaves?

The Fugitive Slave Act Inspires Northern Protest.

The fugitive slave laws of 1793 and 1824 mandated that all states aid in apprehending and returning runaway slaves to their owners. The **1850** was different in two important respects. First, it eliminated jury trials for alleged fugitives. Second, the law required individual citizens, not just state officials, to help return runaways. The act angered many Northerners who believed that the federal government had gone too far in protecting the rights of slaveholders and thereby aroused sympathy for the abolitionist cause.

Before 1850, free blacks led the effort to aid fugitives, including David Ruggles in New York City; William Still in Philadelphia; and, after his own successful escape, Frederick Douglass. Among their staunchest allies were white Quakers such as Amy and Isaac Post in Rochester, Thomas Garrett in Chester County, Pennsylvania, and Levi and Catherine Coffin in Newport, Indiana. Political abolitionists, like wealthy reformer Gerrit Smith, of Peterboro, New York, also aided the cause

Following passage of the Fugitive Slave Act, the number of slave owners and hired slave catchers pursuing fugitives increased dramatically. But so, too, did the number of northern abolitionists helping blacks escape. Once escaped slaves crossed into free territory, most contacted free blacks or sought out Quaker, Baptist, or Methodist meetinghouses whose members might be sympathetic to their cause. They then began the journey along the underground railroad, from house to house or barn to barn, until they found safe haven. A small number of fortunate slaves were led north by fugitives like Harriet Tubman, who returned south repeatedly to free dozens of family members and other enslaved men and women. Abolitionists purchased the freedom of a few others, including sisters Mary and Emily Edmondson who had been sold to slave traders after a failed escape attempt in 1848. Most fugitives followed

Anti-Fugitive Slave Law Convention, Cazenovia, New York, 1850 This rare daguerreotype captures abolitionists, outraged over the Fugitive Slave Law, at a massive protest meeting. Some 2,000 participants met in an apple orchard. Frederick Douglass sits at the left side of the table. The Edmondson sisters, in plaid shawls, stand behind him on either side of Gerrit Smith. The sisters were among fifty former slaves who attended the meeting. Digital image courtesy of the Getty's Open Content Program

disparate paths, depending on "conductors" to get them from one stop to the next. Despite its limits, the underground railroad was an important resource for fugitives seeking refuge in Canada or hoping to blend into free black communities stateside.

Free blacks were endangered by the claim that slaves hid themselves in their midst. In Chester County, Pennsylvania, on the Maryland border, newspapers reported on at least a dozen free blacks who were kidnapped or arrested as runaways in the first three months of 1851. One provision of the Fugitive Slave Act encouraged such arrests: Commissioners were paid $10 for each slave sent back but only $5 if a slave was not returned. Without the right to a trial, a free black could easily be sent south as a fugitive.

At the same time, a growing number of Northerners challenged the federal government's right to enforce the law. Blacks and whites organized protest meetings throughout the free states. At a meeting in Boston in 1851, William Lloyd Garrison denounced the law: "We execrate it, we spit upon it, we trample it under our feet." On July 5, 1852, Frederick Douglass asked a mixed-race audience, "What to the American slave, is your 4th of July? I answer, a day that reveals to him . . . the gross injustice and cruelty to which he is the constant victim." He then declared, "There is not a nation on the earth guilty of practices more shocking and bloody than are the people of these United States at this very hour."

Some abolitionists established vigilance committees to rescue fugitives who had been arrested. In Syracuse in October 1851, Jermaine Loguen, Samuel Ward, and the Reverend Samuel J. May led a well-organized crowd that broke into a Syracuse courthouse and rescued a fugitive known as Jerry. They successfully hid him from authorities before spiriting him to Canada.

Meanwhile Americans continued to debate the law's effects. John Frémont, one of the first two senators from California, helped defeat a federal bill that would have imposed harsher penalties on those who assisted runaways. And Congress felt growing pressure to calm the situation, including from foreign officials who were horrified by the violence required to sustain slavery in the United States. Black abolitionists denounced the Fugitive Slave Act across Canada, Ireland, and England, intensifying foreign concern over the law. Great Britain and France had abolished slavery in their West Indian colonies and could not support what they saw as extreme policies to keep the institution alive in the United States. Yet southern slaveholders refused to compromise further, as did northern abolitionists.

Explore ▶

See Sources 12.2 and 12.3 for two responses to the Fugitive Slave Act.

Pierce Encourages U.S. Expansion.

In the presidential election of 1852, the Whigs and the Democrats tried once again to appeal to voters across the North-South divide by running candidates who either skirted the slavery issue or voiced ambiguous views. The Democrats nominated Franklin Pierce of New Hampshire. A northern opponent of abolition, Pierce had served in Congress from 1833 to 1842 and in the U.S. army during the Mexican-American War. The Whigs rejected President Millard Fillmore, who had angered many by supporting popular sovereignty and vigorous enforcement of the Fugitive Slave Act. They turned instead to General Winfield Scott of Virginia. General Scott had never expressed any proslavery views and had served with distinction in the war against Mexico. The Whigs thus hoped to gain southern support while maintaining their northern base. The Free-Soil Party, too, hoped to expand its appeal by nominating John Hale, a New Hampshire Democrat.

Franklin Pierce's eventual victory left the Whigs and the Free-Soilers in disarray. Seeking a truly proslavery party, a third of southern Whigs threw their support to the Democrats in the election. Many Democrats who had supported Free-Soilers in 1848 were driven to vote for Pierce by their enthusiasm over the admission of California as a free state. But despite the Democratic triumph, that party also remained fragile. The nation now faced some of its gravest challenges under a president with limited political experience and no firm base of support and a cabinet that included men of widely differing views. When confronted with difficult decisions, Pierce received contradictory advice and generally pursued his own expansionist vision.

Early in his administration, Pierce focused on expanding U.S. trade and extending the "civilizing" power of the nation to other parts of the world. Trade with China had declined in the 1840s, but the United States had begun commercial negotiations with Japan in 1846. These came to fruition in 1854, when U.S. emissary Commodore Matthew C. Perry, a renowned naval officer and founder of the Naval Engineer Corps, obtained the first formal mutual trade agreement with Japan. Within four years, the United States had expanded commercial ties and enhanced diplomatic relations with Japan, in large part by supporting the island nation against its traditional enemies in China, Russia, and Europe.

Pierce had rejected Commodore Perry's offer to take military possession of Formosa and other territories near Japan, but he was willing to consider conquests in the Caribbean and Central America. For decades, U.S. politicians, particularly Southerners, had looked to gain control of Cuba, Mexico, and Nicaragua. A "Young America" movement within the Democratic Party imagined manifest destiny reaching southward as well as westward. In hopes of stirring up rebellious Cubans against Spanish rule, some Democrats joined with private adventurers to send three unauthorized expeditions, known as **filibusters**, to invade Cuba. In 1854 the capture of one of the filibustering ships led to an international incident. Spanish officials confiscated the ship, and southern Democrats urged Pierce to

The Fugitive Slave Law Contested

The Fugitive Slave Law was enacted on September 18, 1850, and soon after African Americans in Boston called a meeting to discuss their response (Source 12.2). Having heard rumors of arrests elsewhere, participants demanded the right to defend themselves. On February 15, 1851, local abolitionists, led by Lewis Hayden, rescued fugitive Shadrach Minkins from the Boston federal courthouse and spirited him to Canada. Three days later, President Millard Fillmore issued a proclamation demanding that citizens obey the law or be prosecuted (Source 12.3). Seven black men and two whites were arrested in Boston, but all were acquitted by juries.

Source 12.2

William C. Nell | Meeting of Colored Citizens of Boston, September 30, 1850

The Chairman [Lewis Hayden] announced, as a prominent feature in calling the present meeting—Congress having passed the infamous Fugitive Slave Bill—the adoption of ways and means for the protection of those in Boston liable to be seized by the prowling man-thief. He said that safety was to be obtained only by an united and persevering resistance of this ungodly, anti-republican law. . . .

The following resolutions were submitted, as a platform for vigilant action in the trial hour:—

Resolved, That the Fugitive Slave Bill, recently adopted by the United States Congress, puts in imminent jeopardy the lives and liberties of ourselves and our children; it deprives us of trial by jury, when seized by the infernal slave-catcher, and by high penalties forbids the

assistance of those who would otherwise obey their heart-promptings in our behalf; in making it obligatory upon marshals to become bloodhounds in pursuit of human prey; leaving us no alternative . . . but to be prepared in the emergency for self-defense; therefore, assured that God has no attribute which can take sides with oppressors, we have counted the cost, and as we prefer *liberty* to *life*, we mutually pledge to defend ourselves and each other in resisting this God-defying and inhuman law, at any and every sacrifice, invoking Heaven's defense of the right.

Resolved, That . . . eternal vigilance is the price of liberty, and that they who would be free, themselves must strike the first blow.

Source: "Meeting of the Colored Citizens of Boston," *Liberator*, October 4, 1850.

---

seek an apology and redress from Spain. But many northern Democrats rejected any effort to obtain another slave state, and Pierce was forced to renounce the filibusters.

Other politicians still pressured Spain to sell Cuba to the United States. These included Pierce's secretary of state, William Marcy, and the U.S. ambassador to Great Britain, James Buchanan, as well as the ministers to France and Spain. In October 1854 these ministers met in Ostend, Belgium and sent a letter to Pierce urging the conquest of Cuba. When the **Ostend Manifesto** was leaked to the press, Northerners were outraged. They viewed the episode as "a dirty plot" to gain more slave territory and forced Pierce to give up plans to obtain Cuba. In 1855 a private adventurer named William Walker, who had organized four filibusters to Nicaragua, invaded that country and set himself up as

Source 12.3

President Millard Fillmore | Proclamation 56 Calling on Citizens to Assist in the Recapture of a Fugitive Slave, February 18, 1851

Whereas information has been received that sundry lawless persons, principally persons of color, combined and confederated together for the purpose of opposing by force the execution of the laws of the United States, did, at Boston, in Massachusetts, on the 15th of this month, make a violent assault on the marshal or deputy marshals of the United States for the district of Massachusetts, in the court-house, and did overcome the said officers, and did by force rescue from their custody a person arrested as a fugitive slave, and then and there a prisoner lawfully holden by the said marshal or deputy marshals of the United States, and other scandalous outrages did commit in violation of law:

Now, therefore, to the end that the authority of the laws may be maintained and those concerned in violating them brought to immediate and condign punishment, I have issued this my proclamation, calling on all well-disposed citizens to rally to the support of the laws of their country, and requiring and commanding all officers, civil and military, and all other persons, civil or military, who shall be found within the vicinity of this outrage, to be aiding and assisting by all means in their power in quelling this and other such combinations and assisting the marshal and his deputies in recapturing the above-mentioned prisoner; and I do especially direct that prosecutions be commenced against all persons who shall have made themselves aiders or abettors in or to this flagitious offense.

Source: *The Messages and Papers of the Presidents, 1789–1913* (Washington, DC: U.S. Government Printing Office, 1913), 988.

Interpret the Evidence

1. How did African Americans in Boston justify their right to defend themselves in defiance of the Fugitive Slave Law, and how would they have responded to Fillmore's Proclamation 56?
2. How does President Fillmore characterize the Boston abolitionists who sought to free fugitives like Shadrach Minkins, and what consequences does he propose for flouting the law?

Put It in Context

What do the conflicts over implementation of the Fugitive Slave Law in Boston suggest about the long-term impact of the law?

ruler. He then invited southern planters to come to Nicaragua and establish plantations. Pierce and many Democrats endorsed his plan, but neighboring Hondurans forced Walker from power in 1857 and executed him three years later. Although Pierce's expansionist dreams failed, his efforts heightened sectional tensions.

REVIEW & RELATE

- What steps did legislators take in the 1840s and early 1850s to resolve the issue of the expansion of slavery? Were they successful?
- How were slavery and American imperialist ambitions intertwined in the 1840s and 1850s?

Sectional Crises Intensify

The political crises of the early 1850s created a lively trade in anti-slavery literature. This cultural turmoil, combined with the weakness and fragmentation of the existing political parties, helped give rise to the Republican Party in 1854. The Republican Party soon absorbed enough Free-Soilers, Whigs, and northern Democrats to become a major political force. The events that drove these cultural and political developments included the publication of *Uncle Tom's Cabin*, continued challenges to the Fugitive Slave Act, a battle over the admission of Kansas to the Union, and a Supreme Court ruling in the *Dred Scott* case.

Popularizing Antislavery Sentiment.

The Fugitive Slave Act forced Northerners to reconsider their role in sustaining the institution of slavery. In 1852, just months before Franklin Pierce was elected president, their concerns were heightened by the publication of the novel **Uncle Tom's Cabin** by Harriet Beecher Stowe. Stowe's father, Lyman Beecher, and brother Henry were among the nation's leading evangelical clergy, and her sister Catharine had opposed Cherokee removal and promoted women's education. Stowe was inspired to write *Uncle Tom's Cabin* by passage of the Fugitive Slave Act in 1850. Published in both serial and book forms, the novel created a national sensation.

Uncle Tom's Cabin built on accounts by former slaves as well as tales gathered by abolitionist lecturers and writers, which gained growing attention in the North. The autobiographies of Frederick Douglass (1845), Josiah Henson (1849), and Henry Bibb (1849) set the stage for Stowe's novel. So, too, did the expansion of the antislavery press, which by the 1850s included dozens of newspapers. Antislavery poems and songs also circulated widely and were performed at abolitionist conventions and fund-raising fairs.

Still, nothing captured the public's attention as did *Uncle Tom's Cabin*. Read by millions in the United States and England and translated into French and German, the book reached a mass audience. Its sentimental portrait of saintly slaves and its vivid depiction of cruel masters and overseers offered white Northerners a way to identify with enslaved blacks. Although some African Americans expressed frustration that a white woman's fictional account gained far more readers than their factual narratives, most recognized the book's important contribution to the antislavery cause.

Yet the real-life stories of fugitive slaves could often surpass their fictional counterparts for drama. In May 1854 abolitionists sought to free fugitive slave Anthony Burns from a Boston courthouse, where his master was attempting to reclaim him. They failed to secure his release, and Burns was soon marched to the docks to be shipped south. Twenty-two companies of state militia held back tens of thousands of angry Bostonians who lined the streets. A year later, supporters purchased Burns's freedom from his master, but the incident raised anguished questions among local residents. In a city that was home to so many intellectual, religious, and antislavery leaders, Bostonians wondered how they had come so far in aiding and abetting slavery.

The Kansas-Nebraska Act Stirs Dissent.

Kansas provided the first test of the effects of *Uncle Tom's Cabin* on northern sentiments toward slavery's expansion. As white Americans displaced Indian nations from their homelands, diverse groups of Indians settled in the northern half of the Louisiana Territory. This unorganized region had once been considered beyond the reach of white settlement, but Democratic senator Stephen Douglas of Illinois was eager to have a transcontinental railroad run through his home state. He needed the federal government to gain control of land along the route he proposed and thus argued for the establishment of a vast Nebraska Territory. But to support his plan, Douglas also needed to convince southern congressmen, who sought a route through their own region. According to the Missouri Compromise, states lying above the southern border of Missouri were automatically free. To gain southern support, Douglas sought to reopen the question of slavery in the territories.

In January 1854 Douglas introduced the **Kansas-Nebraska Act** to Congress. The act extinguished Indians' long-held treaty rights in the region and repealed the Missouri Compromise. Two new territories—Kansas and Nebraska—would be carved out of the unorganized lands, and voters in each would determine whether to enter the nation as a slave or a free state (Map 12.2). The act spurred intense opposition from most Whigs and some northern Democrats who wanted to retain the Missouri Compromise line. Months of fierce debate followed, but the bill was ultimately voted into law.

Passage of the Kansas-Nebraska Act enraged many Northerners who considered the dismantling of the Missouri Compromise a sign of the rising power of the South. They were infuriated that the South—or what some now called the "Slave Power"—had again benefited from northern politicians' willingness to compromise. Although few of these opponents considered the impact of the law on Indians, the act also shattered treaty provisions that had protected the Arapaho, Cheyenne, Ponco, Pawnee, and Sioux nations. These Plains Indians lost half the land they had held by treaty as thousands of settlers swarmed into the newly organized territories. In the fall of 1855, conflicts between white settlers and Indians erupted across the Great Plains. The U.S. army then sent six hundred troops to retaliate against a Sioux village, killing eighty-five residents of Blue Water in the Nebraska Territory and triggering continued violence throughout the region.

As tensions escalated across the nation, Americans faced the 1854 congressional elections. The Democrats, increasingly viewed as supporting the priorities of slaveholders, lost badly in the North. But the Whig Party also proved weak, having failed to stop the Slave Power from extending its leverage over federal policies. A third party, the American Party, was founded in the early 1850s and attracted native-born workers and Protestant farmers who were drawn to its anti-immigrant and anti-Catholic message. They continued to seek limits on immigrants' political power and cultural influence. Responding to these political realignments, another new party, led by antislavery Whigs and Free-Soilers—the **Republican Party**—was founded in the spring of 1854. Among its early members was a Whig politician from Illinois, Abraham Lincoln.

Although established only months before the fall 1854 elections, the Republican Party gained significant support in the Midwest, particularly in state and local campaigns. Meanwhile the American Party gained control of the Massachusetts legislature and nearly captured New York. These victories marked the demise of the Whigs and the Second Party System. Unlike the Whig Party, however, with its national constituency, the Republican Party was rooted solely in the North. Like Free-Soilers, the Republicans argued that slavery should not be extended into new territories. But the Republicans also advocated a program of commercial and industrial development and internal improvements to attract a broader base than earlier antislavery parties. The Republican Party attracted both ardent abolitionists and men whose main concern was keeping western territories open to free white men. This latter group was more than willing to accept slavery where it already existed.

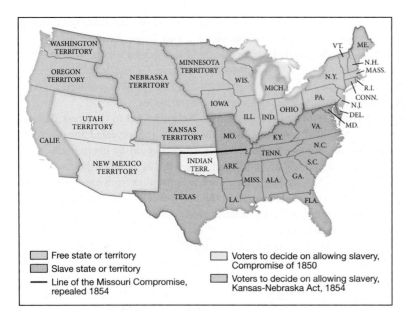

MAP 12.2 Kansas-Nebraska Territory

From 1820 on, Congress attempted to limit sectional conflict. But the Missouri Compromise (1820) and the Compromise of 1850 failed to resolve disagreements over slavery's expansion. The creation of the Kansas and Nebraska territories in 1854 heightened sectional conflict and ensured increased hostilities with Indians in the region.

□ Free state or territory
□ Slave state or territory
— Line of the Missouri Compromise, repealed 1854
□ Voters to decide on allowing slavery, Compromise of 1850
□ Voters to decide on allowing slavery, Kansas-Nebraska Act, 1854

Bleeding Kansas and the Election of 1856. The 1854 congressional elections exacerbated sectional tensions by bringing representatives from a strictly northern party—the Republicans—into Congress. But the conflicts over slavery reached far beyond the nation's capital. After passage of the Kansas-Nebraska Act, advocates and opponents of slavery poured into Kansas in anticipation of a vote on whether the state would enter the Union slave or free.

As Kansas prepared to hold its referendum, settlers continued to arrive daily, making it difficult to determine who was eligible to vote. In 1855 Southerners installed a proslavery government at Shawnee Mission, while abolitionists established a stronghold in Lawrence. Violence erupted when proslavery settlers invaded Lawrence, killing one resident, demolishing newspaper offices, and plundering shops and homes. Fearing that southern settlers in Kansas were better armed than antislavery Northerners in the territory, eastern abolitionists raised funds to ship rifles to Kansas.

In 1856 longtime abolitionist John Brown carried his own rifles to Kansas. Four of his sons already lived in the territory. To retaliate for proslavery attacks on Lawrence, the Browns and two friends kidnapped five proslavery advocates from their homes along Pottawatomie Creek and hacked them to death. The so-called Pottawatomie Massacre infuriated southern settlers, who then drew up the Lecompton Constitution, which declared Kansas a slave state. President Pierce made his support of the proslavery government clear, but Congress remained divided. While Congress deliberated, armed battles continued. In the first six months of 1856, more than fifty settlers—on both sides of the conflict—were killed in what became known as **Bleeding Kansas.**

Fighting also broke out on the floor of Congress. Republican senator Charles Sumner of Massachusetts delivered an impassioned speech against the continued expansion of the Slave Power. He launched scathing attacks on planter politicians like South Carolina senator Andrew Butler. Butler's nephew, Preston Brooks, a Democratic member of the House of Representatives, rushed to defend his family's honor. He assaulted Sumner in the Senate chamber, beating him

John Doy and His Rescue Party, Kansas, 1859   John Doy and his son Charles were captured in Kansas in January 1859 while assisting thirteen slaves to escape their owners. Taken to Missouri, Charles was set free, but his father was sentenced to five years in prison for abducting slaves. Abolitionist friends freed him, and the group (with John Doy seated) posed for this picture when they reached Lawrence. Kansas State Historical Society

senseless with a cane. Sumner, who never fully recovered from his injuries, was considered a martyr in the North. Meanwhile Brooks was celebrated throughout South Carolina.

The presidential election of 1856 began amid an atmosphere poisoned by violence and recrimination. The Democratic Party nominated James Buchanan of Pennsylvania, a proslavery advocate. Western hero John C. Frémont headed the Republican Party ticket. The American Party, in its final presidential contest, selected former president Millard Fillmore as its candidate. The strength of nativism in politics was waning, however, and Fillmore won only the state of Maryland. Meanwhile Frémont attracted cheering throngs as he traveled across the nation. Large numbers of women turned out to see Jessie Frémont, the first presidential candidate's wife to play a significant role in a campaign. Frémont carried most of the North and the West. Buchanan captured the South along with Pennsylvania, Indiana, and Illinois. Although Buchanan won only 45.2 percent of the popular vote, he received a comfortable majority in the electoral college, securing his victory. The nation was becoming increasingly divided along sectional lines, and President Buchanan would do little to resolve these differences.

The *Dred Scott* Decision. Just two days after Buchanan's inauguration, the Supreme Court finally announced its decision in the *Dred Scott* case (see "Comparing American Histories"). Led by Chief Justice Roger Taney, a proslavery Southerner, the majority ruled that a slave was not a citizen and therefore could not sue in court. Indeed, Taney claimed that black men had no rights that a white man was bound to respect. The ruling annulled Scott's suit and meant that he and his wife remained enslaved. But the ruling went further. The **Dred Scott decision** declared that Congress had no constitutional authority to exclude slavery from any territory, thereby nullifying the Missouri Compromise and any future effort to restrict slavery's expansion. The ruling outraged many Northerners, who were now convinced that a Slave Power conspiracy had taken hold of the federal government, including the judiciary.

In 1858, when Stephen Douglas faced reelection to the U.S. Senate, the Republican Party nominated Abraham Lincoln, a successful lawyer from Springfield, Illinois, to oppose him. The candidates participated in seven debates in which they explained their positions on slavery in the wake of the *Dred Scott* decision. Pointing to the landmark ruling, Lincoln asked Douglas how he could favor popular sovereignty, which allowed residents to keep slavery out of a territory, and yet support the *Dred Scott* decision, which protected slavery in all territories. Douglas claimed that if residents did not adopt local legislation to protect slaveholders' property, they could thereby exclude slavery for all practical purposes. At the same time, he accused Lincoln of advocating "negro equality," a position that went well beyond Lincoln's views. Lincoln did support economic opportunity for free blacks, but not political or social equality. Still, the Republican candidate did declare that "this government cannot endure permanently half slave and half free. . . . It will become all one thing or all the other."

The Lincoln-Douglas debates attracted national attention, but the Illinois legislature selected the state's senator. Narrowly controlled by Democrats, it returned Douglas to Washington. Although the senator retained his seat, he was concerned by how far the Democratic Party had tilted toward the South. So when President Buchanan tried to push the Lecompton Constitution through Congress, legitimating the proslavery government in Kansas, Douglas opposed him. The two struggled over control of the party, with Douglas winning a symbolic victory in January 1861 when Kansas was admitted as a free state. By then, however, the Democratic Party had split into southern and northern wings, and the nation was on the verge of civil war.

REVIEW & RELATE

- What factors contributed to the spread of antislavery sentiment in the North beyond committed abolitionists?

- How did the violence in Kansas and the *Dred Scott* decision reflect and intensify the growing sectional divide within the nation?

From **Sectional Crisis** to **Southern Secession**

During the 1850s, a profusion of abolitionist lectures, conventions, and literature swelled antislavery sentiment in the North. Mainstream newspapers regularly covered rescues of fugitives, the *Dred Scott* case, and the bloody crisis in Kansas. Republican candidates in state and local elections also kept concerns about slavery's expansion and southern power alive. Nothing, however, riveted the nation's attention as much as John Brown's raid on the federal arsenal at Harpers Ferry, Virginia in 1859. Less than a year later, Republican Abraham Lincoln captured the White House. In the wake of his election, South Carolina seceded from the Union.

John Brown's Raid. John Brown was committed not only to the abolition of slavery but also to complete equality between whites and blacks. A militant abolitionist and deeply religious man, Brown held views quite similar to those of David Walker, whose 1829 *Appeal* warned that slaves would eventually rise up and claim their freedom by force. Following the bloody battles in Kansas, Brown was convinced that direct action was the only answer. After the Pottawatomie killings, he went into hiding and reappeared back east, where he hoped to initiate an uprising to overthrow slavery.

Brown focused his efforts on the federal arsenal in **Harpers Ferry, Virginia**. With eighteen followers—five African Americans and thirteen whites, including three of his sons—Brown planned to capture the arsenal and distribute arms to slaves in the surrounding area. He hoped this action would ignite a rebellion that would destroy the plantation system. He tried to convince Frederick Douglass to join the venture, but Douglass considered it a foolhardy plan. However, Brown did manage to persuade a small circle of white abolitionists to bankroll the effort.

On the night of October 16, 1859, Brown and his men successfully kidnapped some leading townsmen and seized the arsenal. Local residents were stunned but managed to alert authorities, and state militia swarmed into Harpers Ferry. The next day, federal troops arrived, led by Colonel Robert E. Lee. With troops flooding into the town, Brown and his men were soon under siege, trapped in the arsenal. Fourteen rebels were killed, including two of Brown's sons. On October 18, Brown and three others were captured.

As word of the daring raid spread, Brown was hailed as a hero by many devoted abolitionists and depicted as a madman by southern planters. Southern whites were sure the raid was part of a widespread conspiracy led by power-hungry abolitionists. Federal authorities moved quickly to quell slaveholders' fears and end the episode. Brown rejected his lawyer's advice to plead insanity, and a local jury found him guilty of murder, criminal conspiracy, and treason. He was hanged on December 2, 1859.

John Brown's execution unleashed a massive outpouring of grief, anger, and uncertainty across the North. Abolitionists organized parades, demonstrations, bonfires, and tributes to the newest abolitionist martyr. Even many Quakers and other pacifists viewed John Brown as a hero for giving his life in the cause of emancipation. But most northern politicians and editors condemned the raid as a rash act that could only intensify sectional tensions. **See Primary Source Project 12: Visions of John Brown, page 416.**

Among southern whites, fear and panic greeted the raid on Harpers Ferry, and the execution of John Brown did little to quiet their outrage. By this time, southern intellectuals had developed a sophisticated proslavery argument that, to them, demonstrated the benefits of bondage for African Americans and its superiority to the northern system of wage labor. They argued that slave owners provided care and guidance for blacks from birth to death. Considering blacks too childlike to fend for themselves, proslavery advocates saw no problem with the enslaved providing labor and obedience in return for their care. Such arguments failed to convince abolitionists, who highlighted the brutality, sexual abuse, and shattered families that marked the system of bondage. In this context, Americans on both sides of the sectional divide considered the 1860 presidential election critical to the nation's future.

The Election of 1860. Brown's hanging set the tone for the 1860 presidential campaign. The Republicans met in Chicago five months after Brown's execution and distanced themselves from the more radical wing of the abolitionist movement. The party platform condemned both John Brown and southern "Border Ruffians," who initiated the violence in Kansas. The platform

Republican Party Presidential Ticket, 1860 The Republican Party had no hope of gaining significant votes in the South, so this campaign banner for Abraham Lincoln and Hannibal Hamlin sought to appeal to voters in the North and West. Crowded with imagery to attract the various interests that made up the new party, the banner was displayed at campaign rallies and party offices. Library of Congress, 3a09182

accepted slavery where it already existed, but continued to advocate its exclusion from western territories. Finally, the platform insisted on the need for federally funded internal improvements and protective tariffs. The Republicans nominated Abraham Lincoln as their candidate for president. Recognizing the impossibility of gaining significant votes in the South, the party focused instead on winning large majorities in the Northeast and Midwest.

The Democrats met in Charleston, South Carolina. Although Stephen Douglas was the leading candidate, southern delegates were still angry with him over Kansas being admitted as a free state. When Mississippi senator Jefferson Davis introduced a resolution to protect slavery in the territories, Douglas's northern supporters rejected it. President Buchanan also came out against Douglas, and the Democratic convention ended without choosing a candidate. Instead, various factions met separately. A group of largely northern Democrats met in Baltimore and nominated Douglas. Southern Democrats selected John Breckinridge, the vice president, a slaveholder, and an advocate of annexing Cuba. The Constitutional Union Party, comprised mainly of former southern Whigs, advocated "no political principle other than the Constitution of the country, the union of the states, and the enforcement of the laws." Its members nominated Senator John Bell of Tennessee.

Although Lincoln won barely 40 percent of the popular vote, he carried a clear majority in the electoral college. With the admission of Minnesota and Oregon to the Union in 1858 and 1859, free states outnumbered slave states eighteen to fifteen, and Lincoln won all but one of them. Lincoln did not win a single Southern electoral vote. However, since free states were more populous than slave states, they therefore controlled a large number of electoral votes. Douglas ran second to Lincoln in the popular vote, but Bell and Breckinridge captured more electoral votes than Douglas did because of their success in the South. Despite a deeply divided electorate, Lincoln became president (Map 12.3).

MAP 12.3 The Election of 1860

Four candidates vied for the presidency in 1860, and the voters split along clearly sectional lines. Although Stephen Douglas ran a vigorous campaign and gained votes in all regions of the country, he won a majority only in Missouri. Lincoln triumphed in the North and far West, and Breckinridge in most of the South.

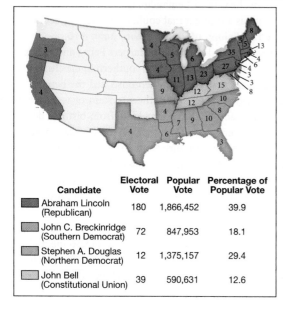

Candidate	Electoral Vote	Popular Vote	Percentage of Popular Vote
Abraham Lincoln (Republican)	180	1,866,452	39.9
John C. Breckinridge (Southern Democrat)	72	847,953	18.1
Stephen A. Douglas (Northern Democrat)	12	1,375,157	29.4
John Bell (Constitutional Union)	39	590,631	12.6

Although many abolitionists were wary of the Republicans, who were willing to leave slavery alone where it existed, most were nonetheless relieved at Lincoln's victory and hoped he would become more sympathetic to their views once in office. Meanwhile, southern whites, especially those in the deep South, were furious that a Republican had won the White House without carrying a single southern state.

The Lower South Secedes.

On December 20, 1860, six weeks after Lincoln's election, the legislature of South Carolina announced that because "a sectional party" had engineered "the election of a man to the high office of President of the United States whose opinions and purposes are hostile to slavery," the people of South Carolina dissolve their union with "the other states of North America." In early 1861, Mississippi, Florida, Alabama, Georgia, Louisiana, and Texas followed suit. Representatives from these states met on February 8 in Montgomery, Alabama, where they adopted a provisional constitution, elected Jefferson Davis as their president, and established the **Confederate States of America** (Map 12.4).

Explore ▶

See Sources 12.4 and 12.5 for two historians' interpretations of why southern states seceded from the Union.

President Buchanan did nothing to stop the secession movement. His cabinet included three secessionists and two unionists, one of whom resigned in frustration over Buchanan's failure to act. But Washington, D.C. was filled with southern sympathizers, who urged caution on an already timid president. Although some Northerners were shocked by the decision of South Carolina and its allies, many others supported their right to leave or believed they would return to the Union when they realized they could not survive economically on their own. Moreover, with Virginia, Maryland, and other Upper South slave states still part of the nation, the secession movement seemed unlikely to succeed.

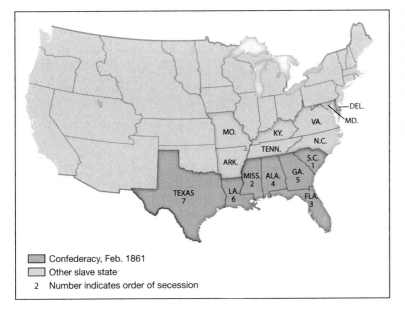

MAP 12.4   The Original Confederacy

Seven states in the Lower South seceded from the United States and formed the Confederate States of America in February 1861. While the original Confederacy was too limited in population and resources to defend itself against the U.S. government, its leaders hoped that other slave states would soon join them.

Confederacy, Feb. 1861
Other slave state
2   Number indicates order of secession

SECONDARY SOURCE ANALYSIS

White Southerners Decide to Secede

Alabama and Georgia became the fourth and fifth states to secede from the United States in winter 1861. Advocates of secession argued that they had voluntarily joined the nation and thus had the right to withdraw when their liberties were threatened. While southerners offered various reasons for seceding, since the 1960s, historians have generally agreed that the protection of slavery lay at the heart of the movement. Yet state-level studies written in the 1970s and 1980s, made two important contributions. First, in several states, including Georgia and Alabama, advocates of secession held only a slight edge among voters. Second, the arguments used by secessionists to win the debate differed from state to state.

Source 12.4

Michael P. Johnson, Georgians Choose Secession, 1977

Secession was the ultimate test of the hegemony of slaveholders. Yet secession was necessary precisely because the hegemony of slaveholders was not secure. According to secessionists, . . . secession was necessary because of the internal divisions within the South [over] the degree to which the slaveholding minority could have its way in a government based ultimately on manhood suffrage. In particular, secessionists feared that many southerners would be receptive to Republican offers of patronage and would become the nucleus of a southern Republican party. . . .

In Georgia, secessionists translated that fear into a double revolution: a revolution for home rule – to eliminate the external threat; and a conservative revolution for those who ruled at home – to prevent the political realization of the internal threat. Men with conservative social and political ideas were instrumental not only in creating the small electoral margin that secessionists enjoyed in Georgia, but also in the definition and direction of the second revolution. The actions of the secession convention, including the new state constitution which they drafted, . . . represented an attempt to preserve the social status quo by reconciling the tension between the slaveholding minority and the enfranchised slaveless majority. . . .

Secession was [thus] driven by political conflict not only between the South and the North but also between the black belt and the upcountry, slaveholders and nonslaveholders, and those who feared democracy and those who valued it.

Source: Michael P. Johnson, *Toward a Patriarchal Republic: The Secession of Georgia* (Baton Rouge: Louisiana State University, 1977), pp. xx–xxi.

In the midst of the crisis, Kentucky senator John Crittenden proposed a compromise that gained significant support. Indeed, Congress approved the first part of his plan, which called for a constitutional amendment to protect slavery from federal interference in any state where it already existed. But the second part of the **Crittenden plan** failed to win Republican votes. It would have extended the Missouri Compromise line (latitude 36°30') to the California border and barred slavery north of that line. South of that line, however, slavery would be protected, including in any territories "acquired hereafter." Fearing that passage would encourage southern planters to again seek territory in Cuba, Mexico, or

Source 12.5

J. Mills Thornton, Alabamans Move toward Secession, 1978

Antebellum Alabama was . . . obsessed with the idea of slavery. . . . [T]he fear of an imminent loss of freedom was a part of the inheritance which Alabama's citizens had received from their Revolutionary forebears. . . . [T]his tradition was lent considerable urgency by a daily familiarity with black slavery, . . . [B]ecause servility excluded one from [citizen]ship, . . an Alabamian . . . [had] to prove his worth - his claim to possess the qualities of a free man - constantly, both to his fellows and to himself. . . . [S]lavery guaranteed, so it was believed, that very few white men would ever have to depend directly upon other white men for their sustenance. . . . [Thus,] the existence of slavery . . . came to seem an essential bulwark of freedom. . . .

[D]uring the 1850s, . . . [Alabama's] Government at all levels became much more active; its expenditures increased enormously. . . .

Control of the political mechanism began slipping from the hands of poorer citizens, as the influence of great planters . . . [increased in] significance. . . .

[A]t this time, however, leadership within the [dominant] Democratic party . . . was passing to a second generation of politicians, less sensitive to the attitudes and apprehensions of the masses. . . . Only the villains offered by the southern rights advocates among them seemed capable of striking fire with the voters. . . . If Republicans controlled the federal government, [they argued], a southerner would be able to go to the territories only if he were willing to abandon a truly egalitarian, democratic world [rooted in slavery] for a hierarchical, elitist one, on the northern model. . . .

Source: J. Mills Thornton, *Politics and Power in a Slave Society: Alabama, 1800–1860*. Baton Rouge: Louisiana State University Press, 1978, pp. xviii, xix, 402.

Examine the Sources

1. How do Johnson and Thornton differ in their understanding of the key issues behind arguments for secession?
2. How might the geographical locations of Georgia and Alabama have shaped Johnson's and Thornton's interpretations?

Put It in Context

In what ways did John Brown's raid, Lincoln's election to the presidency, and the earlier secessions of South Carolina, Mississippi, and Florida influence convention delegates in Alabama and Georgia?

Central America, Republicans in Congress rejected the proposal. Despite the hopes of the Buchanan administration, it was becoming apparent that compromise was impossible.

REVIEW & RELATE

• How and why did John Brown's raid on Harpers Ferry move the country closer to civil war?

• Why did many in the South believe that the election of Abraham Lincoln was cause for secession?

Conclusion: A Nation Divided

Dred Scott did not live to see Abraham Lincoln take the oath of office in March 1861. Following the Supreme Court's 1857 ruling, Scott was returned to Irene Emerson, who had married abolitionist Calvin Chaffee. Unwilling to be the owner of the most well-known slave in America, Chaffee quickly returned Dred Scott and his family to his original owners, the Blow family. The Blows then freed the Scotts. For the next year and a half, before dying of tuberculosis, Dred Scott lived as a free man. Although Harriet and their daughters lived to see slavery abolished, in the spring of 1861 they could not imagine how that goal would be reached.

In 1860 John C. Frémont believed the nation was headed to war; and he was willing, once again, to serve a country he had helped expand. His work as a surveyor and soldier opened new territories to white settlement, and the gold rush then ensured California's admission to the Union. Yet what Frémont and other advocates of manifest destiny saw as U.S. victories had decimated many Indian nations as well as the property rights and livelihoods of many Mexicans. Despite the efforts of the Comanche and other tribes to fend off white encroachment, the U.S. government and white settlers claimed more and more territory. It was these western territories, moreover, that heightened conflicts over slavery and led the nation to the situation it faced in spring 1861.

While some Confederate planters imagined expanding the nation—and slavery—into Cuba, Nicaragua, and other southern regions, Northerners fought any such schemes. Outraged by the Fugitive Slave Act and appalled by Bleeding Kansas, militant activists applauded John Brown's raid at Harpers Ferry. Just as important, more moderate Northerners increasingly opposed slavery and voted for Lincoln in the fall of 1860. By the time Abraham Lincoln took office in March 1861, however, seven southern states had seceded, and the ever-widening political chasm brought the nation face-to-face with civil war.

TIMELINE OF EVENTS

1842	John C. Frémont leads expedition along the Oregon Trail
1848	Gold discovered in California
1850	Compromise of 1850
	Fugitive Slave Act
1852	Harriet Beecher Stowe publishes *Uncle Tom's Cabin*
1854	U.S.-Japanese treaty allows for mutual trading
	Republican Party founded
	Kansas-Nebraska Act
1854–1858	Period of violence in Bleeding Kansas
1857	*Dred Scott* case
1858	Lincoln-Douglas debates
1859	John Brown's raid on Harpers Ferry
November 1860	Abraham Lincoln elected president
December 1860	South Carolina secedes from the Union
January 1861	Mississippi, Florida, Alabama, Georgia, Louisiana, and Texas secede
February 1861	Confederate States of America established
March 1861	Lincoln inaugurated as president

KEY TERMS

Oregon Trail, *392*

gold rush, *394*

Compromise of 1850, *399*

Fugitive Slave Act of 1850, *399*

filibusters, *401*

Ostend Manifesto, *402*

Uncle Tom's Cabin, 404

Kansas-Nebraska Act, *405*

Republican Party, *405*

Bleeding Kansas, *406*

Dred Scott decision, *408*

Harpers Ferry, Virginia, *409*

Confederate States of America, *411*

Crittenden plan, *412*

REVIEW & RELATE

1. Why did Americans go west in the 1830s and 1840s, and what was the journey like?

2. What groups competed for land and resources in the West? How did disease, drought, and violence shape this competition?

3. What steps did legislators take in the 1840s and early 1850s to resolve the issue of the expansion of slavery? Were they successful?

4. How were slavery and American imperialist ambitions intertwined in the 1840s and 1850s?

5. What factors contributed to the spread of antislavery sentiment in the North beyond committed abolitionists?

6. How did the violence in Kansas and the *Dred Scott* decision reflect and intensify the growing sectional divide within the nation?

7. How and why did John Brown's raid on Harpers Ferry move the country closer to civil war?

8. Why did many in the South believe that the election of Abraham Lincoln was cause for secession?

Visions of John Brown

▶ How do the reactions to John Brown's raid on Harpers Ferry illustrate the intensifying conflicts over slavery in the United States?

On October 16, 1859, John Brown led a group of eighteen men on a raid on the federal arsenal at Harpers Ferry, Virginia. The plan failed, and Brown and his surviving accomplices were captured and put on trial. On December 2, a mere seven weeks after the raid began, Brown was executed by hanging.

The raid shocked the nation, not least because John Brown was a white man leading an uprising to free enslaved blacks. Brown's quick trial and execution were designed to calm southern fears and minimize northern support for his actions. Neither goal was accomplished. The northern press and political establishment denounced the raid, but also condemned the brutalities of slavery that inspired it. Although most abolitionists were appalled by Brown's violent methods, they wrote tributes to Brown and organized a "Day of Mourning" for his execution (Sources 12.7 and 12.8). White Southerners and some northern Democrats labeled Brown a terrorist, believing he was part of a vast abolitionist conspiracy to violently overthrow slavery (Sources 12.6 and 12.9). The following sources highlight the competing images of John Brown—painting him as a hero, a saint, a brute, and a fanatic. The 1863 painting suggests the continued importance of his legacy to racial progressives (Source 12.10).

Source 12.6

State Register (Springfield, Illinois) | The Irrepressible Conflict, 1859

While many Northerners shared Brown's antislavery beliefs, most opposed his use of violence. The following editorial in the *State Register* (Springfield, Illinois), a Democratic Party paper, reflects the outrage felt throughout the nation. The *State Register* blamed Republicans for the Harpers Ferry raid, condemning William Seward and Abraham Lincoln for speeches they claimed had fueled the actions of John Brown.

The telegraphic dispatches yesterday morning startled the public with an account of one of the most monstrous villainies ever attempted in this country. It was no less than an effort on the part of a party of abolitionists and negroes to take possession of one of the national arsenals, at Harpers Ferry, with the military stores and the public money there deposited. Under the lead of the most infamous of the Kansas crew of black republican marauders, Ossawatomie Brown, the insurgents, to the number of five or six hundred, attacked and took possession of the whole town of Harpers Ferry, including the government buildings and stores, stopped the mails, imprisoned peaceable citizens, and, before they were dislodged, numbers were killed and wounded on both sides.

It was scarcely credible, when the first dispatch was received yesterday, that the object of the ruffians could be other than plunder, but late dispatches . . . show, conclusively, that the movement was a most extensive one, having for its object the uprising of the negroes throughout the south, a servile war, and its consequences—murder, rapine, and robbery.

The leader chosen was just the man to initiate the work. Bankrupt in fortune and character, an outlaw and an outcast, he was just the man to commence the work which ultra Abolitionism, through its diligent Parkers and Garrisons, hope to reach the millennium of their traitorous designs. Their open-mouthed treason . . . is but the logical sequence of the teachings of Wm. H. Seward and Abraham Lincoln—the one boldly proclaiming an "irrepressible conflict" between certain states of the Union . . . and the other declaring . . . that the Union cannot continue as the fathers made it—part slave and part free states. When such men, by specious demagogism [promoting factionalism], in the name of freedom and liberty, daily labor to weaken the bonds of our glorious governmental fabric, the work of sages and patriots, themselves the holders of black men as slaves, is it to be wondered at that ignorant, unprincipled, and reckless camp followers of the party for which these leaders speak, attempt, practically, to illustrate the doctrines which they preach. . . .

Brown, though a blood-stained ruffian, is a bold man. As a black republican he practices what his leaders preach. As it is urged by statesmen (save the mark!) of his party that there is an "irrepressible conflict," he wants it in tangible, material shape. He believes in blows, not words, and the Harpers Ferry villainy is the first in his line of performance.

Source: "The 'Irrepressible Conflict' Fruits of the Lincoln-Seward Doctrine," *State Register* (Springfield, Illinois), October 20, 1859.

Henry David Thoreau | A Plea for Captain John Brown, 1859

Most abolitionists were quick to condemn John Brown's use of armed force, but Henry David Thoreau rushed to his defense. The transcendentalist author had been introduced to Brown years earlier by Franklin Sanborn, who helped finance the Harpers Ferry raid. On the day Brown was to be hung, Thoreau delivered a speech, "A Plea for Captain John Brown," in front of a public gathering in Concord, Massachusetts. The widely circulated speech helped establish Brown as a martyr for the abolitionist cause.

Little as I know of Captain Brown, I would fain [willingly] do my part to correct the tone and the statements of the newspapers, and of my countrymen generally, respecting his character and actions. It costs us nothing to be just. We can at least express our sympathy with, and admiration of, him and his companions, and that is what I now propose to do. . . .

. . . He was a superior man. He did not value his bodily life in comparison with ideal things. He did not recognize unjust human laws, but resisted them as he was bid. For once we are lifted out of the trivialness and dust of politics into the region of truth and manhood. No man in America has ever stood up so persistently and effectively for the dignity of human nature, knowing himself for a man, and the equal of any and all governments. In that sense he was the most American of us all. . . . He was more than a match for all the judges that American voters, or office-holders of whatever grade, can create. He could not have been tried by a jury of his peers, because his peers did not exist. When a man stands up serenely against the condemnation and vengeance of mankind, rising above them literally *by a whole body*—even though he were of late the vilest murderer, who has settled that matter with himself— the spectacle is a sublime one . . . and we become criminal in comparison. Do yourselves the honor to recognize him. . . .

It was his peculiar doctrine that a man has a perfect right to interfere by force with the slaveholder, in order to rescue the slave. I agree with him. They who are continually shocked by slavery have some right to be shocked by the violent death of the slaveholder, but no others. Such will be more shocked by his life than by his death. I shall not be forward to think him mistaken in his method who quickest succeeds to liberate the slave. I speak for the slave when I say, that I prefer the philanthropy of Captain Brown to that philanthropy which neither shoots me nor liberates me. . . . I do not wish to kill nor to be killed, but I can foresee circumstances in which both these things would be by me unavoidable. We preserve the so-called peace of our community by deeds of petty violence every day. Look at the policeman's billy and handcuffs! Look at the jail! Look at the gallows! Look at the chaplain of the regiment! . . . I know that the mass of my countrymen think that the only righteous use that can be made of Sharpe's rifles and revolvers is to fight duels with them, when we are insulted by other nations, or to hunt Indians, or shoot fugitive slaves with them, or the like. I think that for once the Sharpe's rifles and revolvers were employed in a righteous cause. . . .

The question is not about the weapon, but the spirit in which you use it. No man has appeared in America, as yet, who loved his fellow-man so well, and treated him so tenderly. He [Brown] lived for him. He took up his life and he laid it down for him. . . .

I am here to plead his cause with you. I plead not for his life, but for his character—his immortal life; and so it becomes your cause wholly, and is not his in the least. Some eighteen hundred years ago Christ was crucified; this morning, perchance, Captain Brown was hung. These are the two ends of a chain which is not without its links. He is not Old Brown any longer; he is an angel of light.

Source: James Redpath, *Echoes of Harper's Ferry* (Boston: Thayer and Eldridge, 1860), 2, 30, 37–38, 41–42.

Source 12.8

Reverend J. Sella Martin | Day of Mourning Speech, December 2, 1859

On the day of John Brown's execution, black and white abolitionists around the country held a "Day of Mourning" in his honor. In Boston four thousand people gathered at the Tremont Temple to celebrate Brown's life. There Reverend J. Sella Martin, a former slave and the pastor of the Joy Street Baptist Church, proclaimed his support for Brown and his methods.

I know that John Brown, in thus rebuking our public sin, in thus facing the monarch, has had to bear just what John the Baptist bore. His head today, by Virginia—that guilty maid of a more guilty mother, the American Government—has been cut off, and it has been presented to the ferocious and insatiable hunger, the terrible and inhuman appetite, of this corrupt government. Today, by the telegraph, we have received the intelligence that John Brown has forfeited his life—all this honesty, all this straight-forwardness, all this self-sacrifice has been manifested in Harper's Ferry. . . .

I know that there is some quibbling, some querulousness, some fear, in reference to an out-and-out endorsement of his course. Men of peace principles object to it, in consequence of their religious conviction; politicians in the North object to it, because they are afraid that it will injure their party; pro-slavery men in the South object to it, because it has touched their dearest idol; but I am prepared, my friends . . . in the light of all human history, to approve of the *means*; in the light of all Christian principle, to approve of the *end*. (Applause.) I say this is not the language of rage, because I remember that our Fourth-of-July orators sanction the same thing; because I remember that Concord, and Bunker Hill, and every historic battlefield in this country, and the celebration of those events, all go to approve the means that John Brown has used; the only difference being, that in our battles, in America, means have been used for *white* men and that John Brown has used his means for *black* men. (Applause.) And I say, that so far as principle is concerned, so far as the sanctions of the Gospel are concerned, I am prepared to endorse his end; and I endorse it because God Almighty has told us that we should feel with them that are in bonds as being bound with them. I endorse his end, because every single instinct of our nature rises and tells us that it is right. I find an endorsement of John Brown's course in the large assembly gathered here this evening. . . .

Now, I bring this question down to the simple test of the Gospel. . . . I look at this question as a peace man. I say, in accordance with the principles of peace, that I do not believe the sword should be unsheathed . . . until there is in the system to be assailed such terrible evidences of corruption, that it becomes the *dernier* [last] *resort*. And my friends, we are not to blame the application of the instrument, we are to blame the disease itself. When a physician cuts out a cancer from my face, I am not to blame the physician for the use of the knife; but the impure blood, the obstructed veins, the disordered system, that have caused the cancer, and rendered the use of the instrument necessary.

Source: *Liberator*, December 9, 1859, in *Blacks on John Brown*, ed. Benjamin Quarles (Urbana: University of Illinois Press, 1972), 26–27.

Source 12.9

A Southern Paper Reacts to Brown's Execution, December 3, 1859

The following article appeared in a North Carolina newspaper the day after Brown's execution. It predicts that the North will make Brown a martyr and ridicules the Day of Mourning held in his honor. The article singles out the celebration in Boston (Source 12.7) for particular condemnation and labels its participants treasonous.

I t is to be hoped, with Brown's exit from the world, the excitement at the North will subside. But we must confess that this hope is but of the faintest character. Fanaticism at the North is rampant, and overrides every thing. On yesterday, the godly city of Boston, built up and sustained by the products of negro slave labor, went into mourning, fasting, and prayer, over the condign [deserved] punishment of a negro stealer, murderer, and traitor, and from fifty pulpits the Praise-God-Bare-bones belched forth volumes of blasphemy and treason.

In all the Noo England towns and villages, we may expect to hear that mock funerals have been celebrated, and all kinds of nonsensically lugubrious displays made. (It is a pity that they haven't a witch or two to drown or burn, by way of variety.) We hope that Gov. Wise [of Virginia] will have the gallows on which Brown was hung burned, and give notice of the fact. Our reasons for this wish is this: The Yankees have no objection to mingling money making with their grief, and they will, unless Brown's gallows is known to have been burned, set to work and make all kinds of jimcracks and notions out of what they will call parts of Old John Brown's gallows and sell them. Let the rope which choked him, too, be burned and the fact advertised, or we shall see vast quantities of breast pins, lockets, and bracelets,

containing bits of the "rope which hung Old Brown" for sale. [P. T.] Barnum is already in the market for Old Brown's old clothes, and hopes and expects to make [a good] speculation out of them.

Source: "Execution of John Brown," *Register* (Raleigh, North Carolina), December 3, 1859.

Source 12.10

Currier and Ives | John Brown on His Way to Execution, 1863

In the weeks after Brown's death, newspapers were filled with accounts of his final days and execution. The *New York Tribune* published a story claiming that Brown had kissed a slave child he encountered on his way to the gallows. Although this story was false, it was widely repeated and became the subject of a painting by Louis Ransom. This 1863 Currier and Ives lithograph based on Ransom's painting further cemented the legend.

Library of Congress, 3a06486

419

Interpret the Evidence

1. What language and imagery do the printed sources and the Currier and Ives engraving use to describe Brown? How do the speakers, editors, and engraver seek to persuade their audiences and how do the audiences for each source differ?

2. In what ways do Brown's admirers, such as Henry David Thoreau (Source 12.7) and J. Sella Martin (Source 12.8), support Brown and his use of violence?

3. Critics of Brown used his raid to condemn abolitionism. On what basis did they make more generalized claims of northern guilt (Sources 12.6 and 12.9)?

4. In what ways do these sources characterize Brown before his execution (Sources 12.6 and 12.7) and after (Sources 12.8, 12.9, and 12.10)?

Put It in Context

How did Brown's raid illuminate tensions within the northern antislavery movement and fuel the regional conflicts that led to South Carolina's secession?

Civil War

1861–1865

WINDOW TO THE PAST

Union Soldiers in Camp c. 1863

The Civil War was the first military conflict in U.S. history to be photographically documented. Many photographers took formal portraits of soldiers, individually or in groups, while others captured the bloody aftermath of battles. This picture offers a rare informal glimpse of soldiers in camp. Their range of poses and expressions suggests the various ways that soldiers responded to a lull in the conflict. ▸ To discover more about what this primary source can show us, see Source 13.2 on page 434.

Library of Congress, LC-DIG-ppmsca-34191

After reading this chapter you should be able to:

- Explain why southern states seceded and describe the advantages and disadvantages that marked the Confederacy and the Union at the beginning of the Civil War.

- Describe the changing roles of African Americans, free and enslaved, in the war and the growing sentiment for emancipation in the North.

- Evaluate how the war changed northern and southern political priorities and the lives of soldiers and civilians.

- Identify turning points in the Civil War, including key battles in the eastern and western theaters of war, and explain the factors that led to Union victory and the abolition of slavery.

COMPARING AMERICAN HISTORIES

Born into slavery in 1818, Frederick Douglass became a celebrated orator, editor, and abolitionist in the 1840s. In 1845 Douglass published his autobiography, *Narrative of the Life of Frederick Douglass*, which described his enslavement in Maryland, his defiance against his masters, and his eventual escape to New York in 1838 with the help of Anna Murray, a free black servant.

After marrying in New York, Frederick and Anna moved to New Bedford, Massachusetts, and changed

(left) **Frederick Douglass** Beinecke Rare Book and Manuscript Library, Yale University

(right) **Rose O'Neal Greenhow** Documenting the American South, University Library, The University of North Carolina at Chapel Hill, http://docsouth.unc.edu/fpn/greenhow/frontis.html

their last name to Douglass to avoid capture. In 1841 the American Anti-Slavery Society hired Frederick to present his vivid tale of slave life in public. Four years later, Douglass launched a British lecture tour that attracted enthusiastic audiences. Supporters in Britain purchased his freedom, and Douglass returned to Massachusetts a free man in 1847.

Late that year, Frederick moved to Rochester, New York with Anna and their children to launch his abolitionist paper, the *North Star*. Soon after, he broke with the Garrisonians and embraced the Liberty Party and eventually the Republicans. When war erupted in April 1861, Douglass lobbied President Lincoln relentlessly to make emancipation a war aim.

Initially Douglass feared that Lincoln was more committed to reconstituting the Union than abolishing slavery. But when the president issued the Emancipation Proclamation in January 1863, Douglass spoke enthusiastically on its behalf. He also argued that it was essential for black men to serve in the Union army. When African Americans were finally allowed to join in 1862 to 1863, Douglass helped recruit volunteers but also protested discrimination against black troops and the denial of black civil rights.

Like Douglass, Rose O'Neal was born on a Maryland plantation, but she was white and free. Her father was John O'Neal, a planter who was killed in 1817 when Rose was about four. In her teens, she and her sister moved to Washington, D.C., where their aunt ran a fashionable boardinghouse. Her boarders included John C. Calhoun, whose states' rights views Rose eagerly embraced. Rose was welcomed into elite social circles and in 1835 married Virginian Robert Greenhow, who worked for the State Department.

Rose O'Neal Greenhow quickly became a favorite Washington hostess, entertaining congressmen, cabinet ministers, and foreign diplomats. Ardent proslavery expansionists, the Greenhows supported efforts to acquire Cuba and expand slavery into western territories. When Robert died in 1854, Rose and their four children remained in D.C. and continued to entertain powerful political leaders.

In May 1861, as the Civil War commenced, a U.S. army captain about to join the Confederate cause recruited Greenhow to head an espionage ring in

Washington, D.C. With her close ties to southern sympathizers in the capital, Greenhow gathered intelligence on Union plans. Although she initially avoided suspicion, by August 1861 Greenhow was investigated and placed under house arrest. After continuing to smuggle out letters, she was sent to the Old Capitol Prison in January 1862. When Greenhow again managed to transmit information, she was exiled to Richmond, where Confederate president Jefferson Davis hailed her as a hero. ∎

Comparing the American histories of Frederick Douglass and Rose O'Neal Greenhow illustrates the ways that Americans, black and white, northern and southern, men and women, were shaped by and shaped the war that followed secession. They were among hundreds of thousands of Americans who saw the war as a means to achieve their goals: a free nation, a haven for slavery, or a reunited country. Once conflict erupted at Fort Sumter in April 1861, more southern states seceded although four slave states, reluctantly, remained in the Union. Even with the addition of more states, the Confederacy lagged behind the Union in population, industrial and agricultural production, and railroad lines. These differences became more important as the war unfolded. Initially, however, skilled officers and knowledge of the southern terrain benefited the Confederate army. On the home front, hundreds of thousands of Americans labored on farms and in factories, burgeoning government offices, and hospitals to support the Union or the Confederacy. After 1862, tens of thousands of African Americans joined the Union army, both free blacks and enslaved men freed by Union forces. The next year, the Emancipation Proclamation ensured that a Union victory would eradicate slavery. As the war dragged on, antiwar protests erupted North and South, fueled by inflation, conscription acts, and mounting casualties. Finally in 1865, the greater resources of the North, complemented by General Ulysses S. Grant's hard war strategy, led to Union victory and the final abolition of slavery.

The **Nation Goes** to **War, 1861**

When Abraham Lincoln took office, seven states in the Lower South had already formed the Confederate States of America, and more states threatened to secede. Lincoln had promised not to interfere with slavery where it existed, but many southern whites doubted such assurances. By seceding, southern slaveholders also proclaimed their unwillingness to become a permanent minority in the nation. Still, not all slave states were yet willing to cut their ties to the nation. Northerners, too, disagreed about the appropriate response to secession. Once fighting erupted, however, preparations for war became the primary focus in both the Union and the Confederacy.

The South Embraces Secession. Confederate president Jefferson Davis joined other planters in arguing that Lincoln's victory jeopardized the future of slavery and that secession was therefore a necessity. Advocates of secession contended that the federal government had failed to implement fully the Fugitive Slave Act and the *Dred Scott* decision. They were convinced that a Republican administration would do even less to support southern interests. White Southerners also feared that Republicans might inspire a massive uprising of slaves, and secession allowed whites to maintain control over the South's black population.

Still, when Lincoln was inaugurated, some legislators in the Upper South hoped a compromise could be reached, and the president hoped to bring the Confederates back into the Union without using military force. Most northern merchants, manufacturers, and bankers approved, wanting to maintain their economic ties to southern planters. Yet Lincoln also realized he must demonstrate Union strength to curtail further secessions. He focused on **Fort Sumter** in South Carolina's Charleston harbor, where a small Union garrison was running low on food and medicine. On April 8, 1861, Lincoln dispatched ships to the fort but promised to use force only if the Confederates blocked his peaceful effort to send supplies.

The Confederate government would now have to choose. It could attack the Union vessels and bear responsibility for starting a war or permit a "foreign power" to maintain a fort in its territory. President Davis and his advisers chose the aggressive course, demanding Fort Sumter's immediate and unconditional surrender. The commanding officer refused, and on April 12 Confederate guns opened fire. Two days later, Fort Sumter surrendered. On April 15, Lincoln called for 75,000 volunteers to put down the southern insurrection.

The declaration of war led whites in the Upper South to reconsider secession. Some small farmers and landless whites were drawn to Republican promises of free labor and free soil and remained suspicious of the goals and power of secessionist planters. Yet the vast majority of southern whites, rich and poor, defined their liberty in relation to black bondage. They feared that Republicans would free the slaves and introduce racial amalgamation, the mixing of whites and blacks, in the South.

Explore ▶

See Source 13.1 for a Georgia congressman's views on secession.

Fearing more secessions, Lincoln used the powers of his office to keep the border states that allowed slavery—Maryland, Delaware, Missouri, and Kentucky—in the Union. He waived the right of habeas corpus (which protects citizens against arbitrary arrest and detention), jailed secessionists, arrested state legislators, and limited freedom of the press. However, four other slave states—North Carolina, Virginia, Tennessee, and Arkansas— seceded. Virginia, with its strategic location near the nation's capital, was by far the most significant. Richmond, which would soon become the capital of the Confederacy, was also home to the South's largest iron manufacturer, which could produce weapons and munitions.

While Northerners differed over how to respond when the first seven states seceded, the firing on Fort Sumter prompted most to line up behind Lincoln's call for war. Manufacturers and merchants, once intent on maintaining commercial links with the South, now rushed to support the president, while northern workers, including immigrants, responded to Lincoln's call for volunteers. They assumed that the Union, with its greater resources and manpower, could quickly set the nation right. New York editor Horace Greeley proclaimed, "Jeff Davis and Co. will be swingin' from the battlements at Washington at least by the 4th of July."

Both Sides Prepare for War. At the onset of the war, the Union certainly held a decided advantage in resources and population. The Union states held more than 60 percent of the U.S. population, and the Confederate population included several million slaves who would not be armed for combat. The Union also far outstripped the

Confederacy in manufacturing and even led the South in agricultural production. The North's many miles of railroad track ensured greater ease in moving troops and supplies. And the Union could launch far more ships to blockade southern ports (Figure 13.1).

GUIDED ANALYSIS

Robert Toombs | Supporting Secession in Georgia, 1860

Immediately after Abraham Lincoln's election, several southern states began to discuss secession. Georgia called a special convention to debate the issue on November 13–14, 1860, immediately following the presidential election. One of the principal speakers was Robert Toombs, a U.S. congressman. In the following selection, Toombs argues in favor of secession, and Georgia became the fifth state to secede, two months before Lincoln took office.

Source 13.1

Who in Toombs's view forced the issue of secession?

How does Toombs seek to demonstrate the humane character of slavery?

What actions of the North threatened the security of the South and slavery?

The stern, steady march of events has brought us in conflict with our non-slaveholding confederates upon the fundamental principles of our compact of Union. We have not sought this conflict; we have sought too long to avoid it. . . . The door of conciliation and compromise is finally closed by our adversaries, and it remains only to us to meet the conflict with the dignity and firmness of men worthy of freedom. . . .

. . . The South at all times demanded nothing but equality in the common territories, equal enjoyment of them with their property, to that extended to Northern citizens and their property—nothing more. . . . In 1790 we had less than eight hundred thousand slaves. Under our mild and humane administration of the system they have increased above four millions. The country has expanded to meet this growing want, and Florida, Alabama, Mississippi, Louisiana, Texas, Arkansas, Kentucky, Tennessee, and Missouri have received this increasing tide of African labor; before the end of this century, at precisely the same rate of increase, the Africans among us in a subordinate condition will amount to eleven millions of persons. What shall be done with them? We must expand or perish. . . . The North understand it better—they have told us for twenty years that their object was to pen up slavery within its present limits—surround it with a border of free States, and like the scorpion surrounded with fire, they will make it sting itself to death.

Source: Frank Moore, ed., *The Rebellion Record: A Diary of American Events* (New York: G. P. Putnam and Henry Holt, 1864), 1:362–63, 365.

Put It in Context

Explain the importance of the issue of slavery and expansion to Toombs's arguments regarding secession.

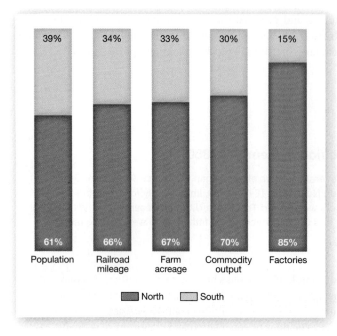

FIGURE 13.1   Economies of the North and South, 1860

This figure provides graphic testimony to the enormous advantages in resources the North held on the eve of the Civil War. The North led the South in population, farm acreage, and railroad mileage as well as factories and commodity output. Over four years of war, how might the differences in each area affect the ability of the Union and the Confederacy to pursue their objectives?

Source: Data from Stanley Engerman, "The Economic Impact of the Civil War," in *The Reinterpretation of American Economic History*, ed. Robert W. Fogel and Stanley Engerman (New York: Harper and Row, 1971).

Yet Union forces were less prepared for war than the Confederates, who had been organizing troops and gathering munitions for months. To match their efforts, Winfield Scott, general in chief of the U.S. army, told Lincoln he would need at least 300,000 men committed to serve for two or three years. Scott believed that massing such huge numbers of soldiers would force the Confederacy to negotiate a peace. But fearing to unnerve Northerners, the president asked for only 75,000 volunteers for three months. Moreover, rather than forming a powerful national army led by seasoned officers, Lincoln left recruitment, organization, and training largely to the states. The result was disorganization and the appointment of officers based more on political connections than military expertise.

Confederate leaders also initially relied on state militia units and volunteers, but they prepared for a prolonged war from the start. Before the firing on Fort Sumter, President Davis signed up 100,000 volunteers for a year's service. The labor provided by slaves allowed a large proportion of white working-age men to volunteer for military service. And Southerners knew they were likely to be fighting mainly on home territory, where they had expert knowledge of the terrain. When the final four states joined the Confederacy, the southern army also gained important military leadership. It ultimately recruited 280 West Point graduates, including Robert E. Lee, Thomas "Stonewall" Jackson, James Longstreet, and others who had proved their mettle in the Mexican-American War.

The South's advantages were apparent in the first major battle of the war. And Confederate troops were also aided by information on Union plans sent by Rose Greenhow. When 30,000 Union troops marched on northern Virginia on July 21, 1861, Confederate forces were ready. At the **Battle of Bull Run** (or **Manassas**), later known as the First Battle of Bull Run, 22,000 Confederates repelled the Union attack. Civilians from Washington who traveled to the battle site to view the combat had to flee for their lives to escape Confederate artillery.

Battle of Wilson's Creek   This colored lithograph depicts the First Iowa Regiment, led by General Nathaniel Lyon, charging Confederate forces at the Battle of Wilson's Creek, Missouri on August 10, 1861. The Confederates won the battle, and Lyon, on the ground here, became the first Union general to die in the war. The lithograph was created in 1893 based on a wartime sketch. Library of Congress, 3g01767

Despite Union defeats at Bull Run and then at Wilson's Creek, Missouri in August 1861, the Confederate army did not launch major strikes against Union forces. Meanwhile the Union navy began blockading the South's deepwater ports. By the time the armies settled into winter camps in 1861–1862, both sides had come to realize that the war was likely to be a long and costly struggle.

REVIEW & RELATE

- What led four more states to join the Confederacy in 1861 and four other slave states to remain in the Union?

- What advantages and disadvantages did each side have at the onset of the war?

Military Conflict and Political Strife, 1861–1862

The Union and the Confederacy faced very different tasks in the war. The South had to defend its territory and force the federal government to halt military action. The North had a more complicated challenge. Initially, northern political leaders believed that secession was driven mainly by slave owners and that high death rates and destruction of property would only alienate southern whites who favored reconciliation. But a policy of conciliation depended on early Union victories. With early defeats, it was clear the North would have to invade the South and isolate it from potential allies abroad. At the same time, most northern politicians believed that the nation could be reunited without abolishing slavery while abolitionists argued that only emancipation could resolve the problems that led to war. Meanwhile, enslaved Southerners immediately looked for ways to loosen their bonds.

The Wartime Roles of African Americans and Indians.

The outbreak of war intensified debates over abolition. Some 225,000 African Americans lived in the free states, and many offered their services in an effort to end slavery. African American leaders in Cleveland proclaimed, "Today, as in the times of '76, we are ready to go forth and do battle in the common cause of our country." But Secretary of War Simon Cameron had no intention of calling up black soldiers.

Northern optimism about a quick victory contributed to the rejection of African American volunteers. Union leaders feared that whites would not enlist if they had to serve alongside blacks. In addition, Lincoln and his advisers were initially wary of letting a war to preserve the Union become a war against slavery, and they feared that any further threat to slavery might drive the four slave states that remained in the Union into the Confederacy. This political strategy, however, depended on quick and overwhelming victories; and with U.S. soldiers posted mainly on the western frontier and a third of officers joining the Confederacy, victories were few. Nonetheless a rush of volunteers allowed Union troops to push into Virginia while the Union navy captured crucial islands along the Confederate coast.

Wherever Union forces appeared, southern slaves began considering freedom as a possibility. Enslaved workers living near battle sites circulated information on Union troop movements. Then, as planters in Virginia began sending male slaves to more distant plantations for fear of losing them, some managed to flee and headed to Union camps. Many slave owners tracked fugitives behind Union lines and demanded their return. Some Union commanders denied slaves entrance or returned them to their masters. However, a few Union officers recognized these fugitives' value: They knew the local geography well, could dig trenches and provide other services, and drained the Confederate labor supply. At the Union outpost at Fort Monroe, Virginia in May 1861, General Benjamin Butler offered fugitive slaves military protection. He claimed them as **contraband** of war: property forfeited by the act of rebellion.

Lincoln endorsed Butler's policy because it allowed the Union to strike at the institution of slavery without proclaiming a general emancipation that might prompt border states where slavery remained legal to secede. Congress expanded Butler's policy in August 1861 by passing a confiscation act. It proclaimed that any owner whose slaves were used by the Confederate army would lose all claim to those slaves. Although it was far from a clear-cut declaration of freedom, the act spurred the hopes of northern abolitionists and many southern slaves.

While Northerners continued to debate African Americans' role in the war effort, the Union army recruited a wide array of other ethnic and racial groups, including American Indians. Unlike blacks, however, Indians did not necessarily all support the Union. The Comanche negotiated with both Union and Confederate agents while raiding the Texas frontier for horses and cattle. The Confederacy gained significant support from slaveholding

Portrait of Loots-Tow-Oots and Wife   This 1868 portrait of Pawnee warrior Loots-Tow-Oots, also known as Rattlesnake and George Esaw, reflects the dual identities carried by American Indians who served in the Civil War. While both he and his wife wear combinations of native and white clothing, Loots-Tow-Oots's Indian feather and leggings offer an especially stark contrast to his Union uniform and cavalry sword. National Anthropological Archives, Smithsonian Institution [GN 01260]

Indians who had earlier been removed from the Southeast. The Cherokee split over the war as they had over removal. General Stand Watie led a pan-Indian force into battle for the Confederates. Initially John Ross joined the Confederates as well, but later he led a group of Cherokee into Union army ranks alongside the Osage, Delaware, Seneca, and other Indian nations. Ely Parker, a Seneca sachem and engineer, became a lieutenant colonel in the Union army, serving with General Ulysses S. Grant.

Indians played crucial roles in a number of important early battles, particularly on the Confederate side. Cherokee and Seminole warriors fought valiantly with Confederates at the Battle of Pea Ridge in Tennessee in March 1862, but were defeated by a smaller but better supplied Union force. In August 1862 Indians contributed to the Confederate victory at the Second Battle of Bull Run and the following month participated in the bloodiest single day of battle in U.S. history at Antietam (Sharpsburg). The Confederate army recruited Mexican-American soldiers as well, hoping to gain control of the West's gold and silver mines. But a Union victory gained by a troop of Colorado miners at Glorieta Pass near Sante Fe, New Mexico ended that Confederate dream.

While both Union and Confederate armies recruited Indian regiments, African Americans were barred from enlisting as soldiers on either side. However, a series of Union military defeats helped transform the attitudes of northern whites. In the spring of 1862, Confederate general Stonewall Jackson won a series of stunning victories against three Union armies in Virginia's Shenandoah Valley. That June and July, General Robert E. Lee fought Union forces under General George B. McClellan to a standstill in the Seven Days Battle near Richmond. Then in August, Lee, Jackson, and General James Longstreet joined together to defeat Union troops at the Second Battle of Bull Run (Map 13.1).

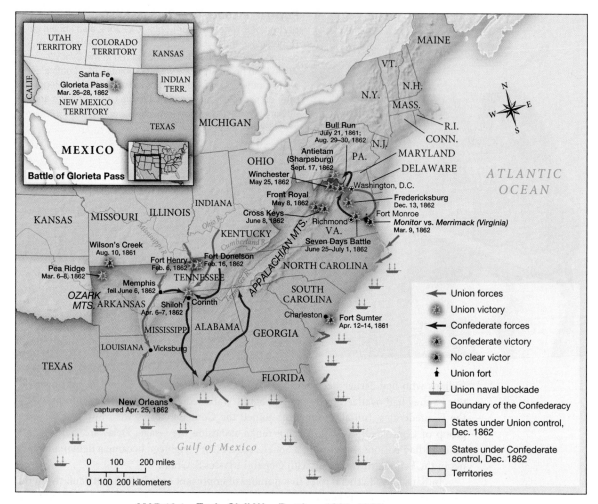

MAP 13.1 Early Civil War Battles, 1861–1862

In 1861 and 1862, the Confederate army stunned Union forces with a series of dramatic victories in Virginia and Missouri. However, the Union army won a crucial victory at Antietam (Sharpsburg); gained control of Confederate territory in Tennessee, Arkansas, and Mississippi; fended off Confederate efforts to gain New Mexico Territory; and established a successful naval blockade of Confederate ports.

As the war turned against the North, the North turned against slavery. In April 1862 Congress had approved a measure to abolish slavery in the District of Columbia, symbolizing a significant shift in Union sentiment. During that bloody summer, Congress passed a second confiscation act, declaring that the slaves of anyone who supported the Confederacy should be "forever free of their servitude, and not again held as slaves." In July Congress also approved a militia act that allowed African Americans to serve in "any military or naval service for which they may be found competent."

Support for the 1862 militia act built on Union victories as well as defeats. In April 1862 a Union blockade led to the capture of New Orleans, while the **Battle of Shiloh** in

Tennessee provided the army entrée to the Mississippi valley. There Union troops came face-to-face with slavery. Few of these soldiers were abolitionists, but many were shocked by what they saw, including instruments used to torture slaves. One Union soldier reported he had seen "enough of the horror of slavery to make one an Abolitionist forever." Southern blacks also provided important intelligence to northern officers, making clear their value to the Union war effort.

Whether in victory of defeat, rising death tolls increased support for African American enlistment. The Battle of Shiloh was the bloodiest battle in American history to that point. Earlier battles had resulted in a few hundred or even a few thousand casualties, but with more than 23,000 casualties, Shiloh raised the carnage to a new level. As the war continued, such brutal battles became routine. The Union army would need every available man—white, black, and Indian—to sustain its effort against the Confederates.

Indian regiments had already proven themselves in battle, and African Americans soon followed suit. In October 1862 a group of black soldiers in the First Kansas Colored Volunteers repulsed Confederates at a battle in Missouri. In the South, white abolitionists serving as Union officers organized former slaves into units like the First South Carolina Volunteers in January 1863. A few months later, another black regiment—the Massachusetts Fifty-fourth—attracted recruits from across the North, including Frederick Douglass's three sons. For the next two years, tens of thousands of African American soldiers fought valiantly in dozens of battles.

Union Politicians Consider Emancipation.
By the fall of 1862, African Americans and abolitionists had gained widespread support for emancipation as a necessary goal of the war. Lincoln and his cabinet realized that embracing abolition as a war aim would likely prevent international recognition of southern independence. As Massachusetts senator Charles Sumner proclaimed, "You will observe that I propose no crusade for abolition. [Emancipation] is to be presented strictly as a measure of military necessity." Still, some Union politicians feared that emancipation might arouse deep animosity in the slaveholding border states and drive them from the Union.

From the Confederate perspective, international recognition was critical. Support from European nations might persuade the North to accept southern independence. More immediately, recognition would ensure markets for southern agriculture and access to manufactured goods and war materiel. Confederate officials were especially focused on Britain, the leading market for cotton and a leading producer of industrial products. President Davis considered sending Rose Greenhow to England to promote the Confederate cause.

Fearing that the British might capitulate to Confederate pressure, abolitionist lecturers toured Britain, reminding residents of their early leadership in the antislavery cause. The Union's formal commitment to emancipation would certainly increase British support for its position and prevent diplomatic recognition of the Confederacy. By the summer of 1862, Lincoln was convinced, but he wanted to wait for a military victory before making a formal announcement regarding emancipation.

Instead, the Union suffered a series of defeats that summer, and Lee marched his army into Union territory in Maryland. On September 17, Longstreet joined Lee in a fierce battle along Antietam Creek as Union troops brought the Confederate advance to a standstill near the town of Sharpsburg. Union forces suffered more than 12,000 casualties and the Confederates more than 10,000, the bloodiest single day of battle in U.S. history. Yet

President Lincoln Presenting the Emancipation Proclamation to His Cabinet In this engraving, Lincoln reads the draft of his Emancipation Proclamation to his cabinet in September 1862. On the left are Secretary of War Edwin Stanton (seated) and Secretary of the Treasury Salmon P. Chase, the two strongest supporters of the proclamation. Postmaster General Montgomery Blair and Attorney General Edward Bates (seated), who opposed the plan, are on the right. Library of Congress, LC-DIG-pga-02502

because Lee and his army were forced to retreat, Lincoln claimed the **Battle of Antietam** as a great victory. Five days later, the president announced his preliminary **Emancipation Proclamation** to the assembled cabinet, promising to free slaves in all seceding states.

On January 1, 1863, Lincoln signed the final edict, proclaiming that slaves in areas still in rebellion were "forever free" and inviting them to enlist in the Union army. Over the next two years, tens of thousands of enslaved men fled southern plantations and fought in the Union Army alongside equal numbers of free blacks who volunteered to ensure the Confederacy's defeat. Still, the proclamation was a moderate document in many ways. Its provisions exempted from emancipation the 450,000 slaves in the loyal border states, as well as more than 300,000 slaves in Union-occupied areas of Tennessee, Louisiana, and Virginia. The proclamation also justified the abolition of southern slavery on military, not moral, grounds. Despite its limits, the Emancipation Proclamation inspired joyous celebrations among free blacks and white abolitionists, who viewed it as the first step toward slavery's final eradication.

REVIEW & RELATE

How and why did the Union and the Confederacy treat American Indian and African American participation in the war differently?

What events occurred to make the Civil War become a war to end slavery?

War Transforms the North and the South

For soldiers and civilians seeking to survive the upheaval of war, political pronouncements rarely alleviated the dangers they faced. The war's extraordinary death tolls shocked Americans on both sides. On the home front, the prolonged conflict created labor shortages and severe inflation in both North and South. The war initially disrupted industrial and agricultural production as men were called to service, but the North recovered quickly by building on its prewar industrial base and technological know-how. In the South, manufacturing increased, with enslaved laborers pressed into service as industrial workers, but this created shortages on plantations. The changed circumstances of the war required women to take on new responsibilities as well. Yet these dramatic transformations also inspired dissent and protest as rising death tolls and rising prices made the costs of war ever clearer.

Life and Death on the Battlefield. Few soldiers entered the conflict knowing what to expect. A young private wrote that his idea of combat had been that the soldiers "would all be in line, all standing in a nice level field fighting, a number of ladies taking care of the wounded, etc., etc., but it isn't so." See Primary Source Project 13: Firsthand Accounts of the Civil War. Improved weaponry turned battles into scenes of bloody carnage. The shift from smoothbore muskets to rifles, which had grooves that spun the bullet, made weapons far more effective at longer distances. The use of minié balls—small bullets with a deep cavity that expanded upon firing—increased fatalities as well. By 1863 Union

Explore ▸

For two images of soldiers in wartime, see Sources 13.2 and 13.3.

army sharpshooters acquired new repeating rifles with metal cartridges. With more accurate rifles and deadlier bullets, the rival armies increasingly relied on heavy fortifications, elaborate trenches, and distant mortar and artillery fire when they could. Still, casualties continued to rise, especially since the trenches served as breeding grounds for disease.

The hardships and discomforts of war extended beyond combat itself. As General Lee complained before Antietam, many soldiers fought in ragged uniforms and without shoes. Rations, too, ran short. Food was dispensed sporadically and was often spoiled. Many Union troops survived primarily on an unleavened biscuit called hardtack as well as small amounts of meat and beans and enormous quantities of coffee. Their diet improved over the course of the war, however, as the Union supply system grew more efficient while Confederate troops subsisted increasingly on cornmeal and fatty meat. As early as 1862, Confederate soldiers began gathering food from the haversacks of Union dead.

For every soldier who died as a result of combat, three died of disease. Measles, dysentery, typhoid, and malaria killed thousands who drank contaminated water, ate tainted food, and were exposed to the elements. And infected soldiers on both sides carried yellow fever and malaria into towns where they built fortifications. Prisoner-of-war camps were especially deadly locales. Debilitating fevers in a camp near Danville, Virginia spread to the town, killing civilians as well as soldiers.

The sufferings of African American troops were particularly severe. The death rate from disease for black Union soldiers was nearly three times greater than that for white Union soldiers, reflecting their poorer health upon enlistment, the hard labor they performed, and the minimal medical care they received in the field. Southern blacks who began their army careers in contraband camps fared even worse, with a camp near Nashville losing a quarter of its residents to death in just three months in 1864.

COMPARATIVE ANALYSIS

Photographers Bring the War Home

The development of battlefield photography in the 1860s offered civilians new perspectives on warfare. Photographs were exhibited in photographers' studios and reproduced as engravings in newspapers across the country. The photographs here offer stark contrasts between soldiers on and off the battlefield. In the first, Union soldiers rest at a camp with sturdy wooden cabins. For this picture, some men stopped in the midst of work while others caroused for the camera. In the second, Union dead lie in front of the Dunker Church on the Antietam battlefield, where more than 3,600 were killed in a single day.

Source 13.2

Union Soldiers in Camp, c. 1863

Library of Congress, LC-DIG-ppmsca-34191

For all soldiers, medical assistance was primitive. Antibiotics did not exist, antiseptics were still unknown, and anesthetics were scarce. Union medical care improved with the **U.S. Sanitary Commission**, which was established by the federal government in June 1861 to promote and coordinate better medical treatment for soldiers. Nonetheless, a commentator accurately described most field hospitals as "dirty dens of butchery and horror," where amputations often occurred with whiskey as the only anesthetic.

As the horrors of war sank in, large numbers of soldiers deserted or refused to reenlist. As volunteers declined and deserters increased, both the Confederate and the Union governments were forced to institute conscription laws to draft men into service.

Battlefield Dead at Antietam, 1862

Library of Congress, LC-DIG-ppmsca-32887

Interpret the Evidence

1. How do the soldiers present themselves in the Union camp photo? How would this photograph have affected viewers on the home front?
2. How might the photograph of the Antietam battlefield affect civilians and influence soldiers like those shown in the Union camp photo?

Put It in Context

How might images like these affect attitudes toward the war among politicians, military leaders, and the public, North and South?

The Northern Economy Expands. As the war dragged on, the North's economic advantages became more apparent. Initially, the effects of the war on northern industry had been little short of disastrous. Raw cotton for textiles disappeared, southern planters stopped ordering shoes, and trade fell off precipitously. By 1863, however, the northern economy was in high gear and could provide more arms, food, shoes, and clothing to its troops as well as for those back home. As cotton production declined, woolen manufacturing doubled; and northern iron and coal production increased 25 to 30 percent during the war. Northern factories turned out weapons and ammunition while shipyards built the fleets that blockaded southern ports.

These economic improvements were linked to a vast expansion in the federal government's activities. War Department orders fueled the industrial surge. It also created the U.S. Military Railroads unit to construct tracks in newly occupied southern territories and granted large contracts to northern railroads to carry troops and supplies. With southern Democrats out of federal office, Congress also raised tariffs on imported goods to protect northern industries. In addition, the government hired thousands of "sewing women," who were contracted to make uniforms for Union soldiers. Other women joined the federal labor force as clerical workers to sustain the expanding bureaucracy and the voluminous amounts of government-generated paperwork.

That paperwork multiplied exponentially when the federal government created a national currency and a national banking system. Before the Civil War, private banks (chartered by the states) issued their own banknotes, which were used in most economic transactions. During the war, Congress revolutionized this system, giving the federal government the power to create currency, issue federal charters to banks, and take on national debt. The government then flooded the nation with treasury bills, commonly called greenbacks. The federal budget mushroomed as well—from $63 million in 1860 to nearly $1.3 billion in 1865. By the end of the war, the federal bureaucracy had become the nation's largest single employer.

Northern manufacturers faced one daunting problem: a shortage of labor. Over half a million workers left their jobs to serve in the Union army, and others were hired by the expanding federal bureaucracy. Manufacturers dealt with the problem primarily by mechanizing more tasks and by hiring more women and children, native-born and immigrant. Combining the lower wages paid to these workers with production speedups, manufacturers improved their profits while advancing the Union cause.

Urbanization and Industrialization in the South. Although Southerners had gone to war to protect an essentially rural lifestyle, the war encouraged the growth of cities and industry. The creation of a large governmental and military bureaucracy brought thousands of Southerners to the Confederate capital of Richmond. As the war expanded, refugees also flooded into Atlanta, Savannah, Columbia, and Mobile.

Industrialization contributed to urban growth as well. With the South unable to buy industrial goods from the North and limited in its trade with Europe, military necessity spurred southern industry. Clothing and shoe factories had "sprung up almost like magic" in Natchez and Jackson, Mississippi. The Tredegar Iron Works in Richmond expanded significantly as well, employing more than 2,500 men, black and white. More than 10,000 people labored in war industries in Selma, Alabama, where one factory produced cannons. With labor in short supply, widows and orphans, enslaved blacks, and white men too old or injured to fight were recruited for industrial work in many cities.

Women Aid the War Effort. Women of all classes contributed to the war effort, North and South. Thousands filled jobs in agriculture, industry, and the government that were traditionally held by men while others assisted the military effort more directly. Most Union and Confederate officials initially opposed women's direct engagement in the war. Yet it was women's voluntary organization of relief efforts that inspired the federal government to establish the U.S. Sanitary Commission. By 1862 tens of thousands of women volunteered funds and assistance through hundreds of local chapters across the North. They

Dr. Mary E. Walker Dr. Mary E. Walker received her medical degree from Syracuse Medical College and became the first female army surgeon. Wearing bloomers (pants under a skirt), she assisted soldiers and civilians in numerous battlefield areas. Captured by Confederate troops in 1864, Walker soon returned to Union ranks. She was the first woman awarded the Medal of Honor for military service. Library of Congress, LC-DIG-ppmsca-19911

Art Collection 3/Alamy Stock Photo

hosted fund-raising fairs, coordinated sewing and knitting circles, rolled bandages, and sent supplies to the front lines. With critical shortages of medical staff, some female nurses and doctors eventually gained acceptance in northern hospitals and field camps. Led by such memorable figures as Clara Barton, Mary Ann "Mother" Bickerdyke, and Dr. Mary Walker, northern women almost entirely replaced men as military nurses by the end of the war.

In the South, too, much of the medical care was performed by women. But without government support, nursing was never recognized as a legitimate profession for women, and most nurses worked out of their own homes. As a result, a Confederate soldier's chances of dying from wounds or disease were greater than those of his Union counterpart. Southern women also worked tirelessly to supply soldiers with clothes, blankets, munitions, and food. But this work, too, was often performed locally and by individuals rather than as part of a coordinated Confederate effort.

Some Union and Confederate women played more unusual roles in the war. A few dozen women joined Rose Greenhow in gathering information for military and political leaders. One of the most effective spies on the Union side was the former fugitive Harriet Tubman, who gathered intelligence in South Carolina, including from many slaves, between 1862 and 1864. Even more women served as couriers, carrying messages across battle lines to alert officers of critical changes in military orders or in the opponent's position. In addition, at least four hundred women disguised themselves as men and fought as soldiers.

Union women also sought to influence wartime policies. Following the Emancipation Proclamation, Elizabeth Cady Stanton, Susan B. Anthony, and Lucy Stone founded the **Women's National Loyal League** and launched a massive petition drive to broaden Lincoln's policy. Collecting 260,000 signatures, two-thirds of them from women, the League demanded a congressional act "emancipating all persons of African descent" everywhere in the nation.

Dissent and Protest in the Midst of War. Dissent roiled some border states from the start of the war. In 1863 and 1864, frustration spread across the North and the South generally with increasing casualties, declining numbers of volunteers, and rising inflation. As the war dragged on, many white Northerners began to wonder whether defeating the Confederacy was worth the cost, and many white Southerners whether saving it was.

From 1861 on, battles raged among residents in the border state of Missouri, with Confederate sympathizers refusing to accept living in a Union state. Pro-southern residents formed militias and staged guerrilla attacks on Union supporters. The militias, with the tacit support of Confederate officials, claimed thousands of lives during the war and forced the Union army to station troops in the area.

By 1863, dissent broadened to include Northerners who earlier embraced the Union cause. Some white Northerners had always opposed emancipation, based on racial prejudice or fear that a flood of black migrants would increase competition for jobs. Then, just two months after the Emancipation Proclamation went into effect, a new law deepened concerns among many working-class Northerners. The **Enrollment Act**, passed by Congress in March 1863, established a draft system to ensure sufficient soldiers for the Union army. While draftees were to be selected by an impartial lottery, the law allowed a person with $300 to pay the government in place of serving or to hire another man as a substitute. Many workers deeply resented the draft's profound inequality.

Dissent turned to violence in July 1863 when the new law went into effect. Riots broke out in cities across the North. In New York City, where inflation caused tremendous suffering and a large immigrant population solidly supported the Democratic Party, implementation of the draft triggered four days of the worst rioting Americans had ever seen. Women and men—including many Irish and German immigrants—attacked Republican draft officials, wealthy businessmen, and the free black community. Between July 13 and 16, rioters lynched at least a dozen African Americans and looted and burned the city's Colored

New York City Draft Riots, July 1863 On July 13 the draft riots in New York City began with an attack on the Colored Orphan Asylum on Fifth Avenue. As the matron led 233 African American children to safety, mobs of white men and women looted the building and set it ablaze. This wood engraving appeared in illustrated weeklies from New York to London. **Granger, NYC**

Orphan Asylum. The violence ended only when Union troops put down the riots by force. By then, more than one hundred New Yorkers, most of them black, lay dead.

By 1864 inflation also fueled protests in the North as it eroded the earnings of rural and urban residents. Women, children, and old men took over much of the field labor in the Midwest, trying to feed their families and the army while struggling to pay their bills. Factory workers, servants, and day laborers felt the pinch as well. With federal greenbacks flooding the market and military production a priority, the price of consumer goods climbed about 20 percent faster than wages. Although industrialists garnered huge profits, workers suffered. A group of Cincinnati seamstresses complained to President Lincoln in 1864 about employers "who fatten on their contracts by grinding immense profits out of the labor of their operatives." At the same time, employers persuaded some state legislatures to prohibit strikes in wartime. The federal government, too, supported business over labor. When workers at the Parrott arms factory in Cold Spring, New York struck for higher wages in 1864, the government declared martial law and arrested the strike leaders.

Northern Democrats saw the widening unrest as a political opportunity. Although some Democratic leaders supported the war effort, many others—whom opponents called **Copperheads**, after the poisonous snake—rallied behind Ohio politician Clement L. Vallandigham in opposing the war. Presenting themselves as the "peace party," these Democrats enjoyed considerable success in eastern cities where inflation was rampant and immigrant workers were caught between low wages and military service. The party was also strong in parts of the Midwest, like Missouri, where sympathy for the southern cause and antipathy to African Americans ran deep.

In the South, too, some whites expressed growing dissatisfaction with the war. Jefferson Davis signed a conscription act in April 1862, a year before Lincoln did so, inciting widespread opposition. Here, too, men could hire a substitute if they had enough money, and an October 1862 law exempted men owning twenty or more slaves from military service. Thus, large planters, many of whom served in the Confederate legislature, had effectively exempted themselves from fighting. As one Alabama farmer fumed, "All they want is to get you pumpt up and go to fight for their infernal negroes, and after you do their fighting you may kiss their hine parts for all they care."

Small farmers were also hard hit by policies that allowed the Confederate army to take whatever supplies it needed. The army's forced acquisition of farm produce intensified food shortages that had been building since early in the war. Moreover, the lack of an extensive railroad or canal system in the South limited the distribution of what food was available.

Food shortages drove up prices on basic items like bread and corn, while the Union blockade and the focus on military needs dramatically increased prices on other consumer goods. As the Confederate government issued ever more treasury notes to finance the war, inflation soared 2,600 percent in less than three years. In spring 1863 food riots led by working-class women erupted in cities across the South, including the Confederate capital of Richmond.

Some state legislatures then tried to control food prices, but Richmond workers continued to voice their resentment. In fall 1863 a group proclaimed, "From the fact that he consumes all and produces nothing, we know that without [our] labor and production the man with money could not exist."

The devastation of the war added to all these grievances. Since most battles were fought in the Upper South or along the Confederacy's western frontier, small farmers in these regions saw their crops, animals, and fields devastated. A phrase that had seemed cynical in 1862—"A rich man's war and a poor man's fight"—became the rallying cry of the southern peace movement in 1864. Secret peace societies flourished mainly among small farmers and in regions, like the western mountains, where plantation slavery did not develop. A secret organization centered in North Carolina provided Union forces with information on southern troop movements and encouraged desertion by Confederates. In mountainous areas, draft evaders and deserters formed guerrilla groups that attacked draft officials and actively impeded the war effort. Women joined these efforts, hiding deserters, raiding grain depots, and burning the property of Confederate officials.

When slaveholders led the South out of the Union in 1861, they had assumed the loyalty of yeomen farmers, the deference of southern ladies, and the privileges of the southern way of life. Far from preserving social harmony and social order, however, the war undermined ties between elite and poor Southerners, between planters and small farmers, and between women and men. Although most white Southerners still supported the Confederacy in 1864 and internal dissent alone did not lead to defeat, it did weaken the ties that bound soldiers to their posts in the final two years of the war.

REVIEW & RELATE

- What were the economic effects of the war on the North and the South?

- How did social conflicts created or heightened by the war fuel dissent and protest in the North and the South?

The Tide of War Turns, 1863–1865

In spring 1863, amid turmoil on the home front, General Robert E. Lee's army defeated a Union force twice its size at Chancellorsville, Virginia. The victory set the stage for a Confederate thrust into Pennsylvania, but Lee's decision to go on the offensive proved the Confederacy's undoing. In July 1863 the Union won two decisive military victories: at Gettysburg, Pennsylvania and Vicksburg, Mississippi. At the same time, the flood of African Americans, including former slaves, into the Union army transformed the very meaning of the war. By 1864, with the momentum favoring the Union, General Ulysses S. Grant implemented policies of hard war that forced the Confederacy to consider surrender.

Key Victories for the Union. In mid-1863 Confederate commanders believed the tide was turning in their favor. Following victories at Fredericksburg and Chancellorsville, General Lee launched an invasion of northern territory. While the Union army maneuvered to protect Washington, D.C., General Joseph Hooker resigned as head of the Union Army of the Potomac. On June 28, Lincoln appointed George A. Meade as the new Union commander, and the general immediately faced a major engagement at the **Battle of Gettysburg** in Pennsylvania. If Confederates won a victory there, European countries might finally recognize the southern nation and force the North to accept peace.

Neither Lee nor Meade set out to launch a battle in this small Pennsylvania town. But Lee was afraid of outrunning his supply lines, and Meade wanted to keep Confederates from gaining control of the roads that crossed at Gettysburg. So between July 1 and July 3, the opposing armies fought a desperate battle with Union troops occupying the high ground and

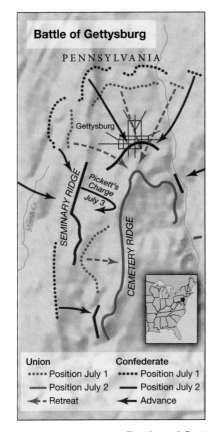

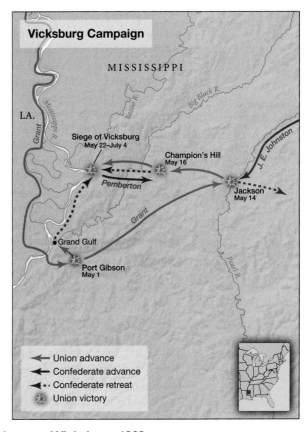

MAP 13.2   Battles of Gettysburg and Vicksburg, 1863

The three-day Battle of Gettysburg and the six-week siege of Vicksburg led to critical victories for the Union. Together, these victories forced General Lee's troops back into Confederate territory and gave the Union control of the Mississippi River. Still, the war was far from over. Confederate troops controlled the southern heartland, and Northerners wearied of the ever-increasing casualties.

Confederate forces launching deadly assaults from below (Map 13.2). Ultimately, Gettysburg proved a disaster for the South: More than 4,700 Confederates were killed, including a large number of officers; another 18,000 were wounded, captured, or missing. Although the Union suffered similar casualties, it had more men to lose, and it could claim victory.

As Lee retreated to Virginia, the South suffered another devastating defeat. Troops under General Grant had been pounding Vicksburg, Mississippi since May 1863. The **siege of Vicksburg** ended with the surrender of Confederate forces on July 4. This victory was even more important strategically than Gettysburg (Map 13.2). Combined with a victory five days later at Port Hudson, Louisiana, the Union army controlled the entire Mississippi valley, the richest plantation region in the South. This series of victories also effectively cut Louisiana, Arkansas, and Texas off from the rest of the Confederacy, ensuring Union control of the West. In November 1863 Grant's troops achieved another major victory at Chattanooga, opening up much of the South's remaining territory to invasion. Thousands of slaves deserted their plantations, and many joined the Union war effort.

That same month, November 1863, President Lincoln spoke at the official dedication ceremony for the National Cemetery at Gettysburg, Pennsylvania. In his **Gettysburg Address**, Lincoln tied the war against slavery to the fulfillment of the nation's founding ideal "that all men are created equal." He insisted that the United States "shall have a new birth of freedom—and that government of the people, by the people, and for the people, shall not perish from the earth." Only in this way, he declared, could Americans ensure that the "honored dead" had not "died in vain."

Explore ▶

Compare two opposing views of why soldiers fought for the Union in Sources 13.4 and 13.5.

As 1864 dawned, the Union had twice as many forces in the field as the Confederacy, whose soldiers were suffering from low morale, high mortality, and dwindling supplies. Although some difficult battles lay ahead, the war of attrition (in which the larger, better-supplied Union forces slowly wore down their Confederate opponents) had begun to pay dividends.

The changing Union fortunes increased support for Lincoln and his congressional allies. Union victories and the Emancipation Proclamation also convinced Great Britain not to recognize the Confederacy as an independent nation. And the heroics of African American soldiers, who engaged in direct and often brutal combat against southern troops, expanded support for emancipation. Republicans, who now fully embraced abolition as a war aim, were nearly assured the presidency and a congressional majority in the 1864 elections.

Northern Democrats still campaigned for peace and the readmission of Confederate states with slavery intact. They nominated George B. McClellan, the onetime Union commander, for president. McClellan attracted working-class and immigrant voters who traditionally supported the Democrats and bore the heaviest burdens of the war. But Democratic hopes for victory in November were crushed when Union general William Tecumseh Sherman captured Atlanta, Georgia just two months before the election. Lincoln and the Republicans won easily, giving the party a clear mandate to continue the war to its conclusion.

African Americans Contribute to Victory. Lincoln's election secured the eventual downfall of slavery. Yet the president and Congress did not eradicate human bondage on their own. From the fall of 1862 on, African Americans enlisted in the Union army and helped ensure that nothing short of universal emancipation would be the outcome of the war. As Private Thomas Long, a former slave serving with the First South Carolina Volunteers, explained: "If we hadn't become sojers, all might have gone back as it was before. . . . But now tings can neber go back, because we have showed our energy and our courage and our naturally manhood."

In the border states, which were exempt from the Emancipation Proclamation, enslaved men were adamant about enlisting since those who served in the Union army were granted their freedom. Because of this provision, slaveholders in these states did everything in their power to prevent their slaves from joining the army. Despite these efforts, between 25 and 60 percent of military-age enslaved men in the four border states stole away and joined the Union army. By the end of the war, nearly 200,000 black men had served officially in the army and navy, and some 37,000 blacks had given their lives for the Union.

Yet despite their courage and commitment, black soldiers felt the sting of racism. They were segregated in camps, given the most menial jobs, and often treated as inferiors by white soldiers and officers. Particularly galling was the Union policy of paying black soldiers less than whites. African American soldiers openly protested this discrimination even after a black sergeant who voiced his views was charged with mutiny and executed by firing squad in February 1864. The War Department finally equalized wages four months later.

Portrait of a Black Union Soldier and Family, c. 1863–1865 Taken after African Americans were allowed to join the Union Army, this daguerreotype captures a Union soldier with his wife and two daughters. He was likely a member of one of the seven Union regiments raised in Maryland, where the picture was discovered. The dresses and hats worn by the wife and daughters suggest the family was free. Library of Congress LC-DIG-ppmsca-36454

One primary concern of African American soldiers was to liberate slaves as Union armies moved deeper into the South. At the same time, thousands of southern slaves headed for Union lines. Even those forced to remain on plantations learned when Union troops were nearby and talked openly of emancipation. "Now they gradually threw off the mask," a slave remembered, "and were not afraid to let it be known that the 'freedom' in their songs meant freedom of the body in this world."

The Final Battles of a Hard War. In the spring of 1864, the war in the East entered its final stage. That March, Lincoln placed General Grant in charge of all Union forces. Grant embarked on a strategy of **hard war**, in which soldiers not only attacked military targets but also destroyed civilian crops, livestock, fields, and property to undermine morale and supply chains. Grant was also willing to accept huge casualties to achieve victory. Over the next year, he led his troops overland through western Virginia in an effort to take Richmond. Meanwhile, General Philip Sheridan devastated "The Breadbasket of the Confederacy" in Virginia's Shenandoah Valley, and General Sherman laid waste to the remnants of the plantation system in Georgia and the Carolinas.

Grant's troops headed toward Richmond, where Lee's army controlled strong defensive positions. The Confederates won a series of narrow, bloody victories, but Grant continued to push forward. Although Lee lost fewer men, they were losses he could not afford given the Confederacy's much smaller population. Combining high casualties with deserters, Lee's army was melting away with each engagement. Although soldiers and civilians—North and South—called Grant "the butcher" for his seeming lack of regard for human life, the Union general was not deterred.

In the fall of 1864, implementing hard war tactics, Sheridan rendered the Shenandoah Valley a "barren waste." Called "the burning" by local residents, Sheridan's soldiers torched fields, barns, and homes and destroyed thousands of bushels of grain along with livestock,

Why Union Soldiers Fought the Civil War

The Civil War was the bloodiest war ever fought by Americans. Hoping for a quick victory, some 75,000 men volunteered to join the Union Army in spring 1861. Yet even as the war dragged on and the death toll rose, hundreds of thousands more rallied to the Union cause. The Confederacy recruited soldiers by reminding them that they had to protect their homeland against northern invaders. In the North, the rationale for taking up arms was less clear, but even those drafted into Union service generally stayed the course, throwing themselves into battle after battle in pursuit of victory. The two historians below offer divergent explanations for why Union soldiers fought.

Source 13.4

Chandra Manning, The Fight Against Slavery (2007)

Enlisted Union soldiers came to the conclusion that winning the war would require the destruction of slavery partly because soldiers' personal observations of the South led many to decide that slavery blighted everything it touched. . . .

Yet more influential than Union soldier's preexisting notions, or even their firsthand observations of the South, were their interactions with actual slaves, which led many to view slavery as a dehumanizing and evil institution that corroded the moral virtue necessary for a population to govern itself. . . .

Hostility to slavery did not necessarily mean support for racial equality. In fact, white Union soldiers strove mightily to keep the issues of slavery and black rights separate. . . .

[Still], contact with slaves and southern society convinced many Union troops that the immoral and blighting institution of slavery was antithetical to republican government, and that

any republican government that tried to accommodate slavery was doomed to eventual failure. . . . [C]lear demands for the destruction of slavery plainly emerged among enlisted Union soldiers, especially those stationed in the slave states who were witnessing slavery with their own eyes for the first time. Even some border state Union soldiers joined the clamor, either because they had witnessed for years the violence that slavery could engender or out of shock and anger that slaveholders in their home states valued the peculiar institution over the Union. Slaves themselves did the most to force emancipation onto the Union agenda, . . . [primarily] by winning over enlisted Union soldiers, who, in the first year of the war, became the first major group after black Americans and abolitionists to call for an end to slavery. . . .

Source: Chandra Manning, *What This Cruel War Was Over: Soldiers, Slavery and the Civil War* (New York: Vintage Books, 2007), pp. 47, 49, 50–51.

shops, and mills. His campaign demoralized civilians in the region and denied Confederate troops crucial supplies.

In the preceding months, Sherman had laid siege to Atlanta, but on September 2 his forces swept around the city and destroyed the roads and rails that connected it to the rest of the Confederacy. When General John B. Hood and his Confederate troops abandoned their posts, Sherman telegraphed Lincoln: "Atlanta is ours, and fairly won." That victory

Source 13.5

Gary Gallagher, The Fight to Save the Union (2011)

The loyal American citizenry fought a war for the Union that also killed slavery. . . . Union always remained the paramount goal, a fact clearly expressed by Abraham Lincoln in speeches and other statements designed to garner the widest popular support for the war effort. . . . That hardpan of unionism held millions of Americans to the task of suppressing the slaveholders' rebellion, even as the human and material cost mushroomed. . . .

[The Union] represented a cherished legacy of the founding generation, a democratic republic with a constitution that guaranteed political liberty and afforded individuals a chance to better themselves economically. From the perspective of loyal Americans, their republic stood as the only hope for a democracy in [the] western world . . . [following] the failed European revolutions of the 1840s. Slaveholding aristocrats who established the Confederacy . . .

posed a direct threat not only to the long-term success of the American republic but also to the broader future of democracy. . . .

Issues related to the institution of slavery precipitated secession and the outbreak of fighting, but the loyal citizenry initially gave little thought to emancipation in their quest to save the Union. By the early summer of 1862, long before black men donned blue uniforms in large numbers, victorious Union armies stood poised to win the war with slavery largely intact…. Eventually, most loyal citizens, though profoundly prejudiced by twenty-first century-standards and largely indifferent toward enslaved black people, embraced emancipation as a tool to punish slaveholders, weaken the Confederacy, and protect the Union from future internal strife.

Source: Gary Gallagher, *The Union War* (Cambridge: Harvard University Press, 2011), pp. 1, 2.

Examine the Sources

1. How do Manning and Gallagher differ in their interpretations of why Union soldiers joined the war effort?
2. Based on evidence in this chapter, including the Primary Source Project, evaluate the main arguments of each author.

Put It in Context

How might the Emancipation Proclamation and the introduction of black troops in the Union Army have affected the way white Union and Confederate soldiers thought about the purpose of the war?

---

cut the South in two, but Sherman continued on. **Sherman's March to the Sea** introduced hard war tactics to Southerners along the three-hundred-mile route from the Atlantic coast north through the Carolinas. His troops cut a path of destruction fifty to sixty miles wide. They confiscated or destroyed millions of pounds of cotton, corn, wheat, and other agricultural items; tore up thousands of miles of railroad tracks; and burned Columbia, the South Carolina capital. As Eleanor Cohen Seixas, whose family had earlier fled to

Columbia for safety, recorded in her journal, "The fires raged fearfully all night" and the "vile Yankees took from us clothing, food, jewels, all our cows, horses, carriages, etc." Despite later claims that Sherman's men ravaged white women, instances of such behavior were rare, although Union soldiers did ransack homes and confiscate food and clothing.

Enslaved blacks hoped that Sherman's arrival marked their emancipation. During his victorious march, nearly 18,000 enslaved men, women, and children fled ruined plantations and sought to join the victorious troops. To their dismay, soldiers refused to take them along. Union soldiers realized that they could not care for this vast number of people and carry out their military operations. Some Union soldiers went further, abusing African American men, raping black women, or stealing their few possessions. Angry Confederates captured many blacks who were turned away, killing some and reenslaving others.

These actions caused a scandal in Washington. In January 1865, Lincoln dispatched Secretary of War Edwin Stanton to Georgia to investigate the charges. At an extraordinary meeting in Savannah, Stanton and Sherman met with black ministers to hear their complaints and hopes. The ministers spoke movingly of the war lifting "the yoke of bondage." Freed blacks, they argued, "could reap the fruit of their own labor" and, if given land, "take care of ourselves, and assist the Government in maintaining our freedom." In response, Sherman issued **Field Order Number 15**, setting aside more than 400,000 acres of captured Confederate land to be divided into small plots for former slaves. The order proved highly controversial, but it offered blacks some hope of significant change.

If many African Americans were disappointed by the actions of Union soldiers in the East, American Indians were even more devastated by developments in the West. Despite Indian nations' substantial aid to Union armies, any hope of being rewarded for their efforts vanished by 1864. Tens of thousands of whites migrated west of the Mississippi during the Civil War, and congressional passage of the Homestead Act in 1864 increased the numbers. At the same time, the U.S. army grew exponentially during the war, using its increased power to assault western Indian nations.

Attacks on Indians were not an extension of hard war policies, but rather a government-sanctioned effort to terrorize native communities. Beginning in 1862, Dakota Sioux went to war with the United States over broken treaties. After being defeated, four hundred warriors were arrested by military officials and thirty-eight executed. In 1863 California Volunteers slaughtered more than two hundred men, women, and children in a Shoshone-Bannock village in Idaho. Meanwhile thousands of white settlers had been flooding into Colorado after gold was discovered in 1858, forcing Cheyenne and Arapaho Indians off their land. In 1864 these Indians were promised refuge at Sand Creek by officers at nearby Fort Lyon. Instead, Colonel John M. Chivington led his Third Colorado Calvary in a rampage that left 125 to 160 Indian men, women, and children dead. The Sand Creek Massacre ensured that white migrants traveling in the region would be subject to Indian attacks for years to come. At the same time, in the Southwest, the Navajo were defeated by U.S. troops and their Ute allies and forced into a four-hundred-mile trek to a reservation in New Mexico.

U.S. army officers considered "winning the West" one way to restore national unity once the Civil War ended. For Indian nations, the increased migration, expanded military presence, and sheer brutality they experienced in 1863 and 1864 boded ill for their future, whichever side won the Civil War.

The War Comes to an End. As the defeat of the Confederacy loomed, the U.S. Congress finally considered abolishing slavery throughout the nation. With intense lobbying by abolitionists, petitioning by the Women's National Loyal League, the valiant efforts of Ohio Congressman James Ashley, and President Lincoln's lobbying of wavering senators, Congress passed the **Thirteenth Amendment** to the U.S. Constitution on January 31, 1865. It prohibited slavery and involuntary servitude anywhere in the United States. Some northern and western states had already enacted laws to ease racial inequities. Ohio, California, and Illinois repealed statutes barring blacks from testifying in court and serving on juries. Then, in May 1865, Massachusetts passed the first comprehensive public-accommodations law in U.S. history, ensuring equal treatment in stores, schools, theaters, and other social spaces. Cities from San Francisco to Cincinnati and New York also desegregated their streetcars.

Still hoping to stave off defeat, southern leaders also began rethinking their racial policies. The Confederate House passed a law to recruit slaves into the army in February 1865, but the Senate defeated the measure. It was too late to make a difference anyway.

In early April 1865, with Sherman heading toward Raleigh, North Carolina, Grant captured Petersburg, Virginia and then drove Lee and his forces out of Richmond. Seasoned African American troops led the final assault on the city and were among the first Union soldiers

Richmond in Ruins, April 1865   This photograph shows the Richmond and Petersburg Railroad Depot following the capture of the Confederate capital by General Grant and his troops in April 1865. The black man sitting amid the devastation no doubt realized that Richmond's fall marked the defeat of the South. Library of Congress, LC-DIG-cwpb-02709

to enter the Confederate capital. On April 9, after a brief engagement at Appomattox Court House, Virginia, Lee surrendered to Grant. Within hours, Lee's troops began heading home. While sporadic fighting continued—Cherokee Stand Watie was the last Confederate general to surrender in June 1865—the back of the Confederate army had been broken.

With Lee's surrender, many Northerners hoped that the reunited nation would be stronger and more just. Jubilation in the North was short-lived, however. On April 14, Abraham Lincoln was shot at Ford's Theatre by a Confederate fanatic named John Wilkes Booth. The president died the next day, leading to great uncertainty about how peace and national unity would be achieved.

REVIEW & RELATE

- What role did African Americans play in the defeat of the South? How did attitudes toward African Americans change in the final year of the war?

- How did the Union win the war against the Confederacy while defeating Indians in the West?

Conclusion: An Uncertain Future

The Civil War devastated and transformed the nation. The deadliest conflict in American history—some 600,000 to 750,000 Americans died in the war—the Civil War freed nearly 4 million Americans who had been enslaved. Soldiers who survived brought new experiences and knowledge back to their families and communities, but many were also marked—like former slaves—by deep physical and emotional wounds. The war transformed the home front as well. Northern and southern women entered the labor force and the public arena in numbers never before imagined. The northern economy flourished and the South became more urbanized, but the Confederacy was left economically ruined. Meanwhile the federal government significantly expanded during the war. It also initiated programs, like the Homestead Act, that fueled migration, intensifying conflicts in the West and devastating numerous Indian nations. Altogether, the Civil War dramatically accelerated the pace of economic, political, and social change, transforming American society both during the war and for decades afterward.

Still, the legacies of the war were far from certain in 1865. Protests during the war reflected a growing sense of class inequalities while the abolition of slavery highlighted ongoing racial disparities. Moreover, even in defeat, white Southerners honored Lee and other "heroes" of the "Lost Cause" with portraits, parades, and statues. Confederate women also worked tirelessly to preserve the memory of ordinary Confederate soldiers and of heroines like Rose O'Neal Greenhow, who had drowned in 1864 while returning from a mission to gain support in Europe.

Victorious Northerners celebrated wartime heroes as well but recognized that much still needed to be done. Frederick Douglass joined other former abolitionists in seeking to enfranchise African American men to secure their rights as freedpeople. He and his colleagues had no illusions about the lengths to which many whites would go to protect their traditional privileges. Yet many northern whites, exhausted by four years of war, hoped to leave the problems of slavery and secession behind. Others sought to rebuild the South quickly to ensure the nation's economic stability. These competing visions—between Northerners and Southerners and within each group—would shape the uncertainties of peace in ways few could imagine at the end of the war.

TIMELINE OF **EVENTS**

1861 Fort Sumter attacked

Slaves declared "contraband"

U.S. Sanitary Commission established

Battle of Bull Run (Manassas)

Confiscation Act passed

1862 Battle of Shiloh

Conscription act signed in South

Battle of Antietam

1863 Emancipation Proclamation signed

Enrollment Act passed in North

New York City draft riots

Battle of Gettysburg

Siege of Vicksburg

Gettysburg Address

1864 Atlanta falls

Sand Creek Massacre

Sherman's "March to the Sea"

1865 More than 200,000 African Americans serve in the Union army and navy

Field Order Number 15

Thirteenth Amendment passed

Lee surrenders to Grant

Lincoln assassinated

KEY **TERMS**

Fort Sumter, *424*

Battle of Bull Run (Manassas), *426*

contraband, *428*

Battle of Shiloh, *430*

Battle of Antietam, *432*

Emancipation Proclamation, *432*

U.S. Sanitary Commission, *434*

Women's National Loyal League, *437*

Enrollment Act, *438*

Copperheads, *493*

Battle of Gettysburg, *440*

siege of Vicksburg, *441*

Gettysburg Address, *442*

hard war, *443*

Sherman's March to the Sea, *445*

Field Order Number 15, *446*

Thirteenth Amendment, *447*

REVIEW & RELATE

1. What led four more states to join the Confederacy in 1861 and four other slave states to remain in the Union?

2. What advantages and disadvantages did each side have at the onset of the war?

3. How and why did the Union and the Confederacy treat American Indian and African American participation in the war differently?

4. What events occurred to make the Civil War become a war to end slavery?

5. What were the economic effects of the war on the North and the South?

6. How did social conflicts created or heightened by the war fuel dissent and protest in the North and the South?

7. What role did African Americans play in the defeat of the South? How did attitudes toward African Americans change in the final year of the war?

8. How did the Union win the war against the Confederacy while defeating Indians in the West?

Firsthand Accounts of the Civil War

▶ Compare the different war experiences revealed here and consider how these experiences changed over the course of the war.

Throughout the Civil War, soldiers and their families kept in close touch by writing letters. The volume of wartime correspondence was immense, with ninety thousand letters a day processed in the Union alone. Other men and women kept journals to record their experiences, which some used as the basis for published reminiscences years later. Soldiers' letters were especially important in capturing the daily experiences of war, from the boredom of encampments to the excitement or horrors of battle to concerns about their families back home (Source 13.7). Soldiers' letters also expressed their views on the causes of the war and their changing understandings of its meaning (Source 13.6). For black soldiers this often meant coming to terms with discrimination by the very government for which they were fighting (Source 13.9). Female volunteers provide another dramatic perspective on the war. Suzy King Taylor, who ran away from a Georgia plantation to work for the Union army, is the only former slave who published her memoirs of the war (Source 13.8). Far more women experienced the war from the home front, but for many Confederate women this often meant living near army outposts and even prisoner-of-war camps (Source 13.10).

The letters and journals reprinted here, from both Northerners and Southerners, represent an array of experiences, including those of soldiers and civilians, women and men, blacks and whites. Covering nearly the whole expanse of the war, they help us trace transformations among soldiers, female volunteers, and civilians.

Source 13.6

Frederick Spooner | Letter to His Brother Henry, April 30, 1861

At the start of the war, many Northerners expected a quick victory, as evidenced in this letter written by seventeen-year-old Frederick Spooner to his older brother Henry. A native of Providence, Rhode Island, Frederick believed the South was weakened by its reliance on slavery. Perhaps inspired by these same beliefs, Henry enlisted in the Union army in 1862 and later practiced law in Rhode Island and served in the U.S. House of Representatives.

Dear Henry,

Your letter was received, and I now sit down in my shirt sleeves (as it is warm) to write in return.

For the last few weeks there has been great excitement here, and nothing has been thought of scarcely except that one subject which now received the undivided attention of the whole loyal North—war.

And well may war, so hideous and disgusting in itself receive such attention when carried on for such noble and just principles as in the present case.

Traitors have begun the conflict, let us continue and end it. Let us settle it now, once and for all.

Let us settle it, even if the whole South has to be made one common graveyard, and their cotton soaked in blood. Let us do it *now* while the whole North is aroused from the inactivity and apparent laziness in which it has been so long.

There are plenty of men, an abundance of money, and a military enthusiasm never before known in the annals of history, all of which combined will do the work nice and clean, and if need be will wipe out that palmetto, pelican, rattlesnake region entirely. The holy cause in which our volunteers are enlisted will urge them on to almost superhuman exertions. The South *may* be courageous but I doubt it, they can *gas* and *hag* [complain and bluster] first rate; they can lie and steal to perfection, but I really do believe that they cannot fight. . . .

But granting them to be brave (which I don't believe can be proven) they have no chance to overturn this government. They haven't the resources, the "almighty dollar," that powerful ally, or formidable enemy—is against them. They have no money—their property has legs and will be continually disappearing.

They have prospered dealing in human flesh—let them now take the results of it.

They have had what *they* consider the *blessings* of slavery—let them now receive the *curses* of it.

They must be put down, conquered, and thoroughly subdued if need be. . . . The fifteen weak states of the South can stand no chance against the nineteen powerful states of the North. . . .

When I began I did not intend to give a lecture or write a composition on the "crisis," . . . but unconsciously I got on the all-absorbing topic at the very commencement, and it was hard work to let go of it.

There hasn't been much studying lately, and it is very hard work to think or write concerning any other subject than that on which I've paused so long.

So therefore excuse my "crisis" beginning.

Source: Nina Silber and Mary Beth Sievens, eds., *Yankee Correspondence: Civil War Letters between New England Soldiers and the Home Front* (Charlottesville: University Press of Virginia, 1996), 55–56.

Source 13.7

John Hines | Letter to His Parents, April 22, 1862

Confederate soldier John Hines describes the Battle of Shiloh in southwestern Tennessee in this letter written to his parents back home in Kentucky. The bloodiest battle up to that point in the war, Shiloh was also Hines's first combat experience. As was common for soldiers on both sides of the conflict, Hines's early enthusiasm for the war and his opinion of the enemy changed with his first taste of battle.

Dear Ma and G. Pa

. . . I was in the battle of Shiloh from beginning to end. It is said to have been the hardest fought battle ever fought on this continent. Persons who were in the battles of Manassas [Bull Run] and Ft. Donelson say they were skirmishes in comparison. . . .

Our squadron was ordered close to the federal [Union] lines on Saturday evening. We stopped close enough to hear their drums beating. We were very tired and hungry. Some of the men not having et [eaten] for 36 hours. I gave a teamster 50 cents for a biscuit. Tied my horse close to me and laid down without taking off boots or pistols and slept soundly until just at dawn the loud peal of some half dozen cannons aroused us. In a few moments we were in our saddles, overcoats and extra equipment lashed to our saddles. In our shirt sleeves, we sat on our horses examining our arms, ready for the coming fray, for we knew we would give the enemy battle if they would stand.

The increased roaring of artillery and an occasional ambulance bearing off wounded soldiers told that, as we say in camp, the ball was open. Before the sun was up we were marching to the scene of action, which was perhaps a mile off. We had not marched very far before we came upon our line of infantry. For three miles in one unbroken line stood our troops, their fixed bayonets glistening in the new sunbeams, for the sun was just coming over the top of a small elevation.

Almost every hill now on both sides looked like a volcano, for the deep mouthed cannon were roaring on every side. Soon the rattle of musketry announced that our vanguard had found the foe. The dark line of men now moved quickly in. After minutes more the volleys of musketry announced that they too had entered the bloody arena. It was really a grand scene now: you could not distinguish a musket shot now, it was one continual roar like the rushing of a storm. . . . A shell or cannonball would tear some of your comrades to pieces and a person could not tell whose turn it might be next.

Being mounted and ordered to different places during the day, I had an opportunity to see everything that happened almost and I can assure you that a battlefield is far from being a pleasant place, laying aside the dangers of being hurt, because you can't get out of hearing the groans of the dying or out of sight of the dead. It seemed to me like my acquaintances were always lying in the most auspicious places. Turn what way we might I could find some ghastly looking face that perhaps an hour ago I had seen rushing to the contest with a smile on his face. . . .

We have again returned to camp which is now outside of the former federal lines and are resting quietly. I've a good slice of cheese and a can of oysters which I took out of a federal tent before setting fire to it. I have nothing to do but think over what has happened in the last few days. . . .

Your affectionate son,
J. H. Hines

Source: Rod Gragg, ed., *The Illustrated Confederate Reader* (New York: HarperCollins, 1989), 99–100.

Source 13.8

Suzy King Taylor | Caring for the Thirty-third U.S. Colored Troops, 1863

In 1862 Suzy King Taylor escaped with other family members to a contraband camp on the Sea Islands. There she married Edward King, a black noncommissioned officer with the Thirty-third U.S. Colored Troops. Since black soldiers did not get their full pay for more than a year, many wives worked for the army as well. Suzy King was hired as a laundress but also served as a teacher, nurse, and cook. This selection is from a memoir of her experiences published in 1902.

Fort Wagner being only a mile from our camp, I went there two or three times a week, and would go up on the ramparts to watch the gunners send their shells into Charleston. . . . Outside of the fort were many skulls lying about. . . . The comrades and I would have quite a debate as to which side the men fought on. . . . They were a gruesome sight, those fleshless heads and grinning jaws, but by this time I had become accustomed to worse things. . . .

It seems strange how our aversion to seeing suffering is overcome in time of war,—how we are able to see the most sickening sights, such as men with their limbs blown off and mangled by the deadly shells without a shudder; and instead of turning away, how we hurry to assist in alleviating their pain, bind up their wounds, and press cool water to their parched lips. . . .

Finally orders were received to prepare to take Fort Gregg. . . .

About four o'clock, July 2, the charge was made. The firing could be plainly heard in camp. . . . When the wounded arrived, or rather began to arrive, the first one brought was Samuel Anderson of our company. He was badly wounded. Then others of our boys, some with their legs off, arm gone, foot off, and wounds of all kinds imaginable. . . .

My work now began. I gave my assistance to alleviate their sufferings. I asked the doctor of the hospital what I could get for them to eat. . . . I had a few cans of condensed milk and some turtle eggs, so I thought I would try to make some custard. . . . This I carried to the men, who enjoyed it very much. My services were given at all times for the comfort of these men. . . . I was enrolled as company laundress, but I did very little of it, because . . . I was employed all the time doing something for the officers and comrades.

Source: Suzy King Taylor, *Reminiscences of my Life in Camp with the 33rd United States Colored Troops, Late 1st S.C. Volunteers* (Boston: By the Author, 1902).

Thomas Freeman | Letter to His Brother-in-Law, March 26, 1864

The Massachusetts Fifty-fourth Colored Infantry, one of the Union's first black units, was recognized for its valor and heroism. The unit was also known for protesting the mistreatment of black soldiers, including a regiment-wide pay boycott to demand equal salaries for black and white soldiers. In this letter to his brother-in-law, Thomas Freeman of Worcester, Massachusetts echoes black soldiers' discontent with discrimination and poor treatment.

Jacksonville, Florida
March 26, 1864

Dear William

I will devote some spare moments I have in writing you a few lines which I hope may find you and all your family the same, also all of my many Friends in Worcester. Since the Regiment Departure from Morris Island I have enjoyed the best of health. . . . The Regiment in general are in Good Health but in Low Spirits and no reason why for they have all to a man done there duty as a soldier. It is 1 year the 1st Day of April since I enlisted and there is men here in the regiment that have been in Enlisted 13 Months and have never received one cent But there bounty and they more or less have family, and 2 thirds have never received any State Aid, and how do you think men can feel to do there duty as Soldiers, but let me say we are not Soldiers but Labourers working for Uncle Sam for nothing but our board and clothes. . . . We never can be Elevated in this country while such rascality is Performed. Slavery with all its horrorrs can not Equalise this for it is nothing but work from morning till night Building Batteries, Hauling Guns, Cleaning Bricks, clearing up land for other Regiments to settle on and if a Man Says he is sick it is the Doctors Priveledge to say yes or no. If you cannot work then you are sent to the Guard House Bucked Gagged and stay so till they see fit to relieve You and if you dont like that some white man will Give you a crack over the Head with his sword. Now do you call this Equality? If so God help such Equality. . . . I want You to consult some counsel in Relation to the Matter and see if a man could not sue for his Discharge . . . and let me know immiedeitely for I am tired of such treatment. Please answer as soon as you can and Oblidge Yours

T. D. Freeman

Source: Nina Silber and Mary Beth Sievens, eds., *Yankee Correspondence: Civil War Letters between New England Soldiers and the Home Front* (Charlottesville: University Press of Virginia, 1996), 47–48.

Eliza Frances Andrews | On Union Prisoners of War, 1865

Eliza Frances Andrews was the daughter of a Georgia planter and a staunch Confederate. In her early twenties when the Civil War began, she kept a journal that included reports on her visits to various army camps. In January 1865 she and a friend visited Captain Bonham at a local fort and met a Yankee prisoner, Peter Louis, who had been transferred from Andersonville Prison because of his skills as a shoemaker. Some 13,000 Union soldiers died at Andersonville.

I expect the poor Yank [Peter Louis] is glad to get away from Anderson on any terms. Although matters have improved somewhat with the cool weather, the tales that are told of the condition of things there last summer are appalling. Mrs. Brisbane heard all about it from Father Hamilton, a Roman Catholic priest from Macon, who has been working like a good Samaritan in those dens of filth and misery. It is a shame to us Protestants that we have let a Roman Catholic get so far ahead of us in this work of charity and mercy. Mrs. Brisbane says Father Hamilton told her that during the summer the wretched prisoners burrowed in the ground like moles to protect themselves from the sun. It was not safe to give them material to build shanties as they might use it for clubs to overcome the guards. These underground huts, he said, were alive with vermin and stank like charnel [burial] houses. Many of the prisoners were stark naked, having not so much as a shirt to their backs. . . . Father Hamilton said that at one time the prisoners died at a rate of 150 a day. . . .

Dysentery was the most fatal disease. . . . My heart aches for the poor wretches, Yankees though they are, and I am afraid God will suffer some terrible retribution to fall upon us for letting such things happen. . . . And yet, what can we do? The Yankees are really more to blame than we, for they won't exchange these prisoners, and our poor, hard-pressed Confederacy had not the means to provide for them when our own soldiers are starving in the field. Oh, what a horrible thing war is when stripped of all its pomp and circumstance!

Source: Eliza Frances Andrews, *The War-Time Journal of a Georgia Girl, 1864–1865* (New York: D. Appleton, 1908), 76–79.

Interpret the Evidence

1. According to these sources, what accounts for the early popular support for the war and when and where does that support appear to diminish?

2. Compare the letters from soldiers Fred Spooner (Source 13.6), John Hines (Source 13.7), and Thomas Freeman (Source 13.9). How did each view the enemy and the causes of the war?

3. In what ways do Suzy King Taylor (Source 13.8) and Eliza Frances Andrews (Source 13.10) defy or confirm contemporary gender roles? How does their race and their status shape these roles?

4. How do the experiences of Suzy King Taylor and Thomas Freeman (Sources 13.8 and 13.9) compare to those of the white writers (Sources 13.6, 13.7, and 13.10)?

Put It in Context

In what ways do these personal sources complement or challenge the more well-known political and military history of the Civil War?

14

Emancipation and Reconstruction

1863–1877

WINDOW TO THE PAST

Sharecropping Agreement, 1870

After the end of slavery, plantation owners needed to find new ways to work their land and former slaves needed to find employment. As a result, freedpeople sought to enter into sharecropping agreements, such as the one shown here, to farm on behalf of landowners because they lacked money and tools and wanted to farm their own land. However, despite their best efforts, they usually found themselves in debt to the white planter-merchants who controlled the accounts and sold them supplies. ▶ To discover more about what this primary source can show us, see Source 14.8 on page 486.

Alabama Department of Archives and History, Montgomery, Alabama

After reading this chapter you should be able to:

- Describe the challenges newly freed African Americans faced and how they responded to them.

- Analyze the influence of the president and Congress on Reconstruction policy and evaluate the successes and shortcomings of the policies they enacted.

- Evaluate the changes that took place in the society and economy of the South during Reconstruction.

- Explain how and why Reconstruction came to an end by the mid-1870s.

COMPARING AMERICAN HISTORIES

Jefferson Franklin Long spent his life improving himself and the lives of others of his race. Born a slave in Alabama in 1836, Long showed great resourcefulness in profiting from the limited opportunities available to him under slavery. His master, a tailor who moved his family to Georgia, taught him the trade, but Long taught himself to read and write. When the Civil War ended, he opened a tailor shop in Macon, Georgia. His business success allowed him to venture into Republican Party politics. Elected as Georgia's first black congressman in 1870, Long fought for the political rights of freed slaves. In his first appearance on the House floor, he opposed a bill that would allow former Confederate officials to return to Congress,

(*left*) **Jefferson Franklin Long** Library of Congress, LC-DIG-cwpbh-556

(*right*) **Andrew Johnson** Library of Congress, 3a53290

noting that many belonged to secret societies, such as the Ku Klux Klan, that intimidated black citizens. Despite his pleas, the measure passed, and Long decided not to run for reelection.

By the mid-1880s, Long had become disillusioned with the ability of black Georgians to achieve their objectives via electoral politics. Instead, he counseled African Americans to turn to institution building as the best hope for social and economic advancement. Long helped found the Union Brotherhood Lodge, a black mutual aid society with branches throughout central Georgia, which provided social and economic services for its members. He died in 1901, as political disfranchisement and racial segregation swept through Georgia and the rest of the South.

Jefferson Long and Andrew Johnson shared many characteristics, but their views on race could not have been more different. Whereas Long fought for the right of self-determination for African Americans, Johnson believed that whites alone should govern. Born in 1808 in Raleigh, North Carolina, Johnson grew up in poverty. At the age of thirteen or fourteen, he became a tailor's apprentice and, after moving to Tennessee in 1826, like Long, opened a tailor shop. The following year, Johnson married and began to prosper, purchasing a farm and a small number of slaves.

As he made his mark in Greenville, Tennessee, Johnson became active in Democratic Party politics. A social and political outsider, Johnson gained support by championing the rights of workers and small farmers against the power of the southern aristocracy. Political success followed, and by the time the Civil War broke out, he was a U.S. senator.

When the Civil War erupted, Johnson remained loyal to the Union even after Tennessee seceded in 1861. President Abraham Lincoln rewarded Johnson by appointing him as military governor of Tennessee. In 1864 the Republican Lincoln chose the Democrat Johnson to run with him as vice president. Less than six weeks after their inauguration in March 1865, Johnson became president upon Lincoln's assassination.

Fate placed Reconstruction in the hands of Andrew Johnson. After four years, the brutal Civil War had come to a close. Yet the hard work of reunion remained. Toward this end, President Johnson oversaw the reestablishment of state governments in the former Confederate states. He considered the southern states as having fulfilled their obligations for rejoining the Union, even as they passed measures that restricted black civil and political rights. Most Northerners reached a different conclusion. Having won the bloody war, they feared losing the peace to Johnson and the defeated South. ■

Comparing the American histories of Andrew Johnson and Jefferson Long highlights hard-fought battles to determine the fate of the postwar South and the meaning of freedom for newly emancipated African Americans. Former slaves sought to reunite their families, obtain land, and seek an education. President Johnson rejected their pleas for assistance to fulfill these aims. However, Congress passed laws to ensure civil rights and extend the vote to African American men, although African American women, like white women, remained disfranchised. In the South, whites attempted to restore their economic and political power over African Americans by resorting to intimidation and violence. By 1877, they succeeded in bringing Reconstruction to an end with the consent of the federal government.

Emancipation

Even before the war came to a close, Reconstruction had begun on a small scale. During the Civil War, blacks remaining in Union-occupied areas, such as the South Carolina Sea Islands, gained some experience with freedom. When Union troops arrived, most southern whites fled, but enslaved workers chose to stay on the land. Some farmed for themselves, but most worked for northern whites who moved south to demonstrate the profitability of free black labor. After the war, however, former plantation owners returned. Rather than work for these whites, freedpeople preferred to establish their own farms. If forced to hire themselves out, they insisted on negotiating the terms of their employment. Wives and mothers often refused to labor for whites at all in favor of caring for their own families. These conflicts reflected the priorities that would shape the actions of freedpeople across the South in the immediate aftermath of the war. For freedom to be meaningful, it had to include economic independence, the power to make family decisions, and the right to control some community decisions.

African Americans Embrace Freedom. When U.S. troops arrived in Richmond, Virginia in April 1865, the city's enslaved population knew that freedom was, finally, theirs. Four days after Union troops arrived, 1,500 African Americans, including a large number of soldiers, packed First African Baptist, the largest of the city's black churches. During the singing of the hymn "Jesus My All to Heaven Is Gone," they raised their voices at the line "This is the way I long have sought." As news of the Confederacy's defeat spread, newly freed African Americans across the South experienced similar emotions. Many years later, Houston H. Holloway, a Georgia slave who had been sold three times before he was twenty years old, recalled the day of emancipation: "I felt like a bird out a cage. Amen. Amen, Amen. I could hardly ask to feel any better than I did that day."

For southern whites, however, the end of the war brought fear, humiliation, and uncertainty. From their perspective, the jubilation of former slaves poured salt in their wounds. In many areas, blacks celebrated their freedom under the protection of Union soldiers. When the army moved out, freedpeople suffered deeply for their enthusiasm. Whites beat, whipped, raped, and shot blacks who they felt had been too joyous in their celebration or too helpful to the Yankee invaders. As one North Carolina freedman testified, the Yankees "tol' us we were free," but once the army left, the planters "would get cruel to the slaves if they acted like they were free."

Newly freed blacks also faced less visible dangers. During the 1860s, disease swept through the South and through the contraband camps that housed many former slaves; widespread malnutrition and poor housing heightened the problem. A smallpox epidemic that spread south from Washington, D.C. killed more than sixty thousand freedpeople.

Despite the dangers, southern blacks eagerly pursued emancipation. They moved; they married; they attended school; they demanded wages; they refused to work for whites; they gathered together their families; they created black churches and civic associations; they held political meetings. Sometimes, black women and men acted on their own, pooling their resources to advance their freedom. At other times, they received help from private organizations—particularly northern missionary and educational associations—staffed mostly by former abolitionists, free blacks, and evangelical Christians.

Emancipated slaves also called on federal agencies for assistance and support. The most important of these agencies was the newly formed Bureau of Refugees, Freedmen, and Abandoned Lands, popularly known as the **Freedmen's Bureau**. Created by Congress in 1865 and signed into law by President Lincoln, the bureau provided ex-slaves with economic and legal resources. The Freedmen's Bureau also aided many former slaves in achieving one of their primary goals: obtaining land. A South Carolina freedman summed up the feeling of the newly emancipated. "Give us our own land and we take care of ourselves," he remarked. "But without land, the old masters can hire or starve us, as they

Explore ▶

See Source 14.1 for freedpeople's views about ownership of land.

please." During the last years of the war, the federal government had distributed to the freedpeople around 400,000 acres of abandoned land from the South Carolina Sea Islands to Florida. Immediately after hostilities ceased, the Freedmen's Bureau made available hundreds of thousands of additional acres to recently emancipated slaves.

Reuniting Families Torn Apart by Slavery.

The first priority for many newly freed blacks was to reunite families torn apart by slavery. Men and women traveled across the South to find family members. Well into the 1870s and 1880s, parents ran advertisements in newly established black newspapers, providing what information they knew about their children's whereabouts and asking for assistance in finding them. Milly Johnson wrote to the Freedmen's Bureau in March 1867, after failing to locate the five children she had lost under slavery. She finally located three of them, but any chance of discovering the whereabouts of the other two disappeared because the records of the slave trader who purchased them burned during the war. Despite such obstacles, thousands of slave children were reunited with their parents in the 1870s.

Husbands and wives, or those who considered themselves as such despite the absence of legal marriage under slavery, also searched for each other. Those who lived on nearby plantations could now live together for the first time. Those whose spouse had been sold to distant plantations had a more difficult time. They wrote (or had letters written on their behalf) to relatives and friends who had been sold with their mate; sought assistance from

GUIDED ANALYSIS

Freedpeople Petition for Land, 1865

A committee of former slaves in Edisto Island, South Carolina wrote President Johnson requesting that they be allowed to purchase land promised them by the government during the Civil War. The president intended to restore the properties to the former rebel landholders and did not respond to the black petitioners.

Source 14.1

Edisto Island S.C. Oct 28th 1865.

> . . . Here is where secession was born and Nurtured Here is were we have toiled nearly all Our lives as slaves and were treated like dumb Driven cattle, This is our home, we have made These lands what they are. we were the only true and Loyal people that were found in posession of these Lands. we have been always ready to strike for Liberty and humanity yea to fight if needs be To preserve this glorious union. Shall not we who Are freedman and have been always true to this Union have the same rights as are enjoyed by Others? Have we broken any Law of these United States? Have we forfieted our rights of property In Land?—If not then! are not our rights as A free people and good citizens of these United States To be considered before the rights of those who were Found in rebellion against this good and just Government.
>
> We have been encouraged by government to take up these lands in small tracts, receiving Certificates of the same—we have thus far Taken Sixteen thousand (16000) acres of Land here on This Island. We are ready to pay for this land When Government calls for it and now after What has been done will the good and just government take from us all this right and make us Subject to the will of those who have cheated and Oppressed us for many years God Forbid! We the freedmen of this Island and of the State of South Carolina–Do therefore petition to you as the President of these United States, that some provisions be made by which Every colored man can purchase land. and Hold it as his own. . . .

In behalf of the Freedmen Committee
Henry Bram. Ishmael. Moultrie. yates. Sampson.

Source: Henry Bram et al. to the President of these United States, 28 Oct. 1865, filed as P-27 1865, Letters Received, series 15, Washington Headquarters, Bureau of Refugees, Freedmen, & Abandoned Lands, Record Group 105, National Archives.

Why do the freedpeople believe their request justified?

Why do they think the former landowners do not deserve the land?

How does this show the importance of land-ownership to them?

Put It in Context

Why was landownership so important to the freed slaves?

Winslow Homer, *A Visit from the Old Mistress*, 1876 Civil War correspondent and artist Winslow Homer visited Virginia in the mid-1870s and visually captured the tensions existing between freedpeople and former owners. Here, a former mistress visits the home of three black women. Although the house is humble, one woman refuses to stand for the "old mistress" and the other two, one holding a free-born child, eye her warily. Smithsonian American Art Museum, Washington, D.C./ Art Resource, NY

government officials, churches, and even their former masters; and traveled to areas where they thought their spouse might reside.

These searches were complicated by long years of separation and the lack of any legal standing for slave marriages. In 1866 Philip Grey, a Virginia freedman, located his wife, Willie Ann, and their daughter Maria, who had been sold away to Kentucky years before. Willie Ann was eager to reunite with her husband, but in the years since being sold, she had remarried and borne three children. Her second husband had joined the Union army and was killed in battle. When Willie Ann wrote to Philip in April 1866, she explained her new circumstances, concluding: "If you love me you will love my children and you will have to promise me that you will provide for them all as well as if they were your own. . . . I know that I have lived with you and loved you then and love you still."

Most black spouses who found each other sought to legalize their relationship. A superintendent for marriages for the Freedmen's Bureau in northern Virginia reported that he gave out seventy-nine marriage certificates on a single day in May 1866. In another case, four couples went right from the fields to a local schoolhouse, still dressed in their work clothes, where the parson married them.

Of course, some former slaves hoped that freedom would allow them to leave unhappy relationships. Having never been married under the law, couples could simply separate and move on. Complications arose, however, if they had children. In Lake City, Florida in 1866, a Freedmen's Bureau agent asked his superiors for advice on how to deal with Madison Day and Maria Richards. They refused to legalize the relationship forced on them under slavery, but both sought custody of their three children. As with white couples in the mid-nineteenth century, the father was granted custody on the assumption that he had the best chance of providing for the children financially.

Freedom to Learn. Seeking land and reuniting families were only two of the many ways that southern blacks proclaimed their freedom. Learning to read and write was another. The desire to learn was all but universal. Slaves had been forbidden to read and write, and with emancipation they pursued what had been denied them. A newly liberated father in Mississippi proclaimed, "If I nebber does nothing more while I live, I shall give my children a chance to go to school, for I considers education [the] next best ting to liberty."

A variety of organizations opened schools for former slaves during the 1860s and 1870s. By 1870 nearly a quarter million blacks were attending one of the 4,300 schools established by the Freedmen's Bureau. Black and white churches and missionary societies sent hundreds of teachers, black and white, into the South to establish schools in former plantation areas. Their attitudes were often paternalistic and the schools were segregated, but the institutions they founded offered important educational resources for African Americans.

Freedmen's Bureau School   This photograph of a one-room Freedmen's Bureau school in North Carolina in the late 1860s shows the large number and diverse ages of students who sought to obtain an education following emancipation. The teachers included white and black northern women sent by missionary and reform organizations as well as southern black women who had already received some education. Granger, NYC

Parents worked hard to keep their children in school during the day. As children gained the rudiments of education, they passed on their knowledge to parents and older siblings whose jobs prevented them from attending school. Still, many adult freedpeople insisted on getting a bit of education for themselves. In New Bern, North Carolina, where many blacks labored until eight o'clock at night, a teacher reported that they then spent at least an hour "in earnest application to study."

Freedmen and freedwomen sought education for a variety of reasons. Some viewed it as a sign of liberation. Others knew that they must be able to read the labor contracts they signed if they were ever to challenge exploitation by whites. Some freedpeople were eager to correspond with relatives, others to read the Bible. Growing numbers hoped to participate in politics, particularly the public meetings organized by blacks in cities across the South. When such gatherings set priorities for the future, the establishment of public schools was high on the list.

Despite the enthusiasm of blacks and the efforts of the federal government and private agencies, schooling remained severely limited throughout the South. A shortage of teachers and of funding kept enrollments low among blacks and whites alike. The isolation of black farm families and the difficulties in eking out a living limited the resources available for education. By 1880, only about a quarter of African Americans were literate.

Freedom to Worship and the Leadership Role of Black Churches.

One of the constant concerns freedpeople expressed was the desire to read the Bible and interpret it for themselves. A few black congregations had existed under slavery, but most slaves were forced to listen to white preachers who claimed that God created slavery.

From the moment of emancipation, freedpeople gathered at churches to celebrate community events. Black Methodist and Baptist congregations spread rapidly across the South following the Civil War. In these churches, African Americans were no longer forced to sit in the back benches or punished for moral infractions defined by white masters. Now blacks invested community resources in their own religious institutions where they filled the pews, hired the preachers, and selected boards of deacons and elders. Churches were the largest structures available to freedpeople in many communities and thus were used by a variety of community organizations. They often served as schools and hosted picnics, dances, weddings, funerals, festivals, and other events that brought blacks together. Church leaders also often served as arbiters of community standards of morality.

In the early years of emancipation black churches also served as important sites for political organizing. Some black ministers worried that political concerns would overwhelm spiritual devotions. Others agreed with the Reverend Charles H. Pearce of Florida, who declared, "A man in this State cannot do his whole duty as a minister except he looks out for the political interests of his people." Whatever the views of ministers, black churches were among the few places where African Americans could express their political views free from white interference.

REVIEW & RELATE

• What were freedpeople's highest priorities in the years immediately following the Civil War? Why?

• How did freedpeople define freedom? What steps did they take to make freedom real for themselves and their children?

National Reconstruction

Presidents Abraham Lincoln and Andrew Johnson viewed Reconstruction as a process of national reconciliation. They sketched out terms by which the former Confederate states could reclaim their political representation in the nation without serious penalties. Congressional Republicans, however, had a more thoroughgoing reconstruction in mind. Like many African Americans, Republican congressional leaders expected the South to extend constitutional rights to the freedmen and to provide them with the political and economic resources to sustain their freedom. Over the next decade, these competing visions of Reconstruction played out in a hard-fought and tumultuous battle over the meaning of the South's defeat and the emancipation of blacks.

Abraham Lincoln Plans for Reunification.

In December 1863, President Lincoln issued the **Proclamation of Amnesty and Reconstruction**, which asked relatively little of the southern states. Lincoln declared that defeated states would have to accept the abolition of slavery, but then new governments could be formed when 10 percent of those eligible to vote in 1860 (which in practice meant white southern men but not blacks) swore an oath of allegiance to the United States. Lincoln's plan granted amnesty to all but the highest-ranking Confederate officials, and the restored voters in each state would elect members to a constitutional convention and representatives to take their seats in Congress. In the next year and a half, Arkansas, Louisiana, and Tennessee reestablished their governments under Lincoln's "Ten Percent Plan."

Republicans in Congress had other ideas. Radical Republicans argued that the Confederate states should be treated as "conquered provinces" subject to congressional supervision. In 1864 Congress passed the Wade-Davis bill, which established much higher barriers for readmission to the Union than did Lincoln's plan. For instance, the Wade-Davis bill substituted 50 percent of voters for the president's 10 percent requirement. Lincoln put a stop to this harsher proposal by using a pocket veto—refusing to sign it within ten days of Congress's adjournment.

Although Lincoln and congressional Republicans disagreed about many aspects of postwar policy, Lincoln was flexible, and his actions mirrored his desire both to heal the Union and to help southern blacks. For example, the president supported the **Thirteenth Amendment**, abolishing slavery, which passed Congress in January 1865 and was sent to the states for ratification. In March 1865, Lincoln signed the law to create the Freedmen's Bureau. That same month, the president expressed his sincere wish for reconciliation between the North and the South. "With malice toward none, with charity for all," Lincoln declared in his second inaugural address, "let us strive on to finish the work . . . to bind up the nation's wounds." Lincoln would not, however, have the opportunity to implement his balanced approach to Reconstruction. When he was assassinated in April 1865, it fell to Andrew Johnson, a very different sort of politician, to lead the country through the process of reintegration.

Andrew Johnson and Presidential Reconstruction.

The nation needed a president who could transmit northern desires to the South with clarity and conviction and ensure that they were carried out. Instead, the nation got a president who substituted his own aims for those of the North, refused to engage in meaningful compromise, and misled the South into believing that he could achieve restoration quickly. In the 1864 election, Lincoln chose Johnson, a southern Democrat, as his running mate in a thinly veiled effort to attract border-state voters. The vice presidency was normally an inconsequential role, so it mattered little to Lincoln that Johnson was out of step with many Republican Party positions.

As president, however, Johnson's views took on profound importance. Born into rural poverty, Johnson had no sympathy for the southern aristocracy. Yet he had been a slave owner, so his political opposition to slavery was not rooted in moral convictions. Instead, it sprang from the belief that slavery gave plantation owners inordinate power and wealth, which came at the expense of the majority of white Southerners, who owned no slaves. Johnson saw emancipation as a means to "break down an odious and dangerous [planter] aristocracy," not to empower blacks. Consequently, he was unconcerned with the fate of African Americans in the postwar South. Six months after taking office, President Johnson rescinded the wartime order to distribute confiscated land to freedpeople in the Sea Islands. He saw no reason to punish the Confederacy's leaders, because he believed that the end of slavery would doom the southern aristocracy. He hoped to bring the South back into the Union as quickly as possible and then let Southerners take care of their own affairs.

Johnson's views, combined with a lack of political savvy and skill, ensured his inability to work constructively with congressional Republicans, even the moderates who constituted the majority. Moderate Republicans shared the prevalent belief of their time that blacks were inferior to whites, but they argued that the federal government needed to protect newly emancipated slaves. Senator Lyman Trumbull of Illinois, for example, warned that without national legislation, ex-slaves would "be tyrannized over, abused, and virtually reenslaved." The moderates expected southern states, where 90 percent of African Americans lived, to extend basic civil rights to the freedpeople, including equal protection, due process of law, and the right to work and hold property.

Nearly all Republicans shared these positions, but the Radical wing of the party wanted to go further. Led by Senator Charles Sumner of Massachusetts and Congressman Thaddeus Stevens of Pennsylvania, this small but influential group advocated suffrage, or voting rights, for African American men as well as the redistribution of southern plantation lands to freed slaves. Stevens called on the federal government to provide freedpeople "a homestead of forty acres of land," which would give them some measure of autonomy. These efforts failed, and the Republican Party proved unable to pass a comprehensive land distribution program that enabled freed blacks to gain economic independence. Nonetheless, whatever disagreements between Radicals and moderates, all Republicans believed that Congress should have a strong voice in determining the fate of the former Confederate states. From May to December 1865, with Congress out of session, they waited to see what Johnson's restoration plan would produce, ready to assert themselves if his policies deviated too much from their own.

At first, it seemed as if Johnson would proceed as they hoped. He appointed provisional governors to convene new state constitutional conventions and urged these conventions to ratify the Thirteenth Amendment, abolishing slavery, and revoke the states' ordinances of secession. He also allowed the majority of white Southerners to obtain amnesty and a pardon by swearing their loyalty to the U.S. Constitution, but he required those who had held more than $20,000 of taxable property—the members of the southern aristocracy—to petition him for a special pardon to restore their rights. Republicans

Mourning at Stonewall Jackson's Gravesite, 1866
Many Northerners were concerned that the defeat of the Confederacy did not lessen white Southerners' devotion to the "Lost Cause" or the heroism of soldiers who fought to maintain a society based on the domination of African Americans. Women, who led the efforts to memorialize Confederate soldiers, are shown at the gravesite of General Stonewall Jackson in Lexington, Virginia. Virginia Military Institute Archives

expected him to be harsh in dealing with his former political foes. Instead, Johnson relished the reversal of roles that put members of the southern elite at his mercy. As the once prominent petitioners paraded before him, the president granted almost all of their requests for pardons.

By the time Congress convened in December 1865, Johnson was satisfied that the southern states had fulfilled his requirements for restoration. Moderate and Radical Republicans disagreed, seeing few signs of change or contrition in the South. Mississippi, for example, rejected ratification of the Thirteenth Amendment. As a result of Johnson's liberal pardon policy, many former leaders of the Confederacy won election to state constitutional conventions and to Congress. Indeed, Georgians elected Confederate vice president Alexander H. Stephens to the U.S. Senate.

Far from providing freedpeople with basic civil rights, the southern states passed a variety of **black codes** intended to reduce African Americans to a condition as close to slavery as possible. Some laws prohibited blacks from bearing arms; others outlawed intermarriage and excluded blacks from serving on juries. The codes also made it difficult for blacks to leave plantations unless they proved they could support themselves. Laws like this were designed to ensure that white landowners had a supply of cheap black labor despite slavery's abolition.

Northerners viewed this situation with alarm. In their eyes, the postwar South looked very similar to the Old South, with a few cosmetic adjustments. If the black codes prevailed, one Republican proclaimed, "then I demand to know of what practical value is the amendment abolishing slavery?" Others wondered what their wartime sacrifices meant if the South admitted no mistakes, was led by the same people, and continued to oppress its black inhabitants. **See Primary Source Project 14: Testing and Contesting Freedom, page 484.**

Johnson and Congressional Resistance.

Faced with growing opposition in the North, Johnson stubbornly held his ground. He insisted that the southern states had followed his plan and were entitled to resume their representation in Congress. Republicans objected, and in December 1865 they barred the admission of southern lawmakers. But Johnson refused to compromise. In January 1866, the president rejected a bill passed by Congress to extend the life of the Freedmen's Bureau for two years. A few months later, he vetoed the Civil Rights Act, which Congress had passed to protect freedpeople from the restrictions placed on them by the black codes. These bills represented a consensus among moderate and Radical Republicans on the federal government's responsibility toward former slaves.

Johnson justified his vetoes on both constitutional and personal grounds. He and other Democrats contended that so long as Congress refused to admit southern representatives, it could not legally pass laws affecting the South. The president also condemned the Freedmen's Bureau bill because it infringed on the right of states to handle internal affairs such as education and economic policies. Johnson's vetoes exposed his racism and his lifelong belief that the evil of slavery lay in the harm it did to poor whites, not to enslaved blacks. Johnson argued that the bills he vetoed discriminated against whites, who would receive no benefits under them, and thus put whites at a disadvantage with blacks who received government assistance. Johnson's private secretary reported in his diary, "The president has at times exhibited a morbid distress and feeling against the Negroes."

Johnson's actions united moderates and Radicals against him. In April 1866, Congress repassed both the Freedmen's Bureau extension and Civil Rights Act over the president's vetoes. In June, lawmakers adopted the **Fourteenth Amendment**, which incorporated many of the provisions of the Civil Rights Act, and submitted it to the states for ratification (see Appendix). Reflecting its confrontational dealings with the president, Congress wanted to ensure more permanent protection for African Americans than simple legislation could provide. Lawmakers also wanted to act quickly, as the situation in the South seemed to be deteriorating rapidly. In May 1866, a race riot had broken out in Memphis,

Explore ▶

See Sources 14.2 and 14.3 for two perspectives on the Freedmen's Bureau.

Tennessee. For a day and a half, white mobs, egged on by local police, went on a rampage, during which they terrorized blacks and burned their homes and churches. "The late riots in our city," the white editor of a Memphis newspaper asserted, "have satisfied all of one thing, that the *southern man* will not be ruled by the *negro*."

The Fourteenth Amendment defined citizenship to include African Americans, thereby nullifying the ruling in the *Dred Scott* case of 1857, which declared that blacks were not citizens. It extended equal protection and due process of law to all persons, not only citizens. The amendment repudiated Confederate debts, which some state governments had refused to do, and it barred Confederate officeholders from holding elective office unless Congress removed this provision by a two-thirds vote. Although most Republicans were upset with Johnson's behavior, at this point they were not willing to embrace the Radical position entirely. Rather than granting the right to vote to black males at least twenty-one years of age, the Fourteenth Amendment gave the states the option of excluding blacks and accepting a reduction in congressional representation if they did so.

Johnson remained inflexible. Instead of counseling the southern states to accept the Fourteenth Amendment, which would have sped up their readmission to the Union, he encouraged them to reject it. In the fall of 1866, Johnson decided to take his case directly to northern voters before the midterm congressional elections. Campaigning for candidates

Memphis Race Riot   A skirmish between white policemen and black Union veterans on May 1, 1866 resulted in three days of rioting by white mobs that attacked the black community of Memphis, Tennessee. Before federal troops restored peace, numerous women had been raped, and forty-six African Americans and two whites had been killed. This illustration from *Harper's Weekly* depicts the carnage. Granger, NYC

who shared his views, he embarked on a swing through the Midwest. Out of touch with northern opinion, Johnson attacked Republican lawmakers and engaged in shouting matches with audiences. On election day, Republicans increased their majorities in Congress and now controlled two-thirds of the seats, providing them with greater power to override presidential vetoes.

Congressional Reconstruction.   When the Fortieth Congress convened in 1867, Republican lawmakers charted a new course for Reconstruction. With moderates and Radicals united against the president, Congress intended to force the former Confederate states not only to protect the basic civil rights of African Americans but also to grant them the vote. Moderates now agreed with Radicals that unless blacks had access to the ballot, they would not be able to sustain their freedom. Extending the suffrage to African Americans also aided the fortunes of the Republican Party in the South by adding significant numbers of new voters. By the end of March, Congress enacted three Military Reconstruction Acts. Together they divided ten southern states into five military districts, each under the supervision of a Union general (Map 14.1). The male voters of each state, regardless of race, were to elect delegates to a constitutional convention; only former Confederate officials were disfranchised. The conventions were required to draft constitutions that guaranteed black suffrage and ratified the Fourteenth Amendment. Within a year, North Carolina, South Carolina, Florida, Alabama, Louisiana, and Arkansas had fulfilled these obligations and reentered the Union.

Debating the Freedmen's Bureau

From the start, the Freedmen's Bureau generated controversy. To its Republican supporters, it helped southern blacks make the transition from slavery to freedom. For most white Southerners and many northern Democrats, however, the bureau was little more than an expensive social welfare program that rewarded idleness in blacks. Both points of view are represented in the following documents. In a report written to the Congressional Joint Committee on Reconstruction, Colonel Eliphalet Whittlesey, the assistant head of the Freedmen's Bureau in North Carolina, outlined the bureau's initial accomplishments. The anti-bureau cartoon reprinted here was created during the height of the conflict over Reconstruction between the Republican Congress and President Andrew Johnson; it was intended to support the election of a Democratic candidate for governor of Pennsylvania, an ally of Johnson.

Source 14.2

Colonel Eliphalet Whittlesey | Report on the Freedmen's Bureau, 1865

All officers of the bureau are instructed—

To aid the destitute, yet in such a way as not to encourage dependence.

To protect freedmen from injustice.

To assist freedmen in obtaining employment and fair wages for their labor.

To encourage education, intellectual and moral. . . .

. . . [W]e have in our camps at Roanoke Island and Newbern, many women and children, families of soldiers who have died in the service, and refugees from the interior during the war, for whom permanent provision must be made. . . . The reports prepared by Surgeon Hogan will show the condition of freedmen hospitals. In the early part of the summer much suffering and mortality occurred for want of medical attendance and supplies. This evil is now being remedied by the employment of surgeons by contract. . . .

Contrary to the fears and predictions of many, the great mass of colored people have remained quietly at work upon the plantations of their former masters during the entire summer. The crowds seen about the towns in the early part of the season had followed in the wake of the Union army, to escape from slavery. After hostilities ceased these refugees returned to their homes, so that but few vagrants can now be found. In truth, a much larger amount of vagrancy exists among the whites than among the blacks. It is the almost uniform report of officers of the bureau that freedmen are industrious.

The report is confirmed by the fact that out of a colored population of nearly 350,000 in the State, only about 5,000 are now receiving support from the government. Probably some others are receiving aid from kind-hearted men who have enjoyed the benefit of their services from childhood. To the general quiet and industry of this people there can be no doubt that the efforts of the bureau have contributed greatly.

Source: *The Reports of the Committees of the House of Representatives Made during the First Session, Thirty-ninth Congress, 1865–1866* (Washington, DC: Government Printing Office, 1866), 186–87, 189.

Source 14.3

Democratic Flier Opposing the Freedmen's Bureau Bill, 1866

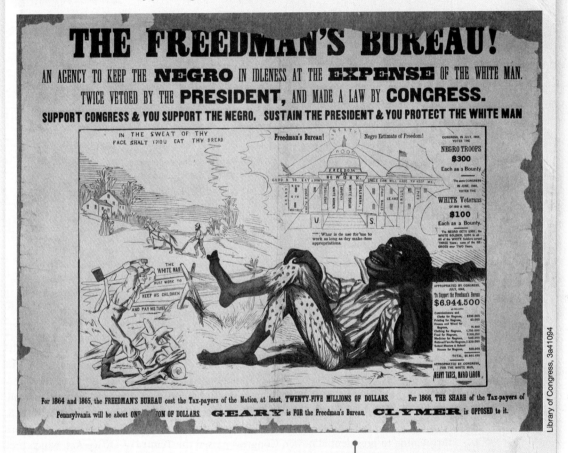

Library of Congress, 3a41094

Interpret the Evidence

1. According to Colonel Whittlesey, what needs does the Freedmen's Bureau address? How does he measure the bureau's success?

2. Why might this portrayal of the Freedmen's Bureau have appealed to some whites, north and south? How would Whittlesey and other bureau supporters have responded?

Put It in Context

How did prevailing racial assumptions shape both the cartoon and the report?

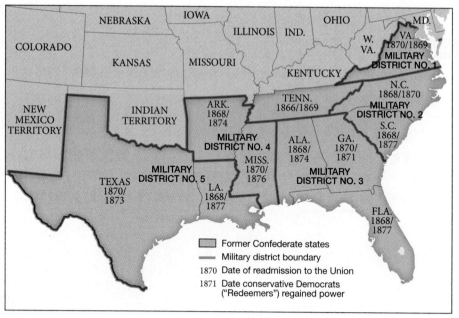

MAP 14.1 Reconstruction in the South

In 1867 Congress enacted legislation dividing the former Confederate states into five military districts. All the states were readmitted to the Union by 1870, and white conservative Democrats (Redeemers) had replaced Republicans in most states by 1875. Only in Florida, Louisiana, and South Carolina did federal troops remain until 1877.

Having ensured congressional Reconstruction in the South, Republican lawmakers turned their attention to disciplining the president. Johnson continued to resist their policies and used his power as commander in chief to order generals in the military districts to soften the intent of congressional Reconstruction. In response, Congress passed the Command of the Army Act in 1867, which required the president to issue all orders to army commanders in the field through the General of the Army in Washington, D.C., Ulysses S. Grant. The Radicals knew they could count on Grant to carry out their policies. Even more threatening to presidential power, Congress passed the **Tenure of Office Act**, which prevented Johnson from firing cabinet officers sympathetic to congressional Reconstruction. This measure barred the chief executive from removing from office any appointee that the Senate had ratified previously without returning to the Senate for approval.

Convinced that the new law was unconstitutional and outraged at the effort to limit his power, the quick-tempered Johnson chose to confront the Radical Republicans directly rather than seek a way around a congressional showdown. In February 1868, Johnson fired Secretary of War Edwin Stanton, a Lincoln appointee and a Radical sympathizer, without Senate approval. In response, congressional Radicals prepared articles of impeachment.

In late February, the House voted 126 to 47 to impeach Johnson, the first president ever to be impeached, or charged with unlawful activity. The case then went to trial in the Senate, where the chief justice of the United States presided and a two-thirds vote was necessary for conviction and removal from office. After a six-week hearing, the Senate fell one vote short of convicting Johnson. Most crucial for Johnson's fate were the votes of seven moderate Republicans who refused to find the president guilty of violating his oath to uphold the Constitution. They were convinced that Johnson's actions were insufficient to merit the enormous step of removing a president from office. Although Johnson remained in office, Congress effectively ended his power to shape Reconstruction policy.

The Republicans had restrained Johnson, and in 1868 they won back the presidency. Ulysses S. Grant, the popular Civil War general, ran against Horatio Seymour, the Democratic governor of New York. Although an ally of the Radical Republicans, Grant called for reconciliation with the South. He easily defeated Seymour, winning nearly 53 percent of the popular vote and 73 percent of the electoral vote.

The Struggle for Universal Suffrage.

In February 1869, Congress passed the **Fifteenth Amendment** to protect black male suffrage, which had initially been guaranteed by the Military Reconstruction Acts. A compromise between moderate and Radical Republicans, the amendment prohibited voting discrimination based on race, but it did not deny states the power to impose qualifications based on literacy, payment of taxes, moral character, or any other standard that did not directly relate to race. Subsequently, the wording of the amendment provided loopholes for white leaders to disfranchise African Americans. The amendment did, however, cover the entire nation, including the North, where states like Connecticut, Kansas, Michigan, New York, Ohio, and Wisconsin still excluded blacks from voting.

The Fifteenth Amendment sparked serious conflicts not only within the South but also among old abolitionist allies. The American Anti-Slavery Society disbanded with emancipation, but many members believed that important work remained to be done to guarantee the rights of freedpeople. They formed the **American Equal Rights Association** immediately following the war, but members divided over the Fifteenth Amendment.

Frances Ellen Watkins Harper   Born a free person of color in Baltimore, Frances Ellen Watkins Harper distinguished herself as a poet, a teacher, and an abolitionist. After the Civil War, she became a staunch advocate of women's suffrage and a supporter of the Fifteenth Amendment, which set her at odds with the suffragists Susan B. Anthony and Elizabeth Cady Stanton.   Documenting the American South, The University of North Carolina at Chapel Hill http://docsouth.unc.edu/neh/brownhal/ill22.html

Some women's rights advocates, including Elizabeth Cady Stanton and Susan B. Anthony, had earlier objected to the Fourteenth Amendment because it inserted the word *male* into the Constitution for the first time when describing citizens. Although they had supported abolition before the war, Stanton and Anthony worried that postwar policies intended to enhance the rights of southern black men would further limit the rights of women. While most African American activists embraced the Fifteenth Amendment, a few voiced concern. At a meeting of the Equal Rights Association in 1867, Sojourner Truth noted, "There is quite a stir about colored men getting their rights, but not a word about colored women."

At the 1869 meeting of the Equal Rights Association, differences over the measure erupted into open conflict. Stanton and Anthony denounced suffrage for black men only, and Stanton now supported her position on racial grounds. She claimed that the "dregs of China, Germany, England, Ireland, and Africa" were degrading the U.S. polity and argued that white, educated women should certainly have the same rights as immigrant and African American men. Black and white supporters of the Fifteenth Amendment, including Frances Ellen Watkins Harper, Wendell Phillips, Abby Kelley, and Frederick Douglass, denounced Stanton's bigotry. Believing that southern black men urgently needed suffrage to protect their newly won freedom, they argued that ratification of the Fifteenth Amendment would speed progress toward the enfranchisement of women, black and white.

This conflict led to the formation of competing organizations committed to women's suffrage. The National Woman Suffrage Association, established by Stanton and Anthony, allowed only women as members and opposed ratification of the Fifteenth Amendment. The American Woman Suffrage Association, which attracted the support of women and men, white and black, supported ratification. Less than a year later, in the spring of 1870, the Fifteenth Amendment was ratified and went into effect.

Since the amendment did not grant the vote to either white or black women, women suffragists attempted to use the Fourteenth Amendment to achieve their goal. In 1875 Virginia Minor, who had been denied the ballot in Missouri, argued that the right to vote was one of the "privileges and immunities" granted to all citizens under the Fourteenth Amendment. In *Minor v. Happersatt*, the Supreme Court ruled against her, and most women were denied national suffrage for decades thereafter.

REVIEW & RELATE

- What was President Johnson's plan for reconstruction? How were his views out of step with those of most Republicans?

- What characterized congressional Reconstruction? What priorities were reflected in congressional Reconstruction legislation?

Remaking the **South**

With President Johnson's power effectively curtailed, reconstruction of the South moved quickly. New state legislatures, ruled by a coalition of southern whites and blacks and white northern migrants, enacted political, economic, and social reforms that improved the overall quality of life in the South. Despite these changes, many black and white Southerners barely eked out a living under the planter-dominated sharecropping system. Moreover, the biracial Reconstruction governments lasted a relatively short time, as conservative whites used a variety of tactics, including terror and race baiting, to defeat their opponents at the polls.

Whites Reconstruct the South.

During the first years of congressional Reconstruction, two groups of whites occupied the majority of elective offices in the South. A significant number of native-born Southerners joined Republicans in forging postwar constitutions and governments. Before the war, some had belonged to the Whig Party and opposed secession from the Union. Western sections of Alabama, Georgia, North Carolina, and Tennessee had demonstrated a fiercely independent strain, and many residents had remained loyal to the Union. Small merchants and farmers who detested large plantation owners also threw in their lot with the Republicans. Even a few ex-Confederates, such as General James A. Longstreet, decided that the South must change and allied with the Republicans. The majority of whites who continued to support the Democratic Party viewed these whites as traitors. They showed their distaste by calling them **scalawags**, an unflattering term meaning "scoundrels."

At the same time, Northerners came south to support Republican Reconstruction. They had varied reasons for making the journey, but most considered the South a new frontier to be conquered culturally, politically, and economically. Some—white and black—had served in the Union army during the war, liked what they saw of the region, and decided to settle there. Some of both races came to provide education and assist the freedpeople in adjusting to their new lives. As a relatively underdeveloped area, the South also beckoned fortune seekers and adventurers who saw opportunities to get rich. Southern Democrats denounced such northern interlopers, particularly whites, as **carpetbaggers**, suggesting that they invaded the region with all their possessions in a satchel, seeking to plunder it and then leave. While Northerners did seek economic opportunity, they were acting as Americans always had in settling new frontiers and pursuing dreams of success. In fact, much of the animosity directed toward them resulted primarily not from their mere presence, but from their efforts to ally with African Americans in reshaping the South.

Black Political Participation and Economic Opportunities.

Still, the primary targets of southern white hostility were African Americans who attempted to exercise their hard-won freedom. Blacks constituted a majority of voters in five states—Alabama, Florida, South Carolina, Mississippi, and Louisiana—while in Georgia, North Carolina, Texas, and Virginia they fell short of a majority. They did not use their ballots to impose black rule on the South, as many white Southerners feared. Only in South Carolina did African Americans control the state legislature, and in no state did they manage to elect a governor. Nevertheless, for the first time in American history, blacks won a wide variety of elected positions. More than six hundred blacks served in state legislatures; another sixteen, including Jefferson Long, held seats in the U.S. House of Representatives; and two from Mississippi were chosen to serve in the U.S. Senate.

Explore ▶

Compare two opposing views of southern Blacks in Reconstruction-era governments in Secondary Sources 14.4 and 14.5.

Former slaves showed enthusiasm for politics in other ways, too. African Americans considered politics a community responsibility, and in addition to casting ballots, they held rallies and mass meetings to discuss issues and choose candidates. Although they could not vote, women attended these gatherings and helped influence their outcome. Covering a Republican convention in Richmond in October 1867, held in the First African

SECONDARY SOURCE ANALYSIS

Race and Reconstruction

Although the Civil War ended slavery, it left deep and unresolved racial tensions that continued to incite conflict. In the years immediately following the war, freedmen were allowed to vote for representatives and to serve in newly formed southern state governments. These developments outraged many white Confederates who insisted that these governments were corrupt and that blacks were especially vulnerable to graft and manipulation. Many prominent historians accepted such views of postwar southern politics until the 1960s, when a younger generation of scholars argued for a reconsideration of race and Reconstruction. (Until the 1970s, the term negro or Negro was used by most scholars to denote African American or black.)

Source 14.4

William A. Dunning, Radical Reconstruction (1907)

. . . [T]he southerners felt that the policy of Congress had no real cause save the purpose of radical politicians to prolong and extend their party power by means of negro suffrage.... It was as inconceivable to the southerners that rational men of the North should seriously approve of negro suffrage *per se* as it had been in 1860 to the northerners that rational men of the South should approve of secession *per se*.

. . . . The registration of voters was so directed as to insure . . . the fullest enrollment of the blacks and the completest exclusion of disfranchised whites. . . . The result of the elections was a group of constituent assemblies whose unfitness for their task was pitiful. . . . [T]he mass of the delegates consisted of whites and blacks whose ignorance and inexperience in respect to political methods were equaled only by the crudeness and distortion of their ideas as to political and social ends.

. . . . But a solitary chance presented itself of escape from the disasters of negro political supremacy: if the freedmen could be won to look for guidance in their new duties to their old masters, all might yet be well. . . . [However], to the emancipated race all the astounding changes of the recent wonder years had come through other sources, and the vague but intoxicating delights of political privilege must, they felt, be enjoyed under the same auspices that had brought them freedom, schools, and the unlimited indulgence of those weird emotions which they called religion.

Source: William Archibald Dunning, *Reconstruction Political and Economic, 1865–1877* (New York: Harper and Brothers Publishers, 1907), pp. 110–11, 112, 114–15.

Baptist Church, the *New York Times* reported that "the entire colored population of Richmond" attended. In addition, freedpeople formed mutual aid associations to promote education, economic advancement, and social welfare programs, all of which they saw as deeply intertwined with politics.

Southern blacks also bolstered their freedom by building alliances with sympathetic whites. These interracial political coalitions produced considerable reform in the South. They created the first public school systems; provided funds for social services, such as poor relief and state hospitals; upgraded prisons; and rebuilt the South's transportation

Source 14.5

John Hope Franklin, The South's New Leaders (1961)

The entrance of Negroes into the political arena was the most revolutionary aspect of the Reconstruction program. Out of a population of approximately four million, some 700,000 qualified as voters, but the most of them were without the qualifications to participate effectively in a democracy. In this they were not unlike the large number of Americans who were enfranchised during the Age of Jackson. . . . None of this is surprising. It had been only two years since emancipation from a system that for more than two centuries had denied slaves most rights as human beings. And it must be remembered that in these two years the former Confederates, in power all over the South, did nothing to promote the social and political education of the former slaves. What is surprising is that there were some—and no paltry number—who in 1867 were able to assume the responsibilities of citizens and leaders.

. . . . One of the really remarkable features of the Negro leadership was the small amount of vindictiveness in their words and their actions. There was no bully, no swagger, as they took their places in the state and federal governments traditionally occupied by the white planters of the South.... Negroes generally wished to see political disabilities removed from the whites. . . . Negroes attempted no revolution in the social relations of the races in the South. . . . Nor did any considerable number of Negroes seek to effect an economic revolution in the South.

Source: John Hope Franklin, *Reconstruction After the Civil War* (Chicago: University of Chicago Press, 1961), pp. 86–7, 88, 89–90, 91.

Examine the Sources

1. How do Dunning and Franklin differ in their interpretations of the role played by African Americans during Reconstruction?
2. Drawing on evidence from this chapter, including the Primary Source Project, how would you evaluate the strengths and weaknesses of Dunning's and Franklin's interpretations?

Put It in Context

How might the fact that these interpretations were written fifty-four years apart (1907/1961) influence their conclusions?

system. Moreover, the state constitutions that the Republicans wrote brought a greater measure of political democracy and equality to the South by extending suffrage to poor white men as well as black men. Some states allowed married women greater control over their property and liberalized the criminal justice system. In effect, these Reconstruction governments brought the South into the nineteenth century.

Obtaining political representation was one way in which African Americans defined freedom. Economic independence constituted a second. Without government-sponsored land redistribution, however, the options for southern blacks remained limited. Lacking capital to purchase farms, most entered into various forms of tenant contracts with large landowners. **Sharecropping** proved the most common arrangement. Blacks and poor whites became sharecroppers for much the same reasons. They received tools and supplies from landowners and farmed their own plots of land on the plantation. In exchange, sharecroppers turned over a portion of their harvest to the owner and kept the rest for themselves.

The benefits of sharecropping proved less valuable to black farmers in practice than in theory. To tide them over during the growing season, croppers had to purchase household provisions on credit from a local merchant, who was often also their landlord. At the mercy of store owners who kept the books and charged high interest rates, tenants usually found themselves in considerable debt at the end of the year. To satisfy the debt, merchants devised a crop lien system in which tenants pledged a portion of their yearly crop to satisfy what they owed. Falling prices for agricultural crops in this period ensured that most indebted tenants did not receive sufficient return on their produce to get out of debt and thus remained bound to their landlords. For many African Americans, sharecropping turned into a form of virtual slavery.

The picture for black farmers was not all bleak, however. About 20 percent of black farmers managed to buy their own land. Through careful management and extremely hard

Exodusters This photograph of two black couples standing on their homestead was taken around 1880 in Nicodemus, Kansas. These settlers, known as Exodusters, had migrated to northwest Kansas following the end of Reconstruction. They sought economic opportunity free from the racial repression sweeping the South. Library of Congress, HABS KANS, 33-NICO, 1-6

work, black families planted gardens for household consumption and raised chickens for eggs and meat. Despite its pitfalls, sharecropping provided a limited measure of labor independence and allowed some blacks to accumulate small amounts of cash.

Following the war's devastation, many of the South's white small farmers, known as yeomen, also fell into sharecropping. Meanwhile, many planters' sons abandoned farming and became lawyers, bankers, and merchants. Despite these changes, one thing remained the same: White elites ruled over blacks and poor whites, and they kept these two economically exploited groups from uniting by fanning the flames of racial prejudice.

Economic hardship and racial bigotry drove many blacks to leave the South. In 1879 former slaves, known as **Exodusters**, pooled their resources to create land companies and purchase property in Kansas on which to settle. They encouraged an exodus of some 25,000 African Americans from the South. Kansas was ruled by the Republican Party and had been home to the great antislavery martyr John Brown. As one hopeful freedman from Louisiana wrote to the Kansas governor in 1879, "I am anxious to reach your state . . . because of the sacredness of her soil washed in the blood of humanitarians for the cause of black freedom." Poor-quality land and unpredictable weather often made farming on the Great Plains hard and unrewarding. Nevertheless, for many black migrants, the chance to own their own land and escape the oppression of the South was worth the hardships. In 1880 the census counted 40,000 blacks living in Kansas.

White Resistance to Congressional Reconstruction.

Despite the Republican record of accomplishment during Reconstruction, white Southerners did not accept its legitimacy. They accused interracial governments of conducting a spending spree that raised taxes and encouraged corruption. Indeed, taxes did rise significantly, but mainly because legislatures funded much-needed educational and social services. Corruption on building projects and railroad construction was common during this time. Still, it is unfair to single out Reconstruction governments and especially black legislators as inherently depraved, as their Democratic opponents acted the same way when given the opportunity. Economic scandals were part of American life after the Civil War. As enormous business opportunities arose in the postwar years, many economic and political leaders made unlawful deals to enrich themselves. Furthermore, southern opponents of Reconstruction exaggerated its harshness. In contrast to revolutions and civil wars in other countries, only one rebel was executed for war crimes (the commandant of Andersonville Prison in Georgia); only one high-ranking official went to prison (Jefferson Davis); no official was forced into exile, though some fled voluntarily; and most rebels regained voting rights and the ability to hold office within seven years after the end of the rebellion.

Most important, these Reconstruction governments had only limited opportunities to transform the South. By the end of 1870, civilian rule had returned to all of the former Confederate states, and they had reentered the Union. Republican rule did not continue past 1870 in Virginia, North Carolina, and Tennessee and did not extend beyond 1871 in Georgia and 1873 in Texas. In 1874 Democrats deposed Republicans in Arkansas and Alabama; two years later, Democrats triumphed in Mississippi. In only three states— Louisiana, Florida, and South Carolina—did Reconstruction last until 1877.

The Democrats who replaced Republicans trumpeted their victories as bringing "redemption" to the South. Of course, these so-called **Redeemers** were referring to the white South. For black Republicans and their white allies, redemption meant defeat.

Visit of the Ku Klux Klan This 1872 wood engraving by the noted magazine illustrator Frank Bellew appeared at the height of Ku Klux Klan violence against freed blacks in the South. This image depicts a black family seemingly secure in their home in the evening while masked Klansmen stand in their doorway ready to attack with rifles. Library of Congress, 3c27756

Democratic victories came at the ballot boxes, but violence, intimidation, and fraud paved the way. In 1865 in Pulaski, Tennessee General Nathan Bedford Forrest organized Confederate veterans into a social club called the **Knights of the Ku Klux Klan (KKK)**. Spreading throughout the South, its followers donned robes and masks to hide their identities and terrify their victims. Gun-wielding Ku Kluxers rode on horseback to the homes and churches of black and white Republicans to keep them from voting. When threats did not work, they beat and murdered their victims. In 1871, for example, 150 African Americans were killed in Jackson County in the Florida Panhandle. A black clergyman lamented, "That is where Satan has his seat." There and elsewhere, many of the individuals targeted had managed to buy property, gain political leadership, or in other ways defy white stereotypes of African American inferiority. Other white supremacist organizations joined the Klan in waging a reign of terror. During the 1875 election in Mississippi, which toppled the Republican government, armed terrorists killed hundreds of Republicans and scared many more away from the polls.

To combat the terror unleashed by the Klan and its allies, Congress passed three **Force Acts** in 1870 and 1871. These measures empowered the president to dispatch officials into the South to supervise elections and prevent voting interference. Directed specifically at the KKK, one law barred secret organizations from using force to violate equal protection of the laws. In 1872 Congress established a joint committee to probe Klan tactics, and its investigations produced thirteen volumes of gripping testimony about the horrors perpetrated by the Klan. Elias Hill, a freedman from South Carolina who had become a Baptist preacher and teacher, was one of those who appeared before Congress. He and his brother lived next door to each other. The Klansmen went first to his brother's house, where, as Hill testified, they "broke open the door and attacked his wife, and I heard her screaming and mourning [moaning]. . . . At last I heard them have [rape] her in the yard." When the Klansmen discovered Elias Hill, they dragged him out of his house and beat, whipped, and threatened to kill him. On the basis of such testimony, the federal government prosecuted some 3,000 Klansmen. Only 600 were convicted, however. As the Klan disbanded in the wake of federal prosecutions, other vigilante organizations arose to take its place.

REVIEW & RELATE

- What role did black people play in remaking southern society during Reconstruction?

- How did southern whites fight back against Reconstruction? What role did terrorism and political violence play in this effort?

The **Unraveling** of **Reconstruction**

The violence, intimidation, and fraud perpetrated by Redeemers does not fully explain the unraveling of Reconstruction. By the early 1870s most white Northerners had come to believe that they had done more than enough for black Southerners, and it was time to focus on other issues. Growing economic problems intensified this feeling. Still reeling from the amount of blood shed during the war, white Americans, north and south, turned their attention toward burying and memorializing the Civil War dead. White America was once again united, if only in the shared belief that it was time to move on, consigning the issues of slavery and civil rights to history.

The Republican Retreat. Most northern whites shared the racial prejudices of their counterparts in the South. Although they had supported protection of black civil rights and suffrage, they still believed that African Americans were inferior to whites and were horrified by the idea of social integration. They began to sympathize with Southern whites' racist complaints that blacks were not capable of governing honestly and effectively.

In 1872 a group calling themselves Liberal Republicans challenged the reelection of President Grant. Financial scandals had racked the Grant administration. This high-level corruption reflected other get-rich-quick schemes connected to economic speculation and development following the Civil War. Outraged by the rising level of immoral behavior in government and business, Liberal Republicans nominated Horace Greeley, editor of the *New York Tribune*, to run against Grant. They linked government corruption to the expansion of federal power that accompanied Reconstruction and called for the removal of troops from the South and amnesty for all former Confederates. They also campaigned for civil service reform, which would base government employment on a merit system and abolish the "spoils system"—in which the party in power rewarded loyal supporters with political appointments—that had been introduced by Andrew Jackson in the 1820s.

The Democratic Party believed that Liberal Republicans offered the best chance to defeat Grant, and it endorsed Greeley. Despite the scandals that surrounded him, Grant remained popular. Moreover, the main body of Republicans "waved the bloody shirt," reminding northern voters that a ballot cast for the opposition tarnished the memory of brave Union soldiers killed during the war. The president won reelection with an even greater margin than he had four years earlier. Nevertheless, the attacks against Grant foreshadowed the Republican retreat on Reconstruction. Among the Democrats sniping at Grant was Andrew Johnson. Johnson had returned to Tennessee, and in 1874 the state legislature chose the former president to serve in the U.S. Senate. He continued to speak out against the presence of federal troops in the South until his death in 1875.

Congressional and Judicial Retreat. By the time Grant began his second term, Congress was already considering bills to restore officeholding rights to former Confederates who had not yet sworn allegiance to the Union. Black representatives, including Georgia congressman Jefferson Long, as well as some white lawmakers, remained opposed to such measures, but in 1872 Congress removed the penalties placed on former Confederates by the Fourteenth Amendment and permitted nearly all rebel leaders the right to vote and hold office. Two years later, for the first time since the start of the Civil War, the Democrats gained a majority in the House of Representatives and prepared to remove the remaining troops from the South.

Republican leaders also rethought their top priority with economic concerns increasingly replacing racial considerations. In 1873 a financial panic resulting from the collapse of the Northern Pacific Railroad triggered a severe economic depression lasting late into the decade. Tens of thousands of unemployed workers across the country worried more about finding jobs than they did about black civil rights. Businessmen, too, were plagued with widespread bankruptcy. When strikes erupted across the country in 1877, most notably the Great Railway Strike, in which more than half a million workers walked off the job, employers asked the U.S. government to remove troops from the South and dispatch them against strikers in the North and West.

While white Northerners sought ways to extricate themselves from Reconstruction, the Supreme Court weakened enforcement of the civil rights acts. In 1873 the *Slaughterhouse* cases defined the rights that African Americans were entitled to under the Fourteenth Amendment very narrowly. Reflecting the shift from moral to economic concerns, the justices interpreted the amendment as extending greater protection to corporations in conducting business than to blacks. As a result, blacks had to depend on southern state governments to protect their civil rights, the same state authorities that had deprived them of their rights in the first place. In *United States v. Cruikshank* (1876), the high court narrowed the Fourteenth Amendment further, ruling that it protected blacks against abuses only by state officials and agencies, not by private groups such as the Ku Klux Klan. Seven years later, the Court struck down the Civil Rights Act of 1875, which had extended "full and equal treatment" in public accommodations for persons of all races.

The Presidential Compromise of 1876. The presidential election of 1876 set in motion events that officially brought Reconstruction to an end. The Republicans nominated the governor of Ohio, Rutherford B. Hayes, who was chosen partly because he was untainted by the corruption that plagued the Grant administration. The Democrats selected their own anticorruption crusader, Governor Samuel J. Tilden of New York.

The outcome of the election depended on twenty disputed electoral votes, nineteen from the South and one from Oregon. Tilden won 51 percent of the popular vote, but Reconstruction political battles in Florida, Louisiana, and South Carolina put the election up for grabs. In each of these states, the outgoing Republican administration certified Hayes as the winner, while the incoming Democratic regime declared for Tilden.

The Constitution assigns Congress the task of counting and certifying the electoral votes submitted by the states. Normally, this is a mere formality, but 1876 was different. Democrats controlled the House, Republicans controlled the Senate, and neither branch would budge on which votes to count. Hayes needed all twenty for victory; Tilden needed only one. To break the logjam, Congress created a fifteen-member Joint Electoral Commission, composed of seven Democrats, seven Republicans, and one independent. Ultimately, a majority voted to count all twenty votes for the Republican Hayes, making him president (Map 14.2).

Still, Congress had to ratify this count, and disgruntled southern Democrats in the Senate threatened a filibuster—unlimited debate—to block certification of Hayes. With the March 4, 1877 date for the presidential inauguration creeping perilously close and no winner officially declared, behind-the-scenes negotiations finally settled the controversy. A series of meetings between Hayes supporters and southern Democrats led to a bargain. According to the agreement, Democrats would support Hayes in exchange for the president appointing a Southerner to his cabinet, withdrawing the last federal troops from the South, and endorsing construction of a transcontinental railroad through the South. This **compromise of 1877** averted a crisis over presidential succession, underscored increased southern Democratic influence within Congress, and marked the end of strong federal protections for African Americans in the South.

MAP 14.2   The Election of 1876

The presidential election of 1876 got swept up in Reconstruction politics. Democrats defeated Republicans in Florida, Louisiana, and South Carolina, but both parties claimed the electoral votes for their candidates. A federal electoral commission set up to investigate the twenty disputed votes, including one from Oregon, awarded the votes and the election to the Republican, Rutherford B. Hayes.

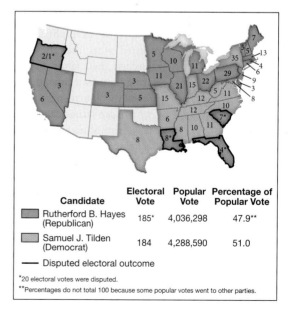

Candidate	Electoral Vote	Popular Vote	Percentage of Popular Vote
Rutherford B. Hayes (Republican)	185*	4,036,298	47.9**
Samuel J. Tilden (Democrat)	184	4,288,590	51.0

—— Disputed electoral outcome

*20 electoral votes were disputed.
**Percentages do not total 100 because some popular votes went to other parties.

Why did northern interest in Reconstruction wane in the 1870s?

What common values and beliefs among white Americans were reflected in the compromise of 1877?

Conclusion: The Legacies of Reconstruction

Reconstruction was, in many ways, profoundly limited. Notwithstanding the efforts of the Freedmen's Bureau, African Americans did not receive the landownership that would have provided them with economic independence and bolstered their freedom from the racist assaults of white Southerners. The civil and political rights that the federal government conferred did not withstand the efforts of former Confederates to disfranchise and deprive the freedpeople of equal rights. The Republican Party shifted its priorities, and Democrats gained enough political power nationally to short-circuit federal intervention, even as numerous problems remained unresolved in the South. Northern support for racial equality did not run very deep, so white Northerners, who shared many of the prejudices of white Southerners, were happy to extricate themselves from further intervention in southern racial matters. Nor was there sufficient support to give women, white or black, the right to vote. Finally, federal courts, with growing concerns over economic rather than social issues, sanctioned Northerners' retreat by providing constitutional legitimacy for abandoning black Southerners and rejecting women's suffrage in court decisions that narrowed the interpretation of the Fourteenth and Fifteenth Amendments.

Despite all of this, Reconstruction did transform the country. As a result of Reconstruction, slavery was abolished and the legal basis for freedom was enshrined in the Constitution. Indeed, blacks exercised a measure of political and economic freedom during Reconstruction that never entirely disappeared over the decades to come. In many areas, freedpeople, exemplified by Congressman Jefferson Franklin Long and many others, asserted what they never could have during slavery—control over their lives, their churches, their labor, their education, and their families. What they could not practice during their own time, their descendants would one day revive through the promises codified in the Fourteenth and Fifteenth Amendments.

African Americans transformed not only themselves; they transformed the nation. The Constitution became much more democratic and egalitarian through inclusion of the Reconstruction amendments. Reconstruction lawmakers took an important step toward making the United States the "more perfect union" that the nation's Founders had pledged to create. Reconstruction established a model for expanding the power of the federal government to resolve domestic crises that lay beyond the abilities of states and ordinary citizens. It remained a powerful legacy for elected officials who dared to invoke it. And Reconstruction transformed the South to its everlasting benefit. It modernized state constitutions, expanded educational and social welfare systems, and unleashed the repressed potential for industrialization and economic development that the preservation of slavery had restrained. Ironically, Reconstruction did as much for white Southerners as it did for black Southerners in liberating them from the past.

TIMELINE OF EVENTS

1863 Lincoln issues Proclamation of Amnesty and Reconstruction

1865 Ku Klux Klan formed

Freedmen's Bureau established

Thirteenth Amendment passed

Lincoln assassinated; Andrew Johnson becomes president

1866 Freedmen's Bureau and Civil Rights Act extended over Johnson's presidential veto

Fourteenth Amendment passed

1867 Military Reconstruction Acts

Command of the Army and Tenure of Office Acts passed

1868 Andrew Johnson impeached

1869 Fifteenth Amendment passed

Women's suffrage movement splits over support of Fifteenth Amendment

1870 250,000 blacks attend schools established by the Freedmen's Bureau

Civilian rule returns to the South

1870–1872 Congress takes steps to curb Ku Klux Klan violence in the South

1873 Financial panic sparks depression

1873–1883 Supreme Court limits rights of African Americans

1875 Civil Rights Act passed

1877 Rutherford B. Hayes becomes president

Reconstruction ends

1879 Black Exodusters migrate from South to Kansas

KEY TERMS

Freedmen's Bureau, *458*

Proclamation of Amnesty and Reconstruction, *463*

Thirteenth Amendment, *463*

black codes, *465*

Fourteenth Amendment, *466*

Tenure of Office Act, *470*

Fifteenth Amendment, *471*

American Equal Rights Association, *471*

scalawags, *473*

carpetbaggers, *473*

sharecropping, *476*

Exodusters, *477*

Redeemers, *477*

Knights of the Ku Klux Klan, *478*

Force Acts, *478*

compromise of 1877, *481*

REVIEW & RELATE

1. What were freedpeople's highest priorities in the years immediately following the Civil War? Why?

2. How did freedpeople define freedom? What steps did they take to make freedom real for themselves and their children?

3. What was President Johnson's plan for reconstruction? How were his views out of step with those of most Republicans?

4. What characterized congressional Reconstruction? What priorities were reflected in congressional Reconstruction legislation?

5. What role did black people play in remaking southern society during Reconstruction?

6. How did southern whites fight back against Reconstruction? What role did terrorism and political violence play in this effort?

7. Why did northern interest in Reconstruction wane in the 1870s?

8. What common values and beliefs among white Americans were reflected in the compromise of 1877?

Testing and Contesting Freedom

▶ How did blacks and whites view emancipation and what role did the federal government play in overseeing the transition from slavery to freedom?

Nine months after the Civil War ended in April 1865, twenty-seven states ratified the Thirteenth Amendment, abolishing slavery throughout the United States. Freedom, however, did not guarantee equal rights or the absence of racial discrimination. Immediately following the North's victory, white southern leaders enacted black codes, which aimed to prevent freedpeople from improving their social and economic status (Source 14.6). Although Lincoln's successor, Andrew Johnson, did not support the codes, he did nothing to overturn them. A southern advocate of limited government, Johnson clashed repeatedly with Congress over Reconstruction. In 1867 the Republican majority in Congress took control and passed the Military Reconstruction Acts, placing the South under military rule and forcing whites to extend equal political and civil rights to African Americans.

Then in 1870, ratification of the Fifteenth Amendment extended suffrage to black men. In alliance with white Republicans, blacks won election to a variety of public offices, including seats in local and state governments. These interracial legislatures improved conditions for blacks and whites, providing funds for public education, hospitals, and other social services. But their opponents succeeded in tarring them with claims of fraud, corruption, wasteful spending, and "Black Rule" (Sources 14.7 and 14.10). Most newly freed blacks were eager to acquire land so they could support themselves, but many were forced to sign

sharecropping agreements with white landowners. Although sharecropping provided some benefits to freed people as well as white landowners, blacks' limited economic and political leverage ensured that these agreements gave more authority to landowners than laborers (Sources 14.7 and 14.8).

By the mid-1870s, many white Northerners sought reconciliation rather than continued conflict while southern whites created vigilante groups like the Ku Klux Klan that used violence to intimidate black and white Republicans. By the mid-1870s, northern magazines as well as southern newspapers began challenging black political rule, further isolating blacks from popular and government support (Sources 14.9 and 14.10). Ultimately, the withdrawal of federal oversight crushed southern Republicanism, leaving African Americans struggling to retain the freedoms they had supposedly gained.

Source 14.6

Mississippi Black Code, 1865

Southern legislatures created black codes primarily to limit the rights of free blacks after emancipation and return them to a condition as close as possible to slavery. Mississippi was one of the first states to enact a black code. Although its laws did legalize marriage for blacks and allowed them to own property and testify in court, its primary intent was to limit freedpeople's mobility and economic opportunities.

*An Act to Confer Civil Rights on Freedmen,
and for other Purposes*

. . . SECTION 2. All freedmen, free negroes and
mulattoes may intermarry with each other, in the
same manner and under the same regulations that
are provided by law for white persons: Provided, that
the clerk of probate shall keep separate records of
the same.

SECTION 3. All freedmen, free negroes or
mulattoes who do now and have herebefore lived
and cohabited together as husband and wife shall be
taken and held in law as legally married, and the
issue shall be taken and held as legitimate for all
purposes; and it shall not be lawful for any freedman,
free negro or mulatto to intermarry with any white
person; nor for any person to intermarry with any
freedman, free negro or mulatto; and any person who
shall so intermarry shall be deemed guilty of felony,
and on conviction thereof shall be confined in the
State penitentiary for life; and those shall be deemed
freedmen, free negroes and mulattoes who are of
pure negro blood, and those descended from a negro
to the third generation, inclusive, though one
ancestor in each generation may have been a white
person.

SECTION 4. In addition to cases in which
freedmen, free negroes and mulattoes are now by
law competent witnesses, freedmen, free negroes or
mulattoes shall be competent in civil cases, when a
party or parties to the suit, either plaintiff or
plaintiffs, defendant or defendants; also in cases
where freedmen, free negroes and mulattoes is or are
either plaintiff or plaintiffs, defendant or defendants.
They shall also be competent witnesses in all
criminal prosecutions where the crime charged is
alleged to have been committed by a white person
upon or against the person or property of a
freedman, free negro or mulatto. . . .

An Act to Amend the Vagrant Laws of the State . . .

SECTION 2. All freedmen, free negroes and mulattoes
in this State, over the age of eighteen years, found on
the second Monday in January, 1866, or thereafter,
with no lawful employment or business, or found
unlawful[ly] assembling themselves together, either
in the day or night time, and all white persons

assembling themselves with freedmen, free negroes
or mulattoes, or usually associating with freedmen,
free negroes or mulattoes, on terms of equality, or
living in adultery or fornication with a freed woman,
freed negro or mulatto, shall be deemed vagrants,
and on conviction thereof shall be fined in a sum not
exceeding, in the case of a freedman, free negro or
mulatto, fifty dollars, and a white man two hundred
dollars, and imprisonment at the discretion of the
court, the free negro not exceeding ten days, and the
white man not exceeding six months. . . .

SECTION 6. The same duties and liabilities
existing among white persons of this State shall
attach to freedmen, free negroes or mulattoes, to
support their indigent families and all colored
paupers; and that in order to secure a support for
such indigent freedmen, free negroes, or mulattoes, it
shall be lawful, and is hereby made the duty of the
county police of each county in this State, to levy a
poll or capitation tax on each and every freedman,
free negro, or mulatto, between the ages of eighteen
and sixty years, not to exceed the sum of one dollar
annually to each person so taxed, which tax, when
collected, shall be paid into the county treasurer's
hands, and constitute a fund to be called the
Freedman's Pauper Fund, . . . for the maintenance of
the poor of the freedmen, free negroes and mulattoes
of this State.

Source: *Laws of the State of Mississippi, Passed at a Regular
Session of the Mississippi Legislature, Held in the City of Jackson,
October, November, and December, 1865* (Jackson, MS, 1866),
82–86, 165–67.

Source 14.7

Richard H. Cain | Federal Aid for Land Purchase, 1868

Richard H. Cain, a free black minister raised in Ohio,
went to South Carolina after the war and served
as a Republican member of the U.S. House of
Representatives for two terms in the 1870s. The
following excerpt comes from a speech Cain made
in 1868 as a representative to the South Carolina
constitutional convention. Cain proposed that the
convention petition Congress for a $1 million loan to
purchase land that could be resold to freedmen at a
reasonable price.

believe the best measure to be adopted is to bring capital to the State, and instead of causing revenge and unpleasantness, I am for even-handed justice. I am for allowing the parties who own lands to bring them into the market and sell them upon such terms as will be satisfactory to both sides. I believe a measure of this kind has a double effect: first, it brings capital, what the people want; second, it puts the people to work; it gives homesteads, what we need; it relieves the Government and takes away its responsibility of feeding the people; it inspires every man with a noble manfulness, and by the thought that he is the possessor of something in the State; it adds also to the revenue of the country. By these means men become interested in the country as they never were before. . . . I will also guarantee that after one year's time, the Freedman's Bureau will not have to give any man having one acre of land anything to eat.

Source: *Proceedings of the South Carolina Constitutional Convention of 1868* (Charleston, SC, 1868), 420–21.

Source 14.8

Willis B. Bocock and Black Laborers, Sharecropping Agreement, 1870

Because Congress did not generally provide freedpeople with land, African Americans lacked the means to start their own farms. At the same time, plantation owners needed labor now that slavery was abolished. Out of mutual necessity, white plantation owners such as Willis B. Bocock entered into sharecropping agreements with blacks to work their farms in exchange for a portion of the crop. Several of the blacks who signed this agreement had previously been enslaved to Bocock.

Contract made the 3rd day of January in the year 1870 between us the free people who have signed this paper of one part, and our employer, Willis P. Bocock, of the other part. . . . We are to furnish the necessary labor . . . and are to have all proper work done, ditching, fencing, repairing, etc., as well as cultivating and saving the crops of all kinds, so as to put and keep the land we occupy and tend in good order for cropping, and to make a good crop ourselves; and to do our fair share of job work about the place. . . . We are to be responsible for the good conduct of ourselves, our hands, and families, and agree that all shall be respectful to employer, owners, and manager, honest, industrious, and careful about every thing . . . and then our employer agrees that he and his manager shall treat us kindly, and help us to study our interest and do our duty. If any hand or family proves to be of bad character, or dishonest, or lazy, or disobedient, or any way unsuitable our employer or manager has the right, and we have the right, to have such turned off. . . .

For the labor and services of ourselves and hands rendered as above stated, we are to have one third part of all the crops, or their net-proceeds, made and secured, or prepared for market by our force. . . .

We are to be furnished by our employer through his manager with provisions if we call for them . . . to be charged to us at fair market prices.

And whatever may be due by us, or our hands to our employer for provisions or any thing else, during the year, is to be a lien on our share of the crops, and is to be retained by him out of the same before we receive our part.

Source: Waldwick Plantation Records, 1834–1971, LPR174, box 1, folder 9, Alabama Department of Archives and History.

Source 14.9

Ellen Parton | Testimony on Klan Violence, 1871

In March 1871, white mobs killed some thirty African Americans in Meridian, Mississippi. Later that month, a joint committee of the United States Congress held hearings on the violence, which included the following testimony by Ellen Parton of Mississippi, a former slave and domestic worker. The Klan suspected that Parton's husband was involved in the Union League, a southern affiliate of the Republican Party. Congress also conducted hearings on the vigilante violence against blacks throughout the South.

Ellen Parton, being sworn, states:

I reside in Meridian; have resided here nine years; occupation, washing and ironing and scouring; Wednesday night was the last night they came to my house; by "they" I mean bodies or companies of men; they came on Monday, Tuesday, and Wednesday. On Monday night they said that they came to do us no harm. On Tuesday night they said they came for the arms; I told them there was none, and they said they would take my word for it. On Wednesday night they came and broke open the wardrobe and trunks, and committed rape upon me; there were eight of them in the house; I do not know how many there were outside; they were white men; there was a light in the house; I was living in Marshal Ware's house; there were three lights burning. Mr. Ware has been one of the policemen of this town. He was concealed at the time they came; they took the claw hammer and broke open the pantry where he was lying; he was concealed in the pantry under some plunder, covered up well; I guess he covered himself up. A man said "here is Marshal's hat, where is Marshal?" I told him "I did not know"; they went then into everything in the house, and broke open the wardrobe; I called upon Mr. Mike Slamon, who was one of the crowd, for protection; I said to him "please protect me tonight, you have known me for a long time." This man covered up his head then; he had a hold of me at this time; Mr. Slamon had an oil-cloth and put it before his face, trying to conceal himself, and the man that had hold of me told me not to call Mr. Slamon's name any more. He then took me in the dining room, and told me that I had to do just what he said: I told him I could do nothing of that sort; that was not my way, and he replied "by God, you have got to," and then threw me down. This man had a black eye, where some one had beaten him; he had a black velvet cap on. After he got through with me he came through the house, and said that he was after the Union Leagues; I yielded to him because he had a pistol drawn; when he took me down he hurt me of course; I yielded to him on that account.

Source: *Report of the Joint Select Committee [of Congress] to Inquire into the Condition of Affairs in the Late Insurrectionary States, Mississippi* (Washington, DC: Government Printing Office, 1872), 1:38–39.

Source 14.10

Thomas Nast | *Colored Rule in a Reconstructed (?) State*, 1874

Thomas Nast began drawing for the popular magazine *Harper's Weekly* in 1859. Nast initially used his illustrations to rouse northern public sentiment for the plight of blacks in the South after the Civil War. By 1874, however, many Northerners had become disillusioned with federal efforts to enforce Reconstruction. Like them, Nash accepted the white southern point of view that "Black Reconstruction" was a recipe for corruption and immorality. The figure of Columbia (at the top right) represents the nation, and the caption captures the view of many Northerners by 1874: "You are Aping the lowest Whites. If you disgrace your Race in this way you had better take Back Seats."

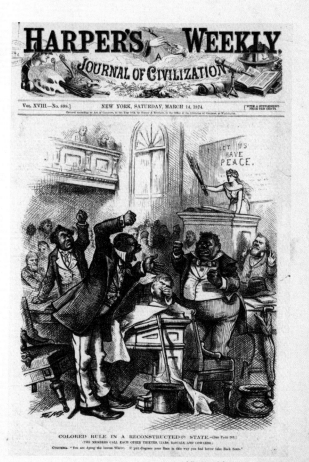

COLORED RULE IN A RECONSTRUCTED (?) STATE.
(THE MEMBERS CALL EACH OTHER THIEVES, LIARS, RASCALS AND COWARDS.)
COLUMBIA. "You are Aping the lowest Whites. If you disgrace your Race in this way you had better take Back Seats."

Interpret the Evidence

1. How did black codes and sharecropping agreements (Sources 14.6 and 14.8) attempt to reimpose bondage on former slaves? How did they differ from pre-Civil War slave laws?

2. Why did freedpeople consider property holding a fundamental right and to what extent did sharecropping agreements allow them to gain some economic benefits from their labor (Sources 14.7 and 14.8)?

3. Contrast the image of South Carolina's black politicians presented in Richard Cain's speech (Source 14.7) and Thomas Nast's cartoon (Source 14.10). What does Nast's cartoon suggest about white northern attitudes toward freedpeople in the South by 1874?

4. Despite the fear and physical danger caused by the Ku Klux Klan, what does the testimony of Ellen Parton (Source 14.9) reveal about black attempts to resist it?

Put It in Context

How much did Reconstruction transform the South and the nation? What were the greatest limitations of federal Reconstruction policies and the greatest challenges to implementing them?

The West

1865–1896

15

WINDOW TO THE PAST

Buffalo Hunting, c. 1875

This image of a buffalo (bison) hunt was rendered on a buffalo hide. Buffalo were an important resource for Native Americans on the Great Plains, and the decline of this resource at the hands of white settlers not only changed the landscape of the West but also irreparably changed the lives of the Indians who lived there.

▶ To discover more about what this primary source can show us, see Source 15.1 on page 498.

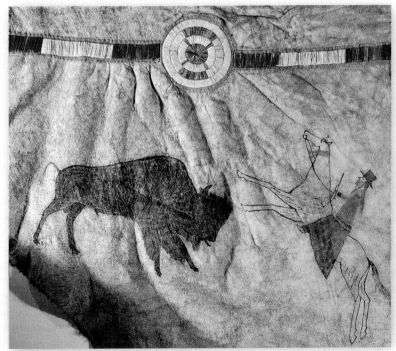

© Werner Forman/TopFoto/The Image Works

After reading this chapter you should be able to:

■ Analyze the motives and incentives that led to settling of the trans-Mississippi West and the technological developments that encouraged it.

■ Evaluate the strategies used by the U.S. government to control the lives of Native Americans in the West and Indians' reactions to these efforts.

■ Compare the roles of the mining and lumber industries in the economic and social development of the West.

■ Summarize the factors that led to the rise of commercial ranching and contrast the image of life in the West for ranchers and farmers with the reality.

■ Analyze the cultural diversity of the far West and the ethnic tensions that followed from this diversity.

COMPARING AMERICAN HISTORIES

Born in 1860, Phoebe Ann Moses grew up east of the Mississippi, seventy miles north of Cincinnati, Ohio. One of seven surviving children, she was sent to an orphanage at the age of nine, after her father died and her mother could not care for all her children. After working for a farm family, she ran away at the age of twelve and found a new home with a recently remarried widow. There, Phoebe Ann learned to ride and hunt and became an expert shot with a rifle. At fifteen, she entered a shooting contest and defeated a professional

(*left*) **Annie Oakley.** Yale Collection of Western Americana, Beinecke Rare Book and Manuscript Library, Yale University

(*right*) **Geronimo.** Library of Congress, 3c24560

marksman, Frank Butler. The two married in 1876. Phoebe Ann changed her professional name to "Annie Oakley," and she and Butler toured the Midwest in an act that featured precision shooting.

In 1884 Oakley and Butler met William F. "Buffalo Bill" Cody in New Orleans. In 1883, as the western frontier began to recede and the U.S. government relocated Native Americans who lived there, Cody attempted to recapture and reinvent the frontier experience by staging "Wild West" shows. A year later, he hired Oakley, with Butler serving as her manager. For the next fifteen years, Oakley was the star of the show. Wearing a fringed skirt, an embroidered blouse, and a broad felt hat, she stood atop her horse and performed amazing feats of marksmanship. Oakley toured Europe and fascinated heads of state and audiences alike with her version of "western authenticity." Fans at home and overseas displayed great nostalgia for a fast-diminishing era. When the census of 1890 reported that no open land was left to settle and thus no western frontier was left to conquer, Oakley's popularity soared. She continued performing in Wild West shows until her death in 1926.

While Annie Oakley portrayed the Wild West, Geronimo had lived it. Born to a Chiricahua Apache family in what was then northern Mexico (present-day Arizona and New Mexico), Geronimo led Apaches in a constant struggle against Spain, Mexico, and the United States. In 1851 a band of Mexicans raided an Apache camp, murdering Geronimo's mother, wife, and three children. After fighting Mexicans, Geronimo clashed with U.S. troops and evaded capture until 1877, when an Indian agent arrested him in New Mexico. Sent to a reservation, Geronimo escaped and for eight years engaged in daring raids against his foes. In 1886 two Chiricahua scouts led the U.S. military to Geronimo. Against an army of five thousand soldiers, the Apache warrior, with a band of eighteen fighters and some women and children, finally surrendered and was eventually relocated by the U.S. government to Fort Sill, Oklahoma.

The once-elusive warrior decided to take advantage of his legendary reputation and America's growing fascination with the mythic West. He sold photos of himself and pieces of his clothing; he appeared at the 1904 World's Fair in St. Louis, selling bows and arrows and autographs; and in 1905 he rode in President Theodore Roosevelt's inaugural parade as an example of a "tamed" Indian. Despite all of this, Geronimo never gave up the idea of returning to his birthplace. As long as the U.S. government prohibited him from going back to his ancestral lands in the Southwest, he considered himself a "prisoner of war." And so he remained until his death in 1909. ■

The American histories of Annie Oakley and Geronimo were profoundly different, yet they both contributed to the creation of a shared story, the myth of the American West. The West has great fascination in American culture. Stories about the frontier have romanticized both cowboys and Indians. These stories have also glorified individualism, self-help, and American ingenuity and minimized cooperation, organization, and the role of foreign influence in developing the West. As the American histories of Annie Oakley and Geronimo make clear, reality presents a more complicated picture of a diverse region initially inhabited by native peoples who were pushed aside by the arrival of white settlers and immigrants. In the areas known as the Great Plains and the far West, women took on new roles, and new cities emerged to accommodate the influx of miners, ranchers, and farmers.

Opening the West

The area west of the Mississippi was not hospitable to farmers and other adventurers lured by the appeal of cheap land and a fresh start. These pioneers demonstrated rugged determination; however, they could not have settled the West on their own. Federal policy and foreign investment played a large role in encouraging and financing the development of the West. Railroads were essential in transforming the region (Map 15.1).

The Great Plains.

In the mid-nineteenth century, the western frontier lay in the **Great Plains**. Lying on both sides of the Rocky Mountains, the Great Plains plateau was a semiarid territory with an average yearly rainfall sufficient to sustain short grasslands but not many trees. Prospects for sedentary farmers in this dry region did not appear promising. In 1878 geologist John Wesley Powell issued a report that questioned whether the land beyond the easternmost portion of the Great Plains could support small farming. Lack of rainfall, he argued, would make it difficult or even impossible for homesteaders to support themselves on family farms of 160 acres. Instead, he recommended that for the plains to prove economically sustainable, settlers would have to work much larger stretches of land, around 2,560 acres (4 square miles). This would provide ample room to raise livestock under dry conditions.

Powell's words of caution did little to diminish Americans' conviction, dating back to Thomas Jefferson, that small farmers would populate the territories brought under U.S. jurisdiction and renew democratic values as they ventured forth. Charles Dana Wilber summed up the view of those who saw no barriers to the expansion of small farmers in the plains. Rejecting the idea that the Great Plains should remain a "perpetual desert," Wilber asserted that "in reality there is no desert anywhere except by man's permission or neglect." Along with millions of others, he had great faith in Americans' ability to turn the Great Plains into a place where Jefferson's republican vision could take root and prosper.

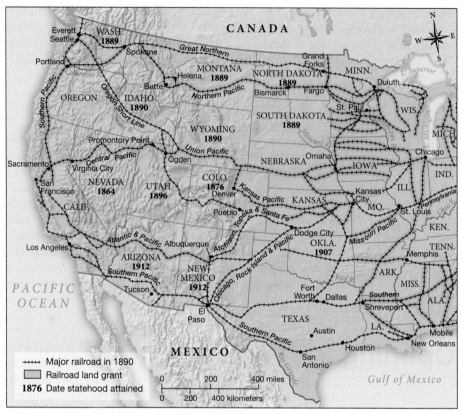

MAP 15.1   The American West, 1860–1900

Railroads played a key role in the expansion and settlement of the American West. The network of railroads running throughout the West opened the way for extensive migration from the East and for the development of a national market. None of this would have been possible without the land grants provided to the railroads by the U.S. government.

Federal Policy and Foreign Investment.

Despite the popular association of the West with individual initiative and self-sufficiency, the federal government played a huge role in facilitating the settlement of the West. National lawmakers enacted legislation offering free or cheap land to settlers and to mining, lumber, and railroad companies. The U.S. government also provided subsidies for transporting mail and military supplies, recruited soldiers to subdue the Indians who stood in the way of expansion, and appointed officials to govern the territories. Through these efforts, the government provided a necessary measure of safety and stability for new businesses to start up and grow as well as interconnected transportation and communication systems to supply workers and promote opportunities to develop new markets across North America.

Along with federal policy, foreign investment helped fuel development of the West. Lacking sufficient funds of its own, the United States turned to Europe to finance the sale of public bonds and private securities. European firms also invested in American mines, with the British leading the way. In 1872 an Englishman wrote that mines in Nevada were

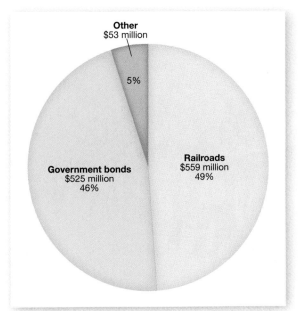

Other
$53 million

5%

Government bonds
$525 million
46%

Railroads
$559 million
49%

FIGURE 15.1   British Foreign Investment in the United States, 1876

British investment was an important source of funding for westward expansion following the Civil War. Nearly half of all British loans went toward financing railroad construction, which required large capital expenditures. The British also invested heavily in government bonds and to a lesser extent in cattle ranching and mining enterprises. Why did American railroads attract so much British investment?

Source: Data from Mina Wilkins, *The History of Foreign Investment in the United States to 1914* (Cambridge, MA: Harvard University Press, 1989), 164.

"more British than American." The development of the western cattle range — the symbol of the American frontier and the heroic cowboy — was also funded by overseas financiers. At the height of the cattle boom in the 1880s, British firms supplied some $45 million to underwrite ranch operations. The largest share of money, however, that flowed from Europe to the United States came with the expansion of the railroads, the most important ingredient in opening the West (Figure 15.1).

The **transcontinental railroad** became the gateway to the West. In 1862 the Republican-led Congress appropriated vast areas of land that railroad companies could use to lay their tracks or sell to raise funds for construction. The Central Pacific Company built from west to east, starting in Sacramento, California. The construction project attracted thousands of Chinese railroad workers. From the opposite direction, the Union Pacific Company began laying track in Council Bluffs, Iowa, and hired primarily Irish workers. In May 1869, the Central Pacific and Union Pacific crews met at Promontory Point, Utah. Workmen from the two companies drove a golden spike to complete the connection. For many Americans recovering from four years of civil war and still embroiled in southern reconstruction, the completion of the transcontinental railroad renewed their faith in the nation's ingenuity and destiny. A wagon train had once taken six to eight weeks to travel across the West. That trip could now be completed by rail in seven days. The railroad allowed both people and goods to move faster and in greater numbers than before. The West was now open not just to rugged pioneers but to anyone who could afford a railroad ticket.

The building of the railroads also provided new business opportunities, albeit more questionable. For example, Union Pacific promoters created a fake construction company called the Crédit Mobilier, which they used to funnel government bond and contract money into their own pockets. They also bribed congressmen to avoid investigation into their sordid dealings. Despite these efforts, in 1872 Congress exposed this corruption.

Railroad Construction Crew   Chinese and other immigrant groups were instrumental in the construction of the transcontinental railroad and other railway lines in the West. This photo shows Chinese workers building the Loma Prieta Lumber Company's railroad near Watsonville, California about 1885. In addition to transporting people, railroads were essential to the western lumber industry, which needed railways to transport timber from forest to sawmill. Pajaro Valley Historical Association

REVIEW & RELATE

What role did the federal government play in opening the West to settlement and economic exploitation?

Explain the determination of Americans to settle in land west of the Mississippi River despite the challenges the region presented.

Indians and Resistance to Expansion

American pioneers may have thought they were moving into a wilderness, but the West was home to large numbers of American Indians. Before pioneers and entrepreneurs could go west to pursue their economic dreams, the U.S. government would have to remove this obstacle to American expansion. Through treaties — most of which Americans broke — and war, white Americans conquered the Indian tribes inhabiting the Great Plains during the nineteenth century. After the native population was largely subdued, those who wanted to reform Indian policy focused on carving up tribal lands and forcing Indians to assimilate into American society.

Indian Civilizations.

Long before white settlers appeared, the frontier was already home to diverse peoples. The many native groups who inhabited the West spoke distinct languages, engaged in different economic activities, and competed with one another for power and resources. The descendants of Spanish conquistadors had also lived in the Southwest and California since the late sixteenth century, pushing the boundaries of the Spanish empire northward from Mexico. Indeed, Spaniards established the city of Santa Fe as the territorial capital of New Mexico years before the English landed at Jamestown, Virginia in 1607.

By the end of the Civil War, around 350,000 Indians were living west of the Mississippi. They constituted the surviving remnants of the 1 million people who had occupied the land for thousands of years before Europeans set foot in America. Nez Percé, Ute, and Shoshone Indians lived in the Northwest and the Rocky Mountain region; Lakota, Cheyenne, Blackfoot, Crow, and Arapaho tribes occupied the vast expanse of the central and northern plains; and Apaches, Comanches, Kiowas, Navajos, and Pueblos made up the bulk of the population in the Southwest. Some of the tribes, such as the Cherokee, Creek, and Shawnee, had been forcibly removed from the East during Andrew Jackson's presidency in the 1830s.

Given the rich assortment of Indian tribes, it is difficult to generalize about Indian culture and society. The tribes each adapted in unique ways to the geography and climate of their home territories, spoke their own language, and had their own history and traditions. Some were hunters, others farmers; some nomadic, others sedentary. In New Mexico, for example, Apaches were expert horsemen and fierce warriors, while the Pueblo Indians built homes out of adobe and developed a flourishing system of agriculture. Also, they cultivated the land through methods of irrigation that foreshadowed modern practices. The Pawnees in the Great Plains periodically set fire to the land to improve game hunting and the growth of vegetation. Indians on the southern plains gradually became enmeshed in the market economy for bison robes, which they sold to American traders (Map 15.2).

The lives of all Indian peoples were affected by the arrival of Europeans, but the consequences of cross-cultural contact varied considerably depending on the history and circumstances of each tribe. Whites trampled on Indian hunting grounds, polluted streams with acid run-off from mines, and introduced Indians to liquor. They inflicted the greatest damage through diseases for which Indians lacked the immunity that Europeans and white Americans had acquired. By 1870, smallpox had wiped out half the population of Plains Indians, and cholera, diphtheria, and measles caused serious but lesser harm. Nomadic tribes such as the Lakota Sioux were able to flee the contagion, while agrarian tribes such as the Mandan suffered extreme losses. As a result, the balance of power among Plains tribes shifted to the more mobile Sioux. Indians were not pacifists, and they engaged in warfare with their enemies in disputes over hunting grounds, horses, and honor. However, the introduction of guns by European and American traders transformed Indian warfare into a much more deadly affair than had existed previously. And by the mid-nineteenth century, some tribes had become so deeply engaged in the commercial fur trade with whites that they had depleted their own hunting grounds.

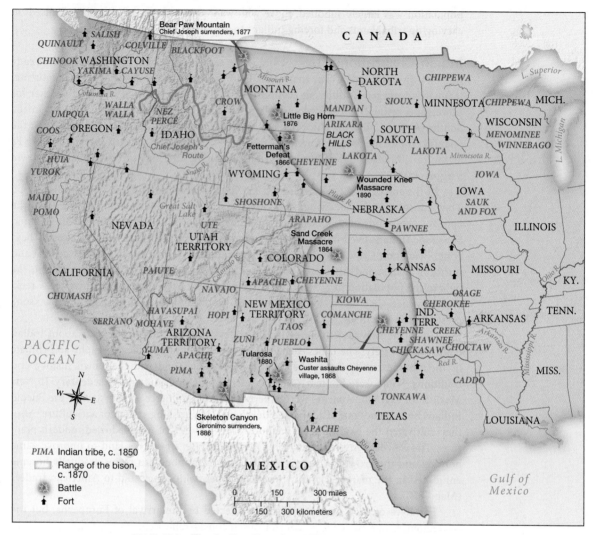

MAP 15.2 The Indian Frontier, 1870

Western migration posed a threat to the dozens of Indian tribes and the immense herds of bison in the region. The tribes had signed treaties with the U.S. government recognizing the right to live on their lands. The presence of U.S. forts did not protect the Indians from settlers who invaded their territories.

Native Americans had their own approach toward nature and the land they inhabited. Most tribes did not accept private ownership of land, as white pioneers did. Indians recognized the concept of private property in ownership of their horses, weapons, tools, and shelters, but they viewed the land as the common domain of their tribe, for use by all members. "The White man knows how to make everything," the Hunkpapa Lakota chieftain Sitting Bull remarked, "but he does not know how to distribute it." This communitarian outlook also reflected native attitudes toward the environment. Indians considered human beings not as superior to the rest of nature's creations, but rather as part of an interconnected world of animals, plants, and natural elements. According to this view, all plants and animals were part of a larger spirit world, which flowed from the power of the sun, the sky, and the earth.

Bison (commonly known as buffalo) played a central role in the religion and society of many Indian tribes. By the mid-nineteenth century, approximately thirty million bison grazed on the Great Plains. Before acquiring guns, Indians used a variety of means to hunt their prey, including bows and arrows and spears. Some rode their horses to chase bison and stampede them over cliffs. The meat from the buffalo provided food; its hide provided material to construct tepees and make blankets and clothes; bones were crafted into tools, knives, and weapons; dried bison dung served as an excellent source of fuel. It is therefore not surprising that the Plains Indians dressed up in colorful outfits, painted their bodies, and danced to the almighty power of the buffalo and the spiritual presence within it.

Explore ▶

See Source 15.1 for a depiction of buffalo hunting.

Indian hunting societies, such as the Lakota Sioux and Apache, contained gender distinctions. The task of riding horses to hunt bison became men's work; women waited for the hunters to return and then prepared the buffalo hides. Nevertheless, women refused to think of their role as passive; they saw themselves as sharing in the work of providing food, shelter, and clothing for the members of their tribe. Similarly, the religious belief that the spiritual world touched every aspect of the material world gave women an opportunity to experience this transcendent power without the mediation of male leaders.

Changing Federal Policy toward Indians.
The U.S. government started out by treating western Indians as autonomous nations, thereby recognizing their stewardship over the land they occupied. In 1851 the **Treaty of Fort Laramie** confined tribes on the northern plains to designated areas in an attempt to keep white settlers from encroaching on their land. A treaty two years later applied these terms to tribes on the southern plains. Indians kept their part of the agreement, but white miners racing to strike it rich did not. They roamed through Indian hunting grounds in search of ore and faced little government enforcement of the existing treaties. In fact, the U.S. military made matters considerably worse. On November 29, 1864, a peaceful band of 700 Cheyennes and Arapahos under the leadership of Chief Black Kettle gathered at Sand Creek, Colorado, supposedly under guarantees of U.S. protection. Instead, Colonel John M. Chivington and his troops launched an attack, despite a white flag of surrender hoisted by the Indians, and brutally killed some 270 Indians, mainly women and children. A congressional investigation later determined that the victims "were mutilated in the most horrible manner." Although there was considerable public outcry over the incident, the government did nothing to increase enforcement of its treaty obligations. In almost all disputes between white settlers and Indians, the government sided with the whites, regardless of the Indians' legal rights. In 1867, the government once again signed treaties with Indian tribes in the southern plains, with similarly devastating results. The **Treaty of Medicine Lodge** provided reservation lands for the Comanche, Kiowa-Apache, and Southern Arapaho to settle. Despite this agreement, white hunters soon invaded this territory and decimated the buffalo herds.

The duplicity of the U.S. government was not without consequences. The Sand Creek massacre unleashed Indian wars throughout the central plains, where the Lakota Sioux led the resistance from 1865 to 1868. After two years of fierce fighting, both sides signed a second Treaty of Fort Laramie, which gave northern tribes control over the "Great Reservation" set aside in parts of present-day Montana, Wyoming, North Dakota, and South Dakota. Another treaty placed the southern tribes in a reservation carved out of western Oklahoma.

One of the tribes that wound up in Oklahoma was the Nez Percé. Originally settled in the corner where Washington, Oregon, and Idaho meet, the tribe was forced to sign a treaty

GUIDED ANALYSIS

Buffalo Hunting, c. 1875

This pictograph from around 1875 portrays a Shoshone man on a buffalo hunt. This drawing was made on a buffalo skin robe quilled by a tribal woman and worn by a hunter.

Source 15.1

Why do you think the person who made this drawing placed such a design on the robe?

What evidence appears to show this Indian has made use of some items from the culture of white settlers?

Why is the buffalo drawn so much larger than the Indian on his horse?

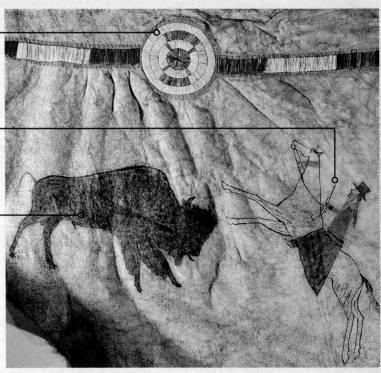

© Werner Forman/TopFoto/The Image Works

Put It in Context

Why did Native Americans in the West have such a close personal connection to the buffalo?

ceding most of its land to the United States and to relocate onto a reservation. In 1877 Chief Joseph led the Nez Percé out of the Pacific Northwest, directing his people in a daring march of 1,400 miles over mountains into Montana and Wyoming as federal troops pursued them. Intending to flee to Canada, the Nez Percé were finally intercepted in the mountains of northern Montana, just thirty miles from the border. Subsequently, the government relocated these northwestern Indians to the southwestern territory of Oklahoma. In 1879 Chief Joseph pleaded with lawmakers in Congress to return his people to their home and urged the U.S. government to live up to the original intent of the treaties. His words carried some weight, and the Nez Percé returned under armed escort to a reservation in Washington.

The treaties did not produce a lasting peace. Though most of the tribes relocated onto reservations, some refused. The Apache chief Victorio explained why he would not resettle his people on a reservation. "We prefer to die in our own land under the tall cool pines," he declared. "We will leave our bones with those of our people. It is better to die fighting than to starve." General William Tecumseh Sherman, commander of the military forces against the Indians, ordered the army to wage a merciless war of annihilation "against all hostile Indians till they are obliterated or beg for mercy." In November 1868, Lieutenant Colonel George Armstrong Custer took Sherman at his word and assaulted a Cheyenne village, killing more than one hundred Indians. Nearly a decade later, in 1876, the Indians, this time Lakota Sioux, exacted revenge by killing Custer and his troops at the **Battle of the Little Big Horn** in Montana. Yet this proved to be the final victory for the Lakota nation, as the army mounted an extensive and fierce offensive against them that shattered their resistance.

Indian Drawing of Battle of Little Big Horn   This ink-on-paper drawing by Amos Bad Heart Buffalo (1869–1913) depicts the June 1876 Battle of Little Big Horn, also known as Custer's Last Stand. It portrays the retreat of Major Marcus Reno's forces. The painted warrior on the white horse who is shooting a soldier from his saddle is Crazy Horse, the Sioux chieftain. Private Collection/The Stapleton Collection/Bridgeman Images

Among the troops that battled the Indians were African Americans. Known as **buffalo soldiers**, they represented a cross section of the postwar black population looking for new opportunities that were now available after their emancipation. Some blacks enlisted to learn how to read and write; others sought to avoid unpleasant situations back home. Cooks, waiters, painters, bakers, teamsters, and farmers signed up for a five-year stint in the army at $13 a month. A few gained more glory than money. In May 1880, Sergeant George Jordan of the Ninth Cavalry led troops under his command to fend off Apache raids in Tularosa, New Mexico, for which he was awarded the Congressional Medal of Honor.

Indian Defeat.

By the late 1870s, Indians had largely succumbed to U.S. military supremacy. The tribes, as their many victories demonstrated, contained agile horsemen and skilled warriors, but the U.S. army was backed by the power of an increasingly industrial economy. Telegraph lines and railroads provided logistical advantages in the swift deployment of U.S. troops and the ability of the central command to communicate with field officers. Although Indians had acquired firearms over the years, the army boasted an essentially unlimited supply of superior weapons. The diversity of Indians and historic rivalries among tribes also made it difficult for them to unite against their common enemy. The federal government exploited these divisions by hiring Indians to serve as army scouts against their traditional tribal foes.

The government devised its policies based on flawed cultural assumptions. Even the most sensitive white administrators of Indian affairs considered Indians a degraded race, in accordance with the scientific thinking of the time. At most, whites believed that Indians could be lifted to a higher level of civilization, which in practice meant a withering away of their traditional culture and heritage. **See Primary Source Project 15: American Indians and Whites in the West, page 520.**

The wholesale destruction of the bison was the final blow to Indian independence. As railroads pushed their tracks beyond the Mississippi, they cleared bison from their path by sending in professional hunters with high-powered rifles to shoot the animals. At the same time, buffalo products such as shoes, coats, and hats became fashionable in the East. By the mid-1880s, hunters had killed more than thirteen million bison. As a result of the relentless move of white Americans westward and conspicuous consumption back east, bison herds were almost annihilated.

Faced with decimation of the bison, broken treaties, and their opponents' superior military technology, Native Americans' capacity to wage war collapsed. Indians had little choice but to settle on shrinking reservations that the government established for them. The absence of war, however, did not necessarily bring them security. In the late 1870s, gold discoveries in the Black Hills of North Dakota ignited another furious rush by miners onto lands supposedly guaranteed to the Lakota people. Rather than honoring its treaties, the U.S. government forced the tribes to relinquish still more land. General Custer's Seventh Cavalry was part of the military force trying to push Indians out of this mining region, when it was annihilated at the Little Big Horn in 1876. Elsewhere, Congress opened up a portion of western Oklahoma to white homesteaders in 1889. Although this land had not been assigned to specific tribes relocated in Indian Territory, more than eighty thousand Indians from various tribes lived there. This government-sanctioned land rush only added to the pressure from homesteaders and others to acquire more land at the expense of the Indians. A decade later, Congress officially ended Indian control of Indian Territory.

Reforming Indian Policy. As reservations continued to shrink under expansionist assault and government acquiescence, a movement arose to reform Indian policy. Largely centered in the East, where few Indians lived, reformers came to believe that the future welfare of Indians lay not in sovereignty but in assimilation. In 1881 Helen Hunt Jackson published *A Century of Dishonor*, her exposé of the unjust treatment the Indians had received. Roused by this depiction of the Indians' plight, groups such as the Women's National Indian Association joined with ministers and philanthropists to advocate the transformation of native peoples into full-fledged Americans.

From today's vantage point, these well-intentioned reformers could be viewed as contributing to the demise of the Indians by trying to eradicate their cultural heritage. Judged by the standards of their own time, however, they wanted to save the Indians from the brutality and corrupt behavior they had endured, and they believed they were acting in the Indians' best interests. The most advanced thinking among anthropologists at the time offered an approach that supported assimilation as the only alternative to extinction. The influential Lewis Morgan, author of *Ancient Society* (1877), concluded that all cultures evolved through three stages: savagery, barbarism, and civilization. Indians occupied the lower rungs, but reformers argued that by adopting white values they could become civilized.

Reformers faced opposition from white Americans who doubted that Indian assimilation was possible. For many Americans, secure in their sense of their own superiority, the decline and eventual extinction of the Indian peoples was an inevitable consequence of what they saw as Indians' innate inferiority. For example, a Wyoming newspaper predicted: "The same inscrutable Arbiter that decreed the downfall of Rome has pronounced the doom of extinction upon the red men of America."

Reformers found their legislative spokesman in Senator Henry Dawes of Massachusetts. As legislative director of the Boston Indian Citizenship Association, Dawes shared Christian reformers' belief that becoming a true American would save both the Indians and the soul of the nation. A Republican who had served in Congress since the Civil War, Dawes had the same paternalistic attitude toward Indians as he had toward freed slaves. He believed that if both degraded groups worked hard and practiced thrift and individual initiative in the spirit of Dawes's New England Puritan forebears, they would succeed. The key for Dawes was private ownership of land.

Passed in 1887, the **Dawes Act** ended tribal rule and divided Indian lands into 160-acre parcels. The act allocated one parcel to each family head. The government held the lands in trust for the Indians for twenty-five years; at the end of this period, the Indians would receive American citizenship. In return, the Indians had to abandon their religious and cultural rites and practices, including storytelling and the use of medicine men. Whatever lands remained after this reallocation — and the amount was considerable — would be sold on the open market, and the profits from the sales would be placed in an educational fund for Indians.

Unfortunately, like most of the policies it replaced, the Dawes Act proved detrimental to Native Americans. Indian families received inferior farmlands and inadequate tools to cultivate them, while speculators reaped profits from the sale of the "excess" Indian lands. A little more than a decade after the Dawes Act went into effect, Indians controlled 77 million acres of land, down sharply from the 155 million acres they held in 1881. Additional legislation in 1891 forced Indian parents to send their children to boarding schools or else face arrest. At these educational institutions, Indian children were given

"American" names, had their long hair cut, and wore uniforms in place of their native dress. The program for boys provided manual and vocational training and that for girls taught domestic skills, so that they could emulate the gender roles in middle-class American families. However, this schooling offered few skills of use in an economic world undergoing industrial transformation.

Indian Assimilation and Resistance.

Not all Indians conformed to the government's attempt at forced acculturation. Some refused to abandon their traditional social practices, and others rejected the white man's version of private property and civilization. Even on reservations, Indians found ways to preserve aspects of their native traditions. Through close family ties, they communicated to sons and daughters their languages, histories, and cultural practices. Parents refused to grant full control of their children to white educators and often made sure that schools were located on or near reservations where they fit into the pattern of their lives. Yet, many others displayed more complicated approaches to survival in a world that continued to view Indians with prejudice. Geronimo and Sitting Bull participated in pageants and Wild West shows but refused to disavow their heritage. Ohiyesa, a Lakota also known as Charles Eastman, went to boarding school, graduated from Dartmouth College, and earned a medical degree from Boston University. He supported passage of the Dawes Act, believed in the virtues of an American education, and worked for the Bureau of Indian Affairs. At the same time, he spoke out against government corruption and fraud perpetrated against Indians. Reviewing his life in his later years, Eastman/Ohiyesa reflected: "I am an Indian and while I have learned much from civilization . . . I have never lost my Indian sense of right and justice."

Disaster loomed for those who resisted assimilation and held on too tightly to the old ways. In 1888 the prophet Wovoka, a member of the Paiute tribe in western Nevada, had a vision that Indians would one day regain control of the world and that whites would disappear. He believed that the Creator had provided him with a **Ghost Dance** that would make this happen. The dance spread to thousands of Lakota Sioux in the northern plains. Seeing the Ghost Dance as a sign of renewed Indian resistance, the army attempted to put a stop to the revival. On December 29, 1890, the Seventh Cavalry chased three hundred ghost dancers to Wounded Knee Creek on the Pine Ridge Reservation in present-day South Dakota. In a confrontation with the Lakota leader Big Foot, a gunshot accidentally rang out during a struggle with one of his followers. The cavalry then turned the full force of their weaponry on the Indians, killing 250 Native Americans, many of them women and children.

The message of the massacre at Wounded Knee was clear for those who raised their voices against Americanization. As Black Elk, a spiritual leader of the Oglala Lakota tribe, asserted: "A people's dream died there. . . . There is no center any longer, and the sacred tree is dead." It may not have been the policy of the U.S. government to exterminate the Indians as a people, but it was certainly U.S. policy to destroy Indian culture and society once and for all.

REVIEW & RELATE

• How and why did federal Indian policy change during the nineteenth century?

• Describe some of the ways that Indian peoples responded to federal policies. Which response do you think offered their greatest chance for survival?

The **Mining** and **Lumber Industries**

Among the settlers pouring into Indian Territory in the Rocky Mountains were miners in search of gold and silver. These prospectors envisioned instant riches that would come from a lucky strike. The vast majority found only backbreaking work, danger, and frustration. Miners continued to face hardship and danger as industrial mining operations took over from individual prospectors, despite the efforts of some miners to fight for better wages and working conditions. By 1900 the mining rush had peaked, and many of the boomtowns that had cropped up around the mining industry had emptied out. Still, mining companies and the workers they attracted forged big cities of diverse peoples and commerce. Closely related to mining, the lumber industry was less demographically diverse but also followed the pattern of domination by big business.

The Business of Mining. The discovery of gold in California in 1848 had set this mining frenzy in motion. Over the next thirty years, successive waves of gold and silver strikes in Colorado, Nevada, Washington, Idaho, Montana, and the Dakotas lured individual prospectors with shovels and wash pans. One of the biggest finds came with the **Comstock Lode** in the Sierra Nevada, where miners extracted around $350 million worth of silver (in 19th century dollars). One of those who came to try to share in the wealth was Samuel Clemens. Like most of his fellow miners, Clemens did not find his fortune in Nevada and soon turned his attention to writing, finally achieving success as the author called Mark Twain.

Like Twain, many of those who flocked to the Comstock Lode and other mining frontiers were men. Nearly half were foreign-born, many of them coming from Mexico or China. Using pans and shovels, prospectors could find only the ore that lay near the surface of the earth and water. Once these initial discoveries were played out, individual prospectors could not afford to buy the equipment needed to dig out the vast deposits of gold and silver buried deep in the earth. As a result, western mining operations became big businesses run by men with the financial resources necessary to purchase industrial mining equipment.

When mining became an industry, prospectors became wageworkers. In Virginia City, Nevada miners labored for $4 a day, an amount that barely covered the expenses of life in a mining boomtown. Moreover, the work was extremely dangerous. Mine shafts extended down more than a thousand feet, and working temperatures regularly exceeded 100 degrees Fahrenheit. Noxious fumes, fires, and floods of scalding water flowed through the shafts, and other threats killed or disabled thousands each year.

Struggling with low pay and dangerous work, western miners sought to organize. In the mid-1860s, unions formed in the Comstock Lode areas of Virginia City and Gold Hill, Nevada. Although these unions had some success, they also provoked a violent backlash from mining companies determined to resist union demands. Companies hired private police forces to help break strikes. Such forces were often assisted by state militias deployed by elected officials with close ties to the companies. For example, in 1892 the governor of Idaho crushed an unruly strike by calling up the National Guard, a confrontation that resulted in the deaths of seven strikers. A year later, mine workers formed one of the most militant labor organizations in the nation, the Western Federation of Miners. Within a decade, it had attracted fifty thousand members, though membership did not extend to all ethnicities. The union excluded Chinese, Mexican, and Indian workers from its ranks.

Life in the Mining Towns.

Life in the Mining Towns. Men worked the mines, but women flocked to the area as well. In Storey County, Nevada, the heart of the Comstock Lode, the 1875 census showed that women made up about half the population. Most employed women worked long hours as domestics in boardinghouses, hotels, and private homes. Prostitution, which was legal, accounted for the single-largest segment of the female workforce. Most prostitutes were between the ages of nineteen and twenty-four, and they entered this occupation because few other well-paying jobs were available to them. The demand for their services remained high among the large population of unmarried men. Yet prostitutes faced constant danger, and many were victims of physical abuse, robbery, and murder.

As early as the 1880s, gold and silver discoveries had played out in the Comstock Lode. Boomtowns, which had sprung up almost overnight, now became ghost towns as gold and silver deposits dwindled. Even more substantial places like Virginia City, Nevada experienced a severe decline as the veins of ore ran out. One revealing sign of the city's plummeting fortunes was the drop in the number of prostitutes, which declined by more than half by 1880. The mining business then shifted from gold and silver to copper, lead, and zinc, centered in Montana and Idaho. As with the early prospectors in California and Nevada, these miners eventually became wageworkers for giant consolidated mining companies. By the end of the nineteenth century, the Amalgamated Copper Company and the American Smelting and Refining Company dominated the industry.

Mining towns that survived became only slightly less rowdy places, but they did settle into more complex patterns of urban living. At its height in the 1870s, Virginia City contained 25,000 residents and was among the largest cities west of the Mississippi River. It provided schools and churches and featured such cultural amenities as theaters and opera houses. Though the population in mining towns remained predominantly young and male, the young men were increasingly likely to get married and raise families. Residents lived in neighborhoods divided by class and ethnicity. For example, in Butte, Montana the west side of town became home to the middle and upper classes. Mine workers lived on

Prostitution on the Frontier Prostitution was one of the main sources of employment for women in frontier mining towns. A legal enterprise, it paid better than other work such as domestic service and teaching. In 1875 in the Comstock region of Nevada, 307 women plied their trade in brothels and saloons similar to the saloon shown here. Bill Manns/REX/Shutterstock

the east side in homes subdivided into apartments and in boardinghouses. The Irish lived in one section; Finns, Swedes, Serbs, Croatians, and Slovenes in other sections. Each group formed its own social, fraternal, and religious organizations to relieve the harsh conditions of overcrowding, poor sanitation, and discrimination. Residents of the east side relied on one another for support and frowned on those who deviated from their code of solidarity. "They didn't try to outdo the other one," one neighborhood woman remarked. "If you did, you got into trouble. . . . If they thought you were a little richer than they were, they wouldn't associate with you." Although western mining towns retained distinctive qualities, in their social and ethnic divisions they came to resemble older cities east of the Mississippi River.

The Lumber Boom. The mining industry created a huge demand for timber, as did the railroad lines that operated in the West. Initially small logging firms moved into the Northwest and California, cut down all the trees they could, sent them to nearby sawmills for processing, and moved on. By 1900, a few large firms came to dominate the industry and acquired vast tracts of forests. Frederick Weyerhaeuser purchased 900,000 acres of prime timberland in the Western Cascades of Oregon, largely bringing an end to the often chaotic competition of small firms that had characterized the industry in its early days. Increasingly, the western lumber industry became part of a global market that shipped products to Hawaii, South America, and Asia.

Loggers and sawmill workers did not benefit from these changes. Exclusively male, large numbers of workers came from Scandinavia, and only a few were Asian or African American. Men died or lost limbs in cutting down the trees, transporting them in the rivers, or processing the wood in sawmills. As lumber camps and mill villages became urbanized, those who gained the most were the merchants and bankers who supplied the goods and capital.

REVIEW & RELATE

- How and why did the nature of mining in the West change during the second half of the nineteenth century?

- How did the mining and lumber industries reshape the frontier landscape?

The **Cattle Industry** and **Commercial Farming**

Like mining and lumber, cattle ranching and farming in the West increasingly became dominated by big business. Foreign investors from England, Scotland, Wales, and South America poured in money to fund the cattle industry and placed day-to-day control of their ranches in the hands of experienced corporate managers. Cowboys functioned as industrial laborers. They worked long hours in tough but boring conditions on the open range. Similarly, commercial farmers who headed west endured great hardships in trying to raise crops in an often inhospitable climate. Extreme weather and falling crop prices, however, forced many ranchers and farmers out of business, and their lands and businesses were snatched up by larger, more consolidated commercial ranching and agricultural enterprises. Despite difficult physical and economic conditions, many of the women and men who ranched and farmed in the West showed grit and determination not only in surviving but in improving their lives as well.

The Life of the Cowboy.

There is no greater symbol of the frontier West than the cowboy. As portrayed in novels and film, the cowboy hero was the essence of manhood, an independent figure who fought for justice and defended the honor and virtue of women. Never the aggressor, he fought to protect law-abiding residents of frontier communities.

This romantic image excited generations of American readers and later movie and television audiences. In reality, cowboys' lives were much more mundane. Rather than working as independent adventurers, they increasingly operated in an industrial setting dominated by large cattle companies. Cowpunchers worked for paltry monthly wages, put in long days herding cattle, and spent part of the night guarding them on the open range.

Explore ▶

See Sources 15.2 and 15.3 for two depictions of cowboy life.

Their major task was to make the 1,500-mile **Long Drive** along the Chisholm Trail. Beginning in the late 1860s, cowboys moved cattle from ranches in Texas through Oklahoma to rail depots in Kansas towns such as Abilene and Dodge City; from there, cattle were shipped by train eastward to slaughterhouses in Chicago. Life along the trail was monotonous, and riders had to contend with bad weather, dangerous work, and disease.

Numbering around forty thousand and averaging twenty-four years of age, the cowboys who rode through the Great Plains from Texas to Kansas came from diverse backgrounds. The majority, about 66 percent, were white, predominantly southerners who had fought for the South during the Civil War. Most of the rest were divided evenly between Mexicans and African Americans, some of whom were former slaves and others Union veterans of the Civil War.

Besides experiencing rugged life on the range, black and Mexican cowboys faced racial discrimination. Jim Perry, an African American who rode for the three-million-acre XIT Ranch in Texas for more than twenty years, complained: "If it weren't for my damned old black face I'd have been boss of one of these divisions long ago." Mexican *vaqueros*, or cowboys, earned one-third to one-half the wages of whites, whereas blacks were usually paid on a par with whites. Because the cattle kingdoms first flourished during Reconstruction, racial discrimination and segregation carried over into the Southwest. On one drive along the route to Kansas, a white boss insisted that a black cowboy eat and sleep separately from whites and shot at him when he refused to heed this order. Nevertheless, the proximity in which cowboys worked and the need for cooperation to overcome the pitfalls of the long drive made it difficult to enforce rigid racial divisions on the open range.

The Rise of Commercial Ranching.

Commercial ranches absorbed cowboys into their expanding operations. Spaniards had originally imported cattle into the Southwest, and by the late nineteenth century some five million Texas longhorn steers grazed in the area. Cattle that could be purchased in Texas for $3 to $7 fetched a price of $30 to $40 in Kansas. The extension of railroads across the West opened up a quickly growing market for beef in the East. The development of refrigerated railroad cars guaranteed that meat from slaughtered cattle could reach eastern consumers without spoiling. With money to be made, the cattle industry rose to meet the demand. Fewer than 40 ranchers owned more than 20 million acres of land. Easterners and Europeans joined the boom and invested money in giant ranches. By the mid-1880s, approximately 7.5 million head of cattle roamed the western ranges, and large cattle ranchers became rich. Cattle ranching had become fully integrated into the national commercial economy.

Then the bubble burst. Ranchers, who were already raising more cattle than the market could handle, increasingly faced competition from cattle producers in Canada and Argentina. Prices spiraled downward. Another source of competition came from homesteaders who moved into the plains and fenced in their farms with barbed wire, thereby reducing the size of the open range. Yet the greatest disaster occurred from 1885 to 1887. Two frigid winters, together with a torrid summer drought, destroyed 90 percent of the cattle on the northern plains of the Dakotas, Montana, Colorado, and Wyoming. Under these conditions, outside capital to support ranching diminished, and many of the great cattle barons went into bankruptcy. This economic collapse consolidated the remaining cattle industry into even fewer hands. The cowboy, never more than a hired hand, became a laborer for large corporations.

Commercial Farming.

Like cowboys, farm families endured hardships to make their living in the West. They struggled to raise crops in an often inhospitable climate in hopes that their yields would be sold for a profit. Falling crop prices, however, led to soaring debt and forced many farmers into bankruptcy and off their land, while others were fortunate enough to survive and make a living.

The federal government played a major role in opening up the Great Plains to farmers, who eventually clashed with cattlemen. The Republican Party of Abraham Lincoln had opposed the expansion of slavery in order to promote the virtues of free soil and free labor for white men and their families. In 1862, during the Civil War, preoccupation with battlefield losses did not stop the Republican-controlled Congress from passing the **Homestead Act**. As an incentive for western migration, the act established procedures for distributing 160-acre lots to western settlers, on condition that they develop and farm their land. What most would-be settlers did not know, however, was that lots of 160 acres were not viable in the harsh, dry climate of the Great Plains.

Reality did not deter pioneers and adventurers. In fact, weather conditions in the region temporarily fooled them. The decade after 1878 witnessed an exceptional amount of rainfall west of the Mississippi. Though not precisely predictable, this cycle of abundance and drought had been going on for millennia. In addition, innovation and technology bolstered dreams of success. Farmers planted hardy strains of wheat imported from Russia that survived the fluctuations of dry and wet and hot and cold weather. Machines produced by industrial laborers in northern factories to the east allowed farmers to plow tough land and harvest its yield. Steel-tipped plows, threshers, combines, and harvesters expanded production greatly, and windmills and pumping equipment provided sources of power and access to scarce water. These improvements in mechanization led to a significant expansion in agricultural production, which helped to lower food prices for consumers.

The people who accepted the challenge of carving out a new life were a diverse lot. The Great Plains attracted a large number of immigrants from Europe, some two million by 1900. Minnesota and the Dakotas welcomed communities of settlers from Sweden and Norway. Nebraska housed a considerable population of Germans, Swedes, Danes, and Czechs. About one-third of the people who migrated to the northern plains came directly from a foreign country.

Railroads and land companies lured settlers to the plains with tales of the fabulous possibilities that awaited their arrival. The federal government had given railroads generous grants of public land on which to build their tracks as well as parcels surrounding the

Cowboy Myths and Realities

William F. Cody, known as "Buffalo Bill," had been a real-life bison hunter in the American West and an army scout in the Indian wars of the 1860s and 1870s. Drawing on his authentic adventures and his heroism, Cody helped romanticize the figures that populated the American frontier, especially the cowboys, through his Wild West shows, a poster from which is shown here. The diary entries of George C. Duffield present a more mundane description of cowboy life. Duffield drove cattle on the open range in 1866 from Texas, where they were bred, to Iowa, where they went to market.

Source 15.2

Poster Advertising Buffalo Bill's Wild West Show, 1893

Newberry Library, Chicago, Illinois, USA/Bridgeman Images

tracks that they could sell off to raise revenue for construction. Western railroads advertised in both the United States and Europe, proclaiming that migrants to the plains would find "the garden spot of the world."

Having enticed prospective settlers with exaggerated claims, railroads offered bargain rates to transport them to their new homes. Families and friends often journeyed together and rented an entire car on the train, known as "the immigrant car," in which

Source 15.3

George C. Duffield | Diary of a Real Cowboy, 1866

12th

Hard Rain & Wind. Big stampede & here we are among the Indians with 150 head of Cattle gone. Hunted all day & the Rain pouring down with but poor success. Dark days are these to me. Nothing but Bread & Coffee. Hands all Growling & Swearing—everything wet & cold. Beeves [steers] gone. Rode all day & gathered all but 35 mixed with 8 other Herds. Last Night 5000 Beeves stampeded at this place & a general mix up was the result. . . .

14th

Last night there was a terrible storm. Rain poured in torrents *all* night & up to 12 AM today. Our Beeves left us in the night but for *once* on the whole trip we found them *all* together near camp at day break. *All* the other droves as far as I can hear are scattered to the four winds. Our Other Herd was all gone. We are now 25 Miles from Ark River & it is Very High. We are water bound by two creeks & but Beef & Flour to eat, am not Homesick but Heart sick. . . .

16th

Last night was a dark Gloomey night but we made it all right. Today it is raining & we have crossed Honey creek & am informed that there is another creek 6 miles ahead swimming. Twelve o clock today it rained one Hour so hard that a creek close by rose 20 ft in the afternoon. All wet.

Source: George C. Duffield, "Driving Cattle from Texas to Iowa, 1866," *Annals of Iowa* 14, no. 4 (1924): 253–54.

Interpret the Evidence

1. What does the placement of Cody's portrait in the poster suggest about the role of white men in the West?
2. How does Duffield's experience of the West differ from that conveyed in the poster?

Put It in Context

Why do you think Americans remember Buffalo Bill's version of the West rather than Duffield's?

they loaded their possessions, supplies, and even livestock. Often migrants came to the end of the rail line before reaching their destination. They completed the trip by wagon or stagecoach.

Commercial advertising alone did not account for the desire to journey westward. Settlers who had made the trip successfully wrote to relatives and neighbors back east and in the old country about the chance to start fresh. Linda Slaughter, the wife of an army doctor in the Dakotas, gushed: "The farms which have been opened in the vicinity of Bismarck have proven highly productive, the soil being kept moist by frequent rains. Vegetables of all kinds are grown with but little trouble."

Those who took the chance shared a faith in the future and a willingness to work hard and endure misfortune. They found their optimism and spirits sorely tested. Despite the company of family members and friends, settlers faced a lonely existence on the vast expanse of the plains. Homesteads were spread out, and a feeling of isolation became a routine part of daily life.

With few trees around, early settlers constructed sod houses. These structures let in little light but a good deal of moisture, keeping them gloomy and damp. A Nebraskan who lived in this type of house jokingly remarked: "There was running water in our sod house. It ran through the roof." Bugs, insects, and rodents, like the rain, often found their way inside to make living in such shelters even more uncomfortable.

If these dwellings were bleak, the climate posed even greater challenges. After the unusually plentiful rainfall in the late 1870s and early 1880s, severe drought followed. Before that, a plague of grasshoppers ravaged the northern plains in the late 1870s, destroying fruit trees and plants. Intense heat in the summer alternated with frigid temperatures in the winter. The Norwegian American writer O. E. Rolvaag, in *Giants in the Earth* (1927), described the extreme hardships that accompanied the fierce weather: "Blizzards from out of the northwest raged, swooped down and stirred up a greyish-white fury, impenetrable to human eyes. As soon as these monsters tired, storms from the northeast were sure to come, bringing more snow."

Women Homesteaders. The women of the family were responsible for making homesteads more bearable. Mothers and daughters were in charge of household duties, cooking the meals, canning fruits and vegetables, and washing and ironing clothing. Despite the drudgery of this work, women contributed significantly to the economic well-being of the family by occasionally taking in boarders and selling milk, butter, and eggs.

In addition, a surprisingly large number of single women staked out homestead claims by themselves. Some were young, unmarried women seeking, like their male counterparts, economic opportunity. Others were widows attempting to take care of their children after their husband's death. One such widow, Anne Furnberg, settled a homestead in the Dakota Territory in 1871. Born in Norway, she had lived with her husband and son in Minnesota. After her husband's death, the thirty-four-year-old Furnberg moved with her son near Fargo and eventually settled on eighty acres of land. She farmed, raised chickens and a cow, and sold butter and eggs in town. The majority of women who settled in the Dakotas were between the ages of twenty-one and twenty-five, had never been married, and were native-born children of immigrant parents. A sample of nine counties in the Dakotas shows that more than 4,400 women became landowners. Nora Pfundheler, a single woman, explained her motivation: "Well I was 21 and had no prospects of doing anything. The land was there, so I took it."

Once families settled in and towns began to develop, women, married and single, directed some of their energies to moral reform and extending democracy on the frontier. Because of loneliness and grueling work, some men turned to alcohol for relief. Law enforcement in newly established communities was often no match for the saloons that

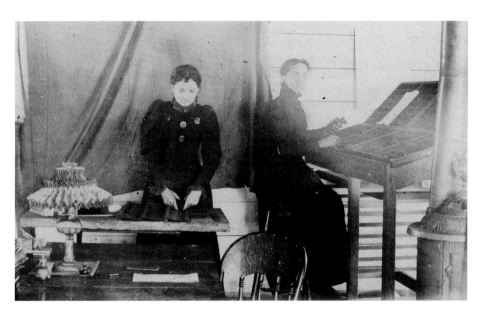

Women at Work in Kansas   Women pioneers in the West worked in a variety of jobs besides homemakers and farmers. In the 1880s, these two women worked as typesetters for the *Kansas Workman*, a weekly newspaper that supported equal rights for workers. Women were often chosen for this job of arranging tiny pieces of lead, inky type because it required sure fingers and sober attention to detail. Kansas State Historical Association

catered to a raucous and drunken crowd. In their roles as wives, mothers, and sisters, many women tried to remove the source of alcohol-induced violence that disrupted both family relationships and public decorum. In Kansas in the late 1870s, women flocked to the state's Woman's Christian Temperance Union, founded by Amanda M. Way. Although they did not yet have the vote, in 1880 these women vigorously campaigned for a constitutional amendment that banned the sale of liquor.

Temperance women also threw their weight behind the issue of women's suffrage. In 1884 Kansas women established the statewide Equal Suffrage Association, which delivered to the state legislature a petition with seven thousand signatures in support of women's suffrage. Their attempt failed, but in 1887 women won the right to vote and run for office in all Kansas municipal elections. Julia Robinson, who campaigned for women's suffrage in Kansas, recalled the positive role that some men played: "My father had always said his family of girls had just as much right to help the government as if we were boys, and mother and he had always taught us to expect Woman Suffrage in our day." Kansas did not grant equal voting rights in state and national elections until 1912, but women obtained full suffrage before then in many western states.

Farming on the Great Plains. Surviving loneliness, drudgery, and bad weather still did not guarantee financial success for homesteaders. In fact, the economic realities of farming on the plains proved formidable. Despite the image of yeomen farmers — individuals engaged in subsistence farming with the aid of wives and children — most agriculture was geared to commercial transactions. Few farmers were independent or self-reliant. Farmers depended on barter and short-term credit. They borrowed from banks to purchase the additional land necessary to make agriculture economically feasible in the semi-arid climate. They also needed loans to buy machinery to help increase production and to sustain their families while they waited for the harvest.

Instead of raising crops solely for their own use, farmers concentrated on the cash crops of corn and wheat. The price of these commodities depended on the vagaries of an international market that connected American farmers to growers and consumers throughout the world. When supply expanded and demand remained relatively stable during the 1880s and 1890s, prices fell. This deflation made it more difficult for farmers to pay back their loans, and banks moved to foreclose.

Under these challenging circumstances, almost half of the homesteaders in the Great Plains picked up and moved either to another farm or to a nearby city. Large operators bought up the farms they left behind and ran them like big businesses. As had been the case in mining, logging, and ranching, western agriculture was increasingly commercialized and consolidated over the course of the second half of the nineteenth century.

The federal government unwittingly aided this process of commercialization and consolidation, to the benefit of large companies. The government sought to make bigger plots of land available in regions where small farming had proved impractical. The Desert Land Act (1877) offered 640 acres to settlers who would irrigate the land, but it brought small relief for farmers because the land was too dry. These properties soon fell out of the hands of homesteaders and into those of cattle ranchers. The Timber and Stone Act (1878) allowed homesteaders to buy 160 acres of forestland at $2.50 an acre. Lumber companies hired "dummy entrymen" to file claims and then quickly transferred the titles and added the parcels to their growing tracts of woodland.

REVIEW & RELATE

- How did market forces contribute to the boom and bust of the cattle ranching industry and commercial farming?

- How did women homesteaders on the Great Plains in the late nineteenth century respond to frontier challenges?

Diversity in the **Far West**

Some pioneers settled on the Great Plains or moved west for reasons beyond purely economic motives. The Mormons, for example, settled in Utah to find a religious home. The West Coast states of Washington, Oregon, and especially California, with their abundant resources and favorable climates, beckoned adventurers to travel beyond the Rockies and settle along the Pacific Ocean. The far West attracted many white settlers and foreign immigrants — especially Chinese — who encountered Spaniards and Mexicans already inhabiting the region. This interweaving among diverse cultural groups sparked clashes that produced more oppression than opportunity for nonwhites.

Mormons.   Unlike miners, cowboys, and farmers, **Mormons** sought refuge in the West for religious reasons. By 1870 the migration of Mormons (members of the Church of Jesus Christ of Latter-Day Saints) into the Utah Territory had attracted more than 85,000 settlers, most notably in Salt Lake City. Originally traveling to Utah under the leadership of Brigham Young in the late 1840s, Mormons had come under attack from opponents of their religion and the federal government for several reasons. Most important, Mormons believed in polygamy, the practice of having more than one wife at a time. Far from seeing the practice as immoral, Mormon doctrine held polygamy as a blessing that would guarantee both husbands and wives an exalted place in the afterlife. Non-Mormons denounced polygamy as a form of involuntary servitude. In reality, only a small minority of Mormon men had multiple wives, and most of these polygamists had only two wives.

Mormons also departed from the mainstream American belief in private property. The church considered farming a communal enterprise. To this end, church elders divided land among their followers, so that, as Brigham Young explained, "each person perform[ed] his several duties for the good of the whole more than for individual aggrandizement."

In the 1870s, the federal government took increased measures to control Mormon practices. In *Reynolds v. United States* (1879), the Supreme Court upheld the criminal conviction of a polygamist Mormon man. Previously in 1862 and 1874, Congress had banned plural marriages in the Utah Territory. Congress went further in 1882 by passing the Edmunds Act, which disfranchised men engaging in polygamy. In 1887 Congress aimed to slash the economic power of the church by limiting Mormon assets to $50,000 and seizing the rest for the federal Treasury. A few years later, under this considerable pressure, the Mormons officially abandoned polygamy.

Related to the attack on polygamy was the question of women's suffrage. In 1870 voters in Utah endorsed a referendum granting women the right to vote, which enfranchised more than seventeen thousand women. Emmeline B. Wells, a Mormon woman who defended both women's rights and polygamy, argued that women "should be recognized as . . . responsible being[s]," capable of choosing plural marriage of their own free will. Opponents of enfranchisement contended that as long as polygamy existed, extending the vote to "enslaved" Mormon women would only perpetuate the practice because they would vote the way their husbands did. This point of view prevailed, and the Edmunds-Tucker Act (1887) rescinded the right to vote for women in the territory. Only with the rejection of polygamy did Congress accept statehood for Utah in 1896. The following year, the state extended the ballot to women.

Californios.

As with the nation's other frontiers, migrants to the West Coast did not find uninhabited territory. Besides Indians, the largest group that lived in California consisted of Spaniards and Mexicans. Since the eighteenth century, these **Californios** had established themselves as farmers and ranchers. The 1848 Treaty of Guadalupe Hidalgo, which ended the Mexican-American War, supposedly guaranteed the property rights of Californios and granted them U.S. citizenship, but reality proved different. Mexican American miners had to pay a "foreign miners tax," and Californio landowners lost their holdings to squatters, settlers, and local officials. By the end of the nineteenth century, about two-thirds of all land originally owned by Spanish-speaking residents had fallen into the hands of Euro-American settlers. By this time, many of these once wealthy Californios had been forced into poverty and the low-wage labor force. The loss of land was matched by a diminished role in the region's government, as economic decline, ethnic bias, and the continuing influx of white migrants combined to greatly reduce the political influence of the Californio population.

Explore ▶

See Sources 15.4 and 15.5 for two different interpretations of the significance of the frontier.

The Significance of the Frontier

The expansion of the American West beyond the Mississippi River to the West Coast has become a symbol of freedom, democracy, and national renewal. Popular novels, films, and television shows have depicted adventurous pioneers rebuilding their lives economically, politically, and spiritually by moving to the vastness of the Great Plains and Far West. In something of a morality play, righteous cowboys spread civilization and maintain law and order so that others might settle peacefully. American Indians, who already inhabited these supposed open lands, were considered enemies of American progress and collateral damage as the government reneged on its treaty obligations and the military defeated them. With the closing of the American frontier according to the 1890 census, historians began commenting on the role the West had played in shaping American society.

Source 15.4

Frederick Jackson Turner, The Significance of the Frontier in American History (1893)

"[W]e have . . . a recurrence of the process of evolution in each western area reached in the process of expansion. Thus American development has exhibited not merely advance along a single line, but a return to primitive conditions on a continually advancing frontier line, and a new development for that area. American social development has been continually beginning over again on the frontier. This perennial rebirth, this fluidity of American life, this expansion westward with its new opportunities, its continuous touch with the simplicity of primitive society, furnish the forces dominating American character. . . . The frontier is the line of most rapid and effective Americanization. The wilderness masters the colonist. It finds him a European in dress, industries, tools, models of travel, and thought. It takes him from the railroad car and puts him in the birch canoe. It strips off the garments of civilization and arrays him in the hunting shirt and moccasin. . . . In short, at the frontier the environment is at first too strong for the man. . . . Little by little he transforms the wilderness, but the outcome is not the old Europe. . . . The fact is that here is a new product that is American. . . . Thus the advance of the frontier has meant a steady movement away from the influence of Europe, a steady growth of independence on American lines."

Source: Frederick Jackson Turner, *The Frontier in American History*. New York: Henry Holt and Company, 1920, 2–3, 4.

Spaniards and Mexicans living in the Southwest met the same fate as the Californios. When Anglo cattle ranchers began forcing Mexican Americans off their land near Las Vegas, New Mexico, a rancher named Juan Jose Herrera assembled a band of masked night riders known as Las Gorras Blancas (The White Caps). According to fliers that they distributed promoting their grievances, the group sought "to protect the rights and interests of the people in general and especially those of the helpless classes." Enemies

Source 15.5

Patricia Nelson Limerick, Deemphasizing the Concept of the Frontier (1987)

"Turner's frontier was a process, not a place. When 'civilization' had conquered 'savagery' at any one location, the process—and the historian's attention—moved on. In rethinking Western history, we gain the freedom to think of the West as a place—as many complicated environments occupied by natives who considered their homelands to be the center, not the edge. . . . Deemphasize the frontier and its supposed end, conceive of the West as a place and not a process, and Western American history has a new look. First, the American West was an important meeting ground, the point where Indian America, Latin America, Anglo-America, Afro-America, and Asia America intersected . . . Second, the working of conquest tied these diverse groups into the same story. Happily or not, minorities and majorities occupied a common ground. Conquest basically involved the drawing of lines on a map, the definition and allocation of ownership (personal, tribal, corporate, state, federal, and international), and the evolution of land from matter to property."

Source: Patricia Nelson Limerick, *The Legacy of Conquest: The Unbroken Path of the American West*. New York: W.W. Norton & Company (1987), 26, 27, 31.

Examine the Sources

1. How do Turner and Limerick differ in their understanding of the frontier and the West?
2. Based on evidence in this chapter, evaluate the main arguments of Turner and Limerick.

Put It in Context

On another page of her book, Limerick writes, "Just as Turner, I take my cues from the present." How does each author's main thesis reflect their "present"?

of "tyrants," they desired a "free ballot and fair court." In 1889 and 1890, as many as seven hundred White Caps burned Anglo fences, haystacks, barns, and homes. In the end, however, Spanish-speaking inhabitants could not prevent the growing number of whites from pouring onto their lands and isolating them politically, economically, and culturally.

Rock Springs Massacre   This engraving depicts the Rock Springs massacre in Wyoming. On September 3, 1885, a mob of white coal miners killed at least 28 Chinese miners, injured 15, and burned 75 homes of Chinese residents. The violence came after years of anti-Chinese sentiment in the western United States. White miners blamed the Chinese for working for lower wages and taking their jobs. Granger

The Chinese. California and the far West also attracted a large number of Chinese immigrants. Migration to California and the West Coast was part of a larger movement in the nineteenth century out of Asia that brought impoverished Chinese to Australia, Hawaii, Latin America, and the United States. The Chinese migrated for several reasons in the decades after 1840. Economic dislocation related to the British Opium Wars (1839–1842 and 1856–1860), along with bloody family feuds and a decade of peasant rebellion from 1854 to 1864, propelled migration. Faced with unemployment and starvation, the Chinese sought economic opportunity overseas.

Chinese immigrants were attracted first by the 1848 gold rush and then by jobs building the transcontinental railroad. By 1880 the Chinese population had grown to 200,000, most of whom lived in the West. San Francisco became the center of the transplanted Chinese population, which congregated in the city's Chinatown. Under the leadership of a handful of businessmen, Chinese residents found jobs, lodging, and meals, along with social, cultural, and recreational outlets. Most of those who came were young, unmarried men who intended to earn enough money to return to China and start anew. The relatively few women who immigrated came as servants or prostitutes.

For many Chinese, the West proved unwelcoming. When California's economy slumped in the mid-1870s, many whites looked to the Chinese as scapegoats. White workingmen believed that Chinese laborers in the mines and railroads undercut their demands for higher wages. They contended that Chinese would work for less because they were racially inferior people who lived degraded lives. Anti-Chinese clubs mushroomed in California during the 1870s, and they soon became a substantial political force in the state. The Workingmen's Party advocated laws that restricted Chinese labor, and it initiated boycotts of goods made by Chinese people. Vigilantes attacked Chinese in the streets and set fire to factories that employed Asians. The Workingmen's Party and the Democratic Party joined forces in 1879 to craft a new state constitution that blatantly discriminated against Chinese residents. In many ways, these laws resembled the Jim Crow laws passed in the South that deprived African Americans of their freedom following Reconstruction (discussed in chapter 16).

Pressured by anti-Chinese sentiment on the West Coast, the U.S. government enacted drastic legislation to prevent any further influx of Chinese. The **Chinese Exclusion Act** of 1882 banned Chinese immigration into the United States and prohibited those Chinese already in the country from becoming naturalized American citizens. The exclusion act, however, did not stop anti-Chinese assaults. In the mid-1880s, white mobs drove Chinese out of Eureka, California; Seattle and Tacoma, Washington; and Rock Springs, Wyoming. These attacks were often organized. In 1885, the Tacoma mayor and police led a mob that rounded up 700 Chinese residents and forced them to leave the city on a train bound for Portland.

REVIEW & RELATE

- What migrant groups were attracted to the far West? What drew them there?

- Explain the rising hostility to the Chinese and other minority groups in the late-nineteenth-century far West.

Conclusion: The **Ambiguous Legacy** of the **West**

The legacy of the pioneering generation of Americans has proven mixed. Men and women pioneers encountered numerous obstacles posed by difficult terrain, forbidding climate, and unfamiliar inhabitants of the land they sought to harness. They built their homes, tilled the soil to raise crops, and mined the earth to remove the metals it contained. They developed cities that would one day rival those back east: San Francisco, Los Angeles, Seattle, and Denver. These pioneers served as the advance guard of America's expanding national and international industrial and commercial markets. As producers of staple crops and livestock and consumers of manufactured goods, they contributed to the expansion of America's factories, railroads, and telegraph communication system. The nation would memorialize their spirit as a model of individualism and self-reliance.

In fact, settlement of the West required more than individual initiative and self-determination. Without the direct involvement of the federal government, settlers would not have received free or inexpensive homesteads and military protection to clear native inhabitants out of their way. Without territorial governors and judges appointed by Washington to preside over new settlements, there would have been even less law, order, and justice than appeared in the rough-and-tumble environment of the West. Railroads, mining, and cattle ventures all relied heavily on foreign investors. Moreover, all the individualism and self-reliance that pioneers brought would not have saved them from the harsh conditions and disasters they faced without banding together as a community and pitching in to create institutions that helped them collectively. Despite their desire to achieve success, various pioneers — farmers, prospectors, cowboys — mostly found it difficult to make it on their own and began working for larger farming, mining, and ranching enterprises, with many of them becoming wageworkers. And for an experience that has been portrayed as a predominantly male phenomenon, settlement of the West depended largely on women.

Pioneers did not fully understand the land and people they encountered. More from ignorance than design, settlers engaged in agricultural, mining, and ranching practices that damaged fragile ecosystems. The settlement of the West nearly wiped out the bison and left Native Americans psychologically demoralized, culturally endangered, and economically impoverished. Some Indians willingly adopted white ways, but most of them fiercely resisted acculturation. Other minorities in the West, such as Mexicans and Chinese, also experienced harsh treatment at the hands of whites and suffered greatly.

TIMELINE OF EVENTS

1848	Gold discovered in California
1851	First Treaty of Fort Laramie
1862	Homestead Act
1864	Sand Creek massacre
1865–1868	Lakota Sioux lead Indian resistance
Late 1860s	Large-scale cattle drives begin
1868	Second Treaty of Fort Laramie
1869	Transcontinental railroad completed
1870s	Gold discovered in Black Hills of North Dakota
1876	Battle of the Little Big Horn
1877	Desert Land Act
	Timber and Stone Act
1881	Helen Hunt Jackson publishes *A Century of Dishonor*
1882	Edmunds Act
	Chinese Exclusion Act
1884	Annie Oakley joins William Cody's Wild West show
1885–1887	Cattle industry collapses
1886	Geronimo captured
1887	Dawes Act
	Kansas women win right to vote in municipal elections
1889–1890	Mexican American White Caps attack Anglo property
1890	Massacre at Wounded Knee
1893	Western Federation of Miners formed

KEY TERMS

Great Plains, *491*

transcontinental railroad, *493*

Treaty of Fort Laramie, *497*

Treaty of Medicine Lodge, *497*

Battle of the Little Big Horn, *499*

buffalo soldiers, *500*

Dawes Act, *501*

Ghost Dance, *502*

Comstock Lode, *503*

Long Drive, *506*

Homestead Act, *507*

Mormons, *512*

Californios, *513*

Chinese Exclusion Act, *517*

REVIEW & RELATE

1. What role did the federal government play in opening the West to settlement and economic exploitation?

2. Explain the determination of Americans to settle in land west of the Mississippi River despite the challenges the region presented.

3. How and why did federal Indian policy change during the nineteenth century?

4. Describe some of the ways that Indian peoples responded to federal policies. Which response do you think offered their greatest chance for survival?

5. How and why did the nature of mining in the West change during the second half of the nineteenth century?

6. How did the mining and lumber industries reshape the frontier landscape?

7. How did market forces contribute to the boom and bust of the cattle ranching industry and commercial farming?

8. How did women homesteaders on the Great Plains in the late nineteenth century respond to frontier challenges?

9. What migrant groups were attracted to the far West? What drew them there?

10. Explain the rising hostility to the Chinese and other minority groups in the late-nineteenth-century far West.

American Indians and Whites in the West

▶ Evaluate the extent to which the U.S. government from 1865 to 1890 balanced its commitment to both continental expansion and equal justice under the law and explain how Native Americans forged strategies in response to U.S. policy.

Views on the relationship between whites and American Indians varied widely in the late-nineteenth-century West, though most shared a basic premise — that Indian cultures and tribal identities did not deserve to be preserved and defended. Some white Americans advocated exterminating the Indians, whereas others sought to assimilate them (Sources 15.6 and 15.7). These attitudes differed significantly by region. Whites who were most likely to encounter Indians were generally the least sympathetic (Source 15.8). Government officials were also divided. The most notable differences were between civilians in the Interior Department who favored peaceful solutions and those in the War Department who were inclined to use military force to resolve conflicts. However, even reform-minded whites often failed to understand or pay heed to actual Indian culture, and they developed many policies that led to the decline of Indian tribal societies. Facing a dominant white American society that could see only two options — eliminating Indian culture outright, or fundamentally changing its core — Indian attitudes ranged from fierce resistance, to accommodation to, in rare cases, assimilation (Sources 15.9 and 15.10).

Source 15.6

James Michael Cavanaugh | Support for Indian Extermination, 1868

James Michael Cavanaugh was originally from Springfield, Massachusetts, but moved to Minnesota in 1854, where he served in Congress for one term. He subsequently moved to Colorado and then Montana and served in the House of Representatives as a Democrat from 1867 to 1871. In the following congressional speech, Cavanaugh explains his attitude toward Indians in a discussion about Indian appropriations with Republican representative Benjamin Butler of Massachusetts.

I will say that I like an Indian better dead than living. I have never in my life seen a good Indian (and I have seen thousands) except when I have seen a dead Indian. I believe in the Indian policy pursued by New England in years long gone. I believe in the Indian policy which was taught by the great chieftain of Massachusetts, Miles Standish. I believe in the policy that exterminates the Indians, drives them outside the boundaries of civilization, because you cannot civilize them. Gentlemen may call this very harsh language; but perhaps they would not think so if they had had my experience in Minnesota and Colorado. In Minnesota the almost living babe has been torn from its mother's womb; and I have seen the child, with its young heart palpitating, nailed to the window-sill. I have seen women who were scalped, disfigured, outraged. In Denver, Colorado Territory, I have seen women and children brought in scalped. Scalped why? Simply because the Indian was "upon the war-path," to satisfy his devilish and barbarous propensities. You have made your treaties with the Indians, but they have not been observed. . . . The Indian will make a treaty in the fall, and in the spring he is again "upon the war-path." The torch, the scalping-knife, plunder, and desolation follow wherever the Indian goes.

But, Mr. Chairman, I will answer the gentleman's question more directly. My friend from Massachusetts [Mr. Butler] has never passed the barrier of the frontier. All he knows about Indians (the gentleman will pardon me for saying it) may have been gathered, I presume, from the brilliant pages of the author of "The Last of the Mohicans," or from the lines of the poet Longfellow in "Hiawatha." The gentleman has never yet seen the Indian upon the war-path. He has never been chased, as I have been, by these red devils—who seem to be the pets of the eastern philanthropists.

Source: U.S. Congress, *The Congressional Globe: Containing the Debates and Proceedings of the Second Session of the Fortieth Congress*, May 28, 1868, 2638.

Helen Hunt Jackson | Challenges to Indian Policy, 1881

Helen Hunt Jackson's book *A Century of Dishonor* severely criticized U.S. policy toward Indians. Jackson sent a copy of her book to every member of Congress. Despite her attack on the government's treatment of Indians and her advocacy of reform, Jackson believed that American Indians could not become citizens until they received proper training from enlightened white teachers.

There is not among these three hundred bands of Indians one which has not suffered cruelly at the hands either of the Government or of white settlers. The poorer, the more insignificant, the more helpless the band, the more certain the cruelty and outrage to which they have been subjected. This is especially true of the bands on the Pacific slope. These Indians found themselves of a sudden surrounded by and caught up in the great influx of gold-seeking settlers, as helpless creatures on a shore are caught up in a tidal wave. There was not time for the Government to make treaties; not even time for communities to make laws. The tale of the wrongs, the oppressions, the murders of the Pacific-slope Indians in the last thirty years would be a volume by itself, and is too monstrous to be believed. . . .

To assume that it would be easy, or by any one sudden stroke of legislative policy possible, to undo the mischief and hurt of the long past, set the Indian policy of the country right for the future, and make the Indians at once safe and happy, is the blunder of a hasty and uninformed judgment. The notion which seems to be growing more prevalent, that simply to make all Indians at once citizens of the United States would be a sovereign and instantaneous panacea for all their ills and all the Government's perplexities, is a very inconsiderate one. To administer complete citizenship of a sudden, all round, to all Indians, barbarous and civilized alike, would be as grotesque a blunder as to dose them all round with any one medicine, irrespective of the symptoms and needs of their diseases. It would kill more than it would cure. . . . All judicious plans and measures for their safety and salvation must embody provisions for their becoming citizens as fast as they are fit, and must protect them till then in every right and particular in which our laws protect other "persons" who are not citizens. . . .

Cheating, robbing, breaking promises—these three are clearly things which must cease to be done. One more thing, also, and that is the refusal of the protection of the law to the Indian's rights of property, "of life, liberty, and the pursuit of happiness."

When these four things have ceased to be done, time, statesmanship, philanthropy, and Christianity can slowly and surely do the rest. Till these four things have ceased to be done, statesmanship and philanthropy alike must work in vain, and even Christianity can reap but small harvest.

Source: Helen Hunt Jackson, *A Century of Dishonor: A Sketch of the United States Government's Dealings with Some of the Indian Tribes* (New York: Harper and Brothers, 1881), 337–38, 340–42.

Source 15.8

Thomas Nast | "Patience until the Indian Is Civilized — So to Speak," 1878

Through his cartoons, artist Thomas Nast crusaded against political corruption and mistreatment of freedpeople in the South. Although generally sympathetic to the rights of American Indians, in this illustration he raises questions about what the federal government should do regarding conflicts between white settlers and Indians in the West. Nast depicts Secretary of the Interior Carl Schurz (left), an Indian reformer, counseling patience to western settlers.

Library of Congress, LC-DIG-ds-01283

Source 15.9

Zitkala-Ša | Life at an Indian Boarding School, 1921

Gertrude Simmons Bonnin, who later took the Indian name Zitkala-Ša, lived on the Yankton Reservation in South Dakota, with her mother and brother until 1884, when missionaries recruited her to attend school so that she would become assimilated into Anglo-American culture. After attending a Quaker school in Wabash, Indiana, Zitkala-Ša briefly attended Earlham College and then taught at the Carlisle Indian Industrial School in Pennsylvania for two years. During that time, she experienced a reawakening of her American Indian heritage and consciousness and began publishing autobiographical accounts criticizing the educational practices of the schools she attended and at which she taught. In 1921 she recounted her own experiences in these Indian schools, including the incident she describes in the following selection.

The first day in the land of apples was a bitter-cold one; for the snow still covered the ground, and the trees were bare. A large bell rang for breakfast, its loud metallic voice crashing through the belfry overhead and into our sensitive ears. The annoying clatter of shoes on bare floors gave us no peace. The constant clash of harsh noises, with an undercurrent of many voices murmuring an unknown tongue, made a bedlam within which I was securely tied. And though my spirit tore itself in struggling for its lost freedom, all was useless.

A paleface woman, with white hair, came up after us. We were placed in a line of girls who were marching into the dining room. These were Indian girls, in stiff shoes and closely clinging dresses. The small girls wore sleeved aprons and shingled hair [haircut with the hair cut short from the back of the head to the nape of the neck]. As I walked noiselessly in my soft moccasins, I felt like sinking to the floor, for my blanket had been stripped from my shoulders. I looked hard at the Indian girls, who seemed not to care that they were even more immodestly dressed than I, in their tightly fitting clothes. . . .

A small bell was tapped, and each of the pupils drew a chair from under the table. Supposing this act meant they were to be seated, I pulled out mine and at once slipped into it from one side. But when I turned my head, I saw that I was the only one seated, and all the rest at our table remained standing. Just as I began to rise, looking shyly around to see how chairs were to be used, a second bell was sounded. All were seated at last, and I had to crawl back into my chair again. I heard a man's voice at one end of the hall, and I looked around to see him. But all the others hung their heads over their plates. As I glanced at the long chain of tables, I caught the eyes of a paleface woman upon me. Immediately I dropped my eyes, wondering why I was so keenly watched by the strange woman. The man ceased his mutterings, and then a third bell was tapped. Every one picked up his knife and fork and began eating. I began crying instead, for by this time I was afraid to venture anything more.

But this eating by formula was not the hardest trial in that first day. Late in the morning, my friend Judéwin gave me a terrible warning. Judéwin knew a few words of English; and she had overheard the paleface woman talk about cutting our long, heavy hair. Our mothers had taught us that only unskilled warriors who were captured had their hair shingled by the enemy. Among our people, short hair was worn by mourners, and shingled hair by cowards!

We discussed our fate some moments, and when Judéwin said, "We have to submit, because they are strong," I rebelled.

"No, I will not submit! I will struggle first!" I answered.

I watched my chance, and when no one noticed I disappeared. I crept up the stairs as quietly as I could in my squeaking shoes—my moccasins had been exchanged for shoes. Along the hall I passed, without knowing whither I was going. Turning aside to an open door, I found a large room with three white beds in it. The windows were covered with dark green curtains, which made the room very dim. Thankful that no one was there, I directed my steps toward the corner farthest from the door. On my hands and knees I crawled under the bed, and cuddled myself in the dark corner.

From my hiding place I peered out, shuddering with fear whenever I heard footsteps near by. Though in the hall loud voices were calling my name, and I knew that even Judéwin was searching for me, I did not open my mouth to answer. Then the steps were quickened and the voices became excited. The sounds came nearer and nearer. Women and girls entered the room. I held my breath and watched them open closet doors and peep behind large trunks. Some one threw up the curtains, and the room was filled with sudden light. What caused them to stoop and look under the bed I do not know. I remember being dragged out, though I resisted by kicking and scratching wildly. In spite of myself, I was carried downstairs and tied fast in a chair.

I cried aloud, shaking my head all the while until I felt the cold blades of the scissors against my neck, and heard them gnaw off one of my thick braids. Then I lost my spirit. Since the day I was taken from my mother I had suffered extreme indignities. People had stared at me. I had been tossed about in the air like a wooden puppet. And now my long hair was shingled like a coward's! In my anguish I moaned for my mother, but no one came to comfort me. Not a soul reasoned quietly with me, as my own mother used to do; for now I was only one of many little animals driven by a herder.

Source: Zitkala-Ša (Gertrude Bonnin), *American Indian Stories* (Washington, DC: Hayworth, 1921), 52–56.

Source 15.10

Chief Joseph | Views on Indian Affairs, 1879

In 1877, following a string of treaties broken by the U.S. government, Chief Joseph led the Nez Percé on a 1,300-mile march from their tribal land in Oregon to Canada, in search of a home. Thirty miles from the Canadian border, they were surrounded by U.S. troops. After his capture, Chief Joseph was taken to Washington, D.C., where he addressed a gathering of cabinet members and congressmen and tried to convince them to return tribal lands to the Nez Percé.

At last I was granted permission to come to Washington and bring my friend Yellow Bull and our interpreter with me. I am glad we came. I have shaken hands with a great many friends, but there are some things I want to know which no one seems able to explain. I can not understand how the Government sends a man out to fight us, as it did General [Nelson A.] Miles, and then breaks his word. Such a government has something wrong about it. I can not understand why so many chiefs are allowed to talk so many different ways, and promise so many different things. . . . I do not understand why nothing is done for my people. I have heard talk and talk, but nothing is done. Good words do not last long unless they amount to something. Words do not pay for my dead people. They do not pay for my country, now overrun by white men. They do not protect my father's grave. They do not pay for all my horses and cattle. Good words will not give me back my children. . . . Good words will not give my people good health and stop them from dying. Good words will not get my people a home where they can live in peace and take care of themselves. I am tired of talk that comes to nothing. It makes my heart sick when I remember all the good words and all the broken promises. . . . Too many misrepresentations have been made, too many misunderstandings have come up between the white men about the Indians. If the white man wants to live in peace with the Indian he can live in peace. There need be no trouble. Treat all men alike. Give them all the same law. Give them all an even chance to live and grow. All men were made by the same Great Spirit Chief. They are all brothers. The earth is the mother of all people, and all people should have equal rights upon it. You might as well expect the rivers to run backward as that any man who was born a free man should be contented when penned up and denied liberty to go where he pleases. If you tie a horse to a stake, do you expect he will grow fat? If you pen an Indian up on a small spot of earth, and compel him to stay there, he will not be contented, nor will he grow and prosper. . . .

I know that my race must change. We can not hold our own with the white men as we are. We only ask an even chance to live as other men live. We ask to be recognized as men. We ask that the same law shall work alike on all men. If the Indian breaks the law, punish him by the law. If the white man breaks the law, punish him also.

Whenever the white man treats the Indian as they treat each other, then we shall have no more wars. . . . For this time the Indian race are waiting and praying. I hope that no more groans of wounded men and women will ever go to the ear of the Great Spirit Chief above, and that all people may be one people.

Source: "An Indian's View of Indian Affairs," *North American Review*, April 1879, 431–33.

Interpret the Evidence

1. Explain why James Michael Cavanaugh (Source 15.6) and Helen Hunt Jackson (Source 15.7) reach different conclusions concerning Indian policy.
2. How does Thomas Nast's illustration (Source 15.8) reflect the historical situation in 1878?
3. What options did Indians have when confronted with white determination to eradicate their culture? What choice does Zitkala-Ša (Source 15.9) make? Why?
4. How does Chief Joseph's experience (Source 15.10) reflect the fundamental contradiction of federal policy toward Indians?
5. Explain which audience would have been most likely to respond positively to each document's argument.

Put It in Context

Imagine that you are an American president in the second half of the nineteenth century and can design Indian policy. Based on what you have read, what would you do, and why? What challenges might you face as you attempted to implement your policy?

Industrial America

1877–1900

16

WINDOW TO THE PAST

What a Funny Little Government, 1900

This image from a cartoon shows the nation's capitol, where Congress meets, taken over by the Standard Oil Trust owned by John D. Rockefeller. Industrialization created large corporations, which through consolidation of functions and the elimination of competition yielded tremendous personal and national wealth. The artist is commenting on the power of big business to control politics. ▶ To discover more about what this primary source can show us, see Source 16.1 on page 556.

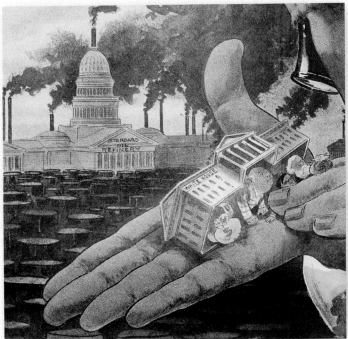

© Collection of the New-York Historical Society, USA/Bridgeman Images

After reading this chapter you should be able to:

- Summarize the causes of American industrialization and evaluate the impact of industrialization on business and the economy.

- Analyze popular doctrines guiding social and economic policy during the industrial age and evaluate prominent critiques of these ideas.

- Describe new lifestyles that emerged from industrialization and explain how Americans reacted to anxieties about changing gender and racial roles that resulted.

- Describe the forces that constrained and influenced national politics in the late 1800s.

COMPARING AMERICAN HISTORIES

In 1848 Will and Margaret Carnegie left Scotland and sailed to America, hoping to find a better life for themselves and their children. Once settled in Pittsburgh, Pennsylvania, the family went to work, including thirteen-year-old Andrew, who found a job in a textile mill. For $1.25 per week, he dipped spools into an oil bath and fired the factory furnace — tasks that left him nauseated by the smell of oil and frightened by the boiler. Nevertheless, like the hero of the rags-to-riches stories that were so popular in his era, Andrew Carnegie persevered, rising from poverty to great wealth through a series of jobs and clever

investments. As a teenager, he worked in a telegraph office. A superintendent of the Pennsylvania Railroad Company noticed Andrew's aptitude and made him his personal assistant and telegrapher. While in this position, Carnegie learned about the railroad industry and purchased stock in a sleeping car company; the returns from that investment tripled his annual salary. Carnegie then became a railroad superintendent in western Pennsylvania, and by the time he was thirty-five, he had grown wealthy from his investments in a wide variety of industries.

Andrew Carnegie eventually founded the greatest steel company in the world and became one of the wealthiest men of his time. He also became one of the era's greatest philanthropists, fulfilling his sense of community obligation by giving away a great deal of his fortune.

John Sherman also believed in public service, but for him it would come through politics. Born in Lancaster, Ohio in 1823, Sherman became a lawyer like his father, an Ohio Supreme Court judge. Like Carnegie, Sherman made shrewd investments that brought him wealth, although not on the same scale as Carnegie.

Sherman decided to enter politics and in 1854 won election from Ohio to the House of Representatives as a member of the newly created Republican Party. He rose up the leadership ranks as Republicans came to national power with the election of Abraham Lincoln to the presidency in 1860. From 1861 to 1896, Sherman held a variety of major political positions, including U.S. senator from Ohio and secretary of the treasury under President Rutherford B. Hayes. After his term as treasury secretary ended, he returned to the Senate and wielded power as one of the top Republican Party leaders. With his background as chair of the Senate Finance Committee and as secretary of the treasury, Sherman was the most respected Republican of his time in dealing with monetary and financial affairs. Sherman believed that government should encourage business. His most famous accomplishment, the Sherman Antitrust Act, which authorized the government to break up organizations that restrained competition, embodied this belief. It enacted limited reforms without harming powerful business interests. ■

(*left*) **Andrew Carnegie.** Library of Congress, 3c20152
(*right*) **John Sherman.** Library of Congress, cwpbh.05141

The American histories of Andrew Carnegie and John Sherman began very differently. Both men played a prominent role in developing the government-business partnership that was crucial to the rapid industrialization of the United States. Carnegie's organization and management skills helped shape the formation of large-scale business. At the same time, Sherman and his fellow lawmakers provided support for that enterprise, using the power of government to reduce risks for businessmen and to increase incentives for economic expansion. They often did so in ways that made politics more corrupt and made politicians less respected. Nevertheless, the public took politics seriously and turned out at the polls in great numbers. Corporate leaders joined with the clergy and writers to defend the established hierarchy of wealth and power. These businessmen used the doctrines of laissez-faire and Social Darwinism to justify their ruthless practices in the name of progress.

Industrialization and big business reshaped the nation. Railroads expanded national and international markets for American factory goods. Innovations and new inventions promoted business consolidation. Industrialization even brought changes to the agricultural South, all within the framework of racial segregation. Great fortunes were made, and the rich showcased their lavish lifestyles. Corporate consolidation also created a new middle class. The men of this group used their leisure to create new social and professional organizations while the women devoted more time to clubs and charitable associations.

America Industrializes

Between 1870 and 1900, the United States grew into a global industrial power. Transcontinental railroads spurred this breathtaking transformation, linking regional markets into a national market; at the same time, railroads themselves served as a massive new market for raw materials and new technologies. Building on advantages developed over the course of the nineteenth century, the Northeast, Midwest, and West led the way in the new economy, while efforts to industrialize the South met with uneven success. Men like Andrew Carnegie became both the heroes and the villains of their age. They engaged in ruthless practices that would lead some to label the new industrialists "robber barons," but they also created systems of industrial organization and corporate management that altered the economic landscape of the country and changed the place of the United States in the world.

The New Industrial Economy.
The industrial revolution of the late nineteenth century originated in Europe. Great Britain was the world's first industrial power, but by the 1870s Germany had emerged as a major challenger for industrial dominance, increasing its steel production at a rapid rate and leading the way in the chemical and electrical industries. The dynamic economic growth and innovation stimulated by industrial competition quickly crossed the Atlantic.

Industrialization transformed the American economy. As industrialization took hold, the U.S. gross domestic product, the output of all goods and services produced annually, quadrupled — from $9 billion in 1860 to $37 billion in 1890. During this same period, the number of Americans employed by industry doubled. Moreover, the nature of industry itself changed, as small factories catering to local markets were displaced by large-scale firms producing for national and international markets. The midwestern cities of Chicago,

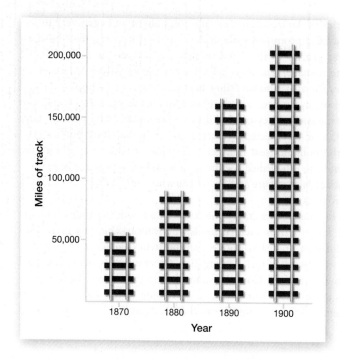

FIGURE 16.1 Expansion of the Railroad System, 1870–1900

The great expansion of the railroads in the late nineteenth century fueled the industrial revolution and the growth of big business. Connecting the nation from East Coast to West Coast, transcontinental railroads created a national market for natural resources and manufactured goods. The biggest surge in railroad construction occurred west of the Mississippi River and in the South. Describe the political and technological forces that promoted enormous railroad expansion from 1870–1900.

Cincinnati, and St. Louis joined Boston, New York, and Philadelphia as centers of factory production, while the exploitation of the natural resources in the West took on an increasingly industrial character. Trains, telegraphs, and telephones connected the country in ways never before possible.

From 1870 to 1913, the United States experienced an extraordinary rate of growth in industrial output: In 1870 American industries turned out 23.3 percent of the world's manufacturing production; by 1913 this figure had jumped to 35.8 percent. In fact, U.S. output in 1913 almost equaled the combined total for Europe's three leading industrial powers: Germany, the United Kingdom, and France. By the end of the nineteenth century, the United States was surging ahead of northern Europe as the manufacturing center of the world.

At the heart of the American industrial transformation was the railroad. Large-scale business enterprises would not have developed without a national market for raw materials and finished products. A consolidated system of railroads crisscrossing the nation facilitated the creation of such a market (Figure 16.1). In addition, railroads were direct consumers of industrial products, stimulating the growth of a number of industries through their consumption of steel, wood, coal, glass, rubber, brass, and iron. Finally, railroads contributed to economic growth by increasing the speed and efficiency with which products and materials were transported.

Before railroads could create a national market, they had to overcome several critical problems. In 1877 railroad lines dotted the country in haphazard fashion. They primarily served local markets and remained unconnected at key points. This lack of coordination stemmed mainly from the fact that each railroad had its own track gauge (the width between the tracks), making shared track use impossible and long-distance travel extremely difficult.

The consolidation of railroads solved many of these problems. In 1886 railroad companies finally agreed to adopt a standard gauge. Railroads also standardized time zones, thus eliminating confusion in train schedules. During the 1870s, towns and cities each set their own time zone, a practice that created discrepancies among them. In 1882 the time in New York City and in Boston varied by 11 minutes and 45 seconds. The following year, railroads agreed to coordinate times and divided the country into four standard time zones. Most cities soon cooperated with the new system, but not until 1918 did the federal government legislate the standard time zones that the railroads had first adopted.

Innovation and Inventions.

As important as railroads were, they were not the only engine of industrialization. American technological innovation created new industries, while expanding the efficiency and productivity of old ones. In 1866 a transatlantic telegraph cable connected the United States and Europe, allowing businessmen on both sides of the ocean to pursue profitable commercial ventures. New inventions also allowed business offices to run more smoothly: Typewriters were invented in 1868, carbon paper in 1872, adding machines in 1891, and mimeograph machines in 1892. As businesses grew, they needed more space for their operations. The construction of towering skyscrapers in the 1880s in cities such as Chicago and New York was made possible by two innovations: structural steel, which had the strength to support tall buildings, and elevators.

Alexander Graham Bell's telephone revolutionized communications. By 1880 fifty-five cities offered local service and catered to a total of 50,000 subscribers, most of them business customers. In 1885, Bell established the American Telephone and Telegraph Company (AT&T), and long-distance service connected New York, Boston, and Chicago. By 1900 around 1.5 million telephones were in operation.

Perhaps the greatest technological innovations that advanced industrial development in the late nineteenth century came in steel manufacturing. In 1859 Henry Bessemer, a British inventor, designed a furnace that burned the impurities out of melted iron and converted it into steel. The open-hearth process, devised by another Englishman, William Siemens, further improved the quality of steel by removing additional impurities from the iron. Railroads replaced iron rails with steel because it was lighter, stronger, and more durable than iron. Steel became the major building block of industry, furnishing girders and cables to construct manufacturing plants and office structures. As production became cheaper and more efficient, steel output soared from 13,000 tons in 1860 to 28 million tons in the first decade of the twentieth century.

Factory machinery needed constant lubrication, and the growing petroleum industry made this possible. A new drilling technique devised in 1859 tapped into pools of petroleum located deep below the earth's surface. In the post–Civil War era, new distilling techniques transformed petroleum into lubricating oil for factory machinery. This process of "cracking" crude oil also generated lucrative by-products for the home, such as kerosene and paraffin for heating and lighting and salve to soothe cuts and burns. After 1900, the development of the gasoline-powered, internal combustion engine for automobiles opened up an even richer market for the oil industry.

Locomotives also benefited from innovations in technology. Improvements included air brakes and automatic coupling devices to attach train cars to each other. Elijah McCoy, a trained engineer and the son of former slaves, was forced because of racial discrimination to work at menial railroad jobs shoveling coal and lubricating train parts every few

Manufacturing of Steel Tubing, 1897 This engraving appeared in the December 18, 1897 issue of *Scientific American* and illustrates the manufacture of steel tubing pipes at the National Tube Works in McKeesport, Pennsylvania. With hot flames in the background, workers are welding rings on a 23-inch pipe. American Stock Archive/ Getty Images

miles to keep the gears from overheating. This experience encouraged him to invent and patent an automatic lubricating device to improve efficiency.

Early innovations resulted from the genius of individual inventors, but by the late nineteenth century technological progress was increasingly an organized, collaborative effort. Thomas Alva Edison and his team served as the model. In 1876 Edison set up a research laboratory in Menlo Park, New Jersey. Housed in a two-story, white frame building, Edison's "invention factory" was staffed by a team of inventors and craftsmen. In 1887 Edison opened another laboratory, ten times bigger than the one at Menlo Park, in nearby Orange, New Jersey. These facilities pioneered the research laboratories that would become a standard feature of American industrial development in the twentieth century.

Out of Edison's laboratories flowed inventions that revolutionized American business and culture. The phonograph and motion pictures changed the way people spent their leisure time. The electric light bulb illuminated people's homes and made them safer by eliminating the need for candles and gas lamps, which were fire hazards. It also brightened city streets, making them available for outdoor evening activities, and lit up factories so that they could operate all night long.

Like his contemporaries who were building America's huge industrial empires, Edison cashed in on his workers' inventions. He joined forces with the Wall Street banker J. P. Morgan to finance the Edison Electric Illuminating Company, which in 1882 provided lighting to customers in New York City. Goods produced by electric equipment jumped in value from $1.9 million in 1879 to $21.8 million in 1890. In 1892, Morgan helped Edison merge his companies with several competitors and reorganized them as the General Electric Corporation, which became the industry leader.

Building a New South. Although the largely rural South lagged behind the North and the Midwest in manufacturing, industrial expansion did not bypass the region. Well aware of global economic trends and eager for the South to achieve its economic potential, southern business leaders and newspaper editors saw industrial development as the key to the creation of a **New South**. Attributing the Confederate defeat in the Civil War to the North's superior manufacturing output and railroad supply lines, New South proponents hoped to modernize their economy in a similar fashion. One of those boosters was Richard H. Edmonds, editor of the *Manufacturers' Record*. He extolled the virtues of the "real South" of the 1880s, characterized by "the music of progress — the whirr of the spindle, the buzz of the saw, the roar of the furnace, the throb of the locomotive." The South of Edmonds's vision would move beyond the regional separatism of the past and become fully integrated into the national economy.

Railroads were the key to achieving such economic integration, so after the Civil War new railroad tracks were laid throughout the South. Not only did this expanded railroad system create direct connections between the North and the South, it also facilitated the growth of the southern textile industry. Seeking to take advantage of plentiful cotton, cheap labor, and the improved transportation system, investors built textile mills throughout the South. Victims of falling prices and saddled with debt, sharecroppers and tenant farmers moved into mill towns in search of better employment. Mill owners preferred to hire girls and young women, who worked for low wages, to spin cotton and weave it on the looms. To do so, however, owners had to employ their entire family, for mothers and fathers would not let their daughters relocate without their supervision. Whatever attraction the mills offered applied only to whites. The pattern of white supremacy emerging in the post-Reconstruction South kept African Americans out of all but the most menial jobs.

Blacks contributed greatly to the construction of railroads in the New South, but they did not do so as free men. Convicts, most of whom were African American, performed the exhausting work of laying tracks through hills and swamps. Southern states used the **convict lease** system, in which blacks, usually imprisoned for minor offenses, were hired out to private companies to serve their time or pay off their fine. The convict lease system brought additional income to the state and supplied cheap labor to the railroads and planters, but it left African American convict laborers impoverished and virtually enslaved.

The South attracted a number of industries besides textile manufacturing. In the 1880s, James B. Duke established a cigarette manufacturing empire in Durham, North Carolina. Nearby tobacco fields provided the raw material that black workers prepared for white workers, who then rolled the cigarettes by machine. Acres of timber pines in the Carolinas, Florida, and Alabama sustained a lucrative lumber industry. Rich supplies of coal and iron in Alabama fostered the growth of the steel industry in Birmingham (Map 16.1).

Despite this frenzy of industrial activity, the New South in many ways resembled the Old South. Southern entrepreneurs still depended on northern investors to supply much of the capital for investment. Investors were attracted by the low wages that prevailed in the South, but low wages also meant that southern workers remained poor and, in many cases, unable to buy the manufactured goods produced by industry. Efforts to diversify agriculture beyond tobacco and cotton were constrained by a sharecropping system based on small, inefficient plots. In fact, even though industrialization did make considerable headway in the South, the economy remained overwhelmingly agricultural. This suited many white southerners who wanted to hold on to the individualistic, agrarian values they

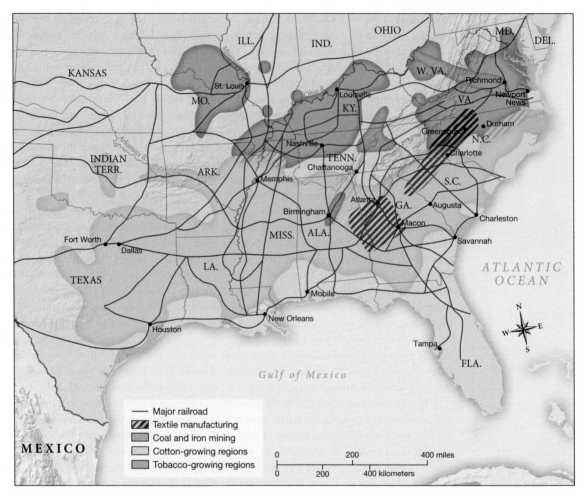

MAP 16.1   The New South, 1900

Although the South remained largely agricultural by 1900, it had made great strides toward building industries in the region. This so-called New South boasted an extensive railway network that provided a national market for its raw materials and manufactured goods, including coal, iron, steel, and textiles. Still, the southern economy in 1900 depended primarily on raising cotton and tobacco.

associated with the Old South. Yoked to old ideologies and a system of forced labor, modernization in the South could go only so far.

Industrial Consolidation.
In the North, South, and West, nineteenth-century industrialists strove to minimize or eliminate competition. To gain competitive advantages and increase profits, industrial entrepreneurs concentrated on reducing production costs, charging lower prices, and outselling the competition. Successful firms could then acquire rival companies that could no longer afford to compete, creating an industrial empire in the process.

Building such industrial empires was not easy, however, and posed creative challenges for business ventures. Heavy investment in machinery resulted in very high fixed costs (or overhead) that did not change much over time. Because overhead costs remained stable, manufacturers could reduce the per-unit cost of production by increasing the output of a product — what economists call "economy of scale." Manufacturers thus aimed to raise the volume of production and find ways to cut variable costs — for labor and materials, for example. Through such savings, a factory owner could sell his product more cheaply than his competitors and gain a larger share of the market.

A major organizational technique for reducing costs and underselling the competition was **vertical integration**. "Captains of industry," as their admirers called them, did not just build a business; they created a system — a network of firms, each contributing to the final product. Men like Andrew Carnegie controlled the various phases of production from top to bottom (vertical), extracting the raw materials, transporting them to the factories, manufacturing the finished products, and shipping them to market. By using vertical integration, Carnegie eliminated middlemen and guaranteed regular and cheap access to supplies. He also lowered inventories and gained increased flexibility by shifting segments of the labor force to areas where they were most needed. His credo became "Watch the costs and the profits will take care of themselves."

Businessmen also employed another type of integration — **horizontal integration**. This approach focused on gaining greater control over the market by acquiring firms that sold the same products. John D. Rockefeller, the founder of the mammoth Standard Oil Company, specialized in this technique. In the mid-1870s, he brought a number of key oil refiners into an alliance with Standard Oil to control four-fifths of the industry. At the same time, the oil baron ruthlessly drove out of business or bought up marginal firms that could not afford to compete with him.

Horizontal integration was also a major feature in the telegraph industry. By 1861 Western Union had strung 76,000 miles of telegraph line throughout the nation. Founded in 1851, the company had thrived during the Civil War by obtaining most of the federal government's telegraph business. The firm had 12,600 offices housed in railroad depots throughout the country and strung its lines adjacent to the railroads. Seeing an opportunity to make money, Wall Street tycoon Jay Gould set out to acquire Western Union. In the mid-1870s, Gould, who had obtained control over the Union Pacific Railway, financed companies to compete with the giant telegraph outfit. Gould finally succeeded in 1881, when he engineered a takeover of Western Union by combining it with his American Union Telegraph Company. Gould made a profit of $30 million on the deal. On February 15, the day after the agreement, the *New York Herald Tribune* reported: "The country finds itself this morning at the feet of a telegraphic monopoly," a business that controlled the market and destroyed competition.

Bankers played a huge role in engineering industrial consolidation. No one did it more skillfully than John Pierpont Morgan. In the 1850s, Morgan started his career working for a prominent American-owned banking firm in London, and in 1861 he created his own investment company in New York City. Morgan played the central role in channeling funds from Britain to support the construction of major American railroads. During the 1880s and 1890s, Morgan orchestrated the refinancing of several ailing railroads. To maintain control over these enterprises, the Wall Street financier placed his allies on their boards of directors and selected the companies' chief operating officers. Morgan then turned his talents for organization to the steel industry. In 1901 he was instrumental in merging Carnegie's company with several competitors in which he had a financial interest. United States Steel, Morgan's creation, became the world's largest industrial corporation, worth $1.4 billion. By the end of the first decade of the twentieth century, Morgan's investment house held more than 340 directorships in 112 corporations, amounting to more than $22 billion in assets, the equivalent of $525 billion in 2015, all at a time when there was no income tax.

The Growth of Corporations.

With economic consolidation came the expansion of corporations. Before the age of large-scale enterprise, the predominant form of business ownership was the partnership. Unlike a partnership, a **corporation** provided investors with "limited liability." This meant that if the corporation went bankrupt, shareholders could not lose more than they had invested. Limited liability encouraged investment by keeping the shareholders' investment in the corporation separate from their other assets. In addition, corporations provided "perpetual life." Partnerships dissolved on the death of a partner, whereas corporations continued to function despite the death of any single owner. This form of ownership brought stability and order to financing, building, and perpetuating what was otherwise a highly volatile and complex business endeavor.

Capitalists devised new corporate structures to gain greater control over their industries. Rockefeller's Standard Oil Company led the way by creating the **trust**, a monopoly formed by a small group of leading stockholders from several firms who manage the consolidated enterprise. To evade state laws against monopolies, Rockefeller created a petroleum trust. He combined other oil firms across the country with Standard Oil and placed their owners on a nine-member board of trustees that ran the company. Subsequently, Rockefeller fashioned another method of bringing rival businesses together. Through a holding company, he obtained stock in a number of other oil companies and held them under his control.

Explore ▶

See Source 16.1 for one cartoonist's interpretation of Rockefeller's power.

Between 1880 and 1905, more than three hundred mergers occurred in 80 percent of the nation's manufacturing firms. Great wealth became heavily concentrated in the hands of a relatively small number of businessmen. Around two thousand businesses, a tiny fraction of the total number, dominated 40 percent of the nation's economy.

In their drive to consolidate economic power and shield themselves from risk, corporate titans generally had the courts on their side. In *Santa Clara County v. Southern Pacific Railroad Company* (1886), the Supreme Court decided that under the Fourteenth Amendment, which originally dealt with the issue of federal protection of African Americans' civil rights, a corporation was considered a "person." In effect, this ruling gave corporations the same right of due process that the framers of the amendment had meant to give to former slaves. In the 1890s, a majority of the Supreme Court embraced this interpretation. The right of due process shielded corporations from prohibitive government regulation of the workplace, including the passage of legislation reducing the number of hours in the workday.

Yet trusts did not go unopposed. In 1890 Congress passed the **Sherman Antitrust Act**, which outlawed monopolies that prevented free competition in interstate commerce. The bill passed easily with bipartisan support because it merely codified legal principles that already existed. Senator Sherman and his colleagues never intended to stifle large corporations, which

Horace Taylor | What a Funny Little Government, 1900

As large firms merged with competitors to form giant companies that dominated the marketplace, opponents of such trusts decried the power that these enterprises wielded over the economy and the political system. Responding to such concerns, Congress passed the Sherman Antitrust Act in 1890, but the law proved weak and was loosely enforced. In the following illustration, cartoonist Horace Taylor, a Democrat, sought to make trusts an issue in the 1900 election by attacking John D. Rockefeller, whose Standard Oil Company embodied the evils of trusts for many critics.

Source 16.1

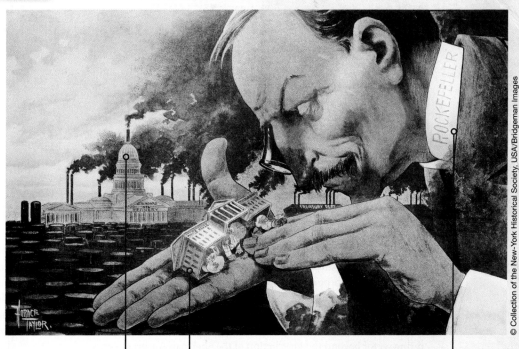

© Collection of the New-York Historical Society, USA/Bridgeman Images

How are the Capitol and Treasury depicted?

What is Rockefeller holding in his hand?

How does this illustration of Rockefeller emphasize the cartoonist's antitrust position?

Put It in Context

What does this cartoon suggest about the relationship between big business and the federal government at the start of the twentieth century?

1899 Sears, Roebuck Catalog The expansion of industrialization and completion of the transcontinental railroad created a national market for manufactured goods and led to the growth of consumer culture. The Chicago-based Sears, Roebuck used its mail-order catalog to attract customers throughout the United States and, as its cover suggests, the world. This colorful 1899 catalog offers the latest in carpets, furniture, china, fashion, and photographic equipment and supplies. Granger

through efficient business practices came to dominate the market. Rather, the lawmakers attempted to limit underhanded actions that destroyed competition. The judicial system further bailed out corporate leaders. In *United States v. E.C. Knight Company* (1895), a case against the "sugar trust," the Supreme Court rendered the Sherman Act virtually toothless by ruling that manufacturing was a local activity within a state and that, even if it was a monopoly, it was not subject to congressional regulation. This ruling left most trusts in the manufacturing sector beyond the jurisdiction of the Sherman Antitrust Act.

The introduction of managerial specialists, already present in European firms, proved the most critical innovation for integrating industry. With many operations controlled under one roof, large-scale businesses required a corps of experts to oversee and coordinate the various steps of production. As the expanding labor force worked to produce a rapidly rising volume of goods, efficiency experts sought to cut labor costs and make the production process operate more smoothly. Frederick W. Taylor, a Philadelphia engineer and businessman, developed the principles of scientific management. Based on his concept of reducing manual labor to its simplest components and eliminating independent action on the part of workers, managers introduced time-and-motion studies. Using a stopwatch, they calculated how to break down a job into simple tasks that could be performed in the least amount of time. From this perspective, workers were no different from the machines they operated. With production soaring, marketing and advertising managers were called upon to devise new techniques to gauge consumer interests and stimulate their demands.

Another vital factor in creating large-scale industry was the establishment of retail outlets that could sell the enormous volume of goods pouring out of factories. As consumer goods became less expensive, retail outlets sprang up to serve the growing market for household items. Customers could shop at department stores — such as Macy's in New York City, Filene's in Boston, Marshall Field's in Chicago, May's in Denver, Nordstrom's in Seattle, and Jacome's in Tucson — where they were waited on by an army of salesclerks. Or they could buy the cheaper items in Frank W. Woolworth's five and ten cent stores, which opened in towns and cities nationwide. Chain supermarkets — such as the Great Atlantic and Pacific Tea Company (A&P), founded in 1869 — sold fruits and vegetables packed in tin cans. They also sold foods from the meatpacking firms of Gustavus Swift and Philip Armour, which shipped them on refrigerated railroad cars. Mail-order catalogs allowed Americans in all parts of the country to buy consumer goods without leaving their home. The catalogs of Montgomery Ward (established in 1872) and Sears, Roebuck (founded in 1886) offered tens of thousands of items. Rural free delivery (RFD), instituted by the U.S. Post Office in 1891, made it even easier for farmers and others living in the countryside to obtain these catalogs and buy their merchandise without having to travel miles to the nearest post office. By the end of the nineteenth century, the industrial economy had left its mark on almost all aspects of life in almost every corner of America.

REVIEW & RELATE

What were the key factors behind the acceleration of industrial development in late-nineteenth-century America?

How did industrialization change the way American businessmen thought about their companies and the people who worked for them?

Laissez-Faire, Social Darwinism, and Their Critics

American industrialization developed as rapidly as it did in large part because it was reinforced by traditional ideas and values. The notion that hard work and diligence would result in success meant that individuals felt justified, even duty-bound, to strive to achieve upward mobility and accumulate wealth. Those who succeeded believed that they had done so because they were more talented, industrious, and resourceful than others. Thus prosperous businessmen regarded competition and the free market as essential to the health of an economic world they saw based on merit. Yet these same businessmen also created trusts that destroyed competition, and they depended on the government for resources and protection. This obvious contradiction, along with the profoundly unequal distribution of wealth that characterized the late-nineteenth-century economy, generated a good deal of criticism of business tycoons and their beliefs.

The Doctrines of Success. Those at the top of the new industrial order justified their great wealth in a manner that most Americans could understand. The ideas of the Scottish economist Adam Smith, in *The Wealth of Nations* (1776), had gained popularity during the American Revolution. Advocating **laissez-faire** ("let things alone"), Smith contended that an "Invisible Hand," guided by natural law, guaranteed the greatest economic success if the government let individuals pursue their own self-interest unhindered by outside and artificial influences. In the late nineteenth century, businessmen and their conservative allies on the Supreme Court used Smith's doctrines to argue against restrictive government regulation. They equated their right to own and manage property with the personal liberty protected by the Fourteenth Amendment. Thus the Declaration of Independence, with its defense of "life, liberty, and the pursuit of happiness," and the Constitution, which enshrined citizens' political freedom, became instruments to guarantee unfettered economic opportunity and safeguard private property.

The view that success depended on individual initiative was reinforced in schools and churches. The McGuffey Readers, widely used to educate children, taught moral lessons of hard work, individual initiative, reliability, and thrift. The popular dime novels of Horatio Alger portrayed the story of young men who rose from "rags to riches." Americans could also hear success stories in houses of worship. Russell Conwell, pastor of the Grace Baptist Church in Philadelphia, delivered a widely printed sermon entitled "Acres of Diamonds," which equated godliness with riches and argued that ordinary people had an obligation to strive for material wealth. "I say that you ought to get rich, and it is your duty to get rich," Conwell declared, "because to make money honestly is to preach the gospel."

If economic success was a matter of personal merit, it followed that economic failure was as well. The British philosopher Herbert Spencer proposed a theory of social evolution based on this premise in his book *Social Statics* (1851). Imagining a future utopia, Spencer wrote, "Man was not created with an instinct for his own degradation, but from the lower he has risen to the higher forms. Nor is there any conceivable end to his march to perfection." In his view, those at the top of the economic ladder were closer to perfection than were those at the bottom. Any effort to aid the unfortunate would only slow the march of progress for society as a whole. Spencer's book proved extremely popular, selling nearly 400,000 copies in the United States by 1900. Publication of Charles Darwin's landmark *On the Origin of Species* (1859) appeared to provide some scientific legitimacy for Spencer's view. The British naturalist argued that plants, animals, and humans progressed or declined because of their ability or inability to adapt favorably to the environment and transmit these characteristics to future generations. The connection between the two men's ideas led some people decades later to label Spencer's theory **"Social Darwinism."**

Doctrines of success, such as Social Darwinism, gained favor because they helped Americans explain the rapid economic changes that were disrupting their lives. Although most ordinary people would not climb out of poverty to middle-class respectability, let alone affluence, they clung to ideas that promised hope. Theories such as Spencer's that linked success with progress provided a way for those who did not do well to understand their failure and blame themselves for their own inadequacies. At the same time, the notion that economic success derived from personal merit legitimized the fabulous wealth of those who did rise to the top.

Capitalists such as Carnegie found a way to soften both the message of extreme competition and its impact on the American public. Denying that the government should help the poor, they proclaimed that men of wealth had a duty to furnish some assistance. In his famous essay **"The Gospel of Wealth"** (1889), Carnegie argued that the rich should act as stewards of the wealth they earned. As trustees, they should administer their surplus income for the benefit of the community. Carnegie distinguished between charity (direct handouts to individuals), which he deplored, and philanthropy (building institutions that would raise educational and cultural standards), which he advocated. Carnegie was particularly generous in funding libraries (he provided the buildings but not the books) because they allowed people to gain knowledge through their own efforts.

Capitalists may have sung the praises of individualism and laissez-faire, but their actions contradicted their words. Successful industrialists in the late nineteenth century sought to destroy competition, not perpetuate it. Their efforts over the course of several decades produced giant corporations that measured the worth of individuals by calculating their value to the organization. As John D. Rockefeller, the master of consolidation, proclaimed, "The day of individual competition in large affairs is past and gone." **See Primary Source Project 16: Debates about Laissez-Faire, page 556.**

Nor did capitalists strictly oppose government involvement. Although industrialists did not want the federal government to take any action that *retarded* their economic efforts, they did favor the use of the government's power to *promote* their enterprises and to stimulate entrepreneurial energies. Thus manufacturers pushed for congressional passage of high tariffs to protect goods from foreign competition and to foster development of the national marketplace. Industrialists demanded that federal and state governments dispatch troops when labor strikes threatened their businesses. They persuaded Washington to provide land grants for railroad construction and to send the army to clear Native Americans and bison from their tracks. They argued for state and federal courts to interpret constitutional and statutory law in a way that shielded property rights against attacks from workers. In large measure, capitalists succeeded not in spite of governmental support but because of it.

Challenges to Laissez-Faire.

Proponents of government restraint and unbridled individualism did not go unchallenged. Critics of laissez-faire created an alternative ideology for those who sought to organize workers and expand the role of government as ways of restricting capitalists' power over labor and ordinary citizens.

Lester Frank Ward attacked laissez-faire in his book *Dynamic Sociology* (1883). Ward did not disparage individualism but viewed the main function of society as "the organization of happiness." Contradicting Herbert Spencer, Ward maintained that societies progressed when government directly intervened to help citizens—even the unfortunate. Rejecting laissez-faire, he argued that what people "really need is more government in its primary sense, greater protection from the rapacity of the favored few."

Some academics supported Ward's ideas. Most notably, economist Richard T. Ely applied Christian ethics to his scholarly assessment of capital and labor. He condemned the railroads for dragging "their slimy length over our country, and every turn in their progress is marked by a progeny of evils." In his book *The Labor Movement* (1886), Ely suggested that the ultimate solution for social ills resulting from industrialization lay in "the union of capital and labor in the same hands, in grand, wide-reaching, co-operative enterprises."

Two popular writers, Henry George and Edward Bellamy, added to the critique of materialism and greed. In *Progress and Poverty* (1879), George lamented: "Amid the greatest accumulations of wealth, men die of starvation." He blamed the problem on rent, which he viewed as an unjustifiable payment on the increase in the value of land. His remedy was to have government confiscate rent earned on land by levying a single tax on landownership. Though he advocated government intervention, he did not envision an enduring role for the state once it had imposed the single tax. By contrast, Bellamy imagined a powerful central government. In his novel *Looking Backward, 2000–1887* (1888), Bellamy attacked industrialists who "maim and slaughter workers by thousands." In his view, the federal government should take over large-scale firms, administer them as workers' collectives, and redistribute wealth equally among all citizens.

Neither Bellamy, George, Ward, nor Ely endorsed the militant socialism of Karl Marx. The German philosopher predicted that capitalism would be overthrown and replaced by a revolutionary movement of industrial workers that would control the means of economic production and establish an egalitarian society. Although his ideas gained popularity among European labor leaders, they were not widely accepted in the United States during this period. Most critics believed that the American political system could be reformed without resorting to the extreme solution of a socialist revolution. They favored a cooperative commonwealth of capital and labor, with the government acting as an umpire between the two.

REVIEW & RELATE

- In the late nineteenth century, how did many Americans explain individual economic success and failure?

- How did the business community view the role of government in the economy at the end of the nineteenth century?

Society and Culture in the Gilded Age

Wealthy people in the late nineteenth century used their fortunes to support lavish lifestyles. For many of them, especially those with recent wealth, opulence rather than good taste was the standard of adornment. This tendency inspired writer Mark Twain and his collaborator Charles Dudley Warner to describe this era of wealth creation as the **Gilded Age**. Glittering on the outside, the enormous riches covered up the unbridled materialism and political rottenness that lay below the surface.

Twain and Warner had the very wealthy in mind when they coined the phrase, but others further down the social ladder found ways to participate in the culture of consumption. The rapidly expanding middle class enjoyed modest homes furnished with mass-produced consumer goods. Women played the central role in running the household, as most wives remained at home to raise children. Women and men often spent their free time attending meetings and other events sponsored by social, cultural, and political organizations. Such prosperity was, however, largely limited to whites. For the majority of African Americans still living in the South, life proved much harder. In response to black aspirations for social and economic advancement, white politicians imposed a rigid system of racial segregation on the South. Although whites championed the cause of individual upward mobility, they restricted opportunities to achieve success to whites only.

Wealthy and Middle-Class Leisure-Time Pursuits.
Industrialization and the rise of corporate capitalism led to the expansion of the wealthy upper class as well as the expansion of the middle class, and new lifestyles emerged. Urban elites lived lives of incredible material opulence. J. P. Morgan, William Vanderbilt, and John D. Rockefeller

built lavish homes in New York City. High-rise apartment buildings also catered to the wealthy. Overlooking Central Park, the nine-story Dakota Apartments boasted fifty-eight suites, a banquet hall, and a wine cellar. Millionaire residents furnished their stately homes with an eclectic mix of priceless art objects and furniture in a jumble of diverse styles. The rich and famous established private social clubs, sent their children to exclusive prep schools and colleges, and worshipped in the most fashionable churches.

Second homes, usually for use in the summer, were no less expensively constructed and decorated. Besides residences in Manhattan and Newport, Rhode Island, the Vanderbilts constructed a "home away from home" in the mountains of Asheville, North Carolina. The Biltmore, as they named it, contained 250 rooms, 40 master bedrooms, and an indoor swimming pool.

The wealthy also built and frequented opera houses, concert halls, museums, and historical societies as testimonies to their taste and sophistication. For example, the Vanderbilts, Rockefellers, Goulds, and Morgans financed the completion of the Metropolitan Opera House in New York City in 1883. When the facility opened, a local newspaper commented about the well-heeled audience: "The Goulds and the Vanderbilts and people of that ilk perfumed the air with the odor of crisp greenbacks." Upper-class women often traveled abroad to visit the great European cities and ancient Mediterranean sites.

Industrialization and the rise of corporate capitalism also brought an array of white-collar workers in managerial, clerical, and technical positions. These workers formed a new, expanded middle class and joined the businesspeople, doctors, lawyers, teachers, and clergy who constituted the old middle class. More than three million white-collar workers were employed in 1910, nearly three times as many as in 1870.

Middle-class families decorated their residences with mass-produced furniture, musical instruments, family photographs, books, periodicals, and a variety of memorabilia collected in their leisure time. They could relax in their parlors and browse through mass-circulation magazines and popular newspapers. Or they could read some of the era's outpouring of fiction, including romances, dime novels, westerns, humor, and social realism, an art form that depicted working-class life.

Explore ▸

See Sources 16.2 and 16.3 for two images of women.

With more money and time on their hands, middle-class women and men were able to devote their efforts to charity. They joined a variety of social and professional organizations that were arising to deal with the problems accompanying industrialization (see Table 16.1). During the 1880s, charitable organizations such as the American Red Cross were established to provide disaster relief. In 1892 the General Federation of Women's Clubs was founded to improve women's educational and cultural lives. Four years later, the National Association of Colored Women organized to help relieve suffering among the black poor, defend black women, and promote the interests of the black race.

During these swiftly changing times, adults became increasingly concerned about the nation's youth and sought to create organizations that catered to young people. Formed before the Civil War in England and expanded to the United States, the Young Men's Christian Association (YMCA) grew briskly during the 1880s as it erected buildings where young men could socialize, build moral character, and engage in healthy physical exercise. The Young Women's Christian Association (YWCA) provided similar opportunities for women.

Leisure-Class Women

The spectacular economic growth in the second half of the nineteenth century spawned a rise in leisure activities. In wealthy and middle-class families, women were central in shaping household consumption. Expected to conform to public standards of female decorum, some young leisure-class women challenged established gender roles in private. Contrast the cover of *The Delineator* (1900), one of America's foremost women's magazines, with the photograph taken by Alice Austen in 1891. In this photograph Austen and her friend, Trude Eccleston, whose father was an Episcopalian minister, are pictured in Eccleston's bedroom.

Source 16.2

The Delineator, 1900

Sarah Fabian-Baddiel/Heritage-Images/The Image Works

African Americans also participated in "Y" activities through the creation of racially separate branches.

Changing Gender Roles. Economic changes led to adjustments in lifestyles and gender roles during the industrial era. Middle-class wives generally remained at home, caring for the house and children, often with the aid of a servant. Whereas in the past

Source 16.3

Alice Austen and Trude Eccleston, 1891

Collection of Historic Richmond Town Staten Island Historical Society.

Interpret the Evidence

1. What do the clothing and activity of the woman on the cover of *The Delineator* suggest about her background?
2. Compare the image of Austen and her friend with the magazine's cover woman. What norms of female behavior are they contesting?

Put It in Context

What social and political trends during the late nineteenth century gave middle-class women increased opportunities to express themselves?

farmers and artisans had worked from the home, now most men and women accepted as natural the separation of the workplace and the home caused by industrialization and urbanization. Although the birthrate and marriage rates among the middle class dropped during the late nineteenth century, wives were still expected to care for their husbands and family first to fulfill their feminine duties. Even though daughters increasingly attended colleges reserved for women, their families viewed education as a means of providing

TABLE 16.1   An Age of Organizations, 1876–1896

Category	Year of Founding	Organization
Charitable	1881	American Red Cross
	1887	Charity Organization Society
	1889	Educational Alliance
	1893	National Council of Jewish Women
Sports/Fraternal	1876	National League of Baseball
	1882	Knights of Columbus
	1888	National Council of Women
	1892	General Federation of Women's Clubs
	1896	National Association of Colored Women
Professional	1883	Modern Language Association
	1884	American Historical Association
	1885	American Economic Association
	1888	American Mathematical Society

refinement rather than a career. One physician summed up the prevailing view that women could only use their brains "but little and in trivial matters" and should concentrate on serving as "the companion or ornamental appendage to man."

Middle-class women threw themselves into the new consumer culture. Department stores, chain stores, ready-made clothes, and packaged goods, from Jell-O and Kellogg's Corn Flakes to cake mixes, competed for the money and loyalty of female consumers. Hairdressers, cosmetic companies, and department stores offered a growing and ever-changing assortment of styles. The expanding array of consumer goods did not, however, decrease women's domestic workload. They had more furniture to dust, fancier meals to prepare, changing fashions to keep up with, higher standards of cleanliness to maintain, and more time to devote to entertaining. Yet the availability of mass-produced goods to assist the housewife in her chores made her role as consumer highly visible, while making her role as worker nearly invisible.

For the more socially and economically independent young women — those who attended college or beauty and secretarial schools — new worlds of leisure opened up. Bicycling, tennis, and croquet became popular sports for women in the late nineteenth century. So, too, did playing basketball, both in colleges and through industrial leagues. Indeed, women's colleges made sports a requirement, to offset the stress of intellectual life and produce a more well-rounded woman.

Middle-class men enjoyed new leisure pursuits, too. During the late nineteenth century 5.5 million men (of some 19 million adult men in the United States) joined fraternal orders, such as the Odd Fellows, Masons, Knights of Pythias, and Elks. These groups

Women Bicyclists   In the 1890s, with improvements in technology, middle-class women had both more leisure time and access to easy-to-ride bicycles. This photograph shows women at an early stage of the bicycle craze before changes in fashion allowed women to wear less-restrictive clothing that permitted exposed ankles and visible bloomers. In 1895, a Nebraska newspaper commented on the larger social implications of women bicyclists: The bicycle took "old-fashioned, slow-going notions of the gentler sex," and replaced them with "some new woman, mounted on her steed of steel." Robert Alexander/Getty Images

offered middle-class men a network of business contacts and gave them a chance to enjoy a communal, masculine social environment otherwise lacking in their lives.

In fact, historians have referred to a "crisis of masculinity" afflicting a segment of middle- and upper-class men in the late nineteenth and early twentieth centuries. Middle-class occupations whittled away the sense of autonomy that men had experienced in an earlier era when they worked for themselves. The emergence of corporate capitalism had swelled the ranks of the middle class with organization men, who held salaried jobs in managerial departments. At the same time, the expansion of corporations and big business stimulated a demand for clerical workers, female as well as male. This offered women many new opportunities to enter the job market. Along with this development, the push for women's rights, especially the right to vote, and women's increasing involvement in civic associations threatened to reduce absolute male control over the public sphere.

Responding to this gender crisis, middle-class men sought ways to exert their masculinity and keep from becoming frail and effeminate. Psychologists like G. Stanley Hall warned that unless men returned to a primitive state of manhood, they risked becoming spiritually paralyzed. To avoid this, went their advice, men should build up their bodies and engage in strenuous activities to improve their physical fitness.

Men turned to sports to cultivate their masculinity. Besides playing baseball and football, they could attend various sporting events. Baseball became the national pastime, and men could root for their home team and establish a community with the thousands of male spectators who filled up newly constructed ballparks. Baseball, a game played by elites in New York City in the 1840s, soon became a commercially popular sport. It spread across the country as baseball clubs in different cities competed with each other. The sport came into its own with the creation of the professional National League in 1876, and the introduction of the World Series in 1903 between the winners of the National League and the American League pennant races.

Boxing also became a popular spectator sport in the late nineteenth century. Bare-knuckle fighting — without the protection of gloves — epitomized the craze to display pure masculinity. A boxing match lasted until one of the fighters was knocked out, leaving both fighters bloody and battered.

During the late nineteenth century, middle-class women and men also had increased opportunities to engage in different forms of sociability and sexuality. Gay men and lesbians could find safe havens in New York City's Greenwich Village and Chicago's North Side for their own entertainment. Although treated by medical experts as sexual "inverts" who might be cured by an infusion of "normal" heterosocial contact, gays and lesbians began to emerge from the shadows of Victorian-era sexual constraints around the turn of the twentieth century. "Boston marriages" constituted another form of relationship between women. The term apparently came from Henry James's book *The Bostonians* (1886), which described a female couple living together in a monogamous, long-term relationship. This conjugal-style association appealed to financially independent women who did not want to get married. Many of these relationships were sexual, but some were not. In either case, they offered women of a certain class an alternative to traditional, heterosexual marriage.

Black America and Jim Crow.

While wealthy and middle-class whites experimented with new forms of social behavior, African Americans faced greater challenges to preserving their freedom and dignity. In the South, where the overwhelming majority of blacks lived, post-Reconstruction governments adopted various techniques to keep blacks from voting. To circumvent the Fifteenth Amendment, southern states devised suffrage qualifications that they claimed were racially neutral, and the Supreme Court ruled in their favor. They instituted the poll tax, a tax that each person had to pay in order to cast a ballot. Poll taxes fell hardest on the poor, a disproportionate number of whom were African American. Disfranchisement reached its peak in the 1890s, as white southern governments managed to deny the vote to most of the black electorate (Map 16.2). Literacy tests officially barred the uneducated of both races, but they were administered in a manner that discriminated against blacks while allowing illiterate whites to satisfy the requirement. Many literacy tests contained a loophole called a "grandfather clause." Under this exception, men whose father or grandfather had voted in 1860 — a time when white men but not black men, most of whom were slaves, could vote in the South — were excused from taking the test.

In the 1890s, white southerners also imposed legally sanctioned racial segregation on the region's black citizens. Commonly known as **Jim Crow** laws (named for a character in a minstrel show, where whites performed in blackface), these new statutes denied African Americans equal access to public facilities and ensured that blacks lived apart from whites. In 1883, when the Supreme Court struck down the 1875 Civil Rights Act (see "congressional and Judicial Retreat," chapter 14), it gave southern states the freedom to adopt

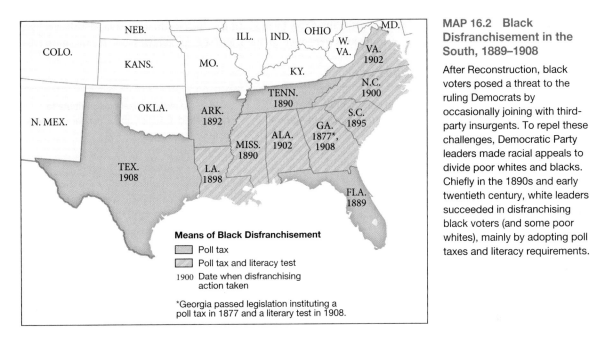

MAP 16.2 Black Disfranchisement in the South, 1889–1908

After Reconstruction, black voters posed a threat to the ruling Democrats by occasionally joining with third-party insurgents. To repel these challenges, Democratic Party leaders made racial appeals to divide poor whites and blacks. Chiefly in the 1890s and early twentieth century, white leaders succeeded in disfranchising black voters (and some poor whites), mainly by adopting poll taxes and literacy requirements.

measures confining blacks to separate schools, public accommodations, seats on transportation, beds in hospitals, and sections of graveyards. In 1896 the Supreme Court sanctioned Jim Crow, constructing the constitutional rationale for legally keeping the races apart. In **Plessy v. Ferguson**, the high court ruled that a Louisiana law providing for "equal but separate" accommodations for "whites" and "coloreds" on railroad cars did not violate the equal protection clause of the Fourteenth Amendment. In its decision, the Court concluded that civil rights laws could not change racial destiny. "If one race be inferior to the other socially," the justices explained, "the Constitution of the United States cannot put them on the same plane." In practice, however, white southerners obeyed the "separate" part of the ruling but never provided equal services. If blacks tried to overstep the bounds of Jim Crow in any way that whites found unacceptable, they risked their lives. Between 1884 and 1900, nearly 1,700 blacks were lynched in the South. Victims were often subjected to brutal forms of torture before they were hanged or shot.

In everyday life, African Americans carried on as best they could. Segregation provided many African Americans with opportunities to build their own businesses; control their own churches; develop their own schools, staffed by black teachers; and form their own civic associations and fraternal organizations. Segregation, though harsh and unequal, did foster a sense of black community, promote a rising middle class, and create social networks that enhanced racial pride. Founded in 1898, the North Carolina Life Insurance Company, one of the leading black-owned and black-operated businesses, employed many African Americans in managerial and sales positions. Burial societies ensured that their members received a proper funeral when they died. As with whites, black men joined lodges such as the Colored Masons and the Colored Odd Fellows, while women participated in the YWCA and the National Association of Colored Women. A small percentage of southern blacks resisted Jim Crow by migrating to the North, where blacks still exercised the right to vote, more jobs were open to them, and segregation was less strictly enforced.

REVIEW & RELATE

- What role did consumption play in the society and culture of the Gilded Age?

- How did industrialization contribute to heightened anxieties about gender roles and race?

National Politics in the Era of Industrialization

Politicians played an important role in the expanding industrial economy that provided new opportunities for the wealthy and the expanding middle class. For growing companies and corporations to succeed, they needed a favorable political climate that would support their interests. Businessmen frequently looked to Washington for assistance. Marcus Alonzo Hanna, a wealthy industrialist, considered Ohio senator John Sherman "our main dependence in the Senate for the protection of our business interests." During this era, the office of the president was a weak and largely administrative post and legislators and judges were highly influenced and sometimes directly controlled by business leaders. For much of this period, the two national political parties battled to a standoff, which resulted in congressional gridlock with little accomplished. Yet spurred by fierce partisan competition, political participation grew among the electorate.

The Weak Presidency. James Bryce, a British observer of American politics, devoted a chapter of his book *The American Commonwealth* (1888) to "why great men are not chosen presidents." He believed that the White House attracted mediocre occupants because the president functioned mainly as an executor. The stature of the office had shrunk following the impeachment of Andrew Johnson and the reassertion of congressional power during Reconstruction (see "Congressional Reconstruction" in chapter 14). Presidents considered themselves mainly as the nation's top administrator. They did not see their roles as formulating policy or intervening on behalf of legislative objectives. With the office held in such low regard, great men became corporate leaders, not presidents.

Perhaps aware that they could expect little in the way of assistance or imagination from national leaders, voters refused to give either Democrats or Republicans solid support. No president between Ulysses S. Grant and William McKinley won back-to-back elections or received a majority of the popular vote. The only two-time winner, the Democrat Grover Cleveland, lost his bid for reelection in 1888 before triumphing again in 1892.

Nevertheless, the presidency attracted accomplished individuals. Rutherford B. Hayes (1877–1881), James A. Garfield (1881), and Benjamin Harrison (1889–1893) all had served ably in the Union army as commanding officers during the Civil War and had prior political experience. The nation greatly mourned Garfield following his assassination in 1881 by Charles Guiteau, a disgruntled applicant for federal patronage. Upon Garfield's death, Chester A. Arthur (1881–1885) became president. He had served as a quartermaster general during the Civil War, had a reputation as being sympathetic to African American civil rights, and had run the New York City Customs House effectively. Grover Cleveland (1885–1889, 1893–1897) first served as mayor of Buffalo and then as governor of New York. All of these men, as even Bryce admitted, worked hard, possessed common sense, and were honest. However, they were uninspiring individuals who lacked qualities of leadership that would arouse others to action.

Congressional Inefficiency.

Congressional Inefficiency. The most important factor in the weakened presidency was the structure of Congress, which prevented the president from providing vigorous leadership. Throughout most of this period, Congress remained narrowly divided. Majorities continually shifted from one party to the other. For all but two terms, Democrats controlled the House of Representatives, while Republicans held the majority in the Senate. Divided government meant that during his term in office no late-nineteenth-century president had a majority of his party in both houses of Congress. Turnover among congressmen in the House of Representatives, who were elected every two years, was quite high, and there was little power of incumbency. The Senate, however, provided more continuity and allowed senators, with six-year terms of office, to amass greater power than congressmen could.

For all the power that Congress wielded, it failed to govern effectively or efficiently. In the House, measures did not receive adequate attention on the floor because the Speaker did not have the power to control the flow of systematic debate. Committee chairmen held a tight rein over the introduction and consideration of legislation and competed with one another for influence in the chamber. Congressmen showed little decorum as they conducted business on the House floor and often chatted with each other or read the newspaper rather than listen to the speakers at the podium.

The Senate, though more manageable in size and more stable in membership (only one-third of its membership stood for reelection every two years), did not function much more smoothly. Senators valued their own judgments and business interests more than party unity. The position of majority leader, someone who could impose discipline on his colleagues and design a coherent legislative agenda, had not yet been created. Woodrow Wilson, the author of *Congressional Government* (1885) and a future president, concluded: "Our government is defective as it parcels out power and confuses responsibility." Under these circumstances, neither the president nor Congress governed efficiently.

The Business of Politics.

The Business of Politics. Many lawmakers viewed politics as a business enterprise that would line their pockets with money. One cabinet officer grumbled, "A Congressman is a hog! You must take a stick and hit him on the snout!" Senators were elected by state legislatures, and these bodies were often controlled by well-funded corporations that generously spread their money around to gain influence. In both branches of Congress, party leaders handed out patronage to supporters regardless of their qualifications for the jobs (a practice known as the spoils system). Modern-day standards of ethical conduct did not exist; nor did politicians see a conflict of interest in working closely with corporations. Indeed, there were no rules to prevent lawmakers from accepting payments from big business. Most congressmen received free passes from railroads and in turn voted on the

Explore ▶

Compare two opposing views of John D. Rockefeller in Sources 16.4 and 16.5.

SECONDARY SOURCE ANALYSIS

Robber Baron or Captain of Industry?

Matthew Josephson did not coin the phrase *Robber Barons*, but the publication of his book of the same name in 1934 provided a vivid description of the greed, ruthlessness, and corruption that characterized the late nineteenth century industrialists and capitalists. Actually, the term Robber Barons first appeared in the 1880s in an anti-railroad pamphlet circulated by agrarian reformers in Kansas. Yet the notion of avaricious Robber Barons did not go unchallenged. While recognizing the dark sides of development of industrialization and big business, later writers, such as Ron Chernow, emphasized the qualities of risk taking, creativity, hard work, and leadership.

Source 16.4

Matthew Josephson, *The Robber Barons* (1934)

"But for the very reason that forces leading to combination were at work in the society, the general effect of the period [1877–1900] was one of strenuous contest for the market, of anarchic, individual appetite and money-lust, of ruinous competition conducted with more terrible instruments than before, out of which a few giant industrialists arose. . . .

With his measured spirit, with his organized might, [John D. Rockefeller] tested men and things. There were men and women of all sorts who passed under his implacable rod, and their tale … has contributed to the legend of the 'white devil' who came to rule over American industry.

A certain widow, a Mrs. [Fred M.] Backus of Cleveland, who had inherited an oil-refinery, had appealed to Mr. Rockefeller to preserve her, 'the mother of fatherless children." And he had promised 'with tears in his eyes that he would stand by her.' But in the end he offered her only $79,000 for a property which had cost $200,000. The whole story of the defenseless widow and her orphans, the stern command, the confiscation of two-thirds of her property, when it came out made a deep stir and moved many hearts."

Source: Matthew Josephson, *The Robber Barons*. New York: Harcourt, Brace & World, Inc., 1962, 254, 267.

companies' behalf. To be fair, most politicians such as Senator Sherman did not see a difference between furthering the legislative agenda of big corporations and promoting the nation's economic interests. Nevertheless, the public held politicians in very low esteem because they resented the influence of corporate money in politics.

The 1890 Congress stands out as an example of fiscal irresponsibility. Known as the **Billion Dollar Congress**, the same Republican legislative majority that passed the Sherman Anti-Trust Act adopted the highest tariff in U.S. history. Sponsored by Ohio congressman William McKinley, a close associate of the industrialist Marcus Hanna, it lavishly protected manufacturing interests. Congress also spent enormous sums on special projects to enrich their constituents and themselves. Republicans spent so much money on extravagant enterprises that they wiped out the federal budget surplus.

Increasingly throughout the 1890s, corporate leaders and their political allies joined together in favor of extending American influence and control over foreign markets and

Source 16.5

Ron Chernow, John D. Rockefeller, Industrial Statesman, 1998

"'If it were true [the Widow Backus story],' Rockefeller later conceded, it 'would represent a shocking instance of cruelty in crushing a defenceless [sic] woman. It is probable that its wide circulation and its acceptance as true by those who know nothing of the facts has awakened more hostility against the Standard Oil Company and against me personally than any charge which has been made.'

. . . While Backus wanted Rockefeller to conduct the negotiations for her plant, he knew nothing about lubricants [lubricating oils and grease] and sent his associates instead. According to Backus, Rockefeller's hirelings bilked her unmercifully. . . . Backus's negotiator . . . later swore that his client, in an estimated inventory of her assets, had written down

$71,000 for plant and goodwill—not much more than Rockefeller finally paid her. Yet she grew incensed over the purchase price and drafted a savage latter to Rockefeller accusing him of double-dealing... [Rockefeller] then pointed out that the $60,000 paid for the property was two to three times the cost of constructing equal or better facilities. . . . In investing her proceeds in Cleveland real estate . . . Backus far from being reduced to filth and misery, became an extremely rich woman. . . . The notion of Rockefeller gleefully ruining a poor widow was such a good story, with so fine a Dickensian ring, that gullible reporters gave it fresh circulation for many years."

Source: Ron Chernow, *Titan: The Life of John D. Rockefeller, Sr.* New York: Random House, 1998, 445–447.

Examine the Sources

1. How do Josephson and Chernow differ in their interpretations of Rockefeller's business practices?
2. Drawing upon evidence in this chapter, evaluate the main arguments of Josephson and Chernow.

Put it in Context

How might the fact that these interpretations were written sixty-four years apart (1934/1998) influence their conclusions?

---

natural resources abroad, especially in Central America and the Pacific regions. They agreed that cyclical fluctuations in the domestic economy required overseas markets to assure high profits. To accomplish this would necessitate building up American military and commercial power (see "The Awakening of Imperialism" in chapter 20).

An Energized and Entertained Electorate. Despite all the difficulties of the legislative process, political candidates eagerly pursued office and conducted extremely heated campaigns. The electorate considered politics a form of entertainment. Political parties did not stand for clearly stated issues or offer innovative solutions; instead, campaigns took on the qualities of carefully staged performances. Candidates crafted their oratory to arouse the passions and prejudices of their audiences, and their managers handed out buttons, badges, and ceramic and glass plates stamped with the candidates' faces and slogans.

1892 Presidential Campaign Plate
Before radio, television, and the Internet,
political parties advertised candidates in a
variety of colorful ways, including banners,
buttons, ribbons, and ceramic and glass plates.
Voters, who turned out in record numbers during
the late nineteenth century, coveted these items.
This plate shows the 1892 Democratic
presidential ticket of Grover Cleveland and Adlai
Stevenson, who won the election. Collection of
Steven F. Lawson

Partisanship helped fuel high political participation. During this period, voter
turnout in presidential elections was much higher than at any time in the twentieth
century. Region, as well as historical and cultural allegiances, replaced ideology as the
key to party affiliation. The wrenching experience of the Civil War had cemented voting loyalties for many Americans. After Reconstruction, white southerners tended to
vote Democratic; northerners and newly enfranchised southern blacks generally voted
Republican. However, geography alone did not shape political loyalties; a sizable contingent of Democratic voters remained in the North, and southern whites and blacks
periodically abandoned both the Democratic and Republican parties to vote for third
parties.

Religion played an important role in shaping party loyalties during this period of
intense partisanship. The Democratic Party tended to attract Protestants of certain sects,
such as German Lutherans and Episcopalians, as well as Catholics. These faiths emphasized
religious ritual and the acceptance of personal sin. They believed that the government
should not interfere in matters of morality, which should remain the province of Christian
supervision on earth and divine judgment in the hereafter. By contrast, other Protestant
denominations, such as Baptists, Congregationalists, Methodists, and Presbyterians, highlighted the importance of individual will and believed that the law could be shaped to eradicate ignorance and vice. These Protestants were more likely to cast their ballots for
Republicans, except in the South, where regional loyalty to the Democratic Party trumped
religious affiliation.

Some people went to the polls because they fiercely disliked members of the opposition party. Northern white workers in New York City or Cincinnati, Ohio, for example, might vote against the Republican Party because they viewed it as the party of African Americans. Other voters cast their ballots against Democrats because they identified them as the party of Irish Catholics, intemperance, and secession.

Although political parties commanded fierce loyalties, the parties remained divided internally. For example, the Republicans pitted "Stalwarts" against "Half Breeds." The Stalwarts presented themselves as the "Old Guard" of the Republican Party, what they called the "Grand Old Party" (GOP). The Half Breeds, a snide name given to them by the Stalwarts, claimed to be more open to new ideas and less wedded to the old causes that the Republican Party promoted, such as racial equality. In the end, however, the differences between the two groups had less to do with ideas than with which faction would have greater power within the Republican Party.

Overall, the continuing strength of party loyalties produced equilibrium as voters cast their ballots primarily along strict party lines. The outcome of presidential elections depended on key "undecided" districts in several states in the Midwest and in New York and nearby states, which swung the balance of power in the electoral college. Indeed, from 1876 to 1896 all winning candidates for president and vice president came from Ohio, Indiana, Illinois, New York, and New Jersey.

REVIEW & RELATE

- What accounted for the inefficiency and ineffectiveness of the federal government in the late nineteenth century?

- How would you explain the high rates of voter turnout and political participation in an era of uninspiring politicians and governmental inaction?

Conclusion: Industrial America

From 1877 to 1900, American businessmen demonstrated a zeal for organization. Prompted by new technology that opened up national markets of commerce and communication, business entrepreneurs created large-scale corporations that promoted industrial expansion. Borrowing from European investors and importing and improving on European technology, by 1900 U.S. industrialists had surpassed their overseas counterparts.

Capitalists made great fortunes and lived luxurious lifestyles, emulating the fashions of European elites. Most corporate leaders did not rise from poverty but instead came from the upper middle class and had access to education and connections. Those like Andrew Carnegie, who rose from rags to riches, were the exceptions. The wealthy explained their success as the result of individual effort and hard work. This idea was reinforced in schoolbooks such as the McGuffey Readers, the novels of Horatio Alger, and religious sermons like those of Russell Conwell.

Although most working Americans did not achieve much wealth during this era of industrialization, they had faith in the possibility of improving their economic positions. Members of the middle class lived less extravagantly than did the wealthy; nonetheless, they enjoyed the comforts of the growing consumer economy. Although Jim Crow restricted the black middle class and a heightened sense of masculinity inhibited opportunities available to white women, both groups managed to carve out ways to lift themselves economically and socially.

In gaining success, the wealthy exchanged individualism for organization, competition for consolidation, and laissez-faire for government support. Without pro-business policies from Washington lawmakers and favorable decisions from the Supreme Court, big business would not have developed as rapidly as it did in this era. To prosper, corporations needed sympathetic politicians — whether to furnish free land for railroad expansion, enact tariffs to protect manufacturers, or protect private property. Even when a public outcry led to the regulation of trusts, the pro-business senator John Sherman and his colleagues shaped the legislation so as to minimize damage to corporate interests. In general, national politicians avoided engaging in fierce ideological conflicts, but they, too, organized. The political parties they fashioned encouraged a high level of political participation among voters.

It remained for those who did not share in the glittering wealth of the Gilded Age to find ways to resist corporate domination. While corporate leaders and the expanding middle class enjoyed the fruits of industrial capitalism, workers, farmers, and reformers sought to remedy the economic, social, and political ills that accompanied industrialization.

TIMELINE OF EVENTS

1859	Charles Darwin publishes *On the Origin of Species*
	Henry Bessemer improves steel production process
1860–1890	U.S. gross domestic product quadruples
1866	Transatlantic telegraph cable completed
1868	Typewriter invented
1870–1900	U.S. becomes a global industrial power
1870–1910	Number of U.S. white-collar workers triples
1870s	John D. Rockefeller takes control of oil refining business
1872	Montgomery Ward established
1876	Thomas Edison establishes research laboratory
1881	James Garfield assassinated
1883	Civil Service Act
1884–1900	1,700 blacks lynched in the South
1885	Alexander Graham Bell founds American Telephone and Telegraph
1886	U.S. railroads adopt standard gauge
	Santa Clara County v. Southern Pacific Railroad Company
1889	Andrew Carnegie publishes "The Gospel of Wealth"
1890	Sherman Antitrust Act
1890s	African Americans disfranchised in the South
1895	*United States v. E.C. Knight Company*
1896	*Plessy v. Ferguson*
1901	United States Steel established

KEY TERMS

New South, *531*

convict lease, *531*

vertical integration, *533*

horizontal integration, *533*

corporation, *534*

trust, *534*

Sherman Antitrust Act, *534*

laissez-faire, *537*

Social Darwinism, *538*

"The Gospel of Wealth," *538*

Gilded Age, *540*

Jim Crow, *546*

Plessy v. Ferguson, 547

Billion Dollar Congress, *550*

REVIEW & RELATE

1. What were the key factors behind the acceleration of industrial development in late-nineteenth-century America?

2. How did industrialization change the way American businessmen thought about their companies and the people who worked for them?

3. In the late nineteenth century, how did many Americans explain individual economic success and failure?

4. How did the business community view the role of government in the economy at the end of the nineteenth century?

5. What role did consumption play in the society and culture of the Gilded Age?

6. How did industrialization contribute to heightened anxieties about gender roles and race?

7. What accounted for the inefficiency and ineffectiveness of the federal government in the late nineteenth century?

8. How would you explain the high rates of voter turnout and political participation in an era of uninspiring politicians and governmental inaction?

Debates about Laissez-Faire

▶ Evaluate the extent to which differing ideas of competition and cooperation influenced views about obtaining wealth in late nineteenth century America.

From the nation's founding, the pursuit of individual opportunity has held a central place among American values. In the late nineteenth century, as big business consolidated and giant trusts came to dominate whole industries, defenders of unfettered big business argued that individual effort and initiative were still the central engine of the American economy. Championing Adam Smith's notion of laissez-faire — the idea that the marketplace should be left to regulate itself — they argued that government should do nothing to constrain the development of industry (Source 16.6). Yet as poverty expanded while a small number of industrialists and financiers accumulated great wealth, reformers questioned whether individualism undermined community, and contended that the government should regulate the free market to promote the greater public welfare (Sources 16.7 and 16.9). With the gap between rich and poor growing, even industrialists realized that if they did not help the poor in some way, the working classes would rise up against them (Source 16.8). Nevertheless, they continued to resist government interference.

Defenders of the status quo argued that individualism must be preserved as the natural order of society. Critics countered that cooperation rather than individual competition made social progress possible and that the government should protect ordinary people from the harm done by greedy capitalists.

Source 16.6

William Graham Sumner | A Defense of Laissez-Faire, 1883

Yale professor William Graham Sumner believed that millionaires deserved their wealth, a notion that appealed to successful industrialists. Men like Andrew Carnegie, he declared, "may fairly be regarded as the naturally selected agents of society." The poor, he argued, also justly deserved their fate. Sumner and other defenders of economic inequality maintained that if the government tried to help these unfortunate losers in the competitive struggle, progress would be halted and civilization would decay.

[It] may be said that those whom humanitarians and philanthropists call the weak are the ones through whom the productive and conservative forces of society are wasted. They constantly neutralize and destroy the finest efforts of the wise and industrious, and are a dead-weight on the society in all its struggles to realize any better things. Whether the people who mean no harm, but are weak in the essential powers necessary to the performance of one's duties in life, or those who are malicious and vicious, do the more mischief, is a question not easy to answer. . . .

The humanitarians, philanthropists, and reformers, looking at the facts of life as they present themselves, find enough which is sad and unpromising in the condition of many members of society. They see wealth and poverty side by side.

They note great inequality of social position and social chances. They eagerly set about the attempt to account for what they see, and to devise schemes for remedying what they do not like. In their eagerness to recommend the less fortunate classes to pity and consideration they forget all about the rights of other classes; they gloss over all the faults of the classes in question, and they exaggerate their misfortunes and their virtues. They invent new theories of property, distorting rights and perpetrating injustice, as any one is sure to do who sets about the re-adjustment of social relations with the interests of one group distinctly before his mind, and the interests of all other groups thrown into the background. When I have read certain of these discussions I have thought that it must be quite disreputable to be respectable, quite dishonest to own property, quite unjust to go one's own way and earn one's own living, and that the only really admirable person was the good-for-nothing. The man who by his own effort raises himself above poverty appears, in these discussions, to be of no account. The man who has done nothing to raise himself above poverty finds that the social doctors flock about him, bringing the capital which they have collected from the other class, and promising him the aid of the State to give him what the other had to work for. In all these schemes and projects the organized intervention of society through the State is either planned or hoped for, and the State is thus made to become the protector and guardian of certain classes. The agents who are to direct the State action are, of course, the reformers and philanthropists. . . . Here it may suffice to observe that, on the theories of the social philosophers to whom I have referred, we should get a new maxim of judicious living: Poverty is the best policy. If you get wealth, you will have to support other people; if you do not get wealth, it will be the duty of other people to support you.

Source: William Graham Sumner, *What the Social Classes Owe Each Other* (New York: Harper and Brothers, 1883), 19–24.

Source 16.7

Edward Bellamy | *Looking Backward, 2000–1887*, 1888

Edward Bellamy's best-selling novel *Looking Backward, 2000–1887*, offered utopian socialist solutions to the problems facing the rapidly industrializing United States. After falling into a medically induced sleep, Bellamy's narrator, Julian West, awakens in the year 2000 to find that many of the social inequities of the late nineteenth century have been resolved.

The records of the period show that the outcry against the concentration of capital was furious. Men believed that it threatened society with a form of tyranny more abhorrent than it had ever endured. They believed that the great corporations were preparing for them the yoke of a baser servitude than had ever been imposed on the race, servitude not to men but to soulless machines incapable of any motive but insatiable greed. Looking back, we cannot wonder at their desperation, for certainly humanity was never confronted with a fate more sordid and hideous than would have been the era of corporate tyranny which they anticipated.

Meanwhile, without being in the smallest degree checked by the clamor against it, the absorption of business by ever larger monopolies continued. In the United States, where this tendency was later in developing than in Europe, there was not, after the beginning of the last quarter of the century, any opportunity whatever for individual enterprise in any important field of industry, unless backed by a great capital. During the last decade of the century, such small businesses as still remained were fast failing survivals of a past epoch, or mere parasites on the great corporations, or else existed in fields too small to attract the great capitalists. Small businesses, as far as they still remained, were reduced to the condition of rats and mice, living in holes and corners, and counting on evading notice for the enjoyment of existence. The railroads had gone on combining till a few great syndicates controlled every rail in the land. In manufactories, every important staple was controlled by a syndicate. These syndicates, pools, trusts, or whatever their name, fixed prices and crushed all competition except when combinations as vast as themselves arose. Then a struggle, resulting in a still greater consolidation, ensued. The great city bazar crushed its country rivals with branch stores, and in the city itself absorbed its smaller rivals till the business of a whole quarter was concentrated under one roof with a hundred former proprietors of shops serving as clerks. Having no business of his own to put his money in, the small capitalist, at the same time that he took service under the corporation, found no other investment for his money but its stocks and bonds, thus becoming doubly dependent upon it.

The fact that the desperate popular opposition to the consolidation of business in a few powerful hands had no effect to check it, proves that there must have been a strong economical reason for it. The small capitalists, with their innumerable petty concerns, had, in fact, yielded the field to the great aggregations of capital, because they belonged to a day of small things and were totally incompetent to the demands of an age of steam and telegraphs and the gigantic scale of its enterprises. To restore the former order of things, even if possible, would have involved returning to the day of stage-coaches. Oppressive and intolerable as was the regime of the great consolidations of capital, even its victims, while they cursed it, were forced to admit the prodigious increase of efficiency which had been imparted to the national industries, the vast economies effected by concentration of management and unity of organization, and to confess that since the new system had taken the place of the old, the wealth of the world had increased at a rate before undreamed of. To be sure this vast increase had gone chiefly to make the rich richer, increasing the gap between them and the poor; but the fact remained that, as a means merely of producing wealth, capital had been proved efficient in proportion to its consolidation. The restoration of the old system with the subdivision of capital, if it were possible, might indeed bring back a greater equality of conditions

with more individual dignity and freedom, but it would be at the price of general poverty and the arrest of material progress. . . .

Early in the last century the evolution was completed by the final consolidation of the entire capital of the nation. The industry and commerce of the country, ceasing to be conducted by a set of irresponsible corporations and syndicates of private persons at their caprice and for their profit, were intrusted to a single syndicate representing the people, to be conducted in the common interest for the common profit. The nation, that is to say, organized as the one great business corporation in which all other corporations were absorbed; it became the one capitalist in the place of all other capitalists, the sole employer, the final monopoly in which all previous and lesser monopolies were swallowed up, a monopoly in the profits and economies of which all citizens shared.

Source: Edward Bellamy, *Looking Backward, 2000–1887* (Boston: Ticknor, 1888), 71–78.

Source 16.8

Andrew Carnegie | The Gospel of Wealth, 1889

Andrew Carnegie, who immigrated to the United States and experienced poverty as a young boy, made his fortune in the steel industry and became one of the richest men in the United States. Recognizing the dangers of widespread poverty among the mass of American workers, Carnegie sought to use philanthropy to provide opportunities for individuals to help themselves, as he explains in the following essay, which is usually referred to as "The Gospel of Wealth."

The best uses to which surplus wealth can be put have already been indicated. Those who would administer wisely must, indeed, be wise; for one of the serious obstacles to the improvement of our race is indiscriminate charity. It were better for mankind that the millions of the rich were thrown into the sea than so spent as to encourage the slothful, the drunken, the unworthy. Of every thousand dollars spent in so-called charity today, it is probable that nine hundred and fifty dollars is unwisely spent—so spent, indeed, as to produce the very evils which it hopes to mitigate or cure. . . .

In bestowing charity, the main consideration should be to help those who will help themselves; to provide part of the means by which those who desire to improve may do so; to give those who desire to rise the aids by which they may rise; to assist, but rarely or never to do all. Neither the individual nor the race is improved by almsgiving. Those worthy of assistance, except in rare cases, seldom require assistance. The really valuable men of the race never do, except in case of accident or sudden change. Every one has, of course, cases of individuals brought to his own knowledge where temporary assistance can do genuine good, and these he will not overlook. But the amount which can be wisely given by the individual for individuals is necessarily limited by his lack of knowledge of the circumstances connected with each. He is the only true reformer who is as careful and as anxious not to aid the unworthy as he is to aid the worthy, and, perhaps, even more so, for in almsgiving more injury is probably done by rewarding vice than by relieving virtue.

[T]he best means of benefiting the community is to place within its reach the ladders upon which the aspiring can rise—free libraries, parks, and means of recreation, by which men are helped in body and mind; works of art, certain to give pleasure and improve the public taste; and public institutions of various kinds, which will improve the general condition of the people; in this manner returning their surplus wealth to the mass of their fellows in the forms best calculated to do them lasting good.

Thus is the problem of rich and poor to be solved. The laws of accumulation will be left free, the laws of distribution free. Individualism will continue, but the millionaire will be but a trustee for the poor, intrusted for a season with a great part of the increased wealth of the community, but administering it for the community far better than it could or would have done for itself. The best minds will thus have reached a stage in the development of the race in which it is clearly seen that there is no mode of disposing of surplus wealth creditable to

thoughtful and earnest men into whose hands it flows, save by using it year by year for the general good. . . . [T]he day is not far distant when the man who dies leaving behind him millions of available wealth, which was free for him to administer during life, will pass away "unwept, unhonored, and unsung," no matter to what uses he leaves the dross which he cannot take with him. Of such as these the public verdict will then be: "The man who dies thus rich dies disgraced."

Such, in my opinion, is the true gospel concerning wealth, obedience to which is destined some day to solve the problem of the rich and the poor, and to bring "Peace on earth, among men good will."

Source: Andrew Carnegie, *The Gospel of Wealth and Other Timely Essays* (New York: Century, 1901), 16–19.

Source 16.9

Henry Demarest Lloyd | Critique of Wealth, 1894

Many academics and writers attacked industrial capitalists, claiming that their excessive wealth came at the expense of workers and the general public. Lawyer and journalist Henry Demarest Lloyd wrote numerous articles for the *Chicago Tribune* exposing corruption in business and politics. A reformer influenced by British socialists, Lloyd supported legislation to ban child labor and to allow women to vote. In his 1894 book *Wealth against Commonwealth,* he denounced ruthless and unsavory competitive practices by industrialists who created monopolies that exploited working people. In the following excerpt, Lloyd raises questions about the fundamental value of industrial capitalism and its threat to social progress.

I f our civilization is destroyed, . . . it will not be by . . . barbarians from below. Our barbarians come from above. Our great money-makers have sprung in one generation into seats of power kings do not know. The forces and the wealth are new, and have been the opportunity of new men. Without restraints of culture, experience, the pride, or even the inherited caution of class or rank, these men, intoxicated, think they are the wave instead of the float, and that they have created the business which has created them. To them science is but a never-ending repertoire of investments stored up by nature for the syndicates, government but a fountain of franchises, the nations but customers in squads, and a million the unit of a new arithmetic of wealth written for them. They claim a power without control, exercised through forms which make it secret, anonymous, and perpetual. . . .

. . . In casting about for the cause of our industrial evils, public opinion has successively found it in "competition," "combination," the "corporations," "conspiracies," "trusts." But competition has ended in combination, and our new wealth takes as it chooses the form of corporation or trust, or corporation again, and with every change grows greater and worse. Under these kaleidoscopic masks we begin at last to see progressing to its terminus a steady consolidation, the end of which is one-man power. The conspiracy ends in one, and one cannot conspire with himself. When this solidification of many into one has been reached, we shall be at last face to face with the naked truth that it is not only the form but the fact of arbitrary power, of control without consent, of rule without representation that concerns us.

Business motivated by the self-interest of the individual runs into monopoly at every point it touches the social life — land monopoly, transportation monopoly, trade monopoly, political monopoly in all its forms, from contraction of the currency to corruption in office. The society in which in half a lifetime a man without a penny can become a hundred times a millionaire is as over-ripe, industrially, as was, politically, the Rome in which the most popular bully could lift himself from the ranks of the legion on to the throne of the Caesars. Our rising issue is with business. Monopoly is business at the end of its journey. It has got there. The irrepressible conflict is now as distinctly with business as the issue so lately met was with slavery. Slavery went first only because it was the cruder form of business. . . .

Our system, so fair in its theory and so fertile in its happiness and prosperity in its first century, is now, following the fate of systems, becoming artificial, technical, corrupt; and, as always happens in human institutions, after noon, power is stealing from the many to the few. Believing wealth to be good, the people believed the wealthy to be good. But, again in history, power has intoxicated and hardened its possessors, and Pharaohs are bred in counting-rooms as they were in palaces. Their furniture must be banished to the world-garret [attic], where lie the out-worn trappings of the guilds and slavery and other old lumber of human institutions.

Source: Henry Demarest Lloyd, *Wealth against Commonwealth* (New York: Harper and Brothers, 1902), 510–12, 515.

Interpret the Evidence

1. Compare the attitudes of William Graham Sumner (Source 16.6) and Andrew Carnegie (Source 16.8) toward whether the wealthy have a responsibility to help the poor.

2. What historical evidence would support or refute the argument for federal intervention against big business found in Edward Bellamy's novel, Looking Backward (Source 16.7)?

3. How do wealthy Americans maintain their power at the expense of everyone else, according to Henry Demarest Lloyd (Source 16.9)?

4. What changes in U.S. society and government might Sumner, Carnegie, Bellamy, and Lloyd recommend for individuals to achieve success?

Put It in Context

Despite their different philosophies, what do these men think about the growth of organizations during the late nineteenth century?

Workers and Farmers in the Age of Organization

1877–1900

WINDOW TO THE PAST

Detail from Walter Huston, "Here Lies Prosperity," 1895

As this cartoon shows, the depression of 1893 had a devastating impact on American workers and farmers. According to critics, the economic policies of President Grover Cleveland and Congress increased the debt of working people and made it more difficult to repay. This situation led to protests and the formation of a new third party — the Populists. ▶ To discover more about what this primary source can show us, see Source 17.2 on page 580.

Detail of "The Situation . . . ," from Miller, *Populist Cartoons.*

After reading this chapter you should be able to:

- Explain how industrialization spurred the formation of labor organizations and how the government, in turn, responded to unionization.

- Analyze how industrialization affected rural life and how farmers responded to these changes.

- Compare the responses of industrial workers and farmers to the rise of big business.

- Explain the causes of the depression of 1893 and its consequences for workers, farmers, and politics.

COMPARING AMERICAN HISTORIES

John McLuckie worked at Andrew Carnegie's steel works in Homestead, Pennsylvania. In this town of some eleven thousand residents, where nearly everyone worked for Carnegie, the popular McLuckie was twice elected mayor and headed the Amalgamated Association of Iron and Steel Workers, one of the largest unions in the country. Although McLuckie earned a relatively decent income for that time, steelworkers and other industrial laborers had little power over the terms and conditions under which they worked. Visiting fraternal lodges and saloons, where steelworkers congregated, he spread the message of standing up to corporate leaders. "The constitution of this country," McLuckie declared,

(*left*) **John McLuckie.**
(*right*) **Mary Elizabeth Lease.** kansasmemory.org, Kansas State Historical Society

"guarantees all men the right to live, but in order to live we must keep up a continuous struggle."

In 1892 McLuckie faced the fight of his life when he battled with Carnegie and his plant manager, Henry Clay Frick, over wages and working conditions at the Homestead plant. Like Carnegie, the owners of a host of industries had created giant organizations that produced great wealth but also reshaped the working conditions of ordinary Americans. Toward the end of the nineteenth century, workers who labored for these industrial giants sought greater control over their employment by organizing unions to increase their power to negotiate with their employers. The events that unfolded in Homestead in 1892 revealed that workers were vastly outmatched in their struggle with management.

Mary Elizabeth Clyens was the daughter of Irish Catholic parents who came to the United States as part of the great wave of Irish immigration that began in the 1840s. Mary was raised in western Pennsylvania but moved to Kansas in 1870 to teach at a Catholic girls' school. There she met and married Charles L. Lease, a pharmacist turned farmer. The couple, however, could not support themselves and their children through farming, and in 1883 the Leases moved to Wichita. In Wichita, Mary found a much wider scope to express her interests and beliefs than she had on the farm. She joined a variety of organizations and worked in support of Irish independence, women's suffrage, and movements to advance the cause of industrial workers and farmers exploited by big business, railroads, and banks.

Lease entered state and national politics through the Populist Party, which formed in 1890 to challenge the power of large corporations and their political allies, promote the interests of small farmers, and create an alliance between farmers and industrial workers. A mesmerizing speaker, she urged her audiences, according to reporters, to "raise less corn and more hell." Lease offered a variety of remedies for late-nineteenth-century America's economic and political ills, including nationalizing railroad and telegraph lines, increasing the currency supply, and expanding popular democracy. She also agitated for women's rights and voiced her determination "to place the mothers of this nation on an equality with the fathers." Following the collapse of the Populist Party in 1896, Lease and her family moved to New York City.

She worked as a journalist, divorced her husband, and remained active as a speaker for educational reform and birth control until her death in 1931. ■

The American histories of John McLuckie and Mary Elizabeth Lease were linked by the economic and political forces that shaped the lives of both factory workers and farmers in industrialized America. Even though the culture of rural America was quite different from that of the nation's industrial towns and cities, farmers and workers faced many of the same problems. Over the course of the late nineteenth century, both groups had seen control over the nature and terms of their work pass from the individual worker or farmer to large corporations and financial institutions. McLuckie and Lease were part of a larger effort by laborers and farmers to fight for their own interests against the concentrated economic and political power of big business and to regain control of their lives and their work. In the 1890s, a severe economic depression made the situation even worse for farmers and industrial workers. Many of them joined the newly formed Populist Party to challenge the two major political parties for failing to represent their concerns.

Working People Organize

Industrialists were not the only ones who built organizations to promote their economic interests. Like their employers, working men and women also saw the benefits of organizing to increase their political and economic leverage. Determined to secure decent wages and working conditions, workers joined labor unions, formed political parties, and engaged in a variety of collective actions, including strikes. However, workers' organizations were beset by internal conflicts over occupational status, race, ethnicity, and gender. They proved no match for the powerful alliance between corporations and the federal government that stood against them, and they failed to become a lasting national political force. Workers fared better in their own communities, where family, neighbors, and local businesses were more likely to come to their aid.

The Industrialization of Labor. The industrialization of the United States transformed the workplace, bringing together large numbers of laborers under difficult conditions. In 1870 few factories employed 500 or more workers. Thirty years later, more than 1,500 companies had workforces of this size. Just after the Civil War, manufacturing employed 5.3 million workers; thirty years later, the figure soared to more than 15.1 million. Most of these new industrial workers came from two main sources. First, farmers like the Leases who could not make a decent living from the soil moved to nearby cities in search of factory jobs. Although mostly white, this group also included blacks who sought to escape the oppressive conditions of sharecropping. Between 1870 and 1890, some 80,000 African Americans journeyed from the rural South to cities in the South and the North to search for employment. Second, the economic opportunities in America drew millions of immigrants from Europe over the course of the nineteenth century. Immigrant workers initially came from northern Europe. However, by the end of the nineteenth century, the number of immigrants from southern and eastern European countries had surpassed those coming from northern Europe.

Inside factories, **unskilled workers**, those with no particular skill or expertise, encountered a system undergoing critical changes, as small-scale manufacturing gave way to larger and more mechanized operations. Immigrants, who made up the bulk of unskilled laborers, had to adjust both to a new country and to unfamiliar, unpleasant, and often dangerous industrial work. A traveler from Hungary who visited a steel mill in Pittsburgh that employed many Hungarian immigrants compared the factories to prisons where "the heat is most insupportable, the flames most choking." Nor were any government benefits — such as workers' compensation or unemployment insurance — available to industrial laborers who were hurt in accidents or laid off from their jobs.

Skilled workers, who had particular training or abilities and were more difficult to replace, were not immune to the changes brought about by industrialization and the rise of large-scale businesses. In the early days of manufacturing, skilled laborers operated as independent craftsmen. They provided their own tools, worked at their own pace, and controlled their production output. This approach to work enhanced their sense of personal dignity, reflected their notion of themselves as free citizens, and distinguished them from the mass of unskilled laborers. Mechanization, however, undercut their autonomy by dictating both the nature and the speed of production through practices of scientific management. Instead of producing goods, skilled workers increasingly applied their craft to servicing machinery and keeping it running smoothly. While owners reaped the benefits of the mechanization and regimentation of the industrial workplace, many skilled workers saw such "improvements" as a threat to their freedom.

Explore ▶

See Source 17.1 for one worker's opinion on mechanization.

Still, most workers did not oppose the technology that increased their productivity and resulted in higher wages. Compared to their mid-nineteenth-century counterparts, industrial laborers now made up a larger share of the general population, earned more money, and worked fewer hours. During the 1870s and 1880s, the average industrial worker's real wages (actual buying power) increased by 20 percent. At the same time, the average workday declined from ten and a half hours to ten hours. From 1870 to 1890, the general price index dropped 30 percent, allowing consumers to benefit from lower prices.

Yet workers were far from content, and the lives of industrial workers remained extremely difficult. Although workers as a group saw improvements in wages and hours, they did not earn enough income to support their families adequately. Also, there were widespread disparities based on job status, race, ethnicity, sex, and region. Skilled workers earned more than unskilled workers. Whites were paid more than African Americans, who were mainly shut out of better jobs. Immigrants from northern Europe, who had settled in the United States before southern Europeans, tended to hold higher-paying skilled positions. Southern factory workers, whether in textiles, steel, or armaments, earned less than their northern counterparts. And women, an increasingly important component of the industrial workforce, earned, on average, only 25 percent of what men did.

Between 1870 and 1900, the number of female wageworkers grew by 66 percent, accounting for about one-quarter of all nonfarm laborers. The majority of employed women, including those working in factories, were single and between the ages of sixteen and twenty-four. Overall, only 5 percent of married women worked outside the home, although 30 percent of African American wives were employed. Women workers were

GUIDED ANALYSIS

John Morrison | Testimony on the Impact of Mechanization, 1883

Like other skilled laborers, New York City machinist John Morrison saw the introduction of machinery that accompanied industrialization as a threat to his identity as a craftsman. In the following excerpt from his testimony before a U.S. Senate committee investigating conflicts between capital and labor, Morrison discusses the source of many skilled workingmen's discontent.

Source 17.1

What are the problems with subdividing the machinist trade?

Why do manufacturers favor subdivision of labor?

Which of these tactics do you think might have benefited skilled workers the most?

Question: Is there any difference between the conditions under which machinery is made now and those which existed ten years ago?

Answer: A great deal of difference.

Question: State the differences as well as you can.

Answer: Well, the trade has been subdivided and those subdivisions have been again subdivided, so that a man never learns the machinist's trade now. Ten years ago he learned, not the whole of the trade, but a fair portion of it. Also, there is more machinery used in the business, which again makes machinery. The different branches of the trade are divided and subdivided so that one man may make just a particular part of a machine and may not know anything whatever about another part of the same machine. In that way machinery is produced a great deal cheaper than it used to be formerly, and in fact, through this system of work, 100 men are able to do now what it took 300 or 400 men to do fifteen years ago. By the use of machinery and the subdivision of the trade they so simplify the work that it is made a great deal easier and put together a great deal faster. There is no system of apprenticeship, I may say, in the business. You simply go in and learn whatever branch you are put at, and you stay at that unless you are changed to another. . . .

Question: Are the machinists here generally contented, or are they in a state of discontent and unrest?

Answer: There is mostly a general feeling of discontent, and you will find among the machinists the most radical workingmen, with the most revolutionary ideas. You will find that they don't so much give their thoughts simply to trade unions and other efforts of that kind, but they go far beyond that; they only look for relief through the ballot or through a revolution, a forcible revolution.

Source: *Report of the Committee of the Senate upon the Relations between Labor and Capital*, 48th Cong. (1885), 755–59.

Put It in Context

How did the introduction of machinery affect skilled workers?

concentrated in several areas. White and black women continued to serve as maids and domestics. Others took over jobs that were once occupied by men. They became teachers, nurses, clerical workers, telephone operators, and department store salesclerks. Other women toiled in manufacturing jobs requiring fine eye-hand coordination, such as cigar rolling and work in the needle trades and textile industry.

Women also turned their homes into workplaces. In crowded apartments, they sewed furs onto garments, made straw hats, prepared artificial flowers, and fashioned jewelry. Earnings from piecework (work that pays at a set rate per unit) were even lower than factory wages, but they allowed married women with young children to contribute to the family income. When sufficient space was available, families rented rooms to boarders, and women provided meals and housekeeping for the lodgers. Some female workers found other ways to balance work with the needs and constraints of family life. To gain greater autonomy in their work, black laundresses began cleaning clothes in their own homes, rather than their white employers' homes, so that they could control their own work hours. In 1881 black washerwomen in Atlanta conducted a two-week strike to secure higher fees from white customers.

Manufacturing also employed many child workers. By 1900 about 10 percent of girls and 20 percent of boys between the ages of ten and fifteen worked, and at least 1.7 million children under the age of sixteen held jobs. Employers often exposed children to dangerous and unsanitary conditions. Most child workers toiled long, hard hours breathing in dust and fumes as they labored in textile mills, tobacco plants, print shops, and coal mines. In Indiana, young boys worked the night shift in dark, windowless glass factories. Children under the age of ten, known as "breaker boys," climbed onto filthy coal heaps and picked out unprocessed material. Working up to twelve-hour days, these children received less than a dollar a day.

Women and children worked because the average male head of household could not support his family on his own pay, despite the increase in real wages. As Carroll D. Wright, director of the Massachusetts Bureau of the Statistics of Labor, reported in 1882, "A family of workers can always live well, but the man with a family of small children to support, unless his wife works also, has a small chance of living properly." For example, in 1883 in Joliet, Illinois, a railroad brakeman tried to support his wife and eight children on $360 a year. A state investigator described the way they lived: "Clothes ragged, children half dressed and dirty. They all sleep in one room regardless of sex. The house is devoid of furniture, and the entire concern is as wretched as could be imagined." Not all laborers lived in such squalor, but many wageworkers barely lived at subsistence level.

Although the average number of working hours dropped during this era, many laborers put in more than 10 hours a day on the job. In the steel industry, blast-furnace operators toiled 12 hours a day, 7 days a week. They received a day off every 2 weeks, but only if they worked a 24-hour shift. Given the long hours and backbreaking work, it is not surprising that accidents were a regular feature of industrial life. Each year tens of thousands were injured on the job, and thousands died as a result of mine cave-ins, train wrecks, explosions in industrial plants, and fires at textile mills and garment factories. Railroad employment was especially unsafe — accidents ended the careers of one in six workers.

Agricultural refugees who flocked to cotton mills in the South also faced dangerous working conditions. Working twelve-hour days breathing the lint-filled air from the processed cotton posed health hazards. Textile workers also had to place their hands into

Chinese American Telephone Operator   The invention of the telephone brought jobs to many Americans, especially women. Yet not all operators were women, as this photograph shows. San Francisco's Chinatown employed workers from its own community, and in this photo a Chinese man works as a telephone operator while a child in a school uniform and another man stand by him. Library of Congress, Prints & Photographs Division, Reproduction number LC-USZC2-3755 (color film copy slide)

heavy machinery to disentangle threads, making them extremely vulnerable to serious injury. Wages scarcely covered necessities, and on many occasions families did not know where their next meal was coming from. North Carolina textile worker J. W. Mehaffry complained that the mill owners "were slave drivers" who "work their employees, women, and children from 6 a.m. to 7 p.m. with a half hour for lunch." Mill workers' meals usually consisted of potatoes, cornbread, and dried beans cooked in fat. This diet, without dairy products and fresh meat, led to outbreaks of pellagra, a debilitating disease caused by niacin (vitamin B3) deficiency.

Although wages and working hours improved slightly for some workers, employers kept the largest share of the increased profits that resulted from industrialization. In 1877 John D. Rockefeller collected dividends at the rate of at least $720 an hour, roughly double what his average employee earned in a year. Despite some success stories, prospects for upward mobility for most American workers remained limited. A manual worker might rise into the ranks of the semiskilled but would not make it into the middle class. And to achieve even this small upward mobility required putting the entire family to work and engaging in rigorous economizing, what one historian called "ruthless underconsumption." Despite their best efforts, most Americans remained part of the working class.

Organizing Unions.   Faced with improving but inadequate wages and with hazardous working conditions, industrial laborers sought to counter the concentrated power of corporate capitalists by joining forces. They attempted to organize **unions** — groups of workers seeking rights and benefits from their employers through their collective efforts. Union organizing was prompted by attitudes that were common among employers. Most employers were convinced that they and their employees shared identical interests, and they believed that they were morally and financially entitled to establish policies on their

workers' behalf. They refused to engage in negotiations with labor unions (a process known as **collective bargaining**). Although owners appreciated the advantages of companies banding together to eliminate competition or to lobby for favorable regulations, similar collective efforts by workers struck them as unfair, even immoral. It was up to the men who supplied the money and the machines — rather than the workers — to determine what was a fair wage and what were satisfactory working conditions. In 1877 William H. Vanderbilt, the son of transportation tycoon Cornelius Vanderbilt, explained this way of thinking: "Our men feel that although I . . . may have my millions and they the rewards of their daily toil, still we are about equal in the end. If they suffer, I suffer, and if I suffer they cannot escape." Needless to say, many workers disagreed.

Industrialists expected their paternalistic values to reduce grievances among their workforce. They sponsored sports teams, set up social clubs, and offered cultural activities. The railroad magnate George Pullman built a model village to house his workers. In return, capitalists demanded unquestioned loyalty from their employees.

Yet a growing number of working people failed to see the relationship between employer and employee as mutually beneficial. Increasingly, they considered labor unions to be the best vehicle for communication and negotiation between workers and owners. Though not the first national workers' organization, the **Noble Order of the Knights of Labor**, founded by Uriah Stephens in 1869, initiated the most extensive and successful campaign after the Civil War to unite workers and challenge the power of corporate capitalists. "There is no mutuality of interests . . . [between] capital and labor," the Massachusetts chapter of the Knights proclaimed. "It is the iron heel of a soulless monopoly, crushing the manhood out of sovereign citizens." In fact, the essential premise of the Knights was that all workers shared common interests that were very different from those of owners.

The Knights did not enjoy immediate success and did not really begin to flourish until Terence V. Powderly became Grand Master of the organization in 1879. Powderly advocated the eight-hour workday, the abolition of child labor, and equal pay for women. Under his leadership, the Knights accepted African Americans, immigrants, and women as members, though they excluded Chinese immigrant workers, as did other labor unions. As a result, the Knights experienced a surge in membership from 9,000 in 1879 to nearly a million in 1885, about 10 percent of the industrial workforce.

Rapid growth proved to be a mixed blessing. As membership grew, Powderly and the national organization exercised less and less control over local chapters. In fact, local chapters often defied the central organization by engaging in strikes, a tactic Powderly had officially disavowed. Nonetheless, members of the Knights struck successfully against the Union Pacific Railroad and the Missouri Pacific Railroad in 1885. The following year, on May 1, 1886, local assemblies of the Knights joined a nationwide strike to press for an eight-hour workday. However, this strike was soon overshadowed by events in Chicago that would prove to be the undoing of the Knights (Figure 17.1).

For months before the general strike, the McCormick Harvester plant in Chicago had been at the center of an often violent conflict over wages and work conditions. On May 3, 1886, police killed two strikers in a clash between union members and strikebreakers who tried to cross the picket lines. In response, a group of anarchists led by the German-born activist August Spies called for a rally in **Haymarket Square** to protest police violence. Consisting mainly of foreign-born radicals, such anarchists believed that

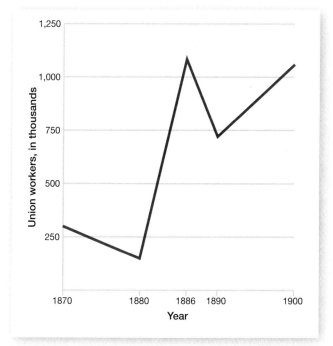

FIGURE 17.1   Union Membership, 1870–1900

Union membership fluctuated widely in the late nineteenth century. After reaching a low point in 1880, the number of union members rebounded. However, membership plummeted after 1886 only to soar again in the 1890s. Explain the rise and fall of union membership from 1880 through 1900.

Source: Data from Richard B. Freeman, "Spurts in Union Growth: Defining Moments and Social Processes," working paper 6012, National Bureau of Economic Research, Cambridge, MA, 1997.

government represented the interests of capitalists and stifled freedom for workers. Anarchists differed among themselves, but they generally advocated tearing down government authority, restoring personal freedom, and forming worker communes to replace capitalism. To achieve their goals, anarchists like Spies advocated the violent overthrow of government.

The Haymarket rally began at 8:30 in the evening of May 4 and attracted no more than 1,500 people, who listened to a series of speeches as rain fell. By 10:30 p.m., when the crowd had dwindled to some 300 people, 180 policemen decided to break it up. As police moved into the square, someone set off a bomb. The police fired back, and when the smoke cleared, seven policemen and four protesters lay dead. Most of the fatalities and injuries resulted from the police crossfire. A subsequent trial convicted eight anarchists of murder, though there was no evidence that any of them had planted the bomb or used weapons. Four of them, including Spies, were executed. Although Powderly and other union leaders denounced the anarchists and the bombing, the incident greatly tarnished the labor movement. Capitalists and their allies in the press attacked labor unionists as radicals prone to violence and denounced strikes as un-American. Following the Haymarket incident, the membership rolls of the Knights plunged to below 500,000. By the mid-1890s, the Knights had fewer than 20,000 members.

As the fortunes of the Knights of Labor faded, the **American Federation of Labor (AFL)** grew in prominence, offering an alternative vision of unionization. Instead of one giant industrial union that included all workers, skilled and unskilled, the AFL organized only skilled craftsmen — the labor elite — into trade unions. In 1886 Samuel Gompers became president of the AFL. Gompers considered trade unions "the business organizations

Women in the Labor Movement, 1884   This wood engraving shows the wives of striking coal miners jeering at Pinkerton detectives as they escort strikebreakers into the mines in Buchtel, Ohio in 1884. It was common for the family and friends of strikers in local communities to rally support on their behalf. Granger.

of the wage earners to attend to the business of the wage earners" and favored the use of strikes. No social reformer, the AFL president concentrated on obtaining better wages and hours for workers so that they could share in the prosperity generated by industrial capitalism. By 1900 the AFL had around a million members. It achieved these numbers by recruiting the most independent, highest-paid, and least replaceable segment of the labor force — white male skilled workers. Unlike the Knights, the AFL had little or no place for women and African Americans in its ranks.

As impressive as the AFL's achievement was, the union movement as a whole experienced only limited success in the late nineteenth century. Only about one in fifteen industrial workers belonged to a union in 1900. Union membership was low for a variety of reasons. First, the political and economic power of corporations and the prospects of retaliation made the decision to sign up for union membership a risky venture. Second, the diversity of workers made organizing a difficult task. Foreign-born laborers came from many countries and were divided by language, religion, ethnicity, and history. Moreover, European immigrants quickly adopted native-born whites' racial prejudices against African Americans. Third, despite severe limitations in social mobility, American workers generally retained their faith in the benefits of the capitalist system. Finally, the government used its legal and military authority to side with employers and suppress militant workers.

Southern workers were the most resistant to union organizing. The agricultural background of mill workers left them with a heightened sense of individualism and isolation.

In addition, their continued connection to family and friends in the countryside offered a potential escape route from industrial labor. Moreover, employers' willingness to use racial tensions to divide working-class blacks and whites prevented them from joining together to further their common economic interests.

Clashes between Workers and Owners.

Despite the difficulties of organizing workers, labor challenged some of the nation's largest industries in the late nineteenth century. Faced with owners' refusal to recognize or negotiate with unions, workers marshaled their greatest source of power: withholding their labor and going on strike. Employers in turn had powerful weapons at their command to break strikes. They could recruit strikebreakers and mobilize private and public security forces to protect their businesses. That workers went on strike against such odds testified to their desperation and courage (Map 17.1).

Workers in the United States were not alone in their efforts to combat industrial exploitation. In England, laborers organized for better wages and working conditions. In 1888 in London, young women who worked at a match factory staged a walkout to protest the exorbitant fines that employers imposed on them for arriving even one minute late to

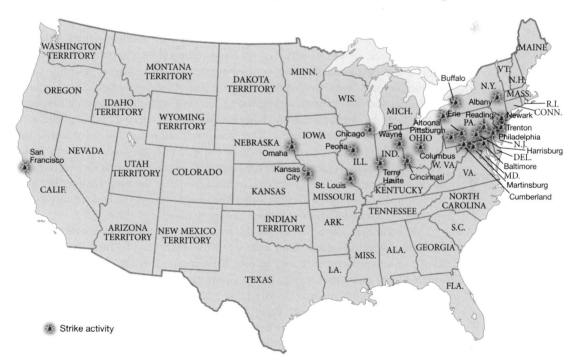

★ Strike activity

MAP 17.1   The Great Railroad Strike

This nationwide strike, precipitated by falling wages during the Depression of 1873, started in West Virginia and Pennsylvania and spread to Chicago, St. Louis, and San Francisco. The strike brought a halt to rail traffic as over 100,000 workers and another half a million sympathizers walked off their jobs. Violence broke out in Pittsburgh, resulting in more than twenty deaths. Federal troops were eventually dispatched to end the strike. Many workers quickly recognized the need to form union to gain power to stand up against employers and the government.

work. With community support, they won their demands. From 1888 to 1890, the number of strikes throughout Europe grew from 188 to 289. In 1890 thousands of workers in Budapest, Hungary rose up to protest unsafe working conditions. European workers also campaigned for the right to vote, which unlike white male American workers, they were denied on economic grounds.

In the United States in the 1890s, labor mounted several highly publicized strikes. Perhaps the most famous was the 1892 **Homestead strike**. Steelworkers at Carnegie's Homestead, Pennsylvania factory near Pittsburgh played an active role in local politics and civic affairs. Residents generally believed that Andrew Carnegie's corporation paid decent wages that allowed them to support their families and buy their own homes. In 1892 craftsmen earned $180 a month, and they appeared to have Carnegie's respect. Others, like John McLuckie, earned less than half that amount, and unskilled workers made even less.

In 1892, with steel prices falling, Carnegie decided to replace some of his skilled craftsmen with machinery, cut wages, save on labor costs, and bust McLuckie's union, the Amalgamated Association of Iron and Steel Workers. Knowing that his actions would provoke a strike and seeking to avoid the negative publicity that would result, Carnegie left the country and went to Scotland, leaving his plant manager, Henry Clay Frick, in charge.

Fiercely anti-union, Frick prepared for the strike by building a three-mile, fifteen-foot-high fence, capped with barbed wire and equipped with searchlights, around three sides of the Homestead factory. A hated symbol of the manager's hostility, the fence became known as "Fort Frick." Along the fourth side of the factory flowed the Monongahela River. Frick had no intention of negotiating seriously with the union on a new contract, and on July 1 he ordered a lockout. Only employees who rejected the union and accepted lower wages could return to work. The small town rallied around the workers, and the union members won a temporary victory. On July 6, barge-loads of armed Pinkerton detectives, hired by Frick to protect the plant, set sail toward the factory entrance alongside the Monongahela. From the shore, union men shot at the barges and set fire to a boat they pushed toward the Pinkertons. When the smoke cleared, the Pinkertons surrendered and hastily retreated onshore as women and men chased after them.

This triumph proved costly for the union. The battle left nine strikers and three Pinkerton detectives dead. Frick convinced the governor of Pennsylvania to send in state troops to protect the factory and the strikebreakers. Frick's efforts to end the strike spurred some radicals to action. Emma Goldman, an anarchist who advocated the violent overthrow of capitalism, declared that a blow against Frick would "strike terror in the enemy's ranks and make them realize that the proletariat of America had its avengers." On July 23, Alexander Berkman, Goldman's partner, who had no connection with the union, entered Frick's office and shot the steel executive in the neck, leaving him wounded but alive. The resulting unfavorable publicity, together with the state's prosecution of the union, broke the strike. Subsequently, steel companies blacklisted the union leaders for life, and McLuckie fled Pennsylvania and wound up nearly penniless in Arizona.

Like Andrew Carnegie, George Pullman considered himself an enlightened employer, one who took good care of the men who worked in his luxury sleeping railcar factory outside Chicago. However, also like the steel titan, Pullman placed profits over personnel. In

The Homestead Steel Strike, 1892   This lithograph depicts the battle between strikers at the Carnegie Steelworks in Homestead, Pennsylvania and Pinkerton detectives brought in to protect the mill and break the strike. The Pinkertons attempted to get to the plant by barge but were repelled by the strikers from the dock. The strike received international attention, and this illustration appeared in the British weekly newspaper *The Graphic* on July 30, 1892. Private Collection/Peter Newark American Pictures/Bridgeman Images

1893 a severe economic depression prompted Pullman to cut wages without correspondingly reducing the rents that his employees paid for living in company houses. This dual blow to worker income and purchasing power led to a fierce strike the following year. The Pullman workers belonged to the American Railway Union, headed by Eugene V. Debs. After George Pullman refused to negotiate, the union voted to go on strike.

In the end, the **Pullman strike** was broken not by the Pullman company but by the federal government. President Grover Cleveland ordered federal troops to get the railroads operating, but the workers still refused to capitulate. Richard Olney, Cleveland's attorney general, then obtained an order from the federal courts to restrain Debs and other union leaders from continuing the strike. The government used the Sherman Antitrust Act to punish unions for conspiring to restrain trade, something it had rarely done with respect to large corporations. Refusing to comply, Debs and other union officials were charged with contempt, convicted under the Sherman Antitrust Act, and sent to jail. The strike collapsed. **See Primary Source Project 17: The Pullman Strike of 1894, page 590.**

Debs remained unrepentant. After serving his jail sentence, he became even more radical. In 1901 he helped establish the Socialist Party of America. German exiles who came to the United States following revolutions in Europe in 1848 had brought with them the revolutionary ideas of the German philosopher Karl Marx. Marx argued that capital and labor were engaged in a class struggle that would end with the violent over-throw of capitalist government and its replacement by communism. Marxist ideas attracted a small following in the United States, mainly among the foreign-born popu-lation. By contrast, other types of European socialists, including the German Social Democratic Party, appealed for working-class support by advocating the creation of a more just and humane economic system through the ballot box, not by violent revolu-tion. Debs favored this nonviolent, democratic brand of socialism and managed to attract a broader base of supporters by articulating socialist doctrines in the language of cooperation and citizenship that many Americans shared. Debsian socialism appealed not only to industrial workers but also to dispossessed farmers and miners in the Southwest and Midwest.

Western miners had a history of labor activism, and by the 1890s they were ready to listen to radical ideas. Shortly after the Homestead strike ended in 1892, silver miners in Coeur d'Alene, Idaho walked out after owners slashed their wages. Employers refused to recognize any union, obtained an injunction against the strike, imported strikebreakers to run the mines, and persuaded Idaho's governor to impose martial law, in which the military took over the normal operation of civilian affairs. The work stoppage lasted four months, resulting in the arrest of six hundred strikers. Although the workers lost, the following year they succeeded in forming the Western Federation of Miners, which continued their fight.

The **Industrial Workers of the World (IWW)**, which emerged largely through the efforts of the Western Federation of Miners, sought to raise wages, improve working con-ditions, and gain union recognition for the most exploited segments of American labor. The IWW, or "Wobblies" as they were popularly known, sought to unite all skilled and unskilled workers in an effort to overthrow capitalism. The Wobblies favored strikes and direct-action protests rather than collective bargaining or mediation. At their rallies and strikes, they often encountered government force and corporation-inspired mob violence. Nevertheless, the IWW had substantial appeal among lumberjacks in the Northwest, dockworkers in port cities, miners in the West, farmers in the Great Plains, and textile workers in the Northeast.

Even though industrialists usually had state and federal governments as well as the media on their side, workers continued to press for their rights. Workers used strikes as a last resort when business owners refused to negotiate or recognize their demands to orga-nize themselves into unions. Although most late-nineteenth-century strikes failed, strik-ing unionists nonetheless called for collective bargaining, higher wages, shorter hours, and improved working conditions—an agenda that unions and their political allies would build on in the future.

Working-Class Leisure in Industrial America.
Despite the hardships indus-trial laborers faced in the late nineteenth century, workers carved out recreational spaces that they could control and that offered relief from their backbreaking toil. For many, Sun-day became a day of rest that took on a secular flavor.

Working-class leisure patterns varied by gender, race, and region. Women did not gen-erally attend spectator sporting events, such as baseball and boxing matches, which catered to men. Nor did they find themselves comfortable in union halls and saloons, where men found solace in drink. Working-class wives preferred to gather to prepare for births, wed-dings, and funerals or to assist neighbors who had suffered some misfortune.

Once employed, working-class daughters found a greater measure of independence and free time by living in rooming houses on their own. Women's wages were only a small fraction of men's earnings, so workingwomen rarely made enough money to support a regular social life. Still, they found ways to enjoy their free time. Some single women went out in groups, hoping to meet men who would pay for drinks, food, or a vaudeville show. Others dated so that they knew they would be taken care of for the evening. Some of the men who "treated" on a date assumed a right to sexual favors in return, and some of these women then expected men to provide them with housing and gifts in exchange for an ongoing sexual relationship. Thus emotional and economic relationships became intertwined.

Around the turn of the twentieth century, dance halls flourished as one of the mainstays of working-class communities. Huge dance palaces were built in the entertainment districts of most large cities. They made their money by offering music with lengthy intermissions for the sale of drinks and refreshments. Women and men also attended nightclubs, some of which were racially integrated. In so-called red-light districts of the city, prostitutes earned money entertaining their clients with a variety of sexual pleasures.

Vaudeville, 1897   The popular comedy team of J. Sherrie Matthews and Harry Bulger performed in vaudeville shows throughout the country. This photo, taken in the San Francisco Bay area, shows Matthews playing the mandolin while Bulger dances. Notice the braid running down the front of Bulger's costume, apparently an attempt to ridicule the Chinese population in the area. In similar fashion, in minstrel shows, the predecessor of vaudeville, whites appeared in blackface to mock African Americans. University of Washington Libraries, Special Collections, UW36672

Not all forms of leisure were strictly segregated along class lines. A number of forms of cheap entertainment appealed not only to working-class women and men but also to their middle-class counterparts. By the turn of the twentieth century, most large American cities featured amusement parks. Brooklyn's Coney Island stood out as the most spectacular of these sprawling playgrounds. In 1884, the world's first roller coaster was built at Coney Island, providing thrills to those brave enough to ride it. In Chicago at the 1893 World's Columbian Exposition, residents enjoyed the new Ferris wheel, which soared 250 feet in the air. Vaudeville houses — with their minstrel shows (whites in blackface) and comedians, singers, and dancers — brought howls of laughter to working-class audiences. Nickelodeons charged five cents to watch short films. Live theater generally attracted more wealthy patrons; however, the Yiddish theater, which flourished on New York's Lower East Side, and other immigrant-oriented stage productions appealed mainly to working-class audiences.

Itinerant musicians entertained audiences throughout the South. Lumber camps, which employed mainly African American men, offered a popular destination for these musicians. Each camp contained a "barrelhouse," also called a honky tonk or a juke joint. Besides showcasing music, the barrelhouse also gave workers the opportunity to "shoot craps, dice, drink whiskey, dance, every modern devilment you can do," as one musician who played there recalled. From the Mississippi delta emerged a new form of music — the blues. W. C. Handy, "the father of the blues," discovered this music in his travels through the delta, where he observed southern blacks performing songs of woe, accompanying themselves with anything that would make a "musical sound or rhythmical effect, anything from a harmonica to a washboard." Meanwhile in New Orleans, an amalgam of black musical forms evolved into jazz. Musicians such as "Jelly Roll" Morton experimented with a variety of sounds, putting together African and Caribbean rhythms with European music, mixing pianos with clarinets, trumpets, and drums. Blues and jazz spread throughout the South.

In mountain valley mill towns, southern whites preferred "old-time" music, but with a twist: they modified the lyrics of traditional ballads and folk songs, originally enjoyed by British settlers, to extol the exploits of outlaws and adventurers. Country music, which combined romantic ballads and folk tunes to the accompaniment of guitars, banjos, autoharps, dulcimers, and organs, emerged as a distinct brand of music by the twentieth century. As with African Americans, in the late nineteenth century working-class and rural whites found new and exciting types of music to entertain them in their leisure. Religious music also appealed to both white and black audiences and drew crowds to evangelical revivals.

Mill workers also amused themselves by engaging in social, recreational, and religious activities. Women visited each other and exchanged confidences, gossip, advice on child rearing, and folk remedies. Men from various factories organized baseball teams that competed in leagues. Managers of a mill in Charlotte, North Carolina admitted that they "frequently hired men better known for their batting averages than their work records."

REVIEW & RELATE

• How did industrialization change the American workplace? What challenges did it create for American workers?

• How did workers resist the concentrated power of industrial capitalists in the late nineteenth century, and why did such efforts have only limited success?

Farmers Organize

Like industrial workers, farmers experienced severe economic hardships and a loss of political power in the face of rapid industrialization. The introduction of new machinery such as the combine harvester, introduced in 1878, led to substantial increases in the productivity of American farms. Soaring production, however, led to a decline in agricultural prices in the late nineteenth century, a trend that was accelerated by increased agricultural production around the world. Faced with an economic crisis caused by falling prices and escalating debt, farmers fought back, creating new organizations to champion their collective economic and political interests.

Farmers Unite.

From the end of the Civil War to the mid-1890s, increased production of wheat and cotton, two of the most important American crops, led to a precipitous drop in the price for these crops. Falling prices created a debt crisis for many farmers. Most American farmers were independent businessmen who borrowed money to pay for land, seed, and equipment. When their crops were harvested and sold, they repaid their debts with the proceeds. As prices fell, farmers increased production in an effort to cover their debts. This tactic led to a greater supply of farm produce in the marketplace and even lower prices. Unable to pay back loans, many farmers lost their property in foreclosures to the banks that held their mortgages and furnished them credit.

To make matters worse, farmers lived isolated lives. Spread out across vast acres of rural territory, farmers had few social and cultural diversions. As the farm economy declined, more and more of their children left the monotony of rural America behind and headed for cities in search of new opportunities and a better life.

Early efforts to organize farmers were motivated by a desire to counteract the isolation of rural life by creating new forms of social interaction and cultural engagement. In 1867, Oliver H. Kelly founded the Patrons of Husbandry to brighten the lonely existence of rural Americans through educational and social activities. Known as **Grangers** (from the French word for "granary"), the association grew rapidly in the early 1870s, especially in the Midwest and the South. Between 1872 and 1874, approximately fourteen thousand new Grange chapters were established.

Grangers also formed farm cooperatives to sell their crops at higher prices and pool their purchasing power to buy finished goods at wholesale prices. The Grangers' interest in promoting the collective economic interests of farmers led to their increasing involvement in politics. Rather than forming a separate political party, Grangers endorsed candidates who favored their cause. Perhaps their most important objective was the regulation of shipping and grain storage prices. In many areas, individual railroads had monopolies on both of these services and, as a result, were able to charge farmers higher-than-usual rates to store and ship their crops. By electing sympathetic state legislators, Grangers managed to obtain regulations that placed a ceiling on the prices railroads and grain elevators could charge. The Supreme Court temporarily upheld these victories in *Munn v. Illinois* (1877). In 1886, however, in *Wabash v. Illinois* the Supreme Court reversed itself and struck down these state regulatory laws as hindering the free flow of interstate commerce.

Another apparent victory for regulation came in 1887 when Congress passed the Interstate Commerce Act, establishing the **Interstate Commerce Commission (ICC)** to regulate railroads. Although big businessmen could not prevent occasional government regulation, they managed to render it largely ineffective. In time, railroad advocates came

Granger Movement, 1876   As the farmer's central placement in this lithograph implies, farmers were the heart of the Granger movement. The title is a variation on the movement's motto, "I Pay for All." A farmer with a plough and two horses stands at the center of the scene providing food for all, while other occupational types positioned around him echo a similar refrain based on their profession. Note the attitude toward the broker implied by the label "I Fleece You All." Library of Congress, LC-DIG-pga-00025

to dominate the ICC and enforced the law in favor of the railway lines rather than the shippers. Implementation of the Sherman Antitrust Act also favored big business. From the standpoint of most late-nineteenth-century capitalists, national regulations often turned out to be more of a help than a hindrance.

By the late 1880s, the Grangers had abandoned electoral politics and once again devoted themselves strictly to social and cultural activities. A number of factors explain the Grangers' return to their original mission. First, prices began to rise for some crops, particularly corn, relieving the economic pressure on midwestern farmers. Second, the passage of regulatory legislation in a number of states convinced some Grangers that their political goals had been achieved. Finally, a lack of marketing and business experience led to the collapse of many agricultural collectives.

The withdrawal of the Grangers from politics did not, however, signal the end of efforts by farmers to form organizations to advance their economic interests. While farmers in the midwestern corn belt experienced some political success and an economic upturn, farmers farther west in the Great Plains and in the Lower South fell more deeply into debt, as the price of wheat and cotton on the international market continued to drop. In both of these regions, farmers organized **Farmers' Alliances**. In the 1880s, Milton George formed the Northwestern Farmers' Alliance. At the same time, Dr. Charles W. Macune organized the much larger Southern Farmers' Alliance. Southern black farmers, excluded from the Southern Farmers' Alliance, created a parallel Colored Farmers' Alliance. The Alliances formed a network of recruiters to sign up new members. No recruiter was more effective than Mary Elizabeth Lease, who excited farm audiences with her forceful and colorful rhetoric, delivering 160 speeches in the summer of 1890 alone. The Southern Farmers' Alliance advocated a sophisticated plan to solve the farmers' problem of mounting debt. Macune devised a proposal for a **subtreasury system**. Under this plan, the federal government would locate offices near warehouses in which farmers could store nonperishable commodities. In return, farmers would receive federal loans for 80 percent of the current market value of their produce. In theory, temporarily taking crops off the market would decrease supply and, assuming demand remained stable, lead to increased prices. Once prices rose, farmers would return to the warehouses, redeem their crops, sell them at the higher price, repay the government loan, and leave with a profit.

The first step toward creating a nationwide farmers' organization came in 1889, when the Northwestern and Southern Farmers' Alliances agreed to merge. Alliance leaders, including Lease, saw workers as fellow victims of industrialization, and they invited the Knights of Labor to join them. They also attempted to lower prevailing racial barriers by bringing the Colored Farmers' Alliance into the coalition. The following year, the National Farmers' Alliance and Industrial Union held its convention in Ocala, Florida. The group adopted resolutions endorsing the subtreasury system, as well as recommendations that would promote the economic welfare of farmers and extend political democracy to "the plain people." These proposals included tariff reduction, government ownership of banks and railroads, and political reforms to extend democracy, such as direct election of U.S. senators.

Finally, the Alliance pressed the government to increase the money supply by expanding the amount of silver coinage in circulation. In the Alliance's view, such a move would have two positive, and related, consequences. First, the resulting inflation would lead to higher prices for agricultural commodities, putting more money in farmers' pockets. Second, the real value of farmers' debts would decrease, since the debts were contracted in pre-inflation dollars and would be paid back with inflated currency. Naturally, the eastern bankers who supplied farmers with credit opposed such a policy. In fact, in 1873 Congress, under the leadership of Senator John Sherman, had halted the purchase of silver by the Treasury Department, a measure that helped reduce the money supply. Later, however, under the Sherman Silver Purchase Act (1890), the government resumed buying silver, but the act placed limits on its purchase and did not guarantee the creation of silver coinage by the Treasury. In the past, some members of the Alliance had favored expanding the money supply with greenbacks (paper money). However, to attract support from western silver miners, Alliance delegates emphasized the free and unlimited coinage of silver. Alliance supporters met with bitter disappointment, though, as neither the Republican nor the Democratic Party embraced their demands. Rebuffed, farmers took an independent course and became more directly involved in national politics through the formation of the Populist Party.

Explore ▶

See Sources 17.2 and 17.3 to compare views of the Populists.

Farmers and Workers Organize: Two Views

Farmers in the Midwest and the South organized to address the problems they faced as a result of industrialization and the growth of big business. The Populists in the 1880s and 1890s tried to deal with various social and economic issues. Compare the following excerpt from the Populist Party platform, adopted on July 4, 1892, in Omaha, Nebraska, with the pro-Populist cartoon that focuses on one source of its grievance.

Source 17.2

Walter Huston | Here Lies Prosperity, 1895

The "money question" became a focus of American politics in the first half of the 1890s and was exacerbated by the depression of 1893. Those who supported the gold standard believed that it provided the basis for a sound and stable economy. Proponents of the unlimited coinage of silver, especially Populists and Democrats such as William Jennings Bryan, asserted that expansion of the money supply would liberate farmers and workers from debt and bring prosperity to more Americans. This cartoon illustrates the "free silver" point of view.

THE SITUATION; THE RESULT OF INTEREST-BEARING BONDS AND SHERMAN.

Source: "The Situation; The Result of Interest Bearing Bonds and Sherman," *Sound Money* (Massillon, OH), August 22, 1895. Reproduced from Worth Robert Miller, *Populist Cartoons: An Illustrated History of the Third Party Movement in the 1890s* (Truman State University Press, 2011).

Source 17.3

Populist Party Platform, 1892

FINANCE—We demand a national currency, safe, sound, and flexible issued by the general government. . . .

1. We demand free and unlimited coinage of silver and gold at the present legal ratio of 16 to 1. . . .
3. We demand a graduated income tax.
4. We believe that the money of the country should be kept as much as possible in the hands of the people, and hence we demand that all State and national revenues shall be limited to the necessary expenses of the government, economically and honestly administered. . . .

TRANSPORTATION—Transportation being a means of exchange and a public necessity, the government should own and operate the railroads in the interest of the people. The telegraph and telephone . . . should be owned and operated by the government in the interest of the people.

LAND—The land, including all the natural sources of wealth, is the heritage of the people, and should not be monopolized for speculative purposes, and alien ownership of land should be prohibited. All land now held by railroads and other corporations in excess of their actual needs, and all lands now owned by aliens should be reclaimed by the government and held for actual settlers only.

EXPRESSION OF SENTIMENTS

1. Resolved, That we demand a free ballot, and a fair count in all elections . . . without Federal intervention, through the adoption by the States of the . . . secret ballot system.
2. Resolved, That the revenue derived from a graduated income tax should be applied to the reduction of the burden of taxation now levied upon the domestic industries of this country. . . .
4. Resolved, That we condemn the fallacy of protecting American labor under the present system, which opens our ports to [immigrants including] the pauper and the criminal classes of the world and crowds out our [American] wage-earners; and we . . . demand the further restriction of undesirable immigration.
5. Resolved, That we cordially sympathize with the efforts of organized workingmen to shorten the hours of labor. . . .
6. Resolved, That we regard the maintenance of a large standing army of mercenaries, known as the Pinkerton system, as a menace to our liberties, and we demand its abolition.

Source: "People's Party Platform," *Omaha Morning World-Herald*, July 5, 1892.

Interpret the Evidence

1. Explain how these two sources emphasize different aspects of Populist grievances.
2. How do these two sources appeal to the same audience in different ways?

Put It in Context

How did the Populists respond to the shifts in economic and political power that occurred at the end of the nineteenth century?

Populists Rise Up.

In 1892 the National Farmers' Alliance moved into the electoral arena as a third political party. The People's Party of America, known as the **Populists**, held its first nominating convention in Omaha, Nebraska in 1892. In addition to incorporating the Alliance's Ocala planks into their platform, they adopted recommendations to broaden the party's appeal to industrial workers. Populists endorsed a graduated income tax, which would impose higher tax rates on higher income levels, the eight-hour workday, and immigration restriction, which stemmed from the unions' desire to keep unskilled workers from glutting the market and depressing wages. Reflecting the influence of women such as Mary Lease, the party endorsed women's suffrage. The party did not, however, offer specific proposals to prohibit racial discrimination or segregation. Rather, the party focused on remedies to relieve the economic plight of impoverished white and black farmers in general.

In 1892 the Populists nominated for president former Union Civil War general James B. Weaver. Although Weaver came in third behind the Democratic victor, Grover Cleveland, and the Republican incumbent, Benjamin Harrison, he managed to win more than 1 million popular votes and 22 electoral votes.

At the state level, Populists performed even better. They elected 10 congressional representatives, 5 U.S. senators, 3 governors, and 1,500 state legislators. Two years later, the party made even greater strides by increasing its total vote by 42 percent and achieving its greatest strength in the South. This electoral momentum positioned the Populists to make an even stronger run in the next presidential election. The economic depression that began in 1893 and the political discontent it generated enhanced Populist chances for success.

REVIEW & RELATE

- Why was life so difficult for American farmers in the late nineteenth century?

- What were the similarities and differences between farmers' and industrial workers' efforts to organize in the late nineteenth century?

The Depression of the 1890s

When the Philadelphia and Reading Railroad went bankrupt in early 1893, it set off a chain reaction that pushed one-quarter of American railroads into insolvency. As a result, on May 5, 1893, "Black Friday," the stock market collapsed in a panic, triggering the **depression of 1893**. Making this situation worse, England and the rest of industrial Europe had experienced an economic downturn several years earlier. In the early 1890s foreign investors began selling off their American stocks, leading to a flow of gold coin out of the country and further damage to the banking system. Hundreds of banks failed, which hurt the businesspeople and farmers who relied on a steady flow of bank credit. By the end of 1894, nearly 12 percent of the American workforce remained unemployed. The depression became the chief political issue of the mid-1890s and resulted in a realignment of power between the two major parties. Rather than capitalizing on depression discontent, however, the Populist Party split apart and collapsed.

Depression Politics.

President Grover Cleveland's handling of the depression, accompanied by protest marches and labor strife, only made a bad situation worse. In the spring of 1894, Jacob Coxey, a Populist reformer from Ohio, led a march on Washington, D.C., demanding that Cleveland and Congress initiate a federal public works program to provide jobs for the unemployed. Though highly critical of the favored few who dominated the federal government, Coxey had faith that if "the people . . . come in a body like this, peaceably to discuss their grievances and demanding immediate relief, Congress . . . will heed them and do it quickly." After traveling for a month from Ohio, Coxey led a parade of some five hundred unemployed people into the nation's capital.

Explore ▶

Compare Sources 17.4 and 17.5 to evaluate different interpretations of the Populists.

Attracting thousands of spectators, **Coxey's army** attempted to mount their protest on the grounds of the Capitol building. In response, police broke up the demonstration and arrested Coxey for trespassing. Cleveland turned a deaf ear to Coxey's demands for federal relief and also disregarded protesters participating in nearly twenty other marches on Washington.

In the coming months, Cleveland's political stock plummeted further. He responded to the Pullman strike in the summer of 1894 by obtaining a federal injunction against the strikers and dispatching federal troops to Illinois to enforce it. The president's action won him high praise from the railroads and conservative business interests, but it showed millions of American workers that the Cleveland administration did not have a solution for ending the suffering caused by the depression. "While the people should patriotically and cheerfully support their Government," the president declared, "its functions do not include the support of the people."

Making matters worse, Cleveland convinced Congress to repeal the Sherman Silver Purchase Act. This angered western miners, who relied on strong silver prices, along with farmers in the South and Great Plains who were swamped by mounting debt. At the same time, the removal of silver as a backing for currency caused private investors to withdraw their gold deposits from the U.S. Treasury. To keep the government financially solvent, Cleveland worked out an agreement with a syndicate led by J. P. Morgan to help sell government bonds, a deal that netted the banker a huge profit. In the midst of economic suffering, this deal looked like a corrupt bargain between the government and the rich.

In 1894 Congress also passed the Wilson-Gorman Act, which raised tariffs on imported goods. Intended to protect American businesses by keeping the price of imported goods high, it also deprived foreigners of the necessary income with which to buy American exports. This drop in exports did not help economic recovery. The Wilson-Gorman Act did include a provision that the Populists and other reformers endorsed: a progressive income tax of 2 percent on all annual earnings over $4,000. No federal income tax existed at this time, so even this mild levy elicited cries of "socialism" from conservative critics, who challenged the tax in the courts. In *Pollack v. Farmers Loan and Trust* (1895), the Supreme Court declared the income tax unconstitutional and denounced it as the opening wedge in "a war of the poor against the rich; a war constantly growing in intensity and bitterness."

With Cleveland's legislative program in shambles and his inability to solve the depression abundantly clear, the Democrats suffered a crushing blow at the polls. In the congressional elections of 1894, the party lost an astonishing 120 seats in the House. This defeat offered a preview of the political shakeup that loomed ahead.

Political Realignment in the Election of 1896.
The presidential election of 1896 marked a turning point in the political history of the nation. Democrats nominated William Jennings Bryan of Nebraska, a farmers' advocate who favored silver coinage.

When he vowed that he would not see Republicans "crucify mankind on a cross of gold," the Populists endorsed him as well.

Republicans nominated William McKinley, the governor of Ohio and a supporter of the gold standard and high tariffs on manufactured and other goods. McKinley's campaign manager, Marcus Alonzo Hanna, an ally of Ohio senator John Sherman, raised an unprecedented amount of money, about $16 million, mainly from wealthy industrialists who feared that the free and unlimited coinage of silver would debase the U.S. currency. Hanna saturated the country with pamphlets, leaflets, and posters, many of them written in the native languages of immigrant groups. He also hired a platoon of speakers to fan out across the country denouncing Bryan's free silver cause as financial madness. By contrast, Bryan raised about $1 million.

The outcome of the election transformed the Republicans into the majority party in the United States. McKinley won 51 percent of the popular vote and 61 percent of the electoral vote. More important than this specific contest, however, was that the election proved critical in realigning the two parties. Voting patterns shifted with the 1896 election, giving Republicans the edge in party affiliation among the electorate not only in this contest but also in presidential elections over the next three decades (Map 17.2).

What happened to produce this critical realignment in electoral power? The main ingredient was Republicans' success in fashioning a coalition that included both corporate capitalists and their workers. Many urban dwellers and industrial workers took out their anger on Cleveland's Democratic Party and Bryan as its standard-bearer for failing to end the depression. In addition, Bryan, who hailed from Nebraska and reflected small-town agricultural America and its values, could not win over the swelling numbers of urban immigrants who considered Bryan's world alien to their experience.

The election of 1896 broke the political stalemate in this age of organization. The core of Republican backing came from industrial cities of the Northeast and Midwest. Republicans won support from their traditional constituencies of Union veterans, businessmen, and African Americans and added to it the votes of a large number of urban wageworkers. The campaign persuaded voters that the Democratic Party represented the party of depression and that Republicans stood for prosperity and progress. They were soon able to

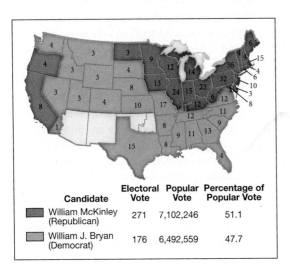

Candidate	Electoral Vote	Popular Vote	Percentage of Popular Vote
William McKinley (Republican)	271	7,102,246	51.1
William J. Bryan (Democrat)	176	6,492,559	47.7

MAP 17.2   The Election of 1896

William McKinley's election in 1896 resulted in a realignment of political power in the United States that lasted until 1932. Republicans became the nation's majority party by forging a coalition of big business and urban industrial workers from the Northeast and Midwest. Democratic strength was confined to the South and to small towns and rural areas of the Great Plains and Rocky Mountain states.

take credit for ending the depression when, in 1897, gold discoveries in Alaska helped increase the money supply and foreign crop failures raised American farm prices. Democrats managed to hold on to the South as their solitary political base.

The Decline of the Populists.
The year 1896 also marked the end of the Populists as a national force, as the party was torn apart by internal divisions over policy and strategy. Populist leaders such as Tom Watson of Georgia did not want the Populist Party to emphasize free silver above the rest of its reform program. Northern Populists, who either had fought on the Union side during the Civil War or had close relatives who did, such as Mary Lease whose father and brother died on the Union side, could not bring themselves to join the Democrats, the party of the old Confederacy. Nevertheless, the Populist Party officially backed Bryan, but to retain its identity, the party nominated Watson for vice president on its own ticket. After McKinley's victory, the Populist Party collapsed.

Losing the presidential election alone did not account for the disintegration of the Populists. Several problems plagued the third party. The nation's recovery from the depression removed one of the Populists' prime sources of electoral attraction. Despite appealing to industrial workers, the Populists were unable to capture their support. The free silver plank attracted silver miners in Idaho and Colorado, but the majority of workers failed to identify with a party composed mainly of farmers. As consumers of agricultural products, industrial laborers did not see any benefit in raising farm prices. Populists also failed to create a stable, biracial coalition of farmers. Most southern white Populists did not truly accept African Americans as equal partners, even though both groups had mutual economic interests.

Wilmington, North Carolina Massacre, 1898   In 1898, Populists in alliance with the Republican Party in Wilmington, N.C. elected a white mayor and a biracial city council. Two days after the election, on November 10, armed members of the defeated Democratic Party, the party of white supremacy, overthrew the new city government. A mob of around 2000 white men, some of whom are pictured above, set fire to the city's black newspaper building. White terrorists killed at least fifteen people and forced more than 2000 blacks to flee the city permanently. The success of this *coup d'état* dealt Populism a mortal blow. Library of Congress, 3a51950

The Agrarian Myth and Populism

The Merriam-Webster dictionary defines populism as a belief in the "rights, wisdom, or virtues of the common people," and those who identify with this label share a common belief in challenging the established political and economic order. In contemporary times the word is associated with politicians on a broad scale of the political spectrum, both on the left and the right. The Populist (or Peoples) Party of the 1890s was a movement that challenged the two major political parties before its demise at the turn of the twentieth century. The Populist Party has attracted contrasting opinions from the scholars that have studied it. One of the debates centers on the Populist idea that yeoman farmers provided the backbone of democracy and in the late nineteenth century were being crushed by conspiratorial capitalists on Wall Street and in the boardrooms of big business.

Source 17.4

Richard Hofstadter, The Agrarian Myth, 1955

"As a businessman, the farmer was appropriately hardheaded; he tried to act upon a cold and realistic strategy of self-interest. As the head of the family, however, the farmer felt that ... when he risked the farm he risked his home – that he was, in short, a single man running a personal enterprise in a world of impersonal forces. It was from this aspect of his situation – seen in the hazy glow of the agrarian myth – that his political leaders in the 1890s developed their rhetoric and some of their concepts of political action.

The utopia of the Populists was in the past, not the future. According to the agrarian myth, the health of the state was proportionate to the degree to which it was dominated by the agricultural class, and this assumption pointed to the superiority of an earlier age. The Populists looked backward with longing to the lost agrarian Eden, to the Republican America of the early years of the nineteenth century in which there were few millionaires, and as they saw it, no beggars when the laborer had excellent prospects and the farmer had abundance, when the statesman still responded to the mood of the people and there was no such thing as money power. What they meant – though they did not express themselves in such terms – was that they would like to restore the conditions prevailing before the development of industrialism and the commercialization of agriculture.... There was in fact a widespread Populist idea that all American history since the Civil War could be understood as a sustained conspiracy of the international money power.... In Populist thought the farmer is not a speculating businessman, victimized by the risk economy of which he is a part, but rather a wounded yeoman preyed upon by those who are alien to the life of folkish virtue."

Source: Richard Hofstadter, *The Age of Reform: From Bryan to F.D.R.* New York: Vintage Books, 1955, 46, 62.

To eliminate Populism's insurgent political threat, southern opponents found ways to disfranchise black and poor white voters. During the 1890s, southern states inserted into their constitutions voting requirements that virtually eliminated the black electorate and greatly diminished the white electorate. Seeking to circumvent the Fifteenth Amendment's prohibition against racial discrimination in the right to vote, conservative white lawmakers adopted regulations based on wealth and education because blacks were disproportionately poor and had lower literacy rates. They instituted poll taxes, which imposed a fee for

Source 17.5

Charles Postel, The Populist Vision, 2007

"The Populist world was too commercially and intellectually dynamic to resemble a traditional society in any meaningful sense of the term. This tells us something important about the nature of late nineteenth-century: the men and women of the Populist movement were modern people. The term *modern* does not mean "good.' Nor is it a value judgment across the political spectrum from right to left. Moreover, to say that the Populists were modern does not imply that they were more modern than, say, their Republican or Democratic opponents. Nor does it imply that all rural people shared the Populists' modern sensibility. On the contrary, the Populists understood that the transformations they sought required the uprooting of ignorance, inertia, and force of habit. Populism formed a unique social movement that represented a distinctly modernizing impulse....

Modernity also implied a particular kind of people with particular types of strivings... Modern men and women ... 'look forward to future developments in their conditions of life and their relations with their fellow men.' The Populists were just this kind of people. They sought to improve their domestic economy and their national government. They sought renewal in local schoolhouses and federal credit systems. They sought to refashion associational ties with neighbors and commercial relations with the world. They sought new techniques, new acreage, and new avenues of spiritual expression."

Source: Charles Postel, *The Populist Vision*. New York: Oxford University Press, 2007, 9, 10.

Examine the Sources

1. How do Hofstadter and Postel differ in their assessments of Populism?
2. Drawing upon evidence in this chapter, how would you evaluate the strengths and weaknesses of Hofstadter and Postel's presentations?

Put It in Context

Evaluate the historical legacy of the Populist Party.

voting, and literacy tests, which asked questions designed to trip up black would-be voters. In 1898 the Supreme Court upheld the constitutionality of these voter qualifications in *Williams v. Mississippi*. Recognizing the power of white supremacy, the Populists surrendered to its appeals.

Tom Watson provides a case in point. He started out by encouraging racial unity but then switched to divisive politics. In 1896 the Populist vice presidential candidate called on citizens of both races to vote against the crushing power of corporations and railroads. By whipping up antagonism against blacks, his Democratic opponents appealed to the racial pride of poor whites to keep them from defecting to the Populists. Chastened by the outcome of the 1896 election and learning from the tactics of his political foes, Watson embarked on a vicious campaign to exclude blacks from voting. "What does civilization owe the Negro?" he bitterly asked. "Nothing! Nothing! NOTHING!!!" Only by disfranchising African Americans and maintaining white supremacy, Watson and other white reformers reasoned, would poor whites have the courage to vote against rich whites.

Nevertheless, even in defeat the Populists left an enduring legacy. Many of their political and economic reforms — direct election of senators, the graduated income tax, government regulation of business and banking, and a version of the subtreasury system (called the Commodity Credit Corporation, created in the 1930s) — became features of reform in the twentieth century. Perhaps their greatest contribution, however, came in showing farmers that their old individualist ways would not succeed in the modern industrial era. Rather than re-creating an independent political party, most farmers looked to organized interest groups, such as the Farm Bureau, to lobby on behalf of their interests.

REVIEW & RELATE

- How did the federal government respond to the depression of 1893?
- What were the long-term political consequences of the depression of 1893?

Conclusion: A Passion for Organization

From 1877 to 1900, industrial workers and farmers joined the march toward organization led by the likes of Carnegie, Rockefeller, and Morgan. These wealthy titans of industry and finance had created the large corporations that transformed the rhythms and meanings of life in workplaces, farms, and leisure activities. Working people such as John McLuckie met the challenges of the new industrial order by organizing unions. Lacking the power of giant companies and confronted by the federal government's use of force to break up strikes, labor unions nevertheless carved out sufficient space for workers to join together in their own defense to resist absolute corporate rule. At the same time, farmers, perhaps the most individualistic workers, and their advocates, such as Mary Elizabeth Lease, created organizations that proposed some of the most forward-looking solutions to remedy the ills accompanying industrialization. Though the political fortunes of the Grangers and Populists declined, their message persisted: Resourceful and determined workers and farmers could, and should, join together to ensure survival not just of the fittest but of the neediest as well.

Under the pressure of increased turmoil surrounding industrialization and a brutal economic depression, the political system reached a crisis in the 1890s. Despite the historic shift in party loyalties brought about by the election of William McKinley, it remained to be seen whether political party realignment could furnish the necessary leadership to address the problems of workers and farmers. The events of the 1890s convinced many Americans, including many in the middle class, that the hands-off approach to social and economic problems that had prevailed in the past was no longer acceptable. In cities and states across the country, men and women took up the cause of reform. They had to wait for national leaders to catch up to them.

TIMELINE OF **EVENTS**

1865–1895	U.S. manufacturing jobs jump from 5.3 million to 15.1 million
1867	Grange founded
1869	Knights of Labor founded
1870–1900	Number of female wageworkers increases by 66 percent
1877	Great Railroad Strike
1879	Terence Powderly becomes leader of Knights of Labor
1880s	Northwestern, Southern, and Colored Farmers' Alliances formed
1886	Haymarket Square violence
	American Federation of Labor founded
1887	Interstate Commerce Act
1889	Northwestern and Southern Farmers' Alliances merge
1890	Sherman Silver Purchase Act
1890s	Southern states restrict blacks' right to vote
1892	Homestead steelworkers' strike
	Populist Party established
1893	Depression triggered by stock market collapse
1894	Pullman strike
	Coxey's army marches to Washington
	Sherman Silver Purchase Act repealed
1896	Populist William Jennings Bryan runs for president
1897	Populist Party declines
1901	Eugene Debs establishes Socialist Party of America

KEY **TERMS**

unskilled workers, *564*

skilled workers, *564*

unions, *567*

collective bargaining, *568*

Noble Order of the Knights of Labor, *568*

Haymarket Square, *568*

American Federation of Labor (AFL), *569*

Homestead strike, *572*

Pullman strike, *573*

Industrial Workers of the World (IWW), *574*

Grangers, *577*

Interstate Commerce Commission (ICC), *577*

Farmers' Alliances, *579*

subtreasury system, *579*

Populists, *582*

depression of 1893, *582*

Coxey's army, *583*

REVIEW & RELATE

1. How did industrialization change the American workplace? What challenges did it create for American workers?

2. How did workers resist the concentrated power of industrial capitalists in the late nineteenth century, and why did such efforts have only limited success?

3. Why was life so difficult for American farmers in the late nineteenth century?

4. What were the similarities and differences between farmers' and industrial workers' efforts to organize in the late nineteenth century?

5. How did the federal government respond to the depression of 1893?

6. What were the long-term political consequences of the depression of 1893?

The Pullman Strike of 1894

▶ Explain the reasons industrial workers sought to organize against their employers and evaluate why they were not more successful in gaining a larger share of economic and political power in the late nineteenth century.

Late-nineteenth-century industrialists exercised massive power over workers and the conditions of labor. Workers organized into unions to secure higher wages, shorter hours, improved safety, and a fairer measure of control of the labor process. Even those corporate owners who were considered sympathetic to the needs of laborers and their families, such as railcar magnate George Pullman, assumed the right to manage their businesses as they saw fit (Source 17.6). Though Pullman had constructed a model town with clean housing and parks for his employees, he refused to heed workers' economic complaints after the depression of 1893 began (Source 17.8).

Yet this power did not go unchallenged. When the American Railway Union (ARU), headed by Eugene V. Debs (Source 17.7), launched a nationwide strike against the Pullman company in May 1894 to improve economic conditions and gain recognition for the union, Pullman refused to negotiate. Rebuffed by Pullman, the union coordinated strike activities across the country from its headquarters in Chicago. Workers refused to operate trains with Pullman cars attached, and when the railroads hired strikebreakers, some 260,000 strikers brought rail traffic to a halt. In response, U.S. attorney general Richard Olney, a member of many railroad boards, obtained a federal injunction ordering strikers back to work, but without success. At Olney's recommendation, President Grover Cleveland ordered federal troops into Chicago

to enforce the injunction. Their clash with strikers resulted in thirteen deaths, more than fifty injuries, hundreds of thousands of dollars in property damages, and the spread of violence to twenty-six states (Source 17.9). After the government arrested union leaders, including Debs, for disobeying the injunction, the strike collapsed in July 1894, and the Supreme Court upheld Debs's imprisonment.

The following sources reveal the points of view from four major combatants in the labor struggle. Explain the reasons industrial workers sought to organize against their employers, and evaluate why they were not more successful in gaining a larger share of economic and political power in the late nineteenth century.

Source 17.6

George Pullman | Testimony before the U.S. Strike Commission, 1894

In July 1894, President Grover Cleveland appointed a commission to investigate the Chicago (Pullman) strike. Although the Cleveland administration played a major role in ending the strike to the detriment of the American Railway Union, the president selected Carroll D. Wright, the U.S. commissioner of labor, to chair the commission. Wright had significant experience investigating labor conditions and collecting statistical data, and he was sympathetic to the plight of workers. George Pullman appeared before the commission to explain his position on the strike.

COMMISSIONER WRIGHT . . . State generally what the idea was of establishing the town [of Pullman] in connection with your manufacturing plant. . . .

PULLMAN [reading from a statement] The object in building Pullman was the establishment of a great manufacturing business on the most substantial basis possible, recognizing, as we did, and do now, that the working people are the most important element which enters into the successful operation of any manufacturing enterprise. We decided to build, in close proximity to the shops, homes for workingmen of such character and surroundings as would prove so attractive as to cause the best class of mechanics to seek that place for employment in preference to others. We also desired to establish the place on such a basis as would exclude all baneful [harmful] influences, believing that such a policy would result in the greatest measure of success, both from a commercial point of view, and also, what was equally important, or perhaps of greater importance, in a tendency toward continued elevation and improvement of the conditions not only of the working people themselves, but of their children growing up about them. . . .

If any lots had been sold in Pullman it would have permitted the introduction of the baneful elements which it was the chief purpose to exclude from the immediate neighborhood of the shops, and from the homes to be erected about them. The plan was to provide homes in the first place for all people who should desire to work in the shops, at reasonable rentals, with the expectation that as they became able and should desire to do so, they would purchase lots and erect homes for themselves within convenient distances, or avail themselves of the opportunity to rent homes from other people who should build in that vicinity. As a matter of fact, at the time of the strike 563 of the shop employees owned their homes, and 461 of that number are now employed in the shops; 560 others at the time of the strike lived outside; and, in addition, an estimated number from 200 to 300 others employed at Pullman were owners of their homes. . . .

Due attention was paid to the convenience and general well-being of the residents by the erection of stores and markets, a church, public schools, a library, and public halls for lectures and amusements; also a hotel and boarding houses. The basis on which rents were fixed was to make a return of 6 percent on the actual investment, which at that time, 1881, was a reasonable return to be expected from such an investment; and in calculating what, for such a purpose, was the actual investment in the dwellings on the one hand and the other buildings on the other, an allowance was made for the cost of the streets and other public improvements, just as it has to be considered in the valuation of any property for renting anywhere, all public improvements having to be paid for by the owner of a lot, either directly or by special assessment, and by him considered in the valuation. The actual operations have never shown a net return of 6 percent, the amount originally contemplated. The investment for several years returned a net revenue of about 4½ percent, but during the last two years additional taxes and heavier repairs have brought the net revenue down to 3.82 percent. . . .

COMMISSIONER NICOLAS WORTHINGTON I wanted to know what you had in mind at the time you made the statement that "it was very clear that no prudent man could submit to arbitration in this matter" when you were referring to your daily losses as a reason why any prudent man could not submit to arbitration?

PULLMAN The amount of the losses would not cut any figure; it was the principle involved, not the amount that would affect my views as to arbitration.

WORTHINGTON Then it was not the amount of losses that the company was then sustaining, but it was the fact that a continuance of the business at the rates that had been paid would entail loss upon the company?

PULLMAN It was the principle that that should not be submitted to a third party. That was a matter that the company should decide for itself. . . .

WORTHINGTON Now, let me ask you if, taking all the revenues of the Pullman company for the last year, so far as you are advised, if the company has lost money or made money during the last year?

PULLMAN The company has made money during the last year.

Source: *Executive Documents of the Senate of the United States*, 53rd Cong. (1894–1895), 529–30, 553.

Source 17.7

Eugene V. Debs | On Radicalism, 1902

American Railway Union leader Eugene Debs served six months in jail after leading the Pullman strike. This experience moved him in more radical directions politically, and he established the Socialist Party. He ran as the party's presidential candidate five times, and in 1905 Debs helped form the Industrial Workers of the World, an organization interested in uniting all workers and challenging the capitalist system. In 1902 he described to the readers of the *Comrade*, a New York socialist newspaper, his thoughts on the Pullman strike and how he became a socialist.

n 1894 the American Railway Union was organized and a braver body of men never fought the battle of the working class.

Up to this time I had heard but little of Socialism, knew practically nothing about the movement, and what little I did know was not calculated to impress me in its favor. I was bent on thorough and complete organization of the railroad men and ultimately the whole working class, and all my time and energy were given to that end. My supreme conviction was that if they were only organized in every branch of the service and all acted together in concert they could redress their wrongs and regulate the conditions of their employment. The stockholders of the corporation acted as one, why not the men? It was such a plain proposition—simply to follow the example set before their eyes by their masters—surely they could not fail to see it, act as one, and solve the problem. . . .

Next followed the final shock—the Pullman strike—and the American Railway Union again won, clear and complete. The combined corporations were paralyzed and helpless. At this juncture there [was] delivered, from wholly unexpected quarters, a swift succession of blows that blinded me for an instant and then opened wide my eyes—and in the gleam of every bayonet and the flash of every rifle *the class struggle was revealed*. This was my first practical lesson in Socialism, though wholly un-aware that it was called by that name.

An army of detectives, thugs, and murderers [was] equipped with badge and beer and bludgeon and turned loose; old hulks of cars were fired; the alarm bells tolled; the people were terrified; the most startling rumors were set afloat; the press volleyed and thundered, and over all the wires sped the news that Chicago's white throat was in the clutch of a red mob; injunctions flew thick and fast, arrests followed, and our office and headquarters, the heart of the strike, was sacked, torn out, and nailed up by the "lawful" authorities of the federal government; and when in company with my loyal comrades I found myself in Cook county jail at Chicago, with the whole press screaming conspiracy, treason, and murder. . . .

. . . But the tempest gradually subsided and with it the bloodthirstiness of the press and "public sentiment." We were not sentenced to the gallows, nor even to the penitentiary—though put on trial for conspiracy—for reasons that will make another story.

The Chicago jail sentences were followed by six months at Woodstock [the Illinois jail where Debs was imprisoned] and it was here that Socialism gradually laid hold of me in its own irresistible fashion. Books and pamphlets and letters from socialists came by every mail and I began to read and think and dissect the anatomy of the system in which workingmen, however organized, could be shattered and battered and splintered at a single stroke. . . .

The American Railway Union was defeated but not conquered—overwhelmed but not destroyed. It lives and pulsates in the Socialist movement, and its defeat but blazed the way to economic freedom and hastened the dawn of human brotherhood.

Source: Eugene V. Debs, *Debs: His Life, Writings, and Speeches* (Chicago: Charles Kerr, 1908), 81–84.

Jennie Curtis | Testimony before the U.S. Strike Commission, 1894

During the Pullman strike, seamstress Jennie Curtis was president of the American Railway Union Local 269, known as the "girls' union." Following a stirring speech by Curtis at an ARU convention, the union agreed to support workers striking against Pullman. In the following excerpt, Curtis explains to Carroll D. Wright, chairman of the congressional commission that later investigated the strike, the dire economic situation employees faced as the company cut back wages and raised rents.

COMMISSIONER WRIGHT State your name, residence, and occupation.

CURTIS Jennie Curtis; reside at Pullman; have been a seamstress for the Pullman company in the repair shops sewing room; worked for them five years.

WRIGHT Are you a member of any labor organization?

CURTIS Yes, sir; I am a member of the American Railway Union.

WRIGHT How long have you been a member of that union?

CURTIS Since about the 8th day of last May.

WRIGHT Do you hold any position in the union?

CURTIS I am president of the girls' union, local, No. 269, at Pullman.

WRIGHT Did you have anything to do with the strike at Pullman, which occurred on the 11th of May, 1894?

CURTIS No, sir.

WRIGHT Had you anything to do with any of the efforts to avoid the strike, or to settle the difficulties?

CURTIS I had not, further than being on a committee which called to see Mr. Pullman and Mr. Wickes, the general manager of the company, to ask for more wages, asking to arbitrate, and such as that.

WRIGHT Were you on those committees, or some of them?

CURTIS Yes, sir; I was.

WRIGHT State briefly what you did as a member serving upon those committees.

CURTIS I was on a committee that went from Pullman to speak for the girls in May before the strike, to ask for more wages. . . .

WRIGHT State what took place at the first interview.

CURTIS We went there and asked, as the men did, for more wages; we were cut lower than any of the men's departments throughout the works; in 1893 we were able to make 22 cents per hour, or $2.25 per day, in my department, and on the day of the strike we could only earn, on an average, working as hard as we possibly could, from 70 to 80 cents a day.

COMMISSIONER JOHN D. KERNAN Can you give us how the wages changed from month to month?

CURTIS Whenever the men were cut in their wages the girls also received a cut. We were cut twice inside of a week in November, 1893, and in January our wages were cut again; that was the last cut we received, and we worked as hard as we possibly could and doing all we could, too. The most experienced of us could only make 80 cents per day, and a great many of the girls could only average 40 to 50 cents per day. . . .

WRIGHT Do you pay rent in Pullman?

CURTIS No, sir; not now.

WRIGHT You pay board?

CURTIS Yes, sir. My father worked for the Pullman company for thirteen years. He died last September, and I paid the rent to the Pullman company up to the time he died; I was boarding at the time of my father's death. He being laid off and sick for three months, owed the Pullman company $60 at the time of his death for back rent, and the company made me, out of my small earnings, pay that rent due from my father.

KERNAN How did they make you do it?

CURTIS The contract was that I should pay $3 on the back rent every pay day; out of my small earnings I could not give them $3 every pay day, and when I did not do so I was insulted and almost put out of the bank by the clerk for not being able to pay it to them. My wages were cut so low that I could not pay my board and give them $3 on the back rent, but if I had $2 or so over my board I would leave it at the bank on the rent. On the day of the strike I still owed them $15, which I am afraid they never will give me a chance to pay back.

Source: *Executive Documents of the Senate of the United States*, 53rd Cong. (1894–1895).

Report from the Commission to Investigate the Chicago Strike, 1895

The commission appointed by President Grover Cleveland to investigate the Pullman strike concluded that strikes were wasteful, disruptive, and unlawful. Blaming both capital and labor for the strike, the commission believed that the Pullman trouble originated because neither the public nor the government had taken adequate measures to control monopolies and corporations and had failed "to reasonably protect the rights of labor and redress its wrongs."

Committee Recommendations Following Investigation of the Chicago Strike

I.

(1) That there be a permanent United States strike commission of three members, with duties and powers of investigation and recommendation as to disputes between railroads and their employees similar to those vested in the Interstate Commerce Commission as to rates, etc. . . .

II.

(1) The commission would suggest the consideration by the States of the adoption of some system of conciliation and arbitration like that, for instance, in use in the Commonwealth of Massachusetts. That system might be reenforced by additional provisions giving the board of arbitration more power to investigate all strikes, whether requested so to do or not, and the question might be considered as to giving labor organizations a standing before the law, as heretofore suggested for national trade unions.

(2) Contracts requiring men to agree not to join labor organizations or to leave them, as conditions of employment, should be made illegal, as is already done in some of our States.

III.

(1) The commission urges employers to recognize labor organizations; that such organizations be dealt with through representatives, with special reference to conciliation and arbitration when difficulties are threatened or arise. It is satisfied that employers should come in closer touch with labor and should recognize that, while the interests of labor and capital are not identical, they are reciprocal.

(2) The commission is satisfied that if employers everywhere will endeavor to act in concert with labor; that if when wages can be raised under economic conditions they be raised voluntarily, and that if when there are reductions reasons be given for the reduction, much friction can be avoided. It is also satisfied that if employers will consider employees as thoroughly essential to industrial success as capital, and thus take labor into consultation at proper times, much of the severity of strikes can be tempered and their number reduced.

Source: *Report on the Chicago Strike of June–July, 1894* by the *United States Strike Commission* (Washington, DC: Government Printing Office, 1895), LII–LIV.

Interpret the Evidence

1. Compare the views of George Pullman (Source 17.6) with those of Jennie Curtis (Source 17.8) concerning whether Pullman treated his workers fairly.

2. How does being a woman affect Jennie Curtis's experiences as a Pullman worker (Source 17.8)?

3. According to Eugene V. Debs (Source 17.7), what is the purpose of labor activism? How does the Pullman strike teach Debs about socialism?

4. By comparison, how do you think Pullman and Debs would have responded to the report on the Pullman strike issued by the commission to investigate the Chicago strike (Source 17.9)?

Put It in Context

Using these sources, evaluate the complex relationship among labor, management, and government at the close of the nineteenth century.

Cities, Immigrants, and the Nation

1880–1914

WINDOW TO THE PAST

"Be Just — Even to John Chinaman, 1893"

This image, from a cartoon supporting the Chinese Exclusion Act (1882), appeared in the satirical magazine *Judge*. The Chinese were singled out for harsh treatment because they competed with white workers for jobs in the West. Of all the immigrants entering the country after the Civil War, the Chinese were most often viewed as incapable of being assimilated. ▶ To discover more about what this primary source can show us, see Source 18.8 on page 625.

After reading this chapter you should be able to:

- Explain the reasons late nineteenth- and early twentieth-century immigrants came to the United States and evaluate how they were received by native-born Americans.

- Explain why farmers, small-town residents, and African Americans from the South migrated to cities, and summarize the challenges and technological changes they encountered.

- Assess the benefits and liabilities of urban political machines and compare those who supported and opposed them.

COMPARING AMERICAN HISTORIES

In the fall of 1905, Beryl Lassin faced a difficult choice. Living in a *shtetl* (a Jewish town) in western Russia, Lassin had few if any opportunities as a young blacksmith. Beryl and his wife, Lena, lived at a dangerous time in Russia. Jews were subject to periodic pogroms, state-sanctioned outbreaks of anti-Jewish violence carried out by local Christians. Beryl also faced a discriminatory military draft that required conscripted Jews to serve twenty-year terms in the army, far longer than Christians. Beryl decided he should quickly follow his wife's brother to the United States. With the understanding that his wife would follow as soon as possible, Beryl set sail for America on October 7, 1905. He was crammed into

the steerage belowdecks with hundreds of other passengers. Ten days later he disembarked in New York harbor at Ellis Island, the processing center for immigrants, where he stood in long lines and underwent a strenuous medical examination to ensure that he was fit to enter the country. Once he proved he had someplace to go, Beryl boarded a ferry across the Hudson that took him to a new life in the United States.

Less than a year later, Lena joined her husband. Over the next decade, the couple had five children. Shortly after the youngest girl was born, Lena died and Beryl, now called Ben, was forced to place his children in a group home and foster care. The children were reunited with their father when Ben remarried, but life was still difficult. To make ends meet, his three eldest boys left school and went to work. Still, Ben's family managed to leave the crowded Lower East Side for Harlem and then the Bronx. Ben preferred to speak in Yiddish and never learned to read English. Nor did he become an American citizen. His children, however, were all citizens because they had been born in the United States.

On June 8, 1912, another immigrant followed a similar route but ended up taking a different journey. Seventeen years old and unmarried, Maria Vik decided to leave her home in rural Hungary. As a Catholic, Maria did not experience the religious persecution that Beryl did. Like many other Hungarians, Maria left to help support her family back in the old country. She had an aunt living in the United States, and she came across with a Hungarian couple who escorted young women for domestic service in America.

Maria, too, landed at Ellis Island and passed the rigorous entry exams. Soon she boarded a train for Rochester in western New York. There she worked as a cook for a German physician, learned English, and led an active social life within the local Hungarian community. She married Karoly (Charles) Takacs, a cabinetmaker from Hungary, who had come to avoid the military draft. Charles became a U.S. citizen in May 1916. By marrying him, Mary, as she was now called, became a citizen as well.

The couple purchased a farm in Middleport, New York. Because so many Hungarians lived in the area,

(*left*) **Beryl Lassin.** Courtesy of Steven F. Lawson
(*right*) **Maria Vik Takacs.** Courtesy of Irene Hewitt

Mary only began to speak more English when the oldest of her four children entered kindergarten.

The American histories of Beryl and Maria took one to the urban bustle of New York City, the other to a quiet rural village in western New York State. However, as different as their lives in America were, neither regretted their choice to immigrate. Like millions of others, they had come to America to build better lives for themselves and their families, and both saw their children and grandchildren succeed in ways that they could have only dreamed of in their native countries. Indeed, two grandchildren of Beryl and Maria, Steven Lawson and Nancy Hewitt, respectively — became historians, got married, and wrote this textbook. The experiences of these families, like countless others, reflect the complicated ways that immigrants' lives were transformed at the same time the nation itself was being transformed. ■

Lassin and Vik were part of a flood of immigrants who entered the United States from 1880 to the outbreak of World War I in 1914. Unlike the majority of earlier immigrants, who had come from northern Europe, most of the more than 20 million people who arrived during this period came from southern and eastern Europe. A smaller number of immigrants came from Asia and Mexico. Most remained in cities, which grew as a result. Urban immigrants were welcomed by political bosses, who saw in them a chance to gain the allegiance of millions of new voters. At the same time, their coming upset many middle- and upper-class city dwellers who blamed these new arrivals for lowering the quality of urban life.

A New Wave of Immigrants

For more than three hundred years following the settlement of the North American colonies, the majority of white immigrants to America were northern European Protestants. Unlike European immigrants who came voluntarily, blacks were brought forcibly from Africa, mainly by way of the West Indies and the Caribbean. Although African Americans originally followed their own religious practices, most eventually converted to Protestantism. By the end of the nineteenth century, however, a new pattern of immigration had emerged, one that included much greater ethnic and religious diversity. These new immigrants often encountered hostility from those whose ancestors had arrived generations earlier, and faced the difficult challenge of retaining their cultural identities while becoming assimilated as Americans.

Immigrants Arrive from Many Lands. Immigration to the United States was part of a worldwide phenomenon. In addition to the United States, European immigrants also journeyed to other countries in the Western Hemisphere, especially Canada, Argentina, Brazil, and Cuba. Others left China, Japan, and India and migrated to Southeast Asia and Hawaii. From England and Ireland, migrants ventured to other parts of the British empire. As with those who came to the United States, these immigrants left their homelands to find new job opportunities or to obtain land to start their own farms. In countries like Australia, New Zealand, and South Africa, white settlers often pushed aside native peoples to make communities for themselves. Whereas most immigrants chose to relocate voluntarily, some made the move bound by labor contracts that limited their movement during the terms of the agreement. Chinese, Mexican, and Italian workers made up a large portion of this group.

The late nineteenth century saw a shift in the country of origin of immigrants to the United States: Instead of coming from northern and western Europe, many now came from southern and eastern European countries, most notably Italy, Greece, Austria-Hungary, Poland, and Russia. Most of those settling on American shores after 1880 were Catholic or Jewish and hardly knew a word of English. They tended to be even poorer than immigrants who had arrived before them, coming mainly from rural areas and lacking suitable skills for a rapidly expanding industrial society. Even after relocating to a new land and a new society, such immigrants struggled to break patterns of poverty that were, in many cases, centuries in the making.

Immigrants came from other parts of the world as well. From 1860 to 1924, some 450,000 Mexicans migrated to the U.S. Southwest. Many traveled to El Paso, Texas, near the Mexican border, and from there hopped aboard one of three railroad lines to jobs on farms and in mines, mills, and construction. Cubans, Spaniards, and Bahamians traveled to the Florida cities of Key West and Tampa, where they established and worked in cigar factories. Although Congress excluded Chinese immigration after 1882, it did not close the door to migrants from Japan. Unlike the Chinese, the Japanese had not competed with white workers for jobs on railroad and other construction projects. Moreover, Japan was a major world power in the late nineteenth century and held American respect by defeating

Angel Island Physical Exam   Beginning in 1910, tens of thousands of Chinese tried to immigrate to the United States through Angel Island in San Francisco Bay. Thousands were detained for long periods until they could prove their identities and demonstrate they had relatives in the country. One of the hurdles they had to overcome was the medical examination. In this photo taken in 1923, a group of Chinese boys waits to see the doctor while a military official inspects one of them. Photo no. 90-G-124-45 National Archives

Russia in the Russo-Japanese War of 1904–1905. Some 260,000 Japanese arrived in the United States during the first two decades of the twentieth century. Many of them settled on the West Coast, where they worked as farm laborers and gardeners and established businesses catering to a Japanese clientele. Nevertheless, Japanese immigrants were considered part of an inferior "yellow race" and encountered discrimination in their West Coast settlements.

Despite the 1882 Chinese Exclusion Act, tens of thousands of Chinese attempted to immigrate, many claiming to be family members of those already in the country. Some first went to Canada or Mexico, but very few managed to cross over the border illegally. In 1910 the government established an immigration station at Angel Island in San Francisco Bay. In contrast to Ellis Island, Angel Island served mainly as a detention center where Chinese immigrants were imprisoned for months, even years, while they sought to prove their eligibility to enter the United States. Nevertheless, over the next thirty years, some 50,000 Chinese successfully passed through Angel Island. This wave of immigration changed the composition of the American population. By 1910 one-third of the population was foreign-born or had at least one parent who came from abroad. Foreigners and their children made up more than three-quarters of the population of New York City, Detroit, Chicago, Milwaukee, Cleveland, Minneapolis, and San Francisco. Immigration, though not as extensive in the South as in the North, also altered the character of southern cities. About one-third of the population of Tampa, Miami, and New Orleans consisted of foreigners and their descendants. The borderland states of Texas, New Mexico, Arizona, and southern California contained similar percentages of immigrants, most of whom came from Mexico (Map 18.1).

These immigrants came to the United States largely for economic, political, and religious reasons. Nearly all were poor and expected to find ways to make money in America. U.S. railroads and steamship companies advertised in Europe and recruited passengers by emphasizing economic opportunities in the United States. Early immigrants wrote to relatives back home extolling the virtues of what they had found, perhaps exaggerating their success.

The importance of economic incentives in luring immigrants is underscored by the fact that millions returned to their home countries after they had earned sufficient money. Of the more than 27 million immigrants from 1875 to 1919, 11 million returned home (Table 18.1). Immigrants facing religious or political persecution in their homeland, like Beryl Lassin, were the least likely to return.

Creating Immigrant Communities.

In cities such as New York, Boston, and Chicago, immigrants occupied neighborhoods that took on the distinct ethnic characteristics of the groups that inhabited them. A cacophony of different languages echoed in the streets as new residents continued to communicate in their mother tongues. The neighborhoods of immigrant groups often were clustered together, so residents were as likely to learn phrases in their neighbors' languages as they were to learn English.

The formation of **ghettos** — neighborhoods dominated by a single ethnic, racial, or class group — eased immigrants' transition into American society. Living within these ethnic enclaves made it easier for immigrants to find housing, hear about jobs, buy food, and seek help from those with whom they felt most comfortable. **Mutual aid societies** sprang

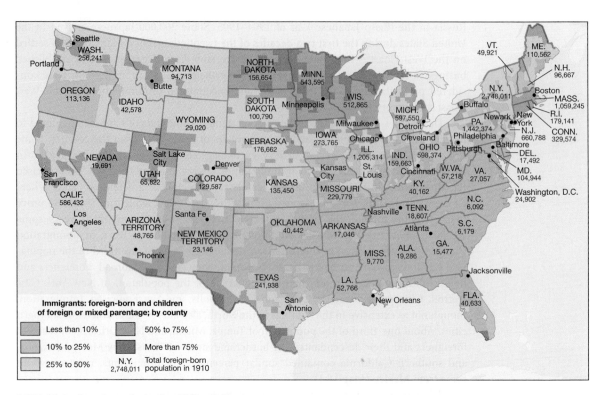

MAP 18.1 Immigrants in the U.S., 1910

By 1910, immigrants had come to the United States from primarily Europe, Asia, Mexico, and Latin America. They tended to settle near their ports of entry in cities, where they usually joined people from their own country who had settled previously. The pattern of settlement varied widely among regions of the country, as the map shows.

up to provide social welfare benefits, including insurance payments and funeral rites. Group members established social centers where immigrants could play cards or dominoes, chat and gossip over tea or coffee, host dances and benefits, or just relax among people who shared a common heritage. In San Francisco's Chinatown, the largest Chinese community in California, such organizations usually consisted of people who had come from the same towns in China. These groups performed a variety of services, including finding jobs for their members, resolving disputes, campaigning against anti-Chinese discrimination, and sponsoring parades and other cultural activities. One society member explained: "We are strangers in a strange country. We must have an organization to control our country fellows and develop our friendship."

The same impulse to band together occurred in immigrant communities throughout the nation. On the West Coast, Japanese farmers joined *kenjinkai*, which not only provided social activities but also helped first-generation immigrants locate jobs and find housing. In Ybor City, Tampa's cigar-making section, mutual aid organizations rose to meet the needs of Spaniards, Cubans, Afro-Cubans, and Italians. El Centro Asturiano constructed a building that contained a 1,200-seat theater, "$4,000 worth of modern lighting

TABLE 18.1   Percentage of Immigrant Departures versus Arrivals, 1875–1914

Year	Arrivals	Departures	Percentage of Departures to Arrivals
1875–1879	956,000	431,000	45%
1880–1884	3,210,000	327,000	10%
1885–1889	2,341,000	638,000	27%
1890–1894	2,590,000	838,000	32%
1895–1899	1,493,000	766,000	51%
1900–1904	3,575,000	1,454,000	41%
1905–1909	5,533,000	2,653,000	48%
1910–1914	6,075,000	2,759,000	45%

fixtures, a cantina, and a well stocked *biblioteca* (library)." Cubans constructed their own palatial clubhouse, El Circulo Cubano, with stained-glass windows, a pharmacy, a theater, and a ballroom. The modest La Union Martí-Maceo catered to Tampa's Afro-Cubans and sponsored its own baseball team. The establishment of such clubs and cultural centers speaks to the commitment of immigrant groups there and elsewhere to enhance their communities.

Besides family and civic associations, churches and synagogues provided religious and social activities for urban immigrants. Between 1865 and 1900, the number of Catholic churches nationwide more than tripled. Like mutual aid societies, churches offered food and clothing to those who were ill or unable to work and fielded sports teams to compete in recreational leagues. Immigrants altered the religious practices and rituals in their churches to meet their own needs and expectations, many times over the objections of their clergy. Various ethnic groups challenged the orthodox practices of the Catholic Church and insisted that their parishes adopt religious icons that they had worshipped in the old country. These included patron saints or protectresses from Old World towns, such as the Madonna del Carmine, whom Italian Catholics in New York's East Harlem celebrated with an annual festival that their priests considered a pagan ritual. Women played the predominant role in running these street festivities. German Catholics challenged Vatican policy by insisting that each ethnic group have its own priests and parishes. Some Catholics, like Mary Vik, who lived in rural areas that did not have a Catholic church in the vicinity, attended services with local Christians from other denominations.

Religious worship also varied among Jews. German Jews had arrived in the United States in an earlier wave of immigration than their eastern European coreligionists. By the early twentieth century, they had achieved some measure of economic success and founded Reform Judaism, with Cincinnati, Ohio as its center. This brand of Judaism relaxed strict standards of worship, including absolute fidelity to kosher dietary laws, and allowed prayers to be said in English. By contrast, eastern European Jews, like Beryl Lassin, observed the traditional faith, maintained a kosher diet, and prayed in Hebrew.

Polish Saloon in Chicago, 1903 The *Polska Scaya* was a saloon located in the heart of one of the Polish neighborhoods in Chicago. Saloons were a central institution of immigrant culture, where men spent a good deal of leisure time. They read newspapers written in their native languages, swapped information about job opportunities, enjoyed time away from overcrowded tenements, discussed politics, and fostered bonds of masculinity exclusive of women. However, the excessive drinking associated with saloons put a severe strain on family health and finances, especially when inebriated husbands and fathers lost their tempers at home or squandered their wages on alcohol. Peter Newark Pictures / Bridgeman Images

With few immigrants literate in English, foreign-language newspapers proliferated to inform their readers of local, national, and international events. Between the mid-1880s and 1920, 3,500 new foreign-language newspapers came into existence. These newspapers helped sustain ethnic solidarity in the New World as well as maintain ties to the Old World. Newcomers could learn about social and cultural activities in their communities and keep abreast of news from their homeland.

Like other communities with poor, unskilled populations, immigrant neighborhoods bred crime. Young men joined gangs based on ethnic heritage and battled with those of other immigrant groups to protect their turf. Adults formed underworld organizations — some of them tied to international criminal syndicates, such as the Mafia — that trafficked in prostitution, gambling, robbery, and murder. Tongs (secret organizations) in New York City's and San Francisco's Chinatowns, controlled the opium trade, gambling, and prostitution in their communities. A survey of New York City police and municipal court records from 1898 concluded that Jews "are prominent in their commission of forgery, violation of corporation ordinance, as disorderly persons (failure to support wife or family), both grades of larceny, and of the lighter grade of assault."

Crime was not the only social problem that plagued immigrant communities. Newspapers and court records reported husbands abandoning wives and children, engaging in drunken and disorderly conduct, or abusing their family. Boarders whom immigrant families took into their homes for economic reasons also posed problems. Cramped spaces created a lack of privacy, and male boarders sometimes attempted to assault the woman of the house while her husband and children were out to work or in school. Finally, generational conflicts within families began to develop as American-born children of immigrants questioned their parents' values. Thus the social organizations and mutual aid societies that immigrant groups established were more than a simple expression of ethnic solidarity and pride. They were also a response to the very real problems that challenged the health and stability of immigrant communities.

Explore ▶

See Source 18.1 for a depiction of one immigrant family's intergenerational conflict.

Hostility toward Recent Immigrants. On October 28, 1886, the United States held a gala celebration for the opening of the Statue of Liberty in New York harbor, a short distance from Ellis Island. French sculptors Frédéric-Auguste Bartholdi and Alexandre-Gustave Eiffel had designed the monument to appear at the Centennial Exposition in Philadelphia in 1876. Ten years overdue, the statue arrived in June 1885, but funds were still needed to finish construction of a base on which the sculpture would stand. Ordinary people dipped into their pockets for spare change, contributing to a campaign that raised $100,000 so that Lady Liberty could finally hold her uplifted torch for all to see. In 1903 the inspiring words of Emma Lazarus, a Jewish poet, were inscribed on the pedestal welcoming new generations of immigrants.

> Give me your tired, your poor,
> Your huddled masses yearning to breathe free,
> The wretched refuse of your teeming shore,
> Send these, the homeless, tempest-tossed to me,
> I lift my lamp beside the golden door!

Despite the welcoming inscription on the Statue of Liberty, many Americans whose families had arrived before the 1880s considered the influx of immigrants from southern and eastern Europe, Mexico, the Caribbean, and Asia at best a necessary evil and at worst a menace. Industrialists counted on immigrants to provide cheap labor. Not surprisingly, existing industrial workers saw the newcomers as a threat to their economic livelihoods and believed that their arrival would result in greater competition for jobs and lower wages. Moreover, even though most immigrants came to America to find work and improve the lives of their families, a small portion antagonized and frightened capitalists and middle-class Americans with their radical calls for the reorganization of society and the overthrow of the government. Of course, the vast majority of immigrants were not radicals, but a large proportion of radicals were recent immigrants. During times of labor-management strife, this fact made it easier for businessmen and their spokesmen in the press to associate all immigrants with anti-American radicalism.

Anti-immigrant fears linked to ideas about race and ethnicity had a long history in the United States. In 1790 Congress passed a statute restricting citizenship to those

Anzia Yerzierska | Immigrant Fathers and Daughters, 1925

Anzia Yerzierska, a Jewish immigrant who came to the United States from Poland around 1890, wrote about the struggles of immigrant families in adjusting to their new world. Her novel *Bread Givers* focuses on the conflict of a Jewish daughter, Sara Smolinski, patterned after herself, and the girl's father, Reb Smolinski, a Talmudic scholar. Intent on taking advantage of new opportunities in America, Sara resists her father's attempts to impose his Old World beliefs about the traditional duties of a subservient female.

Source 18.1

As I came through the door with my bundle, Father caught sight of me. "What's this?" he asked. "Where are you going?"

"I'm going back to work, in New York."

"What? Wild-head! Without asking, without consulting your father, you get yourself ready to go? Do you yet know that I want you to work in New York? Let's first count out your carfare to come home every night. Maybe it will cost so much there wouldn't be anything left from your wages."

"But I'm not coming home!"

"What? A daughter of mine, only seventeen years old, not home at night?"

"I'll go to Bessie or Mashah."

"Mashah is starving poor, and you know how crowded it is by Bessie."

"If there's no place for me by my sisters, I'll find a place by strangers."

"A young girl, alone, among strangers? Do you know what's going on in the world? No girl can live without a father or a husband to look out for her. It says in the Torah, only through a man has a woman an existence. Only through a man can a woman enter Heaven."

"I'm smart enough to look out for myself. It's a new life now. In America, women don't need men to boss them."

"*Blut-und-Eisen!* [Blood and iron!] They ought to put you in a madhouse till you're cured of your crazy nonsense!" . . .

Wild with all that was choked in me since I was born, my eyes burned into my father's eyes. "My will is as strong as yours. I'm going to live my own life. Nobody can stop me. I'm not from the old country. I'm American!"

"You blasphemer!" His hand flung out and struck my cheek. "Denier of God! I'll teach you respect for the law!"

I leaped back and dashed for the door. The Old World had struck its last on me.

Source: Anzia Yerzierska, *Bread Givers* (New York: Persea Books, 1975), 136–38.

How does Sara's father view the father-daughter relationship?

What role does religion play in shaping Sara's father's point of view?

How does Sara view herself as different from her father?

Put It in Context

What pressures did immigrants face in adjusting to their new home?

deemed white. Among those excluded from citizenship were American Indians, who were regarded as savages, and African Americans, most of whom were slaves at the time. In 1857 the Supreme Court ruled that even free blacks were not citizens. From the very beginning of the United States, largely Protestant lawmakers debated whether Catholics and Jews qualified as whites. Although lawmakers ultimately included Catholics and Jews within their definition of "white," over the next two centuries Americans viewed racial categories as not simply matters of skin color. Ethnicity (country or culture of origin) and religion became absorbed into and intertwined with racial categories. A sociological study of Homestead, Pennsylvania published in 1910 broke down the community along the following constructed racial lines: "Slav, English-speaking European, native white, and colored." Russian Jewish immigrants such as Beryl Lassin were recorded as Hebrews rather than as Russians, suggesting that Jewishness was seen by Christian America as a racial identity.

Natural scientists and social scientists gave credence to the idea that some races and ethnic groups were superior and others were inferior. Referring to Darwin's theory of evolution, biologists and anthropologists constructed measures of racial hierarchies, placing descendants of northern Europeans with lighter complexions—Anglo-Saxons, Teutonics, and Nordics—at the top of the evolutionary scale. Those with darker skin were deemed inferior "races," with Africans and Native Americans at the bottom. Scholars attempting to make disciplines such as history more "scientific" accepted these racial classifications. The prevailing sentiment of this era reflected demeaning images of many immigrant groups: Irish as drunkards, Mexicans and Cubans as lazy, Italians as criminals, Hungarians as ignorant peasants, Jews as cheap and greedy, and Chinese as drug addicts. These characteristics supposedly resulted from inherited biological traits, rather than from extreme poverty or other environmental conditions.

Newer immigrants, marked as racially inferior, became a convenient target of hostility. Skilled craftsmen born in the United States viewed largely unskilled workers from abroad who would work for low wages as a threat to their attempts to form unions and keep wages high. Middle-class city dwellers blamed urban problems on the rising tide of foreigners. In addition, Protestant purists felt threatened by Catholics and Jews and believed these "races" incapable or unworthy of assimilation into what they considered to be the superior white, Anglo-Saxon, and Protestant culture.

Nativism—the belief that foreigners pose a serious danger to one's native society and culture—arose as a reactionary response to immigration. In 1887 Henry F. Bowers of Clinton, Iowa founded the American Protective Association. The group proposed restricting Catholic immigration, making English a prerequisite to American citizenship, and prohibiting Catholics from teaching in public schools or holding public offices. New England elites, such as Massachusetts senator Henry Cabot Lodge and writer John Fiske,

Explore ▶

See Sources 18.2 and 18.3 on different perspectives of Chinese immigration.

argued that southern European, Semitic, and Slavic races did not fit into the "community of race" that had founded the United States. In 1893 Lodge and fellow Harvard graduates established the Immigration Restriction League and lobbied for federal legislation that would exclude adult immigrants unable to read in their own language.

Proposals to restrict immigration, however, did nothing to deal with the millions of foreigners already in America. To preserve their status and power and increase the size of the native-born population, nativists embraced the idea of **eugenics**—a pseudoscience

The Chinese in America

The harshest response against immigration came against the Chinese. In the West, violence against the Chinese was commonplace. White workers feared that Chinese laborers would take jobs away from them and contaminate their cities with vice and drugs. Based on racist assumptions of uncivilized Chinese, the exclusion act of 1882 banned Chinese from entering the country. In 1885, not long after passage of this law, one Chinese resident of New York, Saum Song Bo, used the occasion of the celebration of the Statue of Liberty to express disappointment in his adopted country. Soon after, in its decision in *Yick Wo v. Hopkins*, the U.S. Supreme Court affirmed the right of Chinese to equal protection of the law.

Source 18.2

Saum Song Bo | "A Chinese View of the Statue of Liberty" 1885

SIR: A paper was presented to me yesterday for inspection, and I found it to be specially drawn up for subscription among my countrymen toward the Pedestal Fund of the . . . Statue of Liberty. Seeing that the heading is an appeal to American citizens, to their love of country and liberty. . . . But the word liberty makes me think of the fact that this country is the land of liberty for men of all nations except the Chinese. I consider it as an insult to us Chinese to call on us to contribute toward building in this land a pedestal for a statue of Liberty. That statue represents Liberty holding a torch which lights the passage of those of all nations who come into this country. But are the Chinese allowed to come? As for the Chinese who are here, are they allowed to enjoy liberty as men of all other nationalities enjoy it? Are they allowed to go about everywhere free from the insults, abuse, assaults, wrongs and injuries from which men of other nationalities are free?

. . . Whether this statute [Exclusion Act] against the Chinese or the statue to Liberty will be the more lasting monument to tell future ages of the liberty and greatness of this country, will be known only to future generations.

Liberty, we Chinese do love and adore thee; but let not those who deny thee to us, make of thee a graven image and invite us to bow down to it.

Source: Saum Song Bo, "A Chinese View of the Statue of Liberty," *American Missionary* 39, no. 10 (1885): 290.

that advocated "biological engineering" — and supported the selective breeding of "desirable" races to counter the rapid population growth of "useless" races. Accordingly, eugenicists promoted the institutionalization of people deemed "unfit," sterilization of those considered mentally impaired, and the licensing and regulation of marriages to promote better breeding. In pushing for such measures, eugenicists believed that they were following the dictates of modern science and acting in a humane fashion to prevent those deemed unfit from causing further harm to themselves and to society.

Others took a less harsh approach. As had been the case with American Indians, reformers stressed the need for immigrants to assimilate into the dominant culture, embrace the values of individualism and self-help, adopt American styles of dress and grooming, and exhibit loyalty to the U.S. government. They encouraged immigrant

Source 18.3

Yick Wo v. Hopkins, 1886

Mr. Justice [Stanley] Matthews delivered the opinion of the court

[I]n 1880, San Francisco passed a fire-safety ordinance that all laundries operating in wooden buildings be licensed or the owners would risk criminal penalties. After the city government refused to grant licenses to nearly all Chinese laundries while approving those run by whites, Yick Wo, the owner of one rejected establishment, refused to close his business and was prosecuted.

[P]etitioners have complied with every requisite, deemed by the law or by the public officers charged with its administration, necessary for the protection of neighboring property from fire, or as a precaution against injury to the public health. No reason whatever, except the will of the supervisors, is assigned why they should not be permitted to carry on, in the accustomed manner, their harmless and useful occupation, on which they depend for a livelihood. And while this consent of the supervisors is withheld from them and from two hundred others who have also petitioned, all of whom happen to be Chinese subjects, eighty others, not Chinese subjects, are permitted to carry on the same business under similar conditions. The fact of this discrimination is admitted. No reason for it is shown, and the conclusion cannot be resisted, that no reason for it exists except hostility to the race and nationality to which the petitioners belong, and which in the eye of the law is not justified. The discrimination is, therefore, illegal, and the public administration which enforces it is a denial of the equal protection of the laws and a violation of the Fourteenth Amendment of the Constitution. The imprisonment of the petitioners is, therefore, illegal, and they must be discharged.

Source: *Yick Wo v. Hopkins,* 118 U.S. 356, 374 (1886).

Interpret the Evidence

1. Why does Saum Song Bo believe the sentiments of the Statue of Liberty do not apply to the treatment of Chinese?
2. According to Justice Matthews, why does the treatment of Chinese laundrymen violate the Fourteenth Amendment?

Put It in Context

What were American attitudes toward Chinese immigrants in the nineteenth century? What pressures and changes influenced these views?

children to attend public schools, where they would learn to speak English and adopt American cultural rituals by celebrating holidays such as Thanksgiving and Columbus Day and reciting the pledge of allegiance, introduced in 1892. Educators encouraged adult immigrants to attend night classes to learn English.

The Assimilation Dilemma. If immigrants were not completely assimilated, neither did they remain the same people who had lived on the farms and in the villages of Europe, Asia, Mexico, and the Caribbean. Some, like Mary Vik, sought to become full-fledged Americans or at least see that their children did so. Writer Israel Zangwill, an English American Jew, furnished the enduring image of assimilation in his 1908 play *The Melting-Pot.* Zangwill portrayed people from distinct backgrounds entering the cauldron of American life, mixing together, and emerging as citizens identical to their native-born counterparts.

However, the image of America as a **melting pot** worked better as an ideal than as a mirror of reality. Immigrants during this period never fully lost the social, cultural, religious, and political identities they had brought with them. Even if all immigrants had sought full assimilation, which they did not, the anti-immigrant sentiment of many native-born Americans reinforced their status as strangers and aliens. The same year that Zangwill's play was published, Alfred P. Schultz, a New York physician, provided a dim view of the prospects of assimilation in his book *Race or Mongrel*. Schultz dismissed the melting pot theory that public schools could convert the children of all races into Americans. **See Primary Source Project 18: "Melting Pot" or "Vegetable Soup"? page 623.**

Thus most immigrants faced the dilemma of assimilating while holding on to their heritage. Sociologist W. E. B. Du Bois summed up this predicament for one of the nation's earliest transported groups. In *The Souls of Black Folk* (1903), Du Bois wrote that African Americans felt a "two-ness," an identity carved out of their African heritage together with their lives as slaves and free people in America. This "double-consciousness . . . two souls, two thoughts, two unreconciled strivings" also applied to immigrants at the turn of the twentieth century. Immigrants who entered the country after 1880 were more like vegetable soup — an amalgam of distinct parts within a common broth — than a melting pot.

REVIEW & RELATE

- What challenges did new immigrants to the United States face?

- What steps did immigrants take to meet these challenges?

Becoming an Urban Nation

In the half century after the Civil War, the population of the United States quadrupled, but the urban population soared seven-fold. In 1870 one in five Americans lived in cities with a population of 8,000 or more. By 1900 one in three resided in cities of this size. In 1870 only Philadelphia and New York had populations over half a million. Twenty years later, in addition to these two cities, Chicago's population exceeded 1 million; St. Louis, Boston, and Baltimore had more than 500,000 residents; and Cleveland, Buffalo, San Francisco, and Cincinnati boasted populations over 250,000. Urbanization was not confined to the Northeast and Midwest. Denver's population jumped from 4,700 in 1870 to more than 107,000 in 1890. During that same period, Los Angeles grew nearly fivefold, from 11,000 to 50,000, and Birmingham leaped from 3,000 to 26,000. This phenomenal urban growth also brought remarkable physical changes to the cities, as tall buildings reached toward the skies, electric lights brightened the night-time hours, and water and gas pipes, sewers, and subways snaked below the ground.

The New Industrial City. Although cities have long been a part of the landscape, Americans have felt ambivalent about their presence. Many Americans have shared Thomas Jefferson's idea that democratic values were rooted in the soil of small, independent farms. In contrast to the natural environment of rural life, cities have been perceived as artificial creations in which corruption and contagion flourish. In the 1890s, the very identity of Americans seemed threatened as the frontier came to an end. Some agreed with the historian Frederick Jackson Turner, who believed the closing of the western frontier endangered the existence of democracy because it removed the opportunity for the pioneer spirit that built America to regenerate. Rural Americans were especially uncomfortable with the country's increasingly urban life. When the small-town lawyer Clarence Darrow moved to Chicago in the 1880s he was horrified by the "solid, surging sea of human units, each intent upon hurrying by." Still, like Darrow, millions of people were drawn to the new opportunities cities offered.

Urban growth in America was part of a long-term worldwide phenomenon. Between 1820 and 1920, some 60 million people globally moved from rural to urban areas. Most of them migrated after the 1870s, and as noted earlier, millions journeyed from towns and villages in Europe to American cities. Yet the number of Europeans who migrated internally was greater than those who went overseas. As in the United States, Europeans moved from the countryside to urban areas in search of jobs. Many migrated to the city on a seasonal basis, seeking winter employment in cities and then returning to the countryside at harvest time.

Before the Civil War, commerce was the engine of growth for American cities. Ports like New York, Boston, New Orleans, and San Francisco became distribution centers for imported goods or items manufactured in small shops in the surrounding countryside. Cities in the interior of the country located on or near major bodies of water, such as Chicago, St. Louis, Cincinnati, and Detroit, served similar functions. As the extension of railroad transportation led to the development of large-scale industry, these cities and others became industrial centers as well.

Industrialization contributed to rapid urbanization in several ways. It drew those living on farms, who either could not earn a satisfactory living or were bored by the isolation of rural areas, into the city in search of better-paying jobs and excitement. One rural dweller in Massachusetts complained: "The lack of pleasant, public entertainments in this town has much to do with our young people feeling discontented with country life." In addition, while the mechanization of farming increased efficiency, it also reduced the demand for farm labor. In 1896 one person could plant, tend, and harvest as much wheat as it had taken eighteen farmworkers to do sixty years before.

Industrial technology and other advances also made cities more attractive and livable places. Electricity extended nighttime entertainment and powered streetcars to convey people around town. Improved water and sewage systems provided more sanitary conditions, especially given the demands of the rapidly expanding population. Structural steel and electric elevators made it possible to construct taller and taller buildings, which gave cities such as Chicago and New York their distinctive skylines. Scientists and physicians made significant progress in the fight against the spread of contagious diseases, which had become serious problems in crowded cities.

Many of the same causes of urbanization in the Northeast and Midwest applied to the far West. The development of the mining industry attracted business and labor to urban settlements. Cities grew up along railroad terminals, and railroads stimulated urban growth by bringing out settlers and creating markets. By 1900, the proportion of residents in western cities with a population of at least ten thousand was greater than in any other section of the country except the Northeast. More so than in the East, Asians and Hispanics inhabited western urban centers along with whites and African Americans. In 1899

Salt Lake City boasted the publication of two black newspapers as well as the president of the Western Negro Press Association. Western cities also took advantage of the latest technology, and in the 1880s and 1890s electric trolleys provided mass transit in Denver and San Francisco.

Although immigrants increasingly accounted for the influx into the cities across the nation, before 1890 the rise in urban population came mainly from Americans on the move. In addition to young men, young women left the farm to seek their fortune. The female protagonist of Theodore Dreiser's novel *Sister Carrie* (1900) abandons small-town Wisconsin for the lure of Chicago. In real life, mechanization created many "Sister Carries" by making farm women less valuable in the fields. The possibility of purchasing mass-produced goods from mail-order houses such as Sears, Roebuck also left young women less essential as homemakers because they no longer had to sew their own clothes and could buy labor-saving appliances from catalogs.

Similar factors drove rural black women and men into cities. Plagued by the same poverty and debt that white sharecroppers and tenants in the South faced, blacks suffered from the added burden of racial oppression and violence in the post-Reconstruction period. From 1870 to 1890, the African American population of Nashville, Tennessee soared from just over 16,000 to more than 29,000. In Atlanta, Georgia, the number of blacks jumped from slightly above 16,000 to around 28,000.

Economic opportunities were more limited for black migrants than for their white counterparts. African American migrants found work as cooks, janitors, and domestic servants. Many found employment as manual laborers in manufacturing companies — including tobacco factories, which employed women and men; tanneries; and cottonseed oil firms — and as dockworkers. Although the overwhelming majority of blacks worked as unskilled laborers for very low wages, others opened small businesses such as funeral parlors, barbershops, and construction companies or went into professions such as medicine, law, banking, and education that catered to residents of segregated black neighborhoods. Despite considerable individual accomplishments, by the turn of the twentieth century most blacks in the urban South had few prospects for upward economic mobility.

In 1890, although 90 percent of African Americans lived in the South, a growing number were moving to northern cities to seek employment and greater freedom. Boll weevil infestations during the 1890s decimated cotton production and forced sharecroppers and tenants off farms. At the same time, blacks saw significant erosion of their political and civil rights in the last decade of the nineteenth century. Most black citizens in the South were denied the right to vote and experienced rigid, legally sanctioned racial segregation in all aspects of public life. Between 1890 and 1914 approximately 485,000 African Americans left the South. By 1914 New York, Chicago, and Philadelphia each counted more than 100,000 African Americans among their population. An African American woman expressed her enthusiasm about the employment she found in Chicago, where she earned $3 a day working in a railroad yard. "The colored women like this work," she explained, because "we make more money . . . and we do not have to work as hard as at housework," which required working sixteen-hour days, six days a week.

Although many blacks found they preferred their new lives to the ones they had led in the South, the North did not turn out to be the promised land of freedom. Black newcomers encountered discrimination in housing and employment. Residential segregation confined African Americans to racial ghettos. Black workers found it difficult to obtain skilled

African American Family, 1900   Despite the rigid racial segregation and oppression that African Americans faced in the late nineteenth century, some black families found ways to achieve economic success and upward mobility. With its piano and fine furniture, the home of this African American family reflects middle-class conventions of the period. The father is a graduate of Hampton Institute, a historically black university founded after the Civil War to educate freedpeople. Library of Congress, 3a38506

employment despite their qualifications, and women and men most often toiled as domestics, janitors, and part-time laborers.

Nevertheless, African Americans in northern cities built communities that preserved and reshaped their southern culture and offered a degree of insulation against the harshness of racial discrimination. A small black middle class appeared consisting of teachers, attorneys, and small business owners. In 1888 African Americans organized the Capital Savings Bank of Washington, D.C. Ten years later, two black real estate agents in New York City were worth more than $150,000 each, and one agent in Cleveland owned $100,000 in property. The rising black middle class provided leadership in the formation of mutual aid societies, lodges, and women's clubs. Newspapers such as the *Chicago Defender* and *Pittsburgh Courier* furnished local news to their subscribers and reported national and international events affecting people of color. As was the case in the South, the church was at the center of black life in northern cities. More than just religious institutions, churches furnished space for social activities and the dissemination of political information. By the first decade of the twentieth century, more than two dozen churches had sprung up in Chicago alone. Whether housed in newly constructed buildings or in storefronts, black churches provided worshippers freedom from white control. They also allowed members of the northern black middle class to demonstrate what they considered to be respectability and refinement. This meant discouraging enthusiastic displays of "old-time religion," which celebrated more exuberant forms of worship. As the Reverend W. A. Blackwell of Chicago's AME Zion Church declared, "Singing, shouting, and talking [were] the most useless ways of proving Christianity." This conflict over modes of religious expression reflected a larger process that was under way in black communities at the turn of the twentieth century. As black urban communities in the North grew and developed, tensions and divisions emerged within the increasingly diverse black community, as a variety of groups competed to shape and define black culture and identity.

Expand Upward and Outward.

As the urban population increased, cities expanded both up and out. Before 1860, the dominant form of brick and stone construction prevented buildings from rising more than four or five stories. However, as cities became much more populous, land values soared. Steep prices prompted architects to make the most of small, expensive plots of land by finding ways to build taller structures. Architects began using cast-iron columns instead of the thick, heavy walls of brick that limited floor space. The resulting "cloudscrapers" raised the urban skyline to ten stories. The development of structural steel, which was stronger and more durable than iron, turned cloudscrapers into **skyscrapers**, which stretched some thirty stories into the air. With the development of the electric elevator and the radiator, which replaced fireplaces with hot water circulated through pipes, even taller skyscrapers came to loom over downtown business districts in major cities.

Cities also expanded horizontally, as new transportation technology made it possible for residents to move around a much larger urban landscape. In the mid-nineteenth century in cities such as Boston and Philadelphia, pedestrians could still walk from one end of the city to the other within an hour. If residents preferred, they could pay a fare and hop on board a horse-drawn railcar. These vehicles moved slowly and left tons of horse manure in the streets. To avoid such problems, in 1873 San Francisco, followed by Seattle and Chicago, installed a system of cable-driven trolley cars. At first, these trolleys still proved slow and unreliable. But by 1914, advances in transportation converted walking cities into riding cities.

Electricity provided the transportation breakthrough. In 1888 naval engineer Frank J. Sprague completed the first electric trolley line in Richmond, Virginia. Electric-powered streetcars traveled twice as fast as horse-drawn railcars and left little mess on the streets. Subways could run underground without asphyxiating passengers and workmen with a steam engine's smoke and soot. Boston opened the first subway in 1897, followed by New York City in 1904.

Bridges spanning large rivers and waterways also helped extend the boundaries of the inner city. In 1883 the Brooklyn Bridge opened, connecting Manhattan with the city of Brooklyn. Designed and engineered by John Augustus Roebling, and completed by his son Washington and Washington's wife Emily, the bridge had taken thirteen years to construct and cost twenty men their lives. It stretched more than a mile across the East River and was broad enough for a footpath, two double carriage lanes, and two railroad lines. During its first year in operation, more than 11 million people passed over the bridge; today, more than 51 million vehicles cross the bridge each year.

The electrification of public transportation and the construction of bridges made it feasible for some people to live considerable distances from their workplace. In the eighteenth and nineteenth centuries, middle- and upper-class merchants and professionals usually lived near their shops and offices in the heart of the city, surrounded by their employees. After 1880, the huge influx of immigration brought large numbers of impoverished workers to city centers. The resulting traffic congestion and overcrowded housing pushed wealthier residents to seek more open spaces in which to build houses. The new electric trolley lines allowed middle-class urbanites to move miles away from downtown areas. In 1850 the Boston metropolis spread in a radius of two to three miles around the city and had a population of 200,000. In 1900 suburban Boston ringed the city in a ten-mile radius, with a population of more than 1 million. Increasingly, cities divided into two parts: an inner commercial and industrial core housing the working class, and outer communities occupied by a wealthier class of white, older-stock Americans.

How the Other Half Lived.

As the middle and upper classes fled the industrial urban center for the suburbs, the working poor moved in to replace them. They lived in old factories and homes and in shanties and cellars. Because land values were higher in the city, rents were high and the poorest people could least afford them. To make ends meet, families crowded into existing apartments, sometimes taking in boarders to help pay the rent. This led to increased population density and overcrowding in the urban areas where immigrants lived. On New York's Lower East Side, the population density was the highest in the world. Such overcrowding fostered communicable diseases and frustration, giving the area the nicknames "typhus ward" and "suicide ward."

Explore ▶

Compare two historians' interpretations of nativism and who is classified as white in Sources 18.4 and 18.5.

Overcrowding combined with extreme poverty turned immigrant neighborhoods into slums, which were characterized by substandard housing. Impoverished immigrants typically lived in multiple-family apartment buildings called **tenements** (legally defined as containing more than three families). First constructed in 1850, these early dwellings often featured windowless rooms and little or no plumbing and heating. In 1879 a New York law reformed the building codes to require minimal plumbing facilities and to stipulate that all bedrooms (but not all rooms) have a window. Constructed on narrow 25-by-100-foot lots, these five- and six-story buildings included four small apartments on a floor and had only two toilets off the hallway. Tenements stood right next to each other, with only an air shaft separating them. Although these dwellings marked some improvement in living conditions, they proved miserable places to live in — dark, damp, and foul smelling. In 1895 a federal government housing inspector observed that the air shafts provided "imperfect light and ventilation" and that "refuse matter or filth of one kind or another [was] very apt to accumulate at the bottom, giving rise to noxious odors." The air shafts also operated as a conduit for fires that moved swiftly from one tenement to another.

In fact, the density of late-nineteenth-century cities could turn individual fires into citywide disasters. The North Side of Chicago burned to the ground in 1871, and Boston and Baltimore suffered catastrophic fires as well. On April 18, 1906, an earthquake in San Francisco set the city ablaze, causing about 1,500 deaths. Such fires could, however, have long-term positive consequences. The great urban conflagrations encouraged construction of fireproof buildings made of brick and steel instead of wood. In addition, citizens organized fire watches and established municipal fire departments to replace volunteer

SECONDARY SOURCE ANALYSIS

Immigration, Nativism, and Whiteness

Since its founding, the United States has been a nation of immigrants, a haven for people all over the world seeking a better life whether for political, economic, or religious reasons. At the same time, hostility toward foreigners — nativism — has moved in tandem with immigration as an expression of concern that the influx of new arrivals, especially from certain regions of the world, would threaten jobs and debase American culture. From the very beginning of the country, immigration and citizenship were tied to race, but the question remained of which nationalities were white, the predominant race of the Europeans who settled and conquered North America. The meaning of whiteness and who was qualified for citizenship has changed over time, but expressions of nativism remain palpable. In these selections two historians trace nativism, racism, and whiteness from different perspectives.

Source 18.4

John Higham, Nativism and Race, 1955

"What concerns us is the intersection of racial attitudes with nationalistic ones-in other words, the extension to European nationalities of that sense of absolute difference which already divided white Americans from people of other colors. When sentiments analogous to those already discharged against Negroes, Indians, and Orientals spilled over into anti-European channels, a force of tremendous intensity entered the stream of American nativism. The whole story of modern racial ferment, nativist and otherwise, has two levels, one involving popular emotions, the other concerning more or less systematic ideas. Most of the emotions flow from a reservoir of habitual suspicion and distrust accumulated over the span of American history toward human groups stamped by obvious differences of color. The ideas, on the other hand, depend on the speculations of intellectuals on the nature of races. …

However, the evolution of white supremacy into a comprehensive philosophy of life,

grounding human values in the innate constitution of nature, required a major theoretical effort. It was the task of the racethinkers to organize specific antipathies toward dark-hued peoples into a generalized, ideological structure. To the development of racial nativism, the thinkers have made a special contribution. Sharp physical differences between native Americans and European immigrants were not readily apparent; to a large extent they had to be manufactured. A rather elaborate, well-entrenched set of racial ideas was essential before the newcomers from Europe could seem a fundamentally different order of men. Accordingly, a number of race-conscious intellectuals blazed the way for ordinary nativists, and it will be useful to tell their story before turning in later chapters to the popular emotions their ideas helped to orient.

Source: John Higham, *Strangers in the Land: Patterns of American Nativism, 1860–1925*. New Brunswick, New Jersey: Rutgers University Press, 1925, 132, 133.

Source 18.5

Katherine Benton-Cohen, Nativism, Mexicans, and Whiteness, 2009

"In the mid-nineteenth century, "Mexican" and "white" were overlapping categories, not opposite poles in a regional racial system. In this world, Apaches were not Americans, but Mexicans might be. These categories were, however, highly contingent on local conditions… Building national and racial boundaries required the removal and exclusion of some peoples, and the new inclusion of others. In small irrigated farm and ranch communities, the Apache Wars encouraged close settlement patterns and intermarriage among Mexican and European Americans. But race relations in place with different economic systems soon became more problematic. Where Mexicans owned ranches and farms, racial categories were blurry and unimportant. But in the industrial copper-mining town of Bisbee [Arizona], Mexican workers were segregated economically by their lower pay ('Mexican wage') and geographically by new town-planning experiments. To most non-Mexican residents of Bisbee, Mexicans were peon workers or potential public charges, not neighbors or business partners, not co-workers or co-worshippers and certainly not potential marriage partners.

In Cochise County [Arizona], corporations and governments exerted enormous influence over the creation of racial categories. Ideas about masculinity, femininity, nationhood and class colored ordinary people's judgements about race in tangible ways… Mexican could be white, and Italians could fail to be. Rich and poor, immigrant and native, miner and farmer, manager and workers, man and woman: they all fought over how race would be defined and who would benefit from these definitions."

Source: Katherine Benton-Cohen, *Borderline Americans: Racial Division and Labor War in the Arizona Borderlands*. Cambridge, Mass: Harvard University Press, 2009, 7–8, 14.

Examine the Sources

1. How do Higham and Benton-Cohen agree and differ in their views of nativism and whiteness?
2. What evidence can you find in these sources that nativism did not simply fall on a black-white spectrum but that there were racial categories in between white and black, and they were fluid?

Put it in Context

Evaluate the reasons that nativism flourished in the late nineteenth and early twentieth centuries and discuss how it affected different immigrant groups.

companies. An unintended side effect, fires provided cities with a chance to rebuild. Chicago's skyscrapers and its system of urban parks were built on land cleared by fire.

In 1890 Jacob Riis, a Danish immigrant, newspaperman, and photographer, illustrated the brutal conditions endured by tenement families such as Beryl Lassin's on New York's Lower East Side. "In the stifling July nights," he wrote in *How the Other Half Lives*, "when the big barracks are like fiery furnaces, their very walls giving out absorbed heat, men and women lie in restless, sweltering rows, panting for air and sleep." Under these circumstances, Riis lamented, an epidemic "is excessively fatal among the children of the poor, by reason of the practical impossibility of isolating the patient in a tenement." Despite their obvious problems, tenements soon spread to other cities such as Cleveland, Cincinnati, and Boston, and one block might have ten of these buildings, housing as many as four thousand people.

With all the misery they spawned as places to live, tenements also functioned as workplaces. Czech immigrants made cigars in their apartments from six in the morning until nine at night, seven days a week, for about 6 cents an hour. By putting an entire family to work, they could make $15 a week and pay their rent of $12 a month. Clothing contractors in particular saw these tenement **sweatshops** as a cheap way to produce their products. By jamming two or three sewing machines into an apartment and paying workers a fixed amount for each item they produced, contractors kept their costs down and avoided factory regulations.

The Triangle Shirtwaist Company Fire, 1911   On March 25, 1911, fire erupted in the Triangle Shirtwaist factory in lower Manhattan. Most of the company's six hundred garment workers were immigrant women. The building had inadequate fire escapes and blocked exits, which resulted in the high death toll of 146 workers. This catastrophe aroused many New Yorkers to rally around factory reforms. In the aftermath of the fire, Rose Schneiderman, a Polish Jewish immigrant who had led a strike at the Triangle Shirtwaist Company in 1909, addressed a memorial gathering at the Metropolitan Opera House. Bettmann/Getty Images

Even when immigrants left sweatshop apartments and went to work in factories, they continued to face exploitation. The Jewish and Italian clothing workers who toiled in the **Triangle Shirtwaist Company**, located in New York City's Greenwich Village, worked long hours for little pay. In 1911 a fire broke out on the eighth story of the factory and quickly spread to the ninth and tenth floors. The fire engines' ladders could not reach that high, and one of the exits on the ninth floor was locked to keep workers from stealing material. More than 140 people died in the blaze — some by jumping out the windows, but most by getting trapped behind the closed exit door. Following public outrage over the fire and through the efforts of reformers, New York City established a Bureau of Fire Protection, required safety devices in buildings, and prohibited smoking in factories. Furthermore, this tragedy spearheaded legislative efforts to improve working conditions in general, protect women workers, and abolish child labor.

Slums compounded the potential for disease, poor sanitation, fire, congestion, and crime. Living on poor diets, slum dwellers proved particularly vulnerable to epidemics. Cholera, yellow fever, and typhoid killed tens of thousands. Tuberculosis was even deadlier. An epidemic that began in a slum neighborhood could easily spread into more affluent areas of the city. Children suffered the most. Almost one-quarter of the children born in American cities in 1890 did not live to celebrate their first birthdays.

Contributing to the outbreak of disease was faulty sewage disposal, a problem that vexed city leaders. Until the invention of the modern indoor flush toilet in the late nineteenth century, people relied on outdoor toilets, with as many as eight hundred people using a single facility. All too often, cities dumped human waste into rivers that also supplied drinking water. In 1881 the exasperated mayor of Cleveland called the Cuyahoga River "an open sewer through the center of the city." At the same time, the great demand for water caused by the population explosion resulted in lower water pressure. Consequently, residents in the upper floors of tenements had to carry buckets of water from the lower floors. Until cities overcame their water and sanitation challenges, epidemics plagued urban dwellers.

Urban crowding created other problems as well. Traffic moved slowly through densely populated cities. Pedestrians and commuters had to navigate around throngs of people walking on sidewalks and streets, peddlers selling out of pushcarts, and piles of garbage cluttering the walkways. Streets remained in poor shape. In 1889 the majority of Cleveland's 440 miles of streets consisted of sand and gravel. Chicago did not fare much better. In 1890 most road surfaces were covered with wooden blocks, and three-quarters of the city's more than 2,000 miles of streets remained unpaved. Rainstorms quickly made matters worse by turning foul-smelling, manure-filled streets into mud.

Poverty and overcrowding contributed to increased crime. The U.S. murder rate quadrupled between 1880 and 1900, at a time when the murder rates in most European cities were declining. In New York City, crime thrived in slums with the apt names of "Bandit's Roost" and "Hell's Kitchen," and groups of young hoodlums preyed on unsuspecting citizens. Poverty forced some of the poor to turn to theft or prostitution. One twenty-year-old prostitute, who supported her sickly mother and four brothers and sisters, lamented: "Let God Almighty judge who's to blame most, I that was driven, or them that drove me to the pass I'm in." Rising criminality led to the formation of urban police departments, though many law officers supplemented their incomes by collecting graft (illegal payments) for ignoring criminal activities.

- What factors contributed to rapid urban growth in the late nineteenth century?

- How did the American cities of 1850 differ from those of 1900? What factors account for these differences?

Urban Politics at the Turn of the Century

The problems that booming cities faced in trying to absorb millions of immigrants proved formidable and at times seemed insurmountable. From a governmental standpoint, cities had limited authority over their own affairs. They were controlled by state legislatures and needed state approval to raise revenues and pass regulations. For the most part, there were no zoning laws to regulate housing construction. Private companies owned public utilities, and competition among them produced unnecessary duplication and waste. The government services that did exist operated on a segmented basis, with the emphasis on serving wealthier neighborhoods at the expense of the city at large. Missing was a vision of the city as a whole, working as a single unit.

Political Machines and City Bosses.   City government in the late nineteenth century was fragmented. Mayors usually did not have much power, and decisions involving public policies such as housing, transportation, and municipal services often rested in the hands of private developers. Bringing some order out of this chaos, the **political machine** functioned to give cities the centralized authority and services that they otherwise lacked. At the head of the machine was the political **boss**. Although the boss himself (and they were all men) held some public office, his real authority came from leadership of the machine. These organizations maintained a tight network of loyalists throughout city wards (districts), each of which contained designated representatives responsible for catering to the needs of their constituents. Whether Democratic or Republican, political machines did not care about philosophical issues; they were concerned primarily with staying in power.

The strength of political machines rested in large measure on immigrants. The organization provided a kind of public welfare when private charity could not cope satisfactorily with the growing needs of the poor. Machines doled out turkeys on holidays, furnished a load of coal for the winter, provided jobs in public construction, arranged for shelter and meals if tenement houses burned down, and intervened with the police and the courts when a constituent got into trouble. Bosses sponsored baseball clubs, held barbecues and picnics, and attended christenings, bar mitzvahs, weddings, and funerals. For enterprising members of immigrant groups — and this proved especially true for the Irish during this period — the machine offered upward mobility out of poverty as they rose through its ranks. Not all immigrants benefited from political bosses equally, however. In San Francisco, Abe Ruef, whose parents were French Jews, became a political boss around the turn of the twentieth century. His sympathies for immigrants did not extend to the Chinese, however. Following the 1906 earthquake, he led an effort to expel residents of the city's Chinatown.

Boss Abe Reuf   In 1908 Abe Ruef, the political boss of San Francisco, was tried and convicted on charges of bribery and influence peddling. Ruef served four and a half years of a fourteen-year sentence at San Quentin. This photo captures a worried-looking Ruef listening to his attorney, Henry Ach, outside the courthouse during his trial. *Courtesy of the Bancroft Library, University of California, Berkeley, call no. BANC PIC 1905.02623-A*

The poor were not the only group that benefited from connections to political machines. The machine and its functionaries helped businessmen maneuver through the maze of contradictory and overlapping codes regulating building and licenses that impeded their routine course of activities. In addition to assisting legitimate businessmen, the machine facilitated the underworld commerce of vice, prostitution, and gambling by acting as an arbiter to keep this trade within established boundaries — all for a cut of the illegal profits.

In return for these services, the machine received the votes of immigrants and money from businessmen. When challenged by reformers or other political rivals, the machine readily engaged in corrupt election practices to maintain its power. Mobilizing the "graveyard vote," bosses took names from tombstones to pad lists of registered voters. They also hired "repeaters" to vote more than once under phony names and did not flinch from dumping whole ballot boxes into the river or using hired thugs to scare opponents from the polls.

Bosses enriched themselves through graft and corruption. They secured protection money from both legitimate and illegitimate business interests in return for their services. In the 1860s and 1870s, Boss William Marcy Tweed, the head of Tammany Hall, New York City's political machine, swindled the city out of a fortune while supervising the construction of a lavish three-story courthouse in lower Manhattan. The original budget for the building was $250,000, but the city spent more than $13 million on the structure. The building remained unfinished in 1873, when Tweed was convicted on fraud charges and went to jail. In later years, Tammany Hall's George Washington Plunkitt distinguished this kind of "dishonest graft" from the kind of "honest graft" that he practiced. If he received inside information about a future sale of city property, Plunkitt reasoned, why shouldn't he get a head start, buy it at a low price, and then sell it at a higher figure? As he delighted in saying, "I seen my opportunities and I took 'em." Still, courts did not see such behavior so favorably. In 1908, San Francisco's Boss Ruef was convicted of bribery and imprisoned at San Quentin.

The services of political machines came at a high cost. Corruption and graft led to higher taxes on middle-class residents. Moreover, the image of the political boss as a modern-day Robin Hood who stole from the rich and gave to the poor is greatly exaggerated. Much of the proceeds of machine activities went into the private coffers of machine bosses and other functionaries. Trafficking in vice might have run more smoothly under the coordination of the machine, but the safety and health of city residents hardly improved. Most important, although immigrants and the poor did benefit from an informal system of social welfare, the machine had no interest in resolving the underlying causes of their problems. As the dominant urban political party organization, the machine cared little about issues such as good housing, job safety, and sufficient wages. It remained for others to provide alternative approaches to relieving the plight of the urban poor.

Urban Reformers. The men and women who criticized the political bosses and machines — and the corruption and vice they fostered — usually came from the ranks of the upper middle class and the wealthy. Their solutions to the urban crisis typically centered around toppling the political machine and replacing it with a civil service that would allow government to function on the basis of merit rather than influence peddling and cronyism. Both locally and nationally, they pushed for civil service reform. In 1883 Congress responded to this demand by passing the **Pendleton Civil Service Reform Act**, which required federal jobs to be awarded on the basis of merit, as determined by competitive examinations, rather than through political connections. As for the immigrants who supported machine politics, these reformers preferred to deal with them from afar and expected that through proper education they might change their lifestyles and adopt American ways.

Another group of Americans from upper- and middle-class backgrounds put aside whatever prejudices they might have held about working-class immigrants and dealt directly with newcomers to try to solve various social problems. These reformers — mostly young people, and many of them women and college graduates — took up residence in **settlement houses** located in urban slums. Settlement houses offered a variety of services to community residents, including day care for children; cooking, sewing, and secretarial classes; neighborhood playgrounds; counseling sessions; and meeting rooms for labor unions. Settlement house organizers understood that immigrants gravitated to the political machine or congregated in the local tavern not because they were inherently immoral but because these institutions helped mitigate their suffering and, in some cases, offered concrete paths to advancement. Although settlement house workers wanted to Americanize immigrants, they also understood immigrants' need to hold on to remnants of their original culture. By 1900 approximately one hundred settlement houses had been established in major American cities.

Religiously inspired reform provided similar support for slum dwellers. Some Protestant ministers began to argue that immigrants' problems resulted not from chronic racial or ethnic failings but from their difficult environment. Some of them preached Christianity as a "social gospel," which included support for civil service reform, antimonopoly regulation, income tax legislation, factory inspection laws, and workers' right to strike.

Despite the efforts of social gospel advocates and the charitable organizations that arose to help relieve human misery, private attempts to combat the various urban ills, however well-meaning, proved insufficient. The problems were structural, not personal, and one group or even several operating together did not have the resources or power to make urban institutions more efficient, equitable, and humane. If reformers were to succeed in tackling the most significant social problems and make lasting changes in American society and politics, they would have to enlist state and federal governments.

REVIEW & RELATE

- What role did political machines play in late-nineteenth-century cities?

- Who led the opposition to machine control of city politics, and what solutions and alternatives did they offer?

Conclusion: A **Nation** of **Cities**

Immigrants from southern and eastern Europe, as well as from Asia and points south, who came to the United States between the 1880s and 1914 survived numerous hardships as they strove to create better lives for their families. They persevered despite discrimination, overcrowding in slums, and dangerous working conditions, long hours, and low wages. Immigrants joined neighborhood groups — houses of worship, fraternal organizations, burial societies, political machines, and settlement houses — to promote their own welfare. Some achieved success and returned to their homelands. Most of those who remained in the United States, like Mary Vik and Ben Lassin, struggled to earn a living but managed to pave the way for their children and grandchildren to obtain better education and jobs. Mary's granddaughter, Nancy A. Hewitt, earned a Ph.D. in history from the University of Pennsylvania, and Ben's grandson, Steven F. Lawson, earned a doctorate in history from Columbia University. They became university professors and, through their teaching and writing, have tried to preserve their grandparents' legacy.

Immigrants were not the only group on the move in the late nineteenth century. Rural dwellers left their farms seeking new job opportunities as well as the excitement cities provided. Among them, African Americans migrated in search of political freedom and economic opportunity. They relocated from the rural South to the urban South and North, where they continued to encounter discrimination. Yet cities gave them more leeway to develop their own communities and institutions than they had before. And African Americans in the North were allowed to vote, a tool they would use to gain equality in the future. Nevertheless, because of long-standing patterns of racism, supported by law, African Americans would struggle much longer than did white immigrants to obtain equality and justice.

Few public institutions attempted to aid immigrants or racial minorities as they made the difficult transition to urban and industrial life. Yet immigrants did participate in urban politics through the efforts of political bosses and their machines who sought immigrant votes. In return, political machines provided immigrants with rudimentary social and political services. Political machines, however, bred corruption, along with higher taxes to fund their extravagances. Dishonest government prompted middle- and upper-class urban dwellers to take up reform in order to sweep the political bosses out of office and diminish the power of their immigrant supporters, as we will see in the next chapter.

CHAPTER **18** REVIEW

TIMELINE OF EVENTS

KEY TERMS

REVIEW & RELATE

1. What challenges did new immigrants to the United States face?
2. What steps did immigrants take to meet these challenges?
3. What factors contributed to rapid urban growth in the late nineteenth century?
4. How did the American cities of 1850 differ from those of 1900? What factors account for these differences?
5. What role did political machines play in late-nineteenth-century cities?
6. Who led the opposition to machine control of city politics, and what solutions and alternatives did they offer?

"Melting Pot" or "Vegetable Soup"?

▶ Describe and evaluate the competing ideas about race and ethnicity that shaped opinions about immigrants and their place in American society at the turn of the twentieth century.

I n his play *The Melting-Pot* (1908), writer Israel Zangwill created what would become the dominant metaphor of immigrant assimilation. Zangwill portrayed people from different backgrounds entering American society, undergoing a process of assimilation, and becoming citizens virtually indistinguishable from their native-born counterparts. When the play premiered at the Columbia Theater in Washington, D.C., President Theodore Roosevelt, to whom the play was dedicated, was in the audience and reportedly cheered the production. The play went on to become a hit on Broadway the following year.

The reality of immigrant assimilation was more complicated than Zangwill's "melting pot" metaphor suggested (Sources 18.6 and 18.7). There is some truth in Zangwill's metaphor: In the days before radio and television, immigrants absorbed new values, language, style of dress, taste in foods, and sense of humor from schools, newspapers, magazines, and silent movies. However, many of them also valued aspects of their native cultural and social heritages and took pains to preserve cherished traditions and beliefs (Source 18.8). Although immigrants saw the necessity of some degree of assimilation, many were unwilling to become "fully American" if that meant completely abandoning their previous cultural identities. Assimilation also varied by generation, with the children of immigrants becoming more Americanized than their parents.

While many Americans saw assimilation as a requirement of true citizenship, others rejected the very possibility of assimilation, arguing that immigrants were inherently inferior and could not be absorbed into American society (Sources 18.8 and 18.9). Only a few such as Randolph Bourne took the position of what today we call multiculturalism (Source 18.10).

Source 18.6

Israel Zangwill | *The Melting-Pot,* 1908

The Melting-Pot explores the experiences of David Quixano, a Jewish immigrant and musician, as he writes a symphony that puts to music the racial and ethnic harmony created by the assimilation of immigrant groups in America at the turn of the twentieth century. In the following scene, David explains the process of assimilation to his love interest, Vera, and his uncle Mendel.

VERA So your music finds inspiration in America?

DAVID Yes—in the seething of the Crucible.

VERA The Crucible? I don't understand!

DAVID Not understand! You, the Spirit of the Settlement! Not understand that America is God's Crucible, the great Melting-Pot where all the races of Europe are melting and re-forming! Here you stand, good folk, think I, when I see them at Ellis Island, here you stand in your fifty groups, with your fifty languages and histories, and your fifty blood hatreds and rivalries. But you won't be long like that, brothers, for these are the fires of God you've come to—these are the fires of God. A fig for your feuds and vendettas! Germans and

Frenchmen, Irishmen and Englishmen, Jews and Russians—into the Crucible with you all! God is making the American.

MENDEL I should have thought the American was made already—eighty millions of him.

DAVID Eighty millions! Eighty millions! Over a continent! Why, that cockleshell of a Britain has forty millions! No, uncle, the real American has not yet arrived. He is only in the Crucible, I tell you—he will be the fusion of all races, the coming superman. Ah, what a glorious Finale for my symphony—if I can only write it.

Source: Israel Zangwill, *The Melting-Pot: Drama in Four Acts* (New York: Macmillan, 1909), 36–38.

Source: Israel Zangwill, *The Melting-Pot: Drama in Four Acts* (New York: Macmillan, 1909), 36–38.

Source 18.7

"The Mortar of Assimilation — and the One Element That Won't Mix," 1889

Before Zangwill's play appeared, the magazine *Puck* published a cartoon that contains the concept of the melting pot. In it Columbia, the female symbol of the United States, draped in an American flag, is stirring a pot labeled "Citizenship" with a spoon called "Equal Rights." Various nationalities can be seen in the pot, but only one group, the Irish, appears to resist assimilation.

THE MORTAR OF ASSIMILATION — AND THE ONE ELEMENT THAT WON'T MIX.

Newberry Library, Chicago, Illinois, USA/Bridgeman Images

"Be Just — Even to John Chinaman," 1893

The following cartoon appeared in the satirical magazine *Judge* the year after Congress renewed the Chinese Exclusion Act and added provisions requiring the Chinese already living in the United States to carry certificates of identity and residence. A caption beneath the cartoon states: "Judge (*to Miss Columbia*) — 'You allowed that boy to come into your school, it would be inhuman to throw him out now — it will be sufficient in the future to keep his brothers out!'" While the cartoon favors the Chinese Exclusion Act, it presents a more complex message. It accepts the presence of other immigrant groups and Native Americans, shown in stereotyped depictions, suggesting that schooling will turn them into true Americans. It also expresses some sympathy for the Chinese remaining in the country. The cartoon also proposes that some of these earlier immigrants harbored anti-Chinese feelings. Note the Irish American holding up a blackboard that says, "Kick Out the Heathen; He's Got No Vote."

BE JUST—EVEN TO JOHN CHINAMAN.

JUDGE (*to Miss Columbia*) — "You allowed that boy to come into your school, it would be inhuman to throw him out now — it will be sufficient in the future to keep his brothers out !"

Granger, NYC

Alfred P. Schultz | The Mongrelization of America, 1908

Using the fall of Rome as his example, Alfred P. Schultz argued in *Race or Mongrel* that the mixing of races produced a mongrel civilization and inevitably led to the decay of a nation. As one reviewer noted at the time, the author's "apparent object is to check alien immigration into the United States." Like most opponents of the new immigrants, Schultz used arguments based on moral judgments and supposedly sound medical and scientific information.

The influx of these races cannot be without consequences. The surgeons at the ports of immigration observe that the present immigrants have a much higher percent of loathsome diseases, and that, in general physique, it is very much inferior to the immigration of thirty years ago. The history of the races now coming proves beyond doubt their mental inferiority to the races that immigrated before the advent of Slavs and Latins. If immigration is still a blessing, then the sturdy Northern races are in every way preferable to the Southern and Southeastern debris of races that have been. The free admission of these latter prevents the coming of the former, for if content to compete with Slavs and Latins, the Northerners need not migrate as far as the United States. Much more important than the economic effects of immigration are the racial effects of immigration. . . .

Up to the middle of the last century a distinct national character was developing in the United States, and certain distinctive traits were forming. The addition of millions of other races has caused a decomposition which prevented the endurance of these characteristics, and caused this development to cease. . . .

One cause only is sufficiently powerful to cause the decay of a nation. This cause is promiscuousness. A nation is decayed that consists of degenerates, and it consists of degenerates when it no longer constitutes a distinct race. A degenerated race is one that has no longer the same internal worth which it had of old, for the reason that incessant infusions of foreign blood have diluted and weakened the old blood. In other words, a nation is deteriorated that consists of individuals not at all related or very distantly related to the founders of the nation. . . .

The principle that all men are created equal is still considered the chief pillar of strength of the United States. It is a little declamatory phrase, and only one objection can be raised against it, that it does not contain one iota of truth. Every man knows that the phrase is a falsehood. The truth is that all men are created unequal. Even the men of one and the same race are unequal; the inequalities, however, are not greater than the inequalities existing between the individual leaves of one tree, for they are variations of one and the same type. The differences between individuals of distinct races are essential, and, as they are differences that exist between one species and another, they are lasting. The attempts at creating perfect man, man pure and simple, or "The American," by a fusion of all human beings, is similar to the attempt of creating the perfect dog by a fusion of all canine races. Every animal breeder knows that it cannot be done. . . .

The United States is not much less cosmopolitan today than imperial Rome was. The friends of universal uniformity and of eternal peace will say: "Well, as soon as we are equally worthless, we will not know it, and happiness and peace will prevail." The conclusion is false. The mongrels are equally worthless, but there is no harmony in the depraved lot. The instincts of the different races do not entirely disappear, but they cannot develop. The result is internal unhappiness as far as the individual is concerned, and discord, chronic civil war, as far as the state is concerned. Anarchy within the individual, anarchy in the state.

And why should promiscuousness in the United States have a different effect than it had in Rome and elsewhere? The opinion is advanced that the public schools change the children of all races into Americans. Put a Scandinavian, a German, and a Magyar boy in at one end, and they will come out Americans at the other end. Which is like saying, let a pointer, a setter, and a pug enter one end of a tunnel and they will come out three greyhounds at the other end.

Public schools are in our time not educational institutions, but information bureaus, and the cultivation of the memory predominates. The children of every race can be trained to the cultivation of memory, but they cannot all be educated alike. The instincts of the different races are too much out of harmony. It is for this reason that the schools give information, with very little education. Schools cannot accomplish the impossible. To express the same opinion biologically, "All animals cannot be fed with the same fodder." . . .

This is the truth: schools, political institutions, and environment are utterly incapable to produce anything. No man can ever become anything else than he is already potentially and essentially. Education and schools are favourable or detrimental to development. They cannot create. To express it differently, no man can ever learn anything or know anything that he does not know already potentially and essentially. . . . Biologically expressed, this sentence reads as follows: A young pug develops into nothing but an old pug, a young greyhound into nothing but an old greyhound; and never, in all the ages between the creation of the world and doomsday, does a pug develop into a greyhound, no matter what the education, the training, the political institutions, and the environment.

Source: Alfred P. Schultz, *Race or Mongrel* (Boston: L. C. Page, 1908), 254–55, 257–61, 266.

Randolph S. Bourne | Trans-national America, 1916

Not all Americans embraced the melting pot or disparaged immigrants. Randolph Bourne, a journalist and political activist, took a middle position on the issue, dividing those calling for assimilation and those seeking to curtail immigration. In an essay that appeared in the *Atlantic Monthly*, Bourne argued for a "trans-national America," where instead of completely shedding their Old World cultures, immigrants retained the best of their cultural identities within the larger democratic American society.

We are all foreign-born or the descendants of foreign-born, and if distinctions are to be made between us they should rightly be on some other ground than indigenousness. The early colonists came over with motives no less colonial than the later. They did not come to be assimilated in an American melting-pot. They did not come to adopt the culture of the American Indian. They had not the smallest intention of "giving themselves without reservation" to the new country. They came to get freedom to live as they wanted to. They came to escape from the stifling air and chaos of the old world; they came to make their fortune in a new land. They invented no new social framework. Rather they brought over bodily the old ways to which they had been accustomed. Tightly concentrated on a hostile frontier, they were conservative beyond belief. Their pioneer daring was reserved for the objective conquest of material resources. In their folkways, in their social and political institutions, they were, like every colonial people, slavishly imitative of the mother-country. So that, in spite of the "Revolution," our whole legal and political system remained more English than the English, petrified and unchanging, while in England law developed to meet the needs of the changing times.

It is just this English-American conservatism that has been our chief obstacle to social advance. We have needed the new peoples—the order of the German and Scandinavian, the turbulence of the Slav and Hun—to save us from our own stagnation. I do not mean that the illiterate Slav is now the equal of the New Englander of pure descent. He is raw material to be educated, not into a New Englander, but into a socialized American along such lines as those thirty nationalities are being educated in the amazing schools of Gary [Indiana]. I do not believe that this process is to be one of decades of evolution. The spectacle of Japan's sudden jump from medievalism to post-modernism should have destroyed that superstition. We are not dealing with individuals who are to "evolve." We are dealing with their children, who, with that education we are about to have, will start level with all of us. Let us cease to think of ideals like democracy as magical qualities inherent in certain peoples. Let us speak, not of

627

inferior races, but of inferior civilizations. We are all to educate and to be educated. These peoples in America are in a common enterprise. It is not what we are now that concerns us, but what this plastic next generation may become in the light of a new cosmopolitan ideal.

We are not dealing with static factors, but with fluid and dynamic generations. To contrast the older and the newer immigrants and see the one class as democratically motivated by love of liberty, and the other by mere money-getting, is not to illuminate the future. To think of earlier nationalities as culturally assimilated to America, while we picture the later as a sodden and resistive mass, makes only for bitterness and misunderstanding. There may be a difference between these earlier and these later stocks, but it lies neither in motive for coming nor in strength of cultural allegiance to the homeland. . . .

What we emphatically do not want is that these distinctive qualities should be washed out into a tasteless, colorless fluid of uniformity. Already we have far too much of this insipidity—masses of people who are cultural half-breeds, neither assimilated Anglo-Saxons nor nationals of another culture. Each national colony in this country seems to retain in its foreign press, its vernacular literature, its schools, its intellectual and patriotic leaders, a central cultural nucleus. From this nucleus the colony extends out by imperceptible gradations to a fringe where national characteristics are all but lost. Our cities are filled with these half-breeds who retain their foreign names but have lost the foreign savor. This does not mean that they have actually been changed into New Englanders or Middle Westerners. It does not mean that they have been really Americanized. It means that, letting slip from them whatever native culture they had, they have substituted for it only the most rudimentary American—the American culture of the cheap newspaper, the "movies," the popular song, the ubiquitous automobile. The unthinking who survey this class call them assimilated, Americanized. The great American public school has done its work. With these people our institutions are safe.

We may thrill with dread at the aggressive hyphenate [hyphenated American], but this tame flabbiness is accepted as Americanization. The same moulders of opinion whose ideal is to melt the different races into Anglo-Saxon gold hail this poor product as the satisfying result of their alchemy. . . .

. . . Let us face realistically the America we have around us. Let us work with the forces that are at work. Let us make something of this trans-national spirit instead of outlawing it. Already we are living this cosmopolitan America. What we need is everywhere a vivid consciousness of the new ideal. Deliberate headway must be made against the survivals of the melting-pot ideal for the promise of American life.

Source: Randolph S. Bourne, "Trans-national America," *Atlantic Monthly*, July 1916, 87–88, 90, 97.

Interpret the Evidence

1. Explain why Israel Zangwill thinks immigrants will become "real Americans" (Source 18.6).
2. Compare the two cartoons (Sources 18.7 and 18.8). What are their views of the melting pot?
3. Describe Alfred Schultz's view of the melting pot and the possibilities of assimilation (Source 18.9) and explain how he would evaluate the two cartoons.
4. How does Randolph Bourne's vision of America's future (Source 18.10) differ from that of Zangwill (Source 18.6)? On what points might the two men have agreed, and could they have satisfied Schultz (Source 18.9)?

Put It in Context

What are the limitations of the melting pot metaphor for immigrant assimilation?

What metaphor would you choose to describe the assimilation process? Explain your choice.

Progressivism and the Search for Order

1900–1917

WINDOW TO THE PAST

Louis D. Brandeis, Brief for Defendant in Error, *Muller v. Oregon 1908*

This image is of the brief submitted by Louis D. Brandeis to the U.S. Supreme Court in the landmark case of *Muller v. Oregon* (1908). Going beyond legal precedents, the brief marshaled medical and social science evidence about the dangers of long working hours for women outside the home. The brief also raised questions about the best strategy to pursue equality for women. Legal cases like this make excellent sources for exploring social and political history. ▶ To discover more about what this primary source can show us, see Source 19.8 on page 662.

I. THE DANGERS OF LONG HOURS

A. *Causes*

(1) PHYSICAL DIFFERENCES BETWEEN MEN AND WOMEN

The dangers of long hours for women arise from their special physical organization taken in connection with the strain incident to factory and similar work.

Long hours of labor are dangerous for women primarily because of their special physical organization. In structure and function women are differentiated from men. Besides these anatomical and physiological differences, physicians are agreed that women are fundamentally weaker than men in all that makes for endurance: in muscular strength, in nervous energy, in the powers of persistent attention and application. Overwork, therefore, which strains endurance to the utmost, is more disastrous to the health of women than of men, and entails upon them more lasting injury.

Supreme Court of the United States

After reading this chapter you should be able to:

- Compare progressivism with Populism.

- Describe the problems humanitarian progressives tried to address.

- Explain the reasons progressives engaged in moral reform and evaluate how their views of immigrants shaped their efforts.

- Analyze how the notions of efficiency, openness, and accountability influenced the progressives' approach to political and environmental reform.

- Compare the ways in which the federal government handled progressive reform during the administrations of Presidents Theodore Roosevelt, William Howard Taft, and Woodrow Wilson.

COMPARING AMERICAN HISTORIES

Gifford Pinchot grew up on a Connecticut estate where he learned to hunt, fish, and enjoy nature. Yet Pinchot rejected a life of leisure and instead sought to make his mark through public service by working to conserve and protect America's natural resources. After graduating from Yale in 1889, Pinchot had to

(*left*) **Gifford Pinchot.** Library of Congress, LC-DIG-ggbain-04976
(*right*) **Geneva Stratton-Porter.** Indiana Historical Society
P0391 (detail)

study forestry abroad. No American university offered a forestry program, reflecting the predominant view that, for all practical purposes, the nation's natural resources were unlimited. As a consequence, Pinchot took courses at the French National School of Forestry, where the curriculum treated forests as crops that needed care and replenishing.

On his return in 1890, Pinchot began finding likeminded Americans who had begun to see the need to conserve the nation's natural resources and protect its wild spaces. Drawing on his scientific training and his experiences in Europe, Pinchot advocated the use of natural resources by sportsmen and businesses under carefully regulated governmental authority. Appointed to head the Federal Division of Forestry in 1898, Pinchot found a vigorous ally in the White House when Theodore Roosevelt took office in 1901. In 1907 Pinchot began to speak of the need for *conservation*, which he defined as the use of America's natural resources "for the benefit of the people who live here now." This use of resources included responsible business practices in industries such as logging and mining.

Not all environmentalists agreed. In contrast to Pinchot, author and nature photographer Geneva (Gene) Stratton-Porter focused her energies on *preservation*, the protection of public land from any private development. Born in 1863 in Wabash County, Indiana, Stratton-Porter grew up roaming through fields, watching birds, and observing "nature's rhythms." After marrying in 1886, Stratton-Porter took up photography and hiked into the wilderness of Indiana to take pictures of wild birds.

Stratton-Porter built a reputation as a nature photographer. She also published a series of widely read novels and children's books that revealed her vision of the harmony between human beings and nature. She urged readers to preserve the environment so that men and women could lead a truly fulfilling existence on earth and not destroy God's creation. One area on which she and Pinchot agreed was support for national parks. ■

The American histories of Gifford Pinchot and Gene Stratton-Porter reveal the efforts of just two of the many individuals who searched for ways to control the damaging impact of modernization on the United States. From roughly 1900 to 1917, many Americans sought to bring some order out of the chaos accompanying rapid industrialization and urbanization. Despite the magnitude of the issues, those who believed in the need to combat the problems of industrial America possessed an optimistic faith — sometimes derived from religious principles, sometimes from a secular outlook — that they could relieve the stresses and strains that modern life brought. Such people were not bound together by a single, rigid ideology. Instead, they were united by faith in the notion that if people joined together and applied human intelligence to the task of improving the nation, progress was inevitable. So widespread was this hopeful conviction that we call this period the Progressive Era.

In pursuit of progress and stability, some reformers tried to control the behavior of groups they considered a threat to the social order. Equating difference with disorder, many progressives tried to impose white middle-class standards of behavior on immigrant populations. Some sought to eliminate the "problem" altogether by curtailing further immigration from southern and eastern Europe. Others advocated birth control as a means to preserve the lives of childbearing women, but also to promote ethnic and racial engineering. In addition, progressives fought for women's suffrage, consumer protection, regulation of business, and good government reform. Many white progressives, particularly in the South, favored racial segregation and disfranchisement of African Americans. At the same time, however, black progressives and their white allies created organizations dedicated to securing racial equality. Despite their disparate and sometimes conflicting aims, progressives maintained a passion for change as a means of improving the nation.

The **Roots** of **Progressivism**

At the turn of the twentieth century, many Americans believed that the nation was in dire need of reform. Two decades of westward expansion, industrialization, urbanization, and skyrocketing immigration had transformed the country in unsettling ways. In the aftermath of the social and economic turmoil that accompanied the depression of the 1890s, many members of the middle and upper classes were convinced that unless they took remedial measures, the country would collapse under the weight of class conflict. Progressives advocated governmental intervention, yet they sought change without radically altering capitalism or the democratic political system. Not everyone endorsed progressives' goals, however. Conservatives continued to support individualism and the free market as the determinant of political and economic power, and radicals pressed for the socialist reorganization of the economy and the democratization of politics. Yet the public showed widespread support for progressivism by electing the reformers Theodore Roosevelt and Woodrow Wilson as presidents.

Progressive Origins. Progressives contended that old ways of governing and doing business did not address modern conditions. In one sense, they inherited the legacy of the Populist movement of the 1890s. Progressives attacked laissez-faire capitalism, and by regulating monopolies they aimed to limit the power of corporate trusts. Like the Populists, progressives advocated instituting an income tax as well as a variety of initiatives designed to give citizens a greater say in government. However, progressives differed from Populists in fundamental ways. Perhaps most important, progressives were interested primarily in urban and industrial America, while the Populist movement had emerged in direct response to the problems that plagued rural America.

Progressives were heirs to the intellectual critics of the late nineteenth century who challenged laissez-faire and rejected Herbert Spencer's doctrine of the "survival of the fittest." **Pragmatism** greatly influenced progressives. Pragmatists contended that the meaning of truth did not reside in some absolute doctrine but could be discovered only through experience. Ideas had to be measured by their practical consequences. From these critics, progressives derived a skepticism toward rigid dogma and instead relied on human experience to guide social action.

Reformers also drew inspiration from the religious ideals of the **social gospel**. In *Christianity and the Social Crisis* (1907), Walter Rauschenbusch urged Christians to embrace the teachings of Jesus on the ethical obligations for social justice and to put these teachings into action by working among the urban poor. Washington Gladden argued that unregulated private enterprise was "inequitable" and compared financial speculators to vampires "sucking the life-blood of our commerce." Progressive leaders such as Theodore Roosevelt and Gifford Pinchot combined the moral fervor of the social gospel with the rationalism of the gospel of scientific efficiency.

> **Explore ▶**
>
> See Source 19.1 for Walter Rauschenbusch's views on the social responsibility of Christianity.

Pragmatism and the social gospel appealed to members of the new middle class. Before the Civil War, the middle class had consisted largely of ministers, lawyers, physicians, and small proprietors. The growth of large-scale businesses during the second half of the nineteenth century expanded the middle class, which now included men whose professions grew out of industrialization, such as engineering, corporate management, and social work. Progressivism drew many of its most devoted adherents from this new middle class.

Ida B. Wells   Born a slave in Holly Springs, Mississippi, Ida B. Wells rose to become a teacher, writer, editor, and civil rights activist. As an investigative journalist — muckrakers, as they were known at the time — she wrote about and campaigned against lynching. This photograph from 1910 shows Wells around the age of forty-eight. That same year she joined in the founding of the NAACP. Special Collections Research Center, University of Chicago Library

GUIDED ANALYSIS

Walter Rauschenbusch | Christianity and the Social Crisis, 1907

Walter Rauschenbusch was a Protestant theologian and Baptist minister from Rochester, New York, who preached the message of the social gospel in his writings and sermons. He believed that Christianity was revolutionary, that Jesus died to substitute love for selfishness, and that capitalism produced inequality. Establishing the Kingdom of God on earth would mean working to end income inequality, child labor, and other harmful results of industrialization.

Source 19.1

According to Rauschenbusch, what does Christianity demand?

What are the fictions of capitalism?

Why do industrialists deceive the public?

Social religion, too, demands repentance and faith; repentance for our social sins; faith in the possibility of a new social order. . . . In the same way we have to see through the fictions of capitalism. We are assured that the poor are poor through their own fault; that rent and profit are the just dues of foresight and ability; that the immigrants are the cause of corruption in our city politics; that we cannot compete with foreign countries unless our working class will descend to the wages paid abroad. These are all very plausible assertions, but they are lies dressed up in truth. . . . Industrialism as a whole sends out deceptive prospectuses just like single corporations within it. But in the main these misleading theories are the self-deception of those who profit by present conditions and are loath to believe that their life is working harm. It is very rare for a man to condemn the means by which he makes a living, and we must simply make allowance for the warping influence of self-interest when he justifies himself and not believe him entirely.

Source: Walter T. Rauschenbusch, *Christianity and the Social Crisis* (New York: Macmillan, 1907), 349, 350, 351.

Put It in Context

How did the social gospel provide a justification for progressive reform?

Muckrakers. The growing desire for reform at the turn of the century received a boost from investigative journalists known as **muckrakers**. Popular magazines such as *McClure's* and *Collier's* sought to increase their readership by publishing exposés of corruption in government and the shady operations of big business. Filled with details uncovered through intensive research, these articles had a sensationalist appeal that both informed and aroused their mainly middle-class readers. In 1902 journalist Ida Tarbell lambasted the ruthless and dishonest business practices of the Rockefeller family's Standard Oil Company, the model of corporate greed. Lincoln Steffens wrote about machine bosses' shameful rule in many American cities. Ida B. Wells wrote scathing articles and pamphlets condemning the lynching of African Americans. Other muckrakers exposed fraudulent practices in insurance companies, child labor, drug abuse, and prostitution.

REVIEW & RELATE

- What late-nineteenth-century trends and developments influenced the progressives?

- Why did the progressives focus on urban and industrial America?

Humanitarian and Social Justice Reform

Progressivism took many configurations depending on the interests and concerns of its participants. Although many of these reforms overlapped, it is useful to examine them in specific categories. Humanitarian reformers focused on the plight of urban immigrants, African Americans, and the underprivileged. They tried mainly to improve housing and working conditions for impoverished city dwellers. Their motives were not always purely altruistic. Unless living standards improved, many reformers reasoned, immigrants and racial minorities would contaminate the cities' middle-class inhabitants with communicable diseases, escalating crime, and threats to traditional cultural norms. These reformers also supported suffrage for women, whose votes, they believed, would help purify electoral politics and elect candidates committed to social and moral reform.

Female Progressives and the Poor. Women played the leading role in efforts to improve the lives of the impoverished. Jane Addams had toured Europe after graduating from a women's college in Illinois. The Toynbee Hall settlement house (see "Urban Reformers," in chapter 18) in London impressed her for its work in helping poor residents of the area. After returning home to Chicago in 1889, Addams and her friend Ellen Starr established **Hull House** as a center for social reform. Hull House inspired a generation of young women to work directly in immigrant communities. Many were college-educated, professionally trained women who were shut out of jobs in male-dominated professions. Staffed mainly by women, settlement houses became all-purpose urban support centers providing recreational facilities, social activities, and educational classes for neighborhood residents. Calling on women to take up **civic housekeeping**, Addams maintained that women could protect their individual households from the chaos of industrialization and urbanization only by attacking the sources of that chaos in the community at large.

Settlement houses and social workers occupied the front lines of humanitarian reform, but they found considerable support from women's clubs. Formed after the Civil War, these local groups provided middle-class women places to meet, share ideas, and work on common projects. By 1900 these clubs counted 160,000 members. Initially devoted to discussions of religion, culture, and science, club women began to help the needy and lobby for social justice legislation. "Since men are more or less closely absorbed in business," one club woman remarked about this civic awakening, "it has come to pass that the initiative in civic matters has devolved largely upon women." Starting out in towns and cities, club women carried their message to state and federal governments and campaigned for legislation that would establish social welfare programs for working women and their children.

In an age of strict racial segregation, African American women formed their own clubs. They sponsored day care centers, kindergartens, and work and home training projects.

The activities of black club women, like those of white club women, reflected a class bias, and they tried to lift up poorer blacks to ideals of middle-class womanhood. Yet in doing so, they challenged racist notions that black women and men were incapable of raising healthy and strong families. By 1916 the National Association of Colored Women (NACW), whose motto was "lifting as we climb," boasted 1,000 clubs and 50,000 members.

White working-class women also organized, but because of employment discrimination there were few, if any, black female industrial workers to join them. Building on the settlement house movement and together with middle-class and wealthy women, working-class women founded the National Women's Trade Union League (WTUL) in 1903. Recognizing that many women needed to earn an income to help support their families, the WTUL was dedicated to securing higher wages, an eight-hour day, and improved working conditions. Believing women to be physically weaker than men, most female reformers advocated special legislation to protect women in the workplace. They campaigned for state laws prescribing the maximum number of hours women could work, and they succeeded in 1908 when they won a landmark victory in the Supreme Court in *Muller v. Oregon*, which upheld an Oregon law establishing a ten-hour workday for women. These reformers also convinced lawmakers in forty states to establish pensions for mothers and widows. In 1912 their focus shifted to the federal government with the founding of the Children's Bureau in the Department of Commerce and Labor. Headed by Julia Lathrop, the bureau collected sociological data and devised a variety of publicly funded social welfare measures. In 1916 Congress enacted a law banning child labor under the age of fourteen (it was declared unconstitutional in 1918). In 1921 Congress passed the Shepherd-Towner Act, which allowed nurses to offer maternal and infant health care information to mothers. **See Primary Source Project 19: *Muller v. Oregon,* page 660.**

Not all women believed in the idea of protective legislation for women. In 1898 Charlotte Perkins Gilman published *Women and Economics*, in which she argued against the notion that women were ideally suited for domesticity. She contended that women's reliance on men was unnatural: "We are the only animal species in which the female depends on the male for food." Emphasizing the need for economic independence, Gilman advocated the establishment of communal kitchens that would free women from household chores and allow them to compete on equal terms with men in the workplace. Emma Goldman, an anarchist critic of capitalism and middle-class sexual morality, also spoke out against the kind of marriage that made women "keep their mouths shut and their wombs open." These women considered themselves as feminists—women who aspire to reach their full potential and gain access to the same opportunities as men.

Fighting for Women's Suffrage.

Fighting for Women's Suffrage. Before 1900 women did not have the full right to vote, except in a handful of western states. Although the Fourteenth and Fifteenth Amendments extended citizenship to African Americans and protected the voting rights of black men, they left women, both white and black, ineligible to vote. Following Reconstruction, the two major organizations campaigning for women's suffrage at the state and national levels—Susan B. Anthony and Elizabeth Cady Stanton's National Woman Suffrage Association and Lucy Stone and Julia Ward Howe's American Woman Suffrage Association—failed to achieve major victories. In 1890 the two groups combined to form the National American Woman Suffrage Association, and by 1918 women could vote fully in fifteen states and the territory of Alaska (Map 19.1).

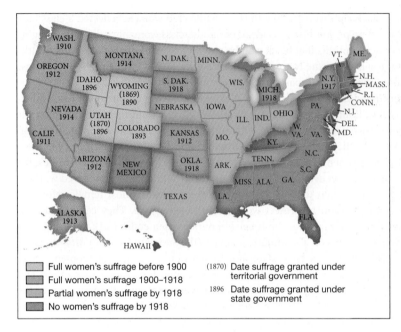

MAP 19.1 Women's Suffrage

Western states and territories were the first to approve women's suffrage. Yet even as western states enfranchised women, most placed restrictions on or excluded African American, American Indian, Mexican American, and Asian American women. States granting partial suffrage allowed women to vote only in certain contests, such as municipal or school board, primary, or presidential elections.

Suffragists included a broad coalition of supporters and based their campaign on a variety of arguments. Reformers such as Jane Addams attributed corruption in politics to the absence of women's maternal influence. In this way, mainstream suffragists couched their arguments within traditional conceptions of women as family nurturers and claimed that men should see women's vote as an expansion of traditional household duties into the public sphere. By contrast, suffragists such as Alice Paul rejected such arguments, asserting that women deserved the vote on the basis of their equality with men as citizens. She founded the National Woman's Party and in 1923 proposed that Congress adopt an Equal Rights Amendment to provide full legal equality to women.

Both male and female opponents fought against women's suffrage. They believed that women were best suited by nature to devote themselves to their families and leave the world of politics to men. Suffrage critics insisted that extending the right to vote to women would destroy the home, lead to the moral degeneracy of children, and tear down the social fabric of the country.

Campaigns for women's suffrage did not apply to all women. White suffragists in the South often manipulated racial prejudice to support female enfranchisement. Outspoken white suffragists such as Rebecca Latimer Felton from Georgia, Belle Kearney from Mississippi, and Kate Gordon from Louisiana contended that as long as even a fraction of black men voted and the Fifteenth Amendment continued to exist, allowing southern white women to vote would preserve white supremacy by offsetting black men's votes. These arguments also had a class component. Poll taxes disfranchised poor whites. Extending the vote to white women would benefit mainly those in the middle class who had enough family income to satisfy restrictive poll tax requirements.

Many middle-class women outside the South used similar reasoning, but they targeted newly arrived immigrants instead of African Americans. Many Protestant women

Suffrage Campaign, 1913 During the Progressive Era, women mounted a determined campaign to gain suffrage from state and federal governments. They employed a variety of tactics, from persuasion through education to direct confrontation and getting arrested. On August 10, 1913, New York women suffragists took the opportunity to promote their cause at the New York Fair held in Yonkers, a suburb of New York City. Women won the right to vote in New York in 1917 and finally succeeded nationally with ratification of the Nineteenth Amendment in 1920. Library of Congress, 3a25016

and men viewed Catholics and Jews from southern and eastern Europe as racially inferior and spiritually dangerous. They blamed such immigrants for the ills of the cities in which they congregated, and some suffragists believed that the vote of middle-class Protestant women would help clean up the mess the immigrants created.

African American women challenged these racist arguments and mounted their own drive for female suffrage. They had an additional incentive to press for enfranchisement. As the target of white sexual predators during slavery and its aftermath, some black women saw the vote as a way to address this problem. "The ballot," Nannie Helen Burroughs, the founder of the NACW remarked, is the black woman's "weapon of moral defense." Although they did not gain much support from white suffragists, by 1916 African American women worked through the NACW and formed suffrage clubs throughout the nation.

The campaign for women's suffrage in the United States was part of an international movement. Victories in New Zealand (1893), Australia (1902), and Norway (1913) spurred on American suffragists. In the 1910s, radical American activists found inspiration in the militant tactics employed by some in the British suffrage movement. Activists such as Alice Paul conducted wide-ranging demonstrations in Washington, D.C., including chaining themselves to the gates of the White House. Although mainstream suffrage leaders denounced these new tactics, they gained much-needed publicity for the movement, which in turn aided the lobbying efforts of more moderate activists. In 1919 Congress passed the Nineteenth Amendment, granting women the vote. The following year, the amendment was ratified by the states.

Progressivism and African Americans.

As with suffrage, social justice progressives faced huge barriers in the fight for racial equality. By 1900 white supremacists in the South had disfranchised most black voters and imposed a rigid system of segregation in education and all aspects of public life, which they enforced with violence. From 1884 to 1900, approximately 2,500 people were lynched, most of them southern blacks. Antiblack violence also took the form of race riots that erupted in southern cities. Farther north, in Springfield, Illinois, a riot broke out in 1908 when the local sheriff tried to protect two black prisoners from a would-be lynch mob. This confrontation triggered two days of white violence against blacks, some of whom fought back, leaving twenty-four businesses and forty homes destroyed and seven people (two blacks and five whites) dead.

As the situation for African Americans deteriorated, black leaders responded in several ways. Booker T. Washington espoused an approach that his critics called accommodation but that he defended as practical. Born a slave and emancipated at age nine, Washington attended Hampton Institute, run by sympathetic whites in his home state of Virginia. School officials believed that African Americans would first have to build up their character and accept the virtues of abstinence, thrift, and industriousness before seeking a more intellectual education. In 1881 Washington founded **Tuskegee Institute** in Alabama, which he modeled on Hampton. In 1895, he received an enthusiastic reception from white business and civic leaders in Atlanta for his message urging African Americans to remain in the South, accept racial segregation, concentrate on moral and economic development, and avoid politics. At the same time, he called on white leaders to protect blacks from the growing violence directed at them.

White leaders in both the South and the North embraced Washington, and he became the most powerful African American of his generation. Although he discouraged public protests against segregation, he emphasized racial pride and solidarity among African Americans. Yet Washington was a complex figure who secretly financed and supported court challenges to electoral disfranchisement and other forms of racial discrimination.

Washington's enormous power did not discourage opposing views among African Americans. Ida B. Wells, like Washington, had been born a slave. In 1878 she took a job in Memphis as a teacher. Six years later, Wells sued the Chesapeake & Ohio Railroad for moving her from the first-class "Ladies Coach" to the segregated smoking car because she was black. She won her case in the lower court, but her victory was reversed by the Tennessee Supreme Court. Undeterred, she began writing for the newspaper *Free Speech*, and when her articles exposing injustices in the Memphis school system got her fired from teaching, she took up journalism full-time.

Unlike Washington, Wells believed that black leaders had to speak out vigorously against racial inequality and lynching. On March 9, 1892, three black men in Memphis were murdered by a white mob. The victims had operated a grocery store that became the target of hostility from white competitors. The black businessmen fought back and shot three armed attackers in self-defense. In support of their actions, Wells wrote, "When the white man . . . knows he runs as great a risk of biting the dust every time his

Afro-American victim does, he will have greater respect for Afro-American life." Subsequently arrested for their armed resistance, the three men were snatched from jail and lynched.

In response to Wells's articles about the Memphis lynching, a white mob burned down her newspaper's building. She fled to Chicago, where she published a report refuting the myth that the rape of white women by black men was the leading cause of lynching. She concluded that racists used this brand of violence to ensure that African Americans would not challenge white supremacy. Wells waged her campaign throughout the North and in Europe. She also joined the drive for women's suffrage, which she hoped would give black women a chance to use their votes to help combat racial injustice.

Explore ▶

See Sources 19.2 and 19.3 for Washington's and Wells's responses to inequality.

W. E. B. Du Bois also rejected Washington's accommodationist stance and urged blacks to demand first-class citizenship. In contrast to Washington's and Wells's families, Du Bois's ancestors were free blacks, and he grew up in Great Barrington, Massachusetts. He earned a Ph.D. in history from Harvard. Du Bois agreed with Washington about advocating self-help as a means for advancement, but he did not believe this effort would succeed without a proper education and equal voting rights. In *The Souls of Black Folk* (1903), Du Bois argued that African Americans needed a liberal arts education. Du Bois contended that a classical, humanistic education would produce a cadre of leaders, the "Talented Tenth," who would guide African Americans to the next stage of their development. Rather than forgoing immediate political rights, African American leaders should demand the universal right to vote. Only then, Du Bois contended, would African Americans gain equality, self-respect, and dignity as a race.

Du Bois was an intellectual who put his ideas into action. In 1905 he spearheaded the creation of the Niagara Movement, a group that first met on the Canadian side of Niagara Falls. The all-black organization demanded the vote and equal access to public facilities for African Americans. By 1909 internal squabbling and a shortage of funds had crippled the group. That same year, however, Du Bois became involved in the creation of an organization that would shape the fight for racial equality throughout the twentieth century: the **National Association for the Advancement of Colored People (NAACP)**. In addition to Du Bois, Ida B. Wells, and veterans of the Niagara Movement, white activists such as Jane Addams joined in forming the organization. Beginning in 1910, the NAACP initiated court cases challenging racially discriminatory voting practices and other forms of bias in housing and criminal justice. Its first victory came in 1915, when its lawyers convinced the Supreme Court to strike down the grandfather clause that discriminated against black voters (*Guinn v. United States*).

African Americans also pursued social justice initiatives outside the realm of politics. Southern blacks remained committed to securing a quality education for their children after whites failed to live up to their responsibilities under *Plessy v. Ferguson*. Black schools remained inferior to white schools, and African Americans did not receive a fair return from their tax dollars; in fact, a large portion of their payments helped subsidize white schools.

Black women played a prominent role in promoting education. For example, in 1901 Charlotte Hawkins Brown set up the Palmer Memorial Institute outside of Greensboro, North Carolina. In these endeavors, black educators received financial assistance from northern philanthropists, white club women interested in moral uplift of the black race,

---

COMPARATIVE ANALYSIS

Addressing Racial Inequality

By the end of the nineteenth century, the former Confederate states had stripped most blacks of the right to vote and instituted legal forms of segregation. In the face of violence, hostility, and widespread discrimination, African American leaders Booker T. Washington and Ida B. Wells developed alternative approaches to the problem of racial inequality. Washington emphasized accommodation within the existing social and political system, whereas Wells insisted that blacks must secure the right to vote.

Source 19.2

Booker T. Washington | The Atlanta Compromise, 1895

The wisest among my race understand that the agitation of questions of social equality is the extremest folly, and that progress in the enjoyment of all the privileges that will come to us must be the result of severe and constant struggle rather than of artificial forcing. No race that has anything to contribute to the markets of the world is long in any degree ostracized. It is important and right that all privileges of the law be ours, but it is vastly more important that we be prepared for the exercise of those privileges. The opportunity to earn a dollar in a factory just now is worth infinitely more than the opportunity to spend a dollar in an opera house. . . . I pledge that in your [white race] effort to work out the great and intricate problem which God has laid at the doors of the South,

you shall have at all times the patient, sympathetic help of my race; only let this be constantly in mind that, while from representations in these buildings of the product of field, of forest, of mine, of factory, letters, and art, much good will come, yet far above and beyond material benefits will be that higher good, that, let us pray God, will come, in a blotting out of sectional differences and racial animosities and suspicions, in a determination to administer absolute justice, in a willing obedience among all classes to the mandates of law. This, coupled with our material prosperity, will bring into our beloved South a new heaven and a new earth.

Source: Booker T. Washington, *The Story of My Life and Work* (Cincinnati: W. W. Ferguson, 1900), 170–71.

---

and religious missionaries seeking converts in the South. By 1910 more than 1.5 million black children went to school in the South, most of them taught by the region's 28,560 black teachers. Thirty-four black colleges existed, and more than 2,000 African Americans held college degrees.

Progressivism and Indians. Like African Americans, Native Americans struggled against injustice. Indian muckrakers criticized government policies and anti-Indian attitudes, but the magazines that exposed the evils of industrialization often ignored their plight. Instead, Indian reformers turned to the *Quarterly Journal*, published by the Society of American Indians, to air their grievances. Carlos Montezuma was the most outspoken critic of Indian policy. A Yavapai tribe member from Arizona, he called for the abolition of the Indian Office as an impediment to the welfare of Native Americans.

Source 19.3

Ida B. Wells | A Critique of Booker T. Washington, 1904

Industrial education for the Negro is Booker T. Washington's hobby. He believes that for the masses of the Negro race an elementary education of the brain and a continuation of the education of the hand is not only the best kind, but he knows it is the most popular with the white South. He knows also that the Negro is the butt of ridicule with the average white American, and that the aforesaid American enjoys nothing so much as a joke which portrays the Negro as illiterate and improvident [shortsighted]; a petty thief or a happy-go-lucky inferior. . . .

There are many who can never be made to feel that it was a mistake thirty years ago to give the unlettered freedman the franchise, their only weapon of defense, any more than it was a mistake to have fire for cooking and heating purposes in the home, because ignorant or careless servants sometimes burn themselves. . . .

Does this mean that the Negro objects to industrial education? By no means. It simply means that he knows by sad experience that industrial education will not stand him in place of political, civil and intellectual liberty, and he objects to being deprived of fundamental rights of American citizenship to the end that one school for industrial training shall flourish. To him it seems like selling a race's birthright for a mess of pottage.

Source: Ida B. Wells, "The Negro Problem from the Negro Point of View," *World Today*, April 1904, 518, 520, 521.

Interpret the Evidence

1. Why does Washington believe that economic development is the key to racial progress?
2. How does Wells challenge Washington's agenda? Why does she insist that industrial education is not enough and political and social reforms are essential to black economic progress?

Put It in Context

How do Washington and Wells reflect, in different ways, the status of African Americans in the United States at the turn of the twentieth century?

Arthur C. Parker, an anthropologist from the eastern tribe of the Seneca, challenged the notion that Indians suffered mainly because of their own backwardness. In scathing articles, he condemned the United States for robbing American Indians of their cultural and economic independence. One Indian who wrote for non-Indian magazines such as *Harper's Weekly* was Zitkala-Ša (see Source 15.9 in chapter 15). This Sioux woman published essays exposing the practices of boarding schools designed to assimilate Indians. Non-Indian anthropologists such as Franz Boas and Ruth Benedict added their voices to those of Indian journalists in attacking traditional views of Native Americans as inferior and uncivilized.

Indian reformers, however, did not succeed in convincing state and federal governments to pass legislation to address their concerns. Nevertheless, activists did succeed in filing thirty-one complaints with the U.S. Court of Claims for monetary compensation for federal payments to which they were entitled but had not received. Like other exploited groups during the Progressive Era, Indians created organizations, such as the Black Hills Treaty Council and others, to pressure the federal government and to publicize their demands.

REVIEW & RELATE

What role did women play in the early-twentieth-century fight for social justice?

How did social reformers challenge discrimination against women, minorities, and Indians?

Morality and Social Control

In many cases, progressive initiatives crossed over from social reform to social control. Convinced that the "immorality" of the poor was the cause of social disorder, some reformers sought to impose middle-class standards of behavior and morality on the lower classes. As with other forms of progressivism, reformers interested in social control were driven by a variety of motives. However, regardless of their motives, efforts to prohibit alcohol, fight prostitution, and combat juvenile delinquency often involved attempts to repress and control the poor. So, too, did protective health measures such as birth control. Some social control progressives went even further in their efforts to impose their own morality, calling for restrictions on immigration, which they saw as a cultural threat.

Prohibition. Prohibition campaigns began long before the Civil War but scored few important successes until 1881, when Kansas became the first state whose constitution banned the consumption of alcohol. Women spearheaded the prohibition movement by forming the **Woman's Christian Temperance Union (WCTU)** in 1874 under the leadership of Frances Willard. Willard built the temperance movement around the need to protect the home. Husbands and fathers who drank excessively were also likely to abuse their wives and children and to drain the family finances. Prohibiting the consumption of alcohol would therefore help combat these evils. At the same time, the quality of family and public life would be improved if women received the right to vote and young children completed their education without having to go to work.

After Willard's death in 1898, the Anti-Saloon League (ASL) became the dominant force in the prohibition movement. Established in 1893, the league grew out of evangelical Protestantism. The group had particular appeal in the rural South, where Protestant fundamentalism flourished. Between 1906 and 1917, twenty-one states, mostly in the South and West, banned liquor sales. However, concern over alcohol was not confined to the South. Middle-class progressives in northern cities, who identified much of urban decay with the influx of immigrants, saw the tavern as a breeding ground for immoral activities. In 1913 the ASL convinced Congress to pass the Webb-Kenyon Act, which banned the transportation of alcoholic beverages into dry states. After the United States entered World War I in 1917, reformers argued that prohibition would help win the war by conserving grain used to make liquor and by saving soldiers from intoxication. The Eighteenth Amendment, ratified in 1919, made prohibition the law of the land until it was repealed in 1933.

Prostitution, Narcotics, and Juvenile Delinquency. Alarmed by the increased number of brothels and "streetwalkers" that accompanied the growth of cities, progressives sought to eliminate prostitution. Some framed the issue in terms of public health, linking prostitution to the spread of sexually transmitted diseases. Others presented it as an effort to protect female virtue. Such reformers were generally interested only in white women, who, unlike African American and Asian women in similar circumstances, were considered sexual innocents coerced into prostitution. Still others claimed that prostitutes themselves were to blame, seeing women who sold their sexual favors as inherently immoral.

Reformers offered two different approaches to the problem. Taking the moralistic solution, Representative James R. Mann of Chicago steered through Congress the White Slave Trade Act (known as the Mann Act) in 1910, banning the transportation of women across state lines for immoral purposes. By contrast, the American Social Hygiene Association, founded in 1914, subsidized scientific research into sexually transmitted diseases, funded investigations to gather more information, and drafted model ordinances for cities to curb prostitution. By 1915 every state had laws making sexual solicitation a crime.

Prosecutors used the Mann Act to enforce codes of traditional racial as well as sexual behavior. In 1910 Jack Johnson, an African American boxer, defeated the white heavyweight champion, Jim Jeffries. His victory upset some white men who were obsessed with preserving their racial dominance and masculine integrity. Johnson's relationships with white women further angered some whites, who eventually succeeded in bringing down the outspoken black champion by prosecuting him on morals charges in 1913.

Moral crusaders also sought to eliminate the use and sale of narcotics. By 1900 approximately 250,000 people in the United States were addicted to opium, morphine, or cocaine — far fewer, however, than those who abused alcohol. On the West Coast, immigration opponents associated opium smoking with the Chinese and tried to eliminate its use as part of their wider anti-Asian campaign. In alliance with the American Medical Association, reformers convinced Congress to pass the Harrison

The Crusade against White Slavery Published by Clifford B. Roe and B. S. Steadwell in 1911, *The Great War on White Slavery* campaigned against prostitution and the criminals who lured impoverished young women into what they called "the human stockyards . . . for girls." As an assistant state's attorney in Chicago, Roe prosecuted more than 150 cases against sex traffickers. He exemplified progressivism's moral reform impulse. © Mary Evans Picture Library/The Image Works

Narcotics Control Act of 1914, prohibiting the sale of narcotics except by a doctor's prescription.

Progressives also tried to combat juvenile delinquency. Led by women, these reformers lobbied for a juvenile court system that focused on rehabilitation rather than punishment for youthful offenders. Despite progressives' sincerity, many youthful offenders doubted their intentions. Young women often appeared before a magistrate because their parents did not like their choice of friends, their sexual conduct, or their frequenting dance halls and saloons. These activities, which violated middle-class social norms, had now become criminalized, even if in a less coercive and punitive manner than that applied to adults.

Birth Control.

The health of women and families occupied reformers such as Margaret Sanger, the leading advocate of birth control. Working as a nurse mainly among poor immigrant women in New York City, she witnessed the damage that unrestrained childbearing produced on women's health. According to Sanger, contraception—the use of artificial means to prevent pregnancy—would save the lives of mothers by preventing unwanted childbearing and avoiding unsafe and illegal abortions, and would keep families from having large numbers of children they could not afford. Moreover, Sanger believed that if women were freed from the anxieties of becoming pregnant, they would experience more sexual enjoyment and make better companions for their spouses. Her arguments for birth control also had a connection to eugenics. Contraception, she believed, would raise the quality of the white race by reducing the chances of immigrant and minority women reproducing so-called unfit children.

Sanger and her supporters encountered enormous opposition. It was illegal to sell contraceptive devices or furnish information about them. Nevertheless, in 1916 Sanger opened up the nation's first birth control clinic in an immigrant section of Brooklyn. The police quickly closed down the facility and arrested Sanger. Undeterred, she continued to agitate for her cause and push to change attitudes toward women's health and reproductive rights.

Immigration Restriction.

Sanger wanted to lessen the problems faced by immigrant women. However, other moral reformers sought to restrict immigration itself. Anti-immigrant sentiment often reflected racial and religious bigotry, as reformers concentrated on preventing Catholics, Jews, and all non-Europeans from entering the United States. Social scientists validated these prejudices by categorizing darker-skinned immigrants as inferior races. The harshest treatment was reserved for Asians. In 1908 President Theodore Roosevelt entered into an executive agreement with Japan that reduced Japanese immigration to the United States. In 1913 the California legislature passed a statute barring Japanese immigrants from buying land, a law that twelve other states subsequently enacted.

In 1917 reformers succeeded in further restricting immigration. Congress passed legislation to ban people who could not read English or their native language from entering the country. The act also denied entry to other undesirables: "alcoholics," "feeble-minded persons," "epileptics," "people mentally or physically defective," "professional beggars," "anarchists," and "polygamists." In barring people considered unfit to enter the country, lawmakers intended to keep out those who could not support themselves and might become public wards of the state and, in the case of anarchists and polygamists, those who threatened the nation's political and religious values.

REVIEW & RELATE

- What practices and behaviors of the poor did social control progressives find most alarming? Why?

- What role did anti-immigrant sentiment play in motivating and shaping progressives' social control initiatives?

Good Government Progressivism

In an effort to diminish the power of corrupt urban political machines and unregulated corporations, progressives pushed for good government reforms, promoting initiatives they claimed would produce greater efficiency, openness, and accountability in government. Many of the progressives' proposed reforms appeared, at least on the surface, to give citizens more direct say in their government; however, a closer look reveals a more complicated picture.

Municipal and State Reform. Cities were at the forefront of government reform during the Progressive Era. Municipal governments failed to keep up with the problems ushered in by accelerated urban growth. Political machines distributed city services within a system bloated by corruption and graft. Upper-middle-class businessmen and professionals fed up with wasteful and inefficient political machines sought to institute new forms of government that functioned more rationally and cost less.

The adoption of the commission form of government was a hallmark of urban reform. Commission governments replaced the old form of a mayor and city council with elected commissioners, each of whom ran a municipal department as if it were a business. By 1917 commissions had spread to more than four hundred cities throughout the country. Governments with a mayor and city council also began to appoint city managers, who functioned as chief operating officers, to foster businesslike efficiency. The head of the National Cash Register Company, who helped bring the city manager system to Dayton, Ohio, praised it for resembling "a great business enterprise whose stockholders are the people."

Reformers also adopted direct primaries so that voters could select candidates rather than allowing a handful of machine politicians to decide elections behind closed doors. To reverse the influence of immigrants clustered in ghettos who supported their own ethnic candidates and to topple the machines that catered to them, municipal reformers replaced district elections with citywide "at-large" elections. Ethnic enclaves lost not only their ward representatives but also a good deal of their influence because citywide election campaigns were expensive, shifting power to those who could afford to run. Working- and lower-class residents of cities still retained the right to vote, but their power was diluted.

In the South, where fewer immigrants lived, white supremacists employed these tactics to build on steps taken in the late nineteenth century to disfranchise African Americans. Southern lawmakers diminished whatever black political power remained by adopting at-large elections and commission governments. Throughout the South, direct primary contests (or "white primaries") were closed to blacks.

If urban progressivism fell short of putting democratic ideals into practice, it did produce a number of mayors who carried out genuine reforms.

Explore ▶

Read Sources 19.4 and 19.5 for two historians' perspectives on southern progressivism.

Elected in 1901, Cleveland mayor Tom L. Johnson implemented measures to assess taxes more equitably, regulate utility companies, and reduce public transportation fares. Samuel "Golden Rule" Jones, who served as Toledo's mayor from 1897 to 1903, supported social justice measures by establishing an eight-hour workday for municipal employees, granting them paid vacations, and prohibiting child labor. Under Mayor Hazen Pingree, who served from 1889 to 1896, Detroit constructed additional schools and recreational facilities and put the unemployed to work on municipal projects during economic hard times.

Progressives also took action at the state level. Robert M. La Follette, Republican governor of Wisconsin from 1901 to 1906, led the way by initiating a range of reforms to improve the performance of state government and increase its accountability to constituents. During his tenure as governor, La Follette dismantled the statewide political machine by instituting direct party primaries, an expanded civil service, a law forbidding direct corporate contributions to political parties, a strengthened railroad regulatory commission, and a graduated income tax. In 1906 La Follette entered the U.S. Senate, where he battled for further reform.

Other states picked up and expanded La Follette's progressive agenda. In 1913 three-quarters of the states ratified the Seventeenth Amendment, which mandated that U.S. senators would be elected by popular vote instead of being chosen by state legislatures. This constituted another effort to remove the influence of money from politics.

Theodore Roosevelt and John Muir, 1903   Taken in 1903, this photograph pictures President Theodore Roosevelt and his associates standing in front of the "Grizzly Giant," a towering sequoia tree over 200 feet in height in Yosemite National Park, California. Roosevelt is in the center, and standing to his front left is John Muir, the founder of the Sierra Club, who convinced Roosevelt to place Yosemite under federal control and establish it as a national park in 1906. Also shown in this photo from left to right are an unidentified secret serviceman; William H. Moody, secretary of the navy; George Pardee, governor of California; Presley Marion Rixey, White House physician; Nicholas Murray Butler, president of Columbia University; William Loeb, Roosevelt's personal secretary; and Benjamin Ide Wheeler, president of the University of California. Theodore Roosevelt Collection Houghton Library, Harvard University, call no. 560.51 1903–115

Conservation and Preservation of the Environment.

The penchant for efficiency that characterized good government progressivism also shaped progressive efforts to conserve natural resources. As chief forester in the Department of Agriculture, Gifford Pinchot emphasized the efficient use of resources and sought ways to reconcile the public interest with private profit motives. His approach often won support from large lumber companies, which had a long-term interest in sustainable forests. Large companies also saw conservation as a way to drive their smaller competitors out of business, as large companies could better afford the additional costs associated with managing healthy forests.

This gospel of efficiency faced a stiff test in California. After the devastating earthquake of 1906, San Francisco officials, coping with water and power shortages, asked the federal government to approve construction of a hydroelectric dam and reservoir in **Hetch Hetchy valley**, located in Yosemite National Park (Map 19.2). Pinchot supported the project because he saw it as the best use of the land for the greatest number of people. The famed naturalist John Muir strongly disagreed. He campaigned to save Hetch Hetchy from "ravaging commercialism" and warned against choosing economic gains over spiritual values.

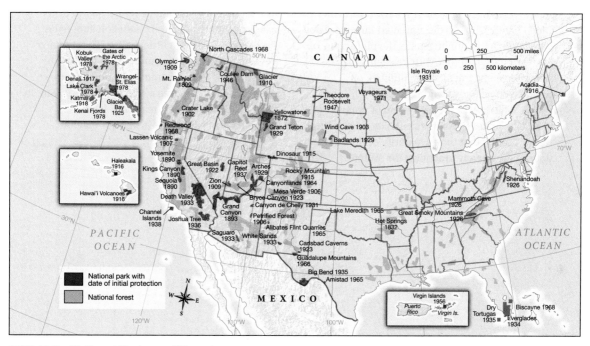

MAP 19.2   National Parks and Forests

In 1872, the federal government created the first national park at Yellowstone, which spread over portions of the future states of Wyoming, Montana, and Idaho. President Theodore Roosevelt added six sites — Crater Lake, Wind Cave, Petrified Forest, Lassen Volcanic, Mesa Verde, and Zion — to the park system. The construction of a dam and reservoir in Yosemite National Park's Hetch Hetchy Valley divided conservationists Gifford Pinchot and John Muir during the Roosevelt administration.

SECONDARY SOURCE ANALYSIS

Progressivism in White and Black

The Progressive Era produced an outpouring of reforms on the local, state, and national levels. Originally viewed as an attempt to spread political and economic democracy, historians have increasingly questioned the motives of progressives and the reforms they championed. In addition, historians have expanded their lens on progressivism to include the efforts of racial and ethnic minorities that previously had been obscured from view. The following document offers two views of southern progressivism and the groups that propelled it.

Source 19.4

C. Vann Woodward, Progressivism for Whites Only, 1951

Southern progressivism was essentially urban and middle class in nature, and the typical leader was a city professional man or businessman, rather than a farmer. Under the growing pressure of monopoly, the small businessmen and urban middle-class overcame their fear of reform and joined hands with the discontented farmers. They envisaged as a common enemy the plutocracy of the Northeast, together with its agents, banks, insurance companies, public utilities, oil companies, pipelines, and railroads.

. . . The direct primary system of nominating party candidates was not invented in Wisconsin in 1903 . . . for by that time a majority of the Southern states were already practicing the system. . . . The joker in the Southern primaries was the fact that they were *white* primaries. Southern progressivism generally was progressivism for white men only. . . . The paradoxical combination of white supremacy and progressivism was not new to the region, but it never ceased to be a cause of puzzlement and confusion above the Potomac—and not a little, below. The paradox nevertheless had its counterpart in the North, where it was not uncommon for one man to champion both progressivism and imperialism. In such instances it was a matter of white supremacy over browns instead of blacks.

Source: C. Vann Woodward, *Origins of the New South, 1877–1913* (Baton Rouge, Louisiana: Louisiana State University Press, 1971), 372, 373.

After a bruising seven-year battle, Pinchot (by this time a private citizen) triumphed. Still, this incursion into a national park helped spur the development of environmentalism as a political movement.

Besides the clash with preservationists, the Hetch Hetchy Dam project reveals another aspect of the progressive conservation movement. Like progressives who focused

Source 19.5

Glenda Elizabeth Gilmore, Southern Black Women and Progressivism, 1996

From the debris of disfranchisement, black women discovered fresh approaches to serving their communities and crafted new tactics to dull the blade of white supremacy. . . . After disfranchisement . . . the political culture black women had created through thirty years of work in temperance organization, Republican Party aid societies, and churches furnished both an ideological basis and an organization structure from which black women could take on those tasks. After black men's banishment from politics, North Carolinas black women added a network of women's groups that crossed denominational and—later party lines— and took a multi-issue approach to civic action. In a nonpolitical guise, black women became the black community's diplomats to the white community. Black women might not be voters, but they could be clients, and in that role they could become spokespeople for and motivators of black citizens. They could claim a distinctly female moral authority and pretend to eschew any political motivation. The deep camouflage of their leadership style—their womanhood— helped them remain invisible as they worked toward political ends. At the same time, they could deliver not votes but hands and hearts through community organization: willing workers in city clean up campaigns, orderly children who complied with state educational requirements and hookworm-infested people eager for treatment at public health fairs.

. . . As much as southern whites plotted to reserve progressivism for themselves, and as much as they schemed to alter the ill-fitting northern version accordingly, they failed. African American women embraced southern white progressivism, reshaped it, and sent back a new model that included black power brokers and grass roots activists. . . . Southern black women initiated every progressive reform that southern white women initiated, a feat they accomplished without financial resources, without the civic protection of their husbands, and without publicity.

Source: Glenda Elizabeth Gilmore, *Gender and Jim Crow: Women and the Politics of White Supremacy in North Carolina: 1896–1920* (Chapel Hill: University of North Carolina Press, 1996), 147, 148, 174.

Examine the Sources

1. Describe one major difference between Woodward's and Gilmore's interpretations of progressivism.
2. Explain how evidence in this chapter can be used to support or refute either Woodward's or Gilmore's interpretation of progressivism.

Put It in Context

Compare northern and southern progressivism and consider how regional factors influenced the development of progressivism.

on urban and political issues, progressive conservationists had a racial bias. Conservationists such as Pinchot may have seen themselves as acting in the public interest, but their definition of "the public" did not include all Americans. In planning for the Hetch Hetchy Dam, progressives did not consult with the Mono Lake Paiutes who lived in Yosemite and who were most directly affected by the project. Conservation was meant to serve the interests of white San Franciscans and not those of the Indian inhabitants of Yosemite.

REVIEW & RELATE

Who gained and who lost political influence as a result of progressive reforms?

How did a commitment to greater efficiency shape progressives' political and environmental initiatives?

Presidential Progressivism

The problems created by industrialization and the growth of big business were national in scope. Recognizing this fact, prominent progressives sought national leadership positions, and two of them, Presidents Theodore Roosevelt and Woodrow Wilson, instituted progressive reforms during their terms. In the process, they reinvigorated the presidency, an office that had declined in power and importance during the late nineteenth century.

Theodore Roosevelt and the Square Deal.
Born into a moderately wealthy New York family, Theodore Roosevelt graduated from Harvard in 1880 and entered government service. In 1898, Roosevelt formed a regiment of soldiers — the "Rough Riders" — and fought in Cuba against Spanish forces. That same year he was elected governor of New York. Elected as William McKinley's vice president in 1900, Roosevelt became president after McKinley's assassination a year later.

Roosevelt brought an activist style to the presidency. He considered his office a **bully pulpit** — a platform from which to promote his programs and from which he could rally public opinion. To this end, he used his energetic and extroverted personality to establish an unprecedented rapport with the American people.

For all his exuberance and energy, President Roosevelt pursued a moderate domestic course. Like his progressive colleagues, he opposed ideological extremism in any form. Roosevelt believed that as head of state he could serve as an impartial arbiter among competing factions and determine what was best for the public. To him, reform was the best defense against revolution.

As president, Roosevelt sought to provide economic and political stability, what he referred to as a "Square Deal." The coal strike that began in Pennsylvania in 1902 gave Roosevelt an opportunity to play the role of impartial mediator and defender of the public good. Miners had gone on strike for an eight-hour workday, a pay increase of 20 percent, and recognition of their union. Union representatives agreed to have the president create a panel to settle the dispute, but George F. Baer, president of the Reading Railroad, which also owned the mines, pledged that he would never agree to the workers' demands. Disturbed by what he considered the owners' "arrogant stupidity," Roosevelt threatened to dispatch federal troops to take over and run the mines. When the owners backed down, the president established a commission that hammered out a compromise, which raised wages and reduced working hours but did not recognize the union.

At the same time, Roosevelt tackled the problems caused by giant business trusts. In February 1902, the president instructed the Justice Department to sue the Northern Securities

Company under the Sherman Antitrust Act. Financed by J. P. Morgan, Northern Securities held monopoly control of the northernmost transcontinental railway lines. In 1904 the Supreme Court ordered that the Northern Securities Company be dissolved, ruling that the firm had restricted competition. With this victory, Roosevelt affirmed the federal government's power to regulate business trusts that violated the public interest. Overall, Roosevelt initiated twenty-five suits under the Sherman Antitrust Act, including litigation against the tobacco and beef trusts and the Standard Oil Company, actions that earned him the title of "trustbuster."

Roosevelt distinguished between "good" trusts, which acted responsibly, and "bad" trusts, which abused their power. Railroads had earned an especially bad reputation with the public for charging higher rates to small shippers and those in remote regions while granting rebates to favored customers, such as Standard Oil. In 1903 Roosevelt helped persuade Congress to pass the Elkins Act, which outlawed railroad rebates. Three years later, the president increased the power of the Interstate Commerce Commission to set maximum railroad freight rates. Also in 1903 Roosevelt secured passage of legislation that established the Department of Commerce and Labor. Within this cabinet agency, the Bureau of Corporations gathered information about large companies in an effort to promote fair business practices.

Soaring in popularity, Roosevelt easily won reelection in 1904. During the next four years, the president applied antitrust laws even more vigorously than before. He steered

"The Jungle" Upton Sinclair's 1906 novel *The Jungle* exposed unsanitary conditions in the meatpacking industry and led to passage of the Meat Inspection Act. In this photo from around 1905, workers at the Swift company process sausages as they roll off machines at ten feet per second. Library of Congress, 3a50293

through Congress various reforms concerning the railroads, such as the Hepburn Act (1906), which standardized shipping rates, and took a strong stand for conservation of public lands. Roosevelt charted a middle course between preservationists and conservationists. He reserved 150 million acres of timberland as part of the national forests, but he authorized the expenditure of more than $80 million in federal funds to construct dams, reservoirs, and canals largely in the West.

Not all reform came from Roosevelt's initiative. Congress passed two notable consumer laws in 1906 that reflected the multiple and sometimes contradictory forces that shaped progressivism. That year, Upton Sinclair published *The Jungle*, a muckraking novel that portrayed the impoverished lives of immigrant workers in Packingtown (Chicago) and the deplorable working conditions they endured. Outraged readers responded to the vivid description of the shoddy and filthy ways the meatpacking industry slaughtered animals and prepared beef for sale. The largest and most efficient meatpacking firms had financial reasons to support reform as well. They were losing money because European importers refused to purchase tainted meat. Congress responded by passing the Meat Inspection Act, which benefited consumers and provided a way for large corporations to eliminate competition from smaller, marginal firms that could not afford to raise standards to meet the new federal meat-processing requirements.

In 1906 Congress also passed the Pure Food and Drug Act, which prohibited the sale of adulterated and fraudulently labeled food and drugs. The impetus for this law came from consumer groups, medical professionals, and government scientists. Dr. Harvey Wiley, a chemist in the Department of Agriculture, drove efforts for reform from within the government. He considered it part of his professional duty to eliminate harmful products (Table 19.1).

Roosevelt initially gave African Americans reason to believe that they, too, would get a square deal. In October 1901, at the outset of his first term, Roosevelt invited Booker T. Washington to a dinner at the White House, outraging white supremacists in the South. Though Roosevelt dismissed this criticism, he never invited another black guest. Also in his first term, Roosevelt supported the appointment of a few black Republicans to federal posts in the South.

Nevertheless, Roosevelt lacked a commitment to black equality and espoused the racist ideas of eugenics then in fashion. He deplored the declining birthrate of native-born white Americans compared with that of eastern and southern European newcomers and African Americans, whom he considered inferior stock. He argued that unless Anglo-Saxon women produced more children, whites would end up committing "race suicide." "If the women flinch from breeding," Roosevelt worried, "the . . . death of the race takes place even quicker."

Once he won reelection in 1904, Roosevelt had less political incentive to defy the white South. He stopped cooperating with southern black officeholders and maneuvered to build the Republican Party in the region with all-white support. However, his most reprehensible action involved an incident that occurred in Brownsville, Texas, in 1906. White residents of the town charged that black soldiers stationed at Fort Brown shot and killed one man and wounded another. Roosevelt ordered that unless the alleged perpetrators stepped forward, the entire regiment would receive dishonorable discharges without a court-martial. Roosevelt never doubted the guilt of the black

TABLE 19.1   **National Progressive Legislation**

1903	Department of Labor and Commerce established to promote fair business practices
	Elkins Act
1906	Pure Food and Drug Act
	Meat Inspection Act; Hepburn Act
1910	White Slave Trade Act
1913	Underwood Act reduces tariffs to benefit farmers
	Sixteenth Amendment (graduated income tax)
	Seventeenth Amendment (election of senators by popular vote)
	Federal Reserve System
1914	Harrison Narcotics Control Act
	Federal Trade Commission
	Clayton Antitrust Act
1916	Adamson Act provides eight-hour workday for railroad workers
	Keating-Owen Act outlaws child labor in firms engaged in interstate commerce
	Workmen's Compensation Act
1919	Eighteenth Amendment (prohibition)
1920	Nineteenth Amendment (women's suffrage)

soldiers, and when no one admitted responsibility, he summarily dismissed 167 men from the military.

Taft Retreats from Progressivism. When Roosevelt decided not to seek another term as president in 1908, choosing instead to back William Howard Taft as his successor, he thought he was leaving his reform legacy in capable hands. A Roosevelt loyalist, Taft easily defeated the Democratic candidate, William Jennings Bryan, who was running for the presidency for the third and final time.

Taft's presidency did not proceed as Roosevelt and his progressive followers had hoped. Taft did not have the charisma or energy of his predecessor and appeared to move in slow motion compared with Roosevelt. Taft proved a weak leader and frequently took stands opposite to those of progressives. After convening a special session of Congress in March 1909 to support lower tariffs, the president retreated in the face of conservative Republican opposition in the Senate. That year, when lawmakers passed the Payne-Aldrich tariff, which raised duties on imports, Taft signed it into law, thereby alienating key progressive legislators.

The situation deteriorated even further in the field of conservation. When Pinchot criticized Taft's secretary of the interior, Richard Ballinger, for returning restricted Alaskan coal mines to private mining companies in 1910, Taft fired Pinchot. Taft did not oppose conservation—he transferred more land from private to public control than did Roosevelt—but his dismissal of Pinchot angered conservationists.

Even more harmful to Taft's political fortunes, Roosevelt turned against his hand-picked successor. After returning from overseas in 1910, Roosevelt became increasingly troubled by Taft's missteps. The loss of the House of Representatives to the Democrats in the 1910 elections highlighted the split among Republicans that had developed under Taft. A year later, relations between the ex-president and the incumbent further deteriorated when Roosevelt attacked Taft for filing antitrust litigation against U.S. Steel for a deal that the Roosevelt administration had approved in 1907. Ironically, Roosevelt, known as a trustbuster, believed that filing more lawsuits under the Sherman Antitrust Act yielded diminishing returns, whereas Taft, the conservative, initiated more antitrust litigation than did Roosevelt.

The Election of 1912.

Convinced that only he could heal the party breach, Roosevelt announced his candidacy for the 1912 Republican presidential nomination. However, despite Roosevelt's widespread popularity among rank-and-file Republicans, Taft still controlled the party machinery and the majority of convention delegates. Losing to Taft on the first ballot, an embittered but optimistic Roosevelt formed a third party to sponsor his run for the presidency. Roosevelt excitedly told thousands of supporters gathered in Chicago that he felt "as strong as a BULL MOOSE," which became the nickname for Roosevelt's new **Progressive Party**.

In accepting the nomination, Roosevelt articulated the philosophy of **New Nationalism**. He argued that the federal government should use its power to fight against the forces of special privilege and for social justice for the majority of Americans. To this end, the Progressive Party platform advocated income and inheritance taxes, an eight-hour workday, the abolition of child labor, workers' compensation, fewer restrictions on labor unions, and women's suffrage.

Roosevelt was not the only progressive candidate in the contest. The Democrats nominated Woodrow Wilson, the reform governor of New Jersey. As an alternative to Roosevelt's New Nationalism, Wilson offered his **New Freedom**. As a Democrat and a southerner (he was born in Virginia), Wilson had a more limited view of government than did the Republican Roosevelt. Wilson envisioned a society of small businesses, with the government's role confined to ensuring open competition among businesses and freedom for individuals to make the best use of their opportunities. Unlike Roosevelt's New Nationalism, Wilson's New Freedom did not embrace social reform and rejected federal action in support of women's suffrage and the elimination of child labor.

If voters considered either Roosevelt's or Wilson's brand of reform too mainstream, they could cast their ballots for Eugene V. Debs, the Socialist Party candidate who had been imprisoned for his leadership in the Pullman strike. He favored overthrowing capitalism through peaceful, democratic methods and replacing it with government ownership of business and industry for the benefit of the working class.

The Republican Party split decided the outcome of the election. The final results gave Roosevelt 27 percent of the popular vote and Taft 23 percent. Together they had a majority, but because they were divided, Wilson became president, with 42 percent of the popular vote and 435 electoral votes. Finishing fourth, Debs did not win any electoral votes, but he garnered around a million popular votes (6 percent).

Woodrow Wilson's New Freedom   Before Woodrow Wilson was elected president in 1912 he had been a college professor of political science and president of Princeton University. Having stepped out of the university's ivory tower into the White House, Wilson was prepared to "educate" his opponents about their economic and civic duties to the nation. How does this political cartoon depict this? Granger

Woodrow Wilson and the New Freedom Agenda.

Once in office, Wilson hurried to fulfill his New Freedom agenda. Even though he differed from Roosevelt about the scope of federal intervention, both men believed in a strong presidency. An admirer of the British parliamentary system, Wilson viewed the president as an active and strong leader whose job was to provide his party with a legislative program. The 1912 elections had given the Democrats control over Congress, and Wilson expected his party to support his New Freedom measures.

Tariff reduction came first. The Underwood Act of 1913 reduced import duties, a measure that appealed to southern and midwestern farmers who sought lower prices on the manufactured goods they bought that were subject to the tariff. The law also incorporated a reform that progressives had adopted from the Populists: the graduated income tax (tax rates that increase at higher levels of income). The ratification of the Sixteenth Amendment in 1913 provided the legal basis for the income tax after the Supreme Court had previously declared such a levy unconstitutional. The graduated income tax was meant to advance the cause of social justice by moderating income inequality. The need to recover revenues lost from lower tariffs provided an additional practical impetus for imposing the tax. Because the law exempted people earning less than $4,000 a year from paying the income tax, more than 90 percent of Americans owed no tax. Those with incomes exceeding this amount paid rates ranging from 1 percent to 6 percent on $500,000 or more.

Also in 1913, Wilson pressed Congress to consider banking reform. Farmers favored a system supervised by the government that afforded them an ample supply of credit at low interest rates. Eastern bankers wanted reforms that would stabilize a system plagued by cyclical financial panics, the most recent in 1907, while keeping the banking system under the private control of bankers. The resulting compromise created the Federal Reserve System. The act established twelve regional banks. These banks lent cash reserves to member banks in their districts at a "rediscount rate," a rate that could be adjusted according to the fluctuating demand for credit. Federal Reserve notes became the foundation for a uniform currency. The Federal Reserve Board, appointed by the president and headquartered in Washington, D.C., supervised the system. Nevertheless, as with other progressive agencies, the experts selected to oversee the new banking system came from within the banking industry itself. Although farmers won a more rational and flexible credit supply, Wall Street bankers retained considerable power over the operation of the Federal Reserve System.

Next, President Wilson took two steps designed to help resolve the problem of economic concentration. First, in 1914 he persuaded Congress to create the Federal Trade Commission. The commission had the power to investigate corporate activities and prohibit "unfair" practices (which the law left undefined). Wilson's second measure directly attacked monopolies. Enacted in 1914, the Clayton Antitrust Act strengthened the Sherman Antitrust Act by banning certain corporate operations, such as price discrimination and overlapping membership on company boards, which undermined economic competition. The statute also exempted labor unions from prosecution under antitrust legislation, reversing the policy initiated by the federal government in the wake of the Pullman strike.

By the end of his second year in office, Wilson had achieved most of his New Freedom objectives. Political considerations, however, soon forced him to widen his progressive agenda and support measures he had previously rejected. With the Republican Party once again united after the electoral fiasco of 1912, Wilson, looking ahead to reelection in 1916, resumed the campaign for progressive legislation. Wilson appealed to Roosevelt's constituency by supporting New Nationalism social justice measures. In 1916 he signed into law the Adamson Act, which provided an eight-hour workday and overtime pay for railroad workers; the Keating-Owen Act, outlawing child labor in firms that engaged in interstate commerce; and the Workmen's Compensation Act, which provided insurance for federal employees in case of injury. In supporting programs that required greater intervention by the federal government, Wilson had placed political expediency ahead of his professed principles. He would later show a similar flexibility when he lent his support to a women's suffrage amendment, a cause he had long opposed.

Despite facing a challenge from a united Republican Party, Wilson won the 1916 election against former New York Governor Charles Evans Hughes with slightly less than 50 percent of the vote. Wilson's reelection owed little to support from African Americans. W. E. B. Du Bois, who backed Wilson in 1912 for pledging to "assist in advancing the interest of [the black] race," had become disillusioned with the president. Born in the South and with deep southern roots, Wilson surrounded himself with white appointees from the South. Despite black protests, Wilson held a screening in the White House of the film *Birth of a Nation*, which glorified the Ku Klux Klan and denigrated African Americans.

Making the situation worse, Wilson introduced racial segregation into government offices and dining facilities in the nation's capital, and blacks lost jobs in post offices and other federal agencies throughout the South. In Wilson's view, segregation and discrimination were in the "best interests" of African Americans.

Still, President Wilson achieved much of the progressive agenda — more, in fact, than he had intended to when he first came to office. By the beginning of his second term, the federal government had further extended regulation over the activities of corporations and banks. Big business and finance still wielded substantial power, but Wilson had steered the government on a course that also benefited ordinary citizens, including passage of social justice measures he had originally opposed.

REVIEW & RELATE

- How did the progressive agenda shape presidential politics in the first two decades of the twentieth century?

- How and why did the role of the president in national politics change under Roosevelt, Taft, and Wilson?

Conclusion: The Progressive Legacy

By the end of the Progressive Era, Americans had come to expect more from their government. They were more confident that their food and medicine were safe, that children would not have to sacrifice their health and education by going to work, that women laborers would not be exploited, and that political officials would be more responsive to their wishes. As a result of the efforts of environmentalists as different as Gifford Pinchot and Gene Stratton-Porter, the nation expanded its efforts both to conserve and to preserve its natural resources. These and other reforms accomplished what Theodore Roosevelt, Woodrow Wilson, and their fellow progressives wanted: to bring order out of chaos.

In challenging laissez-faire and championing governmental intervention, progressives sought to balance individualism with social justice and social control. Despite cloaking many of their political reforms in democratic garb, middle- and upper-class progressives generally were more interested in augmenting their ability to advance their own agenda than in expanding opportunities for political participation for all Americans. Confident that they spoke for the "interests of the people," progressives had little doubt that increasing their own political power would be good for the nation as a whole.

Progressivism was not for whites only, but racial boundaries shaped the progressive movement. Native Americans campaigned and organized to get the federal government to repair its broken promises of justice. Blacks were active participants in progressivism, whether through extending educational opportunities, working in settlement houses, campaigning for women's suffrage, or establishing the NAACP. Nevertheless, racism was also a characteristic of progressivism. White southern reformers generally favored disfranchisement and segregation. Northern whites did not prove much more sympathetic. Immigrants also found themselves unwelcome targets of moral outrage as progressives forced these newcomers to conform to middle-class standards of social behavior. Campaigns for temperance, moral reform, and birth control all shared a desire to mold people deemed inferior into proper citizens, uncontaminated by chronic vice and corruption.

Progressivism was not monolithic and included a range of disparate and overlapping efforts to reorder political, social, moral, and physical environments. Except for the brief existence of the Progressive Party in 1912, reformers did not have a tightly knit organization or a fixed agenda. Leaders were more likely to come from the middle class, but support came from the rich as well as the poor, depending on the issue. Of course, many Americans did not embrace progressive principles, as conservative opponents continued to hold power and to fight against reform. Nevertheless, by 1917 a combination of voluntary changes and government intervention had cleared the way to regulate corporations, increase governmental efficiency, and promote social justice. Progressives succeeded in ameliorating conditions that might have produced violent revolution and more disorder. In time, they would bring their ideas to reordering international affairs.

TIMELINE OF EVENTS

1874   Woman's Christian Temperance Union founded

1889   Jane Addams and Ellen Starr establish Hull House

1890   National American Woman Suffrage Association formed

1895   Booker T. Washington delivers Atlanta address

1900   First commission form of government established in Galveston, Texas

1902   President Roosevelt settles coal strike

1903   National Women's Trade Union League founded

1906   Meat Inspection Act and Pure Food and Drug Act

1908   Race riot in Springfield, Illinois

1909   National Association for the Advancement of Colored People founded

1910   President Taft fires Gifford Pinchot

1912   Roosevelt forms Progressive Party

        Children's Bureau of the Department of Commerce and Labor established

1913   Sixteenth Amendment (graduated income tax) ratified

        Federal Reserve System created

1914   Harrison Narcotics Control Act

        Federal Trade Commission created Clayton Antitrust Act

1916   Keating-Owen Act

        Workmen's Compensation Act

1919   Eighteenth Amendment (prohibition) ratified

1920   Nineteenth Amendment (women's vote) ratified

KEY TERMS

pragmatism, *632*

social gospel, *632*

muckrakers, *633*

Hull House, *634*

civic housekeeping, *634*

suffragists, *636*

Tuskegee Institute, *638*

National Association for the Advancement of Colored People (NAACP), *639*

Woman's Christian Temperance Union (WCTU), *642*

Hetch Hetchy valley, *647*

bully pulpit, *650*

Progressive Party, *654*

New Nationalism, *654*

New Freedom, *654*

REVIEW & RELATE

1. What late-nineteenth-century trends and developments influenced the progressives?

2. Why did the progressives focus on urban and industrial America?

3. What role did women play in the early-twentieth-century fight for social justice?

4. How did social reformers challenge discrimination against women, minorities, and Indians?

5. What practices and behaviors of the poor did social control progressives find most alarming? Why?

6. What role did anti-immigrant sentiment play in motivating and shaping progressives' social control initiatives?

7. Who gained and who lost political influence as a result of progressive reforms?

8. How did a commitment to greater efficiency shape progressives' political and environmental initiatives?

9. How did the progressive agenda shape presidential politics in the first two decades of the twentieth century?

10. How and why did the role of the president in national politics change under Roosevelt, Taft, and Wilson?

Muller v. Oregon, 1908

▸ Explain the social and legal arguments for protecting women workers, and evaluate the tensions in these sources between gender difference and equality.

Women played a major role in progressivism. In pursuing a wide array of reforms, women helped to bring relief from the problems accompanying industrialization and urbanization. In this way they sought to benefit men as well as themselves. Yet to further advance their cause, reformers sometimes chose to emphasize the physical and psychological distinctions between the sexes (Sources 19.6 and 19.8). Unlike the battle for equal suffrage, in the field of labor relations reformers highlighted the weaknesses of women compared to men and argued for women's protection in the workplace. To a large extent, Supreme Court precedents forced them to do so. In 1905 the Court concluded that the government generally had limited power to regulate the private contracts workers entered into with their employers concerning hours and wages. Following this ruling, progressives such as Florence Kelley, the head of the National Consumers League, attempted to find a way to extend labor protections to women by distinguishing them from men.

In 1903 Oregon passed a law that prohibited the employment of women in factories and laundries for more than ten hours a day. Subsequently, Curt Muller, the owner of a laundry, compelled Emma Gotcher to work more than the maximum number of hours. After Gotcher complained, a local judge ruled against Muller, whose appeal wound up in the Supreme Court (Source 19.7). In 1908 the Court upheld the Oregon law (Source 19.9). In this instance, women workers won, but in the long run their victory dealt a blow to women's claim

of equality with men (Source 19.10). *Muller* provided ammunition for employers to discriminate against women on the basis of gender differences in hiring and promotion. Following this case, the Supreme Court in *Bunting v. Oregon* (1917) did extend the ten-hour day to male workers. However, this ruling did not erase the legal distinctions between men and women established in *Muller*.

Source 19.6

Theodore Roosevelt | "On American Motherhood," 1905

On March 13, 1905, President Theodore Roosevelt gave the following speech to the National Congress of Mothers. In the speech he acknowledges that women and men are equal citizens, but he also states that women have a special duty to produce and raise children. He insists that this is not just a family issue but a matter of the preservation of the highest values of the race, by which he meant the white race. His view of women and their role in promoting the general welfare would be echoed in *Muller v. Oregon*.

There are certain old truths which will be true as long as this world endures, and which no amount of progress can alter. One of these is the truth that the primary duty of the husband is to be the home-maker, the breadwinner for his wife and children, and that the primary duty of the woman is to be the helpmate, the housewife, and mother. The woman should have ample educational advantages; but save in exceptional cases the man must be, and she need not be, and generally ought not to be, trained for a lifelong career as the family breadwinner; and, therefore, after a certain point, the training of the two must normally be different because the duties of the two are normally different. This does not mean inequality of function, but it does mean that normally there must be dissimilarity of function. On the whole, I think the duty of the woman the more important, the more difficult, and the more honorable of the two; on the whole I respect the woman who does her duty even more than I respect the man who does his.

No ordinary work done by a man is either as hard or as responsible as the work of a woman who is bringing up a family of small children; for upon her time and strength demands are made not only every hour of the day but often every hour of the night. She may have to get up night after night to take care of a sick child, and yet must by day continue to do all her household duties as well; and if the family means are scant she must usually enjoy even her rare holidays taking her whole brood of children with her. The birth pangs make all men the debtors of all women. Above all our sympathy and regard are due to the struggling wives among those whom Abraham Lincoln called the plain people, and whom he so loved and trusted; for the lives of these women are often led on the lonely heights of quiet, self-sacrificing heroism. . . .

[I]f the average family in which there are children contained but two children the nation as a whole would decrease in population so rapidly that in two or three generations it would very deservedly be on the point of extinction, so that the people who had acted on this base and selfish doctrine would be giving place to others with braver and more robust ideals. Nor would such a result be in any way regrettable; for a race that practised such doctrine—that is, a race that practised race suicide—would thereby conclusively show that it was unfit to exist, and that it had better give place to people who had not forgotten the primary laws of their being.

Source: Theodore Roosevelt, "On American Motherhood," March 13, 1905. http://www.theodorerooseveltcenter.org/Research/Digital-Library/Record.aspx?libID=o280100, 7–10, 21.

William D. Fenton and Henry H. Gilfry | Brief for Plaintiff in Error, *Muller v. Oregon*, 1907

In their brief to the Supreme Court, Muller's attorneys, William D. Fenton and Henry H. Gilfry, argued that women were citizens and therefore deserved the same rights and privileges as men in the workplace. They contended that women had the freedom to enter into contracts with their employers concerning the number of hours they worked. Premised on women's equality, this argument was primarily directed at preventing government intervention in the economy.

It is to be observed also, that this law forbids a woman, whether married or single, from doing what would be perfectly lawful and proper for her brother or husband to contract to do in the same service. The classification is based wholly upon her sex, and without regard to her safety or the safety of those with whom she is working, and without regard to any question of morals or danger to the public health.

. . . The health of men is no less entitled to protection than that of women. For reasons of chivalry, we may regret that all women may not be sheltered in happy homes, free from the exacting demands upon them in pursuit of a living, but their right to pursue any honorable vocation, any business not forbidden as immoral, or contrary to public policy, is just as sacred and just as inviolate as the same right enjoyed by men. In many vocations women far excel, in proficiency, ability and efficiency, the most proficient men. . . .

. . . Women, in increasing numbers, are compelled to earn their living. They enter the various lines of employment hampered and handicapped by centuries of tutelage and the limitation and restriction of freedom of contract. Social customs narrow the field of her endeavor. Shall her hands be further tied by statute ostensibly framed in her interests, but intended perhaps to limit and restrict her employment, and whether intended so or not, enlarging the field and opportunity of her competitor among men?

Source: William D. Fenton and Henry H. Gilfry, "Brief for Plaintiff in Error," *Curt Muller v. State of Oregon*, Supreme Court of the United States, October Term, 1907, No. 107: 13–14, 24, 31.

Louis D. Brandeis | Brief for Defendant in Error, *Muller v. Oregon*, 1908

In defense of the Oregon law restricting women's industrial work to ten hours, Louis Brandeis sought to persuade the Supreme Court that medical and sociological evidence proved that it was reasonable to pass legislation to protect women's health. Brandeis, a lawyer who would later become a Supreme Court justice, together with Josephine Goldmark of the National Consumers League, presented a 113-page brief furnishing excerpts of reports from doctors and industrial commissions attesting to dangers of working long hours on women's health.

The Dangers of Long Hours

A. Causes

(1) *Physical differences between men and women.*

The dangers of long hours for women arise from their special physical organization taken in connection with the strain incident to factory and similar work.

Long hours of labor are dangerous for women primarily because of their special physical organization. In structure and function women are differentiated from men. Besides these anatomical and physiological differences, physicians are agreed that women are fundamentally weaker than men in all that makes for endurance: in muscular strength, in nervous energy, in the powers of persistent attention and application. Overwork, therefore, which strains endurance to the utmost, is more disastrous to the health of women than of men, and entails upon them more lasting injury. . . .

Report of the Massachusetts Bureau of Labor Statistics, 1884

We secured the personal history of these 1,032 of the whole 20,000 working girls of Boston, a number amply sufficient for the scientific purposes of the investigation. . . .

Long hours, and being obliged to stand all day, are very generally advanced as the principal reasons for any lack or loss of health occasioned by the work of the girls. . . . There appears, as far as my

observation goes, quite a predisposition to pelvic disease among the female factory operatives. . . . The necessity for instrumental delivery has very much increased within a few years, owing to the females working in the mills while they are pregnant and in consequence of deformed pelvis. Other uterine diseases are produced, and, in other cases, aggravated in consequence of the same.

The effect of women's overwork on future generations

Report of the Massachusetts Bureau of Labor Statistics, 1871

. . . It is well known that like begets like, and if the parents are feeble in constitution, the children must also inevitably be feeble. Hence, among that class of people, you find many puny, sickly, partly developed children; every generation growing more and more so.

Source: Louis D. Brandeis, "Brief for Defendant in Error," *Curt Muller v. State of Oregon*, Supreme Court of the United States, October Term, 1907, No. 107: 18, 39–40, 51.

David J. Brewer | Opinion, *Muller v. Oregon*, 1908

In his unanimous opinion in *Muller v. Oregon*, Justice David J. Brewer upheld the law and accepted Brandeis's contention that women needed the protection of state legislation in limiting daily working hours to ten. He accepted the sociological jurisprudence fashioned by Brandeis and agreed that women needed special protection based on their innate physical and psychological characteristics.

That woman's physical structure and the performance of maternal functions place her at a disadvantage in the struggle for subsistence is obvious. This is especially true when the burdens of motherhood are upon her. Even when they are not, by abundant testimony of the medical fraternity continuance for a long time on her feet at work, repeating this from day to day, tends to injurious effects upon the body, and, as healthy mothers are essential to vigorous offspring, the physical well-being of woman becomes an object of public interest and care in order to preserve the strength and vigor of the race.

Still again, history discloses the fact that woman has always been dependent upon man. He established his control at the outset by superior physical strength, may, without conflicting with the provisions and this control in various forms, with diminishing intensity, has continued to the present. As minors, though not to the same extent, she has been looked upon in the courts as needing especial care that her rights may be preserved. Education was long denied her, and while now the doors of the schoolroom are opened and her opportunities for acquiring knowledge are great, yet even with that and the consequent increase of capacity for business affairs it is still true that in the struggle for subsistence she is not an equal competitor with her brother. Though limitations upon personal and contractual rights may be removed by legislation, there is that in her disposition and habits of life which will operate against a full assertion of those rights. She will still be where some legislation to protect her seems necessary to secure a real equality of right. Doubtless there are individual exceptions, and there are many respects in which she has an advantage over him; but looking at it from the viewpoint of the effort to maintain an independent position in life, she is not upon an equality. Differentiated by these matters from the other sex, she is properly placed in a class by herself, and legislation designed for her protection may be sustained, even when like legislation is not necessary for men, and could not be sustained. It is impossible to close one's eyes to the fact that she still looks to her brother and depends upon him. Even though all restrictions on political, personal, and contractual rights were taken away, and she stood, so far as statutes are concerned, upon an absolutely equal plane with him, it would still be true that she is so constituted that she will rest upon and look to him for protection; that her physical structure and a proper discharge of her maternal functions—having in view not merely her own health, but the well-being of the race—justify legislation to protect her from the greed as well as the passion of man. The limitations which this statute places upon her contractual powers, upon her right to agree with her employer as to the time she shall labor, are not imposed solely for her benefit, but also largely for the benefit of all. Many words cannot make this plainer. The two sexes differ in structure of body, in the functions to be performed by each, in the amount of physical strength, in the capacity for long continued labor, particularly when done standing, the influence of vigorous health upon the future well-being of the race, the self-reliance which enables one to assert full rights, and in the capacity to maintain the struggle for subsistence. This difference justifies a difference in legislation, and upholds that which is designed to compensate for some of the burdens which rest upon her.

Source: 208 U.S. 412, 420, 421, 422, 423 (1908).

Source 19.10

Louisa Dana Haring | Letter, "Equality Before the Law," 1908

Some women disagreed with Justice Brewer's opinion. As long as women were viewed by law as dependent on and different from men, they would fail to achieve sexual equality. In the following letter to the *Woman's Tribune*, a newspaper whose motto was "Equality Before the Law," Louisa Dana Haring of Chicago criticizes the *Muller* decision.

Dear Madam: The last number of your paper which you kindly sent me is just received, and I want to express appreciation of your editorial about the restriction of the working hours of women. It is the first sensible thing I have seen on the subject. If men want to curtail the hours of work for women, let them see to it that the rates per hour are raised, so as to afford compensation for loss of time. Who ever heard of limiting a working woman in a home (where she often does the rudest, heaviest sort of work) to eight hours of toil a day? If the government is interested in the welfare of women, one would think it would stop discriminating against them in civil service examinations and pay them as well as men when they do work for Uncle Sam!

Source: Louisa Dana Haring, "Unjust to Working Woman," *Woman's Tribune*, May 9, 1908.

Interpret the Evidence

1. How would Theodore Roosevelt's ideas (Source 19.6) have fit into the arguments presented by each side in *Muller* (Sources 19.7 and 19.8)?
2. How does Justice Brewer respond to the arguments in each brief (Source 19.9)?
3. Among women, who would have found Louisa Dana Haring's letter most appealing (Source 19.10)?
4. Comparing these documents, do you think women can be considered equal under the law and still claim special protection?

Put It in Context

How do the arguments for women's suffrage compare with those of limiting working hours for women?

How did women influence the battle for progressive reform?

Empire and Wars

1898–1918

WINDOW TO THE PAST

Detail from Cartoon "A Bigger Job than He Thought For," 1899

This image portrays a cartoon from a newspaper in 1899 opposing the war in the Philippines. The annexation of the island after the War of 1898 led to a rebellion against U.S. military occupation by the Filipinos, a bloody insurrection that lasted for three years. ▶ To discover more about what this primary source can show us, see Source 20.3 on page 679.

Granger, NYC

After reading this chapter you should be able to:

- Analyze the reasons behind U.S. imperialism in the 1890s and early twentieth century.

- Compare the interventions in Cuba and the Philippines and their effects on U.S. attitudes toward nation building.

- Compare Roosevelt's "big stick" diplomacy, Taft's dollar diplomacy, and Wilson's moral diplomacy and identify their benefits and drawbacks.

- Summarize the reasons for U.S. intervention in World War I and evaluate their relative importance.

- Evaluate the domestic effects of World War I on U.S. economics, culture, and politics.

COMPARING AMERICAN HISTORIES

Alfred Thayer Mahan came from a military family. Born in 1840, he grew up in West Point, New York, where his father served as dean of the faculty at the U.S. Military Academy. Seeking to emerge from his father's shadow, Alfred attended the U.S. Naval Academy, receiving his commission in 1861, just as the Civil War was getting under way. His wartime experience convinced him that the navy needed a dramatic overhaul.

After the war, Captain Mahan built his reputation as a military historian and strategist at the U.S. Naval War College. In 1890 he published *The Influence of*

(*left*) **Alfred Thayer Mahan.** Library of Congress, LC-DIG-ggbain-17956

(*right*) **José Martí.** Library of Congress, LC-DIG-hec-08533

Sea Power upon History, in which he argued that great imperial powers in modern history had succeeded because they possessed strong navies and merchant marines. In his view, sea power had allowed these nations to defeat their enemies, conquer territories, and establish colonies. Appearing at a time when European nations were embarking on a new round of empire building, this book had an enormous influence on U.S. imperialists, including Theodore Roosevelt. Mahan's work reinforced the belief of men like Roosevelt that the long-term prospects of the United States depended on the acquisition of strategic outposts in Asia and the Caribbean that could guarantee U.S. access to overseas markets.

As the economic and strategic importance of the Caribbean grew in the minds of imperial strategists such as Mahan and Roosevelt, the Cuban freedom fighter José Martí developed a very different vision of the region's future. Born in 1853, Martí got involved in the fight for Cuban independence from Spain as a teenager. In 1869, at age seventeen, he was arrested for protest activities during a revolutionary uprising against Spain. Sentenced to six years of hard labor, Martí was released after six months and was forced into exile. He returned to Cuba in 1878, only to be arrested and deported again the following year.

Martí settled in the United States, where, along with other Cuban exiles, he continued to promote Cuban independence and the establishment of a democratic republic. He conceived of the idea of Cuba Libre (Free Cuba) not just as a struggle for political independence but also as a social revolution that would erase unfair distinctions based on race and class. Martí united disparate elements in expatriate communities in the United States and the Caribbean under the banner of a single Cuban Revolutionary Party.

When Cubans once again rebelled against Spain in 1895, Martí returned to Cuba to fight alongside his comrades. On May 19, only three months after he had returned to Cuba, Martí died in battle. Cuba ultimately won its independence from Spain, but Martí's vision of Cuba Libre was only partially realized. In 1898 the United States intervened on the side of the Cuban rebels, guaranteeing their victory but not their freedom. ∎

By comparing the American histories of Alfred Thayer Mahan and José Martí, we see disparate understandings of the United States' relationship with the rest of the world. Up until the late nineteenth century, most Americans associated colonialism with the European powers and saw overseas expansion as incompatible with U.S. values. In this context, they shared Martí's point of view. The imperialism espoused by Mahan and others therefore represented a reversal of traditional U.S. attitudes. Supporters of U.S. imperialism saw the acquisition and control of overseas territories, by force if necessary, as essential to the protection of U.S. interests. This perspective would come to dominate U.S. foreign policy in the early twentieth century. Theodore Roosevelt and Woodrow Wilson, progressive presidents who sanctioned intervention in economic and moral issues at home, supported vigorous intervention in world affairs. Many progressives lined up with the imperialists because they supported foreign expansion as part of the inevitable progress of the nation. Just as they used government power to institute economic, political, and social reforms at home, so too did many progressives advocate U.S. intervention to reshape world affairs. Although Roosevelt and Wilson differed in style and approach, in foreign affairs they asserted America's right to use its power to secure order and thwart revolution wherever U.S. interests were seen to be threatened. Having become a major power on the world stage in the early twentieth century, the United States chose to enter World War I, in which rival European alliances battled for imperial domination. The end of the war heightened America's critical role in world affairs but brought neither lasting peace nor the dissolution of empire.

The **Awakening** of **Imperialism**

The United States became a modern imperial power relatively late. In the decades following the Civil War, the U.S. government concentrated most of its energies on settling the western territories, pushing Native Americans aside, and extracting the region's resources. In many ways, westward expansion in the nineteenth century foreshadowed international expansion. The conquest of the Indians reflected a broader imperialistic impulse within the country. Arguments based on racial superiority and the nation's duty to expand became justifications for expansion in North America and overseas. By the end of the nineteenth century — with the nation's internal frontier officially gone according to the 1890 census — sweeping economic, cultural, and social changes led many in the United States to conclude that the time had come for the country to assert its power beyond its borders. In 1893, the influential U.S. historian Frederick Jackson Turner argued that the ending of the frontier necessitated a "wider field" for the "exercise [of] American energy" and reinvigorating the nation's political, economic, and cultural strengths (see "Secondary Source Analysis" in chapter 15). Convinced of the argument for empire advanced by Mahan and other imperialists, U.S. officials led the nation in a burst of overseas expansion from 1898 to 1904, in which the United States acquired Guam, Hawaii, the Philippines, and Puerto Rico; established a protectorate in Cuba; and exercised force to build a canal through Panama. These gains paved the way for subsequent U.S. intervention in Haiti, the Dominican Republic, and Nicaragua.

The Economics of Expansion. The industrialization of the United States and the growth of corporate capitalism stimulated imperialist desires in the late nineteenth century.

Throughout its early history, the United States had sought overseas markets for exports. However, the importance of exports to the U.S. economy increased dramatically in the second half of the nineteenth century, as industrialization gained momentum. In 1870 U.S. exports totaled $500 million. By 1910 the value of U.S. exports had increased threefold to $1.7 billion (Figure 20.1).

The bulk of U.S. exports went to the developed markets of Europe and Canada, which had the greatest purchasing power. Although the less economically advanced nations of Latin America and Asia did not have the same ability to buy U.S. products, businessmen still considered these regions — especially China, with its large population — as future markets for U.S. industries.

The desire to expand foreign markets remained a steady feature of U.S. business interests. The fear that the domestic market for manufactured goods was shrinking gave this expansionist hunger greater urgency. The fluctuating business cycle of boom and bust that characterized the economy in the 1870s and 1880s reached its peak in the depression of the 1890s. The social unrest that accompanied this depression worried business and political leaders about the stability of the country. The way to sustain prosperity and contain radicalism, many businessmen agreed, was to find foreign markets for U.S. goods. Senator William Frye of Maine argued, "We must have the market [of China] or we shall have revolution."

Similar commercial ambitions led many in the United States to covet Hawaii. U.S. missionaries first visited the Hawaiian Islands in 1820. As missionaries tried to convert native islanders to Christianity, U.S. businessmen sought to establish plantations on

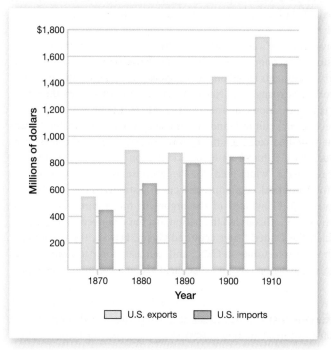

FIGURE 20.1   U.S. Exports and Imports, 1870–1910

As U.S. industrial power expanded at the end of the nineteenth century, exports increased dramatically. Between 1870 and 1910, U.S. exports more than tripled. Imports rose as well but were restrained by protective tariffs. How did the desire for overseas trade influence U.S. expansion overseas?

the islands, especially to grow sugarcane. In exchange for duty-free access to the U.S. sugar market, white Hawaiians signed an agreement in 1887 that granted the United States exclusive rights to a naval base at Pearl Harbor in Honolulu.

The growing influence of white sugar planters on the islands alarmed native Hawaiians. In 1891 Queen Liliuokalani, a strong nationalist leader who voiced the slogan "Hawaii for the Hawaiians," sought to increase the power of the indigenous peoples she governed, at the expense of the sugar growers. In 1893 white plantation owners, with the cooperation of the U.S. ambassador to Hawaii and 150 U.S. marines, overthrew the queen's government. Once in command of the government, they entered into a treaty of annexation with the United States. However, President Grover Cleveland opposed annexation and withdrew the treaty. Nevertheless, planters remained in power and waited for a suitable opportunity to seek annexation.

Cultural Justifications for Imperialism.
Imperialists linked overseas expansion to practical, economic considerations, but race was also a key component in their arguments for empire. Many in the United States and western Europe declared themselves superior to nonwhite peoples of Latin America, Asia, and Africa. Buttressing their arguments with racist studies claiming to demonstrate scientifically the "racial" superiority of white Protestants, imperialists asserted a "natural right" of conquest and world domination.

Imperialists added an ethical dimension to this ideology by contending that "higher civilizations" had a duty to uplift inferior nations. In *Our Country* (1885), the Congregationalist minister Josiah Strong proclaimed the superiority of the Anglo-Saxon, or white northern European, race and the responsibility of the United States to spread the "blessings" of its Christian way of life throughout the world. Secular intellectuals, such as historian John Fiske, praised the English race for settling the United States and predicted that English society and culture would become "predominant" in the less civilized parts of the globe.

As in Hawaii, Christian missionaries served as foot soldiers for the advancing U.S. commercial empire. In fact, there was often a clear connection between religious and commercial interests. For example, in 1895 industrialists John D. Rockefeller Jr. and Cyrus McCormick created the World Student Christian Federation, which dispatched more than five thousand young missionaries throughout the world, many of them women. Likewise, it was no coincidence that China became a magnet for U.S. missionary activity. Many Americans hoped that, under missionary supervision, the Chinese would become consumers of both U.S. ideas and U.S. products.

Gender and Empire.
Gender anxieties provided additional motivation for U.S. imperialism. In the late nineteenth century, with the Civil War long over, many in the United States worried that the rising generation of U.S. men lacked opportunities to test and strengthen their manhood. For example, in 1897 Mississippi congressman John Sharp Williams lamented the waning of "the dominant spirit which controlled in this Republic [from 1776 to 1865] . . . one of honor, glory, chivalry, and patriotism." Such gender anxieties were not limited to elites. The depression of the 1890s hit working-class men hard, causing them to question their self-worth as they lost the ability to support their families. By embracing the imperialist project, they would regain their manly honor.

Explore ▶

See Source 20.1 for part of Kipling's poem in support of white men's imperial ambitions in the Philippines.

GUIDED ANALYSIS

Rudyard Kipling | "The White Man's Burden," 1899

The English writer Rudyard Kipling was a leading exponent of British imperialism. His famous poem "The White Man's Burden" originally appeared in the popular U.S. magazine *McClure's* with the subtitle "The United States and the Philippine Islands." Given this subtitle, the poem can be seen as a direct appeal to U.S. men to join their British counterparts in the global imperial project.

Source 20.1

Take up the White Man's burden—
Send forth the best ye breed—
Go, bind your sons to exile
To serve your captives' need;
To wait, in heavy harness,
On fluttered folk and wild—
Your new-caught sullen peoples,
Half devil and half child. . . .

What does Kipling's characterization of the colonized people suggest about his point of view?

Take up the White Man's burden—
The savage wars of peace—
Fill full the mouth of Famine,
And bid the sickness cease;
And when your goal is nearest
(The end for others sought)
Watch sloth and heathen folly
Bring all your hope to nought. . . .

According to Kipling, why is it appropriate to describe imperialism as a "burden"?

What does the reward for colonizers suggest about his purpose in writing this poem?

Take up the White Man's burden!
Have done with childish days—
The lightly-proffered laurel,
The easy ungrudged praise:
Comes now, to search your manhood
Through all the thankless years,
Cold, edged with dear-bought wisdom,
The judgment of your peers.

Source: Rudyard Kipling, "The White Man's Burden," *McClure's Magazine*, February 1899, 290–91.

Put It in Context

How was the notion of "the white man's burden" used to justify expansion and annexation?

The growing presence of women as political activists in campaigns for suffrage and moral, humanitarian, and governmental reforms was particularly troubling to male identity. Some men warned that dire consequences would result if women succeeded in feminizing politics. Alfred Thayer Mahan believed that women's suffrage would undermine the nation's military security because women lacked the will to use physical force. He asserted that giving the vote to women would destroy the "constant practice of the past ages by which to men are assigned the outdoor rough action of life and to women that indoor sphere which we call the family." For Mahan and others, calling U.S. men to action was often paired with a call for U.S. women to leave the public arena and return to the home.

Males in the United States could reassert their manhood by adopting a militant spirit. Known as **jingoists**, war enthusiasts such as Theodore Roosevelt and Alfred Thayer Mahan saw war as necessary to the development of a generation of men who could meet the challenges of the modern age. "No greater danger could befall civilization than the disappearance of the warlike spirit (I dare say war) among civilized men," Mahan asserted. "There are too many barbarians still in the world." Mahan and Roosevelt promoted naval power, and by 1900 the U.S. fleet contained seventeen battleships and six armored cruisers, making it the third most powerful navy in the world, up from twelfth place in 1880. Having built a powerful navy, the United States would soon find opportunities to use it.

REVIEW & RELATE

- What role did economic developments play in prompting calls for a U.S. empire? What role did social and cultural developments play?

- Why did the United States embark on building an empire in the 1890s and not decades earlier?

The **War** with **Spain**

The United States went to war with Spain over Cuba in 1898 not to defend itself from attack but because U.S. policymakers decided that Cuban independence from Spain was in the United States' economic and strategic interests. Victory over Spain, however, brought the United States much more than control over Cuba. In the peace negotiations following the war, the United States acquired a significant portion of Spain's overseas empire, turning the United States into a major imperial power. To Americans, the war has traditionally been called the Spanish-American War, but this term fails to take into account the significant role played by the Cuban people and subsequently by the Filipinos who were also under Spanish rule.

Revolution in Cuba. The Cuban War for Independence began in 1895 around the concept of Cubanidad — pride of nation. José Martí envisioned that this war of national liberation from Spain would provide land to impoverished peasants and offer genuine racial equality for the large Afro-Cuban population that had been liberated from slavery less than a decade earlier, in 1886. "Our goal," the revolutionary leader declared in 1892, "is not so much a mere political change as a good, sound, and just and equitable system." Black Cubans, such as Antonio Maceo, flocked to the revolutionary cause and constituted a significant portion of the senior ranks in the rebel army.

The insurgents fought a brilliant guerrilla war. Facing some 200,000 Spanish troops, 50,000 rebels ground them down in a war of attrition. Within eighteen months, the

Cuban Revolutionary Soldiers   Under the command of General Maximo Gómez, these Cuban soldiers fought against Spanish forces in 1898. Gómez waged guerrilla warfare for Cuban independence from Spain before the United States entered the war. His army consisted of numerous Afro-Cubans, whose race troubled white U.S. commanders when they occupied Cuba. Granger, NYC

rebellion had spread across the island and garnered the support of all segments of the Cuban population. The Spanish government's brutal attempts to crack down on the rebels only stiffened their resistance. By the end of 1897, the Spanish government recognized that the war was going poorly and offered the rebels a series of reforms that would give the island home rule within the empire but not independence. Sensing victory, the insurgents held out for total separation to realize their vision of **Cuba Libre**, an independent Cuba with social and racial equality.

The revolutionaries had every reason to feel confident as they wore down Spanish troops. First, they had help from the climate. One-quarter of Spanish soldiers had contracted yellow fever, malaria, and other tropical illnesses and remained confined to hospitals. Second, mounting a successful counterinsurgency would have required far more troops than Spain could spare. Its forces were spread too thin around the globe to keep the empire intact. Finally, antiwar sentiment was mounting in Spain, and on January 12, 1898 Spanish troops mutinied in Havana. Speaking for many, a former president of Spain asserted: "Spain is exhausted. She must withdraw her troops and recognize Cuban independence before it is too late."

The War of 1898.   With the Cuban insurgents on the verge of victory, President William McKinley came to favor military intervention as a way to increase U.S. control of postwar Cuba. By intervening before the Cubans won on their own, the United States staked its claim for determining the postwar relationship between the two countries and protecting its vital interests in the Caribbean, including the private property rights of U.S. landowners in Cuba.

The U.S. press, however, helped build support for U.S. intervention not by focusing on economic interests and geopolitics but by framing the war as a matter of U.S. honor. William Randolph Hearst's *New York Journal* competed with Joseph Pulitzer's *New York World* to see which could provide the most lurid coverage of Spanish atrocities. Known disparagingly as **yellow journalism**, these sensationalist newspaper accounts aroused jingoistic outrage against Spain.

On February 15, 1898, the battleship *Maine*, anchored in Havana harbor, exploded, killing 266 U.S. sailors. Newspapers in the United States blamed Spain. The *World* shouted the rallying cry "Remember the *Maine*! To hell with Spain!" Assistant Secretary of the Navy Theodore Roosevelt seconded this sentiment by denouncing the explosion as a Spanish "act of treachery." Why the Spaniards would choose to blow up the *Maine* and provoke war with the United States while already losing to Cuba remained unanswered, but the incident was enough to turn U.S. opinion toward war.

On April 11, 1898, McKinley asked Congress to declare war against Spain. The declaration included an amendment proposed by Senator Henry M. Teller of Colorado declaring that Cuba "ought to be free and independent." Yet the document left enough room for U.S. maneuvering to satisfy the imperial ambitions of the McKinley administration. In endorsing independence, the war proclamation asserted the right of the United States to remain involved in Cuban affairs until it had achieved "pacification." On April 21, the United States officially went to war with Spain.

In going to war, McKinley embarked on an imperialistic course that had been building since the early 1890s. The president signaled the broader expansionist concerns behind the war when, shortly after it began, he successfully steered a Hawaiian annexation treaty through Congress. Businessmen joined imperialists in seizing the moment to create a commercial empire that would catch up to their European rivals.

It was fortunate for the United States that the Cuban insurgents had seriously weakened Spanish forces before the U.S. fighters arrived. The U.S. army lacked sufficient strength to conquer Cuba on its own, and McKinley had to mobilize some 200,000 National Guard troops and assorted volunteers. Theodore Roosevelt resigned from his post as assistant secretary of the navy and organized his own regiment, called "Rough Riders." U.S. forces faced several problems: They lacked battle experience; supplies were inadequate; their uniforms were not suited for the hot, humid climate of a Cuban summer; and the soldiers did not have immunity from tropical diseases.

African American soldiers, who made up about one-quarter of the troops, encountered additional difficulties. As more and more black troops arrived in southern ports for deployment to Cuba, they faced increasingly hostile crowds, angered at the presence of armed African American men in uniform. In Tampa, Florida, where troops gathered from all over the country to be transported to Cuba, racial tensions exploded on the afternoon of June 8. Intoxicated white soldiers from Ohio grabbed a two-year-old black boy from his mother and used him for target practice, shooting a bullet through his shirtsleeve. In retaliation, African American soldiers stormed into the streets and exchanged gunfire with whites, leaving three whites and twenty-seven black soldiers wounded.

Despite military inexperience, logistical problems, and racial tensions, the United States quickly defeated the weakened Spanish military, and the war was over four months after it began. During this war, 460 U.S. soldiers died in combat, far fewer than the more than 5,000 who lost their lives to disease. The subsequent peace treaty ended Spanish rule in Cuba, ceded Puerto Rico and the Pacific island of Guam to the United States, and recognized U.S. occupation of the Philippines until the two countries could arrange a final settlement. As a result of the territorial gains in the war, U.S. foreign-policy strategists could now begin to construct the empire that Mahan had envisioned.

The Pacification of Cuba.

Although Congress had adopted the **Teller Amendment** in 1898 pledging Cuba's independence from Spain, President McKinley and his supporters insisted that Cuban self-rule would come only after pacification. Racial prejudice and cultural chauvinism blinded Americans to the contributions Cubans had made to defeat Spain. One U.S. officer reported to the New York Times: "The typical Cuban I encountered was a treacherous, lying, cowardly, thieving, worthless half-breed mongrel, born of a mongrel spawn of [Spain], crossed upon the fetches of darkest Africa and aboriginal America." José Martí may have been fighting for racial equality, but the U.S. government certainly was not.

Because U.S. officials presumed that Cuba was unfit for immediate freedom, the island remained under U.S. military occupation until 1902. The highlight of Cuba's transition to self-rule came with the adoption of a governing document based on the U.S. Constitution. However, the Cuban constitution came with strings attached. In March 1901, Congress passed the **Platt Amendment**, introduced by Senator Orville Platt of Connecticut, which limited Cuban sovereignty. The amendment prohibited the Cuban government from signing treaties with other nations without U.S. consent, permitted the United States to intervene in Cuba to preserve independence and remove threats to economic stability, and leased Guantánamo Bay to the United States as a naval base. U.S. officials pressured Cuban leaders to incorporate the Platt Amendment into their constitution. When U.S. occupation ended in 1902, Cuba was not fully independent.

The Philippine War.

Even before invading Cuba, the United States had won a significant battle against Spain on the other side of the world. At the outset of the war, the U.S. Pacific Fleet, under the command of Commodore George Dewey, attacked Spanish forces in their colony of the Philippines. Dewey defeated the Spanish flotilla in Manila Bay on May 1, 1898. Two and a half months later, U.S. troops followed up with an invasion of Manila, and Spanish forces promptly surrendered (Map 20.1).

While pacifying Cuba, the U.S. government had to decide what to do with the Philippines. Imperialists viewed U.S. control of the islands as an important step forward in the quest for entry into the China market. The Philippines could serve as a naval station for the merchant marine and the navy to safeguard potential trade with the Asian mainland. Moreover, President McKinley believed that if the United States did not act, another European power would take Spain's place, something he thought would be "bad business and deplorable."

With this in mind, McKinley decided to annex the Philippines. As with Cuba, McKinley and most U.S. citizens believed that nonwhite Filipinos were not yet capable of self-government. Thus, McKinley set out "to educate the Filipinos, and uplift and Christianize them." As was often the case with imperialism, assumptions of racial and cultural superiority provided a handy justification for the pursuit of economic and strategic advantage.

The president's plans, however, ran into vigorous opposition. Anti-imperialists in Congress took a strong stand against annexing the Philippines. Their cause drew support from such prominent Americans as industrialist Andrew Carnegie, social reformer Jane Addams, writer Mark Twain, and labor organizer Samuel Gompers, all of whom joined the

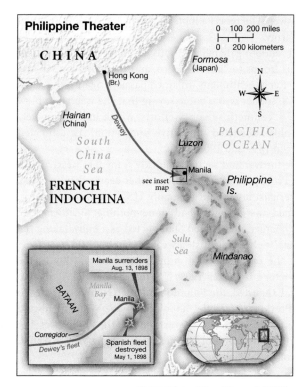

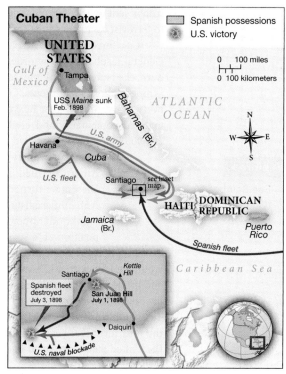

MAP 20.1   The War of 1898

The United States and Spain fought the War of 1898 (sometimes referred to as the Spanish-American War) on two fronts — the Philippines and Cuba. Naval forces led by Admiral George Dewey made the difference in the U.S. victory by defeating the Spaniards first in Manila Bay and then off the coast of Cuba. In Cuba, rebels had seriously weakened the Spanish military before U.S. ground troops secured victory.

Anti-Imperialist League, founded in November 1898. Progressives like Addams who were committed to humanitarian reforms at home questioned whether the United States should exploit colonial people overseas. Some argued that the United States would violate its anticolonialist heritage by acquiring the islands. Union leaders feared that annexation would prompt the migration of cheap laborers into the country and undercut wages. Others worried about the financial costs of supporting military forces across the Pacific. Most anti-imperialists had racial reasons for rejecting the treaty. Like imperialists, they considered Asians to be inferior to Europeans. In fact, many anti-imperialists held an even dimmer view of the capabilities of people of color than did their opponents, rejecting the notion that Filipinos could be "civilized" under U.S. tutelage. **See Primary Source Project 20: Imperialism versus Anti-Imperialism, page 695.**

Despite this opposition, imperialists won out. Approval of the treaty annexing the Philippines in 1898 marked the beginning of problems for the United States. As in Cuba, rebellion had preceded U.S. occupation. At first, the rebels welcomed the Americans as liberators, but once it became clear that U.S. rule would simply replace Spanish rule, the mood changed. Led by Emilio Aguinaldo, insurgent forces fought back against the 70,000 troops sent by this latest colonial power. The rebels adopted guerrilla tactics and resorted to terrorist assaults against the U.S. army.

U.S. forces responded in kind, adopting harsh methods to suppress the uprising. General Jacob H. Smithy ordered his troops to "kill and burn, and the more you kill and burn, the better you will please me." Racist sentiments inflamed passions against the dark-skinned Filipino insurgents. One U.S. soldier wrote home saying that "he wanted to blow every nigger into nigger heaven." U.S. counterinsurgency efforts, which indiscriminately targeted combatants and civilians alike, alienated the native population. An estimated 200,000 Filipino civilians died between 1899 and 1902.

Explore ▶

See Sources 20.2 and 20.3 for two views on the Philippine War.

The country's taste for war and sacrifice quickly waned, as nearly 5,000 Americans died in the Philippine war, far more combat deaths than in Cuba. Dissenters turned imperialist arguments of manly U.S. honor upside down. Anti-imperialists claimed that the war had done nothing to affirm U.S. manhood; rather, they charged, the United States acted as a bully, taking the position of "a strong man" fighting against "a weak and puny child."

Despite growing casualties on the battlefield and antiwar sentiment at home, the conflict ended with a U.S. military victory. In March 1901, U.S. forces captured Aguinaldo and broke the back of the rebellion. Exhausted, the Filipino leader asked his comrades to lay down their arms. In July 1901, President McKinley appointed Judge William Howard Taft of Ohio as the first civilian governor to oversee the government of the Philippines. For the next forty-five years, except for a brief period of Japanese rule during World War II, the United States remained in control of the islands.

REVIEW & RELATE

- Why did the United States go to war with Spain in 1898?

- In what ways did the War of 1898 mark a turning point in the relationship between the United States and the rest of the world?

Extending U.S. Imperialism, 1899–1913

The War of 1898 turned the United States into an imperial nation. Once the war was over, and with its newly acquired empire in place, the United States sought to extend its influence, competing with its European rivals for even greater global power. President Theodore Roosevelt and his successors achieved Captain Mahan's dream of building a Central American canal and wielded U.S. military and financial might in the Caribbean with little restraint. At the same time, the United States took a more active role in Asian affairs.

Theodore Roosevelt and "Big Stick" Diplomacy.   After President McKinley was assassinated in 1901, Vice President Theodore Roosevelt succeeded him as president. A progressive reformer at home, Roosevelt believed that the national government must intervene in economic and social affairs to maintain stability and avoid class warfare. In similar fashion, he advocated using military power to protect U.S. commercial and strategic interests as well as to preserve international order. "It is contemptible for a nation, as for an individual," Roosevelt instructed Congress, "[to] proclaim its purposes, or to take positions which are ridiculous if unsupported by potential force, and then to refuse to provide this force." This Progressive Era interventionist, inspired by Captain Mahan's writings, welcomed his nation's new role as an international policeman.

To fulfill his international agenda, Roosevelt sought to demonstrate U.S. might and preserve order in the Caribbean and Central and South America. The building of the Panama Canal provides a case in point. Mahan considered a canal across Central America as vital because it would provide faster access to Asian markets and improve the U.S. navy's ability to patrol two oceans effectively. The United States took a step toward realizing Mahan's goal in 1901, when it signed the Hay-Pauncefote Treaty with Britain, granting the United States the right to construct such a canal. After first considering Nicaragua, Roosevelt settled on Panama as the prime location. A French company had already begun construction at this site and had completed two-fifths of the operation; however, when it ran out of money, it sold its holdings to the United States.

Before the United States could resume building, it had to negotiate with the South American country of Colombia, which controlled Panama. Secretary of State John Hay and Colombian representatives reached an agreement highly favorable to the United States, which the Colombian government refused to ratify. When Colombia held out for a higher price, Roosevelt accused the Colombians of being "utterly incapable of keeping order" in Panama and declared that transit across Panama was vital to world commerce. In 1903 the president supported a pro-U.S. uprising by sending warships into the harbor of Panama City, an action that prevented the Colombians from quashing the insurrection. Roosevelt signed a treaty with the new government of Panama granting the United States the right to build the canal and exercise "power and authority" over it. In 1914, under U.S. control, the Panama Canal opened to sea traffic.

With the United States controlling Cuba, the Panama Canal, and Puerto Rico, President Roosevelt intended to deter any threats to U.S. power in the region. The economic instability of Central American and Caribbean nations provided Roosevelt with the opportunity to brandish what he called a "big stick" to keep these countries in check and prevent intervention by European powers also interested in the area. In 1904, when the government of the Dominican Republic was teetering on the edge of bankruptcy and threatened to default on $22 million in European loans, Roosevelt sprang into action. He announced U.S. opposition to any foreign intervention to reclaim debts, a position that echoed the principles of the Monroe Doctrine, which in 1823 proclaimed that the United States would not tolerate outside intervention in the Western Hemisphere. Moreover, Roosevelt added his own corollary to the Monroe Doctrine by affirming the right of the United States to intervene in the internal affairs of any country in Latin America or the Caribbean that displayed "chronic wrong-doing" and could not preserve order and manage its own affairs. The **Roosevelt Corollary** proclaimed that the countries of Central America and the Caribbean had to behave according to U.S. wishes or face American military invasion. Accordingly, the president acknowledged that this region was part of the U.S. sphere of influence.

Opening the Door in China.
Roosevelt displayed U.S. power in other parts of the world. His major concern was protecting the **Open Door** policy in China that his predecessor McKinley had engineered to secure naval access to the Chinese market. By 1900 European

COMPARATIVE ANALYSIS

Fighting in the Philippines

After defeating Spain, the United States annexed the Philippines. Despite considerable U.S. opposition to annexation, President William McKinley declared it his duty to uplift an "uncivilized" people (Source 20.2). However, Filipino rebels rejected U.S. occupation and continued their struggle for independence. As the fighting wore on, many Americans turned against the war. In the cartoon, penned by William Carson of the *Saturday Globe* (Utica, New York), in Source 20.3, Uncle Sam is saying to a Filipino insurgent: "Behave, You Fool! Durn Me, If I Ain't Most Sorry I Undertook to Rescue You."

Source 20.2

President McKinley Defends His Decision

When I next realized that the Philippines had dropped into our laps I confess I did not know what to do with them. . . . And one night late it came to me this way . . . 1) That we could not give them back to Spain—that would be cowardly and dishonorable; 2) that we could not turn them over to France and Germany—our commercial rivals in the Orient—that would be bad business and discreditable; 3) that we [could] not leave them to themselves—they are unfit for self-government—and they would soon have anarchy and misrule over there worse than Spain's wars; and 4) that there was nothing left for us to do but to take them all, and to educate the Filipinos, and uplift and civilize and Christianize them, and by God's grace do the very best we could by them, as our fellow-men for whom Christ also died.

Source: General James Rusling, "Interview with President William McKinley," *Christian Advocate*, January 22, 1903, 17.

powers had already dominated foreign access to Chinese markets, leaving scant room for newcomers. When the United States sent 2,500 troops to China in August 1900 to help quell a nationalist rebellion against foreign involvement known as the Boxer uprising, European competitors in return were compelled to allow the United States free trade access to China.

In 1904 the Russian invasion of the northern Chinese province of Manchuria prompted the Japanese to attack the Russian fleet. Roosevelt admired Japanese military prowess, but he worried that if Japan succeeded in driving the Russians out of the area, it would cause "a real shifting of equilibrium as far as the white races are concerned."

Source 20.3

William Carson | "A Bigger Job Than He Thought For," 1899

A BIGGER JOB THAN HE THOUGHT FOR.
UNCLE SAM—Behave, You Fool! Durn Me, If I Ain't Most Sorry I Undertook to Rescue You.

Granger, NYC

Interpret the Evidence

1. As represented by this cartoon, why did Americans turn against the Philippines War?
2. Compare the views presented here about Filipinos. What other sources might you consult to understand American views about Filipinos in this period?

Put It in Context

What role did annexation of the Philippines play in U.S. imperialism?

To prevent that from happening, Roosevelt convened a peace conference in Portsmouth, New Hampshire in 1905. Under the agreement reached at the conference, Japan received control over Korea and parts of Manchuria but pledged to support the United States' Open Door policy. In 1906 the president sent sixteen U.S. battleships on a trip around the globe in a show of force meant to demonstrate that the United States was serious about taking its place as a premier world power.

When Roosevelt's secretary of war, William Howard Taft, became president (1909–1913), he continued his predecessor's foreign policy with slight modification. Proclaiming

Boxer Uprising In 1900 the Society of Righteous and Harmonious Fists, a Chinese militaristic and secret society known as the Boxers, attacked foreign diplomatic offices in Beijing to expel outsiders. This illustration from Hunan province portrays the Boxers killing foreigners and burning Christian books. The Boxers viewed Christian missionaries as cultural enemies. A coalition of multinational forces crushed the uprising. Kharbine-Tapabor/The Art Archive at Art Resource, NY

that he would rather substitute "dollars for bullets," Taft encouraged private bankers to invest money in the Caribbean and Central America, a policy known as **dollar diplomacy**. Yet Taft did not rely on financial influence alone. He dispatched more than 2,000 U.S. troops to the region to guarantee economic stability.

Taft's diplomacy also led to extensive intervention in Nicaragua. In 1909 U.S. fruit and mining companies in Nicaragua helped install a regime sympathetic to their interests. When a group of rebels threatened this pro-U.S. government, Taft invoked the Roosevelt Corollary and sent in U.S. marines to police the country and deter further uprisings. They remained there for another twenty-five years. Under this occupation, U.S. bankers took control of Nicaragua's customs houses and paid off debts owed to foreign investors, a move meant to forestall outside intervention in a nation that was now under U.S. "protection."

REVIEW & RELATE

How did the United States assert its influence and control over Latin America in the early twentieth century?

How did U.S. policies in Latin America mirror U.S. policies in Asia?

Wilson and American Foreign Policy, 1912–1917

When Woodrow Wilson became president in 1913, he pledged to open a new chapter in the United States' relations with Latin America and the rest of the world. Disdaining power politics and the use of force, Wilson vowed to place diplomacy and moral persuasion at the center of U.S. foreign policy. Diplomacy, however, proved less effective than he had hoped. Despite Wilson's stated commitment to the peaceful resolution of international issues, during his presidency the U.S. military intervened repeatedly in Latin America, and U.S. troops fought on European soil in the global conflict that contemporaries called the Great War.

Diplomacy and War. Despite his stated preference for moral diplomacy, Wilson preserved the U.S. sphere of influence in the Caribbean using much the same methods as had Roosevelt and Taft. To protect U.S. investments, the president sent marines to Haiti in 1915, to the Dominican Republic in 1916, and to Cuba in 1917.

The most serious challenge to Wilson's diplomacy came in Mexico. The **Mexican revolution** in 1911 spawned a civil war among various insurgent factions. The resulting instability threatened U.S. interests in Mexico, particularly oil. When Mexicans refused to accept Wilson's demands to install leaders he considered "good men," Wilson withdrew diplomatic recognition from Mexico. In a disastrous attempt to influence Mexican politics, Wilson sent the U.S. navy to the port of Veracruz on April 22, 1914, leading to a bloody clash that killed 19 Americans and 126 Mexicans. The situation worsened after Wilson first supported and then turned against one of the rebel competitors for power in Mexico, General Francisco "Pancho" Villa. In response to this betrayal, Villa and 1,500 troops rode across the border and attacked the town of Columbus, New Mexico. In July 1916, Wilson ordered General John Pershing to send 10,000 army troops into Mexico in an attempt to capture Villa. The operation was a complete failure that only further angered Mexican leaders and confirmed their sense that Wilson had no respect for Mexican sovereignty.

At the same time as the situation in Mexico was deteriorating, a much more serious problem was developing in Europe. On June 28, 1914, a Serbian nationalist, intending to strike a blow against Austria-Hungary, assassinated the Austrian archduke Franz Ferdinand in Sarajevo, the capital of the province of Bosnia. This terrorist attack plunged Europe into what would become a world war. On August 4, 1914, the Central Powers — Germany, the Ottoman empire, and Austria-Hungary — officially declared war against the Allies — Great Britain, France, and Russia. (Italy joined the Allies in 1915.)

For the first three years of the Great War, Wilson kept the United States neutral. Though privately he supported the British, the president urged Americans to remain "impartial in thought as well as action." Peace activists sought to keep Wilson to his word. In 1915 women reformers and suffragists such as Jane Addams and Carrie Chapman Catt organized the Women's Peace Party to keep the United States out of the war.

Explore ▶

Read Sources 20.4 and 20.5 for two historians' arguments about Wilson's handling of neutrality in World War I.

Wilson faced two key problems in maintaining neutrality. First, the United States had closer and more important economic ties with the Allies than with the Central Powers, a disparity that would only grow as the war went on. The Allies purchased more than $750 million in U.S. goods in 1914, a figure that quadrupled over the next three years. By contrast, the Germans bought approximately $350 million worth of U.S. products in 1914; by 1917

SECONDARY SOURCE ANALYSIS

The U.S. Chooses to Enter World War I

The entry of the United States into World War I proved controversial. The war having started in Europe in 1914, the American government under President Woodrow Wilson pledged to remain neutral. Although war hawks such as former President Theodore Roosevelt argued for the United States to join the Allied side, most Americans remained divided and reluctant to join the overseas fight. Wilson won re-election in 1916 on the pledge, "He Kept Us Out of War," but the following year the president persuaded Congress to declare war on Germany and the Central Powers. The causes of U.S. entry into the war are complicated and have been debated by historians, with the focus on Wilson's handling of neutrality and his desire to create a system of international relations based on morality.

Source 20.4

Arthur S. Link | Woodrow Wilson and Neutrality 1963

In the final analysis, American policy was determined by the President and public opinion, which had a great, if unconscious, influence upon him. It was Wilson who decided to accept the British maritime system in the first instance, who set the American government against unrestricted use of the submarine, and who made the final decision for war instead of a continuance of armed neutrality.

. . . [I]f the German leaders had at any time desired a genuinely reasonable settlement and evidenced a willingness to help build a peaceful and orderly postwar world, they would have found a friend in the White House eager to join them in accomplishing these high goals.

The German decision to gamble on all-out victory or complete ruin . . . alone compelled Wilson to break diplomatic relations, to adopt a policy of armed neutrality, and finally to ask for a declaration of war—because American ships were being sunk and American citizens were being killed on the high seas, and because armed neutrality seemed no longer possible. Considerations of America's alleged economic stake in an Allied victory did not influence Wilson's thought during the critical weeks from February 1 to April 2, 1917. Nor did considerations of national interest, or of the great ideological issues at stake in the conflict.

Source: Arthur S. Link, *Woodrow Wilson and the Progressive Era, 1910–1917* (New York: Harper and Row), 1963, 280, 281.

the figure had shrunk to $30 million. Moreover, when the Allies did not have the funds to pay for U.S. goods, they sought loans from private bankers. Initially, the Wilson administration resisted such requests. In 1915, however, Wilson reversed course. Concerned that failure to keep up the prewar level of commerce with the Allies would hurt the country economically, the president authorized private loans. The gap in financial transactions with the rival war powers grew even wider; by 1917 U.S. bankers had loaned the Allies $2.2 billion, compared with just $27 million to Germany.

The second problem facing Wilson arose from Great Britain's and Germany's differing war strategies. As the superior naval power, Britain established a blockade of the North Sea to quarantine Germany and starve it into submission. The British navy violated international law by mining the waters to bottle up the German fleet and keep foreign ships from

Source 20.5

John Whiteclay Chambers II, Woodrow Wilson's Unneutral Neutrality, 2000

Although the president emphasized German violation of neutral rights, neither American tradition nor law nor economic necessity required him to guarantee the right of Americans to travel on armed belligerent ships. Though he couched his policies in terms of international law and principle, Wilson was responsible for defining the growth of trade with Britain as a legitimate and profitable expression of neutral rights. He rejected definitions of other neutrals—Spain, the Netherlands, and the Scandinavian countries—that banned such passenger travel and embargoed guns and ammunition. In addition, he refused to consider the German and British blockades similarly or to hold Germany to a postwar accounting, as he did in the case of Britain. Thus by 1917 Wilson found himself constrained by the framework created by his earlier decisions about American rights.

. . . Wilson's policies reflected the traditional American belief that the ideals of America were the ideals of all humankind and that the other nations must conform to Americans prescriptions and ideals. . . . This global interventionism was new, but it drew on an attitude of superiority that had much earlier become a part of American culture. Germany had to be restrained because it had broken America's rules, disputed its ideals, threatened the rights and property of American citizens, and even challenged its security and hegemony through the proposed military alliance with Mexico.

Source: John Whiteclay Chambers II, *The Tyranny of Change: America in the Progressive Era, 1890–1920*. Second Edition (New Brunswick, New Jersey: Rutgers University Press, 2000), 229, 231.

Examine the Sources

1. Compare Link and Chambers's interpretations of Wilson's handling of neutrality and explain the basis of their disagreement.
2. Based on the evidence in this chapter, who do you think presents a stronger argument and why?

Put It in Context

What would it have cost the United States to refrain from entering World War I? Do you think the decision to go to war was worth the price?

supplying Germany with food and medicines. Although Wilson protested this treatment, he did so weakly. He believed that the British could pay compensation for such violations of international law after the war.

Confronting a strangling blockade, Germany depended on the newly developed U-boat (*Unterseeboot*, or submarine) to counter the British navy. In February 1915, Germany declared a blockade of the British Isles and warned citizens of neutral nations to stay off British ships in the area. U-boats, which were lighter and sleeker than British battleships and merchant marine ships, relied on surprise. This strategy violated the rules of engagement under international maritime law, which required belligerent ships to allow civilians to leave passenger liners and cargo ships before firing. The British complicated the situation for the Germans by flying flags of neutral countries on merchant vessels and arming them with small "defensive" weapons. If U-boats played by the rules and surfaced before inspecting merchant ships, they risked being blown out of the water by disguised enemy guns.

Under these circumstances, U.S. neutrality could not last long. On May 15, 1915, catastrophe struck. Without surfacing and identifying itself, a German submarine off the Irish coast attacked the British luxury liner *Lusitania*, which had departed from New York City en route to England. Although the ship's stated objective was to provide passengers with transport, its cargo contained a large supply of ammunition for British weapons. The U-boat's torpedoes rapidly sank the ship, killing 1,198 people, including 128 Americans.

Outraged Americans called on the president to respond; some, including Theodore Roosevelt, advocated the immediate use of military force. Despite his pro-British sentiments, Wilson resisted going to war. Instead, he held the Germans in "strict accountability" for their action. Wilson demanded that Germany refrain from further attacks against passenger liners and offer a financial settlement to the *Lusitania*'s survivors. Unwilling to risk war with the United States, the Germans consented.

Wilson had only delayed the United States' entry into the war. By pursuing a policy of neutrality that treated the combatants unequally and by insisting that Americans had a right to travel on the ships of belligerent nations, the president diminished the chance that the United States would stay out of the war.

Throughout 1916, Wilson pursued two separate but interrelated policies that embodied the ambivalence that he and the U.S. people shared about the war. On the one hand, with Germany alternating between continued U-boat attacks and apologies, the president sought to build the country's military preparedness in the event of war. He signed into law the National Defense Act, which increased the size of the army, navy, and National Guard. On the other hand, Wilson stressed his desire to remain neutral and stay out of the war. With U.S. public opinion divided on the Great War, Wilson chose to run for reelection as a peace candidate. The Democrats adopted the slogan "He kept us out of war" and also emphasized the president's substantial record of progressive reform. Wilson won a narrow victory against Charles Evans Hughes, the former governor of New York, who wavered between advocating peace and criticizing Wilson for not sufficiently supporting the Allies.

Making the World Safe for Democracy.

As 1917 dawned, the bloody war dragged on. Neither side wanted a negotiated peace because each counted on victory to gain sufficient territory and financial compensation to justify the great sacrifices in human lives and materiel caused by the conflict. Nevertheless, Wilson tried to persuade the belligerents to abandon the battlefield for the bargaining table. On January 22, 1917, he declared that the world needed a "peace without victory," one based on self-determination, freedom of the seas, respect for international law, and the end of hostile alliances. It was a generous vision from a nation that had made few sacrifices.

Germany quickly rejected Wilson's proposal. The United States had never been truly neutral, and Germany's increasingly desperate leaders saw no reason to believe that the situation would change. In 1915 and again in 1916, to prevent the United States from entering the war, Germany had pledged to refrain from using its U-boats against passenger and merchant ships. However, on February 1, 1917 the Germans chose to change course and resume unrestricted submarine warfare, calculating that they could defeat the

Trench Warfare   Trench warfare was at the center of the fighting in World War I. Both sides constructed a network of trenches and dugout shelters and fought from these trenches to wear the enemy down. This photograph snapped by Sergeant Leon H. Caverly on March 22, 1918 shows Red Cross workers in a trench caring for a wounded American soldier. Sgt. Leon H. Caverly/Topical Press Agency/Getty Images

Allies before the United States declared war and its troops could make a substantial difference. In response, Wilson used his executive power to arm merchant ships, bringing the United States one step closer to war.

The country moved even closer to war after the **Zimmermann telegram** became public. On February 24, the British turned over to Wilson an intercepted message from Arthur Zimmermann, the German foreign minister, to the Mexican government. The note revealed that Germany had offered Mexico an alliance in the event that the United States joined the Allies. If the Central Powers won, Mexico would receive the territory it had lost to the United States in the mid-nineteenth century — Texas, New Mexico, and Arizona. When U.S. newspapers broke the story several days later, it inflamed public opinion and provided the Wilson administration another reason to fear a German victory.

In late February and March, German U-boats sank several armed U.S. merchant ships, and on April 2, 1917 President Wilson asked Congress to declare war against Germany and the other Central Powers. After four days of vigorous debate led by opponents of the war — including Senator Robert M. La Follette of Wisconsin and the first female elected representative, Jeanette P. Rankin from Montana — Congress voted to approve the war resolution.

President Wilson had not reached his decision lightly. For three years, he resisted calls for war. In the end, however, Wilson decided that only by going to war would he be able to ensure that the United States played a role in shaping the peace. For the president, the security of the nation rested on respect for law, human rights, and extension of free governments. "The world must be made safe for democracy," he informed Congress in his war message, and he had concluded that the only way to guarantee this outcome was by helping to defeat Germany. This need became even more urgent when in November 1917 the Russian Revolution installed a Bolshevik (Communist) regime that negotiated a separate peace with the Central Powers. (See Map 20.2.)

It would take a while for Americans to make their presence felt in Europe. First, the United States needed a large army, which it created through the draft. The Selective

MAP 20.2   European Alliances, 1914

Pre-war alliances helped precipitate World War I. The assassination of Archduke Ferdinand of Austria-Hungry by a Serbian revolutionary in Sarajevo set the countries in the Austro-Hungarian and German-led Central Alliance against the British-French-Russian Entente, as the map shows.

Service Act of 1917 conscripted 3 million men by war's end. Mobilizing such a large force required substantial time, and the **American Expeditionary Forces (AEF)**, established in 1917 under General Pershing, did not make much of an impact until 1918. Before then, the U.S. navy made the greatest contribution. U.S. warships joined the British in escorting merchant vessels, combating German submarines, and laying mines in the North Sea. The United States also provided crucial funding and supplies to the Allies as their reserves became depleted.

The AEF finally began to make an impact in Europe in May 1918. From May through September, more than 1 million U.S. troops helped the Allies repel German offensives in northern France near the Belgian border. One momentous battle in the Argonne Forest lasted two months until the Allies broke through enemy lines and pushed toward Germany. Nearly 50,000 U.S. troops died in the fierce fighting, and another 230,000 were injured. Like their European counterparts, who suffered a staggering 8 to 10 million casualties, Americans experienced the horrors of war magnified by new technology. Dug into filthy trenches, soldiers dodged rapid machine-gun fire, heavy artillery explosions, and poison gas shells. In the end, however, the AEF succeeded in tipping the balance in favor of the Allies. On November 11, 1918, an exhausted Germany surrendered.

REVIEW & RELATE

- In what ways, if any, did President Wilson's approach to Latin American affairs differ from that of his predecessors?

- Why did President Wilson find it so difficult to keep the United States out of World War I?

Fighting the War at Home

Modern global warfare required full mobilization at home. In preparing to support the war effort, the country drew on recent experience. The progressives' passion for organization, expertise, efficiency, and moralistic control was harnessed to the effort of placing the economy on a wartime footing and rallying the American people behind the war. In the process, the government gained unprecedented control over American life. At the same time, the war effort also produced unforeseen economic and political opportunities.

Government by Commission. Progressives had relied on government commissions to regulate business practices as well as health and safety standards, and in July 1917 the Wilson administration followed suit by establishing the **War Industries Board (WIB)** to supervise the purchase of military supplies and to gear up private enterprise to meet demand. However, the WIB was largely ineffective until March 1918, when the president found the right man to lead it. He chose Wall Street financier Bernard Baruch, who recruited staff from business enterprises that the board regulated. Baruch prodded businesses into compliance mainly by offering lucrative contracts rather than by coercion. Ultimately, the WIB created a government partnership with the corporate sector that would last beyond the war.

Labor also experienced significant gains through government regulation. Shortages of workers and an outbreak of strikes hampered the war effort. In April 1918 Wilson created the **National War Labor Board (NWLB)** to settle labor disputes. The agency consisted of representatives from unions, corporations, and the public. In exchange for obtaining a "no strike pledge" from organized labor, the NWLB supported an eight-hour workday with time-and-a-half pay for overtime, labor's right to collective bargaining, and equal pay for equal work by women.

The NWLB fell short of reaching this last goal, but the war employed more than a million women who had not held jobs before. As military and government services expanded, women found greater opportunities as telephone operators, nurses, and clerical workers. At the same time, the number of women employed as domestic servants declined. Women took over formerly male jobs driving streetcars, delivering ice, assembling airplane motors, operating drill presses, oiling railroad engines, and welding parts. Yet women's incomes continued to lag significantly behind those of men performing the same tasks.

Americans probably experienced the expanding scope of government intervention most directly through the efforts of three new agencies that regulated consumption and travel. Wilson appointed Herbert Hoover to head the Food Administration. Hoover sought to increase the military and civilian food supply mainly through voluntary conservation measures. He generated a massive publicity campaign urging Americans to adopt "wheatless Mondays," "meatless Tuesdays," and "porkless Thursdays and Saturdays." The government also mobilized schoolchildren to plant vegetable gardens to increase food production for the home front.

Consumers saved gas and oil under the prodding of the Fuel Administration. The agency encouraged fuel "holidays" along the line of Hoover's voluntary restrictions and created daylight savings time to conserve fuel by adding an extra hour of sunlight to the end of the workday. The Fuel Administration also offered higher prices to coal companies to increase productivity. Patterns of consumer travel changed under government regulation. The Railroad Administration acted more forcefully than most other agencies. Troop and supply shipments depended on the efficient operation of the railways. The administration controlled the railroads during the war, coordinating train schedules, overseeing terminals and regulating ticket prices, upgrading tracks, and raising workers' wages.

Winning Hearts and Minds.

Winning Hearts and Minds. America's entry into the Great War did not immediately end the significant antiwar sentiment. Consequently, Wilson waged a campaign to rally support for his aims and to stimulate patriotic fervor. To generate enthusiasm and ensure loyalty, the president appointed journalist George Creel to head the **Committee on Public Information (CPI)**, which focused on generating propaganda. Creel recruited a vast network of lecturers to speak throughout the country and spread patriotic messages. The committee coordinated rallies to sell bonds and raise money to fund the war. The CPI persuaded reporters to censor their war coverage, and most agreed in order to avoid government intervention. The agency helped produce films depicting the Allies as heroic saviors of humanity and the Central Powers as savage beasts. The CPI also distributed colorful and sometimes lurid posters emphasizing the depravity of the enemy and the nation's moral responsibility to defeat the Central Powers.

Propaganda did not prove sufficient, however, and Americans remained deeply divided about the war. To suppress dissent, Congress passed the Espionage Act in 1917 and the Sedition Act a year later. Both limited freedom of speech by criminalizing certain forms of expression. The **Espionage Act** prohibited antiwar activities, including interfering with the draft. It also banned the mailing of publications advocating forcible interference with any laws. The **Sedition Act** punished individuals who expressed beliefs disloyal or abusive to the U.S. government, flag, or military uniform. Of the slightly more than two thousand prosecutions under these laws, only a handful concerned charges of actual sabotage or espionage. Most defendants brought to trial were critics who merely spoke out against the war. In 1918, for telling a crowd that the military draft was a form of slavery, the Socialist Party's Eugene V. Debs was tried, convicted, and sentenced to ten years under the Espionage Act. (President Warren G. Harding pardoned Debs in 1921.) The Justice Department also went after the Industrial Workers of the World (IWW), which continued

World War I Posters   Many of the wartime posters were aimed at rallying women to provide help on the home front and mobilizing men to defend women by joining the military. The poster on the left was put out by the Food Administration and the one at the right, illustrated by Fred Spear for the Boston Committee of Public Safety, shows a mother and her infant drowning with the sinking of the *Lusitania* in 1915. *National Archives, 512614 and Galerie Bilderwelt / Bridgeman Images*

to initiate labor strikes during the war. The government broke into the offices of the IWW, ransacked the group's files for evidence of disloyalty, and arrested more than 130 members.

Government efforts to promote national unity and punish those who did not conform prompted local communities to enforce "one hundred percent Americanism." Civic groups banned the playing of German music and operas from concert halls, and schools prohibited teaching the German language. Foods with German origins were renamed — sauerkraut became "liberty cabbage," and hamburgers became "liberty sandwiches." Such sentiments were expressed in a more sinister fashion when mobs assaulted German Americans.

Prejudice toward German Americans was further inflamed by the formation of the **American Protective League (APL)**, a quasi-official association endorsed by the Justice Department. Consisting of 200,000 chapters throughout the country, the APL employed individuals to spy on German residents suspected of disloyal behavior. Most often, APL agents found little more than German immigrants who merely retained attachments to family and friends in their homeland. Gossip and rumor fueled many of the league's loyalty probes.

The repressive side of progressivism came to the fore in other ways as well. Anti-immigrant bias, shared by many reformers, flourished. The effort to conserve manpower and grain supplies bolstered the impulse to control standards of moral behavior, particularly those associated with immigrants, such as drinking. This anti-immigrant prejudice in part explains the ratification of the Eighteenth Amendment in 1919, prohibiting the sale of all alcoholic beverages. Yet not all the moral indignation unleashed by the war resulted in restriction of freedom. After considerable wartime protest and lobbying, women suffragists succeeded in securing the right to vote.

President Wilson's goal "to make the world safe for democracy" appealed to oppressed minorities. They hoped the war would push the United States to live up to its rhetoric and extend freedom at home. Nearly 400,000 African Americans served in the war and more than 40,000 saw combat, but most were assigned to service units and worked in menial jobs. The army remained segregated, and few black officers commanded troops. Despite this discrimination, W. E. B. Du Bois echoed African Americans' hope that their patriotism would be rewarded at the war's end: "We of the colored race have no ordinary interest in the outcome."

The same held true for American Indians. More than ten thousand Indians participated in the war. Recruited from Arizona, Montana, and New York, they fought in the major battles in France and Belgium. Unlike African Americans, they did not fight in segregated units and saw action as scouts and combat soldiers. They gained recognition by communicating messages in their native languages to confuse the Germans listening in. Aware of the contradiction between their troubling treatment historically by the U.S. government and the nation's democratic war aims, they expected that their wartime patriotism would bring them a greater measure of justice. However, like African Americans, they would be disappointed.

Waging Peace. In January 1918, ten months before the war ended, President Wilson presented Congress with his plan for peace. Wilson bundled his ideas in the **Fourteen Points**, principles that he hoped would prevent future wars. Based on his assessment of the causes of the Great War, Wilson envisioned a generous peace treaty that included freedom of the seas, open diplomacy and the abolition of secret treaties, free trade, self-determination for colonial subjects, and a reduction in military spending. More important than any specific measure, Wilson's proposal hinged on the creation of the **League of Nations**, a body of large and small nations that would guarantee peaceful resolution of disputes and back up decisions through collective action, including the use of military force as a last resort.

Following the armistice that ended the war on November 11, 1918, Wilson personally took his message to the Paris Peace Conference, the postwar meeting of the victorious Allied nations that would set the terms of the peace. The first sitting president to travel overseas, Wilson was greeted in Paris by joyous crowds.

For nearly six months, Wilson tried to convince reluctant Allied leaders to accept the central components of his plan. Having exhausted themselves financially and having suffered the loss of a generation of young men, the Allies intended to scoop up the spoils of victory and make the Central Powers pay dearly. The European Allies intended to hold on to their respective colonies regardless of Wilson's call for self-determination, and as a nation that depended on a strong navy, Britain refused to limit its options by discussing freedom of the seas. Perhaps Georges Clemenceau, France's president, best expressed his colleagues' skepticism about Wilson's idealistic vision: "President Wilson and his Fourteen Points bore me. Even God Almighty has only ten!"

During the conference, Wilson was forced to compromise on a number of his principles in order to retain the cornerstone of his diplomacy — the establishment of the League of Nations. He abandoned his hope for peace without bitterness by agreeing to a "war guilt" clause that levied huge economic reparations on Germany for starting the war. He was willing to sacrifice some of his ideals because the league took on even greater importance in the wake of the 1917 Communist revolution in Russia. The president believed that capitalism, as regulated and reformed during the Progressive Era, would raise living conditions throughout the world as it had done in the United States, would prevent the spread of communism, and would benefit U.S. commerce. Wilson needed the league to keep the peace so that war-ravaged and recovering nations had the opportunity to practice economic freedom and political democracy. In the end, the president won agreement for the establishment of his cherished League of Nations. The **Treaty of Versailles,** signed at the royal palace just outside Paris, authorized the league to combat aggression against any member nation through collective military action.

The Failure of Ratification.
In July 1919, after enduring bruising battles in Paris, Wilson returned to Washington, D.C., only to face another wrenching struggle in the Senate over ratification of the Versailles treaty. The odds were stacked against Wilson from the start. The Republicans held a majority in the Senate, and Wilson needed the support of two-thirds of the Senate to secure ratification. Moreover, Henry Cabot Lodge, the Republican chairman of the Senate Foreign Relations Committee, opposed Article X of the League of Nations covenant, which sanctioned collective security arrangements against military aggression. Lodge argued that such an alliance compromised the United States' independence in conducting its own foreign relations. Lodge had at least thirty-nine senators behind him, more than enough to block ratification. Conceding the need to protect the country's national self-interest, the president agreed to modifications to the treaty so that the Monroe Doctrine and America's obligations in the Caribbean and Central America were kept intact. Lodge, however, was not satisfied and insisted on adding fourteen "reservations" limiting compliance with the treaty, including strong language affirming Congress's right to declare war before agreeing to a League of Nations military action.

Wilson's stubbornness more than equaled Lodge's, and the president refused to compromise further over the league. Insisting that he was morally bound to honor the treaty he had negotiated in good faith, Wilson rejected additional changes. Making matters worse, Wilson faced resistance from sixteen lawmakers dubbed "irreconcilables," who opposed the league under any circumstances. Mainly Republicans from the Midwest and West, they voiced the traditional U.S. rejection of entangling alliances.

To break the logjam, the president attempted to rally public opinion behind him. In September 1919, he embarked on a nationwide speaking tour to carry his message directly to the American people. Over a three-week period, he traveled eight thousand miles by train, keeping a grueling schedule that exhausted him. After a stop in Pueblo, Colorado on September 25, Wilson collapsed and canceled the rest of his trip. On October 2, Wilson suffered a massive stroke that nearly killed him. The effects of the stroke, which left him partially paralyzed, emotionally unstable, and mentally impaired, dimmed any remaining hopes of compromise. The full extent of his illness was kept from the public, and his wife, Edith, ran the White House for the next eighteen months.

On November 19, 1919, the Senate rejected the amended treaty. The following year, Wilson had one final chance to obtain ratification, but still he refused to accept reservations despite members of his own party urging compromise. In March 1920, treaty ratification failed one last time, falling just seven votes short of the required two-thirds majority. Had Wilson shown the same willingness to compromise that he had in Paris, the outcome might have been different. In the end, however, the United States never signed the Treaty of Versailles or joined the League of Nations, weakening the league and diminishing the prospects for long-term peace.

REVIEW & RELATE

● What steps did the U.S. government take to control the economy and public opinion during World War I?

● How did President Wilson's wartime policies and his efforts to shape the peace that followed reflect his progressive roots?

Conclusion: A U.S. Empire

In the final decade of the nineteenth century, the United States transformed itself into an imperial power. Presidents McKinley and Roosevelt carried out the strategy outlined by Captain Alfred Thayer Mahan to enlarge the navy, construct a canal linking the Atlantic and Pacific Oceans, and acquire coaling stations and bases in the Pacific to service the fleet. U.S. officials disregarded the nationalistic aspirations of freedom fighters such as José Martí in Cuba and Emilio Aguinaldo in the Philippines in favor of the imperial spoils gained from winning the War of 1898. The United States justified intervention on moral grounds predicated on racist beliefs, much as it had in conquering the Indians during westward expansion. As a fit and manly nation, the United States had the responsibility to uplift inferior peoples to "civilized" standards and make them capable of self-government. This justification quickly wore thin. To crush the rebellion in the Philippines, the military engaged in atrocities that called into question the honor and virtue of the United States. Once it achieved victory in the Philippines, the nation concentrated its efforts on maintaining territories primarily for commercial purposes. Within the few short years from 1898 to 1904, this commercial empire had fallen into place.

The Progressive Era presidents, Roosevelt and Wilson, created and sustained a U.S. empire. They disagreed significantly in approach — Roosevelt favoring force, Wilson preferring negotiations — but in practice they shared a willingness to use military power to protect national interests. These two presidents helped construct the modern American state, an expanded federal government that officially sanctioned cooperation with responsible corporate leaders. This relationship reached its peak during World War I. In mobilizing the home front, the Wilson administration blurred the line between public and private business by expanding the reach of government over the economy and curtailing personal liberty.

In 1917, because of its heavy reliance on trade with foreign countries, especially in Europe, the United States confronted its first major international crisis of the twentieth century. Wilson reluctantly led the country into war to guarantee a world order in which reasonable nations attempted to resolve controversies through negotiation, not violence. The failure of the United States to join the League of Nations, for which the president was largely responsible, shattered that idealistic dream.

The United States retreated from joining an international body offering collective security, but it did not isolate itself from participation in the world. The country emerged from the war in excellent financial shape; it had become the leading foreign creditor, and its industrial capacity had greatly expanded. Tending its commercial empire in the Caribbean and Central America, the United States probed for new markets in Asia and the Middle East. It would take another two decades for policymakers to realize that the country's refusal to support a strong collective response to expansionist aggression posed serious dangers for U.S. commerce and values.

CHAPTER **20** REVIEW

TIMELINE OF **EVENTS**

1880–1900	U.S. creates third most powerful navy
1893	U.S. plantation owners overthrow Queen Liliuokalani of Hawaii
1895–1898	Cuban War for Independence
1898	U.S. battleship *Maine* explodes
	The War of 1898
	Anti-Imperialist League founded
1899–1902	Philippine-American War
1901	Platt Amendment passed
1904	Roosevelt Corollary announced
1909	U.S. intervenes in Nicaragua on behalf of U.S. fruit and mining companies
1914	Panama Canal opens
	World War I begins
1915	German submarine sinks the *Lusitania*
1916	Wilson sends U.S. troops into Mexico to capture Pancho Villa
1917	Zimmermann telegram
	United States enters World War I
	Espionage Act
	War Industries Board established
	Committee on Public Information established
1918	Sedition Act
	National War Labor Board established
	Germany surrenders, ending World War I
1919	Wilson loses battle for ratification of Treaty of Versailles

KEY **TERMS**

jingoists, *671*
Cuba Libre, *672*
yellow journalism, *673*
Teller Amendment, *674*
Platt Amendment, *674*
Anti-Imperialist League, *675*
Roosevelt Corollary, *677*
Open Door, *677*
dollar diplomacy, *680*
Mexican revolution, *681*
Zimmermann telegram, *685*
American Expeditionary Forces (AEF), *686*

War Industries Board (WIB), *687*
National War Labor Board (NWLB), *687*
Committee on Public Information (CPI), *688*
Espionage Act, *688*
Sedition Act, *688*
American Protective League (APL), *689*
Fourteen Points, *690*
League of Nations, *690*
Treaty of Versailles, *691*

REVIEW & RELATE

1. What role did economic developments play in prompting calls for a U.S. empire? What role did social and cultural developments play?

2. Why did the United States embark on building an empire in the 1890s and not decades earlier?

3. Why did the United States go to war with Spain in 1898?

4. In what ways did the War of 1898 mark a turning point in the relationship between the United States and the rest of the world?

5. How did the United States assert its influence and control over Latin America in the early twentieth century?

6. How did U.S. policies in Latin America mirror U.S. policies in Asia?

7. In what ways, if any, did President Wilson's approach to Latin American affairs differ from that of his predecessors?

8. Why did President Wilson find it so difficult to keep the United States out of World War I?

9. What steps did the U.S. government take to control the economy and public opinion during World War I?

10. How did President Wilson's wartime policies and his efforts to shape the peace that followed reflect his progressive roots?

Imperialism versus Anti-Imperialism

▶ Evaluate the differences Americans expressed towards overseas expansion and explain how they shaped their arguments to convince their audience.

On January 16, 1893, the USS *Boston* sailed into Honolulu harbor, in a show of support for U.S. businessmen who were aligned against Queen Liliuokalani, Hawaii's ruling monarch. Liliuokalani sought to overturn the 1887 constitution that had been forced on King Kalākaua. This "Bayonet Constitution," as it came to be known, favored U.S. and other foreign interests and limited the political power of native islanders, the poor, and the monarchy. The day after U.S. forces landed, Liliuokalani abdicated, and a provisional government, the Republic of Hawaii, was set up under the control of U.S. sugar growers. Native Hawaiians continued to rebel against their U.S.-dominated government, and in 1897 representatives from several political groups issued the Hawaiian Memorial (Source 20.6). This petition for self-rule failed, and Hawaii was formally annexed in 1898. In that same year, U.S. territorial acquisitions from the War of 1898 intensified the heated debate over U.S. imperialism and the principles of self-governance and democracy.

The following documents reveal the viewpoints of imperialists, anti-imperialists, and colonized people. Those supporting imperialism could find no greater advocate than Senator Albert Beveridge of Indiana, who served from 1899 to 1911. His speech entitled "The March of the Flag" compared Philippine colonization to U.S. westward expansion across North America and argued that Filipinos were a child-like and savage race incapable of self-governance (Source 20.7). A different view of the Philippine conflict came from a New Hampshire woman who in 1899 wrote to her local newspaper to scold U.S. women for failing to speak out against the "murderous, cowardly, dastardly war" in the Philippines (Source 20.9). Throughout this period — on the Senate floor and in town meeting halls, schoolrooms, national magazines, and local newspapers (Source 20.8) — Americans deliberated the significance and implications of international expansion.

Source 20.6

The Hawaiian Memorial, 1897

Hawaiian political groups sent the following petition (also called a memorial) to the U.S. government as a formal request to remove the provisional government of the Hawaiian Islands, which they viewed as illegitimate. Although the U.S. Senate initially refused to ratify President McKinley's effort to annex Hawaii in 1897, the following year Congress adopted a joint resolution annexing Hawaii as a territory.

To the President, the Congress, and the People of the United States of America:

This Memorial respectfully represents as follows:

1. That your memorialists are residents of the Hawaiian Islands; that the majority of them are aboriginal Hawaiians; and that all of them possess the qualifications provided for electors of representatives in the Hawaiian Legislature by the Constitution and laws prevailing in the Hawaiian Islands at the date of the overthrow of the Hawaiian Constitutional Government, January 17, 1893.

2. That the supporters of the Hawaiian Constitution of 1887 have been, thence to the present time, in the year 1897, held in subjection by the armed forces of the Provisional Government of the Hawaiian Islands, and of its successor, the Republic of Hawaii, and have never yielded and do not acknowledge a spontaneous or willing allegiance or support to said Provisional Government, or to said Republic of Hawaii.

3. That the Government of the Republic of Hawaii has no warrant for its existence in the support of the people of these islands; that it was proclaimed and instituted and has hitherto existed and now exists without considering the rights and wishes of a great majority of the residents, native and foreign-born, of the Hawaiian Islands; and especially that said Government exists and maintains itself solely by force of arms, against the rights and wishes of almost the entire aboriginal population of these islands.

4. That said Republic is not and never has been founded or conducted upon a basis of popular government or republican principles; that its Constitution was adopted by a convention, a majority of whose members were self-appointed, and the balance of whose members were elected by a numerically insignificant minority of the white and aboriginal male citizens and residents of these islands. . . .

5. That the Constitution so adopted by said convention has never been submitted to a vote of the people of these islands, but was promulgated and established over the said islands, and has ever since been maintained only by force of arms, and with indifference to the will of practically the entire aboriginal population, and a vast majority of the whole population of these islands.

6. That the said Government, so existing under the title of the Republic of Hawaii, assumes and asserts the right to extinguish the Hawaiian nationality, heretofore existing, and to cede and convey all rights of sovereignty in and over the Hawaiian Islands and their dependencies to a foreign power, namely, to the United States of America.

7. That your memorialists have learned with grief and dismay that the President of the United States has entered into, and submitted for ratification by the United States Senate, a treaty with the Government of the Republic of Hawaii, whereby it is proposed to extinguish our existence as a nation, and to annex our territory to the United States. . . .

9. That your memorialists humbly but fervently protest against the consummation of this invasion of their political rights; and they earnestly appeal to the President, the Congress, and the people of the United States to refrain from further participating in the wrong so proposed; and they invoke in support of this memorial the spirit of that immortal instrument, the Declaration of American Independence; and especially the truth therein expressed, that governments derive their just powers from the consent of the governed — and here repeat that the consent of the people of the Hawaiian Islands to the forms of government imposed by the so-called Republic of Hawaii, and to said proposed treaty of annexation, has never been asked by and is not accorded, either to said government or to said project of annexation.

10. That the consummation of the project of annexation dealt with in said treaty would be subversive of the personal and political rights of these memorialists and of the Hawaiian people and nation. . . .

11. Wherefore your memorialists respectfully submit that they, no less than the citizens of any American Commonwealth, are entitled to select, ordain, and establish for themselves such forms of government as to them shall seem most likely to effect their safety and happiness. . . .

12. And your memorialists humbly pray the President, Congress, and the people of the United States that no further steps be taken toward the ratification of said treaty, or toward the extinguishment of the Hawaiian nationality, or toward the absorption of the Hawaiian people and territory into the body politic and territory of the United States of America, at least until the Hawaiian people, as represented by those citizens and residents of the Hawaiian Islands

who, under the provisions of the Hawaiian Constitution, promulgated July 7, 1887, would be qualified to vote for representatives in the Legislature, shall have had the opportunity to express, at the ballot-box, their wishes as to whether such project of annexation shall be accepted or rejected.

13. And your memorialists, for themselves, and in behalf of the Hawaiian people and of the residents of the Hawaiian Islands, pledge their faith that if they shall be accorded the privilege of voting upon said questions, at a free and fair election to be held for that purpose, and if a fair count of the votes that shall be cast at such election shall show a majority in favor of such annexation, these memorialists and the Hawaiian people will yield a ready and cheerful acquiescence in said project.

Signed

J. Kalua Kahookano, Samuel K. Pua, F. J. Testa, C. B. Maile, Samuel K. Kamakaia, Citizens' Committee

James Keauiluna Kaulia, President of the Hawaiian Patriotic League

David Kalauokalani, President of the Hawaiian Political Association

Source: "The Hawaiian Memorial," *City and State*, December 2, 1897, 143.

Source 20.7

Albert Beveridge | The March of the Flag, 1898

In September 1898 Albert Beveridge, who was campaigning to become U.S. senator from Indiana, gave a rousing speech supporting the annexation of Spain's former colonies. At the time of this address, the war with Spain had ended, but U.S. troops still occupied the Philippines. Once in office, Beveridge was an ardent supporter of U.S. imperial policies.

Hawaii is ours; Porto Rico is to be ours; at the prayer of her people Cuba finally will be ours; in the islands of the East, even to the gates of Asia, coaling stations are to be ours at the very least; the flag of a liberal government is to float over the Philippines, and may it be the banner that [Zachary] Taylor unfurled in Texas and [John] Fremont carried to the coast.

The Opposition tells us that we ought not to govern a people without their consent. I answer, the rule of liberty that all just government derives its authority from the consent of the governed, applies only to those who are capable of self-government. We govern the Indians without their consent, we govern our territories without their consent, we govern our children without their consent. How do they know [what] our government would be without their consent? Would not the people of the Philippines prefer the just, humane, civilizing government of this Republic to the savage, bloody rule of pillage and extortion from which we have rescued them?

And, regardless of this formula of words made only for enlightened, self-governing people, do we owe no duty to the world? Shall we turn these peoples back to the reeking hands from which we have taken them? Shall we abandon them, with Germany, England, Japan, hungering for them? Shall we save them from those nations, to give them a self-rule of tragedy?

They ask us how we shall govern these new possessions. I answer: Out of local conditions and the necessities of the case, methods of government will grow. If England can govern foreign lands, so can America. If Germany can govern foreign lands, so can America. If they can supervise protectorates, so can America. Why is it more difficult to administer Hawaii than New Mexico or California? Both had a savage and an alien population; both were more remote from the seat of government when they came under our dominion than the Philippines are today.

Will you say by your vote that American ability to govern has decayed; that a century's experience in self-rule has failed of a result? Will you affirm by your vote that you are an infidel to American power and practical sense? Or will you say that ours is the blood of government; ours the heart of dominion; ours the brain and genius of administration? Will you remember that we do but what our fathers did — we but pitch the tents of liberty farther westward, farther southward — we only continue the march of the flag?

The march of the flag! In 1789 the flag of the Republic waved over 4,000,000 souls in thirteen states, and their savage territory which stretched to the Mississippi, to Canada, to the Floridas. The timid minds of that day said that no new territory was needed, and, for the hour, they were right. But Jefferson, through whose intellect the centuries marched; Jefferson, who dreamed of Cuba as an American state; Jefferson, the first Imperialist of the Republic—Jefferson acquired that imperial territory which swept from the Mississippi to the mountains, from Texas to the British possessions, and the march of the flag began!

The infidels to the gospel of liberty raved, but the flag swept on! The title to that noble land out of which Oregon, Washington, Idaho, and Montana have been carved was uncertain; Jefferson, strict constructionist of constitutional power though he was, obeyed the Anglo-Saxon impulse within him, whose watchword then and whose watchword throughout the world today is, "Forward!": another empire was added to the Republic, and the march of the flag went on! . . .

The ocean does not separate us from lands of our duty and desire—the oceans join us, rivers never to be dredged, canals never to be repaired. Steam joins us; electricity joins us—the very elements are in league with our destiny. Cuba not contiguous! Porto Rico not contiguous! Hawaii and the Philippines not contiguous! The oceans make them contiguous. And our navy will make them contiguous.

But the Opposition is right—there is a difference. We did not need the western Mississippi Valley when we acquired it, nor Florida, nor Texas, nor California, nor the royal provinces of the far northwest. We had no emigrants to people this imperial wilderness, no money to develop it, even

no highways to cover it. No trade awaited us in its savage fastnesses [remote places]. Our productions were not greater than our trade. There was not one reason for the land-lust of our statesmen from Jefferson to Grant, other than the prophet and the Saxon within them. But, today, we are raising more than we can consume, making more than we can use. Therefore we must find new markets for our produce.

And so, while we did not need the territory taken during the past century at the time it was acquired, we do need what we have taken in 1898, and we need it now. The resources and the commerce of these immensely rich dominions will be increased as much as American energy is greater than Spanish sloth. In Cuba, alone, there are 15,000,000 acres of forest unacquainted with the ax, exhaustless mines of iron, priceless deposits of manganese, millions of dollars' worth of which we must buy, today, from the Black Sea districts. There are millions of acres yet unexplored.

The resources of Porto Rico have only been trifled with. The riches of the Philippines have hardly been touched by the fingertips of modern methods. And they produce what we consume, and consume what we produce—the very predestination of reciprocity—a reciprocity "not made with hands, eternal in the heavens." They sell hemp, sugar, cocoanuts, fruits of the tropics, timber of price like mahogany; they buy flour, clothing, tools, implements, machinery, and all that we can raise and make. Their trade will be ours in time. Do you indorse that policy with your vote?

Source: Albert J. Beveridge, *The Meaning of the Times and Other Speeches* (Indianapolis: Bobbs-Merrill, 1908), 48–50, 52–53.

"There's Plenty of Room at the Table," 1906

The satirical weekly magazine *Judge* was a strong supporter of President McKinley and the Republican Party. Its illustrations often depicted imperial expansion as good for the U.S. public as well as for colonized nations.

THERE'S PLENTY OF ROOM AT THE TABLE. WHY NOT ASK THE HUNGRY LITTLE FELLOW TO SIT DOWN?

Anti-Imperialism Letter, 1899

What began in 1898 as a conflict to free the Philippines from Spanish control quickly became a struggle to subdue Filipino rebels intent on establishing their own government. The following letter was written to the *Springfield (Massachusetts) Republican* just one month after the new Philippine Republic declared war on the United States. The brutality of the fighting caused many Americans to question the motives and methods of U.S. imperial aspirations.

To The Editor of the Republican:

I cannot longer hold my peace, though only a woman. I am thankful to see today that the business men (some of them, I should say) have started a plan for the cessation of this murderous, cowardly, dastardly war. Also I saw yesterday that Gamaliel Bradford [an American writer and poet] has volunteered to speak in the same just and holy cause wheresoever needed. This is the thing I have longed to see done weeks and weeks ago. The "peace" treaty never would have been ratified if the nation had been waked up to the meaning of its iniquity. Speaking everywhere is needed, such as we had at the beginning of the civil war, giving light to the thousands that now do not care. "It is no business of theirs." "Congress will take care," they say, reading the papers that hurrah for McKinley. What do they know about it? They don't feel the burden much yet. Taxes are bad enough, but those that must come with the McKinley policy long continued, they don't feel yet. It is healthy for all they see out there, none of theirs have died, and it's only the Filipinos mostly that are killed: and we are to be a "bigger country." What the whole country needs is to rouse the people, that they demand that this sin shall cease, that America's shame may be wiped out ere it is too late!

I blush for my sisters who call themselves "Colonial Dames," "Daughters of the Revolution,"

"Abraham Lincoln circle of the Ladies of the Grand Army," and such patriotic sounding titles, where is their claim to such? In all these months of anxiety and anguish never one word of protest have I heard of their breathing! They have gathered for various social reasons and held good times, but the solemn duties and responsibilities that should be their first concern seem to have been utterly ignored. Cannot they be induced to begin likewise an appeal in every place where their orders exist, signed by every woman who has at heart the love of her country and its true honor. Only that something should be done! While we wait the islanders are being murdered by hundreds and a price put on the head of their brave leader!

J. W. P.

Source: Letter to the editor, *Springfield Republican*, March 16, 1899.

Examine the Evidence

1. What purpose do the petitioners of the Hawaiian Memorial (Source 20.6) have in claiming that the provisional government is illegitimate? Why do they think U.S. officials will respond favorably to their arguments?

2. Why does Albert Beveridge claim that it is the United States' duty to colonize the Philippines, and what does he think are the benefits to Americans and Filipinos (Source 20.7)? How does he attempt to convince his audience?

3. Compare the views of the cartoon, "There's Plenty of Room at the Table" (Source 20.8) with those of the letter from J. W. P. (Source 20.9)? How does each attempt to convince a different audience?

4. How do imperialists and anti-imperialists shape their arguments to appeal to either men or women?

Put It in Context

How do imperialists and anti-imperialists reflect the political and economic contexts in which they live?

Why did the arguments of the imperialists prevail over those of anti-imperialists from 1898 to 1904?

The Twenties

1919–1929

WINDOW TO THE PAST

The Case against the Reds, 1920

The panic over the spread of Communism following World War I reflected underlying political, economic, and social fears in the nation. Attorney General A. Mitchell Palmer justified the roundup and deportation of immigrant radicals as essential to stopping the spread of Communism. ▸ To discover more about what this primary source can show us, see Source 21.1 on page 705.

> Like a prairie-fire, the blaze of revolution was sweeping over every American institution of law and order a year ago. It was eating its way into the homes of the American workman, its sharp tongues of revolutionary heat were licking the altars of the churches, leaping into the belfry of the school bell, crawling into the sacred corners of American homes, seeking to replace marriage vows with libertine laws, burning up the foundations of society.
>
> Robbery, not war, is the ideal of communism. This has been demonstrated in Russia, Germany, and in America. As a foe, the anarchist is fearless of his own life, for his creed is a fanaticism that admits no respect of any other creed. Obviously it is the creed of any criminal mind, which reasons always from motives impossible to clean thought. Crime is the degenerate factor in society.

A. Mitchell Palmer, "The Case against the Reds," The Forum, February 1920, 174–75, 185

After reading this chapter you should be able to:

- Explain the causes of the anti-communist panic, labor unrest, and escalating racial tensions following World War I.

- Evaluate the importance of the second industrial revolution, the creation of the consumer culture, urbanization, and the federal government in promoting economic expansion.

- Describe how white and black popular culture challenged traditional morality and gender roles.

- Examine the tensions between nativists and immigrants and fundamentalism and modernism, and explain how these culture wars affected federal policies.

- Explain the dominance of the Republican Party over the Progressive and Democratic Parties and analyze the political flaws that led to the Great Depression.

COMPARING AMERICAN HISTORIES

David Curtis (D. C.) Stephenson's pursuit of the American dream kept him on the move. Born in 1891 to Texas sharecroppers, Stephenson moved with his family to the Oklahoma Territory in 1901. After quitting school at age sixteen, he drifted around for more than a decade, working for a string of newspapers and gaining a reputation as a heavy drinker. In 1915 he married and appeared to settle down; however, he soon lost his newspaper job, abandoned

(left) **D. C. Stephenson.** Indiana Historical Society (detail)
(right) **Ossian Sweet**. Courtesy of the Burton Historical Collection, Detroit Public Library

his pregnant wife, and hit the road working for one newspaper after another in between binges of drunkenness. His wife divorced him, and in 1917 Stephenson joined the army to fight in World War I. Despite a series of drunken brawls and sexual misadventures, he received an honorable discharge in 1919.

Stephenson remarried and settled in Indiana, where he found financial and political success. In 1920 he joined the Ku Klux Klan (KKK), the Reconstruction-era organization that had reemerged in 1915 in Georgia. The newly revived Klan spread beyond the South, targeting African Americans, recent immigrants, Jews, and Catholics as enemies of traditional Protestant family values. Stephenson directed Klan operations in twenty-three states, building a profitable empire on fear, prejudice, and get-rich-quick schemes. A few years later, however, his Klan career ended with his arrest and conviction on rape and second-degree murder charges.

Ossian Sweet also pursued the American dream. Like Stephenson, he rose from humble beginnings. The descendant of slaves, Sweet was born in 1895 and grew up in central Florida. Hoping to shield him from the violence that whites used to keep blacks in their place, Sweet's parents sent him north when he was thirteen years old.

After attending Wilberforce University in Ohio and Howard Medical School in Washington, D.C., Sweet moved to Detroit in 1921 to open a medical practice. He married, and in 1924 the Sweets decided to buy a house in a working-class neighborhood occupied exclusively by whites. Before the Sweets moved in, their white neighbors, with Klan backing, began organizing to keep them out.

When the Sweet family moved into their house on September 8, 1925, they encountered a hostile crowd in the street. Dr. Sweet had brought some backup with him. Armed to resist the mob, the Sweets and their defenders fired their weapons at the crowd after rocks smashed through the upstairs windows of the house. When the shooting stopped and the police restored calm, one white man lay dead and another wounded. Dr. Sweet; his wife, Gladys; and the other nine occupants of his house went on trial on first-degree murder charges. Hired by the NAACP, Clarence Darrow represented the eleven defendants and after two trials — the first ended in a hung jury — won an acquittal in 1926. ■

T he American histories of Ossian Sweet and D. C. Stephenson illustrate the competing forces that shaped the 1920s. Both men achieved a measure of financial success, but they did so in the post–World War I atmosphere of growing social friction and intense racial resentments. When Sweet's parents decided to send him north, they were responding to the racial violence that plagued the South, but they were also demonstrating their belief that a better life was possible for their son. By contrast, Stephenson grew wealthy by tapping into the same racial tensions that shaped the Sweets' lives. Many whites who considered themselves "100 percent Americans," born and bred in small towns or living in sections of cities with homogeneous populations, believed that racial and ethnic minorities threatened their power. The fear of Communist infiltration heightened their concerns over immigration, and changes in morality and gender roles further raised their fears. Although the general prosperity of the period masked the tensions lying beneath the surface, it did not eliminate them. Rampant consumerism concealed the unequal prosperity fostered by Republican policies that later led to the Great Depression. As the experiences of D. C. Stephenson and Ossian Sweet show, the decade following the end of World War I opened up fresh avenues for economic prosperity as well as new sites for cultural clashes exacerbated by the tensions of modern America.

Social Turmoil

The return of peace in 1918 brought with it problems that would persist into the 1920s. Government efforts to suppress opposition to U.S. involvement in World War I fostered an atmosphere of fear and repression that continued after the war. An influenza epidemic that killed hundreds of thousands of Americans and millions of people around the world heightened the climate of anxiety. Finally, the abrupt transition away from a wartime economy produced inflation, labor unrest, and escalating racial tensions.

The Red Scare, 1919–1920. The success of the Bolshevik Revolution in Russia in 1917 and the subsequent creation of the Union of Soviet Socialist Republics terrified officials of capitalist countries in western Europe and the United States. This fear was further exacerbated in 1919 with the creation of the Comintern, an association of Communists who pledged to incite revolution in capitalist countries around the world. This sparked a panic over Communist-inspired radicalism known as the **Red scare**, which set the stage for the suppression of dissent.

In this atmosphere of anxiety, on March 3, 1919, in *Schenck v. United States* the Supreme Court invoked the Espionage Act to uphold the conviction of Charles Schenck, the general secretary of the Socialist Party, for mailing thousands of leaflets opposing the military draft. Delivering the Court's unanimous opinion, Justice Oliver Wendell Holmes argued that during wartime Congress has the authority to prohibit individuals from using words that create "a clear and present danger" to the safety of the country. Although the trial record failed to show that Schenck's leaflets had convinced any young men to resist conscription, the Court upheld his conviction under Holmes's doctrine. Later that year in *Abrams v. United States*, the Court further limited free speech by sustaining the guilty verdict of five anarchists who distributed leaflets denouncing U.S. military efforts to overthrow the Bolshevik regime.

Immediate postwar economic problems further increased the anxiety of American citizens, reinforcing the position of officials who sought to restore order by suppressing radicals. Industries were slow to convert their plants from military to civilian production, and consumer goods therefore remained in short supply. The war had brought jobs and higher wages on the home front, and consumers who had been restrained by wartime rationing were eager to spend their savings. With demand greatly exceeding supply, however, prices soared by 77 percent, frustrating consumers. At the same time, farmers, who had benefited from wartime conditions, faced falling crop prices as European nations resumed agricultural production and the federal government ended price supports.

A series of widespread strikes launched by labor unions in 1919 contributed to the fear that the United States was under assault by sinister, radical forces. As skyrocketing inflation undercut wages and employers launched a new round of union-busting efforts, labor went on the offensive. In 1919 more than four million workers went on strike nationwide. In September, striking Boston policemen left the city unguarded, resulting in widespread looting and violence. Massachusetts governor Calvin Coolidge sent in the National Guard to break the strike and restore order.

Public officials and newspapers decried the violence, but they also greatly exaggerated the peril. Communists and socialists did support some union activities; however, few of the millions of workers who struck for higher wages and better working conditions had ties to extremists. The major prewar radical organization, the Industrial Workers of the World, never recovered from the government harassment that had crippled it during World War I. However, scattered acts of violence allowed government and business leaders to stir up anxieties about the Communist threat. On May 1, 1919, radicals sent more than thirty incendiary devices through the mail to prominent Americans, though authorities defused the bombs before they reached their targets. The following month, bombs exploded in eight cities, including one at the doorstep of the home of A. Mitchell Palmer, the attorney general of the United States.

After the attack on his home, Palmer launched a government crusade to root out and prosecute Communists. Palmer traced the source of radicalism to recent immigrants, mainly those from Russia and eastern and southern Europe. To track down suspected radicals, Palmer selected J. Edgar Hoover to head the General Intelligence Division in the Department of Justice. In November 1919, based on Hoover's research and undercover activities, government agents in twelve cities rounded up and arrested hundreds of foreigners, including the anarchist and feminist Emma Goldman. Goldman and some 250 other people caught in the government dragnet were soon deported to Russia. Over the next few months, the **Palmer raids** continued in more than thirty cities. Authorities seized approximately six thousand suspected radicals, took them to police stations, interrogated them without the benefit of legal counsel, and held them incommunicado without stipulating the charges against them. Of the thousands arrested, the government found reason to deport 556. The raids did not uncover any extensive plots to overthrow the U.S. government, nor did they lead to the arrest of the bombers.

Explore ▶

See Palmer's justification for the raids in Source 21.1.

Americans' initial support of the Palmer raids quickly waned in the face of civil liberty violations that accompanied the raids. In 1920 a group of pacifists, progressives, and constitutional lawyers formed the American Civil Liberties Union (ACLU) to monitor government abridgments of the Bill of Rights. Although the Palmer raids ended, the Red scare extended throughout the 1920s. After Hoover became director of the Bureau of Investigation (later renamed the Federal Bureau of Investigation) in 1921, he continued spying and collecting information on suspected radicals and increasing his power over the next several decades.

Compounding Americans' anxieties, in late 1918 an influenza epidemic struck the United States. Part of a worldwide contagion, the disease infected nearly 20 percent of the U.S. population and killed more than 675,000 people. As the death toll mounted over

---

GUIDED ANALYSIS

A. Mitchell Palmer | The Case against the Reds, 1920

Attorney General A. Mitchell Palmer was a leading architect of the Red scare. In response to the strikes and riots throughout 1919 into early 1920, Palmer organized a series of raids against suspected Communists, anarchists, and other foreign radicals. More than six thousand people were arrested, most of whom were later released. In an article in *Forum* magazine, Palmer defended his actions and described his views on radicalism and its threat to American society.

Source 21.1

According to Palmer, what institutions did revolutionaries threaten?

Why does Palmer think communism is a threat?

Why doesn't Palmer think there is any practical difference between the principles of radicals and their actions?

Like a prairie-fire, the blaze of revolution was sweeping over every American institution of law and order a year ago. It was eating its way into the homes of the American workman, its sharp tongues of revolutionary heat were licking the altars of the churches, leaping into the belfry of the school bell, crawling into the sacred corners of American homes, seeking to replace marriage vows with libertine laws, burning up the foundations of society.

Robbery, not war, is the ideal of communism. This has been demonstrated in Russia, Germany, and in America. As a foe, the anarchist is fearless of his own life, for his creed is a fanaticism that admits no respect of any other creed. Obviously it is the creed of any criminal mind, which reasons always from motives impossible to clean thought. Crime is the degenerate factor in society.

Upon these two basic certainties, first that the "Reds" were criminal aliens, and secondly that the American Government must prevent crime, it was decided that there could be no nice distinctions drawn between the theoretical ideals of the radicals and their actual violations of our national laws. An assassin may have brilliant intellectuality, he may be able to excuse his murder or robbery with fine oratory, but any theory which excuses crime is not wanted in America. This is no place for the criminal to flourish, nor will he do so, so long as the rights of common citizenship can be exerted to prevent him.

Source: A. Mitchell Palmer, "The Case against the Reds," *Forum*, February 1920, 174–75, 185.

Put It in Context

How did the Red Scare shape the politics and culture of the 1920s?

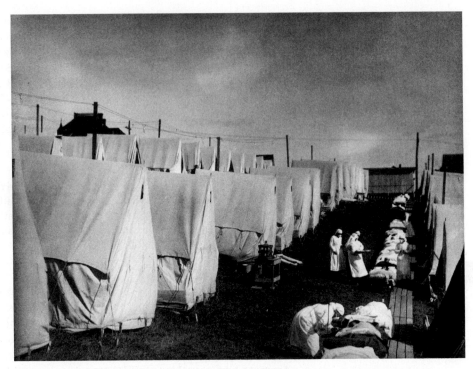

The Influenza Epidemic, Lawrence, Massachusetts, 1918 Nurses take care of
patients suffering from the Spanish influenza epidemic in Lawrence, Massachusetts. This textile
town had experienced an influx of immigrants from southern and eastern Europe around the turn
of the twentieth century and was the scene of major union organizing and labor strife just before
the epidemic struck. Flu victims were removed from crowded residences and relocated to canvas
tents outdoors for what was considered a fresh air cure. Hulton Archive / Getty Images

the course of 1919, terror gripped the nation. Susanna Turner, a volunteer at an emergency
hospital in Philadelphia, recalled: "The fear in the hearts of people just withered them.
They were afraid to go out, afraid to do anything. . . . It was a horror-stricken time." A staggering 50 to 100 million people worldwide are estimated to have died from the flu before it
subsided in 1920.

Racial Violence in the Postwar Era.
Racial strife also heightened postwar
anxieties. Drawn by the promise of wartime industrial jobs, more than 400,000 African
Americans left the South beginning in 1917 and 1918 and headed north hoping to escape
poverty and racial discrimination. (By 1930 another 800,000 blacks had left the South.)
This exodus became known as the **great migration**. During World War I, many blacks
found work in steel production, meatpacking, shipbuilding, and other heavy industries,
but most were relegated to low-paying jobs. Still, as a carpenter earning $95 a month wrote
from Chicago to a friend back in Hattiesburg, Mississippi: "I should have been here 20
years ago. I just begin to feel like a man." Most African American women remained
employed as domestic workers, but more than 100,000 obtained manufacturing jobs.

For many blacks, however, the North was not the "promised land" they expected. Instead, they encountered bitter opposition from white migrants from the South competing for employment and scarce housing. As black and white veterans returned from the war, racial hostilities exploded. In 1919 race riots erupted in twenty-five cities throughout the country, including one in Washington, D.C., which Ossian Sweet witnessed firsthand. The previous year, W. E. B. Du Bois of the NAACP had urged the black community to "close ranks" to fight Germany, but the racial violence against blacks in 1919 embittered him. "By the God of Heaven," Du Bois wrote, "we are cowards and jackasses if now that that war is over, we do not marshal every ounce of our brain and brawn to fight a sterner, longer, more unbending battle against the forces of hell in our own land."

The worst of these disturbances occurred in Chicago. On a hot July day, a black youth swimming at a Lake Michigan beach inadvertently crossed over into an area of water customarily reserved for whites. In response, white bathers shouted at the swimmer to return to the black section of the beach and hurled stones at him. The black swimmer drowned, and word of the incident quickly spread through white and black neighborhoods in Chicago. For thirteen days, mobs of blacks and whites attacked each other, ransacked businesses, and torched homes. Over the course of the riots, at least 15 whites and 23 blacks died, 178 whites and 342 blacks were injured, and more than 1,000 black families were left homeless.

REVIEW & RELATE

● What factors combined to produce the turmoil of the immediate postwar period?

● What factors contributed to the rise in racial tensions that accompanied the transition from wartime to peacetime?

Prosperity, Consumption, and Growth

Despite the turbulence of the immediate postwar period and the persistence of underlying social and racial tensions, the 1920s were a time of vigorous economic growth and urbanization. Between 1922 and 1927, the economy grew by 7 percent a year. Unemployment rates remained low, as producers added new workers in an effort to keep up with increasing consumer demand. Aligning themselves with big business, government officials took an active role in stimulating industrial and economic growth. Although the average purchasing power of wage earners soared, this economic boom left out many Americans from sharing in prosperity.

Government Promotion of the Economy.

The general prosperity of the 1920s owed a great deal to backing by the federal government. Republicans controlled the presidency and Congress, and though they claimed to stand for principles of laissez-faire and opposed various economic and social reforms, they were willing to use governmental power to support large corporations and the wealthy.

Senator Warren G. Harding of Ohio, who was elected president in 1920, declared that he and his party wanted "less government in business and more business in government." Harding's cabinet appointments reflected this goal. Treasury Secretary Andrew Mellon, a banker and an aluminum company titan, believed that the government should stimulate economic growth by reducing taxes on the rich, raising tariffs to protect manufacturers from foreign competition, and trimming the budget. The Republican Congress enacted much of this agenda. During the Harding administration, tax rates for the wealthy, which had skyrocketed during World War I, plummeted from 66 percent to 20 percent. Mellon believed that those on the lower rungs of the economic ladder would prosper once businesspeople invested the extra money they received from tax breaks into expanding production. Supposedly, the wealth would trickle down through increased jobs and purchasing power. At the same time, Republicans turned Progressive Era regulatory agencies such as the Federal Trade Commission and the Federal Reserve Board into boosters for major corporations and financial institutions by weakening enforcement.

Secretary of Commerce Herbert Hoover had an even greater impact than Mellon in cementing the government-business partnership during the 1920s. Hoover believed that the federal government had a role to play in the economy and in lessening economic suffering. Rejecting government control of business activities, however, he insisted on voluntary cooperation between the public and private sectors. Hoover favored the creation of trade associations in which businesses would collaborate to stabilize production levels, prices, and wages. In turn, the Commerce Department would provide helpful data and information to improve productivity and trade.

Hoover's vision fit into a larger Republican effort to weaken unions by promoting voluntary business-sponsored worker welfare initiatives. For example, under the **American Plan**, some firms established health insurance and pension plans for their workers. As early as 1914, Henry Ford provided his autoworkers over twenty-two years old "a share in the profits of the house" equal to a minimum wage of $5 a day, and he cut the workday from nine hours to eight. Already under pressure from such tactics, unions were further damaged by a series of Supreme Court rulings that restricted strikes and overturned hard-won victories such as child labor legislation and minimum wage laws. By 1929 union membership had dropped from approximately five million to three million, or about 10 percent of the industrial labor market.

Teapot Dome Scandal   Clifford K. Berryman, the political cartoonist for the Washington *Evening Star*, illustrates the Teapot Dome scandal, which damaged the Harding administration. Captioned "Juggernaut," this image shows Secretary of the Navy Edward Denby on the left and Secretary of the Interior Albert Fall on the right fleeing from charges of bribery and corruption that a Senate committee brought to light. Granger, NYC

Scandals during the presidency of Warren G. Harding diminished its luster but did not tarnish the shine of Republican economic policy. The **Teapot Dome scandal** grabbed the most headlines. In 1921 Interior Secretary Albert Fall collaborated with Navy Secretary Edwin Denby to transfer potential oil fields to the Interior Department. Fall then parceled out these properties to private companies. As a result, Harry F. Sinclair's Mammoth Oil Company received a lease to develop the Teapot Dome section in Wyoming. In return for this handout, Sinclair delivered more than $300,000 to Fall. In the wake of congressional hearings, Fall and Sinclair were convicted on a number of criminal charges and sent to jail.

Harding's sudden death from a heart attack in August 1923 brought Vice President Calvin Coolidge to the presidency. Coolidge distanced himself from the scandals of his predecessor's administration but reaffirmed Harding's economic policies. "The chief business of the American people is business," President Coolidge remarked succinctly.

Americans Become Consumers.

The 1920s marked a period of economic expansion and general prosperity. National income rose from approximately $63 billion to $88 billion, and per capita income jumped from $641 to $847, an increase of 32 percent. The purchasing power of wage earners climbed approximately 20 percent.

This great spurt of economic growth in the 1920s resulted from the application of technological innovation and scientific management techniques to industrial production (Figure 21.1). Perhaps the greatest innovation came with the introduction of the assembly line. First used in the automobile industry before World War I, the assembly line moved the product to a worker who performed a specific task before sending it along to the next worker. This deceptively simple system, perfected by Henry Ford, saved enormous time

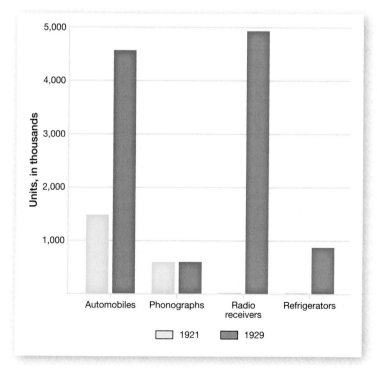

FIGURE 21.1 Production of Consumer Goods, 1921 and 1929

Rising per capita income, lower manufacturing costs, urban electrification, and advertising spurred the production of consumer goods in the 1920s. According to this figure, what were the most popular consumer goods in this period and how did they serve to bring Americans from all regions together?

and energy by emphasizing repetition, accuracy, and standardization. Streamlined production lowered costs, which, in turn, allowed Ford to lower prices.

Besides the automobile, the **second industrial revolution** focused on the production of consumer-oriented goods previously considered luxuries. The electrification of urban homes created demand for a wealth of new labor-saving appliances. Refrigerators, washing machines, toasters, and vacuum cleaners appealed to middle-class housewives whose husbands could afford to purchase them. Wristwatches replaced bulkier pocket watches. Radios became the chief source of home entertainment.

Although such household items changed the lives of many Americans, no single product had as profound an effect on American life in the 1920s as the automobile. Auto sales soared in the 1920s from a total of 1.5 million to 5 million, fueling the growth of related industries such as steel, rubber, petroleum, and glass. In 1929 Ford and his competitors at General Motors, Chevrolet, and Oldsmobile employed nearly 4 million workers, and around one in eight American workers toiled in factories connected to automobile production.

The automobile also changed day-to-day living patterns. Although most roads and highways consisted of dirt and contained rocks and ruts, enough were paved to extend the boundaries of suburbs farther from the city. By the end of the 1920s, around 17 percent of Americans lived in suburbia. Cars allowed families to travel to vacation destinations at greater distances from their homes. Even the roadside landscape changed, as gas stations, diners, and motels sprang up to serve motorists. Each year, vacation resorts on the east and west coasts of Florida attracted thousands of tourists who drove south to enjoy the state's beautiful beaches. Motorists also flocked to national parks in the Rocky Mountains and on the West Coast.

The automobile also provided new dating opportunities for young men and women. At the turn of the twentieth century, a young man courted a woman by going to her home and sitting with her on the sofa or out on the porch under the watchful eyes of her parents and family members. With the arrival of the automobile, couples could move from the couch in the parlor to the backseat of a car, away from adult supervision. Driving to a "lover's lane," the young couple could express their feelings with greater physicality than before.

Although Ford and his fellow manufacturers succeeded in lowering prices, they still had to convince Americans to spend their hard-earned money to purchase their products. Turning for help to the fledgling advertising industry, manufacturers nearly tripled their spending on advertising over the course of the 1920s. Firms pitched their products around price and quality, but they directed their efforts more than ever to the personal psychology of the consumer. Advertisers played on consumers' unexpressed fears, unfulfilled desires, hopes for success, and sexual fantasies. The producers of Listerine mouthwash transformed a product previously used to disinfect hospitals into one that fought the dreaded but made-up disease of halitosis (bad breath). Advertisers told people that they could measure success through consumption. Purchasing a General Electric all-steel refrigerator not only would preserve food longer but also would enhance the owners' reputation among their neighbors.

Although average wages and incomes rose during the 1920s, the majority of Americans did not have the disposable income to afford the bounty of new consumer goods. To resolve this problem, companies extended credit in dizzying amounts. By 1929 consumers purchased 60 percent of their cars and 80 percent of their radios and furniture on credit — mainly through the installment plan. "Buy now and pay later" became the motto of corporate America.

Chevrolet Advertisement, 1920s   The 1920s boom in the production of automobiles posed a challenge for business marketers and advertisers. They had to convince consumers that items once considered as luxuries were now necessities that would improve their lives. Many of these advertisements were directed at middle-class women who, as housewives, managed the family budget. The Chevrolet Motor Company aimed this advertisement at women by appealing to its car's easy handling and low price. Image Courtesy of The Advertising Archives

Urbanization. The growth of cities helped promote the spread of the consumer-oriented economy. Increasingly clustered in urban areas, people had more convenient access to department stores and chain stores. Advertisers targeted city residents because they were easier to reach. Although cities contained plenty of poor people who could not afford to buy items they considered luxuries, a large middle class of shoppers provided a growing market.

The census of 1920 reported that for the first time in U.S. history a majority of Americans lived in cities. In 1910 just over 54 percent of the nation lived in small towns and villages with fewer than 2,500 people. A decade later, only 49 percent inhabited these areas. The end of World War I brought a decline in demand for American agricultural goods, and about six million residents left their farms and villages and moved to cities. By 1930 the percentage of those living in rural America further dropped to 44 percent. The war had pushed large numbers of African Americans out of the rural South for jobs in the cities. Also, with war's end, immigration from southern and eastern Europe resumed.

The West grew faster than any other region of the country, and its cities boomed. From 1910 to 1930, the population of the United States increased by 33.5 percent; at the same time, the population of the West soared by nearly 59 percent. In northern California, the bay area cities of San Francisco, Oakland, and Berkeley nearly doubled in population. Seattle, Portland, Denver, and Salt Lake City also rose in prominence. After the war, western city leaders boasted of the business and employment opportunities and beautiful landscapes that awaited migrants to their urban communities (Map 21.1).

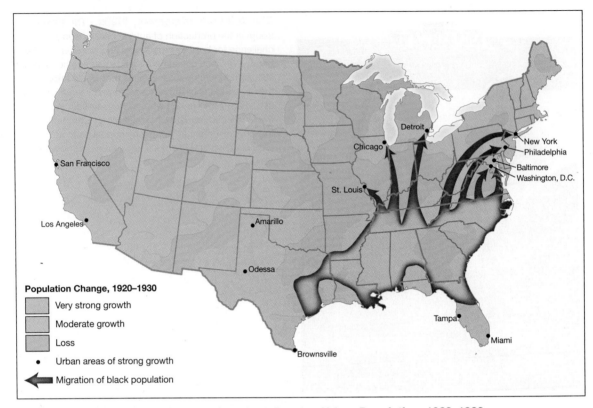

MAP 21.1   The Shift from Rural to Urban Population, 1920–1930

Throughout late nineteenth and early twentieth centuries the population of the nation had shifted from rural to urban areas. In the 1920s this migration continued, especially among African Americans in the South and Latinos in the Southwest and West. Many of these migrants from rural to urban landscapes actually stayed in the same region, particularly Latinos.

Los Angeles stood out for its growth, which skyrocketed from 319,000 residents in 1910 to over 1.2 million in 1930. The mild, sunny climate of southern California attracted midwesterners and northeasterners who were tired of rugged winters. Los Angeles was surrounded by beautiful mountains, and promoters enticed new residents to buy up real estate, which could be purchased cheaply and sold for a big profit. The city offered a dependable public transit system that connected Los Angeles and neighboring counties. During the 1920s, the motion picture industry settled here, and its movies delighted audiences throughout the nation. This urban boom boosted economic growth and, along with it, consumer spending.

Perilous Prosperity.   Prosperity in the 1920s was real enough, but behind the impressive financial indicators flashed warnings that profound danger loomed ahead. Perhaps most important, the boom was accompanied by growing income inequality. A majority of workers lived below the poverty line, and farmers plunged deeper into hard times. Corporate profits increased much faster than wages, resulting in a disproportionate share of the wealth going to the rich. The combined income of the top 1 percent of families was greater

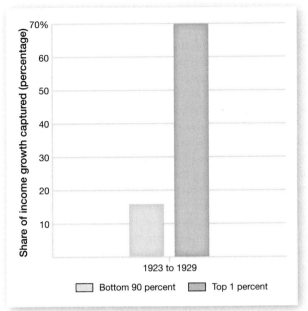

FIGURE 21.2   Income Inequality, 1923–1929

Although the U.S. economy expanded rapidly in the early 1920s, the accumulation of vast wealth among a small percentage of Americans created growing inequality. Explain the dangers this created for the overall economy in the 1920s.

than that of the 42 percent at the bottom (Figure 21.2); 66 percent lived below the income level necessary to maintain an adequate standard of living.

Income inequality was a critical problem because America's new mass-production economy depended on ever-increasing consumption, and higher income groups could consume only so much, no matter how much of the nation's wealth they controlled. While the expansion of consumer credit helped hide this fundamental weakness, the low wages earned by most Americans drove down demand over time. Cutbacks in demand forced manufacturers to reduce production, thereby reducing jobs and increasing unemployment, which in turn dragged down the demand for consumer goods even further. As a result, by 1926 the growth of automobile sales had begun to slow, as did new housing construction — signs of an economy heading for trouble.

At the same time, the wealthy few used their disproportionate wealth to speculate in the stock market and risky real estate ventures. To encourage investments, brokers promoted buying stocks on margin (credit) and required down payments of only a fraction of the market price. Without vigilant governmental oversight, banks and lending agencies extended credit without taking into account what would happen if a financial panic occurred and they were suddenly required to call in all of their loans. To make matters worse, the banking system operated on shaky financial grounds, combining savings facilities with speculative lending operations. With minimal interference from the Federal Trade Commission, businesspeople frequently managed firms in a reckless way that created a high level of interdependence among them. This interlocking system of corporate ownership and control meant that the collapse of one company could bring down many others, while also imperiling the banking houses that had generously financed them.

Rampant real estate speculation in Florida foreshadowed these dangers. In many cases, investors bought properties sight unseen, as speculators and unscrupulous agents worked under the assumption that land values in Florida would continue to increase forever. However, severe storms in 1926 and 1928 abruptly halted the rise in land values. Land prices spiraled downward, speculators defaulted on bank loans, and financial institutions tottered.

Throughout the 1920s, fortunes plummeted for farmers as well. Declining world demand following the end of World War I, together with increased productivity because of the mechanization of agriculture, drove down farm prices and income. Between 1925 and 1929, falling wheat and cotton prices cut farm income in half. The collapse of farm prices had the most devastating effects on tenants and sharecroppers, who were forced off their lands through mortgage foreclosures. Around three million displaced farmers migrated to cities.

Internationally, the United States encountered serious economic obstacles. World War I had destroyed European economies, leaving them ill equipped to repay the $11 billion they had borrowed from the United States. Much of the Allied recovery, and hence the ability to repay debts, depended on obtaining the reparations imposed on Germany at the conclusion of World War I. Germany, however, was in even worse shape than France and Britain and could not meet its obligations. Consequently, the U.S. government negotiated a deal by which the United States provided loans to Germany to pay its reparations and Britain and France reduced the size of Germany's payments. The result was a series of circular payments. American banks loaned money to Germany, which used the money to pay reparations to Britain and France, which in turn used Germany's reparations payments to repay debts owed to U.S. banks. What appeared a satisfactory resolution at the time ultimately proved a calamity. In undertaking this revolving-door solution, U.S. bankers added to the cycle of spiraling credit and placed themselves at the mercy of unstable European economies. Compounding the problem, Republican administrations in the 1920s supported high tariffs on imports, reducing foreign manufacturers' revenues and therefore their nations' tax receipts, making it more difficult for these countries to pay off their debts.

REVIEW & RELATE

- Describe the relationship between business and government in the 1920s.

- Why was a high level of consumer spending so critical to 1920s prosperity, and why was the economic expansion of the 1920s ultimately unsustainable?

Challenges to Social Conventions

While most of the nation ignored growing evidence of the fragility of American prosperity, the social and cultural consequences of the second industrial revolution received considerable attention, as new, distinctly modern cultural patterns emerged. Advertising and credit, two of the mainstays of modern capitalism, sought to bypass the time-honored virtues of saving and living within one's means. Conventional sexual standards came under assault from the growth of the film and automobile industries, which influenced clothing styles and dating practices. In addition to moral and social behavior, traditional racial assumptions came under attack. African American writers and artists condemned racism, drew on their rich racial legacies, and produced a cultural renaissance. Other blacks, led by the Jamaican immigrant Marcus Garvey, rejected the integrationist strategy of the NAACP in favor of black nationalism.

Hollywood   Hollywood's silent movies provided audiences with graphic images of changing sexual values during the 1920s. Rudolph Valentino, pictured in this advertisement for *Blood and Sand* (1922), was the leading male heartthrob of the era. Here he embraces his costar Nita Naldi, who responds with a look of ecstasy to Valentino's touch. Courtesy Everett Collection

Breaking with the Old Morality. Challenges to the virtues of thrift and sacrifice were accompanied by a transformation of the moral codes of late-nineteenth-century America, especially those relating to sex. The entertainment industry played a large role in promoting relaxed attitudes toward sexual relations to a mass audience throughout the nation. The motion picture business attracted women and men to movie palaces where they could see swashbuckling heroes and glamorous heroines.

Originally shown as short films for five cents in nickelodeons, movies appealed to a national audience. By the 1920s, films had expanded into feature-length pictures, Hollywood film studios had blossomed into major corporations, and movies were shown in ornate theaters in cities and towns across the country. The star system was born, and matinee idols influenced fashions and hairstyles. Female stars dressed as "flappers" and wooed audiences. Representing the liberated **new woman**, flappers sported short hair and short skirts, used ample makeup (formerly associated with prostitutes), smoked cigarettes in public, drank illegal alcoholic beverages, and gyrated to jazz tunes on the dance floor.

However, even as Americans enjoyed new entertainment opportunities most remained faithful to traditional values. By 1929 approximately 40 percent of households owned a radio. Shows such as *The General Motors Family* and *The Maxwell House Hour* blended product advertising with family entertainment. *Amos 'n' Andy* garnered large audiences by satirizing black working-class life, which, intentionally or not, reinforced racist stereotypes. In cities like New York and Chicago, immigrants could tune in to foreign-language radio programs aimed at non-English-speaking ethnic groups, which offered listeners an outlet for preserving their identity in the face of the increasing homogeneity fostered by the national consumer culture.

The most spirited challenge to both traditional values and the modern consumer culture came from a diverse group of intellectuals known as the **Lost Generation**. Author Gertrude Stein coined the term to describe the disillusionment that many of her fellow writers and artists felt after the ravages of World War I. Already concerned about the impact of mass culture and corporate capitalism on individualism and free thought, they focused their talents on criticizing what they saw as the hypocrisy of old values and the conformity ushered in by the new. In the novel *This Side of Paradise* (1920), F. Scott Fitzgerald complained that his generation had "grown up to find all Gods dead, all wars fought, all faith in man shaken." In a series of novels, including *Main Street* (1920), *Babbitt* (1922), and *Elmer Gantry* (1927), Sinclair Lewis ridiculed the narrow-mindedness of small-town life, the empty materialism of businessmen, and the insincerity of evangelical

Augusta Savage   Born in Florida, Augusta Savage joined other artists in moving to New York City in the 1920s as part of the Harlem Renaissance. She took formal art classes at the Cooper Union, working mainly in clay. In addition to the sculpture of the young boy here, Savage produced busts of W. E. B. Du Bois and Marcus Garvey. Hansel Mieth/The LIFE Picture Collection/Getty Images

preachers. Journalist Henry Louis (H. L.) Mencken picked up these subjects in the pages of his magazine, *The American Mercury*. From his vantage point in Baltimore, Maryland, he lampooned the beliefs and behavior of Middle America.

Scholars joined literary and social critics in challenging conventional ideas. Sigmund Freud, an Austrian psychoanalyst, shifted emphasis away from culture to individual consciousness. His disciples stressed the role of the unconscious mind and the power of the sex drive in shaping human behavior, beliefs that gained traction not only in university education but also in advertising appeals.

Scholars also discredited conventional wisdom about race. Challenging studies that purported to demonstrate the intellectual superiority of whites over blacks, Columbia University anthropologist Franz Boas argued that any apparent intelligence gap between the races resulted from environmental factors and not heredity. His student Ruth Benedict further argued that the culture of so-called primitive tribes, such as the Pueblo Indians, produced a less stressful and more emotionally connected lifestyle than that of more advanced societies.

The Harlem Renaissance.

The greatest challenge to conventional notions about race came from African Americans. The influx of southern black migrants to the North during and after World War I created a black cultural renaissance, with New York City's Harlem and the South Side of Chicago leading the way. Gathered in Harlem — with a population of more than 120,000 African Americans in 1920 and growing every day — a group of black writers paid homage to the **New Negro**, the second generation born after emancipation. These New Negro intellectuals refused to accept white supremacy. They expressed pride in their race, sought to perpetuate black racial identity, and demanded full citizenship and participation in American society. Black writers and poets drew on themes from African American life and history for inspiration in their literary works.

The poets, novelists, and artists of the **Harlem Renaissance** captured the imagination of blacks and whites alike. Many of these artists increasingly rejected white standards of taste as well as staid middle-class black values. Writers Langston Hughes and Zora Neale Hurston in particular drew inspiration from the vernacular of African American folk life. In 1926 Hughes defiantly asserted: "We younger Negro artists who create now intend to express our dark-skinned selves without fear or shame. If white people are pleased, we are glad. If they are not, it doesn't matter." **See Primary Source Project 21: The New Negro and the Harlem Renaissance, page 733.**

Black music became a vibrant part of mainstream American popular culture in the 1920s. Musicians such as Ferdinand "Jelly Roll" Morton, Louis Armstrong, Edward "Duke" Ellington, and singer Bessie Smith developed and popularized two of America's most original forms of music — jazz and the blues. These unique compositions grew out of the everyday experiences of black life and expressed the thumping rhythms of work, pleasure, and pain. Such music did not remain confined to dance halls and clubs in black communities; it soon spread to white musicians and audiences for whom the hot beat of jazz rhythms meant emotional freedom and the expression of sexuality.

Marcus Garvey and Black Nationalism.

In addition to providing a fertile ground for African American intellectuals, Harlem became the headquarters of the most significant alternative black political vision of the 1920s. In 1916 the Jamaican-born Marcus Mosiah Garvey settled in Harlem and became the leading exponent of black nationalism. In 1914 Garvey had set up the **Universal Negro Improvement Association (UNIA)** in Jamaica, an organization through which he promoted racial separation and pride as well as economic self-help through black business ownership. Unlike the leaders of the NAACP, who sought equal access to American institutions and cooperation with whites, Garvey favored a "Back to Africa" movement that would ultimately repatriate many black Americans to their ancestral homelands on the African continent. His recently acquired Black Star Line steamship company planned to transport passengers between the United States, the West Indies, and Africa. Together with the indigenous black African majority, transplanted African Americans would help overthrow colonial rule and use their power to assist black people throughout the world.

In addition to offering a revival of black cultural heritage and providing an outlet for dreams of economic advancement, Garvey tapped into the racial discontent of African Americans for whom living in the United States had proved so difficult. He denounced what he saw as the accommodationist efforts of the NAACP and declared, "To be a Negro is no disgrace, but an honor, and we of the UNIA do not want to become white." Ironically, the UNIA and D. C. Stephenson's Klan agreed on the necessity of racial segregation, though Garvey never accepted the premise that blacks were inferior. Garvey's appeals to black manhood were accompanied by a celebration of black womanhood. He set up the Black Cross Nurses, and his wife, Amy Jacques Garvey, went beyond her husband's traditional notions of femininity to extol the accomplishments of black women in politics and culture. Garveyism became the first mass African American movement in U.S. history and was especially effective in recruiting working-class blacks. UNIA branches were established in thirty-eight states throughout the North and South and attracted some 500,000 members.

Marcus Garvey   Dressed in military regalia topped off with a plumed hat, the Jamaican immigrant Marcus Garvey embodied the spirit of black nationalism after World War I. His Universal Negro Improvement Association, headquartered in Harlem, attracted a sizable following in the United States, the Caribbean, Central America, Canada, and Africa. Garvey advocated black political and economic independence. NY Daily News Archive via Getty Images

Given his ideas and outspokenness, Garvey soon made powerful enemies. Du Bois and fellow members of the NAACP despised him. The black socialist labor leader A. Philip Randolph, who saw the UNIA program as just another form of exploitative capitalism, labeled Garvey an "unquestioned fool and ignoramus." Yet Garvey's downfall came from his own business practices. Convicted in 1925 of mail fraud related to his Black Star Line, Garvey served two years in federal prison until President Coolidge commuted his term and had the Jamaican citizen deported.

REVIEW & RELATE

• How did new forms of entertainment challenge traditional morality and traditional gender roles?

• Describe the black cultural and intellectual renaissance that flourished in the 1920s.

Culture Wars

Attacks on traditional cultural and racial values did not go uncontested. During this era when technological innovations overturned traditional economic values, when modes of social behavior were in a state of flux, and when white supremacy came under assault, it is not surprising that many segments of the population resisted these changes. Rallying around ethnic and racial purity, Protestant fundamentalism, and family values, defenders of an older America attempted to roll back the tide of modernity. The enactment of prohibition was their greatest victory.

Prohibition. After decades of efforts to combat the use of alcohol, in 1919 the Eighteenth Amendment, banning its manufacture and sale, was ratified. That same year Congress passed the Volstead Act, which set up the legal machinery to enforce the amendment. Supporters claimed that prohibition would promote family stability, improve morals, and prevent crime. They took aim at the ethnic culture of saloons associated with urban immigrants.

Enforcing this attempt to promote traditional values proved to be the problem. In rural areas "moonshiners" took grain and processed it into liquor. In big cities, clubs known as speakeasies offered illegal alcohol and the entertainment to keep their customers satisfied. Treasury Department agents roamed the country destroying stills and raiding speakeasies, but liquor continued to flow. Nevertheless, prohibition did reduce alcohol consumption, but crime flourished. Gangsters paid off police, bribed judges, and turned cities into battlegrounds between rival criminal gangs, reinforcing the notion among small-town and rural dwellers that urban life eroded American values. By the end of the decade, most Americans welcomed an end to prohibition.

Nativists versus Immigrants. Prohibition reflected the surge in nativist (anti-immigrant) and racist thinking that in many ways revealed long-standing prejudices — earlier attempts at temperance reform had been largely aimed at immigrants. The end of World War I brought a new wave of Catholic and Jewish emigration from eastern and southern Europe, triggering religious prejudice among Protestants. Just as immigrants had been linked to socialism and anarchism in the 1880s and 1890s, old-stock Americans associated these immigrants with immoral behavior and political radicalism and saw them as a threat to traditional U.S. culture and values. Moreover, as in the late nineteenth century, native-born workers saw immigrants as a source of cheap labor that threatened their jobs and wages.

The **Sacco and Vanzetti** case provides the most dramatic evidence of this nativism. In 1920 a botched robbery in South Braintree, Massachusetts resulted in the murder of two employees. Police charged Nicola Sacco and Bartolomeo Vanzetti with the crime. These two Italian immigrants shared radical political views as anarchists and World War I draft evaders. The subsequent trial revolved around their foreign birth and ideology more than the facts pertaining to their guilt or innocence. The presiding judge at the trial referred to the accused as "anarchistic bastards" and "damned dagos" (a derogatory term for "Italians"). Convicted and sentenced to death, Sacco and Vanzetti lost their appeals for a new trial. Criticism of the verdict came from all over the world. Workers in Mexico, Argentina, Uruguay, France, and Morocco organized vigils and held rallies in solidarity with the condemned men. Despite such support, the two men were executed in the electric chair in 1927.

The Sacco and Vanzetti case provides an extreme example of 1920s nativism, but the anti-immigrant views that contributed to the two men's conviction and execution were commonplace during the period and shared by Americans across the social spectrum. For example, Henry Ford saw immigrants as a threat to cherished traditions. Ford believed that immigrants were the cause of a decline in U.S. morality. He contended that aliens did not understand "the principles which have made our [native] civilization," and he blamed the influx of foreigners for society's "marked deterioration" during the 1920s. He stirred up anti-immigrant prejudices mainly by targeting Jews. Believing that an international Jewish conspiracy was attempting to subvert non-Jewish societies, Ford serialized in his company newspaper the so-called *Protocols of the Elders of Zion*, an anti-Semitic tract concocted in czarist Russia to justify pogroms against Jews. Ford continued to publish it even after the document was proved a fake.

Ford joined other nativists in supporting legislation to restrict immigration. In 1924 Congress passed the **National Origins Act**, a quota system on future immigration. The measure limited entry by any foreign group to 2 percent of the number of people of that nationality who resided in the United States in 1890. The statute's authors were interested primarily in curbing immigration from eastern and southern Europe. They chose 1890 as the benchmark for immigration because most newcomers from those two regions entered the United States after that year. Quotas established for northern Europe went unfilled, while those for southern and eastern Europe could not accommodate the vast number of people who sought admission. The law continued to bar East Asian immigration altogether. However, immigration from Mexico and elsewhere in the Western Hemisphere was exempted from the quotas of the Nation Origins Act because farmers in the Southwest needed Mexican laborers to tend their crops and pressured the government to excuse them from coverage. In a related measure, in 1924 Congress established the Border Patrol to control the flow of undocumented immigration from Mexico. Nevertheless, *legal* immigration to the United States from Mexico increased during the 1920s.

With immigration of those considered "undesirable" severely if not completely curtailed, some nativist reformers shifted their attention to Americanization, which developed into one of the largest social and political movements in American history. Speaking about immigrants, educator E. P. Cubberly said, "Our task is to break up their groups and settlements, to assimilate and amalgamate these people as a part of our American race, to implant in their children the northern-European conception of righteousness, law and order, and popular government." Business corporations conducted Americanization and naturalization classes on factory floors. Schools, patriotic societies, fraternal organizations, women's groups, and labor unions launched citizenship classes.

In the Southwest and on the West Coast, whites aimed their Americanization efforts at the growing population of Mexican Americans. Subject to segregated education, Mexican Americans were expected to speak English in their classes. Anglo school administrators and teachers generally believed that Mexican Americans were suited only for farmwork and manual trades. For Mexican Americans, therefore, Americanization meant vocational training and preparation for low-status, low-wage jobs.

American Indians fared little better. During World War I, to save money the federal government had ceased appropriating funds for public health programs aimed at benefiting reservation Indians. With the war over, the government failed to restore the funds. Throughout the 1920s, rates of tuberculosis, eye infections, and infant mortality spiked among the Indian population. Boarding schools continued to promote menial service jobs for Indian students. On the brighter side, in 1924 Congress passed the **Indian Citizenship Act** granting citizenship and the right to vote to all American Indians. Nevertheless, most Indians remained outside the economic and political mainstream of American society with meager government help.

Chinese residents also continued to face discrimination and segregation. The Chinese Exclusion Act remained in operation, making it difficult for nurturing family life. By 1920, Chinese men outnumbered Chinese women by seven to one. Furthermore, immigration restrictions prohibited Chinese workingmen from bringing their wives into the country. The 1924 Immigration Act made matters worse by banning all Asian women from entering the country. That same year the Supreme Court upheld the segregation of Chinese children in public schools.

Chinese communities faced problems similar to those experienced by other ethnic groups. Tensions developed between those born in China and their American-born children over assimilation. One Chinese American who grew up in San Francisco noted, "There was endless discussion about what to do about the dilemma of being *caught in between.*" Many Chinese parents prohibited their children from speaking English at home and sent them to Chinese-language schools after public school. Chinese American children found cultural preservation efforts an onerous burden as they increasingly partook in America's growing consumer culture.

Despite attempts at Americanization, ethnic groups did not dissolve into a melting pot and lose their cultural identities. First-generation Americans — the children of immigrants — learned English, enjoyed American popular culture, and dressed in fashions of the day. Yet in cities around the country where immigrants had settled, ethnic enclaves remained intact and preserved the religious practices and social customs of their residents. Americanization may have watered down the "vegetable soup" of American diversity, but it did not eliminate the variety and distinctiveness of its flavors.

Resurrection of the Ku Klux Klan.

Nativism received its most spectacular boost from the reemergence of the Ku Klux Klan in 1915. Originally an organization dedicated to terrorizing emancipated African Americans and their white Republican allies in the South during Reconstruction, the KKK branched out during the 1920s to the North and West. In addition to blacks, the new Klan targeted Catholics and Jews, as well as anyone who was alleged to have violated community moral values. The organization consisted of a cross section of native-born Protestants primarily from the middle and working classes who sought to reverse a perceived decline in their social and economic power. Revived by W. J. Simmons, a former Methodist minister, the new Klan celebrated its founding at Stone Mountain, Georgia, near Atlanta. There, Klansmen bowed to the twin symbols of their cause, the American flag and a burning cross that represented their fiery determination to stand up for Christian morality and against all those considered "un-American." People flocked to the new KKK, and by the mid-1920s, Klan membership totaled more than three million men and women. Not confined to rural areas, the revived Klan counted a significant following in D. C. Stephenson's Indianapolis and Ossian Sweet's Detroit, as well as in Chicago, Denver, Portland, and Seattle. Rural dwellers who had moved into cities with large numbers of black migrants and

Explore ▶

See Sources 21.2 and 21.3 for two perspectives on the KKK.

COMPARATIVE ANALYSIS

Men and Women of the KKK

While the new Ku Klux Klan grew in power and visibility, many Americans also resisted and ridiculed the organization. In the first selection, journalist Gerald Johnson describes the typical KKK member. The second selection, an excerpt from the bylaws of a Maryland chapter of the Women of the Ku Klux Klan, indicates the group's devotion to the responsibilities of traditional womanhood. Nearly half a million women joined the women's auxiliaries of the KKK.

Ku Klux Klan Wedding, 1925

FPG/Hulton Archive/Getty Images

Source 21.2

Gerald W. Johnson │ The Ku Kluxer, 1924

The Ku Klux Klan was swept beyond the racial boundaries of the Negro and flourishes now in the Middle West because it is a perfect expression of the American idea that the voice of the people is the voice of God. The belief that the average klansman is consciously affected by an appeal to his baser self is altogether erroneous. In the voice of the organizer he hears a clarion call to knightly and selfless service. It strikes him as in no wise strange that he should be so summoned; is he not, as an American citizen, of the nobility? Politics has been democratized. Social usage has been democratized. Religion has been most astoundingly democratized. Why, then, not democratize chivalry?

The klansman has already been made, in his own estimation, politically a monarch, socially a peer of the realm, spiritually a high priest. Now the Ku Klux Klan calls him to step up and for the trifling consideration of ten dollars he is made a Roland, a Lancelot, a knight-errant vowed to the succor of the oppressed, the destruction of ogres and magicians, the defense of the faith. Bursting with noble ideals and lofty aspirations, he accepts the nomination. The trouble is that this incantation doesn't work, as none of the others has worked, except in his imagination. King, aristocrat, high priest as he believes himself to be, he is neither royal, noble, nor holy. So, under his white robe and pointed hood he becomes not a Chevalier Bayard [French knight] but a thug.

Source: Gerald W. Johnson, "The Ku Kluxer," *American Mercury*, February 1924, 209–10.

Source 21.3

Women of the Ku Klux Klan, 1927

Objects and Purposes

SECTION 1. The objects of this Order shall be to unite white female persons, native-born Gentile citizens of the United States of America, who owe no allegiance of any nature or degree to any foreign government, nation, institution, sect, ruler, person, or people; whose morals are good; whose reputations and vocations are respectable; whose habits are exemplary; who are of sound minds and 18 years or more of age, under a common oath into a Sisterhood of strict regulation, to cultivate and promote patriotism toward our Civil Government; to practice an honorable clannishness toward each other; to exemplify a practical benevolence; to shield the sanctity of the home and the chastity of womanhood; to maintain forever white supremacy; to teach and faithfully inculcate a high spiritual philosophy through an exalted ritualism, and by a practical devotion to conserve,

protect, and maintain the distinctive institutions, rights, privileges, principles, traditions, and ideals of a pure Americanism.

SEC. 2. To create and maintain an institution by which the present and succeeding generations shall commemorate the great sacrifice, chivalric service, and imperishable achievements of the Ku Klux Klan and the Women of the Reconstruction period of American History, to the end that justice and honor be done the sacred memory of those who wrought through our mystic society during that period, and that their valiant accomplishments be not lost to posterity; to perpetuate their faithful courage, noble spirit, peerless principles, and faultless ideals; to hold sacred and make effective their spiritual purpose in this and future generations, that they be rightly vindicated before the world by a revelation of the whole truth.

Source: Women of the KKK (Maryland) Records, Schlesinger Library, Radcliffe Institute, Harvard University, reprinted in *Modern American Women*, ed. Susan Ware (Boston: McGraw-Hill, 2002), 136–37.

Interpret the Evidence

1. How does Johnson describe the typical KKK member?
2. How do each of these statements identify the central purpose of the KKK?

Put It in Context

Why did the KKK and other nativist groups appeal to so many people during the 1920s?

recent immigrants found solace in Klan vows to preserve "Native, white, Protestant supremacy."

The phenomenal growth of the KKK in the 1920s probably resulted more from the desire to reestablish traditional values than from sheer hostility toward blacks. In the face of challenges to conventional values, a changing sexual morality, and the flaunting of prohibition, wives joined their husbands as devoted followers. Protestant women appreciated the Klan's message condemning abusive husbands and fathers and the group's affirmation of the status of white Protestant women as the embodiment of virtue.

Like the original Klan, its successor resorted to terror tactics. Acting under cover of darkness and concealed in robes and hoods, Klansmen burned crosses to scare their victims, many of whom they beat, kidnapped, tortured, and murdered. To gain greater legitimacy and to appeal to a wider audience, the Klan also participated in electoral politics. The KKK succeeded in electing governors in Georgia and Oregon, a U.S. senator from Texas, numerous state legislators, and other officials in California, Indiana, Michigan, Ohio, and Oklahoma. Politicians routinely joined the Klan to advance their careers, whether they shared its views or not.

Fundamentalism versus Modernism.
Protestant fundamentalists also fought to uphold long-established values against modern-day incursions. Around 1910, two wealthy Los Angeles churchgoers had subsidized and distributed a series of booklets called *The Fundamentals*, informing readers that the Bible offered a true account of the genesis and development of humankind and the world and that its words had to be taken literally. After 1920, believers of this approach to interpreting the Bible became known as "fundamentalists." Their preachers spread the message of old-time religion through carnival-like revivals, and ministers used the new medium of radio to broadcast their sermons. Fundamentalism's appeal was strongest in the Midwest and the South — the so-called Bible belt — where residents felt deeply threatened by the secular aspects of modern life that left their conventional religious teachings open to skepticism and scorn.

Nothing bothered fundamentalist Protestants as much as Charles Darwin's theory of evolution. In *On the Origin of Species* (1859), Darwin replaced the biblical story of creation with a scientific theory of the emergence and development of life that centered on evolution and natural selection. Fundamentalists rejected this explanation and repudiated the views of fellow Protestants who attempted to reconcile Darwinian evolution with God's Word by reading the Bible as a symbolic representation of what might have happened. To combat any other interpretation but the biblical one, in 1925 lawmakers in Arkansas, Florida, Mississippi, Oklahoma, and Tennessee made it illegal to teach in public schools and colleges "any theory that denies the story of the Divine Creation of man as taught in the Bible."

Shortly after the anti-evolution law passed, the town of Dayton, Tennessee decided to take advantage of it to attract new investment to the area. The townspeople recruited John Scopes, a general science high school teacher, to defy the law by lecturing from a biology textbook that presented Darwin's theory. With help from the ACLU, which wanted to challenge the restrictive state statute on the grounds of free speech and academic freedom, Dayton turned an ordinary judicial hearing into the "trial of the century."

The resulting trial brought Dayton more fame, much of it negative, than the planners had bargained for. When court convened in July 1925, millions of people listened over the radio to the first trial ever broadcast. Reporters from all over the country descended on Dayton to keep their readers informed of the proceedings.

Clarence Darrow headed the defense team. A controversial criminal lawyer from Chicago, who in a few months would defend Ossian Sweet, Darrow doubted the existence of God. On the other side, William Jennings Bryan, three-time Democratic candidate for president and secretary of state under Woodrow Wilson, assisted the prosecution. As a Protestant fundamentalist, Bryan believed that accepting scientific evolution would undermine the moral basis of politics and that communities should have the right to determine their children's school curriculum. A minister summed up what the fundamentalists considered to be at stake: "[Darwin's theory] breeds corruption, lust, immorality, greed, and such acts of criminal depravity as drug addiction, war, and atrocious acts of genocide."

The presiding judge, John T. Raulston, ruled that scientists could not take the stand to defend evolution because he considered their testimony "hearsay," given that they had not been present at the creation. The jury took only eight minutes to declare Scopes guilty, but his conviction was overturned by an appeals court on a technicality. Yet fundamentalists remained as certain as ever in their beliefs, and anti-evolution laws stayed in force until the 1970s. The trial had not "settled" anything. Rather, it served to highlight a cultural division over the place of religion in American society that persists to the present day.

REVIEW & RELATE

- What was the connection between anti-immigrant sentiment and the defense of tradition during the 1920s?

- Who challenged the new morality associated with modernization? Why?

Politics and the Fading of Prosperity

These cultural clashes tore the Democratic Party apart, leaving Republicans in command of national politics. As it attracted a growing number of urban immigrants to its ranks alongside its customary base of white southerners, the Democratic Party tried to reconcile the tensions between traditional and modern America. Its failure to do so kept Republicans in power despite growing evidence of their inability to resolve serious economic problems. Although many progressives continued to press for reform, they were all but powerless to prevent the coming economic crisis.

The Battle for the Soul of the Democratic Party.
The 1924 presidential election exposed serious fault lines within the Democratic Party. Since Reconstruction, Democrats had dominated the South, and Republicans ceased to compete for office in the region. Southern Democrats shared fundamentalist religious beliefs and support for prohibition

that usually placed them at odds with big-city Democrats. The northern urban wing of the party also represented immigrants who rejected prohibition as contrary to their cultural practices. These distinctions, however, were not absolute — some rural dwellers opposed prohibition, and some urbanites supported temperance.

Delegates to the 1924 Democratic convention in New York City disagreed over a party platform and a presidential candidate. When northeastern urban delegates attempted to insert a plank condemning the Ku Klux Klan for its intolerance, they lost by a thin margin. The sizable number of convention delegates who either belonged to or had been backed by the Klan ensured the proposal's defeat.

The selection of the presidential ticket proved even more divisive. Urban Democrats favored New York governor Alfred E. Smith. Smith came from an Irish Catholic immi-grant family, had grown up on New York City's Lower East Side, and was sponsored by the Tammany Hall machine. The epitome of everything that rural Democrats despised, Smith also denounced prohibition. After a fierce contest, the pride of New York City lost the nomination to John W. Davis, a West Virginia Protestant and a defender of prohibition. Left deeply divided going into the general election, Davis lost to Calvin Coolidge in a landslide (Map 21.2).

> **Explore ▶**
>
> See Sources 21.4 and 21.5 for two historians' interpretations of the effectiveness of the federal government during Prohibition.

In 1928, however, when the Democrats met in Houston, Texas, the delicate cultural equilibrium within the Democratic Party had shifted in favor of the urban forces. With Stephenson and the Klan discredited and no longer a force in Democratic politics, the del-egates nominated Al Smith as their presidential candidate.

The Republicans selected Herbert Hoover, one of the most popular men in the United States. Affectionately called "the Great Humanitarian" for his European relief efforts after World War I, Hoover served as secretary of commerce during the Harding and Coolidge administrations. His name became synonymous with the Republican prosperity of the 1920s. In accepting his party's nomination for president in 1928, Hoover optimistically

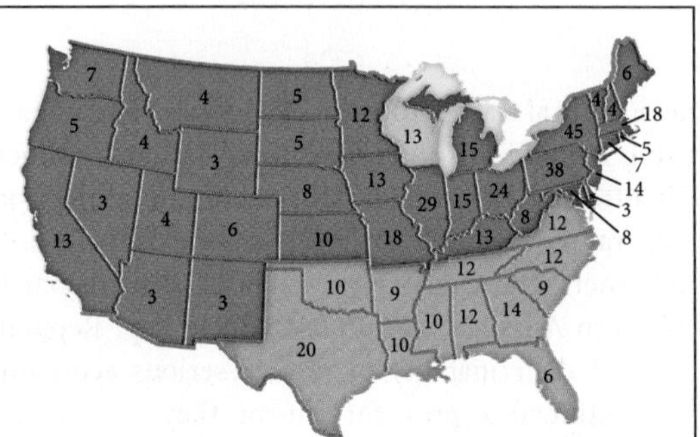

Candidate	Electoral Vote	Popular Vote	Percentage of Popular Vote
Calvin Coolidge (Republican)	382	15,725,016	54.0
John W. Davis (Democrat)	136	8,386,503	28.8
Robert M. La Follette (Progressive)	13	4,822,856	16.6

MAP 21.2   The Election of 1924

Republican Calvin Coolidge, who became president in August 1923 on the death of Warren Harding, continued Harding's policies of limited government regulation and corporate tax cuts. Coolidge easily defeated Democrat John Davis, whose strength was confined to the South. Running as the Progressive Party candidate, Senator Robert La Follette won 16 percent of the popular vote but carried only his home state of Wisconsin, with 13 electoral votes.

declared: "We in America today are nearer to the final triumph over poverty than ever before in the history of the land." A Protestant supporter of prohibition from a small town, Hoover was everything Smith was not.

The outcome of the election proved predictable. Hoover trounced Smith with 58 percent of the popular vote and more than 80 percent of the electoral vote. Despite the weakening economy, Smith lost usually reliable Democratic votes to religious and ethnic prejudices. The New Yorker prevailed only in Massachusetts, Rhode Island, and six southern states but failed to win his home state. A closer look at the election returns showed a significant party realignment under way. Smith succeeded in identifying the Democratic Party with urban, ethnic-minority voters and attracting them to the polls. Despite the landslide loss, he captured the twelve largest cities in the nation, all of which had gone Republican four years earlier. In another fifteen big cities, Smith did better than the Democrat ticket had done in the 1924 election. To break the Republicans' national dominance, the Democrats would need a candidate who appealed to both traditional and modern Americans. Smith's candidacy, though ending in defeat, laid the foundation for future Democratic political success.

Lingering Progressivism.
The Democrats and Republicans were not the only parties that attracted voters in the 1920s. Some voters continued to cast their ballot for the Socialist Party. Others took the opportunity to voice their disapproval of Republican policies by voting for the remaining progressive candidates. Progressives did manage to hold on to seats in Congress, and in 1921 they helped pass the Shepherd-Towner Act, which appropriated federal funds to establish maternal and child centers. Senator Thomas J. Walsh of Montana, a progressive Democrat, led the investigation into the Teapot Dome scandal. But their efforts to restrict the power of the Supreme Court, reduce tax cuts for the wealthy, nationalize railroads, and extend agricultural relief to farmers were rebuffed by conservative legislative majorities. In 1924 reformers nominated Senator Robert M. La Follette of Wisconsin to run for president on a revived Progressive Party ticket, but he came in a distant third. The Progressive Party collapsed soon after La Follette died in 1925.

Still, progressivism managed to stay alive on the local and state levels. Gifford Pinchot, a Roosevelt ally and a champion of conservation, twice won election as governor of Pennsylvania starting in 1922. Social workers continued their efforts to alleviate urban poverty and lobby for government assistance to the poor. Even at the national level, women in the Children's Bureau maintained the progressive legacy by supporting assistance to families and devising social welfare proposals. Progressivism did not disappear during the 1920s, but it did fight an uphill and often losing battle during an age of conservative political ascendancy. Its weakness contributed to the government's failure to check the worst corporate and financial practices, a failure that would play a role in the nation's economic collapse.

Financial Crash.
On October 29, 1929, a day that became known as **Black Tuesday**, stock market prices tumbled. Over the previous five years, the rising market, bolstered by optimistic buyers, earned huge profits for investors, and the value of stocks nearly doubled. In late October, panicked sellers sent stock prices into free fall. Although only 2.5 percent of Americans owned stock, the stock market collapse had an enormous impact on the economy and the rest of the world. Because so much of the stock boom depended

The Impact of Prohibition

Prohibition, which culminated in passage of the Eighteenth Amendment (1919), pitted those who sought to combat what they considered the moral degeneracy of the modern city against those who considered the saloon an institution of immigrant cohesion. Some historians have viewed prohibition as a "pseudo reform," one that distorted the social and humanitarian impulses of the Progressive Era. Still, it should be recalled that Prohibition had a long history as a reform movement dating back to temperance campaigns in the mid- and late-nineteenth centuries that were aimed at promoting the economic and physical well-being of the family, particularly mothers and children. Although most historians render Prohibition a failure, it did have a significant impact on American government and society.

Source 21.4

Andrew Sinclair, The Excesses of Prohibition, 1962

[T]he leaders of the drys [prohibitionists] knew that they could never get a majority of the American people to give up drinking immediately. They hoped that a new generation of teetotalers would grow up from the ranks of the young, and that the protected drys would win converts among the shamed wets [drinkers]

…There was never any serious effort to enforce national prohibition until the early thirties, and by that time it was too late. After less than four years under the Volstead Act, it was clear that "three tremendous popular passions" were being satisfied, "the passion of prohibitionists for law, the passion of the drinking classes for the drink, and the passion for the largest and best-organized smuggling trade that has ever existed for money." Once legalism had turned the possession of alcohol into a popular obsession and the sale of alcohol into a new Gold Rush, enforcement of the liquor laws had no chance.

The failure of the enforcement of the Volstead Act was due to the administrative stupidity, political graft, the federal structure of the United States, an antiquated legal system and the flaws in the act itself. These interlocking and corrigible causes for the failure were overshadowed by one overriding consideration, that the prohibition law could not be adequately enforced in the America of that time.…Indeed, it is doubtful that national prohibition can ever be enforced, even under a dictatorship. Alcoholic drinks have been made in every civilized society in history.…The job of the Prohibition Bureau was to enforce the impossible.

Andrew Sinclair, *Prohibition: The Era of Excess* (Boston: Little, Brown and Company, 1962), 182–83.

Source 21.5

Lisa McGirr, The National State and Crime Control, 2016

The enforcement of Prohibition was notable for its magnitude and it selectivity. Not surprisingly for a movement led at its core by the well-heeled Protestant Anti-Saloon League, enforcement hit working-class, urban immigrant and poor communities hardest. It was, after all, enacted to discipline their leisure in the first place…. Prohibition law enforcement was anything but a dead letter. In the poor communities that bore its brunt, it contributed to a crisis of overcrowded court dockets and prisons.

…Even with its vast corruption, inefficacy, and insufficient funding, Prohibition marked the birth of a qualitatively new and enduring role of the federal state in crime control. The massive, flagrant violations of the law in response to the war on alcohol engendered a new public panic over crime. For the first time crime became a national problem, and a national obsession. The effort to restore law and order resulted in streamlined federal criminal record keeping, professionalized prison administration, new prison growth, and expanded and muscular federal policing, including stronger authority and a broadened purview of the FBI.

… Despite its baleful enforcement, Prohibition and the escalating crime it sparked permanently convinced Americans to look to the federal government for solutions to new national problems. The government did not retreat from its new role in crime control after the end of the war on alcohol. Its punitive approach to recreational narcotics persisted and expanded in new directions…. As broad support for the war on alcohol waned and then collapsed, key antiliquor crusaders turned their energies to the less controversial war against recreational narcotic drugs. With a second twentieth-century drug war contributing to a new crisis of overcrowded prisons and uncounted social costs, there is no better time to revisit the history of national alcohol Prohibition.

Source: Lisa McGirr, *The War on Alcohol: Prohibition and The Rise of the American State* (New York: W.W. Norton & Company, 2016), xiv, xviii, xxi, xxii.

Examine the Sources

1. Describe the major difference or differences between Sinclair's and McGirr's interpretations of Prohibition.
2. How might the difference in the times in which they wrote account for the differences in interpretation between Sinclair and McGirr?

Put It in Context

Evaluate the political and social effects that Prohibition had on the nation.

on generous margin requirements (a down payment of only 5 to 10 percent), when investor-borrowers got caught short by falling prices, they could not repay the financial institutions that had extended them credit. Banks and lending agencies, with their interlocking management and overextension of credit, had difficulty withstanding the turmoil unleashed by the tumbling stock market.

The 1929 crash did not cause the decade-long Great Depression that followed. The seeds for the greatest economic catastrophe in U.S. history had been planted earlier. The causes stemmed from flaws in an economic system that produced a great disparity of wealth, inadequate consumption, overextension of credit both at home and abroad, and the government's unwillingness to relieve the plight of farmers. Republican administrations made matters worse by lowering taxes on the rich and raising tariffs to benefit manufacturers. The Federal Reserve Board exacerbated the situation by keeping interest rates high, thereby making it difficult for people to get loans and repay debts. The failure was not that of the United States alone; the depression affected capitalist nations throughout the world. The stock market collapse crushed whatever confidence the American public had that the unfettered law of supply and demand and laissez-faire economics could ensure prosperity.

REVIEW & RELATE

- How did divisions within the Democratic Party contribute to Republican political dominance in the 1920s?

- What underlying economic weaknesses led to the Great Depression?

Conclusion: The **Transitional Twenties**

The 1920s signaled the tense transition of the United States from a rural, small-town society to an urban, industrial one. Factories roared with the noise of new products aimed at the mass of American consumers. Automobiles, fueled by gasoline, traveled up and down streets and highways. Electricity powered household appliances and ran movie projectors in theaters throughout the nation. People living throughout the country had similar opportunities to buy consumer products and partake in a mass culture made possible by movies and radio. Producing for a mass market, industrial giants like Henry Ford transformed the nature of work and pleasure. The assembly line revolutionized the pace of labor and turned it into a standardized routine. The automobile transformed dating patterns and opened up new opportunities for the exploration of romance and sex.

Yet the roar of consumption and the excitement of breaking the ties of social and cultural conventions proved fleeting. Most Americans lived at or below the poverty line and earned just enough for bare necessities. They could live beyond their means through an ample supply of credit, but their poverty contrasted with the increasing concentration of wealth in the hands of the richest Americans. The stock market crash of 1929 and the ensuing Great Depression exposed the shortcomings of the corporate business world, inadequate oversight by the federal government, and an overreliance on the private sector to look after the nation's economic health.

The weaknesses of the economy were often overshadowed by the clash over cultural differences. Guardians of traditional morality and values worried about the effects of more than fifty years of industrialization, immigration, and urbanization. Issues such as the enforcement of prohibition, the teaching of evolution in the schools, and the debate about whether a Catholic should be elected president dominated political discussion, while efforts to assist farmers and workers were unsuccessful. These battles marked a turning point in U.S. history — the transition from a traditional, rural, Protestant society to an urban, ethnically and religiously diverse one. The widespread popularity of D. C. Stephenson's Ku Klux Klan throughout the South and the North demonstrated that the older America of white, northern European Protestants did not intend to relinquish political or cultural power without a struggle. At the same time, ethnic minorities represented by Al Smith had no intention of backing down. Neither did millions of African Americans, whether they joined the NAACP, as did Ossian Sweet, or supported Marcus Garvey's UNIA. During the next decade, Americans from all backgrounds would battle more than cultural threats; they would fight for their economic survival.

CHAPTER **21** REVIEW

TIMELINE OF **EVENTS**

KEY **TERMS**

REVIEW & RELATE

1. What factors combined to produce the turmoil of the immediate postwar period?

2. What factors contributed to the rise in racial tensions that accompanied the transition from wartime to peacetime?

3. Describe the relationship between business and government in the 1920s.

4. Why was a high level of consumer spending so critical to 1920s prosperity, and why was the economic expansion of the 1920s ultimately unsustainable?

5. How did new forms of entertainment challenge traditional morality and traditional gender roles?

6. Describe the black cultural and intellectual renaissance that flourished in the 1920s.

7. What was the connection between anti-immigrant sentiment and the defense of tradition during the 1920s?

8. Who challenged the new morality associated with modernization? Why?

9. How did divisions within the Democratic Party contribute to Republican political dominance in the 1920s?

10. What underlying economic weaknesses led to the Great Depression?

The New Negro and the Harlem Renaissance

▶ Explain the political and social contexts that shaped the works of New Negro writers, artists, and performers.

In 1925 the editors of the magazine *Survey Graphic* invited Howard University sociologist Alain Locke to compile a special issue dedicated to Harlem. Locke did not suffer from a lack of source material, as the years following World War I had witnessed an unprecedented flowering of political activism and art in this majority-black section of New York City. The issue was an instant success, and Locke expanded it into a book, *The New Negro*, published that same year. Locke's writing confirmed that in the aftermath of World War I, African Americans would not be silent.

The intense activity in 1920s Harlem, which came to be known as the Harlem Renaissance, found expression in many different ways. Followers of Marcus Garvey endorsed not only black pride but also separatism. Democratic socialists such as A. Philip Randolph demanded full economic, political, and social equality for the New Negro (Source 21.6). Black writers broke ground in technique and subject matter. No topic was off-limits. Writers questioned the meaning of the American dream, as well as the significance of their shared African heritage. Poets examined African American history in all of its violence and challenged American blacks to confront the seemingly continuous rise of white supremacy in their home country. Black women challenged the gender conventions of both races. Writers and poets such as Langston Hughes, Claude McKay, Zora Neale Hurston, and Nella Larsen entered the canon of American literature (Sources 21.7 and 21.8).

The following sources offer only a glimpse of the ideas, writing, art (Source 21.9), and music (Source 21.10) that African Americans produced during the post–World War I years.

Source 21.6

A. Philip Randolph and Chandler Owen | "The New Negro — What Is He?" 1919

A. Philip Randolph and Chandler Owen founded the *Messenger* in 1917 to provide an outlet for African American workers. The *Messenger* tackled issues of both race and class from a socialist perspective. It caused great controversy for its coverage of international issues, especially when it opposed U.S. involvement in World War I on pacifist grounds. The following editorial from 1920 elaborates on the definition of the New Negro and argues for fundamental changes in the structure of American life and politics.

In politics, the New Negro, unlike the Old Negro, cannot be lulled into a false sense of security with political spoils and patronage. A job is not the price of his vote. He will not continue to accept political promisory notes from a political debtor, who has already had the power, but who has refused to satisfy his political obligations. The New Negro demands political equality. He recognizes the necessity of selective as well as elective representation. He realizes that so long as the Negro votes for the Republican or Democratic party, he will have only the right and privilege to elect but not to

733

select his representatives. And he who selects the representatives controls the representative. The New Negro stands for universal suffrage.

A word about the economic aims of the New Negro. Here, as a worker, he demands the full product of his toil. His immediate aim is more wages, shorter hours and better working conditions. As a consumer, he seeks to buy in the market, commodities at the lowest possible price.

The social aims of the New Negro are decidedly different from those of the Old Negro. Here he stands for absolute and unequivocal "*social equality*." He realizes that there cannot be any qualified equality. He insists that a society which is based upon justice can only be a society composed of *social equals*. He insists upon identity of social treatment. With respect to intermarriage, he maintains that it is the only logical, sound and correct aim for the Negro to entertain. He realizes that the acceptance of laws against intermarriage is tantamount to the acceptance of the stigma of inferiority. Besides, laws against intermarriage expose Negro women to sexual exploitation, and deprive their offspring, by white men, of the right to inherit the property of their father. Statistics show that there are nearly four million mulattoes in America as a result of miscegenation.

Source: A. Philip Randolph and Chandler Owen, "The New Negro — What Is He?" *Messenger* 2 (August 1920): 73–74.

Source 21.7

Claude McKay | "If We Must Die," 1919

Jamaican-born writer Claude McKay moved to the United States in 1912 and influenced many writers of the Harlem Renaissance. His poems focus primarily on race relations and the lives of working-class African Americans. The following poem is one of his most powerful and well-known works, written in reaction to the violence against African Americans in the summer of 1919.

If we must die, let it not be like hogs
Hunted and penned in an inglorious spot,
While round us bark the mad and hungry dogs,
Making their mock at our accursèd lot.

If we must die, O let us nobly die,
So that our precious blood may not be shed
In vain; then even the monsters we defy
Shall be constrained to honor us though dead!
O kinsmen! we must meet the common foe!
Though far outnumbered let us show us brave,
And for their thousand blows deal one death-blow!
What though before us lies the open grave?
Like men we'll face the murderous, cowardly pack,
Pressed to the wall, dying, but fighting back!

Source: Claude McKay, "If We Must Die," in *Harlem Shadows: The Poems of Claude McKay* (New York: Harcourt, Brace, 1922), 53.

Source 21.8

Langston Hughes | "The Negro Speaks of Rivers," 1921

No figure became more synonymous with the Harlem Renaissance than Langston Hughes. Poems like "The Weary Blues" (1926) and "I, Too, Sing America" (1925) simultaneously gave voice to the historical anxieties that African Americans faced and celebrated the roles of blacks in the arts. Hughes also wrote penetrating essays, such as "The Negro Artist and the Racial Mountain" (1925), which explored how African Americans might best present their art. In this early poem, "The Negro Speaks of Rivers," Hughes ponders his relationship to Africa.

I've known rivers:
I've known rivers ancient as the world and older than the flow of
human blood in human veins.
My soul has grown deep like the rivers.
I bathed in the Euphrates when dawns were young.
I built my hut near the Congo and it lulled me to sleep.
I looked upon the Nile and raised the pyramids above it.
I heard the singing of the Mississippi when Abe Lincoln went down to New Orleans, and I've seen its muddy bosom turn all golden in the sunset.
I've known rivers:
Ancient, dusky rivers.
My soul has grown deep like the rivers.

Source: Langston Hughes, "The Negro Speaks of Rivers," *Crisis*, June 1921, 17.

Aaron Douglas | Illustration, *The New Negro*, 1925

Born in Topeka, Kansas, Aaron Douglas became the leading painter and illustrator of the Harlem Renaissance. He used techniques of modern art to explore themes of race and justice. This illustration appeared in Alain Locke's anthology, *The New Negro*, which contains selections by the major writers of the Harlem Renaissance.

Art ©Heirs of Aaron Douglas/Licensed by VAGA, New York, NY. Photo, Library of Congress, 3b00857

Bessie Smith | "Down-Hearted Blues," 1923

Music, particularly jazz and the blues, played a central role in the Harlem Renaissance. Born in Chattanooga, Tennessee, Bessie Smith became one of the most popular African American performers at venues like Harlem's Cotton Club. Her recording of "Down-Hearted Blues," written by Lovie Austin and Alberta Hunter, sold more than 750,000 copies and made Smith a major star of the burgeoning music industry. Its lyrics demonstrate how Smith used music to communicate ideas about relationships, gender, and sexuality.

Gee, but it's hard to love someone, when that someone don't love you,
I'm so disgusted, heartbroken too,
I've got those down-hearted blues.
Once I was crazy about a man, he mistreated me all the time,
The next man I see, he's got to promise to be mine, all mine.

Trouble, trouble, I've had it all my days,
Trouble, trouble, I've had it all my days,
It seems that trouble's going to follow me to my grave.

If I could only find the man, oh, how happy I would be,
To the Good Lord ev'ry night I pray, please send my man back to me
I've almost worried myself to death wond'ring why he went away,
But just wait and see, he's gonna want me back some sweet day.

World in a jug, the stopper's in my hand,
Got the world in a jug, the stopper's in my hand,
Going to hold it, baby, till you come under my command.

Say, I ain't never loved but three men in my life,
No, I ain't never loved but three men in my life,
'Twas my father, my brother, and the man who wrecked my life.

'Cause he mistreated me and he drove me from his door,
Yes, he mistreated me and he drove me from his door
But the Good Book says you'll reap just what you sow.

Oh, it may be a week and it may be a month or two,
Yes, it may be a week and it may be a month or two,
But the day you quit me, honey, it's coming home to you.

Oh, I walked the floor and I wrung my hands and cried,
Yes, I walked the floor and I wrung my hands and cried,
Had the down-hearted blues and couldn't be satisfied.

Source: Bessie Smith, "Down-Hearted Blues," Columbia A3844, 1923.

Interpret the Evidence

1. Compare the idea of the New Negro as presented by the editors of the *Messenger* (Source 21.6) with the ideas expressed by Claude McKay (Source 21.7).
2. Explain how Langston Hughes appeals to history to lend insight into the experiences of Africans in America (Source 21.8).
3. How does Aaron Douglas illustrate the themes Hughes presents in his poetry (Source 21.9)?
4. Examine whether Bessie Smith's lyrics (Source 21.10) provide evidence of the idea of the New Negro.

Put It in Context

Why did the Harlem Renaissance flourish in the 1920s?

Depression, Dissent, and the New Deal

1929–1940

WINDOW TO THE PAST

A Sharecropper's Family in Washington County, Arkansas, 1935

Photographers captured ordinary Americans as they tried to survive the hardships of the Great Depression. Through stark black-and-white photos they gave representation to those "forgotten Americans" who were, as Franklin Roosevelt put it, "ill-housed, ill-clad, ill-nourished."

▸ To discover more about this primary source can show us, see Source 22.8 on page 772.

Franklin D. Roosevelt Library

After reading this chapter you should be able to:

- Evaluate the Hoover administration's response to the Great Depression and its impact on the rural poor, working people, and minorities.

- Describe the major New Deal programs and assess their positive and negative effects on the groups they were designed to help.

- Explain how the New Deal expanded its scope after 1935 and why it came to an end in 1938.

COMPARING AMERICAN HISTORIES

In 1901, at the age of fifteen, Anna Eleanor Roosevelt saw her uncle Theodore succeed William McKinley as president. Like other girls of her generation, Eleanor was expected to marry and become a "charming wife." Eleanor appeared well on her way toward doing so when she married her distant cousin Franklin Delano Roosevelt in 1905. Over a ten-year period, Eleanor gave birth to six children, further reinforcing her status as a traditional woman of her class.

Two events, however, altered the expected course of her life. First, thirteen years into her marriage Eleanor discovered that her husband was having an affair with her social secretary, Lucy Mercer. She did not divorce him but made it clear that she would stay with him primarily as a mother to their children and a political partner. Second, in 1921 Franklin contracted polio.

(left) **Eleanor Roosevelt.** Library of Congress, 3c08091
(right) **Luisa Moreno.** Courtesy of Vicki L. Ruiz

Although he recovered, he would never walk again or stand without the aid of braces. This physical hardship allowed Eleanor to gain increased political influence with Franklin. After her husband won the presidency in 1932, Eleanor did not function as a typical First Lady. She played a very public role promoting her husband's agenda, and she also took advantage of her own extensive contacts in labor unions, civil rights organizations, and women's groups to advance a variety of causes. In many ways more liberal than her husband, Eleanor was a fierce advocate for the rights of women, minorities, workers, and the poor. Behind the scenes, she pushed her husband to move further to the political left.

Eleanor Roosevelt's proximity to power provided her with a unique position from which to confront the problems of her day. In contrast, Luisa Moreno provides a striking example of an activist whose American story bears little resemblance to that of Roosevelt. A native of Guatemala, Moreno moved to Mexico and then New York City. In the midst of the Great Depression, she worked as a seamstress in a sweatshop to support her young child and unemployed husband. Like tens of thousands of people disillusioned with capitalism, in 1930 she joined the Communist Party but quit several years later.

In 1935 Moreno went to Florida to organize cigar workers for the American Federation of Labor (AFL). Despite numerous successes, she grew tired of the AFL's refusal to recruit unskilled workers and jumped to the United Cannery, Agricultural, Packing, and Allied Workers of America (UCAPAWA), an affiliate of the Congress of Industrial Organizations (CIO).

Moreno also promoted the advancement of Latinos throughout the United States. In 1939 she helped create El Congreso de Pueblos de Habla Española (The Congress of Spanish-Speaking People). Besides championing equal access to jobs, education, housing, and health care, the organization pressed to end the segregation of Latinos in schools and public accommodations. Moreno was not nearly as well-known as Eleanor Roosevelt, but she worked just as hard to fight poverty, exploitation, and racial bigotry on behalf of people whom President Franklin Roosevelt called "the forgotten Americans." ∎

The American histories of Eleanor Roosevelt and Luisa Moreno are very different; both of their lives were shaped in fundamental ways by the same global catastrophe, the Great Depression. Even before the Great Depression, most Americans lived at or near the poverty level, surviving month to month. By 1933, millions of Americans had lost even this tenuous hold on economic security, as unemployment reached a record 25 percent. The Republican administration of President Herbert Hoover depended on private charity and voluntary efforts to meet the needs of downtrodden Americans afflicted by the Depression, but these efforts fell short of the vast need that grew during the Depression and left many frustrated. Proclaiming the establishment of a New Deal for America, Franklin Roosevelt expanded the power of the federal government by initiating relief, recovery, and reform measures, all the while drawing critics on the political left and right. In seeking to break from the past, Roosevelt occasionally overextended his reach, as he did in challenging the Supreme Court. Despite its successes, the New Deal did not end the depression and left minorities and the rural and urban poor still suffering.

The **Great Depression**

Herbert Hoover had the unenviable task of assuming the presidency in 1929 just as the economy was about to crumble. Given his long history of public service, he seemed the right man for the job. Hoover, however, was unwilling to make a fundamental break with conventional economic approaches and proved unable to effectively communicate his genuine concern for the plight of the poor. Despite his sincere efforts, the depression deepened. As this happened, many Americans, made desperate by their economic plight and angered by the inadequate response of their government, took to the streets in protest.

Hoover Faces the Depression. National prosperity was at its peak when the Republican Hoover entered the White House in March 1929. Hoover brought to the presidency a blend of traditional and progressive ideas. He believed that government and business should form voluntary partnerships to work toward common goals. Rejecting the principle of absolute laissez-faire, he nonetheless argued that the government should extend its influence lightly over the economy — to encourage and persuade sensible behavior, but not to impose itself on the private sector.

The Great Depression sorely tested Hoover's beliefs. Having placed his faith in cooperation rather than coercion, the president relied on voluntarism to get the nation through hard economic times. Hoover hoped that management and labor, through gentle persuasion, would hold steady on prices and wages. In the meantime, for those in dire need, the president turned to local communities and private charities. Hoover expected municipal and state governments to shoulder the burden of providing relief to the needy, just as they had during previous economic downturns.

Hoover's remedies failed to rally the country back to good economic health. Initially, businesspeople responded positively to the president's request to maintain the status quo, but when the economy did not bounce back, they lost confidence and defected. Nor did local governments and private agencies have the funds to provide relief to all those who needed it. With tax revenues in decline, some 1,300 municipalities across the country had gone bankrupt by 1933. Benevolent societies and religious groups could handle

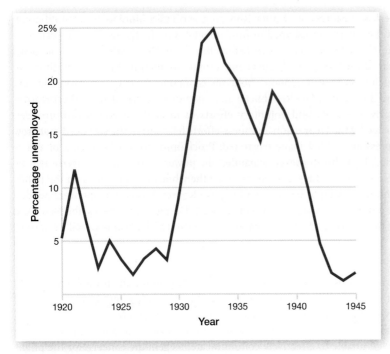

FIGURE 22.1   Unemployment, 1920–1945

Business prosperity and immigration restriction ensured low unemployment during most of the 1920s. When unemployment rose dramatically in the late 1920s, President Hoover failed to handle the crisis. During the 1930s, President Roosevelt's New Deal took initiatives to lower unemployment. What does this figure indicate about the effectiveness of New Deal programs on unemployment?

short-term misfortunes, but they could not cope with the ongoing disaster of mass unemployment (Figure 22.1).

As confidence in recovery fell and the economy sank deeper into depression, President Hoover shifted direction. He persuaded Congress to lower income tax rates and to allocate an unprecedented $423 million for federal public works projects. In 1929 the president signed into law the Agricultural Marketing Act, a measure aimed at raising prices for long-suffering farmers.

Hoover's recovery efforts fell short, however. He retreated from initiating greater spending because he feared government deficits more than unemployment. With federal accounting sheets showing a rising deficit, Hoover reversed course in 1932 and joined with Congress in sharply raising income, estate, and corporate taxes on the wealthy. This effectively slowed down investment and new production, throwing millions more American workers out of jobs. The Hawley-Smoot Act, passed by Congress in 1930, made matters worse. In an effort to replenish revenues and protect American farmers and companies from foreign competition, the act increased tariffs on agricultural and industrial imports. However, other countries retaliated by raising their import duties, which hurt American companies because it diminished demand for American exports.

In an exception to his aversion to spending, Hoover lobbied Congress to create the Reconstruction Finance Corporation (RFC) to supply loans to troubled banks, railroads, and insurance companies. By injecting federal dollars into these critical enterprises, the president and lawmakers expected to produce dividends that would trickle down from the top of the economic structure to the bottom. In 1932 Congress gave the RFC a budget of

$1.5 billion to employ people in public works projects, a significant allocation for those individuals hardest hit by the depression.

This notable departure from Republican economic philosophy failed to reach its goal. The RFC spent its budget too cautiously, and its funds reached primarily those institutions that could best afford to repay the loans, ignoring the companies in the greatest difficulty. Wealth never trickled down. Although Hoover was not indifferent to the plight of others, he was incapable of breaking away from his ideological preconceptions. He refused to support expenditures for direct relief (what today we call welfare) and hesitated to extend assistance for work relief because he believed that it would ruin individual initiative and character.

Hoover and the United States did not face the Great Depression alone; it was a worldwide calamity. By 1933 Germany, France, and Great Britain were all facing mass unemployment. In this climate of extreme social and economic unrest, authoritarian dictators came to power in a number of European countries, including Germany, Italy, Spain, and Portugal. Each claimed that his country's social and economic problems could be solved only by placing power in the hands of a single, all-powerful leader.

Hoovervilles and Dust Storms.
The depression hit all areas of the United States hard. In large cities, families crowded into apartments with no gas or electricity and little food to put on the table. In Los Angeles, people cooked their meals over wood fires in backyards. In many cities, the homeless constructed makeshift housing consisting of cartons, old newspapers, and cloth — what journalists derisively dubbed Hoovervilles. Thousands of hungry citizens wound up living under bridges in Portland, Oregon; in wrecked autos in city dumps in Brooklyn, New York, and Stockton, California; and in abandoned coal furnaces in Pittsburgh.

Soup Kitchen, 1931   At the height of the Great Depression, these unemployed men stand in a long line outside a Chicago soup kitchen waiting for a meal. Without major government relief efforts for the unemployed during the Hoover administration, such men depended mainly on the efforts of charity. In this instance, the notorious gangster Al Capone set up this establishment before going to federal prison for tax evasion in 1932. National Archives photo no. 306-NT-165319c

Rural workers fared no better. Landlords in West Virginia and Kentucky evicted coal miners and their families from their homes in the dead of winter, forcing them to live in tents. Farmers in the Great Plains, who were already experiencing foreclosures, were little prepared for the even greater natural disaster that laid waste to their farms. In the early 1930s, dust storms swept through western Kansas, eastern Colorado, western Oklahoma, the Texas Panhandle, and eastern New Mexico, in an area that came to be known as the Dust Bowl, destroying crops and plant and animal life (Map 22.1). The storms resulted from both climatological and human causes. A series of droughts had destroyed crops and turned the earth into sand, which gusts of wind deposited on everything that lay in their path. Though they did not realize it at the time, plains farmers, by focusing on growing wheat for income, had neglected planting trees and grasses that would have kept the earth from eroding and turning into dust. **See Primary Source Project 22: The Depression in Rural America, page 770.**

As the storms continued through the 1930s, most residents—approximately 75 percent— remained on the plains. Millions, however, headed for California looking for relief from the plague of swirling dirt and hoping to find jobs in the state's fruit and vegetable fields. Although they came from several states besides Oklahoma, these migrants came to be known as "Okies," a derogatory term used by those who resented and looked down on the poverty-stricken newcomers to their communities. John Steinbeck's novel *The Grapes of Wrath* (1939) portrayed the plight of the fictional Joad family as storms and a bank fore-closure destroyed their Oklahoma farm and sent them on the road to California.

Challenges for Minorities. Given the demographics of the workforce, the over-whelming majority of Americans who lost their jobs were white men; yet racial and ethnic minorities, including African Americans, Latinos, and Asian Americans, suffered

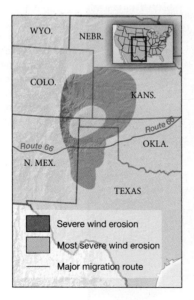

MAP 22.1   The Dust Bowl

Although "Okies" was the term used for the migrants escaping the Dust Bowl and heading to California, as depicted in John Steinbeck's classic novel *Grapes of Wrath*, Oklahoma was not the only state from where they came. Many of those who fled the terrible windstorms also journeyed from their homes in Kansas, Texas, and Colorado. Seen at the time as a natural phenomenon, the dust storms in fact originated from man-made agricultural practices that eroded the soil.

disproportionate hardship. Racial discrimination had kept these groups from achieving economic and political equality, and the Great Depression added to their woes.

Traditionally the last hired and the first fired, blacks occupied the lowest rungs on the industrial and agricultural ladders. "The depression brought everybody down a peg or two," the African American poet Langston Hughes wryly commented. "And the Negroes had but few pegs to fall." Despite the great migration to the North during and after World War I, three-quarters of the black population still lived in the South. Mainly sharecroppers and tenant farmers, black southerners were mired in debt that they could not repay as crop prices plunged to record lows during the 1920s. As white landowners struggled to save their farms by introducing machinery to cut labor costs, they forced black sharecroppers off the land and into even greater poverty. Nor was the situation better for black workers employed at the lowest-paying jobs as janitors, menial laborers, maids, and laundresses. On average, African Americans earned $200 a year, less than one-quarter of the average wage of white factory workers.

The economic misfortune that African Americans experienced was compounded by the fact that they lived in a society rigidly constructed to preserve white supremacy. The 25 percent of blacks living in the North faced racial discrimination in employment, housing, and the criminal justice system, but at least they could express their opinions and desires by voting. By contrast, black southerners remained segregated and disfranchised by law. The depression also exacerbated racial tensions, as whites and blacks competed for the shrinking number of jobs. Lynching, which had declined during the 1920s, surged upward — in 1933 twenty-four blacks lost their lives to this form of terrorism.

Events in Scottsboro, Alabama reflected the special misery African Americans faced during the Great Depression. Trouble erupted in 1931 when two young, unemployed white women, Ruby Bates and Victoria Price, snuck onto a freight train heading to Huntsville, Alabama. Before the train reached the Scottsboro depot, a fight broke out between black and white men on top of the freight car occupied by the two women. After the train pulled in to Scottsboro, the local sheriff arrested nine black youths between the ages of twelve and nineteen. Charges of assault quickly escalated into rape, when the women told authorities that the black men in custody had molested them on board the train.

The defendants' court-appointed attorney was less than competent and had little time to prepare his clients' cases. It probably made no difference, as the all-white male jury swiftly convicted the accused and awarded the harshest of sentences; only the youngest defendant was not given the death penalty. The Supreme Court spared the lives of the **Scottsboro Nine** by overturning their guilty verdicts in 1932 on the grounds that the defendants did not have adequate legal representation and again in 1935 because blacks had been systematically excluded from the jury pool. Although Ruby Bates had recanted her testimony and there was no physical evidence of rape, retrials in 1936 and 1937 produced the same guilty verdicts, but this time the defendants did not receive the death penalty — a minor victory considering the charges. State prosecutors dismissed charges against four of the accused, all of whom had already spent six years in jail. Despite international protests against this racist injustice, the last of the remaining five did not leave jail until 1950.

Explore ▸

See Source 22.1 for a letter from the Scottsboro prisoners.

Scottsboro Nine, 1933 Two years after their original conviction, the Scottsboro defendants discuss their new trial with their attorney Samuel Leibowitz in 1933 while still in prison. Flanked by two guards, they are from the left, Olen Montgomery, Clarence Norris, Willie Robertson, Andrew Wright, Ozie Powell, Eugene Williams, Charlie Weems, and Roy Wright. Haywood Patterson is seated next to Leibowitz. Known as the "Scottsboro Boys," at the time of their arrest they ranged in age from twelve to nineteen. Granger, NYC

Racism also worsened the impact of the Great Depression on Spanish-speaking Americans. Mexicans and Mexican Americans made up the largest segment of the Latino population living in the United States. Concentrated in the Southwest and California, they worked in a variety of low-wage factory jobs and as migrant laborers in fruit and vegetable fields. The depression reduced the Mexican-born population living in the United States in two ways. The federal government, in cooperation with state and local governments and private businesses, deported (or what officials called "repatriation") around one million Mexicans, a majority of whom were American citizens. Los Angeles officials organized more than a dozen deportation trains transporting thousands of Mexicans to the border. Many others returned to Mexico voluntarily when demand for labor in the United States dried up.

The exodus eased off by 1933, as the numbers of migrants no longer posed an economic threat and the Roosevelt administration adopted more humane policies. Those who remained endured growing hardships. Relief agencies refused to provide them with the same benefits as whites. Like African Americans, they encountered discrimination in public schools, in public accommodations, and at the ballot box. Conditions remained harshest for migrant workers toiling long hours for little pay and living in overcrowded

GUIDED ANALYSIS

Plea from the Scottsboro Prisoners, 1932

In 1931, nine black youths were arrested in Scottsboro, Alabama and charged with raping two white women. They were quickly convicted, and eight were sentenced to death. (One of the nine, Roy Wright, was twelve years old, and the prosecution did not seek the death penalty.) In this letter to the editor of the *Negro Worker*, a Communist magazine, the Scottsboro Nine plead their innocence and ask for help. A year had passed since their arrest and trial, which would account for their ages in the following statement recorded as between thirteen to twenty. Only those sentenced to death signed the letter.

Source 22.1

Why do you think they mention their ages?

What tactics did Alabama officials use on the prisoners? What was their purpose?

Why do the Scottsboro prisoners repeatedly emphasize that they were workers?

We have been sentenced to die for something we ain't never done. Us poor boys have been sentenced to burn up on the electric chair for the reason that we is workers—and the color of our skin is black. We like any one of you workers is none of us older than 20. Two of us is 14 and one is 13 years old.

What we guilty of? Nothing but being out of a job. Nothing but looking for work. Our kinfolk was starving for food. We wanted to help them out. So we hopped a freight—just like any one of you workers might a done—to go down to Mobile to hunt work. We was taken off the train by a mob and framed up on rape charges.

At the trial they gave us in Scottsboro we could hear the crowd yelling, "Lynch the Niggers." We could see them toting those big shotguns. Call 'at a fair trial? And while we lay here in jail, the boss-man make us watch 'em burning up other Negroes on the electric chair. "This is what you'll get," they say to us.

Working class boys, we asks you to save us from being burnt on the electric chair. We's only poor working class boys whose skin is black. . . . Help us boys. We ain't done nothing wrong.
[Signed] Andy Wright, Olen Montgomery, Ozie Powell, Charlie Weems, Clarence Norris, Haywood Patterson, Eugene Williams, Willie Robertson

Source: "Scottsboro Boys Appeal from Death Cells to the 'Toilers of the World,'" *The Negro Worker* 2, no. 5 (May 1932): 8–9.

Put It in Context

Why was it unlikely that black men in Alabama could receive a fair trial on the charge of raping a white woman?

and poorly constructed housing. In both fields and factories, employers had little incentive to improve the situation because there were plenty of white migrant workers to fill their positions.

The transient nature of agricultural work and the vulnerability of Mexican laborers made it difficult for workers to organize, but Mexican American laborers engaged in dozens

Mexican Migrant Worker, 1937
This photograph by Dorothea Lange shows a Mexican field worker on the edge of a frozen pea field in the Imperial Valley, California. Leaning on an automobile, he is holding a baby alongside a dilapidated shack. Demand for Mexican labor declined during the Great Depression as displaced farmers from the Dust Bowl moved west to take jobs formerly held by Mexicans. Government deportations further decreased the number of undocumented Mexican laborers in the United States. Library of Congress, 8b38632

of strikes in California and Texas in the early 1930s. Most ended in defeat, but a few, such as a strike of pecan shellers in San Antonio, Texas, led by Luisa Moreno, won better working conditions and higher wages. Despite these hard-fought victories, the condition of Latinos remained precarious.

On the West Coast, Asian Americans also remained economically and politically marginalized. Japanese immigrants eked out livings as small farmers, grocers, and gardeners, despite California laws preventing them from owning land. Many of their college-educated U.S.-born children found few professional opportunities available to them, and they often returned to work in family businesses. The depression magnified the problem. Like other racial and ethnic minorities, the Japanese found it harder to find even the lowest-wage jobs now that unemployed whites were willing to take them. As a result, about one-fifth of Japanese immigrants returned to Japan during the 1930s.

The Chinese suffered a similar fate. Although some 45 percent of Chinese Americans had been born in the United States and were citizens, people of Chinese ancestry remained isolated in ethnic communities along the West Coast. Discriminated against in schools and most occupations, many operated restaurants and laundries. During the depression, those Chinese who did not obtain assistance through governmental relief turned instead to their own community organizations and to extended families to help them through the hard times.

Filipino immigrants had arrived on the West Coast after the Philippines became a territory of the United States in 1901. Working as low-wage agricultural laborers, they were subject to the same kind of racial animosity as other dark-skinned minorities. Filipino farmworkers organized agricultural labor unions and conducted numerous strikes in California, but like their Mexican counterparts they were brutally repressed. In 1934 anti-Filipino hostility reached its height when Congress passed the Tydings-McDuffie

Act. The measure accomplished two aims at once: The act granted independence to the Philippines, and it restricted Filipino immigration into the United States.

Families under Strain.
With millions of men unemployed, women faced increased family responsibilities. Stay-at-home wives had to care for their children and provide emotional support for out-of-work husbands who had lost their role as the family bread-winner. Despite the loss of income, homemakers continued their daily routines of shopping, cooking, cleaning, and child rearing.

Disproportionate male unemployment led to an increase in the importance of women's income. The depression hit male-dominated industries like steel mills and auto-makers the hardest. As a result, men were more likely to lose their jobs than women. Although more women held on to their jobs, their often meager wages had to go further because many now had to support unemployed fathers and husbands. During the 1930s, federal and local governments sought to increase male employment by passing laws to keep married women from holding civil service and teaching positions. Nonetheless, more and more married women entered the workplace, and by 1940 the proportion of women in the job force had grown by about 25 percent.

As had been the case in previous decades, a higher proportion of African American women than white women worked outside the home in the 1930s. By 1940 about 40 percent of African American women held jobs, compared to about 25 percent of white women. Racial discrimination played a key role in establishing this pattern. Black men faced higher unemployment rates than did their white counterparts, and what work was available was often limited to the lowest-paying jobs. As a result, black women faced greater pressure to supplement family incomes. Still, unemployment rates for black women reached as high as 50 percent during the 1930s.

Despite increased burdens, most American families remained intact and discovered ways to survive the economic crisis. They pared down household budgets, made do without telephones and new clothes, and held on to their automobiles for longer periods of time. What money they managed to save they often spent on movies. Comedies, gangster movies, fantasy tales, and uplifting films helped viewers forget their troubles, if only for a few hours. Radio remained the chief source of entertainment, and radio sales doubled in the 1930s as listeners tuned in to soap operas, comedy and adventure shows, news reports, and musical programs.

Organized Protest.
As the depression deepened, angry citizens found ways to express their discontent. Farmers had suffered economic hardship longer than any other group. Even before 1929, they had seen prices spiral downward, but in the early 1930s agricultural income plummeted 60 percent, and one-third of farmers lost their land (Figure 22.2). Some farmers decided that the time had come for drastic action. In the summer of 1932, Milo Reno, an Iowa farmer, created the Farm Holiday Association to organize farmers to keep their produce from going to market and thereby raise prices. Strikers from the association blocked roads and kept reluctant farmers in line by smashing their truck windshields and headlights and slashing their tires. When law enforcement officials arrested fifty-five demonstrators in Council Bluffs, thousands of farmers marched on the jail and forced their release. Despite armed attempts to prevent foreclosures and the intentional

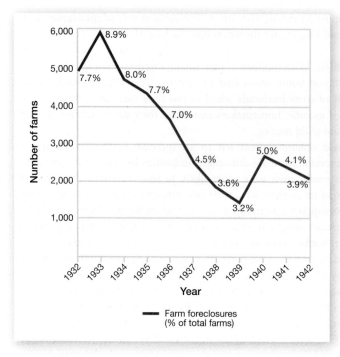

FIGURE 22.2 Farm Foreclosures, 1932–1942

A drop of 60 percent in prices led to a wave of farm foreclosures and rural protests in the early 1930s. From 1934 on, federal programs that promoted rural electrification, crop allotments, commodity loans, and mortgage credits allowed many farmers to retain their land. Is this figure adequate measure of the impact of New Deal programs on tenant farmers and sharecroppers? Explain why or why not.

destruction of vast quantities of farm produce, the Farm Holiday Association failed to achieve its goal of raising prices.

Disgruntled urban residents also resorted to protest. Although the Communist Party remained a tiny group of just over 10,000 members in 1932, it played a large role in organizing the dispossessed. In major cities such as New York, Communists set up unemployment councils and led marches and rallies demanding jobs and food. In Harlem, the party endorsed rent strikes by African American apartment residents against their landlords. Party members did not confine their activities to the urban Northeast. They also went south to defend the Scottsboro Nine and to organize industrial workers in the steel mills of Birmingham and sharecroppers in the surrounding rural areas of Alabama. On the West Coast, Communists unionized seamen and waterfront workers and led strikes. They also recruited writers, directors, and actors in Hollywood.

One of the most visible protests of the early 1930s centered on the Ford factory in Dearborn, Michigan. As the depression worsened after 1930, Henry Ford, who had initially pledged to keep employee wages steady, changed his mind and reduced wages. On March 7, 1932, spearheaded by Communists, three thousand autoworkers marched from Detroit to Ford's River Rouge plant in nearby Dearborn. When they reached the factory town, they faced policemen indiscriminately firing bullets and tear gas, which killed four demonstrators. The attack provoked great outrage. Around forty thousand mourners attended the funeral of the four protesters; sang the Communist anthem, the "Internationale"; and surrounded the caskets, which were draped in a red banner emblazoned with a picture of Bolshevik hero Vladimir Lenin.

Protests spread beyond Communist agitators. The federal government faced an uprising by some of the nation's most patriotic and loyal citizens — World War I veterans. Scheduled to receive a $1,000 bonus for their service, unemployed veterans could not wait until the payment date arrived in 1945. Instead, in the spring of 1932 a group of ex-soldiers from Portland, Oregon set off on a march on Washington, D.C., to demand immediate payment of the bonus by the federal government. By the time they reached the nation's capital, the ranks of this **Bonus Army** had swelled to around twenty thousand veterans. They camped in the Anacostia Flats section of the city, constructed ramshackle shelters, and in many cases moved their families in with them.

Although many veterans eventually returned home, much of the Bonus Army remained in place until late July. When President Hoover decided to clear the capital of the protesters, violence ensued. Rather than engaging in a measured and orderly removal, General Douglas MacArthur overstepped presidential orders and used excessive force to disperse the veterans and their families. The Third Cavalry, commanded by George S. Patton, torched tents and sent their residents fleeing from the city.

In this one-sided battle, the biggest loser was President Hoover. Through four years of the country's worst depression, Hoover had lost touch with the American people. His cheerful words of encouragement fell increasingly on deaf ears. As workers, farmers, and veterans stirred in protest, Hoover appeared aloof, standoffish, and insensitive.

REVIEW & RELATE

- How did President Hoover respond to the problems and challenges created by the Great Depression?

- How did different segments of the American population experience the depression?

The **New Deal**

The nation was ready for a change, and on election day 1932, with hard times showing no sign of abating, Democratic presidential candidate Franklin Delano Roosevelt, the governor of New York, defeated Hoover easily. Roosevelt won 57 percent of the popular votes and garnered an overwhelming 472 electoral votes. He attracted a coalition of the poor: farmers and city dwellers, laborers and immigrants, northerners and southerners (the majority of African Americans did not join the coalition until 1936). Roosevelt's sizable victory provided him with a mandate to take the country in a bold new direction. However, few Americans, including Roosevelt himself, knew exactly what the new president meant to do or what his pledge of a New Deal would mean for the country.

Roosevelt Restores Confidence.

As a presidential candidate, Roosevelt presented no clear, coherent policy. He did not spell out how his plans for the country would differ from Hoover's, but he did refer broadly to providing a "new deal" and bringing to the White House "persistent experimentation." Roosevelt's appeal derived more from the genuine compassion he was able to convey than from the specificity of his promises. In this context, Eleanor Roosevelt's evident concern for people's suffering and her history of activism made Franklin Roosevelt even more attractive.

Franklin Delano Roosevelt Campaigning in Kansas, 1932 New York governor Franklin D. Roosevelt promises a "new deal" to farmers in Topeka, Kansas as he campaigns for president in 1932 as the Democratic candidate. Photographers were careful not to show that Roosevelt was unable to use his legs, which were paralyzed after he contracted polio in 1921. His son James, seated at the left, often propped up his father so that it appeared he could stand on his own, as he is doing in this photograph. Roosevelt forged a coalition of farmers and urban workers and easily defeated the incumbent Hoover. Franklin D. Roosevelt Library

Instead of any fixed ideology, FDR, as he was popularly known, followed what one historian has called "pragmatic humanism." A seasoned politician who understood the need for flexibility, Roosevelt blended principle and practicality. "It is common sense," Roosevelt explained, "to take a method and try it. If it fails, admit it frankly and try another. But above all, try something." More than any president before him, FDR created an expectation among Americans that the federal government would take concrete action to improve their lives. A Colorado woman expressed her appreciation to Eleanor Roosevelt: "Your husband is great. He seems lovable even tho' he is a 'politician.'" The New Deal would take its twists and turns, but Roosevelt never lost the support of the majority of Americans.

Starting with his inaugural address, in which he declared that "the only thing we have to fear is fear itself," Roosevelt took on the task of rallying the American people and restoring their confidence in the future. Using the power of radio to communicate directly, Roosevelt delivered regular fireside chats in which he boosted morale and informed his audience of the steps the government was taking to help solve their problems. Not limited to rhetoric, Roosevelt's **New Deal** would provide relief, put millions of people to work, raise prices for farmers, extend conservation projects, revitalize America's financial system, and rescue capitalism.

Steps toward Recovery.

President Roosevelt took swift action on entering office. In March 1933 he issued an executive order shutting down banks for several days to calm the panic that gripped many Americans in the wake of bank failures and the loss of their life's savings. Shortly after, Congress passed the administration's Emergency Banking Act, which subjected banks to Treasury Department inspection before they reopened, reorganized the banking system, and provided federal funds to bail out banks on the brink of closing. This assertion of federal power allowed solvent banks to reopen. Boosting confidence further, Congress passed the Glass-Steagall Act in June 1933. The measure created the **Federal Deposit Insurance Corporation (FDIC)**, insuring personal savings accounts up to $5,000, and detached commercial banks from investment banks to avoid risky speculation. The president also sought tighter supervision of the stock market. By June 1934 Roosevelt had signed into law measures setting up the Securities and Exchange Commission (SEC) to regulate the stock market and ensure that corporations gave investors accurate information about their portfolios.

The regulation of banks and the stock exchange did not mean that Roosevelt was antibusiness. He affirmed his belief in a balanced budget and sought to avoid a $1 billion deficit by cutting government workers' salaries and lowering veterans' pensions. Roosevelt also tried to keep the budget under control by ending prohibition, which would allow the government to tax alcohol sales and eliminate the cost of enforcement. The Twenty-first Amendment, ratified in 1933, ended the more than decade-long experiment with temperance.

As important as these measures were, the Roosevelt administration had much more to accomplish before those hardest hit by the depression felt some relief. Roosevelt viewed the Great Depression as a crisis analogous to war and adapted many of the bureaus and commissions used during World War I to ensure productivity and mobilize popular support to fit the current economic emergency. Many former progressives lined up behind Roosevelt, including women reformers and social workers who had worked in government and private agencies during the 1920s. At his wife Eleanor's urging, Roosevelt appointed one of them, Frances Perkins, as the first woman to head a cabinet agency — the Department of Labor.

Rehabilitating agriculture and industry stood at the top of the New Deal's priority list. Farmers came first. In May 1933 Congress passed the **Agricultural Adjustment Act**, aimed at raising prices by reducing production. The Agricultural Adjustment Administration (AAA) paid farmers subsidies to produce less in the future, and for farmers who had already planted their crops and raised livestock, the agency paid them to plow under a portion of their harvest, slaughter hogs, and destroy dairy products. By 1935 the program succeeded in raising farm income by 50 percent. Large farmers remained the chief beneficiaries of the AAA because they could afford to cut back production. In doing so, especially in the South, they forced off the land sharecroppers who no longer had plots to farm. Even when sharecroppers managed to retain a parcel of their acreage, AAA subsidies went to the landowners, who did not always distribute the designated funds owed to the sharecroppers. Though poor white farmers felt the sting of this injustice, the system of white supremacy existing in the South guaranteed that blacks suffered most.

The Roosevelt administration exhibited its boldest initiative in creating the **Tennessee Valley Authority (TVA)** in 1933, to bring low-cost electric power to rural areas and help redevelop the entire Tennessee River valley region through flood-control projects. In contrast to the AAA and other farm programs in which control stayed in private hands, the TVA owned and supervised the building and operation of public power plants. For farmers outside the Tennessee River valley, the Rural Electrification Administration helped them obtain cheap electric power starting in 1935, and for the first time tens of thousands of farmers experienced the modern conveniences that electricity brought (though most farmers would not get electric power until after World War II).

Roosevelt and Congress also acted to deal with the soil erosion problem behind the dust storms. In 1933 the Department of the Interior established a Soil Erosion Service, and two years later Congress created a permanent Soil Conservation Service in the Department of Agriculture. Although these measures would prove beneficial in the long run, they did nothing to prevent even more severe storms from rolling through the Dust Bowl in 1935 and 1936.

At the same time, Roosevelt concentrated on industrial recovery. In 1933 Congress passed the National Industrial Recovery Act, which established the **National Recovery Administration (NRA)**. This agency allowed business, labor, and the public (represented by government officials) to create codes to regulate production, prices, wages, hours, and collective bargaining. Designers of the NRA expected that if wages rose and prices remained stable, consumer purchasing power would climb, demand would grow, and businesses would put people back to work. For this plan to work, businesspeople needed to keep prices steady by absorbing some of the costs of higher wages. Businesses that joined the NRA displayed the symbol of the blue eagle to signal their patriotic participation.

However, the NRA did not function as planned, nor did it bring the desired recovery. Businesses did not exercise the necessary restraint to keep prices steady. Large manufacturers dominated the code-making committees, and because Roosevelt had suspended enforcement of the antitrust law, they could not resist taking collective action to force smaller firms out of business. The NRA legislation guaranteed labor the right to unionize, but the agency did not vigorously enforce collective bargaining. The government failed to intervene to redress the imbalance of power between labor and management because Roosevelt depended primarily on big business to generate economic improvement. Moreover, the NRA had created codes for too many businesses, and government officials could not properly oversee them all. In 1935 the Supreme Court delivered the final blow to the NRA by declaring it an unconstitutional delegation of legislative power to the president.

Direct Assistance and Relief.

Economic recovery programs were important, but they took time to take effect, and many Americans needed immediate help. Thus, relief efforts and direct job creation were critical parts of the New Deal. Created in the early months of Roosevelt's term, the Federal Emergency Relief Administration (FERA) provided cash grants to states to revive their bankrupt relief efforts. Roosevelt chose Harry Hopkins, the chief of New York's relief agency, to head the FERA and distribute its initial $500 million appropriation. On the job for two hours, Hopkins had already spent $5 million. He did not calculate whether a particular plan "would work out in the long run," because, as he remarked, "people don't eat in the long run — they eat every day."

National Recovery Administration Eagles   President Roosevelt initiated the National Recovery Administration in 1933 as the centerpiece of his New Deal to stimulate economic growth. The city of Miami Beach employed these bathing beauties to attract conventioneers and vacationers to its hotels. Under the NRA code, they worked a forty-hour week and showed their satisfaction by sporting the NRA blue eagle insignia on their backs. © Bettmann/Getty Images

Harold Ickes, secretary of the interior and director of the Public Works Administration (PWA), oversaw efforts to rebuild the nation's infrastructure. Funding architects, engineers, and skilled workers, the PWA built the Grand Coulee, Boulder, and Bonneville dams in the West; the Triborough Bridge in New York City; 70 percent of all new schools constructed between 1933 and 1939; and a variety of municipal buildings, sewage plants, port facilities, and hospitals.

Explore ▶

See Sources 22.2 and 22.3 for two views of direct relief.

Yet neither the FERA nor the PWA provided enough relief to the millions who faced the winter of 1933–1934 without jobs or the money to heat their homes. In response, Hopkins persuaded Roosevelt to launch a temporary program to help needy Americans get through this difficult period. Both men favored "work relief"—giving people jobs rather than direct welfare payments whenever practical. The Civil Works Administration (CWA) lasted four months, but in that brief time it employed more than 4 million people on about 400,000 projects that built 500,000 miles of roads, 40,000 schools, 3,500 playgrounds, and 1,000 airports.

One of Roosevelt's most successful relief programs was the **Civilian Conservation Corps (CCC)**, created shortly after he entered the White House. The CCC recruited unmarried men between the ages of eighteen and twenty-five for a two-year stint, putting

Letters to Eleanor Roosevelt

During the 1930s Americans wrote to President Roosevelt and the First Lady in unprecedented numbers, revealing their personal desperation and their belief that the Roosevelts would respond to their individual pleas. Though most requested government assistance, not all letter writers favored the New Deal. In the following letters written to Eleanor Roosevelt, high school student Mildred Isbell from Albertville, Alabama asks the First Lady for personal help, while Minnie Hardin of Columbus, Indiana expresses her frustration with direct relief programs.

Source 22.2

Mildred Isbell to Mrs. Roosevelt, January 1, 1936

Dear Mrs. Roosevelt,

My life has been a story to me and most of the time a miserable one. When I was 7 years old my father left for a law school and never returned. This leaving my mother and 4 children. He left us a small farm, but it could not keep us up. For when we went back to mother's people the renters would not give us part, and we were still dependent. I have been shoved to pillar to post that I feel very relieved to get off to my self.

I am now 15 years old and in the 10th grade. I have always been smart but I never had a chance as all of us is so poor. I hope to complete my education, but I will have to quit school I guess if there is no clothes can be bought. (Don't think that we are on the relief.) Mother has been a faithful servent for us to keep us to gather. I don't see how she has made it.

Mrs Roosevelt, don't think I am just begging, but that is all you can call it I guess. There is no harm in asking I guess eather. Do you have any old clothes you have throwed back. You don't realize how honored I would feel to be wearing your clothes. I don't have a coat at all to wear. The clothes may be too large but I can cut them down so I can wear them. Not only clothes but old shoes, hats, hose, and under wear would be appreciated so much. I have three brothers that would appreciate any old clothes of your boys or husband. I wish you could see the part of North Alabama now. The trees, groves, and every thing is covered with ice and snow. It is a very pretty scene. But Oh, how cold it is here. People can hardly stay comfortable.

Sources: Mildred Isbell, letter to Eleanor Roosevelt, January 1, 1936; Minnie Hardin, letter to Eleanor Roosevelt, December 14, 1937, Eleanor Roosevelt Papers, Series 190, Miscellaneous, 1937, Franklin D. Roosevelt Library.

them to work planting forests; cleaning up beaches, rivers, and parks; and building bridges and dams. Participants received $1 per day, and the government sent $25 of the $30 in monthly wages directly to their families, helping make this the most popular of all New Deal programs. The CCC employed around 2.5 million men and lasted until 1942.

New Deal Critics. Despite the unprecedented efforts of the Roosevelt administration to spark recovery, provide relief, and encourage reform between 1933 and 1935, the country remained in depression, and unemployment still hovered around 20 percent. Roosevelt

Source 22.3

Minnie Hardin to Mrs. Roosevelt, December 14, 1937

Mrs. Roosevelt:

I suppose from your point of view the work relief, old age pensions, slum clearance, and all the rest seems like a perfect remedy for all the ills of this country, but I would like for you to see the results, as the other half see them.

We have always had a shiftless, never-do-well class of people whose one and only aim in life is to live without work. I have been rubbing elbows with this class for nearly sixty years and have tried to help some of the most promising and have seen others try to help them, but it can't be done. We cannot help those who will not try to help themselves and if they do try, a square deal is all they need, and by the way that is all this country needs or ever has needed: a square deal for all

and then, let each paddle their own canoe, or sink.

There has never been any necessity for any one who is able to work, being on relief in this locality, but there have been many eating the bread of charity and they have lived better than ever before. I have had taxpayers tell me that their children came from school and asked why they couldn't have nice lunches like the children on relief. The women and children around here have had to work at the fields to help save the crops and several women fainted while at work and at the same time we couldn't go up or down the road without stumbling over some of the reliefers, moping around carrying dirt from one side of the road to the other and back again, or else asleep.

Interpret the Evidence

1. How does each writer explain the source of poverty and the attitudes of poor people?
2. If Minnie Hardin were answering Mildred Isbell's letter, what would she say to her?

Put It in Context

How did the New Deal tackle poverty?

---

found himself under attack from both the left and the right. On the right, conservatives questioned New Deal spending and the growth of big government. On the left, the president's critics argued that he had not done enough to topple wealthy corporate leaders from power and relieve the plight of the downtrodden.

In 1934 officials of the Du Pont Corporation and General Motors formed the American Liberty League. From the point of view of the league's founders, the New Deal was little more than a vehicle for the spread of socialism and communism. The organization spent $1 million attacking what it considered to be Roosevelt's "dictatorial" policies and his assaults on free enterprise. The league, however, failed to attract support beyond a small group of northern industrialists, Wall Street bankers, and disaffected Democrats.

Corporate leaders also harnessed Christian ministers to promote their pro-capitalism, anti–New Deal message. The United States Chamber of Commerce and the National Association of Manufacturers allied with clergymen to challenge "creeping socialism." In 1935 the Reverend James W. Fifield founded Spiritual Mobilization and, from the pulpit of his wealthy First Congregational Church in Los Angeles, praised capitalism as a pillar of Christianity and attacked the "pagan statism" of the New Deal.

Roosevelt also faced criticism from the left. Communist Party membership reached its peak of around 75,000 in 1938, and though the party remained relatively small in numbers, it attracted intellectuals and artists whose voices could reach the larger public. Party members led unionizing drives in both the North and the South and displayed great talent and energy in organizing workers where resistance to unions was greatest. In the mid-1930s, the party followed the Soviet Union's antifascist foreign policy and joined with left-leaning, non-Communist groups, such as unions and civil rights organizations, to oppose the growing menace of fascism in Europe, particularly in Germany and Italy. By the end of the decade, however, the party had lost many members after the Soviet Union reversed its anti-Nazi foreign policy.

The greatest challenge to Roosevelt came from a trio of talented men who reflected diverse beliefs. Francis Townsend, a retired California physician, proposed a "Cure for Depressions." In 1934 he formed the Old-Age Revolving Pensions Corporation, whose title summed up the doctor's idea. Townsend would have the government give all Americans over the age of sixty a monthly pension of $200 if they retired and spent the entire stipend each month. Retirements would open up jobs for younger workers, and the

Father Charles E. Coughlin
Father Charles E. Coughlin spoke at Cleveland Stadium in 1936 on behalf of Ohio congressional candidates who had been endorsed by his National Union for Social Justice. Coughlin, a Catholic priest and a stern critic of President Roosevelt, advocated the nationalization of banks and other industries, protection of worker rights, and monetary reform. Despite Coughlin's outspoken opposition, Roosevelt easily won reelection in 1936. © Bettmann/Getty Images

income these workers received, along with the pension for the elderly, would pump ample funds into the economy to promote recovery. The government would fund the Townsend plan with a 2 percent "transaction" or sales tax. By 1936 Townsend Clubs had attracted about 3.5 million members throughout the country, and one-fifth of all adults in the United States signed a petition endorsing the Townsend plan.

While Townsend appealed mainly to the elderly, Charles E. Coughlin, a priest from the Detroit area, attracted Catholics and a lower-middle-class following. Father Coughlin used his popular national radio broadcasts to talk about economic and political issues. Originally a Roosevelt supporter, by 1934 Coughlin had begun criticizing the New Deal for catering to greedy bankers. He spoke to millions of radio listeners about the evils of the Roosevelt administration, the godless Communists who had allegedly infested it, and international bankers — coded language referring to Jews — who supposedly manipulated it. As the decade wore on, his strident anti-Semitism and his growing fondness for fascist dictatorships abroad overshadowed his economic justice message, and Catholic officials ordered him to stop broadcasting.

Huey Pierce Long of Louisiana posed the greatest political threat to Roosevelt. Unlike Townsend and Coughlin, Long had built and operated a successful political machine, first as governor and then as U.S. senator, taking on the special interests of oil and railroad corporations in his home state. Early on he had backed Roosevelt, but Long found the New Deal wanting. In 1934 Long established the Share Our Wealth society, promising to make "every man a king" by presenting families with a $5,000 homestead and a guaranteed annual income of $2,000. To accomplish this, Long proposed levying heavy income and inheritance taxes on the wealthy. Although the financial calculations behind his bold plan did not add up, Share Our Wealth clubs counted some seven million members. The swaggering senator departed from most of his segregationist southern colleagues by appealing to a coalition of disgruntled farmers, industrial workers, and African Americans. Before Long could help lead a third-party campaign for president, he was shot and killed in 1935.

REVIEW & RELATE

- What steps did Roosevelt take to stimulate economic recovery and provide relief to impoverished Americans during his first term in office?

- What criticisms did Roosevelt's opponents level against the New Deal?

The **New Deal** **Moves** to the **Left**

Facing criticism from within his own party about the pace and effectiveness of the New Deal, and with the 1936 election looming, Roosevelt moved to the left. He adopted harsher rhetoric against recalcitrant corporate leaders; beefed up economic and social programs for the unemployed, the elderly, and the infirm; and revived measures to redress the power imbalance between management and labor. In doing so, he fashioned a New Deal political coalition that would deliver a landslide victory in 1936 and allow the Democratic Party to dominate electoral politics for the next three decades.

Expanding Relief Measures. Even though the New Deal had helped millions of people, millions of others still felt left out, as the popularity of Townsend, Coughlin, and Long indicated. "We the people voted for you," a Columbus, Ohio worker wrote the president in disgust, "but it is a different story now. You have faded out on the masses of hungry, idle people. . . . The very rich is the only one who has benefited from your new deal."

In 1935 the president seized the opportunity to win his way back into the hearts of impoverished "forgotten Americans." Although Roosevelt favored a balanced budget, political necessity forced him to embark on deficit spending to expand the New Deal. Federal government expenditures would now exceed tax revenues, but New Dealers argued that these outlays would stimulate job creation and economic growth, which ultimately would replenish government coffers. Based on the highly successful but short-lived Civil Works Administration, the **Works Progress Administration (WPA)** provided jobs for the unemployed with a far larger budget, starting out with $5 billion. To ensure that the money would be spent, Roosevelt appointed Harry Hopkins to head the agency. Although critics condemned the WPA for employing people on unproductive "make-work" jobs — a criticism not entirely unfounded — overall the WPA did a great deal of good. The agency constructed or repaired more than 100,000 public buildings, 600 airports, 500,000 miles of roads, and 100,000 bridges. The WPA employed about 8.5 million workers during its eight years of operation.

The WPA also helped artists, writers, and musicians. Under its auspices, the Federal Writers Project, the Federal Art Project, the Federal Music Project, and the Federal Theater Project encouraged the production of cultural works and helped bring them to communities and audiences throughout the country. Writers Richard Wright, Ralph Ellison, Clifford Odets, Saul Bellow, John Cheever, Margaret Walker, and many others nourished both their works and their stomachs while employed by the WPA. Some painters, such as Jacob Lawrence, worked in the "easel division"; others created elaborate murals on the walls of post offices and other government buildings. Historians and folklorists researched and prepared city and state guides and interviewed black ex-slaves whose narratives of the system of bondage would otherwise have been lost.

In addition to the WPA, the National Youth Administration (NYA) employed millions of young people. Their work ranged from clerical assignments and repairing automobiles to building tuberculosis isolation units and renovating schools. Heading the NYA in Texas, the young Lyndon B. Johnson worked hard to expand educational and construction projects to unemployed whites and blacks. The Division of Negro Affairs, headed by the Florida educator Mary McLeod Bethune and the only minority group subsection in the NYA, ensured that African American youths would benefit from the programs sponsored by the agency.

Despite their many successes, these relief programs had a number of flaws. The WPA paid participants relatively low wages. The $660 in annual income earned by the average worker fell short of the $1,200 that a family needed to survive. In addition, the WPA limited participation to one family member. In most cases, this meant the male head of the household. As a result, women made up only about 14 percent of WPA workers, and even in the peak year of 1938, the WPA hired only 60 percent of eligible women. With the exception of the program for artists, most women hired by the WPA worked in lower-paying jobs than men.

New Deal Art　The Works Progress Administration, established by the Roosevelt administration in 1935, put Americans to work amid the ongoing depression. The WPA's Federal Art Project employed artists such as Ingrid E. Edwards of Minnesota, whose painting *Communications* features a newspaper boy, a telephone operator, a radio announcer, and a railroad train. Many of these works adorned public buildings. Collection of Minnesota Historical Society. Lent by Fine Arts Collection, Public Buildings Service, U.S. General Services. Gift of Ah-Gwah Ching Archive

Establishing Social Security. The elderly required immediate relief and insurance in a country that lagged behind the rest of the industrialized world in helping its aged workforce. In August 1935, the president rectified this shortcoming and signed into law the **Social Security Act**. The measure provided that at age sixty-five, eligible workers would receive retirement payments funded by payroll taxes on employees and employers. The law also extended beyond the elderly by providing unemployment insurance for those temporarily laid off from work and welfare payments for the disabled who were permanently out of a job as well as for destitute, dependent children of single parents.

The Social Security program had significant limitations. The act excluded farm, domestic, and laundry workers, who were among the neediest Americans and were disproportionately African American. The reasons for these exclusions were largely political. The president needed southern Democrats to support this measure, and as a Mississippi newspaper observed: "The average Mississippian can't imagine himself chipping in to pay pensions for able bodied Negroes to sit around in idleness." The system of financing pensions also proved unfair. The payroll tax, which imposed the same fixed percentage on all incomes, was a regressive tax, one that fell hardest on those with lower incomes. Nor did

TABLE 22.1   Major New Deal Measures, 1933–1938

Year	Legislation	Purpose
1933	National Industrial Recovery Act	Government, business, labor cooperation to set prices, wages, and production codes
	Agricultural Adjustment Act	Paid farmers to reduce production to raise prices
	Civilian Conservation Corps	Jobs for young men in conservation
	Public Works Administration	Construction jobs for the unemployed
	Federal Emergency Relief Act	Relief funds for the poor
	Tennessee Valley Authority	Electric power and flood control to rural areas
	Glass-Steagall Act	Insured bank deposits and separated commercial from investment banking
1934	Securities and Exchange Commission	Regulated the stock market
1935	Social Security Act	Provided retirement pensions, unemployment insurance, aid to the disabled, and payments to women with dependent children
	Wagner Act	Guaranteed collective bargaining for unions
	Works Progress Administration	Provided jobs to 8 million unemployed
1938	Fair Labor Standards Act	Established minimum hourly wage and maximum weekly working hours

Social Security take into account the unpaid labor of women who remained in the home to take care of their children.

Even with its flaws, Social Security revolutionized the expectations of American workers. It created a compact between the federal government and its citizens, and workers insisted that their political leaders fulfill their moral responsibilities to keep the system going. President Roosevelt recognized that the tax formula might not be economically sound, but he had a higher political objective in mind. He believed that payroll taxes would give contributors the right to collect their benefits and that "with those taxes in there, no damn politician can ever scrap my social security program."

Organized Labor Strikes Back. In 1935 Congress passed the **National Labor Relations Act**, also known as the Wagner Act for its leading sponsor, Senator Robert F. Wagner Sr. of New York. The law created the National Labor Relations Board (NLRB), which protected workers' right to organize labor unions without owner interference. During the 1930s, union membership rolls soared from fewer than 4 million workers to more than 10 million, including more than 800,000 women. At the outset of the depression, barely 6 percent of the labor force belonged to unions, compared with 33 percent in 1940.

Government efforts boosted this growth, but these spectacular gains were due primarily to workers' grassroots efforts set in motion by economic hard times. The number of striking workers during the first year of the Roosevelt administration soared from nearly

325,000 to more than 1.5 million. Organizers such as Luisa Moreno traveled the country to bring as many people as possible into the union movement. The most important development within the labor movement occurred in 1935, with the creation of the CIO. After the AFL, which consisted mainly of craft unions, rejected a proposal by John L. Lewis of the United Mine Workers to incorporate industrial workers under its umbrella, Lewis and representatives of seven other AFL unions defected and formed the CIO. Unlike the AFL, the new union sought to recruit a wide variety of workers without respect to race, gender, or region.

In 1937 the CIO mounted a full-scale organizing campaign. More than 4.5 million workers participated in some 4,700 strikes. Unions found new ways to protest poor working conditions and arbitrary layoffs. Members of the United Auto Workers (UAW), a CIO affiliate, launched a **sit-down strike** against General Motors (GM) in Flint, Michigan to win union recognition, higher wages, and better working conditions. Strikers refused to work but remained in the plants, shutting them down from the inside. When the company sent in local police forces to evict the strikers on January 11, 1937, the barricaded workers bombarded the police with spare machine parts and anything that was not bolted down.

Women's Emergency Brigade, 1937   After the United Auto Workers initiated a sit-down strike against General Motors in Flint, Michigan for union recognition, better working conditions, and higher wages, a group of their women relatives, friends, and coworkers formed the Women's Emergency Brigade. In this February 1937 demonstration, they held the clubs that they had used to smash windows at the Chevrolet Plant occupied by the strikers. AP Photo

The community rallied around the strikers, and wives and daughters called "union maids" formed the Women's Emergency Brigade, which supplied sit-downers with food and water and kept up their morale. Neither the state nor the federal government interfered with the work stoppage, and after six weeks GM acknowledged defeat and recognized the UAW.

The following year, the New Deal added a final piece of legislation sought by organized labor. The **Fair Labor Standards Act** (1938) established minimum wages at 40 cents an hour and maximum working hours at forty per week. By the end of the decade "big labor," as the AFL and CIO unions were known, had become a significant force in American politics and a leading backer of the New Deal.

A Half Deal for Minorities. President Roosevelt made significant gestures on behalf of African Americans. He appointed Mary McLeod Bethune and Robert Weaver to staff New Deal agencies and gathered an informal "Black Cabinet" in the nation's capital to advise him on matters pertaining to race. The Roosevelt administration also established the Civil Liberties Unit (later renamed Civil Rights Section) in the Department of Justice, which investigated racial discrimination. Eleanor Roosevelt acted as a visible symbol of the White House's concern with the plight of blacks. In 1939 Eleanor Roosevelt quit the Daughters of the American Revolution, a women's organization, when it refused to allow black singer Marian Anderson to hold a concert in Constitution Hall in Washington, D.C. Instead, the First Lady brought Anderson to sing on the steps of the Lincoln Memorial.

Perhaps the greatest measure of Franklin Roosevelt's impact on African Americans came when large numbers of black voters switched from the Republican to the Democratic Party in 1936, a pattern that has lasted to the present day. "Go turn Lincoln's picture to the wall," a black observer commented after the election. "That debt has been paid in full."

Yet overall the New Deal did little to break down racial inequality. President Roosevelt believed that the plight of African Americans would improve, along with that of all downtrodden Americans, as New Deal measures restored economic health. Black leaders disagreed. They argued that the NRA's initials stood for "Negroes Ruined Again" because the agency displaced black workers and approved lower wages for blacks than for whites. The AAA dislodged black sharecroppers. New Deal programs such as the CCC and those for building public housing maintained existing patterns of segregation. Both the Social Security Act and the Fair Labor Standards Act omitted from coverage jobs that black Americans were most likely to hold. In fact, the New Deal's big labor/big government alliance left out non-unionized industrial and agricultural workers, many of whom were African American and lacked bargaining power.

This pattern of halfway reform persisted for other minorities. Since the end of the Indian wars in 1890, Native Americans had lived in poverty, forced onto reservations where they were offered few economic opportunities and where whites carried out a relentless assault on their culture. By the early 1930s, American Indians earned an average income of less than $50 a year — compared with $800 for whites — and their unemployment rate was three times higher than that of white Americans. For the most part, they lived on lands that whites had given up on as unsuitable for farming or mining. The

Explore ▸

Compare differing interpretations of the New Deal in Sources 22.4 and 22.5.

The Indian New Deal   John Collier, commissioner of Indian affairs under President Roosevelt, favored a New Deal for Native Americans. An advocate for Indian culture, Collier implemented reform legislation that replaced the policy of Indian assimilation with that of self-determination. In this photo he appears with two Native Americans in the Southwest. MPI/Getty Images

policy of assimilation established by the Dawes Act of 1887 had exacerbated the problem by depriving Indians of their cultural identities as well as their economic livelihoods. In 1934 the federal government reversed its course. Spurred on by John Collier, the commissioner of Indian affairs, Congress passed the **Indian Reorganization Act (IRA)**, which terminated the Dawes Act, authorized self-government for those living on reservations, extended tribal landholdings, and pledged to uphold native customs and language.

Although the IRA brought economic and social improvements for Native Americans, many problems remained. Despite his considerable efforts, Collier approached Indian affairs from the top down. One historian remarked that Collier had "the zeal of a crusader who knew better than the Indians what was good for them." The Indian commissioner failed to appreciate the diversity of native tribes and administered laws that contradicted Native American political and economic practices. For example, the IRA required the tribes to operate by majority rule, whereas many of them reached decisions through consensus, which respected the views of the minority. Although 174 tribes accepted the IRA, 78 tribes, including the Seneca, Crow, and Navajo, rejected it.

New Deal or Raw Deal

The Great Depression posed major challenges for the U.S. government and its citizens. Depressions had struck many times throughout American history but none had been so severe or long lasting. Grasping that the economic collapse was not just the ordinary rise and fall of the business cycle, Franklin Roosevelt's New Deal brought the federal government into the lives of Americans to a greater extent than ever before. Yet the New Deal did not end the depression nor did it redistribute wealth and power more equally among the various segments of the population. The key question for historians remains, what did it do and how much reform did it bring to those who needed it most?

Source 22.4

William E. Leuchtenburg, The Roosevelt Reconstruction, 1963

Franklin Roosevelt re-created the modern Presidency. He took an office which had lost much of its prestige and power in the previous twelve years and gave it an importance which went well beyond what even Theodore Roosevelt and Woodrow Wilson had done…. Under Roosevelt, the White House became the focus of all government—the fountainhead of ideas, the initiator of action, the representative of the national interest.

Despite this encroachment of government on traditional business prerogatives, the New Deal could advance impressive claims to being regarded as a "savior of capitalism." Roosevelt's sense of the land, of family, and of the community marked him as a man with deeply ingrained conservative traits. In the New Deal years, the government sought deliberately, in Roosevelt's words, "to energize private enterprise." The RFC financed business, housing agencies underwrote home financing, and public works spending aimed to revive the construction industry. . . . Yet such considerations should not obscure the more important point: that the New Deal, however conservative it was in some respects and however much it owed to the past, marked a radically new departure. . . . The New Deal achieved a more just society by recognizing groups which had been largely unrepresented—staple farmers, industrial workers, particular ethnic groups, and a new intellectual-administrative class. Yet this was still a halfway revolution; it swelled the ranks of the bourgeoisie but left many Americans— sharecroppers, slum dwellers, most Negroes—outside of the new equilibrium.

Source: William E. Leuchtenburg, *Franklin D. Roosevelt and the New Deal, 1932–1940* (New York: Harper & Row, 1963), 327, 336, 347.

Decline of the New Deal.   Roosevelt's shift to the left paid political dividends, and in 1936 the president won reelection by a landslide. His sweeping victory proved to be one of the rare critical elections that signified a fundamental political realignment. Democrats replaced Republicans as the majority party in the United States, overturning thirty-six years of Republican rule. While Roosevelt had won convincingly in 1932, not until 1936 did the president put together a stable coalition that could sustain Democratic dominance for many years to come.

Source 22.5

Barton J. Bernstein, The Conservative Achievements of Liberal Reform, 1969

The liberal reforms of the New Deal did not transform the American system; they conserved and protected American corporate capitalism, occasionally by absorbing parts of threatening programs. There was no significant redistribution of power in American society, only limited recognition of other organized groups, seldom of unorganized peoples. Neither the bolder programs advanced by New Dealers nor the final legislation greatly extended the beneficence of government beyond the middle classes or draw upon the wealth of the few for the needs of the many. Designed to maintain the American system, liberal activity was directed toward essentially conservative goals. Experimentalism was most frequently limited to means; seldom did it extend to ends. Never questioning private enterprise, it operated within safe channels, far short of Marxism or even of native American radicalisms that offered structural critiques and structural solutions.

The New Deal was [not] … "a half-way revolution," as William Leuchtenburg concludes. Not only was the extension of representation to new groups less than full-fledged partnership, but the New Deal neglected many Americans — sharecroppers, tenant farmers, migratory workers and farm laborers, slum dwellers, unskilled workers, and unemployed Negroes. They were left outside the new order. … Yet by the power of rhetoric and through the appeals of political organization, the Roosevelt government managed to win or retain the allegiance of these people. Perhaps this is one of the crueler ironies of liberal politics, that the marginal men trapped in hopelessness were seduced by rhetoric, by the style and movement, of efforts seldom reaching beyond words.

Source: Barton J. Bernstein, "The New Deal: The Conservative Achievements of Liberal Reform," in *Towards a New Past: Dissenting Essays in American History*, edited by Barton J. Bernstein (New York, Vintage Books, 1969), 264, 281.

Examine the Sources

1. Compare the similarities and differences between the Leuchtenburg and Bernstein interpretations of Roosevelt and the New Deal.
2. Based on evidence in this chapter, evaluate the credibility of each interpretation.

Put it in Context

Explain why it was possible for President Roosevelt to get so much of his New Deal legislation passed.

In 1936 Roosevelt trounced Alfred M. Landon, the Republican governor of Kansas, and Democrats increased their congressional majorities by staggering margins. The vote broke down along class lines. Roosevelt won the votes of 80 percent of union members, 81 percent of unskilled workers, and 84 percent of people on relief, compared with only 42 percent of high-income voters. Millions of new voters came out to the polls, and most of them supported Roosevelt's New Deal coalition of the poor, farmers, urban ethnic minorities, unionists, white southerners, and African Americans.

The euphoria of his triumph, however, proved short-lived. An overconfident Roosevelt soon reached beyond his electoral mandate and within two years found himself unable to extend the New Deal. In 1937 Roosevelt devised a **court-packing plan** to ensure support of New Deal legislation and asked Congress to increase the size of the Supreme Court. He justified this as a matter of reform, claiming that the present nine-member Court could not handle its workload. Roosevelt attributed a good deal of the problem to the advanced age of six of the nine justices, who were over seventy years old. Under his proposal, the president would make one new appointment for each judge over the age of seventy who did not retire so long as the bench did not exceed fifteen members. In reality, Roosevelt schemed to "pack" the Court with supporters to prevent it from declaring New Deal legislation such as Social Security and the Wagner Act unconstitutional.

The plan backfired. Conservatives charged Roosevelt with seeking to destroy the separation of powers enshrined in the Constitution among the executive, legislative, and judicial branches. In the end, the president failed to expand the Supreme Court, but he preserved his legislative accomplishments. In a series of rulings, the chastened Supreme Court approved Social Security, the Wagner Act, and other New Deal legislation. Nevertheless, the political fallout from the court-packing fight damaged the president and his plans for further legislative reform.

Roosevelt's court-packing plan alienated many southern Democratic members of Congress who previously had sided with the president. Traditionally suspicious of the power of the federal government, southern lawmakers worried that Roosevelt was going too far toward centralizing power in Washington at the expense of states' rights. Southern Democrats formed a coalition with conservative northern Republicans who shared their concerns about the expansion of federal power and excessive spending on social welfare programs. Their antipathy toward labor unions further bound them. Although they held a minority of seats in Congress, this **conservative coalition** could block unwanted legislation by using the filibuster in the Senate (unlimited debate that could be shut down only with a two-thirds vote). After 1938 these conservatives made sure that no further New Deal legislation passed.

Roosevelt also lost support for New Deal initiatives because of the recession of 1937, which FDR's policies had triggered. When federal spending soared after passage of the WPA and other relief measures adopted in 1935, the president lost his economic nerve for deficit spending. He called for reduced spending, which increased unemployment and slowed economic recovery. In addition, as the Social Security payroll tax took effect, it reduced the purchasing power of workers, thereby exacerbating the impact of reduced government spending. Making the situation worse, pension payments were not scheduled to begin for several years. This "recession within the depression" further eroded congressional support for the New Deal.

The country was still deep in depression in 1939. Unemployment was at 17 percent, with more than 11 million people out of work. Most of those who were poor at the start of the Great Depression remained poor. Recovery came mainly to those who were temporarily impoverished as a result of the economic crisis. The distribution of wealth remained skewed toward the top. In 1933 the richest 5 percent of the population controlled 31 percent of disposable income; in 1939 the latter figure stood at 26 percent.

Against this backdrop of persistent difficult economic times, the president's popularity began to fade. In the midterm elections of 1938, Roosevelt campaigned against

Democratic conservatives in an attempt to reinvigorate his New Deal coalition. His efforts failed and upset many ordinary citizens who associated the tactic with that used by European dictators who had recently risen to power. As the decade came to a close, Roosevelt turned his attention away from the New Deal and increasingly toward a new war in Europe that threatened to engulf the entire world.

REVIEW & RELATE

- Why and how did the New Deal shift to the left in 1934 and 1935?

- Despite the president's landslide victory in 1936, why did the New Deal stall during Roosevelt's second term in office?

Conclusion: New Deal Liberalism

The Great Depression produced enormous economic hardships that the Hoover administration fell far short of relieving. Although Hoover's successor, Franklin Roosevelt, also failed to end the depression, in contrast he provided unprecedented economic assistance to the poor as well as the rich. The New Deal expanded the size of the federal government from 605,000 employees to more than 1 million during the 1930s. Moreover, the New Deal rescued the capitalist system, doing little to alter the fundamental structure of the American economy. Despite subjecting businesses to greater regulation, it left corporations, the stock market, farms, and banks in the hands of private enterprise. Indeed, by the end of the 1930s large corporations had more power over markets than ever before. Income and wealth remained unequally distributed, nearly to the same extent as they had been before Roosevelt took office in 1933.

Roosevelt forged a middle path between reactionaries and revolutionaries at a time when the fascist tyrants Adolf Hitler and Benito Mussolini gained power in Germany and Italy, respectively, and Joseph Stalin ruthlessly consolidated his rule in the Communist Soviet Union. By contrast, the American president expanded democratic capitalism, bringing a broader cross section of society to the decision-making table. Roosevelt's "broker state" of multiple competing interests provided for greater democracy than a government dominated exclusively by business elites. This system did not benefit those who remained unorganized and wielded little power, but marginalized groups — African Americans, Latinos, and Native Americans — did receive greater recognition and self-determination from the federal government. Indeed, these and other groups helped shape the New Deal. As Eleanor Roosevelt's history shows, women played key roles in campaigning for social welfare legislation. Others, like Luisa Moreno, helped organize workers and promoted ethnic pride among Latinos in the face of deportations. African Americans challenged racism and pressured the federal government to distribute services more equitably. American Indians won important democratic and cultural reforms, and though Asian Americans continued to encounter considerable discrimination on the West Coast, they joined to help each other. President Roosevelt also solidified the institution of the presidency as the focal point for public leadership. His cheerfulness, hopefulness, and pragmatism rallied millions of individuals behind him. Even after Roosevelt died in 1945, the public retained its expectation that leadership would come from the White House.

Through his programs and his force of personality, Franklin Roosevelt convinced Americans that he cared about their welfare and that the federal government would not ignore their suffering. However, he was not universally beloved: Millions of Americans despised him because they thought he was leading the country toward socialism, and he did not solve all the problems the country faced — it would take government spending for World War II to end the depression. Still, together with his wife, Eleanor, Franklin Roosevelt conveyed a sense that the American people belonged to a single community, capable of banding together to solve the country's problems, no matter how serious they were or how intractable they might seem.

TIMELINE OF **EVENTS**

1931	Scottsboro Nine tried for rape
1932–1939	Dust Bowl storms
1932	Reconstruction Finance Corporation created
	River Rouge autoworkers' strike
	Farm Holiday Association formed
	Bonus Army marches
1933	Roosevelt moves to stabilize banking and financial systems
	Agricultural Adjustment Act passed
	Federal Emergency Relief Administration created
	Tennessee Valley Authority created
	National Recovery Administration created
	Civilian Conservation Corps created
1934	Indian Reorganization Act passed
	Francis Townsend forms Old-Age Revolving Pensions Corporation
	Huey Long establishes Share Our Wealth movement
	Securities and Exchange Commission created
1935	Charles E. Coughlin organizes National Union for Social Justice
	Works Progress Administration created
	Social Security Act passed
	National Labor Relations Act passed
	Congress of Industrial Organizations founded
1937	Sit-down strike against General Motors
	Roosevelt proposes to increase the size of the Supreme Court
1938	Fair Labor Standards Act passed

KEY **TERMS**

Scottsboro Nine, *743*

Bonus Army, *749*

New Deal, *751*

Federal Deposit Insurance Corporation (FDIC), *751*

Agricultural Adjustment Act, *751*

Tennessee Valley Authority (TVA), *752*

National Recovery Administration (NRA), *752*

Civilian Conservation Corps (CCC), *753*

Works Progress Administration (WPA), *758*

Social Security Act, *759*

National Labor Relations Act, *760*

sit-down strike, *761*

Fair Labor Standards Act, *762*

Indian Reorganization Act (IRA), *763*

court-packing plan, *766*

conservative coalition, *766*

REVIEW & RELATE

1. How did President Hoover respond to the problems and challenges created by the Great Depression?
2. How did different segments of the American population experience the depression?
3. What steps did Roosevelt take to stimulate economic recovery and provide relief to impoverished Americans during his first term in office?
4. What criticisms did Roosevelt's opponents level against the New Deal?
5. Why and how did the New Deal shift to the left in 1934 and 1935?
6. Despite the president's landslide victory in 1936, why did the New Deal stall during Roosevelt's second term in office?

The Depression in Rural America

▶ Describe the challenges faced by rural Americans in the 1930s and explain the responses made by different individuals and groups to those problems.

During the 1930s, rural Americans' lives were devastated by the twin disasters of the Great Depression and, in the Great Plains, the most sustained drought in American history. But both crises only deepened the already difficult problems of many farmers. Agriculture in the South had long been dominated by sharecropping, a system that hampered crop diversification and left many African American tenant farmers vulnerable to exploitation by white landowners. In the Midwest, farmers had spent decades overgrazing pastures and exhausting the soil through overproduction. Prices dropped dramatically throughout the 1920s, and farmers were the only group whose incomes fell during that decade.

When the depression hit, many farmers did not have the resources to stay on their land, and farm foreclosures tripled in the early 1930s. Ferocious dust storms plagued many of the farmers who desperately struggled to hold on to their land (Source 22.6). Sharecroppers, tenant farmers, and former farm owners left their homes to find better opportunities, and a million people left the Great Plains alone (Source 22.8). Many ended up as migrant agricultural laborers in farms and orchards on the West Coast. Feeling overrun by refugees, California passed a law in 1937 making it a misdemeanor to bring into California any indigent person who was not a state resident. This law remained in effect until 1941.

Under the New Deal, the federal government acted in a number of ways to relieve the plight of farmers around the country. The Agricultural Adjustment Act attempted to raise crop prices and stabilize agricultural incomes by encouraging farmers to cut production. In doing so, however, it did little to relieve the plight of African American farmers (Source 22.7). The Farm Credit Act helped some farmers refinance mortgages at a lower rate, the Rural Electrification Administration brought electricity to farm areas previously without it, and the Soil Conservation Service advised farmers on how to properly cultivate their hillsides. The report of the Great Plains Committee (Source 22.10), another Roosevelt creation, detailed additional recommendations for helping the agricultural economy in the Midwest. In contrast, the federal government failed to protect Mexican migrant workers and instead deported a large number of them to Mexico (Source 22.9).

Source 22.6

Ann Marie Low | Dust Bowl Diary, 1934

When massive dust storms swept through the Midwest beginning in the early 1930s, they blew away the topsoil of a once productive farm region and created hazardous living conditions. Residents needed to clean and wash repetitively to perform even simple daily tasks. Ann Marie Low, a young woman living with her family in southeastern North Dakota, describes the difficulty of life in the Dust Bowl.

May 21, 1934, Monday . . .

Saturday Dad, Bud, and I planted an acre of potatoes. There was so much dirt in the air I couldn't see Bud only a few feet in front of me. Even the air in the house was just a haze. In the evening the wind died down, and Cap came to take me to the movie. We joked about how hard it is to get cleaned up enough to go anywhere.

The newspapers report that on May 10 there was such a strong wind the experts in Chicago estimated 12,000,000 tons of Plains soil was dumped on that city. By the next day the sun was obscured in Washington, D.C., and ships 300 miles out at sea reported dust settling on their decks.

Sunday the dust wasn't so bad. Dad and I drove cattle to the Big Pasture. Then I churned butter and baked a ham, bread, and cookies for the men, as no telling when Mama will be back.

May 30, 1934, Wednesday
Ethel got along fine, so Mama left her at the hospital and came to Jamestown by train Friday. Dad took us both home.

The mess was incredible! Dirt had blown into the house all week and lay inches deep on everything. Every towel and curtain was just black. There wasn't a clean dish or cooking utensil. There was no food. Oh, there were eggs and milk and one loaf left of the bread I baked the weekend before. I looked in the cooler box down the well (our refrigerator) and found a little ham and butter. It was late, so Mama and I cooked some ham and eggs for the men's supper because that was all we could fix in a hurry. It turned out they had been living on ham and eggs for two days.

. . . It took until 10 o'clock to wash all the dirty dishes. That's not wiping them—just washing them. The cupboards had to be washed out to have a clean place to put them.

Saturday was a busy day. Before starting breakfast I had to sweep and wash all the dirt off the kitchen and dining room floors, wash the stove, pancake griddle, and dining room table and chairs. There was cooking, baking, and churning to be done for those hungry men. Dad is 6 feet 4 inches tall, with a big frame. Bud is 6 feet 3 inches and almost as big-boned as Dad. We say feeding them is like filling a silo.

Mama couldn't make bread until I carried water to wash the bread mixer. I couldn't churn until the churn was washed and scalded. We just couldn't do anything until something was washed first. Every room had to have dirt almost shoveled out of it before we could wash floors and furniture.

Source: Ann Marie Low, *Dust Bowl Diary* (Lincoln: University of Nebraska Press, 1984), 96–97.

Source 22.7

John P. Davis | A Black Inventory of the New Deal, 1935

African Americans shouldered a double burden during the Great Depression. Already victims of racial oppression, they now fell into even deeper poverty while still experiencing discrimination. Although the New Deal tried to help farmers through the Agricultural Adjustment Administration, which paid farmers to cut back production and cease farming parcels of land, it did little to improve the fortunes of black tenant farmers and sharecroppers, who were often forced off their plots to reduce production. In this excerpt from an article in the NAACP's *Crisis*, John P. Davis criticizes the New Deal's approach to solving the problems of African American farmers in the South.

The Agricultural Adjustment Administration has used cruder methods in enforcing poverty on the Negro farm population. It has made violations of the rights of tenants under crop reduction contracts easy; it has rendered enforcement of these rights impossible. The reduction of the acreage under cultivation through the government rental agreement rendered unnecessary large numbers of tenants and farm laborers. Although the contract with the government provided that the land owner should not reduce the number of his tenants, he did so. . . . Farm laborers are now jobless by the hundreds of thousands, the conservative government estimate of the decline in agricultural employment for the year 1934 alone being a quarter of a million. The larger portion of these are unskilled Negro agricultural workers— now without income and unable to secure work or relief.

But the unemployment and tenant evictions occasioned by the crop reductions policy of the A.A.A. is not all. For the tenants and sharecroppers who were retained on the plantations the government's agricultural program meant reduced income. Wholesale fraud on tenants in the payment of parity checks occurred. Tenants complaining to the Department of Agriculture in Washington have their letters referred back to the locality in which they live and trouble of serious nature often results. Even when this does not happen, the tenant fails to get his check. The remainder of the land he tills on shares with his landlord brings him only the most meagre necessities during the crop season varying from three to five months. The rest of the period for him and his family is one of "root hog or die."

Source: John P. Davis, "A Black Inventory of the New Deal," *Crisis*, May 1935, 141–42.

Source 22.8

A Sharecropper's Family in Washington County, Arkansas, 1935

The Resettlement Administration (later the Farm Security Administration) documented the plight of migrant farmworkers and sharecroppers in numerous photographs. The following photo, taken by the noted photojournalist Arthur Rothstein, depicts a sharecropper's wife and daughters in Washington County, Arkansas, in 1935.

Franklin D. Roosevelt Library

Source 22.9

Martin Torres | Protest Against Maltreatment of Mexican Laborers in California, 1934

While union organizers achieved some gains in the industrial sector, they made little headway in the agricultural fields of California despite guarantees from the National Recovery Administration. In 1934 a delegation from the Confederation of Unions of Mexican Laborers and Peasants in the State of California attended a convention of workers in Mexico and asked for assistance. In response the Mexican organization (the Mexican Regional Confederation of Labor) sent the following letter to Josephus Daniels, the U.S. ambassador to Mexico.

Several months ago ten thousand compatriots in Southern California went on a strike. . . . These compatriots had been receiving ten cents per hour and were demanding thirty and that the children who had been working for five cents should be confined in future only to scholastic labors. The rich farmers of the region were not satisfied; they armed themselves to the teeth and taking advantage of a meeting which was being held by the strikers in the town of V[i]salia, they fired their guns on them, killing two, including a Mexican who, as a member of the Honorary Commission of a nearby town, was engaged in an investigation for the Government of Mexico. The farmer assassins fled. Later, they were tried by jury and were declared free of responsibility in the crime, and in order to celebrate, the following night an orgy was held which

772

lasted till dawn and during which could be heard only the cry of "down with the Mexican greasers!" . . .

For months five thousand Mexicans in the Imperial Valley, California, have been on strike, and under the pretext of their upholding radical ideas, notwithstanding the fact that the N.R.A. has backed the strike, they have been treated worse than beasts by the authorities and farmers. They have been incarcerated, struck, fired upon, put out of their homes with their women and children with clubs, firearms and tear bombs, and many leaders are still under arrest in the prisons of that region. . . .

The Mexican Regional Confederation of Labor consider that the acts which motivated the complaints presented by our compatriots at the XI Convention of our Organization are radically opposed to the liberal purposes of the Honorable President—Mr. Franklin D. Roosevelt—which purposes he has publicly set forth on more than one occasion, and which he has crystallized into action, in some of his principles of Government so faithfully interpreted by you as Ambassador of that Democratic Administration, setting them forth in various addresses which you have made.

[Signed] Martin Torres, April 10, 1934

Source: "Protest Against Maltreatment of Mexican Laborers in California. General Secretary Martin Torres of Mexican Regional Confederation of Labor to United States Ambassador Josephus Daniels," April 20, 1934, in *Decade of Betrayal: Mexican Repatriation in the 1930s*, by Francisco E. Balderrama and Raymond Rodríguez (Albuquerque: University of New Mexico Press, 1995), 65–68.

Source 22.10

Otis Nation | Testimony to the Great Plains Committee, 1937

In 1936 President Roosevelt established the Great Plains Committee to investigate the causes of the Dust Bowl and possible solutions for the region. The committee's report, submitted the following year, outlined how federal, state, and local government agencies could work together to restore the Great Plains to economic health. One of the witnesses the committee called to testify was Otis Nation, an organizer for the Oklahoma Tenant Farmers' Union, whose testimony follows.

Much has been written of our droughts here in Oklahoma, and how they have driven the farmers from the land. But little has been said of the other tentacles that choke off the livelihood of the small owner and the tenant. We do not wish to minimize the seriousness of these droughts and their effects on the farming population. But droughts alone would not have permanently displaced these farmers. The great majority of migrants had already become share-tenants and sharecroppers. The droughts hastened a process that had already begun. We submit the following as the cases for migratory agricultural workers:

1. *High interest rates.* Often a farmer borrows money for periods of 10 months and is charged an interest rate of 10 percent. These rates are charged when crops are good and when they fail. Through such practices the farmer loses his ownership; he becomes a tenant, then a sharecropper, then a migrant.

2. *The tenant and sharecropping system.* When share tenants are charged 33 1/3 percent of all corn or feed crops and 25 percent or more on cotton, plus 10 percent on all money borrowed at the bank, when sharecroppers are charged 50 to 75 percent of all he produces to the landlords, plus 10 percent for the bank's share on money invested; when these robbing practices are carried on in a community or a State, is it surprising that 33,241 farm families have left Oklahoma in the past 5 years?

3. *Land exhaustion, droughts, soil erosion, and the one-crop system of farming.* Lacking capital and equipment, small farmers have been unable to terrace their land or conduct other soil-conservation practices. The tenant and sharecropping system is chiefly responsible for the one-crop system. The landlord dictates what crops are to be planted—invariably cotton—and the tenant either plants it or gets off.

4. *Unstable markets.* Approximately a month and a half before the wheat harvest this year the price for this product was 93 cents here in Oklahoma City. But at harvest time the farmer sold his wheat for 46 cents to 60 cents per bushel, depending on the grade. . . . Kaffir [a grain sorghum] was selling

for $1.30 one month ago, and yesterday we sold some for 85 cents per hundred. . . .

It is obvious to all of us that farm prices are set by speculators. The farmer's losses at the market have contributed in no small part to the farmer losing his place on the land. Higher prices for farm products are quoted when the farmer has nothing to sell.

5. *Tractor farming.* In Creek County, Okla., we have the record of one land-owner purchasing 3 tractors and forcing 31 of his 34 tenants and croppers from the land. Most of these families left the State when neither jobs nor relief could be secured. This is over 10 families per machine, 10 families who must quit their profession and seek employment in an unfriendly, industrialized farming section of Arizona or California. Many of these families were even unable to become

"Joads" [the fictional family in *The Grapes of Wrath*] in these other States, and had to seek relief from an unfriendly national administration and a more unfriendly State administration. . . .

. . . There are no more important problems facing us than the problem of stopping this human erosion and rehabilitating those unfortunates who have already been thrown off the land. Certainly it is un-American for Americans to be starved and dispossessed of their homes in our land of plenty. Those who seek to exploit and harass these American refugees, the migratory workers, are against our principles of democracy.

Source: U.S. Congress, House Select Committee to Investigate the Interstate Migration of Destitute Citizens (Washington, DC: U.S. Government Printing Office, 1940–1941), 2102.

Interpret the Evidence

1. Explain why women like Ann Marie Low faced particular challenges during the Dust Bowl era (Source 22.6).
2. Evaluate John P. Davis's arguments (Source 22.7) about the treatment of black farmers under the New Deal's AAA.
3. In the photograph of the Arkansas family (Source 22.8), how do the subjects seem to react to the Great Depression? Compare their plight to that of black sharecroppers.
4. Why did unions in Mexico believe that Mexican farmworkers in California would receive assistance from the federal government (Source 22.9)? Compare their assumptions with Davis's (Source 22.7).
5. How might Ann Marie Low and John P. Davis have responded to the report of the Great Plains Committee (Source 22.10)?

Put It in Context

Explain how the New Deal changed the structure of American agriculture and evaluate its effects on poor and wealthy farmers.

World War II

1933–1945

WINDOW TO THE PAST

Hiroshima, August 6, 1945

In the months following the death of Franklin D. Roosevelt in April 1945, President Harry S. Truman decided to give the order to drop atomic bombs on the Japanese cities of Hiroshima and Nagasaki. He considered it a military necessity to get Japan to surrender before the U.S. launched an invasion of the Japanese island, which would have resulted in the deaths of tens of thousands of American soldiers. This photograph, taken the day of the bombing, captures the tremendous devastation to Hiroshima. ▶ To discover more about what this primary source can show us, see Source 23.8 on page 809.

AP Photo/Stanley Troutman

After reading this chapter you should be able to:

- Evaluate the key reasons behind U.S. intervention in World War II as well as the arguments of those who opposed it.

- Analyze the effects the war had on the U.S. economy and on the lives of women and families.

- Compare and contrast the treatment of minority groups and their responses on the home front.

- Explain the Allied military strategy in fighting World War II on the European and Pacific fronts, including how it affected the decision to drop the atomic bomb on Japan, U.S-Soviet relations and the Holocaust.

COMPARING AMERICAN HISTORIES

One month after Japan attacked the U.S. naval base at Pearl Harbor on December 7, 1941, President Franklin Roosevelt approved a full-scale effort to develop an atomic bomb. As scientific director of this top-secret program, physicist J. Robert Oppenheimer orchestrated the work of more than 3,000 scientists, technicians, and military personnel at the Los Alamos Laboratories near Santa Fe, New Mexico. The son of German American Jews, Oppenheimer helped Jews gain asylum in the United States when the Nazis started persecuting them in the early 1930s.

(*left*) **J. Robert Oppenheimer.** Agence France Presse/Getty Images
(*right*) **Fred Korematsu.** National Portrait Gallery, Smithsonian Institution/Art Resource, NY

On July 16, 1945, Oppenheimer and his team successfully tested their new weapon. The explosion lit up the predawn sky with a blast so powerful that it broke a window 125 miles away. A mushroom cloud shot up 41,000 feet into the sky over ground zero, where a 1,200-foot-wide crater had formed. Oppenheimer understood that the world had been permanently transformed. Quoting from Hindu scriptures, he remembered thinking at the moment of the explosion, "I am become death, destroyer of worlds." Weeks later, in early August 1945, the United States dropped two atomic bombs on Japan, which resulted in over 200,000 deaths.

While Oppenheimer and his team remained cloistered at Los Alamos, Fred Korematsu and some 112,000 Japanese Americans lived in internment camps, imprisoned for no other reason than their Japanese ancestry. Born in Oakland, California in 1919 to Japanese immigrants, Fred grew up like many first-generation Americans. His parents spoke Japanese at home and maintained the cultural traditions of their native land, while their sons learned English in public school, ate hamburgers, and played football and basketball like other children their age. Following graduation from high school, Korematsu worked on the Oakland docks as a welder.

After the 1941 bombing of Pearl Harbor, residents on the West Coast turned their anger on the Japanese and Japanese Americans living among them. As assimilated as Fred Korematsu and many other Nisei (the U.S.-born children of Japanese immigrants) had become, white Americans doubted their loyalty. As a result, Korematsu soon lost his job.

On March 21, 1942, President Roosevelt issued Executive Order 9066 authorizing military commanders on the West Coast to take any measures necessary to promote national security. On May 9, the military ordered Korematsu's family to report to Tanforan Racetrack in San Mateo, from which they would be transported to internment camps throughout the West. Although the rest of his family complied with the order, Fred refused. Three weeks later, he was arrested and then transferred to the

Topaz internment camp in south-central Utah. Found guilty of violating the original evacuation order, Korematsu received a sentence of five years of probation. When he appealed his conviction to the U.S. Supreme Court in 1944, the high court upheld the verdict. ∎

The American histories of Fred Korematsu and J. Robert Oppenheimer were shaped by the profound changes brought about by war. Korematsu was subjected to the full force of anti-Japanese sentiment that followed the attack on Pearl Harbor, while Oppenheimer played a key role in developing a weapon that he believed would shorten the war.

The war that these two men experienced in such different ways marked a critical point for the United States in the twentieth century. World War II finally ended the Great Depression, cementing the trend toward government intervention in the economy that had begun with the New Deal. With the war fought almost entirely on foreign soil, the United States converted its factories to wartime production and became the "arsenal of democracy," putting millions of Americans to work in the process, including African Americans, other minorities, and women. The war also provided opportunities for African Americans to press for civil rights, while at the same time the government trampled on the civil liberties of Japanese Americans. All Americans contributed to the war effort through rationing and higher taxes. Overseas, soldiers fought fierce battles in Europe, Africa, and Asia. The combined military power of the Allies, led by the United States, Great Britain, and the Soviet Union, finally defeated the Axis nations of Germany, Italy, and Japan, but not until the fighting had killed 60 to 70 million people, more than half of whom were civilians, and ushered in the Atomic Age.

The **Road** toward **War**

The end of World War I did not bring peace and prosperity to Europe. The harsh peace terms imposed on the Central Powers in 1919 left the losers, especially Germany, deeply resentful. The war saddled both sides with a huge financial debt and produced economic instability, which contributed to the Great Depression. In the Far East, Japanese invasions of China and Southeast Asia threatened America's Open Door policy (see "Opening the Door in China" in chapter 20). The failure of the United States to join the League of Nations dramatically reduced the organization's ability to maintain peace and stability. German expansionism in Europe in the late 1930s moved President Roosevelt and the nation toward war, but it took the Japanese attack on Pearl Harbor to bring the United States into the global conflict.

The Growing Crisis in Europe.
Despite its failure to join the League of Nations, the United States did not withdraw from international affairs in the 1920s. It participated in arms control negotiations; signed the Kellogg-Briand Pact, which outlawed war as an instrument of national policy but proved unenforceable; and expanded its foreign

investments in Central and Latin America, Asia, the Middle East, and western Europe. In 1933 a new possibility for trade emerged when the Roosevelt administration extended diplomatic recognition to the Soviet Union (USSR).

Overall, the country did not retreat from foreign affairs so much as it refused to enter into collective security agreements that would restrain its freedom of action. To the extent that American leaders practiced isolationism, they did so mainly in the political sense of rejecting internationalist organizations such as the League of Nations, institutions that might require military cooperation to implement their decisions.

The experience of World War I had reinforced this brand of political isolationism, which was reflected in an outpouring of antiwar sentiments in the late 1920s and early 1930s. Best-selling novels like Ernest Hemingway's *Farewell to Arms* (1929), Erich Maria Remarque's *All Quiet on the Western Front* (1929), and Dalton Trumbo's *Johnny Got His Gun* (1939) presented graphic depictions of the horror and futility of war. Beginning in 1934, Senate investigations chaired by Gerald Nye of North Dakota concluded that bankers and munitions makers — "merchants of death," as one contemporary writer labeled them — had conspired to push the United States into war in 1917. Nye's hearings appealed to popular antibusiness sentiment in Depression-era America.

Following the Nye Committee hearings, Congress passed a series of **Neutrality Acts**, each designed to make it more difficult for the United States to become entangled in European armed hostilities. In 1935 Congress prohibited the sale of munitions to either warring side and authorized the president to warn Americans against traveling on passenger liners of belligerent nations. The following year, lawmakers added private loans to the ban, and in 1937 they required belligerents to pay cash for nonmilitary purchases and ship them on their own vessels — so-called cash-and-carry provisions.

Events in Europe, however, made U.S. neutrality ever more difficult to maintain. After rising to power as chancellor of Germany in 1933, Adolf Hitler revived Germany's economic and military strength despite the Great Depression. Hitler installed National Socialism (Nazism) at home and established the empire of the Third Reich abroad. The *Führer* (leader) whipped up patriotic fervor by scapegoating and persecuting Communists and Jews. To garner support for his actions, Hitler manipulated German feelings of humiliation for losing World War I and having been forced to sign the "war guilt" clause (see "Waging Peace" in chapter 20) and pointed to the disastrous effects of the country's inflation-ridden economy. In 1936 Hitler sent troops to occupy the Rhineland between Germany and France in blatant violation of the Treaty of Versailles.

Hitler did not stop there. Citing the need for more space for the Germanic people to live, he pushed for German expansion into eastern Europe. In March 1938 he forced Austria to unite with Germany. In September of that year Hitler signed the Munich Accord with Great Britain and France, allowing Germany to annex the Sudetenland, the mainly German-speaking, western region of Czechoslovakia. Hitler still wanted more land and was convinced that his western European rivals would not stop him, so in March 1939 he sent German troops to invade and occupy the rest of Czechoslovakia. Hitler proved correct; Britain and France did nothing in response, a policy critics called **appeasement**.

Hitler's Italian ally, Benito Mussolini, joined him in war and conquest. In 1935 Italian troops invaded Ethiopia. The following year, both Germany and Italy intervened in the Spanish civil war, providing military support for General Francisco Franco in his effort to overthrow the democratically elected, socialist republic of Spain. While the United States and Great Britain remained on the sidelines, only the Soviet Union officially assisted the Loyalist defenders of the Spanish republic. In violation of American law, private citizens, many of whom were Communists, volunteered to serve on the side of the Spanish Loyalists and fought on the battlefield as the Abraham Lincoln Brigade. Other sympathetic Americans, such as J. Robert Oppenheimer, provided financial assistance for the anti-Franco government. Despite these efforts, Franco's forces seized control of Spain in early 1939, another victory for Hitler and Mussolini.

The Challenge to Isolationism.
As Europe drifted toward war, public opinion polls revealed that most Americans wanted to stay out of any European conflict. The president, however, thought it likely that, to protect its own economic and political interests, the United States would eventually need to assist the Western democracies. Still, Roosevelt

America First Committee Rally, 1941   Organized in 1940, the America First Committee campaigned against U.S. entry into World War II. One of its leaders, the popular aviator Charles Lindbergh, addressed a rally of 3,000 people in Ft. Wayne, Indiana on October 5, 1941. The isolationist group blamed eastern bankers, British sympathizers, and Jewish leaders for promoting war fever. The committee dissolved soon after this 1941 rally and the Japanese attack on Pearl Harbor. Everett Collection

had to tread lightly in the face of the Neutrality Acts that Congress had passed between 1935 and 1937 and overwhelming public opposition to American involvement in Europe.

Germany's aggression in Europe eventually led to full-scale war. When Germany invaded Poland in September 1939, Britain and France declared war on Germany and Italy. Just before the invasion, the Soviet Union had signed a nonaggression agreement with Germany, which carved up Poland between the two nations and permitted the USSR to occupy the neighboring Baltic states of Latvia, Lithuania, and Estonia. Soviet leader Joseph Stalin had few illusions about Hitler's ultimate design on his own nation, but he concluded that by signing this pact he could secure his country's western borders and buy additional time. (In June 1941 the Germans broke the pact and invaded the Soviet Union.)

Roosevelt responded to the outbreak of war by reaffirming U.S. neutrality. Despite his sympathy for the Allies, which most Americans had come to share, the president stated his hope that the United States could stay out of the war: "Let no man or woman thoughtlessly or falsely talk of America sending its armies to European fields."

With the United States on the sidelines, German forces marched toward victory. By the spring of 1940, German armies had launched a *Blitzkrieg* (lightning war) across Europe, defeating and occupying Denmark, Norway, the Netherlands, Belgium, and Luxembourg. With German victories mounting, committed opponents of American involvement in foreign wars organized the **America First Committee**. America First tapped into the feeling of isolationism and concern among a diverse group of Americans who did not want to get dragged into another foreign war.

The greatest challenge to isolationism occurred in June 1940 when France fell to the German onslaught and Nazi troops marched into Paris. Britain now stood virtually alone, and its position seemed tenuous. The British had barely succeeded in evacuating their forces from France by sea when the German *Luftwaffe* (air force) began a bombing campaign on London and other targets in the Battle of Britain.

The surrender of France and the Battle of Britain drastically changed Americans' attitude toward entering the war. Before Germany invaded France, 82 percent of Americans thought that the United States should not aid the Allies. After France's defeat, in a complete turnaround, some 80 percent of Americans favored assisting Great Britain in some way. However, four out of five Americans polled opposed immediate entry into the war. As a result, the politically astute Roosevelt portrayed all U.S. assistance to Britain as a way to prevent American military intervention by allowing Great Britain to defeat the Germans on its own.

Nevertheless, the Roosevelt administration found acceptable ways of helping Britain. On September 2, 1940, the president sent fifty obsolete destroyers to the British in return for leases on British naval bases in Newfoundland, Bermuda, and the British West Indies. Two weeks later, on September 16, Roosevelt persuaded Congress to pass the Selective Service Act, the first peacetime military draft in U.S. history, which quickly registered more than 16 million men.

This political maneuvering came as Roosevelt campaigned for an unprecedented third term in 1940. He defeated the Republican Wendell Willkie, a Wall Street lawyer who shared Roosevelt's anti-isolationist views. However, both candidates accommodated voters' desire to stay out of the European war, and Roosevelt went so far as to promise American parents: "Your boys are not going to be sent into any foreign war."

Roosevelt's campaign promises did not halt the march toward war. Roosevelt succeeded in pushing Congress to pass the **Lend-Lease Act** in March 1941. With Britain running out of money and its shipping devastated by German submarines, this measure circumvented the cash-and-carry provisions of the Neutrality Acts. The United States would lend or lease equipment, but no one expected the recipients to return the used weapons and other commodities. To protect British ships carrying American supplies, the president extended naval and air patrols in the North Atlantic. In response, German submarines began sinking U.S. ships. By May 1941, Germany and the United States were engaged in an undeclared naval war.

The United States Enters the War.

Financially, militarily, and ideologically, the United States had aligned itself with Britain, and Roosevelt expected that the nation would soon be formally at war. As Germany and Italy successfully expanded their empires, they endangered U.S. economic interests and democratic values. President Roosevelt believed that American security abroad was threatened by the German Nazis and Italian Fascists.

Roosevelt, Churchill, and the Atlantic Charter, 1941.   U.S. President Franklin D. Roosevelt and British Prime Minister Winston Churchill converse aboard the battleship *Prince of Wales* off the coast of Newfoundland on Aug. 10, 1941. The five-day secret meeting produced the Atlantic Charter, a declaration that shaped the Anglo-American alliance of World War II. AP photo

After passage of the Lend-Lease Act, American and British military planners agreed that defeating Germany would become the top priority if the United States entered the war. In August 1941, Roosevelt and British prime minister Winston Churchill met in Newfoundland, where they signed the **Atlantic Charter**, a lofty statement of war aims that included principles of freedom of the seas, self-determination, free trade, and "freedom from fear and want"—ideals that laid the groundwork for the establishment of a postwar United Nations. At the same meeting, Roosevelt promised Churchill that the United States would protect British convoys in the North Atlantic as far as Iceland while the nation waited for a confrontation with Germany that would rally the American public in support of war. The president got what he wanted. After several attacks on American ships by German submarines in September and October, the president persuaded Congress to repeal the neutrality legislation of the 1930s and allow American ships to sail across the Atlantic to supply Great Britain. By December, the nation was close to open war with Germany.

The event that finally prompted the United States to enter the war, however, occurred not in the Atlantic but in the Pacific Ocean. For nearly a decade, U.S. relations with Japan had deteriorated over the issue of China's independence and maintaining the Open Door to Chinese markets. The United States did little to challenge the Japanese invasion and occupation of Manchuria in 1931, but after Japanese armed forces moved farther into China in 1937, the United States supplied arms to China.

Explore ▶

See Source 23.1 for a Japanese American perspective on the bombing of Pearl Harbor.

Relations worsened in 1940 when the Japanese government signed the Tripartite Pact with Germany and Italy, which created a mutual defense agreement among the Axis powers. That same year, Japanese troops invaded northern Indochina, and Roosevelt responded by embargoing sales of products that Japan needed for war. This embargo did not deter the Japanese; in July they occupied the remainder of Indochina to gain access to the region's natural resources. The Roosevelt administration retaliated by freezing Japanese assets and cutting off all trade with Japan.

On the quiet Sunday morning of December 7, 1941, Japan attacked the U.S. Pacific Fleet stationed at Pearl Harbor in Honolulu, Hawaii. This surprise air and naval assault killed more than 2,400 Americans and seriously damaged ships and aircraft. The bombing raid abruptly ended isolationism and rallied the American public behind President Roosevelt, who pronounced December 7 "a date which will live in infamy." The next day, Congress overwhelmingly voted to go to war with Japan, and on December 11 Germany and Italy declared war on the United States in response. In little more than a year after his reelection pledge to keep the country out of war, Roosevelt sent American men to fight overseas. Still, an overwhelming majority of Americans now considered entry into the war as necessary to preserve freedom and democracy against assaults from fascist and militaristic nations.

REVIEW & RELATE

- How did American public opinion shape Roosevelt's foreign policy in the years preceding U.S. entry into World War II?

- What events in Europe and the Pacific ultimately brought the United States into World War II?

GUIDED ANALYSIS

Monica Sone | Memories of Pearl Harbor

Few Americans would forget where they were or how they felt when they first learned of the Japanese attack on Pearl Harbor. The following document describes the experience of Monica Sone, a Nisei who was a student at the University of Washington in December 1941. Sone and her family were eventually placed in an internment camp in Idaho.

Source 23.1

What does this tell you about Sone's relationship to the United States?

On a peaceful Sunday morning, December 7, 1941, Henry, Sumi, and I were at choir rehearsal singing ourselves hoarse in preparation for the annual Christmas recital of Handel's "Messiah." Suddenly Chuck Mizuno, a young University of Washington student, burst into the chapel, gasping as if he had sprinted all the way up the stairs.

"Listen, everybody!" he shouted. "Japan just bombed Pearl Harbor . . . in Hawaii. It's war!"

The terrible words hit like a blockbuster, paralyzing us. Then we smiled feebly at each other, hoping this was one of Chuck's practical jokes. Miss Hara, our music director, rapped her baton impatiently on the music stand and chided him, "Now Chuck, fun's fun, but we have work to do. Please take your place. You're already half an hour late."

But Chuck strode vehemently back to the door. "I mean it, folks, honest! I just heard the news over my car radio. Reporters are talking a blue streak. Come on down and hear it for yourselves."

. . . I felt as if a fist had smashed my pleasant little existence, breaking it into jigsaw puzzle pieces. An old wound opened up again, and I found myself shrinking inwardly from my Japanese blood, the blood of an enemy. I knew instinctively that the fact that I was an American by birthright was not going to help me escape the consequences of this

Why was she worried?

unhappy war.

One girl mumbled over and over again, "It can't be, God, it can't be!" Someone else was saying, "What a spot to be in! Do you think we'll be considered Japanese or Americans?"

A boy replied quietly, "We'll be Japs, same as always. But our parents

Why did Monica and her friends think they would not be treated as Americans?

are enemy aliens now, you know."

A shocked silence followed.

Source: Monica Sone, *Nisei Daughter* (Boston: Little, Brown, 1953), 145–46.

Put It in Context

What does the experience of Japanese Americans during World War II indicate about constitutional guarantees of civil liberties during wartime?

The **Home-Front Economy**

The global conflict had profound effects on the American home front. World War II ended the Great Depression, restored economic prosperity, and increased labor union membership. At the same time, it smoothed the way for a closer relationship between government and private defense contractors, later referred to as the **military-industrial complex**. The war extended U.S. influence in the world and offered new economic opportunities at home. Despite fierce and bloody military battles throughout the world, Americans kept up morale by rallying around family and community.

Managing the Wartime Economy.

To mobilize for war, President Roosevelt increased federal spending to unprecedented levels. Federal government employment during the war expanded to an all-time high of 3.8 million workers, setting the foundation for a large, permanent Washington bureaucracy. War orders fueled economic growth, productivity, and employment. The gross domestic product increased from the equivalent of nearly $900 billion in 1939 (in 1990 prices) to nearly $1.5 trillion (in 1990 prices) at the end of the war (Figure 23.1), union membership rose from around 9 million to nearly 15 million, and unemployment dropped from 8 million to less than 1 million. The armed forces helped reduce unemployment significantly by enlisting 12 million men and women, 7 million of whom had been unemployed.

Prosperity was not limited to any one region. The industrial areas of the Northeast and Midwest once again boomed, as automobile factories converted to building tanks and other military vehicles, oil refineries processed gasoline to fuel them, steel and rubber companies manufactured parts to construct these vehicles and the weapons they carried, and textile and shoe plants furnished uniforms and boots for soldiers to wear. As farmers provided food for the nation and its allies, farm production soared. The economy diversified geographically. Fifteen million Americans—11 percent of the entire population—migrated between 1941 and 1945. The war transformed the agricultural South into a budding industrial region. The federal government poured more than $4 billion in contracts into the South to operate military camps, contract with textile factories to clothe the military, and use its ports to build and launch warships. The availability of jobs in southern cities attracted sharecroppers and tenant farmers, black and white, away from the countryside and promoted urbanization while reducing the region's dependency on the plantation economy.

No region was changed more by the war than the West. The West Coast prospered because it was the gateway to the Pacific war. The federal government established aircraft plants and shipbuilding yards in California, Oregon, and Washington, resulting in extraordinary population growth in Los Angeles, San Diego, San Francisco, Portland, and Seattle. The West's population grew three times as fast as the rest of the nation's. Los Angeles led the way in attracting defense contracts, as its balmy climate proved ideal for test-flying the aircraft that rolled off its assembly lines.

Following the attack on Pearl Harbor, Congress passed the War Powers Act, which authorized the president to reorganize federal agencies any way he thought necessary to win the war. In 1942 the president established the **War Production Board** to oversee the economy. The agency enticed business corporations to meet ever-increasing government orders by negotiating lucrative contracts that helped underwrite their costs, lower their taxes, and guarantee large profits. The government also suspended antitrust enforcement,

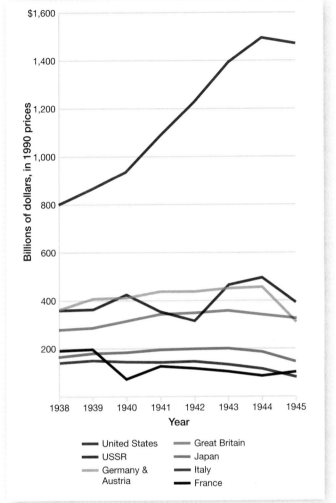

FIGURE 23.1   Real Gross Domestic Product of the Great Powers, 1938–1945

Although World War II stalled or damaged the economic productivity of most of the warring nations, the U.S. economy grew dramatically between 1938 and 1944. With all the battles taking place outside the continental United States, the demand for food, weapons, ships, airplanes, gasoline, and other items by Great Britain and other Allied powers fueled this growth. Explain why the war and not the New Deal succeeded in ending the Great Depression.

Data from Mark Harrison, ed., *The Economics of World War II: Six Great Powers in International Comparison* (Cambridge: Cambridge University Press, 1998), 11.

giving private companies great leeway in running their enterprises. Much of the antibusiness hostility generated by the Great Depression evaporated as the Roosevelt administration recruited business executives to supervise government agencies. Indeed, the close relationship between the federal government and business that emerged during the war produced the military-industrial complex, which would have a vast influence on the future development of the economy.

In the first three years of the war, the United States increased military production by some 800 percent. American factories accounted for more than half of worldwide manufacturing output. By 1945 the United States had produced 86,000 tanks, nearly 300,000 airplanes, 15 million rifles and machine guns, and 6,500 ships.

Financing this enormous enterprise took considerable effort. The federal government spent more than $320 billion, ten times the cost of World War I. To pay for the war, the federal government sold $100 billion in bonds, only about half of what was needed. The rest came from increased income tax rates, which for the first time affected low- and middle-income workers, who had paid little or no tax before. At the same time, the tax rate for the wealthy was boosted to 94 percent. In addition to paying higher taxes, American consumers shouldered the burden of shortages and high prices.

Building up the armed forces was the final ingredient in the mobilization for war. In 1940 about 250,000 soldiers were serving in the U.S. military. By 1945 American forces had grown to more than 12 million men and women through voluntary enlistments and a draft of men between the ages of eighteen and forty-five. The military reflected the diversity of the U.S. population. The sons of immigrants fought alongside the sons of older-stock Americans. Although the military tried to exclude homosexuals, many managed to join the fighting forces. Some 700,000 African Americans served in the armed forces, but civilian and military officials confined them to segregated units in the army, assigned them to menial work in the navy, and excluded them from the marines. The Army Air Corps created a segregated fighting unit trained at Tuskegee Institute in Alabama, and these Tuskegee airmen, like their counterparts among the ground forces, distinguished themselves in battle. Women could not fight in combat, but 140,000 joined the Women's Army Corps, and 100,000 joined the navy's WAVES (Women Accepted for Voluntary Emergency Service). In these and other service branches, women contributed mainly as nurses and performed transportation and clerical duties.

Women also played an important but secretive role in bolstering Allied military efforts. The navy and army recruited thousands of women college students and small-town school teachers to Washington, D.C., where they worked on deciphering German and Japanese diplomatic and military codes. These young, unmarried women worked very long, tedious hours during the week as well as on weekends, and succeeded in providing the U.S. military

Tuskegee Airmen   Twenty black pilots, among those known as the Tuskegee airmen, line up for a photograph, which they signed. The Army Air Corps created two segregated units of African American airmen, the 442nd Bombardment Group and the 99th Pursuit Squadron. The latter flew combat missions in Europe. The success of the Tuskegee airmen contributed to the postwar desegregation of the armed forces. Courtesy National Park Service, Museum Management Program and Tuskegee Institute National Historic Site, TUAI 31.

with secret information of enemy planning. In this way, they joined the efforts already begun by British female codebreakers operating at Bletchley Park, England.

The government relied on corporate executives to manage wartime economic conversion, but without the sacrifice and dedication of American workers, their efforts would have failed. The demands for wartime production combined with the departure of millions of American workers to the military created a labor shortage that gave unions increased leverage. By 1945 the membership rolls of organized labor had grown from 9 million to nearly 14 million. In 1942 the Roosevelt administration established the **National War Labor Board**, which regulated wages, hours, and working conditions and authorized the government to take over plants that refused to abide by its decisions. Unions at first refrained from striking but later in the war organized strikes to protest the disparity between workers' wages and corporate profits. In 1943 Congress responded by passing the Smith-Connally Act, which prohibited walkouts in defense industries and set a thirty-day "cooling-off" period before unions could go out on strike.

New Opportunities for Women.

World War II opened up new opportunities for women in the paid workforce. Between 1940 and the peak of wartime employment in 1944, the number of employed women rose by more than 50 percent, to 6 million. Given severe labor shortages caused by increased production and the exodus of male workers into the armed forces, for the first time in U.S. history married working women outnumbered single

Women Workers during the War   During the war, women worked in industrial jobs in unprecedented numbers. Corporations and the federal government actively recruited women through posters and advertisements and promised women that factory work was something that would benefit them, their families, and their nation. As the Allies neared victory, however, the message changed, and women were urged to prepare to return to the home to open up jobs for returning soldiers. Library of Congress, LC-USZC4-4442

working women. At the start of the war, about half of women employees held poorly paid clerical, sales, and service jobs. Women in manufacturing labored mainly in low-wage textile and clothing factories. During the war, however, the overall number of women in manufacturing grew by 141 percent; in industries producing directly for war purposes, the figure jumped by 463 percent. By contrast, the number of women in domestic service dropped by 20 percent. As women moved into defense-related jobs, their incomes also improved.

As impressive as these figures are, they do not tell the whole story. First, although married women entered the job market in record numbers, most of these workers were older and without young children. Women over the age of thirty-five accounted for 60 percent of those entering the workforce. The government did little to encourage young mothers to work, and few efforts were made to provide assistance for child care for those who did. In contrast to this situation, in Great Britain child care programs were widely available. Second, openings for women in manufacturing jobs did not guarantee equality. Women received lower wages for labor comparable to the work that men performed, and women did not have the same chances for advancement. Typical union benefits, such as seniority, hurt women, who were generally the most recent hires. In fact, some contracts stipulated that women's tenure in jobs previously held by men would last only for the duration of the war.

Gender stereotypes continued to dominate the workforce and society in general. Magazine covers with the image of "Rosie the Riveter," a woman with her sleeves rolled up and her biceps bulging, became a symbol for the recruitment of women, but reality proved different. Women who took war jobs were viewed not so much as war workers but as women temporarily occupying "men's jobs" during the emergency. As the war drew to a close, public relations campaigns shifted gears and encouraged the same women they had recently recruited to prepare to return home. And nearly all of the brilliant women codebreakers in Washington, D.C. were ordered to go back home.

Everyday Life on the Home Front. Morale on the home front remained generally high during the war, as prosperity returned and American casualties proved relatively light compared with those of other allied nations. As in World War I, the government set up an agency, the Office of War Information, to promote patriotism and urge Americans to contribute to the war effort any way they could. Schoolchildren collected scrap metal and rubber to donate to the production of military vehicles and weapons. With rationing in effect and food in short supply, the government encouraged families in towns and cities to grow "victory gardens" for their own fruits and vegetables. Mothers and daughters helped staff USO (United Service Organizations) dances and recreational activities for soldiers headquartered in the United States. Americans also contributed to the war effort by adhering to restrictions on the consumption of consumer goods. Rationing cards restricted purchases of gasoline for cars and for food such as meat, butter, and sugar.

Hollywood kept the American public entertained, and movie attendance reached a record high of more than 100 million viewers. Films portrayed the heroism of soldiers on battlefields in Guadalcanal and Bataan. They celebrated the courage of Russian allies in propaganda epics such as *Mission to Moscow* (1943) and explored the depth of personal and political loyalties in classics such as *Casablanca* (1943). Hollywood stars such as Betty Grable kept up servicemen's spirits by posing for photos that GIs pinned up in their lockers, tents, and equipment.

For many Americans, life went on, but not quite in the same way. Around 15 million Americans moved during the war, with more than half of them relocating out of state. With husbands at war and wives at work, many children became "latchkey kids" who stayed home alone after school until their mothers or fathers returned from their jobs. With less parental supervision, juvenile delinquency rose, resulting in increased teenage arrests for robbery, vandalism, and loitering. In contrast, with the end of the Great Depression and with more young people working, marriage rates increased, and couples wed at a younger age. By 1945 the winding down of the war and the rapidly increasing number of marriages produced the first signs of a "baby boom." At the same time, the stresses of life during wartime, including long separations of husbands and wives, also resulted in higher divorce rates.

REVIEW & RELATE

How did the war accelerate the trend that began during the New Deal toward increased government participation in the economy?

How did the war affect life on the home front for the average American?

Fighting for Equality at Home

The war also had a significant impact on race relations. The fight to defeat Nazism, a doctrine based on racial prejudice and white supremacy, offered African Americans a chance to press for equal opportunity at home. By contrast, Japanese Americans experienced intensified discrimination and oppression as wartime anti-Japanese hysteria led to the internment of Japanese Americans, an erosion of their civil rights. They were freed toward the end of the war, but their incarceration left scars. Finally, Mexican Americans and American Indians benefited from wartime jobs and military service but continued to experience ethnic prejudice.

The Origins of the Civil Rights Movement.

In 1941 A. Philip Randolph, the head of the Brotherhood of Sleeping Car Porters, applied his labor union experience to the struggle for civil rights. He announced that he planned to lead a 100,000-person march on Washington, D.C., in June 1941 to protest racial discrimination in government and war-related employment as well as segregation in the military. Although Randolph believed in an interracial alliance of working people, he insisted that the march should be all-black to show that African Americans could lead their own movement. Inching the country toward war, but not yet engaged militarily, President Roosevelt wanted to avoid any embarrassment the proposed march would bring to the forces supporting democracy and freedom. With his wife, Eleanor, serving as go-between, Roosevelt agreed to meet with Randolph and worked out a compromise. Randolph called off the march, and in return, on June 25, 1941, the president issued Executive Order 8802, creating the **Fair Employment Practice Committee (FEPC)**. Roosevelt refused to order the desegregation of the military, but he set up a committee to investigate inequality in the armed forces. Although the FEPC helped African Americans gain a greater share of jobs in key industries than they had before, the effect was limited because the agency did not have enforcement power.

The march on Washington movement was emblematic of rising civil rights activity. Black leaders proclaimed their own "two-front war" with the symbol of the **Double V** to represent victory against racist enemies both abroad and at home. The National Association for the Advancement of Colored People continued its policy of fighting racial discrimination in the courts. In 1944 the organization won a significant victory in a case from

Texas, *Smith v. Allwright*, which outlawed all-white Democratic primary elections in the traditionally one-party South. As a result of the decision, the percentage of African Americans registered to vote in the South doubled between 1944 and 1948. In 1942 early civil rights activists also founded the interracial Congress of Racial Equality (CORE) in Chicago. CORE protested directly against racial inequality in public accommodations. Its members organized "sit-ins" at restaurants and bowling alleys that refused to serve African Americans. Students at Howard University in Washington, D.C., used the same tactics, with some success, to protest racial exclusion from restaurants and cafeterias in the nation's capital. Although these demonstrations did not get the national attention that postwar protests would, they constituted the prelude to the civil rights movement.

Population shifts on the home front during World War II exacerbated racial tensions, resulting in violence. As jobs opened up throughout the country at military installations and defense plants, hundreds of thousands of African Americans moved from the rural South to the urban South, the North, and the West. Cities could not handle this rapid influx of people and failed to provide sufficient housing to accommodate those who migrated in search of employment. Competition between white and black workers for scarce housing spilled over into tensions in crowded transportation and recreational facilities. In 1943 the stress caused by close wartime contact between the races exploded in more than 240 riots. The most serious one occurred in Detroit, where federal troops had to restore order after whites and blacks fought with each other following an altercation at a popular amusement park that killed thirty-four people.

Struggles for Mexican Americans. Immigration from Mexico increased significantly during the war. To address labor shortages in the Southwest and on the Pacific coast and departing from the deportation policies of the 1930s, in 1942 the United States negotiated an agreement with Mexico for contract laborers (*braceros*) to enter the country for a limited time to work as farm laborers and in factories. *Braceros* had little or no control over their living spaces or working conditions. Not surprisingly, they conducted numerous strikes for higher wages in the agricultural fields of the Southwest and Northwest. Most U.S. residents of Mexican ancestry were, however, American citizens. Like other Americans, they settled into jobs to help fight the war, while more than 300,000 Mexican Americans served in the armed forces.

The war heightened Mexican Americans' consciousness of their civil rights. As one Mexican American World War II veteran recalled: "We were Americans, not 'spics' or 'greasers.' Because when you fight for your country in a World War, against an alien philosophy, fascism, you are an American and proud to be in America." In southern California, newspaper publisher Ignacio Lutero Lopez campaigned against segregation in movie theaters, swimming pools, and other public accommodations. He organized boycotts against businesses that discriminated against or excluded Mexican Americans. Wartime organizing led to the creation of the Unity Leagues, a coalition of Mexican American business owners, college students, civic leaders, and GIs that pressed for racial equality. In Texas, Mexican Americans joined the League of United Latin American Citizens (LULAC), a largely middle-class group that challenged racial discrimination and segregation in public accommodations. Members of the organization emphasized the use of negotiations to redress their grievances, but when they ran into opposition, they resorted to economic boycotts and litigation. The war encouraged LULAC to expand its operations throughout the Southwest.

Navajo Code Talkers, 1943 Private First Class Preston Toledo and Private First Class Frank Toledo, cousins and Navajo Indians, attached to a Marine Artillery Regiment in the South Pacific, relay orders over a field radio in their native language on July 7, 1943. These "code talkers" were among the more than 400 bilingual Navajo soldiers deployed to transmit secret communications in their complex tribal language. PhotoQuest/Getty Images

Mexican American citizens encountered hostility from recently transplanted whites and longtime residents. Tensions were greatest in Los Angeles. A small group of Mexican American teenagers joined gangs and identified themselves by wearing zoot suits — colorful, long, loose-fitting jackets with padded shoulders and baggy pants tapered at the bottom. Not all zoot-suiters were gang members, but many outside their communities failed to make this distinction and found the zoot-suiters' dress and swagger provocative. On the night of June 4, 1943, squads of sailors stationed in Long Beach invaded Mexican American neighborhoods in East Los Angeles and indiscriminately attacked both zoot-suiters and those not dressed in this garb, setting off four days of violence. Mexican American youths tried to fight back. The **zoot suit riots** ended as civilian and military authorities restored order. In response, the Los Angeles city council banned the wearing of zoot suits in public.

American Indians. Some twenty-five thousand Indians served in the military during the war. Although the Iroquois nation challenged the right of the United States to draft Indians, in 1942 it separately declared war against the Axis powers. The armed forces used Navajo soldiers in the Pacific theater to confuse the Japanese by sending coded messages in their tribal language. In addition to those serving the military, another forty thousand Indians worked in defense-related industries. The migration of Indians off reservations opened up new opportunities and fostered increased pride in the part they played in winning the war. Nevertheless, for most Indians the war did not improve their living conditions or remove hostility to their tribal identities.

The Ordeal of Japanese Americans.

World War II marked a significant crossroads for the protection of civil liberties. In general, the federal government did not repress civil liberties as harshly as it had during World War I, primarily because opposition to World War II was not nearly as great. The chief potential for radical dissent came from the Communist Party, but after the Germans attacked the Soviet Union in June 1941, Communists and their sympathizers rallied behind the war effort and did whatever they could to stifle any protest that threatened the goal of defeating Germany. On the other side of the political spectrum, after the attack on Pearl Harbor conservative isolationists in the America First Movement quickly threw their support behind the war.

Of the three ethnic groups associated with the Axis enemy — Japanese, Germans, and Italians — Japanese Americans received by far the worst treatment from the civilian population and state and federal officials. Germans had experienced animosity and repression on the home front during World War I but, like Italian immigrants, had generally assimilated into the wider population. In addition, German Americans and Italian Americans had spread out across the country, while Japanese Americans remained concentrated in distinct geographical pockets along the West Coast. Although German Americans and Italian Americans experienced prejudice, they had come to be considered racially white, unlike Japanese Americans. Nevertheless, the government arrested about 1,500 Italians considered "enemy aliens" and placed around 250 of them in internment camps. It also arrested more than 11,000 Germans, some of them American citizens, who were considered a danger.

The **internment**, or forced relocation and detainment, of Italians and Germans in the United States paled in comparison with that of the Japanese. Nearly all people of Japanese descent lived along the West Coast. Government officials relocated all of those living there — citizens and noncitizens alike — to camps in Arizona, Arkansas, California, Colorado, Idaho, Texas, Utah, and Wyoming. In Hawaii, the site of the Japanese attack on Pearl Harbor, the Japanese population, nearly one-third of the territory's population, was too large to transfer and instead lived under martial law. The few thousand Japanese Americans living elsewhere in the continental United States remained in their homes.

It did not matter that Fred Korematsu had been born in the United States, had a white girlfriend of Italian heritage, and counted whites among his best friends. His parents had come from Japan, and for much of the American public, his racial heritage meant that he was not a true American. As one American general put it early in the war, "A Jap's a Jap. It makes no difference whether he is an American citizen or not." Along with more than 100,000 people of Japanese descent, two-thirds of whom were American citizens, Korematsu spent most of the war in an internment camp. Unlike Nazi concentration camps, these facilities did not work inmates to death or execute them. Yet Japanese Americans lost their freedom and protection under the Bill of Rights and the Fourteenth Amendment. Despite scant evidence that Japanese Americans were disloyal or harbored spies or saboteurs, U.S. officials chose to believe that as a group they threatened national security. The government established a system that questioned German Americans and Italian

Americans on an individual basis if their loyalty came under suspicion. By contrast, U.S. officials identified all Japanese Americans and Japanese resident aliens with the nation that had attacked Pearl Harbor, and incarcerated them. In this respect, the United States was not unique. Following the United States' lead, Canada interned its Japanese population, more than 75 percent of whom held Canadian citizenship.

For their part, Japanese Americans made the best they could out of this situation. They had been forced to dispose of their homes and sell their possessions and businesses quickly, either selling or renting them at very low prices or simply abandoning them. They left their neighborhoods with only the possessions they could carry. They lived in wooden barracks divided into one-room apartments and shared communal toilets, showers, laundries, and dining facilities. The camps provided schools, recreational activities, and opportunities for religious worship, except for Shintoism, the official religion of Japan. Some internees attempted to farm, but the arid land on which the camps were located made this nearly impossible. Inmates who worked at jobs within a camp earned monthly wages of $12 to $19, far less than they would have received outside the camps.

Explore ▶

See Sources 23.2 and 23.3 for two views of Japanese American internment policy.

Japanese Americans responded to their internment in a variety of ways. Many formed community groups, and some expressed their reactions to the emotional upheaval by writing of their experiences or displaying their feelings through artwork. Contradicting beliefs that their ancestry made them disloyal or not real Americans, some 18,000 men joined the army, and many fought gallantly in some of the war's fiercest battles on the European front with the 442nd Regiment, one of the most heavily decorated units in the military. Nisei soldiers were among the first, along with African American troops, to liberate Jews from German concentration camps. Others, like Fred Korematsu, remained in the camps and challenged the legality of President Roosevelt's executive order, which had allowed military officials to exclude Japanese Americans from certain areas and evacuate them from their homes. However, the Supreme Court ruled against him and others. Finally, in December 1944, shortly after he won election to his fourth term as president, Roosevelt rescinded Executive Order 9066.

In contrast to the treatment of Japanese Americans, the status of Chinese Americans improved markedly during the war. With China under Japanese occupation, Congress repealed the Chinese Exclusion Act in 1943, making the Chinese the first Asians who could become naturalized citizens. Chinese American men also fought in integrated military units like their Filipino peers. For the first time, the war opened up jobs to Chinese American men and women outside their ethnic economy.

Despite the violation of the civil liberties of Japanese American citizens, the majority did not become embittered against the United States. Rather, most of the internees returned to their communities after the war and resumed their lives, still intent on pursuing the American dream from which they had been so harshly excluded; however, some 8,000 Japanese Americans renounced their U.S. citizenship and repatriated to Japan in 1945. After briefly moving to Detroit, Korematsu returned to San Leandro, California with his wife and two children. Still, Korematsu had trouble finding regular employment because he had a criminal record for violating the exclusion order. Unlike most inmates of German concentration camps, Korematsu survived, but in the name of national security the government had established the precedent of incarcerating groups deemed "suspect." It took four decades for the U.S. government to admit its mistake and apologize, and in 1988

COMPARATIVE ANALYSIS

Japanese American Internment

In 1942 Charles Kikuchi was an American-born citizen of Japanese descent and a twenty-six-year-old graduate student when he was ordered to relocate to the Tanforan Race Track in San Bruno, California, where he and his family lived in a converted horse stable along with hundreds of others for nine months before moving to Gila River Relocation Center in Arizona. While at Tanforan he kept a vivid diary. In 1943 Kikuchi was released and moved to Chicago. A year later, the Supreme Court ruled that the detention of Japanese Americans did not violate the Constitution. Kikuchi was one of the first to be released because he agreed to move inland, but tens of thousands, like Fred Korematsu, remained interned.

Source 23.2

Charles Kikuchi | Internment Diary, 1942

There was a terrific rainstorm last night and we have had to wade through the "slush alleys" again. Everyone sinks up to the ankles in mud. Some trucks came in today with lumber to build new barracks, but the earth was so soft that the truck sank over the hubs and they had a hell of a time pulling it out. The Army certainly is rushing things. About half of the Japanese have already been evacuated from the restricted areas in this state. Manzanar, Santa Anita, and Tanforan will be the three biggest centers. Now that S.F. [San Francisco] has been almost cleared the American Legion, the Native Sons of the Golden West, and the California Joint Immigration Committee are filing charges that the Nisei [children born in America to Japanese parents] should be disfranchised because we have obtained citizenship under false pretenses and that "we are loyal subjects of Japan" and

therefore never should have been allowed to obtain citizenship. This sort of thing will gain momentum and we are not in a very advantageous position to combat it. I get fearful sometimes because this sort of hysteria will gain momentum.

The S.F. Registrar has made a statement that we will be sent absentee ballots to which Mr. James Fisk of the Joint Immigration Committee protests greatly. Tomorrow I am going to carry a petition around to protest against their protests. I think that they are stabbing us in the back and that there should be a separate concentration camp for these so-called Americans. They are a lot more dangerous than the Japanese in the U.S. ever will or have been.

Source: John Modell, ed., *The Kikuchi Diary: Chronicle from an American Concentration Camp* (Champaign: University of Illinois Press, 1992), 73.

Congress awarded reparations of $20,000 to each of the 60,000 living internees. In 1998 President Bill Clinton awarded Korematsu the Presidential Medal of Freedom — the highest decoration a civilian can receive.

REVIEW & RELATE

- What new challenges and opportunities did the war present to minority groups?

- Why were Japanese Americans singled out as a particular threat to national security?

Source 23.3

Justice Hugo Black | *Korematsu v. United States*, 1944

Our task would be simple, our duty clear, were this a case involving the imprisonment of a loyal citizen in a concentration camp because of racial prejudice. Regardless of the true nature of the assembly and relocation centers—and we deem it unjustifiable to call them concentration camps with all the ugly connotations that term implies—we are dealing specifically with nothing but an exclusion order. To cast this case into outlines of racial prejudice, without reference to the real military dangers which were presented, merely confuses the issue. Korematsu was not excluded from the Military Area because of hostility to him or his race. He was excluded because we are at war with the Japanese Empire, because the properly constituted military authorities feared an invasion of our West Coast and felt constrained to take proper security measures, because they decided that the military urgency of the situation demanded that all citizens of Japanese ancestry be segregated from the West Coast temporarily, and finally, because Congress, reposing its confidence in this time of war in our military leaders—as inevitably it must—determined that they should have the power to do just this. There was evidence of disloyalty on the part of some, the military authorities considered that the need for action was great, and time was short.

Source: *Korematsu v. United States*, 323 U.S. 214, 223–24 (1944).

Interpret the Evidence

1. According to Charles Kikuchi, why did groups such as the American Legion seek to deprive the Nisei of their right to vote?
2. According to Justice Hugo Black, why were Japanese American citizens such as Kikuchi and Korematsu interned? What role did he say racial prejudice played?

Put It in Context

In what ways was internment different from when the United States suppressed civil liberties during World War I?

Global War

World War II pitted the "Grand Alliance" of Great Britain, the Soviet Union, the French government in exile, and the United States against the Axis powers of Germany, Japan, and Italy. From the outset, the United States deployed military forces to contain Japanese aggression, but its most immediate concern was to defeat Germany. Before battles in Europe, Asia, and four other continents concluded, more than 60 million people perished, including 405,000 Americans. Six million Jewish civilians died in the Holocaust, the Nazi regime's genocidal effort to eradicate Europe's Jewish population. Another 9 million civilians—Slavic peoples, Romani, Jehovah's Witnesses, homosexuals, the disabled, and Communists—also were systematically murdered by the Nazis. The Soviet Union experienced the greatest losses—nearly 27 million soldiers and civilians, more than two-fifths of all those killed.

War in Europe. United against Hitler, the Grand Alliance divided over how quickly to mount a counterattack directly on Germany. The Soviet Union, which bore the brunt of the fighting in trying to repel the German army's invasion, demanded the opening of a **second front** through France and into Germany to take the pressure off its forces. The British wanted to fight first in northern Africa and southern Europe, in part to remove Axis forces from territory that endangered their economic interests in the Mediterranean and the Middle East and in part to buy time to rebuild their depleted fighting strength. President Roosevelt understood the Soviet position, but worried about losing public support early in the war if the United States experienced heavy casualties. He approved his military advisers' plans for an invasion of France from England in 1943, but in the meantime he agreed with Churchill to fight the Germans and Italians on the periphery of Europe.

From a military standpoint, this circuitous approach proved successful. In October 1942 British forces in North Africa overpowered the Germans at El Alamein, pushing them out of Egypt and removing their threat to the Suez Canal. The following month, British and American troops landed in Algeria and Morocco. After some early defeats, the combined strength of British and American ground, air, and naval forces drove the Germans out of Africa in May 1943.

These military victories failed to relieve political tensions among the Allies. Although the Soviets had managed to stop the German offensive against Stalingrad, the deepest penetration of enemy troops into their country, Stalin expected the second front to begin as promised in the spring of 1943. He was bitterly disappointed when Roosevelt postponed the cross–English Channel invasion of France until 1944. To Stalin, it appeared as if his allies were looking to gain a double triumph by letting the Communists and Nazis beat each other into submission.

Instead of opening a second front in France, British, American, and Canadian troops invaded Italy from its southern tip in July 1943. Their initial victories quickly led to the removal of Mussolini and his retreat to northern Italy, where he lived under German protection (Map 23.1). Not until June 4, 1944 did the Allies occupy Rome in central Italy and force the Germans to retreat.

To overcome Stalin's dissatisfaction with the postponement of opening the second front, President Roosevelt issued orders to give the Soviets unlimited access to Lend-Lease supplies to sustain their war efforts and to care for their citizens. In November 1943, Roosevelt, Churchill, and Stalin met in Tehran, Iran. Roosevelt and Stalin seemed to get along well. Stalin agreed to deploy troops against Japan after the war in Europe ended, and Roosevelt agreed to open the second front within six months. Churchill joined Roosevelt and Stalin in supporting the creation of an international organization to ensure postwar peace.

This time the Americans and British kept their word, and the Allies finally embarked on the second-front invasion. On June 6, 1944—called **D Day**—more than 1.5 million American, British, and Canadian troops crossed the English Channel in 4,000 boats and landed on the beaches of Normandy, France. Despite deadly machine-gun fire from

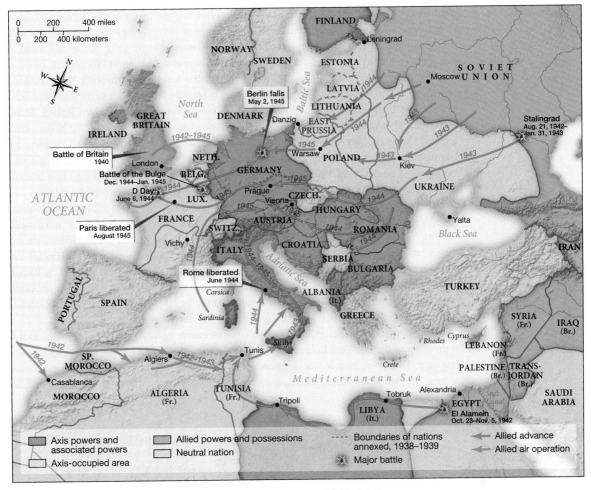

MAP 23.1   World War II in Europe, 1941–1945

By late 1941, the Axis powers had brought most of Europe and the Mediterranean region under their control. But between 1942 and 1945, the Allied powers drove them back. Critical victories at Leningrad and Stalingrad, in North Africa, and on the beaches of Normandy forced the retreat, and then the defeat, of the Axis powers.

German troops placed on higher ground, the Allied forces managed to establish a beachhead. The bravery and discipline of the troops, along with their superior numbers, overcame the Germans and opened the way for the Allies to liberate Paris in August 1944. By the end of the year, the Allies had regained control of the rest of France and most of Belgium.

Amid these Allied victories, Roosevelt ran for a fourth term against Republican challenger Thomas E. Dewey, governor of New York. He dumped from the campaign ticket his vice president, Henry A. Wallace, a liberal on economic and racial issues, and replaced him with Senator Harry S. Truman of Missouri, who was more acceptable to southern voters. Despite his declining health, Roosevelt won easily.

War in the Pacific.

With the Soviet Union bearing the brunt of the fighting in eastern Europe, the United States shouldered the burden of fighting Japan. U.S. military commanders began a two-pronged counterattack in the Pacific in 1942. General Douglas MacArthur, whose troops had escaped from the Philippines as Japanese forces overran the islands in May 1942, planned to regroup in Australia, head north through New Guinea, and return to the Philippines. At the same time, Admiral Chester Nimitz directed the U.S. Pacific Fleet from Hawaii toward Japanese-occupied islands in the western Pacific. If all went well, MacArthur's ground troops and Nimitz's naval forces would combine with General Curtis LeMay's air forces to overwhelm Japan. This strategy was known as **"island-hopping."** Accordingly, American and allied forces would leapfrog over heavily fortified Japanese positions and concentrate their resources on lightly defended Japanese islands that would provide bases capable of sustaining the campaign to attack the nation of Japan.

All went according to plan in 1942. Shortly after the Philippines fell to the Japanese, the Allies won a major victory in May in the Battle of the Coral Sea, off the northwest coast of Australia. The following month, the U.S. navy achieved an even greater victory when it defeated the Japanese in the Battle of Midway Island, northwest of Hawaii. In August, the fighting moved to the Solomon Islands, east of New Guinea, where U.S. forces waged fierce battles at Guadalcanal Island. After six months of heavy casualties on both sides, the Americans finally dislodged the Japanese. By late 1944, American, Australian, and New Zealand troops had put the Japanese on the defensive.

In 1945 the United States mounted its final offensive against Japan. In preparation for an invasion of the Japanese home islands, American marines won important battles on Iwo Jima and Okinawa, two strategic islands off the coast of Japan. The fighting proved costly — on Iwo Jima alone, the Japanese fought and died nearly to the last man while

Fighting in Guadalcanal From August 1942 to February 1943, U.S. Marines and Allied forces fought fierce battles against the Japanese on Guadalcanal, part of the Solomon Islands in the South Pacific. Operating in this tropical environment, the Marines had captured this field gun position from the Japanese and camouflaged it. This victory sparked the Allied offensive in the Pacific Theater. Official Marine Corps Photo #50515

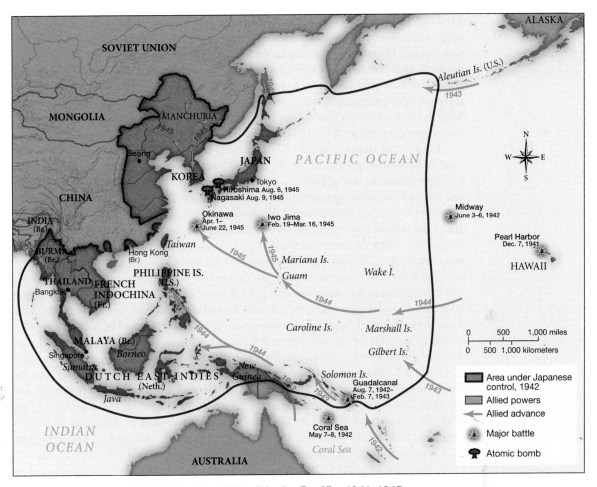

MAP 23.2   World War II in the Pacific, 1941–1945

After bombing Pearl Harbor on December 7, 1941, Japan captured the Philippines and wrenched control of Asian colonies from the British, French, and Dutch and then occupied eastern China. The Allied powers, led by U.S. forces, eventually defeated Japan by winning a series of hard-fought victories on Central Pacific islands and by bombing Hiroshima and Nagasaki.

killing 6,000 Americans and wounding 20,000 others. At the same time, the U.S. Army Air Corps conducted firebomb raids over Tokyo and other major cities, killing some 330,000 Japanese civilians. These attacks were conducted by newly developed B-29 bombers, which could fly more than 3,000 miles and could be dispatched from Pacific island bases captured by the U.S. military. The purpose of this strategic bombing was to destroy Japan's economic capability to sustain the war rather than to destroy their military forces. At the same time, the navy blockaded Japan, further crippling its economy and reducing its supplies of food, medicine, and raw materials (Map 23.2). Still, the Japanese government refused to surrender and indicated its determination to resist by launching *kamikaze* attacks (suicidal airplane crashes) on American warships and airplanes.

Ending the War. With victory in sight in both Europe and the Pacific, the Allies addressed problems of postwar relations. In February 1945 Roosevelt and Churchill met with Stalin in the resort city of Yalta in the Ukraine. There they clashed over the question of the postwar government of Poland and whether to recognize the claim of the Polish government in exile in London, which the United States and Great Britain supported, or that of the pro-Soviet government, which had spent the war in the USSR. The loosely worded **Yalta Agreement**, which resulted from the conference, called for the establishment of permanent governments in Poland and the rest of eastern Europe through free elections.

Despite this controversy, the Allies left Yalta united over other issues. They renewed their commitment to establishing the United Nations, and the Soviets reaffirmed their intention to join the war against Japan three months after Germany's surrender. The Allies also reached a tentative agreement on postwar Germany. The United States, Great Britain, the Soviet Union, and France would divide the country into four zones, each occupied by one of the powers. They would further subdivide Berlin into four sectors because the capital city fell within the Soviet occupation area. As with the accord over Poland, the agreement concerning Germany created tension after the war.

The Yalta Conference concluded just as the final assault against Germany got under way. The Germans had launched one last offensive in mid-December 1944. Mobilizing troops from remaining outposts in Belgium, they attacked Allied forces in the Battle of the Bulge. After an initial German drive into enemy lines, American and British fighting men recovered and sent the Germans retreating across the Rhine River and back into Germany. Pushing from the west, American general Dwight D. Eisenhower stopped at the Elbe River, where he had agreed to meet up with Red Army troops who were charging from the east to Berlin. After an intense assault by the Soviets, the German capital of Berlin fell, and on April 25 Russian and American forces linked up in Torgau on the Elbe River. They achieved this triumph two weeks after Franklin Roosevelt died at the age of sixty-three from a cerebral hemorrhage. On April 30, 1945, with Berlin shattered, Hitler committed suicide in his bunker. A few days earlier, Italian antifascist partisans had captured and executed Mussolini in northern Italy. On May 2, German troops surrendered in Italy, and on May 7 the remnants of the German government formally surrendered. The war in Europe ended the next day.

With the war over in Europe, the United States made its final push against Japan. Since 1942, J. Robert Oppenheimer and his team of scientists and engineers had labored feverishly to construct an atomic bomb. Few people knew about the top-secret **Manhattan Project**, and Congress appropriated $2 billion without knowing its true purpose.

Vice President Harry S. Truman did not learn about the details of the Manhattan Project until Roosevelt's death on April 12, and in July he found out about the first atomic test while en route to a conference in Potsdam, Germany with Stalin and Churchill. He ordered the State Department to issue a vaguely worded ultimatum to the Japanese demanding their immediate surrender or else face annihilation. When Japan indicated that it would surrender if the United States allowed the country to retain its emperor, Hirohito, the Truman administration refused and demanded unconditional surrender. As a further blow to Japan, Stalin was ready to send the Soviet military to attack Japanese troops in Manchuria on August 8, which would seriously weaken Japan's ability to hold out.

On August 6 the *Enola Gay*, an American B-29 bomber, dropped an atomic bomb on Hiroshima. The weapon immediately killed 80,000 civilians, and tens of thousands later died slowly from radiation poisoning. Three days later, on August 9, Japan still had not surrendered, and the Army Air Corps dropped another atomic bomb on Nagasaki, killing more than 100,000 civilians. Five days later, on August 14, Japan announced that it would surrender; the formal surrender was completed on September 2.

At the time, very few Americans questioned the decision to drop atomic bombs on Japan. Truman believed that had Roosevelt been alive, he would have authorized use of the bombs. Newly on the job, Truman hesitated to reverse a decision already reached by his predecessor. He reasoned that his action would save American lives because the U.S. military would not have to launch a costly invasion of Japan's home islands. He also felt justified in giving the order because he sought retaliation for the surprise attack on Pearl Harbor and for Japanese atrocities against American soldiers, especially in the Philippines. **See Primary Source Project 23: The Decision to Drop the Atomic Bomb, page 807.**

Evidence of the Holocaust.

The end of the war revealed the full extent and horror of the **Holocaust** — Germany's calculated and methodical slaughter of certain religious, ethnic, and political groups. As Allied troops liberated Germany and Poland, they saw for themselves the brutality of the Nazi concentration camps that Hitler had set up to execute or work to death 6 million Jews and another 5 million "undesirables" — Slavs, Poles, Gypsies, homosexuals, the physically and mentally disabled, and Communists. At Buchenwald and Dachau in Germany and at Auschwitz in Poland, the Allies encountered the skeletal remains of inmates tossed into mass graves, dead from starvation, illness, and executions. Crematoria on the premises contained the ashes of inmates first poisoned and then incinerated. Troops also freed the "living dead," those still alive but seriously ill and undernourished.

Explore ▶

Compare different perspectives on the Roosevelt administration's response to the Holocaust in Sources 23.4 and 23.5.

These horrific discoveries shocked the public, but evidence of what was happening had appeared early in the war. Journalists like Varian Fry had outlined the Nazi atrocities against the Jews several years before. "Letters, reports, tables all fit together. They add up to the most appalling picture of mass murder in all human history," Fry wrote in the *New Republic* magazine in 1942.

The Roosevelt administration did little in response, despite growing evidence. It chose not to send planes to bomb the concentration camps or the railroad lines leading to them, deeming it too risky militarily and too dangerous for the inmates. "The War Department," its assistant Secretary John J. McCloy wrote the director of the War Refugee Board in defending this decision, "is of the opinion that the suggested air operation is impracticable. It could be executed only by the diversion of considerable air support essential to the success of our forces now engaged in decisive operations and would in any case be of such very doubtful efficacy that it would not amount to a practical project." In a less defensible decision, the Roosevelt administration refused to relax immigration laws to allow Jews and other persecuted minorities to take refuge in the United States, and only 21,000 managed to find asylum. The State Department, which could have modified these policies, was staffed with anti-Semitic officials, and though President Roosevelt expressed sympathy for the plight of Hitler's victims, he believed that winning the war as quickly as possible was the best way to help them.

Nevertheless, even when it had been possible to rescue Jews, the United States balked. In 1939 a German liner, the SS *St. Louis*, embarked from Hamburg with 937 Jewish

SECONDARY SOURCE ANALYSIS

The Roosevelt Administration and the Holocaust

The genocide committed by the Nazis during World War II against six million European Jews stands out for its moral depravity even in the bloodiest world war in human history. In the United States, with a significant Jewish population that supported FDR, the Roosevelt administration had to deal with two problems: refugees seeking asylum and military operations against Nazi death camps. Roosevelt's main goal was to end the global war as quickly as possible and by doing so save more lives, including Jewish prisoners in concentration camps. Because of the profound moral dimensions of the Holocaust, however, the question for historians remains whether Roosevelt could have made a greater effort on behalf of European Jews and others murdered by the Nazis.

Source 23.4

David S. Wyman, FDR Abandoned the Jews, 1984

America's response to the Holocaust was the result of action and inaction on the part of many people. In the forefront was Franklin D. Roosevelt, whose steps to aid Europe's Jews were very limited. If he had wanted to, he could have aroused substantial public backing for a vital rescue effort by speaking out on the issue. If nothing else, a few forceful statements by the President would have brought the extermination news out of obscurity and into the headlines. But he had little to say about the problem and gave no priority to rescue at all.

. . . Even when interested in rescue action, Roosevelt was unwilling to run a political risk for it, as his response to the free-ports plan showed. The WRB's [War Refugee Board] original rescue strategy depended on America's setting an example to other nations by offering to open several temporary havens. The President, by agreeing to only one American camp, signaled that little was expected of any country. A more extensive free-ports program would have strained relations with Congress. It might also have cost votes, and 1944 was an election year.

. . . It appears that Roosevelt's overall response to the Holocaust was deeply affected by political expediency. Most Jews supported him unwaveringly, so an active rescue policy offered little political advantage. A pro-Jewish stance, however, could lose votes. American Jewry's great loyalty to the President thus weakened the leverage it might have exerted on him to save European Jews.

Source: David S. Wyman, *The Abandonment of the Jews: America and the Holocaust, 1941–1945* (New York: Pantheon Books, 1984), 311, 312.

refugees aboard and set sail for Cuba. Blocked from entry by the Cuban government, the ship sailed for the coast of Florida, hoping to gain permission to enter the United States. However, the United States refused, maintaining that the passengers did not have the proper documents required under the Immigration Act of 1924. The ship then headed back to Europe, where the United Kingdom, Belgium, the Netherlands, and France took in the passengers. Unfortunately, in 1940, when the Nazis invaded Belgium, the Netherlands, and France and sent their Jewish residents to concentration camps, an estimated 254 of the *St. Louis* passengers died along with countless others.

Source 23.5

Richard Breitman and Allan J. Lichtman, FDR Did Not Abandon the Jews, 2013

For most of his presidency Roosevelt did little to aid the imperiled Jews of Germany and Europe. He put other policy priorities well ahead of saving Jews and deferred to fears of an anti-Semitic backlash at home. He worried that measures to assist European Jews might endanger his political coalition at home and then a wartime alliance abroad. . . .When he engaged Jewish issues, he maneuvered, often behind the scenes. When he hesitated, other American officials with far less sympathy for Jews set or carried out policies.

Still, at times, Roosevelt acted decisively to rescue Jews, often withstanding contrary pressures from the American public, Congress, and his own State Department. . . . He was a far better president for Jews than any of his political adversaries would have been. Roosevelt defied most Republican opponents and some isolationist Democrats to lead political and military opposition to Nazi Germany's plans for expansion and world domination.

. . .The story of FDR and the Jews is ultimately a tragic one that transcends the achievements and failures of one leader. Even if FDR had been more willing to override domestic opposition and twist arms abroad, he could not have stopped the Nazi mass murder of some six million Jews. For Hitler and his followers, the annihilation of the Jews was not a diversion from the war effort, but integral to its purpose. For America and Britain, the rescue of Jews, even if practical, was ultimately subordinate to the overriding priorities of total war and unconditional surrender of the enemy,

Source: Richard Breitman and Allan J. Lichtman, *FDR and the Jews* (Cambridge, Mass., The Belknap Press of Harvard University Press, 2013), 2, 6–7.

Examine the Sources

1. Specify one major difference between Wyman's and Breitman/Lichtman's interpretation of Franklin D. Roosevelt's response to the Holocaust and explain how these historians use evidence to support their arguments.
2. Based on evidence in this chapter, evaluate the strengths and/or weaknesses of the Wyman and Breitman/Lichtman interpretations.

Put It in Context

Based on what Roosevelt knew about the Holocaust at the time, how much more could he have done?

Although not nearly to the same extent as in the Holocaust, the Japanese also committed numerous war atrocities. Around 50,000 U.S. soldiers and civilians became prisoners of war and about half of them were forced to work as slave laborers. From June 1942 to October 1943, the Japanese constructed a 300-mile railroad between Burma (Myanmar) and Thailand using 60,000 Allied prisoners of war and 200,000 Asian conscripts. Working under inhumane conditions, approximately 13,000 Allied workers and 80,000 Asian laborers died before the railway was completed. About 40 percent of American POWs died in Japanese captivity (in contrast only 1 percent died in Nazi camps).

Holocaust Survivors   When American troops of the 80th Army Division liberated the Buchenwald concentration camp in Germany, they found these emaciated victims of the Holocaust. Elie Wiesel (seventh from the left on the middle bunk next to the vertical post) went on to become an internationally famous writer who wrote about his wartime experiences and won the Nobel Peace Prize. H. Miller/Getty Images

One reason why POWs were treated so poorly was because the Japanese believed that surrender was a cowardly act and those who did so were beneath contempt. Far more than the Americans and their allies, Chinese civilians and native residents of such countries as Burma and the Dutch East Indies (Indonesia) were brutalized and killed by the Japanese occupying forces.

REVIEW & RELATE

How did the Allies win the war in Europe and in the Pacific, and how did tensions among them shape their military strategy and postwar plans?

Why did the United States fail to do more to help victims of the Holocaust?

Conclusion: The Impact of World War II

Franklin Roosevelt initially charted a course of neutrality before the United States entered World War II. Yet Roosevelt believed that the rise of European dictatorships and their expansionist pursuits throughout the world threatened American national security. He saw signs of trouble early, but responding to antiwar sentiment from lawmakers and the American public, Roosevelt waited for a blatant enemy attack before declaring war. The Japanese attack on Pearl Harbor in 1941 provided that justification.

On the domestic front, World War II accomplished what Franklin Roosevelt's New Deal could not. Prosperity and nearly full employment returned only after the nation's factories began supplying the Allies and the United States joined in the fight against the Axis powers. Mobilization for war also furthered the tremendous growth and centralization of power in the federal government that had begun under the New Deal. Washington, D.C. became the chief source of authority to which Americans looked for solutions to problems concerning economic security and financial development. The federal government showed that it would use its authority to expand equal rights for African Americans. The war swung national power against racial discrimination, and various civil rights victories during the war served as precursors to the civil rights movement of subsequent decades. The war also heightened Mexican Americans' consciousness of oppression and led them to organize for civil rights. However, in neither case, nor that of American Indians, did the war erase white prejudice.

At the same time, the federal government did not hesitate to trample on the civil liberties of Japanese Americans. The president succumbed to wartime antagonism against Japanese immigrants and their children. With China a wartime ally, Chinese Americans escaped a similar fate. Yet like white and black Americans, the Nisei displayed their patriotism by distinguishing themselves as soldiers on the battlefields of Europe.

The war brought women into the workforce as never before, providing a measure of independence and distancing them from their traditional roles as wives and mothers. Nevertheless, the government and private employers made it clear that they expected most female workers to give up their jobs to returning servicemen and to become homemakers once the war ended.

Finally, the war thrust the United States onto the world stage as one of the world's two major superpowers alongside the Soviet Union. This position posed new challenges. In sole possession of the atomic bomb, the most powerful weapon on the planet, and fortified by a robust economy, the United States filled the international power vacuum created by the weakening and eventual collapse of the European colonial empires. The fragile alliance that had held together the United States and the Soviet Union shattered soon after the end of World War II. The Atomic Age, which J. Robert Oppenheimer helped usher in with a powerful weapon of mass destruction, and the government oppression that Fred Korematsu endured in the name of national security did not disappear. Rather, they expanded in new directions and shaped the lives of all Americans for decades to come.

CHAPTER 23 REVIEW

TIMELINE OF EVENTS

1933	United States extends diplomatic recognition to the Soviet Union
	Adolf Hitler becomes chancellor of Germany
1935–1937	Neutrality Acts
1939	Germany occupies Czechoslovakia
	Germany and Soviet Union invade Poland; World War II begins
1940	Battle of Britain begins
	Tripartite Pact signed
1941	Lend-Lease Act
	Fair Employment Practice Committee created
	Atlantic Charter signed
	Germany invades Soviet Union
December 7, 1941	Pearl Harbor bombed
December 11, 1941	Germany and Italy declare war on the United States
1942	Congress of Racial Equality established
	Manhattan Project approved
	Roosevelt orders internment of Japanese Americans
1943	Zoot suit riots
June 6, 1944	D Day invasion begins
1945	Final U.S. offensive against Japan, with victories at Iwo Jima and Okinawa
February 1945	Yalta Conference
May 1945	Germany surrenders
August 1945	U.S. drops atomic bombs on Hiroshima and Nagasaki
September 1945	Japan surrenders

KEY TERMS

Neutrality Acts, *778*

appeasement, *778*

America First Committee, *780*

Lend-Lease Act, *781*

Atlantic Charter, *782*

military-industrial complex, *784*

War Production Board, *784*

National War Labor Board, *787*

Fair Employment Practice Committee (FEPC), *789*

Double V, *789*

zoot suit riots, *791*

internment, *792*

second front, *796*

D Day, *796*

"island-hopping", *798*

Yalta Agreement, *800*

Manhattan Project, *800*

Holocaust, *801*

REVIEW & RELATE

1. How did American public opinion shape Roosevelt's foreign policy in the years preceding U.S. entry into World War II?

2. What events in Europe and the Pacific ultimately brought the United States into World War II?

3. How did the war accelerate the trend that began during the New Deal toward increased government participation in the economy?

4. How did the war affect life on the home front for the average American?

5. What new challenges and opportunities did the war present to minority groups?

6. Why were Japanese Americans singled out as a particular threat to national security?

7. How did the Allies win the war in Europe and in the Pacific, and how did tensions among them shape their military strategy and postwar plans?

8. Why did the United States fail to do more to help victims of the Holocaust?

The Decision to Drop the Atomic Bomb

▶ Evaluate the reasons the United States dropped atomic bombs on Hiroshima and Nagasaki.

The Manhattan Project — the code name given to the U.S. atomic program — was formally set up in 1942 under the direction of General Leslie Groves and physicist J. Robert Oppenheimer. The program was a massive undertaking, employing thousands of workers at sites in Chicago; Berkeley, California; Oak Ridge, Tennessee; Hanford, Washington; and, most famously, at the scientific laboratory in Los Alamos, New Mexico. It took $3 billion to create the atomic bombs. The project was so secretive that even Harry Truman didn't learn of it until he became president following Roosevelt's death.

The bombs that exploded over Hiroshima and Nagasaki in August 1945 revolutionized world history. They ended World War II, changed the nature of warfare, and altered the course of international relations. The bombs launched a nuclear arms race that continued throughout the Cold War and unleashed fears of global annihilation. Debates about whether the bombs were necessary began even before they were dropped (Sources 23.6 and 23.7). As a result of the bombing of Hiroshima and Nagasaki, some 200,000 people, mostly civilians, were killed immediately, and even more were stricken with radiation poisoning, burns, and other injuries. More than 80 percent of the buildings in each city were flattened instantly, and permanent shadows were left on walls and pavement (Sources 23.8 and 23.10).

Many aspects of Truman's decision continue to be questioned and debated, especially whether there were reasonable alternatives to dropping the two atomic bombs (Source 23.9).

Source 23.6

Petition to the President of the United States, July 17, 1945

Before the first successful test of the atomic bomb in New Mexico on June 16, 1945, code-named "Trinity," Secretary of War Henry Stimson received a memorandum from the scientific advisory panel of the Manhattan Project, including J. Robert Oppenheimer, which recommended the use of atomic weapons against Japan. However, the day after the test, as the following document shows, seventy scientists involved in the Manhattan Project wrote to President Truman arguing against the bomb's use.

Discoveries of which the people of the United States are not aware may affect the welfare of this nation in the near future. The liberation of atomic power which has been achieved places atomic bombs in the hands of the Army. It places in your hands, as Commander-in-Chief, the fateful decision whether or not to sanction the use of such bombs in the present phase of the war against Japan.

We, the undersigned scientists, have been working in the field of atomic power. Until recently we have had to fear that the United States might be attacked by atomic bombs during this war and that her only defense might lie in a counterattack by the same means. Today, with the defeat of Germany, this danger is averted and we feel impelled to say what follows:

The war has to be brought speedily to a successful conclusion and attacks by atomic bombs may very well be an effective method of warfare. We feel, however, that such attacks on Japan could not be justified, at least not unless the terms which will be imposed after the war on Japan were made public in detail and Japan were given an opportunity to surrender.

If such public announcement gave assurance to the Japanese that they could look forward to a life devoted to peaceful pursuits in their homeland and if Japan still refused to surrender our nation might then, in certain circumstances, find itself forced to resort to the use of atomic bombs. Such a step, however, ought not to be made at any time without seriously considering the moral responsibilities which are involved. . . .

If after this war a situation is allowed to develop in the world which permits rival powers to be in uncontrolled possession of these new means of destruction, the cities of the United States as well as the cities of other nations will be in continuous danger of sudden annihilation. All the resources of the United States, moral and material, may have to be mobilized to prevent the advent of such a world situation. Its prevention is at present the solemn responsibility of the United States—singled out by virtue of her lead in the field of atomic power. . . .

In view of the foregoing, we, the undersigned, respectfully petition: first, that you exercise your power as Commander-in-Chief, to rule that the United States shall not resort to the use of atomic bombs in this war unless the terms which will be imposed upon Japan have been made public in detail and Japan knowing these terms has refused to surrender; second, that in such an event the question whether or not to use atomic bombs be decided by you in the light of the considerations presented in this petition as well as all the other moral responsibilities which are involved.

Source: U.S. National Archives, Record Group 77, Records of the Chief of Engineers, Manhattan Engineer District, Harrison-Bundy file, folder #76.

Source: U.S. National Archives, Record Group 77, Records of the Chief of Engineers, Manhattan Engineer District, Harrison-Bundy file, folder #76.

Source 23.7

President Harry S. Truman | Press Release on the Atomic Bomb, August 6, 1945

After the first atomic bomb, nicknamed "Little Boy," was dropped on Hiroshima, President Truman released the following statement to the public. In it, Truman explains the development of the bomb, its destructive power, and why it was used against Japan. This statement was made before the second bomb was dropped on Nagasaki and before Japan's surrender.

The Japanese began the war from the air at Pearl Harbor. They have been repaid many fold. And the end is not yet. With this bomb we have now added a new and revolutionary increase in destruction to supplement the growing power of our armed forces. In their present form these bombs are now in production and even more powerful forms are in development.

It is an atomic bomb. It is a harnessing of the basic power of the universe. The force from which the sun draws its power has been loosed against those who brought war to the Far East. . . .

We are now prepared to obliterate more rapidly and completely every productive enterprise the Japanese have above ground in any city. We shall destroy their docks, their factories, and their communications. Let there be no mistake; we shall completely destroy Japan's power to make war.

It was to spare the Japanese people from utter destruction that the ultimatum of July 26 was issued at Potsdam. Their leaders promptly rejected that ultimatum. If they do not now accept our terms they may expect a rain of ruin from the air, the like of which has never been seen on this earth. Behind this air attack will follow sea and land forces in such numbers and power as they have not yet seen and with the fighting skill of which they are already well aware. . . .

The fact that we can release atomic energy ushers in a new era in man's understanding of nature's forces. Atomic energy may in the future supplement the power that now comes from coal, oil, and falling water, but at present it cannot be produced on a basis to compete with them commercially. Before that comes there must be a long period of intensive research.

Source: Press Release by the White House, August 6, 1945, Ayers Papers, Truman Library.

Source: Press Release by the White House, August 6, 1945, Ayers Papers, Truman Library.

Hiroshima, August 6, 1945

In this photograph, a survivor stands among the ruins of Hiroshima. The bomb that was dropped on the city destroyed 5 square miles and killed 70,000 to 80,000 people. Three days later, the United States dropped a second atomic bomb on Nagasaki.

AP Photo/Stanley Troutman

U.S. Strategic Bombing Survey, 1946

After the war, President Truman called for a series of surveys on the effectiveness of strategic bombing campaigns in Europe and Asia and on the effects of the atomic bombs on Hiroshima and Nagasaki. The survey on the Pacific war included interviews with Japanese military and government leaders as well as information from Japanese wartime documents. It concluded that the use of the atomic bombs was unnecessary because even without them Japan would have surrendered in the fall of 1945.

4. When Japan was defeated without invasion, a recurrent question arose as to what effect the threat of a home island invasion had had upon the surrender decision. It was contended that the threat of invasion, if not the actual operation, was a requirement to induce acceptance of the surrender terms. On this tangled issue the evidence and hindsight are clear. The fact is, of course, that Japan did surrender without invasion, and with its principal armies intact. Testimony before the Survey shows that the expected "violation of the sacred homeland" raised few fears which expedited the decision to surrender beforehand. Government and Imperial household leaders felt some concern for the "destruction of the Japanese people," but the people were already being shattered by direct air attacks. Anticipated landings were even viewed by the military with hope that they would afford a means of inflicting casualties sufficiently high to improve their chances of a negotiated peace. Preparation of defenses against landings diverted certain resources from dispersal and cushioning moves which might have partially mitigated our air blows. But in Japan's then depleted state, the diversion was not significant. The responsible leaders in power read correctly the true situation and embraced surrender well before invasion was expected. . . .

6. The Hiroshima and Nagasaki atomic bombs did not defeat Japan, nor by the testimony of the enemy leaders who ended the war did they persuade Japan to accept unconditional surrender.

The Emperor [Hirohito], the lord privy seal, the prime minister, the foreign minister, and the navy minister had decided as early as May of 1945 that the war should be ended even if it meant acceptance of defeat on allied terms. The war minister and the two chiefs of staff opposed unconditional surrender. The impact of the Hiroshima attack was to bring further urgency and lubrication to the machinery of achieving peace, primarily by contributing to a situation which permitted the prime minister to bring the Emperor overtly and directly into a position where his decision for immediate acceptance of the Potsdam declaration could be used to override the remaining objectors. Thus, although the atomic bombs changed no votes of the Supreme War Direction Council concerning the Potsdam terms, they did foreshorten the war and expedite the peace. . . .

There is little point in attempting more precisely to impute Japan's unconditional surrender to any one of the numerous causes which jointly and cumulatively were responsible for Japan's disaster. Concerning the absoluteness of her defeat there can be no doubt. The time lapse between military impotence and political acceptance of the inevitable might have been shorter had the political structure of Japan permitted a more rapid and decisive determination of national policies. It seems clear, however, that air supremacy and its exploitation over Japan proper was the major factor which determined the timing of Japan's surrender and obviated any need for invasion.

Based on a detailed investigation of all the facts and supported by the testimony of the surviving Japanese leaders involved, it is the Survey's opinion that certainly prior to 31 December 1945, and in all probability prior to 1 November 1945, Japan would have surrendered even if the atomic bombs had not been dropped, even if Russia had not entered the war, and even if no invasion had been planned or contemplated.

Source: United States Strategic Bombing Survey: Japan's Struggle to End the War, July 1, 1946, Elsey Papers, Truman Library.

Father Johannes Siemes | Eyewitness Account of the Hiroshima Bombing, 1945

Father Johannes Siemes, a German priest living in Japan, wrote the following eyewitness account of the Hiroshima bombing. Siemes lived less than a mile outside the city, and after the attack he went into Hiroshima to look for other priests from his order. He gave this account to Bishop Franklin Corley, an American soldier and one of the first Americans to enter the city.

More than thirty hours had gone by until the first official rescue party had appeared on the scene. We find both children and take them out of the park: six-year old girl who was uninjured, and a twelve-year old girl who had been burned about the head, hands, and legs, and who had lain for thirty hours without care in the park. The left side of her face and the left eye were completely covered with blood and pus, so that we thought that she had lost the eye. When the wound was later washed, we noted that the eye was intact and that the lids had just become stuck together. On the way home, we took another group of three refugees with us. The first wanted to know, however, of what nationality we were. They, too, feared that we might be Americans who had parachuted in. When we arrived in Nagatsuka [a Jesuit monastery in Hiroshima], it had just become dark.

We took under our care fifty refugees who had lost everything. The majority of them were wounded and not a few had dangerous burns. Father Rektor treated the wounds as well as he could with the few medicaments that we could, with effort, gather up. He had to confine himself in general to cleansing the wounds of purulent [consisting of pus] material. Even those with the smaller burns are very weak and all suffered from diarrhea. . . .

Thousands of wounded who died later could doubtless have been rescued had they received proper treatment and care, but rescue work in a catastrophe of this magnitude had not been envisioned; since the whole city had been knocked out at a blow, everything which had been prepared for emergency work was lost, and no preparation had been made for rescue work in the outlying districts. Many of the wounded also died because they had been weakened by under-nourishment and consequently lacked in strength to recover. Those who had their normal strength and who received good care slowly healed the burns which had been occasioned by the bomb. There were also cases, however, whose prognosis seemed good who died suddenly. There were also some who had only small external wounds who died within a week or later, after an inflammation of the pharynx and oral cavity had taken place. . . .

Only several cases are known to me personally where individuals who did not have external burns later died. Father Kleinsorge and Father Cieslik, who were near the center of the explosion, but who did not suffer burns, became quite weak some fourteen days after the explosion. Up to this time small incised wounds had healed normally, but thereafter the wounds which were still unhealed became worse and are to date (in September) still incompletely healed. The attending physician diagnosed it as leucopenia [a decrease in white blood cells]. There thus seems to be some truth in the statement that the radiation had some effect on the blood. I am of the opinion, however, that their generally undernourished and weakened condition was partly responsible for these findings. It was noised about that the ruins of the city emitted deadly rays and that workers who went there to aid in the clearing died, and that the central district would be uninhabitable for some time to come.

Source: Father Johannes Siemes, "Hiroshima, August 6, 1945," *Bulletin of the Atomic Scientists* 1, no. 11 (1946): 5–6.

Interpret the Evidence

1. Compare the arguments of the scientists who opposed dropping the atomic bomb on Japan (Source 23.6) with those put forward by President Truman for dropping the bombs (Source 23.7).

2. According to the strategic bombing survey, what role did the atomic bombs play in defeating Japan (Source 23.9)?

3. How does what you see in the photograph of the day after the bombing of Hiroshima (Source 23.8) compare with the eyewitness account in Source 23.10? Which do you find more powerful and why?

4. What evidence can you find in these documents that atomic power would play a critical role in shaping the postwar world?

Put It in Context

Analyze the political, military, and racial motives behind the United States' decision to drop the atomic bomb on Japan.

What were the alternatives to dropping the atomic bomb and why weren't they used?

The Opening of the Cold War

1945–1961

WINDOW TO THE PAST

Ronald Reagan Testimony before HUAC, 1947

During the Cold War with the Soviet Union, the United States became preoccupied with searching for and punishing Communists at home. In 1947 the House Committee on Un-American Activities investigated alleged communism in Hollywood. The committee heard the testimony of Ronald Reagan, the president of the Screen Actors Guild, who declared that his organization had successfully countered Communist influence. ▶ To discover more about what this primary source can show us, see Source 24.6 on page 843.

> Mr. REAGAN. Well, sir, I would like to say, as Mr. Montgomery and Mr. Murphy have indicated, they have done it very well. I have been alarmed by the misapprehension, the feeling around, that it was a minority fighting against a majority on this issue in our business, and I would like in answering that question to reiterate what those gentlemen have said, that rather 99 percent of us are pretty well aware of what is going on, and I think within the bounds of our democratic rights, and never once stepping over the rights given us by democracy, we have done a pretty good job in our business of keeping those people's activities curtailed. After all, we must recognize them at present as a political party. On that basis we have exposed their lies when we came across them, we have opposed their propaganda, and I can certainly testify that in the case of the Screen Actors Guild we have been eminently successful in preventing them from, with their usual tactics, trying to run a majority of an organization with a well organized minority.
>
> So that fundamentally I would say in opposing those people that the best thing to do is to make democracy work. In the Screen Actors Guild we make it work by insuring everyone a vote and by keeping everyone informed. I believe that, as Thomas Jefferson put it, if all the American people know all of the facts they will never make a mistake.

The U.S. Government Publishing Office

After reading this chapter you should be able to:

- Analyze the causes of the Cold War.
- Explain how the overall strategy of containment changed between 1948 and 1953, and describe in particular how the Korean War affected U.S. Cold War strategy and presidential power.
- Analyze the effects of the Cold War on domestic policy.
- Evaluate how the Eisenhower administration managed containment throughout the world.

COMPARING AMERICAN HISTORIES

George Frost Kennan played a critical role in shaping the postwar confrontation between the United States and the Soviet Union. Kennan's views were based on extensive experience with the Soviets gained during two tours of duty at the U.S. Embassy in Moscow. During the first, from 1933 to 1937, he witnessed countless "enemies of the state" arrested, exiled, or executed in Stalin's purges. His experiences convinced him that there was little basis for a positive relationship between the United States and the Soviet Union.

Kennan's second tour of duty in Moscow, from 1944 to 1946, came at a critical juncture in U.S.-Soviet relations. As the war drew to a close, tensions over the nature of the postwar world escalated, and by 1946 the wartime alliance had collapsed. Against this backdrop,

Kennan warned that Stalin was committed to expanding communism throughout the world and advised President Harry S. Truman to adopt a policy of *containment*. In Kennan's view, all Soviet efforts at expansion should be met with firm resistance. At the same time, the United States should take an active role in rebuilding the economies of war-torn Western European countries, thereby reducing the appeal of communism to their populations. Kennan's concept of containment would become the basis for President Truman's Cold War foreign policy.

Kennan, however, was not a rigid cold warrior. He soon insisted that his containment strategy had been misunderstood. As the Cold War intensified and expanded, Kennan argued that containment would work best through political and economic rather than military means. Increasingly, his views fell out of favor at the State Department, and Kennan left in 1950 in a disagreement with the Truman administration's growing militarization of the conflict with the Soviet Union.

Julius and Ethel Rosenberg were casualties of the Cold War that Kennan helped shape. Accused of passing military secrets to the Soviet Union, they were tried for espionage in an atmosphere of growing anti-Communist fervor. Like other young idealists during the 1930s, Ethel became disillusioned with capitalism, joined the Young Communist League, and took part in labor union organizing in her hometown of New York City. Julius attended the City College of New York, where he, too, joined the Young Communist League. Three years after they met in 1936, Julius and Ethel married and started a family.

During World War II, Julius worked for the Army Signal Corps as an engineer. In 1945 he lost his job after a security investigation revealed his Communist Party membership. Five years later, the federal government charged that during World War II the Rosenbergs had provided classified information about the construction of the atomic bomb to the Soviet Union, charges they denied.

A jury found them guilty on April 5, 1951, and the presiding judge sentenced them to death. Despite an international campaign for clemency and after unsuccessful appeals to the Supreme Court, on June 19,

(*left*) **George Kennan.** Library of Congress, LC-DIG-hec-12925

(*right*) **Ethel Rosenberg.** Tallandier/ Bridgeman Images

1953, the Rosenbergs were executed. Though recent evidence has confirmed Julius Rosenberg's role as a spy, the case against Ethel remains inconclusive.

Without the heightened Cold War climate that then existed in the country, it is likely that neither would have gone to the electric chair. ■

The American histories of both George Kennan and Julius and Ethel Rosenberg revolved around their views of communism and the Soviet Union. Kennan designed an approach to containing Soviet aggression based on his dealings with Stalin. The Rosenbergs believed in communism's promise of social and economic equality and saw the Soviet Union as a defense against Nazi aggression. The lives of Kennan, the Rosenbergs, and all Americans would be profoundly shaped by the epic military and ideological battle between the superpowers as the Cold War expanded from the late 1940s through the 1950s, bringing with it increased interventions abroad, fear of communism within the United States, and changes in the executive power of the presidency.

The **Origins** of the Cold War 1945–1947

The wartime partnership between the United States and the Soviet Union (USSR) was an alliance of necessity. Putting aside ideological differences and a history of mutual distrust, the two nations joined forces to combat Nazi aggression. As long as the Nazi threat existed, the alliance held, but as the war ended and attention turned to the postwar world, the allies became adversaries. The two nations did not engage directly in war, but they entered into a prolonged struggle for political, economic, and military dominance known as the **Cold War**.

Mutual Misunderstandings. The roots of the Cold War stretched back several decades. After the Bolshevik Revolution of 1917, the United States refused to grant diplomatic recognition to the Soviet Union and sent troops to Russia to support anti-Bolshevik forces seeking to overturn the revolution, an effort that failed. At the same time, the American government, fearing Communist efforts to overthrow capitalist governments, sought to wipe out communism in the United States by deporting immigrant radicals during the Red scare (see "The Red Scare, 1919–1920" in chapter 21). The United States continued to deny diplomatic recognition to the USSR until 1933, when President Roosevelt reversed this policy. Nevertheless, relations between the two countries remained uneasy.

World War II brought a thaw in tensions. President Roosevelt went a long way toward defusing Stalin's concerns at the Yalta Conference in 1945. The Soviet leader viewed the Eastern European countries that the USSR had liberated from the Germans, especially Poland, as a buffer to protect his nation from future attacks by Germany. Roosevelt understood Stalin's reasoning and recognized political realities: The Soviet military already occupied Eastern Europe, a state of affairs that increased Stalin's bargaining position. Still, the president attempted to balance Soviet influence by insisting that the Yalta Agreement include a guarantee of free elections in Eastern Europe.

By contrast, Roosevelt's successor, Harry S. Truman, took a much less nuanced approach to U.S.-Soviet relations than his predecessor. Stalin's ruthless purges within the Soviet Union in the 1930s and 1940s convinced Truman that the Soviet dictator was paranoid and extremely dangerous. He believed that the Soviets threatened "a barbarian invasion of Europe," and he intended to deter it. In his first meeting with Soviet foreign minister Vyacheslav Molotov in April 1945, Truman rebuked the Russians for failing to support free elections in Poland. Molotov, recoiling from the sharp tone of Truman's remarks, replied: "I have never been talked to like that in my life."

Despite this rough start, Truman did not immediately abandon the idea of cooperation with the Soviet Union. At the Potsdam Conference in Germany in July 1945, Truman and Stalin agreed on several issues. The two leaders reaffirmed the concept of free elections in Eastern Europe; Soviet troop withdrawal from the oil fields of northern Iran, which bordered the USSR; and the partition of Germany (and Berlin itself) into four Allied occupation zones.

Within six months of the war's end, however, relations between the two countries soured. The United States was the only nation in the world with the atomic bomb and boasted the only economy reinvigorated by the war. As a result, the Truman administration believed that it held the upper hand against the Soviets. With this in mind, the State Department offered the Soviets a $6 billion loan, which the country needed to help rebuild its war-ravaged economy. But when the Soviets undermined free elections in Poland in 1946 and established a compliant government, the United States withdrew the offer. Soviet troops also remained in northern Iran, closing off the oil fields to potential capitalist enterprises. The failure to reach agreement over international control of atomic energy proved the last straw. The United States wanted to make sure it would keep its atomic weapons, while the Soviets wanted the United States to destroy its nuclear arsenal. Clearly, the former World War II allies did not trust each other.

Truman had significantly underestimated the strength of the Soviet position. The Soviets were well on their way toward building their own atomic bomb, negating the Americans' nuclear advantage. The Soviets could also ignore the enticement of U.S. economic aid by taking resources from East Germany and mobilizing the Russian people to rebuild their country's industry and military. Indeed, on February 9, 1946, Stalin delivered a tough speech to rally Russians to make sacrifices to enhance national security. By asserting that communism was "a better form of organization than any non-Soviet social system," he implied, according to George Kennan, that capitalist nations could not coexist with communism and that future wars were unavoidable unless communism triumphed over capitalism.

Whether Stalin meant this speech as an unofficial declaration of a third world war was not clear, but U.S. leaders interpreted it this way. A few days after Stalin spoke, Kennan sent an 8,000-word telegram from the U.S. Embassy in Moscow to Washington, blaming the Soviets for stirring up international tensions and confirming that Stalin could not be trusted. The following month, on March 15, former British prime minister Winston Churchill gave a speech in Truman's home state of Missouri. Declaring that "an iron curtain has descended across the Continent" of Europe, Churchill observed that "there is nothing [the Russians] admire so much as strength, and there is nothing for which they have less respect than for . . . military weakness." This comment reaffirmed Truman's sentiments expressed the previous year: "Unless Russia is faced with an iron fist and strong language another war is in the making." The message was clear: Unyielding resistance to the Soviet Union was the only way to avoid another world war.

Not all Americans agreed with this view. Led by Roosevelt's former vice president Henry Wallace, who served as Truman's secretary of commerce, critics voiced concern about taking a "hard line" against the Soviet Union. Stalin was pursuing a policy of expansion, they agreed, but for limited reasons. Wallace claimed that the Soviets merely wanted to protect their borders by surrounding themselves with friendly countries, just as the United States had done by establishing spheres of influence in the Caribbean. Except for Poland and Romania, Stalin initially accepted an array of governments in Eastern Europe, allowing free elections in Czechoslovakia, Hungary, and, to a lesser extent, Bulgaria. Only as Cold War tensions escalated did the Soviets tighten control over all of Eastern Europe. Critics such as Wallace considered this outcome the result of a self-fulfilling prophecy; by misinterpreting Soviet motives, the Truman administration pushed Stalin to counter the American hard line with a hard line of his own.

Explore ▶

See Source 24.1 for Henry Wallace's criticism of aggressive behavior toward the Soviet Union.

Thus, after World War II, the United States came to believe that the Soviet Union desired world revolution to spread communism, a doctrine hostile to free market individualism. At the same time, the Soviet Union viewed the United States as seeking to make the world safe for capitalism, thereby reducing Soviet chances to obtain economic resources and rebuild its war-shattered economy. Each nation tended to see the other's actions in the most negative light possible and to see global developments as a zero-sum game, one in which every victory for one side was necessarily a defeat for the other.

The Truman Doctrine.

By 1947 U.S.-Soviet relations had reached a new low. International arms control had proved futile, the United States had gone to the United Nations to pressure the Soviets to withdraw from Iran, and the rhetoric from both sides had become warlike. From the American vantage point, Soviet actions to expand communism in Eastern Europe appeared to threaten democracies in Western Europe. By contrast, the Soviets viewed the United States as seeking to extend economic control over nations close to their borders and to weaken communism in the Soviet Union.

Events in Greece allowed Truman to take the offensive and apply Kennan's policy of containment. To maintain access to the Middle East and its Asian colonies, the United Kingdom considered it vitally important to keep Greece within its sphere of influence. In 1946 a civil war broke out in Greece between the right-wing monarchy and a coalition of insurgents consisting of members of the wartime anti-Nazi resistance, Communists, and non-Communist opponents of the repressive government. Exhausted by the war and in desperate financial shape, the British turned to the United States for help.

The Truman administration believed that the presence of Communists among the Greek rebels meant that Moscow was behind the insurgency. In fact, Stalin was not aiding the revolutionaries; the assistance came from the Communist leader of Yugoslavia, Josip Broz (known then as Marshall Tito), who acted independently of the Soviets and would soon break with them. Following Kennan's lead in advocating containment, Truman incorrectly believed that all Communists around the world were ultimately controlled by the Kremlin.

While Truman was convinced that the United States had to intervene in Greece to contain the spread of communism, he still had to convince the Republican-controlled Congress and the American people to go along. To overcome potential opposition to its

GUIDED ANALYSIS

Henry Wallace | The Way to Peace, 1946

By the late 1940s, tensions between the two superpowers threatened to erupt into armed conflict. Opinion within the U.S. government about how to respond to this challenge ranged widely: Some urged cooperation, while others argued for aggressive confrontation with the Soviet Union. In the following selection, Secretary of Commerce Henry Wallace criticizes aggressive responses to the Soviet Union.

Source 24.1

According to Wallace, why do some countries want the United States to confront the Soviet Union?

How does recognition of a nation's spheres of influence affect Wallace's thinking?

What does Wallace indicate the United States would gain from pursuing peace with the Soviet Union?

"Getting tough" never bought anything real and lasting—whether for schoolyard bullies or businessmen or world powers. The tougher we get, the tougher the Russians will get.

Throughout the world there are numerous reactionary elements which had hoped for Axis victory—and now profess great friendship for the United States. Yet, these enemies of yesterday and false friends of today continually try to provoke war between the United States and Russia. They have no real love of the United States. They only long for the day when the United States and Russia will destroy each other. We must not let our Russian policy be guided or influenced by those inside or outside the United States who want war with Russia. This does not mean appeasement. . . .

The real peace treaty we now need is between the United States and Russia. On our part, we should recognize that we have no more business in the political affairs of Eastern Europe than Russia has in the political affairs of Latin America, Western Europe, and the United States. We may not like what Russia does in Eastern Europe. Her type of land reform, industrial expropriation, and suppression of basic liberties offends the great majority of the people of the United States. But whether we like it or not the Russians will try to socialize their sphere of influence just as we try to democratize our sphere of influence. . . .

Russia must be convinced that we are not planning for war against her and we must be certain that Russia is not carrying on territorial expansion or world domination through native Communists faithfully following every twist and turn in the Moscow party line. But in this competition, we must insist on an open door for trade throughout the world. There will always be an ideological conflict—but that is no reason why diplomats cannot work out a basis for both systems to live safely in the world side by side.

Source: Henry Wallace, "The Way to Peace," in *The Annals of America* (Chicago: Encyclopedia Britannica, 1968), 16:372–73.

Put It in Context

Why do you think American foreign policy leaders rejected Wallace's perspective in the postwar period?

plans, the Truman administration exaggerated the danger of Communist influence in Greece. Truman sent Undersecretary of State Dean Acheson to testify before a congressional committee that, "like apples in a barrel infected by one rotten one, the corruption of Greece would infect Iran and all to the east." The administration's presentation of the issues to the American public was even more dramatic. On March 12, 1947, Truman gave a speech to a joint session of Congress that was broadcast over national radio to millions of listeners. He interpreted the civil war in Greece as a titanic struggle between freedom and totalitarianism that threatened the free world. "I believe," the president declared, "that it must be the policy of the United States to support free peoples who are resisting attempted subjugation by armed minorities or by outside pressures." Truman's rhetoric stretched the truth on many counts — the armed minorities to which the president referred had fought Nazi totalitarianism; the Soviets did not supply the insurgents; and the right-wing monarchy, propped up by the military, was hardly democratic. Nevertheless, Truman achieved his goal of frightening both lawmakers and the public, and Congress appropriated $400 million in military aid to fortify the existing governments of Greece and neighboring Turkey.

The **Truman Doctrine**, which pledged to protect democratic countries and contain the expansion of communism, was the cornerstone of American foreign policy throughout the Cold War. The United States committed itself to shoring up governments, whether democratic or dictatorial, as long as they were avowedly anti-Communist. Americans believed that the rest of the world's nations wanted to be like the United States and therefore would not willingly accept communism, which they thought could be imposed only from the outside by the Soviet Union and never reasonably chosen from within.

Although Truman misread Soviet intentions with respect to Greece, Stalin's regime had given him cause for worry. Soviet actions that imposed communism in Poland, along with the USSR's refusal to withdraw troops from the Baltic states of Latvia, Lithuania, and Estonia, reinforced the president's concerns about Soviet expansionism and convinced many in the U.S. government that Stalin had no intention of abiding by his wartime agreements. Difficulties in negotiating with the Soviets about international control of atomic energy further worried American foreign-policy makers about Russian designs for obtaining the atomic bomb.

The Marshall Plan and Economic Containment.

George Kennan's version of containment called for economic and political aid to check Communist expansion. In this context, to forestall Communist inroads and offer humanitarian assistance to Europeans facing homelessness and starvation, the Truman administration offered economic assistance to the war-torn continent. In doing so, the United States also hoped to guarantee increased trade with Europe. In a June 1947 speech that drew heavily on Kennan's ideas, Secretary of State George Marshall sketched out a plan to provide financial assistance to Europe. Although he invited any country, including the Soviet Union, that experienced "hunger, poverty, desperation, and chaos" to apply for aid, Marshall did not expect Stalin to ask for assistance. To do so would require the Soviets to supply information to the United States concerning the internal operations of their economy and to admit to the failure of communism.

Following up Marshall's speech, Truman asked Congress in December 1947 to authorize $17 billion for European recovery. With conservative-minded Republicans still in control of Congress, the president's spending request faced steep opposition. The Soviet Union inadvertently came to Truman's political rescue. Stalin interpreted the proposed **Marshall Plan** of economic assistance as a hostile attempt by the United States to gain influence in Eastern Europe. To forestall this possibility, in late February 1948 the Soviets extinguished the remaining democracy in Eastern Europe by engineering a Communist coup in Czechoslovakia. Congressional lawmakers viewed this action as further proof of Soviet aggression. In April 1948, they approved the Marshall Plan, providing $13 billion in economic assistance to sixteen European countries over the next five years.

Explore ▶

See Sources 24.2 and 24.3 for the reactions of the United States and Soviet Union to the Marshall Plan.

REVIEW & RELATE

- Why did American policymakers believe that containing Communist expansion should be the foundation of American foreign policy?

- What role did mutual misunderstandings and mistrust play in the emergence of the Cold War?

The **Cold War** Hardens, 1948–1953

After 1947 the Cold War intensified. Both sides increased military spending and took measures to enhance their military presence around the world. Fueled by growing distrust, the Soviet Union and the United States engaged in inflammatory rhetoric that added to the danger the conflict posed to world peace. In 1950 the United States, in cooperation with the United Nations, sent troops to South Korea to turn back an invasion from the Communist North. Truman took advantage of Cold War hostilities to expand presidential power through increased military spending and the creation of a vast national intelligence network.

Military Containment. The New Deal and World War II had increased the power of the president and his ability to manage economic and military crises. The Cold War further strengthened the presidency and shifted the balance of governmental power to the executive branch, creating what has been called the **imperial presidency**.

As the Cold War heated up, Congress granted the president enormous authority over foreign affairs and internal security. The National Security Act, passed in 1947, created the Department of Defense as a cabinet agency (replacing the Department of War), consolidated control of the various military services under its authority, and established the Joint Chiefs of Staff, composed of the heads of the army, navy, air force, and marines. To advise the president on military and foreign affairs, the act set up the **National Security Council (NSC)**, a group presided over by the national security adviser and consisting of the secretaries of state, defense, the army, the navy, and the air force and any others the president might appoint.

In addition to this panel, the National Security Act established the Central Intelligence Agency (CIA) as part of the executive branch. The CIA was given the responsibility of coordinating intelligence gathering and conducting espionage abroad to counter Soviet spying operations. Another new intelligence agency, the National Security Agency, created in 1949, monitored overseas communications through the latest technological devices.

Together, these agencies enhanced the president's ability to conduct foreign affairs with little congressional oversight and out of public view.

By 1948 the Truman administration had decided that an economically healthy Germany, with its great industrial potential, provided the key to a prosperous Europe and consequently a depression-proof United States. Rebuilding postwar Germany would also fortify the eastern boundary of Europe against Soviet expansion. In mid-1948 the United States, the United Kingdom, and France consolidated their occupation zones, created the Federal Republic of Germany (West Germany), and initiated economic reforms to stimulate a speedy recovery. The Soviet Union saw a strong Germany as a threat to its national security and responded by closing the access roads from the border of West Germany to Berlin, located in the Soviet zone of East Germany, which effectively cut off the city from the West.

The Soviet blockade of West Berlin turned the Cold War even colder. Without provisions from the United States and its allies in West Germany, West Berliners could not survive. In an effort to break the blockade, Truman ordered a massive airlift, during which American and British planes transported more than 2.5 million tons of supplies to West Berlin. After nearly a year of these flights, the **Berlin airlift** ended in the spring of 1949 when the Russians lifted the blockade.

The Berlin Airlift   This group of West Berliners waits anxiously as an American C-47 cargo plane prepares to land at Tempelhof Airfield to deliver food in July 1948. The Soviets had blockaded ground transportation to the Allied sector of West Berlin, prompting President Truman to airlift supplies. Three years after the war ended, the photograph shows Germany still in ruins. Walter Sanders/The LIFE Picture Collection/Getty Images

The Marshall Plan and the Soviet Union

Shortly after Secretary of State George Marshall proposed the Marshall Plan to grant economic assistance to Europe, France and the United Kingdom invited Soviet leaders to a conference in Paris to discuss their response to General Marshall's offer. The following selections present Marshall's plan and Soviet foreign minister Vyacheslav Molotov's reaction to it.

Source 24.2

George C. Marshall | The Marshall Plan, 1947

The truth of the matter is that Europe's requirements for the next three or four years of foreign food and other essential products—principally from America—are so much greater than her present ability to pay that she must have substantial additional help or face economic, social, and political deterioration of a very grave character.

Aside from the demoralizing effect on the world at large and the possibilities of disturbances arising as a result of the desperation of the people concerned, the consequences to the economy of the United States should be apparent to all. It is logical that the United States should do whatever it is able to do to assist in the return of normal economic health in the world, without which there can be no political stability and no assured peace. Our policy is directed not against any country or doctrine but against hunger, poverty, desperation and chaos. Its purpose should be the revival of a working economy in the world so as to permit the emergence of political and social conditions in which free institutions can exist. Such assistance, I am convinced, must not be on a piecemeal basis as various crises develop. Any assistance that this Government may render in

the future should provide a cure rather than a mere palliative. Any government that is willing to assist in the task of recovery will find full co-operation I am sure, on the part of the United States Government. Any government which maneuvers to block the recovery of other countries cannot expect help from us. Furthermore, governments, political parties, or groups which seek to perpetuate human misery in order to profit therefrom politically or otherwise will encounter the opposition of the United States.

. . . It would be neither fitting nor efficacious for this Government to undertake to draw up unilaterally a program designed to place Europe on its feet economically. This is the business of the Europeans. The initiative, I think, must come from Europe. The role of this country should consist of friendly aid in the drafting of a European program and of later support of such a program so far as it may be practical for us to do so. The program should be a joint one, agreed to by a number, if not all European nations.

Source: Speech by George C. Marshall, "European Initiative Essential to Economic Recovery," June 5, 1947, *Department of State Bulletin* 16, no. 415 (1947): 1159–60.

Source 24.3

Vyacheslav Molotov | Soviet Objections to the Marshall Plan, 1947

When efforts are directed toward Europe helping herself in the first place and developing her economic potentialities as well as the exchange of goods between countries, such efforts are in conformity with the interests of the countries of Europe. When, however, it is stated . . . that the decisive hold on the rehabilitation of the economic life of European countries should belong to the United States and not to the European countries themselves, such a position stands in contradiction to the interests of European countries since it might lead to a denial of their economic independence, which denial is incompatible with national sovereignty.

The Soviet delegation believes that internal measures and the national efforts of each country should have a decisive importance for the countries of Europe and not make calculations for foreign support which should be of secondary importance. The Soviet Union has always counted above all on its own powers and is known to be on a steady way of progress of its economic life.

The first form of cooperation is based on the development of political and economic relations between states possessing equal rights and in that case their national sovereignty does not suffer from foreign interference.

Such is the democratic basis for international cooperation which brings nations closer together and facilitates the task of their mutual aid.

Source: U.S. Department of State, *A Decade of American Foreign Policy: Basic Documents, 1941–1949* (Washington, DC: Department of State Printing Office, 1985), 969.

Interpret the Evidence

1. Why does George Marshall believe the United States should help in the reconstruction of Europe? What roles do self-interest and humanitarianism play?
2. Why does Vyacheslav Molotov think that accepting U.S. assistance would be against the interests of European countries?
3. How do their views differ on the definition of international cooperation?

Put It in Context

How did the Marshall Plan contribute to tensions between the superpowers during the Cold War?

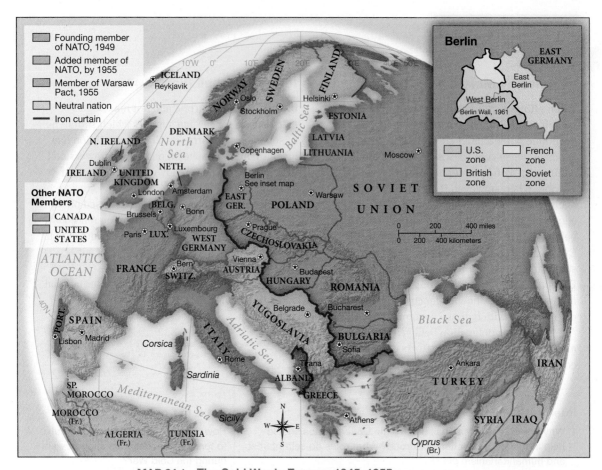

MAP 24.1 The Cold War in Europe, 1945–1955

In 1946, the four major victorious wartime allies divided Germany and Berlin into distinct sectors, leading to increasing conflict. Between 1949 and 1955, the descent of what Winston Churchill called the "iron curtain" of communism and the creation of rival security pacts headed by the United States and the Soviet Union hardened these postwar divisions into the Cold War.

Meanwhile, in November 1948 Truman won election for a second term. He drew opposition from critics on his left and right for his handling of the Cold War, challenging both his aggressiveness toward the Soviets and his increased spending for containment. Nevertheless, most Americans stood behind his anti-Communist foreign policy (see "Truman, the New Deal Coalition, and the Election of 1948" in chapter 25) as the Cold War continued.

The two superpowers kept the conflict alive when each fashioned military alliances to keep the other at bay. In April 1949, the United States joined eleven European countries in the **North Atlantic Treaty Organization (NATO)**. A peacetime military alliance, NATO established a collective security pact in which an attack on one member was viewed as an attack on all (Map 24.1). In 1949 the Russians followed suit by organizing the Council for Mutual Economic Assistance to help their satellite nations rebuild and six years later by creating the Warsaw Pact military alliance, the respective counterparts in Eastern Europe to the Marshall Plan and NATO.

Amid the growing militarization of the Cold War, 1949 brought two new shocks to the United States and its allies. First, in September the Russians successfully tested an atomic bomb. Second, Communist forces within China led by Mao Zedong and Zhou Enlai succeeded in overthrowing the U.S.-backed government of Jiang Jieshi and creating the People's Republic of China. These two events convinced many in the United States that the threat posed by communism was escalating rapidly.

In response, the National Security Council met to reevaluate U.S. strategy in fighting the Cold War. In April 1950 the NSC recommended to Truman that the United States intensify its containment policy both abroad and at home. The document it handed over to the president, entitled **NSC-68**, spelled out the need for action in ominous language. "The Soviet Union, unlike previous aspirants to hegemony," NSC-68 warned, "is animated by a new fanatic faith, antithetical to our own, and seeks to impose its absolute authority over the rest of the world. It is in this context that this Republic and its citizens . . . stand in their deepest peril." NSC-68 proposed that the United States develop an even more powerful nuclear weapon, the hydrogen bomb; increase military spending; and continue to negotiate NATO-style alliances around the globe. Departing from the original guidelines for the CIA, the president's advisers proposed that the United States engage in "covert means" to foment and support "unrest and revolt in selected strategic [Soviet] satellite countries." At home, they added, the government should prepare Americans for the Communist danger by enhancing internal security and civil defense programs.

Truman agreed with many of the principles behind NSC-68 but worried about the cost of funding it. The problem remained a political one. Though the Democrats once again controlled both houses of Congress, there was little sentiment to raise taxes and slash the economic programs established during the New Deal. However, circumstances abruptly changed when, in June 1950, shortly after the president received the NSC report, Communist North Korea invaded U.S.-backed South Korea. In response to this attack, Truman took the opportunity to put into practice key recommendations of NSC-68.

The Korean War. Korea emerged from World War II divided between U.S. and Soviet spheres of influence. Above the 38th parallel, the Communist leader Kim Il Sung ruled North Korea with support from the Soviet Union. Below that latitude, the anti-Communist leader Syngman Rhee governed South Korea. The United States supported Rhee, but in January 1950 Secretary of State Dean Acheson commented that he did not regard South Korea as part of the vital Asian "defense perimeter" protected by the United States against Communist aggression. Truman had already removed remaining American troops from the country the previous year. On June 25, 1950, an emboldened Kim Il Sung sent military forces to invade South Korea, seeking to unite the country under his leadership.

Following the invasion Korea took on new importance to American policymakers. If South Korea fell, the president believed, Communist leaders would be "emboldened to override nations closer to our own shores." Thus the Truman Doctrine was now applied to Asia as it had previously been applied to Europe. This time, however, American financial aid would not be enough. It would take the U.S. military to contain the Communist threat.

U.S. Racial Integration of the Military in Korea, 1950 In 1948, President Truman issued an executive order to desegregate the armed forces. During the Korean War African American soldiers served in integrated combat units. On the top left of this November 20, 1950 photo, Sergeant First Class Major Cleveland, the African American squad leader of this racially integrated unit fighting with the 2nd Infantry Division, points out a Communist-led North Korean position to his machine gun crew. Corbis via Getty Images

Truman did not seek a declaration of war from Congress. Instead, he chose a multinational course of action. With the Soviet Union boycotting the United Nations over its refusal to admit the Communist People's Republic of China, on June 27, 1950, the United States obtained authorization from the UN Security Council to send a peacekeeping force to Korea. Fifteen other countries joined UN forces, but the United States supplied the bulk of the troops, as well as their commanding officer, General Douglas MacArthur. In reality, MacArthur reported to the president, not the United Nations.

Before MacArthur could mobilize his forces, the North Koreans had penetrated most of South Korea, except for the port of Pusan on the southwest coast of the peninsula. In a daring counterattack, on September 15, 1950, MacArthur dispatched land and sea forces to capture Inchon, northwest of Pusan on the opposite coast, to cut off North Korean supply lines. Joined by UN forces pushing out of Pusan, MacArthur's Eighth Army troops chased the enemy northward back over the 38th parallel.

Now Truman had to make a key decision. MacArthur wanted to invade North Korea, defeat the Communists, and unify the country. Instead of sticking to his original goal of containing Communist aggression against South Korea, Truman succumbed to the lure of liberating all of Korea from the Communists. MacArthur received permission to proceed, and on October 9 his forces crossed into North Korea. Within three weeks, UN troops marched through the country until they reached the Yalu River, which bordered China. With the U.S. military massed along their southern perimeter, the Chinese warned that they would send troops to repel the invaders if the Americans crossed the Yalu. Both General MacArthur and Secretary of State Acheson, guided by CIA intelligence, discounted this threat. The intelligence, however, was faulty. Truman approved MacArthur's plan to cross the Yalu, and on November 27, 1950, China sent more than 300,000 troops south into North Korea. Within two months, Communist troops regained control of North Korea, allowing them once again to invade South Korea. On January 4, 1951, the South Korean capital of Seoul fell to Chinese and North Korean troops (Map 24.2).

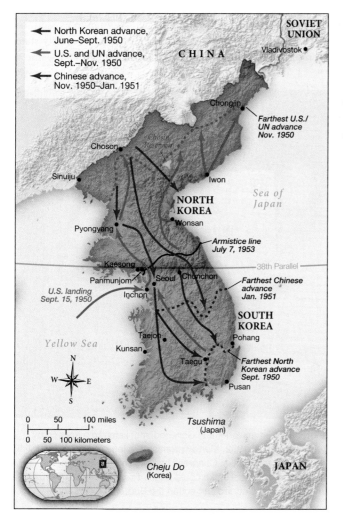

MAP 24.2   The Korean War, 1950–1953

Considered a "police action" by the United Nations, the Korean War cost the lives of nearly 37,000 U.S. troops. Approximately 1 million Koreans were killed, wounded, or missing. Each side pushed deep into enemy territory, but neither could achieve victory. When hostilities ceased in 1953, a demilitarized zone near the original boundary line separated North and South Korea.

By the spring of 1951, the war had degenerated into a stalemate. UN forces succeeded in recapturing Seoul and repelling the Communists north of the 38th parallel. This time, with the American public anxious to end the war and with the presence of the Chinese promising an endless, bloody predicament, the president sought to replace combat with diplomacy. The American objective would be containment, not Korean unification.

Truman's change of heart infuriated General MacArthur, who was willing to risk an all-out war with China and to use nuclear weapons to win. After MacArthur spoke out publicly against Truman's policy by remarking, "There is no substitute for victory," the president removed him from command on April 11, 1951. However, even with the change in strategy and leadership, the war dragged on for two more years, until July 1953, when a final armistice agreement was reached. By that time, the Korean War had cost the United States close to 37,000 lives and $54 billion.

The Korean War and the Imperial Presidency. The Korean War boosted the imperial presidency by allowing the president to bypass Congress and the Constitution to initiate wars in the name of "police actions." The war permitted Truman to expand his powers as commander in chief and augmented the strength of the national security state over which he presided. As a result of the Korean conflict, the military draft became a

Steel Strike, 1952 In this photograph, steelworkers in Gary, Indiana, listen to a speech by CIO president Philip Murray, given on June 22, 1952. Murray promised to lead the union on strike and get a contract for its members. Five years earlier, Congress had passed the Taft-Hartley Act, which hampered union organizing. Before the steel strike could begin, President Truman seized the steel plants and placed them under federal control, an action the Supreme Court soon reversed. © Bettmann/Getty Images

regular feature of American life for young men over the next two decades. The expanded peacetime military was active around the globe, operating bases in Europe, Asia, and the Middle East. During the war, the military budget rose from $13.5 billion to $50 billion, strengthening the connection between economic growth and permanent mobilization to fight the Cold War. The war also permitted President Truman to reshape foreign policy along the lines sketched in NSC-68, including the extension of U.S. influence in Southeast Asia. Consequently, he authorized economic aid to support the French against Communist revolutionaries in Vietnam.

Yet the power of the imperial presidency did not go unchecked. Congress deferred to Truman on key issues of military policy, but on one important occasion the Supreme Court stepped in to restrain him. The central issue grew out of a labor dispute in the steel industry. In 1952 the United Steel Workers of America threatened to go on strike for higher wages, which would have had a serious impact on war production as well as the economy in general. On May 2, after the steel companies refused the union's demands, Truman announced the government seizure and operation of the steel mills to keep them running. He argued that as president he had the "inherent right" to take over the steel plants.

The steel companies objected and brought the matter before the Supreme Court. On June 2, 1952, the Court ruled against Truman. It held that the president did not have the intrinsic authority to seize private property, even during wartime. For the time being, the Supreme Court affirmed some limitations on the unbridled use of presidential power even during periods of war.

REVIEW & RELATE

- What were the causes and consequences of the militarization of the containment strategy in the late 1940s and early 1950s?

- How did the Korean War contribute to the centralization of power in the executive branch?

Combating Communism at Home, 1945–1954

The Korean War heightened fear of the threat of Communist infiltration in American society. In one striking example, the presiding judge in the Rosenbergs' espionage trial sentenced them to death because he believed their actions "caused . . . the Communist aggression in Korea, with the resultant casualties exceeding 50,000." For most of Truman's second administration, fear of Communist subversion within the United States consumed domestic politics. Increasing evidence of Soviet espionage fueled this anti-Communist obsession. Yet in an atmosphere of fear, lawmakers and judges blurred the distinction between actual Soviet spies and political radicals who were merely attracted to Communist beliefs. In the process, these officials trampled on individual constitutional freedoms.

Loyalty and the Second Red Scare.
The postwar fear of communism echoed earlier anti-Communist sentiments. The government had initiated the repressive Palmer raids during the Red scare following World War I, which led to the deportation of immigrants sympathetic to the Communist doctrines of the Russian Revolution (see "The Red Scare, 1919–1920" in chapter 21). In 1938 conservative congressional opponents of the New

Deal established the **House Un-American Activities Committee (HUAC)** to investigate domestic communism, which they tied to the Roosevelt administration. Much of anticommunism, however, was bipartisan. In 1940 Roosevelt signed into law the Smith Act, which prohibited teaching or advocating the "duty, necessity, desirability, or propriety of overthrowing or destroying any government in the United States by force or violence" or belonging to any group with that aim. At the same time, President Roosevelt secretly authorized the FBI to monitor and wiretap individuals suspected of violating the act.

The Cold War produced the second Red scare. Just two weeks after his speech announcing the Truman Doctrine in March 1947, the president signed an executive order creating the **Federal Employee Loyalty Program**. Under this program, a board investigated federal employees to see if "reasonable grounds [existed] to suspect disloyalty." Soviet espionage was, in fact, a cause for legitimate concern. Spies operated in both Canada and the United States during and after World War II, and they had infiltrated the Manhattan Project.

The loyalty board, however, did not focus on espionage. Rather, it concentrated its attention on individuals who espoused dissenting views on a variety of issues. It failed to uncover a single verifiable case of espionage or find even one actual Communist in public service. This lack of evidence did not stop the board from dismissing 378 government employees for their political beliefs and personal behavior. Some employees were fired because they were homosexuals and considered susceptible to blackmail by foreign agents. (Heterosexual men and women who were having extramarital affairs were not treated in the same manner.) The accused rarely faced their accusers and at times did not learn the nature of the charges against them. This disregard for due process of law spread as loyalty boards at state and municipal levels questioned and fired government employees, including public school teachers and state university professors.

Congress also investigated communism in the private sector, especially in industries that shaped public opinion. In 1947 HUAC broadened the anti-Red probe from Washington to Hollywood. Convinced that the film industry had come under Communist influence and threatened to poison the minds of millions of moviegoers, HUAC conducted hearings that attracted much publicity. HUAC cited for contempt ten witnesses, among them directors and screenwriters, for refusing to answer questions about their political beliefs and associations. These and subsequent hearings assumed the form of a ritual. The committee already had information from the FBI about the witnesses; HUAC really wanted the accused to confess their Communist heresy publicly and to show contrition by naming their associates. Those who did not comply were considered "unfriendly" witnesses and were put on an industry blacklist that deprived them of employment. **See Primary Source Project 24: McCarthyism and the Hollywood Ten, page 843.**

HUAC grabbed even bigger headlines in 1948. With Republicans in charge of the committee, they launched a probe of Alger Hiss, a former State Department official in the Roosevelt administration who had accompanied the president to the Yalta Conference. The hearings resulted from charges brought by former Soviet spy Whittaker Chambers that Hiss had passed him classified documents. Hiss denied the allegations, and President Truman dismissed them as a distraction. In fact, Democrats viewed the charges as a politically motivated attempt by Republicans to characterize the Roosevelt and Truman administrations as having been riddled with Communists.

Following Truman's victory in the 1948 presidential election, first-term Republican congressman Richard M. Nixon kept the Hiss affair alive. A member of HUAC, Nixon went to Chambers's farm and discovered a cache of State Department documents that

Chambers had stored for safekeeping. Armed with this evidence, Nixon reopened the case. While the statute of limitations for espionage from the 1930s had expired, the federal government had enough evidence to prosecute Hiss for perjury—lying under oath about passing documents to Chambers. One trial produced a hung jury, but a second convicted Hiss; he was sentenced to five years in prison.

Hiss's downfall tarnished the Democrats, as Republicans charged them with being "soft on communism." It did not matter that Truman was a cold warrior who had advanced the doctrine of containment to stop Soviet expansionism or that he had instituted the federal loyalty program to purge Communists from government. In fact, in 1949 Truman tried to demonstrate his cold warrior credentials by authorizing the Justice Department to prosecute twelve high-ranking officials of the Communist Party for violating the Smith Act. In the 1951 decision in *Dennis v. United States*, the Supreme Court upheld the conviction of the Communist leaders on the grounds that they posed a "clear and present danger" to the United States by advocating the violent overthrow of the government. With no evidence of an immediate danger of a Communist uprising, the justices decided that "the gravity of the [Communist] evil" was enough to warrant conviction.

In 1950 the Truman administration also prosecuted Julius and Ethel Rosenberg. Unlike the *Dennis* case, which involved political beliefs, the Rosenbergs were charged with espionage. When the Russians successfully tested an atomic bomb in 1949, anyone accused of helping them obtain this weapon became "Public Enemy Number One." The outbreak of the Korean War the following year, in which tens of thousands of soldiers died, made the Rosenbergs appear as conspirators to murder. After a lengthy trial in 1951, the couple received the death penalty, rather than a possible thirty-year sentence, undoubtedly because they refused to confess and because the trial took place during the war.

By 1950 the anti-Communist crusade included Democrats and Republicans, liberals and conservatives. Liberals had the most to lose because conservatives could easily brand them as ideologically tainted. In his successful campaign to become a U.S. senator from California in 1950, Richard Nixon had accused his opponent, the liberal Democrat Helen Gahagan Douglas, of being "pink down to her underwear," not quite a Red but close enough. Liberal civil rights and civil liberties groups as well as labor unions were particularly vulnerable to such charges and rushed to rid their organizations of suspected Communists. Such efforts did nothing, however, to slow down conservative attacks. In 1950 Republicans supported legislation proposed by Senator Pat McCarran, a conservative Democrat from Nevada, which required Communist organizations to register with the federal government, established detention camps to incarcerate radicals during national emergencies, and denied passports to American citizens suspected of Communist affiliations. The severity of the entire measure proved too much for President Truman, and he vetoed it. Reflecting the bipartisan consensus on the issue, the Democratic-controlled Congress overrode the veto.

McCarthyism.

Joseph Raymond McCarthy, a Republican senator from Wisconsin, did not create the phenomenon of postwar anticommunism, which was already in full swing from 1947 to 1950, but he served as its most public and feared voice from 1950 until 1954. Senator McCarthy used his position as the head of the Permanent Investigation Subcommittee of the Committee on Government Operations to harass current and former government officials and employees who, he claimed, collaborated with the Communist conspiracy. He had plenty of assistance from members of his own party who considered McCarthy a potent weapon in their battle to reclaim the White House. Robert A. Taft, the respected conservative Republican senator from Ohio, told McCarthy "to keep talking and if one case doesn't work [you] should proceed with another." The press also courted the young senator by giving his charges substantial coverage on the front pages of daily newspapers and then shifting the story to the back pages when McCarthy's claims turned out to be false. McCarthy bullied people, exaggerated his military service, drank too much, and did not pull his punches in making speeches — but his anti-Communist tirades fit into mainstream Cold War politics.

Aware of the power of the Communists-in-government issue, McCarthy gave a speech in February 1950 in Wheeling, West Virginia. Waving sheets of paper in his hand, the senator announced that he had "the names of 205 men known to the Secretary of State as being members of the Communist Party and who nevertheless are still working and shaping the policy of the State Department." McCarthy cared more about the message than about the truth. As he continued campaigning for Republican congressional candidates across the country, he kept changing the number of alleged Communists in the government. When Senator Millard Tydings of Maryland, a Democrat who headed the Senate Foreign Relations Committee, launched an investigation of McCarthy's charges, he concluded that they were irresponsible and unfounded.

This finding did not stop McCarthy; if anything, it emboldened him to go further. He accused Tydings of being "soft on communism" and campaigned against his reelection in 1952. Tydings's defeat in the election scared off many critics from openly confronting McCarthy. McCarthy won reelection to the Senate, and when Republicans once again captured a majority in Congress, he became chair of the Permanent Investigations Subcommittee. Not only did he make false accusations and smear witnesses with anti-Communist allegations, but he also dispatched two aides to travel to Europe and purge what they considered disreputable books from the shelves of overseas libraries sponsored by the State Department.

McCarthy stood out among anti-Communists not for his beliefs but for his tactics. His name became synonymous with anticommunism as well as with manipulating the truth. McCarthy publicly hurled charges so astounding, especially coming from a U.S. senator, that people thought there must be something to them. He specialized in the "multiple untruth," a concoction of allegations so complex and convoluted that it was impossible to refute them simply or quickly. By the time the accusations could be discredited, the damage was already done. The senator bullied and badgered witnesses, called them names, and if necessary furnished phony documents and doctored photographs linking them to known Communists.

In 1954 McCarthy finally went too far. After one of his aides got drafted and the army refused to give him a special commission, McCarthy accused the army of harboring Communists at Camp Kilmer and Fort Monmouth in New Jersey. To sort out these charges and to see whether the army had acted appropriately, McCarthy's own Senate subcommittee conducted an investigation, with the Wisconsin senator stepping down as chair. For two months, the relatively new medium of television broadcast live the army-McCarthy hearings, during which the cameras showed many viewers for the first time how reckless McCarthy had become. As his public approval declined, the Senate decided that it could no longer tolerate McCarthy's outrageous behavior. The famous television journalist Edward R. Murrow ran an unflattering documentary on McCarthy on his evening program on CBS, which further cast doubt on the senator's character and veracity. In December 1954 the Senate voted to censure McCarthy for conduct unbecoming a senator, having violated senatorial decorum by insulting colleagues who criticized him. McCarthy retained his seat on the subcommittee and all his Senate prerogatives, but he never again wielded substantial power. In 1957 he died from acute hepatitis, a disease related to alcoholism.

The anti-Communist consensus did not end with the execution of the Rosenbergs in 1953 or the censure of Joseph McCarthy in 1954. Even J. Robert Oppenheimer, "the father of the atomic bomb," came under scrutiny. In 1954 the Atomic Energy Commission revoked Oppenheimer's security clearance for suspected, though unproven, Communist affiliations. That same year, Congress passed the Communist Control Act, which required "Communist infiltrated" groups to register with the federal government. Federal, state, and municipal governments required employees to take a loyalty oath affirming their allegiance to the United States and disavowing support for any organization that advocated the overthrow of the government. In addition, the blacklist continued in Hollywood throughout the rest of the decade. After the Supreme Court declared racial segregation in public schools unconstitutional in 1954, a number of southern states, including Florida and Louisiana, set up committees to investigate Communist influence in the civil rights movement. In a case concerning civil liberties, the Supreme Court still upheld HUAC's authority to investigate communism and to require witnesses who came before it to answer questions about their affiliations. Yet the Court did put a stop to the anti-Communist momentum. In 1957 the high court dealt a severe blow to enforcement of the Smith Act by ruling in *Yates v. United States* that the Justice Department could not prosecute someone for merely advocating an abstract doctrine favoring the violent overthrow of the government. In response, Congress tried, but failed, to limit the Supreme Court's jurisdiction in cases of this sort.

Even without the presence of Senator Joseph McCarthy, many Americans would have fallen victim to anti-Communist hysteria. J. Edgar Hoover and the FBI did more to fuel the second Red scare than did the Wisconsin senator. Hoover and his bureau did greater damage than McCarthy because they provided the information that Communist-hunters used throughout the government. The FBI was involved in criminal prosecutions in the *Dennis* and *Rosenberg* cases, supplied evidence to congressional committees and loyalty boards, and wiretapped suspected targets and used undercover agents to monitor and harass them. Although attacks against radicals in this period came to be known as **McCarthyism**, the FBI played as important a role in this hysteria as did the senator himself.

REVIEW & RELATE

- Why did fear of Communists in positions of influence escalate in the late 1940s and early 1950s?

- Why was McCarthyism much more powerful than Joseph McCarthy?

The **Cold War Expands, 1953–1961**

With the end of the Korean War in 1953, the United States and the Soviet Union each spent huge sums of money and manpower building up their arsenal of nuclear weapons and military forces. They did not engage directly on the battlefield, but they attempted to spread their influence around the world while protecting their spheres of influence closer to their borders. The growing presence of nuclear weapons hung over diplomatic crises wherever they emerged, occasionally prompting the leaders of the two most powerful nations to seek an accommodation.

Explore ▸

Read differing interpretations
of the causes of the Cold War
in Sources 24.4 and 24.5.

Nuclear Weapons and Containment. In foreign affairs, President Dwight D. Eisenhower perpetuated Truman's containment doctrine while at the same time espousing the contradictory principle of "rolling back" communism in Eastern Europe. However, when Hungarians rose up against their Soviet-backed regime in 1956, the U.S. government did little in response. Rather than pushing back communism, the Eisenhower administration expanded the doctrine of containment around the world by entering into treaties to establish regional defense pacts.

Eisenhower's commitment to fiscal discipline had a profound effect on his foreign policy. The president worried that the alliance among government, defense contractors, and research universities — which he dubbed "the military-industrial complex" — would bankrupt the economy and undermine individual freedom (see "The Home-Front Economy" in chapter 23). With this in mind, he implemented the **New Look** strategy, which placed a higher priority on building a nuclear arsenal and delivery system than on the more expensive task of maintaining and deploying armed forces on the ground throughout the world. Nuclear missiles launched from the air by air force bombers or fired from submarines would give the United States, as Secretary of Defense Charles Wilson asserted, "a bigger bang for the buck." With the nation now armed with nuclear weapons, the Eisenhower administration threatened "massive retaliation" in the event of Communist aggression.

The New Look may have saved money and slowed the rate of defense spending, but it had serious flaws. First, it placed a premium on "brinksmanship," taking Communist enemies to the precipice of nuclear destruction, risking the death of millions, and hoping the other side

Bomb Shelter, 1954   The successful test of an atomic bomb by the Soviets in 1949 followed by the Korean War prompted many Americans to begin preparing for a possible nuclear attack. This Houston, Texas family, including their dog, pose in their bomb shelter stocked with food, first aid supplies, weapons, and ammunition. John Dominis/Getty Images

would back down. Second, massive retaliation did not work for small-scale conflicts. For instance, in the event of a confrontation in Berlin, would the United States launch nuclear missiles toward Germany and expose its European allies in West Germany and France to nuclear contamination? Third, the buildup of nuclear warheads provoked an arms race by encouraging the Soviet Union to do the same. Peace depended on the superpowers terrifying each other with the threat of nuclear annihilation — that is, if one country attacked the other, retaliation was guaranteed to result in shared obliteration. This strategy was known as **mutually assured destruction**, and its acronym — **MAD** — summed up its nightmarish qualities. As each nuclear power increased its capacity to destroy the other many times over, the potential for mistakes and errors in judgment increased, threatening a nuclear holocaust that would leave little to rebuild.

National security concerns occupied a good deal of the president's time. Fearing that a Soviet nuclear attack could wipe out nearly a third of the population before the United States could retaliate, the Eisenhower administration stepped up civil defense efforts. Schoolchildren took part in "duck and cover" drills, in which teachers shouted "Take cover" and students hid under their desks. In the meantime, both the United States and the Soviet Union began producing intercontinental ballistic missiles armed with nuclear warheads. They also stepped up aboveground tests of nuclear weapons, which contaminated the atmosphere with dangerous radioactive particles.

Despite doomsday rhetoric of massive retaliation, Eisenhower generally relied more on diplomacy than on military action. Stalin's death in 1953 and his eventual replacement

by Nikita Khrushchev in 1955 permitted détente, or a relaxation of tensions, between the two superpowers. In July 1955 Eisenhower and Khrushchev, together with British and French leaders, gathered in Geneva to discuss arms control. Nothing concrete came out of this summit, but Eisenhower and Khrushchev did ease tensions between the two nations. In a speech to Communist officials two years later, Khrushchev denounced the excesses of Stalin's totalitarian rule and reinforced hopes for a new era of peaceful coexistence between the Cold War antagonists. In 1958, Vice President Richard Nixon visited the Soviet Union, the first top elected official to do so since the onset of the Cold War, as a sign of warming relations between the two nations. Nixon and Khrushchev attended a U.S. exhibition in Moscow on July 24, 1959, where the two leaders debated the relative merits of capitalism and communism, while looking at an American kitchen that displayed the latest household appliances. This so-called "Kitchen Debate" did not dissuade Khrushchev

Khrushchev Visits the U.S., 1959 During a brief thaw in the Cold War, Soviet Premier Nikita Khrushchev visits the U.S. and tours the country. Here he laughs as he holds up a corn cob during a visit to the farm of Roswell Garst (standing to his right) in Coon Rapids, Iowa on September 23, 1959. Hank Walker/The LIFE Picture Collection/Getty Images

from making a twelve-day visit to the United States later that year. Yet peaceful coexistence remained precarious. Just as President Eisenhower was about to begin his own tour of the Soviet Union in 1960, the Soviets shot down an American U-2 spy plane flying over their country. Eisenhower canceled his trip, and tensions resumed.

Interventions in the Middle East, Latin America, and Africa.

While relations between the Soviet Union and the United States thawed and then cooled during the Eisenhower era, the Cold War advanced into new regions. The efforts of Iranian, Guatemalan, and Cuban leaders to seize control of their countries' resources mirrored the surge of nationalism that swept through former European colonies in the 1950s. Following World War II, revolutionary nationalists in the Middle East, Africa, and Southeast Asia toppled colonial governments and wielded the power of their newly liberated regimes to take charge of their own development. Postwar decolonization and the rise of militant nationalism collided with U.S. Cold War policy, as these non-white nations remained neutral. At the **Bandung Conference** in Indonesia in 1955, twenty-nine Asian and African nations, many of them recently liberated, condemned continued colonization, particularly control in North Africa by France, a close U.S. ally, and asserted their intention to remain non-aligned with either side in the Cold War. The U.S. government took a dim view of this meeting and refused to send representatives. Especially worrisome to the United States, the Communist Chinese government made serious overtures to form closer relations with these nations. The United States frequently took a heavy handed approach when it suspected newly decolonized nations were edging to the side of the Soviets. In a manner first suggested in NSC-68, the Eisenhower administration deployed the CIA to help topple governments considered pro-Communist as well as to promote U.S. economic interests. For example, after Prime Minister Mohammed Mossadegh of Iran nationalized foreign oil corporations in 1953, the CIA engineered a successful coup that ousted his government and installed the pro-American shah Mohammad Reza Pahlavi in his place. Mossadegh was not a Communist, but by overthrowing him American oil companies obtained 40 percent of Iran's oil revenue.

In 1954 the economics of fruit and shipping replaced oil as the catalyst for U.S. intervention into a third-world nation within its own sphere of influence. The elected socialist regime of Jacobo Arbenz Guzmán in Guatemala had seized 225,000 acres of land held by the United Fruit Company, a powerful American company in which Secretary of State John Foster Dulles and his brother, CIA director Allen Dulles, held stock. According to the Dulles brothers, the land's seizure by the Guatemalan government posed a threat to the nearby Panama Canal. Eisenhower allowed the CIA to hatch a plot that resulted in a coup d'état, or government overthrow, that installed a right-wing military regime in Guatemala, which safeguarded both the Panama Canal and the United Fruit Company.

The success of the CIA's covert efforts in Guatemala prompted the Eisenhower administration to plan a similar action in Cuba, ninety miles off the coast of Florida. In 1959 Fidel Castro led an uprising and came to power in Cuba after overthrowing the American-backed dictator Fulgencio Batista. A Cuban nationalist in the tradition of José Martí, Castro sought to regain full control over his country's economic resources, including those owned by U.S. corporations. He appropriated $1 billion worth of American property and signed a trade agreement with the Soviet Union. To consolidate his political rule, Castro jailed opponents and installed a Communist regime. In 1960 President Eisenhower authorized the CIA to design a clandestine operation to overthrow the Castro government, but he left office before the invasion could occur.

The United States and the Soviet Union each tried to gain influence over emerging nations. Many newly independent countries tried to practice neutrality in foreign affairs, accepting aid from both of the Cold War protagonists. Nonetheless, they were often drawn into East-West conflicts.

Such was the case in Egypt, which achieved independence from Great Britain in 1952. Two years later, under General Gamal Abdel Nasser, the country sought to modernize its economy by building the hydroelectric Aswan Dam on the Nile River. Nasser welcomed financial backing from the United States and the Soviet Union, but the Eisenhower administration refused to contribute so long as the Egyptians accepted Soviet assistance. In 1956 Nasser, falling short of funds, sent troops to take over the Suez Canal, the waterway run by Great Britain and through which the bulk of Western Europe's oil was shipped. He intended to pay for the dam by collecting tolls from canal users. In retaliation, Britain and France, the two European powers most affected by the seizure, invaded Egypt on October 29, 1956. Locked in a struggle with Egypt and other Arab nations since its creation in 1948, Israel joined in the attack. The invading forces — all U.S. allies — had not warned the Eisenhower administration of their plans. Coming at the same time as the Soviet crackdown against the Hungarian revolution, the British-French-Israeli assault placed the United States in the difficult position of condemning the Soviets for intervening in Hungary while its anti-Communist partners waged war in Suez. Instead, Eisenhower cooperated with the United Nations to negotiate a cease-fire and engineer a pullout of the invading forces in Egypt. Ultimately, the Soviets proved the winners in this Cold War skirmish. The Suez invasion revived memories of European imperialism and fueled anti-Western sentiments and pan-Arab nationalism (a sense of unity among Arabs across national boundaries), which worked to the Soviets' advantage.

The Eisenhower administration soon moved to counter growing Soviet power in the region. In 1957, to throttle increasing Communist influence in the Middle East, Congress approved the **Eisenhower Doctrine**, which gave the president a free hand to use U.S. military forces in the Middle East "against overt armed aggression from any nation controlled by International Communism." In actuality, the Eisenhower administration proved more concerned with protecting access to oil fields from hostile Arab nationalist leaders than with any Communist incursion. In 1958, when an anti-American, non-Communist regime came to power in Iraq, the president sent 14,000 marines to neighboring Lebanon to prevent a similar outcome there.

Just before Eisenhower left office in January 1961, his administration intervened in a civil war in the newly independent Congo. This former colony of Belgium held valuable mineral resources, which Belgium and the United States coveted. After the Congo's first prime minister, Patrice Lumumba, stated his intentions to remain neutral in the Cold War, President Eisenhower and CIA director Allen Dulles declared him unreliable in the conflict with the Soviet Union. With the support of Belgian military troops and encouragement from the United States, the resource-rich province of Katanga seceded from the Congo in 1960. After the Congolese military, under the leadership of Joseph Mobuto, overthrew Lumumba's government, the CIA launched an operation that culminated in the execution of Lumumba on January 17, 1961. Several years later, Mobuto became president of the country, changed its name to Zaire, and allied with the West.

SECONDARY SOURCE ANALYSIS

Causes of the Cold War

Historians have debated the causes of the Cold War for more than seven decades. Interpretations have cast responsibility on the Soviet Union, the United States, or both. Historians have emphasized a variety of approaches from economic, political, and institutional to cultural, psychological, and ideological. The following excerpts present two schools of thought: the revisionist, first proposed by the historian William Appleman Williams, who argued that the United States was at fault for the Cold War, and the post-revisionist, articulated initially by the historian John Lewis Gaddis, who believed that neither the United States nor the USSR was solely to blame for the cause of the Cold War.

Source 24.4

William Appleman Williams | Expanding the Economic Open Door, 1959

The leaders who succeeded [Franklin] Roosevelt understood neither the dilemma nor the need to alter their outlook. A handful of them thought briefly of stabilizing relations with the Soviet Union on the basis of economic and political agreements, but even that tiny minority saw the future in terms of continued open-door [access to overseas markets] expansion. The great majority rapidly embarked upon a program to force the Soviet Union to accept America's traditional conception of itself and the world. This decision represented the final stage in the transformation of the policy of the open door from a utopian idea into an ideology, from an intellectual outlook for changing the world into one concerned with preserving it in the traditional mold.

American leaders had internalized, and had come to *believe*, the theory and the morality of open-door expansion. Hence they seldom thought it necessary to explain or defend the approach. Instead, they *assumed* the premises and concerned themselves with exercising their apparent freedom to deal with the necessities defined by such an outlook. As far as American leaders were concerned, the philosophy and practice of open-door expansion had become, in both its missionary and economic aspects, *the* view of the world. Those who did not recognize and accept that fact were not only wrong, but they were incapable of thinking correctly.

Source: William Appleman Williams, *The Tragedy of American Diplomacy* (Cleveland: The World Publishing Company, 1959), 150–51.

Early Intervention in Vietnam, 1954–1960. One offshoot of the Korean War was increased U.S. intervention in Vietnam, resulting in profound, long-term consequences. By the 1950s, Vietnamese revolutionaries (the Vietminh) had been fighting for independence from the French for decades. They were led by Ho Chi Minh, a revolutionary who had studied Communist doctrine in the Soviet Union but was not controlled by the Soviets. In fact, he modeled his 1945 Vietnamese Declaration of Independence on that of the United States. In 1954 the Vietminh defeated the French at the Battle of Dien Bien Phu. With the backing of the United States, the Soviet Union, and China, both sides agreed to divide Vietnam at the seventeenth parallel and hold free elections to unite the country in 1956.

Source 24.5

John Lewis Gaddis | Competing Ideologies, 1972

Moscow's position would not have seemed so alarming to American officials . . . had it not been for the Soviet Union's continued commitment to an ideology dedicated to the overthrow of capitalism throughout the world. Hopes that the United States might cooperate successfully with the USSR after the war had been based on the belief, encouraged by Stalin himself, that the Kremlin had given up its former goal of exporting Communism. . . . It seems likely that Washington policy makers mistook Stalin's determination to ensure Russian security through spheres of influence for a renewed effort to spread communism outside the borders of the Soviet Union. . . . But [Stalin] failed to make the limited nature of his objectives clear.

Revisionists are correct in emphasizing the importance of internal constraints, but they have defined them too narrowly: by focusing so heavily on economics, they neglect the profound impact of the domestic political system on the conduct of American foreign policy. . . . The delay in opening the second front, nonrecognition of Moscow's sphere of influence in Eastern Europe, and the decision to retain control of the atomic bomb can all be explained far more plausibly by citing the Administration's need to maintain popular support for its policies rather than by dwelling upon requirements of the economic order . . . , Stalin's paranoia, together with the bureaucracy of institutionalized suspicion with which he surrounded himself, made the situation much worse.

Source: John Lewis Gaddis, *The United States and the Origins of the Cold War, 1941–1947* (New York: Columbia University Press, 1972), 354–55, 359.

Examine the Sources

1. Describe one major difference between Williams's and Gaddis's interpretations of the causes of the Cold War.
2. Based on evidence in this chapter, evaluate the strengths and weaknesses of each interpretation.

Put It in Context

Explain why the Cold War began so soon after World War II ended.

President Dwight Eisenhower, who had brought the Korean War to a close in 1953, believed that if Vietnam fell to the Communists, the rest of Southeast Asia and Japan would "go over very quickly" like "a row of dominoes," threatening American strategic power in the Far East as well as free access to Asian markets. Convinced that Ho Chi Minh and his followers would win free elections, in 1955 the Eisenhower administration supported the anti-French, anti-Communist Ngo Dinh Diem to lead South Vietnam and then backed his regime's refusal to hold national elections in 1956. The anti-Communist interests of the United States had trumped its democratic promises. With the country now permanently divided, Eisenhower funneled economic aid to Diem to undertake needed land reforms that would strengthen his government and weaken the appeal of Ho Chi Minh.

The Battle of Dien Bien Phu, 1954   This photograph shows Vietnamese soldiers resting in a trench at Dien Bien Phu, site of the pivotal battle at which French colonial forces were defeated. Fighting began on March 13, 1954, and ended on May 7, when French troops surrendered. This photo, like most of those taken of the battle, was restaged shortly after the action, mainly for propaganda purposes.   AFP/Getty Images

The president also dispatched CIA agents and military advisers to support the South Vietnamese government. However, Diem used most of the money to consolidate his power rather than implement reforms, which only widened opposition to his regime from Communists and non-Communists alike. This prompted Ho Chi Minh in 1959 to support the creation in the South of the National Liberation Front, or **Vietcong**, to wage a military insurgency against Diem. By the end of the decade, the Eisenhower administration had created a major diplomatic problem with no clear plan for its resolution.

REVIEW & RELATE

- In what ways did the Eisenhower administration continue the Cold War policies of President Truman? In what ways did it depart from his predecessor?

- How did U.S. intervention in Vietnam reflect the policy of containment?

Conclusion: The **Cold War** and **Anticommunism**

Anticommunism remained a potent weapon in political affairs as long as the Cold War operated in full force. When George Kennan designed the doctrine of containment in 1946 and 1947, he had no idea that it would lead to permanent military alliances such as NATO or to a war in Korea. He viewed the Soviet Union as an unflinching ideological enemy, but he believed that it should be contained through economic rather than military means. Despite his launching of the Marshall Plan and providing aid to the Greeks through the Truman Doctrine, President Truman soon departed from Kennan's vision by militarizing containment. Beginning with NATO and continuing with the Korean War, the Truman administration put into operation around the world the heightened military plans called for by NSC-68. Hard-line Cold War rhetoric portrayed the struggle as a battle between good and evil. Born out of different perceptions of national interests and mutual misunderstandings of the other side's actions, the Cold War became frozen in the language of competing moralistic assumptions and self-righteousness. Within this context, though some Americans rallied to obtain clemency for the Rosenbergs, most considered that they got just what they deserved.

The Eisenhower administration continued the policy of containment inherited from Truman. Eisenhower brought the Korean War to an end and attempted to slow down the rate of military spending. Nevertheless, in the name of checking Communist aggression, his administration did not hesitate to intervene in Latin America, the Middle East, Africa, and Southeast Asia. Both the United States and the Soviet Union built up their nuclear arsenals and developed speedier ways by air and sea to deliver these deadly weapons against each other. Occasionally, foreign crises riveted the attention of Americans on the perils of atomic brinksmanship with the Soviets, but the sheer horror of the possibility of nuclear war helped the two major Cold War powers avoid escalating existing conflicts into nuclear destruction. Such brinksmanship did little to quell mounting fears of Communist infiltration and espionage at home in the United States. Those fears led to a second Red scare, as well as a strengthened presidency, one given more powers with which to combat communism and maintain national security. Cold War spending helped boost the American economy, but the renewed prosperity it brought masked some serious trouble brewing at home over civil rights and teenage culture.

CHAPTER 24 REVIEW

TIMELINE OF EVENTS

1938	House Un-American Activities Committee (HUAC) established
1945	Potsdam Conference
1946	Kennan telegram outlines containment strategy
	Churchill's "iron curtain" speech
1947	Truman Doctrine articulated National Security Act passed
	Central Intelligence Agency (CIA) established
	Truman creates Federal Employee Loyalty Program
1948–1949	Berlin blockade and airlift
	Alger Hiss affair
1948	Marshall Plan approved
1949	National Security Agency established
	Communists win Chinese civil war North Atlantic Treaty Organization (NATO) formed
	Soviet Union successfully tests atomic weapon
1950–1953	Korean War
1950–1954	McCarthy's anti-Communist crusade
1950	NSC-68 issued
1953	Julius and Ethel Rosenberg executed for espionage
	U.S. supports overthrow of Iranian government
1954	French defeated in Vietnam
	U.S. supports overthrow of Guatemalan government
1955	U.S. supports Ngo Diem in South Vietnam
1855	Bandung Conference of Non-Aligned Nations
1956	Suez crisis
1958	U.S. troops sent to Lebanon
1959	Fidel Castro takes power in Cuba
	The Vietcong formed
1961	U.S. intervenes in the Congo

KEY TERMS

Cold War, *815*

Truman Doctrine, *819*

Marshall Plan, *820*

imperial presidency, *820*

National Security Council (NSC), *820*

Berlin airlift, *821*

North Atlantic Treaty Organization (NATO), *824*

NSC-68, *825*

House Un-American Activities Committee (HUAC), *830*

Federal Employee Loyalty Program, *830*

McCarthyism, *833*

New Look, *834*

mutually assured destruction (MAD), *835*

Bandung Conference, *836*

Eisenhower Doctrine, *837*

Vietcong, *840*

REVIEW & RELATE

1. Why did American policymakers believe that containing Communist expansion should be the foundation of American foreign policy?

2. What role did mutual misunderstandings and mistrust play in the emergence of the Cold War?

3. What were the causes and consequences of the militarization of the containment strategy in the late 1940s and early 1950s?

4. How did the Korean War contribute to the centralization of power in the executive branch?

5. Why did fear of Communists in positions of influence escalate in the late 1940s and early 1950s?

6. Why was McCarthyism much more powerful than Joseph McCarthy?

7. In what ways did the Eisenhower administration continue the Cold War policies of President Truman? In what ways did it depart from his predecessor?

8. How did U.S. intervention in Vietnam reflect the policy of containment?

McCarthyism and the Hollywood Ten

▶ Evaluate the power of McCarthyism by explaining why so few people challenged McCarthy, HUAC, and other anti-Communist investigators.

In 1947 the House Un-American Activities Committee (HUAC) began a headline-grabbing investigation of Hollywood, hoping to expose Communist influence in the Screen Writers Guild and pro-Communist messages in films. HUAC first called a number of "friendly" witnesses, such as actors Ronald Reagan (Source 24.6) and Gary Cooper, writer Ayn Rand, and movie studio heads Walt Disney and Jack Warner. These witnesses affirmed the presence of Communists in the film industry, though they were careful also to affirm their own anti-Communist beliefs. HUAC then called ten "unfriendly" witnesses who were suspected of being Communists (Source 24.7). They invoked the First Amendment's protection of free speech (or the right not to speak) and free association and refused to answer the committee's questions. The "Hollywood Ten," as they became known, included one director and nine writers, and all were held in contempt of Congress and given fines and jail sentences.

Over the next ten years, thousands of writers, actors, directors, producers, and technicians were blacklisted and lost their jobs (Sources 24.8 and 24.10). Although some were able to continue working under pseudonyms (especially writers), others had to leave the United States to find work; many were forced to look for employment outside the entertainment industry. There were personal consequences, too: Some marriages and families broke apart from the strain, and a few individuals were even driven to suicide. Nevertheless, others fought back. The cartoonist Herbert Lawrence Block (Herblock) ridiculed the attack on civil liberties (Source 24.9).

Source 24.6

Ronald Reagan | Testimony before HUAC, 1947

Ronald Reagan's acting career began in the late 1930s and included numerous starring roles, mostly in B movies. During World War II, he served in the Public Relations Unit of the Army Air Corps, where he helped produce hundreds of training films. Reagan was the president of the Screen Actors Guild during HUAC's Hollywood investigations, and he testified before the committee. Robert Stripling was the committee's chief investigator.

MR. STRIPLING Mr. Reagan, what is your feeling about what steps should be taken to rid the motion-picture industry of any Communist influences, if they are there?

MR. REAGAN Well, sir . . . 99 percent of us are pretty well aware of what is going on, and I think within the bounds of our democratic rights, and never once stepping over the rights given us by democracy, we have done a pretty good job in our business of keeping those people's activities curtailed. After all, we must recognize them at present as a political party. On that basis we have exposed their lies when we came across them, we have opposed their propaganda, and I can certainly testify that in the case of the Screen Actors Guild we have been eminently successful in preventing them from, with their usual tactics, trying to run a majority of an organization with a well organized minority.

So that fundamentally I would say in opposing those people that the best thing to do is to make democracy work. In the Screen Actors Guild we make it work by insuring everyone a vote and by keeping everyone informed. I believe that, as Thomas Jefferson put it, if all the American people know all of the facts they will never make a mistake.

Whether the party should be outlawed, I agree with the gentlemen that preceded me that that is a matter for the Government to decide. As a citizen I would hesitate, or not like, to see any political party outlawed on the basis of its political ideology. We have spent 170 years in this country on the basis that democracy is strong enough to stand up and fight against the inroads of any ideology. However, if it is proven that an organization is an agent of a power, a foreign power, or in any way not a legitimate political party, and I think the Government is capable of proving that, if the proof is there, then that is another matter.

I do not know whether I have answered your question or not. I . . . would like at this moment to say I happen to be very proud of the industry in which I work; I happen to be very proud of the way in which we conducted the fight. I do not believe the Communists have ever at any time been able to use the motion-picture screen as a sounding board for their philosophy or ideology. I think that will continue as long [as] the people in Hollywood continue as they are, which is alert, conscious of it, and fighting.

Source: House Un-American Activities Committee, *Hearings Regarding the Communist Infiltration of the Motion Picture Industry*, 80th Cong., 1st sess. (Washington, DC: Government Printing Office, 1947), 216–17.

Source 24.7

John Howard Lawson | Testimony before HUAC, 1947

Playwright and screenwriter John Howard Lawson was a founding member of the Screen Writers Guild. He was also a member of the American Communist Party and served as the party's cultural commissar in Hollywood, and many of his films included leftist political themes. In 1947 Lawson appeared before HUAC. The following selection shows several attempts by the committee to force Lawson's compliance. Like the other Hollywood Ten, Lawson was imprisoned and blacklisted for refusing to answer HUAC's questions or detail his political affiliations.

MR. LAWSON I am glad you have made it perfectly clear that you are going to threaten and intimidate the witnesses, Mr. Chairman. (The chairman pounding gavel.)

MR. LAWSON I am an American and I am not at all easy to intimidate, and don't think I am. (The chairman pounding gavel.)

MR. STRIPLING Mr. Lawson, I repeat the question. Have you ever held any position in the Screen Writers Guild?

MR. LAWSON I have stated that the question is illegal. But it is a matter of public record that I have held many offices in the Screen Writers Guild. I was its first president, in 1933, and I have held office on the board of directors of the Screen Writers Guild at other times. . . .

MR. STRIPLING Mr. Lawson, are you now, or have you ever been a member of the Communist Party of the United States?

MR. LAWSON In framing my answer to that question I must emphasize the points that I have raised before. The question of communism is in no way related to this inquiry, which is an attempt to get control of the screen and to invade the basic rights of American citizens in all fields.

MR. McDOWELL Now, I must object—

MR. STRIPLING Mr. Chairman— (The chairman pounding gavel.)

MR. LAWSON The question here relates not only to the question of my membership in any political organization, but this committee is attempting to establish the right— (The chairman pounding gavel.)

MR. LAWSON (continuing) Which has been historically denied to any committee of this sort, to invade the rights and privileges and immunity of American citizens, whether they be Protestant, Methodist, Jewish, or Catholic, whether they be Republicans or Democrats or anything else.

THE CHAIRMAN (pounding gavel) Mr. Lawson, just quiet down again. Mr. Lawson, the most pertinent question that we can ask is whether or not you have ever been a member of the Communist Party. Now, do you care to answer that question?

MR. LAWSON You are using the old technique, which was used in Hitler Germany in order to create a scare here—

THE CHAIRMAN (pounding gavel) Oh—

MR. LAWSON In order to create an entirely false atmosphere in which this hearing is conducted— (The chairman pounding gavel.)

MR. LAWSON In order that you can then smear the motion-picture industry, and you can proceed to the press, to any form of communication in this country.

THE CHAIRMAN You have learned—

MR. LAWSON The Bill of Rights was established precisely to prevent the operation of any committee which could invade the basic rights of Americans. . . .

THE CHAIRMAN (pounding gavel) We are going to get the answer to that question if we have to stay here for a week. Are you a member of the Communist Party, or have you ever been a member of the Communist Party?

MR. LAWSON It is unfortunate and tragic that I have to teach this committee the basic principles of American—

THE CHAIRMAN (pounding gavel) That is not the question. That is not the question. The question is: Have you ever been a member of the Communist Party?

MR. LAWSON I am framing my answer in the only way in which any American citizen can frame his answer to a question which absolutely invades his rights.

THE CHAIRMAN Then you refuse to answer that question; is that correct?

MR. LAWSON I have told you that I will offer my beliefs, affiliations, and everything else to the American public, and they will know where I stand.

THE CHAIRMAN (pounding gavel) Excuse the witness—

MR. LAWSON As they do from what I have written.

THE CHAIRMAN (pounding gavel) Stand away from the stand—

MR. LAWSON I have written Americanism for many years, and I shall continue to fight for the Bill of Rights, which you are trying to destroy.

THE CHAIRMAN Officers, take this man away from the stand—(Applause and boos.)

THE CHAIRMAN (pounding gavel) There will be no demonstrations. No demonstrations, for or against. Everyone will please be seated.

Source: House Un-American Activities Committee, *Hearings Regarding the Communist Infiltration of the Motion Picture Industry*, 80th Cong., 1st sess. (Washington, DC: Government Printing Office, 1947), 292–95.

Source 24.8

The Waldorf Statement and the Introduction of the Blacklist, 1947

After the Hollywood Ten were cited for contempt, the movie studios established a policy of blacklisting "unfriendly" witnesses called before congressional committees. After meeting at the Waldorf Astoria in New York, on December 3, 1947, the Motion Picture Association of America issued the following statement.

Members of the Association of Motion Picture Producers deplore the action of the 10 Hollywood men who have been cited for contempt by the House of Representatives. We do not desire to prejudge their legal rights, but their actions have been a disservice to their employers and have impaired their usefulness to the industry.

We will forthwith discharge or suspend without compensation those in our employ, and we will not reemploy any of the 10 until such time as he is acquitted or has purged himself of contempt and declares under oath that he is not a Communist.

On the broader issue of alleged subversive and disloyal elements in Hollywood, our members are likewise prepared to take positive action.

We will not knowingly employ a Communist or a member of any party or group which advocates the overthrow of the government of the United States by force or by any illegal or unconstitutional methods.

In pursuing this policy, we are not going to be swayed by hysteria or intimidation from any source. We are frank to recognize that such a policy involves dangers of hurting innocent people. Creative work at its best cannot be carried on in an atmosphere of fear. We will guard against this danger, this risk, this fear.

The absence of a national policy, established by Congress, with respect to employment of Communists in private industry makes our task difficult. Ours is a nation of laws. We request Congress to enact legislation to assist American industry to rid itself of subversive, disloyal elements.

Nothing subversive or un-American has appeared on the screen, nor can any number of Hollywood investigations obscure the patriotic services of the 30,000 loyal Americans employed in Hollywood who have given our government invaluable aid to war and peace."

Source: "Film Industry's Policy Defined," *Daily Variety*, November 26, 1947, 3.

Herblock | "Fire!" 1949

Editorial cartoonist Herbert Lawrence Block, who wrote under the name "Herblock," was a fierce critic of McCarthyism — both the man and the movement — and coined the term *McCarthyism* in March 1950, weeks after Senator McCarthy's first anti-Communist speech in Wheeling, West Virginia. The cartoon "Fire!" was published in June 1949 by the *Washington Post*.

A 1949 Herblock Cartoon, © The Herb Block Foundation

Source 24.10

Lillian Hellman | Letter to HUAC, 1952

Playwright Lillian Hellman, who was known for her devotion to leftist causes, was called to testify before HUAC in May 1952. Before her appearance, Hellman wrote the following letter to John Wood, the chairman of HUAC, explaining her willingness to answer questions about herself as long as she was not asked to testify against anyone else. Her request was denied. Hellman was blacklisted after invoking the Fifth Amendment during her HUAC appearance.

Dear Mr. Wood:

As you know, I am under subpoena to appear before your committee on May 21, 1952.

I am most willing to answer all questions about myself. I have nothing to hide from your committee and there is nothing in my life of which I am ashamed. I have been advised by counsel that under the fifth amendment I have a constitutional privilege to decline to answer any questions about my political opinions, activities, and associations, on the grounds of self-incrimination. I do not wish to claim this privilege. I am ready and willing to testify before the representatives of our Government as to my own opinions and my own actions, regardless of any risks or consequences to myself.

But I am advised by counsel that if I answer the committee's questions about myself, I must also answer questions about other people and that if I refuse to do so, I can be cited for contempt. My counsel tells me that if I answer questions about myself, I will have waived my rights under the fifth amendment and could be forced legally to answer questions about others. This is very difficult for a layman to understand. But there is one principle that I do understand: I am not willing, now or in the future, to bring bad trouble to people who, in my past association with them, were completely innocent of any talk or any action that was disloyal or subversive. I do not like subversion or disloyalty in any form and if I had ever seen any I would have considered it my duty to have reported it to the proper authorities. But to hurt innocent people whom I knew many years ago in order to save myself is, to me, inhuman and indecent and dishonorable. I cannot and will not cut my conscience to fit this year's fashions, even though I long ago came to the conclusion that I was not a political person and could have no comfortable place in any political group.

I was raised in an old-fashioned American tradition and there were certain homely things that were taught to me: To try to tell the truth, not to bear false witness, not to harm my neighbor, to be loyal to my country, and so on. In general, I respected these ideals of Christian honor and did as well with them as I knew how. It is my belief that you will agree with these simple rules of human decency and will not expect me to violate the good American tradition from which they spring. I would, therefore, like to come before you and speak of myself.

I am prepared to waive the privilege against self-incrimination and to tell you everything you wish to know about my views or actions if your committee will agree to refrain from asking me to name other people. If the committee is unwilling to give me this assurance, I will be forced to plead the privilege of the fifth amendment at the hearing.

A reply to this letter would be appreciated.

Sincerely yours,
Lillian Hellman

Source: House Un-American Activities Committee, *Hearings Regarding Communist Infiltration of the Hollywood Motion-Picture Industry*, 82nd Cong., 2nd sess. (Washington, DC: Government Printing Office, 1952), 3545–46.

Interpret the Evidence

1. Explain how Ronald Reagan (Source 24.6) views the threat communism poses to American society and how that threat should be handled.
2. Assess the way movie producers (Source 24.8) draw the line between artistic expression and blacklisting.
3. Explain how the Herblock cartoon (Source 24.9) defines "un-American."
4. Compare the testimonies of John Howard Lawson and Lillian Hellman (Sources 24.7 and 24.10). What are their chief objections to testifying before HUAC?

Put It in Context

Why did anti-Communist investigations dominate politics after World War II?

Troubled Innocence

1945–1961

25

WINDOW TO THE **PAST**

The Desegregation of Central High School, 1957

After two decades of economic depression and world war, the 1950s saw a return of peace and prosperity. However, for African Americans the 1950s were a time of challenges and conflicts. This photo of Elizabeth Eckford walking through a hostile crowd in Little Rock, Arkansas exhibits the dignity of one teenager in the struggle for racial equality. ▶ To discover more about what this primary source can show us, see Document 25.8 on page 882.

©The Commercial Appeal / Zuma Press

After reading this chapter you should be able to:

- Explain the problems of converting from World War II to peacetime and describe the causes and effects of the postwar economic boom.

- Analyze how the 1950s popular culture reflected the expanding consumer-oriented economy and explain the challenges to mainstream culture posed by teenagers, women, and the Beat generation.

- Examine the growth of the civil rights movement and identify the strategies used to challenge segregation and discrimination in the 1950s.

- Evaluate the impact of President Eisenhower's domestic policies and accomplishments on the Republican Party and the nation.

COMPARING AMERICAN HISTORIES

Alan Freed shook up American youth culture in the 1950s by rebranding existing black music and making it popular with white teenagers. In 1951, at the age of twenty-nine, Aldon (Alan) James Freed was spinning records as a disc jockey, or "deejay," at a Cleveland, Ohio radio station. He played rhythm and blues, an African American music style considered "race music." Calling himself Moondog, Freed howled like a dog and used sound effects to rattle his radio listeners. Although he initially appealed mainly to a black

(left) **Alan Freed.** Michael Ochs Archives/Getty Images
(right) **Grace Metalious.** Everett Collection

audience, Freed's radio show and live concerts of music he dubbed rock 'n' roll soon attracted white teenagers.

In 1954 Freed moved to New York City, where his evening rock 'n' roll radio broadcast became a number one hit. Three years later, he hosted a nationally televised rock 'n' roll program, but only briefly. The American Broadcasting Company canceled Freed's show after four telecasts because of outrage from affiliate stations in the South after the black singer Frankie Lymon was shown dancing with a white girl.

The television incident was only the start of Freed's professional problems. In 1960 Freed was brought before a congressional committee investigating "payola," a common practice among deejays of receiving gifts from record companies in exchange for playing their records. His career sank further when, in 1962, Freed was convicted of commercial bribery by New York State. Impoverished and struggling with alcoholism, Freed died in 1965 at the age of forty-three.

Like Alan Freed, Grace Metalious sent shock waves through American popular culture in the 1950s. Metalious grew up in poverty in Manchester, New Hampshire. In 1943, while still a teenager, she married and became a mother and housewife. In 1956 Metalious published her first novel, *Peyton Place*, and the book sold more than three million copies the first year. Considered provocative and racy because of its discussion of sex, rape, and incest, the novel punctured myths about the straitlaced life of small-town America. It criticized small-minded conformity that enforced a double standard of sexual behavior on women.

Despite the book's popularity, Metalious was never seen as a serious writer. Detractors described her as an untalented author who disseminated filth. Metalious could not reconcile her success with the criticism she received and, like Alan Freed, increasingly turned to alcohol for comfort. In 1964, just eight years after publication of *Peyton Place*, she died at age thirty-nine of cirrhosis of the liver. Both Metalious and Freed challenged notions of conventional taste, and both found their lives upended by the backlash their work inspired. ■

The American histories of Alan Freed and Grace Metalious, both of whom attacked conformity, were made possible by the emergence of a mass-consumption economy fueled by technological innovation. The end of World War II had produced economic, social, and political challenges for Americans; however, the economic boom of the 1950s allowed many Americans to overcome them. A large number of families moved into the middle class and out to suburbia. Yet not everyone felt satisfied, and critics expressed their disapproval in diverse ways. Young people challenged their parents' culture. Writers and musicians experimented with freer forms of artistic expression and attacked the conformity they associated with mainstream America. And African Americans and other minorities challenged racial segregation directly in the Supreme Court and through powerful community protests.

Peacetime Transition and the **Boom Years**

The notoriety of Grace Metalious and Alan Freed came at a time of renewed economic growth and prosperity in the United States. Although confronted with family upheaval, labor disruptions, and economic constraints immediately following the war, by 1950 Americans had more disposable income than they had enjoyed in decades. While Truman struggled to hold together the New Deal coalition, consumers responded enthusiastically to the wide range of products that advertisers promised would improve their lives. The search for the good life propelled middle-class families from cities to the suburbs. At the same time, a postwar baby boom added millions of children to the population and created a market to supply them with goods from infancy and childhood to adolescence.

Peacetime Challenges, 1945–1948. Before Americans could work their way toward prosperity, they faced considerable challenges. Immediately after the war, consumers experienced shortages and high prices, businesses complained about tight regulations, and labor unions sought higher wages and a greater voice in companies' decision making. The return to peace also occasioned debates about whether married women should continue to work outside the home.

By mid-1946, 9 million American soldiers had returned to a changed world. The war had exerted pressures on traditional family life as millions of women had left home to work jobs that men had vacated. Most of the 150,000 women who served in the military received their discharge, and like their male counterparts they hoped to obtain employment. Many other women who had tasted the benefits of wartime employment also wanted to keep working and were reluctant to give up their positions to men.

The war disrupted other aspects of family life as well. During the war, husbands and wives had spent long periods apart, resulting in marital tensions and an increased divorce rate. The relaxation of parental authority during the war led to a rise in juvenile delinquency, which added to the anxieties of adults. In 1948 the noted psychiatrist William C. Menninger observed, "While we alarm ourselves with talk of . . . atom bombs, we are complacently watching the disintegration of our family life." Some observers worried that the very existence of the traditional American family was in jeopardy.

Economic Conversion and Labor Discontent. Even before the war ended, the U.S. government took some steps to meet postwar economic challenges. In 1944, for example, Congress passed the **Servicemen's Readjustment Act**, commonly known as the **GI Bill**, which offered veterans educational opportunities and financial aid as they adjusted to civilian life. Nevertheless, veterans, like other Americans, faced shortages in the supply of housing and consumer goods and high prices for available commodities.

President Harry Truman ran into serious difficulty handling these and other problems. In the years immediately following the war, real incomes fell, undermined by inflation and reduced overtime hours. As corporate profits rose, workers in the steel, automobile, and fuel industries struck for higher wages and a greater voice in company policies. Truman responded harshly. Labor had been one of Franklin Roosevelt's strongest allies, but his successor put that relationship in jeopardy. In 1946 the federal government took over railroads and threatened to draft workers into the military until they stopped striking. Truman took a tough stance, but in the end union workers received a pay raise, though it did little to relieve inflation.

Political developments forced Truman to change course with the labor unions. In the 1946 midterm elections, Republicans won control of Congress. Stung by this defeat, Truman sought to repair the damage his anti-union policies had done to the Democratic Party coalition. In 1947 Congress passed the **Taft-Hartley Act**, which hampered the ability of unions to organize and limited their power to strike if larger national interests were seen

The GI Bill   The GI Bill provided a variety of benefits for World War II veterans. Not only did it pay for veterans to get a high school, vocational, or college degree, it also offered low-cost home mortgages and low-interest loans for business and farm ventures. The government distributed this 1945 lithograph to make GIs aware of some of these benefits. Granger

to be at stake. Seeking to regain labor's support, Truman vetoed the measure. Congress, however, overrode the president's veto, and the Taft-Hartley Act became law.

Truman, the New Deal Coalition, and the Election of 1948.

Truman's handling of domestic and foreign affairs brought out several challengers for the 1948 election. Much of the opposition came from his own party. From the left, former Democratic vice president Henry Wallace ran on the Progressive Party ticket, backed by disgruntled liberals who opposed Truman's hardline Cold War policies. From the right, Democratic governor Strom Thurmond of South Carolina campaigned mainly on preserving racial segregation in the South and headed up the States' Rights Party, known as the Dixiecrats. Both Wallace and Thurmond threatened to take Democratic votes from the president. However, Truman's strongest challenge came from the popular Republican governor of New York, Thomas E. Dewey. Indeed, political pundits and public opinion polls predicted that Truman would lose the 1948 presidential election.

Truman confounded expectations by winning the presidency. His victory resulted from his vigorous campaign style and the complacency of his Republican opponent, who placed too much faith in opinion polls. In addition, Wallace and Thurmond failed to draw significant votes away from Truman, demonstrating the continuing power of the New Deal coalition. Truman succeeded in holding together the coalition of labor, minorities, farmers, and liberals and winning enough votes in the South to come out ahead.

By this time, most liberals had moved closer to the political center. Rejecting what they considered the ideological dogmatism of the extreme left and right, they favored a strong anti-Communist policy abroad and supported a brand of reform capitalism at home that encouraged economic growth rather than a redistribution of wealth to lift Americans into the middle class. In doing so, they also sought to avoid the political fallout from charges of Communist sympathizers-in-government hurled by Republicans.

Economic Boom.

While the United States faced political challenges, the economy flourished in the decade and a half after the Second World War. Between 1945 and 1960 the gross national product (GNP) soared 250 percent and per capita income (total income divided by the population) grew 35 percent. During this fifteen-year period, the average real income (actual purchasing power) for American workers increased by as much as it had during the fifty years preceding World War II. Equally striking, 60 percent of Americans achieved middle-class status, and the number of salaried office workers rose 61 percent. Factory workers also experienced gains. Union membership leaped to the highest level in U.S. history, reaching nearly 17 million.

The affluence of the 1950s was much more equally distributed than the prosperity of the 1920s had been. As the middle class grew, the top 5 percent of wealthy families dropped in the percentage of total income they earned from 21.3 percent to 19 percent. Though poverty remained a persistent problem, the rate of poverty decreased, falling from 34 percent in 1947 to 22.1 percent in 1960 (Figure 25.1). A college education served as a critical marker of middle-class status. Traditionally, colleges and universities had been accessible only to the upper class. That began to change between 1940 and 1960 as the number of high school students who entered college more than doubled.

The market for consumer goods skyrocketed. TV sets became a household staple in the 1950s, and by 1960, 87 percent of Americans owned a television. Americans also

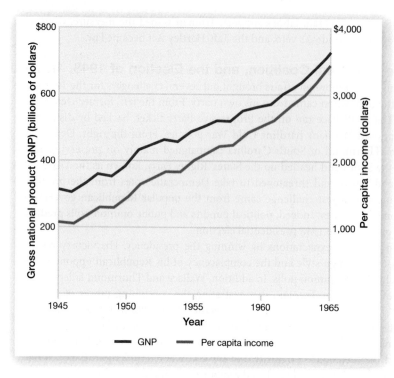

FIGURE 25.1   Economic Growth, 1945–1965

As industries shifted from war equipment to consumer goods, productivity remained high. More Americans entered the middle class in the two decades following World War II, while rising union membership ensured higher incomes for the working class. As a result, the purchasing power of most Americans increased in the immediate postwar period. What factors promoted the growth of the middle class in the 1950s?

continued to purchase automobiles—75 percent owned a car. With gas supplies plentiful and the price per gallon less than 30 cents, automakers concentrated on size, power, and style to compete for buyers. With more cars on the road, motel chains such as Holiday Inn sprang up along the highways. Fast-food establishments proliferated to feed motorists and their families.

Baby Boom. During the postwar years, with traditional gender roles largely rein-stated and the economy booming, nuclear families began to grow. In 1955 Illinois gover-nor Adlai Stevenson told the women graduates at Smith College that they could do their part to maintain a free society as wives and mothers. Educated women had an important role to play in maintaining a household that boosted their husband's morale. The mothers of these female college gradu-ates had suffered through the Great Depression, when keeping the birthrate low was one way to assist the family. That was about to change.

Explore ▶

See Source 25.1 for Adlai Stevenson's speech at Smith explaining why a woman's place is in the home.

In the 1940s and 1950s the average age at marriage was younger than it had been in the 1930s. On average, men married for the first time at the age of just under twenty-three, and 49 percent of women married by nineteen. Couples also produced children at an astonishing rate. In the 1950s, the growth rate in the U.S. population approached that of India (Figure 25.2).

Marriage and parenthood reflected a culture spurred by the Cold War. Public officials and the media urged young men and women to build nuclear families in which the father held a paying job and the mother stayed at home and raised her growing family. Doing

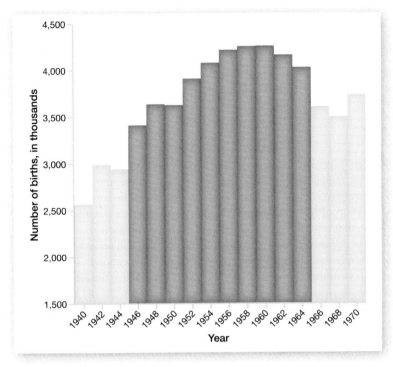

FIGURE 25.2   The Baby Boom, 1946–1964

The U.S. population increased dramatically in the postwar decades. Economic prosperity made it easier to support large families, women's early age at marriage contributed to high fertility, and improved health care led to the survival of more children. As this figure shows, the baby boom experienced its peak in the 1950s. How much did the baby boom influence the flourishing of teenage culture that arose in the same period?

so would strengthen the moral fiber of the United States in its battle against Soviet communism.

Parents could also look forward to their children surviving diseases that had resulted in many childhood deaths in the past. In the 1950s, children received vaccinations against diphtheria, whooping cough, and tuberculosis before they entered school. The most serious illness affecting young children remained the crippling disease of polio, or infantile paralysis. In 1955 Dr. Jonas Salk developed a successful injectable vaccine against the disease. On April 12, 1955, news bulletins interrupted scheduled television programs to announce Salk's breakthrough, and, as one writer recalled, "citizens rushed to ring church bells and fire sirens, shouted, clapped, sang, and made every kind of joyous noise they could." By the mid-1960s polio was no longer a public health menace in the United States.

Changes in Living Patterns. With larger families and larger family incomes came an increased demand for better housing. The economic and demographic booms encouraged migration out of the cities so that growing families could have their own homes, greater space, and a healthier environment. To meet this demand, the federal government provided Americans opportunities to purchase their own homes. The Federal Housing Administration, created in the 1930s, provided long-term mortgages to qualified buyers at low interest rates. After the war, the Veterans Administration offered even lower mortgage rates and did not require substantial down payments for ex-GIs. The federal government also cooperated by building highways that allowed drivers to commute to and from the suburbs. By 1960 nearly 60 million people, one-third of the nation's population, lived in suburbs.

Adlai E. Stevenson | "A Purpose for Modern Woman," 1955

Adlai E. Stevenson was governor of Illinois and Democratic presidential candidate in 1952 and 1956. A liberal Democrat, he nevertheless shared the conventional view of the relationship between the sexes. In his 1955 commencement address at all-female Smith College, he argued that women, however educated they were, should embrace their duty as housewives.

Source 25.1

According to Stevenson, what role do educated housewives have to play?

Why does he believe educated women feel frustrated?

What does he think women can accomplish?

Women, especially educated women, have a unique opportunity to influence us, man and boy, and to play a direct part in the unfolding drama of our free society. But I am told that nowadays the young wife or mother is short of time for such subtle arts, that things are not what they used to be; that once immersed in the very pressing and particular problems of domesticity, many women feel frustrated and far apart from the great issues and stirring debates for which their education has given them understanding and relish. Once they read Baudelaire. Now it is the *Consumers' Guide*. Once they wrote poetry. Now it's the laundry list. Once they discussed art and philosophy until late in the night. Now they are so tired they fall asleep as soon as the dishes are finished. . . . They had hoped to play their part in the crisis of the age. But what they do is wash the diapers. . . .

In modern America the home is not the boundary of a woman's life. There are outside activities aplenty. But even more important is the fact, surely, that what you have learned and can learn will fit you for the primary task of making homes and whole human beings in whom the rational values of freedom, tolerance, charity and free inquiry can take root.

Source: Adlai E. Stevenson, "A Purpose for Modern Woman," *Woman's Home Companion*, September 1955, 30–31. Reprinted by permission of Adlai Stevenson III.

Put It in Context

How were women's roles influenced by economic and social developments after World War II?

William Levitt, a thirty-eight-year-old veteran from Long Island, New York, devised the formula for attracting home buyers to the suburbs. In 1948, Levitt remarked: "No man who owns his own house and lot can be a Communist. He has too much to do." After World War II, Levitt, his father, and his brother saw opportunity in the housing crunch and pioneered the idea of adapting Henry Ford's mass-production principles to the housing industry. To build his subdivision of **Levittown** in Hempstead, Long Island, twenty miles from Manhattan, he bulldozed 4,000 acres of potato fields and brought in trucks that dumped piles of building materials at exact intervals of sixty feet. Specialized crews then moved from pile to pile, each performing their assigned job. In July 1948, Levitt's workers constructed 180 houses a week, or 36 a day, in two shifts. Mass-production methods kept prices low, and Levitt quickly sold his initial 17,000 houses and soon built other subdivisions in Pennsylvania and New Jersey. With Levitt leading the way, the annual production of new single-family homes nearly doubled from 937,000 in 1946 to 1.7 million in 1950.

Although millions of Americans took advantage of opportunities to move to the suburbs, Levitt closed his subdivisions to African Americans. He was supported by the Federal Housing Authority, which guaranteed financing for sales of housing in all-white communities. Many whites moved out of the cities to distance themselves from the growing number of southern blacks who migrated north during World War II and the influx of Puerto Ricans who came to the United States after the war, and they did not welcome these minorities to their new communities. Many communities in the North adopted restrictive covenants, which prohibited resale of homes to blacks and members of other minority groups, including Hispanics, Jews, and Asian Americans. Although the Supreme Court outlawed restrictive covenants in *Shelley v. Kraemer* (1948), housing discrimination remained prevalent in urban and suburban neighborhoods. Real estate brokers steered minority buyers away from white communities, and banks refused to lend money to black purchasers who sought to move into white locales, an illegal policy called redlining.

Nevertheless, a few African Americans succeeded in cracking suburban racial barriers, but at great risk. In August 1957, a black couple, William Myers, an electrical engineer, and his wife Daisy, managed to buy a house in Levittown, Pennsylvania. However, once the Myers moved in they faced two weeks of intimidation and assaults from mobs of disapproving white community residents. When local police refused to protect them, the governor dispatched state troopers to keep them safe. Although the Myers succeeded in remaining in Levittown, their experience underscored the racially discriminatory housing practices that existed in the North.

No sections of the nation expanded faster than the West and the South. Attracted by the warmer climate and jobs in the defense, petroleum, and chemical industries, transplanted Americans swelled the populations of California, Texas, and Florida. The advent of air conditioning also made such moves much more feasible. California's population increased the most, adding nearly six million new residents

William and Daisy Myers Integrate Levittown, 1957 Daisy Myers serves coffee to her husband William in their new $12,150 ranch-style house in Levittown, Pennsylvania. The first black family to move into this all-white community, on August 19, 1957, the Myers braved two weeks of threatening protests by their new neighbors and proclaimed: "We're here to stay," and they did. AP Photo/Sam Myers

between 1940 and 1960, including a large influx of Asians and Latinos. In 1957, in a sign of the times, New York City lost two of its baseball teams, the New York Giants and the Brooklyn Dodgers, to San Francisco and Los Angeles. This migration to the **Sun Belt**, as the southern and western states would be called, transformed the political and social landscapes of the nation.

REVIEW & RELATE

How did the conversion from war to peacetime affect the economy, society, and politics in the United States?

What factors contributed to the economic and population growth of the 1950s, and how did they contribute to suburbanization and the growth in the Sun Belt?

The **Culture** of the **1950s**

In the 1950s, new forms of popular culture developed as the United States confronted difficult political, diplomatic, and social issues. Amid this turmoil, television played a large role in shaping people's lives, reflecting their desire for success and depicting the era as a time of innocence. The rise of teenage culture as a powerful economic force also influenced this portrayal of the 1950s. Teenage tastes and consumption patterns reinforced the impression of a simpler and more carefree time. Religion painted a similar picture, as attendance at houses of worship rose. Still, the decade held a more complex social reality. Cultural rebels—writers, actors, and musicians—emerged to challenge mainstream values. Even women did not always act the suburban parts that television and society assigned them, and religion seemed to serve more of a communal, social function than an individual, spiritual one.

The Rise of Television. Few postwar developments had a greater impact on American society and politics than the advent of television. The three major television networks—the Columbia Broadcasting System (CBS), the National Broadcasting Company (NBC), and the American Broadcasting Company (ABC)—offered programs nationwide that appealed to mainstream tastes while occasionally challenging the public with serious drama, music, and documentaries. During the 1950s, television networks began to feature presidential campaign coverage, from the national nominating conventions to election-day vote tallies, and political advertisements began to fill the airwaves.

If many Americans recall the 1950s as a time of innocence, they have in mind television shows aimed at children, such as *Howdy Doody*, *Superman*, *Hopalong Cassidy*, *The Cisco Kid*, and *The Lone Ranger*. In the course of a half hour, the shows pitted good versus evil; honesty and decency inevitably triumphed. These youth-oriented television programs showcased a simple world of moral absolutes.

In similar fashion, adults enjoyed evening television shows that depicted old-fashioned families entertaining themselves, mediating quarrels peacefully, and relying on the wisdom of parents. In *The Adventures of Ozzie and Harriet*, the Nelsons raised two clean-cut sons. In *Father Knows Best*, the Andersons—a father and mother and their three children—lived a tranquil life in the suburbs, and the father solved whatever dilemmas arose. The same held true for the Cleaver family on *Leave It to Beaver*. Television portrayed working-class families in grittier fashion on shows such as *The Life of Riley*, whose lead character worked at a factory, and *The Honeymooners*, whose male protagonists were a bus driver and a sewer worker. Nevertheless, like their middle-class counterparts, these families stayed together and worked out their problems despite their more challenging financial circumstances.

By contrast, African American families received little attention on television. Black female actors usually appeared as maids, and the one show that featured an all-black cast, *The Amos 'n' Andy Show*, highlighted the racial stereotypes of the period. American Indians faced similar difficulties. Few appeared on television, and those who did served mainly as targets for "heroic" cowboys defending the West from "savage" Indians. One exception was Tonto, the Lone Ranger's sidekick. Played by Jay Silverheels, a Canadian Mohawk, he challenged the image of the hostile Indian by showing his loyalty to his white partner and his commitment to the code of "civilized" justice.

Wild Ones on the Big Screen.

If parents expected young people to behave like Ozzie and Harriet Nelson's sons, the popular culture industry provided teenagers with alternative role models. In *Rebel Without a Cause* (1955), actor James Dean portrayed a seventeen-year-old filled with anguish about his life. A sensitive but misunderstood young man, he muses that he wants "just one day when I wasn't all confused . . . [when] I wasn't ashamed of everything . . . [when] I felt I belonged some place." *The Wild One* (1954), which starred Marlon Brando, also popularized youthful angst. The leather-outfitted leader of a motorcycle gang, Brando rides into a small town, hoping to shake it up. When asked by a local resident, "What are you rebelling against?" he coolly replies, "Whaddya got?" Real gangs did exist on the streets of New York and other major cities. Composed of working-class youth from various ethnic and racial backgrounds, these gangs were highly

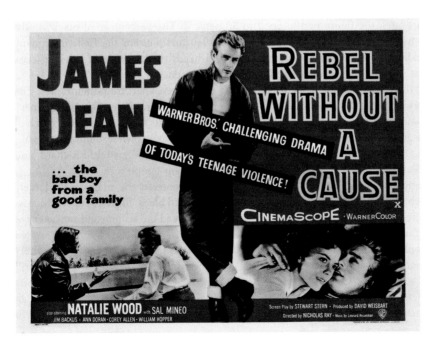

Rebel Without a Cause,
1955   James Dean starred in the movie *Rebel Without a Cause*, playing Jim Stark, a troubled teenager seeking an escape from his middle-class, suburban life. The movie explored the conflict between parents and teenagers, what we call today "the generation gap." Dean's outfit of leather jacket and blue jeans and his anguished demeanor both reflected and shaped teenage culture. Everett Collection

organized, controlled their neighborhood turfs, and engaged in "rumbles" (fights) with intruders. A romanticized version of these battles appeared on Broadway with the production of *West Side Story* (1957), which pitted a white gang against a Puerto Rican gang in a musical rendering of *Romeo and Juliet*.

Hollywood rarely portrayed women as rebels, but instead as mothers, understanding girlfriends, and dutiful wives. If they sought a career, like many of the women played by actor Doris Day, they pursued it only as long as necessary to meet the right man. Yet the film industry did offer a more tantalizing woman, a sexual being who displayed her attributes to seduce and outwit men. Marilyn Monroe in *The Seven Year Itch* (1955) and Elizabeth Taylor in *Cat on a Hot Tin Roof* (1958) revealed that women also had a powerful libido, though in the end they became domesticated or paid a terrible price.

The Influence of Teenage Culture. In 1941 *Popular Science* magazine coined the term *teenager*, and by the middle of the next decade members of this age group viewed themselves not as prospective adults but as a distinct group with its own identity, patterns of behavior, and tastes. Postwar prosperity provided teenagers with money to support their own choices and styles. In 1959 *Life* magazine found that teenagers had $10 billion at their disposal, "a billion more than the total sales of GM [General Motors]." **See Primary Source Project 25: Teenagers in Postwar America, page 880.**

Teenagers owned 10 million record players, more than 1 million TV sets, and 13 million cameras. They spent 16 percent of their disposable income on entertainment, particularly the purchase of rock 'n' roll records. The comic book industry also attracted a huge audience among teenagers by selling inexpensive, illustrated, and easy-to-read pulp fiction geared toward romance and action adventure.

Public high schools reinforced teenage identity. Following World War II, high school attendance exploded. In 1930, 50 percent of working-class children attended high school; thirty years later, the figure had jumped to 90 percent. The percentage of black youths attending high school also grew, doubling from 1940 to 1960. For the first time, many white middle-class teenagers saw the fashions and heard the language of working-class youths close up and both emulated and feared what they encountered.

More than anything else, rock 'n' roll music set teenagers apart from their elders. The pop singers of the 1940s and early 1950s—such as Frank Sinatra, Perry Como, Rosemary Clooney, and Patti Page, who had appealed to both adolescents and parents—lost much of their teenage audience after 1954 to rock 'n' roll, with its heavy downbeat and lyrics evoking teenage passion and sexuality. Black artists such as Chuck Berry, Little Richard, and Antoine "Fats" Domino popularized the sound of classic, up-tempo rock.

Although blacks pioneered the sound, the music entered the mainstream largely through white artists who added rural flavor to rhythm and blues. Born in Tupelo, Mississippi and living in Memphis, Tennessee, Elvis Presley adapted the fashion and sensuality of black performers to his own style. Elvis's snarling singing and pelvic gyrations excited young people, both black and white, while upsetting their parents. In an era when matters of sex remained private or were not discussed at all and when African Americans were still treated as second-class citizens, a white man singing "black" music and shaking his body to its frenetic tempo caused alarm. When Elvis sang on the popular *Ed Sullivan Show* in 1956, cameras were allowed to show him only from the waist up to uphold standards of decency.

The Lives of Women. Throughout the 1950s, movies, women's magazines, mainstream newspapers, and medical and psychological experts informed women that only by embracing domesticity could they achieve personal fulfillment. Dr. Benjamin Spock's best-selling *Common Sense Book of Baby and Child Care* (1946) advised mothers that their children would reach their full potential only if wives stayed at home and watched over their offspring. In another best seller, *Modern Women: The Lost Sex* (1947), Ferdinand Lundberg and Marynia Farnham called the independent woman "a contradiction in terms." A 1951 study of corporate executives found that most businessmen viewed the ideal wife as one who devoted herself to her husband's career. College newspapers described female undergraduates who were not engaged by their senior year as distraught. Certainly many women professed to find domestic lives fulfilling, but not all women were so content. Many experienced anxiety and depression. Far from satisfied, these women suffered from what the social critic Betty Friedan would later call "a problem that has no name," a malady that derived not from any personal failing but from the unrewarding roles women were expected to play.

Not all women fit the stereotype. Although most married women with families did not work during the 1950s, the proportion of working wives doubled from 15 percent in 1940 to 30 percent in 1960, with the greatest increase coming among women over the age of thirty-five. Married women were more likely to work if they were African American or

Women in the Home and in the Workplace   In the 1950s married women were encouraged to stay at home. Modern appliances like this refrigerator (left) supposedly made housework less difficult, but wives had to spend a great deal of time keeping it fully stocked and attending to other household chores. With all the new devices at their disposal, wives were expected to keep the home neat and spotless, while caring for their children. But not all married women stayed at home and tended the family. Margaret Chase Smith (above) was an influential Republican senator from Maine who took on Senator Joseph McCarthy in Congress and challenged his harsh anti-Communist methods. Here she is engaged in serious deliberations with Democratic majority leader Lyndon B. Johnson at a Senate hearing in 1957. (left) George Marks/Retrofile/Getty Images (above) Robert W. Kelley/The LIFE Picture Collection/Getty Images

came from working-class immigrant families. Moreover, women's magazines offered readers a more complex message than domesticity. Alongside articles about and advertisements directed at stay-at-home mothers, these periodicals profiled career women, such as Maine senator Margaret Chase Smith, the African American educator Mary McLeod Bethune, and sports figures such as the golf and tennis great Babe (Mildred) Didrikson Zaharias. At the same time, working women played significant roles in labor unions, where they fought to reduce disparities between men's and women's income and provide a wage for housewives, recognizing the importance of their unpaid work to maintaining families. Many other women joined clubs and organizations like the Young Women's Christian Association (YWCA), where they engaged in charitable and public service activities. Some participated in political organizations, such as Henry Wallace's Progressive Party, and peace groups, such as the Women's International League for Peace and Freedom, to campaign against the violence caused by racial discrimination at home and Cold War rivalries abroad.

Religious Revival.
Along with marriage and the family, religion experienced a revival in the postwar United States. The arms race between the United States and the Soviet Union heightened the dangers of international conflict for ordinary citizens, and the social and economic changes that accompanied the Cold War intensified personal anxiety. Churchgoing underscored the contrast between the United States, a religious nation, and the "godless" communism of the Soviet Union. The link between religion and Americanism prompted Congress in 1954 to add "under God" to the pledge of allegiance and to make "In God We Trust" the national motto.

Americans worshipped in growing numbers. Between 1940 and 1950, church and synagogue membership rose by 78 percent, and more than 95 percent of the population professed a belief in God. Yet religious affiliation appeared to reflect a greater emphasis on togetherness than on specific doctrinal beliefs. It offered a way to overcome isolation and embrace community in an increasingly alienating world. "The people in the suburbs want to feel psychologically secure, adjusted, at home in their environment," theologian Will Herberg explained. "Being religious and joining a church is . . . a fundamental way of 'adjusting' and 'belonging.'"

Television spread religiosity into millions of homes. The Catholic bishop Fulton J. Sheen spoke to a weekly television audience of ten million and alternated his message of "a life worth living" with attacks on atheistic Communists. The Methodist minister Norman Vincent Peale, also a popular TV figure, combined traditional religious faith with self-help remedies prescribed in his best-selling book *The Power of Positive Thinking* (1952). The Reverend Billy Graham, from Charlotte, North Carolina, preached about the unhappiness caused by personal sin at huge outdoor crusades in baseball parks and large arenas, which were broadcast on television. Americans derived a variety of meanings from their religious experiences, but many embraced Americanism as their national religion. A good American, one magazine proclaimed, could not be "un-religious."

Beats and Other Nonconformists.
As many Americans migrated to the suburbs, spent money on leisure and entertainment, and cultivated religion, a small group of young poets, writers, intellectuals, musicians, and artists attacked mainstream politics and culture. Known as **Beats** (derived from "beaten down"), they offered stinging critiques of what they considered the sterility and conformity of white middle-class society. In 1956

The Beat Generation   The literary rebels of the Beat Generation questioned the dominant values of the 1950s. They attacked materialism and conventional sexual morality. They explored Eastern religions as an alternative to Christianity and Judaism, and experimented with psychedelic drugs to reach a higher consciousness. This photograph captures the rebels-to-be as they attended Columbia University in the mid-1940s. From left to right are Hal Chase, Jack Kerouac, Allen Ginsberg, and William S. Burroughs. Allen Ginsberg/CORBIS/Corbis via Getty Images

Allen Ginsberg began his epic poem *Howl* (1956) with the line "I saw the best minds of my generation destroyed by madness, starving hysterical naked." In his novel *On the Road* (1957), Jack Kerouac praised the individual who pursued authentic experiences and mind-expanding consciousness through drugs, sexual experimentation, and living in the moment. At a time when whiteness was not just a skin color but a standard of beauty and virtue, the Beats and authors such as Norman Mailer looked to African Americans as cultural icons, embracing the spontaneity and coolness they attributed to inner-city blacks. The Beats formed their own artistic enclaves in New York City's Greenwich Village and San Francisco's North Beach and Haight-Ashbury districts.

The Beat writers frequently read their poems and prose to the rhythms of jazz, reflecting both their affinity with African American culture and the innovative explorations taking place in music. From the big bands of the 1930s and 1940s, postwar jazz musicians formed smaller trios, quartets, and quintets and experimented with sounds more suitable for serious listening than for dancing. The bebop rhythms of trumpeter Dizzy Gillespie and alto saxophonist Charlie Parker revolutionized jazz, as did trumpeter Miles Davis and tenor saxophonist John Coltrane, who experimented with more complex and textured forms of this music and took it to new heights. Like rock 'n' roll musicians, these black artists broke down racial barriers as their music attracted white audiences.

Homosexuals also attempted to live nonconformist lifestyles, albeit clandestinely. According to studies by researcher Dr. Alfred Kinsey of Indiana University, homosexuals made up approximately 10 percent of the adult population. During World War II, gay men and lesbians had the opportunity to meet other homosexuals in the military and in venues that attracted gay soldiers. Though homosexuality remained taboo and public displays of same-sex sexuality were criminalized, politically radical gay men organized against homophobia after the war. In 1951 they formed the Mattachine Society in Los Angeles, which then spread to the East Coast. In 1954 a group of lesbians founded the Daughters of Bilitis in San Francisco. Because of police harassment, most homosexuals refused to reveal their sexual orientation, which made sense practically but reduced their ability to counter anti-homosexual discrimination.

Kinsey also shattered myths about conformity among heterosexuals. In *Sexual Behavior in the Human Female* (1953), he revealed that 50 percent of the women he interviewed had had sexual intercourse before marriage, and 25 percent had had extramarital affairs. Kinsey's findings were supported by other data. Between 1940 and 1960, the frequency of out-of-wedlock births among all women rose from 7.1 newborns to 21.6 newborns per thousand women of childbearing age. The sexual relations that Grace Metalious depicted in *Peyton Place* merely reflected what many Americans practiced but did not talk about. The brewing sexual revolution went public in 1953 with the publication of *Playboy* magazine, founded by Hugh Hefner. Through a combination of serious articles and photographs of nude women, the magazine provided its chiefly male readers with a guide to pursuing sexual pleasure and a sophisticated lifestyle.

Like Metalious, many writers denounced the conformity and shallowness they found in suburban America. Novelist Sloan Wilson wrote about the alienating experience of suburban life in *The Man in the Gray Flannel Suit* (1955). In J. D. Salinger's novel *Catcher in the Rye* (1951), the young protagonist, Holden Caulfield, mocks the phoniness of the adult world while ending up in a mental institution. Journalists and scholars joined in the criticism. Such critics often overstated the conformity that characterized the suburbs by minimizing the ethnic, religious, and political diversity of their residents. Yet they tapped into a growing feeling, especially among a new generation of young people, of the dangers of a mass culture based on standardization, compliance, and bureaucratization.

REVIEW & RELATE

- What trends in American popular culture did the television shows and popular music of the 1950s reflect?

- How did artists, writers, and social critics challenge the mainstream politics and culture of the 1950s?

The **Growth** of the **Civil Rights Movement**

African Americans wanted what most other Americans desired after World War II—the opportunity to make a decent living, buy a nice home, raise a healthy family, and get the best education for their children. Yet blacks faced much greater obstacles than did whites in obtaining these dreams, particularly in the Jim Crow South. Determined to eliminate racial injustices, black Americans mounted a

Explore ▶

See Sources 25.2 and 25.3
for two views of the meaning
and importance of the civil
rights movement.

campaign against white supremacy in the decades after World War II. African Americans increasingly viewed their struggle as part of an international movement of black people in Africa and other nonwhites in the Middle East and Asia to obtain their freedom from Western colonial rulers. Embracing similar hopes, Asian Americans and Latinos pursued their own struggles for equality.

The Rise of the Southern Civil Rights Movement.

With the war against Nazi racism over, African Americans expected to win first-class citizenship in the United States. During World War II, blacks waged successful campaigns to pressure the federal government to tackle discrimination and organizations such as the Congress of Racial Equality (CORE) and the NAACP attacked racial injustice (see "The Origins of the Civil Rights Movement" in chapter 23). African American veterans returned home to the South determined to build on these victories, especially by extending the right to vote. Yet African Americans found that most whites resisted demands for racial equality.

In 1946 violence surfaced as the most visible evidence of many white people's determination to preserve the traditional racial order. A race riot erupted in Columbia, Tennessee, in which blacks were killed and black businesses were torched. In South Carolina, Isaac Woodard, a black veteran still in uniform and on his way home on a bus, got into an argument with the white bus driver. When the local sheriff arrived, he pounded Woodard's face with a club, permanently blinding the ex-GI. In Mississippi, Senator Theodore Bilbo, running for reelection in the Democratic primary, told white audiences that they could keep blacks from voting "by seeing them the night before" the election. Groups such as the NAACP and the National Association of Colored Women demanded that the president take action to combat this reign of terror.

In December 1946, President Truman responded by issuing an executive order creating the President's Committee on Civil Rights. While the committee conducted its investigation, in April 1947, Jackie Robinson became the first black baseball player to enter the major leagues. This accomplishment proved to be a sign of changes to come.

After extensive deliberations, the committee, which consisted of blacks and whites, northerners and southerners, issued its report, *To Secure These Rights*, on October 29, 1947. Placing the problem of "civil rights shortcomings" within the context of the Cold War, the report argued that racial inequality and unrest could only aid the Soviets in their global anti-American propaganda efforts. "The United States is not so strong," the committee asserted, "the final triumph of the democratic ideal not so inevitable that we can ignore what the world thinks of us or our record." A far-reaching document, the report called for racial desegregation in the military, interstate transportation, and education, as well as extension of the right to vote. The following year, under pressure from African American activists, the president signed an executive order to desegregate the armed forces.

School Segregation and the Supreme Court.

Led by the NAACP, African Americans also launched a prolonged assault on school segregation. First the association filed lawsuits against states that excluded blacks from publicly funded law schools and universities. After victories in Missouri and Maryland, the group's chief lawyer, Thurgood Marshall, convinced the Supreme Court in 1950 to disband the separate law school that Texas had established for blacks and admit them to the University of Texas Law School. At

The Civil Rights Movement and Its Opponents

As the civil rights movement began to tear down the walls of racial segregation and disfranchisement, southern segregationists resisted these efforts. In 1956, 101 southern congressman issued a manifesto, which is excerpted in the first document here, rejecting the *Brown v. Board of Education* (1954) Supreme Court decision. By 1960 the pace of the civil rights movement had quickened, and young people formed organizations such as the Student Nonviolent Coordinating Committee (SNCC) to challenge racial inequality and white supremacy. In the second document, Ella Baker, a longtime activist and adviser to SNCC, sketches out her views on the meaning of the movement.

Source 25.2

The Southern Manifesto, 1956

We regard the decision of the Supreme Court in the school cases as a clear abuse of judicial power. It climaxes a trend in the Federal Judiciary undertaking to legislate, in derogation of the authority of Congress, and to encroach upon the reserved rights of the states and the people. . . .

This unwarranted exercise of power by the Court, contrary to the Constitution, is creating chaos and confusion in the States principally affected. It is destroying the amicable relations between the white and Negro races that have been created through ninety years of patient effort by the good people of both races. It has planted hatred and suspicion where there has been heretofore friendship and understanding.

Without regard to the consent of the governed, outside agitators are threatening immediate and revolutionary changes in our public-school systems. If done, this is certain to destroy the system of public education in some of the States. . . .

We pledge ourselves to use all lawful means to bring about a reversal of this decision which is contrary to the Constitution and to prevent the use of force in its implementation.

Source: "Declaration of Constitutional Principles," *Congressional Record*, 84th Congress, 2d Session, March 12, 1956, 4460–61.

Source 25.3

Ella Baker | "Bigger Than a Hamburger," 1960

The Student Leadership Conference made it crystal clear that current sit-ins and other demonstrations are concerned with something much bigger than a hamburger or even a giant-sized Coke.

Whatever may be the difference in approach to their goal, the Negro and white students, North and South, are seeking to rid America of the scourge of racial segregation and discrimination—not only at lunch counters, but in every aspect of life.

In reports, casual conversations, discussion groups, and speeches, the sense and the spirit of the following statement that appeared in the initial newsletter of the students at Barber-Scotia College, Concord, N.C., were re-echoed time and again: "We want the world to know that we no longer accept the inferior position of second-class citizenship. We are willing to go to jail, be ridiculed, spat upon, and even suffer physical violence to obtain First Class Citizenship."

By and large, this feeling that they have a destined date with freedom, was not limited to a drive for personal freedom, or even freedom for the Negro in the South. Repeatedly it was emphasized that the movement was concerned with the moral implications of racial discrimination for the "whole world" and the "Human Race."

This universality of approach was linked with a perceptive recognition that "it is important to keep the movement democratic and to avoid struggles for personal leadership."

It was further evident that desire for supportive cooperation from adult leaders and the adult community was also tempered by apprehension that adults might try to "capture" the student movement. The students showed willingness to be met on the basis of equality, but were intolerant of anything that smacked of manipulation or domination.

This inclination toward group-centered leadership, rather than toward a leader-centered group pattern of organization, was refreshing indeed to those of the older group who bear the scars of the battle, the frustrations and the disillusionment that come when the prophetic leader turns out to have heavy feet of clay.

Source: Ella Baker, "Bigger Than a Hamburger," *Southern Patriot*, June 1960, 4.

Interpret the Evidence

1. Why do the signers of the Southern Manifesto condemn the *Brown* decision?
2. According to Ella Baker, why are the goals of the civil rights movement "bigger than a hamburger"?
3. How does Baker define "rights" differently than the signers of the Southern Manifesto?

Put It in Context

How did the new generation of young civil rights activists challenge both southern segregationists and older civil rights advocates?

the same time, the Court eliminated separate facilities for black students at the University of Oklahoma graduate school and ruled against segregation in interstate rail transportation.

Before African Americans could attend college, they had to obtain a first-class education in public schools. All-black schools typically lacked the resources provided to white schools, and the NAACP understood that southern officials would never live up to the "separate but equal doctrine" asserted in *Plessy v. Ferguson* (1896). African Americans sought to integrate schools not because they wanted their children to sit next to white students and adopt their ways, but because they believed that integration offered the best and quickest way to secure quality education.

On May 17, 1954, in ***Brown v. Board of Education of Topeka, Kansas***, the Supreme Court overturned *Plessy*. In a unanimous decision read by Chief Justice Earl Warren, the Court concluded that "in the field of public education the doctrine of 'separate but equal' has no place. Separate educational facilities are inherently unequal." This ruling undercut the legal foundation for segregation and officially placed the law on the side of those who sought racial equality. Nevertheless, the ruling did not end the controversy; in fact, it led to more battles over segregation. In 1955 the Court issued a follow-up opinion calling for implementation with "all deliberate speed." But it left enforcement of *Brown* to federal district courts in the South, which consisted mainly of white southerners who espoused segregationist views. As a result, southern officials emphasized "deliberate" rather than "speed" and slowed the implementation of the *Brown* decision.

The Montgomery Bus Boycott.

The *Brown* decision encouraged African Americans to protest against other forms of racial discrimination. In 1955 in Montgomery, Alabama, the Women's Political Council, a group of middle-class and professional black women, petitioned the city commission to improve bus service for black passengers. Among other things, they wanted blacks not to have to give up their seats to white passengers who boarded the bus after black passengers did. Their requests went unheeded until December 1, 1955, when Rosa Parks, a black seamstress and an NAACP activist, refused to give up her seat to a white man. Parks's arrest rallied civic, labor, and religious groups and sparked a bus boycott that involved nearly the entire black community. Instead of riding buses, black commuters walked to work or joined car pools. White officials refused to capitulate and fought back by arresting leaders of the **Montgomery Improvement Association**, the organization that coordinated the protest. Other whites hurled insults at blacks and engaged in violence. After more than a year of conflict, the Supreme Court ruled in favor of the complete desegregation of Montgomery's buses.

Out of this landmark struggle, Martin Luther King Jr. emerged as the civil rights movement's most charismatic leader. His personal courage and power of oratory could inspire nearly all segments of the African American community. Twenty-six years old at the time of Parks's arrest, King was the pastor of the prestigious Dexter Avenue Baptist Church. Though King was familiar with the nonviolent methods of the Indian revolutionary Mohandas Gandhi and the civil disobedience of the nineteenth-century writer Henry David Thoreau, he drew his inspiration and commitment to these principles mainly from black church and secular leaders such as A. Philip Randolph and Bayard Rustin. King understood how to convey the goals of the civil rights movement to sympathetic white Americans, but his vision and passion grew out of black communities. At the outset of the Montgomery bus boycott, King noted proudly of the boycott: "When the history books are written in future generations, the

Montgomery Bus Boycott, 1956   Two months after African American residents of Montgomery, Alabama, began their boycott of the city buses to protest segregation and mistreatment, the black community kept up its boycott despite violence and intimidation. Black women had made up the majority of bus riders, and this photograph, taken on February 1, 1956, shows many of them walking to work or to stores for shopping. Don Cravens/The LIFE Images Collection/Getty Images

historians will have to pause and say 'There lived a great people—a Black people—who injected new meaning and dignity into the veins of civilization.'"

The Montgomery bus boycott made King a national civil rights leader, but it did not guarantee him further success. In 1957 King and a like-minded group of southern black ministers formed the **Southern Christian Leadership Conference (SCLC)** to spread nonviolent protest throughout the region, but except in a few cities, such as Tallahassee, Florida, additional bus boycotts did not take hold.

White Resistance to Desegregation. Segregationists responded forcefully to halt black efforts to eliminate Jim Crow. In 1956, 101 southern congressmen issued a manifesto denouncing the 1954 *Brown* opinion and pledging to resist it through "lawful means." Other southerners went beyond the law. In 1957 a federal court approved a plan submitted by the Little Rock, Arkansas School Board to integrate Central High School. However, the state's governor, Orval Faubus, obstructed the court ruling by sending the state National Guard to keep out nine black students chosen to attend Central High. Faced with blatant state resistance to federal authority, President Eisenhower placed the National Guard under federal control and sent in the 101st Airborne Division to restore order after a mob blocked the students from entering the school. These black pioneers, who became known as the **Little Rock Nine**, attended classes for the year under the protection of the National Guard but still encountered considerable harassment from white students. In defiance of the high court, other school districts, such as Prince Edward County, Virginia, chose to close their public schools rather than desegregate. By the end of the decade, public schools in the South remained mostly segregated.

The white South used other forms of violence and intimidation to preserve segregation. The third incarnation of the Ku Klux Klan (KKK) appeared after World War II to strike back at growing African American challenges to white supremacy. This terrorist group threatened, injured, and killed blacks they considered "uppity." Following the *Brown* decision, segregationists also formed the White Citizens' Council (WCC). The WCC drew members largely from businessmen and professionals. Rather than condoning violence, the WCC generally intimidated blacks by threatening to fire them from jobs or denying them credit from banks. In Alabama, WCC members launched a campaign against radio stations playing the kind of rock 'n' roll music that Alan Freed popularized in New York City because they believed that it fostered close interracial contact.

White Citizens Council, New Orleans, 1960   In November 1960, the White Citizens Council of Greater New Orleans staged a rally at school board offices to protest the integration of two local elementary schools. Among the boisterous crowd of 5000 women and men, two small children stand on chairs waving the Confederate flag, a symbol of resistance to racial equality. Bettmann/Getty Images.

The WCC and the KKK created a racial climate in the deep South that encouraged whites to believe they could get away with murder to defend white supremacy. In the summer of 1955, Emmett Till, a fourteen-year-old from Chicago who was visiting his great-uncle in Mississippi, was killed because he allegedly flirted with a white woman in a country store. Although the two accused killers were brought to trial, an all-white jury quickly acquitted them.

The Sit-Ins.   With boycotts petering out and white violence rising, African Americans, especially high school and college students, developed new techniques to confront discrimination, including sit-ins, in which protesters seat themselves in a strategic spot and refuse to move until their demands are met or they are forcibly evicted. These mass protests did not really get off the ground until February 1960, when four students at North Carolina A&T University in Greensboro initiated sit-ins at the whites-only lunch counters in Woolworth and Kress department stores. Their demonstrations sparked similar efforts throughout the Southeast (Map 25.1).

A few months after the sit-ins began, a number of participants formed the **Student Nonviolent Coordinating Committee (SNCC)**. The organization's young members sought not only to challenge racial segregation in the South but also to create interracial communities based on economic equality and political democracy. This generation of black and white sit-in veterans came of age in the 1950s at a time when Cold War democratic rhetoric and the Supreme Court's *Brown* decision raised their expectations for racial equality. Yet these young activists often saw their hopes dashed by southern segregationist resistance, including the murder of Emmett Till, which both horrified and helped mobilize them to fight for black equality.

> **Explore ▶**
>
> For differing perspectives on when the civil rights movement began, read Sources 25.4 and 25.5.

The Civil Rights Movement and Minority Struggles in the West.

World War II also sparked a migration of African Americans to the West as part of the larger population movement to the Sun Belt. From 1940 to 1960, the black population in the region jumped from 4.9 to 5.4 percent of the total population and numbered more

MAP 25.1 Lunch Counter Sit-Ins, February–April 1960

After starting slowly in the late 1950s, lunch counter sit-ins exploded in 1960 following a sit-in by college students in Greensboro, North Carolina. Within three months, sit-ins erupted in fifty-eight cities across the South. The participation of high school and college students revitalized the civil rights movement and led to the formation of the Student Nonviolent Coordinating Committee in April 1960.

than 1.2 million. Encountering various forms of racial discrimination, African Americans waged boycotts and sit-ins of businesses that refused blacks equal service in Lawrence, Kansas and Albuquerque, New Mexico. Perhaps the most significant protest occurred in Oklahoma City. In August 1958, the teenagers of the NAACP Youth Council and their adult adviser, Clara M. Luper, led sit-ins to desegregate lunch counters in downtown stores. Having succeeded in integrating a dozen facilities, the movement waged a six-year struggle to end discrimination in public accommodations throughout the city.

Like African Americans, other groups in the postwar West struggled for equality. For Mexican Americans World War II inspired such challenges. In southern California, Unity Leagues formed to protest segregation, and they often joined with African American groups in seeking equality. In 1947, the League of United Latin American Citizens (LULAC)

SECONDARY SOURCE ANALYSIS

When Did the Civil Rights Movement Begin?

The "classical" phase of the civil rights movement spans the years from *Brown v. Board of Education* (1954) to the death of Martin Luther King, Jr. (1968). Critics of this timeline contend that it places too much emphasis on national events and national leaders, almost all of whom were men. Instead they find a longer civil rights movement that stretches back to the 1930s and 1940s and includes women, working people, and radicals. The following debate between two historians raises the larger question of when historical periods begin and end.

Source 25.4

Jacquelyn Dowd Hall, The Long Civil Rights Movement, 2005

Another force also rose from the caldron of the Great Depression and crested in the 1940s: a powerful social movement sparked by the alchemy of laborites, civil rights activists, progressive New Dealers, and black and white radicals, some of whom were associated with the Communist party . . . signals the movement's commitment to building coalitions, the expansiveness of the social democratic vision, and the importance of its black radical and laborite leadership. A national movement with a vital southern wing, civil rights unionism was not just a precursor of the modern civil rights movement. It was its decisive first phase.

The link between race and class lay at the heart of the movement's political imagination. . . . [C]ivil rights unionists sought to combine protection from discrimination with universalistic social welfare policies and individual rights with labor rights. For them, workplace democracy, union wages, and fair and full employment went hand in hand with open, affordable housing, political enfranchisement, educational equity, and an enhanced safety net, including health care for all. . . . Extending the New Deal and reforming the South were two sides of the same coin. . . . To challenge the southern Democrats' congressional stranglehold, the movement had to enfranchise black and white southern workers and bring them into the house of labor, thus creating a constituency on which the region's emerging pro-civil rights, pro-labor politicians could rely.

Source: Jacquelyn Dowd Hall, "The Long Civil Rights Movement and the Political Uses of the Past," *Journal of American History* 91 (March 2005), 1245–46.

---

won a case in federal court in *Mendez v. Westminster* prohibiting separate public schools for Mexican-American students. Spurred on by such efforts, Mexican Americans in 1949 succeeded in electing Edward Roybal to the Los Angeles City Council, the first American of Mexican descent to serve on that body since 1888. In Texas LULAC succeeded through litigation and boycotts in desegregating movie theaters, swimming pools, restaurants, and other public accommodations. LULAC also brought an end to discrimination in jury selection. Once Jackie Robinson integrated baseball in 1947, he opened the way for

Source 25.5

Steven F. Lawson, The Short Civil Rights Movement, 2011

There was a genuine movement for social change in the South during the New Deal era, but it took on a different shape from the civil rights movement that followed in the next two decades. Civil rights unions . . . performed the work of extending civil rights and laid the groundwork for what followed, but this remained distinct from the civil rights movement. . . . Class mattered more than race, and critics targeted capitalism as the source of black oppression. . . . [O]nly through a restructuring of corporate capitalism would genuine economic democracy emerge and white supremacy collapse. Although African American progressives actively participated in unions…, the leadership and membership of these organizations in the South consisted mainly of whites. . . . These activists were courageous, visionary, and essential, but they composed only a tiny fraction of the southern population. Their influence should be neither ignored nor exaggerated.

. . . By the time of the *Brown* decision and [Emmett] Till's murder, African Americans possessed the institutional structures necessary to mobilize to close the gap between their expectations of change and the brutal reality of white supremacy. At the national level the NAACP led the way, followed by the SCLC, CORE, and SNCC. Indeed, after *Brown*, state-led efforts to destroy the NAACP, considered the most radical of black organizations by southern white authorities, spurred the creation of new protest organizations locally and throughout the South. Black churches, civic associations, and informal community networks added organizational muscle to the demands for racial equality during the 1950s and 1960s. Without these structures…, the yearning for civil rights would not have grown into a movement, and people would not have taken action against the power of state-supported white supremacy.

Source: Steven F. Lawson, "Long Origins of the Short Civil Rights Movement, 1954-1968," in *Freedom Rights: New Perspectives on the Civil Rights Movement*, edited by Daniel McGuire and John Dittmer (Lexington, Kentucky: University Press of Kentucky, 2011), 14–15, 19, 22–23.

Examine the Sources

1. Describe the major difference between the Hall and Lawson interpretations of when the civil rights movement began.
2. Despite this difference, what similarities in their arguments can you find?

Put It in Context

Historians often look for major turning points, after which there was notable change from before. Why does it matter what turning points historians select for when the civil rights movement began and ended?

Afro-Hispanic ballplayers. Two years later, Orestes "Minnie" Miñoso, an Afro-Cuban, made it to the major leagues and the Cleveland Indians.

World War II had advanced civil rights for the Chinese. In 1943 Congress repealed the exclusion law and followed up by passing the War Brides Act in 1945, which resulted in the admission of 6,000 Chinese women to the United States. However, the fall of China to the Communists in 1949 and the beginning of the Korean War the next year posed new challenges to Chinese communities on the West Coast. Although organizations such as the Six Companies of San Francisco denounced Communist China and pledged their loyalty to the United States, Cold War witch-hunts targeted the Chinese. With the Chinese Communists fighting against the United States in Korea, some regarded Chinese people in America with suspicion. "People would look at you in the street and think," one Chinese woman recalled, " 'Well you're one of the enemy.' " The federal government established a "Confession Program" by which Chinese people illegally in the country would be allowed to stay if they came forward, acknowledged their loyalty to the United States, and provided information about friends and relatives. Some 10,000 Chinese in San Francisco participated in this program.

World War II had also advanced civil rights for the Chinese. In 1943 Congress repealed the exclusion law and followed up by passing the War Brides Act in 1945, which resulted in the admission of 6,000 Chinese women to the United States. However, the fall of China to the Communists in 1949 and the beginning of the Korean War the next year posted new challenges to Chinese communities on the West Coast. Although organizations such as the Six Companies of San Francisco denounced Communist China and pledged their loyalty to the United States, Cold War witch-hunts targeted the Chinese. With the Chinese Communists fighting against the United States in Korea, some regarded Chinese people in America with suspicion. "People would look at you in the street and think," one Chinese woman recalled, " 'Well you're one of the enemy.' " The federal government established a "Confession Program" by which Chinese people illegally in the country would be allowed to stay if they came forward, acknowledged their loyalty to the United States, and provided information about friends and relatives. Some 10,000 Chinese in San Francisco participated in this program.

Despite these hardships, the Chinese made great economic strides. Chinatowns shrank in population as their upwardly mobile residents moved to the suburbs. By 1959 Chinese Americans had a median family income of $6,207, compared with $5,660 for all Americans.

During the late 1940s and 1950s, Japanese Americans attempted to rebuild their lives following their wartime evacuation and internment. Overall, they did remarkably well. Although many returned to the West Coast and found their neighborhoods occupied by other ethnic groups and their businesses in other hands, they took whatever jobs they could find and stressed education for their children. The McCarran-Walter Immigration Act of 1952 made it possible for Japanese aliens to become U.S. citizens. In addition, California repealed its Alien Land Law of 1913, which prohibited noncitizen Japanese from purchasing land. In 1955 about 40,000 Japanese Americans lived in Los Angeles, a figure slightly higher than the city's prewar population. Like other Americans, they began moving their families to suburbs such as Gardena, a half-hour ride from downtown Los Angeles. Still, the federal government neither apologized for its wartime treatment of the Japanese nor awarded them financial compensation for their losses; this would happen three decades later.

REVIEW & RELATE

- What strategies did African Americans adopt in the 1940s and 1950s to fight segregation and discrimination? How did other minorities pursue equality?

- How and why did white southerners resist efforts to end segregation?

Domestic Politics in the **Eisenhower Era**

Despite the existence of civil rights protesters, rock 'n' roll upstarts, intellectual dissenters, and sexual revolutionaries, the 1950s seemed to many a tranquil, even dull period. This impression owes a great deal to the leadership of President Dwight D. Eisenhower. Serving two terms from 1953 to 1961, Eisenhower, or "Ike" as he was affectionately called, convinced the majority of Americans that their country was in good hands regardless of political turbulence at home and heated international conflicts abroad. By 1960, however, the nation was ready for a new generation of leadership.

Modern Republicanism. President Eisenhower, a World War II hero, radiated strength and trust, qualities the American people found very attractive as they rebuilt their lives and established families in the 1950s. In November 1952, Eisenhower coasted to victory over the Democratic candidate Adlai Stevenson, winning 55 percent of the popular vote and 83 percent of the electoral vote. The Republicans managed to win slim majorities in the Senate and the House, but within two years the Democrats regained control of Congress.

Eisenhower adopted what one of his speechwriters called **Modern Republicanism**, which tried to fit the traditional Republican Party ideals of individualism and fiscal restraint within the broad framework of Franklin Roosevelt's New Deal. As Eisenhower wrote to his brother, "Should any political party attempt to abolish social security, unemployment insurance, and eliminate labor laws and farm programs, you would not hear of that party again in our political history." With Democrats in control of Congress after 1954, Republicans agreed to raise Social Security benefits and to include coverage for some ten million additional workers. Congress and the president retained another New Deal mainstay, the minimum wage, and increased it from 75 cents to $1 an hour. Departing from traditional Republican criticism of big government, the Eisenhower administration added the Department of Health, Education, and Welfare to the cabinet in 1953. In 1956 the Eisenhower administration sponsored the **National Interstate and Defense Highway Act**, which provided funds for the construction of 42,500 miles of roads throughout the country, boosting both suburbanization and national defense. In addition, in 1958 Eisenhower signed into law the National Defense Education Act, which provided aid for instruction in science, math, and foreign languages and graduate fellowships and loans for college students. He portrayed the new law as a way to catch up with the Soviets, who the previous year had successfully launched the first artificial satellite, called *Sputnik*, into outer space.

For six of Eisenhower's eight years in office, the president had to work with Democratic majorities in Congress. Overall, he managed to forge bipartisan support for his proposals. Nowhere was this more significant than with civil rights legislation. Under his administration's leadership, Republicans joined with Democrats, led by Senate Majority Leader Lyndon B. Johnson, to pass the first pieces of civil rights legislation since Reconstruction. In 1957 and 1960, Eisenhower signed into law two bills that extended the authority of the federal government to file court challenges against southern election officials who blocked African Americans from registering to vote. However, southern Democratic senators thwarted Congress from passing even stronger voting measures or acts that would have enforced school desegregation.

Eisenhower administration policy, however, did not work to the benefit of American Indians. The federal government reversed many of the reforms instituted during the New Deal. In the 1950s the Bureau of Indian Affairs (BIA) adopted the policy of termination and relocation of Indian tribes. Those tribes deemed to have achieved the most "progress," such as the Flatheads of Montana, the Klamaths of Oregon, and the Hoopas of northern California, were treated as ordinary American citizens, which resulted in termination of their federal benefits and transfer of their tribal lands to state and local governments. The National Congress of American Indians fought unsuccessfully against this program.

The government also relocated Indians to urban areas. Between 1952 and 1960, the BIA encouraged more than 30,000 Indians to move from their reservations to cities. The Indian population of Los Angeles grew to 25,000, including members of the Navajo, Sioux, and Cherokee nations. Although thousands of Indians took advantage of the relocation program, many had difficulty adjusting to urban life and fell into poverty.

The Eisenhower administration also repatriated undocumented Mexican laborers. The *bracero* program instituted in 1942 (see "Struggles for Mexican Americans" in chapter 23), had not eliminated illegal immigration from Mexico into the United States as large agricultural growers sought more cheap labor. Although some who came legally through the program stayed beyond the period allowed, far more Mexicans simply crossed the border illegally, seeking work. Mexico complained about these illegal immigrants because it needed a larger supply of agricultural workers, and American labor groups protested that illegal immigrants took jobs away from Americans. In 1954, Eisenhower's Immigration and Naturalization Service rounded up undocumented Mexicans, mainly in Texas and California, and returned them to Mexico. Those deported often suffered harsh conditions, and seven deportees drowned after they jumped ship. "Operation Wetback," as the program was dubbed using a derogatory term for Mexicans, forced an estimated 250,000 to 1.3 million Mexicans to leave the United States.

After winning a second term in 1956, Eisenhower clashed with the Democratic majority in Congress over spending. He vetoed bills that increased expenditures for public housing, public works projects, and urban renewal in an attempt to keep the budget balanced. Yet under Eisenhower the country overcame two recessions, the middle class grew in size, and inflation remained low. Nonetheless, for forty million Americans poverty, not prosperity, remained the reality.

The Election of 1960. Even after serving two terms in office, Eisenhower remained popular. However, he could not run for a third term, barred by the Twenty-second Amendment (1951), and Vice President Richard M. Nixon ran as the Republican candidate for president in 1960. Unlike Eisenhower, Nixon was not universally liked or respected. His reputation for unsavory political combat drew the scorn of Democrats, especially liberals. Moreover, Nixon had to fend off charges that Republicans, as embodied in the seventy-year-old Eisenhower, were out-of-date and out of new ideas.

Running as the Democratic candidate for president in 1960, Senator John F. Kennedy of Massachusetts promised to instill renewed "vigor" in the White House and get the country moving again. Yet Kennedy did not differ much from his Republican rival on domestic and foreign policy issues. While Kennedy employed a rhetoric of high-minded change, he had not compiled a distinguished or courageous record in the Senate. Moreover,

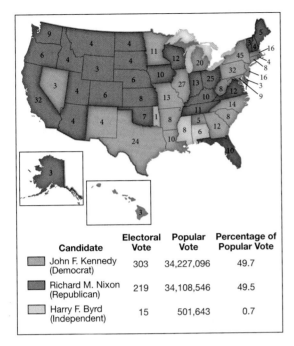

MAP 25.2 The Election of 1960

The 1960 presidential candidates differed little on major policy issues. John F. Kennedy gained the White House by winning back black voters who had supported Eisenhower, gaining crucial support from Catholic voters across the country, and appearing more presidential on the first televised debate in history. Still, his margin of victory was razor thin.

Candidate	Electoral Vote	Popular Vote	Percentage of Popular Vote
John F. Kennedy (Democrat)	303	34,227,096	49.7
Richard M. Nixon (Republican)	219	34,108,546	49.5
Harry F. Byrd (Independent)	15	501,643	0.7

his family's fortune had paved the way for his political career, and he had earned a well-justified reputation in Washington as a playboy and womanizer.

The outcome of the 1960 election turned on several factors. The country was experiencing a slight economic recession, reviving memories in older voters of the Great Depression, which had begun with the Republican Herbert Hoover in power. In addition, presidential candidates faced off on television for the first time, participating in four televised debates. TV emphasized visual style and presentation. In the first debate, with Nixon having just recovered from a stay in the hospital and looking haggard, Kennedy convinced a majority of viewers that he possessed the presidential bearing for the job. Nixon performed better in the next three debates, but the damage had been done. Still, Kennedy had to overcome considerable religious prejudice to win the election. No Catholic had ever won the presidency, and the prejudices of Protestants, especially in the South, threatened to divert critical votes from Kennedy's Democratic base. While many southern Democrats did support Nixon, Kennedy balanced out these defections by gaining votes from the nation's Catholics, especially in northern states rich in electoral votes (Map 25.2).

Race also exerted a critical influence. Nixon and Kennedy had similar records on civil rights, and if anything, Nixon's was slightly stronger. However, on October 19, 1960, when Atlanta police arrested Martin Luther King Jr. for participating in a restaurant sit-in, Kennedy sprang to his defense, whereas Nixon kept his distance. Kennedy telephoned the civil rights leader's wife to offer his sympathy and used his influence to get King released from jail. As a result, King's father, a Protestant minister who had intended to vote against the Catholic Kennedy, now endorsed the Democrat. In addition to the elder King, Kennedy won back for Democrats 7 percent of black voters who had supported Eisenhower in 1956. Kennedy triumphed by a margin of less than 1 percent of the popular vote, underscoring the importance of the African American electorate.

REVIEW & RELATE

• Why did Eisenhower adopt a moderate domestic agenda? What were his most notable domestic accomplishments and failures?

• Why did Kennedy win the 1960 presidential election?

Conclusion: Postwar Politics and Culture

Following the end of World War II and a bumpy period of reconversion, the return of peace and prosperity fostered a baby boom that sent families scrambling for new housing and increasingly away from the cities. Suburbs grew as housing developers such as William Levitt built affordable, mass-produced homes and as the federal government provided new highways that allowed suburban residents to commute to their urban jobs. With increased income, consumers purchased the latest models in automobiles as well as newly introduced televisions, reshaping how they spent their leisure time. As the wartime and baby boom generations entered their teenage years, their sheer numbers and general affluence helped make them a significant economic and cultural force. They poured their dollars into clothes, music, and other forms of entertainment, which reinforced their identity as teenagers and set them apart from adults.

The increasingly distinct teenage culture owed a great deal to African Americans, who contributed to the development of rock 'n' roll and revolutionized jazz and thereby influenced cultural challenges from teenage rebels and the beats. Yet African Americans remained most focused on tearing down the legal and institutional foundations of white supremacy. First in the courts and then in the streets, they confronted segregation and disfranchisement in the South. By the end of the 1950s, African Americans had persuaded the Supreme Court to reverse the doctrine of "separate but equal" that buttressed Jim Crow; they also won significant victories in desegregating buses in Montgomery, schools in Little Rock, and lunch counters in Greensboro. Black teenagers reinvigorated the civil rights movement through their boldness and energy, opening the path for even greater racial changes in the coming decade. Other minority groups, inspired by the civil rights movement, pursued first-class citizenship for themselves. In addition to struggles over racial equality, the 1950s witnessed serious tensions at home. Teenage cultural rebellion, sexual revolution, and McCarthyite witch-hunts, in addition to a bloody war in Korea, confronted the citizens of Alan Freed's and Grace Metalious's America. Nevertheless, the popular image of the 1950s as a tranquil and innocent period persists, with President Eisenhower remaining a symbol for the age. He provided moderate leadership that helped the country adjust to dramatic changes. His critics complained that the nation had lost its spirit of adventure, misplaced its ability to distinguish between community and conformity, failed to live up to ideals of racial and economic justice, and relinquished its primary place in the world. Nevertheless, most Americans emerging from decades of depression and war felt satisfied with the new lives they were building: They still liked Ike.

When the Republican Eisenhower left office in 1961, a new decade began with a Democratic president in charge. Yet the challenges that Eisenhower had faced and the diplomatic, social, and cultural forces that propelled them had not diminished. During the following years, many of the young people who had benefited from the peace and prosperity of the 1950s would lead the way in questioning the role of the United States in world affairs and its commitment to democracy, freedom, and equality at home.

TIMELINE OF **EVENTS**

1940–1960 Migration to Sun Belt swells region's population

1944 Servicemen's Readjustment Act (GI Bill)

1945–1960 U.S. gross national product soars 250 percent; 60 percent of Americans achieve middle-class status; union membership reaches new high

1947 Taft-Hartley Act

President's Committee on Civil Rights issues *To Secure These Rights*

Jackie Robinson becomes the first black baseball player to enter the major leagues

1954–1958 Eisenhower adopts Modern Republicanism and expands domestic programs

1954 *Brown v. Board of Education of Topeka, Kansas* Supreme Court ruling

Operation Wetback

1955–1956 Montgomery bus boycott

1955 Jonas Salk develops polio vaccine

Emmett Till murdered

1956 Grace Metalious publishes *Peyton Place*

National Interstate and Defense Highway Act

1957 Martin Luther King Jr. and other black ministers form Southern Christian Leadership Council (SCLC)

School desegregation in Little Rock, Arkansas, enforced

Soviet Union launches *Sputnik*

1960 Student Nonviolent Coordinating Committee (SNCC) formed

KEY **TERMS**

Servicemen's Readjustment Act (GI Bill), *852*

Taft-Hartley Act, *852*

Levittown, *856*

Sun Belt, *858*

Beats, *862*

To Secure These Rights, *865*

Brown v. Board of Education of Topeka, Kansas, *868*

Montgomery Improvement Association, *868*

Southern Christian Leadership Conference (SCLC), *869*

Little Rock Nine, *869*

Student Nonviolent Coordinating Committee (SNCC), *870*

Modern Republicanism, *875*

National Interstate and Defense Highway Act, *875*

REVIEW & RELATE

1. How did the conversion from war to peacetime affect the economy, society, and politics in the United States?

2. What factors contributed to the economic and population growth of the 1950s, and how did they contribute to suburbanization and the growth in the Sun Belt?

3. What trends in American popular culture did the television shows and popular music of the 1950s reflect?

4. How did artists, writers, and social critics challenge the mainstream politics and culture of the 1950s?

5. What strategies did African Americans adopt in the 1940s and 1950s to fight segregation and discrimination? How did other minorities pursue equality?

6. How and why did white southerners resist efforts to end segregation?

7. Why did Eisenhower adopt a moderate domestic agenda? What were his most notable domestic accomplishments and failures?

8. Why did Kennedy win the 1960 presidential election?

Teenagers in Postwar America

▶ Examine how teenagers affected the U.S. economy, culture, and politics in the postwar period (1945–1961).

"There are many different opinions about just what is the most exclusive club in America these days," observed Dick Clark in his 1959 book *Your Happiest Years* (Source 25.6). But for Clark, the most exclusive and important club was the one he called "Teenagers of America, Inc." Still, for Clark and most other Americans that club was exclusively white—African American, Latino, and Asian teenagers rarely appear in a positive light. Indeed, Clark's appraisal of American society in 1959 may have been self-serving—after all, his career hinged largely on appealing to teen audiences—but he was not alone in his belief in the significance of teenagers in postwar American society.

Even now, pop culture often portrays the 1950s as a simpler time when girls wore poodle skirts and swooned over Elvis Presley (Source 25.7), while boys raced hot-rod cars and took their dates to the malt shop. In this vision, teens were concerned with little more than increasing their popularity, "going steady," and watching *American Bandstand*. As the following documents illustrate, there is much to support this interpretation of postwar teen culture. Young people made rock 'n' roll into an enduring and lucrative entertainment industry, shaped the advertising and manufacture of products, and were the focus of numerous television shows and movies.

But there are other, more complicated images of teen life in this era. For one, juvenile delinquency was seen by many as a serious problem. Actor James Dean's *Rebel Without a Cause* competed with singer Pat Boone's squeaky-clean haircut and white shoes. In 1959 actor Sandra Dee portrayed both a perky Malibu surfer in *Gidget* and an unwed pregnant teen in *A Summer Place*. Teens also grew up under the looming threat of the Cold War, the Korean War, and McCarthyism. African Americans helped popularize rock 'n' roll, but in Little Rock, Arkansas, and elsewhere in the South, black teenagers risked their lives to desegregate public schools (Source 25.8).

The following sources consider different aspects of teen life and postwar culture in the 1950s. They also illustrate teenagers in the 1950s who had more on their minds than just dating and having a good time (Sources 25.9 and 25.10).

Source 25.6

Dick Clark | *Your Happiest Years*, 1959

By 1959 Dick Clark was a nationally popular disc jockey and host of television's *American Bandstand*. Always seen in a suit and tie, Clark, with his clean-cut good looks, projected a more wholesome vision of rock 'n' roll than did many of his contemporaries, such as Alan Freed. Clark's advice book for teenagers includes instructions on manners, makeup, and getting along with parents and other teens, as well as advice on romantic relationships.

We've mentioned before that it is very important to build a wide circle of friends, both fellows and girls. There are two reasons for this, but one is basic to dating. That is, the more fellows or girls you meet, the better the possibility that one or two might consider you what we called "date bait." The other reason, and it's a long shot, is that having a wide circle of friends, you meet more different types of people and learn how to adjust to them. This pays off after the teen years are past and you are either at work or away at school. But in order to get yourself into this teenage world of dating, let's just say you'll grow very lonely if you lock yourself away from eligible fellows or girls.

You've joined the staff of the school paper, or you are a member of a crowd of fellows that seem to attract a liberal following of the fair sex to your athletic contests. Or, on the distaff [female] side, you've a fine collection of girl friends—they're especially fine if they have at least one or two brothers of dating age. If you haven't quite reached that stage of teenage paradise yet, there are such events as community dances, or mixed school or church activities, that bring manly blips on your radarscope. In other words, you've gotten out of your shell and into the teenage swim. Don't be shy. You know that all the other fellows and girls your own age feel the same way you do. Remember, no self-pity. Braces on your teeth can't dim the glow of a sparkling personality, and neither can a shortage of new dresses or suits be an alibi for what is really a lack of effort on your part. Your fellow teenagers are eager to find sincere friends, and if you can prove that you are one then you definitely classify as "date bait." There is a phrase that I heard from General Carlos P. Romulo, the Philippines' famed patriot and Ambassador to the United States, and I think it applies here. "A stranger," the General said, "is a friend that I haven't met." It's a wonderful application of the Golden Rule, and it's one sentence that can carry a teenager through a lot of embarrassing uncertainty.

Accepting your fellow teenagers as friends, known or unknown, is another step toward that all-important phone call or whispered conference in the hall at school. You know the one I mean. It may begin, "Uh, Margie . . . uh, this Saturday night . . . uh, well, some of us were. . . ." And a date is born.

Source: Dick Clark, *Your Happiest Years* (New York: Random House, 1959), 100–101.

Source 25.7

Charlotte Jones | Letter on Elvis, 1957

Nothing highlighted the growing generation gap more than rock 'n' roll. When Elvis Presley burst onto the music scene in the mid-1950s, adults criticized his music and gyrating hips, while teenage boys dressed to imitate his style, and teenage girls screamed and fainted at his concerts. In 1957 Charlotte Jones, an admiring fan, wrote the following letter to the conservative newspaper columnist George Sokolsky in response to Sokolsky's criticism of Presley's popularity.

There are too many people saying that Elvis is going to die out. When Elvis dies out is when the sun quits burning.

You say everybody is forgotten that is once great; George Washington has never been forgotten and nobody can be as great a president or as long remembered as he. Nobody can ever take his place or do what he did. Well, it's the same with Elvis. He'll always be remembered and nobody has ever [done] or ever will do the same thing as Elvis has.

Elvis is the king of popularity and we (teens of America) love him and we'll see he lives forever. Not his body but his name. Adults won't admit he's so great, because they're jealous! They know that their top singers weren't as great as Elvis. They're mad because their taste isn't quite as good as ours.

Look at James Dean, been dead for a year and he's bigger now than he ever was.

God gifted Elvis to us and you oughta thank him, not tear down the greatest thing the world has ever known: Elvis Presley!!!!!!

Scornfully yours,
Charlotte Jones

P.S.: And if you're over 30, you're old. You're certainly not young.

Source: George E. Sokolsky, "Teenager Puts Rap on Suggestion Elvis on Way Out," *Milwaukee Sentinel*, March 11, 1957, 5.

The Desegregation of Central High School, 1957

In 1957 nine black teenagers attempted to desegregate Central High School in Little Rock, Arkansas, pursuant to a federal court order. This photograph captures fifteen-year-old Elizabeth Eckford, one of the Little Rock Nine, surrounded by an angry white crowd on the first day of school. The photo also shows an enraged white student, Hazel Bryan, shouting at her to go home. Neither Eckford nor the other black students managed to attend school that day, but they entered Central High after President Eisenhower sent in federal troops to protect them.

Lloyd Dinkins/The Commercial Appeal /Landov

Gloria Lopez-Stafford | A Mexican American Childhood in El-Paso, Texas, 1949

Born in 1937, Gloria Lopez-Stafford grew into her teenage years in the 1950s. While African Americans were fighting for integrated schools in neighboring Arkansas, Lopez-Stafford and her friends attended interracial schools. Still, as she relates in the following excerpt from her memoir, attending classes with whites did not necessarily satisfy Mexican American youths.

"Remember the Alamo!"

The banner slogan was draped across the blackboard of my social studies class in El Paso, Texas. The black letters jumped off the white background. The slogan on the banner was appropriate because the elementary school was named after Sam Houston, first president of the Texas Republic. . . .

It was September and we were going to the auditorium to see the movie, *The Battle of the Alamo*. Texas history was the course of study for the year and the whole week before the film we made salt maps of the state. I was very proud of my carved Ivory soap model of the Alamo. . . .

That year, my class at Houston School was about half Anglo and half Mexican. . . . *The Battle of the Alamo* was an old film, very dark and gray. The battle brought together small, overdressed Mexican men and big white men dressed in buckskins. As you probably know, the battle was fierce and it was won by a villain named Antonio López de Santa Anna. He was portrayed as a small ruthless man who made martyrs of the Anglos that day at the Alamo. There were 187 Anglos killed and 600 Mexicans killed.

After the film was over, the dark shades on the windows were lifted and the lights turned on. I felt uncomfortable as I looked around the auditorium. . . . I avoided the looks of my friends because I couldn't understand my confused feelings. I felt sick. I was painfully aware of being Mexican. And it wouldn't be the last time that year.

. . . I walked back quietly until my friend Linda ran up to me. Linda's family was from Monterrey [Mexico] and she didn't live far from me.

"Gloria, who did you cheer for?" she asked in a quiet tone. I looked at her and looked around before I answered. "The Mexicans," I replied softly. Linda shrieked, "Me too." . . .

When we were back in the classroom, the teacher stood in front of the room directly beneath the banner. She was a slender, very white woman with sky blue eyes. . . . "The men at the Alamo were heroes—true Texans," she said in a soft voice. . . .

"Yeah. And Texas is for Texans," yelled a voice at the back of the classroom. . . . Even though I was born in Mexico, I had been a Texan since I was two years old. I am also a Mexican. Joe pushed me from behind and uttered a chant of mockery. My friend José across the aisle slugged him. He gestured to Joe with his fists to leave me alone. . . . Angry and confused, I put my head down so that no one could see me cry.

Source: Gloria López-Stafford, *A Place in El Paso: A Mexican American Childhood* (Albuquerque: University of New Mexico Press, 1996), 3–5.

"Why No Chinese American Delinquents?" 1955

Asian Americans had faced a great deal of prejudice from whites, especially on the West Coast. However, after World War II, the hard work and striving of Japanese and Chinese Americans to succeed reversed the traditional prejudices of many white Americans toward them, especially the younger generation. As the following magazine article shows, whereas teenagers in general were a source of concern for older Americans, Chinese teenagers were perceived as a "model minority."

Not long ago, a New York City judge wrote to the *New York Times* saying that not in the seventeen years he had been on the bench had a Chinese-American teen-ager been brought before him on a juvenile-delinquency charge. The judge said that he queried his colleagues on the matter and they, too, expressed their astonishment. They said that not one of the estimated 10,000 Chinese-American teenagers, to their knowledge, had ever been haled into court on a depredation, narcotics, speeding, burglary, vandalism, stickup, purse-snatching or mugging accusation. A check with San Francisco, where there is a large colony of Chinese-Americans, tells the same story. The same holds true of Chicago, where the police report "excellent" behavior on the part of Chinese-American youngsters.

P. H. Chang, Chinese consul-general in New York City, was asked to comment on this warm and amazing return. He said simply, "I have heard this story many times from many judges. They tell me that none of our people are ever brought before them for juvenile delinquency. They were surprised, but I was not. Why?

"I will tell you why I think this is so. Filial piety, the love for parents, is a cardinal virtue my people have brought over from the China that was once free. A Chinese child, no matter where he lives, is brought up to recognize that he cannot shame his parents. To do so would relegate him to worse than oblivion, for his parents would disown him and he would be cast free and alone from our traditions that go back many, many centuries.

"Before a Chinese child makes a move, be stops to think what the reaction on his parents will be. Will they be proud or will they be ashamed? That is the sole question he asks himself. The answer comes readily, and thus he knows what is right and wrong.

"Above all other things, the Chinese teen-ager is anxious to please his parents before he pleases himself. Our family households work on the theory that the parents are wise and seasoned, and if the children follow the same course, they can do no wrong."

Today, there are some 100,000 Chinese-Americans in the United States, of whom 90 per cent live in New York City, Chicago and San Francisco. Most are small businessmen in the import trade who deal with their own people in their own communities. Most, no matter whether wealthy or poor, maintain a strict, family-style home. Mealtimes are ceremonial affairs which must be attended by every member of the family. Holidays are celebrated in family style. Schooling, the reverence for religion and decorum, plus reverence for elders and family tradition, are the prime movers in developing the child from infancy.

Source: "Why No Chinese American Delinquents? Maybe It's Traditional Respect for Parents," *Saturday Evening Post*, April 30, 1955, 12.

Interpret the Evidence

1. Analyze which information in these documents confirms or challenges commonly held beliefs about teenagers in the 1950s.
2. Compare the assumptions about adults and teenagers in Sources 25.6 and 25.10. How do they differ, either in tone or in content, from those written *by* teens (Sources 25.7 and 25.9)?
3. Evaluate what Sources 25.7 and 25.10 tell us about generational differences.
4. Assess what these sources, especially 25.8, tell us about racial and ethnic differences among teenagers in the postwar era.

Put It in Context

How did the economy, politics, and culture of the postwar period (1945–1960) influence teen life in this era?

Liberalism and Its Challengers

1960–1973

26

WINDOW TO THE PAST

Nancy Ellin, Letter Describing Freedom Summer, 1964

In 1964, white and black volunteers spent a summer in Mississippi attempting to register voters and establishing Freedom Schools. Often surrounded by danger, they wrote letters to family and friends, such as the letter here, explaining the work they did, problems they encountered, and the courage of local blacks. ▶ To discover more about what this primary source can show us, see Source 26.7 on page 921.

                                                                    June 30

Dear Dr. and Mrs. Ellin,

It was nice to get your letter today; we hope you will write often. I'm sure Joe will write to you any minute now, but I thought I might as well, too.

We got here OK, though we were frightened most of the way, quite unnecessarily. It was the people who came down in integrated cars who had the unpleasant time - refused service, cars following them, etc. We came down with a very nice girl who just graduated from Smith and who did quite a bit of driving.

We are currently hard at work getting the Freedom Schools organized. Joe and another boy have everyone typing up stencils of the Constitution, the Declaration of Independence, etc. The school enrollment is over 150; we are having official registration Thursday. The philosophy is to take everyone who comes; we will be teaching adults in the evening. There are 10 teachers, 8 more expected from New York City on Thursday. We also intend to recruit a few local people.

I, too, am sorry things came to such a pass. We felt terrible about causing you all such anguish, but we felt the decision was ours to make, and though we were very afraid and doubtful at Oxford, we made the decision to come. You must know that you were not the only parents who were worried, and some kids did drop out, one from our group, in fact, who was underage and couldn't get his parents' consent. Now that we are here we feel more than ever that coming here was the right things to do. Even if we don't teach a singlechild (and I think the odds are heavily against that) we still will have accomplished

After reading this chapter you should be able to:

- Evaluate President Kennedy's approaches to liberalism at home and in foreign affairs.

- Explain how the civil rights movement succeeded in convincing the federal government to enact the Civil Rights Act of 1964 and the Voting Rights Act of 1965.

- Describe the major legislative accomplishments of the Great Society.

- Explain why U.S. intervention in Vietnam escalated in the 1960s.

- Examine the challenges to liberalism from the political left and right and analyze their similarities and differences.

COMPARING AMERICAN HISTORIES

As attorney general of California at the outset of World War II, Earl Warren helped convince President Franklin D. Roosevelt to order the relocation of 110,000 Japanese Americans. After the war, as governor, he continued to fight against perceived threats to national security by joining the anti-Communist crusade. In 1953 President Dwight D. Eisenhower appointed Warren to be chief justice

(left) **Earl Warren.** Collection of the Supreme Court of the United States

(right) **Bayard Rustin.** Library of Congress, 3c18986

of the United States, a choice that many observers saw as a safe conservative pick.

As chief justice, however, Warren defied expectations and instead led the Supreme Court in a liberal direction. In 1954 Warren wrote the landmark opinion ordering school desegregation in *Brown v. Board of Education of Topeka, Kansas.* The Warren Court did not shrink from controversy, and its rulings expanding the rights of accused criminals, banning prayer in public school classrooms, and upholding birth control as a right of privacy evoked harsh criticism from the police, religious fundamentalists, and conservative politicians.

Unlike Earl Warren, Bayard Rustin worked outside of regular political and social channels to achieve change. Rustin joined the Young Communist League in the 1930s because of its commitment to economic justice, racial equality, and international peace. As a committed pacifist, however, Rustin quit the organization in 1941 when the party supported U.S. intervention in World War II and retreated on its fight against racial discrimination during the war.

In 1942 Rustin helped found the Congress of Racial Equality (CORE), an interracial organization that pioneered nonviolent, direct-action protests against racial bias. Rustin was imprisoned from 1943 to 1946 for declining to perform alternative service after he refused to register for the military draft. Following his release, in 1947 Rustin helped plan and lead the Journey of Reconciliation, which challenged segregation on interstate buses in the South. In the 1950s and 1960s, he became an adviser to Martin Luther King Jr. and a major strategist in the civil rights movement in his own right.

Rustin remained active in various causes throughout his life. One of his last efforts was perhaps his most personal: the struggle against antigay prejudice. As a homosexual, Rustin had to conceal his sexual identity at a time when the public and his political allies rejected homosexuals. In the 1980s, as the gay liberation movement grew more vocal, Rustin spoke out for tolerance and equality until his death in 1987. ■

The American histories of Earl Warren and Bayard Rustin demonstrate the complexity of social change. The federal government had the power to encourage social movements by interpreting the Constitution, enacting legislation, and enforcing the law in a manner that eliminated barriers to racial, sexual, and political equality. Yet federal action likely would not have happened without the pressure applied by activists like Rustin. As president, Lyndon Johnson took action with his Great Society programs, but his escalation of the war in Vietnam divided his party and generated opposition from young activists on the left. At the same time, efforts to promote equality and social justice, along with the military stalemate in Vietnam, produced a strong reaction from conservatives who sought to roll back liberal gains; pursue their own policies of small government, low taxes, and self-help; and bring about a quick but honorable end to the war.

The **Politics** of **Liberalism**

Hoping to build on the legacy of the New Deal, liberals sought to increase the role of the federal government in the economy, education, and health care. Most liberals supported a staunchly anti-Communist foreign policy, differing with Republicans more over means than over ends. Indeed, when Democrats recaptured the White House in 1960, they seized opportunities in Cuba and Southeast Asia to vigorously challenge the expansion of Soviet influence.

Kennedy's New Frontier. With victory in World War II and the revival of economic prosperity, liberal thinkers regained confidence in capitalism. Many saw the postwar American free-enterprise system as different from the old-style capitalism that had existed before Franklin Roosevelt's New Deal. In their view, this new "reform capitalism," or democratic capitalism, created abundance for all and not just for the elites. Rather than pushing for the redistribution of wealth, liberals now called on the government to help create conditions conducive to economic growth and increased productivity. The liberal economist John Kenneth Galbraith thus argued in *The Affluent Society* (1958) that increased public investments in education, research, and development were the key to American prosperity and progress.

These ideas guided the thinking of Democratic politicians such as Senator John F. Kennedy of Massachusetts. Elected president in 1960, the forty-three-year-old Kennedy brought good looks, charm, a beautiful wife, and young children to the White House. Kennedy pledged a **New Frontier** to battle "tyranny, poverty, disease, and war," but lacking strong majorities in Congress, he contented himself with making small gains on the New Deal's foundation. Congress expanded unemployment benefits, increased the minimum wage, extended Social Security benefits, and raised appropriations for public housing, but Kennedy's caution disappointed many liberals.

Kennedy, the Cold War, and Cuba. The Kennedy administration showed greater zeal in fighting the Cold War abroad. The president believed that reform capitalism, which worked well in the United States, should become a global model. Communism, like fascism before it, posed a fundamental threat to American interests and to other countries' ability to emulate the economic miracle of the United States. The faith of liberals in U.S. ingenuity, willpower, technological superiority, and moral righteousness encouraged them to reshape the "free world" in America's image.

President Kennedy's first Cold War battle took place in Cuba. Before his election, Kennedy learned of a secret CIA plan, devised by the Eisenhower administration, to topple Fidel Castro from power. After becoming president, Kennedy approved the scheme that Eisenhower had set in motion.

The operation ended disastrously. On April 17, 1961, the invasion force of between 1,400 and 1,500 Cuban exiles, trained by the CIA, landed by boat at the Bay of Pigs on Cuba's southwest coast. Kennedy refused to provide backup military forces for fear of revealing the U.S. role in the attack. Castro's troops defeated the insurgents in three days. CIA planners had underestimated Cuban popular support for Castro, falsely believing that the invasion would inspire a national uprising against the Communist regime. The Kennedy administration had blundered into a bitter foreign policy defeat (Map 26.1).

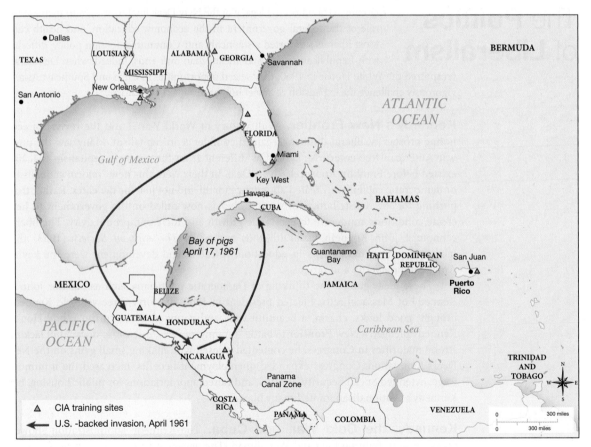

MAP 26.1 The Bay of Pigs Invasion, 1961

President Kennedy launched the Bay of Pigs invasion on April 17, 1961 to topple the Communist regime of Fidel Castro. The CIA secretly trained Cuban exiles in locations in the southern United States, Central America, and the Caribbean. After three days of fighting, the invasion failed and turned Castro into a national hero, thereby strengthening his leadership. Fearing further U.S. aggression, Castro turned to the Soviet Union to install missiles in Cuba for protection.

Two months later, Kennedy met Soviet leader Nikita Khrushchev at a summit meeting in Vienna. Khrushchev took advantage of the president's embarrassing defeat in Cuba to press his own demands. After the confrontational summit meeting increased tensions between the superpowers, Kennedy persuaded Congress to increase the defense budget, dispatch additional troops to Europe, and bolster civil defense. In August, the Soviets responded by constructing a wall through Berlin, making it more difficult for refugees to flee from East Berlin to West Berlin.

Despite the Bay of Pigs disaster, the United States continued its efforts to topple the Castro regime. Such attempts were uniformly unsuccessful, but a wary Castro invited the Soviet Union to install short- and intermediate-range missiles in Cuba to protect the country against any U.S. incursion. On October 22, 1962, Kennedy went on national television to inform the American people that the Soviets had placed missiles in Cuba. The Kennedy administration decided to blockade Cuba to prevent Soviet ships from supplying the deadly warheads that would make the missiles fully operational. If Soviet ships defied the blockade, the president would order air strikes on its island neighbor. Ordinary Americans nervously contemplated the very real possibility of nuclear destruction.

On the brink of nuclear war, both sides chose compromise. Khrushchev agreed to remove the missiles, and Kennedy pledged not to invade Cuba and secretly promised to dismantle U.S. missile sites in Turkey aimed at the Soviet Union. The world breathed a sigh of relief, and Kennedy and Khrushchev, having stepped back from the edge of nuclear holocaust, worked to ease tensions further. In 1963 they signed a Partial Nuclear Test Ban Treaty—which prohibited atmospheric but not underground testing—and installed an electronic "hot line" to ensure swift communications between Washington and Moscow.

Explore ▶

See Source 26.1 for one cartoonist's commentary on the Soviet removal of missiles from Cuba.

Kennedy sought to balance his hardline, anti-Communist policies with new outreach efforts to inspire developing nations to follow a democratic path. The Peace Corps program sent thousands of volunteers to teach and advise developing nations, and Kennedy's Alliance for Progress supplied economic aid to emerging democracies in Latin America.

REVIEW & RELATE

- How did President Kennedy's domestic agenda reflect the liberal political ideology of the early 1960s?

- Evaluate Kennedy's and Khrushchev's actions in the Cuban Missile Crisis. How was war averted?

The **Civil Rights Movement Intensifies, 1961–1968**

At home, the most critical issue facing the nation in the early 1960s was the intensification of the civil rights movement. As a candidate, Kennedy had promised vigorous action on civil rights, but as president he did little to follow through on his promises. With southern Democrats occupying key positions in Congress and threatening to block any civil rights proposals, Kennedy sought to mollify this critical component of his political base. Following Kennedy's death in 1963, President Johnson succeeded in breaking the legislative logjam and signed into law three major pieces of civil rights legislation.

Edmund Valtman | The Cuban Missile Crisis, 1962

For thirteen days in October 1962, the world held its breath while U.S. president John F. Kennedy and Soviet premier Nikita Khrushchev traded threats over the presence of nuclear weapons in Cuba. Khrushchev eventually backed down and removed the missiles. Two days after the crisis ended, the following cartoon by Edmund Valtman appeared in the *Hartford Times*.

Source 26.1

Why might Khrushchev tell Castro, "This hurts me more than it hurts you!"?

What does the placement of the missiles suggest about their importance to Cuba?

What does the position of both characters suggest about the power relationship between Castro and Khrushchev?

Library of Congress, Prints & Photographs Division, drawing by Edmund S. Valtman, LC-USZ62-130423

Put It in Context

How did the Cuban missile crisis affect Kennedy's and Khrushchev's thinking about the Cold War?

He did so under considerable pressure from the civil rights movement. At the height of their triumphs, however, many civil rights activists became increasingly skeptical of non-violence and integration and turned to the racial nationalism and self-determination of black power.

Freedom Rides.

The Congress of Racial Equality took the offensive on May 4, 1961. Similar to Bayard Rustin's efforts in the 1940s, CORE mounted racially integrated **Freedom Rides** to test whether facilities in the South were complying with the 1960 Supreme Court ruling that outlawed segregated bus and train stations serving passengers who were travel-ing interstate. CORE alerted the Justice Department and the FBI of its plans, but the riders received no protection when Ku Klux Klan–dominated mobs in Anniston and Birming-ham, Alabama attacked two of its buses, seriously wounding several activists.

After safety concerns forced CORE to forgo the rest of the trip, members of the Stu-dent Nonviolent Coordinating Committee (SNCC) rushed to Birmingham to continue the bus rides. The Kennedy administration urged them to reconsider, but Diane Nash, an SNCC founder, explained that although the group realized the peril of resuming the jour-ney, "we can't let them stop us with violence. If we do, the movement is dead." When the replenished busload of riders reached Montgomery on May 20, they were brutally assaulted by a mob. Dr. Martin Luther King Jr. subsequently held a rally in a Montgomery church, where white mobs threatened the lives of King and the Freedom Riders inside the building. Faced with the prospect of serious bloodshed, the Kennedy administration dis-patched federal marshals to the scene and persuaded the governor to call out the Alabama National Guard to ensure the safety of everyone in the church.

The president and his brother, Attorney General Robert Kennedy, worked out a com-promise to let the rides continue with minimal violence, and with minimal publicity. The Cold War worked in favor of the protesters. With the Soviet Union publicizing the violence against Freedom Riders in the South, the Kennedy administration attempted to preserve America's image abroad by persuading the Interstate Commerce Commission to issue an order prohibiting segregated transportation facilities. Still, southern whites resisted. When Freedom Riders encountered opposition in Albany, Georgia in the fall of 1961, SNCC workers remained in Albany and helped local leaders organize residents against segregation and other forms of racial discrimination. Even with the assistance of Dr. King and the Southern Christian Leadership Conference (SCLC), the Albany movement stalled.

Kennedy Supports Civil Rights.

Despite the setback in Albany, the civil rights movement kept up pressure on other fronts. In September 1962 Mississippi governor Ross Barnett tried to thwart the registration of James Meredith as an undergraduate at the Uni-versity of Mississippi. Barnett's obstruction precipitated a riot on campus, and President Kennedy dispatched army troops and federalized the Mississippi National Guard to restore order, but not before two bystanders were killed.

The following year, King and the SCLC joined the Reverend Fred Shuttlesworth's movement in Birmingham, Alabama, in its battle against discrimination, segregation, and police brutality. With the white supremacist Eugene "Bull" Connor in charge of law enforcement, civil rights protesters, including children from age six to sixteen, encoun-tered violent resistance, vicious police dogs, and high-powered water hoses. Connor ordered mass arrests, including Dr. King's, prompting the minister to write his famous

"Letter from Birmingham Jail," in which he justified the use of nonviolent direct action. Seeking to defuse the crisis, President Kennedy sent an emissary in early May 1963 to negotiate a peaceful solution that granted concessions to Birmingham blacks and ended the demonstrations. On Sunday, September 15, 1963, however, the Ku Klux Klan dynamited Birmingham's Sixteenth Street Baptist Church, a freedom movement staging ground. The blast killed four young girls attending services.

Even before this brutal bombing, the president had finally embraced the nation's duty to guarantee equal rights regardless of race. On June 11, 1963, shortly after negotiating the Birmingham agreement, Kennedy delivered a nationally televised address. He acknowledged that the country faced a "moral crisis" heightened by the events in Birmingham, and he noted the difficulty of preaching "freedom around the world" while "this is a land of the free except for Negroes." He proposed congressional legislation to end segregation in public accommodations, increase federal power to promote school desegregation, and broaden the right to vote.

Events on the day Kennedy delivered his powerful speech reinforced the need for swift action. Earlier that morning, Alabama governor George C. Wallace stood in front of the administration building at the University of Alabama to block the entrance of two black undergraduates. To uphold the federal court decree ordering their admission, Kennedy deployed federal marshals and the Alabama National Guard, and Wallace, having dramatized his point, stepped aside. However, victory soon turned into tragedy. That evening Medgar Evers, the head of the NAACP in Mississippi, was shot and killed in the driveway of his Jackson home by the white supremacist Byron de la Beckwith. (Following two trials, de la Beckwith remained free until 1994, when he was retried and convicted for Evers's murder.)

Nonetheless, Congress was still unwilling to act. To increase pressure on lawmakers, civil rights organizations held the **March on Washington for Jobs and Freedom** on August 28, 1963, carrying out an idea first proposed by A. Philip Randolph in 1941 (see "The Origins of the Civil Rights Movement" in chapter 23). With Randolph as honorary chair, his associate Bayard Rustin directed the proceedings as 250,000 black and white peaceful protesters rallied in front of the Lincoln Memorial. Two speakers in particular caught the attention of the crowd. John Lewis, the chairman of SNCC, expressed the frustration of militant blacks with both the Kennedy administration and Congress. "The revolution is at hand. . . . We will not wait for the President, nor the Justice Department, nor Congress," Lewis asserted. "But we will take matters into our own hands." In a more conciliatory tone, King delivered a speech expressing his dream for racial and religious brotherhood. Still, King issued a stern warning to "those who hope that the Negro needed to blow off steam and will now be content. . . . There will be neither rest nor tranquility in America until the Negro is granted his citizenship rights."

If civil rights leaders hoped to elicit additional support from the Kennedy administration, their hopes were dashed. On November 22, 1963, Lee Harvey Oswald shot President Kennedy as he rode in an open motorcade in Dallas, Texas. The assassination prompted an outpouring of public grief. In death, Kennedy achieved immense popularity, yet he left many problems unresolved. His legislative agenda, including civil rights, remained unfulfilled. It was up to Vice President Lyndon Johnson to step into the breach.

Freedom Summer and Voting Rights.
Following Kennedy's death, President Johnson took charge of the pending civil rights legislation. Under his leadership, a bipartisan coalition passed the **Civil Rights Act of 1964**. The law prohibited discrimination in

Women and the March on Washington for Jobs and Freedom, 1963   Although black women played central roles in grassroots organizing within the civil rights movement, they received far less attention on the national stage than did male leaders, such as Martin Luther King Jr. and A. Philip Randolph. At the historic 1963 March on Washington, women, black and white, turned out in large numbers, as this photograph shows, but they were not chosen to give any of the major speeches or march at the front of the line with the leading men. Wally McNamee / Getty Images

public accommodations, increased federal enforcement of school desegregation and the right to vote, and created the Community Relations Service, a federal agency authorized to help resolve racial conflicts. The act also contained a final measure to combat employment discrimination on the basis of race and sex.

Yet even as President Johnson signed the Civil Rights Act into law on July 2, black freedom forces launched a new offensive to secure the right to vote in the South. The 1964 act contained a voting rights provision but did little to address the main problems of the discriminatory use of literacy tests and poll taxes and the biased administration of registration procedures that kept the majority of southern blacks from registering. Beatings, killings, acts of arson, and arrests became a routine response to voting rights efforts. Although the Justice Department filed lawsuits against recalcitrant voter registrars and police officers, the government refused to send in federal personnel or instruct the FBI to safeguard vulnerable civil rights workers.

To focus national attention on this problem, SNCC, CORE, the NAACP, and the SCLC launched the **Freedom Summer** project in Mississippi. They assigned eight hundred volunteers from around the nation, mainly white college students, to work on voter registration drives and in "freedom schools" to improve education for rural black youngsters. White supremacists fought back against what they perceived as an enemy invasion. In late June 1964, the Ku Klux Klan, in collusion with local law enforcement officials, killed three civil rights workers. This tragedy focused national attention, and President Johnson pressed the usually uncooperative FBI to find the culprits, which it did. However, civil rights workers continued to encounter white violence and harassment throughout Freedom Summer. **See Primary Source Project 26: Freedom Summer, page 920.**

One outcome of the Freedom Summer project was the creation of the **Mississippi Freedom Democratic Party (MFDP)**. Because the regular state Democratic Party excluded blacks, the civil rights coalition formed an alternative Democratic Party open to everyone. In August 1964 the mostly black MFDP sent a delegation to the Democratic National Convention, meeting in Atlantic City, New Jersey, to challenge the seating of the all-white delegation from Mississippi. One MFDP delegate, Fannie Lou Hamer, who had lost her job for her voter registration activities, offered passionate testimony that was broadcast on television. Johnson then hammered out a compromise that gave the MFDP two at-large seats, seated members of the regular delegation who took a loyalty oath, and prohibited racial discrimination in the future by any state Democratic Party. While both sides rejected the deal, four years later an integrated delegation, which included Hamer, represented Mississippi at the Democratic National Convention in Chicago.

Freedom Summer highlighted the problem of disfranchisement, but it took further demonstrations in Selma, Alabama to resolve it. After state troopers shot and killed a black voting rights demonstrator in February 1965, Dr. King called for a march from Selma to the capital, Montgomery, to petition Governor Wallace to end the violence and allow blacks to vote. On Sunday, March 7, as black and white marchers left Selma, the sheriff's forces sprayed them with tear gas, beat them, and sent them running for their lives. A few days later, a white clergyman who had joined the protesters was killed by a group of white thugs. On March 21, following another failed attempt to march to Montgomery, King finally led protesters on the fifty-mile hike to the state capital, where they arrived safely four days later. Still, after the march, the Ku Klux Klan murdered a white female marcher from Michigan.

Events in Selma prompted President Johnson to take action. On March 15 he addressed a joint session of Congress and told lawmakers and a nationally televised audience that the black "cause must be our cause too." On August 6, 1965, the president signed the **Voting Rights Act**, which banned the use of literacy tests for voter registration, authorized a federal lawsuit against the poll tax (which succeeded in 1966), empowered federal officials to register disfranchised voters, and required seven southern states to submit any voting changes to Washington before they went into effect. With strong federal enforcement of the law, by 1968 a majority of black southerners and nearly two-thirds of black Mississippians could vote (Figure 26.1).

However, these civil rights victories had exacted a huge toll on the movement. SNCC and CORE had come to distrust Presidents Kennedy and Johnson for failing to provide protection for voter registration workers. Furthermore, Johnson's attempt to broker a compromise at the 1964 Atlantic City Convention convinced MFDP supporters that the liberal president had sold them out. The once united movement showed signs of cracking.

From Civil Rights to Black Power.
Increasingly after 1964, SNCC and CORE began exploring new ways of seeking freedom through strategies of black self-determination and self-defense. They were greatly influenced by Malcolm X. Born Malcolm Little, he had engaged in a life of crime, which landed him in prison. Inside jail, he converted to the Nation of Islam, a religious sect based partly on Muslim teachings and partly on the belief that white people were devils (not a doctrine associated with orthodox Islam). After

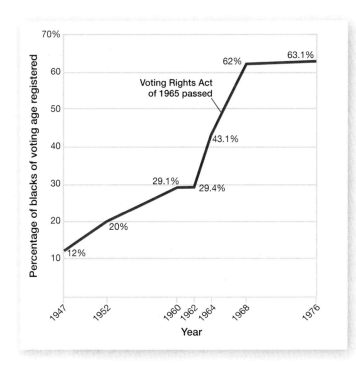

FIGURE 26.1   Black Voter Registration in the South, 1947–1976

After World War II, the percentage of black adults registered to vote in the South slowly but steadily increased, largely as a result of grassroots voting drives. Despite the Kennedy administration's support for voter registration drives, a majority of southern blacks remained prohibited from voting in 1964. The passage of the 1965 Voting Rights Act removed barriers such as literacy tests and poll taxes, strengthened the federal government's enforcement powers, and enabled more than 60 percent of southern blacks to vote by the late 1960s. Compare the growth of black voter registration during the Eisenhower (1953–1961), Kennedy (1961–1963), and Johnson (1963–1969) administrations.

Source: Data from David Garrow, *Protest at Selma* (New Haven, CT: Yale University Press, 1978), and U.S. Department of Commerce, Bureau of the Census, *Statistical Abstract of the United States*, 1976.

his release from jail, Malcolm rejected his "slave name" and substituted the letter X to symbolize his unknown African forebears. Minister Malcolm helped convert thousands of disciples in black ghettos by denouncing whites and encouraging blacks to embrace their African heritage and beauty as a people. Favoring self-defense over nonviolence, he criticized civil rights leaders for failing to protect their communities. After 1963, Malcolm X broke away from the Nation of Islam, visited the Middle East and Africa, and accepted the teachings of traditional Islam. He moderated his anti-white rhetoric but remained committed to black self-determination. He had already influenced the growing number of disillusioned young black activists when, in 1965, members of the Nation of Islam murdered him, apparently in revenge for challenging the organization.

Black militants, echoing Malcolm X's ideas, challenged racial liberalism. They renounced the principles of integration and nonviolence in favor of black power and self-defense. Instead of welcoming whites within their organizations, black radicals believed that African Americans had to assert their independence from white America. In 1966 SNCC expelled white members and created an all-black organization. Stokely Carmichael, SNCC's chairman, proclaimed "black power" as the central goal of the freedom struggle and linked the cause of African American freedom to revolutionary conflicts in Cuba, Africa, and Vietnam.

Black power emerged against a backdrop of riots in black ghettos, which erupted across the nation starting in the mid-1960s: in Harlem and Rochester, New York, in 1964; in Los Angeles in 1965; and in Cleveland, Chicago, Detroit, Newark, and Tampa in the following two years. Urban blacks, many in the North and West, faced problems of high unemployment, dilapidated housing, and police mistreatment that civil rights legislation had done nothing to correct. While many whites perceived the ghetto uprisings solely as an exercise in criminal behavior, many blacks viewed the violence as an expression of political discontent—as rebellions, not riots. The Kerner Commission, appointed by

Malcolm X, 1963 While civil rights leaders campaigned for racial integration and equality through nonviolent protests in the South, Malcolm X questioned their tactics and goals. A charismatic minister in the Nation of Islam, he preached a fiery message of black nationalism and self-defense, ideas that later merged into the ideology of black power. Though his message drew criticism from liberal whites and black civil rights leaders, Malcolm X appealed to many African Americans, as demonstrated here at a rally in New York City's Harlem on June 29, 1963. AP Photo

President Johnson to assess urban disorders and chaired by Governor Otto Kerner of Illinois, concluded in 1968 that white racism remained at the heart of the problem: "Our nation is moving toward two societies, one black, one white—separate and unequal."

New groups emerged to take up the cause of black power. In 1966 Huey P. Newton and Bobby Seale, college students in Oakland, California, formed the **Black Panther Party**. Dressed in black leather, sporting black berets, and carrying guns, the Panthers appealed mainly to black men. They did not, however, rely on armed confrontation and bravado alone. The Panthers established day care centers and health facilities, often run by women, which gained the admiration of many in their communities. Much of this good work was overshadowed by violent confrontations with the police, which led to the deaths of Panthers in shootouts and the imprisonment of key party officials. By the early 1970s, government crackdowns on the Black Panthers had destabilized the organization and reduced its influence.

The assassination of Martin Luther King Jr. in 1968 furthered black disillusionment. King was shot and killed by James Earl Ray in Memphis, where he was supporting demonstrations by striking sanitation workers. In the wake of his murder, riots erupted in hundreds of cities throughout the country. Little noticed amid the fiery turbulence, President Johnson signed into law the 1968 Fair Housing Act, the final piece of civil rights legislation of his term.

REVIEW & RELATE

• How did civil rights activists pressure state and federal government officials to enact their agenda?

• How were the civil rights and black power movements similar and in what ways were they different?

Federal Efforts toward Social Reform, 1964–1968

President Johnson's liberal accomplishments reached beyond civil rights, and he drew on Kennedy's legacy and his own considerable political skills to win passage of the most important items on the liberal agenda. While Johnson pressed ahead in the legislative arena, Chief Justice Earl Warren's Supreme Court issued rulings that extended social justice to minorities and the

President Johnson Signs Medicare into Law, 1965   On July 30, 1965, President Johnson signed the Medicare bill, the health insurance program for elderly Americans. The ceremony took place at the Truman Library in Independence, Missouri, and former President Harry S. Truman received the first Medicare card. In 1945, Truman had first proposed national health insurance, but Congress rejected it. Standing to the right immediately behind Johnson (seated on the left) and Truman (seated on the right) are (from left to right) Lady Bird Johnson, the president's wife; Vice President Hubert Humphrey; and Bess Truman, the former president's wife. LBJ Library photo

economically oppressed and favored those who believed in a firm separation of church and state, free speech, and a right to privacy.

The Great Society. In an address at the University of Michigan on May 22, 1964, President Johnson sketched out his dream for the **Great Society**, one that "rests on abundance and liberty for all. It demands an end to poverty and racial injustice, to which we are totally committed in our time. But that is just the beginning."

Besides poverty and race, he outlined three broad areas in need of reform: education, the environment, and cities. Toward this end, the Elementary and Secondary School Act (1965) was the most far-reaching federal law ever passed. It provided federal funds directly to public schools to improve their quality. The Model Cities program (1966) set up the Department of Housing and Urban Affairs, which coordinated efforts at urban planning and rebuilding neighborhoods in decaying cities. The Department of Transportation sought to ensure a fast, safe, and convenient transportation system. In addition, the president pushed Congress to pass hundreds of environmental protection laws, including those dealing with air and water pollution, waste disposal, the use of natural resources, and the preservation of wildlife and wilderness areas. Still, it was the War on Poverty that garnered the most attention.

The opening salvo of the War on Poverty came with passage of the Economic Opportunity Act of 1964. Through this measure, Johnson wanted to offer the poor "a hand up, not a handout." Among its major components, the law provided job training, food stamps, rent supplements, redevelopment of depressed rural areas, remedial education (later to include the preschool program Head Start), a domestic Peace Corps called Volunteers in Service to America (VISTA), and a Community Action Program that empowered the poor to shape policies affecting their own communities. Between 1965 and 1968, expenditures targeted for the poor doubled, from $6 billion to $12 billion. The antipoverty program helped reduce the proportion of poor people from 20 percent in 1963 to 13 percent five years later, and it helped reduce the rate of black poverty from 40 percent to 20 percent during this same period.

Johnson intended to fight the War on Poverty through the engine of economic growth, which would create new jobs for the unemployed without redistributing wealth. With this in mind, he persuaded Congress to enact significant tax cuts. Johnson's tax cut, which applied across the board, stimulated the economy and sent the gross national product soaring from $591 billion in 1963 to $977 billion by the end of the decade. Despite the gains made, many liberals believed that Johnson's spending on the War on Poverty did not go far enough. Whatever the shortcomings, Johnson campaigned on his antipoverty and civil rights record in his bid to recapture the White House in 1964. His Republican opponent, Senator Barry M. Goldwater of Arizona, personified the conservative right wing of the Republican Party. The Arizona senator condemned big government, supported states' rights, and accused liberals of not waging the Cold War forcefully enough. His aggressive conservatism appealed to his grassroots base in small-town America, especially in southern California, the Southwest, and the South. His tough rhetoric, however, scared off moderate Republicans, resulting on election day in a landslide for Johnson as well as considerable Democratic majorities in Congress.

Flush with victory, Johnson pushed Congress to move quickly. Working together, they achieved impressive results. To cite only a few examples, the Eighty-ninth Congress

TABLE 26.1   Major Great Society Measures, 1964–1968

Year	Legislation or Order	Purpose
1964	Civil Rights Act	Prohibited discrimination in public accommodations, education, and employment
	Economic Opportunity Act	Established War on Poverty agencies: Head Start, VISTA, Job Corps, and Community Action Program
1965	Elementary and Secondary Education Act	Federal funding for elementary and secondary schools
	Medical Care Act	Provided Medicare health insurance for citizens sixty-five years and older and Medicaid health benefits for the poor
	Voting Rights Act	Banned literacy tests for voting, authorized federal registrars to be sent into seven southern states, and monitored voting changes in these states
	Executive Order 11246	Required employers to take affirmative action to promote equal opportunity and remedy the effects of past discrimination
	Immigration and Nationality Act	Abolished quotas on immigration that reduced immigration from non-Western and southern and eastern European nations
	Water Quality Act	Established and enforced federal water quality standards
	Air Quality Act	Established air pollution standards for motor vehicles
	National Arts and Humanities Act	Established National Endowment of the Humanities and National Endowment of the Arts to support the work of scholars, writers, artists, and musicians
1966	Model Cities Act	Approved funding for the rehabilitation of inner cities
1967	Executive Order 11375	Expanded affirmative action regulations to include women
1968	Civil Rights Act	Outlawed discrimination in housing

(1965–1967) subsidized health care for the elderly and the poor by creating Medicare and Medicaid, expanded voting rights for African Americans in the South, raised the minimum wage, and created national endowments for the fine arts and the humanities. The 1965 Immigration Act repealed discriminatory national origins quotas established in 1924, resulting in a shift of immigration from Europe to Asia and Central and South America (Table 26.1).

The Warren Court. The Warren Court reflected this high tide of liberalism. The Court affirmed the constitutionality of the Voting Rights Act. In 1967, the justices overturned state laws prohibiting interracial marriages. A year later, fourteen years after the *Brown* decision, they ruled that school districts in the South could no longer maintain racially exclusive schools and must desegregate immediately. In a series of cases, the Warren Court ensured fairer legislative representation for blacks and whites by removing the disproportionate power that rural districts had held over urban districts.

The Supreme Court's most controversial rulings dealt with the criminal justice system, religion, and private sexual practices. Strengthening the rights of criminal defendants, the justices ruled in *Gideon v. Wainwright* (1963) that states had to provide indigents accused of felonies with an attorney, and in *Miranda v. Arizona* (1966) they ordered the police to advise suspects of their constitutional rights. The Court also moved into new, controversial territory concerning school prayer, contraception, and pornography. In 1962 the Court outlawed a nondenominational Christian prayer recited in New York State schools as a violation of the separation of church and state guaranteed by the First Amendment. Three years later, in *Griswold v. Connecticut*, the justices struck down a state law that banned the sale of contraceptives because such laws, they contended, infringed on an individual's right to privacy. In a 1966 case the justices ruled that states could not prohibit what they deemed pornographic material unless it was "utterly without redeeming social value," a standard that opened the door for the dissemination of sexually explicit books, magazines, and films. These verdicts unleashed a firestorm of criticism, especially from religious groups that accused the Warren Court of undermining traditional values of faith and decency.

REVIEW & RELATE

What problems and challenges did Johnson's Great Society legislation target?

In what ways did the Warren Court's rulings advance the liberal agenda?

The **Vietnam War,** 1961–1969

While substantial progress was made on civil rights and liberal reforms at home, the Kennedy and Johnson administrations enjoyed far less success in fighting communism abroad. Following the overthrow of French colonial rule in Vietnam in 1954, the Cold War spread to Southeast Asia, where the United States applied the doctrine of containment (see "Early Intervention in Vietnam, 1954–1960" in chapter 24). Mistaking the situation in Vietnam as a war of outside Communist aggression, the United States deployed hundreds of thousands of troops to fight in what was, instead, a civil war.

Kennedy's Intervention in South Vietnam. President Kennedy believed that if Communists toppled one regime in Asia it would produce a "domino effect," with one country after another falling to the Communists. Kennedy, a World War II veteran, also believed that aggressive nations that attacked weaker ones threatened world peace unless they were challenged.

Kennedy's containment efforts in Vietnam ran into difficulty because the United States did not control the situation on the ground. The U.S.-backed president of South Vietnam, Ngo Dinh Diem, had spent more than $1 billion of American aid on building up military and personal security forces to suppress political opposition rather than implement the land reform that he had promised. In 1961 Kennedy sent military advisers to help the South Vietnamese fight the Communists, but the situation deteriorated in 1963 when the Catholic Diem prohibited the country's Buddhist majority from holding religious celebrations. In protest, Buddhist monks committed suicide by setting themselves on fire, a grisly display captured on television news programs in the United States. With political opposition mounting against Diem and with the war going poorly, the Kennedy administration endorsed a military coup to replace the Diem government with one more capable of fighting Communists. On November 1, 1963, the coup leaders removed Diem from office, assassinated the deposed president and key members of his regime, and installed a military government.

Diem's death, however, did little to improve the worsening war against the Communists. The National Liberation Front (Vietcong), Communist political and military forces living in South Vietnam and sponsored by Ho Chi Minh, had more support in the rural countryside than did the South Vietnamese government. The rebels promised land reform and recruited local peasants opposed to the corruption and ruthlessness of the Diem regime. The Kennedy administration committed itself to supporting Diem's successor, but by late November 1963 Kennedy seemed torn between sending more American troops and finding a way to negotiate a peace.

Johnson Escalates the War in Vietnam.

When Lyndon Johnson took office after Kennedy's assassination, there were 16,000 American military advisers in Vietnam. Privately, Johnson harbored reservations about fighting in Vietnam, but he feared appearing soft on communism and was concerned that a demonstration of weakness would jeopardize congressional support for his domestic plans. Although Johnson eventually concluded that more U.S. forces had to be sent to Vietnam, he waited for the right moment to rally Congress and the American public behind an escalation of the war.

That moment came in August 1964. On August 2, North Vietnamese gunboats attacked an American spy ship sixty miles off the North Vietnamese coast in the Gulf of Tonkin. Two days later, another U.S. destroyer reported coming under torpedo attack, but because of stormy weather the second ship was not certain that it had been fired on. Neither ship suffered any damage. Despite the considerable uncertainty about what actually happened with the second ship, Johnson seized the opportunity to urge Congress to authorize military action. On August 7 Congress passed the **Gulf of Tonkin Resolution**, which provided the president with unlimited power to make military decisions regarding Vietnam.

After winning election in 1964, President Johnson stepped up U.S. military action. In March 1965, with North Vietnamese forces flooding into the South, the president initiated a massive bombing campaign called Operation Rolling Thunder. For more than three years, American planes dropped a million tons of bombs on North Vietnam, more than the total amount the United States used in World War II. Despite this massive firepower, the operation proved ineffective. A largely agricultural country, North Vietnam did not have the type of industrial targets best suited for air attacks. It stored its vital military resources underground and was able to reconstruct rudimentary bridges and roads to maintain the flow of troops into the South within hours after U.S. bombers had pounded them.

Responding to the need to protect American air bases and the persistent ineffectiveness of the South Vietnamese military, Johnson deployed ever-increasing numbers of ground troops to Vietnam. Troop levels rose from 16,000 in 1963, to 380,000 in 1966, 485,000 in 1967, and 536,000 in 1968. The U.S. military also deployed napalm bombs, which spewed burning jellied gasoline, and Agent Orange, a chemical that denuded the Vietnamese countryside and produced long-term adverse health effects for those who came in contact with it, including American soldiers. These attacks added to the resentment of South Vietnamese peasants and helped the Vietcong gain new recruits.

The United States confronted a challenging guerrilla war in Vietnam. The Vietcong fought at night and blended in during the day as ordinary residents of cities and villages. They did not provide a visible target, and they recruited women and men of all ages,

My Lai Massacre, 1968   On March 16, 1968, U.S. army soldiers killed hundreds of unarmed civilians—most of them women, children, and the elderly—in the village of My Lai. The soldiers left bodies piled in ditches that ran around the village. The massacre became public in 1969, but only one soldier was convicted by a military tribunal. Ronald S. Haeberle/The LIFE Images Collection/Getty Images

making it difficult for U.S. ground forces to distinguish friend from foe. In the end, the U.S. military effort alienated the population they were designed to safeguard.

On the ground, frustration also bred racism, as many American soldiers could not relate to the Vietnamese way of life and dismissed the enemy as "gooks." This attitude helped push some troops over the line between legitimate warfare and murder. Frustrated by rising casualties from an enemy they could not see, some American soldiers indiscriminately burned down villages and killed noncombatant civilians. Such contemptible behavior peaked in March 1968 when an American platoon murdered between 347 and 504 unarmed Vietnamese civilians in the village of My Lai, an event that came to be known as the My Lai massacre.

The My Lai carnage came in the wake of the **Tet Offensive**. On January 31, 1968, the Buddhist New Year of Tet, some 67,000 Communist forces mounted a surprise offensive throughout South Vietnam that targeted major population centers (Map 26.2). For six hours, a suicide squadron of Vietcong surrounded the U.S. Embassy in Saigon. U.S. forces finally repelled the Tet Offensive, but the battle proved psychologically costly to the United States. Following it, the most revered television news anchor of the era, Walter Cronkite of CBS, turned against the war and expressed the doubts of a growing number of viewers when he announced: "To say that we are mired in stalemate seems the only reasonable, yet unsatisfactory conclusion."

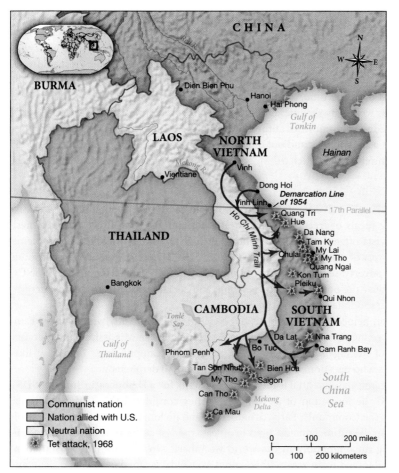

MAP 26.2   The Vietnam War, 1968

The United States wielded vastly more military personnel and weaponry than the Vietcong and North Vietnamese but faced a formidable challenge in fighting a guerrilla war in a foreign country. Massive American bombing failed to defeat the North Vietnamese or stop their troop movements and supply lines along the Ho Chi Minh Trail. The 1968 Tet Offensive demonstrated the shortcomings in the U.S. strategy.

Tet marked the beginning of the end of the war's escalation. On March 31, 1968, President Johnson ordered a halt to the bombing campaign and called for peace negotiations. He also stunned the nation by announcing that he would not seek reelection. By the time Johnson left the White House in 1969, peace negotiations had stalled and some 36,000 Americans had died in combat, along with 52,000 South Vietnamese troops. The escalation of the war had exacted another high price as well: It created a crisis of public confidence in government and turned many ordinary Americans into dissenters against the political establishment.

REVIEW & RELATE

• Why did Kennedy and Johnson escalate the Vietnam War?

• How did the reality of the war on the ground compare with the political and military assumptions for fighting it?

Challenges to the Liberal Establishment

Even at its peak in the 1960s, liberalism faced major challenges from both the left and the right. Young activists became impatient with what they saw as the slow pace of social progress and were increasingly distressed by the escalation of the Vietnam War. At the same time, the right was disturbed by the failure of the United States to win the war as well as by the liberal reforms they believed diminished individual initiative and benefited racial minorities at the expense of the white middle class. Conservatives depicted the left as unpatriotic and out of step with mainstream American values. By 1969 liberalism was in retreat, and Richard M. Nixon, a political conservative, had captured the White House.

The New Left. The civil rights movement had inspired many young people to activism. Combining ideals of freedom, equality, and community with direct-action protest, civil rights activists offered a model for those seeking to address a variety of problems, including the threat of nuclear devastation, the loss of individual autonomy in a corporate society, racism, poverty, sexism, and environmental degradation. The formation of SNCC in 1960 illuminated the possibilities for personal and social transformation and offered a movement culture founded on democracy.

Tom Hayden helped apply the ideals of SNCC to predominantly white college campuses. After spending the summer of 1961 registering voters in Mississippi and Georgia, the University of Michigan graduate student returned to campus eager to recruit like-minded students who questioned America's commitment to democracy.

Hayden became an influential leader of the **Students for a Democratic Society (SDS)**, which advocated the formation of a "New Left." They considered the "Old Left," which revolved around the Communist Party, as autocratic and no longer relevant. "We are people of this generation," SDS proclaimed, "bred in at least modest comfort, housed now in universities, looking uncomfortably to the world we inherit." In its **Port Huron Statement** (1962), SDS condemned mainstream liberal politics, Cold War foreign policy, racism, and research-oriented universities that cared little for their undergraduates. It called for the adoption of "participatory democracy," which would return power to the people. In an ironic twist, the framers of the manifesto picked up the rhetoric of the moderate Republican president, Dwight Eisenhower, in condemning the military-industrial complex (see "Nuclear Weapons and Containment" in chapter 24). "Not only is ours the first generation to live with the possibility of world-wide cataclysm," the statement declared, "it is the first to experience the actual social preparation for cataclysm, the general militarization of American society." The attack on the military-industrial complex and the unrestrained power of the executive branch to conduct foreign and military policy would become a staple of New Left protest.

The New Left, however, never consisted of one central organization; after all, many protesters challenged the very idea of centralized authority. In fact, SDS did not initiate the New Left's most dramatic early protest. In 1964 the University of California at Berkeley banned political activities just outside the main campus entrance in response to CORE protests against racial bias in local hiring. When CORE defied the prohibition, campus police arrested its leader, prompting a massive student uprising. Student activists then formed the **Free Speech Movement (FSM)**, which held rallies in front of the administration building,

The Berkeley Free Speech Movement Mario Savio, a student leader at the University of California at Berkeley and a Freedom Summer volunteer, stands among demonstrators sitting in at Sproul Hall on December 3, 1964, to protest university curbs on free speech. A day earlier, Savio had declared: "There's a time when the operation of the machine becomes so odious . . . you've got to put your bodies upon the gears . . . and you've got to make it stop." AP Photo/ Robert Houston

culminating in a nonviolent, civil rights–style sit-in. When California governor Edmund "Pat" Brown dispatched state and county police to evict the demonstrators, students and faculty joined in protest and forced the university administration to yield to FSM's demands for amnesty and reform. By the end of the decade, hundreds of demonstrations had erupted on campuses throughout the nation.

The Vietnam War accelerated student radicalism, and college campuses provided a strategic setting for antiwar activities. Like most Americans in the mid-1960s, undergraduates had only a dim awareness of U.S. activity in Vietnam. Yet all college men were eligible for the draft once they graduated and lost their student deferment. As more troops were sent to Vietnam, student concern intensified.

Protests escalated in 1966 when President Johnson authorized an additional 250,000-troop buildup in Vietnam. With induction into the military a looming possibility, student protesters launched a variety of campaigns and demonstrations. Others resisted the draft by fleeing to Canada, and still others engaged in various forms of civil disobedience. Most college students, however, were not activists—between 1965 and 1968, only 20 percent of college students attended demonstrations. Nevertheless, the activist minority received extensive media attention and helped raise awareness about the difficulty of waging the Vietnam War abroad and maintaining domestic tranquility at home.

By the end of 1967, as the number of troops in Vietnam approached half a million, protests increased. Antiwar sentiment had spread to faculty, artists, writers, businesspeople, and elected officials. In April Martin Luther King Jr. delivered a powerful antiwar address at Riverside Church in New York City. "The world now demands," King declared, "that we admit that we have been wrong from the beginning of our adventure in Vietnam,

SELECTIVE SERVICE SYSTEM

NOTICE OF CLASSIFICATION

This is to certify that

STEVEN F. LAWSON

(First name)   (Middle initial)   (Last name)

Selective Service No.

| 50 | 22 | 45 | 246 |

1A

is classified in Class_____**1A**_____

until _____
by Local Board unless otherwise
checked below:

☐ by Appeal Board
   vote of _____ to _____
☐ by President

AUG 1 9 1970

(Date of mailing)

V. Dells

(Member, Executive Secretary, or clerk of
local board)

Steven F. Lawson

(Registrant's signature)

SSS Form 110 (Rev. 5-25-67)
(Previous printings are obsolete)
(Approval not required)

(Fold along this line)

Draft Card In 1963 Steven F. Lawson reached the age of eighteen and registered with his draft board, but as a college undergraduate he received a student deferment (II-S). With draft calls climbing due to the escalation of the Vietnam War, Lawson like many others was reclassified to I-A status— "available for military service." When a draft lottery was introduced in 1969, he drew a high number and was not drafted. Courtesy of Steven F. Lawson

that we have been detrimental to the life of the Vietnamese people." As protests spread and the government clamped down on dissenters, some activists substituted armed struggle for nonviolence. SDS split into factions, with the most prominent of them, the Weathermen, going underground and adopting violent tactics.

The Counterculture.

The New Left's challenge to liberal politics attracted many students, and the **counterculture's** rejection of conventional middle-class values of work, sexual restraint, and rationality captivated even more. Cultural rebels emphasized living in the present, seeking immediate gratification, expressing authentic feelings, and reaching a higher consciousness through mind-altering drugs. Despite differences in approach, both the New Left and the counterculture expressed concerns about modern technology, bureaucratization, and the possibility of nuclear annihilation and sought new means of creating political, social, and personal liberation.

Rock 'n' roll became the soundtrack of the counterculture. In 1964 Bob Dylan's song "The Times They Are A-Changin' " became an anthem for youth rebellion. That same year, the Beatles, a British quartet influenced by 1950s black and white rock 'n' rollers, toured the United States and revolutionized popular music. Originally singing melodic compositions of teenage love and angst, the Beatles embraced the counterculture and began writing songs about alienation and politics, flavoring them with the drug-inspired sounds of psychedelic music. Although most of the songs that reached the top ten on the record charts did not undermine traditional values, the music of groups like the Beatles, the Rolling Stones, the Who, the Grateful Dead, Jefferson Airplane, and the Doors spread counterculture messages.

The counterculture viewed the elimination of sexual restrictions as essential for transforming personal and social behavior. The 1960s generation did not invent sexual freedom, but it did a great deal to shatter time-honored moral codes of monogamy, fidelity, and moderation. Promiscuity—casual sex, group sex, extramarital affairs, public nudity—and open-throated vulgarity tested public tolerance. Yet within limits, the broader culture reflected these changes. The Broadway production of the musical *Hair* showed frontal nudity, the movie industry adopted ratings of "X" and "R" that made films with nudity and profane language available to a wider audience, and new television comedy shows featured sketches with risqué content.

With sexual conduct in flux, society had difficulty maintaining the double standard of behavior that privileged men over women. The counterculture gave many women a chance to enjoy sexual pleasure that had long been denied them. The availability of birth control pills for women, introduced in 1960, made much of this sexual freedom possible. Although sexual liberation still carried more risks for women than for men, increased openness in discussing sexuality allowed many women to gain greater control over their bodies and their relationships.

Liberation Movements. The varieties of political protest and cultural dissent emboldened other oppressed groups to emancipate themselves. Women, Latinos, Indians, and gay Americans all launched liberation movements.

Despite passage of the Nineteenth Amendment in 1920, which gave women the right to vote, women did not have equal access to employment, wages, or education or control over reproduction. Nor did they have sufficient political power to remove these obstacles to full equality. Yet by 1960 nearly 40 percent of all women held jobs, and women made up 35 percent of college enrollments. The social movements of the 1960s—civil rights, the New Left, and the counterculture—attracted large numbers of women. Groups like SNCC empowered female staff in community-organizing projects, and women also played central roles in antiwar efforts, leading many to demand their own movement for liberation.

Explore ▶

See Sources 26.2 and 26.3 for statements on Chicano and American Indian protests.

The women's liberation movement also built on efforts of the federal government to address gender discrimination. In 1961 President Kennedy appointed the **Commission on the Status of Women**. The commission's report, *American Women*, issued in 1963, reaffirmed the primary role of women in raising the family but cataloged the inequities women faced in the workplace. In 1963 Congress passed the Equal Pay Act, which required employers to give men and women equal pay for equal work. The following year, the 1964 Civil Rights Act opened up further opportunities when it prohibited sexual bias in employment and created the Equal Employment Opportunity Commission (EEOC).

COMPARATIVE ANALYSIS

Chicano and Native American Freedom Movements

In April 1969, a group of students met at the University of California at Santa Barbara and formed the Movimiento Estudiantil Chicano de Aztlán (MEChA; Chicano Student Movement of Aztlán). MEChA organizers drafted "El Plan de Santa Barbara," excerpted in Document 26.2, which set out their basic philosophy and objectives. The same year, eighty-nine California college students representing a number of different tribes of American Indians seized Alcatraz Island located in San Francisco Bay and presented their grievances, which are excerpted in Source 26.3, to the American government. They claimed that under a Sioux Treaty of 1868, Alcatraz belonged to the Indians.

Source 26.2

Chicano Student Movement of Aztlán, 1969

For decades Mexican people in the United States struggled to realize the "American Dream." And some—a few—have. But the cost, the ultimate cost of assimilation, required turning away from *el barrio* [one's neighborhood] and *la colonia* [one's community]. In the meantime, due to the racist structure of this society, to our essentially different life style, and to the socioeconomic functions assigned to our community by Anglo-American society—as suppliers of cheap labor and a dumping ground for the small-time capitalist entrepreneur—the *barrio* and *colonia* remained exploited, impoverished, and marginal.

As a result, the self-determination of our community is now the only acceptable mandate for social and political action; it is the essence of Chicano commitment. Culturally, the word *Chicano*, in the past a pejorative and class-bound adjective, has now become the root idea of a new cultural identity for our people. It also reveals a growing solidarity and the development of a common social praxis [customary conduct]. The widespread use of the term *Chicano* today signals a rebirth of pride and confidence. *Chicanismo* simply embodies an ancient truth: that man is never closer to his true self as when he is close to his community.

Chicanismo draws its faith and strength from two main sources: from the just struggle of our people and from an objective analysis of our community's strategic needs. We recognize that without a strategic use of education, an education that places value on what we value, we will not realize our destiny. Chicanos recognize the central importance of institutions of higher learning to modern progress, in this case, to the development of our community. But we go further: we believe that higher education must contribute to the information of a complete man who truly values life and freedom.

Source: Carlos Muñoz Jr., *Youth, Identity, Power: The Chicano Movement* (London: Verso, 1989), 191–92.

In 1963 Betty Friedan published a landmark book, *The Feminine Mystique*, which questioned society's prescribed gender roles and raised the consciousness of mostly college-educated women. In *The Feminine Mystique*, she described the post-college isolation and alienation experienced by her female friends who got married and stayed home to care for their children. However, not all women saw themselves reflected in Friedan's book.

The Alcatraz Proclamation, 1969

We, the native Americans, re-claim the land known as Alcatraz Island in the name of all American Indians *by right of discovery*.

We wish to be fair and honorable in our dealings with the Caucasian inhabitants of this land, and hereby offer the following treaty:

We will purchase said Alcatraz Island for 24 dollars ($24) in glass beads and red cloth, a precedent set by the white man's purchase of a similar island about 300 years ago. We know that $24 in trade goods for these 16 acres is more than was paid when Manhattan Island was sold, but we offer that land values have risen over the years. Our offer of $1.24 per acre is greater than the 47 cents per acre the white men are now paying the California Indians for their land. We will give to the inhabitants of this island a portion of that land for their own, to be held in trust by the American Indian Government—for as long as the sun shall rise and the rivers go down to the sea—to be administered by the Bureau of Caucasian Affairs (BC). We will further guide the inhabitants in the proper way of living. We will offer them our religion, our education, our life-ways in order to help them achieve our level of civilization and thus raise them and all their white brothers up from their savage and unhappy state. We offer this treaty in good faith and wish to be fair and honorable in our dealings with the white men.

. . . In the name of all Indians, therefore, we reclaim this island for Indian nations, for all these reasons. We feel this claim is just and proper, and that this land should rightfully be granted to us for as long as the rivers run and the sun shall shine.

Signed, Indians of All Tribes, November 19, 1969, San Francisco, California

Source: Camilla Townsend, ed., *American Indian History: A Documentary Reader* (Malden, MA: Wiley-Blackwell, 2009), 186–88.

Interpret the Evidence

1. Why does MEChA focus on the use of the term *Chicano*, and what does it hope to gain by its usage?
2. Why do the Alcatraz protesters believe they are being fair to the United States?
3. What connections do Chicano and Indian protesters make between cultural awareness and political activism?

Put It in Context

How did the civil rights and black power movements influence other freedom movements?

Many working-class women and those from African American and other minority families had not had the opportunity to attend college or stay home with their children, and younger college women had not yet experienced the burdens of domestic isolation.

Nevertheless, in October 1966, Betty Friedan and like-minded women formed the **National Organization for Women (NOW)**. With Friedan as president, NOW dedicated

Explore ▸

Compare two historians' perspectives on second wave feminism in Sources 26.4 and 26.5.

itself to moving society toward "true equality for all women in America, and toward a fully equal partnership of the sexes." NOW called on the EEOC to enforce women's employment rights more vigorously and favored passage of an Equal Rights Amendment (ERA), paid maternity leave for working women, the establishment of child care centers, and reproductive rights. Although NOW advocated job training programs and assistance for impoverished women, it attracted a mainly middle-class white membership. Some blacks were among its charter members, but most African American women chose to concentrate first on eliminating racial barriers that affected black women and men alike. Some union women also continued to oppose the ERA, and antiabortion advocates wanted to steer clear of NOW's support for reproductive rights.

Young women, black and white, had also faced discrimination, sometimes in unexpected places. Even within the civil rights movement women were not always treated equally, often being assigned clerical duties. Men held a higher status within the antiwar movement because women were not eligible for the draft. Ironically, men's claims of moral advantage justified many of them in seeking sexual favors. "Girls say yes to

The Miss America Pageant Protest, 1968 In fighting for gender equality, the women's movement that emerged in the 1960s challenged all aspects of the male-dominated culture that considered women as sex objects. On September 7, 1968, feminists targeted the Miss America contest in Atlantic City, New Jersey. Protesters believed the pageant degraded women by producing a sex-driven ideal of femininity. An unidentified member of the Women's Liberation Party drops a brassiere, a garment protesters considered an instrument "of female torture," in the trash barrel.

guys who say no," quipped draft-resisting men who sought to put women in their traditional place.

As a result of these experiences, radical women formed their own, mainly local organizations. They created "consciousness-raising" groups that allowed them to share their experiences of oppression in the family, the workplace, the university, and movement organizations. These women's liberationists went beyond NOW's emphasis on legal equality and attacked male domination, or patriarchy, as a crucial source of women's subordination. They criticized the nuclear family and cultural values that glorified women as the object of male sexual desires, and they protested creatively against discrimination. In 1968 radical feminists picketed the popular Miss America contest in Atlantic City, New Jersey, and set up a "Freedom Trash Can" into which they threw undergarments and cosmetics. Radical groups such as the Redstockings condemned all men as oppressors and formed separate female collectives to affirm their identities as women. In contrast, other feminists attempted to build the broadest possible coalition. In 1972 Gloria Steinem, a founder of NOW, established *Ms.* magazine in hope of attracting readers from across the feminist political spectrum. The magazine featured women's art and poetry alongside articles on sisterhood, child rearing, and abortion.

In 1973 feminists won a major battle in the Supreme Court over a woman's right to control reproduction. In **Roe v. Wade**, the high court ruled that states could not prevent a woman from obtaining an abortion in the first three months of pregnancy but could impose some limits in the next two trimesters. In furthering the constitutional right of privacy for women, the justices classified abortion as a private medical issue between a patient and her doctor. This decision marked a victory for a woman's right to choose to terminate her pregnancy, but it also stirred up a fierce reaction from women and men who considered abortion to be the murder of an unborn child.

Latinas joined the feminist movement, often forming their own organizations, but they, like black women, also joined men in struggles for racial equality and advancement. During the 1960s, the size of the Spanish-speaking population in the United States tripled from three million to nine million. Hispanic Americans were a diverse group who hailed from many countries and backgrounds. In the 1950s, Cesar Chavez had emerged as the leader of oppressed Mexican farmworkers in California. In seeking the right to organize a union and gain higher wages and better working conditions, Chavez shared King's nonviolent principles. In 1962 Chavez formed the National Farm Workers Association, and in 1965 the union called a strike against California grape growers, one that attracted national support and finally succeeded after five years.

Younger Mexican Americans, especially those in cities such as Los Angeles and other western *barrios* (ghettos), supported Chavez's economic goals but challenged older political leaders who sought cultural assimilation. Borrowing from the Black Panthers, Mexican Americans formed the Brown Berets, a self-defense organization. In 1969 some 1,500 activists gathered in Denver and declared themselves *Chicanos*, a term that expressed their cultural pride and identity. Chicanos created a new political party, **La Raza Unida (The United Race)**, to promote their interests, and the party and its allies sponsored demonstrations to fight for jobs, bilingual education, and the creation of Chicano studies programs in colleges. Chicano and other Spanish-language communities also took advantage of the protections of the Voting Rights Act, which in 1975 was amended to include sections of the

Native American Power   A group of Native Americans, one named Tim Williams (a chief of the Klamath River Hurek tribe) in full headdress and ceremonial attire, approaches Alcatraz Island located in San Francisco Bay, California. They are part of Native American protests that lasted from November 1969 to June 1971 to reclaim the island and the federal prison it houses from the U.S. government. Ralph Crane/The LIFE Picture Collection/Getty Images.

country—from New York to California to Florida and Texas—where Hispanic literacy in English and voter registration were low.

In similar fashion, Puerto Ricans organized the Young Lords Party (YLP). Originating in Chicago in 1969, the group soon spread to New York City. Like the Black Panthers, the organization established inner-city breakfast programs and medical clinics. The YLP supported bilingual education in public schools, condemned U.S. imperialism, favored independence for Puerto Rico, and supported women's reproductive rights.

American Indians also joined the upsurge of activism and self-determination. By 1970 some 800,000 people identified themselves as American Indians, many of whom lived in poverty on reservations. They suffered from inadequate housing, high alcoholism rates, low life expectancy, staggering unemployment, and lack of education. Conscious of their heritage as the first Americans, they determined to halt their deterioration by asserting "red" pride and established the **American Indian Movement (AIM)** in 1968. The following year, Indians occupied the abandoned prison island of Alcatraz in San Francisco Bay, where they remained until 1971. Among their demands, they offered to buy the island for $24 in beads and cloth—a reference to the purchase of Manhattan Island in 1626—and turn it into an Indian educational and cultural center. In 1972 AIM occupied the headquarters of the Federal Bureau of Indian Affairs in Washington, D.C. AIM demonstrators also seized the village of Wounded Knee, South Dakota, the scene of the 1890 massacre of Sioux residents by the U.S. army, to dramatize the impoverished living conditions on reservations. They held on for more than seventy days with eleven hostages until a shootout with the FBI ended the confrontation, killing one protester and wounding another.

The results of the red power movement proved mixed. Demonstrations focused media attention on the plight of American Indians but did little to halt their downward spiral. Nevertheless, courts became more sensitive to Indian claims and protected mineral and fishing rights on reservations.

Asian American college students on the West Coast fought their own liberation struggle. At the University of California, Berkeley, and San Francisco State University, they participated in demonstrations against the Vietnam War and racism. In 1968 Asian American students at San Francisco State joined the Third World Liberation Front and, along with the Black Student Union, went on strike for five months, succeeding in the establishment of programs in Asian American and Black studies.

The children of newly arrived Chinese immigrants faced different problems, doing poorly in public schools that taught exclusively in English. Established in 1969, the Chinese for Affirmative Action filed a lawsuit against San Francisco school officials for discriminating against students with limited English-language skills. In *Lau v. Nichols* (1974), the Supreme Court upheld the group's claim, accelerating opportunities for bilingual education.

During this period many Japanese American high school and college students learned for the first time about their parents' and grandparents' internment during World War II. Like other activists, they expressed pride in their ethnic heritage and joined in efforts to publicize the injustices that earlier generations had endured. The activism of this third generation of Japanese helped convince the moderate Japanese American Citizens League in 1970 to endorse reparations for the internees, the first step in an ultimately successful two-decade effort.

Unlike African Americans, Chicanos, American Indians, and Asian Americans, homosexuals were not distinguished by the color of their skin. Estimated at 10 percent of the population, gays and lesbians remained largely invisible to the rest of society. In the 1950s, gay men and women created their own political and cultural organizations and frequented bars and taverns outside mainstream commercial culture, but most lesbians and gay men, like Bayard Rustin, hid their identities. It was not until 1969 that they took a major step toward asserting their collective grievances in a very visible fashion. Police regularly cracked down on gay bars like the Stonewall Tavern in New York City's Greenwich Village. But on June 27, 1969, gay patrons battled back. The *Village Voice* called the **Stonewall riots** "a kind of liberation, as the gay brigade emerged from the bars, back rooms, and bedrooms of the Village and became street people." In the manner of black power, the New Left, and radical feminists, homosexuals organized the Gay Liberation Front, voiced pride in being gay, and demanded equality of opportunity regardless of sexual orientation.

As with other oppressed groups, gays achieved victories slowly and unevenly. In the decades following the 1960s, gay men and lesbians faced discrimination in employment, could not marry or receive domestic benefits, and were subject to violence for public displays of affection.

The Revival of Conservatism.
These diverse social movements did a great deal to change the political and cultural landscapes of the United States, but they did not go unchallenged. Many mainstream Americans worried about black militancy, opposed liberalism, and were even more dismayed by the radical offshoots they spawned. Conservatives soon attracted support from many Americans who did not see change as progress. Many believed that the political leadership of the nation did not speak for them about what constituted a great society.

The brand of conservatism that emerged in the 1960s united libertarian support for a laissez-faire political economy with opposition to social welfare policies and moralistic concerns for defeating communism and defending religious devotion, moral decency, and family values. Unlike earlier conservatives, the new generation believed that the United States had to escalate the struggle against the evil of godless communism anywhere it posed a threat in the world, but they opposed internationalism as represented in the United Nations.

Conservative religious activists who built grassroots organizations to combat liberalism joined forces with political and intellectual conservatives such as William F. Buckley, the founder of the *National Review*, an influential journal of conservative ideas. The Reverend Billy Joe Hargis's Christian Crusade and Dr. Frederick Charles Schwartz's Christian Anti-Communist Crusade, both formed in the early 1950s, promoted conspiracy theories about how the eastern liberal establishment intended to sell the country out to the Communists by supporting the United Nations, foreign aid, Social Security, and civil rights. The John Birch Society packaged these ideas in periodicals and radio broadcasts throughout the country and urged readers and listeners to remain vigilant to attacks against their freedom.

In the late 1950s and early 1960s, the conservative revival grew, mostly unnoticed, at the grassroots level in the suburbs of southern California and the Southwest. Bolstered by the postwar economic boom that centered around military research and development, these towns in the Sun Belt attracted college-educated engineers, technicians, managers, and other professionals from the Midwest (or Rust Belt) seeking new economic opportunities. These migrants brought with them Republican loyalties as well as traditional conservative political and moral values. Women played a large part in conservative causes, especially in protesting against public school curricula that they perceived as un-Christian and un-American. Young housewives built an extensive network of conservative study groups.

In addition, the conservative revival, like the New Left, found fertile recruiting ground on college campuses. In October 1960 some ninety young conservatives met at William Buckley's estate in Sharon, Connecticut to draw up a manifesto of their beliefs. "In this time of moral and political crisis," the framers of the Sharon Statement declared, "the foremost among the transcendent values is the individual's use of his God-given free will, whence derives his right to be free from the restrictions of arbitrary force." Based on this essential principle, the manifesto affirmed the conservative doctrines of states' rights, the free market, and anticommunism. Participants at the conference formed the **Young Americans for Freedom (YAF)**, which six months later boasted 27,000 members. In 1962 the YAF filled Madison Square Garden to listen to a speech by the one politician who excited them: Republican senator Barry M. Goldwater of Arizona.

Goldwater's book *The Conscience of a Conservative* (1960) attacked New Deal liberalism and advocated abolishing Social Security; dismantling the Tennessee Valley Authority, the government-owned public power utility; and eliminating the progressive income tax. His firm belief in states' rights put him on record against the ruling in *Brown v. Board of Education* and prompted him to vote against the Civil Rights Act of 1964, positions that won him increasing support from conservative white southerners. However, Goldwater's advocacy of small government did not prevent him from supporting increased military spending to halt the spread of communism. The senator may have anticipated growing concerns about government excess, but his defeat in a landslide to Lyndon Johnson in the 1964 presidential election indicated that most voters perceived Goldwater's brand of conservatism as too extreme.

The election of 1964 also brought George C. Wallace onto the national stage as a leading architect of the conservative revival. As Democratic governor of Alabama, the segregationist Wallace had supported states' rights and opposed federal intervention to reshape social and political affairs. Wallace began to attract white northerners fed up with rising black militancy, forced busing to promote school integration, and open housing laws to desegregate their neighborhoods. Running in the Democratic presidential primaries in 1964, the Alabama governor garnered 34 percent of the votes in Wisconsin, 30 percent in Indiana, and 43 percent in Maryland.

More so than Goldwater, Wallace united a populist message against the political establishment with concern for white working-class Americans. Wallace voters identified with the governor as an "outsider." Many of them also backed Wallace for attacking privileged college students who, he claimed, mocked patriotism, violated sexual taboos, and looked down on hardworking, churchgoing, law-abiding Americans. How could "all those rich kids—from the fancy suburbs," one father wondered, "[avoid the draft] when my son has to go over there and maybe get his head shot off?" Each in his own way, George Wallace and Barry Goldwater waged political campaigns against liberals for undermining the economic freedom of middle- and working-class whites and coddling what they considered "racial extremists" and "countercultural barbarians."

REVIEW & RELATE

How did organizations on the left challenge social, cultural, and economic norms in the 1960s?

What groups were attracted to the 1960s conservative movement? Why?

Race and Class in Second Wave Feminism

The civil rights and black liberation movements helped inspire the re-emergence of feminism in the 1960s and 1970s, but the ongoing relationship between feminism and race-based liberation movements was complicated and often fraught. This was especially true for the women's liberation movement, which in the 1960s was one wing of second wave feminism (the first wave originated in the 19th century and culminated in the adoption of the women's suffrage amendment in 1920). Second wave feminism attracted multiple generations of women that espoused diverse solutions to various forms of sexism. While many scholars highlight the tensions and conflicts between white feminists and women activists of color , they often differ on the degree of antagonism and the extent of common ground.

Source 26.4

Anne Valk, Feminist Interactions, 2008

By the late 1960s a distinct movement to end women's gender-based oppression emerged that was philosophically and strategically tied to, but also separate from, contemporaneous struggles for black liberation. . . . As this predominantly white women's movement evolved to fight for reproductive and sexual freedom, its participants drew on—and reacted to—the ideas and approaches generated within movements . . . [such as] African American liberation. At the same time, participants in campaigns for racial liberation and economic justice responded to arguments and priorities advanced within women's liberation organizations, adopting and adapting some while rejecting others. . . . But . . . women of color . . . resisted the notion of a universal sisterhood and contended that no single approach could guarantee the liberation of all women, . . . Black feminism also challenged white feminists and proponents of racial liberation to understand the intersectional nature of racism, sexism, and class oppression.

. . . . Although acknowledging the important influence that the civil rights, student, and anti-war movements played on the emergence of second-wave feminism, [early] studies have typically treated the histories of these movements separately. As a result, much of this scholarship has obscured the continuous and fruitful interactions that occurred even when each movement declared its independence from the others. . . . Many recent studies, however, have focused on African American's women's activism for racial and sexual liberation, thereby challenging the view that feminism was exclusively a white women's movement; yet even this scholarship treats black and white women's activities as largely separate and generally antagonistic. . . . [T]his book acknowledges the divisions that occurred between various movements and groups, but still aims to understand the cross-fertilization of ideas that took place. . . . [It] includes both women who explicitly identified themselves as feminists and . . . those who fought to elevate women's status in their own communities and in the larger society through movements for economic justice and black liberation.

Source: Anne Valk, *Radical Sisters: Second-Wave Feminism and Black Liberation in Washington, D.C.* (Urbana: University of Illinois Press, 2008), 3, 4–5.

Source 26.5

Linda Gordon, Race, Class, and Feminism, 2014

One fissure within women's liberation . . . was never bridged; its dominant white and middle-class composition gave rise to accusations of racism and privilege directed at it. The confidence, the articulateness, even the vocabularies of the college-educated women who dominated many feminist groups in the 1970s often functioned to silence working-class women. . . . Sisterhood talk and a one size-fits-all feminist program were harmless; in reflecting the class and race upbringings and cultures of those who dominated the movement, middle-class women built walls around themselves. Despite their best intentions and despite their conscious opposition to racism, their priorities and assumptions sometimes blinded them to the situation of women of color and poorer women. . . . Middle-class whites did not take sufficiently into account the situation of women who experienced racism, low wages, ill health, and dangerous neighborhoods. Those poor and working-class women, in turn, frequently felt that the women's liberation movement did not represent them—even though many of them were feminist in the generic sense that they recognized women as disadvantaged.

Source: Linda Gordon, "The Women's Liberation Movement," in *Feminism Unfinished: A Short, Surprising History of American Women's Movements*, by Dorothy Sue Cobble, Linda Gordon, and Astrid Henry (New York: Liveright Publishing Corporation, 2014), 92–3.

Examine the Sources

1. Where do Valk and Gordon agree and differ in their understandings of the relations between white women and women of color in second wave feminism and women's liberation?

2. Drawing upon evidence in this chapter, how would you evaluate the strengths and weaknesses of Valk's and Gordon's interpretations?

Put It in Context

How did racial and gender differences shape the New Left and the distinct liberation movements that emerged in the 1960s and 1970s?

Conclusion: Liberalism and Its **Discontents**

The presidencies of John Kennedy and Lyndon Johnson marked the high point of liberal reform as well as Cold War military intervention. Kennedy's New Frontier and Johnson's Great Society expanded the power of the national state to provide both compassionate government and bureaucratic regulation. Liberalism permitted greater freedom for racial, ethnic, and sexual minorities; expanded educational opportunities for the disadvantaged; reduced poverty; extended health care for the elderly; and began to clean up the environment. However, these expensive programs drew opposition from conservatives who saw big government as a threat to fiscal responsibility and individual liberty. Kennedy and Johnson's escalation of the Vietnam War fractured the liberal consensus of the 1960s and overshadowed their domestic accomplishments.

Kennedy and Johnson did not achieve their liberal agenda by themselves. The civil rights movement, with activists like Bayard Rustin, forced the federal government into action. In addition, Earl Warren's Supreme Court affirmed the constitutionality of major pieces of reform legislation and charted a new course for expanding the guarantees of the Bill of Rights.

Although the Vietnam War tarnished liberalism, the struggles of African Americans, Asian Americans, women, Chicanos, Indians, and gays continued. Indeed, the civil rights movement spurred other exploited groups to seek greater freedom, and they flourished in the late 1960s and early 1970s despite the waning of liberalism.

Liberalism began to unravel during the 1960s as its policies and programs prompted powerful attacks from radicals and conservatives alike. Indeed, over the next twenty-five years conservatives mobilized the American electorate and gained power by attacking liberal political, economic, and cultural values.

TIMELINE OF **EVENTS**

1960	Young Americans for Freedom founded
1961	Kennedy sends military advisers to South Vietnam
	Bay of Pigs invasion
	Freedom Rides
	Soviets build Berlin Wall
1962	Port Huron Statement
	Cuban missile crisis
1963–1968	U.S. troops in Vietnam rise from 16,000 to 536,000
1963	Betty Friedan publishes *The Feminine Mystique*
	Partial Nuclear Test Ban Treaty
	March on Washington for Jobs and Freedom
	John F. Kennedy assassinated; Lyndon B. Johnson becomes president
1964–1966	Great Society domestic programs enacted
1964	Civil Rights Act of 1964
	Freedom Summer
	Gulf of Tonkin Resolution
1965	Operation Rolling Thunder begins
	Voting Rights Act
1966	Black Panther Party formed
	National Organization for Women (NOW) formed
1968	American Indian Movement (AIM) founded
	Martin Luther King Jr. assassinated
	Tet Offensive begins
1969	Stonewall Riots
1973	*Roe v. Wade* Supreme Court decision

KEY **TERMS**

New Frontier, *887*

Freedom Rides, *891*

March on Washington for Jobs and Freedom, *892*

Civil Rights Act of 1964, *892*

Freedom Summer, *893*

Mississippi Freedom Democratic Party (MFDP), *894*

Voting Rights Act, *894*

Black Panther Party, *896*

Great Society, *898*

Gulf of Tonkin Resolution, *901*

Tet Offensive, *902*

Students for a Democratic Society (SDS), *904*

Port Huron Statement, *904*

Free Speech Movement (FSM), *904*

counterculture, *906*

Commission on the Status of Women, *907*

National Organization for Women (NOW), *909*

Roe v. Wade, *909*

La Raza Unida (The United Race), *910*

American Indian Movement (AIM), *912*

Stonewall riots, *913*

Young Americans for Freedom (YAF), *915*

REVIEW & RELATE

1. How did President Kennedy's domestic agenda reflect the liberal political ideology of the early 1960s?

2. Evaluate Kennedy's and Khrushchev's actions in the Cuban Missile Crisis. How was war averted?

3. How did civil rights activists pressure state and federal government officials to enact their agenda?

4. How were the civil rights and black power movements similar and in what ways were they different?

5. What problems and challenges did Johnson's Great Society legislation target?

6. In what ways did the Warren Court's rulings advance the liberal agenda?

7. Why did Kennedy and Johnson escalate the Vietnam War?

8. How did the reality of the war on the ground compare with the political and military assumptions for fighting it?

9. How did organizations on the left challenge social, cultural, and economic norms in the 1960s?

10. What groups were attracted to the 1960s conservative movement? Why?

Freedom Summer

▶ Explain the aims of civil rights workers in Mississippi in 1964 and evaluate the extent to which they achieved them.

n June 1964 white college students gathered at the Western College for Women in Oxford, Ohio to train for a massive voter registration project in Mississippi (Source 26.6). Freedom Summer, as it was called, was organized by the Student Nonviolent Coordinating Committee, the Congress of Racial Equality, the National Association for the Advancement of Colored People, and the Southern Christian Leadership Conference. Working under an umbrella organization, the Congress of Federated Organizations (COFO), the project focused on political rights, particularly the right to vote. COFO set up freedom schools, which taught voter literacy, organizing techniques, and basic reading and writing skills (Source 26.7). The decision to use white volunteers was a deliberate one to put more activists on the ground and, more important, draw national attention to the cause. The activities of Freedom Summer volunteers provoked violence and resistance (Source 26.8). Perhaps the most well-known acts of violence were the murders of three civil rights workers: James Chaney, a local black activist; and Michael Schwerner and Andrew Goodman, two northern whites.

Also, black activists formed the interracial Mississippi Freedom Democratic Party (MFDP), which sent its own delegates to the Democratic National Convention in Atlantic City, New Jersey and sought official recognition by the convention to replace the all-white delegation (Source 26.9). Offered a compromise, the MFDP refused it and returned home but supported Lyndon Johnson's election (Source 26.10).

Although few black Mississippians successfully registered to vote and the MFDP was denied official recognition at the Democratic National Convention, Freedom Summer did publicize the plight of black communities in Mississippi and throughout the South, and this publicity contributed to the passage of the Voting Rights Act of 1965.

Source 26.6

Prospectus for Mississippi Freedom Summer, 1964

Civil rights organizers carefully prepared for Freedom Summer, knowing that such a large campaign against intransigent disfranchisement in Mississippi would require extensive planning and coordination. The following selection is from an internal document of the Student Nonviolent Coordinating Committee that summarizes the purpose and strategies of Freedom Summer. It highlights the goals of voter registration and freedom schools.

t has become evident to the civil rights groups involved in the struggle for freedom in Mississippi that political and social justice cannot be won without the massive aid of the country as a whole, backed by the power and authority of the federal government. Little hope exists that the political leaders of Mississippi will steer even a moderate course in the near future . . . ; in fact, the contrary seems true: as the winds of change grow stronger, the threatened political elite of Mississippi becomes more intransigent and fanatical in its support of the status quo.

. . . A program is planned for this summer which will involve the massive participation of Americans dedicated to the elimination of racial oppression. Scores of college students, law students, medical students, teachers, professors, ministers, technicians, folk artists, and lawyers from all over the country have already volunteered to work in Mississippi this summer—and hundreds more are being recruited. . . .

Why this summer?

Mississippi at this juncture in the movement has received too little attention—that is, attention to what the state's attitude really is. . . . Either the civil rights struggle has to continue, as it has for the past few years, with small projects in selected communities with no real progress on any fronts, or [there must be a] task force of such a size as to force either the state and the municipal governments to change their social and legal structures, or the Federal Government to intervene on behalf of the constitutional rights of its citizens.

Since 1964 is an election year, the clear-cut issue of voting rights should be brought out in the open. Many SNCC and CORE workers in Mississippi hold the view that Negroes will never vote in large numbers until Federal marshals intervene. . . . [M]any Americans must be made to realize that the voting rights they so often take for granted involve considerable risk for Negroes in the South. . . . Major victories in Mississippi, recognized as the stronghold of racial intolerance in the South, would speed immeasurably the breaking down of legal and social discrimination in both North and South. . . .

Direction of the Project: . . .

Voter Registration: This will be the most concentrated level of activity. Voter registration workers will be involved in an intensive summer drive to encourage as many Negroes as possible to register. . . . Finally, registration workers will assist in the campaigns of Freedom candidates who are expected to run for seats in all five of the State's congressional districts and for the seat of Senator John Stennis, who is up for re-election.

Freedom Schools:

1. *General Description.* About 25 Freedom Schools are planned, of two varieties: day schools in about 20–25 towns (commitments still pending in some communities) and one or two boarding, or residential, schools on college campuses. Although the local communities can provide school buildings, some furnishings, and staff housing (and, for residential schools, student housing), all equipment, supplies, and staff will have to come from outside. . . . In the schools, the typical day will be hard study in the morning, an afternoon break (because it's too hot for an academic program), and less formal evening activities.

Source: Prospectus for the Mississippi Freedom Summer, Miller (Michael J.) Civil Rights Collection, McCain Library and Archives, University of Southern Mississippi.

Source 26.7

Nancy Ellin | Letter Describing Freedom Summer, 1964

Setting up freedom schools throughout Mississippi was a key project of Freedom Summer. The schools in Hattiesburg were staffed by many northern white volunteers, including Nancy and Joseph Ellin. Both originally from New York City, Nancy and Joseph met at Yale University. The following selection is from a letter written by Nancy to Joseph's parents shortly after Nancy and Joseph arrived in Mississippi.

June 30

Dear Dr. and Mrs. Ellin,

. . . We got here OK, though we were frightened most of the way, quite unnecessarily. It was the people who came down in integrated cars who had the unpleasant time—refused service, cars following them, etc. We came down with a very nice girl who just graduated from Smith [College] and who did quite a bit of driving.

We are currently hard at work getting the Freedom Schools organized. Joe and another boy have everyone typing up stencils of the Constitution, the Declaration of Independence, etc. The school enrollment is over 150; we are having official registration Thursday. The philosophy is to take everyone who comes; we will be teaching adults in the evening. There are 10 teachers, 8 more expected from New York City on Thursday. We also intend to recruit a few local people.

. . . We felt terrible about causing you all such anguish, but we felt the decision was ours to make, and though we were very afraid and doubtful at Oxford [in Ohio], we made the decision to come. You must know that you were not the only parents who were worried, and some kids did drop out, one from our group, in fact, who was underage and couldn't get his parents' consent. Now that we are here we feel more than ever that coming here was the right thing to do. Even if we don't teach a single child (and I think the odds are heavily against that) we still will have accomplished something in showing the people of Hattiesburg that they should not hate whites. Even our own group leaders, Carolyn and Arthur Reese, who are Detroit Negroes (schoolteachers), were very anti-white until Oxford, Ohio. Things here are pretty horrible. The Negro section, where we are, smells and looks more than a little like India. The house we are staying in (free) is pretty good-sized but very dilapidated—creaky floors, etc. It has a bathroom— some don't. Our landlady is registered; her husband has tried but hasn't made it yet. Everyone agrees that things here would be much worse right this minute if it weren't for our presence and the pressure exerted on the [government] on our behalf by our rich Northern parents. Negroes in the movement tend to lose their jobs. We feel—rightly or wrongly—that our place is here, in the heart of the struggle. No man is an island. . . .

. . . Another job we have before us is organizing the library—there are tremendous quantities of books. We haven't had much contact yet, aside from smiles and handshakes, with the regular Negro community, so I haven't much else to report. The leaders we have met are terrific.

Thank Mary and everyone for praying for us.

Love,
Nancy

Source: Letter from Joseph and Nancy Ellin to Dr. and Mrs. Ellin, Joseph and Nancy Ellin Freedom Summer Collection, McCain Library and Archives, University of Southern Mississippi.

White Southerners Respond to Freedom Summer, 1964

As Freedom Summer activists began arriving in Mississippi, newspapers throughout the South ran editorials and articles condemning the volunteers. The following article appeared in a South Carolina newspaper and is representative of the ways in which white southerners characterized Freedom Summer. It mentions the National Council of Churches, a federation of white and black Christian churches that supported many civil rights and peace causes in the postwar era, including Freedom Summer.

This week the vanguard of a youthful army left the rolling hill country of southwestern Ohio, where volunteers had spent several weeks being indoctrinated and incensed, for the flat Delta land of Mississippi. The Summer Project, a joint effort of the Student Non-Violent Coordinating Committee (SNICK) and the National Council of Churches, was on the march. . . .

"The real aim of SNICK and the other more extreme Negro organizations is to secure the military occupation of Mississippi by federal troops." This is not the expressed judgment of Mississippi Governor Paul Johnson or even of Senator James Eastland. The words are those of Joseph Alsop, the liberal columnist. Mr. Alsop, however much he may desire civil rights for Negroes, knows that no good can come from this Summer Project, controlled as it is by the most militant of the many civil rights groups and the one whose ranks include, according to Mr. Alsop, more than a few dedicated Communists.

. . . The crusade leaders say publicly that the main thrust of the summer invasion will be directed at voter discrimination in Mississippi, where only 6.6 percent of Negroes of voting age are registered to vote. Such an effort, conducted with forbearance and directed at helping the Negro improve himself, might produce some good. Judging by the record, however,

SNICK is short on forbearance and uncommonly long on making trouble. Nor is the National Council of Churches likely to provide much in the way of restraint.

"The main problem at this point," [according to the Council,] "is the concentration of wealth among the few, e.g., on an average, 5 percent of the farms control 50 percent of all the farmland."

Voting? This has nothing to do with voting. The Council is speaking of agrarian reform of the sort that socialists promote.

From this, the goals of the Summer Project appear to be two-fold: first, indoctrination in socialist economics; second, military occupation of Mississippi if that can be arranged. This is no longer a struggle of black and white. If the reports of even the most liberal observers are to be believed, the Reds predominate and the nation can anticipate a long, hot summer indeed.

Source: "'Freedom' to the Delta," *Charleston Post*, June 24, 1964.

Source 26.9

Fannie Lou Hamer | Address to the Democratic National Convention Credentials Committee, 1964

At the 1964 Democratic National Convention, Mississippi Freedom Democratic Party (MFDP) members attempted to unseat the official all-white Mississippi delegation. Fannie Lou Hamer testified before the credentials committee in front of a national television audience, but that coverage ended when President Johnson quickly held a press conference to divert attention from the controversy. In the following selection, Hamer tells of her arrest in Winona, Mississippi as she traveled home from a voter registration workshop.

I was carried to the county jail and put in the booking room. They left some of the people in the booking room and began to place us in cells.

And it wasn't too long before three white men came to my cell. One of these men was a state highway patrolman and he asked me where I was from. And I told him Ruleville. He said, "We are going to check this." And they left my cell and it wasn't too long before they came back. He said, "You's from Ruleville all right," and he used a curse word. And he said, "We are going to make you wish you was dead."

I was carried out of that cell into another cell where they had two Negro prisoners. The state highway patrolmen ordered the first Negro to take the blackjack [police baton]. The first Negro prisoner ordered me, by orders from the state highway patrolman, for me to lay down on a bunk bed on my face.

And I laid on my face and the first Negro began to beat. And I was beat by the first Negro until he was exhausted. I was holding my hands behind me at that time on my left side, because I suffered from polio when I was six years old. After the first Negro had beat until he was exhausted, the state highway patrolman ordered the second Negro to take the blackjack. The second Negro began to beat and I began to work my feet, and the state highway patrolman ordered the first Negro [who] had beat me to sit on my feet—to keep me from working my feet. I began to scream and one white man got up and began to beat me in my head and tell me to hush.

One white man—my dress had worked up high—he walked over and pulled my dress, I pulled my dress down, and he pulled my dress back up.

. . . All of this is on account of we want to register, to become first-class citizens. And if the Freedom Democratic Party is not seated now, I question America. Is this America, the land of the free and the home of the brave, where we have to sleep with our telephones off of the hooks because our lives be threatened daily, because we want to live as decent human beings, in America? Thank you.

Source: Megan Parker Brooks and David W. Houck, eds., *The Speeches of Fannie Lou Hamer: To Tell It Like It Is* (Jackson: University Press of Mississippi, 2011), 44–45.

Lyndon B. Johnson | Monitoring the MFDP Challenge, 1964

To maintain party unity and white southern support, President Johnson instructed Senator Hubert Humphrey of Minnesota, a respected liberal, to work out a compromise over the MFDP challenge. In this telephone conversation on August 9, 1964 with Walter Reuther, the head of the United Auto Workers and a power broker at the convention, an irritated Johnson explains his reasoning for working out a deal.

JOHNSON If you and Hubert Humphrey have got any leadership, you'd get Joe Rauh [MFDP lawyer] off that damn television. The only thing that can really screw us good is to seat that group of challengers from Mississippi. . . . He said he's going to take it to the convention floor. Now there's not a damn vote that we get by seating these folks. What we want to do is elect some Congressmen to keep 'em from repealing this [1964 Civil Rights] act. And who's seated at this convention don't amount to a damn. Only reason I would let Mississippi [all-white delegation] come in is because I don't want to run off fourteen border states, like Oklahoma and Kentucky. . . . Incidentally this Governor [Mississippi governor Paul Johnson] has done everything I've asked him to do in Mississippi. We've broken that case [the Chaney, Schwerner, and Goodman murders]. I talk to him two or three times a week. Now he's not for [me]. But I can't say that he hasn't listened to us and he hasn't cooperated.

REUTHER Exactly. . . . We'll lose Mississippi, but the impact on the other Southern states—

JOHNSON That's all I'm worried about. . . . I've got to carry Georgia. . . . I've got to carry Texas. . . . We don't want to cut off our nose to spite our face. If they give us four years, I'll guarantee the Freedom delegation somebody representing views like that will be seated four years from now. But we can't do it all before breakfast.

Source: Michael R. Beschloss, ed., *Taking Charge: The Johnson White House Tapes, 1963–1964* (New York: Simon and Schuster, 1997), 510–11.

Interpret the Evidence

1. Describe the role white volunteers played in the Freedom Summer project (Source 26.7) and explain the advantages and disadvantages they brought to Mississippi.

2. Examine the arguments the *Charleston Post* (Source 26.8) made to discredit Freedom Summer. Compare these arguments to the goals for the project as expressed in the Freedom Summer Prospectus (Source 26.6).

3. Evaluate the testimony of Fannie Lou Hamer (Source 26.9) as a means to gain support for the Mississippi Freedom Democratic Party.

4. Explain President Johnson's views toward seating the MFDP delegation (Source 26.10) and evaluate whether they were consistent with his vision of the Great Society.

Put It in Context

Evaluate the successes and failures of Freedom Summer.

The Swing toward Conservatism

1968–1980

WINDOW TO THE PAST

Phyllis Schlafly, "What's Wrong with 'Equal Rights' for Women?" 1972

The conservative writer and political organizer Phyllis Schlafly spoke out forcefully against the women's liberation movement and its supposedly antifamily values. Believing that American women were happy and fulfilled raising families, she used her *Report* to rally readers against the Equal Rights Amendment and other aspects of feminism. ▸ To discover more about what this primary source can show us, see Source 27.7 on page 955.

The Phyllis Schlafly Report

VOL. 5, NO. 7   Box 618, ALTON, ILLINOIS 62002   FEBRUARY, 1972

What's Wrong With "Equal Rights" for Women?

After reading this chapter you should be able to:

- Compare how President Nixon handled the Vietnam War and the Cold War.

- Evaluate the extent to which President Nixon shaped conservatism and the forces that led to his downfall.

- Evaluate President Carter's successes and failures in domestic and foreign politics.

- Explain how liberal activists addressed the issues of clean energy, equal rights for women, racial equality, and nuclear proliferation in the 1970s.

- Explain the rise of the New Right and compare it to Richard Nixon's approach to conservatism.

COMPARING AMERICAN HISTORIES

For many years Allan Bakke wanted to become a physician, but his life took many detours before he tried to accomplish his ambition. Born in Minnesota in 1940, Bakke grew up in a white middle-class family, earned a degree in mechanical engineering, and served in Vietnam. When his tour of duty was over, Bakke returned home and began working as an engineer in Sunnydale, California.

Finally in 1972 Bakke applied to two California medical schools and was turned down, probably because at age thirty-two he was considered too old. The next year, he applied to twelve schools but was rejected by all of them, including the University of

(left) **Allan Bakke**. © Bettmann/Getty Images
(right) **Louise Day Hicks** AP Photo

California at Davis. Bakke learned that of the one hundred available spaces in the incoming class, the university awarded sixteen spots to minorities, as part of its affirmative action policy to recruit a more racially and ethnically diverse student body. Contending that the policy amounted to reverse discrimination, he sued the University of California at Davis for violating his constitutional rights of equal protection under the Fourteenth Amendment. He provided evidence that he had higher qualifications than some of the minority students accepted into the medical school. "I realize that the rationale for these quotas is that they attempt to atone for past racial discrimination," Bakke complained. "But insisting on a new racial bias in favor of minorities is not a just situation." In 1978, in *Regents of the University of California v. Bakke*, the U.S. Supreme Court ruled in his favor, and Bakke successfully completed his studies and graduated with a medical degree.

Like Allan Bakke, Louise Day Hicks fought against liberal notions of racial justice, thereby rallying support for conservatism. In contrast to Bakke, however, she waged a noisy and divisive campaign for her principles. Born in 1916, Louise Day grew up in a relatively comfortable Irish Catholic home in South Boston. The daughter of a prominent judge, Hicks never moved far away from her working-class Irish community. Yet she crossed boundaries that most women of her age and neighborhood did not reach. After marrying John Hicks in 1942 and having children, she graduated from Boston University Law School in 1955, one of only nine women enrolled in her class of 232.

In 1961, Hicks entered the political arena, winning election to the Boston School Committee as "the only mother on the ballot." She became identified with the cause that would define her public career: opposition to school desegregation. Unlike the South, the North did not decree racial segregation by law, but segregation existed in schools because of public policies that reinforced housing segregation and kept blacks from moving into white ethnic neighborhoods. Nevertheless, Hicks refused to acknowledge the existence of this kind of segregation and lashed out at "racial agitators" and "pseudo-liberals."

In the late 1960s and 1970s, she rode to higher office on the white backlash to racial integration, first as a congresswoman and then as president of the Boston City Council. When a federal judge ordered busing to desegregate city schools in 1974, Hicks founded Restore Our Alienated Rights (ROAR). The group's protests created a good deal of havoc but failed to stop the court ruling. Though all this, Hicks remained a Democrat, but many of her white, working-class supporters in Boston and elsewhere joined the growing conservative coalition shaping the Republican Party. ◼

The American histories of Allan Bakke and Louise Day Hicks reveal the profound political importance of ordinary Americans in the larger context of the rise of conservatism in the late 1960s and 1970s. Elected in 1968 in the conservative backlash to radical dissent, Richard Nixon ended the war in Vietnam and withdrew from the war on poverty. The rise of conservatism did not eliminate the impact of liberal achievements from the 1960s, and the Watergate scandal briefly interrupted conservative success. However, New Right conservatism continued to grow throughout the 1970s by meshing the traditional economic conservatism of lower taxes, deregulation, and anti-unionism with the concerns of religious conservatives over family values and the racial resentments of white voters.

Nixon: War and Diplomacy, 1969–1974

In winning the presidency in 1968, Richard Nixon paid close attention to international affairs. Having pledged to end the war in Vietnam, it took him another four years to do so. Nixon was a fierce anti-Communist, but he considered himself a realist in foreign affairs. He was concerned more with a stable world order than with promoting American ideals. Nixon and Secretary of State Henry Kissinger worked to establish closer relations with both the People's Republic of China and the Soviet Union. While the Soviet Union and China competed for influence in Asia, Nixon exploited this conflict to keep these nuclear powers divided. His administration succeeded in bringing a thaw in Cold War relations, but he was less successful in navigating Arab-Israeli hostilities in the Middle East, a misstep that caused pain for consumers of gasoline and oil at home.

The Election of 1968.

1968 was a turbulent year. In February, police shot indiscriminately into a crowd gathered for civil rights protests at South Carolina State University in Orangeburg, killing three students. In March, student protests at Columbia University led to a violent confrontation with the New York City police. On April 4, the murder of Martin Luther King Jr. sparked an outburst of rioting by blacks in more than one hundred cities throughout the country. The assassination of Democratic presidential aspirant Robert Kennedy in June further heightened the mood of despair. Adding to the unrest, demonstrators gathered in Chicago in August at the Democratic National Convention to press for an antiwar plank in the party platform. Thousands of protesters were beaten and arrested by Chicago police officers. Many Americans watched in horror as television networks broadcast the bloody clashes, but a majority of viewers sided with the police rather than the protesters.

Similar protests occurred around the world. In early 1968, university students outside Paris protested educational policies and what they perceived as their second-class status. When students at the Sorbonne in Paris joined them in the streets, police attacked them viciously. In June, French president Charles de Gaulle sent in tanks to break up the strikes but also instituted political and economic reforms. Protests also erupted during the spring in Prague, Czechoslovakia, where President Alexander Dubček vowed to reform the Communist regime by initiating "socialism with a human face." In August the Soviet Union sent its military into Prague to crush the reforms, bringing this brief experiment in freedom remembered as the "Prague Spring" to a violent end. During the same year, student-led demonstrations erupted in Yugoslavia, Poland, West Germany, Italy, Spain, Japan, and Mexico.

It was against this backdrop of global unrest that Richard Nixon ran for president against the Democratic nominee Hubert H. Humphrey and the independent candidate, George C. Wallace, the segregationist governor of Alabama and a popular archconservative. To outflank Wallace on the right, Nixon declared himself the "law and order" candidate, a phrase that became a code for reining in black militancy. To win southern supporters, he pledged to ease up on enforcing federal civil rights legislation and oppose forced busing to achieve racial integration in schools. He criticized antiwar protesters and promised to end the Vietnam War with honor. Seeking to portray the Democrats as the party of

Explore ▶

See Source 27.1 for a
statement by Richard Nixon
on his conservative agenda.

social and cultural radicalism, Nixon geared his campaign message to the "silent majority" of voters — what one political analyst characterized as "the unyoung, the unpoor, and unblack." This conservative message appealed to many Americans who were fed up with domestic uprisings and war abroad.

Although Nixon won 301 electoral votes, 110 more than Humphrey, none of the three candidates received a majority of the popular vote (see Map 27.1, page 930). Yet Nixon and Wallace together garnered about 57 percent of the popular vote, a dramatic shift to the right compared with Lyndon Johnson's landslide victory just four years earlier. The New Left had given way to an assortment of old and new conservatives, overwhelmingly white, who were determined to contain, if not roll back, the Great Society.

The Failure of Vietnamization.
Vietnam plagued Nixon as it had his Democratic predecessor. Despite intimations during the campaign that he had a secret plan to end the war, Nixon's approach to Vietnam turned out to look much the same as Johnson's. Henry Kissinger, who served first as national security adviser and then as secretary of state, continued peace talks with the North Vietnamese, which had been initiated by Johnson. Over the next four years, Nixon and Kissinger devised a strategy that removed U.S. ground forces and turned over greater responsibility for the fighting to the South Vietnamese army, a process called **Vietnamization**.

Vietnamization did not mean an end to U.S. belligerence in the region, however. In 1969, at the same time that American troop levels were being drawn down, the president ordered secret bombing raids in Cambodia, a neutral country adjacent to South Vietnam that contained enemy forces and parts of the Ho Chi Minh Trail. Meant to pressure the North Vietnamese into accepting U.S. peace terms, the bombing accomplished little. In April 1970

Richard Nixon | Speech Accepting the Republican Nomination for President, August 8, 1968

After a decade of upheaval, the 1968 Republican candidate Richard Nixon, as the following passage from his address at the Republican National Convention shows, appealed to conservatives by supporting their demands for a smaller federal government, maintaining law and order, and cutting expenditures for social welfare programs.

Source 27.1

[T]o those who say that law and order is the code word for racism, there and here is a reply:

Our goal is justice for every American. If we are to have respect for law in America, we must have laws that deserve respect.

Just as we cannot have progress without order, we cannot have order without progress, and so, as we commit to order tonight, let us commit to progress.

How does Nixon reply to the claim that "law and order" is a code term for racism?

And this brings me to the clearest choice among the great issues of this campaign.

For the past five years we have been deluged by government programs for the unemployed; programs for the cities; programs for the poor. And we have reaped from these programs an ugly harvest of frustration, violence and failure across the land.

According to Nixon, what is the source of the nation's economic and social problems?

And now our opponents will be offering more of the same—more billions for government jobs, government housing, government welfare.

I say it is time to quit pouring billions of dollars into programs that have failed in the United States of America. . . .

But for those who are able to help themselves—what we need are not more millions on welfare rolls—but more millions on payrolls in the United States of America.

Instead of government jobs, and government housing, and government welfare, let government use its tax and credit policies to enlist in this battle the greatest engine of progress ever developed in the history of man—American private enterprise.

Let us enlist in this great cause the millions of Americans in volunteer organizations who will bring a dedication to this task that no amount of money could ever buy. . . .

Black Americans, no more than white Americans, they do not want more government programs which perpetuate dependency.

They don't want to be a colony in a nation.

They want the pride, and the self-respect, and the dignity that can only come if they have an equal chance to own their own homes, to own their own businesses, to be managers and executives as well as workers, to have a piece of the action in the exciting ventures of private enterprise.

How does Nixon view African Americans?

Source: Richard M. Nixon, "Address Accepting the Presidential Nomination at the Republican National Convention in Miami Beach, Florida," August 8, 1968, in John T. Woolley & Gerhard Peters, *The American Presidency Project*, http://www.presidency.ucsb.edu/ws/?pid=25968.

Put It in Context

How does Nixon's speech reflect conservative ideology?

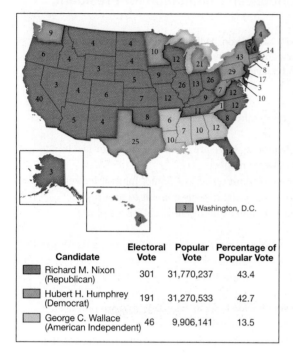

MAP 27.1   The Election of 1968

Democratic presidential candidate Hubert Humphrey lost across the South as white voters turned to Republican Richard Nixon or segregationist George Wallace. Many working-class whites in the North and West also shifted their allegiance to these "law and order" candidates, rejecting the civil rights and antipoverty agendas promoted by President Johnson and blaming Democrats for the turmoil over the Vietnam War.

Candidate	Electoral Vote	Popular Vote	Percentage of Popular Vote
Richard M. Nixon (Republican)	301	31,770,237	43.4
Hubert H. Humphrey (Democrat)	191	31,270,533	42.7
George C. Wallace (American Independent)	46	9,906,141	13.5

Nixon ordered the invasion of Cambodia, which destabilized the country and eventually brought to power the Communist organization Khmer Rouge, which later slaughtered two million Cambodians. In 1971 the United States sponsored the South Vietnamese invasion of Laos, a neighboring country that harbored North Vietnamese troops and supply lines, which again yielded no battlefield gains. Finally, in December 1972, shortly before Christmas, the United States carried out a massive eleven-day bombing campaign of targets in North Vietnam meant to force the North Vietnamese government to come to a peace accord.

The intense bombing of North Vietnam did end formal U.S. involvement in the war. An agreement signed on January 27, 1973 stipulated that the United States would remove all American troops, the North Vietnamese would return captured U.S. soldiers, and North and South Vietnam would strive for peaceful national unification. Despite this agreement, peace had not been achieved. The war in Vietnam continued, and in 1975 North Vietnamese and Vietcong forces captured Saigon, resulting in a Communist victory. This outcome came at a terrible cost. Some 58,000 American soldiers, 215,000 South Vietnamese soldiers, 1 million North Vietnamese and Vietcong soldiers, and an estimated 4 million South and North Vietnamese civilians were killed in the conflict.

The Nixon administration's war efforts generated great controversy at home. The invasion of Cambodia touched off widespread campus demonstrations in May 1970. At Kent State University in Ohio, four student protesters were shot and killed by the National Guard. Large crowds of antiwar demonstrators descended on Washington in 1969 and 1971, though the president refused to heed their message. Nevertheless, the American public, and not just radicals, had turned against the war. By 1972 more than 70 percent of those polled believed that the Vietnam War was a mistake. Growing numbers of Vietnam veterans also

The Fall of Saigon, 1975   On April 29, 1975, the day before Communist troops took control of Saigon, crowds of South Vietnamese, many of whom had supported the United States, scramble to climb the wall of the U.S. Embassy. They were making a desperate attempt to get to evacuation helicopters, but with space limited on available aircraft, many of these people were left behind. AP Photo/Neal Ulevich

spoke out against the war. Contributing to this disillusionment, in 1971 the *New York Times* and the *Washington Post* published a classified report known as the ***Pentagon Papers***. This document confirmed that the Kennedy and Johnson administrations had misled the public about the origins and nature of the Vietnam War. Congress reflected growing disapproval for the war by repealing the Gulf of Tonkin Resolution in 1970 after the Cambodian invasion. In 1973 Congress passed the **War Powers Act**, which required the president to consult with Congress within forty-eight hours of deploying military forces and to obtain a declaration of war from Congress if troops remained on foreign soil beyond sixty days.

The Cold War Thaws.
Although the Vietnam War remained controversial for Nixon, his efforts toward easing tensions with the country's Cold War adversaries proved more successful, through a policy known as **détente**. Via secret maneuvering, Kissinger prepared the way for Nixon to visit mainland China in 1972. After blocking the People's Republic of China's admission to the United Nations for twenty-two years, the United States announced that it would no longer oppose China's entry to the world organization. This cautious renewal of relations opened up possibilities of mutually beneficial trade between the two countries.

The closer relations between China and the United States worried the USSR. Although both were Communist nations, the Soviet Union and China had pursued their own ideological and national interests. To check growing Chinese influence with the United States, Soviet premier Leonid Brezhnev invited President Nixon to Moscow in May 1972, the first time an American president had visited the Soviet Union since 1945. The main topic of discussion concerned arms control, and with the Soviet Union eager to make a deal in the aftermath of Nixon's trip to China, the two sides worked out the historic **Strategic Arms Limitation Treaty (SALT I)**, the first to curtail nuclear arms production during the Cold War. The pact restricted the number of antiballistic missiles that each nation could deploy and froze the number of intercontinental ballistic missiles and submarine-based missiles for five years.

Throughout the world, the United States preferred to support dictatorship over democracy when its strategic or economic interests were at stake. In Chile, the United States overthrew the democratically elected socialist president Salvador Allende after he nationalized U.S. properties. In 1973 the Central Intelligence Agency (CIA) backed an operation that led to the murder of Allende, and the coup brought nearly two decades of dictatorial rule to that country. Under Nixon's leadership, the United States also supported repressive regimes in Nicaragua, South Africa, the Philippines, and Iran.

Crisis in the Middle East and at Home.
Nixon's diplomatic initiatives, however, failed to resolve festering problems in the Middle East. Since its victory in the Six-Day War of 1967, Israel had occupied territory once controlled by Egypt and Syria as well as the former Palestinian capital of Jerusalem. On October 6, 1973, during the start of the Jewish High Holidays of Yom Kippur, Egyptian and Syrian troops, fortified with Soviet arms, launched a surprise attack on Israel. An Israeli counterattack, reinforced by a shipment of $2 billion of American weapons, repelled Arab forces, and the Israeli military stood ready to destroy the Egyptian army. To avoid a complete breakdown in the balance of power, the United States and the Soviet Union agreed to broker a cease-fire that left the situation the same as before the war.

U.S. involvement in the struggle between Israel and its Arab enemies exacerbated economic troubles at home. On October 17, 1973, in the midst of the Yom Kippur War, the Organization of Petroleum Exporting Countries (OPEC) imposed an oil embargo on the United States as punishment for its support of Israel. As a result of the embargo, the price of oil skyrocketed. The effect of high oil prices rippled through the economy, leading to increased inflation and unemployment. The crisis lasted until May 1974, when OPEC lifted its embargo following six months of diplomacy by Kissinger.

REVIEW & RELATE

- Compare Nixon's policies toward Vietnam with those toward the Soviet Union and China.
- How did Nixon's Middle East policy affect Americans at home?

Nixon and Politics, 1969–1974

Nixon won the presidency in 1968 by forging a conservative coalition behind him and blaming liberals for the radical excesses of the 1960s. Nixon won reelection in 1972, but his victory was short-lived. In an effort to ensure electoral success, the Nixon administration engaged in illegal activities that subsequently came to light and forced the president to resign.

Pragmatic Conservatism. On the domestic front, Nixon had pledged during his 1968 campaign to "reverse the flow of power and resources from the states and communities to Washington." He kept his promise by dismantling Great Society social programs, cutting funds for the War on Poverty, and eliminating the Office of Economic Opportunity. In 1972 the president adopted a program of revenue sharing, which transferred federal tax revenues to the states to use as they wished. Hoping to rein in the liberal Warren Court, Nixon nominated conservative justices to the Supreme Court.

However, in several areas Nixon departed from conservatives who favored limited government. In 1970 he persuaded Congress to pass the Environmental Protection Act, which strengthened federal oversight of industrial activities affecting the natural environment throughout the country. In 1972 the federal government increased its responsibility for protecting the health and safety of American workers through the creation of the Occupational Safety and Health Administration (OSHA). The Consumer Products Safety Commission was established to provide added safety for the buying public. In addition, the president signed a law banning cigarette advertising on radio and television because of the link between smoking and cancer.

Nixon also applied a pragmatic approach to racial issues. In general, he supported "benign neglect" concerning the issue of race and rejected new legislative attempts to use busing to promote school desegregation. In this way, Nixon courted southern conservatives in an attempt to deter George Wallace from mounting another third-party challenge in 1972. Still, Nixon moved back to the political center with efforts that furthered civil rights. Expanding **affirmative action** programs begun under the Johnson administration, he adopted plans that required construction companies and unions to recruit minority workers according to their percentage in the local labor force. His support of affirmative action was part of a broader approach to encourage "black capitalism," a concept designed to convince African Americans to seek opportunity within the free-enterprise system rather than through government handouts. Moreover, in 1970 Nixon signed the extension of the 1965 Voting Rights Act, thereby renewing the law that had provided suffrage to the majority of African Americans in the South. The law also lowered the voting age from twenty-one to eighteen for national elections. Support for the measure reflected the impact of the Vietnam War: If young men could fight at eighteen, then they should be able to vote at eighteen. In 1971 the Twenty-sixth Amendment was ratified to lower the voting age for state and local elections as well.

The Nixon administration also veered away from the traditional Republican free market philosophy by resorting to wage and price controls to curb rising inflation brought on, for the most part, by increased military spending during the Vietnam War. In 1971 the president by executive order declared a ninety-day freeze on wages and prices, placed a temporary 10 percent surtax on imports, and let the value of the dollar drop on the international market, leading to increased U.S. exports. Taken together, these measures stabilized consumer prices, reduced unemployment, and boosted the gross national product. Although these proved to be only short-term gains, they improved Nixon's prospects for reelection.

The Nixon Landslide and Watergate Scandal, 1972–1974. By appealing to voters across the political spectrum, Nixon won a monumental victory in 1972. The president invigorated the "silent majority" by demonizing his opponents and encouraging

Vice President Spiro Agnew to aggressively pursue his strategy of polarization. Agnew called protesters "kooks" and "social misfits" and attacked the media and Nixon critics with heated rhetoric. As Nixon had hoped, George Wallace ran in the Democratic primaries. Wallace won impressive victories in the North as well as the South, but his campaign ended after an assassination attempt left him paralyzed. With Wallace out of the race, the Democrats helped Nixon look more centrist by nominating George McGovern, a liberal antiwar senator from South Dakota.

Winning in a landslide, Nixon captured more than 60 percent of the popular vote and nearly all of the electoral votes. Nonetheless Democrats retained control of Congress. However, Nixon would have little time to savor his victory, for within the next two years his conduct in the campaign would come back to destroy his presidency.

In the early hours of June 17, 1972, five men broke into Democratic Party headquarters in the Watergate apartment complex in Washington, D.C. What appeared initially as a routine robbery turned into the most infamous political scandal of the twentieth century. It was eventually revealed that the break-in had been authorized by the Committee for the Re-Election of the President in an attempt to steal documents from the Democrats.

President Nixon may not have known in advance the details of the break-in, but he did authorize a cover-up of his administration's involvement. Nixon ordered his chief of staff, H. R. Haldeman, to get the CIA and FBI to back off from a thorough investigation of the incident. To silence the burglars at their trials, the president promised them $400,000 and hinted at a presidential pardon after their conviction.

Nixon embarked on the cover-up to protect himself from revelations of his administration's other illegal activities. Several of the Watergate burglars belonged to a secret band of operatives known as "the plumbers," which had been formed in 1971 and authorized by the president to find and plug up unwelcome information leaks from government officials. On their first secret operation, the plumbers broke into the office of military analyst Daniel Ellsberg's psychiatrist to look for embarrassing personal information with which to discredit Ellsberg, who had leaked the *Pentagon Papers*. The president had other unsavory matters to hide. In an effort to contain leaks about the administration's secret bombing of Cambodia in 1969, the White House had illegally wiretapped its own officials and members of the press.

Watergate did not become a major scandal until after the election. The trial judge forced one of the burglars to reveal the men's backers. This revelation led two *Washington Post* reporters, Bob Woodward and Carl Bernstein, to investigate the link between the administration and the plumbers. With the help of Mark Felt, a top FBI official whose identity long remained secret and whom the reporters called "Deep Throat," Woodward and Bernstein succeeded in exposing the true nature of the crime. The Senate created a special committee in February 1973 to investigate the scandal. White House counsel John Dean, whom Nixon had fired, testified about discussing the cover-up with the president and his closest advisers. His testimony proved accurate after the committee learned that Nixon had secretly taped all Oval Office conversations. When the president refused to release the tapes to a special prosecutor, the Supreme Court ruled against him.

With Nixon's cover-up revealed, and impeachment and conviction likely, Nixon resigned on August 9, 1974. The scandal took a great toll on the administration: Attorney General John Mitchell and Nixon's closest advisers, H. R. Haldeman and John Ehrlichman,

Nixon Watergate Burglars, 1973   Four of seven defendants charged with breaking into the Democratic National Committee offices at the Watergate complex take a break with their attorney during their trial. Standing outside the federal courthouse from left to right are: Virgilio Gonzales, Frank Sturgis, attorney Henry Rothblatt, Bernard Barker, and Eugenio Martinez. E. Howard Hunt, G. Gordon Liddy, and James McCord are not pictured. All were convicted. Wally McNamee / Corbis via Getty Images

resigned, and twenty-five government officials went to jail. Watergate also damaged the office of the president, leaving Americans wary and distrustful.

Vice President Gerald Ford served out Nixon's remaining term. The Republican representative from Michigan had replaced Vice President Spiro Agnew after Agnew resigned in 1973 following charges that he had taken illegal kickbacks while governor of Maryland. Ford chose Nelson A. Rockefeller, the moderate Republican governor of New York, as his vice president; thus, neither man had been elected to the office he now held. President Ford's most controversial and defining act took place shortly after he entered the White House. Explaining to the country that he wanted to quickly end the "national nightmare" stemming from Watergate, Ford pardoned Nixon for any criminal offenses he might have committed as president. Rather than healing the nation's wounds, this preemptive pardon polarized Americans and cost Ford considerable political capital. Ford also wrestled with a troubled economy as Americans once again experienced rising prices and high unemployment.

REVIEW & RELATE

- Describe the conservative coalition that brought Nixon to power.

- How did Nixon appeal to conservatism and how much did he depart from it?

The **Presidency** of **Jimmy Carter, 1976–1980**

Though deeply disillusioned by Vietnam and the Watergate scandal, most Americans hoped that, with these disasters behind them, better times lay ahead. This was not to be. Under the leadership of the Democratic president Jimmy Carter, the economy worsened as oil-producing nations in the Persian Gulf and Latin America raised the price of petroleum. Carter's efforts to revive the economy and rally the country behind energy conservation were ineffective. In foreign policy President Carter sought to negotiate with the Soviets over arms reduction while at the same time challenging them to do more to protect human rights. In practice, Carter found this balancing act difficult to sustain, and despite his desire to find ways to cooperate with the Soviets, relations between the superpowers deteriorated over the course of his term in office. Despite successful diplomatic efforts in the Middle East, trouble in the Persian Gulf added to the Carter administration's woes.

Jimmy Carter and the Limits of Affluence.

Despite his political shortcomings, Gerald Ford received the Republican presidential nomination in 1976 and ran against James Earl (Jimmy) Carter, a little-known former governor of Georgia, who used his "outsider" status to his advantage. Shaping his campaign with Watergate in mind, Carter stressed personal character over economic issues. As a moderate, post-segregationist governor of Georgia, Carter won the support of the family of Martin Luther King Jr. and other black leaders. Carter needed all the help he could get and eked out a narrow victory.

The greatest challenge Carter faced once in office was a faltering economy. America's consumer-oriented economy depended on cheap energy, a substantial portion of which came from sources outside the United States (Figure 27.1). By the 1970s, four-fifths of the world's oil supply came from Saudi Arabia, Iran, Iraq, and Kuwait, all members of the Arab-dominated **Organization of Petroleum Exporting Countries (OPEC)**. The organization had been formed in 1960 by these Persian Gulf countries together with Venezuela, and it used its control of petroleum supplies to set world prices. In 1973, during the Nixon administration, OPEC imposed an oil embargo on the United States as punishment for its support of Israel during the

Gas Shortages, 1973   A gas station owner in Perkasie, Pennsylvania lets his customers know he is out of gas. OPEC's 1973 oil embargo during the Yom Kippur War caused gas shortages and soaring prices in the United States. Motorists scrambling to find available supplies at gas stations created long lines. AP Photo

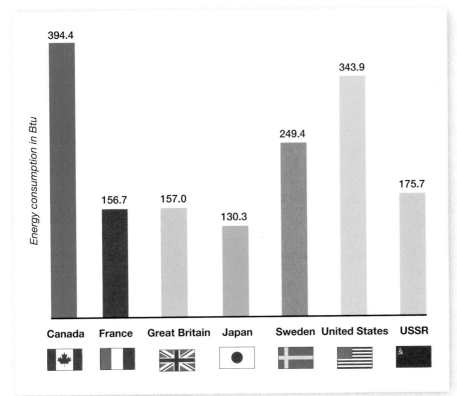

FIGURE 27.1 Global Per Capita Energy Consumption

Next to Canada, in 1980 the United States consumed the largest amount of energy per capita, measured in British thermal units (Btu), among the major industrialized nations in the world. The source of most of this energy came (and still comes) from such fossil fuels as coal and oil. Greenhouse gas emissions from this fuel production and consumption have created an environmental hazard in the above nations, and those like China and India that experienced rapid industrialization in the decades following 1980. Besides industrialization, what other factors influence per capita energy consumption?

Yom Kippur War with Egypt and Syria. The price of oil skyrocketed as a result. By the time Carter became president, the cost of a barrel of oil had jumped to around $30. American drivers who had paid 30 cents a gallon for gas in 1970 paid more than four times that amount ten years later.

Energy concerns helped reshape American industry. With energy prices rising, American manufacturers sought ways to reduce costs by moving their factories to nations that offered cheaper labor and lower energy costs. This outmigration of American manufacturing had two significant consequences. First, it weakened the American labor movement, particularly in heavy industry. In the 1970s, union membership dropped from 28 to 23 percent of the workforce and continued to decline over the next decade. Second, this process of deindustrialization accelerated a significant population shift that had begun during World War II from the old industrial areas of the Northeast and the Midwest (the Rust Belt) to the South and the Southwest (the Sun Belt), where cheaper costs and lower wages were enormously attractive to businesses (Map 27.2). Only 14 percent of southern workers were unionized in a region with a long history of opposition to labor organizing. Consequently, Sun Belt cities such as Houston, Atlanta, Phoenix, and San Diego flourished, while the steel and auto towns in Ohio, Michigan, and Pennsylvania decayed.

These monumental shifts in the American economy produced widespread pain. Higher gasoline prices affected all businesses that relied on energy, leading to serious

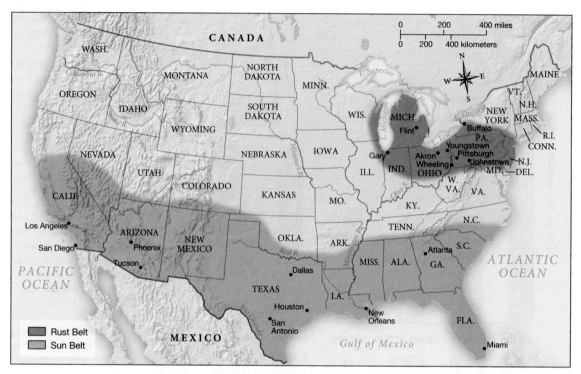

MAP 27.2 The Sun and Rust Belts

Dramatic economic and demographic shifts during the 1970s led to industrial development and population growth in the "Sun Belt" in the South and Southwest at the expense of the "Rust Belt" in the Northeast and Midwest. As manufacturers sought cheap, non-unionized labor, they moved factories to the South or overseas while defense industries and agribusiness fueled growth from Texas to California.

inflation. To maintain their standard of living in the face of rising inflation and stagnant wages, many Americans went into debt, using a new innovation, the credit card, to borrow collectively more than $300 billion. The American economy had gone through inflationary spirals before, but they were usually accompanied by high employment, with wages helping to drive up prices. In the 1970s, however, rising prices were accompanied by growing unemployment, a situation that economists called "stagflation." Traditionally, remedies to control inflation increased unemployment, yet most unemployment cures also spurred inflation. With both occurring at the same time, economists were confounded, and many Americans felt they had lost control over their economy.

President Carter tried his best to find a solution. To reduce dependency on foreign oil, in 1977 Carter devised a plan for energy self-sufficiency, which he called the "moral equivalent of war." Critics called the proposal weak. A more substantial accomplishment came on August 4, 1977, when Carter signed into law the creation of the Department of Energy, with responsibilities covering research, development, and conservation of energy. In 1978, he backed the **National Energy Act**, which set gas emission standards for automobiles and provided incentives for installing alternate energy systems, such as solar and wind power, in homes and public buildings. He also supported congressional legislation to spend $14 billion for public sector jobs as well as to cut taxes by $34 billion, which reduced unemployment but only temporarily.

In many other respects Carter embraced conservative principles. Believing in fiscal restraint, he rejected liberal proposals for national health insurance and more expansive employment programs. Instead, he signed into law bills deregulating the airline, banking, trucking, and railroad industries, measures that appealed to conservative proponents of free market economics.

The Perils of Détente.
In the area of foreign policy Carter departed from Nixon. Whereas Nixon was a realist who considered the U.S. role in world affairs as an exercise in power politics, Carter was an idealist who made human rights a cornerstone of his foreign policy. Unlike previous presidents who had supported dictatorial governments as long as they were anti-Communist, Carter intended to hold such regimes to a higher moral standard. Thus the Carter administration cut off military and economic aid to repressive regimes in Argentina, Uruguay, and Ethiopia. Still, Carter was not entirely consistent in his application of moral standards to diplomacy. Important U.S. allies around the world such as the Philippines, South Korea, and South Africa were hardly models of democracy, but national security concerns kept the president from severing ties with them.

One way that Carter tried to set an example of responsible moral leadership was by signing an agreement to return control of the Panama Canal Zone to Panama at the end of 1999. The treaty that President Theodore Roosevelt negotiated in 1903 gave the United States control over this ten-mile piece of Panamanian land forever. Panamanians resented this affront to their sovereignty, and Carter considered the occupation a vestige of colonialism.

The president's pursuit of détente with the Soviet Union was less successful. In 1978 the Carter administration extended full diplomatic recognition to China. After the fall of China to the Communists in 1949, the United States had supported Taiwan, an island off the coast of China, as an outpost of democracy against mainland China. In abandoning Taiwan by recognizing China, Carter sought to drive a greater wedge between China and the Soviet Union. Nevertheless, Carter did not give up on cooperation with the Soviets. In June 1979 Carter and Soviet leader Leonid Brezhnev signed **SALT II**, a new strategic arms limitation treaty. Six months later, however, the Soviet Union invaded Afghanistan to bolster its pro-Communist Afghan regime. President Carter viewed this action as a violation of international law and a threat to Middle East oil supplies, and he therefore persuaded the Senate to drop consideration of SALT II. In addition, Carter obtained from Congress a 5 percent increase in military spending, reduced grain sales to the USSR, and led a boycott of the 1980 Olympic Games in Moscow.

Of perhaps the greatest long-term importance was President Carter's decision to authorize the CIA to provide covert military and economic assistance to Afghan rebels resisting the Soviet invasion. Chief among these groups were the ***mujahideen***, or warriors who wage jihad. Although portrayed as freedom fighters, these Islamic fundamentalists (including a group known as the Taliban) did not support democracy in the Western sense. Among the mujahideen who received assistance from the United States was Osama bin Laden, a Saudi Arabian Islamic fundamentalist.

Afghan Mujahideen, January 1980 On December 25, 1979, Soviet troops invaded Afghanistan to suppress mujahideen guerrillas who were trying to overthrow the nation's secular, pro-Soviet regime. These rebel forces were among the guerrillas who defeated the Soviets after a decade of warfare and eventually established an Islamic theocracy. © Pascal Manoukian/Sygma/via Getty Images

In ordering these CIA operations, Carter ignored recent revelations about questionable intelligence practices. Responding to presidential excesses stemming from the Vietnam War and the Watergate scandal, the Senate had held hearings in 1975 into clandestine CIA and FBI activities at home and abroad. Led by Frank Church of Idaho, the Senate Select Committee to Study Governmental Operations with Respect to Intelligence Activities (known as the Church Committee) issued reports revealing that both intelligence agencies had illegally spied on Americans and that the CIA had fomented revolution abroad, contrary to the provisions of its charter. Despite the Church Committee's findings, Carter revived some of these murky practices to combat the Soviets in Afghanistan.

Challenges in the Middle East. Before President Carter attempted to restrain the Soviet Union in Afghanistan, he did have some notable diplomatic successes. Five years after the 1973 Yom Kippur War, with relations between Israel and its Arab neighbors in a deadlock, Carter invited the leaders of Israel and Egypt to the United States. Following two weeks of discussions in September 1978 at the presidential retreat at Camp David, Maryland, Israeli prime minister Menachem Begin and Egyptian president Anwar Sadat reached an agreement on a "framework for peace." For the first time in its history, Egypt would extend diplomatic recognition to Israel in exchange for Israel's agreement to return the Sinai peninsula to Egypt, which Israel had captured and occupied since 1967. Carter facilitated Sadat's acceptance of the **Camp David accords** by promising to extend foreign aid to Egypt. The treaty, however, left unresolved controversial issues between Israelis and Arabs concerning the establishment of a Palestinian state and control of Jerusalem.

Whatever success Carter had in promoting peace in the Middle East suffered a serious setback in the Persian Gulf nation of Iran. In 1953 the CIA had helped overthrow Iran's democratically elected president, replacing him with a monarch and staunch ally, Mohammad Reza Pahlavi, the shah of Iran. For more than two decades, the shah ruled Iran with U.S. support, seeking to construct a modern, secular state allied with the United States. In doing so, he used repressive measures against Islamic fundamentalists, deploying his secret police to imprison, torture, and exile dissenters. In 1979 revolutionary forces headed by Ayatollah Ruholla Khomeini, an Islamic fundamentalist exiled by the shah, overthrew his government. Khomeini intended to end the growing secularism in Iran and reshape the nation according to strict Islamic law.

When the deposed shah needed treatment for terminal cancer, President Carter invited him to the United States for medical assistance as a humanitarian gesture, despite warnings from the Khomeini government that it would consider this invitation a hostile action. On November 4, 1979, the ayatollah ordered fundamentalist Muslim students to seize the U.S. Embassy in Tehran and hold its fifty-two occupants hostage until the United States returned the shah to Iran to stand trial. President Carter retaliated by freezing all Iranian assets in American banks, breaking off diplomatic relations, and imposing a trade embargo. In response, Khomeini denounced the United States as "the Great Satan." As the impasse dragged on and with the presidential election of 1980 fast approaching, Carter became desperate. After a failed U.S. rescue attempt, Khomeini's guards separated the hostages, making any more rescue efforts impossible. Further humiliating the president, Khomeini released the hostages on January 20, 1981, the inauguration day of Carter's successor, Ronald Reagan.

REVIEW & RELATE

- How effective was President Carter in domestic politics?

- How did events in the Middle East, the Persian Gulf, and Afghanistan challenge the objectives of the Carter administration?

The **Persistence** of **Liberalism** in the **1970s**

Despite the growing conservatism, political activism did not die out in the 1970s. Many of the changes sought by liberals and radicals during the 1960s had entered the political and cultural mainstreams in the 1970s. The counterculture, with its long hairstyles and colorful clothes, also entered the mainstream, and rock continued to dominate popular music. Some Americans experimented with recreational drugs, and the remaining sexual taboos of the 1960s fell. Many parents became resigned to seeing their daughters and sons living with boyfriends or girlfriends before getting married. And many of those same parents engaged in extramarital affairs or divorced their spouses. The divorce rate increased by 116 percent in the decade after 1965; in 1979 the rate peaked at 23 divorces per 1,000 married couples.

Popular Culture. The antiwar movement and counterculture influenced popular culture in many ways. Rock musicians such as Bruce Springsteen, Jackson Browne, and

Billy Joel sang of loss, loneliness, urban decay, and adventure. The film *M*A*S*H* (1970), though dealing with the Korean War, was a thinly veiled satire of the horrors of the Vietnam War, and in the late 1970s filmmakers began producing movies specifically about Vietnam and the toll the war took on ordinary Americans who served there. The television sitcom *All in the Family* gave American viewers the character of Archie Bunker, an opinionated, white, blue-collar worker, in a comedy that dramatized the contemporary political and cultural wars as conservative Archie taunted his liberal son-in-law with politically incorrect remarks about minorities, feminists, and liberals.

Women's Movement.   In the 1970s the women's movement gained strength, but it also attracted powerful opponents. The 1973 Supreme Court victory for abortion rights in *Roe v. Wade* did not end the controversy. In 1976 Congress responded to abortion opponents by passing legislation prohibiting the use of federal funds for impoverished women seeking to terminate their pregnancies.

Feminists engaged in other debates in this decade, often clashing with more conservative women. The National Organization for Women (NOW) and its allies succeeded in getting thirty-five states out of a necessary thirty-eight to ratify the **Equal Rights Amendment (ERA)**, which prevented the abridgment of "equality of rights under law . . . by the United States or any State on the basis of sex." In response, other women activists formed their own movement to block ratification. Phyllis Schlafly, a conservative activist, founded the Stop ERA organization to prevent the creation of a "unisex society." Despite the inroads made by feminists, traditional notions of femininity appealed to many women and to male-dominated legislatures. The remaining states refused to ratify the ERA, thus killing the amendment in 1982, when the ratification period expired.

Despite the failure to obtain ratification of the ERA, feminists achieved significant victories. In 1972 Congress passed the Educational Amendments Act. Title IX of this law prohibited colleges and universities that received federal funds from discriminating on the basis of sex, leading to substantial advances in women's athletics. Many more women sought relief against job discrimination through the Equal Employment Opportunity Commission, resulting in major victories. NOW membership continued to grow, and the number of battered women's shelters and rape crisis centers multiplied in towns and cities across the country. Women saw their ranks increase on college campuses, in both undergraduate and professional schools. Women also began entering politics in greater numbers, especially at the local and state levels. At the national level, women such as Shirley Chisholm and Geraldine Ferraro of New York, Louise Day Hicks of Massachusetts, Barbara Jordan of Texas, and Patricia Schroeder of Colorado won seats in Congress. At the same time, women of color sought to broaden the definition of feminism to include struggles against race and class oppression as well as sex discrimination. In 1974 a group of black feminists, led by author Barbara Smith, organized the Combahee River Collective and proclaimed: "We . . . often find it difficult to separate race from class from sex oppression because in our lives they are most often experienced simultaneously." Chicana and other Latina feminists also sought to extend women's liberation beyond the confines of the white middle class. In 1987 feminist poet and writer Gloria Anzaldúa wrote: "Though I'll defend my race and culture when they are attacked by non-mexicanos . . . I abhor some of my culture's ways, how it cripples its women . . . our strengths used against us, lowly [women] bearing humility with dignity."

Explore ▶

See Sources 27.2 and 27.3 for two views of feminism by women of color.

Environmentalism. Another outgrowth of 1960s liberal activism that flourished in the 1970s was the effort to clean up and preserve the environment. The publication of Rachel Carson's *Silent Spring* in 1962 had renewed awareness of what Progressive Era reformers called conservation. Carson expanded the concept of conservation to include ecology, which addressed the relationships of human beings and other organisms to their environments. By exploring these connections, she offered a revealing look at the devastating effects of pesticides on birds and fish, as well as on the human food chain and water supply.

This new environmental movement not only focused on open spaces and national parks but also sought to publicize urban environmental problems. By 1970, 53 percent of Americans considered air and water pollution to be one of the top issues facing the country, up from only 17 percent five years earlier. Responding to this shift in public opinion, in 1971 President Nixon established the **Environmental Protection Agency (EPA)** and signed the Clean Air Act, which regulated auto emissions.

Not everyone embraced environmentalism. As the EPA toughened emission standards, automobile manufacturers complained that the regulations forced them to raise prices and hurt an industry that was already feeling the threat of foreign competition, especially from Japan. Workers were also affected, as declining sales forced companies to lay off employees. Similarly, passage of the Endangered Species Act of 1973 pitted timber companies in the Northwest against environmentalists. The new law prevented the federal government from funding any projects that threatened the habitat of animals at risk of extinction.

Several disasters heightened public demands for stronger government oversight of the environment. In 1978 women living near Love Canal outside Niagara Falls, New York complained about unusually high rates of illnesses and birth defects in their community. Investigations revealed that their housing development had been constructed on top of a toxic waste dump. This discovery spawned grassroots efforts to clean up this area as well as other contaminated communities. In 1980 President Carter and Congress responded by

Three Mile Island Nuclear Power Plant, 1979   On March 28, 1979, the Three Mile Island nuclear power plant, outside Harrisburg, Pennsylvania, started leaking radioactive steam that contaminated the surrounding area. The governor called for a voluntary evacuation within a twenty-mile distance. The cooling tower of the nuclear plant stands behind an abandoned playground, where children had been playing only days earlier. AP Photo/Barry Thumma

Women of Color and Feminism

Although women of color participated in predominantly white feminist groups, they faced economic and social problems that middle-class white women did not. At the first National Chicana Conference, participants highlighted issues that ranged beyond gender while advocating sexual freedom, legalized abortion, free child care, and cultural self-determination. The black feminist Combahee River Collective contended that sexism had many sources: capitalism, racism, patriarchy, and enforced heterosexuality. Both groups proclaimed racial solidarity with men of color but recognized the difficulties of forging alliances with them.

Source 27.2

Workshop Resolutions, First National Chicana Conference, 1971

SEX AND THE CHICANA

. . . I. Sex is good and healthy for both Chicanos and Chicanas and we must develop this attitude.

II. We should destroy the myth that religion and culture control our sexual lives.

III. We recognize that we have been oppressed by religion and that the religious writing was done by *men* and interpreted by *men*. Therefore, for those who desire religion, they should interpret their Bible, or Catholic rulings according to their own feelings, what they think is right, without any guilt complexes.

IV. Mothers should teach their sons to respect women as human beings who are equal in every respect. *No double standard.*

V. Women should go back to the communities and form discussion and action groups concerning sex education.

VI. Free, legal abortions and birth control for the Chicano community, controlled by *Chicanas.* As Chicanas we have the right to control our own bodies. . . .

RESOLUTIONS:

. . . Whereas: The need for self-determination and the right to govern their own bodies is a necessity for the freedom of all people, therefore, BE IT RESOLVED: That the National Chicana Conference go on record as supporting free family planning and free and legal abortions for all women who want or need them.

III. Whereas: Due to socio-economic and cultural conditions, Chicanas are often heads of households, i.e., widows, divorcees, unwed mothers, or deserted mothers, or must work to supplement family income, and

Whereas: Chicana motherhood should not preclude educational, political, social, and economic advancement, and

Whereas: There is a critical need for a 24-hour child-care center in Chicano communities, therefore,

BE IT RESOLVED: That the National Chicana Conference go on record as recommending that every Chicano community promote and set up 24-hour day-care facilities, and that it be further resolved that these facilities will reflect the concept of La Raza as the united family, and on the basis of brotherhood (La Raza), so that men, women, young and old assume the responsibility for the love, care, education, and orientation of all the children of Aztlan [ancestral homeland of pre-Columbian Mexicans].

Source: Mirta Vidal, *Chicanas Speak Out, Women: New Voice of La Raza* (New York: Pathfinder Press, 1971), 13–16, http://library.duke.edu/digitalcollections/wlmpc_wlmms01005/.

Source 27.3

Combahee River Collective | *A Black Feminist Statement*, 1977

The major source of difficulty in our political work is that we are not just trying to fight oppression on one front or even two, but instead to address a whole range of oppressions. We do not have racial, sexual, heterosexual, or class privilege to rely upon, nor do we have even the minimal access to resources and power that groups who possess any one of these types of privilege have.

. . . The reaction of black men to feminism has been notoriously negative. They are, of course, even more threatened than black women by the possibility that black feminists might organize around our own needs. They realize that they might not only lose valuable and hard-working allies in their struggles but that they might also be forced to change their habitually sexist ways of interacting with and oppressing black women. Accusations that black feminism divides the black struggle are powerful deterrents to the growth of an autonomous black women's movement.

One issue that is of major concern to us and that we have begun to publicly address is racism in the white women's movement. As black feminists we are made constantly and painfully aware of how little effort white women have made to understand and combat their racism, which requires among other things that they have a more than superficial comprehension of race, color, and black history and culture. Eliminating racism in the white women's movement is by definition work for white women to do, but we will continue to speak to and demand accountability on this issue.

Source: Zillah R. Eisenstein, ed., *Capitalist Patriarchy and the Case for Socialist Feminism* (New York: Monthly Press, 1978), 367–69, 371–72.

Interpret the Evidence

1. In what ways were Chicana and African American feminist views of the sources of sexism the same, and in what ways were they different?

2. Why do these African American feminists criticize their white counterparts?

Put It in Context

How did racial and ethnic diversity within the feminist movement shape women's issues in the 1970s?

Boston Anti-busing March, 1975 Boston City Council member Louise Day Hicks (in center) arrives to address a large demonstration in South Boston's Columbus Park to protest federal court-ordered busing of black students to all-white neighborhood schools, Joining her were some men dressed in Revolutionary War era outfits. In 1976, Hicks was elected first women president of the city council. Spencer Grant/Getty Images

passing the Comprehensive Environmental Response, Compensation, and Liability Act (known as Superfund) to clean up sites contaminated with hazardous substances. Further inquiries showed that the presence of such poisonous waste dumps disproportionately affected minorities and the poor. Critics called the placement of these waste locations near African American and other minority communities "environmental racism" and launched a movement for environmental justice.

The most dangerous threat came in March 1979 at the Three Mile Island nuclear power plant near Harrisburg, Pennsylvania. A broken valve at the plant leaked coolant and threatened the meltdown of the reactor's nuclear core. As officials quickly evacuated residents from the surrounding area, employees at the plant narrowly averted catastrophe by fixing the problem before an explosion occurred. Grassroots activists protested and raised public awareness against the construction of additional nuclear power facilities.

Racial Struggles Continue. The civil rights struggle also did not end with the 1960s. The civil rights coalition of organizations that banded together in the 1960s had disintegrated, but the National Association for the Advancement of Colored People remained active, as did local organizations in communities nationwide. Following passage of the 1965 Voting Rights Act, electoral politics became the new form of activism. By 1992 there were more than 7,500 black elected officials in the United States. Many of them had participated in the civil rights movement and subsequently worked to gain for their constituents the economic benefits that integration and affirmative action had not yet achieved. During this time, the number of Latino American and Asian American elected officials also increased.

The issue of school busing highlighted the persistence of racial discrimination. In the fifteen years following the landmark 1954 decision in *Brown v. Board of Education of Topeka, Kansas,* few schools had been integrated. Starting in 1969, the U.S. Supreme Court ruled that genuine racial integration of the public schools must no longer be delayed. In 1971 the Court went even further in *Swann v. Charlotte-Mecklenburg Board of Education* by requiring school districts to bus pupils to achieve integration. Cities such as Charlotte,

North Carolina; Lexington, Kentucky; and Tampa, Florida, embraced the ruling and carefully planned for it to succeed.

However, the decision was more controversial in other municipalities around the nation and it exposed racism as a national problem. In many northern communities racially discriminatory housing policies created segregated neighborhoods and, thus, segregated schools. When white parents in the Detroit suburbs objected to busing their children to inner-city, predominantly black schools, the Supreme Court in 1974 departed from the *Swann* case and prohibited busing across distinct school district boundaries. This ruling created a serious problem for integration efforts because many whites were fleeing the cities and moving to the suburbs where few blacks lived.

As the conflict over school integration intensified, violence broke out in communities throughout the country. In Boston, Massachusetts, busing opponents led by Louise Day Hicks tapped into the racial and class resentments of the largely white working-class population of South Boston, which was paired with the black community of Roxbury for busing, leaving mainly middle- and upper-class white communities unaffected. In the fall of 1974, battles broke out inside and outside the schools. Despite the violence, schools stayed open, and for the next three decades Boston remained under court order to continue busing.

Along with busing, affirmative action generated fierce controversy, as the case of Allan Bakke showed. From 1970 to 1977, with the acceleration of affirmative action programs, the number of African Americans attending college doubled, constituting nearly 10 percent of the student body, a few percentage points lower than the proportion of blacks in the national population. Though blacks still earned lower incomes than the average white family, black family income as a percentage of white family income had grown from 55.1 percent in 1965 to 61.5 percent ten years later. African Americans, however, still had a long way to go to catch up with whites. The situation was even worse for those who did not reach middle-class status: About 30 percent of African Americans slid deeper into poverty during the decade.

Despite the persistence of economic inequality, many whites believed that affirmative action placed them at a disadvantage with blacks in the educational and economic marketplaces. In particular, many white men condemned policies that they thought recruited blacks at their expense. Polls showed that although most whites favored equal treatment of blacks, they disapproved of affirmative action as a form of "reverse discrimination."

The furor over affirmative action did not end with the *Bakke* case, and over the next three decades affirmative action opponents succeeded in narrowing the use of racial considerations in employment and education. However, they did so without Allan Bakke, who chose to live a private life with his family rather than campaign against affirmative action.

REVIEW & RELATE

- How and why did the social and cultural developments of the 1960s continue to create conflict and controversy in the 1970s?

- Evaluate the strengths and weaknesses of liberalism in the 1970s.

The **New Right** Rises

The backlash against affirmative action and the ERA confirmed that liberal reformers were losing ground to conservatives. By the end of the 1970s, liberalism had become identified with special interests and elitism. At the same time, the pragmatic conservatism of Richard Nixon was being displaced by a harder edged brand of conservatism called the

Explore ▶

Read Sources 27.4 and 27.5
for two different perspectives
on the New Right.

New Right. The New Right was founded on the budding conservatism of the 1960s as represented in the Sharon Statement and the presidential candidacy of Barry Goldwater (see "The Revival of Conservatism" in chapter 26). In the 1970s it expanded for a variety of reasons: the revolt against higher taxes, the backlash against the growth of the federal government, the disillusionment of former liberal intellectuals, and the growth of the Christian Right.

Tax Revolt. In the 1970s, working- and middle-class white resentment centered on big government spending and higher taxes. During that decade, taxation claimed 30 percent of the gross national product, up 6 percent from 1960. Although Americans still paid far less in taxes than their counterparts in Western Europe, Americans objected to raising state and federal taxes. Leading the tax revolt was the Sun Belt state of California. In a 1978 referendum, California voters passed Proposition 13, a measure that reduced property taxes and placed strict limits on the ability of local governments to raise them in the future. In the wake of Proposition 13, a dozen states enacted similar measures.

Economic conservatives also set their sights on reducing the federal income tax. They supported cutting personal and corporate taxes by a third in the belief that reducing taxes would encourage new investment and job creation. "Supply-side" economists argued that lowering tax rates would actually boost tax receipts: With lower taxes, companies and investors would have more capital to invest, leading to expanded job growth; with

Tax Revolt in California, 1978. California residents gather in support of Proposition 13, a state constitutional amendment that proposed a cap on property tax rates. The amendment also required a two-thirds vote by any local or state government to increase taxes in the future. The initiative passed overwhelmingly by a state-wide vote on June 6, 1978. Tony Korody / Sygma via Getty Images

increased employment, more people would be paying taxes. At the same time, supply-side conservatives called for reduced government spending, especially in the social service sector, to ensure balanced budgets and to eliminate what they saw as unnecessary spending on domestic programs.

Neo-Conservatism.

The New Right also benefited by the defection of disillusioned liberals. Labeled **neoconservatives**, intellectuals such as Irving Kristol, Norman Podhoretz, and Nathan Glazer reversed course and condemned the Great Society programs that they had originally supported. They believed that federal policies, such as affirmative action, had aggravated rather than improved the problems government planners intended to solve. They considered the New Left's opposition to the Vietnam War and its disapproval of foreign intervention a threat to national security.

Christian Conservatism.

Perhaps the greatest spark igniting the New Right came from religious and social conservatives, mainly evangelical Christians and Catholics. Evangelicals considered themselves to have been "born again"—literally experiencing Jesus Christ's saving presence inside of them. By the end of the 1970s, evangelical Christians numbered around 50 million, about a quarter of the population. The Christian Right opposed abortion, gay rights, and sex education; attacked Supreme Court rulings banning prayer in the public schools; denounced Charles Darwin's theory of evolution in favor of divine creationism; supported the traditional role of women as mothers and homemakers; and backed a hardline, anti-Communist stand against the Soviet Union. Certainly not all evangelical Christians held all of these beliefs; for example, President Carter, a born-again Christian, did not. Still, conservative Christians believed that the liberals and radicals of the 1960s had spread the secular creed of individual rights and personal fulfillment at the expense of established Christian values.

Social conservatives worried that the traditional nuclear family was in danger, as households consisting of married couples with children declined from 30 percent in the 1970s to 23 percent thirty years later, and the divorce rate soared. The number of unmarried couples living together doubled over the last quarter of the twentieth century. In 1970, 26.4 percent of infants were born to single mothers; by 1990 the rate had risen to 43.8. This increase was part of a trend in developed countries worldwide. Moreover, social conservatives united in fierce opposition to abortion, which the Supreme Court legalized in *Roe v. Wade* (see "Liberation Movements" in chapter 26). They argued that an unborn fetus is a person and therefore has a right to life protected by the Constitution.

The direct impetus pushing conservative evangelicals into politics came when the Internal Revenue Service (IRS) removed tax-exempt status from a fundamentalist Christian college. Bob Jones University in South Carolina defended racial segregation on biblical grounds, but under pressure from the federal government began admitting some African American students in the mid-1970s. However, the school continued practicing discrimination by prohibiting interracial dating. In 1976, when the IRS revoked the university's tax-exempt status, conservative Christians charged that the federal government was interfering with religious freedom. This sparked a grassroots political campaign to rally Christian evangelicals around a host of grievances.

Since the 1950s, Billy Graham, a charismatic Southern Baptist evangelist from North Carolina, had used television to conduct nationwide crusades. Television became an even greater

SECONDARY SOURCE ANALYSIS

The Rise of the New Right

Historians have attempted to trace the politicization of conservative Christians in the 1970s as part of a longer progression. Some have focused on the early Cold War period when Christian conservatives backed the Republican Party for its hardline anticommunist stand. Others pay greater attention to the late 1960s and early 1970s when Christian conservatives began to play a more active role in the Republican Party in opposition to feminism, abortion, gay rights, and a variety of other social issues. Still other historians emphasize the racial concerns that galvanized the New Right, as evidenced in the independent presidential candidacy of George Wallace, segregationist governor of Alabama, in 1968. In the excerpts below, two historians offer different perspectives on the New Right.

Source 27.4

Dan T. Carter, George Wallace, Race, and the New Right, 1996

Historians of the American left have made much of the way in which the civil rights movement influenced the social movements of the 1960s and 1970s, inspiring, for example, the women's rights movement and the politics of sexual liberation. But the movement's counterrevolutionary effects are equally important. In the three decades following the emergence of George Wallace, the rhetoric of racial politics evolved: from the issues of public accommodations to school desegregation, busing, housing, quotas, and struggles over job discrimination, and proposals for economic affirmative action.

. . . Economic and social conservatives— particularly those who have been lifelong opponents of racial bigotry—have bridled at the attempt to link what neoconservatives have called the 'new majoritarianism' of the 1980s with the politics of race. Nevertheless, I think it is fair to say that even though the streams of racial and economic conservatism have sometimes flowed in separate channels, they ultimately joined in the political coalition that reshaped American politics from the 1970s through the mid-1990s. . . . [George] Wallace's sensitivity to being "looked down on" and his identity as a beleaguered white southerner strengthened his appeal to white ethnic minorities and working class Americans.

Source: Dan T. Carter, *From George Wallace to Newt Gingrich: Race in the Conservative Counterrevolution, 1963–1994* (Baton Rouge: Louisiana State University Press, 1996), xiii–xiv, 12.

instrument in the hands of New Right Christian preachers in the 1970s and 1980s. The Reverend Pat Robertson of Virginia founded the Christian Broadcasting Network, and ministers such as Jerry Falwell used the airwaves to great effect. What distinguished Falwell and Robertson from earlier evangelists like Graham was their fusion of religion and electoral politics. In 1979 Falwell founded the Moral Majority, an organization that backed political candidates who supported a "family values" social agenda. Within two years of its creation, the Moral Majority counted four million members who were eager to organize in support of New Right politicians. The New Right also lined up advocacy groups such as the American Enterprise Institute and the Heritage Foundation to generate and promote conservative ideals. The alliance of economic, intellectual, and religious conservatives offered a formidable challenge to liberalism.

See Primary Source Project 27: The New Right and Its Critics, page 954.

Source 27.5

Daniel K. Williams, The Christian Right, 2010

During . . . the late 1960s, conservative Protestants succeeded not only in making alliances with Republican politicians, but in changing the agenda of the party. This time, they focused more on the culture wars than the Cold War. Conservative Protestants who mobilized against feminism, abortion, pornography, and gay rights acquired control of the Republican Party, partly because of their long-standing alliances with Republican politicians, but perhaps more important because of the united front that they presented, and because of demographic and political shifts that favored evangelicals.... The sexual revolution, sex education, race riots, the counterculture, increases in drug use, and the beginning of the feminist movement convinced them that the nation had lost its Christian identity and that the family was under attack.

The end of the civil rights movement facilitated the formation of the Christian political coalition, because it enabled fundamentalists and evangelicals who had disagreed over racial integration to come together. After the passage of federal civil rights legislation and the end of nationally publicized civil rights marches, fundamentalists such as Jerry Falwell accepted the reality of racial integration and began forging political alliances with mainstream Republicans who would have been embarrassed by their segregationist rhetoric only a few years earlier. At the same time, moderate evangelicals who had once cautiously supported the civil rights movement reacted in horror to the race riots and began taking more conservative stances on civil rights. Both fundamentalists and evangelicals embraced Richard Nixon's call for "law and order."

Source: Daniel Williams, *God's Own Party: The Making of the Christian Right* (New York: Oxford University Press: 2010), 3, 5, 6.

Examine the Sources

1. Describe the major difference between Carter's and Williams's interpretations of the New Right.
2. Based on evidence in this chapter, evaluate the extent to which this difference reflects a contrast of perspectives as opposed to a disagreement over facts.

Put It in Context

To what extent was the rise of the New Right in the 1970s a reaction to racial, moral, and economic concerns?

REVIEW AND RELATE

- Explain the rise of the New Right in the 1970s.

- How did Christian evangelicals influence the New Right?

Conclusion: The **Swing** toward **Conservatism**

The election of President Richard M. Nixon signaled discontent with the liberal policies and radical excesses of the 1960s. However, this conservative victory proved short-lived, as Nixon was forced to resign in disgrace as a result of the Watergate scandal. Before his resignation in 1973, Nixon had displayed a pragmatic conservatism that dismantled parts of the Great Society while at the same time signing into law measures that extended environmental protection and voting rights, including those for eighteen-year-olds. He issued executive orders expanding affirmative action and resorted to wage and price controls to recover from an economic crisis.

The return of Democrats to the White House in 1977 did not restore 1960s-style liberalism. The presidential administration of Jimmy Carter acknowledged the conservative notions of limited government and a deregulated market economy while embracing key conservative social values, such as faith in God and prayer. Although Carter departed from conservatives on some key issues concerning the economy, race, and gender, he did not portray himself as the heir of the liberal ideals promoted by Franklin Roosevelt, Harry Truman, and Lyndon Johnson.

The movement toward conservatism grew slowly and sporadically. Nixon's pragmatic conservatism may have stalled in Washington, D.C., but in cities and states around the nation conservatives with a more rigid ideological bent than Nixon rallied their forces. The 1970s marked the rise of the New Right, which joined defectors from liberalism and exponents of conservative free market, anti-government principles with white members of the working class resentful of racial change, anti-abortion advocates, and proponents of right-wing Christian beliefs. The New Right sought to transform the politics of resentment toward the culture of the 1960s into the politics of revivalism, convincing many that traditional values once again might guide the nation. The move to the right, however, did not stifle dissent. For much of the 1970s, Democrats controlled Congress and although the Supreme Court shifted in a more conservative direction, the Court did not reject the precedents established by the Warren Court. The justices upheld abortion rights and, in the case initiated by Allan Bakke, they limited affirmative action but did not overturn its constitutional foundation. Civil rights reformers, feminists, environmentalists, and antinuclear activists continued to press their concerns and achieve victories. Nevertheless, racial problems persisted as conservatives attacked affirmative action and school busing to promote integration. Many of these battles shifted northward, as white, working-class, grassroots activists such as Louise Day Hicks fought against busing in particular and more generally against liberal elites, who, they believed, ignored them.

In foreign affairs, President Nixon ushered in a period of détente with the Soviet Union and the opening of diplomatic relations with Communist China. He brought an end to American military participation in Vietnam, but did so with less than honor. Throughout the rest of the world, Nixon pursued a muscular foreign policy, which often left the United States siding with dictators. His Middle East strategy in the 1973 Yom Kippur War produced a damaging gasoline crisis at home, which would be felt for years. Jimmy Carter built on Nixon's spirit of cooperation with the Soviet Union and China, only to see it end with renewed conflict with the Soviets. Where Nixon and previous presidents had failed, Carter succeeded in brokering a peace treaty between Egypt and Israel. However, his popularity plummeted after Iranian revolutionaries seized the American Embassy in Teheran and held its fifty-two occupants hostage for 444 days despite a failed rescue attempt.

Conservatism experienced its political ups and downs in the 1970s, but by the end of the decade it stood on the edge of transforming the political landscape of the nation. It remained for Ronald Reagan to lead the New Right forward.

CHAPTER **27** REVIEW

TIMELINE OF **EVENTS**

KEY **TERMS**

REVIEW & RELATE

1. Compare Nixon's policies toward Vietnam with those toward the Soviet Union and China.
2. How did Nixon's Middle East policy affect Americans at home?
3. Describe the conservative coalition that brought Nixon to power.
4. How did Nixon appeal to conservatism and how much did he depart from it?
5. How effective was President Carter in domestic politics?
6. How did events in the Middle East, the Persian Gulf, and Afghanistan challenge the objectives of the Carter administration?
7. How and why did the social and cultural developments of the 1960s continue to create conflict and controversy in the 1970s?
8. Evaluate the strengths and weaknesses of liberalism in the 1970s.
9. Explain the rise of the New Right in the 1970s.
10. How did Christian evangelicals influence the New Right?

The New Right and Its Critics

▶ Analyze the arguments of the proponents and critics of the New Right and compare the respective audiences they are aimed at reaching.

The New Right had much in common with its Old Right forebear. Both stood for small government, lower taxes, and deregulation of the economy (Source 27.6). Each viewed labor unions as a danger to free enterprise and believed in a states' rights approach to handling civil rights conflicts. In foreign affairs they took a strong anti-Communist position in challenging the Soviet Union. During the 1950s, groups of conservative religious crusaders put forth right-wing political principles within a Christian framework, but the stridency of their critiques and their penchant for conspiracy theories pushed them to the fringes of political acceptability.

The grassroots conservative movement that propelled Barry Goldwater into national prominence in 1964 gained momentum in the 1970s. It forged a national coalition of economic and social conservatives; militant anti-Communists; and disaffected Democrats, especially in the South. Linking them was their hostility to Great Society programs, Vietnam War protesters, inner-city uprisings, affirmative action, feminism, and challenges to traditional cultural values (Sources 27.7 and 27.9). The New Right coalition that emerged in the 1970s differed in one key respect from its conservative predecessor: It successfully incorporated the religious right as a main partner. By 1980, the political landscape had moved to the right, and Christian conservatives, unlike those in the 1950s, were considered respectable and legitimate.

Defenders of liberalism did not remain silent in the face of conservative arguments. They attacked New Right economics for its trickle-down tax cuts, which benefited the wealthy at the expense of the poor and the middle class, and for failing properly to fund education, scientific research and technological development, energy conservation, and environmental protection. They also criticized social conservatives for opposing the Equal Rights Amendment (Source 27.8) and denounced the Moral Majority for attempting to impose its religious values on a secular society (Source 27.10).

Source 27.6

Proposition 13, California, 1978

Howard Jarvis, a conservative Republican lobbyist, spearheaded a taxpayer revolt in California for lower, fixed property taxes. He devised Proposition 13 and gained sufficient signatures to place it on the ballot as a referendum initiative. In 1978 California voters adopted the measure by an overwhelming majority and set off a national movement for property tax relief.

Section 1.

(a) The maximum amount of any ad valorem [according to value] tax on real property shall not exceed one percent (1%) of the full cash value of such property. The one percent (1%) tax to be collected by the counties and apportioned according to law to the districts within the counties. . . .

Section 2.

. . . (b) The fair market value base may reflect from year to year the inflationary rate not to exceed two percent (2%) for any given year or reduction as shown in the consumer price index or comparable data for the area under taxing jurisdiction.

Section 3.

From and after the effective date of this article, any changes in State taxes enacted for the purpose of increasing revenues collected pursuant thereto whether by increased rates or changes in methods of computation must be imposed by an Act passed by not less than two-thirds of all members elected to each of the two houses of the Legislature, except that no new ad valorem taxes on real property, or sales or transaction taxes on the sales of real property may be imposed.

Section 4.

Cities, Counties and special districts, by a two-thirds vote of the qualified electors of such district, may impose special taxes on such district, except ad valorem taxes on real property or a transaction tax or sales tax on the sale of real property within such City, County or special district.

Source: Howard Jarvis Taxpayers Association, "The Original Proposition 13," accessed December 4, 2015, http://www.hjta.org/propositions/proposition-13/.

Source 27.7

Phyllis Schlafly | "What's Wrong with 'Equal Rights' for Women?" 1972

A long-standing conservative activist, Phyllis Schlafly was an attorney, wife, and mother of six children. She had campaigned for Barry Goldwater in 1964 and successfully led the antifeminist forces against the Equal Rights Amendment in the 1970s. In the excerpt below she explains her views on women.

Of all the classes of people who ever lived, the American woman is the most privileged. We have the most rights and rewards, and the fewest duties. Our unique status is the result of a fortunate combination of circumstances.

1. We have the immense good fortune to live in a civilization which respects the family as the basic unit of society. This respect is part and parcel of our laws and our customs. It is based on the fact of life—which no legislation or agitation can erase—that women have babies and men don't.

If you don't like this fundamental difference, you will have to take up your complaint with God because He created us this way. The fact that women, not men, have babies is not the fault of selfish and domineering men, or of the establishment, or of any clique of conspirators who want to oppress women. It's simply the way God made us. . . .

The Financial Benefits of Chivalry

2. The second reason why American women are a privileged group is that we are the beneficiaries of a tradition of special respect for women which dates from the Christian Age of Chivalry. The honor and respect paid to Mary, the Mother of Christ, resulted in all women, in effect, being put on a pedestal. . . .

In other civilizations, such as the African and the American Indian, the men strut around wearing feathers and beads and hunting and fishing (great sport for men!), while the women do all the hard, tiresome drudgery including the tilling of the soil (if any is done), the hewing of wood, the making of fires, the carrying of water, as well as the cooking, sewing and caring for babies.

This is not the American way because we were lucky enough to inherit the traditions of the Age of Chivalry. In America, a man's first significant purchase is a diamond for his bride, and the largest financial investment of his life is a home for her to live in. American husbands work hours of overtime to buy a fur piece or other finery to keep their wives in fashion, and to pay premiums on their life insurance policies to provide for her comfort when she is a widow (benefits in which he can never share). . . .

The Real Liberation of Women

3. The third reason why American women are so well off is that the great American free enterprise system has produced remarkable inventors who have lifted the backbreaking "women's work" from our shoulders.

In other countries and in other eras, it was truly said that "Man may work from sun to sun, but woman's work is never done." . . . Our American free enterprise system has given us the gigantic food and packaging industry and beautiful supermarkets, which provide an endless variety of foods, prepackaged for easy carrying and a minimum of waiting. In America, women have the freedom from the slavery of standing in line for daily food.

Thus, household duties have been reduced to only a few hours a day, leaving the American woman with plenty of time to moonlight. She can take a full or part-time paying job, or she can indulge to her heart's content in a tremendous selection of interesting educational or cultural or homemaking activities. . . .

Women's Libbers Do NOT Speak for Us

The "women's lib" movement is *not* an honest effort to secure better jobs for women who want or need to work outside the home. This is just the superficial sweet-talk to win broad support for a radical "movement." Women's lib is a total assault on the role of the American woman as wife and mother, and on the family as the basic unit of society.

Source: *The Phyllis Schlafly Report* 5, no. 7 (February 1972): 1–4.

Source 27.8

Gloria Steinem, Testimony on the Equal Rights Amendment, May 6, 1970

Gloria Steinem is a feminist writer, founding editor of *MS.* Magazine, and political activist. In 1970, she testified before the Senate Committee on the Equal Rights Amendment.

During 12 years of working for a living, I have experienced much of the legal and social discrimination reserved for women in this country. I have been refused service in public restaurants, ordered out of public gathering places, and turned away from apartment rentals; all for the clearly stated, sole reason that I am a woman. And all without the legal remedies available to blacks and other minorities. I have been excluded from professional groups, writing assignments on so-called "unfeminine" subjects such as politics, full participation in the Democratic Party, jury duty, and even from such small male privileges as discounts on airline fares. Most important to me, I have been denied a society in which women are encouraged, or even allowed to think of themselves as first-class citizens and responsible human beings.

... The truth is that all our problems stem from the same sex based myths.... Like racial myths, they have been reflected in our laws. Let me list a few.

That woman are biologically inferior to men. In fact, an equally good case can be made for the reverse. Women live longer than men, even when the men are not subject to business pressures. Women survived Nazi concentration camps better, keep cooler heads in emergencies currently studied by disaster-researchers, are protected against heart attacks by their female sex hormones, and are so much more durable at every stage of life that nature must conceive 20 to 50 percent more males in order to keep the balance going. However, I don't want to prove the superiority of one sex to another. That would only be repeating a male mistake.

...Women suffer this second class treatment from the moment they are born. They are expected to be, rather than achieve, to function biologically rather than learn. A brother, whatever his intellect, is more likely to get the family's encouragement and education money, while girls are often pressured to conceal ambition and intelligence, to "Uncle Tom."

...Another myth, that children must have full-time mothers. American mothers spend more time with their homes and children than those of any other society we know about. In the past, joint families, servants, a prevalent system in which grandparents raised the children, or family field work in the agrarian systems—all these factors contributed more to child care than the labor-saving devices of which we are so proud.

The truth is that most American children seem to be suffering from too much mother, and too little father. Part of the program of Women's Liberation is a return of fathers to their children. If laws permit women equal work and pay opportunities, men will then be relieved of their role as sole breadwinner. Fewer ulcers, fewer hours of meaningless work, equal responsibility for his own children: these are a few of the reasons that Women's Liberation is Men's Liberation too.

Source: *The "Equal Rights" Amendment, Hearings before the Subcommittee on Constitutional Amendments of the Committee on the Judiciary United States Senate Ninety-First Congress, Second Session, on S. J. Res. 61 5–7 May 1970* (Washington, D. C.: U. S. Government Printing Office, 1970), 335–7.

Paul Weyrich | Building the Moral Majority, 1979

Paul Weyrich, a conservative Republican from Wisconsin and founder of the Heritage Foundation think tank, orchestrated the formation of the Moral Majority. A devout Catholic, he sought to unite Christians in a crusade against abortion and other liberal causes, as the following excerpt shows.

Because of the strong political reaction against abortion, the necrophiliac agenda for euthanasia, limiting the number of children a family may have (population control) and other overt antifamily schemes has been slowed down considerably. . . .

What the right-to-life movement has managed to put together on the abortion issue is only a sample of what is to come when the full range of family and educational issues becomes the focus of debate in the 1980s.

The homosexual rights advocates, genetic engineers and militant secular humanists who insist on their religion in the schools had better understand what is happening.

The threat to the family has caused leaders of various denominations to put aside their sectarian differences and, for the first time in decades, agree on basic principles worth fighting for. . . . [T]he pro-family movement is a recognition that the moral majority must be put together as a coalition—because our very right to worship as we choose, to bring up our families in some kind of moral order, to educate our children free from the interference of the state, to follow the commands of Holy Scripture and the Church are at stake.

Source: Paul Weyrich, "Building the Moral Majority," *Conservative Digest*, August 1979, 18–19.

A. Bartlett Giamatti | The Moral Majority Threatens Freedom, 1981

One of the Moral Majority's sharpest critics was A. Bartlett Giamatti, a Renaissance scholar, president of Yale University (1978–1986), and subsequently commissioner of Major League Baseball. In an excerpt from the speech he originally gave to Yale's incoming freshman class in 1981, Giamatti attacked the Religious Right for its dogmatism and threat to personal freedom.

A self-proclaimed "Moral Majority," and its satellite or client groups, cunning in the use of a native blend of old intimidation and new technology, threatens the values [of freedom]. Angry at change, rigid in the application of chauvinistic slogans, absolutistic in morality, its members threaten through political pressure or public denunciation whoever dares to disagree with their authoritarian positions. . . .

From the maw of this "morality" come those who presume to know what justice for all is; come those who presume to know what books are fit to read; which television programs are fit to watch; which textbooks will serve for all the young; come spilling those who presume to know what only God knows, which is when human life begins. . . . There is no debate, no discussion, no dissent. They know. There is only one set of overarching political and spiritual and social beliefs; whatever view does not conform to these views is by definition relativistic, negative, secular, immoral, against the family, anti-free enterprise, un-American. What nonsense.

. . . For what [these groups] claim they espouse—love of country, a regard for the sanctity of life and the importance of the family, a belief in high standards of personal conduct, a conviction that we derive our values from a transcendent being, a desire to assert that free enterprise is better than state ownership and state control—are not evil or pernicious beliefs. Quite the contrary. They are the kernels of beliefs held dear, in various ways, by me and by millions of other Americans. You should not scorn these ideas simply because some extremists claim, whether sincerely or hypocritically, to have captured these beliefs for themselves. The point is, the rest of us hold to ideas of family, country, belief in God, *in different ways*. The right to differ, and to see things differently, is our concern.

Source: A. Bartlett Giamatti, "A Liberal Education and the New Coercion," *A Free and Ordered Space: The Real World of the University* (New York: W. W. Norton, 1990), 110–17.

Interpret the Evidence

1. Explain the goals of Proposition 13 (Document 27.6), and how its provisions attempt to achieve them.
2. Compare Phyllis Schlafly's (Document 27.7) views of American women with those of Gloria Steinem (Document 27.8). Why do they reach different conclusions?
3. Describe the perceived dangers that united religious conservatives in the Moral Majority (Document 27.9).
4. Compare the ideas of A. Bartlett Giamatti (Document 27.10) and the Moral Majority (Document 27.9). Describe the areas of disagreement and agreement.

Put It in Context

How did the New Right shape the political and social landscapes of the United States in the 1970s?

The Triumph of Conservatism, the End of the Cold War, and the Rise of the New World Order

28

1980–1992

WINDOW TO THE PAST

United States Conference of Catholic Bishops, Pastoral Letter on War and Peace, 1983

Many Americans worried over President Reagan's buildup of the U.S. nuclear arsenal against the Soviet Union and called on both sides to initiate a nuclear weapons freeze. In 1983 U.S. Catholic bishops wrote this pastoral letter with recommendations to lessen the threat of nuclear war. ▶ To discover more about what this primary source can show us, see Source 28.3 on page 975.

2. We support efforts to achieve deep cuts in the arsenals of both superpowers; efforts should concentrate first on systems which threaten the retaliatory forces of either major power.

3. We support early and successful conclusion of negotiations of a comprehensive test ban treaty.

4. We urge new efforts to prevent the spread of nuclear weapons in the world, and to control the conventional arms race, particularly the conventional arms trade.

After reading this chapter you should be able to:

- Assess the impact of Reaganomics and the ability of Presidents Reagan and Bush to deliver on the New Right's agenda.

- Analyze Ronald Reagan's role in ending the Cold War and fighting international terrorism.

- Describe how George H. W. Bush managed the end of the Cold War, and evaluate how he established a New World Order between the United States and the rest of the world.

COMPARING AMERICAN HISTORIES

As secretary of state, George Pratt Shultz presided over the end of the Cold War. A skilled mediator, Shultz believed in hard-nosed diplomacy, asserting that "negotiations are a euphemism for capitulation if the shadow of power is not cast across the bargaining table." Upon graduating from Princeton with an economics degree in 1942, the twenty-two-year-old Shultz joined the Marine Corps and served in the Pacific during World War II. After the war, he earned a Ph.D. in industrial economics and taught at the Massachusetts Institute of Technology and the University of Chicago. In 1955 he joined President Eisenhower's Council of Economic Advisors, the first

(left) **George Shultz.** U.S. Department of State
(right) **Barbara Deming.** Kanaga, Consuelo (1894–1978)/Brooklyn Museum of Art, New York, USA/Gift of Wallace B. Putnam from the Estate of the Artist/Bridgeman Images

of many government posts he would fill in the Kennedy, Johnson, and Nixon administrations before he left government for the corporate world.

In 1982 Shultz returned to Washington to serve as President Ronald Reagan's secretary of state. Like Reagan, Shultz believed that the United States needed to reassert itself as a global power and rebound from the insecurity and self-doubt that followed the Vietnam War. The president believed that a tough approach would bring peace, and he revived the fiery rhetoric and military preparedness of the darkest days of the Cold War. As an economist, Shultz doubted that the Soviet Union was financially able to sustain its military strength, and his predictions proved correct. Faced with an escalating arms race, a fresh group of Soviet leaders decided to pursue peaceful relations.

While President Reagan and Secretary of State Shultz advocated confrontation with the Soviet Union, Barbara Deming challenged their efforts and devoted her life to promoting peace in a far different manner. Born in 1917 to a middle-class family living in New York City, Deming graduated from Bennington College and became an outspoken proponent of nuclear disarmament, feminism, civil rights, and pacifism. Her radical political beliefs and her recognition that she was a lesbian at the age of sixteen placed her outside the social and cultural mainstream. She lived in a women's commune and mobilized women to demonstrate for peaceful coexistence with the Soviet Union.

In the 1980s, Deming applied her pacifist beliefs against Reagan and Shultz's muscular approach to fighting the Cold War. As part of a worldwide campaign against the deployment of nuclear weapons, she joined the Women's Encampment for a Future of Peace and Justice, which opened in western New York in 1983 next to an army depot that stored nuclear missiles. On July 30, 1983, Deming led a march of seventy-five female activists into the small town of Waterloo. "Four miles into our walk," she recalled, "our way was blocked by several hundred townspeople brandishing American flags and chanting, 'Commies, go home!'" The marchers then sat down in nonviolent protest, and the police arrested Deming and fifty-three other protesters. Demonstrations continued throughout the rest of the summer, inspiring protests in other American communities and throughout Europe. ■

T he American histories of George Shultz and Barbara Deming were shaped by decades of conflict between the United States and the Soviet Union. Both Shultz and Deming believed that the conflict was one of the defining issues of their times, and both were convinced that their approach was the best way to achieve lasting global peace. Advised by Secretary of State Schultz, President Ronald Reagan employed harsher anti-Soviet rhetoric than at any time since the early 1960s and accelerated the buildup of the military. However, similarly to how cold warrior Richard Nixon opened up diplomatic relations with Communist China, so too Reagan seized the moment to end the Cold War. Yet to achieve this result, he needed the cooperation of Soviet leader Mikhail Gorbachev, as well as the global efforts of peace activists who contributed to reducing the prospects of nuclear war. With the collapse of the Soviet Union and its empire, the United States became the world's sole superpower. At the same time, the United States had to operate in an increasingly globalized world and face tests of its strength in Central America, the Middle East, and the Persian Gulf.

Not only did Reagan transform diplomatic relationships with the Soviet Union, he reshaped the nation's political priorities. The president implemented anti-union measures and signed legislation granting large tax cuts as well as reductions in spending for programs that helped the poor and needy. His administration also relaxed government regulations over business and succeeded in tipping the Supreme Court to the right through its conservative appointments. Social conservatives, too, made headway during the 1980s by defeating the Equal Rights Amendment.

The **Reagan Revolution**

The election of former California governor Ronald Reagan as president in 1980 reflected the spectacular growth in political power of the New Right. Reagan pushed the conservative economic agenda of lower taxes and business deregulation alongside the New Right's concern for traditional religious and family values. His presidency installed conservatism as the dominant political ideology for the remainder of the twentieth century.

Reagan and Reaganomics.

Ronald Reagan's presidential victory in 1980 consolidated the growing New Right coalition and reshaped American politics for a generation to come. The former movie actor had transformed himself from a New Deal Democrat into a conservative Republican politician when he ran for governor of California in 1966. As governor, he implemented conservative ideas of free enterprise and small government and denounced Johnson's Great Society for threatening private property and individual liberty. His support for conservative economic and social issues carried him to the presidency.

Explore ▶

For Ronald Reagan's view of America, see Source 28.1.

Reagan handily beat Jimmy Carter and John Anderson, a moderate Republican who ran as an independent candidate (Map 28.1). The high unemployment and inflation of the late 1970s worked in Reagan's favor. Reagan appealed to a coalition of conservative Republicans and disaffected Democrats, promising to cut taxes and reduce spending, to relax federal supervision over civil rights programs, and to end what was left of expensive Great Society measures and affirmative action. The 1980 and subsequent presidential elections demonstrated the rising political, economic, and social influence of the American South and West, especially

GUIDED ANALYSIS

Ronald Reagan | First Inaugural Address, January 20, 1981

In the 1980s, as the nation reeled in the aftermath of Watergate and the Vietnam War as well as the more immediate crises of oil shortages and stagflation, Ronald Reagan promised voters that better times were coming. In his first inaugural address, Reagan reasserted his pledges to lower taxes, reduce the size of the federal government, and restore American pride. By 1984 Reagan and his supporters were ready to claim victory, seeing in the return of economic growth vindication of their ideas and optimism.

Source 28.1

The business of our nation goes forward. These United States are confronted with an economic affliction of great proportions. We suffer from the longest and one of the worst sustained inflations in our national history. It distorts our economic decisions, penalizes thrift, and crushes the struggling young and the fixed-income elderly alike. It threatens to shatter the lives of millions of our people.

Idle industries have cast workers into unemployment, human misery, and personal indignity. Those who do work are denied a fair return for their labor by a tax system which penalizes successful achievement and keeps us from maintaining full productivity. . . .

In this present crisis, government is not the solution to our problem; government is the problem. From time to time, we've been tempted to believe that society has become too complex to be managed by self-rule, that government by an elite group is superior to government for, by, and of the people. Well, if no one among us is capable of governing himself, then who among

us has the capacity to govern someone else? All of us together, in and out of government, must bear the burden. The solutions we seek must be equitable, with no one group singled out to pay a higher price. . . .

It is my intention to curb the size and influence of the Federal establishment and to demand recognition of the distinction between the powers granted to the Federal Government and those reserved to the States or to the people. All of us need to be reminded that the Federal Government did not create the States; the States created the Federal Government.

Now, so there will be no misunderstanding, it's not my intention to do away with government. It is rather to make it work—work with us, not over us; to stand by our side, not ride on our back. Government can and must provide opportunity, not smother it; foster productivity, not stifle it.

Source: Michael Waldman, ed., *My Fellow Americans: The Most Important Speeches of America's Presidents, from George Washington to George W. Bush* (Naperville, IL: Sourcebooks, 2003), 247–49.

Interpret the Evidence

1. According to Reagan, what are the sources of the nation's economic problems?
2. How does Reagan view the role of government in the economy and the relationship between federal and state governments?

Put It in Context

Why did conservatism rise to political power in the 1980s?

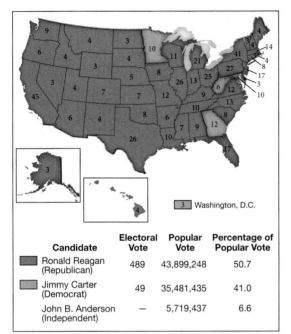

Candidate	Electoral Vote	Popular Vote	Percentage of Popular Vote
Ronald Reagan (Republican)	489	43,899,248	50.7
Jimmy Carter (Democrat)	49	35,481,435	41.0
John B. Anderson (Independent)	—	5,719,437	6.6

MAP 28.1   The Election of 1980

Ronald Reagan won 50.7 percent of the popular vote in the 1980 election, but his margin of victory over Jimmy Carter was much greater in the electoral vote. Reagan won the votes of the South and many disaffected Democrats in the urban North. A third-party candidate, John Anderson of Illinois, won 6.6 percent of the popular vote, demonstrating significant disapproval with both major parties.

as these regions continued their rapid population growth by drawing migrants from other areas of the nation. Finally, he energized members of the religious right, who flocked to the polls to support Reagan's demands for voluntary prayer in the public schools, defeat of the Equal Rights Amendment, and a constitutional amendment to outlaw abortion. In fact, the religious right attracted its most ardent supporters from the burgeoning population of the South and West.

In his inaugural address, Reagan underscored his conservative approach to government. "It's not my intention to do away with government," the president declared. "It is rather to make it work—work with us, not over us; to stand by our side, not ride on our back. Government can and must provide opportunity, not smother it; foster productivity, not stifle it." With this in mind, his first priority was stimulating the stagnant economy. The president's strategy, known as **Reaganomics**, reflected the ideas of supply-side economists and conservative Republicans. Reagan subscribed to the idea of trickle-down economics in which the gains reaped at the top of a strong economy would trickle down to the benefit of those below, thus reducing the need for large government social programs. Stating that "government is not the solution to our problem; government is the problem," Reagan asked Congress for a huge income tax cut of 30 percent over three years, a reduction in spending for domestic programs of more than $40 billion, and new monetary policies to lower rising rates for loans.

The president did not operate in isolation from the rest of the world. He learned a great deal from Margaret Thatcher, the British prime minister who took office two years before Reagan. Thatcher combated inflation by slashing welfare programs, selling off publicly owned companies, and cutting back health and education programs. An advocate of supply-side economics, Thatcher reduced income taxes on the wealthy by more than 50 percent to encourage new investment. West Germany also moved toward the right under Chancellor Helmut Kohl, who reined in welfare spending. In the 1980s Reaganomics and Thatcherism dominated the United States and the two most powerful nations of Western Europe.

In March 1981 Reagan survived a nearly fatal assassin's bullet. More popular than ever after his recovery, the president persuaded the Democratic House and the Republican Senate to pass his economic measures in slightly modified form in the **Economic Recovery Tax Act**. These cuts in taxes and spending did not produce the immediate results Reagan sought—unemployment rose to 9.6 percent in 1983 from 7.1 percent in 1980. However, the government's tight money policies, as engineered by the Federal Reserve Board, reduced inflation from 14 percent in 1980 to 4 percent in 1984. By 1984 the unemployment rate had

Ronald Reagan Campaigns for President, 1980 Pledging to make America great again, Republican presidential candidate Ronald Reagan greets supporters at a senior citizens' retirement community in Seal Beach, California. During his 1980 campaign, Reagan expressed the cardinal tenet of antigovernment conservatism: "Government is like a baby, an alimentary canal with a big appetite at one end and no sense of responsibility at the other." AP Photo/Walter Zeboski

fallen to 7.5 percent, while the gross national product grew by a healthy 4.3 percent, an indication that the recession, and the stagflation that came with it, had ended.

The success of Reaganomics came at the expense of the poor and the lower middle class. The president reduced spending for food stamps, school lunches, Aid to Families with Dependent Children (welfare), and Medicaid, while maintaining programs that middle-class voters relied on, such as Medicare and Social Security. However, rather than diminishing the government, the savings that came from reduced social spending went into increased military appropriations. Together with lower taxes, these expenditures benefited large corporations that received government military contracts and favorable tax write-offs.

As a result of Reagan's economic policies, financial institutions and the stock market earned huge profits. The Reagan administration relaxed antitrust regulations, encouraging corporate mergers to a degree unseen since the Great Depression. Fueled by falling interest rates, the stock market created wealth for many investors. The number of millionaires doubled during the 1980s, as the top 1 percent of families gained control of 42 percent of the nation's wealth and 60 percent of corporate stock. Reflecting this phenomenal accumulation of riches, television produced melodramas depicting the lives of oil barons (such as *Dallas* and *Dynasty*), whose characters lived glamorous lives filled with intrigue and extravagance. In *Wall Street* (1987), a film that captured the money ethic of the period, the main character utters the memorable line summing up the moment: "Greed, for lack of a better word, is good. Greed is right. Greed works."

At the same time that a small number of Americans grew wealthier, the gap between the rich and the poor widened. Contrary to the promises of Reaganomics, the wealth did not trickle down. During the 1980s, the nation's share of poor people rose from 11.7 percent to 13.5 percent, representing 33 million Americans. Severe cutbacks in government social programs such as food stamps worsened the plight of the poor. Poverty disproportionately affected women and minorities. The number of homeless people grew to as many as 400,000 during the 1980s. The middle class also diminished from a high of 53 percent of families in the early 1970s to 49 percent in 1985.

The Reagan administration's relaxed regulation of the corporate sector also contributed to the unbalanced economy. The president aided big business by challenging labor unions. In 1981 air traffic controllers went on strike to gain higher wages and improved safety conditions. In response, the president fired the strikers who refused to return to work, and in their place he hired new controllers. Reagan's anti-union actions both reflected and encouraged a decline in union membership throughout the 1980s, with union membership falling to 16 percent, its lowest level since the New Deal. Without union protection, wages failed to keep up with inflation, further increasing the gap between rich and poor.

Reagan continued the business deregulation initiated under Carter. Federal agencies concerned with environmental protection, consumer product reliability, and occupational safety saw their key functions shifted to the states, which made them less effective. Reagan also extended banking deregulation, which encouraged savings and loan institutions (S&Ls) to make risky loans to real estate ventures. When real estate prices began to tumble, savings and loan associations faced collapse and Congress appropriated over $100 billion to rescue them. Notwithstanding deregulation and small-government rhetoric, the number of federal government employees actually increased under Reagan by 200,000.

Reagan's landslide victory over Democratic candidate Walter Mondale in 1984 sealed the national political transition from liberalism to conservatism. Voters responded overwhelmingly to the improving economy, Reagan's defense of traditional social values, and his boundless optimism about America's future. Despite the landslide, the election was notable for the nomination of Representative Geraldine Ferraro of New York as Mondale's Democratic running mate, the first woman to run on a major party ticket for national office.

Reagan's second term did not produce changes as significant as did his first term. Democrats still controlled the House and in 1986 recaptured the Senate. The Reagan administration focused on foreign affairs and the continued Cold War with the Soviet Union, thus escalating defense spending. Most of the Reagan economic revolution continued as before, but with serious consequences. Supply-side economics failed to support the increase in military spending: The federal deficit mushroomed, and by 1989 the nation was saddled with a $2.8 trillion debt, a situation that jeopardized the country's financial independence and the economic well-being of succeeding generations.

The president further reshaped the future through his nominations to the U.S. Supreme Court. Starting with the choice of Sandra Day O'Connor, the Court's first female justice, in 1981, Reagan's appointments moved the Court in a more conservative direction. The elevation of Associate Justice William Rehnquist to chief justice in 1986 reinforced this trend, which would have significant consequences for decades to come.

The Implementation of Social Conservatism.
Throughout his two terms, President Reagan pushed the New Right's social agenda. Conservatives blamed political

liberalism for what they saw as a decline in family values. Their solution was a renewed focus on conservative Christian principles. In addition to trying to remove evolution and sex education from the classroom and bring in prayer, the New Right stepped up its opposition to abortion and imposed limits on reproductive rights. The Reagan administration required family planning agencies seeking federal funding to notify parents of children under age eighteen before dispensing birth control, cut off financial aid to international organizations supporting abortion, and provided funds to promote sexual abstinence. Despite these efforts, conservatives could not convince the Supreme Court to overturn *Roe v. Wade*. However, they did see the Equal Right Amendment go down to defeat in 1982 when it failed to get the required two-thirds approval from the states (see "Women's Movement" in chapter 27).

Social conservatives also felt threatened by more tolerant views of homosexuality. The gay rights movement, which began in the 1960s, strengthened during the 1970s as thousands of gay men and lesbians made known their sexual orientation, fought discrimination, and expressed pride in their sexual identity. Then, in the early 1980s, physicians traced an outbreak of a deadly illness among gay men to a virus that attacked the immune system (human immunodeficiency virus, or HIV), making it vulnerable to infections that were usually fatal. This disease, called **acquired immune deficiency syndrome (AIDS)**, was transmitted through bodily fluids during sexual intercourse, through blood transfusions, and by intravenous drug use. Scientists could not explain why the disease initially showed up

ACT UP Protest, 1988 Amid the AIDS epidemic in the gay community, the militant group AIDS Coalition to Unleash Power (ACT UP) campaigned for better funding of programs to fight the disease. This photo shows ACT UP protesters blocking the entrance to the headquarters of the Food and Drug Administration in Rockville, Maryland on Oct. 11, 1988. A police officer steps into the group, and some fifty of the protesters were arrested. AP Photo/J. Scott Applewhite

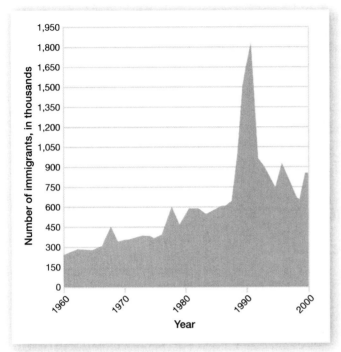

FIGURE 28.1 Immigrant Arrivals to the United States, 1960–2000

Immigration to the United States rose dramatically in the 1970s and 1980s, peaking in the early 1990s. Between 1970 and 2000, nearly 21 million immigrants arrived in the United States, mainly from Mexico, Central America, the Caribbean, and eastern and southern Asia. How do you explain the rise in immigration after 1965?

Source: Data from 2000 Statistical Yearbook of the Immigration and Naturalization Service.

among gay men in the United States; however, New Right critics insisted that AIDS was a plague visited on sexual deviants by an angry God. As the epidemic spread beyond the gay community, gay rights organizers and their heterosexual allies raised research money and public awareness. By the early 1990s, medical advances had begun to extend the lives of AIDS patients and manage the disease.

Increased immigration also troubled social conservatives as another reflection of the general societal breakdown. The number of immigrants to the United States rose dramatically in the 1970s and 1980s following the relaxation of foreign quota restrictions after 1965 (Figure 28.1). During these decades, immigrants came mainly from Mexico, Central America, the Caribbean, and eastern and southern Asia and tended to settle in California, Florida, Texas, New York, and New Jersey. Like those who came nearly a century before, most sought economic opportunity, political freedom, and escape from wars. By 1990 one-third of Los Angeles's and New York City's populations were foreign-born, figures similar to the high numbers of European immigrants at the turn of the twentieth century.

As happened during previous immigration waves, many Americans whose ancestors had immigrated to the United States generations earlier expressed hostility toward the new immigrants. The New Right provoked traditional fears that immigrants took away jobs and depressed wages, and questioned whether these culturally diverse people could assimilate into American society. In 1986 the Reagan administration departed from many of his conservative anti-immigrant supporters and, with bipartisan congressional support, fashioned a compromise that extended amnesty to undocumented aliens residing in the United States for a specified period and allowed them to acquire legal status. At the same time, the **Immigration Reform and Control Act** penalized employers who hired new illegal workers. The measure allowed Reagan and the Republicans to appeal to Latino voters in the Sun Belt states while convincing the New Right that the administration intended to halt further undocumented immigration.

REVIEW & RELATE

- What was Reaganomics, and what were its most important long-term consequences?
- How did conservative ideas shape the social, cultural, and political landscape of the 1980s and 1990s?

Reagan and the End of the Cold War, 1981–1988

As Ronald Reagan entered the White House determined to pose a direct challenge to liberalism, so too did he intend to confront the Soviets. Reagan and Secretary of State George Shultz believed that détente would become feasible only after the United States achieved military supremacy over the Soviet Union. Reagan also took strong measures to fight communism around the globe, from Central America to the Middle East. Yet military superiority alone would not defeat the Soviet Union. A shift of leadership within the USSR, as well as a worldwide protest movement for nuclear disarmament, helped bring an end to the Cold War and prepare the way for the dissolution of the Soviet empire.

"The Evil Empire." In running for president in 1980, Reagan wrapped his hard-line anti-Communist message in the rhetoric of peace. "I've called for whatever it takes to be so strong that no other nation will dare violate the peace," he told the Veterans of Foreign Wars Convention on August 18, 1980. Once in the White House, Reagan left no doubt about his anti-Communist stance. He called the Soviet Union "the evil empire," regarding it as "the focus of evil in the modern world." The president planned to confront that evil with both words and deeds, backing up his rhetoric with a massive military buildup.

In a show of moral and economic might, Reagan proposed the largest military budget in American history. The defense budget grew by about 7 percent per year, increasing from $157 billion in 1981 to around $282 billion in 1988. Reagan clearly intended to win the Cold War by outspending the Soviets, even if it meant running up huge deficits that greatly burdened the U.S. economy.

The president sought to expand the Cold War by developing new weapons to be deployed in outer space. He proposed the Strategic Defense Initiative (SDI), which in theory would use sky-based lasers to shoot down enemy missiles. Critics dubbed this program "Star Wars," and even Secretary of State Shultz privately called it "lunacy." The SDI was never carried out, though the government spent $17 billion on research.

Reagan was unyielding in his initial dealings with the Soviet Union, and negotiations between the superpowers moved slowly and unevenly. The Reagan administration's initial "zero option" proposal called for the Soviets to dismantle all of their intermediate-range missiles in exchange for the United States agreeing to refrain from deploying any new medium-range missiles. The administration presented this option merely for show, expecting the Soviets to reject it. However, in 1982, after the Soviets accepted the principle of "zero option," Reagan sent negotiators to begin Strategic Arms Reduction Talks (START). Influenced by antinuclear protests in Europe, which had a great impact on European governments, the Americans proposed shelving the deployment of 572 Pershing II and cruise missiles in Europe in return for the Soviets' dismantling of Eastern European–based intermediate-range ballistic missiles that were targeted at Western Europe. The Soviets viewed this offer as perpetuating American nuclear superiority and rejected it.

Relations between the two superpowers deteriorated in September 1983 when a Soviet fighter jet shot down a South Korean passenger airliner, killing 269 people. The Soviets charged that the plane had veered off course and violated their airspace. Although the disaster resulted mainly from Soviet mistakes, Reagan chose to condemn this attack as further proof of the malign intentions of the USSR. The United States sent additional missiles to bases in West Germany, Great Britain, and Italy; in response, the Soviets abandoned the disarmament talks and replenished their nuclear arsenal in Czechoslovakia and East Germany. More symbolically, the Soviets boycotted the 1984 Olympic Games in Los Angeles, in retaliation for the U.S. boycott of the Olympics in Moscow four years earlier. As the two adversaries swung from peace talks to threats of nuclear confrontation, one European journalist observed: "The second Cold War has begun."

Human Rights and the Fight against Communism.
The Reagan administration extended its firm Cold War position throughout the world, emphasizing anticommunism often at the expense of human rights. The president saw threats of Soviet intervention in Central America and the Middle East, and he aimed to contain them. Reagan exploited the fear of communism in Central America and the Caribbean, where for nearly a century the United States had guarded its sphere of influence. During the 1980s, the United States continued its economic isolation of Cuba via the trade embargo, and it sought to prevent other Communist or leftist governments from emerging in Central America and the Caribbean.

In the late 1970s Nicaraguan revolutionaries, known as the National Liberation Front or Sandinistas, had overthrown the tyrannical government of General Anastasio Somoza, a brutal dictator. President Jimmy Carter, who had originally supported Somoza's overthrow, halted all aid to Nicaragua in 1980 after the Sandinistas began nationalizing foreign companies and drawing closer to Cuba. Under Reagan, Secretary of State Shultz suggested a U.S. invasion of Nicaragua, reflecting the administration's belief that the revolution in Nicaragua had been sponsored by Moscow. Instead Reagan adopted a more indirect approach. In 1982 he authorized the CIA to train approximately two thousand guerrilla forces outside the country, known as Contras (Counterrevolutionaries), to overthrow the Sandinista government. Although Reagan praised the Contras as "the moral equivalent of our Founding Fathers," the group consisted of pro-Somoza reactionaries as well as anti-Marxist democrats who blew up bridges and oil dumps, burned crops, and killed civilians. In 1982 Congress, unwilling to support such actions, passed the **Boland Amendment**, which prohibited direct aid to the Contras. In the face of congressional opposition, Reagan and his advisers came up with a plan that would secretly fund the efforts of their military surrogates in Nicaragua. Reagan ordered the CIA and the National Security Council (NSC) to raise money from anti-Communist leaders abroad and wealthy conservatives at home. This effort, called "Project Democracy," raised millions of dollars, and by

1985 the number of Contra troops had swelled from 10,000 to 20,000. In violation of federal law, CIA director William Casey also authorized his agency to continue training the Contras in assassination techniques and other methods of subversion.

Elsewhere in Central America, the Reagan administration supported a corrupt right-wing government in El Salvador that, in an effort to put down an insurgency, sanctioned military death squads and killed forty thousand people during the 1980s. Despite the failings and abuses of the El Salvadoran government, Reagan insisted that Communist regimes in Nicaragua and Cuba were behind the Salvadoran insurgents. The United States sent more than $5 billion in aid to El Salvador and trained its military leaders to combat guerrilla forces.

While many Americans supported Reagan's strong anti-Communist stance, others opposed to the president's policy mobilized protests. Marches, rallies, and teach-ins were organized in cities and college campuses nationwide. U.S.-sponsored wars also drove many people to flee their dangerous, poverty-stricken countries and seek asylum in the United States. Between 1984 and 1990, 45,000 Salvadorans and 9,500 Guatemalans applied for asylum in the United States, but because the United States supported the established governments in those two nations, nearly all requests for refugee status were denied. Approximately five hundred American churches and synagogues established a sanctuary movement to provide safe haven for those fleeing Central American civil wars. Other Americans, especially in California and Texas, began to view the influx of refugees from Central America with alarm. This immigration, both legal and illegal, meant an increase in medical and educational costs for state and local communities, which taxpayers considered a burden.

In addition to financing guerrilla wars in Central America, on October 25, 1983 Reagan sent 7,000 marines to invade the tiny Caribbean island of Grenada. After a coup toppled the leftist government of Maurice Bishop, who had received Cuban and Soviet aid, the United States stepped in, ostensibly to protect American medical school students in Grenada from political instability following the coup. A pro-American government was installed. The swift action in Grenada boosted Reagan's popularity.

Reagan's eagerness to fight communism extended around the world, and his administration supported repressive governments in the Middle East, Asia, Latin America, and Africa. Reagan embraced the distinction made by his ambassador to the United Nations, Jeane Kirkpatrick, between non-Communist "authoritarian" nations, which were acceptable, and Communist "totalitarian" regimes, which were not. Reagan considered the South African government an example of an acceptable authoritarianism, even though it practiced apartheid (white supremacy and racial separation) and torture. The fact that the South African Communist Party had joined the fight against apartheid reinforced Reagan's desire to support the white-minority, anti-Communist government. Interested in the country's vast mineral wealth, Reagan opted for what he called "constructive engagement" with South Africa, rather than condemn its racist practices. The Reagan administration did so even as protesters across the United States and the world spoke out against South Africa's repressive white-majority government and campaigned for divestment of public and corporate funds from South African companies. After years of pressure from the divestment movement on college campuses and elsewhere, in 1986 Congress passed the Comprehensive Anti-Apartheid Act, which prohibited new trade and investment in South Africa. President Reagan vetoed it, but Congress overrode the president's veto.

Antiapartheid Protest, Cornell University   In 1986 students on college campuses such as Cornell protested apartheid in South Africa. They constructed shantytowns to highlight the poverty of nonwhite South Africans. Their immediate goal was to persuade their universities to remove their investments in companies that did business in South Africa. David Lyons

Fighting International Terrorism. Two days before the Grenada invasion in 1983, the U.S. military suffered a grievous blow halfway around the world. In the tiny country of Lebanon, wedged between Syrian occupation on its northern border and the Palestine Liberation Organization's (PLO) fight against Israel to the south, a civil war raged between Christians and Muslims. Reagan believed that stability in the region was in America's national interest. With this in mind, in 1982 the Reagan administration sent 800 marines, as part of a multilateral force that included French and Italian troops, to keep the peace. On October 23, 1983, a suicide bomber drove a truck into a marine barracks, killing 241 soldiers. Reagan withdrew the remaining troops.

The removal of troops did not end threats to Americans in the Middle East. Terrorism had become an ever-present danger, especially since the Iranian hostage crisis in 1979–1980. In 1985, 17 American citizens were killed in terrorist assaults, and 154 were injured. In June 1985, Shi'ite Muslim extremists hijacked a TWA airliner in Athens with 39 Americans on board and flew it to Beirut. That same year, commandos of the Palestine Liberation Organization hijacked the Italian liner *Achille Lauro*, which was cruising from Egypt to Israel. One of the 450 passengers, the wheelchair-bound, elderly Jewish American Leon Klinghoffer, was murdered and thrown overboard. After three days, Egyptian authorities negotiated an end to the terrorist hijacking.

In response to the 1985 PLO cruise ship attack, the Reagan administration targeted the North African country of Libya for retaliation. Its military leader, Muammar al-Qaddafi, supported the Palestinian cause and provided sanctuary for terrorists. The

Reagan administration had placed a trade embargo on Libya, and Secretary of State Shultz remarked: "We have to put Qaddafi in a box and close the lid." In 1986, after the bombing of a nightclub in West Berlin killed 2 American servicemen and injured 230, Reagan charged that Qaddafi was responsible. In late April the United States retaliated by sending planes to bomb the Libyan capital of Tripoli. Following the bombing, Qaddafi took a much lower profile against the United States. Reagan had demonstrated his nation's military might despite the retreat from Lebanon (Map 28.2).

In the meantime, the situation in Lebanon remained critical as the strife caused by civil war led to the seizing of American hostages. By mid-1984, seven Americans in Lebanon had been kidnapped by Shi'ite Muslims financed by Iran. Since 1980, Iran, a Shi'ite nation, had been engaged in a protracted war with Iraq, which was ruled by military leader Saddam Hussein and his Sunni Muslim party, the chief rival to the Shi'ites. With relations between the United States and Iran having deteriorated in the aftermath of the 1979 coup, the Reagan administration backed Iraq in this war. The fate of the hostages in Lebanon, however, motivated Reagan to make a deal with Iran. In late 1985 Reagan's national security

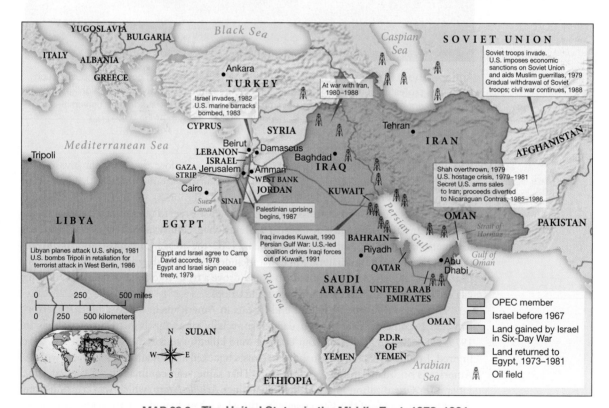

MAP 28.2　The United States in the Middle East, 1978–1991

The United States has historically needed access to the rich oil reserves of the Middle East. From the 1970s to the 1990s, both Democratic and Republican administrations were committed to the security of Israel, supportive of Afghan rebels fighting Soviet invaders, and opposed to the rising power of Islamic regimes. These principles often led to contradictory policies that further embroiled the United States in Middle East affairs.

adviser, Robert McFarlane, negotiated secretly with an Iranian intermediary for the United States to sell antitank missiles to Iran in exchange for the Shi'ite government using its influence to induce the Muslim kidnappers to release the hostages.

Had the matter ended there, the secret deal might never have come to light. However, NSC aide Lieutenant Colonel Oliver North developed a plan to transfer the proceeds from the arms-for-hostages deal to fund the Contras in Nicaragua and circumvent the Boland Amendment, which prohibited direct aid to the rebels. Despite opposition from Secretary of State Shultz, Reagan liked North's plan, although the president seemed vague about the details, and some $10 million to $20 million of Iranian money flowed into the hands of the Contras.

In 1986 information about the **Iran-Contra affair** came to light. **See Primary Source Project 28: The Iran-Contra Affair, page 992.** In the summer of 1987, televised Senate hearings exposed much of the tangled, covert dealings with Iran. In 1988 a special federal prosecutor indicted NSC adviser Vice Admiral John Poindexter (who had replaced McFarlane), North, and several others on charges ranging from perjury to conspiracy to obstruction of justice. Reagan took responsibility for the transfer of funds to the Contras, but he managed to weather the political crisis.

The Nuclear Freeze Movement.
Despite his tough talk and military buildup, Reagan was not immune to public pressure. Rising protests against nuclear weapons in the United States and Europe in the early 1980s revealed a public increasingly anxious about the possibility of nuclear confrontation with the Soviet Union. At the end of the Carter administration, the United States had promised NATO that it would station new missiles in England, Italy, West Germany, and Belgium. Coupled with his confrontational stance against the Soviet Union, Reagan's decision to implement this policy sparked enormous protest. One such protest came in 1981 when peace activists set up camp at Greenham Common in England outside of one of the military bases prepared to house the arriving missiles, one of twenty such camps in England. The peace camp at Greenham Common, where protesters sang, danced, and performed skits to affirm women's solidarity for peace, became the model for the Women's Encampment for a Future of Peace and Justice at Seneca Falls, where Barbara Deming and other activists staged demonstrations. Thus, women came together not only to promote disarmament but also to empower themselves and create supportive communities dedicated to peace.

These activities were part of a larger **nuclear freeze movement** that began in 1980. Its proponents called for a "mutual freeze on the testing, production, and deployment of nuclear weapons and of missiles and aircraft designed primarily to deliver nuclear weapons." Grassroots activists also held town meetings throughout the United States to mobilize ordinary citizens to speak out against nuclear proliferation. In 1982 some 750,000 people rallied in New York City's Central Park to support a nuclear freeze resolution presented at the United Nations. Despite opposition from the United States and its NATO allies, measures favoring the freeze easily passed in the UN General Assembly. In the 1982 elections, peace groups placed nonbinding, nuclear freeze referenda on local ballots, which passed with wide majorities. The nuclear freeze movement's momentum carried over to Congress, where the House of Representatives narrowly rejected an "immediate freeze" by only two votes.

Explore ▶

See Sources 28.2 and 28.3 to read about two nuclear freeze efforts.

Demonstrations in the United States and in Europe influenced Reagan. According to a 1982 public opinion poll, 57 percent of Americans favored an

The Nuclear Freeze Movement

In 1982, 30 percent of American voters considered nuclear freeze referenda in ten states and thirty-seven cities and counties. The nuclear freeze movement called on the United States and the Soviet Union to mutually halt the production, testing, and deployment of nuclear weapons. A nonbinding referendum in New Jersey passed overwhelmingly in every county. In addition to initiating ballot measures, the nuclear freeze campaign won the support of the Catholic Church, which issued a pastoral letter in 1983.

Source 28.2

New Jersey Referendum on Nuclear Freeze, 1982

Public Question No. 1: Freeze on Nuclear Arms Escalation

Do you support a mutual United States–Soviet Union nuclear weapons "freeze" and urge the government of the United States:

(1) to propose to the government of the Soviet Union that both countries immediately agree to a mutual, verifiable halt of all further testing, production and deployment of nuclear warheads, missiles, and delivery systems as a first step toward mutual, balanced reduction, and

(2) to apply the money saved to human needs and tax reduction?

Interpretive Statement

"This non-binding referendum, if approved by the public, would demonstrate the voters' support of a nuclear weapons freeze and would direct the Secretary of State to transmit the results of these voters' opinions on this question to the President of the United States, the Speaker of the House of Representatives and President of the United States Senate no later than twenty (20) days after the conclusion of the election."

Source: "New Jersey Nuclear Freeze Ballot," 1982, http://www
.njelections.org/election-results/1982-public-questions.pdf.

immediate nuclear freeze. Reagan acknowledged that he was more inclined to reconsider deploying missiles abroad because European leaders felt pressure from protesters in their home countries. Ironically, the president credited Europeans' sentiments on the matter while claiming to ignore widespread efforts of domestic opponents such as Barbara Deming. However, the freeze movement inside and outside the United States created a favorable climate in which the president and Soviet leaders could negotiate a genuine plan for nuclear disarmament by the end of the decade.

Source 28.3

United States Conference of Catholic Bishops | Pastoral Letter on War and Peace, 1983

What are we saying? Fundamentally, we are saying that the decisions about nuclear weapons are among the most pressing moral questions of our age. While these decisions have obvious military and political aspects, they involve fundamental moral choices. In simple terms, we are saying that good ends (defending one's country, protecting freedom, etc.) cannot justify immoral means (the use of weapons which kill indiscriminately and threaten whole societies). We fear that our world and nation are headed in the wrong direction. More weapons with greater destructive potential are produced every day. More and more nations are seeking to become nuclear powers. In our quest for more and more security we fear we are actually becoming less and less secure. . . .

On Promoting Peace

1. We support immediate, bilateral verifiable agreements to halt the testing, production, and deployment of new nuclear weapons systems.

This recommendation is not to be identified with any specific political initiative.

2. We support efforts to achieve deep cuts in the arsenals of both superpowers; efforts should concentrate first on systems which threaten the retaliatory forces of either major power.

3. We support early and successful conclusion of negotiations of a comprehensive test ban treaty.

4. We urge new efforts to prevent the spread of nuclear weapons in the world, and to control the conventional arms race, particularly the conventional arms trade.

5. We support, in an increasingly interdependent world, political and economic policies designed to protect human dignity and to promote the human rights of every person, especially the least among us.

Source: "The Challenge of Peace: God's Promise and Our Response," United States Conference of Catholic Bishops, 1983.

Interpret the Evidence

1. What did voters in New Jersey hope to accomplish with a nonbinding referendum? Do you think the nonbinding nature of the measure made much difference to the outcome of the vote?
2. Why did the Catholic Church take such a strong position in support of the nuclear freeze? How do its goals compare with those of the New Jersey referendum?

Put It in Context

What impact did the nuclear freeze movement have on the Cold War?

The Road to Nuclear De-escalation. Ronald Reagan won reelection in 1984 by a landslide. Following his enormous victory, the popular Reagan softened his militant stance and became more amenable to negotiating with the USSR. Reagan espoused conservative principles during his presidency, but he refused to let rigid dogma interfere with more pragmatic considerations to foster peace. Having earned political capital from his long fight against communism, he was prepared, as president, to spend it. By the time President Reagan left office, little remained of the Cold War.

Women's Peace Encampment Vigil On October 24, 1983, protesters from the Women's Encampment for a Future of Peace and Justice held a candlelight vigil outside the Seneca Army Depot in Romulus, New York. Originally organized by feminist women, the protests also drew men. Together they campaigned to shut down the base, which was used as a munitions storage and disposal facility. In 1995 the military closed the depot. AP Photo/Jim McKnight

In the mid-1980s, powerful changes were sweeping through the Soviet Union, which helped bring the Cold War to a close. In September 1985, Mikhail Gorbachev became general secretary of the Communist Party and head of the Soviet Union. Gorbachev introduced a program of economic and political reform. Through **glasnost** (openness) and **perestroika** (restructuring), the Soviet leader hoped to reduce massive state control over the declining economy and to extend democratic elections, as well as freedom of speech and freedom of the press. Gorbachev understood that the success of his reforms depended on reducing Cold War tensions with the United States and slowing the arms escalation that was bankrupting the Soviet economy. Gorbachev's *glasnost* brought the popular American musical performer Billy Joel to the Soviet Union in August 1987, staging the first rock concert in the country.

The changes that Gorbachev brought to the internal affairs of the Soviet Union carried over to the international arena. From 1986 to 1988, the Soviet leader negotiated in person with the American president, something that had not happened during Reagan's first term. In 1986 at a summit in Reykjavik, Iceland, the two leaders agreed to cut the number of strategic nuclear missiles in half. In 1987 the two sides negotiated an Intermediate Nuclear Forces Treaty, which provided for the destruction of existing intermediate-range missiles and on-site inspections to ensure compliance. The height of détente came in December

Explore ▶

Compare Sources 28.4 and 28.5 for two historians' interpretations of the end of the Cold War.

1987, when Gorbachev traveled to the United States to take part in the treaty-signing ceremony. Reagan no longer referred to the USSR as "the evil empire," and Gorbachev impressed Americans with his personal charm and by demonstrating the media savvy associated with American politicians. The following year, Reagan flew to the Soviet Union, hugged his new friend Mikhail at Lenin's Tomb, and told reporters, "They've changed," referring to the once and not-so-distant "evil empire." Citizens of the two adversarial nations breathed a collective sigh of relief; at long last, the icy terrain of the Cold War appeared to be melting.

REVIEW & RELATE

- How did anticommunism shape Ronald Reagan's foreign policy?

- What role did ordinary citizens play in prompting the superpowers to move toward nuclear de-escalation?

The **Presidency** of George H. W. Bush, 1989–1993

After Reagan left office, his two-term vice president, George H. W. Bush, generally carried on his conservative legacy at home and abroad. While sharing most of Reagan's views, Bush called for a "kinder, gentler nation" in dealing with social justice and the environment. When Bush became president in 1989, he also encountered a very different Soviet Union from the one Ronald Reagan had faced a decade earlier and one that produced new challenges. The USSR was undergoing an internal revolution, which allowed Bush and the United States to take on a new role in a world that was no longer divided between capitalist and Communist nations and their allies. Globalization became the hallmark of the post–Cold War era, replacing previously dualistic economic and political systems, with mixed consequences. Following the collapse of the old world order, local and regional conflicts long held in check by the Cold War broke out along religious, racial, and ethnic lines.

"Kinder and Gentler" Conservatism. In his 1988 presidential campaign against Michael Dukakis, the Democratic governor of Massachusetts, Bush defended conservative principles when he promised, "Read my lips: No new taxes." The Republican candidate attacked Dukakis for his liberal positions and accused him of being soft on crime. Bush also affirmed his own opposition to abortion and support for gun rights and the death penalty.

However, once in office Bush had to deal with problems that he inherited from his predecessor. Reagan's economic programs and military spending had left the nation with a mounting federal budget deficit and fears over inflation. Attempts to ward off inflation by raising interest rates had slowed economic growth. Then the real estate market faltered, exacerbating (if not causing) the S&L collapse. To make matters worse, oil prices spiked in 1990 President Bush ordered the invasion of Iraq (see below, "Managing Conflict After the Cold War"). As a result, the nation fell back into recession. Unemployment rose from 5.3 percent when Bush took office in 1989 to 7.5 percent by 1992, and state and local governments had difficulty paying for the educational, health, and social services that the Reagan and Bush administrations had transferred to them. To reverse the downward spiral, Bush abandoned his "no new taxes" pledge. In 1990 he supported a deficit reduction package that included more than $130 billion in new taxes, which failed to solve the economic problems and angered Reagan conservatives. He also departed from anti-Washington conservatives when he signed the Americans with Disabilities Act (1990), extending a range of protections to some 40 million Americans with physical and mental handicaps.

Bush had a mixed record on the environment. In 1989 the oil tanker *Exxon Valdez* struck a reef off the coast of Alaska, dumping nearly 11 million gallons of oil into Prince William Sound. This disaster created pressure for stricter environmental legislation. Thus, in 1990 the president signed the Clean Air Act, which reduced emissions from automobiles and power plants. However, Bush refused to go further, and in 1992 he opposed international efforts to limit carbon dioxide emissions, greenhouse gases that contribute to climate change.

Bush courted conservatives in his nomination of Clarence Thomas in 1991 to fill the Supreme Court vacancy left by Justice Thurgood Marshall, the first African American justice. Thomas belonged to a rising group of conservative blacks who shared Republican views supporting private enterprise and the free market system and opposing affirmative action. As chief of the Equal Employment Opportunity Commission (EEOC) under

Anita Hill Testifies Against the Supreme Court Nomination of Clarence Thomas, 1991 Anita F. Hill is sworn-in to testify before the Senate Judiciary Committee on the confirmation of Clarence Thomas to the U.S. Supreme Court by chairman Joseph Biden, a Democrat from Delaware, on October 11, 1991. Hill claimed Thomas had sexually harassed her when she had worked for him in the early 1980s. There was no woman serving on the Judiciary Committee at that time. Rex Features via AP Images

Reagan, Thomas had generally weakened the agency's enforcement of racial and gender equality in the workplace. He also opposed abortion and denounced welfare. During the course of Thomas's Senate confirmation hearing, Anita Hill, Thomas's assistant at the EEOC, testified before the Senate Judiciary Committee and a nationally televised audience that Thomas had made unwanted sexual advances to her on and off the job, which she quit in 1983. Hill's charges of sexual harassment did not stop his advancement. Following his confirmation battle, Thomas became one of the most conservative members of the Court. Nevertheless, membership in women's political associations — such as Emily's List, founded in 1984, and the Fund for a Feminist Majority, founded in 1987 — soared following Hill's testimony.

The Breakup of the Soviet Union.
Bush's first year in office coincided with upheavals in the Soviet-controlled Communist bloc, with Poland leading the way. In 1980 Polish dockworker Lech Walesa had organized **Solidarity**, a trade union movement that conducted a series of popular strikes that forced the Communist government to recognize the group. Solidarity had ten million members and attracted various opponents of the Communist regime, including working-class democrats, Catholics, and nationalists who favored breaking ties with the Soviet Union. In 1981 Soviet leaders, disturbed by Solidarity's growing strength, forced the Polish government to crack down on the organization, arrest Walesa, and ban Solidarity. However, in 1989 Walesa and Solidarity were still alive and seized on the changes ushered in by Mikhail Gorbachev's *glasnost* in the USSR to press their demands for democracy in Poland. This time, the Soviets refused to intervene, and Poland conducted its first free elections since the beginning of the Cold War, electing Lech Walesa as president of the country. In July 1989, Gorbachev further broke from the past and announced that the Soviet Union would respect the national sovereignty of all the nations in the Warsaw Pact, which the Soviet Union had controlled since the late 1940s.

Gorbachev's proclamation spurred the end of communism throughout Eastern Europe. Within the next year, Soviet-sponsored regimes fell peacefully in Hungary and Czechoslovakia, replaced by elected governments. Bulgaria held free elections, which brought reformers to power. Only in Romania did Communist rulers put up a fight. There, it took a violent popular uprising to topple the brutal dictator Nicolae Ceausescu. The Baltic states of Latvia, Lithuania, and Estonia, which the Soviets had incorporated into the USSR at the outset of World War II, also regained their independence, sparking the political breakup of the Soviet Union itself.

Perhaps the most striking symbolism in the dismantling of the Soviet empire came in Germany, a country that had been divided between East and West states since 1945. With Communist governments collapsing around them, East Germans demonstrated against the regime of Erich Honecker. With no Soviet help forthcoming, Honecker decided to open the border between East and West Germany. On November 9, 1989, East and West Germans flocked to the Berlin Wall and jubilantly joined workers in knocking down the concrete barricade that divided the city. A year later, East and West Germany merged under the democratic, capitalist Federal Republic of Germany.

Gorbachev also brought an end to the costly nine-year Soviet-Afghan War. When the Soviets withdrew their last troops on February 15, 1989, they left Afghanistan in shambles. One million Afghans had perished, and another 5 million fled the country for Pakistan and Iran, resulting in the political destabilization of Afghanistan. Following a civil war, the Taliban, a group of Sunni Muslim fundamentalists, came to power in the mid-1990s and established a theocratic regime that, among other things, strictly regulated what women could wear in public and denied them educational and professional opportunities. The Taliban also provided sanctuary for many of the mujahideen rebels who had fought against the Soviets, including Osama bin Laden, who would use the country as a base for his al-Qaeda organization to promote terrorism against the United States.

Meanwhile, the Soviet Union disintegrated. Free elections were held in 1990, which ironically threatened Gorbachev's own power by bringing non-Communists to local and national political offices. Although an advocate of economic reform and political openness, Gorbachev remained a Communist and was committed to preserving the USSR. Challenges to Gorbachev came from both ends of the political spectrum. Boris Yeltsin, his former protégé, led the non-Communist forces that wanted Gorbachev to move more quickly in adopting capitalism; on the other side, hard-line generals in the Soviet army disapproved of Gorbachev's reforms and his cooperation with the United States. On August 18, 1991, a group of hard-core conspirators staged a coup against Gorbachev, placed him under house arrest, and surrounded the parliament building with troops. Yeltsin, the president of the Russian Republic, rallied fellow legislators and Muscovites against the plotters and brought the uprising to a peaceful end. Several months later, in early December, Yeltsin and the leaders of the independent republics of Belarus and Ukraine formed the Commonwealth of Independent States (CIS), consisting of the Russian Federation and eleven of fifteen former Soviet states. Shortly after, the CIS removed the hammer and sickle, the symbol of communism, from its flag.

Under these circumstances, on December 25, 1991 Gorbachev resigned. The next day, the Soviet legislative body passed a resolution dissolving the USSR. With the Soviet Union dismantled, Yeltsin, as head of the Russian Federation and the CIS, expanded the democratic and free market reforms initiated by Gorbachev (Map 28.3).

Before Gorbachev left office, he completed one last agreement with the United States to curb nuclear arms. In mid-1991, just before conspirators staged their abortive coup, Gorbachev met with President Bush, who had traveled to Moscow to sign a strategic arms reduction treaty. Under this pact, each side agreed to reduce its bombers and missiles by one-third and to trim its conventional military forces. This accord led to a second strategic arms reduction treaty, signed in 1993. Gorbachev's successor, Boris Yeltsin, met with Bush in January 1993, and the two agreed to destroy their countries' stockpile of multiple-warhead intercontinental missiles within a decade.

Globalization and the New World Order.

With the end of the Cold War, cooperation replaced economic and political rivalry between capitalist and Communist nations in a new era of **globalization** — the extension of economic, political, and cultural interconnections among nations, through commerce, migration, and communication. In 1976 the major industrialized democracies had formed the Group of Seven (G7). Consisting of the United States, the United Kingdom, France, West Germany, Italy, Japan, and Canada, the G7 nations met annually to discuss common problems related to issues of global concern, such as trade, health, energy, the environment, and economic and social development. After the fall of communism, Russia joined the organization, which became

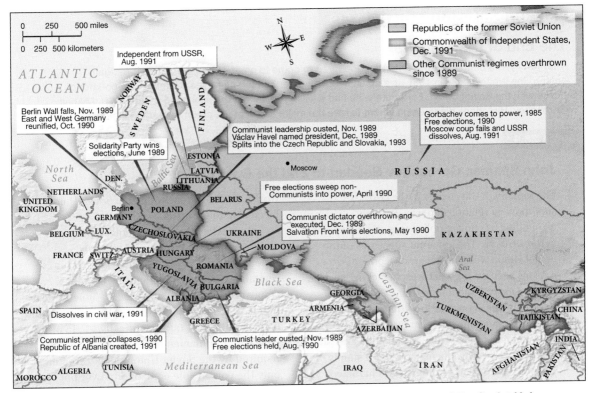

MAP 28.3   The Fall of Communism in Eastern Europe and the Soviet Union, 1989–1991

The collapse of Communist regimes in Eastern Europe was due in part to political and economic reforms initiated by Soviet premier Mikhail Gorbachev, including agreements with the United States to reduce nuclear arms. These changes inspired demands for free elections that were supported by popular uprisings, first in Poland and then in other former Soviet satellites.

known as G8. This group of countries represented only 14 percent of the globe's population but produced 60 percent of the world's economic output.

Globalization was accompanied by the extraordinary growth of multinational (or transnational) corporations—companies that operate production facilities or deliver services in more than one country. Between 1970 and 2000, the number of such firms soared from 7,000 to well over 60,000. By 2000 the 500 largest corporations in the world generated more than $11 trillion in revenues, owned more than $33 trillion in assets, and employed 35.5 million people. American companies left their cultural and social imprint on the rest of the world. Walmart greeted shoppers in more than 1,200 stores outside the United States, and McDonald's changed global eating habits with its more than 1,000 fast-food restaurants worldwide. As American firms penetrated other countries with their products, foreign companies changed the economic landscape of the United States. For instance, by the twenty-first century Japanese automobiles, led by Toyota and Honda, captured a major share of the American market, surpassing Ford

SECONDARY SOURCE ANALYSIS

The End of the Cold War

After forty years of conflict, the Cold War appeared to come to an abrupt end. President Reagan entered the White House in 1981 as a staunch cold warrior and left eight years later as a negotiator of peace with the Soviet Union. Fortunately, he had a willing partner in the new head of the USSR, Mikhail Gorbachev. Historians disagree on whom to give the major share of the credit for ending the hostilities.

Source 28.4

John Spanier, Gorbachev Needed to End the Cold War, 1992

The rapidity of the change in the two superpowers relationship was certainly astounding. . . . Soviet policy was at a high point in the 1970s . . . The apparent successes of the Soviet Union were, however, deceptive. Two reasons account for what was, in fact, a flawed policy. One was the failure of the Soviet economy. The economic growth rate, 5 percent in the 1960s, and only 2 percent by the early 1970s, was standing still at virtually 0 percent a decade later. Capable of producing a plentiful supply of weapons, the Soviet economy was characterized by a an absence of consumer goods and food. . . . A second reason for the Soviet turnabout was the cost of . . . [its] foreign policy. . . . The continuous arms buildup across the board and Moscow's expansionist activities in the third world produced fear and suspicion of Soviet intentions. . . . The Reagan administration's hard-line policies made Soviet foreign policy even more costly, thereby contributing to

Gorbachev's awareness that the Soviet Union faced a systemic crisis.

Gorbachev therefore changed priorities and launched his program of *glasnost* (openness) and *perestroika* (restructuring) to revitalize Soviet society and the economy. . . . Opposition to Gorbachev was . . . fueled by the fear that the loosening of central controls could be harmful, if not fatal, politically. . . . In other words, the fundamental structural reforms required by the Soviet Union might threaten not only the party's sole control of power but also Moscow's imperial control over its own vast country. . . . The Soviet Union faced the real possibility of becoming the Soviet *Disunion* . . . the Soviet political system had become the greatest obstacle to economic modernization. That is why, preoccupied at home, Gorbachev needed to end the Cold War.

Source: John Spanier, *American Foreign Policy Since World War II*, *Twelfth Revised Edition* (Washington, D.C., 1992), 346, 347, 349, 350.

and General Motors, once the hallmark of the country's superior manufacturing and salesmanship.

Globalization also affected popular culture and media. In the 1990s reality shows, many of which originated in Europe, became a staple of American television. At the same time, American programs were shown as reruns all over the world. As cable channels proliferated, American viewers of Hispanic or Asian origin could watch programs in their native languages. The Cable News Network (CNN), the British Broadcasting Corporation (BBC), and Al Jazeera, an Arabic-language television channel, competed for viewers with specially designed international broadcasts.

Source 28.5

Beth Fischer, Reagan Ends the Cold War, 1997

. . . Washington did not merely respond to changes within the Soviet Union. In fact, the Reagan administration began seeking rapprochement with the Kremlin *before* the Soviets began to reform. The White House switched to a more conciliatory policy toward Moscow in (3) January 1984 – fifteen months before Gorbachev became leader of the Soviet Union, and more than two years before the introduction of *glasnost* and *perestroika*.

. . . [T]he Reagan administration's stated policy toward Moscow was especially hard-line through October 1983. . . . Only ten weeks later, however, Washington reversed course. On January 16, 1984, President Reagan delivered an address on super-power relations that proved to be a turning point in his administration's approach to the Kremlin. With this speech, Reagan began seeking a rapprochement. . . .

Reagan warned of the dangers of war, and declared that the United States posed no threat to the security of the Soviet Union. Throughout 1984 and 1985, others within the administration echoed Reagan's calls for "cooperation and understanding" between the superpowers, and underscored that Washington "posed no threat" to Soviet security.

The policy changes that Reagan introduced in 1984 are striking for a number of reasons. Most importantly, they are remarkable because they were implemented before the Soviets began to reform. [in 1984] . . . the old guard within the Kremlin was still fighting the cold war. The conventional view that Washington responded to changes within the Soviet Union is therefore inaccurate.

Source: Beth A. Fischer, *The Reagan Reversal: Foreign Policy and the end of the Cold War* (Columbia: University of Missouri Press, 1997), 2, 3. 4.

Examine the Sources

1. Where do Spanier and Fischer agree and disagree in their interpretations of the end of the Cold War?
2. Based on the evidence in this chapter, explain whose interpretation you find more convincing.

Put It in Context

What are the problems of writing history so close to the events that are taking place?

Globalization also had some negative consequences. Organized labor in particular suffered a severe blow. By 2004 union membership in the United States had dropped to 12.5 percent of the industrial workforce. Fewer and fewer consumer goods bore the label "Made in America," as multinational companies shifted manufacturing jobs to low-wage workers in developing countries. Many of these foreign workers earned more than the prevailing wages in their countries, but by Western standards their pay was extremely low. There were few or no regulations governing working conditions or the use of child labor, and many foreign factories resembled the sweatshops of early-twentieth-century America. Not surprisingly, workers in the United States could not compete in this market.

Furthermore, China, which by 2007 had become a prime source for American manufacturing, failed to regulate the quality of its products closely. Chinese-made toys, including the popular Thomas the Train, showed up in U.S. stores with excessive lead paint and had to be returned before endangering millions of children.

Globalization also posed a danger to the world's environment. As poorer nations sought to take advantage of the West's appetite for low-cost consumer goods, they industrialized rapidly, with little concern for the excessive pollution that accompanied their efforts. The desire for wood products and the expansion of large-scale farming eliminated one-third of Brazil's rain forests. The health of indigenous people suffered wherever globalization-related manufacturing appeared. In Taiwan and China, chemical byproducts of factories and farms turned rivers into polluted sources of drinking water and killed the rivers' fish and plants.

The older industrialized nations added their share to the environmental damage. Besides using nuclear power, Americans consumed electricity and gas produced overwhelmingly from coal and petroleum. The burning of fossil fuels by cars and factories released greenhouse gases, which has raised the temperature of the atmosphere and the

Globalization, 1980s   Following the efforts of Presidents Nixon, Ford, and Carter to normalize relations with Communist China, companies established commercial enterprises there, including American fast-food chain restaurants. Here a Chinese soldier, standing beside a replica of Colonel Sanders, picks up his order at the bike ride-up window of a Kentucky Fried Chicken restaurant. © Dave Bartruff/CORBIS

oceans and contributed to the phenomenon known as global warming or climate change. Most scientists believe that global warming threatens the stability of animal species and of human societies across the planet. However, after the industrialized nations of the world signed the Kyoto Protocol in 1998 to curtail greenhouse-gas emissions, the U.S. Senate refused to ratify it. Critics of the agreement maintained that it did not address the newly emerging industrial countries that polluted heavily and thus was unfair to the United States.

Globalization also highlighted health problems such as the AIDS epidemic. By the outset of the twenty-first century, approximately 33.2 million people worldwide suffered from the disease, though the number of new cases diagnosed annually had dropped to 2.5 million from more than 5 million a few years earlier. Africa remained the continent with the largest number of AIDS patients and the center of the epidemic. Increased education and the development of more effective pharmaceuticals to treat the illness reduced cases and prolonged the lives of those affected by the disease. Though treatments were more widely available in prosperous countries like the United States, agencies such as the United Nations and the World Health Organization, together with nongovernmental groups such as Partners in Health, were instrumental in offering relief in developing countries.

Managing Conflict after the Cold War. The end of the Cold War left the United States as the only remaining superpower. Though Reagan's Cold War defense spending had created huge deficits, the United States emerged from the Cold War with its economic and military strength intact. With the power vacuum created by the breakup of the Soviet Union, the question remained how the United States would use its strength to preserve world order and maintain peace.

Events in China showed the limitations of American military might. In May 1989 university students in Beijing and other major cities in China held large-scale protests to demand political and economic reforms in the country. Some 200,000 demonstrators consisting of students, intellectuals, and workers gathered in the capital city's huge Tiananmen Square, where they constructed a papier-mâché figure resembling the Statue of Liberty and sang songs borrowed from the African American civil rights movement. Deng Xiaoping, Mao Zedong's successor, cracked down on the demonstrations by declaring martial law and dispatching the army to disperse the protesters. Peaceful activists were mowed down by machine guns and stampeded by tanks. Rather than displaying toughness, President Bush merely issued a temporary ban on sales of weapons and nonmilitary items to China. When outrage over the Tiananmen Square massacre subsided, the president restored normal trade relations.

Flexing military muscle in Panama, however, was more feasible for the Bush administration than doing so in China. During the 1980s, the United States had developed a precarious relationship with Panamanian general Manuel Noriega. Although Noriega channeled aid to the Contras with the approval and support of the CIA, he angered the Reagan administration by maintaining close ties with Cuba. Noriega cooperated with the U.S. Drug Enforcement Agency in halting shipments of cocaine from Latin America headed for the United States at the same time that he helped Latin American drug kingpins launder their profits. In 1988 two Florida grand juries indicted the Panamanian leader on charges of drug smuggling and bribery, pressuring President Reagan to cut off aid to Panama and to ask Noriega to resign. Not only did Noriega refuse to step down, but he also nullified the results of the 1989 presidential election in Panama and declared himself the nation's "maximum leader."

After the United States tried unsuccessfully to foment an internal coup against Noriega, in 1989 the Panamanian leader proclaimed a "state of war" between the United States and his country. On December 28, 1989, President Bush launched Operation Just Cause, sending some 27,000 marines to invade Panama. Bush justified the invasion as necessary to protect the Panama Canal and the lives of American citizens, as well as to halt the drug traffic promoted by Noriega. In reality, the main purpose of the mission was to overthrow and capture the Panamanian dictator. In Operation Just Cause, the United States easily defeated a much weaker enemy. The U.S. government installed a new regime, and the marines captured Noriega and sent him to Florida to stand trial on the drug charges. In 1992 he was found guilty and sent to prison.

The Bush administration deployed much more military force in Iraq. Maintaining a steady flow of oil from the Persian Gulf was vital to U.S. strategic interests. During the prolonged Iraq-Iran War in the 1980s, the Reagan administration had switched allegiance from one belligerent to the other to ensure that neither side emerged too powerful. Though the administration had orchestrated the arms-for-hostages deal with Iran, it had also courted the Iraqi dictator Saddam Hussein. U.S. support for Hussein ended in 1990, after Iraq sent 100,000 troops to invade the small oil-producing nation of Kuwait, on the southern border of Iraq.

President Bush responded aggressively. He warned the Iraqis that their invasion "will not stand." Oil was at the heart of the matter. Hussein needed to revitalize the Iraqi economy, which was devastated after a decade of war with Iran. Bush feared that the Iraqi dictator would also attempt to overrun Kuwait's neighbor Saudi Arabia, an American ally, thereby giving Iraq control of half of the world's oil supply. Bush was also concerned that an emboldened Saddam Hussein would then upset the delicate balance of power in the Middle East and pose a threat to Israel by supporting the Palestinians. The Iraqis were rumored to be quickly developing nuclear weapons, which Hussein could use against Israel.

Rather than act unilaterally, President Bush organized a multilateral coalition against Iraqi aggression. Secretary of State James Baker persuaded the United Nations to adopt a resolution calling for Iraqi withdrawal from Kuwait and imposing economic sanctions. Thirty-eight nations, including the Arab countries of Egypt, Saudi Arabia, Syria, and Kuwait, contributed 160,000 troops, roughly 24 percent of the 700,000 allied forces that were deployed in Saudi Arabia in preparation for an invasion if Iraq did not comply.

With military forces stationed in Saudi Arabia, Bush gave Hussein a deadline of January 15, 1991 to withdraw from Kuwait or else risk attack. However, the president faced serious opposition at home against waging a war for oil. Demonstrations occurred throughout the nation, and most Americans supported the continued implementation of economic sanctions, which were already causing serious hardships for the Iraqi people. In the face of widespread opposition, the president requested congressional authorization for military operations against Iraq. After long debate, Congress narrowly approved Bush's request.

Saddam Hussein let the deadline pass. On January 16, **Operation Desert Storm** began when the United States launched air attacks on Baghdad and other key targets in Iraq. After a month of bombing, Hussein still refused to capitulate, so a ground offensive

Gulf War Protests, 1991   The United States gave Iraq a January 15, 1991 deadline to withdraw from Kuwait or face military force. Protesters at the University of South Florida in Tampa favored continued diplomatic efforts. They carry signs that refer to the January 15 deadline, which also is the birthday of Martin Luther King Jr., a critic of U.S. militarism. Courtesy of Steven Lawson and Nancy Hewitt

was launched on February 24, 1991. More than 500,000 allied troops moved into Kuwait and easily drove Iraqi forces out of that nation; they then moved into southern Iraq. Although Hussein had confidently promised that the U.S.-led military assault would encounter the "mother of all battles," the vastly outmatched Iraqi army, worn out from its ten-year war with Iran, was quickly defeated. Desperate for help, Hussein ordered the firing of Scud missiles on Israel to provoke it into war, which he hoped would drive a wedge between the United States and its Arab allies. Despite sustaining some casualties, Israel refrained from retaliation. The ground war ended within one hundred hours, and Iraq surrendered. An estimated 100,000 Iraqis died; by contrast, 136 Americans perished (see Map 28.2).

With the war over quickly, President Bush resisted pressure to march to Baghdad and overthrow Saddam Hussein. Bush's stated goal had been to liberate Kuwait; he did not wish to fight a war in the heart of Iraq. The administration believed that such an expedition would involve house-to-house, urban guerrilla warfare. Marching on Baghdad would also entail battling against Hussein's elite Republican Guard, not the weaker conscripts who had put up little resistance in Kuwait. Bush's Arab allies opposed expanding the war, and the president did not want to risk losing their support. Finally, getting rid of Hussein might make matters worse by leaving Iran and its Muslim fundamentalist rulers the dominant power in the region.

Operation Desert Storm preserved the U.S. lifeline to oil in the Persian Gulf and succeeded because of its limited military objectives. President Bush and his advisers understood that the United States had triumphed because it had pieced together a genuine coalition of nations, including Arab ones, to coordinate diplomatic and military action. Military leaders had a clear and defined mission — the liberation of Kuwait — as well as adequate troops and supplies. When they carried out their purpose, the war was over. However, American withdrawal later allowed Saddam Hussein to slaughter thousands of Iraqi rebels, including Kurds and Shi'ites, to whom Bush had promised support. In effect, the Bush administration had applied the Cold War policy of limited containment in dealing with Hussein.

This successful U.S. military intervention in the Middle East provided President Bush an opportunity to address other explosive issues in the region. Following the end of the Iraq war, Bush set in motion the peace process that brought the Israelis and Palestinians together to sign a 1993 agreement providing for eventual Palestinian self-government in the Gaza Strip and the West Bank. In doing so, the United States for the first time officially recognized Yasser Arafat, the head of the PLO, whom both the Israelis and the Americans had considered a terrorist.

In several areas of the globe, the move toward democracy that had begun in the late 1980s proceeded peacefully into the 1990s. The oppressive, racist system of apartheid fell in South Africa, and antiapartheid activist Nelson Mandela was released after twenty-seven years in prison to become president of the country in 1994. In 1990 Chilean dictator Augusto Pinochet stepped down as president of Chile and ceded control to a democratically elected candidate. That same year, the pro-Communist Sandinista government lost at the polls in Nicaragua, and in 1992 the ruling regime in El Salvador signed a peace accord with the rebels.

The 1992 Election.

Despite his successes abroad, Bush's popularity plunged at home. After the president dispatched American troops and defeated Iraqi military forces in Kuwait in 1991, his approval rating stood at a whopping 89 percent. In sharp contrast, Bush's poll number plummeted to 34 percent in 1992. This precipitous decline resulted mainly from his inability to revive the sagging economy.

Bush ran for reelection against Governor William Jefferson (Bill) Clinton of Arkansas. Learning from the mistakes of Michael Dukakis as well as the successes of Reagan, Clinton ran as a centrist Democrat who promised to reduce the federal deficit by raising taxes on the wealthy and who supported conservative social policies such as the death penalty, tough measures against crime, and welfare reform. Though he did pledge to extend health care and opposed discrimination against homosexuals, Clinton relied on his mainstream southern Democratic credentials to deflect any claims that he was a liberal. Bush also faced a challenge from the independent candidate Ross Perot, a wealthy self-made businessman from Texas, whose campaign against rising government deficits won 19 percent of the popular vote, mostly at Bush's expense. In turn, Clinton defeated the incumbent by a two-to-one electoral margin.

REVIEW & RELATE

- What role did George H. W. Bush play in shaping the post-Cold War world?

- How did the end of the Cold War contribute to the growth of globalization?

Conclusion: Conservative Ascendancy and the End of the Cold War

The election of President Ronald Reagan represented the culmination of conservative ideas first set in motion by Republican Barry Goldwater's campaign for the White House in 1964. He emerged out of southern California where the movement to lower property taxes, increase community control over school curricula, rein in student protesters, disband affirmative action, and dismantle liberal programs had gained momentum in the 1960s and 1970s. First as governor of California and then as president, Reagan spearheaded the New Right movement. Although Reagan did not have a Republican-controlled Congress to work with throughout his presidency (Republicans held the Senate but not the House), he did succeed in reshaping government policies along more conservative lines.

Yet, Reagan's New Right regime bestowed a mixed legacy. The Reagan-Bush administrations reduced inflation and revived economic growth. But they also burdened the country with worrisome budget deficits, and with fiscal and monetary policies that encouraged widespread, imprudent speculation on Wall Street and increased the power of giant corporations over political and economic life.. Tax and spending cuts further enriched the wealthy but hurt the poor and the middle class. Americans learned about the dangers to the environment and took some measures to correct them, but generally refused to alter their lifestyles. African Americans and women broke through barriers that denied them equal access to education and politics, but they confronted white male opposition to further progress.

Conservatives came to power amid major changes occurring in foreign affairs, most notably the proliferation and then the cessation of the Cold War. Some unlikely people were responsible for ending the Cold War. President Reagan, a militant anti-Communist crusader, together with his pragmatic and steady secretary of state, George Shultz, guided the United States through a policy of heightened military preparedness to push the Soviet Union toward peace. It was a dangerous gambit, but it worked; diplomacy rather than armed conflict prevailed. Reagan's Cold War strategy succeeded in part because during the 1980s a leader amenable to peace, Mikhail Gorbachev, governed the Soviet Union. He envisioned the end of the Cold War as a means of bringing political and economic reform to his beleaguered and bankrupt nation. What Reagan and Gorbachev began, their successors, George H. W. Bush and Boris Yeltsin, completed: the Cold War came to a conclusion, and the Soviet Union dismantled its empire and incorporated a measure of democracy and capitalism into Russia.

The activism of ordinary people around the world also helped transform the relationship between the superpowers. Antinuclear protesters in Western Europe and the United States, including Barbara Deming and the Seneca Falls Women's Encampment, kept up pressure on Western leaders to make continued nuclear expansion unacceptable. In Eastern Europe, Polish dockworker Lech Walesa and other fighters for democracy broke from the Soviet orbit and tore down the bricks and barbed-wire fences of the iron curtain.

The United States emerged as the winner of the Cold War, thereby gaining dominance as the world's sole superpower. Yet this did not necessarily guarantee peace. In assuming this preeminent role, the United States faced new threats to international security from governments and insurgents seeking to rebuild nations along ethnic and religious lines in the Middle East and the Persian Gulf. The collapse of the Soviet empire created a power vacuum that would be filled by a variety of unchecked and combustible local and regional forces intent on challenging the political and economic dominance of the United States. President Bush responded to such crises in Iraq and Panama decisively, but his response to China's crackdown at Tiananmen Square was far more tepid.

At the same time, globalization presented new opportunities and posed additional challenges. It promoted more international cooperation and freer trade among nations. Globalization also fostered greater communication and cultural exchanges around the world. However, globalization brought many problems as well. Rapid industrialization and exploration of new sources of wealth accelerated the environmental dangers of air and water pollution, climate change, and the destruction of primeval forests. As globalization shrank the world economically and culturally, the United States became the chief target of those who wanted to contain the influence of Western values. Terrorism, which transcended national borders, replaced communism as the leading enemy of the United States and its allies.

TIMELINE OF EVENTS

1981	Passage of the Economic Recovery Tax Act
1982	Boland Amendment passed
	750,000 attend nuclear freeze rally in New York City
	Ratification period expires for Equal Rights Amendment
1983	Suicide bomb attack in Lebanon kills 241 U.S. soldiers
	U.S. invasion of Grenada
1987	Senate hearings on Iran-Contra affair
	Intermediate Nuclear Forces Treaty signed
1989	Tiananmen Square protests
	Fall of the Berlin Wall
1990	Bush signs Americans with Disabilities Act and Clean Air Act
1990–1991	Soviet Union dismantled
1991	U.S. pushes Iraq out of Kuwait
1993	Second Strategic Arms Reduction Treaty signed

KEY TERMS

Reaganomics, *963*
Economic Recovery Tax Act, *963*
acquired immune deficiency syndrome (AIDS), *966*
Immigration Reform and Control Act, *968*
Boland Amendment, *969*
Iran-Contra affair, *973*
nuclear freeze movement, *973*
glasnost, 976
perestroika, 976
Solidarity, *979*
globalization, *980*
Operation Desert Storm, *986*

REVIEW & RELATE

1. What was Reaganomics, and what were its most important long-term consequences?
2. How did conservative ideas shape the social, cultural, and political landscape of the 1980s and 1990s?
3. How did anticommunism shape Ronald Reagan's foreign policy?
4. What role did ordinary citizens play in prompting the superpowers to move toward nuclear de-escalation?
5. What role did George H. W. Bush play in shaping the post-Cold War world?
6. How did the end of the Cold War contribute to the growth of globalization?

The Iran-Contra Affair

▶ Evaluate the role President Reagan and his administration played in secretly funding anti-revolutionary forces in Nicaragua and explain whether you think Congress reached the correct conclusion about the president's responsibility.

On November 3, 1986, the Lebanese magazine *Ash-Shiraa* revealed a secret arms-for-hostages deal between the United States and Iran. As the affair unfolded, it was revealed that the profits from these arms sales had been illegally diverted to aid anti-Sandinista rebels (called Contras) in Nicaragua. For the next year, the Iran-Contra affair, as it was known, played out in the press as questions of governmental conspiracy, abuse of power, and a White House cover-up swirled around the Reagan administration.

Since the early 1980s, the CIA had been funding, arming, and training groups of dissident forces opposing the leftist Nicaraguan government. After Congress passed the Boland Amendment, which prohibited further aid to the Contras, the Reagan administration then looked for other ways to continue its support for the rebels, eventually funneling money from the Iranian arms sales (Sources 25.6 and 25.7).

Less than a month after the story broke, President Reagan appointed a three-person commission to investigate the allegations. Unsatisfied with the commission's work, the U.S. Senate and House of Representatives established a joint investigative committee and held hearings in the summer of 1987 (Sources 28.9 and 28.10). Both the presidential commission and the congressional committee concluded that neither Reagan nor Vice President George H. W. Bush was aware of the illegal funding of the Contras, though Reagan was sharply criticized

as a poor administrator who needed to exert more control over his staff (Source 28.8).

Several of Reagan's top officials were eventually indicted on a variety of felony accounts, including lying to Congress, destroying evidence, and obstructing justice. In all, eleven men were convicted or pleaded guilty. In late 1992, then-President George H. W. Bush pardoned six men indicted or convicted as part of the Iran-Contra affair.

Source 28.6

The Boland Amendments, 1982 and 1984

Alarmed at the CIA's involvement in the Nicaraguan civil war, Congress passed a measure in 1982 to limit funding and support for these activities. Offered by Edward Boland, a Democratic representative from Massachusetts, the Boland Amendment prohibited the CIA or any other government agency from providing military aid or advice to the Contra rebels. When the Reagan administration found ways to evade the amendment, in 1984 Congress adopted a stronger version as part of an appropriations bill.

1982 Amendment

A substitute amendment to the Harkin amendment [which also prohibited support of military activity in Nicaragua] to prohibit the CIA or Defense Department to use funds of the bill to furnish military equipment, military training or advice, or other support for military activities, to any group or individual, not part of a country's armed forces, for the purpose of overthrowing the government of Nicaragua or provoking a military exchange between Nicaragua and Honduras. The Harkin amendment has prohibited support of any military activity in Nicaragua.

Source: House Amendment 974, 97th Congress (1981–1982).

1984 Amendment

No appropriations or funds made available pursuant to this joint resolution to the Central Intelligence Agency, the Department of Defense, or any other agency or entity of the United States involved in intelligence activities may be obligated or expended for the purpose or which could have the effect of supporting, directly or indirectly, military or paramilitary operations in Nicaragua by any nation, group, organization, movement or individual.

Source: Pub. L. No. 98–441, 98 Stat. 1699 (Oct. 3, 1984).

Source 28.7

CIA Freedom Fighter's Manual, 1983

The CIA's support for the Contras included training in sabotage to disrupt Nicaraguan government and society. In 1983 the CIA prepared the Freedom Fighter's Manual and air-dropped thousands of pamphlets over Nicaragua. Promising "minimal risk for the combatant," the manual's advice ranged from passive and mundane techniques—such as showing up late for work, spreading false rumors, and plugging up toilets with sponges—to more aggressive methods of sabotage, shown here.

PUT NAILS ON ROADS AND HIGHWAYS

REGAR CLAVOS EN LOS CAMINOS Y CARRETERAS

PUT DIRT INTO GASOLINE TANKS

TIERRA

ECHARLE TIERRA AL TANQUE DE GASOLINA

COLOCAR CLAVOS JUNTO A LOS NEUMÁTICOS DE VEHÍCULOS ESTACIONADOS

PUT NAILS NEXT TO THE TIRES OF PARKED VEHICLES

ECHAR AGUA EN EL TANQUE DE GASOLINA

AGUA

PUT WATER IN GASOLINE TANKS

Ronald Reagan | Speech on the Iran-Contra Affair, 1987

President Reagan appointed a commission headed by Senator John Tower to investigate the allegations concerning the sale of arms to Iran in exchange for the release of hostages in Lebanon and the subsequent channeling of funds to support the Contras in Nicaragua. The commission's report, released in February 1987, concluded that while Reagan should have been more directly aware of the actions of his advisers, he was not aware of the illegal diversion of funds to the Contras. A few weeks after the Tower Commission released its report, President Reagan went on television and spoke about the Iran-Contra affair.

First, let me say I take full responsibility for my own actions and for those of my administration. As angry as I may be about activities undertaken without my knowledge, I am still accountable for those activities. As disappointed as I may be in some who served me, I'm still the one who must answer to the American people for this behavior. And as personally distasteful as I find secret bank accounts and diverted funds—well, as the Navy would say, this happened on my watch.

Let's start with the part that is the most controversial. A few months ago I told the American people I did not trade arms for hostages. My heart and my best intentions still tell me that's true, but the facts and the evidence tell me it is not. As the Tower board reported, what began as a strategic opening to Iran deteriorated, in its implementation, into trading arms for hostages. This runs counter to my own beliefs, to administration policy, and to the original strategy we had in mind. There are reasons why it happened, but no excuses. It was a mistake. . . .

Now, another major aspect of the Board's findings regards the transfer of funds to the Nicaraguan contras. The Tower board wasn't able to find out what happened to this money, so the facts here will be left to the continuing investigations of the court-appointed Independent Counsel and the two congressional investigating committees. I'm confident the truth will come out about this matter,

as well. As I told the Tower board, I didn't know about any diversion of funds to the contras. But as President, I cannot escape responsibility.

Much has been said about my management style, a style that's worked successfully for me during 8 years as Governor of California and for most of my Presidency. The way I work is to identify the problem, find the right individuals to do the job, and then let them go to it. I've found this invariably brings out the best in people. They seem to rise to their full capability, and in the long run you get more done. . . .

Now, what should happen when you make a mistake is this: You take your knocks, you learn your lessons, and then you move on. That's the healthiest way to deal with a problem. This in no way diminishes the importance of the other continuing investigations, but the business of our country and our people must proceed. I've gotten this message from Republicans and Democrats in Congress, from allies around the world, and—if we're reading the signals right—even from the Soviets. And of course, I've heard the message from you, the American people. You know, by the time you reach my age, you've made plenty of mistakes. And if you've lived your life properly—so, you learn. You put things in perspective. You pull your energies together. You change. You go forward.

Source: "Address to the Nation on the Iran Arms and Contra Aid Controversy," March 4, 1987, http://www.pbs.org/wgbh/americanexperience/features/primary-resources/reagan-iran-contra.

Oliver North | Testimony to Congress, July 1987

As the Iran-Contra affair intensified, Lieutenant Colonel Oliver North appeared before the joint congressional committee in the summer of 1987 and admitted his role as a chief operator in the Iran-Contra affair. He also confessed that he had lied to Congress and had shredded incriminating documents, but he defended himself as a soldier in service to his country. North was eventually indicted and convicted on three felony counts, though his conviction was overturned on appeal.

QUESTION: Is it correct to say that following the enactment of the Boland Amendment, our support for the war in Nicaragua did not end and that you were the person in the United States Government who managed it?

ANSWER: Starting in the spring of 1984, well before the Boland proscription of no appropriated funds made available to the D.O.D. [Department of Defense] and the C.I.A. etc., I was already engaged in supporting the Nicaraguan resistance and the democratic outcome in Nicaragua. I did so as part of a covert operation. It was carried out starting as early as the spring of '84, when we ran out of money and people started to look in Nicaragua, in Honduras and Guatemala, El Salvador, and Costa Rica for some sign of what the Americans were really going to do, and that that help began much earlier than the most rigorous of the Boland proscriptions. And yes, it was carried out covertly, and it was carried out in such a way as to insure that the heads of state and the political leadership in Nicaragua—in Central America—recognized the United States was going to meet the commitments of the President's foreign policy.

And the President's foreign policy was that we are going to achieve a democratic outcome in Nicaragua and that our support for the Nicaraguan freedom fighters was going to continue, and that I was given the job of holding them together in body and soul. And it slowly transitioned into a more difficult task as time went on and as the C.I.A. had to withdraw further and further from that support, until finally we got to the point in October when I was the only person left talking to them. . . .

QUESTION: Do you know whether or not the President was aware of your activities seeking funds and operational support for the contras, from third countries?

ANSWER: I do not know.

QUESTION: Were you ever—

ANSWER: I assumed that he did.

QUESTION: . . . What was the basis of your assumption?

ANSWER: Just that there was a lot going on and it was very obvious that the Nicaraguan resistance survived—I sent forward innumerable documents, some of which you've just shown us as exhibits, that demonstrated that I was keeping my superiors fully informed, as to what was going on.

Source: "Iran-Contra Hearings: 'I Came Here to Tell You the Truth'; The Colonel States His Case: Country and Orders above All," *New York Times*, July 8, 1987, A8.

Source 28.10

George Mitchell | Response to Oliver North, 1987

Maine senator George Mitchell joined the joint House and Senate committee investigating the Iran-Contra affair in 1987. During Oliver North's testimony, Mitchell listened to North's characterization of his activities and support for the Contras as the true patriotic course of action. In Mitchell's response to North, he discusses the meaning of patriotism in a democratic society.

You have talked here often and eloquently about the need for a democratic outcome in Nicaragua. There is no disagreement on that. There is disagreement as how best to achieve that objective. Many Americans agree with the President's policy; many do not. Many patriotic Americans, strongly anti-Communist, believe there's a better way to contain the Sandinistas, to bring about a democratic outcome in Nicaragua and to bring peace to Central America.

And many patriotic Americans are concerned that in the pursuit of democracy abroad we not compromise it in any way here at home. You and others have urged consistency in our policies, you have said repeatedly that if we are not consistent our allies and other nations will question our reliability. That is a real concern. But if it's bad to change policies, it's worse to have two different policies at the same time: one public policy and an opposite policy in private. It's difficult to conceive of a greater inconsistency than that. It's hard to imagine anything that would give our allies more cause to consider us unreliable than that we say one thing in public and secretly do the opposite. And that's exactly what was done when arms were sold to Iran and arms were swapped for hostages.

. . . You talked about your background and it was really very compelling, and is obviously one of the reasons why the American people are attracted to you.

Let me tell you a story from my background. Before I entered the Senate, I had the great honor of serving as a federal judge. In that position I had great power. The one I most enjoyed exercising was the power to make people American citizens. From time to time I presided at what we call naturalization ceremonies; they're citizenship ceremonies. These are people who came from all over the world, risked their lives, sometimes left their families and their fortunes behind to come here. They had gone through the required procedures, and I, in the final act, administered to them the oath of allegiance to the United States, and I made them American citizens. To this moment, to this moment it was the most exciting thing I've ever done in my life.

Ceremonies were always moving for me because my mother was an immigrant, my father the orphan son of immigrants. Neither of them had any education, and they worked at very menial tasks in our society. But because of the openness of America, because of equal justice under law in America, I sit here today a United States Senator. And after every one of these ceremonies I made it a point to speak to these new Americans, I asked them why they came, how they came, and their stories, each of them, were inspiring. I think you would be interested and moved by them given the views you have expressed on this country.

And when I asked them why they came they said several things, mostly two. The first is they said we came because here in America everybody has a chance, opportunity. And they also said over and over again, particularly people from totalitarian societies, we came here because here in America you can criticize the government without looking over your shoulder. Freedom to disagree with the government.

Now, you have addressed several pleas to this committee, very eloquently. None more eloquent than last Friday when in response to a question by Representative [Richard] Cheney you asked that Congress not cut off aid to the Contras for the love of God and for the love of country. I now address a plea to you. Of all the qualities which the American people find compelling about you, none is more impressive than your obvious deep devotion to this country. Please remember that others share that devotion and recognize that it is possible for an American to disagree with you on aid to the Contras and still love God and still love this country just as much as you do.

Although he's regularly asked to do so, God does not take sides in American politics. And in America, disagreement with the policies of the government is not evidence of lack of patriotism.

. . . Indeed, it is the very fact that Americans can criticize their government openly and without fear of reprisal that is the essence of our freedom, and that will keep us free.

Now, I have one final plea. Debate this issue forcefully and vigorously as you have and as you surely will, but, please, do it in a way that respects the patriotism and the motives of those who disagree with you, as you would have them respect yours.

Source: Iran-Contra Investigation, Joint Hearings Part II, July 10, 13, and 14, 1987: Continued Testimony of Oliver L. North and Robert C. McFarlane, 31–46.

Interpret the Evidence

1. Compare the 1982 and 1984 versions of the Boland Amendment (Source 28.6). How does the wording of the second version clarify Congress's original intent?
2. What, if anything, surprises you about the Freedom Fighter's Manual (Source 28.7)? Why would it focus on these specific activities, and do you think they were effective?
3. Evaluate Reagan's explanation of his Iran-Contra involvement (Source 28.8) and compare it to Oliver North's testimony (Source 28.9).
4. How does Senator George Mitchell (Source 28.10) define patriotism differently than Oliver North (Source 28.9)?

Put It in Context

Compare the Iran-Contra affair with Watergate ("The Nixon Landslide and Watergate Scandal, 1972–1974" in chapter 27). How did Reagan's presidency survive such a scandal when Nixon's did not?

29

The Challenges of a Globalized World

1993 to the present

WINDOW TO THE PAST

President Bush Declares Victory in Iraq, May 1, 2003

On May 1, 2003, in a speech to the American people, President George W. Bush declared that the United States had prevailed in overthrowing the Iraqi dictator, Saddam Hussein. Although the work of reconstruction remained, the president proclaimed that combat operations had ended. However, his statement proved premature, as American forces remained fighting in Iraq for another eight years. ▶ To discover more about what this primary source can show us, see Source 29.2 on page 1012.

Thank you all very much. Admiral Kelly, Captain Card, officers and sailors of the U.S.S. *Abraham Lincoln*, my fellow Americans: Major combat operations in Iraq have ended. In the battle of Iraq, the United States and our allies have prevailed. And now our coalition is engaged in securing and reconstructing that country.

National Archives and Records Administration

After reading this chapter you should be able to:

- Assess the impact of computer technology, globalization, and immigration on the United States.

- Evaluate President Clinton's responses to domestic and global issues.

- Explain the impact of the 9/11 attacks on President Bush's foreign policy and describe his compassionate conservatism at home.

- Analyze the reasons for Barack Obama's election as president and explain the challenges that faced his administration.

- Explain how Donald Trump won the presidency.

COMPARING AMERICAN HISTORIES

William Henry Gates III started tinkering with computers at age thirteen. In the late 1960s, computers were big, bulky machines that filled entire rooms. As a teenager in 1969, the enterprising Gates and some friends set up a business to make computerized traffic counters to gauge the speed of vehicles, for which they earned $20,000.

His brilliant mind and entrepreneurial inclinations led Gates to enroll at Harvard and then to drop out after spending more time at the university's computer center than he did in class. In 1974 he became interested in microcomputers as an alternative to large conventional computers. A year

later, Gates formed a computer software company called Microsoft, envisioning the microcomputer on office desktops and in homes throughout America.

Bill Gates succeeded beyond all expectations. In 1980 Microsoft collaborated with International Business Machines (IBM) to create a software package for IBM's new line of personal computers. Microsoft quickly joined the financial boom and in 1986 became a publicly traded company on the New York Stock Exchange. Within a decade, Gates became the richest man in America, and like industrial titans a century earlier, he donated generously to fund philanthropic activities worldwide.

Despite the enormous benefits of computer technology, the digital revolution has also been used for malicious purposes. On September 11, 2001 (9/11), operatives from the international terrorist network al-Qaeda, who communicated through e-mail and cell phones and trained on computerized flight simulators, attacked the World Trade Center and the Pentagon. Kristen Breitweiser was a young housewife and mother living in suburban New Jersey on that fateful day. Her husband, Ron, a senior vice president at an investment management service, worked in Tower Two of the World Trade Center. When one of the planes commandeered by terrorists crashed into the building, her husband was killed, leaving her a widow with a two-year-old daughter. Breitweiser's loss transformed her from a stay-at-home mother into a grieving victim and a political activist.

She started attending meetings of the Victim Compensation Fund established by the federal government following 9/11. She met Mindy Kleinberg, Lorie Van Auken, and Patty Casazza, other widows from New Jersey. The "Jersey Girls," as they became known, addressed concerns over victims' compensation but soon confronted larger political issues. In 2002 they successfully campaigned to pressure the White House and Congress to form a national commission to investigate how the 9/11 attacks could have happened and what the federal government might have done to prevent them.

The commission's final report in 2004 disappointed Breitweiser. She called the report "hollow"

(left) **Bill Gates.** James Leynse/Corbis via Getty Images

(right) **Kristen Breitweiser.** Reuters/Hyungwon Kang

and criticized President Bush for not fully and openly cooperating with the investigation. Although Breitweiser had voted for Bush in the 2000 election and considered herself a conservative, her rapid political education following 9/11 turned her against his candidacy in 2004. She also spoke out against the Iraq War, which the administration had initiated in 2003 in response to the 9/11 attacks. ∎

The American histories of Bill Gates and Kristen Breitweiser were deeply affected by the twin forces of digital technology and terror that dominated life at the start of the twenty-first century. Computers, the Internet, and cell phone technology reformulated commerce and social relations, furthering the globalization that emerged after the Cold War. Google, the Web, Facebook, and Twitter became household words and broke down domestic and global barriers that earlier technologies had not penetrated. Computer technology revolutionized political communication and organization, mobilized ordinary citizens into action, and expanded opportunities for disgruntled and oppressed citizens of foreign countries to overthrow despotic rulers. Computers fostered the growth of big business mergers by allowing large companies to operate globally in quick and efficient fashion. To encourage international trade, the United States signed free trade agreements to open up foreign markets. Still, new technology posed unintended risks. Driven by new computer models for trading in financial securities, the stock market grew highly volatile, and downturns in the economy became greater in intensity and scope. At the same time, the 9/11 attacks placed the United States and its allies on a permanent war footing, resulting in wars against terrorism in Iraq and Afghanistan and increased surveillance of suspected terrorists and citizens alike. Amid these upheavals, Americans broke new ground by electing their first black president. Still, despite ending the Great Recession, passing health care legislation, extending marriage equality, and removing troops from Iraq, the nation faced historic burdens of racism and the increasing polarization of American politics. The 2016 election of Donald Trump as president underscored the political, economic, and cultural divisions that continued to rip the country apart and highlighted the challenges digital technology posed for national unity and security.

Transforming American Business and Society

The 1990s marked a period of great economic growth and technological advancement in the United States. Computers stood at the center of the technological revolution of the late twentieth and early twenty-first centuries, allowing both small and large businesses to reach new markets and transform the workplace. Digital technology also altered the way individuals worked, purchased goods and services, communicated, and spent their leisure time. As the Internet connected Americans to the rest of the world, corporate leaders embraced globalization as the key to economic prosperity. They put together business mergers so that their companies could operate more powerfully in the international market. Government officials generally supported their efforts by reducing regulations on business and financial practices. Globalization not only thrust American business enterprises outward but also brought a new population of immigrants to the United States.

The Computer Revolution.
The first working computers were developed for military purposes during World War II and the Cold War and were enormous in size and cost. Engineers began to resolve the size issue with the creation of transistors. Invented in the late 1940s, these small electronic devices came into widespread use in running computers during the 1960s. The design of integrated circuits in the 1970s led to the production of microcomputers in which a silicon chip the size of a nail head did the work once performed by huge computers. Bill Gates was not the only one to recognize the potential market of microcomputers for home and business use. Steve Jobs, like Gates a college dropout, founded Apple Computer Company in 1976, turned it into a publicly traded corporation, and became a multimillionaire.

Microchips and digital technology found a market beyond home and office computers. Over the last two decades of the twentieth century, computers came to operate everything from standard appliances such as televisions and telephones, to new electronic devices such as CD players, fax machines, and cell phones. Computers controlled traffic lights on the streets and air traffic in the skies. They changed the leisure patterns of youth: Many

IBM 405: The Early Computer, 1955 The IBM 704, a large-scale computer with a high-speed electronic calculator, was introduced in 1954 and installed at Lawrence Livermore National Laboratory in April 1955. The 704 was considered as "pretty much the only computer that could handle complex math." LLNL/Science Source

young people preferred to play video games indoors than to engage in outdoor activities. Consumers purchased goods online, and companies such as Amazon sold merchandise through the Internet without any retail stores. Soon computers became the stars of movies such as *The Matrix* (1999), *A.I. Artificial Intelligence* (2001), and *Iron Man* (2008).

The Internet—an open, global series of interconnected computer networks that transmit data, information, electronic mail, and other services—grew out of military research in the 1970s, when the Department of Defense constructed a system of computer servers connected to one another throughout the United States. The main objective of this network was to preserve military communications in the event of a Soviet nuclear attack. At the end of the Cold War, the Internet was repurposed for nonmilitary use, linking government, academic, business, and organizational systems. In 1991 the World Wide Web came into existence as a way to access the Internet and connect documents and other resources to one another through hyperlinks. In 2017 about 88 percent of people in the United States used the Internet, up from 50 percent in 2000. Internet use worldwide leapt ten fold, from nearly 361 million people in 2000 to nearly 4 billion in 2017.

Business Consolidation.

The incredible growth of the computer industry led to increased business consolidation, making it possible for large firms to keep control of their far-flung operations by communicating instantly within the United States and throughout the world. The federal government aided the merger process by relaxing financial regulation. Media companies took the greatest advantage of this situation. For example, in 1990 the giant Warner Communications merged with Time Life to create an entertainment empire that included a film studio (Warner Brothers), a television cable network (Home Box Office), a music company (Atlantic Records), a baseball team (the Atlanta Braves), and several magazines (*Time*, *Sports Illustrated*, and *People*).

Other mergers mirrored the trend in the media: The estimated number of business mergers rose from 1,529 in 1991 to 4,500 in 1998. The market value of these transactions in 1998 was approximately $2 trillion, compared with $600 billion for 1989, the previous peak year for consolidation. Corporate consolidation brought corporate malfeasance, as some chief executives abused their power by expanding their companies too quickly and making risky financial deals, which put workers and stockholders in jeopardy.

The Changing American Population.

As the technological revolution transformed the U.S. economy and society, an influx of immigrants began to alter the composition of the American population. Since passage of the Immigration Act of 1965, which repealed discriminatory national origins quotas established in 1924, the country had experienced a wave of immigration comparable to that at the turn of the twentieth century. As the population of the United States grew from 202 million to 300 million between 1970 and 2006, immigrants accounted for some 28 million of the increase. They came to the United States for much the same reasons as those arriving earlier: to seek economic opportunity and to find political and religious freedom.

Most newcomers in the 1980s and 1990s arrived from Latin America and South and East Asia. Relatively few Europeans (approximately 2 million) moved to the United States, though their numbers increased after the collapse of the Soviet empire in the early 1990s. Poverty and political unrest pushed migrants out of Mexico, Central America, and the Caribbean. At the beginning of the twenty-first century, Latinos (35 million) had

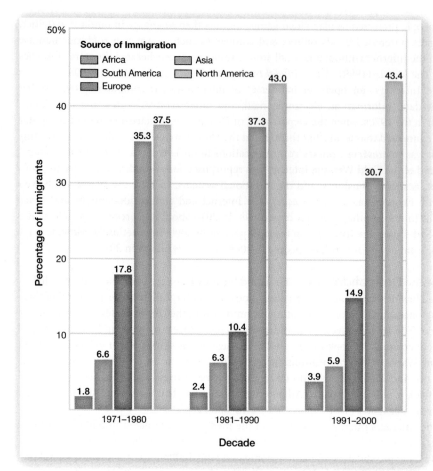

FIGURE 29.1 Immigrant Growth by Home Region, 1991–2015

In the late twentieth and early twenty-first centuries, immigration to the United States increased significantly, especially from East and South Asia. North America (which in this figure includes Mexico, Central America, and the Caribbean) formed the second largest group of immigrants, while Africans arrived in small but growing numbers. Compare each region's percentage of immigration in 1991 with 2015 and present the conclusions you can draw.

Source: Data from *2015 Yearbook of Immigration Statistics, Office of Immigration Statistics, U.S. Department of Homeland Security, December 2016.*

surpassed African Americans (34 million) as the nation's largest minority group. However, with the arrival of Caribbean and African immigrants, black America was also becoming more diverse.

In addition to the 16 million immigrants who came from south of the U.S. border, another 9 million headed eastward from Asia, including Chinese, South Koreans, and Filipinos, together with refugees from Vietnam and Cambodia. By 2010 an estimated 3.18 million Indians from South Asia lived in the United States, most arriving after the 1960s. Indian Americans became the third-largest Asian American group behind Chinese and Filipinos. Another 1 to 2 million people came from predominantly Islamic nations such as Pakistan, Lebanon, Iraq, and Iran (Figure 29.1).

Like their predecessors, new immigrants formed ethnic and religious enclaves. California displayed this fresh face of immigration most vividly. Latinos and Asians had long settled there, and by 2016, 27 percent of the state's population was foreign-born. The majority of Californians consisted of Latinos, Asian Americans, and African Americans, with whites in the minority. In addition to California, immigrants also flocked to the

Southwest and to northeastern and midwestern cities like New York City, Jersey City, Chicago, and Detroit. However, now they also fanned out across the Southeast, adding to the growing populations of Atlanta, Raleigh-Durham, Charlotte, Columbia, and Memphis and providing these cities with an unprecedented ethnic mixture. Like immigrants before them, they created their own businesses, spoke their own languages, and retained their own religious and cultural practices.

Explore ▶

See Source 29.1 for one immigrant's experience in low-wage factory work.

Immigrants also encountered hostility from many native-born Americans. Some workers felt threatened by newcomers who took jobs, both commercial and agricultural, at lower wages. Middle-class taxpayers complained that the flood of impoverished immigrants placed the burden on them to fund the social services — schools, welfare, public health — that the newcomers required. Some children and grandchildren of earlier immigrants had now assimilated into American culture and resented foreigners who pushed for bilingual education and signs and instructions in their native languages. Immigration critics also griped about the influx of illegal residents among the immigrant population. In contrast, some conservative Republicans like President Ronald Reagan, former governor of California, along with agribusiness and other corporate interests that relied on cheap immigrant labor, opposed immigration restrictions.

REVIEW & RELATE

● How did computers change life in the United States at the turn of the millennium?

● How has globalization affected business consolidation and immigration in recent decades?

Political Divisions and Globalization in the Clinton Years

The first president born after 1945, President Bill Clinton had to deal with the challenges facing the post–Cold War world. He embraced globalization as the key to economic prosperity and showed his readiness to promote and defend U.S. national security. Despite achieving general prosperity and peace, Clinton could not escape the political polarization that divided the American electorate, and his tenure in office only intensified this schism.

Domestic and Economic Policy during the Clinton Administration.

Born in Arkansas in 1946, William Jefferson (Bill) Clinton served five terms as Democratic governor of his home state. As governor, Clinton spoke out for equal opportunity, improved education, and economic development. After defeating President George H. W. Bush in 1992, Clinton entered the White House brimming with energy.

In 1993, Clinton sought to reverse a number of Reagan-Bush policies. He persuaded Congress to raise taxes on wealthy individuals and corporation, while his administration reduced defense spending following the end of the Cold War. Taken together, these measures stimulated a robust economic growth of 4 percent annually, established over 22 million jobs, lowered the national debt, and created a budget surplus. Clinton further departed from his Republican predecessors by signing executive orders expanding federal assistance for legal abortion. Demonstrating that women's rights were not incompatible with family

Bo Yee | The New American Sweatshop, 1994

Bo Yee came to the United States from Hong Kong and worked as a seamstress. When her employer laid off workers without paying back wages, Yee joined with a local immigrant women's organization to fight for outstanding payments. In a 1994 interview she described conditions in the California garment factory where she was paid $5 to create dresses that retailed for $175.

Source 29.1

Why did Yee come to the United States?

I started working at a factory a month after I got here. I immigrated to the US because of my two sons. They were not going to be happy in Hong Kong after the 1997 changeover [the transfer of Hong Kong from the United Kingdom to China]. My husband did not want to come to the US but he did come in 1985.

I started working at Lucky Sewing Company in June 1986. Working there was like being a prisoner in a sealed cage. All the windows were locked. They wouldn't let you go to the bathroom. They had "No loud talking" signs posted. There were about 20 of us there working ten hours a day, seven days a week, endlessly, without rest. Most of the workers were from mainland China, although some came from Hong Kong and there were a few Latinos. The boss' wife created a tense, competitive atmosphere between the workers. She would praise some people and downgrade others. Because of my experience, I can work faster than newer workers from China who are not as skillful. They would sacrifice their lunch and break time to catch up. I hated the way the boss made us compete. There were three of us in one department who had to produce 200 pieces. They would push us to see who could finish first. They were getting people to exploit themselves. How disgusting! I hate this!

How did Yee's boss get workers to exploit themselves?

I couldn't communicate with the Latino workers, but you can have fun without speaking each other's language. You motion. You use body language and whatever method you can. The relations with Latinos were better. We were not forced to compete with each other.

How did working in this factory change Yee's opinion of the United States?

I thought America was a very advanced country, but working in sweatshops here, I see that the garment industry is very backward compared to Hong Kong.

Source: Miriam Ching Yoon Louie, *Sweatshop Warriors: Immigrant Women Workers Take On the Global Factory* (Cambridge, MA: South End Press, 2001), 49–50.

Put It in Context

Compare the factory Yee describes to sweatshops that existed a century earlier in the United States as described in chapter 18.

values, Clinton also approved the 1993 Family and Medical Leave Act, which allowed parents to take up to twelve weeks of unpaid leave to care for newborn children without risk of losing their jobs. The president had less success opening the military to gays and lesbians, though many already served secretly. His policy of "don't ask, don't tell" permitted homosexuals to serve in the armed forces so long as they kept their sexual orientation a secret, a compromise that failed to end discrimination. The Clinton administration's most stinging defeat came when Congress failed to pass universal medical coverage.

Clinton tried to appeal to voters across the political spectrum on other issues. He signed a tough anticrime law that funded the recruitment of an additional 100,000 police officers to patrol city streets, while supporting gun control legislation. Although the prison population had been on the rise before the 1990s, Clinton's anticrime bill accelerated the rate of incarceration and had a disproportionate effect on African Americans and Latinos. Managing to overcome the powerful lobby of the National Rifle Association, in 1993 Clinton signed the Brady Bill, which imposed a five-day waiting period to check the background of gun buyers.

To expand the nation's economy even further, Clinton embraced the economic regional cooperation of Europe. In 1993 western European nations formed the European Union (EU), which encouraged free trade and investment among member nations. In 1999 the EU introduced a common currency, the euro, which nineteen nations have now adopted. Clinton encouraged the formation of similar economic partnership in North America. In 1993, together with the governments of Mexico and Canada, the U.S. Congress ratified the **North American Free Trade Agreement (NAFTA)**. The agreement removed tariffs and other obstacles to commerce and investment among the three countries to encourage trade. NAFTA produced noteworthy gains: Between 1994 and 2004, trade among NAFTA nations increased by nearly 130 percent. Although Mexico has seen a significant drop in poverty rates and a rise in real income, NAFTA has harmed workers in the United States to a certain extent. From 1994 to 2007, net manufacturing jobs dropped by 3,654,000 as U.S. companies outsourced their production to Mexico, taking advantage of its low wage and benefits structure. However, many more manufacturing jobs were lost to automation.

Clinton also actively promoted globalization through the World Trade Organization (WTO). Created in 1995, the WTO consists of more than 150 nations and seeks "to ensure that trade flows as smoothly, predictably and freely as possible." The policies of the WTO generally benefit wealthier nations, such as the United States. From 1978 to 2000, the value of U.S. exports and imports jumped from 17 percent to 25 percent of the gross domestic product.

Despite his free-trade economic policies, conservatives were fiercely opposed to Clinton on several fronts. Right-wing talk radio hosts criticized the president and his wife, Hillary Rodham Clinton, a lawyer and leader in the effort to reform health care. Conservatives blamed the Clintons for all they considered wrong in society — feminism, abortion, affirmative action, and secularism. Opponents raised questions about his and his wife's pre-presidential dealings in a controversial real estate development project known as Whitewater, which prompted the appointment in 1994 of a special prosecutor to investigate allegations of impropriety.

Facing conservative antagonism, the president and the Democratic Party fared poorly in the 1994 congressional elections, losing control of both houses of Congress for the first

Celebrating the Contract with America   On April 7, 1995, Speaker of the House Newt Gingrich holds up a copy of the *Contract with America* on the steps of the U.S. Capitol. The document helped Republicans win the mid-term congressional elections in 1994, the first time they controlled both houses of Congress since 1953. Gingrich is joined by some 160 House Republicans to celebrate the completion of the Republicans' 100-day promise of change. However, their legislative efforts to achieve the contract's proposals were mixed.   Richard Ellis/AFP/ Getty Images

time since 1952. Republicans, led by House Minority Leader Newt Gingrich of Georgia, championed the **Contract with America**. This document embraced conservative principles, including a constitutional amendment for a balanced budget, reduced welfare spending, lower taxes, and term limits for lawmakers. The election underscored the increasing electoral influence of white evangelical Christians, who voted in large numbers for Republican candidates.

Stung by this defeat, Clinton tried to outmaneuver congressional Republicans by shifting rightward and championing welfare reform. In 1996 he signed the **Personal Responsibility and Work Opportunity Reconciliation Act**. It replaced the Aid to Families with Dependent Children provision of the Social Security law, the basis for welfare in the United States since the New Deal, with a new measure that required adult welfare recipients to find work within two years or lose the benefits provided to families earning less than $7,700 annually. The law also placed a lifetime limit of five years on these federal benefits. Also in 1996, the president approved the Defense of Marriage Act, which denied married same-sex couples the federal benefits granted to heterosexual married couples, including Social Security survivor's benefits.

In adopting such positions as welfare reform and antigay legislation, Clinton angered many of his liberal supporters but ensured his reelection in 1996. Running against Republican senator Robert Dole of Kansas and the independent candidate Ross Perot, Clinton captured 49 percent of the popular vote and 379 electoral votes. Dole received 41 percent of the vote, and Perot came in a distant third.

Declining support from his liberal base did not seriously undermine President Clinton, but more mundane, sexual indiscretions nearly brought him down. Starting in 1995, Clinton had engaged in consensual sexual relations with Monica Lewinsky, a twenty-two-year-old White House intern. Clinton denied these charges under oath and before a national television audience, but when Lewinsky testified about the details of their sexual encounters, the president recanted his earlier statements. After an independent prosecutor concluded that Clinton had committed perjury and obstructed justice, the Republican-controlled House voted to impeach the president on December 19, 1998. However, on February 12, 1999, Republicans in the Senate failed to muster the necessary two-thirds vote to convict Clinton on the impeachment charges.

Despite his impeachment, Clinton left the country in more prosperous shape than he had found it. At the height of the sex scandal in 1998, the unemployment rate fell to 4.3 percent, the lowest level since the early 1970s. The rate of home ownership reached a record-setting 66 percent. As the "misery index" — a compilation of unemployment and inflation — fell, the gross domestic product grew by more than $250 billion. In 1999 the stock market's Dow Jones average reached a historic high of 10,000 points. That same year the president signed into law a measure that freed banks to merge commercial, investment, and insurance services, prohibited since 1933 under the Glass-Steagall Act, giving them enormous leeway in undertaking profitable but risky ventures. The Clinton administration boasted that its economic policies had succeeded in canceling the Reagan-Bush budget deficit, yielding a surplus for the fiscal year 2000. This boom, however, did not affect everyone equally. African Americans and Latinos lagged behind whites economically; and the gap between rich and poor widened as the wealthiest 13,000 American families earned as much income as the poorest 20 million.

Global Challenges.
Clinton faced numerous foreign policy challenges during his two terms in office. As the first president elected in the post–Cold War era, Clinton could approach trouble spots without the rigid anti-Communist views of his predecessors. No longer did the problems facing the United States result from customary military aggression by one nation against another; rather, the greatest threats came from the implosion of national governments into factionalism and genocide, as well as the dangers posed by Islamic extremists.

President Clinton responded boldly to violence in the Balkans, an area considered vital to U.S. national security. In 1989 Yugoslavia splintered after the crumbling of the ruling Communist regime. The predominantly Roman Catholic states of Slovenia and Croatia declared their independence from the largely Russian Orthodox Serbian population in Yugoslavia. In 1992 the mainly Muslim territory of Bosnia-Herzegovina also broke away, despite protests by its substantial Serbian population (Map 29.1). A civil war erupted between Serb and Croatian minorities and the Muslim-dominated Bosnian government. Supported by Slobodan Milošević, the leader of the neighboring province of Serbia, Bosnian Serbs wrested control of large parts of the region and slaughtered tens of thousands of Muslims through what they euphemistically called **ethnic cleansing**. In 1995 Clinton sponsored NATO bombing raids against the Serbs, dispatched 20,000 American troops as

MAP 29.1 The Breakup of Yugoslavia, 1991–2008
With the collapse of Communist control of Yugoslavia in 1989, the country splintered along ethnic and religious lines, eventually forming seven separate nations. A civil war between Serbia and Croatia ended in 1995, but Serbs then attacked Muslims in Bosnia and Kosovo.

part of a multilateral peacekeeping force, and brokered a peace agreement. In 1999 renewed conflict erupted when Milošević's Serbian government attacked the province of Kosovo to eliminate its Albanian Muslim residents. Clinton and NATO initiated air strikes against the Serbs and placed troops on the ground, actions that preserved Kosovo's independence.

The United States faced an even graver danger from Islamic extremists intent on waging a religious struggle (jihad) against their perceived enemies and establishing a transnational Muslim government, or caliphate. The United States' close relationship with Israel placed it high on the list of terrorist targets, along with pro-American Muslim governments in Egypt, Pakistan, and Indonesia. In 1993 Islamic militants orchestrated the bombing of the World Trade Center's underground garage, killing six people and injuring more than one thousand. Five years later, terrorists blew up American embassies in Kenya and Tanzania, killing hundreds and injuring thousands of local workers and residents. In retaliation, Clinton ordered air strikes against terrorist bases in Sudan and Afghanistan. However, the danger persisted. In 2000 al-Qaeda terrorists blew a gaping hole in the side of the USS *Cole*, a U.S. destroyer anchored in Yemen, killing seventeen American sailors. Terrorism would continue to bedevil the United States.

REVIEW & RELATE

- How did conflicts between Democrats and Republicans affect President Clinton's accomplishments?

- How did the end of the Cold War shape President Clinton's foreign policies?

The **Presidency** of George W. Bush

In 2000 Americans celebrated the new millennium, looking forward with hope for the future. Yet this hope soon waned. Within three years, the country endured a bruising presidential election, experienced unprecedented terrorism at home, and engaged in two wars abroad. President George W. Bush left the country as politically divided as his predecessor had.

Bush and Compassionate Conservatism. In 2000 the Democratic candidate, Vice President Al Gore, ran against George W. Bush, the Republican governor of Texas and son of the forty-first president. Gore ran on the coattails of the Clinton prosperity while Bush campaigned as a "compassionate conservative." Also in the race was Ralph Nader, an anti-corporate activist who ran under the banner of the Green Party, a party formed in 1991 to support grassroots democracy, environmentalism, social justice, and gender equality.

Nader's candidacy drew votes away from Gore, but fraud and partisanship hurt the Democrats even more. Gore won a narrow plurality of the popular vote (48.4 percent, compared with 47.8 percent for Bush and 2.7 percent for Nader). However, Bush won a slim majority of the electoral votes: 271 to 267. The key state in this Republican victory was Florida, where Bush outpolled Gore by fewer than 500 popular votes. Counties with high proportions of African Americans and the poor, who were more likely to support Gore, encountered significant difficulties and outright discrimination in voting. When litigation over the recount reached the U.S. Supreme Court in December 2000, the Court, which included conservative justices appointed by Ronald Reagan and George H. W. Bush, proclaimed Bush the winner.

George W. Bush did not view his slim, contested victory cautiously. Rather, he appealed to his conservative political base by governing as boldly as if he had received a resounding electoral mandate. While Republicans still controlled the House, the Democrats had gained a one-vote majority in the Senate.

The president promoted the agenda of the evangelical Christian wing of the Republican Party. He spoke out against gay marriage, abortion, and federal support for stem cell research, a scientific procedure that used discarded embryos to find cures for diseases. Bush created a special office in the White House to coordinate faith-based initiatives, providing religious institutions with federal funds for social service activities without violating the First Amendment's separation of church and state.

Attending to the faithful made for good politics. At the turn of the twenty-first century, a growing number of churchgoers were joining megachurches. These congregations, mainly Protestant, each contained 2,000 or more worshippers. Between 1970 and 2005, the number of megachurches jumped from 50 to more than 1,300, with California, Texas, and Florida taking the lead. The establishment of massive churches was part of a worldwide movement, with South Korea home to the largest congregation. Joel Osteen — the evangelical pastor of Lakewood Church in Houston, Texas, the largest megachurch in the United States — drew average weekly audiences of 43,000 people, with sermons available in English and Spanish. Such religious leaders held sway with large groups of voters who could be mobilized to significant political effect.

While courting such people of faith, Bush did not neglect economic conservatives. The Republican Congress gave the president tax-cut proposals to sign in 2001 and 2003, measures that favored the wealthiest Americans. Yet to maintain a balanced budget, the cardinal principle of fiscal conservatism, these tax cuts would have required a substantial reduction in spending, which Bush and Congress chose not to do. Furthermore, continued deregulation of business encouraged unsavory activities that resulted in corporate scandals and risky financial practices.

At the same time, Bush showed the compassionate side of his conservatism. His cabinet appointments reflected racial, ethnic, and sexual diversity. They included African Americans as secretary of state (Colin Powell) and national security adviser (Condoleezza Rice, who later succeeded Powell as secretary of state). Compassionate conservatism also included educational reform, especially for those attending school in underprivileged areas. In addition, in 2003 Bush signed into law the Medicare Prescription Drug, Improvement, and Modernization Act, which aimed to lower the cost of prescription drugs to some 40 million senior citizens enrolled in Medicare.

The Iraq War. President Bush ultimately spent little of his presidency focusing on domestic issues because events originating abroad vaulted him into the role of wartime president. To make up for his lack of experience in foreign affairs, Bush relied heavily on Vice President Richard (Dick) Cheney, Secretary of Defense Donald Rumsfeld, and

President Bush at Ground Zero On September 14, 2001, President George W. Bush toured the wreckage of the destroyed World Trade Center. Standing on a pile of rubble, he heard firefighters, police officers, and other rescuers shout, "USA, USA." He responded: "I can hear you. The rest of the world hears you. And the people who knocked these buildings down will hear all of us soon." Courtesy George W. Bush Presidential Library and Museum. (P7365-23a)

Condoleezza Rice. The president's closest advisers sought to reshape critical parts of the post–Cold War world through preemptive force, most notably in the Persian Gulf.

After the attacks on the World Trade Center and the Pentagon on September 11, 2001, in which four commercial jets were hijacked and used as weapons, ultimately killing 2,996 people, Bush launched a war on terror, one that led to protracted and costly conflicts in Afghanistan and Iraq and the erosion of civil liberties at home. As part of that effort, in 2002 Congress created a cabinet-level superagency, the Department of Homeland Security, responsible for developing a national strategy against further terrorist threats. Two years later, Congress also enacted into law a key recommendation of the national commission that Breitweiser and the Jersey Girls pressured the government to establish. In 2004 Congress created the Office of the Director of National Intelligence to coordinate the work of security agencies more effectively.

In the immediate aftermath of the September 11 terrorist attacks, Bush acted decisively. The president dispatched U.S. troops to Afghanistan, whose Taliban leaders refused to turn over Osama bin Laden and other terrorists operating training centers in the country. A combination of anti-Taliban warlords and U.S. military forces toppled the Taliban regime and installed a pro-American government; however, the elusive bin Laden escaped into a remote area of Pakistan.

On the home front, the war on terror prompted passage of the **Patriot Act** in October 2001. The measure eased restrictions on domestic and foreign intelligence gathering and expanded the authority of law enforcement and immigration officials in detaining and deporting immigrants suspected of terrorism-related acts. The act gave law enforcement agencies nearly unlimited authority to wiretap telephones, retrieve e-mail messages, and search the medical, financial, and library borrowing records of individuals, including U.S. citizens, suspected of involvement in terrorism overseas or at home. The computer age had provided terrorist networks like al-Qaeda with the means to communicate quickly across national borders through electronic mail and cell phones and to raise money and launder it into safe bank accounts online. Computer technology also gave U.S. intelligence agencies ways to monitor these communications and transactions.

Amid rising anti-Muslim sentiments, the overwhelming majority of Americans supported the Patriot Act. In the weeks and months following September 11, some people committed acts of violence against mosques, Arab American community centers and businesses, and individual Muslims and people they thought were Muslims. Despite some criticism of the harsh provisions of the Patriot Act, in 2006 Congress renewed the act with only minor changes.

President Bush and his advisers sought to expand the war on terror beyond defeating the Taliban in Afghanistan. They envisioned a larger plan to reshape the politics of the Middle East and Persian Gulf regions along pro-American lines. In doing so, the United States and its European allies would ensure the flow of cheap oil to satisfy the energy demands of consumers in these countries. Furthermore, by replacing authoritarian regimes with democratic governments in places like Iraq and Afghanistan, the Bush administration envisioned a domino effect that would lead to the toppling of reactionary leaders throughout the region. In crafting this strategy, the Bush administration departed from the well-established, post–World War II policy of containing enemies short of going to war. Instead, the **Bush Doctrine** proposed undertaking preemptive war against despotic governments deemed a threat to U.S. national security, even if that danger was not imminent.

Embracing this doctrine, President Bush declared in January 2002 that Iraq was part of an "axis of evil," along with Iran and North Korea. Bush considered Saddam Hussein, the Iraqi dictator, a sponsor of terrorism and sought to remove him from power. The Iraqi leader was considered too undependable to protect U.S. oil interests in the region. Removing him, Bush believed, would also open a path to overthrowing the radical Islamic government of neighboring Iran, which had embarrassed the United States in 1979 and remained its sworn enemy.

Over the next two years, Bush convinced Congress and a majority of the American people that Iraq presented an immediate danger to the security of the United States. He did so by falsely connecting Saddam Hussein to the 9/11 al-Qaeda terrorists. The president also accused Iraq of being well advanced in building and stockpiling "weapons of mass destruction," despite evidence to the contrary. Further, the Bush administration manipulated questionable intelligence information to defend its claims. **See Primary Source Project 29: The Uses of September 11, page 1034.**

In March 2003, after a congressional vote of approval, U.S. military aircraft unleashed massive bombing attacks on Baghdad. In the 1991 Gulf War (see "Managing Conflict after the Cold War" in chapter 28), the first President Bush had responded to the Iraqi invasion of Kuwait by leading a broad coalition of nations, including Arab countries. In 2003 the United States did not wait for any overt act of aggression and created merely a nominal alliance of nations, with only Great Britain supplying significant combat troops. Nevertheless, within weeks Hussein went into hiding, prompting Bush to declare that "major combat operations" had ended in Iraq.

This triumphant declaration proved premature, although Hussein was captured several months later. Despite the presence of 130,000 U.S. and 30,000 British troops, the war dragged on. More American soldiers (over 4,000) died after the president proclaimed victory than had died during the invasion. The perception of the United States as an occupying power destabilized Iraq, leading to a civil war between the country's Shi'ite Muslim majority, which had been persecuted under Saddam Hussein, and its Sunni minority, which Hussein represented. In the northern part of the nation, the Kurdish majority, another group brutalized by Hussein, also battled Sunnis. Moreover, al-Qaeda forces, which previously had been absent from the country, joined the fray.

Explore ▶

Compare President Bush's optimistic view of the war's end with a reporter's description of life in war-torn Iraq the following year in Sources 29.2 and 29.3.

At the same time, Bush instituted the policy of incarcerating suspected al-Qaeda rebels in the U.S. military base in Guantánamo, Cuba, without due process of the law. The facility housed more than six hundred men classified as "enemy combatants," who were subject to extreme interrogation and were deprived of legal counsel.

Amid a protracted war in Iraq, President Bush won reelection in 2004 by promising to stay the course and deter further terrorism. Although the Democratic presidential candidate, Senator John Kerry of Massachusetts, criticized Bush's handling of Iraq, Bush eked out a victory; however, this time, unlike four years before, the president won a majority of the popular vote (50.7 percent).

Bush's Second Term. Over the next four years President Bush's credibility suffered. Several issues — sectarian violence in Iraq, mounting death tolls, and the failures of the

Two Perceptions of New Orleans Looting Some members of the media were guilty of racial profiling in their reporting of the aftermath of Hurricane Katrina. Compare the original caption for the photo on the left ("A young man walks through chest-deep floodwater after looting a grocery store in New Orleans") with the one on the right ("Two residents wade through chest-deep water after finding bread and soda from a local grocery store after Hurricane Katrina came through the area in New Orleans"). Racial identity appears to be the only distinction between who was "looting" and who was "finding." *(above)*: AP Photo/Dave Martin; *(right)*: Chris Graythen/Getty Images

U.S.-supported Iraqi government—turned the majority of Americans against the war. Little changed, however, as American troops remained in Iraq and Afghanistan. The war on terror had become a permanent part of life in the United States, much like the national security state during the Cold War.

With turmoil also continuing in the Persian Gulf, the threat of nuclear proliferation grew. Iraq did not have nuclear weapons, but Iran sought to develop nuclear capabilities. Iranian leaders claimed that they wanted nuclear technology for peaceful purposes, but the Bush administration believed that Iran's real purpose was to build nuclear devices to attack Israel and establish its supremacy in the region.

Bush's handling of a major natural disaster further diminished his popularity. On August 29, 2005, **Hurricane Katrina** slammed into the Gulf coast states of Louisiana and Mississippi. This powerful storm devastated New Orleans, a city with a population of nearly 500,000, a majority of whom were African American. The flood surge caused poorly maintained levees to break, deluging large areas of the city and trapping 50,000

The War in Iraq

After U.S. forces ousted Saddam Hussein, on May 1, 2003, President Bush addressed the nation from the USS *Abraham Lincoln* and proclaimed that major combat operations in Iraq had ended. However, civil war broke out between rival religious sects of Sunni and Shi'ite Muslims. Many Iraqis viewed the United States as an occupying power despite efforts to reconstruct the war-torn nation and promote free elections. In an e-mail to friends in the United States, *Wall Street Journal* correspondent Farnaz Fassihi presents a frank assessment of the deteriorating conditions in Baghdad in September 2004.

Source 29.2

George W. Bush | Declaration of Victory in Iraq, May 1, 2003

Major combat operations in Iraq have ended. In the battle of Iraq, the United States and our allies have prevailed. And now our coalition is engaged in securing and reconstructing that country. . . .

Operation Iraqi Freedom was carried out with a combination of precision and speed and boldness the enemy did not expect and the world had not seen before. From distant bases or ships at sea, we sent planes and missiles that could destroy an enemy division or strike a single bunker. Marines and soldiers charged to Baghdad across 350 miles of hostile ground, in one of the swiftest advances of heavy arms in history. You have shown the world the skill and the might of the American Armed Forces. . . . America is grateful for a job well done. . . .

We have difficult work to do in Iraq. We're bringing order to parts of that country that remain dangerous. We're pursuing and finding leaders of the old regime, who will be held to account for their crimes. We've begun the search for hidden chemical and biological weapons and already know of hundreds of sites that will be investigated. We're helping to rebuild Iraq, where the dictator built palaces for himself instead of hospitals and schools. And we will stand with the new leaders of Iraq as they establish a Government of, by, and for the Iraqi people.

The transition from dictatorship to democracy will take time, but it is worth every effort. Our coalition will stay until our work is done. And then we will leave, and we will leave behind a free Iraq.

Source: *Public Papers of the Presidents of the United States: George W. Bush, 2003* (Washington, DC: U.S. Government Printing Office), 410–13.

residents. Not only did local and state officials respond slowly and ineptly to the crisis, but so, too, did the federal government.

In the days after the storm hit, chaos reigned in New Orleans. Evacuees were housed in the Superdome football stadium and a municipal auditorium without adequate food, water, and sanitary facilities. The flooding killed at least 1,800 residents of the Gulf coast, New Orleans's population dropped by around 130,000 residents, and critics blamed the president

Source 29.3

Farnaz Fassihi | Report from Baghdad, 2004

Being a foreign correspondent in Baghdad these days is like being under virtual house arrest. Forget about the reasons that lured me to this job: a chance to see the world, explore the exotic, meet new people in far away lands, discover their ways, and tell stories that could make a difference.

Little by little, day-by-day, being based in Iraq has defied all those reasons. I am house bound. I leave when I have a very good reason to and a scheduled interview. I avoid going to people's homes and never walk in the streets. I can't go grocery shopping any more, can't eat in restaurants, can't strike a conversation with strangers, can't look for stories, can't drive in anything but a full armored car, can't go to scenes of breaking news stories, can't be stuck in traffic, can't speak English outside, can't take a road trip, can't say I'm an American, can't linger at checkpoints, can't be curious about what people are saying, doing, feeling. And can't and can't. There has been one too many close calls, including a car bomb so near our house that it blew out all the windows. So now my most pressing concern every day is not to write a

kick-ass story but to stay alive and make sure our Iraqi employees stay alive. In Baghdad I am a security personnel first, a reporter second. . . .

Iraqis like to call this mess "the situation." When asked "how are things?" they reply: "the situation is very bad."

What they mean by situation is this: the Iraqi government doesn't control most Iraqi cities, there are several car bombs going off each day around the country killing and injuring scores of innocent people, the country's roads are becoming impassable and littered by hundreds of landmines and explosive devices aimed to kill American soldiers, there are assassinations, kidnappings, and beheadings. The situation, basically, means a raging barbaric guerilla war. . . . As for reconstruction: firstly it's so unsafe for foreigners to operate that almost all projects have come to a halt. After two years, of the $18 billion Congress appropriated for Iraq reconstruction only about $1 billion or so has been spent and a chunk has now been reallocated for improving security, a sign of just how bad things are going here.

Source: Lisa Grunwald and Stephen J. Adler, eds., *Women's Letters: America from the Revolutionary War to the Present* (New York: Dial Press, 2005), 758–60.

Interpret the Evidence

1. From President Bush's perspective, what had the United States accomplished in Iraq?
2. How does Fassihi's report challenge the Bush administration's views on the Iraq War?

Put It in Context

How did the September 11 attacks influence the decision to invade Iraq?

for his lack of leadership and slow response to the disaster. Overall, Hurricane Katrina was as much a human-made disaster as a natural one.

REVIEW & RELATE

- How did President Bush put compassionate conservatism into action?
- How did the war on terror affect American foreign policy in the Bush administration?

The **Challenges** **Faced** by **President** **Barack Obama**

The world was economically interconnected and fully concerned with combating terror when a severe recession began in 2008. Looking for new hope, many Americans rallied behind the presidential candidacy of Barack Obama. Obama's election reflected sweeping demographic changes in the United States and ushered in reforms, but his victory did not eliminate the deep political and cultural divisions in the nation or eradicate pervasive economic and social inequality.

The Great Recession. In 2008 the boom times of the previous decade came to a sudden halt. The stock market's Dow Jones average, which had hit a high of 14,000, fell 6,000 points, the steepest percentage drop since 1931. Americans who had invested their money in the stock market lost trillions of dollars. The gross domestic product fell by about 6 percent, a loss too great for the economy to absorb quickly. Millions of Americans lost their jobs as consumer spending decreased, and many forfeited their homes when they could no longer afford to pay their mortgages. Unemployment jumped from 4.9 percent in January 2008 to 7.6 percent a year later. Confronted by this spiraling disaster, President Bush approved a $700 billion bailout plan to rescue the nation's largest banks and brokerage houses.

The causes of the **Great Recession** were many and had developed over a long period. Since the Reagan presidency, the federal government had relaxed regulation of the financial industry, including repeal of the Glass-Steagall Act during the Clinton administration. Also, the Federal Reserve Bank encouraged excessive borrowing by keeping interest rates very low and relaxed its oversight of Wall Street practices that placed ordinary investors' money at risk. Investment houses developed elaborate computer models that produced new and risky kinds of financial instruments, which went unregulated and whose complex nature few people understood. Insurance companies such as American International Group marketed so-called credit default swaps as protection for risky securities, exacerbating the financial crisis.

Consumers also shared some of the blame. Many took advantage of risky but easily accessible mortgage policies that appealed to borrowers with low incomes or poor credit ratings. When the housing market collapsed, many homeowners found themselves owing banks and mortgage companies much more than their homes were worth and wound up in foreclosure.

The economy might have experienced a less severe downturn if there had been greater economic equality to bolster consumer spending. But this was not the case. Wealth remained concentrated in relatively few hands. In 2007 the top 1 percent of households owned 34.6 percent of all privately held wealth, and the next 19 percent held 50.5 percent. The other 80 percent of Americans owned only 15 percent of the wealth, and the gap between rich and poor continued to widen. This maldistribution of wealth made it extremely difficult to support an economy that required ever-expanding purchasing power and produced steadily rising personal debt (Figure 29.2).

With the interdependence of economies through globalization, the Great Recession spread rapidly throughout the world. Great Britain's banking system teetered on the edge of collapse. Other nations in the European Union (EU), most notably Greece and Spain,

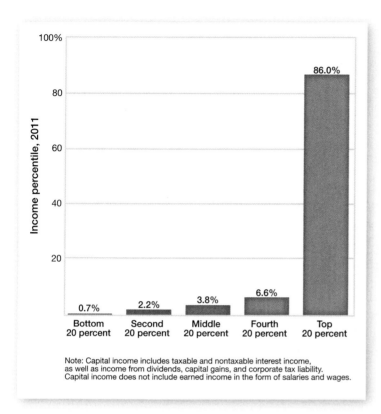

FIGURE 29.2   Wealth Inequality (Capital Income), 2011

The decline of American manufacturing and the expansion of the low-wage service sector, combined with the rise of high-tech industries and unregulated investment banking, led to growing disparities of wealth in the early twenty-first century. Disparities exist even within the top 20th percentile, as the top 1 percent controlled more than half of all capital income in 2011. Compare the top 20 percent and the bottom 20 percent of Americans with respect to capital income.

Note: Capital income includes taxable and nontaxable interest income, as well as income from dividends, capital gains, and corporate tax liability. Capital income does not include earned income in the form of salaries and wages.

verged on bankruptcy and had to be rescued by stronger EU nations. In providing financial assistance to its member states, the EU required countries such as Greece to slash spending for government services and to lower minimum wages. Even in China, where the economy had boomed as a result of globalization, businesses shut down and unemployment rose as global consumer demand for its products declined.

Obama and Domestic Politics.

In the midst of the Great Recession, the United States held the 2008 presidential election. The Republican candidate, John McCain, was a Vietnam War hero and a senator from Arizona. His Democratic opponent, Barack Obama, had served a mere four years in the Senate from Illinois. For their vice presidential running mates, McCain chose Sarah Palin, the first-term governor of Alaska, and Obama selected Joseph Biden, the senior senator from Delaware.

In the end, Obama overcame lingering racial prejudices in the country by speaking eloquently about his background as an interracial child, the son of an immigrant from Kenya and the grandson of a World War II veteran from Kansas. As important, the former community organizer succeeded in building a nationwide, grassroots political movement through digital technology. He raised an enormous amount of campaign money from ordinary donors through the Internet and used Web sites and text messaging to mobilize his supporters. Obama won the presidential election most of all because the public blamed

A Political Cartoonist's View of the Presidential Election of Barack Obama, 2008
Published by politico.com on November 6, 2008, two days after the election of Barack Obama,
this cartoon drawn by Matt Wuerker captures the joyous response of many Americans, black and
white, to the victory of the first African American president. The symbolic connection between
President Abraham Lincoln and President Obama was remarked upon often by political
commentators. © Matt Wuerker/Cartoonist Group

the Bush administration for the recession, and Obama offered hope for economic recovery. Obama captured 53 percent of the popular vote, obtaining a majority of votes from
African Americans, Latinos, women, and the young, who turned out in record numbers,
and a comfortable 365 electoral votes. The Democrats also scored big victories in the
House and Senate.

Despite the persistence of racism, President Obama achieved notable victories during
his first term in office. He continued the Bush administration's bailout of collapsing banks
and investment firms and expanded it to include American automobile companies, which
within three years bounced back, became profitable again, and began paying back the government for the bailout. In 2009 the president supported passage of an economic stimulus
plan that provided federal funds to state and local governments to create jobs and keep
their employees, including teachers, on the public payroll. More controversially, President
Obama pushed Congress to pass the **Patient Protection and Affordable Care Act**

("Obamacare") in 2010, a reform measure mandating that all Americans had to obtain health insurance or face a tax penalty and that no one could be denied coverage for a pre-existing condition. He also signed into law repeal of President Clinton's "don't ask, don't tell" policy, which discriminated against gays in the military.

Obama also took action to address the divisive issue of immigration. Congress had failed to pass the Development, Relief, and Education for Alien Minors (DREAM) Act, first introduced in 2001, which would have provided an opportunity for the children of undocumented immigrants in the United States to gain legal residency status. To protect these so-called "dreamers," in 2012 the president instituted the **Deferred Action for Childhood Arrivals (DACA)** policy, which allows children who have entered the country illegally to receive a renewable two-year extension of their residence in the U.S. along with eligibility for work permits.

Despite many policy accomplishments, President Obama continued to encounter vigorous political opposition. Most Republican lawmakers refused to support his economic stimulus and health care reform bills. A group of Republican conservatives formed the **Tea Party movement** and attacked the president as a "socialist" for what they perceived as an effort to expand federal control over the economy and diminish individual liberty with the health care act. The rise of the Tea Party intensified the partisanship within the country and added to the growing gridlock in Washington, D.C. The Tea Party flexed its electoral muscle in the 2010 midterm elections, successfully campaigning for Republican congressional and gubernatorial candidates who supported its positions. As a result, Republicans regained control of the House while the Democratic majority in the Senate narrowed.

Obama also encountered political difficulties from the left. Although the president saved the financial system from collapse, at the end of 2011 unemployment remained higher than 8 percent (a drop from its high of 10.2 percent). With millions of people still out of work, a resurgent Wall Street rewarded its managers and employees with big financial bonuses. Large corporations earned millions of dollars in profits but did not create new jobs. In 2011 protesters in cities around the nation launched the **Occupy Wall Street movement**, which attacked corporate greed, economic inequality, and government ineffectiveness. Many in the movement were inspired to act by declining tax revenues that led to crippling state budget deficits and massive cuts in spending on education, social services, and infrastructure. Many young people faced high unemployment and crushing student loan debts.

With unemployment remaining high, economic growth moving at a slow pace, and a number of European nations unable to pay mounting debts, the economy loomed as the top issue in the 2012 presidential election. The Republican nominee, Mitt Romney, the former governor of Massachusetts, appealed to conservative voters by opposing Obama's health care reform and by embracing the social agenda of the Christian Right. Despite the slower-than-expected economic recovery, Barack Obama won reelection by holding together his coalition of African American, Latino, female, young, and lower-income voters.

During President Obama's second term, the economy showed greater improvement. The unemployment rate dropped to 4.9 percent in February 2016, the lowest figure in eight years. From 2010 to 2014, the gross domestic product grew steadily by an average of more than 2 percent, and the strengthening economy cut the budget deficit significantly.

However, as the economy recovered from recession, real wages declined and income and wealth inequality widened. The top 1 percent gained about 95 percent of the income growth since 2009, and the top 10 percent held its highest share of income since World War I. One reason for this widening gap was that since 2000 the United States lost 5 million good-paying manufacturing jobs, and many of the jobs created by the recovery were low-wage service positions, whereas the wealthiest Americans benefited from the soaring stock market and rising capital gains. Making the problem worse, union membership continued its long-term decline, thereby eliminating the major opportunity for workers to increase their wages.

In two other areas, gay rights and the environment, the Obama administration made great strides in its second term. Initially Obama had supported civil unions rather than gay marriage, but in 2012 he declared his support for same-sex marriage. The following year, the Supreme Court struck down the 1996 Defense of Marriage Act, thereby extending recognition of gay marriage. Finally, in 2015, in **Obergefell v. Hodges** the Court legalized same-sex marriage nationwide. With respect to the environment, the Obama administration took climate change seriously, encouraged fuel efficiency and clean energy

Same-Sex Marriage   A gay couple exchange rings during their wedding ceremony on August 11, 2012, in Cedar Springs, Washington. The state of Washington allowed same-sex marriage three years before the U.S. Supreme Court, in 2015, ruled it legal nationwide under the Equal Protection Clause of the Fourteenth Amendment. AP Photo/The News Tribune, Peter Haley

Black Lives Matter   After the police shooting of Michael Brown, an unarmed, eighteen-year-old African American in Ferguson, Missouri, in 2014, the Black Lives Matter movement held protests calling for greater police accountability and comprehensive reform of the criminal justice system. The Brown shooting was only one of several highly publicized killings of African Americans around that time. This photo was taken on November 23, 2014, when Black Lives Matter demonstrators marched in St. Louis, near Ferguson.   Jewel Samad/Getty Images

production, bolstered the Environmental Protection Agency, and extended protection of significant cultural and natural landmarks.

Racial conflicts also continued to erupt despite the presence of an African American in the White House. Blacks had long-standing grievances with the criminal justice system, and the acquittal in 2013 of a white man in the shooting of Trayvon Martin, an unarmed black youth in Sanford, Florida, triggered outrage. Moreover, whereas most whites saw police officers as protectors, blacks viewed them with suspicion or as threats to their safety. A series of police killings of unarmed blacks in Ferguson, Missouri; Cleveland, Ohio; Staten Island, New York; and Baltimore, Maryland, renewed these fears and launched a movement that came to be known as **Black Lives Matter**. Technology helped spread its message through Twitter and social networking. As a result of federal investigations, in 2015 the Justice Department found a pattern of systemic racism and excessive use of force in the Ferguson and Cleveland police departments and negotiated settlements that instituted reforms. But here, too, persistent problems remained.

Obama and the World. Throughout Obama's two terms, his administration faced serious tests of its international leadership. In 2008 the president had appointed Hillary Clinton, the former First Lady and a senator from New York, as his secretary of state. The U.S. military increased combat troop withdrawals from Iraq and turned over security for the country to the newly elected Iraqi government. At the same time, the Obama administration stepped up the war in Afghanistan by increasing U.S. troop levels, which led to a rise in casualties. Then in 2011, he achieved a dramatic success when U.S. special forces killed Osama bin Laden in his hideout in Pakistan. By 2016, with John Kerry now his secretary of state, the president had withdrawn most combat soldiers from Afghanistan. Yet Iraq remained unstable in the absence of a strong American military presence, and the outcome of the war against the Taliban in Afghanistan remained uncertain. Despite bin Laden's death, radical jihadists continued to pose a serious danger.

Other international challenges continued as well. From 2006 to 2013, a hostile North Korea tested a series of nuclear weapons. During this period, instability in other parts of Asia, the Middle East, and the Persian Gulf also heightened U.S. security concerns and underscored the difficulties of achieving lasting peace in these regions (Map 29.2).

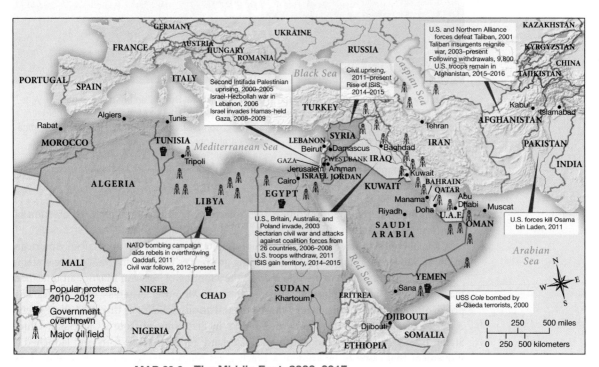

MAP 29.2 The Middle East, 2000–2017

Since 2000 the Middle East has been marked by both terrorism and democratic uprisings. After 9/11 the United States tried to transform Iraq and Afghanistan by military might, which led to prolonged wars. Yet popular rebellions in 2011, led by young people and fueled by new technology, created hope that change was possible. However, as of 2016 the military had regained power in Egypt, and Libya had descended into civil war. Syria remained involved in a brutal civil war. The terrorist, military organization ISIS captured sections of Syria as well as territory in Iraq, but in 2017 they were driven out of most of this territory by Syrian government, Russian, and American-backed military forces.

In 2011 the situation briefly looked more hopeful. In a period known as the Arab Spring, great changes swept across the Middle East, as young people, armed mainly with cell phones and connected through social media networks, peacefully toppled pro-Western but despotic governments in Egypt and Tunisia and convinced the leader of Yemen to step down. In Libya armed rebels succeeded in overthrowing the anti-American dictator Muammar al-Qaddafi.

However, many of these changes in the Middle East did not last. The military returned to power in Egypt, and civil war consumed Libya and Syria. Even more dangerous was the rise of a new militant organization in the region known as the **Islamic State of Iraq and Syria (ISIS)**, an offshoot of al-Qaeda that grew out of the sectarian violence following the overthrow of Saddam Hussein in Iraq. ISIS took over parts of Syria and Iraq, prompting the United States and some Arab nations to launch air strikes against its forces.

The ongoing civil war in Syria had profound effects on the rest of the world. Starting in 2010, millions of Syrians fled their homes, and tens of thousands sought refuge in Western Europe and the United States. This movement of refugees, greater than at any time since World War II, overwhelmed those European countries to which they first came — Greece, Hungary, and the Czech Republic. Hungary constructed fences to stop the flow of migrants, while the EU split over how to manage the crisis. In 2015 President Obama pledged to accept 10,000 additional Syrian refugees into the United States during 2016, but that number paled in comparison to the numbers who needed safe havens. Meanwhile, the humanitarian crisis of providing food, shelter, and medical attention to the refugees remained largely unresolved.

Explore ▶

Read Sources 29.4 and 29.5 for two different interpretations of President Obama.

From the outset of his first term in 2009, President Obama fought the war against terror by stepping up the use of remote-controlled armed drones (unmanned, aerial vehicles) against al-Qaeda and ISIS leaders in Pakistan, Afghanistan, Yemen, and Somalia. Although some top terrorist leaders were killed, drone attacks also resulted in significant civilian deaths.

At home, antiterrorist surveillance provoked growing controversy. Under the Patriot Act, the National Security Agency (NSA) began collecting and storing phone records of U.S. citizens. The NSA did not listen to the calls, but it drew on this bulk data to track suspected terrorists. The existence of this massive, clandestine operation came to light in 2013, when Edward Snowden, an intelligence analyst contracted by the NSA, leaked the information to the *Guardian* newspaper before seeking refuge abroad. In doing so, he ensured public scrutiny of the balance between national security and individual privacy. Snowden's revelations led Congress to pass legislation curtailing this practice in 2015.

On other foreign issues, President Obama launched bold departures. In 2014 he set in motion the normalization of diplomatic relations with Cuba and, the following year, along with several other world powers, negotiated an agreement with Iran on restricting its nuclear program. In contrast, relations with Russia deteriorated. In 2014 Russia, led by Vladimir Putin, annexed its former territory of the Crimea and in 2015 provided military support for pro-Russian separatists in Ukraine. In response the United States and the EU imposed economic sanctions on Russia but declined to take military action. Later in 2015 Russia sent military forces to Syria to support the government of the dictator Bashar al-Assad, a long-time ally, and fight his opponents, both ISIS and rebels backed by the United States.

The Election of Barack Obama

The election of Barack Obama as president in 2008 raised great expectations among Americans, black and white. The first African American president faced the difficult challenge of proving to whites that he would be the president of all the people — a "post-racial" president—while at the same time assuring blacks that he would continue to fight for their interests and further the legacy of the civil rights movement. In attempting to achieve this delicate balance, Obama drew criticism from some African Americans, including intellectuals, who believed he was sacrificing black interests on the altar of racial unity.

Source 29.4

Frederick C. Harris, Decline of Black Politics, 2012

... With the election of Barack Obama as the forty-fourth president of the United States, one could easily draw the conclusion that black America reached the pinnacle of political empowerment--a journey that has taken blacks from one of the most marginalized groups in American history (alongside Native Americans) to a key constituency that helps to elect a man of African descent to lead the nation. ... Far from black America gaining greater influence in American politics, Obama's ascendency to the White House actually signals a decline of a politics aimed at challenging racial inequality head on.

... In the age of Obama ... the majority of black voters have struck a bargain with Obama. In exchange for the president's silence on community-focused interests, black voters are content with a governing philosophy that helps "all people" and a politics centered on preserving the symbol of a black president and family in the White House.... Indeed, the symbol of a black president is not a trivial matter. Yet, the grand bargain granting black pride in exchange for silence on race-specific issues and the marginalization of targeted policies by the Obama administration have left much to be desired.

Source: Frederick C. Harris, *The Price of the Ticket: Barack Obama and the Rise and Decline of Black Politics* (Oxford: Oxford University Press, 2012), x, xii.

The United States faced global economic and environmental challenges as well. As China flourished economically, American workers lost jobs, and the Chinese amassed a nearly $200 billion trade surplus with the United States. In addition, the growth of manufacturing and the market economy in China resulted in the rising consumption of oil and gasoline. The increase in carbon emissions in China and other parts of Asia contributed to the problem of climate change, which ultimately threatens the delicate balance between the natural environment and human societies across the planet. Global warming during the twentieth and into the twenty-first century has resulted mainly from emissions of greenhouse gases into the atmosphere and the erosion of the ozone layer. As temperatures climb,

Source 29.5

Randall Kennedy, The Importance of Symbolism, 2011

Most African Americans eschew the demanding racial politics of Obama's detractors on the black left.... Blacks have, for the most part, been remarkably savvy, patient, and loyal in terms of their relationship to the Obama administration. They appreciate that Obama must accommodate a wide range of competing demands. They expect him to do what he can, consistent with political practicalities, to push the country's agenda in a progressive direction. ... [T]hey defer to Obama because they trust him.

... [T]ime and again people of all sorts have demonstrated the transcendent importance of symbolism in their lives: the liberty to sit anywhere on a bus unhampered by a color line or the freedom to eat a hamburger at a lunch counter unburdened by caste restrictions. Most African Americans gratefully appreciate that the simple fact of a black man occupying the presidency has irrevocably transformed the United States. ... Having received so little for so long, blacks are happy to have someone in the White House with whom they can fully identify and who fully identifies with them, even if he is unwilling to advance any set of federal initiatives that could plausibly be labeled a "black agenda."

Source: Randall Kennedy, *The Persistence of the Color Line: Racial Politics and the Obama Presidency* (New York: Pantheon Books, 2011), 33, 34, 35.

Examine the Sources

1. Describe the similarities and differences in Harris's and Kennedy's interpretations of President Obama's relationship with African Americans.
2. How does the fact that Harris and Kennedy are interpreting current events present both opportunities and problems for them?

Put It in Context

What difference did it make for race relations for an African American to get elected president?

---

they cause the melting of glaciers, a rise in the sea level, extreme fluctuations of weather with severely damaging storms, and famines. Disruptions in industrial and agricultural production caused by storms and the subsequent expense of rebuilding have already had a negative impact on the U.S. and world economies. Recognizing the increasing dangers of global warming, in December 2015 the United States joined 194 nations, including China and India, in signing the Paris Climate Agreement to reduce greenhouse gas emissions produced from fossil fuels.

In the context of international debates over terrorism, refugees, and global warming, controversies continued in the United States over immigration. However the issue is resolved, by the end of the twenty-first century the population of the United States will look much different than it did at the beginning. In 2012 the U.S. Census Bureau reported that nonwhite babies made up the majority of births for the first time. If the current trends in immigration and birthrates continue, the percentage of Latinos and Asian Americans in the nation will increase, while that of whites and blacks will decline. In addition, the racial and ethnic composition of the population has been transformed through intermarriage. In 2010 the Census Bureau disclosed that one of seven new marriages, or 14.6 percent, was interracial or interethnic. In 1961, when Barack Obama was born, the figure for interracial marriages was less than 0.1 percent. Thus, in an increasingly globalized nation, debates over immigration, race, and citizenship have taken new forms and significance.

REVIEW & RELATE

- What were the causes and consequences of the Great Recession?

- What effects did the election and presidency of Barack Obama have on American politics, society, and the United States' relationship to the world?

The **Presidency** of **Donald Trump**

As Barack Obama's second term drew to a close in 2016, Americans elected Donald Trump to succeed him. It was an unexpected result. The Republican Trump defeated the Democratic candidate Hillary Rodham Clinton, preventing her from becoming the first woman elected president. Despite this triumph, Trump and the Republican-controlled Congress found governing difficult.

The 2016 Election A New York City real estate tycoon and a Democrat-turned-Republican, Trump had never held political office or engaged in public service. He had gained widespread publicity as a reality television host on *The Apprentice*, where each week he told one of the contestants, "You're fired." In contrast, Hillary Clinton had an extensive record of public and political service: First Lady, U.S. senator from New York, and secretary of state.

After waging hard-fought primaries, Trump and Clinton faced off against each other in the general election. Running as an antiestablishment outsider, Trump adopted the slogan "Make America Great Again," reflecting the Republican Party's knee-jerk opposition to Obama's agenda. Trump embraced right-wing, nativist populism against Mexican and Muslim immigrants and opposed free trade agreements that he concluded shipped jobs overseas, As part of his "America First" stance, he criticized international military alliances such as NATO, a major component of U.S. foreign policy since World War II.

His nativist rhetoric echoed the beliefs of the **alternative right (alt-right)**, a group of people loosely gathered around the banner of white nationalism, including neo-Nazis, the Ku Klux Klan, and whites who believed they were losing ground to racial minorities. Obama's presidency had brought to a boil the racial resentments of the alt-right and provided fuel for Trump's candidacy. Even before running for president, Trump had called into question Obama's U.S. citizenship, despite substantial proof to the contrary, claiming that he had been born in Kenya and therefore was ineligible to become president. During the campaign, Trump appealed to white racial bitterness by attacking an American-born judge of Latino heritage and the Muslim parents of a war hero who criticized Trump for his racial and religious intolerance. He also stoked the flames of ethnic prejudice by calling unauthorized Mexican immigrants "rapists" and promising to build a wall between the U.S. and Mexican border and make the Mexican government pay for it.

Trump did not operate in a vacuum. Throughout western Europe anti-immigrant, right-wing nationalist parties were gaining ground. In a 2016 referendum, voters in the United Kingdom chose to withdraw from the European Union, a move known as Brexit (British exit). Nativist, anti-Muslim parties grew stronger in France, Germany, Austria, the Netherlands, and Scandinavia, though none gained control of their governments.

In her campaign, Clinton ran on a progressive platform that focused on the growing inequality of wealth and measures such as campaign finance reform, affordable college education, and a path to citizenship for unauthorized immigrants. Yet more than specific policies, Clinton made Trump's fitness for high office the main issue — his mocking of opponents, sexist and racially-tinged remarks, and his seeming lack of desire to educate himself in depth about domestic and international issues.

Trump in turn attacked Clinton's stamina, service as secretary of state, and judgment. Trump charged that she had illegally transmitted classified State Department material via a private e-mail server, posing a threat to national security, and that she had erased the supposedly classified e-mails to cover this up. The FBI investigated and reported that although Clinton had acted unwisely, she was guilty of no crime. Nevertheless, Trump led his campaign rallies in chants of "Lock her up," and promised to put her in jail if he won.

A new matter of e-mails surfaced late in the campaign, when WikiLeaks published e-mails stolen from the accounts of the Democratic National Committee and Clinton's campaign director, John Podesta. In the end, seventeen U.S. intelligence agencies concluded that Russian state-sponsored agents had hacked the accounts and given the e-mails to WikiLeaks — the website that previously had published classified CIA documents. In this instance, Russian hackers had pilfered the records in an attempt to promote negative publicity about the Clinton campaign and sow discord within the American electorate. For his part, Trump praised Putin as a strong leader and refused to acknowledge Russian meddling, despite official intelligence reports.

Most pollsters remained confident that Clinton would become the first woman president. The returns on Election Day proved them wrong. Although Clinton won the popular vote by nearly 3 million ballots, she lost in the Electoral College, 304-227. Trump captured six states that Obama had won in 2012, and the outcome turned on a total of 78,000 votes in Pennsylvania, Michigan, and Wisconsin. Trump had run a populist, anti-establishment, anti-politician campaign, which appealed to an electorate fed up with politics-as-usual and gridlock in Washington, D.C. His nativist agenda, along with sexist and white-identity appeals, resonated especially with older white men, residents of small towns and rural areas, workers who had lost their jobs to automation and globalization, and those who had less than a college education. For her part, Clinton had run a campaign that struggled to connect with voters, and she was unable to retain the broad coalition of support that she needed, particularly in the swing states. Even a majority of white women (53 percent) gave

Trump a slight edge, though Clinton did remain overwhelming popular among African American women.

Working-class and middle-class economic grievances certainly played a role in Trump's victory, but exit polls showed that those who ranked the economy as the most important issue voted for Clinton. Instead, racial and cultural resentments proved most significant in the outcome. White attitudes toward African Americans, immigrants, and Muslims were the main indicators in determining support for Trump. The president-elect did not create these racial, ethnic, and religious resentments but he exploited and legitimized them.

The Trump Presidency Once in the White House, Trump did not reverse course and become more "presidential." Rather, he continued to subvert the norms of American politics. He persisted in using his Twitter account to insult those who disagreed with him, including fellow Republicans. He viewed all criticism as personal, and attacked the mainstream media as "the enemy of the American people," claiming it promoted "fake news." He also engaged in a Twitter war with North Korea's dictator Kim Jong-un (Trump called him "little rocket man"), who seemed determined to develop his country into a nuclear power. Trump's tweets made the conduct of diplomacy very difficult and confused foreign leaders, allies and adversaries alike. At the same time, however, with American military support ISIS suffered defeats in Iraq and Syria, forcing it to withdraw from major cities under its control.

President Trump had mixed success in achieving his legislative agenda. Congress narrowly rejected his signature campaign promise to repeal and replace the Affordable Care Act, which would have cost tens of millions of Americans health coverage. The president was more successful in winning ratification of his appointment of Neil Gorsuch, an arch-conservative, to the Supreme Court, thereby returning conservatives to the majority on the bench after the death of Antonin Scalia. He also gained passage of a Republican tax cut law that disproportionately favors corporations and the wealthy, thereby abandoning his economic populist campaign pledge to work mainly for the working and middle classes.

Trump achieved more by issuing executive orders to forward his agenda. After several false starts, he managed to put into effect a ban on immigrants from primarily Muslim nations. He revoked Obama's DACA order allowing so-called "Dreamers," who had been brought to the country by their undocumented immigrant parents, to remain indefinitely. In addition, his administration revoked the provisional residency permits of more than 200,000 immigrants from El Salvador, Haiti, and Honduras who had fled to the U.S. following natural disasters in their countries. The children subsequently born into these families were American citizens, and the deportation of one or both of their parents would create a humanitarian crisis.

Trump also used his executive power to weaken health-care coverage as well as protections for consumers and the environment. He appointed individuals to head Cabinet offices and regulatory agencies who favored limited governance and privatization of public services, while denying scientific evidence of man-made global warning. He withdrew the United States from the Paris Climate Agreement; rolled back Obama-initiated trade and travel relations with Cuba; and decertified the Iran Nuclear Agreement. Indeed, Trump dedicated much of his first year in office to erasing Obama's presidency. Having first denied Obama's American citizenship, Trump sought to wipe out his predecessor's accomplishments from the historical record.

While these policies provoked outrage, the Trump presidency fueled greater controversy over issues of race and Russia. Trump appointed one of his top campaign advisors, Stephen K. Bannon, as the White House chief strategist. Bannon had headed *Breitbart News*, a website that catered to the alt-right. White nationalists became emboldened by Trump's election and Bannon's appointment. At a rally in Charlottesville, Virginia, Nazis and Ku Klux Klan members paraded across the University of Virginia campus mocking Jews and other minorities. They were there to oppose removal of Confederate monuments, which offended most African Americans for honoring the war to maintain slavery. When an anti-fascist protester was run down and killed by an automobile driven by a white nationalist, President Trump squandered the moral authority of his office by equating the white nationalist demonstrators with those who opposed them.

Of greater concern to his presidency was the investigation into Russian interference in the 2016 election. Two congressional committees and a special prosecutor appointed by the Justice Department, Robert Mueller, looked into Russian hacking and possible collusion between members of the Trump campaign and Kremlin–sponsored operatives seeking to damage Hillary Clinton's campaign. One of the targets of the investigation was General Michael Flynn, who was forced to resign as National Security Advisor shortly after taking office. He subsequently pled guilty to lying to the FBI about his contacts with Russia. Investigators also learned that Russian agents had used Facebook, Twitter, and Google accounts to spread false news about Clinton, specifically targeting voters in battleground states such as Wisconsin and Michigan. No one could say for sure whether the Russian efforts influenced the decisions of voters, but their activities did create an unfavorable climate of opinion against the Democratic candidate. These revelations notwithstanding, Trump refused to acknowledge Russian intervention as a threat to national security and accused the media and his liberal opponents of attempting to delegitimize his election.

Overall, despite some legislative successes along with unemployment at a low 4.1 percent and the stock market soaring to record highs, Trump remained deeply unpopular. His erratic temperament and his rejection of presidential norms of behavior cast doubts about his fitness to govern. Thus, in January 2018, polls shows the majority of Americans (55 percent) disapproved of Trump's performance, making him the least popular second-year president in modern history.

Women Reshape the Political Culture   Trump's election spurred women to challenge pervasive patterns of sexual harassment and misbehavior throughout American society and culture. The release of the "Hollywood Access" video during the presidential campaign, in which Trump is heard talking about how he groped women's genitalia backstage at the beauty pageants he hosted, was augmented by charges from more than fifteen women that Trump had sexually assaulted them. Although he denied the allegations and won the election, his misogynist behavior and rhetoric mobilized a

Women's March on Washington, D.C., 2017   About 500,000 demonstrators gather in the nation's capital on January 21, 2017, a day after President Trump's inauguration, to attend the Women's March on Washington. Refusing to remain silent after the election of a man they considered a misogynist, marchers supported a wide range of goals including gender equality, reproductive freedom, racial equality, worker rights, immigration reform, health care expansion, and environmental protection.   Mario Tama/Getty Images

large number of women to protest. On January 21, 2017, the day after President Trump's inauguration, millions of women and male allies marched in Washington, D.C. and major cities around the nation and the world to reject Trump's views and affirm that "women's rights are human rights." His election also inspired many women to run for political office.

The rage against Trump and his defeat of the first female, major-party, candidate for president sparked a collective uprising against sexual degradation of women. "When Trump won the election, I felt a crushing sense of powerlessness," one woman declared. "And then I realized that I had to do something." Social media provided an outlet for women's frustrations. Originated by Tarana Burke, an African American social activist, and promoted by the actress Alyssa Milano, the **#MeToo** movement linked tens of millions of women who shared on Twitter and Facebook their stories of rape, sexual harassment, and sexual assault. As a result, by the end of 2017, numerous women had come forward with complaints of sexual misconduct by media, entertainment, and sports celebrities, corporate executives, and politicians of both parties, leading in many cases to the swift firing or resignation of these men. Many incidents of sexual abuse remain unpunished; however, women show no sign of letting up in challenging and upending societal tolerance for inappropriate sexual conduct.

REVIEW AND RELATE

• Explain how Donald Trump was elected president and describe the differences between campaigning for office and governing.

• Explain how Trump's election mobilized women to challenge inappropriate sexual behavior.

Conclusion: Technology and **Terror** in a **Global Society**

Since 1993 Americans have faced new forms of globalization, new technologies, and new modes of warfare. The computer revolution begun by Bill Gates and others helped change the way Americans gather information, communicate ideas, purchase goods, and conduct business. It has also shaped national and international conflicts. The September 11, 2001 attacks on the World Trade Center and the Pentagon demonstrated that terrorists could use computers and digital equipment to wreak havoc on the most powerful nation in the world. Shortly thereafter, Kristen Breitweiser used the Internet to mobilize public support for the families of 9/11 victims. And Barack Obama's 2008 presidential campaign, protesters demonstrating against various Middle East dictatorships, and the leaders of the Tea Party and Occupy Wall Street movements also wielded technology to promote their causes. On the other hand, in the interest of combating terrorism, the U.S. government has used this technology to monitor the activities of citizens it considers a threat to national security, thereby raising concerns about civil liberties.

The Bush administration responded to the 9/11 terrorist attacks by fighting wars in Iraq and Afghanistan. President Obama ended the Iraq war and steadily withdrew troops from Afghanistan, but neither administration was able to build stable governments in these countries. The rise of ISIS, which grew out of the fighting in Iraq, posed an even greater danger than did al-Qaeda to stability in the Middle East and the spread of terrorism throughout the world. At the same time, the United States and its allies faced a militarily revitalized Russia seeking to extend its influence in Ukraine and Syria, once again heightening the prospect of confrontation between the world's major nuclear powers.

Along with the computer revolution, globalization has encouraged vast economic transformations throughout the world. Presidents as politically different as Bill Clinton and George W. Bush supported deregulation, free trade, and other policies that fostered corporate mergers and allowed businesses to reach beyond U.S. borders for cheap labor, raw materials, and new markets. While the 1990s witnessed the fruits of the new global economy, in 2008 the dangers of financial speculation and intertwined national economies became strikingly clear with the onset of the Great Recession. This economic collapse has underscored the inequalities of wealth that continue to widen, aggravated by racial, ethnic, and gender disparities.

The Obama administration succeeded in ending the worst features of the recession and at the same time managed to extend health care coverage to the country's most vulnerable citizens. Yet Obama faced increased partisan congressional gridlock that made further reforms concerning immigration, job creation, racial justice, energy consumption, and the environment impossible. Indeed, it took the federal courts to extend marriage equality nationwide.

The election of Donald Trump in 2016 demonstrates that despite the accomplishments of the Obama administration, many Americans feel left out or are fearful of that progress. Trump waged a political campaign based on racial, economic, and cultural grievances that carried over from the campaign into his presidency. These divisions in the nation remain sharper than at any time since the turbulent 1960s.

Nevertheless, it should be kept in mind that throughout its history, the United States has shown great strength in finding solutions to its problems. The nation has incorporated diverse populations into its midst, redefined old cultural identities and created new ones, expanded civil rights and civil liberties, extended economic opportunities, and joined other nations to fight military aggression and address other international concerns. The nation will have to draw on these strengths and continue to innovate and adapt to change if it expects to exert leadership in the world and maintain its greatness into the twenty-first century.

TIMELINE OF **EVENTS**

1975	Microsoft formed
1976	Apple Computer Company formed
1980–1990s	Immigration surges from Mexico, Central America, the Caribbean, and South and East Asia
1991	World Wide Web created
1994	Contract with America announced; Republicans win control of Congress
1996	Personal Responsibility and Work Reconciliation Act passed
	Defense of Marriage Act passed
1998	President Clinton impeached
2000	Supreme Court rules in favor of George W. Bush in contested presidential election
2001	September 11 attacks on World Trade Center and Pentagon
	U.S. troops invade Afghanistan; Patriot Act passed
2003–2011	War in Iraq
2005	Hurricane Katrina
2008	Great Recession begins
	Barack Obama elected president
	Tea Party movement formed
2010	Patient Protection and Affordable Care Act ("Obamacare")
2011	Osama bin Laden killed
	Occupy Wall Street movement formed
	Black Lives Matter movement formed
2012	Deferred Action for Childhood Arrivals (DACA) policy
2015	Supreme Court legalizes same-sex marriage nationwide
	Obama pledges to take 10,000 Syrian refugees
	Agreement signed by 195 nations to lower greenhouse gas emissions
2016	Donald Trump elected president
2017	Women's March on Washington and formation of #MeToo movement

KEY **TERMS**

North American Free Trade Agreement (NAFTA), *1005*

Contract with America, *1006*

Personal Responsibility and Work Opportunity Reconciliation Act, *1006*

ethnic cleansing, *1007*

Patriot Act, *1011*

Bush Doctrine, *1011*

Hurricane Katrina, *1013*

Great Recession, *1016*

Patient Protection and Affordable Care Act (Obamacare), *1018*

Deferred Action for Childhood Arrivals (DACA), *1019*

Tea Party movement, *1019*

Occupy Wall Street movement, *1019*

Obergefell v. Hodges, *1020*

Black Lives Matter, *1021*

Islamic State of Iraq and Syria (ISIS), *1023*

Alt Right, *1026*

#MeToo movement, *1030*

REVIEW & **RELATE**

1. How did computers change life in the United States at the turn of the millennium?
2. How has globalization affected business consolidation and immigration in recent decades?
3. How did conflicts between Democrats and Republicans affect President Clinton's accomplishments?
4. How did the end of the Cold War shape President Clinton's foreign policies?
5. How did President Bush put compassionate conservatism into action?
6. How did the war on terror affect American foreign policy in the Bush administration?
7. What were the causes and consequences of the Great Recession?
8. What effects did the election and presidency of Barack Obama have on American politics, society, and the United States' relationship to the world?
9. Explain how Donald Trump was elected president and describe the differences between campaigning for office and governing.
10. Explain how Trump's election mobilized women to challenge inappropriate sexual behavior.

The Uses of September 11

▶ **How do the authors of these primary sources use the 9/11 attacks for different purposes?**

The terrorist attacks on the morning of September 11, 2001 killed three thousand people and left the American nation reeling. Millions spent that morning and the days that followed glued to their television sets, watching repeated images of the World Trade Center, the Pentagon, and scattered wreckage in Pennsylvania. Police and firefighters flocked to the Pentagon and Ground Zero to aid in rescue and recovery efforts. Rumors began circulating immediately about various terrorist groups or nations that might be responsible, and it was quickly discovered that the terrorist organization al-Qaeda, under the direction of Osama bin Laden, had carried out the attacks.

Americans reacted to the events in various ways, and official responses were immediate. The Bush administration launched the war on terror, which included the creation of the Department of Homeland Security, passage of the Patriot Act, and the invasion of Afghanistan, actions that resulted in heightened government surveillance of both its citizens and adversaries (Source 29.9). In the aftermath of the attacks, more than eighty thousand Arabs and Muslims living in the United States were fingerprinted and registered with the federal government (Sources 29.7 and 29.8). President Bush, believing that Saddam Hussein was linked to al-Qaeda, ordered an American invasion of Iraq in the spring of 2003.

In the wake of the 9/11 attacks, individuals and communities nationwide responded with an outpouring of grief (Source 29.6). Throughout the nation, communities held ceremonies, candlelight vigils, and marches. Impromptu memorials appeared in New York City and Washington, D.C., and photos of the missing filled subway stations and parks. In 2011, ten years after the attacks, the National September 11 Memorial and Museum opened and presented personal stories and artifacts to find meaning in the events of that day (Source 29.10).

Source 29.6

Diana Hoffman | "The Power of Freedom," 2002

The September 11 attacks inspired thousands of poems, essays, and songs that expressed sorrow for the victims and resolve that the tragedy would make America a stronger nation. The following poem by Diana Hoffman, which reflects these sentiments, appeared on a memorial Web site in 2002.

I know you're celebrating
what your evil deeds have wrought
But with the devastation
something else you've also brought
For nothing is more powerful
than Americans who unite
Who put aside their differences
and for freedom fight
Each defenseless victim whose
untimely death you caused
And every fallen hero

whose brave life was lost
Has only served to strengthen
our national resolve
Each freedom-loving citizen
will surely get involved
You've galvanized our nation
into a force so strong
We'll end your reign of terror
although the fight is long
For every heart that's broken
ten million will stand tall
and every tear that's falling
is the mortar for it all
And when this war is over
one thing I know is sure
Our country will be greater
and our freedom will endure

Source: Diana Hoffman, "The Power of Freedom," Never Forgotten Poems, accessed October 16, 2015, http://911neverforget.tripod.com/neverforgotten/id3.html.

Source 29.7

Khaled Abou El Fadl | Response to September 11, 2001

Arab Americans and Muslims became targets of violence, racial profiling, surveillance, and even deportation in the wake of the September 11 attacks. Khaled Abou El Fadl is a law professor at the University of California at Los Angeles and a leading expert on Islamic law. In the following reflection, he recalls how he felt on September 11 and how being a Muslim shaped his response to the attacks.

My reaction very soon after it happened was anguished hope that Muslims were not involved in this. And actually I remember very distinctly sort of a degree of feeling ashamed about having that hope, because you would like to respond to something like this at a human and universal level. You would like to feel like, Muslim or not Muslim, this is just terrible, period. It's really irrelevant who has done this. But because of what I knew, what it's going to mean for Muslims, I knew that the sort of hyphenation of whether a Muslim did this or not was going to make a big difference for me, for my friends, for my family, for my son. That's a reality. And the agony of it has not subsided because the worst fears, that this is going to open a door of much suffering for many human beings, has fully materialized. . . .

The word *fear* describes everything. There is fear of fellow citizens being killed. There is fear that you yourself will be the subject of a terrorist attack. Terrorism doesn't have an exemption clause for Arabs or Muslims. If I was on that plane that day, the fact that I was Arab or Muslim wouldn't have made an iota of difference. So you run the risk of being the victim of a terrorist attack as much as any other member of society. But you now also run the risk of being blamed for it, just simply by the fact that you're Arab or Muslim. . . .

We belong on this plane and on our seat, you don't. You're here because we allow you to be here. It's as if it's a privilege. You're different, it's a privilege that you are allowed on this plane. And when I started wearing suits and ties consistently, regardless of how long or short the flight is, I've noticed that the treatment has gotten better. But it's always anxiety producing, not just for the normal security concerns, but because it's an unknown sum. You just don't know whether you're going to run into someone who's going to say something rude, something hurtful, whether you're going to sit next to someone who asks to change seats, which has happened to me, because they don't feel comfortable sitting next to you. Every time you pick up something from your travel bag, or you take out a magazine, or take out a book, they look like they're going to have a heart attack. Or constantly staring at you. It's just, it's an extremely anxiety producing experience and the irony of it is that if, God forbid, there is a terrorist attack, and I am on a plane, I'm just like everyone else, I die just like everyone else.

Source: "Face to Face: Stories from the Aftermath of Infamy," ITVS Interactive, accessed October 15, 2015, http://archive.itvs.org/facetoface/stories/khaled.html.

Anti-Muslim Discrimination, 2011

The terrorist attacks on September 11 incited anti-Muslim sentiment among many Americans. Although President Bush made it clear that the enemy was al-Qaeda and not Muslims in general, the passage of the Patriot Act and the roundup and deportation of Arab and Muslim immigrants reflected an underlying hostility to Muslim Americans. This cartoon, which appeared in a Florida newspaper, compares discrimination against Muslims to the prejudice that Japanese Americans experienced during World War II.

© Tribune Content Agency, LLC. All Rights Reserved. Reprinted with permission.

Edward Snowden | Interview, 2014

The attacks on September 11 created the need for more reliable intelligence gathering. The latest advances in computer technology aided in this effort. However, as time passed, many critics worried that the government had exceeded the limits of legitimate constitutional bounds and posed a threat to individual freedom. Edward Snowden worked as an intelligence contractor for the National Security Administration (NSA). Following 9/11, the NSA was one of many government agencies conducting information on suspected terrorists. In 2013 Snowden leaked thousands of classified documents to the *Guardian* newspaper revealing the NSA's worldwide secret surveillance program, including the gathering of bulk data on the telephone conversations of many Americans. In the following interview with the *Guardian*, Snowden explains his motivations.

W e constantly hear the phrase "national security" but when the state begins . . . broadly intercepting the communications, seizing the communications by themselves, without any warrant, without any suspicion, without any judicial involvement, without any demonstration of probable cause, are they really protecting national security or are they protecting state security?

What I came to feel—and what I think more and more people have seen at least the potential for—is that a regime that is described as a national security agency has stopped representing the public interest and has instead begun to protect and promote state security interests. And the idea of western democracy as having state security bureaus, just that term, that phrase itself, "state security bureau," is kind of chilling. . . .

Generally, it's not the people at the working level you need to worry about. It's the senior officials, it's the policymakers who are shielded from accountability, who are shielded from oversight and who are allowed to make decisions that affect all of our lives without any public input, any public debate, or any electoral consequences because their decisions and the consequences of the decisions are never known.

Because of the advance of technology, storage becomes cheaper and cheaper year after year and when our ability to store data outpaces the expense of creating that data, we end up with things that are no longer held for short-term periods, they're held for long-term periods and then they're held for a longer term period. At the NSA for example, we store data for five years on individuals. And that's before getting a waiver to extend that even further.

Source: Alan Rusbridger and Ewen MacAskill, "Edward Snowden Interview," *Guardian*, July 18, 2014, mhttp://www.theguardian .com/world/2014/jul/18/-sp-edward-snowden-nsa-whistleblower- interview-transcript, accessed December 14, 2015.

Alice M. Greenwald | Message from the Director of the 9/11 Memorial Museum

After eight years of construction, the National September 11 Memorial and Museum opened to the public on May 21, 2014, at the site of the World Trade Center attacks. The museum documents the history of the events surrounding 9/11 and does so through exhibits of artifacts and personal stories. By 2016, more than 4 million people had visited the museum. In the following statement, the director of the museum explains its historical mission.

O ur visitors have a voice in this Museum, reinforcing the idea that each of us is engaged in the making of history. Whether telling one's own 9/11 story, recording a remembrance for someone who was killed in the attacks, or adding an opinion about some of the more challenging questions raised by 9/11, visitors can contribute their own stories to the Museum in our on-site recording studio. What they record will be added to the Museum archive, and excerpts may be integrated into media exhibits on an ongoing basis.

The core creative team responsible for the 9/11 Museum spent years deliberating over how to shape a memorial museum that would offer a safe environment in which to explore difficult history.

While the events of 9/11 are the foundation of the experience, the Museum does more than facilitate learning. It is a place where an encounter with history connects visitors to the shared human impacts of this event, transforming what can seem like the anonymous abstractions of terrorism and mass murder into a very personal sense of loss.

As much about "9/12" as it is about 9/11, the Museum provides a case study in how ordinary people acted in extraordinary circumstances, their acts of kindness, compassion and generosity of spirit demonstrating the profoundly constructive effect we can have on each other's lives by the choices we make, even in the face of unspeakable destruction. The 9/11 Memorial Museum takes you on a journey into the heart of memory as an agent of transformation, empowering each of us to seek a deeper understanding of what it means to be a human being living in an interdependent world at the start of the 21st century.

Source: Alice M. Greenwald, "Message from the Museum Director," 2014, 9/11 Memorial, http://www.911memorial.org/message-museum-director, accessed October 16, 2015.

Interpret the Evidence

1. Compare and contrast the audiences that Diana Hoffman (Source 29.6) and Khaled Abou El Fadl (Source 29.7) aim at reaching.

2. Why does the cartoonist in Source 29.8 compare the Muslim experience following September 11 to that of Japanese Americans interned in World War II camps?

3. How does Edward Snowden justify his actions in leaking classified documents from the NSA (Source 29.9)? How does his behavior signify that for many Americans the lessons of 9/11 are lessening in importance and other considerations have become more significant?

4. How does the 9/11 Memorial Museum draw on history to chronicle September 11 (Source 29.10)? What would you include in the museum for the sake of historical accuracy?

Put It in Context

How did the attacks on September 11 change America?

THE DECLARATION OF INDEPENDENCE

In Congress, July 4, 1776.

The unanimous Declaration of the thirteen United States of America

When in the course of human events, it becomes necessary for one people to dissolve the political bands which have connected them with another, and to assume, among the powers of the earth, the separate and equal station to which the laws of nature and of nature's God entitle them, a decent respect to the opinions of mankind requires that they should declare the causes which impel them to the separation.

We hold these truths to be self-evident, that all men are created equal; that they are endowed by their Creator with certain unalienable rights; that among these, are life, liberty, and the pursuit of happiness. That, to secure these rights, governments are instituted among men, deriving their just powers from the consent of the governed; that, whenever any form of government becomes destructive of these ends, it is the right of the people to alter or to abolish it, and to institute a new government, laying its foundation on such principles, and organizing its powers in such form, as to them shall seem most likely to effect their safety and happiness. Prudence, indeed, will dictate that governments long established, should not be changed for light and transient causes; and, accordingly, all experience hath shown, that mankind are more disposed to suffer, while evils are sufferable, than to right themselves by abolishing the forms to which they are accustomed. But, when a long train of abuses and usurpations, pursuing invariably the same object, evinces a design to reduce them under absolute despotism, it is their right, it is their duty, to throw off such government and to provide new guards for their future security. Such has been the patient sufferance of these colonies, and such is now the necessity which constrains them to alter their former systems of government. The history of the present King of Great Britain is a history of repeated injuries and usurpations, all having, in direct object, the establishment of an absolute tyranny over these States. To prove this, let facts be submitted to a candid world: He has refused his assent to laws the most wholesome and necessary for the public good.

He has forbidden his governors to pass laws of immediate and pressing importance, unless suspended in their operation till his assent should be obtained; and, when so suspended, he has utterly neglected to attend to them.

He has refused to pass other laws for the accommodation of large districts of people, unless those people would relinquish the right of representation in the legislature; a right inestimable to them, and formidable to tyrants only.

He has called together legislative bodies at places unusual, uncomfortable, and distant from the depository of their public records, for the sole purpose of fatiguing them into compliance with his measures.

He has dissolved representative houses repeatedly for opposing, with manly firmness, his invasions on the rights of the people.

He has refused, for a long time after such dissolutions, to cause others to be elected; whereby the legislative powers, incapable of annihilation, have returned to the people at large for their exercise; the state remaining in the mean-time exposed to all the danger of invasion from without, and convulsions within.

He has endeavoured to prevent the population of these States; for that purpose, obstructing the laws for naturalization of foreigners, refusing to pass others to encourage their migration hither, and raising the conditions of new appropriations of lands.

He has obstructed the administration of justice, by refusing his assent to laws for establishing judiciary powers.

He has made judges dependent on his will alone, for the tenure of their offices, and the amount and payment of their salaries.

He has erected a multitude of new offices, and sent hither swarms of officers to harass our people, and eat out their substance.

He has kept among us, in times of peace, standing armies, without the consent of our legislature.

He has affected to render the military independent of, and superior to, the civil power.

He has combined, with others, to subject us to a jurisdiction foreign to our Constitution, and unacknowledged by our laws; giving his assent to their acts of pretended legislation:

For quartering large bodies of armed troops among us:

For protecting them by a mock trial, from punishment, for any murders which they should commit on the inhabitants of these States:

For cutting off our trade with all parts of the world:

For imposing taxes on us without our consent:

For depriving us, in many cases, of the benefit of trial by jury:

For transporting us beyond seas to be tried for pretended offences:

For abolishing the free system of English laws in a neighboring province, establishing therein an arbitrary government, and enlarging its boundaries, so as to render it at once an example and fit instrument for introducing the same absolute rule into these colonies:

For taking away our charters, abolishing our most valuable laws, and altering, fundamentally, the powers of our governments:

For suspending our own legislatures, and declaring themselves invested with power to legislate for us in all cases whatsoever.

He has abdicated government here, by declaring us out of his protection, and waging war against us.

He has plundered our seas, ravaged our coasts, burnt our towns, and destroyed the lives of our people.

He is, at this time, transporting large armies of foreign mercenaries to complete the works of death, desolation, and tyranny, already begun, with circumstances of cruelty and perfidy scarcely paralleled in the most barbarous ages, and totally unworthy the head of a civilized nation.

He has constrained our fellow citizens, taken captive on the high seas, to bear arms against their country, to become the executioners of their friends, and brethren, or to fall themselves by their hands.

He has excited domestic insurrections amongst us, and has endeavored to bring on the inhabitants of our frontiers, the merciless Indian savages, whose known rule of warfare is an undistinguished destruction of all ages, sexes, and conditions.

In every stage of these oppressions, we have petitioned for redress; in the most humble terms; our repeated petitions have been answered only by repeated injury. A prince, whose character is thus marked by every act which may define a tyrant, is unfit to be the ruler of a free people.

Nor have we been wanting in attention to our British brethren. We have warned them, from time to time, of attempts made by their legislature to extend an unwarrantable jurisdiction over us. We have reminded them of the circumstances of our emigration and settlement here. We have appealed to their native justice and magnanimity, and we have conjured them, by the ties of our common kindred, to disavow these usurpations, which would inevitably interrupt our connections and correspondence. They, too, have been deaf to the voice of justice and consanguinity. We must, therefore, acquiesce in the necessity which denounces our separation, and hold them as we hold the rest of mankind, enemies in war, in peace, friends.

We, therefore, the representatives of the United States of America, in general Congress assembled, appealing to the Supreme Judge of the world for the rectitude of our intentions, do, in the name, and by authority of the good people of these colonies, solemnly publish and declare, that these united colonies are, and of right ought to be, free and independent states: that they are absolved from all allegiance to the British Crown, and that all political connection between them and the state of Great Britain is, and ought to be, totally dissolved; and that, as free and independent states, they have full power to levy war, conclude peace, contract alliances, establish commerce, and to do all other acts and things which independent states may of right do. And, for the support of this declaration, with a firm reliance on the protection of Divine Providence, we mutually pledge to each other our lives, our fortunes, and our sacred honor.

The foregoing Declaration was, by order of Congress, engrossed, and signed by the following members:

JOHN HANCOCK

New Hampshire
Josiah Bartlett
William Whipple
Matthew Thornton

Massachusetts Bay
Samuel Adams
John Adams
Robert Treat Paine
Elbridge Gerry

Rhode Island
Stephen Hopkins
William Ellery

Connecticut
Roger Sherman
Samuel Huntington
William Williams
Oliver Wolcott

New York
William Floyd
Phillip Livingston
Francis Lewis
Lewis Morris

New Jersey
Richard Stockton
John Witherspoon
Francis Hopkinson
John Hart
Abraham Clark

Pennsylvania
Robert Morris
Benjamin Rush
Benjamin Franklin
John Morton
George Clymer
James Smith
George Taylor

James Wilson
George Ross
Caesar Rodney
George Read
Thomas M'Kean

Maryland
Samuel Chase
William Paca
Thomas Stone
Charles Carroll, of Carrollton

North Carolina
William Hooper
Joseph Hewes
John Penn

South Carolina
Edward Rutledge
Thomas Heyward, Jr.

Thomas Lynch, Jr.
Arthur Middleton

Virginia
George Wythe
Richard Henry Lee
Thomas Jefferson
Benjamin Harrison
Thomas Nelson, Jr.
Francis Lightfoot Lee
Carter Braxton

Georgia
Button Gwinnett
Lyman Hall
George Walton

Resolved, That copies of the Declaration be sent to the several assemblies, conventions, and committees, or councils of safety, and to the several commanding officers of the continental troops; that it be proclaimed in each of the United States, at the head of the army.

THE ARTICLES OF CONFEDERATION AND PERPETUAL UNION

Agreed to in Congress, November 15, 1777.
Ratified March 1781.

Between the states of New Hampshire, Massachusetts Bay, Rhode Island and Providence Plantations, Connecticut, New York, New Jersey, Pennsylvania, Delaware, Maryland, Virginia, North Carolina, South Carolina, Georgia.*

Article 1

The stile of this confederacy shall be "The United States of America."

Article 2

Each State retains its sovereignty, freedom and independence, and every power, jurisdiction, and right, which is not by this confederation expressly delegated to the United States, in Congress assembled.

Article 3

The said states hereby severally enter into a firm league of friendship with each other for their common defence, the security of their liberties and their mutual and general welfare; binding themselves to assist each other against all force offered to, or attacks made upon them, or any of them, on account of religion, sovereignty, trade, or any other pretence whatever.

Article 4

The better to secure and perpetuate mutual friendship and intercourse among the people of the different states in this union, the free inhabitants of each of these states, paupers, vagabonds, and fugitives from justice excepted, shall be entitled to all privileges and immunities of free citizens in the several states; and the people of each State shall have free ingress and regress to and from any other State, and shall enjoy therein all the privileges of trade and commerce, subject to the same duties, impositions, and restrictions, as the inhabitants thereof respectively; provided, that such restrictions shall not extend so far as to prevent the removal of property, imported into any State, to any other State of which the owner is an inhabitant; provided also, that no imposition, duties, or restriction, shall be laid by any State on the property of the United States, or either of them. If any person guilty of, or charged with treason, felony, or other high misdemeanor in any State, shall flee from justice and be found in any of the United States, he shall, upon demand of the governor or executive power of the State from which he fled, be delivered up and removed to the State having jurisdiction of his offence. Full faith and credit shall be given in each of these states to the records, acts, and judicial proceedings of the courts and magistrates of every other State.

Article 5

For the more convenient management of the general interests of the United States, delegates shall be annually appointed, in such manner as the legislature of each State shall direct, to meet in Congress, on the 1st Monday in November in every year, with a power reserved to each State to recall its delegates, or any of them, at any time within the year, and to send others in their stead for the remainder of the year.

*This copy of the final draft of the Articles of Confederation to taken from the Journals, 9:907–925, November 15, 1777.

No State shall be represented in Congress by less than two, nor by more than seven members; and no person shall be capable of being a delegate for more than three years in any term of six years; nor shall any person, being a delegate, be capable of holding any office under the United States, for which he, or any other for his benefit, receives any salary, fees, or emolument of any kind.

Each State shall maintain its own delegates in a meeting of the states, and while they act as members of the committee of the states.

In determining questions in the United States, in Congress assembled, each State shall have one vote.

Freedom of speech and debate in Congress shall not be impeached or questioned in any court or place out of Congress: and the members of Congress shall be protected in their persons from arrests and imprisonments, during the time of their going to and from, and attendance on Congress, except for treason, felony, or breach of the peace.

Article 6

No State, without the consent of the United States, in Congress assembled, shall send any embassy to, or receive any embassy from, or enter into any conference, agreement, alliance, or treaty with any king, prince, or state; nor shall any person, holding any office of profit or trust under the United States, or any of them, accept of any present, emolument, office or title, of any kind whatever, from any king, prince, or foreign state; nor shall the United States, in Congress assembled, or any of them, grant any title of nobility.

No two or more states shall enter into any treaty, confederation, or alliance, whatever, between them, without the consent of the United States, in Congress assembled, specifying accurately the purposes for which the same is to be entered into, and how long it shall continue.

No state shall lay any imposts or duties which may interfere with any stipulations in treaties entered into by the United States, in Congress assembled, with any king, prince, or state, in pursuance of any treaties already proposed by Congress to the courts of France and Spain.

No vessels of war shall be kept up in time of peace by any State, except such number only as shall be deemed necessary by the United States, in Congress assembled, for the defence of such State or its trade; nor shall any body of forces be kept up by any State, in time of peace, except such number only as, in the judgment of the United States, in Congress assembled, shall be deemed requisite to garrison the forts necessary for the defence of such State; but every State shall always keep up a well regulated and disciplined militia, sufficiently armed and accoutred, and shall provide, and constantly have ready for use, in public stores, a due number of field pieces and tents, and a proper quantity of arms, ammunition and camp equipage.

No State shall engage in any war without the consent of the United States, in Congress assembled, unless such State be actually invaded by enemies, or shall have received certain advice of a resolution being formed by some nation of Indians to invade such State, and the danger is so imminent as not to admit of a delay till the United States, in Congress assembled, can be consulted; nor shall any State grant commissions to any ships or vessels of war, nor letters of marque or reprisal, except it be after a declaration of war by the United States, in Congress assembled, and then only against the kingdom or state, and the subjects thereof, against which war has been so declared, and under such regulations as shall be established by the United States, in Congress assembled, unless such State be infested by pirates, in which case vessels of war may be fitted out for that occasion, and kept so long as the danger shall continue, or until the United States, in Congress assembled, shall determine otherwise.

Article 7

When land forces are raised by any State for the common defence, all officers of or under the rank of colonel, shall be appointed by the legislature of each State respectively, by whom such forces shall be raised, or in such manner as such State shall direct; and all vacancies shall be filled up by the State which first made the appointment.

Article 8

All charges of war and all other expences, that shall be incurred for the common defence or general welfare, and allowed by the United States, in Congress assembled, shall be defrayed out of a common treasury, which shall be supplied by the several states, in proportion to the value of all land within each State, granted to or surveyed for any person, as such land and the buildings and improvements thereon shall be estimated according to such mode as the United States, in Congress assembled, shall, from time to time, direct and appoint.

The taxes for paying that proportion shall be laid and levied by the authority and direction of the legislatures of the several states, within the time agreed upon by the United States, in Congress assembled.

Article 9

The United States, in Congress assembled, shall have the sole and exclusive right and power of determining on peace and war, except in the cases mentioned in the 6th article; of sending and receiving ambassadors; entering into treaties and alliances, provided that no treaty of commerce shall be made, whereby the legislative power of the respective states shall be restrained from imposing such imposts and duties on foreigners as their own people are subjected to, or from prohibiting the exportation or importation of any species of goods or commodities whatsoever; of establishing rules for deciding, in all cases, what captures on land or water shall be legal, and in what manner prizes, taken by land or naval forces in the service of the United States, shall be divided or appropriated; of granting letters of marque and reprisal in times of peace; appointing courts for the trial of piracies and felonies committed on the high seas, and establishing courts for receiving and determining, finally, appeals in all cases of captures; provided, that no member of Congress shall be appointed a judge of any of the said courts.

The United States, in Congress assembled, shall also be the last resort on appeal in all disputes and differences now subsisting, or that hereafter may arise between two or more states concerning boundary, jurisdiction or any other cause whatever; which authority shall always be exercised in the manner following: whenever the legislative or executive authority, or lawful agent of any State, in controversy with another, shall present a petition to Congress, stating the matter in question, and praying for a hearing, notice thereof shall be given, by order of Congress, to the legislative or executive authority of the other State in controversy, and a day assigned for the appearance of the parties by their lawful agents, who shall then be directed to appoint, by joint consent, commissioners or judges to constitute a court for hearing and determining the matter in question; but, if they cannot agree, Congress shall name three persons out of each of the United States, and from the list of such persons each party shall alternately strike out one, the petitioners beginning, until the number shall be reduced to thirteen; and from that number not less than seven, nor more than nine names, as Congress shall direct, shall, in the presence of Congress, be drawn out by lot; and the persons whose names shall be so drawn, or any five of them, shall be commissioners or judges to hear and finally determine the controversy, so always as a major part of the judges who shall hear the cause shall agree in the determination;

and if either party shall neglect to attend at the day appointed, without shewing reasons which Congress shall judge sufficient, or, being present, shall refuse to strike, the Congress shall proceed to nominate three persons out of each State, and the secretary of Congress shall strike in behalf of such party absent or refusing; and the judgment and sentence of the court to be appointed, in the manner before prescribed, shall be final and conclusive; and if any of the parties shall refuse to submit to the authority of such court, or to appear or defend their claim or cause, the court shall nevertheless proceed to pronounce sentence or judgment, which shall, in like manner, be final and decisive, the judgment or sentence and other proceedings begin, in either case, transmitted to Congress, and lodged among the acts of Congress for the security of the parties concerned: provided, that every commissioner, before he sits in judgment, shall take an oath, to be administered by one of the judges of the supreme or superior court of the State where the cause shall be tried, "well and truly to hear and determine the matter in question, according to the best of his judgment, without favour, affection, or hope of reward:" provided, also, that no State shall be deprived of territory for the benefit of the United States.

All controversies concerning the private right of soil, claimed under different grants of two or more states, whose jurisdictions, as they may respect such lands and the states which passed such grants, are adjusted, the said grants, or either of them, being at the same time claimed to have originated antecedent to such settlement of jurisdiction, shall, on the petition of either party to the Congress of the United States, be finally determined, as near as may be, in the same manner as is before prescribed for deciding disputes respecting territorial jurisdiction between different states.

The United States, in Congress assembled, shall also have the sole and exclusive right and power of regulating the alloy and value of coin struck by their own authority, or by that of the respective states; fixing the standard of weights and measures throughout the United States; regulating the trade and managing all affairs with the Indians not members of any of the states; provided that the legislative right of any State within its own limits be not infringed or violated; establishing and regulating post offices from one State to another throughout all the United States, and exacting such postage on the papers passing through the same as may be requisite to defray the expences of the said office; appointing all officers of the land forces in the service of the United States, excepting regimental officers; appointing all the officers of the naval forces, and commissioning all officers whatever in the service of the United States; making rules for the government and regulation of the said land and naval forces, and directing their operations.

The United States, in Congress assembled, shall have authority to appoint a committee to sit in the recess of Congress, to be denominated "a Committee of the States," and to consist of one delegate from each State, and to appoint such other committees and civil officers as may be necessary for managing the general affairs of the United States, under their direction; to appoint one of their number to preside; provided that no person be allowed to serve in the office of president more than one year in any term of three years; to ascertain the necessary sums of money to be raised for the service of the United States, and to appropriate and apply the same for defraying the public expences; to borrow money or emit bills on the credit of the United States, transmitting, every half year, to the respective states, an account of the sums of money so borrowed or emitted; to build and equip a navy; to agree upon the number of land forces, and to make requisitions from each State for its quota, in proportion to the number of white inhabitants in such State; which requisitions shall be binding; and thereupon, the legislature of each State shall appoint the regimental officers, raise the men, and cloathe, arm, and equip them in a soldier-like manner, at the expence of the United States; and the officers and men so cloathed, armed, and equipped, shall march to the place appointed and within the time agreed on by the United States, in Congress assembled; but if the United States, in Congress assembled, shall, on consideration of circumstances, judge proper that any State should not raise men, or should raise a smaller number than its quota, and that any other State should raise a greater number of men than the quota thereof, such extra number shall be raised, officered, cloathed, armed, and equipped in the same manner as the quota of such State, unless the legislature of such State shall judge that such extra number cannot be safely spared out of the same, in which case they shall raise, officer, cloathe, arm, and equip as many of such extra number as they judge can be safely spared. And the officers and men so cloathed, armed, and equipped, shall march to the place appointed and within the time agreed on by the United States, in Congress assembled.

The United States, in Congress assembled, shall never engage in a war, nor grant letters of marque and reprisal in time of peace, nor enter into any treaties or alliances, nor coin money, nor regulate the value thereof, nor ascertain the sums and expences necessary for the defence and welfare of the United States, or any of them: nor emit bills, nor borrow money on the credit of the United States, nor appropriate money, nor agree upon the number of vessels of war to be built or purchased, or the number of land or sea forces to be raised, nor appoint a commander in chief of the army or navy, unless nine states assent to the same; nor shall a question on any other point, except for adjourning from day to day, be determined, unless by the votes of a majority of the United States, in Congress assembled.

The Congress of the United States shall have power to adjourn to any time within the year, and to any place within the United States, so that no period of adjournment be for a longer duration than the space of six months, and shall publish the journal of their proceedings monthly, except such parts thereof, relating to treaties, alliances or military operations, as, in their judgment, require secrecy; and the yeas and nays of the delegates of each State on any question shall be entered on the journal, when it is desired by any delegate; and the delegates of a State, or any of them, at his, or their request, shall be furnished with a transcript of the said journal, except such parts as are above excepted, to lay before the legislatures of the several states.

Article 10

The committee of the states, or any nine of them, shall be authorized to execute, in the recess of Congress, such of the powers of Congress as the United States, in Congress assembled, by the consent of nine states, shall, from time to time, think expedient to vest them with; provided, that no power be delegated to the said committee, for the exercise of which, by the articles of confederation, the voice of nine states, in the Congress of the United States assembled, is requisite.

Article 11

Canada acceding to this confederation, and joining in the measures of the United States, shall be admitted into and entitled to all the advantages of this union; but no other colony shall be admitted into the same, unless such admission be agreed to by nine states.

Article 12

All bills of credit emitted, monies borrowed and debts contracted by, or under the authority of Congress before the assembling of the United States, in pursuance of the present confederation, shall be deemed and considered as a charge against the United States, for payment and satisfaction whereof the said United States and the public faith are hereby solemnly pledged.

Article 13

Every State shall abide by the determinations of the United States, in Congress assembled, on all questions which, by this confederation, are submitted to them. And the articles of this confederation shall be inviolably observed by every State, and the union shall be perpetual; nor shall any alteration at any time hereafter be made in any of them, unless such alteration be agreed to in a Congress of the United States, and be afterwards confirmed by the legislatures of every State.

These articles shall be proposed to the legislatures of all the United States, to be considered, and if approved of by them, they are advised to authorize their delegates to ratify the same in the Congress of the United States; which being done, the same shall become conclusive.

THE CONSTITUTION OF THE UNITED STATES*

Agreed to by Philadelphia Convention, September 17, 1787. Implemented March 4, 1789.

Preamble

We the people of the United States, in order to form a more perfect union, establish justice, insure domestic tranquility, provide for the common defense, promote the general welfare, and secure the blessings of liberty to ourselves and our posterity, do ordain and establish this Constitution for the United States of America.

Article I

Section 1. All legislative powers herein granted shall be vested in a Congress of the United States, which shall consist of a Senate and a House of Representatives.

Section 2. The House of Representatives shall be composed of members chosen every second year by the people of the several States, and the electors in each State shall have the qualifications requisite for electors of the most numerous branch of the State Legislature.

No person shall be a Representative who shall not have attained to the age of twenty-five years, and been seven years a citizen of the United States, and who shall not, when elected, be an inhabitant of that State in which he shall be chosen.

Representatives and direct taxes shall be apportioned among the several States which may be included within this Union, according to their respective numbers, *which shall be determined by adding to the whole number of free persons, including those bound to service for a term of years and excluding Indians not taxed, three-fifths of all other persons.* The actual enumeration shall be made within three years after the first meeting of the Congress of the United States, and within every subsequent term of ten years, in such manner as they shall by law direct. The number of Representatives shall not exceed one for every thirty thousand, but each State shall have at least one Representative; and until such enumeration shall be made, *the State of New Hampshire shall be entitled to choose three, Massachusetts eight, Rhode Island and Providence Plantations one, Connecticut five, New York six, New Jersey four, Pennsylvania eight, Delaware one, Maryland six, Virginia ten, North Carolina five, South Carolina five, and Georgia three.*

*Passages no longer in effect are in italic type.

When vacancies happen in the representation from any State, the Executive authority thereof shall issue writs of election to fill such vacancies.

The House of Representatives shall choose their Speaker and other officers; and shall have the sole power of impeachment.

Section 3. The Senate of the United States shall be composed of two Senators from each State, *chosen by the legislature thereof,* for six years; and each Senator shall have one vote.

Immediately after they shall be assembled in consequence of the first election, they shall be divided as equally as may be into three classes. The seats of the Senators of the first class shall be vacated at the expiration of the second year, of the second class at the expiration of the fourth year, and of the third class at the expiration of the sixth year, so that one-third may be chosen every second year; and if vacancies happen by resignation or otherwise, during the recess of the legislature of any State, the Executive thereof may make temporary appointments until the next meeting of the legislature, which shall then fill such vacancies.

No person shall be a Senator who shall not have attained to the age of thirty years, and been nine years a citizen of the United States, and who shall not, when elected, be an inhabitant of that State for which he shall be chosen.

The Vice-President of the United States shall be President of the Senate, but shall have no vote, unless they be equally divided.

The Senate shall choose their other officers, and also a President pro tempore, in the absence of the Vice-President, or when he shall exercise the office of President of the United States.

The Senate shall have the sole power to try all impeachments. When sitting for that purpose, they shall be on oath or affirmation. When the President of the United States is tried, the Chief Justice shall preside: and no person shall be convicted without the concurrence of two-thirds of the members present.

Judgment in cases of impeachment shall not extend further than to removal from the office, and disqualification to hold and enjoy any office of honor, trust or profit under the United States: but the party convicted shall nevertheless be liable and subject to indictment, trial, judgment and punishment, according to law.

Section 4. The times, places and manner of holding elections for Senators and Representatives shall be prescribed in each State by the legislature thereof; but the Congress may at any time by law make or alter such regulations, except as to the places of choosing Senators.

The Congress shall assemble at least once in every year, and such meeting *shall be on the first Monday in December, unless they shall by law appoint a different day.*

Section 5. Each house shall be the judge of the elections, returns and qualifications of its own members, and a majority of each shall constitute a quorum to do business; but a smaller number may adjourn from day to day, and may be authorized to compel the attendance of absent members, in such manner, and under such penalties, as each house may provide.

Each house may determine the rules of its proceedings, punish its members for disorderly behavior, and with the concurrence of two-thirds, expel a member.

Each house shall keep a journal of its proceedings, and from time to time publish the same, excepting such parts as may in their judgment require secrecy; and the yeas and nays of the members of either house on any question shall, at the desire of one fifth of those present, be entered on the journal.

Neither house, during the session of Congress, shall, without the consent of the other, adjourn for more than three days, nor to any other place than that in which the two houses shall be sitting.

Section 6.   The Senators and Representatives shall receive a compensation for their services, to be ascertained by law and paid out of the treasury of the United States. They shall in all cases except treason, felony and breach of the peace, be privileged from arrest during their attendance at the session of their respective houses, and in going to and returning from the same; and for any speech or debate in either house, they shall not be questioned in any other place.

No Senator or Representative shall, during the time for which he was elected, be appointed to any civil office under the authority of the United States, which shall have been created, or the emoluments whereof shall have been increased, during such time; and no person holding any office under the United States shall be a member of either house during his continuance in office.

Section 7.   All bills for raising revenue shall originate in the House of Representatives; but the Senate may propose or concur with amendments as on other bills.

Every bill which shall have passed the House of Representatives and the Senate, shall, before it become a law, be presented to the President of the United States; if he approve he shall sign it, but if not he shall return it with objections to that house in which it shall have originated, who shall enter the objections at large on their journal, and proceed to reconsider it. If after such reconsideration two-thirds of that house shall agree to pass the bill, it shall be sent, together with the objections, to the other house, by which it shall likewise be reconsidered, and, if approved by two-thirds of that house, it shall become a law. But in all such cases the votes of both houses shall be determined by yeas and nays, and the names of the persons voting for and against the bill shall be entered on the journal of each house respectively. If any bill shall not be returned by the President within ten days (Sundays excepted) after it shall have been presented to him, the same shall be a law, in like manner as if he had signed it, unless the Congress by their adjournment prevent its return, in which case it shall not be a law.

Every order, resolution, or vote to which the concurrence of the Senate and House of Representatives may be necessary (except on a question of adjournment) shall be presented to the President of the United States; and before the same shall take effect, shall be approved by him, or being disapproved by him, shall be repassed by two-thirds of the Senate and House of Representatives, according to the rules and limitations prescribed in the case of a bill.

Section 8.   The Congress shall have power

To lay and collect taxes, duties, imposts, and excises, to pay the debts and provide for the common defense and general welfare of the United States; but all duties, imposts and excises shall be uniform throughout the United States;

To borrow money on the credit of the United States;

To regulate commerce with foreign nations, and among the several States, and with the Indian tribes;

To establish an uniform rule of naturalization, and uniform laws on the subject of bankruptcies throughout the United States;

To coin money, regulate the value thereof, and of foreign coin, and fix the standard of weights and measures;

To provide for the punishment of counterfeiting the securities and current coin of the United States;

establish post offices and post roads;

To promote the progress of science and useful arts by securing for limited times to authors and inventors the exclusive right to their respective writings and discoveries;

To constitute tribunals inferior to the Supreme Court;

To define and punish piracies and felonies committed on the high seas and offences against the law of nations;

To declare war, grant letters of marque and reprisal, and make rules concerning captures on land and water;

To raise and support armies, but no appropriation of money to that use shall be for a longer term than two years;

To provide and maintain a navy;

To make rules for the government and regulation of the land and naval forces;

To provide for calling forth the militia to execute the laws of the Union, suppress insurrections and repel invasions;

To provide for organizing, arming, and disciplining the militia, and for governing such part of them as may be employed in the service of the United States, reserving to the States respectively the appointment of the officers, and the authority of training the militia according to the discipline prescribed by Congress;

To exercise exclusive legislation in all cases whatsoever, over such district (not exceeding ten miles square) as may, by cession of particular States, and the acceptance of Congress, become the seat of the government of the United States, and to exercise like authority over all places purchased by the consent of the legislature of the State, in which the same shall be, for erection of forts, magazines, arsenals, dock-yards, and other needful buildings;—and

To make all laws which shall be necessary and proper for carrying into execution the foregoing powers, and all other powers vested by this Constitution in the government of the United States, or in any department or officer thereof.

Section 9. *The migration or importation of such persons as any of the States now existing shall think proper to admit shall not be prohibited by the Congress prior to the year one thousand eight hundred and eight; but a tax or duty may be imposed on such importation, not exceeding ten dollars for each person.*

The privilege of the writ of habeas corpus shall not be suspended, unless when in cases of rebellion or invasion the public safety may require it.

No bill of attainder or ex post facto law shall be passed.

No capitation, or other direct, tax shall be laid, unless in proportion to the census or enumeration herein before directed to be taken.

No tax or duty shall be laid on articles exported from any State.

No preference shall be given by any regulation of commerce or revenue to the ports of one State over those of another; nor shall vessels bound to, or from, one State be obliged to enter, clear, or pay duties in another.

No money shall be drawn from the treasury, but in consequence of appropriations made by law; and a regular statement and account of the receipts and expenditures of all public money shall be published from time to time.

No title of nobility shall be granted by the United States: and no person holding any office of profit or trust under them, shall, without the consent of the Congress, accept of any present, emolument, office, or title, of any kind whatever, from any king, prince, or foreign state.

Section 10. No State shall enter into any treaty, alliance, or confederation; grant letters of marque and reprisal; coin money; emit bills of credit; make anything but gold and silver coin a tender in payment of debts; pass any bill of attainder, ex post facto law, or law impairing the obligation of contracts, or grant any title of nobility.

No State shall, without the consent of Congress, lay any imposts or duties on imports or exports, except what may be absolutely necessary for executing its inspection laws: and the net produce of all duties and imposts, laid by any State on imports or exports, shall be for the use of the treasury of the United States; and all such laws shall be subject to the revision and control of the Congress.

No State shall, without the consent of Congress, lay any duty of tonnage, keep troops, or ships of war in time of peace, enter into any agreement or compact with another State, or with a foreign power, or engage in war, unless actually invaded, or in such imminent danger as will not admit of delay.

Article II

Section 1. The executive power shall be vested in a President of the United States of America. He shall hold his office during the term of four years, and, together with the Vice-President, chosen for the same term, be elected as follows:

Each State shall appoint, in such manner as the legislature thereof may direct, a number of electors, equal to the whole number of Senators and Representatives to which the State may be entitled in the Congress; but no Senator or Representative, or person holding an office of trust or profit under the United States, shall be appointed an elector.

The electors shall meet in their respective States, and vote by ballot for two persons, of whom one at least shall not be an inhabitant of the same State with themselves. And they shall make a list of all the persons voted for, and of the number of votes for each; which list they shall sign and certify, and transmit sealed to the seat of government of the United States, directed to the President of the Senate. The President of the Senate shall, in the presence of the Senate and House of Representatives, open all the certificates, and the votes shall then be counted. The person having the greatest number of votes shall be the President, if such number be a majority of the whole number of electors appointed; and if there be more than one who have such majority, and have an equal number of votes, then the House of Representatives shall immediately choose by ballot one of them for President; and if no person have a majority, then from the five highest on the list said house shall in like manner choose the President. But in choosing the President the votes shall be taken by States, the representation from each State having one vote; a quorum for this purpose shall consist of a member or members from two-thirds of the States, and a majority of all the States shall be necessary to a choice. In every case, after the choice of the President, the person having the greatest number of votes of the electors shall be the Vice-President. But if there should remain two or more who have equal votes, the Senate shall choose from them by ballot the Vice-President.

The Congress may determine the time of choosing the electors, and the day on which they shall give their votes; which day shall be the same throughout the United States.

No person except a natural-born citizen, *or a citizen of the United States at the time of the adoption of this Constitution,* shall be eligible to the office of President; neither shall any person be eligible to that office who shall not have attained to the age of thirty-five years, and been fourteen years a resident within the United States.

In cases of the removal of the President from office or of his death, resignation, or inability to discharge the powers and duties of the said office, the same shall devolve on the Vice-President, and the Congress may by law provide for the case of removal, death, resignation, or inability, both of the President and Vice-President, declaring what officer shall then act as President, and such officer shall act accordingly, until the disability be removed, or a President shall be elected.

The President shall, at stated times, receive for his services a compensation, which shall neither be increased nor diminished during the period for which he shall have been elected, and he shall not receive within that period any other emolument from the United States, or any of them.

Before he enter on the execution of his office, he shall take the following oath or affirmation:—"I do solemnly swear (or affirm) that I will faithfully execute the office of the President of the United States, and will to the best of my ability preserve, protect and defend the Constitution of the United States."

Section 2.   The President shall be commander in chief of the army and navy of the United States, and of the militia of the several States, when called into the actual service of the United States; he may require the opinion, in writing, of the principal officer in each of the executive departments, upon any subject relating to the duties of their respective offices, and he shall have power to grant reprieves and pardons for offenses against the United States, except in cases of impeachment.

He shall have power, by and with the advice and consent of the Senate, to make treaties, provided two-thirds of the Senators present concur; and he shall nominate, and by and with the advice and consent of the Senate, shall appoint ambassadors, other public ministers and consuls, judges of the Supreme Court, and all other officers of the United States, whose appointments are not herein otherwise provided for, and which shall be established by law: but Congress may by law vest the appointment of such inferior officers, as they think proper, in the President alone, in the courts of law, or in the heads of departments.

The President shall have power to fill up all vacancies that may happen during the recess of the Senate, by granting commissions which shall expire at the end of their next session.

Section 3.   He shall from time to time give to the Congress information of the state of the Union, and recommend to their consideration such measures as he shall judge necessary and expedient; he may, on extraordinary occasions, convene both houses, or either of them, and in case of disagreement between them, with respect to the time of adjournment, he may adjourn them to such time as he shall think proper; he shall receive ambassadors and other public ministers; he shall take care that the laws be faithfully executed, and shall commission all the officers of the United States.

Section 4.   The President, Vice-President and all civil officers of the United States shall be removed from office on impeachment for, and on conviction of, treason, bribery, or other high crimes and misdemeanors.

Article III

Section 1.   The judicial power of the United States shall be vested in one Supreme Court, and in such inferior courts as the Congress may from time to time ordain and establish. The judges, both of the Supreme and inferior courts, shall hold their offices during good behavior, and shall, at stated times, receive for their services a compensation which shall not be diminished during their continuance in office.

Section 2.   The judicial power shall extend to all cases, in law and equity, arising under this Constitution, the laws of the United States, and treaties made, or which shall be made, under their authority;—to all cases affecting ambassadors, other public ministers and consuls;—to all cases of admiralty and maritime jurisdiction;—to controversies to which the United States shall be a party;—to controversies between two or more States;—between a State and citizens of another State;—between citizens of different States;—between citizens of the same State claiming lands under grants of different States, and between a State, or the citizens thereof, and foreign states, citizens or subjects.

In all cases affecting ambassadors, other public ministers and consuls, and those in which a State shall be party, the Supreme Court shall have original jurisdiction. In all the other cases before mentioned, the Supreme Court shall have appellate jurisdiction, both as to law and fact, with such exceptions, and under such regulations, as the Congress shall make.

The trial of all crimes, except in cases of impeachment, shall be by jury; and such trial shall be held in the State where said crimes shall have been committed; but when not committed within any State, the trial shall be at such place or places as the Congress may by Law have directed.

Section 3.   Treason against the United States shall consist only in levying war against them, or in adhering to their enemies, giving them aid and comfort. No person shall be convicted of treason unless on the testimony of two witnesses to the same overt act, or on confession in open court.

The Congress shall have power to declare the punishment of treason, but no attainder of treason shall work corruption of blood, or forfeiture except during the life of the person attainted.

Article IV

Section 1.   Full faith and credit shall be given in each State to the public acts, records, and judicial proceedings of every other State. And the Congress may by general laws prescribe the manner in which such acts, records, and proceedings shall be proved, and the effect thereof.

Section 2.   The citizens of each State shall be entitled to all privileges and immunities of citizens in the several States.

A person charged in any State with treason, felony, or other crime, who shall flee from justice, and be found in another State, shall on demand of the executive authority of the State from which he fled, be delivered up, to be removed to the State having jurisdiction of the crime.

No Person held to service or labor in one State, under the laws thereof, escaping into another, shall, in consequence of any law or regulation therein, be discharged from such service or labor, but shall be delivered up on claim of the party to whom such service or labor may be due.

Section 3.   New States may be admitted by the Congress into this Union; but no new State shall be formed or erected within the jurisdiction of any other State; nor any State be formed by the junction of two or more States, or parts of States, without the consent of the legislatures of the States concerned as well as of the Congress.

The Congress shall have power to dispose of and make all needful rules and regulations respecting the territory or other property belonging to the United States; and nothing in this Constitution shall be so construed as to prejudice any claims of the United States, or of any particular State.

Section 4.   The United States shall guarantee to every State in this Union a republican form of government, and shall protect each of them against invasion; and on application of the legislature, or of the executive (when the legislature cannot be convened), against domestic violence.

Article V

The Congress, whenever two-thirds of both houses shall deem it necessary, shall propose amendments to this Constitution, or, on the application of the legislatures of two-thirds of the several States, shall call a convention for proposing amendments, which, in either case, shall be valid to all intents and purposes, as part of this Constitution, when ratified by the legislatures of three-fourths of the several States, or by conventions in three-fourths thereof, as the one or the other mode of ratification may be proposed by the Congress; *provided that no amendments which may be made prior to the year one thousand eight hundred and eight shall in any manner affect the first and fourth clauses in the ninth section of the first article;* and that no State, without its consent, shall be deprived of its equal suffrage in the Senate.

Article VI

All debts contracted and engagements entered into, before the adoption of this Constitution, shall be as valid against the United States under this Constitution, as under the Confederation.

This Constitution, and the laws of the United States which shall be made in pursuance thereof; and all treaties made, or which shall be made, under the authority of the United States, shall be the supreme law of the land; and the judges in every State shall be bound thereby, anything in the Constitution or laws of any State to the contrary notwithstanding.

The Senators and Representatives before mentioned, and the members of the several State legislatures, and all executive and judicial officers, both of the United States and of the several States, shall be bound by oath or affirmation to support this Constitution; but no religious test shall ever be required as a qualification to any office or public trust under the United States.

Article VII

The ratification of the conventions of nine States shall be sufficient for the establishment of this Constitution between the States so ratifying the same.

Done in convention by the unanimous consent of the States present, the seventeenth day of September in the year of our Lord one thousand seven hundred and eighty-seven and of the Independence of the United States of America the twelfth. In witness whereof we have hereunto subscribed our names.

GEORGE WASHINGTON, President and Deputy from Virginia

New Hampshire
John Langdon
Nicholas Gilman

Massachusetts
Nathaniel Gorham
Rufus King

Connecticut
William Samuel
Johnson
Roger Sherman

New York
Alexander Hamilton

New Jersey
William Livingston
David Brearley
William Paterson
Jonathan Dayton

Pennsylvania
Benjamin Franklin
Thomas Mifflin
Robert Morris
George Clymer
Thomas FitzSimons
Jared Ingersoll
James Wilson
Gouverneur Morris

Delaware
George Read
Gunning Bedford, Jr.
John Dickinson
Richard Bassett
Jacob Broom

Maryland
James McHenry
Daniel of St. Thomas Jenifer
Daniel Carroll

Virginia
John Blair
James Madison, Jr.

North Carolina
William Blount
Richard Dobbs Spaight
Hugh Williamson

South Carolina
John Rutledge
Charles Cotesworth
Pinckney
Charles Pinckney
Pierce Butler

Georgia
William Few
Abraham Baldwin

AMENDMENTS TO THE CONSTITUTION

(including six unratified amendments)

Amendment I   [Ratified 1791]

Congress shall make no law respecting an establishment of religion, or prohibiting the free exercise thereof; or abridging the freedom of speech, or of the press; or the right of the people peaceably to assemble, and to petition the government for a redress of grievances.

Amendment II   [Ratified 1791]

A well-regulated militia being necessary to the security of a free State, the right of the people to keep and bear arms shall not be infringed.

Amendment III   [Ratified 1791]

No soldier shall, in time of peace, be quartered in any house without the consent of the owner, nor in time of war, but in a manner to be prescribed by law.

Amendment IV   [Ratified 1791]

The right of the people to be secure in their persons, houses, papers, and effects, against unreasonable searches and seizures, shall not be violated, and no warrants shall issue but upon probable cause, supported by oath or affirmation, and particularly describing the place to be searched, and the persons or things to be seized.

Amendment V   [Ratified 1791]

No person shall be held to answer for a capital, or otherwise infamous crime, unless on a present-ment or indictment of a grand jury, except in cases arising in the land or naval forces, or in the militia, when in actual service in time of war or public danger; nor shall any person be subject for the same offence to be twice put in jeopardy of life or limb; nor shall be compelled in any criminal case to be a witness against himself, nor be deprived of life, liberty, or property, without due process of law; nor shall private property be taken for public use without just compensation.

Amendment VI   [Ratified 1791]

In all criminal prosecutions, the accused shall enjoy the right to a speedy and public trial, by an impartial jury of the State and district wherein the crime shall have been committed, which district shall have been previously ascertained by law, and to be informed of the nature and cause of the accusation; to be confronted with the witnesses against him; to have compulsory process for obtaining witnesses in his favor, and to have the assistance of counsel for his defence.

Amendment VII   [Ratified 1791]

In suits at common law, where the value in controversy shall exceed twenty dollars, the right of trial by jury shall be preserved, and no fact tried by a jury shall be otherwise reexamined in any court of the United States, than according to the rules of the common law.

Amendment VIII   [Ratified 1791]

Excessive bail shall not be required, nor excessive fines imposed, nor cruel and unusual punishments inflicted.

Amendment IX   [Ratified 1791]

The enumeration in the Constitution, of certain rights, shall not be construed to deny or disparage others retained by the people.

Amendment X   [Ratified 1791]

The powers not delegated to the United States by the Constitution, nor prohibited by it to the States, are reserved to the States respectively, or to the people.

Unratified Amendment

[Reapportionment Amendment (proposed by Congress September 25, 1789, along with the Bill of Rights)]

After the first enumeration required by the first article of the Constitution, there shall be one Representative for every thirty thousand, until the number shall amount to one hundred, after which the proportion shall be so regulated by Congress, that there shall be not less than one hundred Representatives, nor less than one Representative for every forty thousand persons, until the number of Representatives shall amount to two hundred; after which the proportion shall be so regulated by Congress, that there shall not be less than two hundred Representatives, nor more than one Representative for every fifty thousand persons.

Amendment XI   [Ratified 1798]

The judicial power of the United States shall not be construed to extend to any suit in law or equity, commenced or prosecuted against one of the United States by citizens of another State, or by citizens or subjects of any foreign state.

Amendment XII   [Ratified 1804]

The electors shall meet in their respective States, and vote by ballot for President and Vice-President, one of whom, at least, shall not be an inhabitant of the same State with themselves; they shall name in their ballots the person voted for as President, and in distinct ballots the person voted for as Vice-President, and they shall make distinct lists of all persons voted for as President, and of all persons voted for as Vice-President, and of the number of votes for each, which lists they shall sign and certify, and transmit sealed to the seat of government of the United States, directed to the President of the Senate;—the President of the Senate shall, in the presence of the Senate and House of Representatives, open all the certificates and the votes shall then be counted;—the person having the greatest number of votes for President shall be the President, if such number be a majority of the whole number of electors appointed; and if no person have such majority, then from the persons having the highest numbers not exceeding three on the list of those voted for as President, the House of Representatives shall choose immediately, by ballot, the President. But in choosing the President, the votes shall be taken by States, the representation from each State having one vote; a quorum for this purpose shall consist of a member or members from two-thirds of the States, and a majority of all the States shall be necessary to a choice. And if the House of Representatives shall not choose a President whenever the right of choice shall devolve upon them, before *the fourth day of March* next following, then the Vice-President shall act as President, as in the case of the death or other constitutional disability of the President.

The person having the greatest number of votes as Vice-President shall be the Vice-President, if such number be a majority of the whole number of electors appointed; and if no person have a majority, then from the two highest numbers on the list the Senate shall choose the Vice-President; a quorum for the purpose shall consist of two-thirds of the whole number of Senators, and a majority of the whole number shall be necessary to a choice. But no person constitutionally ineligible to the office of President shall be eligible to that of Vice-President of the United States.

Unratified Amendment

[Titles of Nobility Amendment (proposed by Congress May 1, 1810)]

If any citizen of the United States shall accept, claim, receive or retain any title of nobility or honor or shall, without the consent of Congress, accept and retain any present, pension, office or emolument of any kind whatever, from any emperor, king, prince or foreign power, such person shall cease to be a citizen of the United States, and shall be incapable of holding any office of trust or profit under them or either of them.

Unratified Amendment

[Corwin Amendment (proposed by Congress March 2, 1861)]

No amendment shall be made to the Constitution which will authorize or give to Congress the power to abolish or interfere, within any State, with the domestic institutions thereof, including that of persons held to labor or service by the laws of said State.

Amendment XIII   [Ratified 1865]

Section 1. Neither slavery nor involuntary servitude, except as a punishment for crime whereof the party shall have been duly convicted, shall exist within the United States, or any place subject to their jurisdiction.

Section 2. Congress shall have power to enforce this article by appropriate legislation.

Amendment XIV   [Ratified 1868]

Section 1. All persons born or naturalized in the United States, and subject to the jurisdiction thereof, are citizens of the United States and of the State wherein they reside. No State shall make or enforce any law which shall abridge the privileges or immunities of citizens of the United States; nor shall any State deprive any person of life, liberty, or property, without due process of law; nor deny to any person within its jurisdiction the equal protection of the laws.

Section 2. Representatives shall be appointed among the several States according to their respective numbers, counting the whole number of persons in each State, excluding Indians not taxed. But when the right to vote at any election for the choice of Electors for President and Vice-President of the United States, Representatives in Congress, the executive and judicial officers of a State, or the members of the legislature thereof, is denied to any of the *male* inhabitants of such State, being *twenty-one* years of age and citizens of the United States, or in any way abridged, except for participation in rebellion, or other crime, the basis of representation therein shall be reduced in the proportion which the number of such male citizens shall bear to the whole number of *male* citizens *twenty-one* years of age in such State.

Section 3. No person shall be a Senator or Representative in Congress, or Elector of President and Vice-President, or hold any office, civil or military, under the United States, or under any State, who, having previously taken an oath, as a member of Congress, or as an officer of the

United States, or as a member of any State legislature, or as an executive or judicial officer of any State, to support the Constitution of the United States, shall have engaged in insurrection or rebellion against the same, or given aid or comfort to the enemies thereof. Congress may, by a vote of two-thirds of each house, remove such disability.

Section 4.   The validity of the public debt of the United States, authorized by law, including debts incurred for payment of pensions and bounties for services in suppressing insurrection or rebellion, shall not be questioned. But neither the United States nor any State shall assume or pay any debt or obligation incurred in aid of insurrection or rebellion against the United States, or any claim for the loss or emancipation of any slave; but all such debts, obligations, and claims shall be held illegal and void.

Section 5.   The Congress shall have power to enforce, by appropriate legislation, the provisions of this article.

Amendment XV   [Ratified 1870]

Section 1.   The right of citizens of the United States to vote shall not be denied or abridged by the United States or by any State on account of race, color, or previous condition of servitude.

Section 2.   The Congress shall have power to enforce this article by appropriate legislation.

Amendment XVI   [Ratified 1913]

The Congress shall have power to lay and collect taxes on incomes, from whatever source derived, without apportionment among the several States, and without regard to any census or enumeration.

Amendment XVII   [Ratified 1913]

Section 1.   The Senate of the United States shall be composed of two Senators from each State, elected by the people thereof, for six years; and each Senator shall have one vote. The electors in each State shall have the qualifications requisite for electors of [voters for] the most numerous branch of the State legislatures.

Section 2.   When vacancies happen in the representation of any State in the Senate, the executive authority of such State shall issue writs of election to fill such vacancies: Provided, that the Legislature of any State may empower the executive thereof to make temporary appointments until the people fill the vacancies by election as the Legislature may direct.

Section 3.   *This amendment shall not be so construed as to affect the election or term of any Senator chosen before it becomes valid as part of the Constitution.*

Amendment XVIII

[Ratified 1919; repealed 1933 by Amendment XXI]

Section 1.   *After one year from the ratification of this article the manufacture, sale, or transportation of intoxicating liquors within, the importation thereof into, or the exportation thereof from the United States and all territory subject to the jurisdiction thereof, for beverage purposes, is hereby prohibited.*

Section 2.   *The Congress and the several States shall have concurrent power to enforce this article by appropriate legislation.*

Section 3.   *This article shall be inoperative unless it shall have been ratified as an amendment to the Constitution by the legislatures of the several States, as provided by the Constitution, within seven years from the date of the submission thereof to the States by the Congress.*

Amendment XIX   [Ratified 1920]

Section 1.   The right of citizens of the United States to vote shall not be denied or abridged by the United States or by any State on account of sex.

Section 2.   Congress shall have the power to enforce this article by appropriate legislation.

Unratified Amendment

[Child Labor Amendment (proposed by Congress June 2, 1924)]

Section 1.   *The Congress shall have power to limit, regulate, and prohibit the labor of persons under eighteen years of age.*

Section 2.   *The power of the several States is unimpaired by this article except that the operation of State laws shall be suspended to the extent necessary to give effect to legislation enacted by Congress.*

Amendment XX   [Ratified 1933]

Section 1.   The terms of the President and Vice-President shall end at noon on the 20th day of January, and the terms of Senators and Representatives at noon on the 3rd day of January, of the years in which such terms would have ended if this article had not been ratified; and the terms of their successors shall then begin.

Section 2.   The Congress shall assemble at least once in every year, and such meeting shall begin at noon on the 3rd day of January, unless they shall by law appoint a different day.

Section 3.   If, at the time fixed for the beginning of the term of the President, the President-elect shall have died, the Vice-President-elect shall become President. If a President shall not have been chosen before the time fixed for the beginning of his term, or if the President-elect shall have failed to qualify, then the Vice-President-elect shall act as President until a President shall have qualified; and the Congress may by law provide for the case wherein neither a President-elect nor a Vice-President-elect shall have qualified, declaring who shall then act as President, or the manner in which one who is to act shall be selected, and such person shall act accordingly until a President or Vice-President shall have qualified.

Section 4.   The Congress may by law provide for the case of the death of any of the persons from whom the House of Representatives may choose a President whenever the right of choice shall have devolved upon them, and for the case of the death of any of the persons from whom the Senate may choose a Vice-President whenever the right of choice shall have devolved upon them.

Section 5.   Sections 1 and 2 shall take effect on the 15th day of October following the ratification of this article.

Section 6. This article shall be inoperative unless it shall have been ratified as an amendment to the Constitution by the Legislatures of three-fourths of the several States within seven years from the date of its submission.

Amendment XXI [Ratified 1933]

Section 1. The eighteenth article of amendment to the Constitution of the United States is hereby repealed.

Section 2. The transportation or importation into any State, Territory, or Possession of the United States for delivery or use therein of intoxicating liquors, in violation of the laws thereof, is hereby prohibited.

Section 3. This article shall be inoperative unless it shall have been ratified as an amendment to the Constitution by conventions in the several States, as provided in the Constitution, within seven years from the date of the submission thereof to the States by the Congress.

Amendment XXII [Ratified 1951]

Section 1. No person shall be elected to the office of the President more than twice, and no person who has held the office of President, or acted as President, for more than two years of a term to which some other person was elected President shall be elected to the office of President more than once. But this article shall not apply to any person holding the office of President when this Article was proposed by the Congress, and shall not prevent any person who may be holding the office of President, or acting as President, during the term within which this Article becomes operative from holding the office of President or acting as President during the remainder of such term.

Section 2. This article shall be inoperative unless it shall have been ratified as an amendment to the Constitution by the legislatures of three-fourths of the several States within seven years from the date of its submission to the States by the Congress.

Amendment XXIII [Ratified 1961]

Section 1. The District constituting the seat of Government of the United States shall appoint in such manner as the Congress may direct: A number of electors of President and Vice-President equal to the whole number of Senators and Representatives in Congress to which the District would be entitled if it were a State, but in no event more than the least populous State; they shall be in addition to those appointed by the States, but they shall be considered for the purposes of the election of President and Vice-President, to be electors appointed by a State; and they shall meet in the District and perform such duties as provided by the twelfth article of amendment.

Section 2. The Congress shall have the power to enforce this article by appropriate legislation.

Amendment XXIV [Ratified 1964]

Section 1. The right of citizens of the United States to vote in any primary or other election for President or Vice-President, for electors for President or Vice-President, or for Senator or Representative in Congress, shall not be denied or abridged by the United States or any State by reason of failure to pay any poll tax or other tax.

Section 2. The Congress shall have the power to enforce this article by appropriate legislation.

Amendment XXV   [Ratified 1967]

Section 1.   In case of the removal of the President from office or of his death or resignation, the Vice-President shall become President.

Section 2.   Whenever there is a vacancy in the office of the Vice-President, the President shall nominate a Vice-President who shall take office upon confirmation by a majority vote of both Houses of Congress.

Section 3.   Whenever the President transmits to the President pro tempore of the Senate and the Speaker of the House of Representatives his written declaration that he is unable to discharge the powers and duties of his office, and until he transmits to them a written declaration to the contrary, such powers and duties shall be discharged by the Vice-President as Acting President.

Section 4.   Whenever the Vice-President and a majority of either the principal officers of the executive departments or of such other body as Congress may by law provide, transmit to the President pro tempore of the Senate and the Speaker of the House of Representatives their written declaration that the President is unable to discharge the powers and duties of his office, the Vice-President shall immediately assume the powers and duties of the office as Acting President.

Thereafter, when the President transmits to the President pro tempore of the Senate and the Speaker of the House of Representatives his written declaration that no inability exists, he shall resume the powers and duties of his office unless the Vice-President and a majority of either the principal officers of the executive department[s] or of such other body as Congress may by law provide, transmit within four days to the President pro tempore of the Senate and the Speaker of the House of Representatives their written declaration that the President is unable to discharge the powers and duties of his office. Thereupon Congress shall decide the issue, assembling within forty-eight hours for that purpose if not in session. If the Congress, within twenty-one days after receipt of the latter written declaration, or, if Congress is not in session, within twenty-one days after Congress is required to assemble, determines by two-thirds vote of both Houses that the President is unable to discharge the powers and duties of his office, the Vice-President shall continue to discharge the same as Acting President; otherwise, the President shall resume the powers and duties of his office.

Amendment XXVI   [Ratified 1971]

Section 1.   The right of citizens of the United States, who are eighteen years of age or older, to vote shall not be denied or abridged by the United States or by any State on account of age.

Section 2.   The Congress shall have power to enforce this article by appropriate legislation.

Unratified Amendment

[Equal Rights Amendment (proposed by Congress March 22, 1972; seven-year deadline for ratification extended to June 30, 1982)]

Section 1.   *Equality of rights under the law shall not be denied or abridged by the United States or by any State on account of sex.*

Section 2.   *The Congress shall have the power to enforce, by appropriate legislation, the provisions of this article.*

Section 3.   *This amendment shall take effect two years after the date of ratification.*

Unratified Amendment

[D.C. Statehood Amendment (proposed by Congress August 22, 1978)]

Section 1. *For purposes of representation in the Congress, election of the President and Vice-President, and article V of this Constitution, the District constituting the seat of government of the United States shall be treated as though it were a State.*

Section 2. *The exercise of the rights and powers conferred under this article shall be by the people of the District constituting the seat of government, and as shall be provided by Congress.*

Section 3. *The twenty-third article of amendment to the Constitution of the United States is hereby repealed.*

Section 4. *This article shall be inoperative, unless it shall have been ratified as an amendment to the Constitution by the legislatures of three-fourths of the several states within seven years from the date of its submission.*

Amendment XXVII   [Ratified 1992]

No law, varying the compensation for the services of the Senators and Representatives, shall take effect, until an election of Representatives shall have intervened.

Admission of States to the Union

State	Year of Admission	State	Year of Admission
Delaware	1787	Michigan	1837
Pennsylvania	1787	Florida	1845
New Jersey	1787	Texas	1845
Georgia	1788	Iowa	1846
Connecticut	1788	Wisconsin	1848
Massachusetts	1788	California	1850
Maryland	1788	Minnesota	1858
South Carolina	1788	Oregon	1859
New Hampshire	1788	Kansas	1861
Virginia	1788	West Virginia	1863
New York	1788	Nevada	1864
North Carolina	1789	Nebraska	1867
Rhode Island	1790	Colorado	1876
Vermont	1791	North Dakota	1889
Kentucky	1792	South Dakota	1889
Tennessee	1796	Montana	1889
Ohio	1803	Washington	1889
Louisiana	1812	Idaho	1890
Indiana	1816	Wyoming	1890
Mississippi	1817	Utah	1896
Illinois	1818	Oklahoma	1907
Alabama	1819	New Mexico	1912
Maine	1820	Arizona	1912
Missouri	1821	Alaska	1959
Arkansas	1836	Hawaii	1959

Presidents of the United States

President	Term	President	Term
George Washington	1789–1797	Benjamin Harrison	1889–1893
John Adams	1797–1801	Grover Cleveland	1893–1897
Thomas Jefferson	1801–1809	William McKinley	1897–1901
James Madison	1809–1817	Theodore Roosevelt	1901–1909
James Monroe	1817–1825	William H. Taft	1909–1913
John Quincy Adams	1825–1829	Woodrow Wilson	1913–1921
Andrew Jackson	1829–1837	Warren G. Harding	1921–1923
Martin Van Buren	1837–1841	Calvin Coolidge	1923–1929
William H. Harrison	1841	Herbert Hoover	1929–1933
John Tyler	1841–1845	Franklin D. Roosevelt	1933–1945
James K. Polk	1845–1849	Harry S. Truman	1945–1953
Zachary Taylor	1849–1850	Dwight D. Eisenhower	1953–1961
Millard Fillmore	1850–1853	John F. Kennedy	1961–1963
Franklin Pierce	1853–1857	Lyndon B. Johnson	1963–1969
James Buchanan	1857–1861	Richard M. Nixon	1969–1974
Abraham Lincoln	1861–1865	Gerald R. Ford	1974–1977
Andrew Johnson	1865–1869	Jimmy Carter	1977–1981
Ulysses S. Grant	1869–1877	Ronald Reagan	1981–1989
Rutherford B. Hayes	1877–1881	George H. W. Bush	1989–1993
James A. Garfield	1881	Bill Clinton	1993–2001
Chester A. Arthur	1881–1885	George W. Bush	2001–2009
Grover Cleveland	1885–1889	Barack Obama	2009–2017
President Term		Donald J. Trump	2017-Present

GLOSSARY OF KEY TERMS

acquired immune deficiency syndrome (AIDS)
Immune disorder that reached epidemic proportions in
the United States in the 1980s. (p. 965)

Adams-Onís Treaty Treaty negotiated by John Quincy
Adams and signed in 1819 by which Spain ceded all
of its lands east of the Mississippi River to the United
States. (p. 291)

affirmative action Programs meant to overcome
historical patterns of discrimination against minorities
and women in education and employment. By establishing guidelines for hiring and college admissions, the
government sought to advance equal opportunities for
minorities and women. (p. 933)

Agricultural Adjustment Act New Deal legislation
that raised prices for farm produce by paying farmers
subsidies to reduce production. Large farmers reaped
most of the benefits from the act. The Supreme Court
declared it unconstitutional in 1936. (p. 751)

Alamo Texas fort captured by General Santa Anna
on March 6, 1836, from rebel defenders. Sensationalist
accounts of the siege of the Alamo increased popular
support in the United States for Texas independence.
(p. 68)

Albany Congress June 1754 meeting in Albany, New
York, of Iroquois and colonial representatives meant to
facilitate better relations between Britain and the Iroquois
Confederacy. Benjamin Franklin also put forward a plan
for colonial union that was never implemented. (p. 144)

Alien and Sedition Acts 1798 security acts passed
by the Federalist-controlled Congress. The Alien Act
allowed the president to imprison or deport noncitizens; the Sedition Act placed significant restrictions on
political speech. (p. 234)

Alt right A movement consisting of white nationalists,
including neo-Nazis, members of the Ku Klux Klan,
right-wing media, and whites who believed that they were
losing ground to racial minorities. In 2016, they supported the election to the presidency of Donald Trump, who
appealed to their nativist sentiments. (p. 1026)

America First Committee Isolationist organization
founded by Senator Gerald Nye in 1940 to keep the
United States out of World War II. (p. 780)

American Anti-Slavery Society (AASS) Abolitionist
society founded by William Lloyd Garrison in 1833
that became the most important northern abolitionist
organization of the period. (p. 340)

American Colonization Society (ACS) Organization
formed in 1817 to establish colonies of freed slaves and
freeborn blacks in Africa. The ACS was led by a group of
white elites whose primary goal was to rid the nation of
African Americans. (p. 253)

American Equal Rights Association Group of black
and white women and men formed in 1866 to promote
gender and racial equality. The organization split in 1869
over support for the Fifteenth Amendment. (p. 471)

American Expeditionary Forces (AEF) Established in
1917 after the United States entered World War I. These
Army troops served in Europe under the command of
General John J. Pershing. (p. 686)

American Federation of Labor (AFL) Trade union
federation founded in 1886. Led by its first president,
Samuel Gompers, the AFL sought to organize skilled
workers into trade-specific unions. (p. 569)

American Indian Movement (AIM) An American
Indian group, formed in 1968, that promoted "red
power" and condemned the United States for its
continued mistreatment of Native Americans. (p. 912)

American Plan Voluntary program initiated by businesses in the early twentieth century to protect worker
welfare. The American Plan was meant to undermine
the appeal of labor unions. (p. 708)

American Protective League (APL) An organization of private citizens that cooperated with the Justice
Department and the Bureau of Investigation during
World War I to spy on German residents suspected of
disloyal behavior. (p. 689)

American System Plan proposed by Henry Clay
to promote the U.S. economy by combining federally
funded internal improvements to aid farmers with federal tariffs to protect U.S. manufacturing and a national
bank to oversee economic development. (p. 289)

American system of manufacturing Production
system focused on water-powered machinery, division of labor, and the use of interchangeable parts.

The introduction of the American system in the early nineteenth century greatly increased the productivity of American manufacturing. (p. 267)

Anti-Imperialist League An organization founded in 1898 to oppose annexation of the Philippines. Some feared that annexation would bring competition from cheap labor; others considered Filipinos racially inferior and the Philippines unsuitable as an American territory. (p. 675)

Antifederalists Opponents of ratification of the Constitution. Antifederalists were generally more rural and less wealthy than the Federalists. (p. 225)

Appeal . . . to the Colored Citizens of the World
Radical abolitionist pamphlet published by David Walker in 1829. Walker's work inspired some white abolitionists to take a more radical stance on slavery. (p. 339)

Appeasement The policy of England and France in 1938 that allowed the Nazis to annex Czechoslovak territory in exchange for Hitler promising not to take further land, a pledge he soon violated. (p. 778)

Articles of Confederation Plan for national government proposed by the Continental Congress in 1777 and ratified in March 1781. The Articles of Confederation gave the national government limited powers, reflecting widespread fear of centralized authority. (p. 193)

Atlantic Charter August 1941 agreement between Franklin Roosevelt and Winston Churchill that outlined potential war aims and cemented the relationship between the United States and Britain. (p. 781)

Aztecs Spanish term for the Mexica, an indigenous people who built an empire in present-day Mexico in the centuries before the arrival of the Spaniards. The Aztecs built their empire through conquest. (p. 4)

Bacon's Rebellion 1676 uprising in Virginia led by Nathaniel Bacon. Bacon and his followers, many of whom were former servants, were upset by the Virginia governor's unwillingness to send troops to intervene in conflicts between settlers and Indians and by the lack of representation of western settlers in the House of Burgesses. (p. 51)

Bandung Conference A conference of twenty-nine Asian and African nations held in Indonesia in 1955, declared their neutrality in the Cold War struggle between the United States and the Soviet Union and condemned colonialism. (p. 836)

Battle of Antietam Fought in September 1862, this Civil War battle was the bloodiest single day in U.S. military

history, but it gave Abraham Lincoln the victory he sought before announcing the Emancipation Proclamation. (p. 288)

Battle of Bull Run (Manassas) First major battle of the Civil War at which Confederate troops routed Union forces in July 1861. (p. 284)

Battle of Bunker Hill Early Revolutionary War battle in which British troops narrowly defeated patriot militias, emboldening patriot forces. (p. 179)

Battle of Fallen Timbers Battle at which U.S. General Anthony Wayne won a major victory over a multi-tribe coalition of American Indians in the Northwest Territory in 1794. (p. 284)

Battle of Gettysburg Key July 1863 battle that helped turn the tide for the Union. The Union victory at Gettysburg, combined with a victory at Vicksburg that same month, positioned the Union to push farther into the South. (p. 296)

Battle of Horseshoe Bend In 1814, Tennessee militia led by Andrew Jackson fought alongside Cherokee warriors to defeat Creek forces allied with Britain during the War of 1812. (p. 287)

Battle of Oriskany In one of the bloodiest Revolutionary War battles, a force of German-American farmers and Oneida Indians deterred British troops and their Indian allies in central New York State, leaving British forces further east vulnerable to attack by the Continental Army. (p. 190)

Battle of Saratoga Key Revolutionary War battle fought at Saratoga, New York. The patriot victory there in October 1777 provided hope that the colonists could prevail and increased the chances that the French would formally join the patriot side. (p. 190)

Battle of Shiloh April 1862 battle in Tennessee that provided the Union entrance to the Mississippi valley. Shiloh was the bloodiest battle in American history to that point. (p. 287)

Battle of the Little Big Horn 1876 battle in the Montana Territory in which Lieutenant Colonel George Armstrong Custer and his troops were massacred by Lakota Sioux. (p. 499)

Battle of Yorktown Decisive battle in which the surrender of British forces on October 19, 1781, at Yorktown, Virginia, effectively sealed the patriot victory in the Revolutionary War. (p. 200)

Beats A small group of young poets, writers, intellectuals, musicians, and artists who attacked mainstream American politics and culture in the 1950s. (p. 862)

benign neglect British colonial policy from about 1700 to 1760 that relaxed supervision of internal colonial affairs as long as the North American colonies produced sufficient raw materials and revenue; also known as *salutary neglect*. (p. 154)

Beringia Land bridge that linked Siberia and Alaska during the Wisconsin period. Migrants from northeast Asia used this bridge to travel to North America. (p. 3)

Berlin airlift During the Berlin blockade by the Soviets from 1948 to 1949, the U.S. and British governments dispatched their air forces to transport food and supplies to West Berlin. (p. 821)

Bill of Rights The first ten amendments to the Constitution. These ten amendments helped reassure Americans who feared that the federal government established under the Constitution would infringe on the rights of individuals and states. (p. 226)

Billion Dollar Congress The Republican-controlled Congress of 1890 that spent huge sums of money to promote business and other interests. (p. 550)

black codes Racial laws passed in the immediate aftermath of the Civil War by southern legislatures. The black codes were intended to reduce free African Americans to a condition as close to slavery as possible. (p. 465)

Black Death The epidemic of bubonic plague that swept through Europe beginning in the mid-fourteenth century and wiped out roughly half of Europe's population. (p. 10)

Black Lives Matter Social protest movement begun in the wake of the shooting death of Trayvon Martin by an armed civilian in 2013. Organized by protestors around the social media hashtag Black Lives Matter, the movement expanded throughout the nation after police killings of unarmed African Americans in Ferguson, Missouri; Staten Island, New York; Cleveland, Ohio; and Baltimore, Maryland in 2014 and 2015. (p. 1021)

Black Panther Party Organization founded in 1966 by Huey P. Newton and Bobby Seale to advance the black power movement in black communities. (p. 896)

Black Tuesday October 29, 1929, crash of the U.S. stock market. The 1929 stock market crash marked the beginning of the Great Depression. (p. 727)

Bleeding Kansas The Kansas Territory during a period of violent conflicts over the fate of slavery in the mid-1850s. The violence in Kansas intensified the sectional division over slavery. (p. 406)

Boland Amendment 1982 act of Congress prohibiting direct aid to the Nicaraguan Contra forces. (p. 968)

Bonus Army World War I veterans who marched on Washington, D.C., in 1932 to demand immediate payment of their service bonuses. President Hoover refused to negotiate and instructed the U.S. army to clear the capital of protesters, leading to a violent clash. (p. 749)

boss Leader of a political machine. Men like "Boss" George Washington Plunkitt of New York's Tammany Hall wielded enormous power over city life. (p. 618)

Boston Massacre 1770 clash between colonial protesters and British soldiers in Boston that led to the death of five colonists. The bloody conflict was used to promote the patriot cause. (p. 159)

Brown v. Board of Education of Topeka, Kansas Landmark 1954 Supreme Court case that overturned the "separate but equal" principle established by *Plessy v. Ferguson* and applied to public schools. Few schools in the South were racially desegregated for more than a decade. (p. 868)

buffalo soldiers African American cavalrymen who fought in the West against the Indians in the 1870s and 1880s and served with distinction. (p. 500)

bully pulpit Term used by Theodore Roosevelt to describe the office of the presidency. Roosevelt believed that the president should use his office as a platform to promote his programs and rally public opinion. (p. 650)

Bush Doctrine President George W. Bush's proposal to engage in preemptive war against despotic governments, such as Iraq, deemed to threaten U.S. national security, even if the danger was not imminent. (p. 1011)

Californios Spanish and Mexican residents of California. Before the nineteenth century, Californios made up California's economic and political elite. Their position, however, deteriorated after the conclusion of the Mexican-American War in 1848. (p. 513)

Camp David accords 1978 peace accord between Israel and Egypt facilitated by the mediation of President Jimmy Carter. (p. 940)

carpetbaggers Derogatory term for white Northerners who moved to the South in the years following the Civil War. Many white Southerners believed that such migrants were intent on exploiting their suffering. (p. 473)

Chinese Exclusion Act 1882 act that banned Chinese immigration into the United States and prohibited those Chinese already in the country from becoming naturalized American citizens. (p. 517)

Church of England National church established by Henry VIII after he split with the Catholic Church. (p. 40)

civic housekeeping Idea promoted by Jane Addams for urban reform by using women's traditional skills as domestic managers; caregivers for children, the elderly, and the needy; and community builders. (p. 634)

Civil Rights Act of 1964 Wide-ranging civil rights act that, among other things, prohibited discrimination in public accommodations and employment and increased federal enforcement of school desegregation. (p. 892)

Civilian Conservation Corps (CCC) New Deal work program that hired young, unmarried men to work on conservation projects. The CCC employed about 2.5 million men and lasted until 1942. (p. 753)

Coercive Acts (Intolerable Acts) 1774 act of Parliament passed in response to the Boston Tea Party. The Coercive Acts were meant to force the colonists into submission, but they only resulted in increased resistance. Colonial patriots called them the Intolerable Acts. (p. 163)

Cold War The political, economic, and military conflict, short of direct war on the battlefield, between the United States and the Soviet Union that lasted from 1945 to 1991. (p. 815)

collective bargaining The process of negotiation between labor unions and employers. (p. 568)

Columbian exchange The biological exchange between the Americas and the rest of the world. Although the initial impact of the Columbian exchange was strongest in the Americas and Europe, it was soon felt all over the world. (p. 20)

Commission on the Status of Women Commission appointed by President Kennedy in 1961. The commission's 1963 report, *American Women*, highlighted employment discrimination against women and recommended legislation requiring equal pay for equal work regardless of sex. (p. 907)

committee of correspondence Type of committee first established in Massachusetts to circulate concerns and reports of protests and other events to leaders in other colonies in the aftermath of the Sugar Act. (p. 155)

Committee on Public Information (CPI) Committee established in 1917 to create propaganda and promote censorship to generate enthusiasm for World War I and stifle antiwar dissent. (p. 688)

Common Sense Pamphlet arguing in favor of independence written by Thomas Paine and published in 1776. *Common Sense* was widely read and had an important impact on the debate over declaring independence from Britain. (p. 180)

Compromise of 1850 Series of acts following California's application for admission as a free state. Meant to quell sectional tensions over slavery, the act was intended to provide something for all sides but ended up fueling more conflicts. (p. 399)

Compromise of 1877 Compromise between Republicans and southern Democrats that resulted in the election of Rutherford B. Hayes. Southern Democrats agreed to support Hayes in the disputed presidential election in exchange for his promise to end Reconstruction. (p. 481)

Comstock Lode Massive silver deposit discovered in the Sierra Nevada in the late 1850s. (p. 503)

Confederate States of America Nation established in 1861 by the eleven slave states that seceded between December 1860 and April 1861. (p. 411)

conquistadors Spanish soldiers who were central to the conquest of the civilizations of the Americas. Once conquest was complete, conquistadors often extracted wealth from the people and lands they now ruled. (p. 22)

conservative coalition Alliance of southern Democrats and conservative northern Republicans in Congress that thwarted passage of New Deal legislation after 1938. (p. 766)

Continental Congress Congress convened in Philadelphia in 1774 in response to the Coercive Acts. The delegates hoped to reestablish the freedoms colonists had enjoyed in earlier times. (p. 164)

contraband Designation assigned to escaped slaves by Union general Benjamin Butler in May 1861. By designating slaves as property forfeited by the act of rebellion, the Union was able to strike at slavery without proclaiming a general emancipation. (p. 286)

Contract with America A document that called for reduced welfare spending, lower taxes, term limits for lawmakers, and a constitutional amendment for a balanced budget. In preparation for the 1994 midterm congressional elections, Republicans, led by Representative Newt Gingrich, drew up this proposal. (p. 1006)

convict lease The system used by southern governments to furnish mainly African American prison labor to plantation owners and industrialists and to raise revenue for the states. In practice, convict labor replaced slavery as the means of providing a forced labor supply. (p. 531)

Copperheads Northern Democrats who did not support the Union war effort. Such Democrats enjoyed considerable support in eastern cities and parts of the Midwest. (p. 293)

corporation A form of business ownership in which the liability of shareholders in a company is limited to their individual investments. The formation of corporations in the late nineteenth century greatly stimulated investment in industry. (p. 534)

Corps of Discovery Expedition organized by the U.S. government to explore the Louisiana Territory. Led by Meriwether Lewis and William Clark, the expedition set out in May 1804 and journeyed to the Pacific coast and back by 1806 with the aid of interpreters like Sacagawea. (p. 257)

cotton gin Machine invented by Eli Whitney in 1793 to deseed short-staple cotton. The cotton gin dramatically reduced the time and labor involved in deseeding, facilitating the expansion of cotton production in the South and West. (p. 267)

counterculture Young cultural rebels of the 1960s who rejected conventional moral and sexual values and used drugs to reach a higher consciousness. These so-called hippies bonded together in their style of clothes and taste in rock 'n' roll music. (p. 906)

court-packing plan Proposal by President Franklin Roosevelt in 1937 to increase the size of the Supreme Court and reduce its opposition to New Deal legislation. Congress failed to pass the measure, and the scheme increased resentment toward Roosevelt. (p. 766)

Coxey's army 1894 protest movement led by Jacob Coxey. Coxey and five hundred supporters marched from Ohio to Washington, D.C., to protest the lack of government response to the depression of 1893. (p. 583)

Crittenden plan A political compromise over slavery which failed after seven southern states seceded from the Union in early 1861. It would have protected slavery from federal interference where it already existed and extended the Missouri Compromise line to California. (p. 412)

Crusades Eleventh- and twelfth-century campaigns to reclaim the Holy Land for the Roman Catholic Church. The Crusades were, on the whole, a military failure, but they did stimulate trade and inspire Europeans to seek better connections with the larger world. (p. 10)

Cuba Libre Vision of Cuban independence developed by José Martí, who hoped that Cuban independence would bring with it greater social and racial equality. (p. 672)

cult of domesticity New ideals of womanhood that emerged alongside the middle class in the 1830s and 1840s that advocated women's relegation to the domestic sphere where they could devote themselves to the care of children, the home, and hard-working husbands. (p. 323)

D Day June 6, 1944, invasion of German-occupied France by Allied forces. The D Day landings opened up a second front in Europe and marked a major turning point in World War II. (p. 796)

Dawes Act 1887 act that ended federal recognition of tribal sovereignty and divided Indian land into 160-acre parcels to be distributed to Indian heads of household. The act dramatically reduced the amount of Indian-controlled land and undermined Indian social and cultural institutions. (p. 501)

Declaration of Independence Document declaring the independence of the colonies from Great Britain. Drafted by Thomas Jefferson and then debated and revised by the Continental Congress, the Declaration was made public on July 4, 1776. (p. 182)

Declaration of Sentiments Call for women's rights in marriage, family, religion, politics, and law issued at the 1848 Seneca Falls convention. It was signed by 100 of the 300 participants. (p. 343)

Deferred Action for Childhood Arrivals (DACA) This policy, initiated under the administration of Barack Obama in 2012, allows children who entered the country illegally to receive a two-year extension of their residency in the U.S. along with eligibility for work permits. (p. 1019)

Democratic-Republicans Political party that emerged out of opposition to Federalist policies in the 1790s. The Democratic-Republicans chose Thomas Jefferson as their presidential candidate in 1796, 1800, and 1804. (p. 233)

Democrats and National Republicans Two parties that resulted from the split of the Democratic-Republicans in the early 1820s. Andrew Jackson emerged as the leader of the Democrats. (p. 304)

depression of 1893 Severe economic downturn triggered by railroad and bank failures. The severity of the depression, combined with the failure of the federal government to offer an adequate response, led to the realignment of American politics. (p. 582)

deskilling The replacement of skilled labor with unskilled labor and machines. (p. 329)

détente An easing of tense relations with the Soviet Union during the Cold War. This process moved unevenly through the 1970s and early 1980s but accelerated when Soviet leader Mikhail Gorbachev came to power in the mid-1980s. (p. 931)

dollar diplomacy Term used by President Howard Taft to describe the economic focus of his foreign policy. Taft hoped to use economic policies and the control of foreign assets by American companies to influence Latin American nations. (p. 680)

Double V The slogan African Americans used during World War II to state their twin aims to fight for victory over Fascism abroad and victory over racism at home. (p. 789)

Dred Scott decision 1857 Supreme Court case centered on the status of Dred Scott and his family. In its ruling, the Court denied the claim that black men had any rights and blocked Congress from excluding slavery from any territory. (p. 408)

Dunmore's Proclamation 1775 proclamation issued by the British commander Lord Dunmore that offered freedom to all enslaved African Americans who joined the British army. The proclamation heightened concerns among some patriots about the consequences of independence. (p. 179)

Economic Recovery Tax Act Act signed into law by President Ronald Reagan in 1981, that slashed income and estate taxes especially on those in the highest income brackets. (p. 963)

Eisenhower Doctrine A doctrine guiding intervention in the Middle East. In 1957 Congress granted President Dwight Eisenhower the power to send military forces into the Middle East to combat Communist aggression. Eisenhower sent U.S. marines into Lebanon in 1958 under this doctrine. (p. 837)

Emancipation Proclamation January 1, 1863, proclamation that declared all slaves in areas still in rebellion "forever free." While stopping short of abolishing slavery, the Emancipation Proclamation was, nonetheless, seen by blacks and abolitionists as a great victory. (p. 289)

Embargo Act 1807 act that prohibited American ships from leaving their home ports until Britain and France repealed restrictions on U.S. trade. The act had a devastating impact on American commerce. (p. 261)

encomienda System first established by Christopher Columbus by which Spanish leaders in the Americas received land and the labor of all Indians residing on it. From the Indian point of view, the encomienda system amounted to little more than enslavement. (p. 15)

Enlightenment European cultural movement that emphasized rational and scientific thinking over traditional religion and superstition. Enlightenment thought appealed to many colonial elites. (p. 125)

Enrollment Act March 1863 Union draft law that provided for draftees to be selected by an impartial lottery. A loophole in the law that allowed wealthy Americans to escape service by paying $300 or hiring a substitute created widespread resentment. (p. 292)

Enterprise of the Indies Christopher Columbus's proposal to sail west across the Atlantic to Japan and China. In 1492 Columbus gained support for the venture from Ferdinand and Isabella of Spain. (p. 15)

Environmental Protection Agency (EPA) Federal agency established by Richard Nixon in 1971 to regulate activities that resulted in pollution or other environmental degradation. (p. 943)

Equal Rights Amendment (ERA) A proposed amendment that prevented the abridgment of "equality of rights under law . . . by the United States or any State on the basis of sex." Not enough states had ratified the amendment by 1982, when the ratification period expired, so it was not adopted. (p. 942)

Erie Canal Canal built in the early 1820s that made water transport from the Great Lakes to New York City possible. The success of the Erie Canal inspired many similar projects and ensured New York City's place as the premier international port in the United States. (p. 290)

Espionage Act 1917 act that prohibited antiwar activities, including opposing the military draft. It punished speech critical of the war as well as deliberate actions of sabotage and spying. (p. 685)

ethnic cleansing Ridding an area of a particular ethnic minority to achieve ethnic homogeneity. In the civil war between Serbs and Croatians in Bosnia from 1992 to 1995, the Serbian military attempted to eliminate the Croatian population through murder, rape, and expulsion. (p. 1007)

eugenics The pseudoscience of producing genetic improvement in the human population through selective breeding. Proponents of eugenics often saw ethnic and racial minorities as genetically "undesirable" and inferior. (p. 605)

Exodusters Blacks who migrated from the South to Kansas in 1879 seeking land and a better way of life. (p. 477)

Fair Employment Practice Committee (FEPC) Committee established in 1941 to help African Americans gain a greater share of wartime industrial jobs. (p. 789)

Fair Labor Standards Act 1938 law that provided a minimum wage of 40 cents an hour and a forty-hour workweek for employees in businesses engaged in interstate commerce. (p. 762)

Farmers' Alliances Regional organizations formed in the late nineteenth century to advance the interests of farmers. The most prominent of these organizations were the Northwestern Farmers' Alliance, the Southern Farmers' Alliance, and the Colored Farmers' Alliance. (p. 579)

Federal Deposit Insurance Corporation (FDIC) Federal agency created in 1933 through New Deal legislation, that insured bank deposits up to $5000, a figure that would substantially rise over the years. (p. 751)

Federal Employee Loyalty Program Program established by President Truman in 1947 to investigate federal employees suspected of disloyalty and Communist ties. (p. 830)

Federalists Supporters of ratification of the Constitution, many of whom came from urban and commercial backgrounds. (p. 225)

Field Order Number 15 Order issued by General William Sherman in January 1865 setting aside more than 400,000 acres of Confederate land to be divided into plots for former slaves. Sherman's order came in response to pressure from African American leaders. (p. 306)

Fifteenth Amendment Amendment to the Constitution prohibiting the abridgment of a citizen's right to vote on the basis of "race, color, or previous condition of servitude." From the 1870s on, southern states devised numerous strategies for circumventing the Fifteenth Amendment. (p. 471)

filibusters Unauthorized military expeditions launched by U.S. adventurers to gain control of Cuba, Nicaragua, and other Spanish territories in the 1850s. (p. 401)

Force Acts Three acts passed by the U.S. Congress in 1870 and 1871 in response to vigilante attacks on southern blacks. The acts were designed to protect black political rights and end violence by the Ku Klux Klan and similar organizations. (p. 478)

Fort Sumter Union fort that guarded the harbor in Charleston, South Carolina. The Confederacy's decision to fire on the fort and block resupply in April 1861 marked the beginning of the Civil War. (p. 283)

Fourteen Points The core principles President Woodrow Wilson saw as the basis for lasting peace, including freedom of the seas, open diplomacy, and self-determination for colonial peoples. (p. 690)

Fourteenth Amendment Amendment to the Constitution defining citizenship and protecting individual civil and political rights from abridgment by the states. Adopted during Reconstruction, the Fourteenth Amendment overturned the *Dred Scott* decision. (p. 466)

Free Speech Movement (FSM) Movement protesting policies instituted by the University of California at Berkeley that restricted free speech. In 1964 students at Berkeley conducted sit-ins and held rallies against these policies. (p. 904)

Freedmen's Bureau Federal agency created in 1865 to provide ex-slaves with economic and legal resources. The Freedmen's Bureau played an active role in shaping black life in the postwar South. (p. 458)

Freedom Rides Integrated bus rides through the South organized by CORE in 1961 to test compliance with Supreme Court rulings on segregation. (p. 891)

Freedom Summer 1964 civil rights project in Mississippi launched by SNCC, CORE, the SCLC, and the NAACP. Some eight hundred volunteers, mainly white college students, worked on voter registration drives and in freedom schools to improve education for rural black youngsters. (p. 893)

Free-Soil Party Party founded by political abolitionists in 1848 to expand the appeal of the Liberty Party by focusing less on the moral wrongs of slavery and more on the benefits of providing economic opportunities for northern whites in western territories. (p. 345)

Fugitive Slave Act of 1850 Act strengthening earlier fugitive slave laws, passed as part of the Compromise of 1850. The Fugitive Slave Act provoked widespread anger in the North and intensified sectional tensions. (p. 399)

gag rule Rule passed by the House of Representatives in 1836 to table, or postpone action on, all antislavery petitions without hearing them read to stifle debate over slavery. It was renewed annually until it was rescinded in 1844. (p. 369)

ghettos Neighborhoods dominated by a single ethnic, racial, or class group. (p. 599)

Ghost Dance Religious ritual performed by the Paiute Indians in the late nineteenth century. Following a vision he received in 1888, the prophet Wovoka believed that performing the Ghost Dance would cause whites to disappear and allow Indians to regain control of their lands. (p. 502)

Gilded Age Term coined by Mark Twain and Charles Dudley Warner to describe the late nineteenth century. The term referred to the opulent and often ostentatious lifestyles of the era's superrich. (p. 540)

glasnost Policy of political "openness" initiated by Soviet leader Mikhail Gorbachev in the 1980s. Under *glasnost*, the Soviet Union extended democratic elections, freedom of speech, and freedom of the press. (p. 976)

globalization The extension of economic, political, and cultural relationships among nations, through commerce, migration, and communication. Globalization expanded in the late twentieth century because of free trade agreements and the relaxation of immigration restrictions. (p. 980)

Glorious Revolution 1688 rebellion that forced James II from the English throne and replaced him with William and Mary. The Glorious Revolution led to greater political and commercial autonomy for the British colonies. (p. 74)

gold rush The rapid influx of migrants into California after the discovery of gold in 1848. Migrants came from all over the world seeking riches. (p. 394)

"The Gospel of Wealth" 1889 essay by Andrew Carnegie in which he argued that the rich should act as stewards of the wealth they earned, using their surplus income for the benefit of the community. (p. 538)

Grangers Members of an organization founded in 1867 to meet the social and cultural needs of farmers. Grangers took an active role in the promotion of the economic and political interests of farmers. (p. 577)

Great Awakening Series of religious revivals in colonial America that began in 1720 and lasted to about 1750. (p. 127)

great migration Population shift of more than 400,000 African Americans who left the South beginning in 1917–1918 and headed north and west hoping to escape poverty and racial discrimination. During the 1920s another 800,000 blacks left the South. (p. 706)

Great Plains Semiarid territory in central North America. (p. 491)

Great Recession The severe economic decline in the United States and throughout the world that began in 2008, leading to bank failures, high unemployment, home foreclosures, and large federal deficits. (p. 1016)

Great Society President Lyndon Johnson's vision of social, economic, and cultural progress in the United States. (p. 898)

Gulf of Tonkin Resolution 1964 congressional resolution giving President Lyndon Johnson wide discretion in the use of U.S. forces in Vietnam. The resolution followed reported attacks by North Vietnamese gunboats on two American destroyers. (p. 901)

Haitian Revolution Revolt against French rule by free and enslaved blacks in the 1790s on the island of Saint Domingue. The revolution led in 1803 to the establishment of Haiti, the first independent black-led nation in the Americas. (p. 256)

hard war The strategy promoted by General Ulysses S. Grant in which Union forces destroyed civilian crops, livestock, fields, and property to undermine Confederate morale and supply chains. (p. 306)

Harlem Renaissance The work of African American writers, artists, and musicians that flourished following World War I through the 1920s. (p. 717)

Hartford Convention 1814 convention of Federalists opposed to the War of 1812. Delegates to the convention considered a number of constitutional amendments, as well as the possibility of secession. (p. 286)

Haymarket Square Site of 1886 rally and violence. In the aftermath of the events in Haymarket Square, the union movement in the United States went into temporary decline. (p. 568)

Hetch Hetchy valley Site of a controversial dam built to supply San Francisco with water and power in the aftermath of the 1906 earthquake. The dam was built over the objections of preservationists such as John Muir. (p. 647)

Holocaust The Nazi regime's genocidal effort to eradicate Europe's Jewish population during World War II, which resulted in the deaths of six million Jews. (p. 802)

Homestead Act 1862 act that established procedures for distributing 160-acre lots to western settlers, on condition that they develop and farm their land, as an incentive for western migration. (p. 507)

Homestead strike 1892 strike by steelworkers at Andrew Carnegie's Homestead steel factory. The strike collapsed after a failed assassination attempt on Carnegie's plant manager, Henry Clay Frick. (p. 572)

Hopewell people Indian people who established a thriving culture near the Mississippi River in the early centuries C.E. (p. 7)

horizontal integration The ownership of as many firms as possible in a given industry by a single owner. John D. Rockefeller pursued a strategy of horizontal integration when he bought up rival oil refineries. (p. 533)

horticulture A form of agriculture in which people work small plots of land with simple tools. (p. 4)

House Un-American Activities Committee (HUAC) U.S. House of Representatives committee established in 1938 to investigate domestic communism. After World War II, HUAC conducted highly publicized investigations of Communist influence in government and the entertainment industry. (p. 830)

House of Burgesses Local governing body in Virginia established by the English crown in 1619. (p. 48)

Hull House This settlement house, based on Toynbee Hall in England, was established by Jane Addams and Ellen Starr in Chicago in 1889. It served as a center of social reform and provided educational and social opportunities for working-class poor and immigrant women and their children. (p. 634)

Hurricane Katrina Storm that hit the Gulf coast states of Louisiana, Mississippi, and Alabama in 2005. The hurricane caused massive flooding in New Orleans after levees broke. Federal, state, and local government responses to the storm were inadequate and highlighted racial and class inequities. (p. 1013)

Immigration Reform and Control Act Law signed by President Ronald Reagan in 1986, which extended amnesty to undocumented immigrants in the United States for a specified period and allowed them to obtain legal status. At the same time the law penalized employers who hired new illegal workers. (p. 967)

imperial presidency Term used to describe the growth of presidential powers during the Cold War, particularly with respect to war-making powers and the conduct of national security. (p. 820)

import duty Tax imposed on goods imported into the colonies, paid by the importer rather than directly by the consumer; also known as a *tariff*. (p. 155)

impressment The forced enlistment of civilians into the army or navy. The impressment of residents of colonial seaports into the British navy was a major source of complaint in the eighteenth century. (p. 131)

Incas Andean people who built an empire in the centuries before the arrival of the Spaniards. At the height of their power in the fifteenth century, the Incas controlled some sixteen million people. (p. 6)

indentured servants Servants contracted to work for a set period of time without pay. Many early migrants to the English colonies indentured themselves in exchange for the price of passage to North America. (p. 48)

Indian Citizenship Act 1924 legislation that extended the right to vote and citizenship to all Indians. (p. 721)

Indian Removal Act 1830 act by which Indian peoples in the East were forced to exchange their lands for territory west of the Mississippi River. Andrew Jackson was an ardent supporter of Indian removal. (p. 308)

Indian Reorganization Act (IRA) 1934 act that ended the Dawes Act, authorized self-government for those living on reservations, extended tribal landholdings, and pledged to uphold native customs and language. (p. 763)

Industrial Workers of the World (IWW) Organization that grew out of the activities of the Western Federation of Miners in the 1890s and formed by Eugene V. Debs. Known as Wobblies, the IWW attempted to unite all skilled and unskilled workers in an effort to overthrow capitalism. (p. 574)

internment The relocation of persons seen as a threat to national security to isolated camps during World War II. Nearly all people of Japanese descent living on the West Coast were forced to sell or abandon their possessions and relocate to internment camps during the war. (p. 792)

Interstate Commerce Commission (ICC) Regulatory commission established by Congress in 1887. The commission investigated interstate shipping, required railroads to make their rates public, and could bring lawsuits to force shippers to reduce "unreasonable" fares. (p. 577)

Intolerable Acts *See* Coercive Acts.

Iran-Contra affair Ronal Reagan administration scandal involving the funneling of funds from an illegal arms-for-hostages deal with Iran to the Nicaraguan Contras in the mid-1980s. (p. 973)

Islamic State of Iraq and Syria (ISIS) Jihadist terrorist group originally founded in 1999, which gained strength from the sectarian violence that grew out of the 2003 U.S. invasion of Iraq. The group captured territory in Iraq and Syria and claimed responsibility for terrorist attacks in Paris, San Bernardino, California, and Lebanon. (p. 1023)

Island Hopping This strategy, employed by the U.S. in World War II in the Pacific, directed American and Allied forces to avoid heavily fortified Japanese islands and concentrate on less heavily defended islands in preparation for a combined air, land, and sea invasion of Japan. (p. 798)

Jamestown The first successful English colony in North America. Settled in 1607, Jamestown was founded by soldiers and adventurers under the leadership of Captain John Smith. (p. 46)

Jay Treaty 1796 treaty that required British forces to withdraw from U.S. soil, required American repayment of debts to British firms, and limited U.S. trade with the British West Indies. (p. 230)

Jim Crow Late-nineteenth-century statutes that established legally defined racial segregation in the South. Jim Crow legislation helped ensure the social and economic inferiority of southern blacks. (p. 546)

jingoists Superpatriotic supporters of the expansion and use of military power. Jingoists such as Theodore Roosevelt longed for a war in which they could demonstrate America's strength and prove their own masculinity. (p. 671)

Judiciary Act Act passed in 1801 by the Federalist-controlled Congress to expand the federal court system by creating sixteen circuit (regional) courts, with new judges appointed for each, just before Democratic-Republicans took control of the presidency and Congress. (p. 258)

Kansas-Nebraska Act 1854 act creating the territories of Kansas and Nebraska out of what was then Indian land. The act stipulated that the issue of slavery would be settled by a popular referendum in each territory. (p. 405)

King William's War 1689–1697 war that began as a conflict over competing French and English interests on the European continent but soon spread to the American frontier. Both sides pulled Indian allies into the war. (p. 78)

Knights of the Ku Klux Klan (KKK) Organization formed in 1865 by General Nathan Bedford Forrest to enforce prewar racial norms. Members of the KKK used threats and violence to intimidate blacks and white Republicans. (p. 478)

La Raza Unida (The United Race) A Chicano political party, formed in 1969, that advocated job opportunities for Chicanos, bilingual education, and Chicano cultural studies programs in universities. (p. 910)

laissez-faire French for "let things alone." Advocates of laissez-faire believed that the marketplace should be left to regulate itself, allowing individuals to pursue their own self-interest without any government restraint or interference. (p. 537)

League of Nations The international organization proposed by Woodrow Wilson after the end of World War I to ensure world peace and security in the future through mutual agreement. The United States failed to join the league because Wilson and his opponents in Congress could not work out a compromise. (p. 690)

Lend-Lease Act March 1941 law permitting the United States to lend or lease military equipment and other commodities to Great Britain and its allies. Its passage marked the end of American neutrality before the U.S. entered World War II. (p. 780)

Levittown Suburban subdivision built in Long Island, New York, in the 1950s in response to the postwar housing shortage. Subsequent Levittowns were built in Pennsylvania and New Jersey. (p. 856)

Liberator Radical abolitionist newspaper launched by William Lloyd Garrison in 1831. Through the *Liberator*,

Garrison called for immediate, uncompensated emancipation of slaves. (p. 340)

Liberty Party Antislavery political party formed in 1840. The Liberty Party, along with the Free-Soil Party, helped place slavery at the center of national political debates. (p. 344)

Little Rock Nine Nine African American students who, in 1957, became the first black students to attend Central High School in Little Rock, Arkansas. Federal troops were required to overcome the resistance of white officials and to protect the students. (p. 869)

Long Drive Cattle drive from the grazing lands of Texas to rail depots in Kansas. Once in Kansas, the cattle were shipped eastward to slaughterhouses in Chicago. (p. 506)

Lost Generation A term used by the writer Gertrude Stein to describe the writers and artists disillusioned with the consumer culture of the 1920s. (p. 715)

Louisiana Purchase U.S. government's 1803 purchase from France of the vast territory stretching from the Mississippi River to the Rocky Mountains and from New Orleans to present-day Montana, doubling the size of the nation. (p. 256)

loyalist A colonial supporter of the British during the Revolutionary War. Loyalists came from all economic backgrounds and had a variety of motives for siding with the British. (p. 183)

Manhattan Project Code name for the secret program to develop an atomic bomb. The project was launched in 1942 and directed by the United States with the assistance of Great Britain and Canada. (p. 800)

manifest destiny Term coined by John L. O'Sullivan in 1845 to describe what he saw as the nation's God-given right to expand its borders. Throughout the nineteenth century, the concept of manifest destiny was used to justify U.S. expansion. (p. 375)

Marbury v. Madison 1803 Supreme Court decision that established the authority of the Supreme Court to rule on the constitutionality of federal laws. (p. 258)

March on Washington for Jobs and Freedom August 28, 1963, rally by civil rights organizations in Washington, D.C., that brought increased national attention to the movement. (p. 892)

market revolution Innovations in agriculture, industry, communication, and transportation in the early 1800s fueled increased efficiency and productivity and linked northern industry with western farms and southern plantations. (p. 319)

Marshall Plan Post–World War II European economic aid package developed by Secretary of State George Marshall. The plan helped rebuild Western Europe and served American political and economic interests in the process. (p. 820)

Maya People who established large cities in the Yucatán peninsula. Mayan civilization was strongest between 300 and 800 C.E. (p. 6)

Mayflower Compact Written constitution created by the Pilgrims upon their arrival in Plymouth. The Mayflower Compact was the first written constitution adopted in North America. (p. 56)

McCarthyism Term used to describe the harassment and persecution of suspected political radicals. Senator Joseph McCarthy was one of many prominent government figures who helped incite anti-Communist hysteria in the early 1950s. (p. 833)

McCulloch v. Maryland 1819 Supreme Court decision that reinforced the federal government's ability to employ an expansive understanding of the implied powers clause of the Constitution. (p. 260)

Me Too Movement The social movement of black and white women-spurred on by the election of Donald Trump as president-linked tens of millions of women through social media networks in opposition to sexual harassment and abuse in workplaces and educational institutions. In 2017, it conducted massive marches throughout the U. S. and the world. (p. 1030)

melting pot Popular metaphor for immigrant assimilation into American society. According to this ideal, all immigrants underwent a process of Americanization that produced a homogeneous society. (p. 608)

mercantilism Economic system centered on the maintenance of a favorable balance of trade for the home country, with more gold and silver flowing into that country than flowed out. Seventeenth- and eighteenth-century British colonial policy was heavily shaped by mercantilism. (p. 83)

Metacom's War 1675–1676 conflict between New England settlers and the region's Indians. The settlers were the eventual victors, but fighting was fierce and casualties on both sides were high. (p. 62)

Mexican revolution 1911 revolution in Mexico, which led to nearly a decade of bloodshed and civil war. (p. 681)

Middle Passage The brutal voyage of slave ships laden with human cargo from Africa to the Americas. The voyage was the middle segment in a triangular journey that began in Europe, went first to Africa, then to the Americas, and finally back to Europe. (p. 87)

military-industrial complex The government-business alliance related to the military and national defense that developed out of World War II and greatly influenced future development of the U.S. economy. (p. 782)

Mississippi Freedom Democratic Party (MFDP) Political party formed in 1964 to challenge the all-white state Democratic Party for seats at the 1964 Democratic presidential convention and run candidates for public office. Although unsuccessful in 1964, MFDP efforts led to subsequent reform of the Democratic Party and the seating of an interracial convention delegation from Mississippi in 1968. (p. 894)

Missouri Compromise 1820 act that allowed Missouri to enter the Union as a slave state and Maine to enter as a free state and established the southern border of Missouri as the boundary between slave and free states throughout the Louisiana Territory. (p. 296)

Modern Republicanism The political approach of President Dwight Eisenhower that tried to fit traditional Republican Party ideals of individualism and fiscal restraint within the broad framework of the New Deal. (p. 873)

Monroe Doctrine Assertion by President James Monroe in 1823 that the Western Hemisphere was part of the U.S. sphere of influence. Although the United States lacked the power to back up this claim, it signaled an intention to challenge Europeans for authority in the Atlantic world. (p. 292)

Montgomery Improvement Association Organization founded in Montgomery, Alabama, in 1955 to coordinate the boycott of city buses by African Americans. (p. 868)

Mormons Religious sect that migrated to Utah to escape religious persecution; also known as the Church of Jesus Christ of Latter-Day Saints. (p. 512)

muckrakers Investigative journalists who specialized in exposing corruption, scandal, and vice. Muckrakers helped build public support for progressive causes. (p. 633)

mujahideen Religiously inspired Afghan rebels who resisted the Soviet invasion of Afghanistan in 1979. (p. 939)

multiplier effect The diverse changes spurred by a single invention, including other inventions it spawns and the broader economic, social, and political transformations it fuels. (p. 265)

mutual aid societies Voluntary associations that provide a variety of economic and social benefits to their members. (p. 599)

mutually assured destruction (MAD) Defense strategy built around the threat of a massive nuclear retaliatory strike. Adoption of the doctrine of mutually assured destruction contributed to the escalation of the nuclear arms race during the Cold War. (p. 835)

Nat Turner's rebellion 1831 slave uprising in Virginia led by Nat Turner. Turner's rebellion instilled panic among white Southerners, leading to tighter control of African Americans and reconsideration of the institution of slavery. (p. 364)

National Association for the Advancement of Colored People (NAACP) Organization founded by W. E. B. Du Bois, Ida B. Wells, Jane Addams, and others in 1909 to fight for racial equality. The NAACP strategy focused on fighting discrimination through the courts. (p. 639)

National Energy Act Legislation signed into law by President Jimmy Carter in 1978, which set gas emissions standards for automobiles and provided incentives for installing alternative energy systems, such as wind and solar power. (p. 938)

National Interstate and Defense Highway Act 1956 act that provided funds for construction of 42,500 miles of roads throughout the United States. (p. 873)

National Labor Relations Act 1935 act (also known as the Wagner Act) that created the National Labor Relations Board (NLRB). The NLRB protected workers' right to organize labor unions without owner interference. (p. 760)

National Organization for Women (NOW) Feminist organization formed in 1966 by Betty Friedan and like-minded activists. (p. 908)

National Origins Act 1924 act establishing immigration quotas by national origin. The act was intended to severely limit immigration from southern and eastern Europe as well as prohibit all immigration from East Asia. (p. 720)

National Recovery Administration (NRA) New Deal agency established in 1933 to create codes to regulate production, prices, wages, hours, and collective bargaining. The NRA failed to produce the intended results and was eventually ruled unconstitutional. (p. 752)

National Republicans *See* Democrats and National Republicans.

National Road Road constructed using federal funds that ran from western Maryland through southwestern Pennsylvania to Wheeling, West Virginia; also called the Cumberland Road. Completed in 1818, the road was part of a larger push to improve the nation's infrastructure. (p. 265)

National Security Council (NSC) Council created by the 1947 National Security Act to advise the president on military and foreign affairs. The NSC consists of the national security adviser and the secretaries of state, defense, the army, the navy, and the air force. (p. 820)

National War Labor Board (NWLB) Government agency created in 1918 to settle labor disputes. The NWLB consisted of representatives from unions, corporations, and the public. (p. 687)

National War Labor Board Board established in 1942 to oversee labor-management relations during World War II. The board regulated wages, hours, and working conditions and authorized the government to take over plants that refused to abide by its decisions. (p. 786)

nativism The belief that foreigners pose a serious danger to a nation's society and culture. Nativist sentiment rose in the United States as the size and diversity of the immigrant population grew. (p. 605)

nativists Anti-immigrant Americans who launched public campaigns against foreigners in the 1840s. Nativism emerged as a response to increased immigration to the United States in the 1830s and 1840s, particularly the large influx of Catholic immigrants. (p. 335)

Navigation Acts Acts passed by Parliament in the 1650s and 1660s that prohibited smuggling, established guidelines for legal commerce, and set duties on trade items. In the 1760s, British authorities sought to fully enforce these laws, leading to resistance by colonists. (pp. 84, 154)

neoconservatives Disillusioned liberals who condemned the Great Society programs they had originally supported. Neoconservatives were particularly concerned about affirmative action programs, the domination of campus discourse by New Left radicals, and left-wing

criticism of the use of American military and economic might to advance U.S. interests overseas. (p. 949)

Neutrality Acts Legislation passed between 1935 and 1937 to make it more difficult for the United States to become entangled in overseas conflicts. The Neutrality Acts reflected the strength of isolationist sentiment in 1930s America. (p. 778)

New Deal The policies and programs that Franklin Roosevelt initiated to combat the Great Depression. The New Deal represented a dramatic expansion of the role of government in American society. (p. 751)

New Freedom Term used by Woodrow Wilson to describe his limited-government, progressive agenda. Wilson's New Freedom was offered as an alternative to Theodore Roosevelt's New Nationalism. (p. 654)

New Frontier President John F. Kennedy's domestic agenda. Kennedy promised to battle "tyranny, poverty, disease, and war," but, lacking strong majorities in Congress, he achieved relatively modest results. (p. 887)

New Jersey Plan A proposal to the 1787 Constitutional Convention that highlighted the needs of small states by creating one legislative house in the federal government and granting each state equal representation in it. (p. 223)

New Light clergy Colonial clergy who called for religious revivals and emphasized the emotional aspects of spiritual commitment. The New Lights were leaders in the Great Awakening. (p. 124)

New Look The foreign policy strategy implemented by President Dwight Eisenhower that emphasized the development and deployment of nuclear weapons in an effort to cut military spending. (p. 834)

New Nationalism Agenda articulated by Theodore Roosevelt in his 1912 presidential campaign. Roosevelt called for increased regulation of large corporations, a more active role for the president, and the extension of social justice using the power of the federal government. (p. 654)

New Negro 1920s term for the second generation of African Americans born after emancipation and who stood up for their rights. (p. 716)

New Right The conservative coalition of old and new conservatives, as well as disaffected Democrats. The New Right came to power with the election of Ronald Reagan in 1980. (p. 948)

New South Term popularized by newspaper editor Henry Grady in the 1880s, a proponent of the modernization of the southern economy. Grady believed that industrial development would lead to the emergence of a "New South." (p. 531)

new woman 1920s term for the modern, sexually liberated woman. The new woman, popularized in movies and magazines, flouted traditional morality. (p. 715)

Noble Order of the Knights of Labor Labor organization founded in 1869 by Uriah Stephens. The Knights sought to include all workers in one giant union. (p. 568)

Non-Intercourse Act Act passed by Congress in 1809 allowing Americans to trade with every nation except France and Britain. The act failed to stop the seizure of American ships or improve the economy. (p. 283)

North American Free Trade Agreement (NAFTA) Free trade agreement approved in 1993 by the United States, Canada, and Mexico. (p. 1005)

North Atlantic Treaty Organization (NATO) Cold War military alliance intended to enhance the collective security of the United States and Western Europe. (p. 824)

Northwest Ordinance Act of the confederation congress that provided for the survey, sale, and eventual division into states of the Northwest Territory. The 1787 act clarified the process by which territories could become states. (p. 213)

NSC-68 April 1950 National Security Council document that advocated the intensification of the policy of containment both at home and abroad. (p. 825)

nuclear freeze movement 1980s protests calling for a mutual freeze on the testing, production, and deployment of nuclear weapons and of missiles and aircraft designed primarily to deliver nuclear weapons. (p. 976)

nullification The doctrine that individual states have the right to declare federal laws unconstitutional and, therefore, void within their borders. South Carolina attempted to invoke the doctrine of nullification in response to the tariff of 1832. (p. 306)

Obergefell v. Hodges The 2015 U.S. Supreme Court decision legalizing same-sex marriage throughout the nation. (p. 1019)

Occupy Wall Street A loose coalition of progressive and radical forces that emerged in 2011 in New York City and around the country to protest corporate greed and federal policies that benefit the very wealthy. (p. 1019)

Old Light clergy Colonial clergy from established churches who supported the religious status quo in the early eighteenth century. (p. 124)

Open Door 1899 policy in which Secretary of State John Hay informed the nations occupying China that the United States had the right of equal trade in China. (p. 677)

Operation Desert Storm Code name of the 1991 allied air and ground military offensive that pushed Iraqi forces out of Kuwait. (p. 986)

Oregon Trail The route west from the Missouri River to the Oregon Territory. By 1860, some 350,000 Americans had made the three- to six-month journey along the trail. (p. 392)

Organization of Petroleum Exporting Countries (OPEC) Organization formed by oil-producing countries to control the price and supply of oil on the global market. (p. 936)

Ostend Manifesto This 1854 letter from U.S. ambassadors and the Secretary of State to President Franklin Pierce urged him to conquer Cuba. When it was leaked to the press, Northerners voiced outrage at what they saw as a plot to expand slave territories. (p. 402)

Palmer raids Government roundup of some 6,000 suspected alien radicals in 1919–1920, ordered by Attorney General A. Mitchell Palmer and his assistant J. Edgar Hoover. The raids resulted in the deportation of 556 immigrants. (p. 704)

panic of 1819 The nation's first severe recession. The panic of 1819 lasted four years and resulted from irresponsible banking practices and the declining demand abroad for American goods, including cotton. (p. 293)

panic of 1837 Severe economic recession that began shortly after Martin Van Buren's presidential inauguration. The panic of 1837 started in the South and was rooted in the changing fortunes of American cotton in Great Britain. (p. 373)

Patient Protection and Affordable Care Act (Obamacare) Passed in 2010, this law expanded health insurance to millions of Americans previously uncovered through a variety of measures including extension of Medicaid, setting up of health-insurance exchanges, allowing children to remain under their parents' coverage until the age of twenty-six, and preventing insurance companies from excluding coverage based on pre-existing conditions. (p. 1018)

patriarchal family Model of the family in which fathers have absolute authority over wives, children, and servants. Most colonial Americans accepted the patriarchal model of the family, at least as an ideal. (p. 111)

Patriot Act 2001 law passed in response to the September 11 terror attacks. It eased restrictions on domestic and foreign intelligence gathering and expanded governmental power to deport immigrants. (p. 1011)

Peace of Paris 1763 peace treaty that brought the Seven Years' War to a close. Under the terms of the treaty, Britain gained control of North America east of the Mississippi River and of present-day Canada. (p. 147)

Pendleton Civil Service Reform Act 1883 act that required federal jobs to be awarded on the basis of merit through competitive exams rather than through political connections. (p. 320)

Pentagon Papers Classified report on U.S. involvement in Vietnam leaked to the press in 1971. The report confirmed that the Kennedy and Johnson administrations had misled the public about the origins and nature of the Vietnam War. (p. 931)

Pequot War 1636–1637 conflict between New England settlers, their Narragansett allies, and the Pequots. The English saw the Pequots as both a threat and an obstacle to further English expansion. (p. 59)

perestroika Policy of economic "restructuring" initiated by Soviet leader Mikhail Gorbachev. Gorbachev hoped that by reducing state control he could revive the Soviet economy. (p. 976)

Personal Responsibility and Work Opportunity Reconciliation Act 1996 act reforming the welfare system in the United States. The law required adults on the welfare rolls to find work within two years or lose their welfare benefits. (p. 1006)

Petticoat Affair 1829 political conflict over Andrew Jackson's appointment of John Eaton as secretary of war. Eaton was married to a woman of allegedly questionable character, and the wives of many prominent Washington politicians organized a campaign to snub her. (p. 306)

Pietists German Protestants who decried the power of established churches and urged individuals to follow their hearts rather than their heads in spiritual matters. Pietism had a profound influence on the leaders of the Great Awakening. (p. 126)

Pilgrims Group of English religious dissenters who established a settlement at Plymouth, Massachusetts, in 1620. Unlike more mainstream Protestants, the Pilgrims were separatists who aimed to sever all connections with the Church of England. (p. 55)

Pinckney Treaty 1796 treaty that defined the boundary between U.S. and Spanish territory in the South and opened the Mississippi River and New Orleans to U.S. shipping. (p. 233)

Planters Southern whites who owned the largest plantations and forged a distinct culture and economy around the institution of slavery. (p. 355)

Platt Amendment 1901 act of Congress limiting Cuban sovereignty. American officials pressured Cuban leaders to incorporate the amendment into the Cuban constitution. (p. 674)

Plessy v. Ferguson 1896 Supreme Court ruling that upheld the legality of Jim Crow legislation. The Court ruled that as long as states provided "equal but separate" facilities for whites and blacks, Jim Crow laws did not violate the equal protection clause of the Fourteenth Amendment. (p. 547)

political machine Urban political organizations that dominated many late-nineteenth-century cities. Machines provided needed services to the urban poor, but they also fostered corruption, crime, and inefficiency. (p. 618)

Populists The People's Party of America, formed in 1892. The Populists sought to appeal to both farmers and industrial workers. (p. 582)

Port Huron Statement Students for a Democratic Society manifesto written in 1962 that condemned liberal politics, Cold War foreign policy, racism, and research-oriented universities. It called for the adoption of "participatory democracy." (p. 904)

Powhatan Confederacy Large and powerful Indian confederation in Virginia. The Jamestown settlers had a complicated and contentious relationship with the leaders of the Powhatan Confederacy. (p. 47)

pragmatism Philosophy that holds that truth can be discovered only through experience and that the value of ideas should be measured by their practical consequences.

Pragmatism had a significant influence on the progressives. (p. 632)

Proclamation Line of 1763 Act of Parliament that restricted colonial settlement west of the Appalachian Mountains. The Proclamation Line sparked protests from rich and poor colonists alike. (p. 149)

Proclamation of Amnesty and Reconstruction 1863 proclamation that established the basic parameters of President Abraham Lincoln's approach to Reconstruction. Lincoln's plan would have readmitted the South to the Union on relatively lenient terms. (p. 463)

Progressive Party Third party formed by Theodore Roosevelt in 1912 to facilitate his candidacy for president. Nicknamed the "Bull Moose Party," the Progressive Party split the Republican vote, allowing Democrat Woodrow Wilson to win the election. (p. 654)

proprietary colonies Colonies granted to individuals, rather than held directly by the crown or given to chartered companies. Proprietors of such colonies, such as William Penn of Pennsylvania, had considerable leeway to distribute land and govern as they pleased. (p. 74)

Protestantism Religious movement initiated in the early sixteenth century that resulted in a permanent division within European Christianity. Protestants differed with Catholics over the nature of salvation, the role of priests, and the organization of the church. (p. 39)

Pueblo revolt 1680 uprising of Pueblo Indians against Spanish forces in New Mexico that led to the Spaniards' temporary retreat from the area. The uprising was sparked by mistreatment and the suppression of Indian culture and religion. (p. 76)

Pullman strike 1894 strike by workers against the Pullman railcar company. When the strike disrupted rail service nationwide, threatening the delivery of the mail, President Grover Cleveland ordered federal troops to get the railroads moving again. (p. 573)

Puritans Radical English Protestants who hoped to reform the Church of England. The first Puritan settlers in the Americas arrived in Massachusetts in 1630. (p. 56)

Reaganomics Ronald Reagan's economic policies based on the theories of supply-side economists and centered on tax cuts and cuts to domestic programs. (p. 963)

Red scare The fear of Communist-inspired radicalism in the wake of the Russian Revolution. The Red scare following World War I culminated in the Palmer raids on suspected radicals. (p. 703)

Redeemers White, conservative Democrats who challenged and overthrew Republican rule in the South during Reconstruction. (p. 477)

redemptioners Immigrants who borrowed money from shipping agents to cover the costs of transport to America, loans that were repaid, or "redeemed," by colonial employers. Redemptioners worked for their "redeemers" for a set number of years. (p. 91)

Regulators Local organizations formed in North and South Carolina to protest and resist unpopular policies. After first seeking redress through official institutions, Regulators went on to establish militias and other institutions of self-governance. (p. 150)

Renaissance The cultural and intellectual flowering that began in Italy in the fifteenth century and then spread north. The Renaissance occurred at the same time that European rulers were pushing for greater political unification of their states. (p. 10)

republican motherhood In the 1790s, some leaders supported women's education so that they could instruct their sons in principles of republican government. (p. 219)

Republican Party Party formed in 1854 that was committed to stopping the expansion of slavery and advocated economic development and internal improvements. Although their appeal was limited to the North, the Republicans quickly became a major political force. (p. 405)

Roe v. Wade The 1973 Supreme Court opinion that affirmed a woman's constitutional right to abortion. (p. 909)

Roosevelt Corollary 1904 addition to the Monroe Doctrine that affirmed the right of the United States to intervene in the internal affairs of Caribbean and Latin American countries to preserve order and protect American interests. (p. 677)

Sacco and Vanzetti case 1920 case in which Nicola Sacco and Bartolomeo Vanzetti were convicted of robbery and murder. The trial centered on the defendants' foreign birth and political views, rather than the facts pertaining to their guilt or innocence. (p. 719)

SALT II 1979 strategic arms limitation treaty agreed on by President Jimmy Carter and Soviet leader Leonid Brezhnev. After the Soviet Union invaded Afghanistan, Carter persuaded the Senate not to ratify the treaty. (p. 939)

scalawags Derisive term for white Southerners who supported Reconstruction. (p. 473)

Scottsboro Nine Nine African American youths convicted of raping two white women in Scottsboro, Alabama, in 1931. The Communist Party played a key role in defending the Scottsboro Nine and in bringing national and international attention to their case. (p. 743)

Second Continental Congress Assembly of colonial representatives that served as a national government during the Revolutionary War. Despite limited formal powers, the Continental Congress coordinated the war effort and conducted negotiations with outside powers. (p. 179)

second front Beginning in 1942, Josef Stalin wanted an immediate invasion by U.S., British, and Canadian forces into German-occupied France to take pressure off the Soviet forces fighting the Germans on the eastern front. The attack in western Europe did not begin until 1944, fostering resentment in Stalin. (p. 796)

Second Great Awakening Evangelical revival movement that began in the South in the early nineteenth century and then spread to the North. The social and economic changes of the first half of the nineteenth century were a major spur to religious revivals, which in turn spurred social reform movements. (p. 329)

second industrial revolution Revolution in technology and productivity that reshaped the American economy in the early twentieth century. (p. 710)

Second Party System When the Whig Party formed in 1834, they posed the first significant challenge to Democratic Party control in two decades. (p. 368)

Second Seminole War 1835–1842 war between the Seminoles, including fugitive slaves who had joined the tribe, and the U.S. government over whether the Seminoles would be forced to leave Florida and settle west of the Mississippi River. Despite substantial investments of men, money, and resources, it took seven years for the United States to achieve victory. (p. 369)

Sedition Act 1918 act appended to the Espionage Act. It punished individuals for expressing opinions deemed hostile to the U.S. government, flag, or military. (p. 688)

Servicemen's Readjustment Act (GI Bill) 1944 act that offered educational opportunities and financial aid to veterans as they readjusted to civilian life. Known as the GI Bill, the law helped millions of veterans build new lives after the war. (p. 852)

settlement houses Community centers established by urban reformers in the late nineteenth century. Settlement house organizers resided in the institutions they created and were often female, middle-class, and college educated. (p. 620)

sharecropping A system that emerged as the dominant mode of agricultural production in the South in the years after the Civil War. Under the sharecropping system, sharecroppers received tools and supplies from landowners in exchange for a share of the eventual harvest. (p. 476)

Shays's Rebellion 1786 rebellion by western Massachusetts farmers caused primarily by economic turmoil in the aftermath of the Revolutionary War. (p. 222)

Sherman Antitrust Act 1890 act that outlawed monopolies that prevented free competition in interstate commerce. (p. 534)

Sherman's March to the Sea Hard war tactics employed by General William Tecumseh Sherman to capture Atlanta and huge swaths of Georgia and the Carolinas, devastating this crucial region of the Confederacy in 1864. (p. 306)

siege of Vicksburg After a prolonged siege, Union troops forced Confederate forces to surrender at Vicksburg, Mississippi, leading to Union control of the rich Mississippi River valley. (p. 306)

sit-down strike A strike in which workers occupy their place of employment. In 1937 the United Auto Workers conducted sit-down strikes in Flint, Michigan, against General Motors to gain union recognition, higher wages, and better working conditions. The union won its demands. (p. 761)

skilled workers Workers with particular training and skills. Skilled workers were paid more and were more difficult for owners to replace than unskilled workers. (p. 564)

skyscrapers Buildings more than ten stories high that first appeared in U.S. cities in the late nineteenth century. Urban crowding and high prices for land stimulated the drive to construct taller buildings. (p. 612)

slave laws A series of laws that defined slavery as a distinct status based on racial identity and which passed that status on through future generations. (p. 96)

Social Darwinism The belief associated with the late nineteenth and early twentieth centuries and popularized by Herbert Spencer, that drew upon some of the ideas of Charles Darwin. Stressing individual competition and the survival of the fittest, Social Darwinism was used to justify economic inequality, racism, imperialism, and hostility to federal government regulation. (p. 538)

social gospel Religious movement that advocated the application of Christian teachings to social and economic problems. The ideals of the social gospel inspired many progressive reformers. (p. 632)

Social Security Act Landmark 1935 act that created retirement pensions for most Americans, as well as unemployment insurance. (p. 759)

Solidarity Polish trade union movement led by Lech Walesa. During the 1980s, Solidarity played a central role in ending Communist rule in Poland. (p. 979)

Sons of Liberty Boston organization first formed to protest the Stamp Act. The Sons of Liberty spread to other colonies and played an important role in the unrest leading to the American Revolution. (p. 156)

Southern Christian Leadership Conference (SCLC) Organization founded in 1957 by Martin Luther King Jr. and other black ministers to encourage nonviolent protests against racial segregation and disfranchisement in the South. (p. 869)

spectral evidence Evidence given by spirits acting through possessed individuals. A number of the accused in the 1692 Salem witch trials were convicted on the basis of spectral evidence. (p. 108)

spoils system Patronage system introduced by Andrew Jackson in which federal offices were awarded on the basis of political loyalty. The system remained in place until the late nineteenth century. (p. 155)

Stamp Act 1765 act of Parliament that imposed a duty on all transactions involving paper items. The Stamp Act prompted widespread, coordinated protests and was eventually repealed. (p. 913)

Stonewall riots The 1969 violence between gays and New York City police after the police raided the Stonewall Inn, a gay bar in Greenwich Village whose patrons fought the police in response to harassment. This encounter helped launch the gay liberation movement. (p. 913)

Stono rebellion 1739 uprising by African and African American slaves in South Carolina. In the aftermath of the uprising, white fear of slave revolts intensified. (p. 98)

Strategic Arms Limitation Treaty (SALT I) 1972 agreement between the United States and Soviet Union to curtail nuclear arms production during the Cold War. The pact froze for five years the number of antiballistic missiles (ABMs), intercontinental ballistic missiles (ICBMs), and submarine-based missiles that each nation could deploy. (p. 932)

Student Nonviolent Coordinating Committee (SNCC) Civil rights organization that grew out of the sit-ins of 1960. The organization focused on taking direct action and political organizing to achieve its goals. (p. 870)

Students for a Democratic Society (SDS) Student activist organization formed in the early 1960s that advocated the formation of a "New Left" that would overturn the social and political status quo. (p. 904)

subtreasury system A proposal by the Farmers' Alliances in the 1880s for the federal government to extend loans to farmers and store their crops in warehouses until prices rose and they could buy back and sell their crops to repay their debts. (p. 579)

suffragists Supporters of voting rights for women. Campaigns for women's suffrage gained strength in the late nineteenth and early twentieth centuries and culminated in ratification of the Nineteenth Amendment in 1920. (p. 636)

Sugar Act 1764 act of Parliament that imposed an import tax on sugar, coffee, wines, and other luxury items. The Sugar Act sparked colonial protests that would escalate over time as new revenue measures were enacted. (p. 155)

Sun Belt The southern and western part of the United States. After World War II, millions of Americans moved to the Sun Belt, drawn by the region's climate and jobs in the defense, petroleum, and chemical industries. (p. 856)

sweatshops Small factories or shops in which workers toiled under adverse conditions. Business owners, particularly in the garment industry, turned tenement apartments into sweatshops. (p. 616)

Taft-Hartley Act 1947 law that curtailed unions' ability to organize. It prevented unions from barring employment to non-union members and authorized the federal government to halt a strike for eighty days if it interfered with the national interest. (p. 852)

Tariff of Abominations White Southerners' name for the 1828 Congressional tariff act that benefited northern manufacturers and merchants at the expense of agriculture, especially southern plantations. (p. 306)

Tea Party movement A loose coalition of conservative and libertarian forces that arose around 2008. Generally working within the Republican Party, the Tea Party advocates small government, low taxes, and reduced federal deficits. (p. 1019)

Teapot Dome scandal Oil and land scandal during the Warren Harding administration that highlighted the close ties between big business and the federal government in the early 1920s. (p. 709)

Tejanos Mexican residents of Texas. Although some Tejano elites allied themselves with American settlers, most American settlers resisted the adoption of Tejano culture. (p. 368)

Teller Amendment Amendment to the 1898 declaration of war against Spain stipulating that Cuba should be free and independent. The amendment was largely ignored in the aftermath of America's victory. (p. 674)

temperance The movement to moderate and then ban the sale and consumption of alcohol. The American temperance movement emerged in the early nineteenth century as part of the larger push for improving society from the 1820s to the 1850s. (p. 331)

tenements Multifamily apartment buildings that housed many poor urban dwellers at the turn of the twentieth century. Tenements were crowded, uncomfortable, and dangerous. (p. 613)

Tennessee Valley Authority (TVA) New Deal agency that brought low-cost electricity to rural Americans and redeveloped the Tennessee River valley through flood-control projects. The agency built, owned, and supervised a number of power plants and dams. (p. 752)

Tenure of Office Act Law passed by Congress in 1867 to prevent President Andrew Johnson from removing cabinet members sympathetic to the Republican Party's approach to congressional Reconstruction without Senate approval. Johnson was impeached, but not convicted, for violating the act. (p. 470)

Tet Offensive January 31, 1968, offensive mounted by Vietcong and North Vietnamese forces against population centers in South Vietnam. The offensive was turned back, but it shocked many Americans and increased public opposition to the war. (p. 902)

Thirteenth Amendment Amendment to the Constitution abolishing slavery. The Thirteenth Amendment was passed in January 1865 and sent to the states for ratification. (p. 308, 463)

three-fifths compromise Compromise between northern and southern delegates to the 1787 Constitutional Convention to count enslaved persons as three-fifths of a free person in apportioning representation in the House of Representatives and taxation by the federal government. (p. 24)

To Secure These Rights Report issued by President Harry Truman's Committee on Civil Rights in 1947 that advocated extending racial equality. Among its recommendations was the desegregation of the military, which Truman instituted by executive order in 1948. (p. 865)

Townshend Act 1767 act of Parliament that instituted an import tax on a range of items including glass, lead, paint, paper, and tea. The Townshend Act prompted a boycott of British goods and contributed to violence between British soldiers and colonists. (p. 158)

Trail of Tears The forced march of some 15,000 Cherokees from Georgia to Indian Territory. Inadequate planning, food, water, sanitation, and medicine led to the deaths of thousands of Cherokees. (p. 372)

transcendentalism A movement founded by Ralph Waldo Emerson in the 1830s that proposed that individuals look inside themselves and to nature for spiritual and moral guidance rather than to the dogmas of formal religion. Transcendentalism attracted a number of important American writers and artists to its vision. (p. 333)

transcontinental railroad A railroad linking the East and West Coasts of North America. Completed in 1869, the transcontinental railroad facilitated the flow of migrants and the development of economic connections between the West and the East. (p. 493)

Treaty of Fort Laramie 1851 treaty that sought to confine tribes on the northern plains to designated areas in an attempt to keep white settlers from encroaching on their land. In 1868, the second Treaty of Fort Laramie gave northern tribes control over the "Great Reservation" in parts of present-day Montana, Wyoming, North Dakota, and South Dakota. (p. 497)

Treaty of Fort Stanwix 1784 treaty in which U.S. commissioners coerced Iroquois delegates into ceding vast tracts of land in western New York and the Ohio River Valley to the United States. (p. 213)

Treaty of Ghent Accord signed in December 1814 ending the War of 1812 and returning to U.S. and Britain the lands each controlled before the war. (p. 288)

Treaty of Greenville 1795 treaty signed following the Battle of Fallen Timbers through which Indians in the Northwest Territory were forced to ceded vast tracts of land to the United States. (p. 233)

Treaty of Guadalupe Hidalgo 1848 treaty ending the Mexican-American War. By the terms of the treaty, the United States acquired control over Texas north and east of the Rio Grande plus the New Mexico territory, which included present-day Arizona and New Mexico and parts of Utah, Nevada, and Colorado. The treaty also ceded Alta California, which had declared itself an independent republic during the war, to the United States. (p. 379)

Treaty of Medicine Lodge 1867 treaty that provided reservation lands for the Comanche, Kiowa-Apache and Southern Arapaho to settle. Despite this agreement, white hunters soon invaded this territory and decimated the buffalo herd. (p. 497)

Treaty of New Echota 1836 treaty in which a group of Cherokee men agreed to exchange their land in the Southeast for money and land in Indian Territory. Despite the fact that the treaty was obtained without tribal sanction, it was approved by the U.S. Congress. (p. 371)

Treaty (Peace) of Paris 1783 treaty that formally ended the conflict between Britain and its North American colonies. The newly established United States gained benefits from the treaty. (p. 201)

Treaty of Versailles Signed in 1919, this treaty officially ended World War I. President Woodrow Wilson went to France and played a major role in drafting the treaty, which established a League of Nations to prevent future wars. However, the U.S. Senate refused to ratify the treaty. (p. 691)

Triangle Shirtwaist Company Site of an infamous industrial fire in New York City in 1911. Inadequate fire safety provisions in the factory led to the deaths of 146 workers. (p. 617)

Truman Doctrine U.S. pledge to contain the expansion of communism around the world. Based on the idea of containment, the Truman Doctrine was the cornerstone of American foreign policy throughout the Cold War. (p. 819)

Trust Business monopolies formed in the late nineteenth and early twentieth centuries through mergers and consolidation that inhibited competition and controlled the market. (p. 534)

Tuscarora War War launched by Tuscarora Indians from 1711 to 1715 against European settlers in North Carolina and their allies from the Yamasee, Catawba, and Cherokee nations. The Tuscaroras forfeited their lands when they signed the peace treaty and many then joined the Iroquois Confederacy to the north. (p. 80)

Tuskegee Institute African American educational institute founded in 1881 by Booker T. Washington. Following Washington's philosophy, the Tuskegee Institute focused on teaching industrious habits and practical job skills. (p. 638)

U.S. Sanitary Commission Federal organization established in June 1861 to improve and coordinate the medical care of Union soldiers. Northern women played a key role in the work of the commission. (p. 290)

Uncle Tom's Cabin Novel published in 1852 by Harriet Beecher Stowe. Meant to publicize the evils of slavery, the novel struck an emotional chord in the North and was an international best seller. (p. 404)

underground railroad A series of routes from southern plantation areas to northern free states and Canada along which abolitionist supporters, known as conductors, provided hiding places and transportation for runaway slaves seeking freedom. (p. 340)

unions Groups of workers seeking rights and benefits from their employers through their collective efforts. (p. 567)

Universal Negro Improvement Association (UNIA) Organization founded by Marcus Garvey in 1914 to promote black self-help, pan-Africanism, and racial separatism. (p. 718)

unskilled workers Workers with little or no specific expertise. Unskilled workers, many of whom were immigrants, made up the vast majority of the late-nineteenth-century industrial workforce. (p. 564)

utopian societies Communities formed in the first half of the nineteenth century to embody alternative social and economic visions and to create models for society at large to follow. (p. 336)

Valley Forge Site of Continental Army winter encampment in 1777–1778. Despite the harsh conditions, the Continental Army emerged from its encampment at Valley Forge as a more effective fighting force. (p. 192)

vertical integration The control of all elements in a supply chain by a single firm. For example, Andrew Carnegie, a vertically integrated steel producer, sought to own suppliers of all the raw materials used in steel production. (p. 533)

Vietcong The popular name for the National Liberation Front (NLF) in South Vietnam, which was formed in 1959. The Vietcong waged a military insurgency against the U.S.-backed president, Ngo Dinh Diem, and received support from Ho Chi Minh, the leader of North Vietnam. (p. 840)

Vietnamization President Richard Nixon's strategy of turning over greater responsibility for the fighting of the Vietnam War to the South Vietnamese army. (p. 928)

Virginia and Kentucky Resolutions Resolutions passed by legislatures in Virginia and Kentucky that declared the Alien and Sedition Acts (1798) "void and of no force" in their states. (p. 234)

Virginia Plan Plan put forth at the beginning of the 1787 Constitutional Convention that introduced the ideas of a strong central government, a bicameral legislature, and a system of representation based on population. (p. 223)

Voting Rights Act 1965 act that eliminated many of the obstacles to African American voting in the South and resulted in dramatic increases in black participation in the electoral process. (p. 894)

Walking Purchase 1737 treaty that allowed Pennsylvania to expand its boundaries at the expense of the Delaware Indians. The treaty, quite possibly a forgery, allowed the British to add territory that could be walked off in a day and a half. (p. 121)

War Industries Board (WIB) Government commission created in 1917 to supervise the purchase of military supplies and oversee the conversion of the economy to meet wartime demands. The WIB embodied a government-business partnership that lasted beyond World War I. (p. 687)

War of the Spanish Succession 1702–1713 war over control of Spain and its colonies; also called Queen Anne's War. Although the Treaty of Utrecht that ended the war in 1713 was intended to bring peace through the establishment of a balance of power, imperial conflict continued to escalate. (p. 78)

War Powers Act 1973 act that required the president to consult with Congress within forty-eight hours of deploying military forces and to obtain a declaration of war from Congress if troops remained on foreign soil beyond sixty days. (p. 931)

War Production Board Board established in 1942 to oversee the economy during World War II. The War Production Board was part of a larger effort to convert American industry to the production of war materials. (p. 785)

Watergate Scandal and cover-up that forced the resignation of Richard Nixon in 1974. The scandal revolved around a break-in at Democratic Party headquarters in 1972 and subsequent efforts to conceal the administration's involvement in the break-in. (p. 934)

Whig Party Political party formed in the 1830s to challenge the power of the Democratic Party. The Whigs attempted to forge a diverse coalition from around the country by promoting commercial interests and moral reforms. (p. 368)

Whiskey Rebellion Uprising by western Pennsylvania farmers who led protests against the excise tax on whiskey in the early 1790s. (p. 231)

white supremacy An ideology promoted by southern planters and intellectuals that maintained that all whites, regardless of class or education, were superior to all blacks. (p. 367)

Wilmot Proviso 1846 proposal by Democratic congressman David Wilmot of Pennsylvania to outlaw slavery in all territory acquired from Mexico. The proposal was defeated, but the fight over its adoption foreshadowed the sectional conflicts of the 1850s. (p. 379)

Woman's Christian Temperance Union (WCTU) Organization founded in 1874 to campaign for a ban on the sale and consumption of alcohol. In the late nineteenth century, under Frances Willard's leadership, the WCTU supported a broad social reform agenda. (p. 642)

Women's National Loyal League Organization founded by abolitionist women during the Civil War to press Lincoln and Congress to enact universal emancipation. (p. 291)

Works Progress Administration (WPA) New Deal agency established in 1935 to put unemployed Americans to work on public projects ranging from construction to the arts. (p. 758)

XYZ affair 1798 incident in which French agents demanded bribes before meeting with American diplomatic representatives. (p. 234)

Yalta Agreement Agreement negotiated at the 1945 Yalta Conference by Roosevelt, Churchill, and Stalin about the fate of postwar eastern Europe. The Yalta Agreement did little to ease growing tensions between the Soviet Union and its Western allies. (p. 800)

Yamasee War A pan-Indian war from 1715 to 1717 led by the Yamasee who intended, but failed, to oust the British from South Carolina. (p. 80)

yellow journalism Sensationalist news accounts meant to provoke an emotional response in readers. Yellow journalism contributed to the growth of public support for American intervention in Cuba in 1898. (p. 673)

yeoman farmers Southern independent landowners who did not own slaves. Although yeomen farmers had connections to the South's plantation economy, many realized that their interests were not always identical to those of the planter elite. (p. 365)

Young Americans for Freedom (YAF) A group of young conservatives from college campuses formed in 1960 in Sharon, Connecticut. The group favored free market principles, states' rights, and anticommunism. (p. 916)

Zimmermann telegram 1917 telegram in which Germany offered Mexico an alliance in the event that the United States entered World War I. The telegram's publication in American newspapers helped build public support for war. (p. 685)

zoot suit riots Series of riots in 1943 in Los Angeles, California, sparked by white hostility toward Mexican Americans. White sailors attacked Mexican American teenagers who dressed in zoot suits—suits with long jackets with padded shoulders and baggy pants tapered at the bottom. (p. 791)

Chapter 1

Source Project 1: 1.4 Camilla Townsend, ed. and trans., *American Indian History: A Documentary Reader* (Malden, MA: Wiley-Blackwell, 2009), 29–30. Used with permission from the author.

Chapter 2

Source Project 2: 2.2 *Marie de L'Incarnation, Correspondance,* ed. Dom Guy Oury (Abbaye de Saint-Pierre, 1971), trans. Natalie Zemon Davis, *Women on the Margins: Three Seventeenth-Century Lives* (Cambridge, MA: Harvard University Press, 1995), 111–12. Used with permission.

Chapter 3

Source Project 3: 3.4 James A. Henretta, "Families and Farms: Mentalité in Pre-Industrial America," *William and Mary Quarterly* 35:1 (1978), pp. 4–5. Copyright © 1978 by Omohundro Institute of Early American History and Culture. Used with permission.

Chapter 8

Source Project 8: 8.7 W. Raymond Wood and Thomas D. Thiessen, eds., *Early Fur Trade on the Northern Plains: Canadian Traders among the Mandan and Hidatsa Indians, 1738–1818* (Norman: University of Oklahoma Press, 1985), 232–33. Copyright © 1985 by University of Oklahoma Press. Used with permission.

Chapter 13

Source Project 13: 13.6 Nina Silber and Mary Beth Sievens, eds., *Yankee Correspondence: Civil War Letters between New England Soldiers and the Home Front* (Charlottesville: University Press of Virginia, 1996), 55–56. Copyright © 1996 by the Rhode Island Historical Society. Used with permission. 13.7: "Letter to His Parents," April 22, 1862, by John Hines, Hines Family Collection, MMS 91, Library Special Collections, Western Kentucky University, Bowling Green. Courtesy of Kentucky Library & Museum, Western Kentucky University.

Chapter 17

Source Project 17: 17.4 Richard Hofstadter, Excerpt(s) from AGE OF REFORM, copyright © 1955 by Richard Hofstadter. Used by permission of Alfred A. Knopf, an imprint of the Knopf Doubleday Publishing Group, a division of Penguin Random House LLC. All rights reserved.

Chapter 18

Source Project 18: 18.1 Anzia Yerzierska, excerpts from *Bread Givers,* pp. 21–22. Copyright © 1925 by Doubleday & Co., Inc., renewed 1952 by Anzia Yerzierska. Reprinted with the permission of Persea Books, Inc (New York), www.perseabooks.com. All rights reserved.

Chapter 22

Source Project 22: 22.5 Barton J. Bernstein, "The New Deal: The Conservative Achievements of Liberal Reform," in *Towards a New Past: Dissenting Essays in American History* by Barton J. Bernstein, Lloyd C. Gardner and Eugene D. Genovese, copyright © 1968 by Penguin Random House LLC. Copyright © renewed 1996 by Barton J. Bernstein, Lloyd C. Gardner and Eugene D. Genovese. Used by permission of Pantheon Books, an imprint of the Knopf Doubleday Publishing Group, a division of Penguin Random House LLC. All rights reserved. 22.6: Ann Marie Low, *Dust Bowl Diary* (Lincoln: University of Nebraska Press, 1984), 96–97. Copyright © 1984 by the University of Nebraska Press. Reprinted by permission of the University of Nebraska Press. 22.7: John P. Davis, "A Black Inventory of the New Deal," *Crisis,* May 1935, 141–42. Copyright © 1935 by Crisis Publishing. The publisher wishes to thank the Crisis Publishing Co., Inc., the publisher of the magazine of the National Association for the Advancement of Colored People, for the use of this material first published in the May 1935 issue of Crisis Magazine. 22.9: Francisco E. Balderrama and Raymond Rodríguez, "Protest Against Maltreatment of Mexican Laborers in California. General Secretary Martin Torres of Mexican Regional Confederation of Labor to United States Ambassador Josephus Daniels," April 20, 1934, in *Decade of Betrayal: Mexican Repatriation in the 1930s.* (Albuquerque: University of New Mexico Press, 1995), 65–68. Copyright © 1995 by University of New Mexico Press. Used with permission.

Chapter 23

Source Project 23: 23.1 Monica Sone, From *Nisei Daughter.* Copyright © 1953 and renewed 1981 by Monica Sone. Used by permission of Little, Brown and Company.

Chapter 24

Source Project 24: 24.1 Henry Wallace, "The Way to Peace," in *The Annals of America* (Chicago: Encyclopedia Britannica, 1968), 16:372–73. Reprinted from Annals of America © 1968, 1976 Encyclopedia Britannica, Inc.

INDEX

Letters in parentheses following page numbers refer to figures *(f)*, illustrations *(i)*, maps *(m)*, sources *(s)*, and tables *(t)*.